Nineteenth-Century Literature Criticism

Guide to Gale Literary Criticism Series

For criticism on	Consult these Gale series
Authors now living or who died after December 31, 1999	*CONTEMPORARY LITERARY CRITICISM (CLC)*
Authors who died between 1900 and 1999	*TWENTIETH-CENTURY LITERARY CRITICISM (TCLC)*
Authors who died between 1800 and 1899	*NINETEENTH-CENTURY LITERATURE CRITICISM (NCLC)*
Authors who died between 1400 and 1799	*LITERATURE CRITICISM FROM 1400 TO 1800 (LC)* *SHAKESPEAREAN CRITICISM (SC)*
Authors who died before 1400	*CLASSICAL AND MEDIEVAL LITERATURE CRITICISM (CMLC)*
Authors of books for children and young adults	*CHILDREN'S LITERATURE REVIEW (CLR)*
Dramatists	*DRAMA CRITICISM (DC)*
Poets	*POETRY CRITICISM (PC)*
Short story writers	*SHORT STORY CRITICISM (SSC)*
Black writers of the past two hundred years	*BLACK LITERATURE CRITICISM (BLC)* *BLACK LITERATURE CRITICISM SUPPLEMENT (BLCS)*
Hispanic writers of the late nineteenth and twentieth centuries	*HISPANIC LITERATURE CRITICISM (HLC)* *HISPANIC LITERATURE CRITICISM SUPPLEMENT (HLCS)*
Native North American writers and orators of the eighteenth, nineteenth, and twentieth centuries	*NATIVE NORTH AMERICAN LITERATURE (NNAL)*
Major authors from the Renaissance to the present	*WORLD LITERATURE CRITICISM, 1500 TO THE PRESENT (WLC)* *WORLD LITERATURE CRITICISM SUPPLEMENT (WLCS)*

ISSN 0732-1864

Volume 87

Nineteenth-Century Literature Criticism

Excerpts from Criticism of the
Works of Novelists, Philosophers, and Other
Creative writers Who Died between 1800
and 1899, from the First Published Critical
Appraisals to Current Evaluations

Juliet Byington and Suzanne Dewsbury
Editors

Gianna Barberi
Associate Editor

GALE GROUP

Detroit
New York
San Francisco
London
Boston
Woodbridge, CT

STAFF

Lynn M. Spampinato, Janet Witalec, *Managing Editors, Literature Product*
Kathy D. Darrow, *Product Liaison*
Juliet Byington, Suzanne Dewsbury, *Editors*
Mark W. Scott, *Publisher, Literature Product*

Gianna Barberi, *Associate Editor*
Patti A. Tippett, *Technical Training Specialist*
Deborah J. Morad, Kathleen Lopez Nolan, *Managing Editors, Literature Content*
Susan M. Trosky, *Director, Literature Content*

Maria L. Franklin, *Permissions Manager*
Edna Hedblad, Kimberly F. Smilay, *Permissions Specialists*
Debra Freitas, Shalice Shah, *Permissions Assistants*

Victoria B. Cariappa, *Research Manager*
Tracie A. Richardson, *Project Coordinator*
Andrew Guy Malonis, Barbara McNeil, Gary J. Oudersluys, Maureen Richards, Cheryl L. Warnock, *Research Specialists*
Tamara C. Nott, *Research Associate*
Tim Lehnerer, Ron Morelli, *Research Assistants*

Dorothy Maki, *Manufacturing Manager*
Stacy L. Melson, *Buyer*

Mary Beth Trimper, *Composition and Prepress Manager*
Evi Seoud, *Assistant Production Manager*
Gary Leach, *Composition Specialist*

Randy Bassett, *Image Database Supervisor*
Robert Duncan, *Imaging Specialist*
Michael Logusz, *Graphic Artist*
Pamela A. Reed, *Imaging Coordinator*
Kelly A. Quin, *Imaging Editor*

Library of Congress Catalog Card Number
ISBN 0-7876-4542-7
ISSN 0732-1864
Printed in the United States of America

Contents

Preface

Since its inception in 1981, *Nineteeth-Century Literature Criticism* (*NCLC*) has been a valuable resource for students and librarians seeking critical commentary on writers of this transitional period in world history. Designated an "Outstanding Reference Source" by the American Library Association with the publication of is first volume, *NCLC* has since been purchased by over 6,000 school, public, and university libraries. The series has covered more than 300 authors representing 29 nationalities and over 17,000 titles. No other reference source has surveyed the critical reaction to nineteenth-century authors and literature as thoroughly as *NCLC*.

Scope of the Series

NCLC is designed to introduce students and advanced readers to the authors of the nineteenth century and to the most significant interpretations of these authors' works. The great poets, novelists, short story writers, playwrights, and philosophers of this period are frequently studied in high school and college literature courses. By organizing and reprinting commentary written on these authors, *NCLC* helps students develop valuable insight into literary history, promotes a better understanding of the texts, and sparks ideas for papers and assignments. Each entry in *NCLC* presents a comprehensive survey of an author's career or an individual work of literature and provides the user with a multiplicity of interpretations and assessments. Such variety allows students to pursue their own interests; furthermore, it fosters an awareness that literature is dynamic and responsive to may different opinions.

Every fourth volume of *NCLC* is devoted to literary topics that cannot be covered under the author approach used in the rest of the series. Such topics include literary movements, prominent themes in nineteenth-century literature, literary reaction to political and historical events, significant eras in literary history, prominent literary anniversaries, and the literatures of cultures that are often overlooked by English-speaking readers.

NCLC continues the survey of criticism of world literature begun by Gale's *Contemporary Literary Criticism* (*CLC*) and *Twentieth-Century Literary Criticism* (*TCLC*).

Organization of the Book

An *NCLC* entry consists of the following elements:

- The **Author Heading** cites the name under which the author most commonly wrote, followed by birth and death dates. Also located here are any name variations under which an author wrote, including transliterated forms for authors whose native languages use nonroman alphabets. If the author wrote consistently under a pseudonym, the pseudonym will be listed in the author heading and the author's actual name given in parenthesis on the first line of the biographical and critical information. Uncertain birth or death dates are indicated by question marks. Single-work entries are preceded by a heading that consists of the most common form of the title in English translation (if applicable) and the original date of composition.

- The **Introduction** contains background information that introduces the reader to the author, work, or topic that is the subject of the entry.

- A **Portrait of the Author** is included when available.

- The list of **Principal Works** is ordered chronologically by date of first publication and lists the most important works by the author. The genre and publication date of each work is given. In the case of foreign authors whose works have been translated into English, the list will focus primarily on twentieth-century translations, selecting those works most commonly considered the best by critics. Unless otherwise indicated, dramas are dated by first performance, not first publication. Lists of **Representative Works** by different authors appear with topic entries.

■ Reprinted **Criticism** is arranged chronologically in each entry to provide a useful perspective on changes in critical evaluation over time. The critic's name and the date of composition or publication of the critical work are given at the beginning of each piece of criticism. Unsigned criticism is preceded by the title of the source in which it appeared. All titles by the author featured in the text are printed in boldface type. Footnotes are reprinted at the end of each essay or excerpt. In the case of excerpted criticism, only those footnotes that pertain to the excerpted texts are included. Criticism in topic entries is arranged chronologically under a variety of subheadings to facilitate the study of different aspects of the topic.

■ A complete **Bibliographical Citation** of the original essay or book precedes each piece of criticism.

■ Critical essays are prefaced by brief **Annotations** explicating each piece.

■ An annotated bibliography of **Further Reading** appears at the end of each entry and suggests resources for additional study. In some cases, significant essays for which the editors could not obtain reprint rights are included here. Boxed material following the further reading list provides references to other biographical and critical sources on the author in series published by Gale.

Indexes

Each volume of *NCLC* contains a **Cumulative Author Index** listing all authors who have appeared in a wide variety of reference sources published by the Gale Group, including *NCLC*. A complete list of these sources is found facing the first page of the Author Index. The index also includes birth and death dates and cross references between pseudonyms and actual names.

A **Cumulative Nationality Index** lists all authors featured in *NCLC* by nationality, followed by the number of the *NCLC* volume in which their entry appears.

A **Cumulative Topic Index** lists the literary themes and topics treated in the series as well as in *Classical and Medieval Literature Criticism, Literature Criticism from 1400 to 1800, Twentieth-Century Literary Criticism,* and the *Contemporary Literary Criticism* Yearbook, which was discontinued in 1998.

An alphabetical **Title Index** accompanies each volume of *NCLC*, with the exception of the Topics volumes. Listings of titles by authors covered in the given volume are followed by the author's name and the corresponding page numbers where the titles are discussed. English translations of foreign titles and variations of titles are cross-referenced to the title under which a work was originally published. Titles of novels, dramas, nonfiction books, and poetry, short story, or essay collections are printed in italics, while individual poems, short stories, and essays are printed in roman type within quotation marks.

In response to numerous suggestions from librarians, Gale also produces an annual paperbound edition of the *NCLC* cumulative title index. This annual cumulation, which alphabetically lists all titles reviewed in the series, is available to all customers. Additional copies of this index are available upon request. Librarians and patrons will welcome this separate index; it saves shelf space, is easy to use, and is recyclable upon receipt of the next edition.

Citing *Nineteenth-Century Literature Criticism*

When writing papers, students who quote directly from any volume in the Literary Criticism Series may use the following general format to footnote reprinted criticism. The first example pertains to material drawn from periodicals, the second to material reprinted from books.

Kim McQuaid, "William Apes, Pequot: An Indian Reformer in the Jackson Era," *The New England Quarterly,* 50 (December 1977): 605-25; excerpted and reprinted in *Nineteenth-Century Literature Criticism,* vol. 73, ed. Janet Witalec (Farmington Hills, Mich.: The Gale Group, 1999), 3-4.

Richard Harter Fogle, *The Imagery of Keats and Shelley: A Comparative Study* (Archon Books, 1949), 211-51; excerpted and reprinted in *Nineteenth-Century Literature Criticism,* vol. 73, ed. Janet Witalec (Farmington Hills, Mich.: The Gale Group, 1999), 157-69.

Suggestions are Welcome

Readers who wish to suggest new features, topics, or authors to appear in future volumes, or who have other suggestions or comments are cordially invited to call, write, or fax the Managing Editor:

Managing Editor, Literary Criticism Series
The Gale Group
27500 Drake Road
Farmington Hills, MI 48331-3535
1-800-347-4253 (GALE)
Fax: 248-699-8054

Acknowledgments

The editors wish to thank the copyright holders of the excerpted criticism included in this volume and the permissions managers of many book and magazine publishing companies for assisting us in securing reproduction rights. We are also grateful to the staffs of the Detroit Public Library, the Library of Congress, the University of Detroit Mercy Library, Wayne State University Purdy/Kresge Library Complex, and the University of Michigan Libraries for making their resources available to us. Following is a list of the copyright holders who have granted us permission to reproduce material in this volume of *NCLC*. Every effort has been made to trace copyright, but if omissions have been made, please let us know.

COPYRIGHTED EXCERPTS IN *NCLC*, VOLUME 87, WERE REPRODUCED FROM THE FOLLOWING PERIODICALS:

American Literature, v. 62, September, 1990. Copyright © 1990 by Duke University Press, Durham, NC. Reproduced by permission.—*CLA Journal*, v. XIV, March, 1971; v. XXIV, June, 1982. Copyright 1971, 1982 by The College Language Association. Both reproduced by permission of the College Language Association.—*Eighteenth-Century Fiction*, v. 5, 1993. © McMaster University 1993. Reproduced by permission.—*The French Review*, v. xxvii, February, 1964. Copyright 1964, renewed 1992 by the American Association of Teachers of French; v. lviii, October, 1984. Copyright 1984 by the American Association of Teachers of French. Both reproduced by permission.—*The Journal of Narrative Technique*, v. 26, Fall, 1996, for "Face Value and the Value of Face in 'Les Liaisons dangereuses': The Rhetoric of Form and the Critic's Seduction" by Sandra Camargo. Copyright © 1996 by The Journal of Narrative Technique. Reproduced by permission of the publisher and the author. —*Legacy*, v. 5, Fall, 1988. Copyright © The University of Nebraska Press 1988. Reproduced by permission.—*MLN*, v. 111, September, 1996. Copyright © 1996. Reproduced by permission of The Johns Hopkins University Press.—*The New Criterion*, v. 12, March, 1994. "Seductive Monsters: Laclos's 'Liaisons Dangereuses,'" by Renee Winegarten. Copyright © 1994 by The Foundation for Cultural Review. Reproduced by permission of the author.— *Obsidian*, v. 7, Summer/Winter, 1981, "Roots of Our Literary Culture: George Moses Horton and Biblical Protest" by Sondra O'Neale. Reproduced by permission of the author.—*Studies in Eighteenth-Century Culture*, v. 18, 1988. Copyright © 1988 American Society for Eighteenth-Century Studies. All rights reserved. Reproduced by permission of The Johns Hopkins University Press.—*Studies in Romanticism*, v. 36, Winter, 1997. Copyright 1997 by the Trustees of Board University. Reproduced by permission.—*Studies on Voltaire and The Eighteenth Century*, n. 267, 1989 for "Male Bonding and Female Isolation in Laclos's 'Les Liasions dangereuses'" by Peter V. Conroy, Jr. Reproduced by permission by the author.—*Symposium*, v. 24, Summer, 1980. Copyright © 1980 Helen Dwight Reid Educational Foundation. Reproduced with permission of the Helen Dwight Reid Educational Foundations, published by Heldref Publications, 1319 13th Street NW, Washington, DC 20006-1307.—*The University of Toronto Quarterly*, v. 58, Spring, 1989. © University of Toronto Press, 1989. Reproduced by permission of University of Toronto Press Incorporated.—*The Victorian Newsletter*, n. 55, Spring, 1979, for "Tractarian Aesthetics: Analogy and Reserve in Keble and Newman" by G. B. Tennyson. Reproduced by permission of The Victoria Newsletter and the author.—*Victorian Studies*, v. 30, Summer, 1987. Reproduced by permission of the Trustees of Indiana University.—*The Wordsworth Circle*, v. 29, Spring, 1998. © 1998 Marilyn Gaull. Reproduced by permission of the editor.—*Yale French Studies*, n. 76, 1989 for "Trading Genres: Epistolarity and Theatricality in 'Britannicus' and 'Les Liaisons dangereuses'," by Elizabeth MacArthur. Copyright © Yale French Studies 1989. Reproduced by permission of the publisher and author.

COPYRIGHTED EXCERPTS IN *NCLC*, VOLUME 87, WERE REPRODUCED FROM THE FOLLOWING BOOKS:

Baker, Dorothy Z. From *Poetics in the Poem: Critical Essays on American Self-Reflexive Poetry*. Edited by Dorothy Z. Baker. Peter Lang, 1997. © 1997 Peter Lang Publishing, Inc., New York. All rights reserved. Reproduced by permission.—Barrell, John. From *The Infection of Thomas De Quincey: A Psychopathology of Imperialism*. Yale University Press, 1991. Copyright © 1991 by Yale University. All rights reserved. Reproduced by permission.—Clej, Alini. From *A Genealogy of the Modern Self: Thomas De Quincey and the Intoxication of Writing*. Stanford University Press, 1995. © 1995 by the Board of Trustees of the Leland Stanford Junior University. Reproduced by permissions.—Convoy, Jr., Peter V. From *Intimate, Intrusive, and Triumphant: Readers in the 'Liaisons Dangereuses'*. Edited by William M. Whitby. John Benjamins Publishing Company, 1987. Copyright © 1987. John Benjamins B. V. Reproduced by permission.—De Luca, V.

PHOTOGRAPHS APPEARING IN *NCLC*, VOLUME 87, WERE RECEIVED FROM THE FOLLOWING SOURCES:

Thomas De Quincey
1785-1859

English essayist, critic, and novelist. For additional information on De Quincey's life and works, see *NCLC,* Volume 4.

INTRODUCTION

A versatile essayist and accomplished critic, De Quincey used his own life as the subject of his most acclaimed work, the *Confessions of an English Opium-Eater* (1822), in which he chronicled his fascinating and horrifying addiction to opium. The *Confessions* are an insightful depiction of drug dependency and an evocative portrait of an altered psychological state. De Quincey is recognized as one of the foremost prose writers of his day; his ornate style, while strongly influenced by the Romantic authors he knew and emulated, owes much to his vivid imagination and desire to recreate his own intense personal experiences.

BIOGRAPHICAL INFORMATION

De Quincey's life as a child figures prominently in the *Confessions.* He was a frail, sensitive boy who was tyrannized by an older brother. When he was seven, his beloved older sister, Elizabeth, died. In his later writings, De Quincey maintained that her death shaped his destiny because his grief caused him to seek solace in an imaginary world. This tendency to escape into reverie foreshadowed the importance of dreams and introspection to his work. At ten, he was sent to grammar school where he fared well academically but, according to his autobiographical writings, was deeply unhappy. At seventeen, he ran away from school with a copy of William Wordsworth's *Lyrical Ballads* and a collection of Greek plays. He later described his feeling of liberation in terms Wordsworth had attributed to the spirit of revolutionary France: "the senselessness of joy." For several months he wandered throughout the country, and then traveled to London, where he hoped to study the English Romantic poets. His life during this period was one of self-imposed deprivation, and he eventually returned home. His mother, in an effort to tame her son, enrolled him at Oxford. At the university, he excelled academically but was socially isolated. De Quincey experimented with opium for the first time at Oxford: a classmate prescribed the drug for a toothache and De Quincey found that he enjoyed its effects. By 1813 De

Quincey was, in his own estimation, a "regular and confirmed" opium addict. At Oxford, he abandoned poetry and, inspired by his studies of German thought, decided to become "the first founder of a true philosophy." Whether or not opium was the cause, De Quincey, after submitting a brilliant paper, failed to appear for his final oral examination and left Oxford without completing his degree. While still at Oxford, De Quincey had written Wordsworth a glowing letter, and the poet, in turn, invited him to visit. The offer both thrilled and terrified the young man, and he chose to meet Samuel Taylor Coleridge first. Coleridge shared De Quincey's interest in metaphysics and opium but warned him about the evils of the drug. When De Quincey met Wordsworth, the poet invited him to join the Lake District's literary circle. De Quincey moved nearby, and became a frequent visitor to the Wordsworth household. De Quincey married and seemed content with family life until his opium addiction overpowered him. He had thought the drug would enhance his abilities as a philosopher; instead, he lay in bed listlessly, unable to think or move. His wife devoted herself to his recovery and, with her support, he obtained a position as editor of the *Westmoreland Gazette.* The simple, local newspaper soon featured De Quincey's vivid accounts of grisly murder trials, as well as essays on philology, politics, and German philosophy. De Quincey's subject matter and erratic work habits angered his employers and he was asked to resign. De Quincey agreed to leave, firmly believing that a regular routine was incompatible with the habits of a philosopher. However, because his financial situation was dire and he had a large family to support, he sought out Charles Lamb, who introduced De Quincey to London's journalistic circles and De Quincey was invited to write for *London Magazine.* The publisher encouraged him to write about the subject he knew most intimately—his opium addiction. In September, 1821, the first half of *Confessions of an English Opium-Eater* appeared anonymously in *London Magazine,* and the complete *Confessions* was published as a single volume in 1822. With its publication, De Quincey was immediately established as a major Romantic prose author. Following his stay in London, De Quincey moved to Edinburgh, where he wrote for several journals. He disliked writing for periodicals and often stated that he composed only for money. However, the essays that were published during this period display De Quincey's virtuosity as a prose writer and his interest in a wide array of subjects. De Quincey died in 1859.

MAJOR WORKS

The *Confessions of an English Opium-Eater* and its "sequel," *Suspiria de Profundis* (1845) are intensely personal chronicles of De Quincey's experiences with opium, both its physical and psychological effects. In these autobiographical writings, De Quincey attributes to his opium reveries a visionary power that informs his understanding of creativity and literary style. De Quincey published his expanded version of the *Confessions* in 1856, but this version is considered obscure and stylized. His numerous essays, which initially appeared in periodicals in the Lake District, London, and Edinburgh, treat a large variety of issues, both parochial and international: Britain's imperial conflicts in Asia and northern Africa, criminal violence, theological history, Enlightenment philosophy, as well as numerous more explicitly literary reviews. Among these literary essays, De Quincey's essay on William Shakespeare, "On the Knocking on the Door in Macbeth," has received acclaim as an outstanding piece of psychological criticism, and his critique of Wordsworth's *Lyrical Ballads* is considered a brilliant analysis of the poet's creative process. De Quincey's attention to the psychological aspects of literary, political, and domestic life stands as an important precursor to twentieth-century inheritors of the Romantic tradition. In addition, De Quincey published essays that sketched personal portraits of other Romantic authors; his reminiscences of his interactions with Coleridge and Wordsworth offer largely sympathetic insights into their literary circle.

CRITICAL RECEPTION

Some critics consider De Quincey's *Suspiria de Profundis* the supreme prose fantasy of English literature. Initially, the public believed that the confessions were fictional, to which the author responded by stating that the papers "were drawn up with entire simplicity and fidelity to the facts." Critics often point to the diffuseness of his style, which some believe to be the result of carelessness rather than a conscious artistic device. At the time of his death, his expertise as a literary critic was underestimated, though his prose talent had long been acknowledged. As a critic, he sometimes revealed more prejudice and narrow-mindedness than insight: he found Johann Wolfgang von Goethe's novel, *Wilhelm Meister's Apprenticeship,* immoral and cited evidence of plagiarism in the works of his friend Coleridge. Many recent critics have emphasized De Quincey's complex relationship with British imperialism: his horror and anxiety about the depravity and chaos that he associated with the Orient and his staunchly conservative political views seem to contrast sharply with his Romantic tendencies. Critic John Barrell claims that this tension permeates De Quincey's writing in various forms and is met by attempts to expel "hybridity." Although many critics disdain the ornateness of De Quincey's writing and complain of its digressive tendencies, others find that his essays display an acute psychological awareness. The impassioned prose of his autobiographical works recreates both his youthful dreams and later drug-induced meditations. De Quincey believed that these dreams chronicle the soul's development and provide readers with insight into their own minds. By explicitly addressing the role of visionary experience in the creative process, De Quincey helped to forge a new kind of prose, one which rivaled Romantic poetry in its intensity and evocation of "grandeur." According to contemporary scholars, his literary strengths and the tensions that mark his work situate him within the realm of modernity. In this way, De Quincey exemplifies the Romantic prose writer and at the same time heralds the emergence of a new understanding of literature and subjectivity.

PRINCIPAL WORKS

Confessions of an English Opium-Eater (autobiography) 1822 [revised edition 1856]
"On the Knocking on the Door in Macbeth" (essay) 1823
"On Murder Considered as One of the Fine Arts" (essay) 1827

Klosterheim; or, The Masque (novel) 1832
"The Logic of Political Economy" (essay) 1844
Suspiria de Profundis (autobiography) 1845
"The English Mail-Coach" (essay) 1849
The Collected Writings of Thomas De Quincey. 14 vols.
　　[ed. David Masson] (autobiography, criticism, and
　　essays) 1889-90
The Uncollected Writings of Thomas De Quincey. 2 vols.
　　(criticism and essays) [ed. James Hogg] 1890
The Posthumous Works of Thomas De Quincey. 2 vols.
　　[ed. A. J. Japp] (criticism and essays) 1891

CRITICISM

V. A. De Luca (essay date 1980)

SOURCE: "The Giant Self: *Suspiria de Profundis*" in
Thomas De Quincey: The Prose of Vision, University of
Toronto Press, 1980, pp. 57-83.

[*In the following essay, De Luca discusses the sequel to*
Confessions of an Opium-Eater *as a blending of autobiography and myth.*]

There is little precedent in other major Romantic writers
for the strangely late onset of De Quincey's chief phase as
an imaginative artist, a phase that begins with the *Suspiria
de Profundis* of his sixtieth year and continues for a dozen
years more. A last and climactic bout with the powers of
opium, a struggle always fecund to his imagination,
partially explains this phenomenon.[1] But whatever the
external circumstances, this mid-winter spring of De
Quincey's career is peculiarly appropriate, for a pattern of
tentative beginnings and late flowering is intrinsic to all of
his best work. Such a pattern is visible in the *Confessions,*
for example, in the way that the common day of experience at school and in London leads to and is absorbed by
the unearthly gleam of opium's revelations, or in **'The
Revolt of the Tartars,'** where the prosaic history of the
tribe modulates into a myth of divine guidance. The phases
of his literary career seem to follow the same sort of
progression; it is as if De Quincey feels compelled to
circle warily about his central theme of the imagination's
power, occasionally approaching it and retreating, only to
rush upon it at last, allowing it to transfigure his art.

Suspiria de Profundis initiates the culminating phase of
this progression, and De Quincey clearly intended it to occupy a crowning place in his work. Its subtitle in the
original version published in *Blackwood's Magazine* in
March-July 1845 is 'A Sequel to the *Confessions of an
English Opium-Eater,*' and the new work supersedes, at
least in intention, the earlier one that established his literary reputation. In a letter sent to his friend Professor Lush-

ington in 1846 De Quincey calls it 'very greatly superior
to the first [*Confessions*], . . . the ne plus ultra, as regards
the feeling and the power to express it, which I can ever
hope to attain.'[2] Attempting to assimilate and transcend the
earlier *Confessions,* the *Suspiria* also seems intended as a
kind of repository for every piece of 'impassioned' or
visionary prose that De Quincey was subsequently to write.
As a list of titles found among his papers after his death
indicates, he applied the general title *Suspiria de Profundis* not only to the pieces published in 1845 but also to
The English Mail-Coach of 1849, to 'The Daughter of
Lebanon,' appended to the revised *Confessions* of 1856,
as well as to other pieces not published in his lifetime,
some of them now lost.[3] The *Suspiria* of 1845 thus seems
to represent the central core of a canonical structure, an
arch of autobiography and vision, raising the life of the
English opium-eater to the level of myth.[4] It is, to be sure,
an unfinished arch, for De Quincey completed only one of
the work's four intended sections and later raided the work
freely, distributing parts of it among the heterogeneous
materials gathered to form the ***Autobiographic Sketches***
of 1853. Yet both in its aspirations to canonical stature and
in its incompleteness the *Suspiria* is reminiscent of other
Romantic works of similar scope and intent such as
Blake's *Four Zoas,* Wordsworth's *Recluse,* or Keats's *Hyperion,* great myths of fall and redemption which their
authors can neither finish nor leave behind but which live
on in successive versions of themselves. Like these, De
Quincey's work is more moving for its lack of completion
than any finished work could be, more revealing of the
open-endedness of Romantic myth-making.

I THE 'INTRODUCTORY NOTICE'

Like Wordsworth's *Recluse,* the *Suspiria* aspires to becoming a grand philosophical poem (though in prose), marrying personal history, visionary experiences, and a universal
healing doctrine. The principal difference between the two
works is in their plans of organization; whereas Wordsworth expected to confine his personal history to a prefatory poem, *The Prelude,* De Quincey plans to preserve the
linearity of personal narrative throughout the work, though
interrupting this narrative line with presentations of vision
and transcendental speculation at appropriate intervals.
Thus at the end of the 'Introductory Notice' to the *Suspiria* he insists

> . . . that the whole course of this narrative resembles,
> and was meant to resemble, a *caduceus* wreathed about
> with meandering ornaments, or the shaft of a tree's
> stem hung round and surmounted with some vagrant
> parasitical plant. The mere medical subject of the opium
> answers to the dry, withered pole, which shoots all the
> rings of the flowering plants, and seems to do so by
> some dexterity of its own; whereas, in fact, the plant
> and its tendrils have curled round the sullen cylinder
> by mere luxuriance of *theirs* . . . The true object in my
> 'Opium Confessions' [De Quincey apparently means

by this the *Suspiria* pieces that follow as well as his earlier work] is not the naked physiological theme . . . [but] those parasitical thoughts, feelings, digressions, which climb up with bells and blossoms round about the arid stock; ramble away from it at times with perhaps too rank a luxuriance; but at the same time . . . spread a glory over incidents that for themselves would be—less than nothing.

(SP 157-9)

Although De Quincey is quite misleading when he speaks of 'medical subjects' and 'physiological themes' (for opium never enters the work as we have it in any medical context at all), the general meaning is plain enough. Just as the linear course of life becomes wreathed in an incremental growth of dreams, so too will the narrative line provide a central thread from which a series of digressive sorties into the imagination are to be launched. Yet some of De Quincey's language in this explanation suggests a disquieting prospect as to the formal success of such a cunning mixture of autobiographical continuity and timeless vision. The attractions of vision dangerously overbalance the interest in the life itself, which becomes a 'dry withered pole,' an 'arid stock,' 'less than nothing.' That De Quincey himself realized this danger appears from the twice-repeated reference to the 'parasitical' growth of vision upon life, a growth of 'perhaps too rank a luxuriance,' as if this growth tended to smother whatever value the depiction of a personal history might offer.

Although the formal coherence of the work may be endangered by an imbalance between its visionary and its experiential elements, a valid basis remains for the copresence and linkage of these elements. The visionary power demands experience as its precondition, and the depiction of visionary states demands autobiographical narration for a proper understanding of those states. In the *Suspiria,* as written, the pains of opium have no particular importance at all, but the splendour and grand significance of dreams everywhere receive prominence:

Among the powers in man which suffer by this too intense life of the *social* instincts, none suffers more than the power of dreaming. Let no man think this is a trifle. The machinery for dreaming planted in the human brain was not planted for nothing. That faculty, in alliance with the mystery of darkness, is the one great tube through which man communicates with the shadowy. And the dreaming organ, in connection with the heart, the eye and the ear, compose the magnificent apparatus which forces the infinite into the chambers of a human brain, and throws dark reflections from eternities below all life upon the mirrors of the sleeping mind.

(SP 149)

As the mediating link between the finite and the infinite, between time and eternity, the dream dignifies its creator, who temporarily houses the infinite in his own finite

corporeality, and it raises the substance of his experience, garnered from 'the heart, the eye, and the ear,' to a higher power, converting it into the fabric of eternal vision. Experience thus has the growth of imagination as its goal, and transformed experience is the subject contemplated by the developed imagination in dreams, a reciprocal relation strictly within the range of Wordsworthian conceptions, however unlike Wordsworth De Quincey's funereal embroiderings of the theme may be.

Given this particular strand of interest in the 'Introductory Notice,' it is natural that some of De Quincey's most important remarks in it should centre upon overtly Wordsworthian themes, especially the connection between meditative solitude and imaginative power.[5] The grandeur of dreams unfolds, he maintains, in inverse proportion to the degree of one's involvement in the external multiplicities of social life, and the familiar Wordsworthian complaint against a world too much with us strongly enters his discussion: 'To reconcentrate [thought and feeling] into meditative habits, a necessity is felt by all observing persons for sometimes retiring from crowds. No man ever will unfold the capacities of his own intellect who does not at least checker his life with solitude. How much solitude, so much power' (SP 149). In this formulation De Quincey finds the essential guideline for the path he is to follow in the *Suspiria,* particularly in the long autobiographical section of Part I, 'The Affliction of Childhood.' His child-hero must become bereft of a primal connection with outward things, most starkly through the loss of others whom he loves, in order to enter a solitude which he will fill with his imaginings. In this he is like the Wordsworthian child of the 'Intimations' ode and the 'spots of time' passages of *The Prelude,* who often retires from social activities and sometimes literally becomes lost as he moves about 'in the worlds unrealized.' The pain of life, which is loss, and the glory of life, the power of dreaming and imagining, become inseparably joined through the mediation of solitude, which is the outward token of pain and glory both. In this way De Quincey reconciles the emphasis on a descent into grief and the apparently contradictory but even more potent emphasis on an ascent out of experiential loss into the glories of vision. Whether this reconciliation can dispel all the formal difficulties inherent in a work that aims to proceed by rambling casually through alternative states of sequential personal history and visionary displays, it at least enables De Quincey to embark coherently on an autobiographical account that transcends personal anecdotage and aspires to the status of visionary myth.

II 'THE AFFLICTION OF CHILDHOOD'

In 'The Affliction of Childhood' De Quincey locates the crisis in his experience not at the turn between adolescence and manhood, as in the *Confessions,* but at the earliest point of conscious awareness, and hence this new autobiographical account bears a revisionary relation to his first version of personal history. The *Confessions* of 1822 takes its hero into the world of experience but allows an aura of innocence to linger about that world, so that the climactic episode, the hero's love for Ann, represents simultaneously both the culmination of this innocence and yet the goal of an arduous experiential journey. Placed at the centre of the work, this episode suggests a moment somehow in time and yet before the onset of loss and solitude. In the *Confessions* it is thus possible for innocence and connective bonds with others to assume tangible shapes in a populous world of experience. Thus Ann of Oxford Street is a realized human figure in a way that De Quincey's sister Elizabeth, the corresponding figure of lost love in the *Suspiria,* can never be, and not simply because the latter dies in childhood. The bond of love which Elizabeth shares with her brother is so confined to the remotest period of childhood and broken so early that its status in the adult's consciousness verges on the mythical and the time of its flourishing becomes Edenic. Solitude now becomes not a condition of adulthood but one that takes dominion in the earliest stages of conscious life, and almost all of De Quincey's lifetime, including his childhood, becomes empty space in which a self-sustained imagination has scope to expand. The *via negativa* towards visionary grandeur thus starts early in the *Suspiria,* rather than later, as in the *Confessions,* a sign of the *Suspiria*'s more ambitious attempt to confer a special mythic glory on autobiographical experience.

'The Affliction of Childhood' thus grants brief space to that evocation of a society dwelling in innocence, such as figured so importantly in the first half of the *Confessions.* This evocation rests simply in a modest account of the child's early background in a family comfortably supported by trade:

> We, the children of the house, stood in fact, upon the very happiest tier in the scaffolding of society for all good influences. The prayer of Agar—'Give me neither property nor riches'—was realized for us. That blessing had we, being neither too high nor too low: high enough we were to see models of good manners; obscure enough to be left in the sweetest of solitudes. Amply furnished with the nobler benefits of wealth, *extra* means of health, of intellectual culture, and of elegant enjoyment, on the other hand, we knew nothing of its social distinctions. Not depressed by the consciousness of privations too sordid, not tempted into restlessness by the consciousness of privileges too aspiring, we had no motives for shame, we had none for pride.
>
> (SP 162)

Possessing no taint of shame or pride, the environment described here suggests Eden before the Fall, the 'happy rural seat' associated in English literature from the time of Chaucer with the virtues and comforts of the provincial middle class. Moulded in such an environment by 'the gentlest of sisters, not by horrid, pugilistic brothers' (SP 163), the child dwells in a pastoral of innocence free from the intrusions of pain and strife.

The death of De Quincey's younger sister Jane disturbs this idyll, but only momentarily, for it becomes assimilated into the atmosphere of the natural pastoral in which the child continues to dwell: 'I was sad for Jane's absence. But still in my heart I trusted that she would come again. Summer and winter came again—crocuses and roses; why not little Jane?' (SP 166). If little Jane is a part of nature, the elder sister Elizabeth is like nature itself, and with the death of Elizabeth the young De Quincey seems to lose an entire world. It is important and perhaps surprising to note that, despite all his declarations of extravagant love for this sister and of grief for her loss, De Quincey presents no complete description of her, no concrete example of her virtues, and no specific instance of the affectionate regard which she is presumed to have had for her younger brother. Whatever the young boy's feeling for the actual Elizabeth may have been in 1792, the lack of circumstantial description in 'The Affliction of Childhood' enforces our sense of her representativeness, as if she were the humanized embodiment of that domestic pastoral of innocence in which De Quincey lived as a child. As his 'leader and companion' she fulfils his 'necessity of being loved' (SP 170, 169), for as leader she represents the benevolent tutelary environment, and as companion she serves as the recipient of his own emotional generosity. In this early state of the child's imaginative development transcendence is located in a human figure. In a metaphoric expression of this transcendence Elizabeth is endowed with 'a *tiara* of light or a gleaming *aureola*'; she is a 'pillar of fire,' De Quincey says, 'that didst go before me to guide and to quicken,' a 'lamp lighted in Paradise' (SP 167, 170).

The news that Elizabeth must die strikes the child like 'God's thunderbolt' (SP 171), the first manifestation of another kind of divine presence that works by power, not by love, that dwells in infinity, not concentrated in the finite human form. The second manifestation occurs when De Quincey visits the chamber where his dead sister is laid out:

> Nothing met my eyes but one large window wide open, through which the sun of midsummer at noonday was showering down torrents of splendor. The weather was dry, the sky was cloudless, the blue depths seemed the express types of infinity; and it was not possible for eye to behold or for heart to conceive any symbols more pathetic of life and the glory of life.
>
> (SP 172)

The description registers a remarkable transference of qualities from the dead Elizabeth to the vivid skyscape.

Life, departed from his sister, returns in emblems quintessentially 'pathetic of life'; the ineffable light which once surrounded her is replaced by the glorious light of the sun at its zenith. Somewhat later, as the child contemplates her breathless corpse, the breath returns in cosmic form in the rising swell of a 'solemn wind.' 'It was a wind that had swept the fields of mortality for a hundred centuries. Many times since, upon a summer day, when the sun is about the hottest, I have remarked the same wind arising and uttering the same hollow, solemn, Memnonian, but saintly swell: it is in this world the one sole *audible* symbol of eternity' (SP 175). In other words, the image of Elizabeth is replaced by an array of cosmic images suggesting eternal life and glory, images at once closer to inanimate nature and, in the imagination, to a divine presence than the human beloved afforded. When his sister's death removes the focal point of De Quincey's imaginative desires, they project themselves upon all of the visible cosmos, finding a more absolute expression of the infinite in a nature stripped bare of meaningful human presence.

At this point in the narrative a speculative digression intervenes. The death of a child in the fullness of June somehow strikes De Quincey's imagination as singularly appropriate, and he seeks to justify this paradoxical connection as emanating from a deep psychological principle. 'Often I have been struck with the important truth,' he says, 'that far more of our deepest thoughts and feelings pass to us through perplexed combinations of *concrete* objects, pass to us as *involutes* (if I may coin that word) in compound experiences incapable of being disentangled, than ever reach us *directly,* and in their own abstract shapes' (SP 173). This observation, manifestly relevant to the symbol-making in De Quincey's writings in general, helps to explain here the remarkable transformation that has come over the child in his sister's bedroom. In this instance Elizabeth's death in June enters an 'involute' of feeling derived from associations of Bible-reading in early childhood. These readings awakened visions of the perpetual summer of Oriental climates, visions which propagated a chain of associations: palm trees, Palm Sunday, Jerusalem, and, finally, Christ's Passion and Resurrection: 'There it was, indeed, that the human had risen on wings from the grave; but, for that reason, there also it was that the divine had been swallowed up by the abyss; the lesser star could not rise, before the greater would submit to eclipse' (SP 174-5). Three patterns of cyclic return inform the imaginative power of this involute experience: the imaginative pattern of the Christian myth, with its story of death and rebirth; the pattern of individual memory, which, in the adult writer, recovers the loves of childhood while retaining the sense of the loss of those loves; and the pattern of nature, which recreates in the stasis of summer vegetation a beauty equivocally poised in counter-processes of death and growth. The involute feeling tightly binds De Quincey's contemplation of death to a notion of resurrection; the presence of this feeling is like a privileged moment that contains all of the successive stages in a redemptive cycle simultaneously.

But these contraries are perhaps too tightly wound together, and the imaginative energy needed to hold the various elements in simultaneous juxtaposition is too demanding for the child's consciousness, which suddenly snaps and enters a trance state. The energies of imagination generated by the consciousness of contraries now propels him forward in vision on an infinite flight beyond contraries altogether:

> Instantly, . . . when my eye filled with the golden fulness of life, the pomps and glory of the heavens outside, and turning when it settled upon the frost which overspread my sister's face, instantly a trance fell upon me. A vault seemed to open in the zenith of the far blue sky, a shaft which ran up forever. I, in spirit, rose as if on billows that also ran up the shaft forever; and the billows seemed to pursue the throne of God; but *that* also ran before us and fled away continually. The flight and the pursuit seemed to go on for ever and ever. Frost, gathering frost, some Sarsar wind of death, seemed to repel me.
>
> (SP 176)

J. Hillis Miller, who considers the whole scene in Elizabeth's chamber as the paradigmatic depiction of the disappearance of God in De Quincey's writings, describes the deity of this passage as one 'who plays hide and seek with man, and always withdraws into a further deep of space and time as we approach closer to his throne.'[6] Although the suggestions of resurrection in the involute passage must surely qualify Miller's assessment of the whole scene as emblematic of the divine withdrawal, modern readers attuned to contemporary literature of spiritual alienation are likely to accept his view in this instance. Yet a reading derived from a Romantic context might bring to bear other associations, the Wordsworthian moment, for example,

> when the light of sense
> Goes out, but with a flash that has
> Revealed the invisible world; . . .
> . . . whether we be young or old,
> Our destiny, our being's heart and home,
> Is with infinitude, and only there;
> With hope it is, hope that can never die,
> Effort, and expectation, and desire,
> And something evermore about to be.
>
> (*The Prelude,* (II [1850], 600-8)

Geoffrey Hartman's general theory of Wordsworth's consciousness, that 'nature itself led him beyond nature'[7] to an apocalyptic awareness of the imagination's sublime autonomy, is a notion applicable as well to the progress of vision here. De Quincey's 'light of sense' is not only the summer sun 'showering down torrents of splendor' but

Elizabeth herself, nature in human form, whose passing allows De Quincey an extraordinary visionary autonomy. 'The Affliction of Childhood' has thus progressed from the living light of Elizabeth to the natural but portentous light of the sky, and finally to the visionary shaft of light emanating from a God whose retreat acts as a lure to draw the spirit of the child ever farther out from the bonds of mortality. The progress patently enacts the stages of the mystic progress or 'epistrophe' from sense to spirit,[8] a point corroborated by a passage immediately following the description of the trance:

> Oh flight of the solitary child to the solitary God— flight from ruined corpse to the throne that could not be ruined!—how rich wert thou in truth for after years. Rapture of grief that, being too mighty for a child to sustain, foundest a happy oblivion in a heaven-born dream, and within that sleep didst conceal a dream, whose meanings in after years, when slowly I deciphered, suddenly there flashed upon me new light.
>
> (SP 176)

In a note De Quincey explicitly acknowledges his debt to Plotinus for the first line of this passage and thus enforces the context of imaginative quest in which the whole vision should be read. It is a context characteristically Romantic, suggestive of aspiration towards the transcendent, yet open-ended, even tentative. The open-endedness modifies the absolutism of Neoplatonic systems, but the Neoplatonic element counteracts any tendency to interpret the vision merely as a depiction of God's estrangement.

De Quincey's full appreciation of the vision is, however, a fruit of 'after years.' The visionary flight of the child ends on a more tentative note. The Sarsar wind of death counters the upward surge, and whether representing the child's mortal limitations or a sudden terror at the prospect of infinite vision (a point which De Quincey will later develop in his essay **'System of the Heavens'**), it returns him to his sister's chamber. The suggestion of a play of contraries on a new and higher level—the evolution of 'some mighty relation between God and death' (I, 42)— appears only in the version of 1853. The tentativeness implies that the visionary moment in the chamber of death is only a foretaste of the child's imaginative development now that solitude has come upon him. For at the funeral services he rebels at the liturgical suggestions that Elizabeth has been transformed into a higher thing and transferred to a better world (SP 181). His desire for the restoration of the living Elizabeth he has known indicates a reluctance to let go of the lost domestic idyll of innocence.

The rest of 'The Affliction of Childhood' shows the child attempting to invest a freely roaming imagination in forms adequate to the strength of his desire. The scenes in church which close the installment of March 1845 provide,

through architecture, picture, and music, an organizing form to engage the imagination already diffused in the forms of nature:

> The sides of the windows were rich with storied glass; through the deep purples and crimsons streamed the golden light; emblazonries of heavenly illumination mingling with the earthly emblazonries of what is grandest in man . . . There were the martyrs that had borne witness to the truth through flames . . . There were the saints who, under intolerable pangs, had glorified God by meek submission to his will.
>
> (SP 185)

This scene offers more than the solace to be gained from moralizing depictions. The beauties of natural light and human art join in the stained glass to cancel the martyrs' pain, though they do so by augmenting its visual intensity. Once again, as in Elizabeth's chamber, an externally presented involute of contrary elements prompts the child's own visionary efforts. Awakened by the pictorial art of the stained glass, the imaginative eye of the child paints a story of its own making upon the vision of clouds and sky, glimpsed through the central window where the glass is clear; the clouds become beds of dying children, and their drift through the sky becomes an ascent into the heavens, where a benevolent God, no longer retreating, reaches down to meet them (SP 186).

As a visionary experience this is inadequate; not only is the conversion of clouds into beds mechanical (and visually most awkward), but, unlike the earlier trance, there is no flight of the visionary child towards God, only the sentimental piety of levitating children observed by an earthbound eye. What the child has created is another pictorial exemplum, and the power of simple pictorial projection is beginning to interfere with more sophisticated modes of imagination. Fortunately during the whole creation of this visual experience another form of art is present, the tumultuous music pouring from the church organ:

> But not the less the blare of the tumultuous organ wrought its own separate creations. And oftentimes in anthems, when the mighty instrument threw its vast columns of sound, fierce yet melodious, over the voices of the choir-when it rose high in arches, as might seem, surmounting and overriding the strife of the vocal parts, and gathering by strong coercion the total storm into unity—sometimes I seemed to walk triumphantly upon those clouds which so recently I had looked up to as mementos of prostrate sorrow, and even as ministers of sorrow in its creations; yes, sometimes under the transfigurations of music I felt of grief itself as of a fiery chariot for mounting victoriously above the causes of grief.
>
> (SP 186)

As in so many Romantic works the ear proves mightier than the eye, and this time it is the child who rises, not the objects of his vision. The visual display of the windows, even the display of ascending children shown to the inner eye, are prefigurative visions, pointing to the child's ultimate unification with God in some indefinite future. But music is reflexive rather than figurative in significance; it moves towards the unification of its own self-created oppositions independent of any external reference, and thus can function as the precise equivalent of the free imagination's self-fulfilling operation, made sensually manifest to the child for the first time. In its temporal aspect it carries the child, like Elijah, to the triumphant consummation of those portents first glimpsed in the chamber of his sister; in its spatial aspects, both actual (the locations of choir and organ in the church) and metaphoric (the 'vast columns of sound,' 'high in arches'), it becomes the very architectural structure of the heavenly mansion imaginatively attained.

The experience in church, resolves, in a limited fashion, the paradoxical nature of the visionary flight undertaken in the young De Quincey's first trance. There his imagination sought fulfilment in a goal of absolute transcendence, the throne of God, but this goal is unattainable in any finite quest, though it is this unavailability that guarantees the increase of the child's autonomous imaginative strength. The church and its music at last provide a locus of outward forms to engage and absorb the imaginative energies liberated by the loss of Elizabeth. Yet this receptive function in no way diminishes the autonomy of the child's solitary quest, for the music spells out in sound a self-renewing movement of imagination that is intrinsically his own. Though music carries the child on a chariot of sound, as earlier the billows of his trance carried him towards the throne of God, the vehicle here is the glory attained, a self-fulfilled sublimity. The vehicle none the less still remains external to his imagination, and since the boy cannot remain forever in church, a dangerous freedom returns as his imagination once more roams in solitude. 'Solitude, though silent as light, is, like light, the mightiest of agencies; for solitude is essential' (**SP** 188). This is beautiful but disquieting, and it is not surprising that it begins to turn into a death-wish, a longing for the ultimate solitude disguised as reunion:

> . . . There is a necessity that, if too much left to itself in solitude, finally [grief] will descend into a depth from which there is no reascent: into a disease which seems no disease; into a languishing which, from its very sweetness, perplexes the mind, and is fancied to be very health. Witchcraft has seized upon you—nymph-holepsy has struck you. Now you rave no more. You acquiesce; nay, you are passionately delighted in your condition. Sweet becomes the grave, because you hope immediately to travel thither.
>
> (**SP** 196-7)

Such a repose would be a denial of the imaginative quest altogether, and it is a sign of imaginative strength that the child soon turns away from this preoccupation.

The turning away involves putting on 'the harness of life' (**SP** 199) and entering into the normal routine of ordinary childhood occupations, as described in the April 1845 issue of *Blackwood's*. The problem of an unfixed imaginative excess still remains, and it becomes an aesthetic problem for De Quincey as author as well as an existential problem for the child. 'The Affliction of Childhood' begins at this point to move with a disastrous wobble, mingling eloquent apostrophes to the imaginative and moral capacities of children with anecdotes that belong in the nursery. The 'heart overflowing with love' (**SP** 203) now invests its bounty of grief upon the penning up of Newfoundland dogs and the deaths of kittens and kitchen spiders (**SP** 199-206). It becomes apparent that De Quincey does not know what to do with his visionary theme while pursuing his commitment to a consecutive account of the 'arid stock' of his ordinary life experiences. The theme of imagination is either an obstacle to a truly interesting account of childhood episodes, or, as is more likely, these episodes simply are inadequate to De Quincey's increasing concern, the quest for a fulfilling visionary experience.

Thus a new official direction for the work becomes established openly as 'The Affliction of Childhood' draws to a close, a direction which corresponds to the types of cyclic return, glimpsed in the involute experiences in Elizabeth's chamber:

> Ups and downs you will see, heights and depths, in our fiery course together, such as will sometimes tempt you to look shyly and suspiciously at me, your guide, and the ruler of the oscillations. Here . . . the reader has reached the lowest depths in my nursery afflictions. From that point, according to the principles of *art* which govern the movement of these Confessions, I had meant to launch him upwards through the whole arch of ascending visions which seemed requisite to balance the sweep downwards, so recently described in his course.
>
> (**SP** 222)

The 'lowest depths' mentioned here are merely the trivial sorrows of the nursery, and one begins to wonder 'shyly and suspiciously' how much 'descent' has actually occurred in 'The Affliction of Childhood'. Having paid his dues to anecdotal autobiography, the 'ruler of the oscillations' feels no compunction in leaping an interval of twelve years in order to arrive at Oxford and the youth's first experience with opium. Opium brings on dreams that arrest the reverberations of experiences previously described and reconstitute them with greater intensity:

> Again I was in the chamber with my sister's corpse, again the pomps of life rose up in silence, the glory of

summer, the frost of death. Dream formed itself mysteriously within dream; within these Oxford dreams remoulded itself continually the trance in my sister's chamber . . . Once again arose the swell of the anthem, the burst of the Hallelujah chorus, the storm, the trampling movement of the choral passion, the agitation of my own trembling sympathy, the tumult of the choir, the wrath of the organ. Once more I, that wallowed, became he that rose up to the clouds. And now in Oxford all was bound up into unity; the first state and the last were melted into each other as in some sunny glorifying haze.

(SP 224-5)

As 'The Affliction of Childhood' returns to its point of departure, the celebration of the grandeur of dreams, the rationale of this autobiographical narration becomes clear. It traces not only an increasingly insistent desire for transcendence but also an increasing awareness in the imaginer that the location of this transcendence lies within himself, within the spectrum of his own experience. As a product of his own imagination and a recapitulation of his own past, the dream testifies to the grandeur of the dreamer, not of some external absolute. Yet it is as final a reward as union with that retreating figure of an absolute God would have been, for the dreamer views his own past transfigured into a consummate pattern, in which the 'first state and the last,' like the apocalyptic Alpha and Omega, are bound together in unity. In these dreams the very capacity for vision becomes the subject of vision ('Dream formed within dream') and every moment of discovered pattern, every involute glimpsed along the way, becomes a prophetic microcosm of this encompassing pattern which the imagination fulfils for itself. In this way the youth's quest ends not in some otherworldly attainment but in a state which repeats the events of the quest itself and raises them to a higher power. At this point De Quincey is impelled to abandon autobiographical continuity in order to elaborate on the metaphysics of his discovery, enlarging its significance by projecting it through metaphor and myth. *Suspiria de Profundis* now changes from a work describing the growth of the visionary faculty in an individual to one in which the products of this growth are set forth for all to behold.

III MYTHS OF THE GIANT SELF

The four semi-didactic, semi-visionary prose-poems which conclude Part I of *Suspiria de Profundis* repeat, amplify, and summarize themes that have appeared before. Each piece forms an independent and self-sufficient variation on the theme of the whole, and De Quincey suggests that together they 'may be viewed as in the nature of choruses winding up the overture contained in Part I' (SP 236). *Suspiria de Profundis* obviously aspires in some way to the condition of music, as if the whole work were an attempted expansion in words of its own central emblem, the grand

organ concert first heard in the church services and then reheard in dreams. In this kind of autobiography the 'chorus' of set-pieces performs a function corresponding to that of dreams in the subject's life: while it teaches that living experience deploys itself in an aesthetic pattern, it is in itself the climax of the pattern. The dream provides the visionary synthesis that testifies to the subject's strength of imagination and rescues him from an absurd condition composed of banality and fruitless pain; the prose-poems likewise rescue autobiographical narrative from its potential tendency to submerge thematic interest in an accumulation of trivial incident and detail.

The starting-point for the expanding circles of speculation that pervade these pieces lies in De Quincey's notion of the connection between early experiences of sorrow and a compensatory grandeur of imaginative power in later life. In this latter part of the *Suspiria* De Quincey neither forgets the loss of his sister nor lets us forget it, as frequent allusions to 'the deep, deep tragedies of infancy' (SP 236) make plain. Nevertheless his main concern with the resulting personal gain is even more apparent here than it was in 'The Affliction of Childhood.' In a piece called **'The Dark Interpreter,'** apparently written for the *Blackwood's* series of 1845 and then discarded, De Quincey seems to regard the experience of loss as a kind of moral and psychological tonic to strengthen his own development: 'Pain driven to agony, or grief driven to frenzy, is essential to the ventilation of profound natures . . . A nature which is profound in excess but also introverted in excess, so as to be in peril of wasting itself in interminable reverie, cannot be awakened sometimes without afflictions that go to the very foundations, heaving, stirring, yet finally harmonizing.'[9] In the 'Finale' of Part I, 'Savannah-la-Mar,' an even more ambitious role is assigned to grief, one that confirms the implicit movement of the *Suspiria* away from contemplation of the loveliness of the vanished past and towards the prospective grandeur of the self: 'O, deep is the plowing of grief! But oftentimes less would not suffice for the agriculture of God. Upon a night of earthquake he builds a thousand years of pleasant habitations for man. Upon the sorrow of an infant he raises oftentimes from human intellects glorious vintages that could not else have been' (SP 255-6). These suggestions of a millennium founded upon cataclysm, peculiarly Blakean in their combination of agricultural and apocalyptic imagery, are now appropriated to the history of the self. They strikingly indicate the scope of De Quincey's aspirations as nothing less audacious than the attainment of transcendence and spiritual resurrection in this life, an attainment based upon a knowing of all the modes of human experience. This is made explicit in the most programmatic of the *Suspiria* pieces, 'Levana and Our Ladies of Sorrow,' in which the allegorical Ladies, each representing a phase of De Quincey's personal history, proclaim the purpose of their stern influence over him: 'So shall he be accomplished in the furnace, so shall he see the things that ought *not* to be seen, sights that are abominable, and secrets that are unutterable. So shall he read elder truths, sad truths, grand truths, fearful truths. So shall he rise again *before* he dies. And so shall our commission be accomplished which from God we had—to plague his heart until we had unfolded the capacities of his spirit' (SP 246). De Quincey italicizes 'before' explicitly to dissociate this rising from the traditional Christian ascent out of the earthly vale of tears, an ascent which is of course post-mortem. De Quincey gives his official allegiance to Christianity, but his imagination is at all times Romantic in its metaphysics and thus frequently revisionary in its relation to orthodox beliefs.

One example of this spiritual rising before death has already appeared in the *Suspiria,* the opium-dreams at Oxford described at the end of 'The Affliction of Childhood,' dreams which recapitulate past experience, render it synchronic, and cast over it 'some sunny glorifying haze' of transfiguration. In the prose-poems that follow the 'The Affliction of Childhood' the focus of De Quincey's attention begins to shift from the theme of grief *per se* to this visionary power of perceiving the diachronic order of personal experience as a synchronic pattern. It is a pattern so radiant in its unity and balance that to contemplate it is in itself the glory and reward of experience, the resurrection of the spirit in this life. In 'The Palimpsest,' the first of the four pieces which conclude Part I, De Quincey compares this mode of perception to the phenomenon of the palimpsest manuscript, an objective record of successive pasts gathered together upon a single surface:

> In our own heaven-created palimpsest, the deep memorial palimpsest of the brain, there are not and cannot be . . . incoherencies. The fleeting accidents of a man's life and its external shows may indeed be irrelate and incongruous; but the organizing principles which fuse into harmony, and gather about fixed predetermined centres, whatever heterogeneous elements life may have accumulated from without, will not permit the grandeur of human unity greatly to be violated, or its ultimate repose to be troubled, in the retrospect from dying moments, or from other great convulsions.
>
> (SP 233)

The homing tendency of the 'fleeting accidents' of life, propagated by the journey of experience, finally make that journey self-justifying; in the palimpsest of retrospective vision, the 'grandeur of human unity' is inseparably linked to the proliferation of past experiences, as their traces left on the memory at last converge.

An anecdote from 'The Palimpsest' describing the reported visions of a child on the point of drowning vividly communicates the theory of the simultaneity of the past and the glory conferred on those who behold this pattern:

> At a certain stage of [her] descent, a blow seemed to strike her, phosphoric radiance sprang forth from her eyeballs; and immediately a mighty theatre expanded within her brain. In a moment, in the twinkling of an eye, every act, every design of her past life, lived again, arraying themselves not a succession, but as parts of a coexistence. Such a light fell upon the whole path of her life backwards into the shades of infancy, as the light, perhaps, which wrapt the destined Apostle on his road to Damascus. Yet that light blinded for a season; but hers poured celestial vision upon the brain, so that her consciousness became omnipresent at one moment to every feature in the infinite review.
>
> (SP 234-5)

What is striking about this passage is not the commonplace notion that drowning people see their whole lives flash before their eyes, but that emphasis upon light and expanded vision: 'phosphoric radiance,' 'celestial vision,' 'a mighty theatre expanding,' 'infinite review.' The implied comparison of the child's vision to that of St Paul is especially bold; the apostle is blinded, but the child's vision becomes clear and god-like, 'celestial' and 'omnipresent'; and the radiance emanating from one's individual life seen as a whole becomes implicitly parallel to the radiance emanating from Christ. Such a passage, describing the discovery of incarnate divinity in the depths of the self, remarkably inverts the young boy's vision in the chamber of his dead sister. In the former vision there was an ascent into the heavens in pursuit of a retreating God, but here there is a descent into translucent depths to find an adequate divinity in the totality of self-discovery.

Behind the overt double-myth of the four visionary pieces—the diachronic myth of experiential loss and imaginative resurrection, the synchronic myth of life seen as a multi-faceted design in a moment of total apprehension—there is yet another that encompasses these.[10] This myth, not stated directly, is deducible from the series of metaphors that express the overt themes. The sequence of images that, each in its turn, dominates the four pieces tells a tale of its own, indeed the only tale of which we can share the experience, for the dreamer's experience of the mystic moment of simultaneity is really unavailable to us in literary form. Our vision, instead, is of a palimpsest manuscript, three majestic Ladies of Sorrow, a giant form projected against the sky, a great city drowned by God and explored by human vision. The three latter images all involve grand personified figures of mysterious power, and the first and last present images of multifoliate forms, the work of many generations of hands. All of these images have as their common denominator the sensed presence of a giant composite form, at once human and divine, like Blake's universal man, Albion, one who incorporates past, present, and future, and of whom each individual man is a microcosm.[11] Such a myth makes comprehensible De Quincey's glorification of the pattern of the individual life as apolcalyptic, a glorification that might otherwise seem solipsistic and unearned. In 'The Palimpsest of the Human Brain' the myth is presented obliquely, although the anecdote about the drowning child approaches it more openly; 'Levana and Our Ladies of Sorrow' and 'The Apparition of the Brocken' present directly dream-visions of giant, archetypal figures; and 'Savannah-la-Mar' combines some of the obliquity of 'The Palimpsest' with direct invocations of the power of human vision and divine order. The first of these pieces offers in the image of the palimpsest not the presence of the Giant Man himself but the cumulative record of his imaginative products as seen in the successive stages of literary development:

> In the illustration imagined by myself, from the case of some individual palimpsest, the Grecian tragedy had seemed to be displaced, but was *not* displaced, by the monkish legend; and the monkish legend had seemed to be displaced, but was *not* displaced, by the knightly romance. In some potent convulsion of the system, all wheels back into its earliest elementary stage. The bewildering romance, light tarnished with darkness, the semi-fabulous legend, truth celestial mixed with human falsehoods, these fade even of themselves, as life advances. The romance has perished that the young man adored; the legend has gone that deluded the boy; but the deep, deep tragedies of infancy . . . these remain lurking below all, and these lurk to the last.
>
> (**SP** 235-6)

The various literary forms recovered from the palimpsest— Attic tragedy, a saint's life, and chivalric romance—are all close in outlook and derivation to a religious or mythic consciousness, and they represent successive stages of its development in the Western poetic tradition. De Quincey skillfully associates the various stages of individual human development (particularly his own) with those of the imagination as it unfolds in history: the feeling of primal loss with pagan tragedy, the imaginative religiosity of the child with devotional legend, the questing impulse of the youth with romance.[12] The history of the individual imagination is thus a microcosm of the history of imagination in general, itself a giant organic form with perpetually accessible origins.

The metaphor of the giant figure becomes explicit in the next piece, 'Levana and Our Ladies of Sorrow,' now made personal in import, though grandly transcending the significance of De Quincey's own private woes. The figure of Levana, the Roman goddess of childhood education, becomes representative of the whole process of a resurrection of the spirit through the experience of grief (**SP** 238), and her ministers, the three Ladies of Sorrow, similarly become Romantic analogues of ancient and traditional mythic forces: 'these are the Sorrows; and they are three in number, as the *Graces* are three, who dress man's life with beauty: the *Parcae* are three, who weave the dark arras of man's life in their mysterious loom always with

colors sad in part, sometimes angry with tragic crimson and black; the *Furies* are three, who visit with retributions called from the other side of the grave offenses that walk upon this' (**SP** 239). For De Quincey sorrow represents his fate and his nemesis, but it also holds for him the grace of an elegiac beauty that inspires his song. These figures thus associate the various influential powers of traditional myth with a power of special significance to the writer as an individual. Furthermore, it appears that each of them is representative of a phase of De Quincey's own life. Thus the first of the Sorrows, the *Mater Lachrymarum* corresponds to the period of childhood loss and to a religion-haunted landscape: 'And I knew by childish memories that she could go abroad upon the winds, when she heard that sobbing of litanies, or the thundering of organs, and when she beheld the mustering of summer clouds' (**SP** 241). The second, the *Mater Suspiriorum,* is associated with what De Quincey calls 'The Parish Worlds,' the unredeemed present of terrestrial wandering and imprisonment in time; and the third, the *Mater Tenebrarum,* with 'The Kingdom of Darkness,' the realm where the dreamer shall see 'the things that ought *not* to be seen, sights that are abominable, and secrets that are unutterable' (**SP** 246). This dark kingdom is apparently the apocalyptic realm of demonic horror, not described directly in the ***Suspiria*** but already described in 'The Pains of Opium' in the ***Confessions*** of 1822.

Evidently to fix precisely the symbolic significance of these figures is not an easy task. They are deities or influential presences, avatars of the ancient Graces, Furies, Fates, and Muses all coalesced, and at the same time they are allegorical emblems representing successive temporal phases of an individual consciousness, as well as actual dream images (**SP** 240). If they signify, in discursive terms, the operative forces that enable De Quincey to attain a visionary imagination, in so far as they appear in the actual verbal presentation they are themselves the vision that we behold:

> But the third sister, who is also the youngest! Hush! whisper whilst we talk of *her*! Her kingdom is not large, or else no flesh should live; but within that kingdom all power is hers. Her head, turreted like that of Cybèle, rises almost beyond the reach of sight. She droops not; and her eyes rising so high *might* be hidden by distance. But, being what they are, they cannot be hidden; through the treble veil of crape which she wears, the fierce light of a blazing misery, that rests not for matins or for vespers, for noon of day or noon of night, for ebbing or for flowing tide, may be read from the very ground.
>
> (**SP** 244)

This description of the *Mater Tenebrarum* clearly does not reduce the figure to a mere emblem for a discursive equivalent of, say, opium addiction. All of De Quincey's considerable stylistic powers—the insistent prose rhythms, the parallels and antitheses, the striking pictorial details (the towering headdress, the blazing eyes)—certainly direct the reader here to more than a mundane understanding of an allegorical figure. They evoke, rather, a sharing of the writer's awe before his own visionary creation of a giant power. Although the outline of 'Levana and Our Ladies of Sorrow' is programmatic, the piece fulfils itself in generating huge and mighty forms whose power to fascinate is autonomous even if their source is in the phases of the writer's personal experience.

The emergence of the Giant Man as the true hero of the *Suspiria* is clarified in 'The Apparition of the Brocken.' This piece describes an imaginary ascent of the Brocken, a mountain in North Germany, where, under certain atmospheric conditions, spectators may observe gigantic silhouettes of themselves projected against distant mountains and clouds. The ascent takes place on Whitsunday, which commemorates the pentecostal visit of the Holy Spirit to the apostles and suggests an inspiration even more hallowed than that bestowed by Levana and her ministers. This hallowed ascent, however, reveals not the traditional vision of the celestial spheres but rather a vision of the self writ large upon them. As the projected figure mimics the actions of the observer, 'you are now satisfied,' De Quincey says, 'that the apparition is but a reflex of yourself; and, in uttering your secret feelings to *him,* you make this phantom the dark symbolic mirror for reflection to the daylight what else must be hidden forever' (SP 251). Like the Ladies of Sorrow, the Brocken apparition is both a projection of the self and a mythic giant; he is a protean figure who mimics the actions of all who ascend the mountain, one who reflects the motions of grief and Christian devotion on Whitsunday but who has also reflected in ages past the 'bloody rites' of Druidism once performed on the summit of the mountain (SP 249). De Quincey thus associates the apparition not only with the private world of the individual dreamer but also with the larger sphere of man's typological consciousness, the human imagination which has been able to encompass the horror of demonic idolatry and the repose of Christian peace.

The myth of the giant form, for which the Brocken spectre is a convenient external emblem, finds its internal reflection in the figure of the Dark Interpreter, who appears in De Quincey's dreams:

> He is originally a mere reflex of my inner nature. But as the apparition of the Brocken sometimes is disturbed by storms or by driving showers, so as to dissemble his real origin, in like manner the Interpreter sometimes swerves out of my orbit, and mixes a little with alien natures. I do not always know him in these cases as my own parhelion. What he says, generally, is but that which *I* have said in daylight, and in meditation deep

enough to sculpture itself on my heart. But sometimes, as his face alters, his words alter; and they do not always seem such as I have used, or *could* use.

(SP 251)

The Dark Interpreter is primarily the voice of the self in dreams, that inevitable 'I' who is their protagonist, but he maintains an 'otherness' that removes him from full identity with the dreamer.[13] His utterances are unrecognizable, not because they conform to a Freudian notion of desires forbidden to the knowledge of the conscious self, but because he represents the dreamer's imagination at the outer verge of its individuality, at the point of transaction with large and autonomous powers which assert their presence in the sleeping mind.

The clear image of the giant form achieved in 'The Apparition of the Brocken' is disturbed by the complexity of the 'Finale: Savannah-la-Mar,' which in its attempt to sweep all the major preceding themes of the *Suspiria* into its brief compass offers a difficulty scarcely matched elsewhere in De Quincey's writings. As the action of the *Suspiria* starts in effect with 'God's thunderbolt,' his removal of Elizabeth, in 'Savannah-la-Mar' the work returns in an enormously magnified way to its origins:

> God smote Savannah-la-mar, and in one night, by earthquake, removed her, with all her towers standing and population sleeping, from the steadfast foundations of the shore to the coral floors of ocean. And God said,—'Pompeii did I bury and conceal from men through seventeen centuries: this city I will bury, but not conceal. She shall be a monument to men of my mysterious anger, set in azure light through generations to come; for I will enshrine her in a crystal dome of my tropic seas.' This city, therefore, like a mighty galleon with all her apparel mounted, streamers flying, and tackling perfect, seems floating along the noiseless depths of ocean; and oftentimes in glassy calms, through the translucid atmosphere of water that now stretches like an air-woven awning above the silent encampment, mariners from every clime look down into her courts and terraces, count her gates, and number the spires of her churches. She is one ample cemetery, and *has* been for many a year; but in the mighty calms that brood for weeks over tropic latitudes, she fascinates the eye with a *Fata-Morgana* revelation, as of human life still subsisting in submarine asylums sacred from the storms that torment our upper air.

(SP 253-4)

Savannah-la-Mar in its submerged state is the coalesced form of many opposites reconciled in a harmonious balance, an involute like the death-in-summer described in 'The Affliction of Childhood.' It has the multitudinousness of a city—courts and terraces, gates and spires—tempered, however, by silence, stasis, and the soft monochromatic suffusions of 'azure light.' Forever fixed and stationary, it seems to float like a galleon; the waters that cover it become an 'atmosphere,' a 'crystal dome,' like an 'air-woven awning' or second sky; an 'ample cemetery,' it suggests 'human life still subsisting'; the product of cataclysm and 'mysterious anger,' it has now become an asylum 'sacred from the storms that torment our upper air.' If the city has experienced a death in summer, it is now a summer-in-death, as its location in the eternal warmth of the tropics fittingly suggests.

On one level De Quincey's dream-descent to Savannah-la-Mar, accompanied by the Dark Interpreter, is a descent to a transformed memory of his dead sister, for it was her passing that generated the mutually involved associations of death and summer, descent into the grave and visionary ascent through a 'translucid atmosphere.' The image of the sunken city combines these associations, as it curiously combines associations of the corpse of the beloved and the paradisal city which receives her; like the New Jerusalem of Revelation, Savannah-la-Mar is to some degree 'a city yet a woman' (note De Quincey's use of feminine pronouns in referring to it). More obviously, of course, it is an elaborated version of the 'mighty theatre' of the past recaptured, seen by the drowning girl in the 'Palimpsest' anecdote, an image of the variety of life arrayed in a simultaneous order. It becomes a vision of the past as life englobed in crystal, and hence the dreamer's descent may also suggest a visionary return to his own past experience, harmonized by the ordering powers of imagination. But autobiographical associations are scarcely overt in this vision, and the clear resemblance of Savannah-la-Mar to Atlantis and other lost golden isles symbolizing the happy spot of early days universalizes its significance.[14] Most generally, then, Savannah-la-Mar suggests a synthesis of all pasts, once existing vitally in time, now Edenic in the mythic memory, and this memory is like the covering waters, separating yet joining the 'here-and-now' surface and the deep visionary image.

De Quincey's image of the drowned city becomes in its own way a kind of giant form, an inclusive emblem for the totality of human productions and desires, fusing disguised references to personal memory with allusions to ultimate losses and hopes on a universal scale.[15] It is, to be sure, a passive version of this form, a product and not a producer, and in this sense it differs from the images of the Ladies of Sorrow and the Brocken apparition. Those figures function simultaneously as referential emblems for the products of experience and as visionary depictions of a giant power, the creative force behind experience, but in 'Savannah-la-Mar' De Quincey separates the emblems of the desired and the desirer, the created and the creative. The creative role falls partially to the dreamer and his double, the Dark Interpreter, who are privileged to explore the drowned city and philosophize definitively upon its significance, but the ultimate creative force in the work is that God whose giant power and mysterious purpose bring Savannah-la-Mar to its present state of timeless repose.

'Creative' may seem an inappropriate term to apply to a power that operates by visitations of destruction, and the Dark Interpreter seeks to explain God's plan by a rather enigmatic argument concerning the relation between human and divine time:

> The time which *is* contracts into a mathematic point; and even that point persists a thousand times before we can utter its birth. All is finite in the present; and even that finite is infinite in its velocity of flight towards death. But in God there is nothing finite; but in God there is nothing transitory; but in God there *can* be nothing that tends to death. Therefore, it follows, that for God there can be no present. The future is the present of God, and to the future it is that he sacrifices the human present. Therefore it is that he works by earthquake. Therefore it is that he works by grief.

(SP 255)

All of this may simply mean that God destroys man in order to bring him to heaven all the sooner, but the vision of the drowned city provides associations which enrich and transfigure so bald a formulation. Savannah-la-Mar dwells in a time that is not, a suspended state that incorporates past and future, death and living beauty, a prophetic facsimile for the dreamer of that vision of eternity which awaits the whole cosmos when the present of man and the present of God shall be one. But as a living, terrestrial city every moment of its existence rushed it towards that moment of pure disaster when before and after fell away into non-being. The same melancholy situation confronts every man in so far as he is subject to the anxieties of time-bound existence; each present moment of existence is like a last stand on rapidly shrinking ground, a stand on the brink of two abysses, a past which is all loss and a future which is all threat. But in the divine present of God the perspective is quite different, for the abyss is filled with healing and preserving waters that invest the entire corpus of time with a harmonious beauty. If the human future is the present of God, then it follows that our present must be for him the past, not of course in the sense that it is a memorial record of his experience, but in the way that a narrative written in the past tense must seem to its author, beyond contingency when completed, yet with all its events copresent in the sheaves of pages that comprise it.

When Savannah-la-Mar awakes at last so that its bells and organs 'will utter a *jubilate* repeated by the echoes of Paradise' (SP 254), the event will signal an end to all contingency, the moment when, as J. Hillis Miller has said, 'all presents have flowed into the past' and the whole course of human history arrays itself as a timeless presence.[16] God is thus the supreme artist, and his acts of destruction are in fact acts of creation ('Therefore he works by grief'), for they release events from the anxieties of time so that they may take their place in a panorama of incomparable beauty. It should be clear now how relevant this divine activity is to De Quincey's belief in the beautiful simultaneity of events as seen in dreams and vision. The divine vision of human history is precisely analogous to the dreamer's vision of the sunken city, the metropolis of human contingencies which has undergone a sea-change into a panorama of perfection, and every such vision of the past in the *Suspiria* is a type of the divine vision. If the personal past, the cumulative product of the individual's loves and acts, is a microcosm of the giant and cumulative product of all human experience, the shaping imagination that endows that product with beauty is a microcosm of the giant form of God's imagination. De Quincey becomes the power he is seeking, rising before he dies not so much as one saved, but as one saving, as the artist who can make us see the vicissitudes of human life through the integrating faculties of the divine eye.

The essential thematic design of Part I of the *Suspiria* is now complete; it traces the story of an imagination which, having lost the beloved human figure in whom it originally invested its entire strength, reaches out in search of new rooting, finding it first in the church music, then in the Oxford dreams, and finally in the literary myth of a giant self. In the self-evident art of the visionary *Suspiria* pieces, with their intricate subtleties of argument and metaphor and their sonorities of verbal music, this myth of capable power becomes a reality. The design is Wordsworthian in its beginnings, for Wordsworth's early 'spots of time' involve almost entirely moments of sundering or sudden discontinuity with a consequent release of psychic energy. In its later phases, however, the design of the *Suspiria* acquires something of a Blakean character; it becomes increasingly concerned with the individual poet's imagination and experience as a microcosm of the whole of human existence, viewed as timeless in the divine vision (although De Quincey's visionary impulse, unlike Blake's, is quite devoid of ethical concerns and aspires toward a quite un-Blakean attainment of final stasis).

Although this movement from Wordsworthian to Blakean modes (to label them conveniently) gives to Part I of the *Suspiria* a powerful effect of crescendo, the balance of autobiographical concerns and yearnings for apocalyptic vision poses great danger to the unity and even the feasibility of the *Suspiria de Profundis* as a projected whole. The visions which bring Part I to its climax prophesy the attainment of a state where the pattern of the individual life and the pattern of the universal vision become equivalent, but in order to demonstrate this equivalence and not merely to assert it De Quincey must work his way through the rest of his autobiographical history, through the 'Pariah Worlds' and the 'Kingdom of Darkness.' The visionary luxuriance of the climactic prose-poems of Part I makes it easy to forget that the personal narrative has brought us only to De Quincey's middle childhood, to which it must

return rather anticlimactically. De Quincey's eagerness to display his visionary and metaphysical pattern causes him to present the climax too soon, or else the 'Finale' of Part I is not really a finale, but only a visionary way-station, as it were, on the course of a continuing autobiographical narrative, with the true culmination yet to come. But what can any such vision offer that has not been offered already, what can surpass the apocalyptic theodicy of 'Savannah-la-Mar'? In the '*caduceus*' passage from the 'Introductory Notice' De Quincey has promised 'digressions, which climb up with bells and blossoms round the arid stock [of personal history], ramble away from it at times with perhaps too rank a luxuriance'; is this an indication that each of the four projected parts of the *Suspiria* is to receive its own crowning wreath of metaphysical speculations and visions? It is difficult to guess how such a plan could be managed without awkwardness and redundance. The problem is fundamental; De Quincey's commitment to autobiographical continuity and his fascination with transcendent vision, however intrinsically connected on the thematic level, war with one another on the aesthetic level and cripple the potential of the *Suspiria* to fulfil its own thematic postulates.

In the somewhat shapeless and perhaps fragmentary second part of the *Suspiria,* called 'The Vision of Life,' De Quincey conscientiously attempts to continue the story of his youth with anecdotes about his days at school, which he later transfers, rightly, to the *Autobiographic Sketches* of 1853. It is in some ways an altogether fresh start, for it dissociates itself from the theme of Part I, the visionary return of the past, and directs its interest towards a more conventionally autobiographical theme, the progressive development of personal experience in ordinary life. The new emphasis appears in a remark that 'as "in to-day already walks to-morrow," so in the past experience of a youthful life may be seen dimly the future' (SP 258). This 'past experience' is now prologue not to visionary triumphs but to events surmised 'in troubled vision, by a young man who stands upon the threshold of manhood' (SP 258), scenes of 'the *strife* which besets us, strife from conflicting opinions, positions, passions, interests' (SP 259). The future, not the past, now becomes the arena of suffering, and dream-visions not published in De Quincey's lifetime, such as 'The Princess and the Pomegranate' and 'Who is this Woman That Beckoneth and Warneth Me,' both dealing with ominous portents of the future, may have been intended as part of another 'chorus' of visionary pieces designed to suit this portion of the *Suspiria*.[17] De Quincey's imagination cannot shake itself free, however, of the memory of beautiful and suffering female figures, and he concludes 'The Vision of Life,' not with a narration of his masculine hero engaging in the strife of the world, but with a rambling account of three generations of lovely women, blighted by disease and unrequited love. The ostensible excuse for this account is to show 'the past viewed not *as* the past, but by a spectator who steps back ten years deeper into the rear, in order that he may regard it as a future' (**SP** 278), an aim which associates the anecdote with the general emphasis in Part II. In fact, however, De Quincey shows himself far less interested in experimenting with a temporal point of view than in multiplying wilted flowers as a sentimental indulgence. This dismal straying from the course suggests strongly that De Quincey is either bored with the task of providing a detailed account of his life or uncertain of the value such an account might have.

Significantly ***Suspiria de Profundis*** never appeared anywhere in the Collective Edition published in De Quincey's lifetime, and in the final version, which according to its publisher in 1871 had received the 'benefit of the Author's revision and correction' (XIII, 333), all traces of autobiographical narrative including 'The Affliction of Childhood' itself have been removed, leaving only the dream-visions and metaphysical speculations. But even in 1845 De Quincey's eye is clearly fixed upon the glamour of the visionary experience, a glamour that dims the ordinary events of personal history. In the next few years of his literary career the interest in self-exploration is to become submerged or deflected in such mythic disguises as **'Joan of Arc'** and **'The Spanish Military Nun.'** Meanwhile, with new-found powers of imagination he devotes himself to a more extensive and externally oriented exploration of the cosmos ruled by the apocalyptic power briefly glimpsed in 'Savannah-la-Mar.' It is a fruitful pursuit, leading as it does to **'The English Mail-Coach'** of 1849, the chief document in establishing De Quincey's claim to a place among the major English writers in the visionary tradition. ***Suspiria de Profundis*** remains a heroic attempt, a bold assertion *in propria persona* of De Quincey's worth as an imaginative man, but it founders on the refractoriness of personal experiential detail to the thrust of a visionary consciousness.

Notes

1. See [Edward] Sackville West, *A Flame in Sunlight* [*The Life and Work of Thomas de Quincey* (London: Cassell 1936)], pp 270-5.

2. H. A. Page (pseudonym of A. H. Japp), *Thomas De Quincey: His Life and Writings, with Unpublished Correspondence* (London: John Hogg 1877), I, 339.

3. For a more detailed account of the *Suspiria's* complicated history of publication see Masson's introductory note to the series (XIII, 331-3) and [H. A.] Eaton, *Thomas De Quincey* [*A Biography* (New York: Oxford University Press 1936)], pp 427-8n.

4. This tendency to make autobiography mythic is most compactly seen in a kind of prospectus to the work as whole, attached as a note to 'Leavana and

Our Ladies of Sorrow.' In announcing the quadrapartite scheme of the *Suspiria,* each part devoted to a phase of personal experience, De Quincey assigns to these phases resonant titles such as 'The Pariah Worlds' and 'The Kingdom of Darkness,' as if they were regions of a visionary landscape (SP 246n).

5. Cf Ralph Haven Wolfe, 'Priest and Prophet: Thomas De Quincey and William Wordsworth in their Personal and Literary Relationship' (unpublished diss. Indiana 1961), pp 154-5.

6. [J. Hillis] Miller, *The Disappearance of God* [*Five Nineteenth-Century Writers* (Cambridge, Mass: Harvard University Press 1963)], p 23.

7. Geoffrey Hartman, *Wordsworth's Poetry, 1787-1814* (New Haven: Yale University Press 1964), p 33.

8. The most useful account of this Neoplatonic 'epistrophe' or spiritual return, in its relation to Romanticism, appears in M. H. Abrams, *Natural Supernaturalism: Tradition and Revolution in Romantic Literature* (New York: Norton 1971), pp 148ff.

9. *Posthumous Works of Thomas De Quincey,* ed Alexander H. Japp (London: Heinemann 1891), I, 12.

10. Judson S. Lyon, *Thomas De Quincey* (New York: Twayne 1969), also sees two organizing clusters of concern in the *Suspiria,* one theoretical (pertaining to dreams) and one 'mythical' (centering on lost pariah figures) (pp 97-8). My own sense that the *Suspiria's* underlying myth is concerned with personal imaginative strength is of course diametrically opposed to Lyon's.

11. Blake is cited here and elsewhere in this chapter for illustrative reasons. One senses the presence of the universal man in these visions not through some adventitious comparison with Blake (of whom De Quincey knew probably only a little) but rather in the likely influence of the ancient mystical tradition of the macrocosmic man, the cabbalic 'Adam Kadmon,' which both Blake and De Quincey, among other Romantics, put to use in their imagery. See Abrams, *Natural Supernaturalism,* pp 158 ff, for a useful discussion of this tradition of the cosmic man.

12. A curious analogue to this process occurs in some speculations of Marx, which try to account for the charm that ancient literature retains in an industrial age. Marx associates the 'childhood' of civilization with individual childhood and suggests that one's nostalgia for the latter extends itself to the former. See Peter Demetz, *Marx, Engels, and the Poets,* trans Jeffrey L. Sammons (Chicago: University of Chicago Press 1967), pp 68-9.

13. The notion of the Dark Interpreter as a 'second self' appears in [Lane] Cooper, *The Prose Poetry of Thomas De Quincey* [(Leipzig: Verlag von Dr. Seele

1902)], pp 45-6; [Françoise] Moreux sees in the Dark Interpreter the archetypal figure of the underworld guide (*Thomas De Quincey* [*: la vie, l'homme, l'oeuvre* (Paris: Presses Universitaires de France 1964)], p 491), whereas [Roger J.] Porter views the figure as a 'mediator between the destructive and redemptive powers in De Quincey' ('The Double Self [:Autobiography and Literary Form in Gibbon, De Quincey, Gosse and Edwin Muir' (unpublished diss. Yale 1967)],' p 144).

14. Northrop Frye notes the resemblance of Savannah-la-Mar to Atlantis in 'The Drunken Boat,' *Romanticism Reconsidered,* ed Northrop Frye (New York: Columbia University Press 1963), p 18.

15. Cf. the analogous (but more macabre) city in the sea of Poe, which Georges Poulet considers as a metaphor for the dream world (*Studies in Human Time* [trans Ellioff Coleman (Baltimore: Johns Hopkins University Press 1956)], p 330).

16. See Miller, *The Disappearance of God,* p 73.

17. See *Posthumous Works,* I, 16-23.

Texts and Abbreviations

The standard edition of De Quincey's works is *The Collected Writings of Thomas De Quincey,* edited by David Masson, 14 volumes (Edinburgh: Adam and Charles Black 1889-90). All quotations from De Quincey except those specifically noted below or in my notes are taken from this edition and are cited in the text by volume and page number.

Quotations from the following works of De Quincey are cited in the text by the appropriate abbreviation and page number:

C The Confessions of an English Opium-Eater (London: Taylor and Hessey 1822). This is the first edition of the original version of the *Confessions.*

D A Diary of Thomas De Quincey, 1803, edited by Horace A. Eaton (London: Noel Douglas, n.d.)

SP Confessions of an English Opium-Eater and Suspiria de Profundis (Boston: Ticknor, Reed, and Fields 1853). This volume contains the first reprint of the original *Blackwood's Edinburgh Magazine* series of the *Suspiria:* 57 (March, April, June 1845), 269-85, 489-502, 739-51; 58 (July 1845), 43-55).

D. D. Devlin (essay date 1983)

SOURCE: "The Art of Prose," in *De Quincey, Wordsworth and the Art of Prose,* Macmillan Press, 1983, pp. 101-21.

[*In the following essay, Devlin examines De Quincey's claims regarding "the hidden capacities of prose" to express passion and "grandeur."*]

'To walk well, it is not enough that a man abstains from dancing.'

I

In the 'General Preface' of 1853 to James Hogg's Edinburgh edition of his collected works, De Quincey drew attention to the variety of his prose and to the originality of his prose-poems or impassioned prose. He made three divisions of what he had written; the largest section of his work was made up of what he called 'essays', which he defined as writings 'which address themselves to the understanding as an insulated faculty'. Essays present a problem and try to solve it, and the only questions to be asked are 'what is the success obtained?' and (as a separate question) 'What is the executive ability displayed in the solution of the problem?' Even today nearly all these essays are entertaining, informative and lively; but there was nothing new in De Quincey's way of treating such external subjects, and the only originality is to be found in De Quincey's use of paradox for polemical purposes. The second division of his work consisted of what he called 'Autobiographic Sketches', and for these he claimed little 'beyond that sort of amusement which attaches to any real story, thoughtfully and faithfully related'. At times, however, the narrative rose 'into a far higher key'; for these moments he asked from the reader 'a higher consideration', and, in fact, they occurred when the narrative ceased for a while; when no story carried the reader forward, when nothing of external interest could appeal to him, when simply there was 'nothing on the stage but a solitary infant, and its solitary combat with grief—a mighty darkness, and a sorrow without a voice'. Such moments, claims De Quincey, have far more than mere amusement to offer; in them he has tried 'to see and measure these mystical forces which palsy him', and has attempted 'to pierce the haze which so often envelops, even to himself, his own secret springs of action and reserve'. Such passages are scarcely to be distinguished (another example in De Quincey of distinction without difference?) from the third division of his prose; 'a far higher class of compositions' in which he ranks the **Confessions** 'and also (but more emphatically) the **Suspiria de Profundis**'. And here De Quincey lays claim to originality; both works are 'modes of impassioned prose ranging under no precedents that I am aware of in any literature'. The only confessions of the past that have interested men are those of St. Augustine and Rousseau. 'The very idea of breathing a record of human passion . . . argues an impassioned theme' and 'impassioned, therefore, should be the tenor of the composition'. But in St. Augustine's *Confessions* there is only one 'impassioned passage' (on the death of his young friend in the fourth Book); in Rousseau's *Confessions* 'there is not even so much. In the whole work there is nothing grandly affecting but the character and the inexplicable misery of the writer.'[1]

De Quincey makes 'haughtier pretensions' for originality in the conception of these writings than for their execution; but the new areas of experience which he explored could not be separated from the prose which revealed them. No one, indeed, insisted more than De Quincey that 'manner blends inseparably with substance' and that matter and style, mind and style, even character and style, were indissolubly bonded or, to use one of his own favourite words, 'coadunated'. 'Were a magnificent dedication required,' he writes, 'were a *Defensio pro Populo Anglicano* required, Southey's is not the mind, and, by a necessary consequence, Southey's is not the style, for carrying such purposes into full and memorable effect.' Style, he claims elsewhere, is an indirect expression of a writer's 'nature and moral feelings'. The prevailing tone of Charles Lamb's style 'was in part influenced (or at least sustained) by his disgust for all which transcended the naked simplicity of truth'. Above all, in any writing where the thoughts are subjective, 'in that same proportion does the very essence become identical with the expression, and the style become confluent with the matter'.[2]

Even as a child De Quincey had been aware of how difficult it was in the ordinary language of men to communicate, for example, his 'solitary combat with grief':

> My mother was predisposed to think ill of all causes that required many words: I, predisposed to subtleties of all sorts and degrees, had naturally become acquainted with cases that could not unrobe their apparellings down to that degree of simplicity. If in this world there is one misery having no relief, it is the pressure on the heart from the *Incommunicable*. And, if another Sphinx should arise to propose another enigma to man—saying, What burden is that which only is insupportable by human fortitude? I should answer at once—*It is the burden of the Incommunicable.*
>
> (Masson, III, 315)

At that time nothing which offered itself to his rhetoric 'gave any but the feeblest and most childish reflection of my past sufferings'. Later his impassioned prose would communicate all that he now found incommunicable; not simply the sufferings of childhood, but its dreams, sudden intuitions, forebodings, its inexplicable sorrows and sudden memories, its half hints of connections between past and present and future. De Quincey makes it clear that his 'dreaming tendencies' were 'constitutional and not dependent on laudanum'. When he tells of his childhood dreams of 'terrific grandeur' it is because he believes that 'psychological experiences of deep suffering or joy first attain their entire fulness of expression when they are reverberated from dreams'.[3]

De Quincey's dreams, and the word includes waking visionary moments, are the best known things about his childhood, but he communicated more than these. Two incidents in his life before he reached his second birthday left 'stings in my memory so as to be remembered at this day'; that is, sixty years later. One was, indeed, a remarkable dream; but the other was 'the fact of having connected a profound sense of pathos with the reappearance very early in the spring of some crocuses'. Childhood, says De Quincey, enjoys 'a limited privilege of strength':

> The heart in this season of life is apprehensive; and where its sensibilities are profound, is endowed with a special power of listening for the tones of truth—hidden, struggling or remote.
>
> (Masson, I, 121-2)

Infancy is a separate and distinct period of a man's life, but it is also 'part of a larger world that waits for its final complement in old age'. In the second chapter of his *Autobiography,* 'The Affliction of Childhood', he tells of the death of his much loved elder sister Elizabeth at the age of nine, when De Quincey himself was six years old; but the chapter has a preliminary paragraph before he begins to describe his sister and his deep love for her:

> About the close of my sixth year, suddenly the first chapter of my life came to a violent termination; that chapter which, even within the gates of recovered Paradise, might merit a remembrance. *'Life is Finished!'* was the secret misgiving of my heart; for the heart of infancy is as apprehensive as that of maturest wisdom in relation to any capital wound inflicted on the happiness. *'Life is Finished! Finished it is!'* was the hidden meaning that, half-unconsciously to myself, lurked within my sighs; and, as bells heard from a distance on a summer evening seem charged at times with an articulate form of words, some monitory message, that rolls round unceasingly, even so for me some noiseless and subterraneous voice seemed to chant continually a secret word, made audible only to my own heart—that 'now is the blossoming of life withered for ever'. Not that such words formed themselves vocally within my ear, or issued audibly from my lips: but such a whisper stole silently to my heart.
>
> (Masson, I, 28)

The chapter ends with two short passages entitled 'Dream-Echoes of these Infant Experiences' and 'Dream-Echoes Fifty Years Later'; the afflictions of childhood becomes the afflictions of manhood. The first passage describes an episode twelve years after the death of his sister, when De Quincey was at Oxford and had tasted opium and experienced the extra power of opium dreams: 'And now first the agitation of my childhood reopened in strength; now first they swept in upon the brain with power and the grandeur of recovered life'[4]

> So feeling comes in aid
> Of feeling, and diversity of strength
> Attend us, if but once we have been strong.

In the second passage he refers to 'the transfigurings worked upon troubled remembrances by retrospects so vast as those of fifty years'.

To describe the hidden meanings that half-consciously lurked within his sighs, or explain the pathos of the crocuses, or describe 'the tones of truth' and the eruptions of memory and the transfigurings wrought by dreams upon the apprehensions and scarcely understood experiences of childhood, needed a very different kind of prose that could accommodate 'subtleties of all sorts and degrees'; a prose which by the very nature of the subject could not (as his mother wished) be brief or be expressive in a small compass. One of many extended musical metaphors describes what De Quincey wished to do in prose, and shows him doing it:

> A song, an air, a tune,—that is, a short succession of notes revolving rapidly upon itself,—how could that, by possibility, offer a field of compass sufficient for the development of great musical effects! The preparation pregnant with the future; the remote correspondence; the questions, as it were, which to a deep musical sense are asked in one passage and answered in another; the iteration and ingemination of a given effect, moving through subtle variations that sometimes disguise the theme, sometimes fitfully reveal it, sometimes throw it out tumultuously to the blaze of daylight: these and ten thousand forms of self-conflicting musical passion,— what room could they find, what opening, what utterance, in so limited a field as an air or song?

> (Masson, X, 136)

A 'remote correspondence' or the 'ingemination of a given effect' could not be achieved either by an automatically antithetic prose where in no sentence is there 'any dependency on what goes before', or by the 'lifeless mechanism' of eighteenth-century prose. Dr. Johnson's prose never 'GROWS a truth before your eyes whilst in the act of delivering it. His prose offers no process, no evolution, no movement of self-conflict or preparation'; only distinctions, 'a definite outline of limitation', antitheses and the dissipating of some 'casual perplexity'.[5] The capitalised 'GROWS' suggests that De Quincey will need to create a prose that is (he uses the word) organic and exploratory.

De Quincey needed first of all to insist that prose was an art and the equal of poetry. There had been great prose-writers in the past, but on the subject of prose style De Quincey had found 'nothing of any value in modern writers' and 'not much as regards the grounds and ultimate principles' in the Greek and Roman rhetoricians. For too long readers and critics had assumed that there could never be rules or a theory of prose since prose was considered to be merely 'the negation of verse'; and that to be a writer of prose meant only 'the privilege of being inartificial', and a dispensation from 'the restraints of metre'.

> But this is ignorance, though a pretty common ignorance. To walk well, it is not enough that a man abstains from dancing. Walking has rules of its own the more

difficult to perceive or to practise as they are less broadly *prononcés*. To forbear singing is not, therefore, to speak well or to read well: each of which offices rests upon a separate art of its own. Numerous laws of transition, connexion, preparation, are different for a writer in verse and a writer in prose. Each mode of composition is a great art; well executed, is the highest and most difficult of arts.

> (Masson, VI, 100)

It is the fluency and plasticity of prose, its slow preparation of great effects, its ability to follow the subtlest contours of experience, its power to be 'dark with Cassandra meanings', which De Quincey wants to establish. To achieve these ends the writer will have to observe 'the two capital secrets in the art of prose composition'. The first of these is 'the philosophy of transition and connection, or the art by which one step in an evolution of thought is made to arise out of another: all fluent and effective composition depends on the *connections*'. The second follows from this and is 'the way in which sentences are made to modify each other; for the most powerful effects in written eloquence arise out of this reverberation'. No sentence must be an independent whole. And length of sentence is no security, for 'German prose tends to such immoderate length of sentences that no effect of inter-modification can ever be apparent': the Germans have 'no eloquence'.[6] The art of prose is the art of being eloquent. Eloquence is poetry and power; it is the literature of powerfully moved feelings of any sort. The art of prose depends on that art of 'connexions' (De Quincey never tires of the word) which will recreate for the reader the unity imposed by dreams or memory on the randomness of experience.

Most of what De Quincey has to say about prose-style or the art of prose is description of his own impassioned prose or the eloquent prose of other writers. He is so anxious to insist on the hidden capacities of prose, its ability as great as poetry's to describe the most complex feelings and to move the reader, that he can sometimes seem to reject all other kinds of prose; 'for, unless on a question which admits some action of the feelings', he claims that 'style, properly defined, is impossible'. All prose, says De Quincey, must be judged by its appropriateness, and therefore its effectiveness. In the house of prose there are many mansions; some are bigger and more beautiful than others, but all are fit and useful for some purpose. Addison has an apt grace in a certain line of composition, 'but it is only one line among many, and it is far from being among the highest'.

Governing everything De Quincey says about prose is the traditional notion of decorum. No prose style is 'absolutely good—good unconditionally, no matter what the subject'. For too long readers have assumed that a simple prose was the best prose and was adequate for any subject; Swift,

Defoe and Addison are therefore selected as models. But simple, good prose of this kind was very common in the eighteenth century. The fact that hundreds of religious writers managed effective simple prose should surprise no one, since all that the subject required was 'plain good sense, natural feeling, unpretendingness' and some skill in 'putting together the clockwork of sentences'. Their subject rightly rejected all ornament. 'All depends upon the subject.' The 'unelevated and *unrhythmical*' style of Addison or Swift can manage many things; the prose of *Gulliver's Travels,* for example, is '*purposely* touched slightly with that dulness of circumstantiality which besets the excellent, but somewhat dull, race of men,—old sea-captains'. But 'grand impassioned subjects insist upon a different treatment; and there it is that the true difficulties of style commence', and there it is that 'Master Jonathan would have broke down irrecoverably'.[7] The simple style is right for simple things;

> [but] there is a style transcending these and all other modes of simplicity by infinite degrees, and in the same proportion impossible to most men: the rhythmical—the continuous—what in French is called the *soutenu;* which to humbler styles stands in the relation of an organ to a shepherd's pipe. This also finds its justification in its subject; and the subject which *can* justify it must be of a corresponding quality—loftier, and, therefore, rare.
>
> (Masson, III, 51)

Everything is subject to the laws of decorum; but a writer of any talent and sense will consciously and inevitably obey such laws, because (style and subject being one) having 'no grand impassioned subject' he could neither wish nor need nor be able to deal with such a subject. Southey's mind, for example, was 'not sustained by the higher modes of enthusiasm', and therefore he had not the style to plead passionately against oppression. 'His style is *therefore* good, because it has been suited to his themes,' and his themes were not of a kind 'to allow a thought of eloquence, or of the periodic style which a perfect eloquence instinctively seeks'. The direct style of Charles James Fox is good and is justified by its subject; he was 'simple in his manners, simple in his style, simple in his thought'. Addison was incapable of 'impassioned grandeur' and of 'any expression of sympathy with the lovely, the noble, or the impassioned'.[8] In every case De Quincey finds that the limits of the writer's style are the limits of his world.

II

But De Quincey had new and larger worlds to explore and conquer. His own experiences and dreams in childhood his deep, deep memories and the later pains of his opium dreams had convinced him of the 'one uninterrupted bond of unity running through the entire succession of experiences, first and last'; his profoundest conviction was of

'the dark sympathy, which runs underground, connecting remote events like a ground-swell in the ocean'; and his wish was to reveal in his prose the else 'undiscoverable web of dependency of one thing on another'.[9] This conviction of remote correspondences, of 'filaments fine but inseverable' which gave a unity and coherence where to the eye of vulgar logic none existed, showed itself in many other ways than in his own impassioned prose. It led him, appropriately, to a richly sympathetic account of Coleridge's conversation. What most impressed De Quincey was the way in which Coleridge could traverse 'the most spacious fields of thought by transitions the most just and logical':

> What I mean by saying that his transitions were 'just' is by way of contradistinction to that mode of conversation which courts variety through links of *verbal* connexions. Coleridge, to many people . . . seemed to wander; and he seemed then to wander the most when, in fact, his resistance to the wandering instinct was greatest—viz., when the compass and huge circuit by which his illustrations moved travelled farthest into remote regions before they began to revolve. Long before this coming round commenced most people had lost him, and naturally enough supposed that he had lost himself. They continued to admire the separate beauty of the thoughts, but did not see their relations to the dominant theme.
>
> (Masson, II, 152-3)

What De Quincey admires here is that poetic logic which Coleridge had said was 'as severe as that of science; and more difficult, because more subtle, more complex, and dependent on more and more fugitive causes'.[10] De Quincey, using the word as Coleridge had used it, declared that he had 'a logical instinct for feeling in a moment the secret analogies or parallelisms that connected things else apparently remote'; and in his autobiography said that he neglected 'harsher logic', and connected the separate sections of his sketches 'not by ropes and cables, but by threads of aerial gossamer'. The same concern for connections, for the 'filaments' which create unity, explains his reluctance to comment much on individual lines of verse; a certain line is 'not a good line *when insulated*' but is better 'in its connexion with the entire succession of which it forms part'.[11] And the same passion for the unity born of connections explains De Quincey's surprising enthusiasm for Ricardo and political economy; 'it is eminently an organic science' for every part 'acts on the whole as the whole again reacts on and through each part'.[12]

De Quincey, then, wished to explore new worlds of experience and needed a new prose for the purpose. He had found no help, he said, in either modern writers on prose or in the ancient rhetoricians, and was therefore obliged 'to collect my opinions from the great artists and practitioners' rather than from the theorists. He found the examples he needed in three places: in Greek prose-writers, especially Herodotus and Demosthenes; in some English seventeenth-century writers such as Sir Thomas Browne and Jeremy Taylor; and in Burke.

Herodotus and Demosthenes had one great advantage: they wrote in Greek; and

> the Greek is, beyond comparison, the most plastic of languages. It was a material which bent to the purposes of him who used it beyond the material of other languages; it was an instrument for a larger compass of modulations; and it happens that the peculiar theme of an orator imposes the very largest which is consistent with a prose diction. One step further in passion, and the orator would become a poet.
>
> (Masson, III, 63-4)

De Quincey believed that in his own prose he had, indeed, taken that 'one step further in passion'; he wanted above all to make English prose 'an instrument for a larger compass of modulations', a language 'plastic' enough to follow the very contours of his own subtle, complex, barely communicable experiences.

Herodotus was his favourite. De Quincey seems to be thinking of his own digressive method in dozens of magazine articles and biographical sketches when he says of Herodotus that he was 'a writer whose works do actually, in their major proportion, not essentially concern that subject to which by their translated title they are exclusively referred; or even that part which *is* historical often moves by mere anecdotes or personal sketches'.[13] But, of course, De Quincey sees Herodotus as the 'Father of Prose', as 'the leader of prose composition'. 'And if it is objected that Herodotus was *not* the eldest of prose writers, doubtless, in an absolute sense, no man was.' But 'Herodotus was to prose composition what Homer, six hundred years earlier, had been to Verse'. He was 'a great liberal artist' in prose, 'an *intellectual* potentate'[14] who established prose as an art with separate laws of its own, 'laws of transition, connexion, preparation'. Herodotus was a *power* in literature. Isocrates is condemned; his style is not organic; he 'cultivated the *rhythmus* of his periods' and to this end sacrificed 'the freedom and natural movement of his thoughts'. Demosthenes, in spite of his many gifts, rarely pursued a theme with 'the requisite fulness of development or illustration'. His faults can be blamed on his audience who, 'being always on the fret,—kept the orator on the fret'. He could not, dared not, be eloquent; 'hence arose short sentences; hence the impossibility of the long, voluminous sweeps of beautiful rhythmus'. His style is spirited and animated but not full of 'continuous grandeur'. He had to keep 'the *immediate*—the instant' before his eye and could not quit 'the direct path of the question' even for any purpose of 'ultimate effect'.

'Continuous grandeur' was to be found in certain prose writers of the seventeenth century. De Quincey found that

'Donne, Chillingworth, Sir Thomas Browne, Jeremy Taylor, Milton, South, Barrow form a *pleïad,* a constellation of seven golden stars such as no literature can match in their own class'. They provide the 'highest efforts of eloquence in all English literature'.[15] It is not simply the grandeur or musicality of their prose which appeals to De Quincey, but its continuity. The innumerable musical images which he uses to describe its effect are not attempts to praise the mere sound and sonority of seventeenth-century periods, but to suggest the complex, organic, musical structure which organises separate items into a rich unity. Every single separate sentence is, indeed, 'a subject for complex art'; but 'it is in the *relation* of sentences that the true life of composition resides'. Sentences, he says, must have 'logic and sensuous qualities—rhythm, for instance, or the continuity of metaphor';[16] as a piece of music has a theme which recurs in a dozen different ways enriched, elaborated, extended, disguised, but through it all 'lurks to the last'. De Quincey argued that very often, and especially when the matter is the very feelings of the writer, the manner *is* the matter. His own matter was very often the continuity of experience, the slow preparation of effects, the transubstantiation through memory of childhood incidents, the revelation of connections. Seventeenth-century prose provided examples of the art of preparation and connections; of an eloquence which 'prolongs itself, repeats itself, propagates itself'. Jeremy Taylor's prose is 'all alive with the subtlety of distinctions'; but this is happily matched and balanced by 'the commanding passion and intensity' of his theme, which gives 'a final unity to the tumultuous motions of his intellect'.

> *Human life,* for example, *is short; human happiness is frail;* how trite, how obvious a thesis? Yet, in the beginning of the *Holy Dying,* upon that simplest of themes how magnificent a descant! Variations the most original upon a ground the most universal . . .
>
> (Masson, X, 125)

Where but in Sir Thomas Browne, exclaims De Quincey, is it possible to find 'music so Miltonic, an intonation of such solemn chords' as are struck in *Urn-Burial;* but these chords are simply the beginning of 'a melodious ascent as of a prelude to some impassioned requiem'.[17]

Burke had much in common with these earlier prose-writers, but was an even more congenial revelation of the resources of prose since he moved 'among moving things and uncertainties, as compared with the more stationary aspects of moral philosophy'. In his writings there is process, evolution, preparation, and always some 'oblique glance' at 'remote affinities'. At the very moment of writing, 'every truth, be it what it may, every thesis of a sentence, *grows* in the very act of unfolding it'. Whatever he begins with receives 'a new determination or inflexion at every clause'. His prose is perpetually creative; and, as with Jeremy Taylor, the connections, coherence and unity of his writing are provided by continuity of metaphor. In both writers 'the fancy' (by which De Quincey means the imagination) 'is the express organ of the judgment'. In some writers the metaphors are 'mere embellishments':

> Now, on the contrary, in Taylor and Burke, everything figurative is part and parcel of the process of thinking, and incarnated with the thought; it is not a separate descant *on* what they think, but a part of the organ, by which they think . . . no passage can be produced from either of them, in which the imagery does no more than repeat and reflect the naked unillustrated thought, but that there is some latent feature, or relation of the truth revealed by the imagery, which could not have been revealed without it.

Burke was 'overmastered by the weight of the truth he was communicating'; and so it was 'the necessity of his understanding, dealing with subtle truths, that required a perpetual light of analogy, (the *idem in altero*) for making them apprehensible'.[18]

Not all prose-writers of the seventeenth century merit the same praise as De Quincey gives to his *pleïad*. Bacon suffers from 'the shorthand style of his composition, in which the connexions are seldom fully developed'. Burton is too 'disjointed'; he is 'not so much fanciful as capricious; his motion is not the motion of freedom, but of lawlessness; he does not dance but caper'.[19] For De Quincey, who insists strongly that a writer's mind and style are inseparable, a 'disjointed' style would make it impossible for him to communicate his sense of the connectedness of things, his instinct for secret analogies. A disjointed or simple style can communicate only disjointed or simple things. De Quincey himself is seldom (in the modern sense of the word) a witty writer; a book that is 'aphoristic', he says, is a book 'without a plan'. (He applies the same criticism to long poems. Pope's *Essay on Criticism* is 'a collection of independent maxims . . . having no natural order or logical dependence', and therefore no power of connections in the thought.) A simple style, 'the *style coupé* as opposed to the *style soutenu*' prefers 'the subsultory to the continuous' and therefore cannot explore the subtleties of a subject.

> In order to be brief a man must take a short sweep of view; his range of thought cannot be extensive; and such a rule, applied to a general method of thinking, is fitted rather to aphorisms and maxims, as upon a known subject, than to any process of investigation as upon a subject yet to be fathomed.
>
> (Masson, X, 166)

Fox's style was simple because there were 'no waters in *him* turbid with new crystallizations; everywhere the eye could see to the bottom'.[20] The 'general terseness' of Junius and his short sentences would have been impossible if he had been forced into 'a wider compass of thought' or into

a 'higher subject'. The simplicity and clarity of maxim or aphorism are easy 'where new growths are not germinating', but they can be purchased at too high a rate. Without that elaborate prose which is necessary to growth and full expression, 'much truth and beauty must perish in germ'. (Bacon, says De Quincey, was merely an acorn; Jeremy Taylor was an oak.) Its music may, indeed, be 'dark with Cassandra meaning'; but 'who complains of a prophet for being a little darker in speech than a post-office directory'.[21]

It is not only written prose that De Quincey considers, but the prose of conversation. In 'the velocities and contagious ardour' of conversation, there was likely to be even less distinction between a man's mind and interests and their necessary reflection in his language. Conversation, too, was an art; but by conversation De Quincey means something closer to the Platonic dialectic than the negative energy (as he saw it) of even so mighty a talker as Dr. Johnson. And conversation could make creative thinking perhaps more possible than written prose; it was certainly congenial to De Quincey and his purpose:

> I felt (and in this I could not be mistaken, as too certainly it was a fact of my own experience) that in the electric kindling of life between two minds . . . there sometimes arise glimpses and shy revelations of affinity, suggestion, relation, analogy, that could not have been approached through any avenues of methodical study.

And again he used his favourite musical imagery:

> Great organists find the same effect of inspiration, the same result of power creative and revealing, in the mere movement and velocity of their own voluntaries . . . these *impromptu* torrents of music create rapturous *fioriture,* beyond all capacity in the artist to register, or afterwards to imitate.
>
> (Masson, X, 268-9)

De Quincey praises the best conversation for being organic, for being an example of what he calls 'organology'. The great (though rare) gift of conversation, and the reason why he valued it, was that in it 'approximations are more obvious and easily effected between things too remote for a steadier contemplation'. I have already quoted De Quincey's description of Coleridge's conversation; elsewhere he writes that the distinguishing feature of his talk was its 'power of vast combination': he 'gathered into focal concentration the largest body of objects *apparently* disconnected'.[22] On the other hand Southey's 'epigrammatic form of delivering opinions has a certain effect of *clenching* a subject'; it is 'the style of his mind' which leads him to adapt 'a trenchant, pungent, aculeated form of terse, glittering, stenographic sentences', ending with a 'contentious aphorism' which informs the reader that 'the record is closed'.[23]

A description by Thomas Hood of De Quincey's own talk makes him sound like Coleridge and shows how close for De Quincey the connection was between writing and talking:

> I have found him at home, quite at home in the midst of a German Ocean of literature, in a storm, flooding all the floor, the table and the chairs—billows of books, tossing, tumbling, surging open—on such occasions I have willingly listened by the hour, whilst the philosopher, standing with his eyes fixed on one side of the room, seemed to be less speaking than reading from 'a handwriting on the wall'. Now and then he would diverge for a Scotch mile or two, to the right or left . . . but he always came safely back to the point where he had left, not lost the scent, and thence hunted his topic to the end.[24]

Disjointed, discontinuous, aphoristic prose or talk was not suitable for noting the 'links uniting remote incidents which else seemed casual and disconnected'; a simple prose would not wait for De Quincey's truths to unfold themselves. It could not treat of a moment in childhood that 'reproduces itself in some future perplexity' and which years later would 'come back in some reversionary shape'. It could not show how the child was father of the man, or follow the movement of dreams or the eruptions of memory through involutes, 'the almost infinite intricacy of their movements'. And again De Quincey uses the analogy of music to describe the 'organic' prose which his subjects demanded:

> A curve is long in showing its elements of fluxion; we must watch long in order to compute them; we must wait in order to know the law of their relations and the music of the deep mathematical principles which they obey. A piece of music, again, from the great hand of Mozart or Beethoven, which seems a mere anarchy to the dull, material mind, to the ear which is instructed by a deep sensibility reveals a law of controlling power, determining its movements, its actions and reactions, such as cannot be altogether hidden, even when as yet it is but dimly perceived.[25]

De Quincey's search is always for the law that explains and gives coherence to the richness and seeming randomness of separate experiences and 'connects the scattered phenomena into their rigorous unity'.

Nothing can be creatively understood in a limited prose. When De Quincey comments on prose-writers he finds that the inadequacy of their prose reflects the limits of their imaginative intelligence. It is in comments on Lamb and Hazlitt that De Quincey makes most clear his belief in the inseparability of manner and matter in prose, and in the capacity and resourcefulness of prose to do what his great contemporaries were doing in verse. Hazlitt was neither an eloquent writer nor a comprehensive thinker, and his failures could be seen in his prose:

> Hazlitt was not eloquent, because he was discontinuous. No man can be eloquent whose thoughts are abrupt, insulated, capricious, and (to borrow an impressive word from Coleridge) non-sequacious. Eloquence resides not in separate or fractional ideas, but in the relations of manifold ideas, and in the mode of their evolution from each other. It is not indeed enough that the ideas should be many, and their relations coherent; the main condition lies in the *key* of the evolution, in the *law* of the succession. The elements are nothing without the atmosphere that moulds, and the dynamic forces that combine.

> (Masson, V, 231)

All De Quincey's favourite pejorative adjectives are here and all his favourite terms of praise; and the reference to Coleridge reminds us of the very different subjects and different prose which De Quincey has in mind. The '*key* of the evolution' and 'the *law* of the succession' are the necessary subtle logic of poetry which Coleridge discovered from his schoolmaster at Christ's Hospital and which is the necessary condition of all eloquent writing in verse or prose. De Quincey wants a prose that 'moulds' and 'combines' all the fragments into a unity. Subtle truths require 'a perpetual light of analogy'; but Hazlitt does not provide the continuity of metaphor which might provide this light, since 'his brilliancy is seen chiefly in separate splinterings of phrase or image' which 'spread no deep suffusions of colour'. It could not be otherwise, because his thoughts 'were of the same fractured and discontinuous order as his illustrative images—seldom or never self-diffusive'. Hazlitt had no principles upon any subject. He viewed all things 'under the angle which chance circumstances presented, never from a central station'; he was at the mercy of every random impulse, and so his 'eternal paradoxes' have not even 'a momentary consistency amongst each other', but are always 'shifting, collapsing, moulding and unmoulding themselves like the dancing pillars of sand of the deserts'.[26] Lamb, it is true, did not agree with de Quincey's comments on Hazlitt; but, then, Lamb's prose suffered in the same way. His mind, like Hazlitt's in its 'movement and style of feeling', was 'discontinuous and abrupt'. He necessarily confined himself to 'short flights' since his own 'constitution of intellect sinned by this very habit of discontinuity'. He shrank from 'the continuous, from the sustained, from the elaborate'; when he writes, his sentiment does not 'propagate itself'. De Quincey finds that other features of Lamb's mind would have argued this weakness in his prose by analogy; he was totally insensible to music, to the complex structure of music and therefore of prose composition.

'The English Mail-Coach'[27] is an example of the new areas of experience which De Quincey made fit subjects for prose, and of the prose 'without precedent in any literature' that could encompass and express them. The article, in two parts, had originally appeared in *Blackwood's Magazine* in 1849, four years after the *Suspiria de Profundis* with which it naturally belongs. When De

Quincey prepared the article for the Collective Edition of his writings in 1854 he divided it into its present three sections and De Quincey's editor notes that 'great care was bestowed in the revision. Passages that had appeared in the magazine articles were omitted; new sentences were inserted; and the language was retouched throughout'.[28] In spite of this care, De Quincey mentions in a 'Postscript' added in 1854 (but not usually included in modern editions) that not all readers had understood the article:

> To my surprise, however, one or two critics, not carelessly in conversation, but deliberately in print, professed their inability to apprehend the meaning of the whole, or to follow the links of the connexion between its several parts. I am myself as little able to understand where the difficulty lies, or to detect any lurking obscurity, as these critics found themselves to unravel my logic.
>
> (Masson, XIII, 328)

He then goes on to make clear the 'logic' and 'links of connexion' which will establish (to use phrases from elsewhere in his work) 'the close convergence of the several parts' and will demonstrate how the whole essay is 'a coherent work of art'.

The three sections of **'The English Mail-Coach'** are 'The Glory of Motion', 'The Vision of Sudden Death' and 'Dream-Fugue', to which De Quincey appended the explanatory sub-title, 'Founded on the Preceding Theme of Sudden Death'. The several titles hint already at the 'logic' and 'connexions' of the parts; the words 'glory', 'vision' and 'dream' make clear that De Quincey is dealing with heightened states of awareness. (Wordsworth in 'Strange Fits of Passion' had dared to tell his story only in 'the Lover's ear' who alone would understand the interconnections and associations of things under the influence of deep feeling.) He explains that the whole paper had its origin in the second section, 'The Vision of Sudden Death':

> Thirty-seven years ago, or rather more, accident made me, in the dead of night, and of a night memorably solemn, the solitary witness of an appalling scene, which threatened instant death in a shape the most terrific to two young people whom I had no means of assisting, except in so far as I was able to give them a most hurried warning of their danger; but even *that* not until they stood within the very shadow of catastrophe, being divided from the most frightful of deaths by scarcely more, if more at all, than seventy seconds.
>
> (Masson, XIII, 328-9)

From this scene, he says, 'the whole of this paper radiates as a natural expansion'; and in the two final pages of 'The Vision of Sudden Death' De Quincey makes clear how and why this radiating will occur.

De Quincey had been helpless to avert the threatening collision of the two coaches and when it happened he was sure that the woman had been killed. As the coaches collided and then separated he looked back on the scene which 'wrote all its records on my heart for ever'. A few lines later he is sure that the sight of the woman throwing her arms 'wildly to heaven will never depart from my dreams'; in the closing lines of the section a curve in the road removed the scene from his eyes and 'swept it into my dreams for ever'. In his 'Postscript' De Quincey adds that it was swept into 'a rolling succession of dreams, each one as tumultuous and changing as a musical fugue'. It is natural, therefore, that the final section should recount these dreams or nightmares.

If this had been all, every reader could have unravelled the logic and followed the thread of transition and connection; for in his dreams all the 'elements of the scene blended, under the law of association'. But there were other elements in the dream which readers failed to understand because by no associations could they be connected with 'The Vision of Sudden Death': 'Waterloo, I understand, was the particular feature of the "Dream-Fugue" which my censors were least able to account for'. The explanation does not lie, as De Quincey might have pleaded, in the thought that for thousands of men Waterloo offered visions of sudden and violent death: De Quincey's law of association is tauter and its logic more subtle than this. It is found in that phrase in the 'Postscript' where he says that it was from the second section that 'the whole of this paper radiates as a natural expansion'. The 'whole' of his paper includes the relaxed, even chatty, first section in which De Quincey explains that it was via the regular mail-coach services from London that news of great national victories such as Waterloo was carried to the provinces. His imagination had already been seized by this in the first section: 'The mail-coach it was that distributed over the face of the land, like the opening of apocalyptic vials, the heart-shaking news of Trafalgar, of Salamanca, of Vittoria, of Waterloo.' Such excited imaginings had already done something to heighten the state of consciousness which, in the second section, the beauty of the night and dawn and the sudden threatening danger raised still further.

The general title of the article, **'The English Mail-Coach'**, is an accurate one; the elements in the dreams are to be traced back to happenings and feelings in section one which preceded by at least several hours the vision and near disaster of the second section. Even on the very first page of the opening section De Quincey had already hinted at how the article would end:

> But, finally, that particular element in this whole combination which most impressed myself, and through which it is that to this hour Mr. Palmer's mail-coach system tyrannises over my dreams by terror and terrific beauty, lay in the awful political mission which at that time it fulfilled.
>
> (Masson, XIII, 272)

The disparate elements in the first two sections are picked up again in the 'Dream-Fugue', and, in De Quincey's excellent phrase, 'the whole is gathered into unity by a reflex act of meditation'.

De Quincey explains two other apocalyptic elements in his dreams, two other examples of separate experiences which, when recurring in dreams, because 'symbolically significant'. In his dreams the mail-coach galloped through a vast cathedral; and a sculpture of a dying trumpeter suddenly rose to his feet and 'unslinging his stony trumpet, carried it, in his dying anguish, to his stony lips'. De Quincey explains these by association: the vision of the cathedral derived from a section of the road on which the mail-coach was travelling when the collision happened, where the trees met overhead in arches to suggest a vast nave; and the incident of the dying trumpeter was 'secretly suggested by my own imperfect effort to seize the guard's horn and to blow a warning blast'.

The three parts of **'The English Mail-Coach'** make an extended, subtle, elaborate 'spot of time' or 'involute'. The whole is 'organic—i.e. . . . . each acts upon all, and all react upon each', and its art is in the connections of the several parts. To catch and make real for us the shades and shapes, the hints and 'hieroglyphic suggestion' of dreams, De Quincey fashioned a fluid prose that was accurate but, of necessity, not precise; a prose of 'atmosphere' (his word) that could mould and communicate with power his own 'gleams of original feeling, [his] startling suggestions of novel thought'.

Notes

1. [David Masson (ed.), *The Collected Writings of Thomas De Quincey* (14 vols.) (London, 1896)], I, 9-15.

2. Ibid. II, 346; III, 51; X, 230.

3. Ibid. I, 49.

4. Ibid.

5. Ibid. X, 270-2.

6. Ibid. II, 65.

7. Ibid. V, 91; III, 51; XI, 17.

8. Ibid. II, 346; XI, 36; XI, 21.

9. Ibid. III, 413; [A. H. Japp (ed.), *The Posthumous Works of Thomas De Quincey* (London, 1893)], II, 134-5.

10. *Biographia Literaria,* ch. 1.

11. Masson, XI, 469.

12. Ibid. III, 431.

13. Ibid. VI, 100.

14. Ibid. VI, 101-2.

15. Ibid. III, 266.

16. Ibid. X, 258-9.

17. Ibid. V, 234; X, 108; X, 105.

18. Stuart M. Tave (ed.), *New Essays by De Quincey* (Princeton, 1966) pp. 202-3.

19. Masson, X, 109 n.; 102.

20. Ibid. XI, 36.

21. Ibid. XI, 37.

22. Ibid. V, 204.

23. Ibid. II, 328-9.

24. [James Hogg, *De Quincey and His Friends* (London, 1895)], pp. 53-4.

25. Japp, *Posthumous Works,* II. 108.

26. Tave, *New Essays by De Quincey,* 203, 193; Masson, III, 83.

27. Masson, XIII, 270-330.

28. Ibid. XIII, 270 n.

John C. Whale (essay date 1984)

SOURCE: "Literature as Resistance and Power," in *Reluctant Autobiography,* Barnes & Noble Books, 1984, pp. 40-77.

[*In the following essay, Whale claims that De Quincey's autobiographical writings reveal a fertile tension between the power of imagination and the truth of past experience.*]

RESISTANCE

In De Quincey's difficult situation as a journalist his progress in the act of composition could be both thwarted and encouraged by the varying degrees of intimacy and publicity connected with his context. An alignment of public and private responsibilities created a dichotomy in his appraisal of his own imaginative powers. This dichotomy is also present in his critical writings on other authors. De Quincey's work as a literary critic reveals how imaginative 'power' is in his view related to difficulty and suffering. The apparently negative experience of composition could eventually turn out to have been creative.

One of De Quincey's fundamental concerns as an autobiographer—his notion of fidelity to past experience—could be threatened by capricious acts of memory or consolidated by affirmative acts of memory. The experience of composition constituted a revelatory context because the medium of language could radically compromise directness of communication, at the very least by providing the possibility of ambiguities. In the same way that De Quincey managed to operate as a magazine writer in the formal compromise of the public pact so, too, a fruitful compromise could arise out of this opposition from language itself. De Quincey's critical statements are informed by his experience of composition and they show how, ultimately, a source of power lay in this opposition: the resistance provided De Quincey with a dynamic foundation on which to structure his reluctant autobiography.

De Quincey's conception of a work of literature rests, to a large extent, on his belief that the act of composition is a revelatory context, and that at their best certain types of literature (those most congenial to his own interests) convey the writer's own sense of this to the reader. It is for this reason that he celebrates Burke's prose as opposed to Johnson's:

> For one moment, reader, pause upon the spectacle of two contrasted intellects, Burke's and Johnson's: one an intellect essentially going forward, governed by the very necessity of growth, by the law of motion in advance; the latter essentially an intellect retrogressive, retrospective, and throwing itself back on its own steps . . . The result from these original differences of intellectual constitution . . . is, that Dr. Johnson never, in any instance, GROWS a truth before your eyes whilst in the act of delivering it or moving towards it. All that he offers up to the end of the chapter he had when he began. But to Burke, such was the prodigious elasticity of his thinking, . . . the mere act of movement became the principle or cause of movement. Motion propagated motion, and life threw off life. The very violence of a projectile as thrown by *him* caused it to rebound in fresh forms, fresh angles, splintering, coruscating, which gave out thoughts as new (and as startling) to himself as they are to his reader.[1]

It might seem strange to find De Quincey opposed to a retrospective vision, but the characteristic nature of his experience of autobiographical writing would seem to lie in that ambivalent and seemingly contradictory phrase 'necessity of growth'. While Burke's elasticity of thinking implies an openness, it also involves a potentially hazardous submission. In such a phrase De Quincey combines an organic with a mechanical appreciation of the creative process.

This kind of combined response from De Quincey derives from his experience as a periodical and newspaper writer. The distinction between Burke and Johnson appears in the context of a debate on style as it is governed by oratory and conversation. De Quincey's evaluation of Burke's apparently spontaneous movement is imbued with the past experience of his own career, and a realisation of a particular type of literature and a particular type of effect. Using an analogy which stresses the mechanical side of his appreciation De Quincey explains the principle governing his own context:

> Like boys who are throwing the sun's rays into the eyes of a mob by means of a mirror, you must shift your lights and vibrate your reflections at every possible angle, if you would agitate the popular mind extensively. Every mode of intellectual communication has its separate strength and separate weakness,—its peculiar embarrassments, compensated by peculiar resources.[2]

The extent to which De Quincey writes of a mechanical part being played in literary production qualifies, but does not necessarily contradict, his promotion of the organic concept. The mechanical opposition provided by language is, in fact, conducive to revelatory acts of imagination. It is the combination of these two aspects which is crucial in De Quincey's critical thinking:

> Style may be viewed as an *organic* thing and as a *mechanic* thing. By organic, we mean that which, being acted upon, reacts, and which propagates the communicated power without loss. By mechanic, that which, being impressed with motion, cannot throw it back without loss, and therefore soon comes to an end. The human body is an elaborate system of organs; it is sustained by organs. But the human body is exercised as a machine, and as such may be viewed . . . Now, the use of words is an organic thing, in so far as language is connected with thoughts, and modified by thoughts. It is a mechanic thing in so far as words in combination determine or modify each other.[3]

This combination of organic and mechanic leads De Quincey to an understanding of how spontaneity and self-consciousness in art can happily co-exist. It is particularly from his insistence on the mechanic side, however, that De Quincey comes to a full appreciation of self-consciousness. In an autobiographical work it can provide a further means of self-definition. As we saw earlier, a text can convey this self-consciousness of the writer in opposition to his craft. In an autobiographical work the act of composition could lead to another reassessment of the original past experience. This would seem to constitute an analogous situation to that described by Wordsworth in a famous statement from his *Preface to the Lyrical Ballads*, 1802:

> I have said that Poetry is the spontanous overflow of powerful feelings: it takes its origin from emotion recollected in tranquillity: the emotion is contemplated till by a species of reaction the tranquillity gradually disappears, and an emotion, similar to that which was before the subject of contemplation, is gradually produced, and does itself actually exist in the mind.[4]

Considering De Quincey's case we may say that this secondary emotion rather than being conducive to and present in composition, as Wordsworth argues for himself, is actually produced by the writer's recognition of resistance in composition. Because this recognition is of resistance, and often of difficulty, it tends to obscure its affinity with Coleridge's fine perception of creativity in his attempt to define the distinguishing characteristic of poetry: 'What is this? It is that pleasurable emotion, that peculiar state and degree of excitement, which arises in the poet himself in the act of composition'.[5] Geoffrey Hill has written that, 'Readers of the *Biographia Literaria* may note that Coleridge's concern is not so much with thought as with "the mind's self-experience in the act of thinking"',[6] and that this 'self-experience' is most clearly realised by the process of '"win[ning one's] way up against the stream"'.[7] De Quincey possessed a kindred sort of concern especially as regards the peculiar difficulties of autobiographical writing. Contemplating the popular style of his own age he felt that he was denied this kind of 'self-experience':

> Direct objective qualities it is always by comparison easy to measure; but the difficulty commences when we have to combine with this outer measurement of the object another corresponding measurement of the subjective or inner qualities by which we apply the measure; that is, when besides the objects projected to a distance from the spectator, we have to allow for variations or disturbances in the very eye which surveys them. The eye cannot see itself; we cannot project from ourselves, and contemplate as an object, our own contemplating faculty, or appreciate our own appreciating power.[8]

The possibility which De Quincey considers here, of being confined within his own subjective viewpoint, is one to which he was not always willing to accede. It was precisely this power of self-projection which solaced his subjective literary explorations, and which he was eager to recognise in other writers. Indeed, he frequently argues that an appreciation of 'our appreciating power' is the life-force of subjective literature. Again, he emphasises the extent to which this is a necessary, inevitable result, predetermined by the writer's situation, rather than a sought-after and self-inspired achievement:

> To hang upon one's thoughts as an object of conscious interest, to play with them, to watch and pursue them through a maze of inversions, evolutions, and harlequin changes, implies a condition of society . . . like that in the monastic ages, forced to introvert its energies from mere defect of books.[9]

This kind of situation, where external realities which could aid the writer in his aim of self-definition are denied, led De Quincey to an awareness of the important part which could be played in the act of self-definition by the resistance offered by language itself. It appeared to be a closed circuit where the writer was forced to find all the material within himself, though he was aided by the discrepancy between the thought or feeling and the adequacy of the particular word or words to describe it. His own knowledge of this experience made him draw a firm distinction between subjective and objective literature. But far from lamenting the nature of the former, he was ready to assert its peculiarity and praise its benefits. Again, writing of his own age he states:

> The excess of external materials has sometimes oppressed their creative power, and sometimes their meditative power. The exuberance of *objective* knowledge—that knowledge which carries the mind to materials existing *out* of itself, such as natural philosophy, chemistry, physiology, astronomy, geology, where the mind of the student goes for little and the external object for much—has had the effect of weaning men from subjective speculation, where the mind is all in all and the alien object next to nothing, and in that degree has weaned them from the culture of style.[10]

It is De Quincey's own knowledge of an insulated position which makes him aware of the extent to which form and content cannot be dissociated. Although, in that last quotation, he appears to refer to style as if it can be considered separately, he does so to correct an audience which is dependent on such separations.

It is in his emphasis on this resistance offered in the particular context of almost completely subjective writing that De Quincey offers his most valuable commentaries on the workings of the imagination. When this debate between form and content necessarily converges on autobiographical writing the urgency of De Quincey's address to his audience highlights the importance of that type of writing for him as a manifestation of his own identity:

> There arises a case entirely different, where style cannot be regarded as a *dress* or alien covering, but where style becomes the *incarnation* of the thoughts. The human body is not the dress or apparel of the human spirit: far more mysterious is the mode of their union. Call the two elements A and B; then it is impossible to point out A as existing aloof from B, or *vice versa*. A exists in and through B; B exists in and through A . . . Imagery is sometimes not the mere alien apparelling of a thought, and of a nature to be detached from the thought, but it is the coefficient that, being superadded to something else, absolutely *makes* the thought as a *third* and separate existence.
>
> In this third case, our English tendency to undervalue style goes more deeply into error than in the other two. In those two we simply underrate the enormous services that are or might be rendered by style to the interests of truth and human thinking; but in the third case we go near to abolish a mode of existence . . . There are many ideas . . . which are only to be arrested and realized by a signal *effort*—by a struggle and *nisus* both of reflection and of large combination.[11]

The importance placed on 'signal *effort*' here, and the depth of sympathy in the repetition of 'existence' should intensify concern for De Quincey's achievement of popularising the Romantic theory of the organic conception of language. In his recognition that such an incarnation 'absolutely *makes* the thought as a *third* and separate existence', De Quincey intimates the extent to which he associates this organic concept with the revelatory capacity of the act of composition. It is a recognition of the vital but necessarily separate entity of a work of art. It is separate because of the resistance offered by language to the pre-conceived idea. It is vital because the resistance demands an amalgam which is not simply a compromise, but a union which creates a new statement. The autobiographical implications of this are that the autobiographical statement is seen to exist in its own right, not simply as an extension or a reference back to the non-literary life of the writer: and that this recognition is accompanied by a further act of self-definition precisely because of this separation.

The process of writing is also revelatory because it articulates experiences which have not been linked together and drawn out into coherency. In the very mechanics of composition, in the demand for unity and the desire for continuity, De Quincey realises that subjective material is brought to a stage where it is recognisably different from the experience in its pre-literary form. This discovery is intimately linked to his appreciation of the organic capacity of language. Using an analogy of refracted light which is significantly similar to the one he used to describe the requisite tactics of a popular writer, and which captures well an appreciation of the mechanical in physical alignment with the organic, De Quincey again seeks to affirm his knowledge of the peculiarity of subjective writing:

> he who has to treat a vague question, such as Cicero calls a *quaestio infinita,* where everything is to be furnished out of his own peculiar feelings, or his own way of viewing things . . . soon finds that the manner of treating it not only transcends the matter, but very often, and in a very great proportion, *is* the matter. In very many subjective exercises of the mind,—as, for instance, in that class of poetry which has been formally designated by this epithet (meditative poetry, we mean . . .), the problem before the writer is to project his own inner mind; to bring out consciously what yet lurks by involution in many unanalysed feelings; in short, to pass through a prism and radiate into distinct elements what previously had been even to himself but dim and confused ideas intermixed with each other. Now, in such cases, the skill with which detention or conscious arrest is given to the evanescent, external projection to what is internal, outline to what is fluxionary, and body to what is vague,—all this depends entirely on the command over language as the one sole means of embodying ideas; and in such cases the style, or, in the largest sense, *manner,* is confluent with the matter.[12]

De Quincey acknowledges, when making a similar statement, his indebtedness to Wordsworth for enunciating the idea that language is 'the *incarnation* of thoughts'. But it is in his deviation from this mainstream Romantic doctrine, promulgated by his close associates Wordsworth and Coleridge, that De Quincey has dissatisfied his critics. He continued to make distinctions between rhetoric and eloquence, between 'the literature of knowledge and the literature of power', which are thought to exclude too extensively from the organic concept.

By viewing language as resistance, because of its ability to transform in the process of clarifying preconceived experiences, De Quincey seems to have viewed it as an intermediary agent to which the literary statement or effect was the necessary consequence. Language is in many respects an outside agent reacting against the assimilation of personal experience. De Quincey's considerations of 'style' as opposed to 'content' do not simply represent a naïve contradiction of the organic doctrine mentioned above, but contain the evidence of his autobiographical experience. It is as a means, as an intermediary which is capable of affecting the mind of the reader (who can also be the author) that language reveals its revelatory capacity, its 'external projection' which creates, orders and clarifies. This is especially true of feelings, as De Quincey well knew:

> But to feel is not to feel consciously. Many a man is charmed by one cause who ascribes the effect to another. Many a man is fascinated by the artifices of composition who fancies that it is the subject which has operated so potently.[13]

The inference to be drawn from De Quincey's appreciation of the revelatory nature of the act of composition is that it involved both an organic re-creation and a mechanical, external resistance.

De Quincey's numerous comments upon rhetoric and didactic poetry testify to his belief in language as an indirect means of communicating literary content. The very strengths of these types of literature, as he understands them, rely upon a profound comprehension of this indirectness. De Quincey's descriptions of the seventeenth century prose writers Sir Thomas Browne and Jeremy Taylor show that he valued their works particularly for their quality of capturing that same self-consciousness in the act of writing evident in Burke and Coleridge. His descriptions of their work illustrate his discussions on rhetoric and eloquence. Significantly, he praises Browne and Taylor for their ability to move between both 'rhetoric' and 'eloquence', and stresses how the imaginative life of their work is achieved through the alternating opposition of these two 'types': 'in them only, are the two opposite forces of eloquent passion and rhetorical fancy brought into an exquisite equilibrium,—approaching, receding,—attracting, repelling,—blending, separating,—chasing and chased as in a fugue'.[14] Referring to Jeremy Taylor alone he observes:

> that one remarkable characteristic of his style which we have already noticed, viz. the everlasting strife and fluctuation between his rhetoric and his eloquence, which maintain their alternations with force and inevitable recurrence, like the systole and diastole, the contraction and expansion, of some living organ.[15]

Again we have an example of opposition which results in a mechanical exercise of an organic medium. 'Rhetoric' for De Quincey usually means an intellectual mind-play with a given subject, whereas 'eloquence' refers to an urgency of emotion which contains the same evidence of a dramatic enactment of the mind of the writer. His definition of these two is saturated with Wordsworthian overtones:

> By Eloquence we understand the overflow of powerful feelings upon occasions fitted to excite them. But Rhetoric is the art of aggrandizing and bringing out into strong relief, by means of various and striking thoughts, some aspect of truth which of itself is supported by no spontaneous feelings, and therefore rests upon artificial aids.[16]

Although De Quincey often uses these two terms separately and exclusively his preference was for an interrelation between them. Where one is lacking he is apt to censure. He labels Florian and Chateaubriand as 'elegant sentimentalists' precisely because they are eloquent, but never rhetorical. As a result, and most important of all, in them there is 'no flux and reflux of thought, half-meditative, half capricious'.[17] There is no doubt, in De Quincey's mind, that this motion, as evidence of imaginative life, is the most important factor in assessing a work of art. But it is in the combination of an element which 'overflows' and necessitates communication, and an element which simply brings out 'into relief . . . aspects of truth' that De Quincey contemplates a more profound dichotomy of thought about the imagination which brings him closer to Wordsworth. The terms in which Wordsworth describes the *Lyrical Ballads* closely resemble De Quincey's statements:

> I have said that each of these poems has a purpose. I have also informed my Reader what this purpose will be found principally to be: namely to illustrate the manner in which our feelings and ideas are associated in a state of excitement. But speaking in less general language, it is to follow the fluxes and refluxes of the mind when agitated by the great and simple affections of our nature.[18]

The dichotomy is evident here in Wordsworth's drawing together of a 'purpose' and the passive action of 'following'. He is claiming both a referential veracity and a deliberate construction. These two qualities are by no means mutually exclusive, but they might present some difficulty by requiring the imagination to perform a double function of creating a new truth at the same time as illuminating an old one. De Quincey's formulation of the terms 'rhetoric' and 'eloquence' seems to have been at least partly inspired by a need to satisfy his recognition of this double action of the imagination; its combined process involving a mechanical as well as an organic aspect. His reference to rhetoric's ability of 'bringing out into strong relief . . . some aspects of truth', constitutes a reliance upon the idea of mechanical combination which conforms

to an eighteenth century conception of the imagination, represented by Burke's statement that: 'the power of the imagination is incapable of producing anything absolutely new; it can only vary the disposition of those ideas which it has received from the senses'.[19] De Quincey's reference to eloquence as 'the overflow of powerful feelings' confirms his belief in the imagination as a vital force, and thereby reveals his allegiance to the Romantic attitude. In his demand for both sides he was, of course, attempting to formulate for himself a satisfactory explanation of the double action of the imagination analogous to that which Coleridge stated in his *Biographia Literaria,* and which has been described by M. H. Abrams in the following terms:

> despite Coleridge's intoxication with the alchemical change wrought in the universe by his discovery of the organic analogy, he did not hesitate to save, and to incorporate into his own theory, the mechanical philosophy he so violently opposed. Mechanism is false, not because it does not tell the truth, but because it does not tell the whole truth.[20]

De Quincey's terms remain distinct and individual from Coleridge's, however, tending to be more appropriate to the imaginative compromise of his career as a periodical journalist, and to his specialist needs as an autobiographer, as much as to his professed mistrust of Coleridge's distinctions with their metaphysical implications.

Granted that the creative process could for him both create and illuminate according to this double action, De Quincey's comments on didactic poetry and rhetoric, with their emphasis on indirectness might be found to be disconcerting. Here the imaginative effect or 'power' is elicited from the resistance or opposition provided by the subject matter, and not a direct consequence of it. It is as if the subject exercises its difficulty in order to promote the real imaginative concern of the writer. In the act of overcoming this difficulty the imaginative powers are stimulated. This suggests the nature of De Quincey's career as a newspaper and a periodical writer where he was forced into composition, often reluctantly, and where his translations and plunderings from other works, in the best instances, show how he overcame such tedious labours by imaginatively re-creating them in a process of 'rifacimento'. It is this background which partly accounts for the following pronouncement upon the 'true idea of didactic poetry':

> Either the poet selects an art which furnishes the *occasion* for a series of picturesque exhibitions . . . and in that case it is true that he derives part of his power from the art which he delivers,—not, however, from what is essential to the art, but from its accidents and adjuncts: either he does this, or else . . . so far from seeking in his subject for any part of his *power,* he seeks in *that* only for the *resistance* with which he

contends by means of the power derived from the verse and the artifices of style.[21]

By '*resistance*' here De Quincey has more in mind than the mere consolation afforded by a difficult intellectual exercise; and this would seem to be substantiated by his discussion of the justification of Virgil's *Eclogues*. The first possible justification he considers is: 'As a *difficult* and intractable subject, by way of a *bravura,* or passage of execution'.[22] But this is followed by the serious qualification that: 'This is not a very elevated form of poetic art, and too much like rope-dancing'.[23] Clearly, resistance alone, and especially for its own sake, is not to be considered of high merit: it is to be a means to an end. According to De Quincey then, art is to be achieved as an indirect effect of difficulty and, as we have seen before, must contain a form of revelation, which in an autobiographer's situation may be equated with a further level of self-awareness. It is this act of indirect revelation which dictates his appreciation of didactic poetry. The power of this type of work still depends upon its ability to communicate the 'flux and reflux' of a mind agitated upon the subject. To this extent it 'follows', as Wordsworth says, and is therefore an act of imagination. An ultimate directness or full explicitness would travesty this power of imitation, and so De Quincey states quite categorically:

> No poetry can have the function of teaching. It is impossible that a variety of species should contradict the very purpose which contradistinguishes its *genus* . . . Poetry, or any one of the fine arts (all of which alike speak through the genial nature of man and his agitated sensibilities), can teach only as nature teaches, as forests teach, as the sea teaches, as infancy teaches— viz., by deep impulse, by hieroglyphic suggestion. Their teaching is not direct or explicit, but lurking, implicit, masked in deep incarnations. To teach formally and professedly is to abandon the very differential character and principle of poetry. If poetry could condescend to teach anything it would be truths moral or religious. But even these it can utter only through symbols and actions.[24]

De Quincey's idea of imaginative power as a by-product of resistance overcome conforms to the nature of his enforced periodical writings. It can be seen that it is also in keeping with an appreciation of art as imitation, which first began with Aristotle's notion of *mimesis*. But it is through De Quincey's emphasis upon the impure or difficult medium of language that this idea of imitation is articulated by him in the term '*idem in alio*', which again finds a close parallel in Wordsworth's 'similitude in dissimilitude'.[25] With De Quincey our attention is focused first of all on this difference and so our appreciation of his work as an autobiographer should begin with a denial of any expectation of his autobiography being simply a directly revelatory statement. On the contrary, the revelatory capacity of his autobiography is understood to operate upon a profound recognition that the very disparity between the written word and the experience to which it refers, is conducive to a sharper, conscious appreciation of that experience. In De Quincey's autobiography acts of self-discovery, far from being inconsistent with a highly-wrought, elaborate prose, are thought to be the necessary consequences of artifice. In this sense, too, the autobiographical statement is neither single nor direct. It is with these complexities that De Quincey's autobiography can enact its important function of defining and analysing thoughts and feelings which do not usually come within the range of such conscious scrutiny:

> The unevolved thoughts which pass through the youngest—the rudest—the most inexperienced brain, are innumerable; not detached—voluntary thoughts, but thoughts inherent in what is seen, talked of, experienced, or read of. To evolve these, to make them apprehensible by others, and often even to bring them within their own consciousness, is very difficult to most people; . . . and the power, by which this difficulty is conquered, admits of endless culture: and, amongst the modes of culture, is that of written composition. . . . the direct purpose is to exercise the mind in unravelling its own thoughts, which else lie huddled and tangled together in a state unfit for use, and but dimly developed to the possessor's own consciousness.[26]

Although autobiographical writing undertakes this important action of 'unravelling' fleeting and complexly combined experiences, De Quincey forthrightly denies that it is an easy task. On the contrary, he considers it to be the province of a specialist involved in a delicate and refined activity. At least, this seems to be the implication of his word 'culture', and his reaction against the normal state of unanalysed experiences. He appears to be advocating that such an ability is to be acquired only after numerous attempts: it is a skill which requires a concerted effort if it is to be perfected.

It is by realising the possibilities of artistic elaboration that the sharpest, the most important references can be made to real experience. The benefit of a mature literary autobiography is not simply that its artistic quality therapeutically distances or harmonises the original experiences, but that its sophistication provides an ordered and sensitive counter which can more accurately define those experiences. De Quincey's fastidious concern for rhythm in his prose, which has traditionally supported his literary reputation, and his demand for a musical continuity in the most 'impassioned' passages of his autobiographical writings, are founded upon his realisation that the very distancing ornamentation of art is more conducive to the assessment of 'real' feelings. This would explain both his dislike of an English tradition of naïve confession, which he voices in the opening to his own *Confessions of an English Opium-Eater,* and his contempt for the various forms of realism which were popular in his time. He reacted strongly against the contemporary delight, and faith, in circumstantial details: he objected to the current practice in biographical and autobiographical writing of giving 'the inevitable roll-call of a man's life'. The reasons for this point of view, as we have seen, lie in De Quincey's faith in the viability of art as an indirect form of imitation. It is a point of view which he seems to have shared with Coleridge. Both men used the same analogy of waxwork figures to illustrate their point; De Quincey when describing the distanced, abstracted nature of Greek drama,[27] Coleridge when attempting to define the nature of imitation itself: 'If there be likeness to nature without any check of difference, the result is disgusting, and the more complete the delusion, the more loathsome the effect'.[28] The more artistically achieved the representation the greater the possibility it provides for viewing the experience. There is no disgust to obstruct the view; the distance acts cathartically and allows the reader, after the immediate recognition of difference, to return all the more eagerly to consider the correspondence to the experience in view.

It is for this reason that De Quincey reacts against a directly confessional utterance: he realises that such a method might obtrude upon the sensibility of his reader and thereby cut him off from the possibility of acting in a sympathetic or mediatory capacity. De Quincey's carefully constructed prose (especially that in **'The English Mail-Coach'**) which deliberately declares its own elaborateness, thus performs for him a double function, of registering the earnestness and 'impassioned' feeling of the writer at the same time as invoking the sympathetic attention of the reader. In such a way this very elaborateness is argued to be a 'natural' technique: 'Metre is naturally and necessarily adopted in cases of impassioned themes, for the very obvious reason that rhythmus is both a cause of impassioned feeling, an ally of such feeling, and a natural effect of it';[29] De Quincey's attention to style in the special province of subjective literature is in keeping with the requirements of his task as an autobiographer. The very literary complexity of his work, according to the critical statements we have examined, furthered his aim of a mediated vision which could be both objective and yet demand sympathy from the reader. By saying that 'rhythmus is both a cause of impassioned feeling, an ally of such feeling, and a natural effect of it', De Quincey is also taking into account the idea of self-awareness in the act of composition. The rhythmic aspect of style, as he described it in Burke, contains its own principle of motion, and in that sense it is an ally to De Quincey in offsetting the more resistant difficulties of composition. The continuity afforded by rhythm allows for, even dictates, the progression of the autobiographical statement. It is exactly this kind of continuity which De Quincey fails to find in Hazlitt and Lamb. Of the latter's prose he says: 'It does not prolong itself—it does not repeat itself—it does not propagate itself'.[30] It is this self-propagating style which

De Quincey seems to find most congenial to that type of writing which seeks to communicate the very movement of the mind of the writer upon the subject:

> No man can be eloquent whose thoughts are abrupt, insulated, capricious, and (to borrow an impressive word from Coleridge) non-sequacious. Eloquence resides not in separate or fractional ideas, but in the relations of manifold ideas, and in the mode of their evolution from each other. It is not indeed enough that the ideas should be many, and their relations coherent; the main condition lies in the *key* of the evolution, in the *law* of the succession. The elements are nothing without the atmosphere that moulds, and the dynamic forces that combine.[31]

Again, he refers to the process of combination as 'dynamic', a term which can be thought to signify its importance in the creation of something not simply combined but new. It is in the difficulty of achieving such a modulation (which involves a submission to that '*law* of succession') that a further level of self-consciousness is added to the act of autobiography.

Even though such a harmonised and continuous effect often successfully carries the varied fluctuations of the autobiographer's act of exploration, and his attempt to convey that very continuity, De Quincey occasionally seems to deliberately interrupt it. He intrudes with a further level of commentary which makes direct appeals to the reader and which makes explicit the reference to the nature of the text and its aims. As we shall see in Chapter Four, this further level of commentary performs a number of functions for De Quincey, not least being a mediatory agent which offers an opportunity for apology, justification and explanation. But for our present purpose of '*resistance*', it is also a register of difficulty and a concession to the compromise of the periodical context; it can mediate the autobiographical vision but it is also inherent in De Quincey's literary situation.

De Quincey compared the function of the chorus in Greek drama to the Dark Interpreter of his dreams; an analogy could be drawn between his idea of the chorus and the function he performs in making these direct appeals and explanations to the reader. He refutes the moral function of the chorus in order to place the emphasis on sympathy:

> One great error which remains to be removed is the notion that the chorus either did support, or was meant to support, the office of a moral teacher. The chorus simply stood on the level of a sympathizing spectator, detached from the business and the crash of catastrophe; and its office was to guide or interpret the sympathies of the audience.[32]

While De Quincey's direct interruptions to the reader are often detached from the narrative chronology or the rhythmical progression mentioned above, they often draw attention to the immediate predicament of the act of composition. Frequently they show De Quincey's recognition of his context—the necessity to cater for the readership of the various magazines. To this extent this further level of commentary was enforced; but it also provided a mediating alternative to the rhythmical continuum of the autobiographical statement. It could thus aid De Quincey and the reader, as well as providing a shared experience located in the technique. De Quincey could turn this to his advantage, both subtly manipulating and openly challenging his reader. His description of the characteristic style of Demosthenes recognises this kind of situation (the periodical compromise), is aware of some of the possibilities, but does not speculate on how they can be turned to his advantage:

> It is one which grew naturally . . . from the composition of his audience. His audience . . . being, in fact, always on the fret,—kept the orator always on the fret. Hence arose short sentences; hence the impossibility of the long, voluminous sweeps of beautiful rhythmus which we find in Cicero; hence the animated form of apostrophe and crowded interrogations to the audience. This robs him of a large variety of structure applied to the logic, or the embellishment, or the music of his composition. His style is full of life, but not . . . full of pomp and continuous grandeur. On the contrary, as the necessity of rousing attention, or of sustaining it, obliged the Attic orator to rely too much on the *personality* of direct question to the audience . . . In all things, the *immediate*—the instant—the *praesaens praesentissimum,* was kept steadily before . . . [him] . . . by the mere coercion of self-interest.[33]

That phrase 'the *personality* of direct question to the audience' illuminates De Quincey's own role and technique of creating a literary personality. He recognised, especially in Lamb, a new form of contemporary writing which made a special demand upon the reader by requiring him to recognise such a personality. In his essay **'Charles Lamb'** De Quincey wrote:

> There is in modern literature a whole class of writers . . . standing within the same category: some marked originality of character in the writer becomes a co-efficient with what he says to a common result; you must sympathise with this *personality* in the author before you can appreciate the most significant parts of his views.[34]

The sympathy demanded by the familiar essayist seems to have been born out of a compromise operating against the dictates of the writer, but eventually acknowledged as a source of comfort, and a possible new tactic with which to manipulate the reader.

The significance De Quincey places on the idea of 'resistance' may be viewed as a search for a viable means of communication; not simply overcoming the compromise we have noticed, but being born out of it and successfully

exploiting it as a means of power. The difficulties of composition are not, for De Quincey, one of the peripheral effects which linger in the finished product, but an integral and important part of his material. As we shall see later, in an analysis of his *Suspiria de Profundis,* a good deal of his autobiography concerns itself with the problems of its own genesis. Similarly, De Quincey finds in his appreciation of the mechanical or aggregating part played in creativity, a correspondent power of revelation and creation to the acknowledged organic factor. The resonances of this are most pertinent to his aim of defining his past self: clarification and accurate reconstructions of subjective experiences lead to a new sense of identity; but they are also felt as a fruitful alternative or an extra specific illustration in the formulation of the mainstream Romantic aesthetic. De Quincey's critical statements are central not as theoretical speculations, but as informants of his own practice as an autobiographer. Granted that his compromised situation could be a source of strength, it now remains to analyse its effects, or in De Quincey's words, to assess its 'power'.

POWER

The revelatory aspect of De Quincey's autobiographical writings, their ability to deliver new 'truths' to their audience—'to bring out consciously what yet lurks by involution in many unanalyzed feelings'[35] works in conjunction with a plea for the reader to imagine the difficulties involved in this task. In De Quincey's case the psychological or analytic aspect of subjective writing joins with an equally strong principle to make the reader not simply understand, but sympathise. The 'power' of De Quincey's autobiographical writings is the product of a rare combination of two types of literature which are more usually separate according to his own most famous critical distinction:

> In that great social organ which, collectively, we call literature, there may be distinguished two separate offices that may blend and often *do* so, but capable, severally, of a severe insulation, and naturally fitted for reciprocal replusion. There is first, the literature of *knowledge;* and secondly, the literature of *power.* The function of the first is—to teach; the function of the second is—to *move:* the first is a rudder; the second, an oar or sail. The first speaks to the mere discursive understanding; the second speaks ultimately . . . to the higher understanding or reason, but always *through* affections of pleasure and sympathy.[36]

Although this statement concentrates on the separation of the two types the initial admission at least allows for the possibility of creating an autobiography which is analytic yet demands the imaginative sympathy which may be equated with 'power'.

The revelatory capacity of De Quincey's autobiographical writings would seem to depend on that skill of the autobiographer which deciphers, discovers, rather than that which creates. This seems to be confirmed in another instance where De Quincey concerns himself with the same distinction between the effects of his two types of literature:

> The true antithesis to knowledge, in this case, is not *pleasure,* but *power.* All that is literature seeks to communicate power; all that is not literature, to communicate knowledge. Now, if it be asked what is meant by communicating power, I, in my turn, would ask by what name a man would designate the case in which I should be made to feel vividly, and with a vital consciousness, emotions which ordinary life rarely or never supplies occasions for exciting, and which had previously lain unwakened, and hardly within the dawn of consciousness—as myriads of modes of feeling are at this moment in every human mind for want of a poet to organize them? I say, when these inert and sleeping forms *are* organized, when these possibilities *are* actualized, is this conscious and living possession of mine *power,* or what is it?[37]

The emphasis here is on illumination rather than creation, and in De Quincey's use of the word 'organize', we might again consider him to be referring to the dynamic capacity of combination which is capable of 'realizing' or throwing into relief new possibilities because of the effect of juxtaposition. The revelatory capacity of autobiography might be considered to exist in this opportunity it allows for conscious scrutiny. Its extraordinary quality resides not so much in the experiences it discovers as in the potency of its aspect which makes such scrutiny possible. The autobiography is thus democratic as regards its material, but specialist in its technique. Sigmund K. Procter recognised in his study of De Quincey's literary 'theory' that:

> His definition is in psychological terms and carries virtually no suggestion of the supernatural. High as he conceives the poet's function to be, he engages in no worship of the power. He tends to exalt the effect achieved by poetry, not the poet as an individual. Above all, he does not look upon the poet as one charged with the expression of the ego.[38]

By using the word 'organize' De Quincey is again exhibiting this tendency; it is a question of degree rather than an essential difference. It is this emphasis on degree which is most pertinent to his task as an autobiographer, in articulating subconscious or fleeting experiences:

> It is astonishing how large a harvest of new truths would be reaped simply through the accident of a man's feeling, or being made to feel, more *deeply* than other men. He sees the same objects, neither more nor fewer, but he sees them engraved in lines far stronger and more determinate: and the difference in the strength makes the whole difference between consciousness and subconsciousness.[39]

For De Quincey, it was Wordsworth who exemplified this quality in a writer; he was thus responsible for bringing 'many a truth into life, both for the eye and for the understanding'.[40] Although De Quincey refers to 'the eye . . . and the understanding' here, it is not to those two that his attentions are usually directed. He is more interested in the emotive force attendant upon the discovery, and the conviction which supports it as a truth. The 'great distinction of Wordsworth', he wrote, 'is the extent of his sympathy with what is *really* permanent in human feelings, and also the depth of his sympathy'.[41] It is the insistence first of all on feelings, and a reaction against the 'mere understanding' which characterises the nature of De Quincey's communication of personal discoveries. Feeling is both the cause of the discovery and the means by which it is conveyed through sympathy. When De Quincey writes of 'power' in this context of psychological discovery he seems to be describing the effect on his own feelings as much as the value of the discovery either to himself or to others. Of course, the discovery, by drawing experiences out to be observed by the conscious mind, allows an individual to locate and distinguish the forces which are operating within, and so to that extent allows for greater control. De Quincey senses the degree to which people are governed by unconscious impulses, the existence of which may not always be known. 'Power' in this sense might refer to the secret springs of action upon which conscious behaviour depends:

> And of this let everyone be assured—that he owes to the impassioned books which he has read many a thousand more of emotions than we can consciously trace back to them. Dim by their origination, these emotions yet arise in him, and mould him through life, like forgotten incidents of his childhood.[42]

When De Quincey relates his experience of discovering one of these 'moulding emotions' he is concerned to register the excitement of the discovery rather than to document it scientifically. Although an analytic skill is required to locate and define the discovery in question, it is secondary to the purpose of communicating the imaginative impact that has occurred.

This impact is primarily one of excitement because the discovery has opened up new possibilities. De Quincey's use of the word 'power' relates to the fact that the range of experience has been expanded by the act of discovery. This explains his enthusiasm and his delight at Wordsworth's example. Autobiography, as we have seen, as well as being a vehicle to convey these new possibilities, also adds to them because of the revelatory nature of the act of composition. In this double sense it explores the possibilities of subjective contemplation and is pleased to find new sources of action, new types of feeling and new evidence of vital processes operating within an individual. Autobiography is a means of constantly expanding the depths of personality rather than simply a means of fixing to allow for rational investigation. It is this felt depth of personality which excites De Quincey rather than the external space of the world of nature. His reaction to *King Lear* shows how literary 'power' is connected to the expansion of subjective horizons:

> when I am thus suddenly startled into a feeling of the infinity of the world within me, is this power, or what may I call it? Space, again, what is it in most men's minds? The lifeless form of the world without us, a postulate of the geometrician, with no more vitality or real existence to their feelings than the square root of two . . . Henceforth, therefore, I shall use the antithesis power and knowledge as the most philosophical expression for literature (that is, Literae Humaniores) and anti-literature (that is, Literae didacticae.)[43]

This insistence on feelings and the reaction against 'knowledge' has been noted by the two main critics of De Quincey's own critical abilities—Sigmund K. Procter and John E. Jordan. The latter declares that 'the *primum mobile* . . . as generally in [his] criticism, was that something "produced to my feelings an effect"',[44] while Procter asserts that, 'he chose an anti-intellectualistic solution to the problem of knowledge, thus turning what was a defeat for the pretensions of reason into a victory for the claims of the feelings'.[45] Though De Quincey's distinction above is obviously extreme, he is reacting more against the non-vital aspect of the world as it manifested itself in his time, than absolutely decrying the possibilities of the geometrician or the external world in general. He speaks to the English public from a specific angle—stimulating the new literature-seeking public in one of his **'Letters to a Young Man Whose Education Has Been Neglected'**. He was well aware of the importance of the natural world to Wordsworth, though his references to its importance for himself are very limited. Nevertheless, there is one which satisfies his relation to the natural world which at the same time stresses the nature of the society to which he belongs: on one occasion he contemplates living in isolation in the forests of Canada; the reason is that:

> in England, and in all moderate climates, we are too slightly reminded of nature or the focus of nature. Great heats, or great colds . . . or great hurricanes, as in the West Indian latitudes, recall us continually to the sense of a powerful presence, investing our paths on every side; whereas, in England, it is possible to forget that we live amongst greater agencies than those of men and human institutions. Man, in fact, "too much man", as Timon complained most reasonably in Athens, was then, and is now, our greatest grievance in England.[46]

In his *Suspiria de Profundis* De Quincey similarly reacts against what he calls 'the vortex of the merely human',[47] that is the morbid, demoralising influence of contemporary city life. The 'merely human' refers to a potential grandeur which has not been realised. In its revelatory capacity autobiography reaches beyond the everyday world of habit and dull routine and makes known new possibilities. It is

claimed that by making people feel vividly as opposed to an appeal 'to the mere discursive understanding'[48] life or literature effects an expansion of personality:

> Were it not that human sensibilities are ventilated and continually called out into exercise by the great phenomenon of infancy, or of real life as it moves through chance and change, or of literature as it recombines these elements in the mimicries of poetry . . . it is certain that, like any animal power or muscular energy falling into disuse, all such sensibilities would gradually droop and dwindle. It is in these great *moral* capacities of man that the literature of power, as contradistinguished from that of knowledge, lives and has its field of action.[49]

De Quincey's emphasis on feelings as the essential constituents of his notion of *'power'* need not detract from the moral responsibility of his work. This was no casual or vague belief on his part; as we have already seen, his distinction between genius and talent (which is a product of his experience as a periodical journalist) also rests on this belief in the morally invigorating effect of deep feeling:

> genius is that mode of intellectual power which moves in alliance with the *genial* nature—i.e. with the capacities of pleasure and pain,—whereas talent has no vestige of such an alliance, and is perfectly independent of all human sensibilities. Consequently, genius is a voice of breathing that represents the *total* nature as well as his knowing and distinguishing nature . . . Genius is the language which interprets the synthesis of the human spirit with the human intellect, each acting through the other; whilst talent speaks only from the insulated intellect. And hence also it is that, besides its relation to suffering and enjoying, genius always implies a deeper relation to virtue and vice; whereas talent has no shadow of a relation to *moral* qualities.[50]

While true to De Quincey's experience of the act of composition, due to its attention to 'suffering and enjoying', this statement is not confined to his own insular position. By placing it against its mature intellectual background we can see again how the periodical compromise provides an alternative context in which to culture the imagination rather than simply 'compromising' it. This background gives us the material for a sharper assessment of the type of 'power' which could be produced in that compromise as a result of a fruitful kind of resistance.

The important moral function De Quincey assigns to the feelings in artistic production and effect finds some authority and justification in Kant's *Critique of Aesthetic Judgement* and his pre-Critical work *Observations on the Feeling of the Beautiful and Sublime*. A section of the latter was translated by De Quincey and appeared in *The London Magazine* in 1824. As T. Goldthwait has written in the introduction to his translation of Kant's earlier work,[51] the importance of the Sublime lies in its function of 'uniting

. . . aesthetic with moral experiences'[52] and it 'emerges as an important moral component of the person'.[53] Kant also provides a subjective viewpoint for this moral/aesthetic union: '*The various feelings of enjoyment* or of displeasure rest not so much upon the nature of the external things that arouse them as upon each person's own description to be moved by these to pleasure or pain'.[54] The starting-point of Kant's analysis is to investigate the response of the beholder, the capacity to feel either the effects of the sublime or the beautiful. According to Kant, 'the sublime *moves*', and 'the mien of a man who is undergoing the full feeling of the sublime is earnest, sometimes rigid and astonished'.[55]

This emphasis on the beholder, and the central concern with the effects of the sublime (that is to say, how it registers itself) help to explain Procter's assertion that 'One principal difference between De Quincey's literary theory and that of Wordsworth and Coleridge is that De Quincey occupies himself almost exclusively with an analysis of final effects'.[56] As a result, Procter concludes, De Quincey 'ignores for the most part the process and the agencies by which power is communicated', and therefore he tends 'to value literature . . . as communication rather than expression'.[57] Although this, as we have seen, is not strictly true, both the response of the beholder and direct communication would seem to be the natural emphases of De Quincey the autobiographer. The former may be equated in a special sense with the autobiographer's ability to behold his past self and to be conscious of himself in the very act of composition. The latter coincides with his concern for fidelity to past experience.

In Kant, therefore, De Quincey inherited an example of how his own moral sense could be reconciled to a subjective vision which relied on feelings, and feelings which were compatible with a principle of revelation and expansion. By arguing for the sublime as a moral force, Kant may have allowed De Quincey to see how feelings of awe and astonishment could accord with an exploration of his own personality which was not restricted to the 'merely human'.

De Quincey's own ideas of the sublime (which are first evident in the diary he wrote as a seventeen year old)[58] show that he was also aware and perhaps dissatisfied with the native tradition of aesthetic theory which concerned itself with the distinction between the sublime and the beautiful. The peculiarly modern relevance of the sublime for him reveals itself in his reaction against the classical notion propounded by Longinus:

> Let it be remembered that, of all powers which act upon man through his intellectual nature, the very rarest is that which we moderns call the *sublime*. The Grecians had apparently no word for it, unless it were

that which they meant by [To semnon]: for [hypsos] was a comprehensive expression for all qualities which gave a character of life or animation to the composition.[59]

Dissatisfied with most of the eighteenth century attempts on this subject, and seeking an aesthetic distinction which would accord with the revelatory nature of his autobiographical vision, and the mixture of mechanical combination and organic incarnation which occurred in its composition, De Quincey may have found congenial examples in Burke and Wordsworth. As John E. Jordan has briefly noted,[60] there is an affinity between one of De Quincey's descriptions of the '*dark* sublime' and Burke's idea of terror as one of the causes of the sublime. There are, however, more similarities, and more significant ones for our purpose of defining De Quincey's autobiographical concerns. When considering terror as a cause of the sublime Burke hints at its moral force by drawing attention to the religious nature of the experience:

> not pleasure, but a sort of delightful horror, a sort of tranquillity tinged with terror; which, as it belongs to self-preservation, is one of the strongest of all the passions. Its object is the sublime. Its highest degree I call *astonishment;* the subordinate degrees are awe, reverence, and respect, which by the very etymology of the words, shew from what source they are derived.[61]

De Quincey would have sympathised not simply with Burke's notion of terror, but his belief in the greater power of emotions involving pain and suffering:

> The passions which belong to self-preservation, turn on pain and danger; they are delightful when we have an idea of pain and danger, without being actually in such circumstances; this delight I have not called pleasure, because it turns on pain, and because it is different enough from any idea of positive pleasure. Whatever excites this delight, I call *sublime*. The passions belonging to self-preservation are the strongest of all the passions.[62]

In De Quincey's autobiography, as we shall see, 'sublime' events in his past experience can be viewed in retrospect with this kind of 'delight' which Burke describes. This delight is heightened because such events may be able to locate and explain the power motivating his subsequent life. In attempting to describe these 'sublime' events of his past life, surprising or astonishing links of continuity may be revealed. The autobiography is both a statement about the nature of his past (how it is considered by the writer at that point) and a further means of redefinition. The element of revelation or discovery which promotes the feelings of astonishment and surprise thus exists on more than one level. Alongside these the autobiography also attempts to operate on a more analytic or rational basis, but this usually follows as a consequence to the experience of discovery. These two elements are to some extent separate because the nature of the revelatory element is of a sort which possesses the whole attention of the writer. It is the power of this irrational or rather non-rational kind which 'possesses' the writer, which accords with the idea of the sublime as described by both Burke and Wordsworth.

When Burke describes the effect of the sublime produced by nature, he declares that one of the distinguishing features of 'astonishment' is its exclusive, prepossessing quality:

> The passion caused by the great and sublime in *nature,* when those causes operate most powerfully, is astonishment; and astonishment is that state of the soul, in which all its motions are suspended, with some degree of horror. In this case the mind is so entirely filled with its object, that it cannot entertain any other, nor by consequence, reason on that object which employs it. Hence arises the great power of the sublime, that, far from being produced by them, it anticipates our reasonings, and hurries us on by an irresistable force.[63]

Wordsworth in his uncompleted *The Sublime and the Beautiful* echoes Burke's description of 'astonishment' and carries further the implications of the exclusion of the rational faculty which takes place in an experience of the sublime: 'For whatever suspends the comparing power of the mind and possesses it with a feeling or image of intense unity, without a conscious contemplation of the parts, has produced that state of mind which is the consummation of the sublime'.[64] Characteristically Wordsworth sees the necessity for this suspended effect to be of temporary duration, allowing then for the action of rational and moral considerations. He seems to sense the danger of the power of the sublime:

> But if the Power contemplated be of that kind which neither admits of the notion of resistance or participation, then it may be confidently said that, unless the apprehension which it excites terminate in repose, there can be no sublimity, and that this sense of repose is the result of reason and the moral law.[65]

Both these statements about the 'suspending' effect of the sublime seem, to the two writers concerned, more appropriate to the awe-inspiring effects of the external natural world, though, of course, in *The Prelude* Wordsworth traces the growth of this in an intimate involvement with his imaginative and moral life. In De Quincey's case revealed depths of personality correspond to these heights and depths of the natural world. In Burke's discussion of the sublime he would have found an alternative sort of sublime effect which concerned itself with the expanding dimensions of minutiae—which looked as if inwards rather than to the outside world. This introspective aspect of sublime astonishment which Burke delineates would be compatible with De Quincey's own subjectively-defined, autobiographical exploration, especially in the sense in which it describes an expanding depth:

> Greatness of dimension is a powerful cause of the sublime. This is too evident, and the observation too common, to need any illustration; it is not so common to consider in what ways greatness of dimension, vastness of extent or quantity has the most striking effect . . . we are more struck at looking down from a precipice, than looking up at an object of equal height . . . when we attend to the infinite divisibility of matter, when we pursue animal life into these excessively small, and yet organised beings, that escape the nicest inquisition of the sense, when we push our discoveries yet downward, and consider those creatures so many degrees yet smaller, and the still diminishing scale of existence, in tracing which the imagination is lost as well as the sense, we become amazed and confounded at the wonders of minuteness; nor can we distinguish in its effect this extreme of littleness from the vast itself.[66]

Burke's interest in 'the infinite divisibility of matter' parallels De Quincey's fascination with the divisibility not of tangible realities but emotional and intellectual ones. And it is firmly linked to his experience of composition and the stress which he places on 'combination'. In his later life he could write: 'It is not, it has not been, perhaps it never will be, understood—how vast a thing is combination'.[67] It is precisely this 'vast' quality which characterises 'combination' and which is dependent upon his awareness of 'divisibility'. Combination is such a potent force with De Quincey because it makes him all the more conscious of new depths and possibilities in his own past experience and his means of communicating it. As he says 'all words cover ideas, and many a word covers a choice of ideas, and very many ideas split into a variety of modifications'.[68]

Naturally De Quincey could find such a knowledge to be both comforting and frightening. The sublime experience in representing a suspension of the rational or comparing, quantifying faculty of the mind, constituted a release from the 'merely human'. As far as it dissolved the firm boundaries and clear outlines of his past experience and occasionally offered no prospect of conclusion or final assessment it was a threat to his own identity. In the former aspect it triumphed not only over the dull routine or 'morbid stimulation' of London life, but also over his awareness of the false promises, the delusive openings of creative experience. As we saw in the last chapter, his comments about the workings of his own imagination show how perilously close he thought it to powers of a disruptive and anarchic kind. The 'power' of the sublime as it truly registers itself is thus doubly important to him because of his knowledge of the false nature of such experiences: the power of introspection could be wasted by counterfeit attractions of the imagination.

Likewise, the expansion provided by a sublime moment forms part of De Quincey's reaction against the strong impression he has of mundane, habitual experience amounting to no more than a shadow or an illusion. His central concern as an autobiographer is to provide a continuity of experience; to be self-conscious and aware of the passage of time, feeling vividly the various levels and intensities of his life. How strongly he valued the expansive nature of a 'sublime' moment can be estimated from his consideration of this other side of his experience:

> Generally, that is, for a million against a unit, the awful mystery by which the fearful powers of death, and sorrow, and pain, and sin are locked into parts of a whole; so as, in fact, to be repetitions, reaffirmations of each other under a different phase—this is nothing, does not exist. Death sinks to a mere collective term—a category—a word of convenience for purposes of arrangement. You depress your hands, and behold, the system disappears; you raise them, it appears. This is nothing—a cipher, a shadow. Clap your hands like an Arabian girl, and all comes back. Unstop your ears, and it is muffled. To and fro; it is and is not—is not and is. And mighty heaven that such a mockery should cover the whole vision of life! It is and is not; and on to the day of your death you will still have to learn what is the truth.
>
> The eternal now through the dreadful loom is the overflowing future poured back into the capacious reservoir of the past. All the active element lies in that infinitesimal *now*. The future is not except by relation; the past is not at all, and the present but a sign of the nexus between the two.[69]

In this fragment from his *Posthumous Works* De Quincey might seem to verge on the ludicrous or melodramatic because he is dealing emotively with an idea which is usually considered as a logical platitude. Like Burke's effect of the 'sublime' De Quincey's sense of imaginative power is closely linked to a logical, investigatory ability. He may start out with analytic intentions and then be pleasantly rewarded when the powers of such a method are found to be inadequate. In the extract above it is the normal acceptance of time which appears as a mockery, an inadequate correlative to imaginative experiences—unable to register depth of feeling. When he refers to 'a mere collective term' and 'but a sign' he challenges a tacit acceptance or general understanding which does not convey the sense of dimension, the prospect which brings it alive in the mind.

De Quincey claimed that opium produced, even more dramatically, a sense of time which operated beyond the normal categories. While space and time are both altered by the effect of the drug, and it is this effect which constitutes the 'power', De Quincey's apprehension of that power seems to have been intimately associated with his logical or quantifying faculty. He seems thrilled to find the power overriding his understanding and, to some extent, relies upon this to define and communicate it:

> In the *Opium Confessions* I touched a little upon the extraordinary power connected with opium (after long

use) of amplifying the dimensions of time. Space, also, it amplifies by degrees that are sometimes terrific . . . Time becomes infinitely elastic, stretching out to such immeasurable and vanishing *termini* that it seems ridiculous to compute the sense of it.[70]

Although he claims here that 'it seems ridiculous to compute the sense of it', it would appear that just such an attempt at computation is, for De Quincey, both a natural response and a means of experiencing the full extent of the 'amplification'. As Burke recognised, the greatness of dimension which is a cause of the sublime and can result from attention to the minute details of the natural world confounds both the imagination and the 'sense'. In De Quincey's case the distinction between these two often seems to be sharply maintained, though, of course, they do work in combination with each other. In *Suspiria de Profundis,* for example, it is De Quincey's alter ego—the so-called 'Dark Interpreter' of his dreams—who suggests to him the following computation of time:

> Put into a Roman clepsydra one hundred drops of water; let these run out as the sand in an hour-glass, every drop measuring the hundredth part of a second, so that each shall represent but the three-hundred-and-sixty-thousandth part of an hour. Now, count the drops as they race along; and, when the fiftieth of the hundred is passing, behold! forty-nine are not, because already they have perished, and fifty are not, because they are yet to come. You see, therefore, how narrow, how incalculably narrow, is the true and actual present.[71]

This apparent narrowness is analogous to his previous 'mere category': both cases show how the mind cannot respond to the notion of time simply by using the standard process of logic. The intellectual or analytic intention of the mind resists and fails to accommodate the depth which is felt in the imaginative experience. The sublime moment informs the 'mere category' by expanding the narrowness of the present, and thus transcends the traditional linear progression.

It is in retrospect that De Quincey manipulates an analytic skill in order to imaginatively recreate sublime moments from his past. Even though it was precisely this part of his mind which was confounded in the original experience, it is now the use of this skill which dramatically recaptures the effect for the reader, and which is a necessary factor in controlling literary communication of complex, simultaneous, though brief psychological processes. The sublime moment is thus contained within a logical framework which accepts the usual methods of chronology and investigation. In this way 'power' is often given a greater credibility and authority, as well as being more easily understood. This is as much a concession to the reader as it is a necessary preliminary to conscious scrutiny. The logical framework mediates the primarily emotive force of the sublime moment, both for the autobiographer and for the reader.

Apart from these considerations, however, the analytic framework, though consequent to the original experience, now provides a valuable check upon it, often balancing, even correcting its extreme nature. This is especially so when as in *Suspiria de Profundis* De Quincey considers the involuntary acts of his own consciousness—the effects of opium and sudden intrusions of memory. Although such 'moments' provide an expansion which accords with the sublime idea we have been following, they also possess something of an arbitrary and separate nature. When De Quincey describes such an experience: 'and yet suddenly, at a silent command, at the signal of a blazing rocket sent up from the brain, the pall draws up, and the whole depths of the theatre are exposed',[72] he is aware of the degree to which 'at a silent command' contains a threat to his ability to impose his own self-conscious identity upon his experience by an act of will.

Similarly, De Quincey realises the dangers attendant upon the very process of bringing subconscious intrusions under a conscious scrutiny; of analysing sublime moments which would otherwise have been temporary, and confined to imaginative experience. His recognition of this danger was probably emphasised by his public context. The seriousness of his task, and the responsibility which it necessitated, can be gauged from his comments upon 'confession':

> the practice of confession is undoubtedly the most demoralising practice known to any Christian society. Innocent young persons, whose thoughts would never have wandered out upon any impure images or suggestions, have their . . . curiosity sent roving upon unlawful quests: they are instructed to watch what else would pass undetained in the mind, and would pass unblameably, on the Miltonic principle . . . Nay, which is worse of all, unconscious or semi-conscious thoughts and feelings or natural impulses, rising, like a breath of wind . . . are now brought powerfully under the focal light of the consciousness: and whatsoever is once made the subject of consciousness, can never again have the privilege of gay, careless thoughtlessness—the privilege by which the mind, like the lamps of a mail-coach, moving rapidly through the midnight woods, illuminate, for one instant . . . This happy privilege is forfeited for ever.[73]

With this in mind De Quincey seems to carry out his self-explorations with a good deal of caution, carefully limiting the extent of any logical investigation. Just as the 'power' of the sublime moment must be mediated and, at times, regarded with suspicion, so the objective, rationalising function of his autobiography should be kept in check by being subordinated to the aims of imaginative recreation and correspondence to past experience. Accuracy of objective categorisation is thus balanced by an attempt at experiential veracity. The movement of the autobiography is between these two; modulating and redefining these two extremes of the autobiographer's previous vision and present technique.

This close association of analytic introspection and imaginative expansion provides the limits in which De Quincey's own literature of 'power' functions. Analysis defines and mediates important imaginative events from the past, and provides an instrument for further revelations which may take place in the present act of composition. Most importantly of all, perhaps, it is able to give definition to, and render accessible to a magazine audience the nature and the intensity of imaginative 'power'. When the analytic basis to the autobiographical statement is cut short or seen to be inadequate, it secures the emphasis placed on that 'power', and does not appear as a failure.

In 1836 De Quincey spoke of German philosophy as owing its popularity, and to some extent its usefulness, to the barriers which it seemed to put in the way of rational inquiry. It is against the context of strict logic that he can see the possibilities of imaginative expansion:

> In [its] dark places lies, indeed, the secret of its attraction. Were light poured into them, it would be seen that they are *culs-de-sac,* passages that lead to nothing; but, so long as they continue dark, it is not known whither they lead . . . Were it known that upon every path a barrier faces you insurmountable to human steps . . . the popularity of this philosophy would expire at once; for no popular interest can long be sustained by speculations which . . . are known to be essentially negative and essentially finite. Man's nature has something of infinity within itself, which requires a corresponding infinity in its objects.[74]

In De Quincey's autobiography the logical sense restrains and disciplines, but does not act in opposition to a sense of imaginative power. De Quincey seems to believe that there is a necessary compromise which allows the imagination to flourish alongside the discursive understanding: the two interact to the ultimate benefit of the former. In exploring the subjective infinity to which he refers above, De Quincey realises that a mediated vision promotes a stronger sense of that infinity. The full power of his own 'visionary' experiences can most profitably be communicated to his magazine audience by using a recognisably familiar context. The sublime moments can then be sympathetically (and therefore imaginatively) appreciated, at the same time as they are authenticated and credibilised.

The autobiography thus carries out its revelatory purpose within very specific confines. The limitations imposed upon this purpose are a joint product of the periodical context and the specialist requirements of De Quincey the autobiographer. An interaction with a fairly well defined audience was sometimes conducive to the promotion of imaginative sympathy. The periodical compromise could thus cultivate the autobiographical vision at the same time as particularising it, offering a familiar though potentially dramatic relationship between writer and reader. De

Quincey could turn this situation to his advantage, finding it in some ways analogous to the fruitful nature of conversation:

> I felt (and in this I could not be mistaken, as too certainly it was a fact of my own experience) that in the electric kindling of life between two minds,—and far less from the kindling natural to conflict . . . than from the kindling through sympathy with the object discussed in its momentary coruscation of shifting phases,—there sometimes arise glimpses and shy revelations of affinity, suggestion, relation, analogy, that could not have been approached through any avenues of methodical study. Great organists find the same effect of inspiration, the same result of power creative and revealing, in the mere movement and velocity of their own voluntaries. . . . these *impromptu* torrents of music create rapturous *fioriture,* beyond all capacity in the artist to register, or afterwards to imitate. The reader must be well aware that many philosophic instances exist where a change in the degree makes a change in the kind.[75]

Again, a 'power creative and revealing' is found where it might not have been expected, suddenly presenting itself to the writer, whose task it now becomes to articulate the imaginative effect of its presentation. The difficulty of imitation arises because, as we have seen, it is the extent, the strength of that effect which distinguishes it. De Quincey makes this clear, not only in his statement that 'a change in the degree makes a change in the kind', but in his continued use of that word 'power'.

De Quincey's various critical statements show how much the periodical context exerted its pressures on his own subjective writings. From the resistance which it offered he was able to find both a source of autobiographical revelation and a means of stabilising the most imaginatively invigorating moments from his past. De Quincey's famous distinction between 'the literature of knowledge and the literature of power', which has serious limitations as a useful theoretical terminology, can be examined positively with regard to his autobiographical explorations. His use of the term 'power' might be located in the larger aesthetic debate between the sublime and the beautiful, in which he took a sizeable interest. The singularity of his achievement, however, rests not in the extremities of that debate, but in the viability of presenting the sublime alongside familiarity, in order to support an autobiographical purpose. The methods and techniques De Quincey used in such a presentation form the subject of the next chapter.

Notes

1. Thomas De Quincey, *The Collected Writings of Thomas De Quincey,* David Masson (ed.) (14 vols., Edinburgh, 1889-90), vol. X, pp. 269-270.

2. Ibid., p. 139.

3. Ibid., pp. 163-164.

4. William Wordsworth, *Preface to the Lyrical Ballads,* 1802, R. L. Brett and A. R. Jones (eds.) (London, 1963), p. 266.

5. S. T. Coleridge, *Coleridge's Shakespearean Criticism,* Thomas Middleton Raysor (ed.) (London, 1930), vol. 1, pp. 163-164.

6. Geoffrey Hill, 'Poetry as Menace and Atonement', *The University of Leeds Review,* vol. 21 (1978), p. 70.

7. Ibid.

8. Masson, vol. X, p. 153.

9. Ibid., p. 97.

10. Ibid., p. 220.

11. Ibid., p. 262.

12. Ibid., pp. 226-227.

13. Ibid., p. 139.

14. Ibid., pp. 104-105.

15. Ibid., p. 108.

16. Ibid., p. 92.

17. Ibid., p. 121.

18. Wordsworth, *Preface to the Lyrical Ballads,* p. 247.

19. Edmund Burke, 'On Taste', *The Works of The Right Honourable Edmund Burke* (London, 1801), vol. I, p. 96.

20. M. H. Abrams, *The Mirror and the Lamp* (New York, 1953), p. 175.

21. Masson, vol. X, p. 27.

22. Ibid., vol. XI, p. 220.

23. Ibid.

24. Ibid., pp. 88-89.

25. Wordsworth, *Preface to the Lyrical Ballads,* p. 265.

26. Thomas De Quincey, *The Uncollected Writings of Thomas De Quincey,* James Hogg (ed.) (London, 1890), vol. I, pp. 193-194.

27. Masson, vol. X, p. 369.

28. S. T. Coleridge, 'On Poesy or Art', in *Biographia Literaria,* J. Shawcross (ed.) (Oxford, 1967), vol. II, p. 256.

29. Masson, vol. X, p. 172.

30. Ibid., vol. V, p. 234.

31. Ibid., p. 231.

32. Ibid., vol. X, p. 359.

33. Ibid., pp. 329-330.

34. Ibid., vol. V, p. 217.

35. Ibid., vol. X, p. 226.

36. Ibid., vol. XI, p. 54.

37. Ibid., vol. X, p. 48.

38. Sigmund K. Procter, *Thomas De Quincey's Theory of Literature* (London, 1943), p. 154.

39. Masson, vol. XI, p. 315.

40. Ibid.

41. Ibid., p. 321.

42. Ibid., pp. 59-60.

43. Ibid., vol. X, p. 49.

44. John E. Jordan, *Thomas De Quincey, Literary Critic* (Berkeley and Los Angeles, 1952), p. 263.

45. Procter, *Thomas De Quincey's Theory of Literature,* p. 43.

46. Hogg (ed.), *Uncollected Writings,* vol. 1, p. 128.

47. Masson, vol. XIII, p. 334.

48. Ibid., vol. XI, p. 56.

49. Ibid.

50. Ibid., pp. 382-383.

51. Immanuel Kant, *Observations on the Feeling of the Beautiful and Sublime,* translated by John T. Goldthwatt (Berkeley and Los Angeles, 1965).

52. Ibid., pp. 36-37.

53. Ibid., p. 18.

54. Ibid., p. 45.

55. Ibid., p. 47.

56. Procter, *Thomas De Quincey's Theory of Literature,* pp. 143-144.

57. Ibid.

58. Horace A. Eaton (ed.), *A Diary of Thomas De Quincey, 1803* (New York, 1927), p. 163.

59. Masson, vol. X, p. 400.

60. Jordan, *Thomas De Quincey, Literary Critic,* p. 60.

61. Edmund Burke, 'On the Sublime and Beautiful', *The Works of the Right Honourable Edmund Burke,* vol. 1, p. 262.

62. Ibid., pp. 142-143.

63. Ibid., pp. 149-150.

64. William Wordsworth, 'The Sublime and the Beautiful', *The Prose Works of William Wordsworth,* W. J. B. Owen and Jane Worthington Smyser (eds.) (Oxford, 1974), vol. II, pp. 353-354.

65. Ibid., p. 355.

66. Burke, 'On the Sublime and Beautiful', pp. 171-172.

67. Thomas De Quincey, *The Posthumous Works of Thomas De Quincey,* A. H. Japp (ed.) (London, 1893), vol. II, p. 62.

68. Masson, vol. VIII, p. 274.

69. Japp (ed.), *Posthumous Works,* vol. I, p. 228.

70. Masson, vol. XIII, p. 338.

71. Ibid., p. 360.

72. Ibid., p. 348.

73. Hogg (ed.), *Uncollected Writings,* vol. II, pp. 67-68.

74. Ibid., vol. I, p. 99.

75. Masson, vol. X, pp. 268-269.

John Barrell (essay date 1991)

SOURCE: "Introduction: This/That/the Other," in *The Infection of Thomas De Quincey: A Psychopathology of Imperialism,* Yale University Press, 1991, pp. 1-24.

[*In the following essay, Barrell reads De Quincey's essays and autobiographical sketches as manifestations of an imperialist anxiety about the "Orient."*]

> A 'compromised' person is one who has been in contact with people or things supposed to be capable of conveying infection. As a general rule the whole Ottoman empire lies constantly under this terrible ban.
>
> A. W. Kinglake, *Eothen,* 14n.

> He described the present state of Syria as perfectly impracticable for travellers, or at least highly dangerous, from the united obstacles of marauders and pestilence. He saw a party of deserters marched in near Damascus, chained to each other, and occasionally a man free from plague joined hand in hand with one who was infected.
>
> The Hon. Mrs Damer, *Diary of a Tour,* 1: 22.

I

Thomas De Quincey became a 'regular and confirmed' opium addict in 1813; before that, for ten years, he had used the drug, usually if not invariably in the form of laudanum, on a weekly rather than on a daily basis. When in London he would take it on Saturday nights, and with the idea of indulging in one of two competing pleasures. He went to the opera; or he became a *flâneur* for the evening, a watcher of the poor in their hours of relaxation. Most people, he acknowledges, 'are apt to show their interest in the concerns of the poor chiefly by sympathy with their distresses and sorrows', but 'I at that time was disposed to express mine by sympathising with their pleasures'. Saturday night was the best time for experiencing this sympathetic pleasure, for then the poor, released from the bondage of labour, would congregate in family parties to 'purchase their Sunday's dinner' (so Mayhew explains) at the great street-markets of the metropolis. De Quincey's 'sympathy' was such that on Saturday nights he too began to feel that he was 'released from some yoke of bondage, had some wages to receive, and some luxury of repose to enjoy'. He would, accordingly, knock back his laudanum and 'wander forth, without much regarding the direction or the distance', to all those parts of London where this Saturday night spectacle could be enjoyed (3: 392; Mayhew 1: 10).

This early account of the pleasures of the *flâneur* communicates a very specific sense of the developing modern metropolis. Those that De Quincey calls the 'poor' are the working poor, probably largely employed as outworkers, and paid only on Saturday afternoons or evenings when they take their work to the warehouse. The market-traders must therefore work late on Saturday nights (and also on Sunday mornings) if the poor are to be able to purchase the necessities of life. It is the regularity and uniformity of the working week—regular even in its irregularities, its St Monday, its Friday-night 'ghoster'—that produces this sudden and regular visibility of 'the poor' at a certain time in certain places—and that offers De Quincey the opportunity of 'witnessing, upon as large a scale as possible' this 'spectacle' of early nineteenth-century metropolitan life.[1]

No less interesting is the nature and scope of what De Quincey represents as his sympathy with the poor. 'If wages were a little higher,' he writes, 'or were expected to be so—if the quartern loaf were a little lower, or it was reported that onions or butter were falling—I was glad; yet, if the contrary were true, I drew from opium some means of consolation' (3: 393). There is no pretence that this is a general concern for the well-being of the poor; their pleasures he could use, but he had no need of their sadness. Their job, therefore, was to remain cheerful and acquiescent even in adversity; and to a mind soaked in laudanum, they readily gave the impression of being so:

> sometimes there might be heard murmurs of discontent: but far oftener expressions . . . of patience, of hope, and of reconciliation to their lot. Generally speaking, the impression left upon my mind was that the poor are practically more philosophic than the rich; that they show a more ready and cheerful submission to what they consider as irremediable evils or irreparable losses.
>
> (3: 392-3)

The consolations provided by these Saturday nights, it seems, were as much political as personal, and they are consolations familiar to those brought up within the class structure of Britain. The pleasure is not at all to pretend to be *one of* an inferior class; it is to pretend to be *like* them, fundamentally the same, but different in all that really concerns one's sense of identity and self-esteem. The search for a common human nature becomes the search for a means of reassurance, of making safe what seems to be threatening in the poor, in the 'masses', in the enormous numbers of the working class that the timetable of modern life sometimes permits to congregate together. Especially at those moments it becomes important to believe, as De Quincey puts it, that 'the most hostile sects unite, and acknowledge a common link of brotherhood' (3: 393).

De Quincey's own fear of the working class is elsewhere very evident. They were 'Jacobins'—he could still use the word in the 1850s to describe those whom he had first recognised as the inferiors and enemies of his own class when he was an eight-year-old schoolboy during the Terror. Grevel Lindop describes how in 1842 De Quincey wrote to Blackwood, of *Blackwood's Magazine,* about an essay he was writing on revolutionary movements and the working class. He had kept the 'working poor' under surveillance, he explained, for many years. He had listened carefully to what they said; he had taken every opportunity to encourage them into 'the express manifestation' of their 'true secret dispositions'. 'To a man I look upon the working poor, Scottish or English, as latent Jacobins—*biding their* time' (L345). In the article **'On the Approaching Revolution in Great Britain'**, a jeremiad published in 1831 in anticipation of the passing of the Reform Bill, he disclosed that he had also been keeping his eye on the class of 'petty shopkeepers', who were just as bad:

> I have observed them much, and long . . . no symptom has escaped me for the last sixteen years . . . the result of my observations is, that, with the exception here and there of an individual, bribed, as it were, to reserve and duplicity, by his dependence on some great aristocratic neighbour, this order of men is as purely Jacobinical, and disposed to revolutionary counsels, as any that existed in France at the time of their worst convulsions.
>
> (B30 1831 323)

And in an essay of uncertain date, on Judas Iscariot, he writes of the same class:

> They receive, and with dreadful fidelity they give back, all Jacobinical impulses. . . . In times of fierce political agitation these are the men who most of all are kept *au courant* of the interior councils and policy amongst the great body of acting conspirators.
>
> (8: 182n.)

This is the other side of the jovial *flânerie* amongst the families of the poor, the market-traders, the small shopkeepers of London: a fearful suspicion, a paranoia, that in the apparently routine and good-natured transactions of a Saturday-night shopping trip, conspiratorial words are being whispered, glances exchanged. While De Quincey is watching the poor, they are watching out, for the moment to strike; and as they have no real grievances, the revenge they are contemplating is stimulated by nothing but a 'plebeian envy', a 'low-minded jealousy against the aristocracy' (B30 1831 324).[2]

The need to denounce these petty shopkeepers may have been influenced by the habit, noticed by De Quincey, of referring to them in Scotland as '*merchants*'. De Quincey's father, a member of high bourgeois society in Manchester, had described himself as a merchant, and Thomas himself had announced, in the ***Opium-Eater,*** his pride in being the 'son of a plain English merchant'. But the devaluation of the term in Scotland, where Thomas spent the last half of his life, was a threat to whatever degree of social distinction he had inherited as his birthright. That birthright had always been problematic, however, and in England especially, where the disdain for 'trade', however lucrative, and however much an unacknowledged component of the fortunes of those who passed as 'landed', had always represented the De Quinceys as inferior to the polite and leisured classes that he and his mother wanted so badly to be part of. It was those ambitions that had led De Quincey's mother to decorate the family name—originally plain 'Quincey'—with what he calls 'the aristocratic *De*'. When even she had abandoned it, he retained it, as if to reassure himself that, though apparently a hack writer, permanently on the run from his creditors, he was a member of some *noblesse de plume* (8: 182n.; 1971 61; 1: 30; 3: 459).

The double vision that for De Quincey seems to have characterised the spectacle of the poor is clear enough in the **Opium-Eater** itself, where he describes his happy and hazy wanderings. He begins that description by assuring us that 'the pleasures of the poor . . . can never become oppressive to contemplate', but by the very next paragraph they have become precisely that: to the 'opium-eater, when in the divinest state incident to his enjoyment . . . crowds become an oppression'. The more opium he took, the more the spectacle of mass society produced the fears he had been trying to make safe; and if they disappeared in the evening, they were to return, years later, in a different but still recognisable form at night. There may seem to be a vast geographical and psychic distance between the cheerful bustle of a London street-market on a Saturday night, and the terrifying oriental imagery of the opium dreams, but De Quincey saw in one the representation and displacement of the other. Whatever else they were, the dreams were dreams of the terrors of 'mass society', which De Quincey often rationalised into a fear of popular Jacobinism—of those 'myriads of murderous levellers', for example, who had emerged from the 'dark recesses' and 'gloomy dens' of Paris, and 'wallowed in the blood of illustrious victims' (3: 392, 394; B28 1830 705).

'The human face tyrannised over my dreams'; this tyranny, a kind of dream-dictatorship of the proletariat, was the result not only of the wandering from market to market, but of the continual search, when De Quincey was in London, to find, among the endlessly multiplied faces of the metropolitan crowd, the one face of Ann, the prostitute and 'pariah' who had befriended him on his first trip to London as a teenager, and with whom he had then lost touch.[3] 'I suppose that, in the literal and unrhetorical use of the word *myriad*, I must, on my different visits to London, have looked into many *myriads* of female faces'; and the search 'pursued in the crowds of London', was

pursued also 'through many a year in dreams'. On the last occasion that he saw Ann, he had been worried about the difficulty of attempting to find her again in 'the great Mediterranean of Oxford Street', and his later dreams literalised for him the expression 'a sea of faces' (3: 394, 375, 222, 368). As a result of this 'searching for Ann amongst fluctuating crowds' (*fluctus*, a wave), he writes, the 'human face began to reveal itself' upon the 'rocking waves' of an ocean:

> the sea appeared paved with innumerable faces, upturned to the heavens; faces, imploring, wrathful, despairing; faces that surged upwards by thousands, by myriads, by generations: infinite was my agitation; my mind tossed, as it seemed, upon the billowy ocean, and weltered upon the weltering waves.
>
> (3: 441)

This sense of the sheer terrifying numberlessness of the world's population, of its 'hunger-bitten myriads', of 'surplus' or 'redundant' people (7: 257-8), re-emerges in the preamble to the opium dreams as a terror inspired by 'the enormous population of Asia'. 'The difficulty in India is in individualizing your man', wrote the Baptist missionary Joshua Russell (265); and De Quincey like most other Europeans conceived of Asia beyond the Tigris as a place where people seemed to run into each other, to replicate each other, to compose one mass without divisions or features. 'South-eastern Asia is, and has been for thousands of years, the part of the earth most swarming with human life, the great *officina gentium*. Man is a weed in those regions'. The phrase '*officina gentium*', 'factory where people are made', is also used by De Quincey, in an incident we shall look at later, to describe a factory, full of 'Jacobins', that frightened him in childhood. Differently construed, it is probably this phrase that Disraeli had in mind when, in 1838, he described England's aspirations to be 'the workshop of the World'; and the phrase may once have proposed a kind of equivalence between the 'mass society' of the industrial nations, and an idea of Asia as '*swarming* with *human* life'—with human beings who are evoked only to be dehumanised.[4] In a late essay on China, De Quincey found in Canton, a city where the myriads were oriental, a final realisation of his nightmares: Canton, the city where Englishmen are 'cut to pieces' whenever they wander out alone; and the city which, as De Quincey acknowledged, was the creation of Europe, and of the European 'factories' there, as the trading warehouses were called (3: 442; 1857 7).

This terror of society in the mass, of what he calls in an earlier essay on China the 'monstrous aggregations of human beings . . . in the suburbs of mighty cities', is certainly not, as De Quincey sometimes suggests, the whole of what is displaced and represented as oriental in the description of the opium dreams and its elaborate preamble (B50 1841 688). It was the bit, perhaps, that he could most easily own up to, could acknowledge to himself, at the time when he was writing the ***Opium-Eater.*** Nor were humans growing like weeds, or swarming like ants or bees, the only 'unimaginable horror' to take on an oriental character in De Quincey's writing about his dreams. The turbaned 'Malay' who had once called in at Dove Cottage; the imagery of Hindu theology; the Hindu caste system; the vastness of space and time in India and China; the fauna of everywhere from Egypt to China, but chiefly snakes and crocodiles; pagodas, pyramids, forests, reeds, mud, the Ganges, the Nile, the Euphrates, and so on and so on—all these came together to form, in De Quincey's head, an eclectic visual style he described as the 'barbaresque', a cabinet of oriental curiosities, partly terrifying just because its contents were so unpredictably miscellaneous (14: 48-9, 55-9).

At one point De Quincey himself represents his 'oriental imagery' as composing, precisely, a *collection:*

> under the connecting feeling of tropical heat and vertical sunlights, I brought together all creatures, birds, beasts, reptiles, all trees and plants, usages and appearances, that are found in all tropical regions, and assembled them together in China or Hindostan. From kindred feelings, I soon brought Egypt and her gods under the same law.
>
> (3: 442)

What is being evoked here is perhaps not so much the random collection of oriental curios in the haphazard way of the mid-eighteenth-century virtuoso; it is the beginnings of the large-scale, scientific collecting of the nineteenth-century museum age, with its aspiration to represent *everything*—'*all* creatures . . . *all* trees and plants'—in its galleries and in its botanical and its zoological gardens.[5] Just as the experiences of urban society which find expression in this dream imagery speak to us of a very specific moment in the economic, social and cultural history of Britain, so does that imagery itself. The 'barbaresque' Hindu divinities, for example, had been elaborately depicted in Thomas Maurice's *History of Hindostan* (1795-9) and Edward Moor's *Hindu Pantheon* (1810). In rather less elaborate form they had illustrated Sir William Jones's essay 'The Gods of Greece, Italy, and India' in the *Asiatic Researches,* which De Quincey had read when a boy, and in which he would have read the first serious essays of British orientalists in India. The antiquities collected by the Napoleonic expedition to Egypt—hitherto regarded as too inhospitable a country for regular collectors—were confiscated by the British in 1801 and brought to England in 1802, to form the real basis of the collection of Egyptian antiquities in the British Museum. The Chinese imagery, more generalised, seems to derive from the *chinoiserie* of eighteenth-century garden design and interior décor: pagodas, and tables and sofas 'instinct with life' because carved with the heads and feet of animals.

In short, this oriental imagery is the imagery of an early but well-established imperialist culture, an imagery which had been collected and become familiar to the British imagination, to this degree and in this combination, only in the very last years of the eighteenth century and the opening decades of the nineteenth. Its availability depended on the combination of military, naval, mercantile and scholarly endeavours and acquisitions which was especially typified by the activities of the Asiatic Society in Bengal around 1800; but the increase of British 'interest' in Asia further east than India, for example, and the increasing awareness in Britain of the Ottoman Empire as sick but surviving competitor in the Near East, were contributing their own ingredients to this miscellaneous oriental soup. These ingredients did not come only or mainly as material objects—animals, ornaments, exhibits; they came as narratives too, circulated by newspapers, by engravings, and by melodramas, pantomimes and plays. At the centre of these narratives was a succession of oriental characters drawn from fictions such as the *Arabian Nights,* or from barely less fictionalised accounts of history and politics—Nadir Shah, Siraj-ud-daula, Haider Ali, Tipu Sultan, Ali Pacha, Runjeet Singh—'oriental despots' who were the forerunners in the European imagination of Khomeini, Ghadaffi, and Saddam Hussein—all individualised by the different ferocities imputed to them, but more or less identical to each other in their power to thrill the nursery and the theatre, and to enrage the drawing-room and the club.

The various ingredients, material and immaterial, of the oriental soup, had only two things in common. They were images of an exotic world east of the Mediterranean and still only haphazardly penetrated, not to put too fine a point on it, by western European power; and they were especially serviceable, as forms, images, ideas which could be used to represent 'unimaginable horrors', precisely because the East entered the western European imagination as an unknown, empty space—empty of everything, that is, except its appropriable resources, imaginative as well as material. Of all those resources, the abundantly decorated surfaces of the artefacts of Turkey, Egypt, Persia, India and China, intricately abstract or flamboyantly figurative, were perhaps particularly valuable and easy to appropriate. So crowded, to western eyes, were the surfaces of oriental objects, covered with decoration and imagery not understood and not thought worth understanding, that they could become the very opposite of what they appeared to be—blank screens on which could be projected whatever it was that the inhabitants of Europe, individually or collectively, wanted to displace, and to represent as other to themselves.

II

In De Quincey's writing, however, there is often a particular process or scheme of displacement at work, one

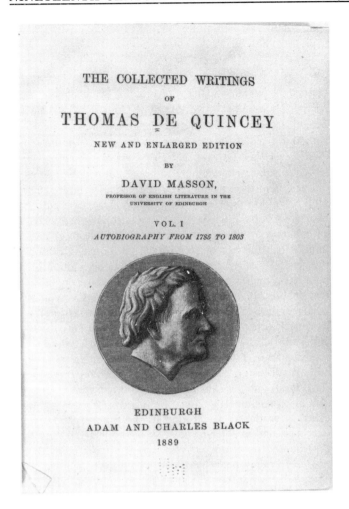

THE COLLECTED WRITINGS
OF
THOMAS DE QUINCEY
NEW AND ENLARGED EDITION
BY
DAVID MASSON,
PROFESSOR OF ENGLISH LITERATURE IN THE
UNIVERSITY OF EDINBURGH

VOL. I
AUTOBIOGRAPHY FROM 1785 TO 1803

EDINBURGH
ADAM AND CHARLES BLACK
1889

which suggests that a simple binary model, of self and other, might not always be adequate for thinking about the uses and dangers of the oriental to the western imagination. An especially interesting example—interesting because it seems to occur playfully, anecdotally, as if nothing very much is at risk—occurs in his discussion of the highly differentiated topography of John Palmer's mail-coaches, in the first section of the long essay **'The English Mail-Coach'**.[6] The essay either records or invents a fascinating moment in the history of class division, the moment when—according to De Quincey—it became a fashionable, a sparkish thing to do, for young gentlemen to travel on the outside of the coach, next or near to the coachman, rather than on the inside, the traditional and more expensive refuge of the genteel. The fashion took hold, according to De Quincey, at some time in the first decade of the nineteenth century, when he was an undergraduate at Oxford. Before that time, the relation between the division of space on the coach and the division of class among the passengers had apparently been unambiguous; those on the outside were, precisely, outsiders, 'Pariahs' as De Quincey puts it. When the fashion

became established, and young gentlemen took to travelling on the outside, the insiders attempted to behave as if the usual etiquette which governed the behaviour of the two types of passenger at inns and staging-posts, and which kept them apart at meal times especially, could still universally be applied. This attempt was strongly resisted by the sparkish young gents.

The division was reinforced by the simple binary terminology in which it was described. In addition to 'insider' and 'outsider', the politics of the first decade of the nineteenth century made available the terms 'aristocrat' and 'democrat'. And because since the early and middle 1790s to be a 'democrat' was to be allied, in the eyes of 'aristocrats', with the un-English, Francophile, and therefore treasonous politics of revolution, De Quincey can describe the relations between insiders and outsiders in terms of treason and the suspicion of treason. No insider would have dreamed, he tells us, of exchanging one word of civility with an outsider: 'even to have kicked an outsider', he writes, 'might have been held to attaint the foot concerned in that operation, so that, perhaps, it would have required an act of Parliament to restore its purity of blood'. If outsiders attempted the treasonous act of breakfasting with insiders, the act would have been so incomprehensible as to be regarded as 'a case of lunacy . . . rather than of treason'. Though the outsiders were 'gownsmen', they were 'constructively', by virtue of where they sat, 'raff' or 'snobs'—varsity slang for (mere) townsmen—there is a reference here to the controversial crime of 'constructive treason', and a suggestion that, by sitting outside, the young Oxford gentlemen 'lose caste'. In spite of all this, however, the young gentlemen managed to effect 'a perfect Revolution' in 'mail-coach society'.[7]

Characteristically, or so it will soon appear, De Quincey attempts to heal the breach between insider and outsider by treating it, in the first place, as not really a breach at all, there being no real class difference between the two varieties of passenger; and then by looking round for a third object which both the first two can agree to regard as other to themselves. He remembers a coach from Birmingham, some 'tawdry', 'plebian', 'jacobinical' '"Tallyho" or "Highflyer"', which once had the temerity to race against the mail. 'The connexion of the mail with the state and executive government' enables him to argue that for 'such a Birmingham thing . . . to challenge us . . . has an air of sedition'; and for it actually to win would have been 'treason'. It is not enough, however, to represent the 'poor Brummagem brute' as plebeian, even as Jacobinical; to complete the processes of identification and abjection in which he is engaged, the rival coach must be orientalised. It had, noted De Quincey scornfully, 'as much writing and painting on its sprawling flanks as would have puzzled a decipherer from the tombs of Luxor'. The accusation of un-Englishness, expressed in the terms 'pariah' and 'traitor', and originally used to distinguish between insiders and outsiders on the Royal Mail, is now used to unite them, by being levelled at the oriental and treasonous 'Brummagem coach'. It is a characteristic of true Englishness, we are reminded—of the Englishness of the polite classes—that they practise understatement, by contrast with the plethora of meaningless signification which characterises the East, and which has come to be connected, somehow, with the tawdry, the gimcrack, and with whatever other vulgarities are conjured up by 'Brummagem'. The connection of all these terms—pariah, vulgar, traitorous, un-English—is finally underlined when the triumph of the English mail-coach, in leaving the Birmingham vehicle far behind, is enjoyed by all except 'a Welsh rustic', who for the playful purposes of the essay can be regarded as a true, because foreign and plebeian, outsider (13: 273-83).

The process we have been observing begins by identifying an apparently exhaustive binary: there is a self, and there is an other, an inside and an outside, an above and a below. The self is constituted by the other, and it requires that other to mark out its own limit, its own definition; yet the two are implacably hostile, and their confrontation appears unavoidable, for there is no third term, no other identity conceivable, nowhere else to go. This is the situation we are presented with at the start of **'The English Mail-Coach'**, and if De Quincey himself starts off on the outside, and so apparently in the place of the other, that is only an early indication of how easily the distinction is about to be, not abolished exactly, but accommodated. The scheme of this accommodation is given in the title of this chapter: the terms self and other can be thought of as superseded by 'this' and 'that', in a narrative which now says, there is *this* here, and it is different from *that* there, but the difference between them, though in its own way important, is as nothing compared with the difference between the two of them considered together, and that third thing, way over there, which is truly *other* to them both.

I could borrow Gayatri Spivak's distinction here between a 'self-consolidating other' and an 'absolute other', for what is involved is precisely an act of consolidation of the self. If I prefer my own way of putting it, that is because it seems to dramatise how what at first seems 'other' can be made over to the side of the self—to a subordinate position on that side—only so long as a new, and a newly absolute 'other' is constituted to fill the discursive space that has thus been evacuated. In an essay on the mutiny, rebellion or war of independence in India in 1857, De Quincey describes his writing as a matter of 'putting this and that together'; and the phrase seems to make the point that to talk of 'this' and 'that' is always to suppose or to require 'the other', a continually reinvented third term which acknowledges that whenever two things have been 'put together', something else has been pushed aside (Spivak 1985b 131; U1: 311-12; 1: 102).[8]

There is a whole historical and geopolitical system in De Quincey's works which is constructed by using the same spatial scheme as is at work in **'The English Mail-Coach'**. There is a 'this', and there is a something hostile to it, something which lies, almost invariably, to the east; but there is an East beyond that East, where something lurks which is equally threatening to both, and which enables or obliges them to reconcile their differences. The translation of the London poor, experienced as oppressive, into 'the enormous population of Asia', may already have provided an example of the process used to make safe more serious threats than the one offered by the 'Brummagem thing' to the genteel mail-coach. It may be the representation of the poor as oriental, when they are experienced as 'oppressive', that enables them to be experienced also as 'sympathetic': whatever is bad about them is characterised as exotic, as extrinsic, as not really them at all, with the effect that they are separated from, and contrasted with, their own representation as oriental. There are the cities of London and Westminster; there is the East End; and there is the East. It is by this means that the limited class solidarity essential to an imperial power, and especially to its ruling class, is produced, for it enables the differences between one class and another to be fully acknowledged, and then represented as almost trivial, when compared with the civilisation they both share, but which is emphatically not shared by whatever oriental other, the sepoys or the dervishes, is in season at the time (see Kiernan, 316-17). Here are some more examples.

FRENCH HISTORY

The village where Joan of Arc was born, Domrémy, stands on the Meuse, which divides France from the territories of the Dukes of Bar and Lorraine. Despite its significance as a political frontier, the river did not divide the populations; it was crossed by bridges and ferries, there was a good deal of intermarriage between the left bank and the right, and so, 'like other frontiers, it produced a *mixed* race, representing the *cis* and the *trans*'. 'The Dukes of Bar and Lorraine had for generations pursued the policy of eternal warfare with France on their own account, yet also of eternal amity and league with France in case anybody else presumed to attack her'. This river was a frontier, therefore, only when no third party was to be taken into consideration. There was however another frontier, to the east—the mountains of the Vosges, covered with vast, impenetrable and mysterious woods. This formed the true 'eastern frontier' of France and Lorraine alike, the dividing line between two Empires of East and West, not unlike 'the desert between Syria and the Euphrates' (5: 390, 394-5).

GREEK HISTORY

In the time of Herodotus, Persia was the sole enemy of Greece, and at that time the whole of the known world consisted of the Persian Empire, and of the countries more or less within the orbit of Greek civilisation or knowledge. In that sense the known world was divided between Greece and Persia, and it is easy to think of the 'terrific collisions' between the two as engrossing all that there then was of history and the world. But if the Greeks, seen in this light, had an interest in the defeat of Persia, they had still greater interest in the stability of the Great King and his Empire. For in another light Persia was 'a great resisting mass interjacent between Greece and the unknown enemies to the north-east or east'. The sense of uncertainty, caused by ignorance of what 'fierce, unknown races' lay eastwards of Persia or in the easternmost reaches of the Persian Empire, meant that the Great King could also be seen 'as a common friend against some horrid enemy from the infinite deserts of Asia', though to be sure he appeared more often to the Greeks as an enemy than as a friend (10: 176-7).

ROMAN HISTORY

The garden of Greenhay, a small country house to the south of Manchester, was divided from the surrounding countryside by the Cornbrook, a stream crossed by a small bridge at the front gate of the garden. The territory on one side of this stream belonged to Romulus, on the other side to his scornful brother Remus, and the two territories may have corresponded to the kingdoms of Gombroon and Tigrosylvania. The brothers were engaged in continual conflict with each other. The northern boundary of the area formed by their two conjoint territories was the River Medlock, and the bridge over this river was held at one time or another by Carthaginians and by various other enemies of Rome—Goths, Vandals—in equal need of deletion. In their long-continued war with these peoples, the Roman brothers were always if uneasily united (1: 69-117).

BYZANTINE HISTORY

Because of the habit of regarding the Roman Empire as in a state of more or less permanent decline from as early as the reign of Commodus, and because of the hostility of the refined and effeminate Byzantine Court to the simple and manly Crusaders, 'we have all been accustomed to speak of the Byzantine Empire with scorn'. This is a great mistake; for though in many respects western Christendom and the Byzantine Empire appear as binary opposites, masculine and feminine, Roman and Greek, in another light they must be seen as united in their resistance to the formidable powers of the further East. However effete the Byzantine Empire may have been, its forces were capable in the seventh century of crossing the Tigris deep into

Persia; more recently, it has been the 'capital bulwark' against the forward march of 'Mahometanism', the 'great aegis', indeed, of western Christendom (7: 255-6).

THE HISTORY OF 'FRANKISTAN'

But then again, and in yet another light, Christendom and the 'Mahometan nations' should not be seen as in all respects exhaustively and irrevocably antagonistic. Both have this in common, that they subscribe to true religions; 'true', not in the sense that both have equal access to the absolute truth, for when all is said and done, Christians are Christians and masculine, and Muslims are emasculated infidels. But the religions of both are, truly, *religions* and not mere superstitions: they are both, as the Muslims say, 'religions of the book'; they are monotheisic, and they consist in a body of doctrine and of moral teaching, and not simply in a set of ritual observances. And even if we do think of Christendom and Islam as ineluctable opposites, and as connected only by their hostilities, they have become familiar to each other, even companionable, by that very opposition. This is true, at least, of the Ottomans, Arabs and Moors. To these peoples, and to European Christendom, we might apply the collective name *Frankistan,* to differentiate them from the peoples of southern and eastern Asia, whether the effeminate 'Mohammedans' of Bengal, or the 'Hindoos' and Buddhists, for example, with their 'foul', 'monstrous idolatries', and (especially) the 'pollution' of 'Hindoo polytheism'. This process of *rapprochement* between Christendom and western Islam has been accelerated in the nineteenth century, as a result of the decay of the Ottoman Empire (according to De Quincey, 'cancered', 'crazy', and 'paralytic'), and the growth of steam power, science, and European travel and trade to the Levant. 'Asia Minor, Egypt, Syria—all that lies west of the Tigris', is coming 'within the network of Christian civilisation', and has been 'taken under the *surveillance* of the great Christian powers' (1: 373; 7: 275; 8: 207-43, 308; J1: 41, 290; J2: 12n.; 7: 212; B48 1840 559-62).[9]

III

The kind of imaginary geography represented by De Quincey's 'this/that/the other' formula had its historical equivalent in British imperial policy or (for they were not always the same thing) the policy of the East India Company: the attempts to 'play off' Muslim against Hindu, or Sikh against Muslim, are obvious examples, and so is the tortuous policy of the Company towards Afghanistan. Here is the *Edinburgh Review,* pronouncing on imperial policy in 1840:

> It is of vital importance to British India that Afghanistan should be interposed as an effectual barrier between the great Mahomedan power of Central Asia—urged on by Muscovite intrigue, and supported, whenever a favour-

able opportunity may offer, by Muscovite troops—and all that is inflammable within the peninsula.

(E71 1840 339)

The 1838 invasion of Afghanistan—the country to which the terms 'barrier-state', 'buffer-state', were first applied—was only the clearest instance of that 'monomaniac' zeal which, as Henry Lushington pointed out, could entertain no other conception of the country than that its destiny was to be a 'barrier to British India' (Lushington 55).[10]

In Afghanistan, indeed, to which between 1840 and 1844 De Quincey devoted no less than three essays, two competing 'systems of diplomatic calculation' were kept from colliding with each other only by the buffers interposed by the inhabitants and the geography of that country: it was here that in the 1830s and early 1840s British imperialism met itself coming back, as it were. For as it gazed eastward from Britain, the Tigris appeared as the last ditch between a manageable and an entirely hostile other; but as it gazed westward from India, the Indus became the 'river of separation' between a vulnerable and over-extended empire and the fantasised rapacity of Persia and Russia. In two essays from the early 1840s, by no means untypical of mid-century writing on the imperial theme, De Quincey attempts to 'arrange', to 'settle and determine the idea of Persia'—the other large country, besides Afghanistan, between the Tigris and the Indus—not according to any Persian notion of that country, but according to what it might be convenient for a version of British foreign policy to believe. 'The Turkish or western chambers' of 'Southern (or Mahometan) Asia,' he announces, 'may be viewed as reaching to the Tigris; the middle, or Persian part, from the Tigris to the desert on the west frontier of Affghanistan; the third or Affghan chamber to the Indus'. The Indus is thus proclaimed as 'the true natural eastern boundary of Cabul or Affghanistan'; and the same river, before the annexation of Sind and the Punjab carried the frontier still further west, was often represented as the 'natural boundary' of India—the more natural because one of its other names, the 'Attok', so the traveller G. T. Vigne explained, 'is derived from Atkana, or Atukna, signifying in Hindustani, *to stop;* no pious Hindoo will venture to go beyond it of his own accord, for fear of losing caste' (B52 1842 280; B48 1840 562; E71 1840 355; Vigne 1840 30).[11]

This is not the occasion to attempt a discussion of the effects on the imperial imagination of these complementary yet also competing systems of geography—systems which at times the British sought to impose by force on the imaginations of others. But the attempt to annex Afghanistan, and the continued anxiety about the security of the North-West frontier, must have contributed much to that sense of divided positionality which—as Homi Bhabha in particular has argued—became a characteristic of the British in the mid-nineteenth century, in Britain as well as in India. De Quincey, who shared Tory doubts about the wisdom of sending the expeditionary force to Kabul, probably suffered less than many from this particular symptom of ambivalence, the dis-orientation produced by the discovery of enemies to the west as well as to the east. He attacked the Afghanistan campaign on the grounds that it was an attempt to raise 'a powerful barrier' against 'enemies who might gather from the *west*' (my emphasis), but who had never been clearly identified (B56 1844 139). His own horror of the Orient was so great that for him the primary geopolitical significance of the Indus was probably as an additional line of defence, keeping the Hindus where they belonged. 'Such is the wonderful attachment to the British uniform', wrote Vigne, 'that in the late expedition to Afghanistan, the native Sepahis [sepoys], many of them Rajpoots, cheered loudly when they saw the British flag flying at Bukkur, and passed the bridge over the Indus with enthusiasm' (Vigne 1840 30-1). That image alone is enough to explain De Quincey's hostility to the Afghanistan adventure: the image of Hindus, in arms, crossing the Forbidden River, advancing towards the Tigris and Frankistan, and threatening to reclaim *that* barrier state for the *other*.

IV

The scheme we have been examining has clear affinities to the rhetorical figure Barthes described, in relation to the politics of class, as 'inoculation'. This consists in 'admitting the accidental evil of a class-bound institution the better to conceal its principal evil'. His more general, supplementary description of inoculation is for our purposes more useful: 'one immunizes the contents of the collective imagination by means of a small inoculation of acknowledged evil; one thus protects it against the risk of a generalized subversion' (Barthes 150). The apparently mixed metaphor here, which seems to identify political opposition and disease, is particularly appropriate to De Quincey's scheme, which figures the oriental as infection, and also as rebel, mutineer or subversive immigrant. De Quincey's life was terrorised by the fear of an unending and interlinked chain of infections from the East, which threatened to enter his system and to overthrow it, leaving him visibly and permanently 'compromised' and orientalised. 'It is well known', he writes,

> that the very reason why the Spanish beyond all nations became so gloomily jealous of a Jewish cross in the pedigree was because, until the vigilance of the Church rose in ferocity, in no nation was such a cross so common. The hatred of fear is ever the deepest. And men hated the Jewish taint, as once in Jerusalem they hated the leprosy, because, even whilst they raved against it, the secret proofs of it might be detected amongst their own kindred; even as in the Temple, whilst once a Hebrew king rose in mutiny against the priesthood (2 Chron. xxvi. 16-20), suddenly the leprosy that dethroned him blazed out upon his forehead.

(13: 210)

The 'oriental leprosy', 'oriental cholera', 'oriental typhus fever', the 'plague of Cairo', the 'cancerous kisses' of the Egyptian crocodile: the fear and hatred projected on to the East kept threatening to return in one such form or another, as in dreams they did return; and it is against these that De Quincey inoculates himself, taking something of the East into himself, and projecting whatever he could not acknowledge as his out into a farther East, an East *beyond* the East.[12] The Eurocentric nomenclature of imperialism is absolutely to the point here, in its definitions of a treacherous but sometimes manageable 'Near East', a terrifying 'Far East', and between them an ambiguous and hard to locate 'Middle East', which seems (like the Middle West in America) to wander around the continent on its own tectonic plate, turning up here or there according to need—a kind of itinerant barrier or buffer between what can possibly be allowed in, and what must be kept out at all costs.

The process of inoculation we have been examining in De Quincey's geopolitical schemata is rather less successful, however, than Barthes suggests. It never *immunises* against the infections of the East; at best it enables the patient to shake them off for a time, or gives him the illusion of having done so, but always with the fear that they will return in a more virulent form, as supergerms now themselves immune from the attacks of antibodies. The process of inoculation involves simultaneously protecting someone against a disease and infecting them with it, and the troubling ambiguity of this process is often visible in the very language in which it is described. 'The finished and accomplished surgeon', writes De Quincey, explaining why he refused to pick a quarrel with one, 'carries a pocket-case of surgical instruments,—lancets, for instance, that are loaded with *virus* in every stage of contagion. Might he not inoculate me with *rabies,* with *hydrophobia,* with the plague of Cairo'? (5: 353). To be inoculated *against* the disease is at the same time to be inoculated *with* it, and in De Quincey's case the process was accompanied by a higher than usual degree of risk; for he already had the disease he was attempting to immunise himself against. As we will see, the disease was always an external materialisation of an internal psychic anxiety, something first projected and rejected, then taken back in; and there was no guarantee that he might not rediscover that disorder in the East he had ingested as well as in the East he had thrown away.[13]

A case in point is his use of opium. To begin with, the phrase 'English Opium-Eater' itself can be read as an example of inoculation. The use of opium was associated in the English imagination with every Asian country from Turkey, through Persia and India, to China, but to describe oneself as an 'eater' of opium was to claim kinship with a recognisably Turkish identity—a kinship qualified, however, and hopefully made safe, by the adjective

'English' (L249). At one point in the ***Opium-Eater***—we can worry about the precise point later—De Quincey playfully describes his long experience of 'East Indian and Turkish' opium as a sequence of medical experiments conducted 'for the general benefit of the world'. He tells us of various surgeons who for the purposes of research had inoculated themselves with cancer, plague, and hydrophobia. Like these, De Quincey had 'inoculated' himself 'with the poison of eight thousand drops of laudanum per day', in search of 'happiness', and against the return of the 'misery', the 'blank desolation', the 'settled and abiding darkness' which had first made him a habitual user of the drug. By day the opium drove the misery away; by night it returned, by the agency of the opium itself, and more virulent than ever (3: 406, 231).

It cannot have helped that the practice of inoculation itself, no less famously than the practice of taking opium, had been borrowed from the Turks—the method of protecting oneself against the oriental was itself oriental—and no one knew better than De Quincey that his inoculations rarely provided the immunisation they promised. The opening section of **'The English Mail-Coach'**, his most light-hearted rehearsal of the 'this/that/the other' scheme, seems to function as the architectural plan for a system of fortification which is normally to be found only as an archaeological ruin, as the trace of an overwhelming defeat at the hands of a persistent and ferocious invader. We have seen how, in the first part of the essay, insiders and outsiders are brought together by the identification of something truly outside, plebeian and oriental. But no sooner has this rearrangement been managed, than De Quincey discovers (we shall see how later) that the coachman perched up beside him on the box of the mail-coach itself, loyally dressed in the King's livery, has been transfigured into an Egyptian crocodile, quite close enough to threaten De Quincey with his 'cancerous kisses' (13: 289).

Likewise, the vast sea of the metropolitan poor, the 'myriads' of human faces that tyrannised over De Quincey's dreams, were transformed at one stage in the description of the opium dreams into the 'abominable head of the crocodile . . . multiplied into ten thousand repetitions'—and this at the point where the crocodile takes over from the Chinese as the worst possible thing to find yourself next to, and to be forced to live with. Or still worse, the coachman appears as the very proof of the dangers of inoculation—part man, part reptile, a horrifying mixture of human and inhuman, English and oriental, a crocodile grafted on to a man, the product of 'the horrid inoculation upon each other of incompatible natures'. In botany, 'inoculation' can involve the grafting of one genus or species on to another, and that is exactly what has happened here. The appearance of the coachman as crocodile is one *mise en scène*—one of many, as we shall see—of De Quincey's horrified discovery that his is (to use Homi

Bhabha's term) a *hybrid* identity; that his relation with an imaginary East, like that of an imperial power with its colonial 'dependencies', is a relation (at best) of symbiotic interdependence, and can no longer be thought of in terms of a safe transaction between a self and an other (3: 443; 13: 291n.; Bhabha 20-2).[14]

The continual attempt to create places of safety, the continual return of an 'alien nature' which has been so carefully expelled, the repeated rediscovery of hybridity, of cultural/racial impurity, is described by De Quincey in these terms

> The dreamer finds housed within himself—occupying, as it were, some separate chamber in his brain—holding, perhaps, from that station a secret and detestable commerce with his own heart—some horrid alien nature. What if it were his own nature repeated,—still, if the duality were distinctly perceptible, even that—even this mere numerical double of his own consciousness—might be a curse too mighty to be sustained. But how if the alien nature contradicts his own, fights with it, perplexes and confounds it? How, again, if not one alien nature, but two, but three, but four, but five, are introduced within what once he thought the inviolable sanctuary of himself? These, however, are horrors from the kingdom of anarchy and darkness, which, by their very intensity, challenge the sanctity of concealment, and gloomily retire from exposition.

> (13: 92n.)

An 'alien nature', once its presence within one has been suspected, can sometimes be represented, it seems, as a repetition or a 'double' of one's own nature, not the self, exactly, but not the other, either—a 'that' to one's own 'this'. To treat it like this is to produce a psychic economy which is bearable, but barely so; the self may still be a kind of sanctuary, though hardly an inviolable one. It may be, however, that the 'alien nature' is so very alien as to be the enemy of one's own, in which case it will have to be represented as beyond the *cordon sanitaire* which defines what can be accepted as one's own nature, and which constitutes that nature. But what if it won't go quietly? or what if it has the power of reproducing itself infinitely, so that as each alien nature is tamed, domesticated, recuperated, another appears in the very place, the very chamber of the brain, the very sanctuary which has just been swept, swabbed down, disinfected, fumigated?[15]

The oriental is for De Quincey a name for that very power, that process of endless multiplication whereby the strategy of self-consolidation, of the recuperation or domestication of the other, always involves the simultaneous constitution of a new threat, or a new version of the old, in the space evacuated by the first. The Orient is the place of a malign, a luxuriant or virulent productivity, a breeding-ground of images of the inhuman, or of the no less terrifyingly half-human, which cannot be exterminated, except at the cost

of exterminating one's self, and which cannot be kept back beyond the various Maginot lines, from the Vosges to the Tigris, that De Quincey attempts to defend against the 'horrid enemy from Asia'. In the *Opium-Eater* he speaks of the Chinese and 'the barrier of utter abhorrence placed between myself and *them*', but though the abhorrence was real enough, there was no barrier at all, and no 'between'. Clive, writes Macaulay (1: 508-9), 'was no sooner matched against an Indian intriguer, than he became himself an Indian intriguer'. De Quincey was all the figures from the Orient that appear in his writings. He *was* Chinese; he *was* the Malay that haunted his dreams; he *was* the crocodile. In one of his essays on Roman history he repeats the story told by a late Roman historian—he treats it as absurd, as an example of the 'anecdotage' of Rome in decline—of how Julius Caesar so enjoyed tickling the 'catastrophes' (the posteriors) of crocodiles (presumably he had some in a pool) that he 'anointed himself with crocodile fat, by which means he humbugged the crocodiles, ceasing to be Caesar, and passing for a crocodile, swimming and playing amongst them'. Like Caesar, De Quincey had become smeared with the fat of crocodiles, the mud of the Nile, the oil of opium, with whatever varieties of slime the Orient afforded, and so he had ceased to be *himself* (6: 439).

V

So far, the question of what anxieties, fears, terrors are figured by the oriental in De Quincey's dream narratives has received only one answer—his fear of the urban poor. He himself, however, gives other answers to the question: the visions, he suggests in the final preface to the *Opium-Eater,* are expressions of a fear of losing a woman, or they are repetitions of the story of how she is already lost. In this light, as we have seen, the myriads of faces seem to have meaning only as the manifestation of some 'shadowy malice' which occludes the sight of the 'lost Pariah woman'—'Ann the Outcast'; a nightmare vision self-consciously repaired in De Quincey's **'Autobiography'**, where the early death of his sister Elizabeth is represented as her absorption, 'high in heaven', into 'a gleaming host of faces'. In other discussions of the origin and meaning of his dreams, he acknowledges that 'some of the phenomena developed in my dream-scenery, undoubtedly, do but repeat the experiences of my childhood; and others seem likely to have been growths and fructifications from seeds at that time sown'. At another time there seems to be no content in the dreams worth considering that is not a displacement of De Quincey's 'nursery experience', as he calls it, or his 'nursery afflictions' (3: 222; 1: 50; 1985 92; 13: 339-40).

I have offered, in this introductory chapter, to write an account of De Quincey's fear of the Orient, and of the means by which he attempts to cope with that fear. What I have actually written, it will soon be apparent, is largely an account of his 'nursery afflictions', or of the mythic melodrama he created from his childhood memories and his adult fantasies. Only in the last five chapters will we discover De Quincey turning his attention to various 'Eastern Questions'—the recent history of the Ottoman Empire, the Opium Wars, the first Afghan War, the Kandyan wars in Sri Lanka, the Indian 'mutiny'—as matters of general public concern. It is, I hope to show, especially but by no means exclusively in the myth of his own childhood, as it is elaborated in his autobiographical writings, and as it re-emerges—by way of repeated patterns of imagery and structures of narrative—in his stories and essays, that most of the material is to be found which is pertinent to an account of De Quincey's terror of almost all things oriental. The scenery of that mythic melodrama is as much and as eclectically oriental as the scenery of the opium dreams themselves: the corpses that litter the stage are discovered against a backdrop of various eastern landscapes, from an orientalised East End to a demonised Far East; behind every palm-tree lurks an eastern assassin, human, animal or microbiological. The cast are all members of De Quincey's own family, some appearing as the terrified victims of the Orient, and some as its terrifying embodiment.

But this fear of the oriental, which at times will appear as a displacement of some primal and private terror, is also just what it appears to be: a fear of the 'modes of life', the 'manners', of a vaguely differentiated but universally abhorrent Asia. De Quincey himself seems to suggest that this fear, just because it is 'deeper than I can analyse' (3: 442), must be standing for the fear of something else; but this book will avoid (I hope) the attempt to establish a hierarchy of precedence, an organisation into the manifest and the latent, the surface and the depth, among the various objects of fear his writings disclose. One part of my argument will be that in De Quincey's writings the guilt of childhood is made over to a troop of wild animals and assassins who are especially terrifying because they are oriental; and that the peoples of the Orient—the Kandyans, the Hindus, the Chinese, the Malays—become especially objects of terror to De Quincey, just because they are used to represent the bogeymen and bogeywomen of his earliest years. It is equally possible, however, to conceive of the guilt which finds expression in the narratives of De Quincey's childhood as a fully social guilt, a guilt at his own participation in the imperialist fantasies that become so all-pervasive in the national imagination from the 1820s and 1830s, and which, because it cannot be avowed, can find a voice and can be rationalised only by being displaced. It seems best, indeed, to think of the relation between childhood and the oriental in De Quincey's writings as a relation between two forms of guilt, personal and political, in which each can be a displaced version of the other, and in which each aggravates the other in an ascending spiral of fear and of violence. . . .

Notes

1. I am indebted to Raphael Samuel for information on the Saturday night markets in London. When Monday was treated as a day of rest, or 'holy day', it was referred to by artisans, labourers and their critics as 'St. Monday'. The term 'ghoster' may be anachronistic in the context of De Quincey: when East-End artisans of the 1880s and 1890s worked very late on Friday evening, or even all night, to complete their piecework by Saturday, they described themselves as working a 'ghoster'. The practice, if not the term, must have been as common at the beginning of the century as at the end.

2. For another example of De Quincey claiming to converse with 'poor men', and discovering that almost all are 'jacobins at heart', see 'Anti-Corn-Law Deputation to Sir Robert Peel', B52 1842 272. A hatred of Jacobinism, and a disposition to regard as Jacobin all political positions (and especially Brougham's) that could not be accommodated within the Tory party, is a feature of De Quincey's writing as early as 1818, if he is indeed the author of *Close Comments upon a Straggling Speech* (De Quincey 1818; attributed by Axon). For more of De Quincey's views on Jacobinism before 1830, see 1966, 51-2, 78, 284, and 366 and 391, where Lord Brougham's Jacobinism is again unmasked (as it is also in 'The Present Cabinet in Relation to the Times', B29 1831 148-9, 153-6). De Quincey's fear of Jacobinism was reawakened, though not immediately, by the events in France in 1830. His *Blackwood's* article 'French Revolution' of September 1830 (542-58) is relatively temperate; but in a series of articles thereafter his fear of popular Jacobinism became intense: see 'France and England' (B28 1830 699-718; 'Political Anticipations' (B28 1830 719-36); 'The Late Cabinet' (B28 1830 960-81); 'The Present Cabinet in Relation to the Times' (B29 1831 143-58); 'On the Approaching Revolution in Great Britain' (B30 1831 313-29); 'The Prospects for Britain' (B31 1832 369-91); 'Mrs Hannah More' (T4 1833 293-321). In 'Hints for the Hustings', Chartism is unmasked as another form of 'the fierce Jacobinism which growls for ever in the lower strata of our . . . domestic population' (B48 1840 309-13). In 'Secession from the Church of Scotland' (1844), we hear of 'Christianity prostituted to the service of Jacobinism' (14: 259).

3. On the figure of London as labyrinth in De Quincey's writings, see J. H. Miller 24-5.

4. Disraeli made the remark in a speech in the House of Commons on March 15th 1838.

5. For cabinets of curiosities and oriental collections, see Impey and MacGregor 251-80; for the early

history of the British Museum, see E. Miller, esp. 19-90, 191-244; for a general history of the development of museums as institutions, see Murray.

6. For Palmer's coaches, see Copeland 109-14.

7. 'Raffs', according to Grose, is 'an appellation given by the gownsmen of the university of Oxford to the inhabitants of that place'. It was at Cambridge, according to the Oxford English Dictionary (OED), that townsmen were called 'snobs'. Other early to mid-nineteenth-century meanings of 'snob' include a person of the lower classes; an ostentatious person without breeding; one who seeks to associate with those of a higher class. 'Raffs', more generally, refers to the lowest class of society. In a note to the passage (13: 275n.) De Quincey suggests that the application of the term 'snobs' to shoemakers did not become current until some ten years after the incidents described in 'The English Mail-Coach'.

8. For a useful survey of theories of colonial discourse, see Parry.

9. For Frankistan, or 'Frangistan', see also Lindsay 283.

10. There are several other such imaginary tripartite geopolitical divisions of the globe in De Quincey's writings. For example, if a belief in the unity of God is a crucial test, then Persia in the period of Xerxes and of Herodotus should be seen as belonging with the Jews of Israel to its west, rather than with the superstitious peoples of the further East. At that period Asia can be understood as divided by the river Tigris into Asia *cis*-Tigritana; and Asia *trans*-Tigritana; and although the Persian Empire was established on both sides of the river (7: 178), *true* Persia was to be found between the two great rivers, that is to say, it was cis-Tigritanian (J2: 242). For contemporary attitudes to the Afghanistan campaign, see Bearce 191-9. For another account of the differences that structure De Quincey's imaginary Orient see Maniquis 96-7.

11. In De Quincey's essay 'The Opium Question with China in 1840', he too had talked of 'a monomania in this country as regards the Emperor of Russia' and his ambitions in south central Asia (14: 203). De Quincey's *Blackwood's* article 'Affghanistan' is a review of Lushington's book (B56 1844). The main sources of De Quincey's knowledge of Afghanistan in the earlier articles were the writings of Burnes and Elphinstone's *Caubul:* by 1844 he is aware also of Eyre's, Havelock's and Nash's accounts of the war, as well as Lushington's. In 'The Prospects for Britain' (B31 1832 577-81, 89-90), the supposed territorial ambitions of Russia are regarded as altogether more dangerous, though it is conceded that Russia is (perhaps) 'the "hammer" employed by the Supreme Ruler for crushing the Mohammedan faith'. By 1842, such anxieties are dismissed as 'mere phantoms of crazy fear' (B52 1842 271); see also below, pp.183-4. In De Quincey's essay 'National Temperance Movements' (1845) Bokhara has come to fill the intermediate position, barrier between everywhere and everything, that had also been filled by Afghanistan; see 14: 277 and n. For other European accounts of the Indus as Forbidden River, see for example Moore 1910 435n., J. Burnes 11-13.

12. 'Farther East'—the phrase is W. H. Russell's—'I am once more on my way to the East—another and a farther East' (1: 1; i.e. farther than the Crimea, Russell's previous assignment).

13. For a different use of inoculation, as it were in the reverse direction, see 1857 12, where De Quincey despairs at the fact that the ignorant Chinese have never been 'inoculated' with true (i.e. with European) science.

14. The economic dependence of Britain on the East was a fact that came to be acknowledged by De Quincey in 1857, if not before: 'Without tea, without cotton, Great Britain, no longer great, would collapse into a very anomalous sort of second-rate power' (U2: 25); see also for example Osborn 10. This issue is an organising theme of Nigel Leask's forthcoming essay on De Quincey (see Acknowledgements).

15. On the 'inexhaustible power of self-reproduction' of the oriental images in De Quincey's opium dreams, see J. H. Miller 68ff. . . .

Works Cited

Roland Barthes, *Mythologies,* selected and translated by Annette Lavers, London (Paladin) 1973.

George D. Bearce, *British Attitudes towards India 1784-1858,* London (Oxford University Press) 1961.

Homi K. Bhabha, 'The Commitment to Theory', *New Formations* no. 5, Summer 1988.

Lieut. Alexander Burnes, *Travels into Bokhara; being the Account of a Journey from India to Cabool, Tartary, and Persia; also Narrative of a Voyage on the Indus. &c.,* 3 vols, London (John Murray) 1834, reprinted in facsimile, ed. James Lunt. Karachi (Oxford University Press) 1973.

Lieut.-Col. Sir Alexander Burnes, *Cabool: being a Personal Narrative of a Journey to, and Residence in that City, in the Years 1836, 7, and 8,* London (John Murray) 1842.

James Burnes, *A Narrative of a Visit to the Court of Sinde: A Sketch of the History of Cutch, . . . and Some Remarks on the Medical Topography of Bhooj,* Bombay (Summachar Press) and Edinburgh (John Stark) 1831.

John Copeland, *Roads and their Traffic, 1750-1850,* Newton Abbot (David and Charles) 1968.

The Hon. Mrs G. L. Damer, *Diary of a Tour in Greece, Turkey, Egypt, and the Holy Land,* 2 vols, London (Henry Colburn) 1841.

[Thomas De Quincey?], *Close Comments upon a Straggling Speech,* Kendal (Airey and Bellingham) 1818.

[Thomas De Quincey], *The Stranger's Grave,* London (for Longman, Hurst, Rees, Orme, Brown and Green) 1823.

[Thomas De Quincey], *The Peasant of Portugal: a Tale of the Peninsular War* (1827), London (Aporia Press) 1985.

[Thomas De Quincey], *The Caçadore: A Story of the Peninsular War* (1828), London (Aporia Press) 1988.

China, by Thomas De Quincey: A Revised Reprint of Articles from 'Titan', with Preface and Additions, Edinburgh (James Hogg) and London (R. Groombridge) 1857.

The Collected Writings of Thomas De Quincey, ed. David Masson, 14 vols, Edinburgh (Adam and Charles Black) 1889-90.

The Uncollected Writings of Thomas De Quincey, ed. James Hogg, 2 vols, London (Swan Sonnenschein) 1890.

The Posthumous Works of Thomas De Quincey, ed. Alexander H. Japp, 2 vols, London (William Heinemann) 1891-3.

A Diary of Thomas De Quincey, 1803, ed. Horace A. Eaton, London (Noel Douglas), no date [1928].

'Niels Kilm, being an incomplete translation, by Thomas De Quincey, from the Danish of Ludvig Holberg, now edited from the manuscript by S. Musgrove', *Auckland University College Bulletin,* no. 42, English series no. 5, 1953.

New Essays by De Quincey: his Contributions to the Edinburgh Saturday Post and the Edinburgh Evening Post, 1827-8, ed. Stuart M. Tave, Princeton (Princeton University Press) 1966.

Thomas De Quincey, *Recollections of the Lakes and the Lake Poets,* ed. David Wright, Harmondsworth (Penguin Books) 1970.

Thomas De Quincey, *Confessions of an English Opium Eater,* ed. Alethea Hayter, Harmondsworth (Penguin Books) 1971.

Thomas De Quincey, *Confessions of an English Opium-Eater and Other Writings,* ed. Grevel Lindop, Oxford and New York (Oxford University Press) 1985.

Lord Beaconsfield's Correspondence with his Sister 1832-1852, London (John Murray) 1886.

The Hon. Mountstuart Elphinstone, *An Account of the Kingdom of Caubul, and its Dependencies in Persia, Tartary, and India: comprising a view of the Afghan Nation, and a History of the Douraunee Monarchy,* London (for Longman, Hurst, Rees, Orme, and Brown and J. Murray) 1815.

Lieutenant Vincent Eyre, *The Military Operations at Cabul, which ended in the Retreat and Destruction of the British Army, January 1842* (1843), 2nd edn, London (John Murray) 1843.

A Dictionary of Buckish Slang, University Wit, and Pickpocket Eloquence. Compiled Originally by Captain Grose, London (for C. Chappel) 1811.

Captain Henry Havelock, *Narrative of the War in Affghanistan. In 1838-9,* 2 vols, London (Henry Colburn) 1840.

Oliver Impey and Arthur MacGregor (eds), *The Origin of Museums: The Cabinet of Curiosities in Sixteenth- and Seventeenth-Century Europe,* Oxford (Clarendon Press) 1985.

Sir William Jones, 'The Gods of Greece, Italy, and India', *Asiatic Researches,* vol. 1, 1789.

V. G. Kierman, *The Lords of Human Kind: Black Man, Yellow Man, and White Man in an Age of Empire* (1969), London (Century Hutchinson; The Cresset Library) 1988.

A. W. Kinglake, *Eothen* (1844), new edn, London (Longman, Brown, Green and Longmans) 1851.

Grevel Lindop, *The Opium-Eater. A Life of Thomas De Quincey,* London (J. M. Dent) 1981.

Lord Lindsay (Alexander William Crawford), *Letters on Egypt, Edom, and the Holy Land* (1838), 4th edn, London (Henry Colburn) 1847.

Henry Lushington, *A Great Country's Little Wars; or England, Affghanistan, and Sinde,* London (J. W. Parker) 1844.

Thomas Babington Macaulay, *Critical and Historical Essays* (1843), 2 vols, London (J. M. Dent) and New York (E. P. Dutton) 1907.

Robert M. Maniquis, 'Lonely Empires: Personal and Public Visions of Thomas De Quincey', in Eric Rothstein and Joseph Anthony Wittreich, Jr. (eds) *Literary Monographs,* vol. 8, Madison (University of Wisconsin Press) 1976.

Thomas Maurice, *The History of Hindostan, its Arts, and its Sciences,* 3 vols, London (for the author) 1795-8.

Henry Mayhew, *London Labour and the London Poor* (1851), 2nd edn, 4 vols (1861-2), reprinted in facsimile, London (Frank Cass) 1967.

Edward Miller, *That Noble Cabinet: A History of the British Museum,* London (André Deutsch) 1973.

J. Hillis Miller, *The Disappearance of God: Five Nineteenth-Century Writers,* Cambridge Mass. (Harvard University Press) 1975.

Edward Moor, *The Hindu Pantheon,* London (Joseph Johnson) 1810.

The Poetical Works of Thomas Moore, ed. A. D. Godley, London (Henry Frowde, for Oxford University Press) 1910.

David Murray, *Museums, Their History and Their Use,* Glasgow (John MacLehose) 1904.

Charles Nash (ed.) *History of the War in Affghanistan, from its Commencement to its Close . . . from the Journal and Letters of an Officer of High Rank,* London (Thomas Brooks) 1843.

Benita Parry, 'Problems in Current Theories of Colonial Discourse', *Oxford Literary Review,* vol. 9, nos. 1-2, (1987) 27-58.

My Diary in India, in the Year 1858-9, 2 vols, London (Routledge, Warne and Routledge) 1860.

'Overdeterminations of Imperialism: David Ochterlony and the Ranee of Sirmoor', in *Europe and Its Others,* vol. 1, Colchester (University of Essex) 1985.

G. T. Vigne, *A Personal Narrative of a Visit to Ghuzni, Kabul, and Affghanistan, and of a Residence at the Court of Dost Mohamed,* &c., London (Whittaker) 1840.

Travels in Kashmir, Ladak, Iskardo, &c., 2 vols, London (Henry Colburn) 1842.

Alina Clej (essay date 1995)

SOURCE: "Prodigal Narratives," in *A Genealogy of the Modern Self: Thomas De Quincey and the Intoxication of Writing,* Stanford University Press, 1995, pp. 76-89.

[*In the following essay, Clej analyzes De Quincey's confessional narratives and essays through the trope of prodigiality and the figure of the pariah.*]

The prodigal narrative that stands at the center of De Quincey's early confessions is his reckless flight from school, the "fatal error" that will follow him throughout his life and for which he can find no excuse. This youthful act of disobedience estranged him from his family (and from his mother's financial support) and left him to fend for himself. This he soon did by squandering his small trust fund (a large sum went as an anonymous gift to Coleridge), which brought him to a state of insolvency that he maintained more or less consistently for the rest of his life. Although he tried occasionally to measure his "debt" (or "delinquency") against that of Coleridge, and sometimes shifted his debts onto him (the anonymous donation inaugurates this practice), De Quincey preferred to accumulate debts as part of his way of embracing prodigality. On a symbolic level De Quincey's confessional narratives, which are by no means limited to the *Confessions,* constitute his main form of prodigal expenditure. As a compulsive narrator, De Quincey can constantly solicit and outrun the credit of his audience.

The relatively simple scenario put forth in the *Confessions,* which explains away De Quincey's prodigality as a matter of juvenile whimsey, is complicated in *Suspiria de Profundis* and the *Autobiographic Sketches* through an additional scenario. In the chapter "The Affliction of Childhood," which appears in slightly different versions in both texts, De Quincey's act of disobedience described in *Confessions* is anticipated by the dark period of despair that followed Elizabeth's death—the moment when the six-year-old De Quincey suddenly realizes that "Life is finished!" and that the "lamp of Paradise" kept alive by her "reflection" has been irrevocably extinguished (*CW,* I: 36). This episode inevitably modifies the first impression conveyed in the early *Confessions* by giving a deeper meaning to De Quincey's childish behavior. His desperate flight from school, his "inexplicable error," could now be viewed as a reenactment of his previous experience of sudden separation and loss. There are also many indications in De Quincey's work that he was never able to complete his mourning and that his mysterious attacks of melancholia, not to mention his opium addiction, were partly related to this initial loss. Yet this excuse, with the mitigation it may offer, is never produced in the first edition of *Confessions.*

Critics have generally assumed that De Quincey was driven out of his childhood paradise by the tragic event of his sister's death, which also ended an ideal state of innocence and harmony between self and world.[1] De Quincey's prodigal narratives are seen as an attempt to come to terms with this "original" trauma and the "psychic wounds" it left behind, on the implicit assumption that autobiography represents a rewriting of the subject's existential trials.[2] The omission of Elizabeth's death from De Quincey's early *Confessions* is at the very least intriguing. It suggests either an extreme reticence on De Quincey's part or the desire to leave the impression of an unsolved mystery. Or perhaps the elements of the famous deathbed scene were simply not available to De Quincey when he was writing his first confessions. At any rate, the image of an original purity and happiness in the writer's life prior to his sister's death is largely a fictional construct. As De Quincey remarks, undermining this idyllic phase in his life, "No Eden of lakes and forest-lawns, such as the *mirage* suddenly evokes in Arabian sands . . . could leave behind it the mixed impression of so much truth combined with so much absolute delusion" (*CW,* I: 55). Furthermore, it is De Quincey who leads us to believe he was not simply hurled into the world of experience by his tragic loss, but rather "launched" himself in it by reenacting the Fall.

In *Suspiria de Profundis,* as in his later *Autobiographic Sketches,* the famous scene in which De Quincey "steals" into the room where his dead sister is laid out in order to see her one more time is clearly described as an act of transgression. Inside the room the child experiences a visionary trance that ends as he imagines or actually hears the sound of footsteps on the stairs—an image that, like the reverberating echo in St. Paul's Cathedral, will haunt him throughout his life. The child is "alarmed" lest he be "detected" and forbidden access to the room. He therefore slinks away like "a guilty thing," after hastily "kiss[ing] the lips that [he] should kiss no more" (*S*: 107).

The nature of the transgression is obscured by a complex set of associations. In one sense the child appears to violate an original mystery. The hushed chamber communicating through an open window with the infinity of the summer sky creates a sacred space in which the mysteries of death and life are symbolically conjoined. The funeral room bathed in sunlight becomes related through a digressive association with the scene of Christ's death and resurrection in Jerusalem, the *"omphalos* of mortality," where "the divine had been swallowed up by the abyss" (*S*: 104-5). From this perspective the violation could refer to the mystery of the Host.[3] Some critics have also suggested that De Quincey's transgression is related to an incestuous longing that makes him feel partly responsible for his sister's death.[4]

In either sense (pagan or Christian) the child's intrusion is immediately censured by a sinister omen, a "hollow, solemn, Memnonian wind" that rises in the sky, boding lasting banishment from divine grace.[5] "A vault seemed to open in the zenith of the far blue sky, a shaft which ran up for ever. I in spirit rose as if on billows that also ran up the shaft for ever; and the billows seemed to pursue the throne of God; but *that* also ran before us and flew away continually" (*S*: 105-7). The vision of endless pursuit and infinite regress, which mirrors De Quincey's prodigal economies, seems to be inaugurated by this imaginary instance of violation. Because of the imminent sound of steps outside the room, De Quincey's last contact with his sister is "mutilated" and "tainted" with fear, marred by a sense of incompleteness and misdoing. He is left with an irremediable sense of guilt and longing, arguably the "sorrow" that constitutes the professed, voiceless—and unvoiceable—object of his confessions, the "wound in [his] infant heart" that cannot heal, the loss that he may be secretly mourning.

From a psychoanalytic point of view one could establish a parallelism between the child's "wound" and the figure of the "crypt" in Nicholas Abraham and Maria Torok's interpretation of this psychoanalytic emblem. According to this view the "crypt" or the gaping wound points to "a memory . . . buried *without legal burial place*," a "segment of painfully lived Reality, whose unutterable nature dodges all work of mourning."[6] Whether autobiographical facts justify De Quincey's sense of guilt or his persistent melancholia is in practical terms impossible to determine because De Quincey is the main source for his early biography.[7] What concerns us here is the play of guilt as a

signifier in De Quincey's narratives of prodigality. His writings accumulate and exchange the marks of guilt, what in psychoanalytic terms would be called the symptoms of repression. How does this accumulation and exchange function, and what is its purpose?

Characteristically, in evoking his guilt, which the address "To the Reader" shows is not openly acknowledged, De Quincey avoids a specifically Christian frame of reference. His description of his fault in terms of physical stigmas ("worm" or "wound") conjures up an archaic sense of evil, that of defilement, defined as "a 'something' that infects, a dread that anticipates the unleashing of the avenging wrath of the interdiction."[8] At the same time, expressions like "sorrow" and "grief" used to describe the same obscure fault bring it closer to the Greek notion of *hamartia,* which was conceived as a "fatal error" or "tragic blindness" and ultimately an "excusable fault."[9] The implicit identification with Oedipus—who like De Quincey is sustained in his later torments by "the sublime piety of his two daughters"—allows De Quincey to play on the ambiguity of his own guilt by confusing the distinction between voluntary and involuntary acts. In his essay **"The Theban Sphinx,"** De Quincey maintains that "Oedipus was loaded with an insupportable burthen of pariah participation in pollution and misery, to which his will had never consented" (*CW,* 6: 142) in the same way that the Opium-Eater is overwhelmed by the "burthen of horrors" brought upon him by the darker side of his addiction (*C,*: 62).[10] This fatal predicament makes Oedipus the epitome of what De Quincey calls *piacularity,* which, like "hereditary sin," denotes "an evil to which the party affected has not consciously concurred," but which, unlike "hereditary sin," "expresses an evil personal to the individual, and not extending itself to the race" (*CW,* 6: 142).

The idea of an external, quasi-material contamination of evil, emphasized by De Quincey's notion of *piacularity*—a fault for which the individual bears little or no responsibility—seems perfectly suited to the Opium-Eater's ineffable sense of guilt.[11] From this perspective opium appears to embody the very idea of the alien (and alienating) nature of evil. One could say that by deliberately ingesting the drug (the *pharmakon*), sometimes in excessive quantities, De Quincey constitutes himself as *pharmakos,* as criminal and scapegoat.[12]

The archaic understanding of evil as a form of possession by alien, uncontrollable forces, or in the Greek sense as possession by a fatal destiny, may explain De Quincey's treatment of his "original" transgression as a form of misfortune for which he is as much to be pitied as blamed. De Quincey's use of the words "sorrow" and "grief" to refer to the pain that allegedly afflicted him long after his sister's death is marked by the ambiguity of the Greek *hamartia,* a fault either "suffered" or "done." Moreover, sorrow, grief, or passion—the express objects of De Quincey's confessions ("impassioned prose")—carry the same ambivalence as their Greek equivalent *pathos.* They can refer to the violent act of the perpetrator or the passive suffering of the victim; De Quincey can adopt these two postures at once without apparent contradiction.

Through his trials De Quincey seems to enact some form of sacrificial drama that "draws the superabundance of grace from the abundance of sin," to use Ricoeur's phrase, but one in which "grace" has a dubious value. This is apparent in De Quincey's use of Christ's passion to allude to his own suffering. But in his version of the Christian topos of *imitatio Christi* the elements of the sacred story become sorely confused. In the episode of his swoon in Oxford Street during a nocturnal walk, De Quincey describes himself as a dying Christ. He had reached, he says, "the crisis of [his] fate" and would have "sunk to a point of exhaustion from which all re-ascent . . . would soon have become hopeless" if it hadn't been for the "saving hand" of Ann (the streetwalker) (*C:* 22).

His hyperbolic agony is alleviated by "a glass of port wine and spices" (as opposed to the biblical vinegar) administered by Ann, his "benefactress" and "Magdalen." In this inverted image the prostitute becomes the savior (the "saving hand") and the instrument of resurrection, while De Quincey performs the role of a helpless Christ. At the end of a period of enforced withdrawal from opium, he describes himself as "agitated, writhing, throbbing, palpitating, shattered; and much, perhaps, in the situation of him who has been racked" (*C:* 78). Yet "the most innocent sufferer," with whom De Quincey compares his torments, is not Christ, as one might have expected, but a civilian traveler of the time of James I, a certain William Lithgow, who gives a powerful account of his sufferings on the rack at Malaga.

De Quincey's obsessive assumption of suffering (and guilt symptoms) or debts (he is a "debtor for life") may "imitate" Christ's passion, but it has none of the redemptive value that such an "imitation" traditionally has in religious confessions. In his case excessive suffering and abjection are not the prelude to a rebirth of the self, but turn out to be yet another posture through which he tries to market his confessional self. In the absence of the climactic moment of conversion (the transcendence of the sinful self), De Quincey's prodigality circles upon itself by a self-contained mechanism that produces as much as it tends to efface the confessional subject. In the end confessing reckless expenditure becomes a form of self-investment in which "interest" (the "thrilling interest" of the confession) is generated as a gratuitous though calculated by-product of an economic regulation of the self.

The excesses of the Opium-Eater transform him into an "exemplary sufferer" in much the same way as a monstrous criminal may acquire an almost sacred aura. In a draft of a political essay De Quincey comments on the particular advantages of being an indicted criminal:

> Standing in that position, he becomes sacred to us all. . . . What a lull, what an awful sabbath of rest is created for him in the midst of his own wicked agitations, and *by* his own agitations! For it is his own crimes which have procured him this immunity. It is because he had become too bad to be borne, it is because he has become insufferable, and from the moment when the outraged law has laid her sacred hand of attachment upon him, that she will suffer no one to question him but herself.[13]

The Opium-Eater grounds his glory in the dubious act of violating and flirting with the law. Throughout his writings De Quincey effectively conflates the image of the scapegoat with that of the Byronic hero-criminal. Given his understanding of *pathos,* De Quincey can sympathize with or impersonate the victim and the criminal and often plays both roles in his endless meanderings through the world of experience.[14]

De Quincey's favorite image for this ambiguous figure is the pariah, whose degradation and marginality are the result of an obscure taboo and whose miserable fate generates a special kind of pathos. Pariahs, from the early Pelasgi and the Jews to medieval lepers, gypsies, and the Pyrenean Cagots, occasion a kind of sacred awe produced by "some dreadful taint of guilt, real or imputed, in ages far remote" (*CW,* 1: 101). According to De Quincey pariahs can also be found in modern times, except that most people ignore their presence due to their "sensuous dulness." "In the very act of facing or touching a dreadful object, they will utterly deny its existence," like the hardened unbelievers denounced by the Scriptures: "Having ears, they hear not; and, seeing, they do not understand" (*CW,* 1: 101). De Quincey's impassioned appeal to faith has nothing to do with religion, however, but is directed instead to newspaper accounts and to what De Quincey calls the "horrible burden of misery" that they contain—to the pathos of everyday life. This somewhat banalized pathos, framed by an aura of magnificence, best exemplifies De Quincey's understanding of "impassioned prose."

In his writings De Quincey identifies with a wide range of pariah figures: Ahasuerus, the wandering Jew, bound on an "endless pilgrimage of woe" (*CW,* 1: 43); Oedipus, trudging along public roads, "aged, blind, and a helpless vagrant" (*CW,* 6: 146); Ann, the streetwalker with whom De Quincey, the "peripatetic" philosopher, associates in his night rambles through London (*C:* 20). In all these variations on the theme of exile and estrangement De Quincey is at once the outcast and the repentant prodigal son.

When trying to explain De Quincey's curious involvement with pariah figures, we first need to remember the extent to which his middle-class audience shared his sympathies. In the effusiveness with which he embraces—at an imaginary level—the fate of the underdog, De Quincey is no doubt a creature of his times. Compassion, the emotional expenditure, often displaced to isolated or "picturesque" victims (beggars, gypsies, or prostitutes) served throughout the nineteenth century to assuage the social guilt produced by the widespread exploitation of both indigenous and colonized workers.[15] De Quincey's persistent identification with social outsiders is by no means a sign of enlightened tolerance; if anything, it constitutes the counterpart of his class prejudices and racial intolerance.[16] The "dreadful taint of guilt" of the pariah, whose source remains a "secret," is but a reflection of De Quincey's (and his readers') own bad conscience and vague fears of the masses, an ideological malaise that may explain the Romantic (Gothic) infatuation with tales of crime and revenge.[17]

Nothing seems to suit De Quincey's sensibility better than the idea of being haunted by invisible enemies. Like a pariah (Oedipus), De Quincey is plagued by an obscure curse (if not the "curse of the Law" itself). He appears to relish the feeling of persecution and punishment, like all melancholiacs do.[18] This dubious pleasure is particularly evident in his masochistic surrender to the cruel fantasies of his elder brother described in *Autobiographic Sketches* or in the impish enjoyment he derived from being harried by creditors. According to his daughter: "It was an accepted fact among us that he was able when saturated with opium to persuade himself and delighted to persuade himself (the excitement of terror was a real delight to him) that he was dogged by dark and mysterious foes."[19] De Quincey's excitement and delight in terror—the hallmark of the sublime—inform both his confessional writings and his Gothic stories, which are related in more ways than one.

De Quincey's prodigality contaminates a whole range of characters both real and imaginary, and the story of estrangement and loss that articulates his confessions reemerges in various guises throughout his writings. The curious figure of the innocent criminal is omnipresent in De Quincey's prodigal narratives, which irrespective of setting or historical context tell the same story of inexplicable woe. One temptation is to find the "real" object of De Quincey's confessions, the "original" fault that explains his addiction, concealed in the fictional texture of these repetitive narratives. Another temptation is to see in them a "mythical" rewriting of De Quincey's childhood "afflictions" and adult phobias.[20]

The problem is that De Quincey both encourages and thwarts these critical impulses by undermining the distinc-

tion between truthful and fictional discourses.[21] The risk of confusion is made particularly explicit in De Quincey's postscript to **"The Spanish Military Nun,"** a picaresque tale set in Spain and South America at the beginning of the sixteenth century and purportedly based on the memoirs of a young nun turned soldier.

> There are some narratives which, though pure fictions from first to last, counterfeit so vividly the air of grave realities that, if deliberately offered for such, they would for a time impose upon everybody. In the opposite scale there are other narratives, which, whilst rigorously true, move amongst characters and scenes so remote from our ordinary experience, and through a state of society so favorable to an adventurous cast of incidents, that they would everywhere pass for romances, if served from the documents which attest their fidelity to facts.
>
> (*CW,* 13: 238)

To illustrate these paradoxes, De Quincey recounts the case of an "artless young rustic" (by all appearances De Quincey's future wife Margaret) who after having read *The Vicar of Wakefield* (which De Quincey had lent her) imagines that all the characters in the novel are real and hence can "sue and be sued."

De Quincey's novella, **"The Spanish Military Nun,"** raises the question of fictionality and deception in more ways than one. The heroine's literal travesty, which disguises "the two main perils [of] her sex, and her monastic dedication," offers ample opportunity for both illusion and imposture. Catalina, or Kate, as De Quincey often calls her, maybe thinking of Kate Wordsworth, is twice in a position of becoming a bridegroom, and the second time the bride to be is so lovely that had Catalina been "really Peter [Diaz]," as she pretended to be, and not just a "sham Peter," she would certainly have been smitten with that "innocent child." The situation is even more confusing when after killing the Portuguese cavalier, she "becomes *falsely* accused (because accused by lying witnesses) of an act which she really *did* commit" (*CW,* 13: 218).

The same absurd situation appears in the *Confessions,* where De Quincey finds himself "accused, or at least suspected," by his Jewish creditors of "counterfeiting his own self" (*C:* 55). But if De Quincey was able to provide proof of his identity, Catalina could not reveal "the secret of her sex," which would have exonerated her from the crime, without shedding light on the other dubious "transactions" in her life that would have attracted the attention of the Inquisition. De Quincey not only identifies with his heroine's guilty predicament—"I love this Kate, bloodstained as she is"—but also defends her acts against the background of "the exaggerated social estimate of all violence" that appears to "translate" the "ethics of a police-office" into that of God-fearing people. There is in De Quincey's eyes something perfectly legitimate about Catalina's violence, whose errors he maintains "never took a shape of self-interest or deceit" (*CW,* 13: 199).

In spite of the overall frothy tone De Quincey uses to retell Kate's story, there are many intimations of doom in which an attentive reader could easily recognize the lineaments of De Quincey's own prodigal narrative. Catalina's escape from the convent is curiously similar to De Quincey's elopement from Manchester Grammar School. Like De Quincey, who wakes up to the morning "which was to launch [him] into the world" and expose him to a "hurricane, and perfect hail-storm of affliction" (*C:* 9), Catalina "pull[s] ahead right out of St. Sebastian's cove into the main ocean of life" to embark upon "her sad and infinite wanderings" (*CW,* 13: 165). Also like De Quincey, Catalina suffers from an "afflicted conscience" and "fearful remembrances"—the death of De Quincey's sister paralleling the killing of Catalina's brother—and is beset by nightmares.

The most remarkable parallel, however, is between Kate's collapse after her ascent of the Andes, when she finds herself "in critical danger of perishing for want of a little brandy" or a draught of laudanum, and De Quincey's swoon in Oxford Street. For a moment it is unclear "whether the jewelly star of [Catalina's] life had descended too far down the arch towards setting for any chance of reascending by *spontaneous* effort," that is, "without some stimulus from earthly vineyards" (*CW,* 13: 206). In the same way, De Quincey describes in his *Confessions* the "crisis of [his] fate," the conviction that "without some powerful and reviving stimulus" he would have "sunk to a point of exhaustion from which all re-ascent . . . would soon have become hopeless" (*C:* 22). Ann offered the providential "glass of port wine and spices" that saved his life.

On even closer inspection Catalina's story, with its ups and downs dramatically figured by her symbolic ascent and descent of the Andes, reveals the fluctuations of De Quincey's prodigal economy, the "oscillating experience" of the opium eater and perpetual debtor. Although opium makes only a fleeting appearance in the story, the obsession with debts and credits pervades the whole narrative. America appears from the very beginning as an inexhaustible source of profit for the Spanish hidalgos and for storytellers like De Quincey:

> And with a view to new leases of idleness, through new generations of slaves, it was (as many people think) that Spain went so heartily into the enterprises of Cortez and Pizarro. A sedentary body of Dons, without needing to uncross their thrice-noble legs, would thus levy eternal tributes of gold and silver upon eternal mines, through eternal successions of nations that had been, and were to be, enslaved.

> (*CW,* 13: 160)

In the meantime aristocratic daughters could be pawned away, "quartered . . . for life upon nunneries," so "their papas, being hidalgos," could make the "magnificent purchase of eternal idleness" (*CW,* 13: 160). As a result, Catalina, whose life has thus been brokered, is always ready to compensate herself for this original injustice by attacking or slaying any personal offender (unfortunately, she could not dispatch her father, as he well deserved). She also levies money on her uncle for assuming to bore her "gratis" and on the king of Spain's contingency box to repay herself the trouble of having to leave his sinking ship and swim to the shore of his majesty's colony. As the bookkeeper of a Peruvian draper, she serves two clients, one who has "credit unlimited" and one who has "*no* credit" and whom she ends up killing in a duel. As a way out the draper offers her marriage to the relative of the deceased man, that is, the client who happens to have unlimited credit, a solution Catalina spurns to pursue her adventures.

The paradox that informs De Quincey's prodigal economy is by now apparent in Catalina's extravagant story—there can be no recovery without loss, no hope of return without previous estrangement. Catalina's many losses are requited in the end by her lavish reinstatement as a heroine in her home country, and her trespasses will all be forgiven by Christ, the ultimate bearer of human debts. In the meantime De Quincey has indebted himself to his readers for being unable to complete his story in two parts as he had originally promised and for having to protract the narrative into a third part.

That De Quincey could picture himself as a woman comes as no surprise given his biographical profile. Like Catalina, who became the "wee pet" of the St. Sebastian nuns, De Quincey was doted on as a young child by his female entourage. When De Quincey has Catalina put on a pair of trousers for the first time, he mentions how at age four he was still "retaining hermaphrodite relations of dress as to wear a petticoat above [his] trousers" (*CW,* 13: 167). It is not the first time that De Quincey exchanges identity with a woman, nor will it be the last. In **"The Spanish Military Nun"** De Quincey takes clear advantage of Catalina's superior "energy and indomitable courage" to pay back some old debts. The "female servant" of the convent whom Catalina pierces with a dreadful look for having "*wilfully*" given her a push recalls the female servant at Greenhay who treated little Jane harshly a couple of days before her death. The brother whom Catalina kills by mistake may be seen as a double of William, the tyrannical brother whom De Quincey resented but was unable to subdue. And the lavish welcome bestowed upon Catalina by the pope and the king of Spain on her return from the New World may be read as an imaginary compensation for De Quincey's measly treatment by his mother and guardians after his youthful escapade.[22] At the same time De Quincey insinuates that prodigal extravagance in the name of the empire can always be forgiven.[23]

This biographical reading is complicated by one further fictional layer. As De Quincey tells us in a digression, while Kate is left suspended on the high ridge of the Andes, struggling alone with her "afflicted conscience," the heroine's condition actually resembles the plight of the "Ancient Mariner" in Coleridge's poem. According to De Quincey "The Rime of the Ancient Mariner" offers three models of interpretation (*CW*, 13: 195). For the unsophisticated reader the Mariner's story is just a "baseless fairy tale." A more advanced reader will see in the Mariner's visions not mere inventions, but the result of an actual delirium caused by a "pestilential fever." Only the wise reader can see beyond the signs of "bodily affection" to the real source of the Mariner's troubles—his "penitential sorrow," which echoes the "penitential loneliness" evoked in Wordsworth's *White Doe*.

The Nemesis that follows the Mariner, "as if he were a Cain, or another Wandering Jew," is the result of his reckless killing of "the creature that, on all earth, loved him best"—the albatross. Catalina's curse turns out to be the same as that of the Mariner. "She, like the mariner, had slain the one sole creature that loved her upon the whole wide earth; she, like the mariner, for this offence, had been hunted into frost and snow—very soon will be hunted into delirium; and from *that* (if she escapes with life) will be hunted into the trouble of a heart that cannot rest" (*CW*, 13: 196).

Oedipus, Catalina, the Ancient Mariner, and De Quincey thus seem to share the same persecution syndrome for an unwitting crime, an accident of fate that transforms them into eternal exiles or pariahs. The difficulty of assessing the significance of De Quincey's fictional personae is certainly not that of finding analogies between De Quincey's prodigality as described in his confessions and that of his characters; the true difficulty is establishing a causal relation between these analogues. Is De Quincey attracted by the story of Oedipus and the Ancient Mariner because of his own prodigal experiences, or are his experiences inspired by these fictional characters? If so, is De Quincey's curse opium or literature, more specifically Coleridge, whose addiction De Quincey emulates?

De Quincey does his best to confuse his readers as to the "real" origin of his stories. The travesty in **"The Spanish Military Nun"** applies not only to the nun, but to De Quincey, who had freely adapted Catalina's story as told by Alexis de Valon from the *Revue des deux mondes* without mentioning his source. The Frenchman's presence is visible only in the figure of Catalina's anonymous detractor, whom De Quincey vehemently upbraids in the passionate defense of his heroine. In its complex mixture of fact and fiction, the case of **"The Spanish Military Nun"** seems to challenge the very limits of the reader's credulity. De Quincey is defending the character of his imaginary Catalina, which is based on the purloined portrait of a supposedly historical person, while effacing all traces that could support his defense.

As David Masson observes in his explicatory note to **"The Spanish Military Nun"** De Quincey never saw Catalina's memoirs on which the Frenchman's story was presumably grounded and obviously could not invoke them as evidence for her character. The origin of De Quincey's story has been effectively erased in the same way that Catalina symbolically disappears in De Quincey's epilogue to **"The Spanish Military Nun"** swallowed up by the sea or as Oedipus vanishes at the end of **"The Theban Sphinx,"** leaving "no trace or visible record" (*CW*, 6: 150). In the meantime, however, De Quincey's dream of perfect invisibility has been punctured by his editor, leaving the reader to muse on De Quincey's own stake in travesty and "bloodstained" pariahs.

Notes

1. See Miller, pp. 18-23.

2. Barrell assumes that De Quincey reconstructs his childhood experiences through a series of narratives ("narratives of trauma" and "narratives of reparation") in which his "nursery afflictions" and adult phobias are both reenacted and transcended (pp. 20-22).

3. For a parallel interpretation of this scene see Black, "Confession, Digression, Gravitation."

4. See Barrell, pp. 26-28.

5. For the Romantic reevaluation of the legendary figure of Memnon, see Hayter, p. 85.

6. Abraham and Torok, "A Poetics of Psychoanalysis," p. 4.

7. The existing accounts of De Quincey's life draw extensively on his own writings for documenting his childhood and youth.

8. Ricoeur, p. 33.

9. See ibid., pp. 114-16.

10. Both Antigone and Oedipus tend to view Oedipus's crimes as unfortunate acts that the hero has "suffered" rather than "done." Oedipus declares at one point: "I have burdened myself with an alien misfortune; yes, I am burdened with it in spite of myself. Let the divinity be witness! Nothing of all that was purposed [*authaireton*]." *Oedipus at Colonus*, ll. 522-23.

11. In *The Infection of Thomas De Quincey,* Barrell discusses at length images of pollution and contamination as indicative of De Quincey's fear of the Orient. This exotic evil covers a much more familiar one.

12. See Derrida, "Plato's Pharmacy," pp. 128-34.

13. Thomas De Quincey, The Wordsworth Trust, Grasmere, England.

14. De Quincey's strange fascination with murder—of which the half-ironic, half-serious essay "On Murder Considered as One of the Fine Arts" is a quizzical proof—gives a certain lurid tinge to his fatal predicament.

15. For an in-depth historical analysis of the emergence of philanthropy in England and western Europe see Haskell.

16. For a discussion of De Quincey's attitude toward Muslims and Jews see Barrell, p. 69.

17. See ibid., pp. 3-8. See also Praz, *The Romantic Agony,* pp. 95-186.

18. Freud, "Mourning and Melancholia," p. 246.

19. Quoted by Eaton, p. 374n. De Quincey's attacks of anxiety were not without practical benefits. As his daughter comments, the persuasion that he was terrorized by invisible enemies "gave a sanction to his conscience for getting away from the crowded discomforts of a home without any competent head." Terror, like opium eating, is a convenient escape from the constraints of reality. In the same way, assuming the identity of the eternal debtor delivered him from all financial obligations. This strategy of denial can be traced back to De Quincey's childhood. "Professing the most absolute bankruptcy from the very beginning," a tactic he used in defending himself against his elder, tyrannical brother, William, was also a way of making sure he "never could be made miserable by unknown responsibilities" (*CW,* I: 60). In a similar way, as a child De Quincey "had a perfect craze for being despised" and doted on what he called his "general idiocy" in order to gain "freedom from anxiety" and to be left alone.

20. See Barrell, pp. 20-22.

21. See Searle's distinction between "serious" and "nonserious" statements in terms of the speaker's commitment to the truth of his or her utterance. "What distinguishes fiction from lies," in Searle's view, "is the existence of a separate set of conventions which enable the author to go through the motions of making statements which he knows to be not true even though he has no intention to deceive" (pp. 65-67).

22. In his discussion of this story Barrell discovers similar parallelisms and attributes them to De Quincey's desire for "liberating himself from all guilty thoughts towards Elizabeth and William" (pp. 78-80). I am questioning in this chapter the biographical validity of De Quincey's guilt.

23. Two of De Quincey's sons had served in the British army overseas—Horace in China, where he died of a fever in 1842, and Paul Frederick in the Sikh War.

Abbreviations

Works cited frequently have been identified by the following abbreviations:

Works by Thomas De Quincey

C Confessions of an English Opium-Eater (1821). In Grevel Lindop, ed., *Confessions of an English Opium-Eater and Other Writings.* Oxford: Oxford University Press, 1985.

C1856 Confessions of an English Opium-Eater: Author's Revised and Enlarged Edition of 1856. In David Masson, ed., *The Collected Writings of Thomas De Quincey,* vol. 3. London: Adam and Charles Black, 1890.

CW The Collected Writings of Thomas De Quincey. David Masson, ed. 14 vols. London: Adam and Charles Black, 1889-90.

D A Diary of Thomas De Quincey (1803). Horace A. Eaton, ed. London: Noel Douglas, 1927.

M De Quincey Memorials. A. H. Japp, ed. 2 vols. London: Heinemann, 1891.

PW The Posthumous Works of Thomas De Quincey. A. J. Japp, ed. 2 vols. London: William Heinemann, 1891.

RL Recollections of the Lakes and the Lake Poets. David Wright, ed. Harmondsworth: Penguin Books, 1970.

S Suspiria de Profundis (1845). In Grevel Lindop, ed., *Confessions of an English Opium-Eater and Other Writings.* Oxford: Oxford University Press, 1985.

UW The Uncollected Works of Thomas De Quincey. 2 vols. James Hogg, ed. London: Swan Sonnenschein, 1892.

Works by Others

AC Augustine. *Confessions.* R. S. Pine-Coffin, trans. Harmondsworth: Penguin Books, 1961.

BL Coleridge, Samuel Taylor. *Biographia Literaria.* James Engell and W. Jackson Bate, eds. 2 vols. Bollingen Series, no. 75. Princeton: Princeton University Press, 1983.

Hogg De Quincey and His Friends. James Hogg, ed. London: Sampson Low, Marston, 1895.

Japp Thomas De Quincey: His Life and Writings. A. H. Japp, ed. London: John Hogg, 1890.

OC Baudelaire, Charles. *Oeuvres complètes.* Bibliothèque de la Pléiade. 2 vols. Paris: Gallimard, 1975.

P Wordsworth, William. *The Prelude; or, Growth of a Poet's Mind* (1805). Ernest de Selincourt, ed., 2d ed. Rev.

Helen Darbishire. Oxford: Clarendon Press, 1959. This edition was corroborated with *The Fourteen-Book Prelude by William Wordsworth.* W. J. B. Owen, ed. Ithaca: Cornell University Press, 1985.

PE Burke, Edmund. *A Philosophical Enquiry into the Origin of Our Ideas of the Sublime and Beautiful.* James T. Boulton, ed. Notre Dame, Ind.: University of Notre Dame Press, 1968.

PL Milton, John. *Paradise Lost.* In John Milton, *The Complete Poems and Major Prose.* Merritt Y. Hughes, ed. Indianapolis: Odyssey Press, 1957.

Po. Aristotle. *Poetics.* Richard Janko, trans. Indianapolis: Hackett, 1987.

PWW Wordsworth, William. *The Prose Works of William Wordsworth.* W. J. B. Owen and Jane Worthington Smyser, eds. 3 vols. Oxford: Clarendon Press, 1974.

SE Freud, Sigmund. *The Standard Edition of the Complete Psychological Works of Sigmund Freud.* Trans. James Strachey. 24 vols. London: Hogarth Press, 1953-74.

Works Cited

Abraham, Nicholas, and Maria Torok. "A Poetics of Psychoanalysis: 'The Lost Object—Me.' " *Sub-stance,* no. 43: 3-18.

Barrell, John. *The Infection of Thomas De Quincey: A Psychopathology of Imperialism.* New Haven, Conn.: Yale University Press, 1991.

Black, Joel D. "Confession, Digression, Gravitation: Thomas De Quincey's German Connection." In Robert Lance Snyder, ed., *Thomas De Quincey: Bicentenary Studies,* pp. 308-38. Norman: University of Oklahoma Press, 1981.

Derrida, Jacques. "Plato's Pharmacy." In Derrida, *Dissemination,* pp. 61-173. Trans. Barbara Johnson. Chicago: University of Chicago Press, 1981.

Freud, Sigmund. "Mourning and Melancholia." In *The Standard Edition of the Complete Psychological Works of Sigmund Freud.* 24 vols., vol. 14, pp. 237-59. Trans. James Strachey. London: Hogarth Press, 1953-74.

Haskell, Thomas L. "Capitalism and the Origins of the Humanitarian Sensibility." Parts 1 and 2. *American Historical Review* 90, no. 2 (April 1985): 339-61; no. 3 (June 1985): 547-66.

Hayter, Alethea. *Opium and the Romantic Imagination: Addiction and Creativity in De Quincey, Coleridge, Baudelaire and Others.* Wellingborough, Northamptonshire, Eng.: Crucible, 1988.

Miller, J. Hillis. *The Disappearance of God: Five Nineteenth-Century Writers.* Cambridge, Mass.: Harvard University Press, 1963.

Praz, Mario. *The Romantic Agony.* New York: Meridian Books, 1956.

Ricoeur, Paul. *The Symbolism of Evil.* Trans. Emerson Buchanan. Boston: Beacon Press, 1967.

Searle, John. "The Logical Status of Fictional Discourse." In Searle, *Expression and Meaning: Studies in the Theory of Speech Acts,* pp. 58-75. Cambridge, Eng.: Cambridge University Press, 1979.

Daniel Sanjiv Roberts (essay date 1997)

SOURCE: "De Quincey's Discovery of *Lyrical Ballads*: The Politics of Reading," in *Studies in Romanticism,* Vol. 36, No. 4, Winter, 1997, pp. 511-40.

[*In the following essay, Roberts examines De Quincey's reading of Wordsworth and Coleridge's poetry within the context of De Quincey's literary life and the development of his political views.*]

Thomas De Quincey's early reading of *Lyrical Ballads* has been widely hailed as the germinal event of his literary career. Biographers and critics have focused on De Quincey's astonishing recognition, at the age of fifteen, of Wordsworth as the predominant poetic figure of his age.[1] By the age of seventeen, De Quincey had declared to Wordsworth his unsurpassed admiration for "those two enchanting volumes" of the second edition of *Lyrical Ballads;* and in 1834, over three decades on, he still regarded his discovery of *Lyrical Ballads* as "the greatest event in the unfolding of my own mind."[2] The testimony of De Quincey's **Diary** of 1803, his youthful correspondence with Wordsworth, and his later absorption into the poet's family circle all testify to the extraordinary precognition of De Quincey's first reading of *Lyrical Ballads.* Yet, despite the seminal importance accorded to De Quincey's early reading of *Lyrical Ballads* and to the Wordsworth/ Coleridge influence derived therefrom, critics and biographers have been surprisingly tardy in addressing the prior issue of mediation involved in such a textual encounter.[3] The canonical status of *Lyrical Ballads* as a foundational text of English romanticism has perhaps tended to obscure the mediatory aspects of De Quincey's reading experience. It has been assumed that the young De Quincey's discovery of *Lyrical Ballads* was made in some more or less direct fashion, the elemental simplicity and genius of the poems achieving an instant impact on the imaginative and sensitive boy. It is not my intention to challenge here the premises of Coleridge's and Wordsworth's genius, or of De Quincey's imaginativeness as a reader—both of which I hold to be essential for an appropriate understanding of De Quincey's reading of *Lyrical Ballads*—but to suggest in addition that "genius" and "imagination" are themselves not unconditioned, and that it may require greater circumstantial attention than previously granted to understand why De Quincey's imaginative sympathy was so finely attuned to the reception of *Lyrical Ballads.*

In the following paper I shall attempt to uncover some of the likely contexts in which De Quincey encountered *Lyrical Ballads* and to suggest thereby a more politicized view of his childhood reading and imagination than has hitherto obtained. My procedure will be to expose some of the contradictions involved in De Quincey's own versions of events, and to question the biographical traditions based on this evidence. Beginning from De Quincey's retrospective account of his encounter in 1801 with the Liverpool literary circle including William Roscoe and James Currie, I will indicate that De Quincey's attitude to them involves an implicit but suppressed connection with *Lyrical Ballads* and that such an attitude is crucially revelatory of the shifting ideological significance of the work for De Quincey. It will be shown that De Quincey's attitude also points to a further unexplored relation between Currie's popular and influential edition of Burns in 1800 and the second edition of *Lyrical Ballads* as companion manifestoes for a new conception of poetry with political implications that were strikingly similar but not identical between the two works. Another contextual reference for De Quincey's reading of *Lyrical Ballads* which has not been adequately examined by critics lies in the influence of reviews, particularly that of the notorious *Edinburgh Review* of which De Quincey was clearly aware. I shall conclude by examining two episodes from De Quincey's early life and autobiography, his visit to Ireland in 1800, and his flight from the Manchester Grammar School in 1802 to indicate the place of *Lyrical Ballads* in terms of his developing political consciousness during this time. Such a procedure, I trust, will help reinscribe De Quincey's reading of *Lyrical Ballads* in an ideological context from which it has been so far held exempt.

In general, the biographical obfuscation I am suggesting may be related to the concept of "Romantic Ideology," now familiar to students of romanticism, whereby an earlier significance of a work is reinterpreted through the lens of a later ideology.[4] My concern is specifically with De Quincey's revisionist attitude to his reading of *Lyrical Ballads*. An important distinction to be made here is between the evidences of the private contemporary records of De Quincey's reading of *Lyrical Ballads* and his later public representations of the event. Though in his various later recollections De Quincey is consistently appreciative of the importance of his early reading of *Lyrical Ballads*, it is a significant omission that he does not seek to explain the *circumstances* of his reading of the work. We are told for instance that "We are Seven" had been "handed about in manuscript" while he was on a school holiday, but whose "manuscript" copy this was, and who had shown it to him, are not mentioned (Jordan 36). While the 1803 *Diary* shows him eagerly accessing information about Coleridge and Wordsworth from persons such as Miss Barcroft, Mr. Bree and others (190-91), his subsequent

reminiscences tend to consign these sources to oblivion. The teasingly undeclared "private source," mentioned in the 1834 essay on Coleridge, to whom he had been obliged for Coleridge's name, is immediately castigated for his "profane way of dealing with a subject so hallowed in my own thoughts" (*R* 34). Thus his later accounts tend to obscure the ethos in which his acquaintance with *Lyrical Ballads* was made in favor of a purely self-centered account emphasizing his own conviction in the "hallowed" nature of his subject, in contrast to the "profane" attitude of his informant(s). The religious metaphor tends to push the event into the realm of divine revelation, rather than suggesting a humanly achieved mediation. So also, his boast in the 1856 ***Confessions*** that he was alone "in all Europe" in quoting Wordsworth in 1802 was more than slightly off the mark.[5] In fact, the popularity of *Lyrical Ballads* had necessitated a third edition of the collection in that year. Thus De Quincey's account seeks to assume greater credit for the originality of his reading than the facts warranted. Such a self-promoting attitude may be seen to involve a deliberate suppression of the radical ambience of *Lyrical Ballads* as originally encountered by De Quincey.

In his introduction to De Quincey's ***Diary,*** Eaton has commented on the strange apparent absence of political engagement in the ***Diary*** to suggest that De Quincey at this time was "living in a world of thought and feeling almost entirely." Eaton here seems to be following De Quincey's lead in representing his adolescence (particularly in the context of his admiration for Wordsworth's poetry) as a period during which "my whole heart had been so steadily fixed on a different world from the world of our daily experience, that, for some years, I had never looked into a newspaper" (*R* 225). Eaton is however puzzled by the supposed lack of political interest on De Quincey's part in the light of his later career, so that it would seem that De Quincey misses the significance of the political events of the early 1800's which are taken to mark the incipient growth of nationalism as well as the radicalization of English class-politics, and which would culminate in the reform movement that was to engage so much of De Quincey's journalistic writing:

> Bonaparte is discussed as if he were an intellectual problem; he reads a message to Parliament from the king, or a speech of Fox without any intimation that they were moving in a great national drama into which he might eventually be drawn.

> (*D* 17)

As Eaton points out, De Quincey's 1803 ***Diary*** is coterminous with the resumption of Anglo-French warfare and the beginning of the Napoleonic war that was to last until 1815. While Coleridge was launching his career in the *Morning Post* with the letters to Fox that were to earn him the sobriquet of "apostate," De Quincey, it would appear, was turning to dreams and introspection rather than to newspapers. De Quincey's seemingly detached attitude to politics prompts the influential conclusion that his admiration of *Lyrical Ballads* is located in a subjectively determined context of "imagination," without recourse to a public realm.

Recent criticism has done much to uncover the political dimension of *Lyrical Ballads,* particularly as this was theorized in the Prefatory remarks added to the second edition of 1800.[6] Grevel Lindop has hinted acutely that Mrs. Quincey's evangelically-minded strictures on Thomas to read "neither infidels nor Jacobins" might well have been prompted by "West Country gossip about the 'Jacobin' Coleridge" (*Opium-Eater* 58). It is important to realize just what a political figure Coleridge in particular did in fact cut in the 1790's and 1800's when De Quincey first encountered the two poets through reading and hearsay. By 1796 Coleridge had already made a name for himself as a radical lecturer in Bristol and had published various political pamphlets; early in that year he had embarked on a tour of the Midlands, preaching to several Dissenting congregations in towns such as Birmingham, Sheffield, Nottingham and Manchester, and advertising his forthcoming journal entitled *The Watchman*. Yet the facts surrounding De Quincey's first knowledge of Coleridge have not elicited biographical speculation despite his leading statement in his 1834 essay on Coleridge that his curiosity in discovering the names of the authors of *Lyrical Ballads* had been defeated for two years until the publication of the second edition, which carried Wordsworth's name on the title page, whilst for Coleridge's he had been "'indebted' to a private source," which however he does not name (*R* 34).

It is worth noting that during the summer of 1801—shortly after the appearance of the second edition of *Lyrical Ballads*—De Quincey was at Everton near Liverpool and was experiencing his first taste of a "literary society" in the liberal Whig circle frequented by William Clarke, a family friend and an erstwhile business contact of Thomas' late father. This was the society he was later to castigate—in the **"Autobiography of an English Opium-Eater,"** published serially in *Tait's Edinburgh Magazine*—as the pretentious literary coterie whose narrow view of literature was contrasted with his own great devotion to the authors of *Lyrical Ballads:*

> to me, who, in that year, 1801, already knew of a grand renovation of poetic power—of a new birth in poetry, interesting not so much to England as to the human mind—it was secretly amusing to contrast the little artificial usages of their petty traditional knack with the natural forms of a divine art—the difference being pretty much as between an American lake, Ontario, or Superior, and a carp pond or a tench preserve.
>
> (*M* 2: 129)

The Liverpool literary society described by De Quincey consisted of "Mr. Roscoe, Dr. Currie (who had just at that time published his Life and Edition of Burns), and Mr. Shepherd of Gatacre, the author of some works on Italian literature (particularly a Life of *Poggio Bracciolini*) and since then, well known to all England by his Reform politics" (*M* 2: 123). It should be remembered here that the essay is written in 1837. De Quincey's mention of the subsequent fame (or infamy) achieved by Shepherd on account of his "Reform politics" should put us on guard that the description of the literary society in question is after all a post-Reform Bill account of an earlier experience of the fifteen-year-old De Quincey. While De Quincey's reminiscence indicates an irritation with the politics of the Liverpool society, it is important to remind ourselves that the source of this irritation is more likely to be the retrospective wisdom gained from De Quincey's later experience in political journalism of the Reform period than his views at the time of his meeting with the Liverpool circle.

De Quincey's biographers have recorded this introduction to a "literary society" as significant but have failed to notice that his representation of the Liverpool literary society as utterly oblivious to the poetic revolution he could see in *Lyrical Ballads* was deceptively at odds with the facts of the case. As early as 1796, William Roscoe had written to Reverend John Edwards, a Unitarian minister at Birmingham and a correspondent of Coleridge's, describing his acquaintance with and admiration for Coleridge's works, the 1796 *Poems on Various Subjects,* the *Conciones ad Populum* and *The Watchman,* the last of which was the object of his particular concern on account of Coleridge's resolution to discontinue the journal in 1796. In order to promote Coleridge's talents as a political journalist, Roscoe offered to help set up a career for him in Liverpool. Coleridge's awareness of this missive and of Roscoe's literary success with the latter's then popular biography of Lorenzo the Magnificent is recorded in his letter of 22 August 1796 to Josiah Wade. This signalled the beginning of a literary acquaintance that has not been accorded much attention from Coleridge's biographers, but which reveals Coleridge's willingness to continue links with "radical" friendships beyond the 1790's. In July 1800, Coleridge visited Liverpool for over a week and wrote enthusiastically to Poole that he had seen "a great deal of Dr. Currie, Roscoe, Rathbone (Colebrook Reynold's Brother-in-law) & other literati." Coleridge describes Currie as a "genuine philosopher" and Roscoe as "a republican with all the feelings of prudence & all the manners of good sense—so that he is beloved by the Aristocrats themselves."[7] Though William Roscoe and the Liverpool intelligentsia are now almost forgotten outside Liverpool city history and the DNB,[8] in 1796 they had been instrumental in starting a new public library named the Athenaeum at Liverpool which Coleridge described to Poole as "most magnificent" (*CL* 1: 608). Mrs. Quincey, in writing to Thomas on 20 May 1801, advises him not to bring books to Liverpool since he would have access to Clarke's Greek and Latin authors, as well as the "noble library" of Liverpool which she describes as a "new institution, comprising a great collection."[9] Among the Liverpool worthies, Roscoe and Currie were among the first well known literary characters De Quincey encountered, though De Quincey did not accord Roscoe much importance in his *Literary Reminiscences* except by way of disparagement. According to De Quincey, Roscoe's verse displayed "the most timid and blind servility to the narrowest of conventional usages, conventional ways of viewing things, conventional forms of expression"; and regarding Currie's famed edition of Burns he prided himself on having "talked, then, being a school-boy, with and against the first editor of Burns" (*M* 2: 130, 135).

De Quincey was to spend the entire summer at Everton and to return to Manchester only by the end of August 1801. In July 1801, Coleridge was proposing to Southey a stay at Liverpool where they might meet Roscoe and Currie whom he promises that Southey would "like as men far, far better than as writers" (*CL* 2: 746). Thus Coleridge's letters reveal his continuing friendship with the radical Liverpool literary society at the very time when De Quincey made their acquaintance. Moreover, they would have known by 1800 from Coleridge of his part in the first edition of *Lyrical Ballads* and must certainly have been discussing in 1801, at the time of De Quincey's acquaintance with them, the new edition brought out by Wordsworth earlier that year without acknowledgement by name to Coleridge.[10] Lindop's description of De Quincey's smug attitude of superiority to the Liverpool literati on account of his knowledge of Wordsworth and *Lyrical Ballads* (53) is clearly based on De Quincey's later reminiscences and is discordant with the facts of the case. Such a version of events is influenced more by De Quincey's revisionist politics than by the evidence of the early records. In fact De Quincey's early knowledge of *Lyrical Ballads* renders it all the more likely that the topic of the new two-volume edition under Wordsworth's name had arisen between Thomas and the Liverpool circle during their literary discussions. From one of them De Quincey would probably also have learned of Coleridge's yet unknown part in *Lyrical Ballads*. This then would have been the "private source" mentioned above to whom De Quincey was obliged for Coleridge's name.

Roscoe's letter to Edwards has not been quoted outside the biography of 1833 written by his son Henry Roscoe, and deserves to be quoted at some length for an idea of Coleridge's significance to an early literary admirer in the 1790's, one of whose immediate circle—if not he himself—was likely to have introduced Coleridge's name to De Quincey:

> I had, some time since, the favour of a letter from you, intended to have been delivered by Mr. Coleridge, but had not the pleasure of seeing him, as I believe he altered his intended route, and did not pay a visit to Liverpool.
>
> I read with great pleasure his *Conciones ad Populum,* which I think contain marks of that disinterested ardour in the cause of liberty, and that abhorrence of violence and bloodshed under whatever pretence they may be resorted to, which in times like the present are so particularly necessary to be inculcated. Mr. Coleridge is one of the few individuals who have perceived the absurdity of the maxim, that it is lawful and expedient to shed the blood of those by whom it is likely that blood will be shed, and which thus authorises the commission of an immediate and actual crime, for the purpose of preventing one which is remote and uncertain, the pretexts of tyrants and of anarchists, at all times and in all countries.
>
> It was with much concern I found he had adopted the resolution of discontinuing his periodical paper of the "Watchman." I conceive he did not give it a sufficient trial, and that if he had persevered he would have found the extent of its circulation increase. Periodical works of this nature are generally slow in taking root, but when once established are very lucrative; and I have no doubt but the paper in question would, if continued, have been of very extensive utility.
>
> With the little volume of Mr. Coleridge's poems I have been greatly delighted—his genius is of the highest class. The characteristics of a fervid imagination and a highly cultivated taste are visible in every page. I must, however, be allowed to remark, that where excellence is so abundant selection might be employed to advantage. He ought not, for a moment, to forget that he writes for immortality, which many have attained by condensing their excellencies, and many have lost by diffusing them through too large a mass. There are few authors who would not lose a considerable share of their reputation were the public in possession of all they wrote.
>
> It would give me much pleasure to be informed, that Mr. Coleridge's prospects in life are such as are likely to give free scope to the exertions of those uncommon talents of which he is possessed; and I shall esteem myself much obliged by any information you can give me respecting him.
>
> His concluding address to his "Watchman" deeply affected me, as it spoke the regret of a virtuous mind disappointed in its efforts to do good. I have since heard that Bristol is not a place likely to reward his merits. If so, might you not recommend it to him to pay a visit to Liverpool, where I know many who would be happy to see him, and who would have a particular pleasure in promoting any plan which he might suggest for rendering his talents advantageous to his country and to himself?[11]

The letter is a flattering one and Coleridge, who was out of regular work, and had a month to go before a proposal to tutor Charles Lloyd would come in, might well have been tempted and certainly gratified. He had, however, turned down an offer of newspaper work in London and had declared his love for Bristol and commitment to the pursuit of philosophy and the Muse against an aversion for "local & temporary politics" such as a newspaper job would entail (*CL* 1: 227). Already, Coleridge was in correspondence with Wordsworth and had received his manuscript of "Salisbury Plain" with the request to make his comments on it before passing it on to Cottle for publication, while by April of that year Wordsworth had read Coleridge's *Poems* and remarked favorably on "Religious Musings." It was clearly to Coleridge's millennialist view of revolution that Wordsworth was responding at this time while in turn Coleridge was aware of Wordsworth's influential visit to revolutionary France and already thought him to be "the best poet of the age" (*CL* 1: 216-17). By the time of Roscoe's letter to Edwards therefore, Coleridge's career was already moving in the direction of the association which would produce the 1798 *Lyrical Ballads*. Roscoe's letter in contrast seeks to suppress Coleridge's Muse and to return Coleridge to the active public life he was now preparing to leave. While Coleridge's genius is allowed to be of the "highest class" his publication is indiscriminate and excessive, and it is his political journalism that Roscoe seeks to encourage.

In their probable revelation of Coleridge's part in *Lyrical Ballads* to the young De Quincey, the Liverpool radicals may well have also revealed something of Coleridge's radical past. Moreover, the preference of such a person as Roscoe for Coleridge's public and radical career over his poetic one might serve to explain De Quincey's later statement in 1834 that his debt of knowledge regarding Coleridge's co-authorship of *Lyrical Ballads* had been "discharged [. . .] ill, for I quarrelled with my informant for what I considered his profane way of dealing with a subject so hallowed in my own thoughts" (*R* 34). Here De Quincey's near devotion to Coleridge's literary productions might well have been ruffled by the somewhat condescending attitude Roscoe had adopted to his poetry. This would explain De Quincey's later irritation at Roscoe's poetic abilities in contrast to the "grand renovation of poetic power" he discerned in the efforts of Wordsworth and Coleridge.

De Quincey's reminiscence of the Liverpool literary society suggests a further connection with Wordsworth and Coleridge which has not been investigated hitherto. As we have seen, Coleridge visited the Liverpool group in early 1800 as the second edition of *Lyrical Ballads* was taking shape. By this time, Currie had recently brought out his new edition of Burns's *Works,* including his "Life of Burns," with prefatory "Remarks on the Character and Condition of the Scottish Peasantry" and a "Criticism on the Writings of Burns." This publication was issued for the benefit of Burns's widow and children, and it was to prove the standard edition of Burns for several decades, running into numerous separate editions as well as providing the basis for many others.[12] In 1801, Mrs. Quincey was writing to Thomas: "I am reading Dr. Currie's 'Life of Burns,' not without a sharply jealous eye to the Doctor's Jacobinism(!)" (Japp, *Memorials* 1: 62). It was after Coleridge's return to Grasmere however and only by September 1800 that discussion began with Wordsworth for a critical Preface to *Lyrical Ballads* which would explain the principles of their poetry to the public. On the face of it, there was no real need for a preface since the first edition had proved itself on the market, and even the reviews had been mainly favorable. As has been shown, moreover, the poems of *Lyrical Ballads* were not as "original" to the reading public as Wordsworth's Preface had made out.[13] I would suggest that there is a remarkable similarity between the prefaces issued by Currie and Wordsworth, and that Wordsworth's self-representation of poetic character in the Preface to *Lyrical Ballads* could have been powerfully influenced by Currie's portrayal of Burns, as understood by him from Coleridge. Significantly, Wordsworth's *Commonplace Book* shows that by 29 September 1800 he had transcribed various fragments from Burns using the second volume of Currie's edition, so it is clear that he received and read the work at this time.[14]

Yet though the resemblances between Wordsworth's and Currie's prefaces are strong, there are important differences between the two works. Although Wordsworth later claimed in his *Letter to a Friend of Robert Burns* (1816) that he well remembered "the sorrow with which, by my own fire-side, I first perused Dr. Currie's Narrative, and some of the letters, particularly those composed in the latter part of the poet's life,"[15] it is worth nothing as well that no immediate account of his reading of Currie's edition of Burns has survived, and by contrast Coleridge's letter to Thomas Poole after his return to Grasmere and *en route* to Keswick enthused "I would have you by all means order the late Edition in four Volumes of Burns's Works—the Life is written by Currie, and a masterly specimen of philosophical Biography it is" (*CL* 1: 607). It would seem likely then that Coleridge had introduced the work to Wordsworth before Poole, but if there was any disagreement between them at that time on the nature of the service to Burns's reputation performed by Currie, this has not survived either.

De Quincey's attack in 1837 on the Liverpool Whigs, Currie, Roscoe and Shepherd concentrated on the reputation accorded to Robert Burns in Currie's edition of the poet. As I would suggest, this accusation reveals a political agenda which cannot be understood without reference to *Lyrical Ballads*. When De Quincey published the essay in 1837 in *Tait's,* there was an angry reply from Shepherd whom De Quincey had described as being ambitious of the title of a buffoon and whom he had expected to be by then merely "a name and a shadow" (*M* 2: 128, 135). Shepherd, who was still very much on this side of the grave, accused De Quincey of grievous inaccuracy with facts and took particular exception to De Quincey's portrayal of the politics allegedly professed by the Liverpool Whigs. According to De Quincey, Currie's view of Burns in 1801 was decidedly aristocratic in tendency; so much so that he faulted the Scottish poet with ingratitude to his patrons while the fifteen-year-old Thomas alone in that company made a "solitary protestation on behalf of Burns's Jacobinism." This statement predictably drew the indignation of Shepherd who considered the entire episode a fabrication, and drew attention to an apparent contradiction in De Quincey's account on the point that "Mr. Shepherd continued to draw from the subject some scoff or growl at Mr. Pitt and the Excise" (*M* 2: 135). In his letter to the editor of *Tait's,* Shepherd demanded to know, "Why should I growl at the excise, except for the harshness of the excise board in its treatment of Burns?"[16] Yet it is worth enquiring why De Quincey represents himself as being a champion of the Jacobinical Burns at a time when the radical Shepherd found reason to blame the poet. But first it is necessary to take a closer look at Currie's edition of Burns in its own context, and to consider its possible relation with Wordsworth and Coleridge.

The main thrust of Currie's representation of Burns lay in his affirmation of Burns's already popular reputation as a Scottish peasant-poet: "Burns was in reality what he has been represented to be, a Scottish peasant" (1: 2). Just as Wordsworth was to choose the human situation of "low and rustic life,"[17] and to base that experience in his residence at Grasmere, Currie described Burns's poetic evolution in terms of his association with the Scottish peasantry. And just as Wordsworth had sought to recover the "very language of men" in his poetry, so did Currie emphasize Burns's use of the Scottish dialect:

> His declared purpose was to paint the manners of rustic life among his "humble compeers," and it is not easy to conceive, that this could have been done with equal humour and effect, if he had not adopted their idiom. There are some indeed who will think the subject too low for poetry. Persons of this sickly taste will find their delicacies consulted in many a polite and learned author [. . .].
>
> (1: 334)

Yet though the resemblances between Wordsworth's *Preface* and Currie's presentation of Burns are strong, there are several differences between the two works. An important variance from Wordsworth in Currie's portrayal of Burns, lay in his "natural" derivation of Burns from the rural milieu in contrast with Wordsworth's more conscious adoption of that originary space. Burns's marvel, of course, lay in the fact that a peasant of an assumed lowly level of

education, and of rustic "manners" and language could produce such poetry, and Currie's essay dealt with the particular circumstances which qualified Burns for poetic endeavor. Far from providing a simplistic account of imagination as a rural commodity, however, Currie argued that the Scottish peasantry, despite their apparent rusticity, were in fact well educated and intelligent, unlike most of their counterparts in other regions of Europe:

> A slight acquaintance with the peasantry of Scotland, will serve to convince an unprejudiced observer that they possess a degree of intelligence not generally found among the same class of men in other countries of Europe. In the very humblest condition of the Scottish peasants, every one can read, and most persons are more or less skilled in writing and arithmetic; and under the disguise of their uncouth appearance, and of their peculiar manners and dialect, a stranger will discover that they possess a curiosity, and have obtained a degree of information corresponding to these acquirements.
>
> (1: 4)

The loyalty of the Scottish peasantry is asserted against the disaffection of the working classes in other parts of Britain, where the radicalization of the working class so well described by E. P. Thompson[18] was already underway:

> Since the Union, Scotland, though the seat of two unsuccessful attempts to restore the house of Stewart to the throne, has enjoyed a comparative tranquillity, and it is since this period that the present character of her peasantry has been in a great measure formed, though the political causes affecting it are to be traced to the previous acts of her separate legislature.
>
> (1: 3)

Despite the known liberalism of the Liverpool circle and the fears of Mrs. Quincey regarding Currie's "Jacobinism," in fact Currie's presentation of Burns, as Davis has recently argued, tends to deflect Burns's political concerns, particularly his Jacobinism and Scottish nationalism, by its deployment of an overriding medical discourse which renders the work politically acceptable in terms of wider British national and colonial interests (43-60). De Quincey's comment that Currie had stifled the Jacobinical aspect of Burns's work is thus a most astute one, even if, as we shall see, it carries its own revisionist agenda.

Currie's equation between disaffection and the lack of educational opportunities suggests one of the paths taken by the radical movement from "Jacobinism" to Reform in the post-Revolutionary era. As in Wordsworth's Preface, education is a central theme of Currie's text; but while Wordsworth appears to favor a non-curricular education in his emphasis on the "beautiful and permanent forms of nature" (245) and in such poems as "Expostulation and Reply" and "The Tables Turned," Currie turns more practically to the "legal provision for parochial schools" which he finds have been enforced in Scotland for a similarly long period as in the "Protestant Cantons of Switzerland" and even more suggestively "in the counties of Westmoreland and Cumberland" (1: 353-54). Here Currie's reference to the inhabitants of the Lake District is an indirect compliment to the experiment he knew to be attempted by Wordsworth and Coleridge in *Lyrical Ballads,* and, in return, his allusion to the peasantry of Switzerland is later taken up by Coleridge in his characterization of the "stronger local attachments and enterprizing spirit of the Swiss, and other mountaineers, [which] applies to a particular mode of pastoral life, under forms of property, that permit and beget manners truly republican, not to rustic life in general, or to the absence of artificial cultivation." Currie's more formal understanding of "education" is in this case akin to Coleridge's later qualifications of the *Preface* which emphasized the imprudence of Wordsworth's identification of himself with the "low and rustic" subjects of his poetry: "Education, or original sensibility, or both, must pre-exist, if the changes, forms, and incidents of nature are to prove a sufficient stimulant."[19]

De Quincey's portrayal of Currie's political sympathies as being out of tune with Burns's "peculiarly wild and almost ferocious spirit of independence, [which] came a generation too soon" (*M* 2:132) seeks to appropriate to himself an extraordinarily foresightful revolutionary zeal which Currie as a republican Whig ironically lacked. De Quincey attempts to read Burns, who died in 1796, as a champion of "revolutionary reform" such as the Liverpool society prided themselves on supporting:

> In this day, he would have been forced to do that, clamorously called upon to do that, and would have found his pecuniary interest in doing that, which in his own generation merely to attempt doing loaded him with the reproach of Jacobinism. It must be remembered that the society of Liverpool wits on whom my retrospect is now glancing were all Whigs—all, indeed, fraternizers with French Republicanism. Yet so it was that—not once, not twice, but daily almost, in the numerous conversations naturally elicited by this Liverpool monument to Burns's memory—I heard every one, clerk or layman, heartily agreeing to tax Burns with ingratitude and with pride falsely directed, because he sate uneasily or restively under the bridle-hand of his noble self-called *"patrons."* Aristocracy, then, the essential spirit of aristocracy—this I found was not less erect and clamorous amongst partisan democrats— democrats who were such merely in a party sense of supporting his Majesty's Opposition against his Majesty's Servants—than it was or could be among the most bigoted of the professed feudal aristocrats.

> (*M* 2: 132-33)

It is worth noting that De Quincey's remarks are published in the liberal *Tait's* magazine (rather than his usually-favored *Blackwood's*) and that they are part of his continuing politico-literary reminiscing, between the articles on

Coleridge in 1834 and those on Wordsworth in 1839. De Quincey's criticism of the modern Whig party is thus attached to his reminiscences of Currie's failure to defend Burns's "Jacobinism" at a time when a present-day Tory like himself had (even as a boy) risen to Burns's defense.

As we have seen, De Quincey's account of the Liverpool society had its discrepancies to an actual survivor of that period like Shepherd.[20] What is more important to us however is De Quincey's willingness to identify himself with a youthful "Jacobinism." Like Wordsworth and Coleridge, De Quincey admits to a youthful revolutionary sympathy but distances himself from the false modern claimants to the revolutionary inheritance who would argue Reform in the name of Revolution. Just as De Quincey's reminiscences represent the familiar view of Wordsworth and Coleridge as early revolutionaries whose zeal had been tempered by experience, so also they conversely represent the Liverpool circle as false revolutionaries, whose early commitment to revolutionary principles was suspect. While the true revolutionaries, Wordsworth and Coleridge, were now identified with the Tory party, it was the false revolutionaries, such as Currie and Roscoe, who were now crying Reform as sustainers of a radical tradition. De Quincey thus reverses the common criticisms of the Lake poets as apostates, by accusing the Liverpool circle of political inconsistency. Moreover, De Quincey's representation of himself as a Jacobinical defender of Burns brings into question the nature of his sympathy with the "poetic revolution" he had first discerned in *Lyrical Ballads.*

Eaton's judgment that by 1803, De Quincey "was living in a world of thought and feeling almost entirely" has obscured the keen interest shown by De Quincey in various critical issues and publishing details surrounding the literary works that he was reading at the time. Modern scholarship has done much to reveal the radical nature of the literary milieu of the 1790's and the 1800's, and of the political provenance of such a work as *Lyrical Ballads.* Such a background is worth considering through the literary interests pursued by De Quincey in the **Diary.** De Quincey's later representations of his reading of *Lyrical Ballads* suggest a revelatory quality at the expense of the details of mediation and context through which these poems were made available to him. An important reference to the powerful medium of review literature which has not drawn adequate editorial comment is De Quincey's note of 14 May 1803, mentioning his "talk with Mr. W[right] about *Edinburgh Review;*—about Coleridge— Wordsworth—Southey—Cottle—Longman and Rees [. . .]" (*D* 171). Longman and Rees as well as Cottle were of course importantly associated with the early publications of the Lake poets, and the reference to the *Edinburgh Review* in this connection is highly suggestive. It may be remembered that Jeffrey's famous attack on the Lake poets had begun in the very first issue of *Edinburgh Review* for October 1802 in the course of a review of Southey's *Thalaba*. Also to be noted is the fact that De Quincey is reading Southey's *Thalaba* during the period covered by the *Diary*. The reference to Jeffrey's damning review which treated Southey's work as a product of Wordsworth's theory in the 1800 Preface, might hence have grown out of De Quincey's interest in Southey. In fact, the connection between Southey, Coleridge and Wordsworth may well have been drawn for him by Jeffrey's review because his list of poets made in April 1803 places the three of them together: a collocation which may be obvious to modern students of romanticism, but may not have been so obvious to a seventeen-year-old in Everton near Liverpool in 1803, without knowledge of the earlier association between Southey and Coleridge and of the contemporary residence of the three poets in the Lake District.[21] Again, it is important not to underestimate the role of such a character as Wright, whose profession as a bookseller would have acquainted him with important details of the literary reception of the Lake poets. Jeffrey's attack on the "sect of poets" which included Wordsworth, Coleridge and Southey had crucially admitted "a very considerable portion of poetical talent" among them, but had condemned their ability "to seduce many into an admiration of the false taste (as it appears to us) in which most of their productions are composed."[22] De Quincey's later letter to Wordsworth of 31 March 1804 in reply to the latter's complaint about the parody of "The Idiot Boy" published by Peter Bayley does make it clear that he had read (at least by then) the offending article by Jeffrey:

> Wherever indeed (as in the solemn and *profound* analysis of your poetry by the Scotch reviewers) I have seen men impressed with a sincere belief that you had founded a school of poetry adverse to the canons of true taste, I have always felt any momentary indignation at their arrogance overbalanced by compassion for the delusions they are putting upon themselves and the disordered taste which such a belief argues.
>
> (Jordan 39-40)

De Quincey's reference to the issue of "taste" identifies the cutting edge of Jeffrey's criticisms of the Lake school: not that they were not talented poets, but that their talents had been misused to "seduce" a large number of readers to a "false taste" in poetry.

Apart from the reference to *Edinburgh Review,* De Quincey's *Diary* shows several indications of being engaged in the crucial issue of literary value that Jeffrey's famous review symptomatized. This was the old debate which had rumbled through the eighteenth century about the respective merits of the "ancients" versus the "moderns" that new literary productions such as Wordsworth's and Coleridge's had raised afresh. Robert Mayo has shown how in many vital respects the poems in *Lyri-*

cal Ballads "not only conformed to the modes of 1798, and reflected popular tastes and attitudes, but enjoyed a certain popularity in the magazines themselves" (486). Thus Jeffrey's influential criticism of the Lake poets was directed against their attempt, in the manner of much of the new poetry appearing in the journals of the day, to invoke a new subject matter and style. Though Jeffrey's criticisms of Burns were to appear rather later in 1809, they were, given his particular critical orientation, completely predictable in essence. In particular, Wordsworth's attempt to turn from a received "poetic" diction and form to the situations and language of "low and rustic life" was for Jeffrey an heretical attempt to subvert the received canons of "taste" and "feeling." In this context, it is worth noting that De Quincey's list of favorite poets in 1803 includes Burns along with the Lake poets, and his *Diary* also records a comparison of Southey and Burns (*D* 145, 160).

Considering De Quincey's *Diary* with the preceding background in mind, we may now notice the many references to the Jeffreyan debate about the comparative merits of "ancient" versus "modern," "classical" versus "English" literature that are strewn through its pages. I quote a single example:

> we talk about classical knowledge, which Mr. W. regrets not having paid more attention to;—he says he supposes I have a knowledge of the ancient languages . . . which I assent to;—he mentions Lord Monboddo;—I take occasion thence of speaking of his unqualified admiration of the ancients—Horne Tooke's lashes on him and his compeer Harris—of asserting the superiority of *modern* to *ancient* lore—though in genera[l] terms.
>
> (*D* 198)[23]

De Quincey's reference to Horne Tooke indicates his awareness of Tooke's radical critique in *The Diversions of Purley* which Marilyn Butler has described as having taken "to a political extreme those efforts to democratize language which are specially characteristic of the last three decades of the century."[24] Like *The Diversions of Purley,* Wordsworth's *Preface* to *Lyrical Ballads* was clearly an argument in favor of returning the notion of linguistic propriety to the vernacular usage rather than the privileged medium associated with the learning of the upper classes. This was also the aspect of the Lake poets' ideology that was singled out for quotation and ridicule by Jeffrey in his review of *Thalaba* in 1802:

> One of their own authors in deed, has very ingeniously set forth, (in a kind of manifesto that preceded one of their most flagrant acts of hostility), that is [sic] was their capital object "to adapt to the uses of poetry, the ordinary language of conversation among the middling and lower orders of the people."

For the politically liberal Jeffrey, the Lake poets clearly exemplified a radically anti-institutional critique of society:

A splenetic and idle discontent with the existing institutions of society, seems to be at the bottom of all their serious and peculiar sentiments. Instead of contemplating the wonders and the pleasures which civilization has created for mankind, they are perpetually brooding over the disorders by which its progress has been attended. They are filled with horror and compassion at the sight of poor men spending their blood in the quarrels of princes, and brutifying their sublime capabilities in the drudgery of unremitting labour. For all sorts of vice and profligacy in the lower orders of society, they have the same virtuous horror, and the same tender compassion.

Such a tendency is attributed by Jeffrey to the influence on the Lake poets of the "great modern reformers" of Germany, and more specifically to "the great apostle of Geneva." One of the elements of their productions is described as:

The antisocial principles, and distempered sensibility of Rousseau—his discontent with the present constitution of society—his paradoxical morality, and his perpetual hankerings after some unattainable state of virtue and perfection.[25]

In this connection, it is worth noting that among the various literary discussions De Quincey mentions in the *Diary* is one

with Mr. Bentejak about Rousseau's *Emile—Julia—Social Contract.* Mr. B. Said it was generally believed Rousseau did not write the "Confessions" in the *Emile.*

(*D* 93)

Even if the young De Quincey's response to *Lyrical Ballads* was certainly antithetical to the critique issued by Jeffrey, it might appear that the latter was in fact strongly instrumental in contextualizing the work for the young reader. On account of his critical support for the "moderns" in the eighteenth-century literary debate mentioned above, De Quincey's reading of Jeffrey serves to contextualize *Lyrical Ballads* for himself against the grain of Jeffrey's argument. Jeffrey's tirade against the presumptuous attempt at literary innovation by the Lake poets would have paradoxically rendered them favorable to the strong supporter of the "moderns" (in literature) in the young De Quincey.

I hope to have shown by now that the unconditioned realm of "thought and feeling" suggested by Eaton is not an appropriate description of De Quincey's early writings in the *Diary* nor of his state of mind in approaching *Lyrical Ballads.* By way of a conclusion to this section I would like to examine De Quincey's 1803 description of the operation of a "press-gang" to suggest some of the converse ways in which his reading of *Lyrical Ballads* was shaping the nature of his political experience at this time. The forced consignment of men (termed "impressment") to

military service during the war with France naturally aroused much discontent and it is significant to note De Quincey's youthful participation in this sense of popular outrage:

Among the men was one who hid his face to conceal his emotions: his two sisters stood on the pier among the crowd—weeping and telling his story to the spectators. Immediately a general exclamation ran along— "Ay that's poor Jack—the boatman"—who is he? I said. "Ay! bless him! he's neither father nor mother; he's quite desolate." On this general tribute of sympathy and affection, the poor fellow, who had hitherto hid his face to stifle or conceal his grief, could bear it no longer; but, sobbing aloud, lifted up his eyes and fixed them with such mingling expressions of agony— gratitude—mournful remembrance on his friends— relations—and his dear countrymen (whom very likely he was now gazing at for the last time) as roused indignation against the pressers and pity for the pressed in every bosom; and not an Englishman stood by . . . that did not manifest the sensibility of his nation. Never did I behold such exquisite sorrow contendg with such manliness of appearance

The look, with which he look'd
Shall never pass away.

Eaton has remarked of this description that it is made "with a certain romantic air as if the scene might have come from one of the many novels he had been so busily reading" (*D* 17, 162). The comment is just in that De Quincey's perception is strongly influenced by literary sources, but I would suggest that in the particular emphasis on "low" life rather than high tragedy, De Quincey's real model is *Lyrical Ballads,* which of course commands the highest literary appreciation to be found in the *Diary.* Indeed the quotation with which De Quincey ends the description (unidentified by Eaton) comes from "The Ancient Mariner" (247-48), describing the fixed gaze of the Mariner's dead shipmates: "The look with which they look'd on me, / Had never passed away" (*LB* 20). The radically abolitionist sensibility of Coleridge's poem is well fitted to lament the fate of forced impressment that meets the boatman.[26] De Quincey's application of Coleridge's description to the sorrowful countenance of the boatman suggests the feelings of guilt and complicity evoked in the viewers by Jack's plight.

In some of the particularities of composition as well, it is obvious that the closer comparison to De Quincey's style must be sought in *Lyrical Ballads* rather than in the gothic novels he was then devouring in an addictive manner but without much evidence of critical sympathy. For example, the slightly inconsequential reply from bystanders to De Quincey's question, "who is he?": "Ay! bless him! he's neither father nor mother; he's quite desolate" reminds us of the repeated use of questioning in poems such as "We are Seven" and "The Idiot Boy" to yield replies which, though not strictly engaging the questions, still provide at a further level an answer to them:

> "How many are you then," said I,
> "If they two are in Heaven?"
> The little Maiden did reply,
> "O Master! we are seven."

(LB 68)

As in Wordsworth's poem, De Quincey takes on the role of interlocuter and purports to record his conversation in a faithful register to the idea of "low" life thus represented. Moreover, it is the very inconsequentiality of the reply that provides the poignancy to the representation. The question of original identity posed by De Quincey ("Who is he?") is shown to be meaningless against the apparent lack or loss of parental origins displayed by the subject. This was the nub of Jeffrey's grouse against the Lake poets, that the mean social position of Wordsworth's characters was the ruin of his poetic abilities.

De Quincey's character takes on in this manner the elemental simplicity and communal significance of the marginal and desolate characters thronging the pages of *Lyrical Ballads* in such portraits as the Female Vagrant, Simon Lee, Lucy, Ruth or the Ancient Mariner, whose origins are mysterious but whose elemental existence seems simply to be taken for granted. Just as these characters are nameless or carry a symbolically commonplace name, so the boatman is identified by only his first name, Jack, and his profession, but is otherwise left undefined by nomenclatural means. Another similarity with *Lyrical Ballads* is evident in the delicate touch provided by the unsustained aversion of countenance to express a "manly" sorrow, Jack's hiding of his face "to stifle or conceal his grief," which reminds us of a poem such as "The Last of the Flock":

> He saw me, and he turned aside,
> As if he wished himself to hide:
> Then with his coat he made essay
> To wipe those briny tears away.

(LB 79)

Such a moment of private sorrow, undistinguished by the prominence of the character, but providing in the unguarded instant of grief, when Jack is able to "bear it no longer," the kind of insight into human nature celebrated in Wordsworth's 1800 Preface, suggests once more the true influence on De Quincey, of those characteristic situations of "low" life which constitute the particular poetic moment of *Lyrical Ballads*.

THE REVOLUTIONARY ETHIC OF *LYRICAL BALLADS*

De Quincey's retrospectively-claimed ultra-Jacobinical reading of Burns (more radical than the liberal Whigs,

Currie and Shepherd) suggests the extremely politicized tendency of his reading at this stage, in contrast to the imputation of a depoliticized world of imagination that he was supposed to be inhabiting at the time. In the following section I would like to proceed from the above understanding of De Quincey's early political interests to an ideological examination of two early episodes in De Quincey's childhood from the viewpoints of his contemporary records as well as of his later representations of these events. The two episodes I am examining are De Quincey's visit to Ireland in early 1800, and his flight from the Manchester Grammar School in 1802. As I shall show, though De Quincey later reinscribes both events from a mature post-revolutionary point of view, his contemporary descriptions of these events evidence a marked transformation developing in De Quincey's thought during this time.

Even apart from his discussions of the politics of Burns's political reputation, De Quincey's reminiscences of and correspondence with Lord Altamont, an Irish peer, on the issue of the Irish Act of Union in 1800, indicate his interest in popular and political issues at this time. The English response to the French revolutionary threat and the Rebellion of 1798 had been to dissolve the separate Irish parliament in return for a largely ineffectual Irish representation at Westminster. Pitt's earlier measures of Catholic relief had failed by 1795 to fulfill the expectations raised, leading to the increasing radicalization of Irish political feeling. Attempts to suppress the revolutionary enthusiasm of the Society of United Irishmen in 1794 led to its reconstitution as a secret society which would become openly republican and predominantly Catholic under Theobald Wolfe Tone. The Rebellion of 1798 reflected the fragmentation and the growing sectarianism of Irish political life. The Irish willingness to draw on French support to achieve its revolutionary ends pointed also to the important links which existed between Irish republicanism and English radicalism in the early nineteenth century.[27] It is worth examining De Quincey's interest in this political matter for some indication of the nature of his political sympathies at the time, and of how these might have been transformed into the ideological stance which he associates with his reading of *Lyrical Ballads*.

Writing to his mother from Ireland, the young De Quincey was attempting to balance the English reports of the Rebellion with the very different ones of the local population:

> As to the rebellion in Ireland, the English, I think, use the *amplifying,* and the Irish the *diminishing hyperbole;* the former view it with a *magnifying glass,* the latter with a *microscope.* In England, I remember, we heard such horrid accounts of murders, and battles, and robberies, and here everybody tells me the country *is* in as quiet a state as England, and *has* been so for some time past.

Yet De Quincey's suspicions are clearly aroused by the Irish accounts of the Rebellion which he considers as being deliberately underplayed: "What makes me suspect the truth of these smooth-tongued messengers is that the rebellion, even at its greatest height, they affect to treat with indifference. . . ."[28] In a letter to Thomas dated 22 September 1800, Altamont refers to Thomas as being "so good and zealous an Englishman," no doubt on account of the opinions he expressed to the former on this issue. Popular Irish feeling on the score of England would have been at a low, and it would appear that De Quincey had had occasion in discussion to rise to the defense of his country. Altamont himself, as one of the Irish peers who had gone over to the English parliament, would have been compromised by popular feeling. His letters to De Quincey reveal him to be an English supporter on the issue of the French Revolution and its effect on Ireland:

> I never hear of anything like another Revolution in France without trembling for the effect it may have upon us here; for our rebellions and the French invasion have left bad effects, which it will take many years wholly to wipe out
>
> (Japp, *Memorials* 1: 42, 49).

De Quincey's early association with Westport and Lord Altamont thus show him to be a "zealous [. . .] Englishman" on the issue of the Irish Union, favoring the measures taken by Pitt to suppress the Irish radical movement.

As with his reminiscences of the Liverpool literary society, De Quincey's later account of the Irish Rebellion reveals several significant variations from what the early documents suggest. De Quincey's recollections of these events in his 1834 "Autobiographic Sketches" for *Tait's* claim his "profoundest sympathies" for the Act (*M* 1: 217). In describing the nature of his sympathy De Quincey crucially enlists the aid of Wordsworth's republican sonnet "On the Extinction of the Venetian Republic" to a reversionary significance:

> Wordsworth's fine sonnet on the extinction of the Venetian Republic had not then been published, else the last two lines would have expressed my feelings. After admitting that changes had taken place in Venice, which in manner challenged and presumed this last mortal change, the poet goes on to say, that all this long preparation for the event could not break the shock of it. Venice, it is true, had become a shade; but, after all,
>
> "Men we are, and must grieve when even the shade
> Of that which once was great has pass'd away."
>
> But here the previous circumstances were far different from those of Venice. *There* we saw a superannuated and paralytic state, sinking at any rate into the grave, and yielding, to the touch of military violence, that only which a brief lapse of years must otherwise have yielded to internal decay. *Here,* on the contrary, we saw a young eagle, rising into power, and robbed prema-

turely of her natural honours, only because she did not comprehend their value, or because at this great crisis she had no champion. Ireland, in a political sense, was surely then in her youth, considering the prodigious developments she has since experienced in population, and in resources of all kinds.

De Quincey's retrospective appeal (in 1834) to Wordsworthian republicanism to express his sentiments on the issue of the Irish Union tends to reinscribe the event in the light of his later influence. Furthermore De Quincey represents Westport and Altamont as being secretly in sympathy with the revolutionary movement opposed to the Union:

> Yet oftentimes it seemed to me, when I introduced the subject, and sought to learn from Lord Altamont the main grounds which had reconciled him and other men, anxious for the welfare of Ireland, to a measure which at least robbed her of some splendour, and, above all, robbed her of a name and place amongst the independent states of Europe—that neither father nor son was likely to be displeased should some great popular violence put force upon the recorded will of Parliament, and compel the two Houses to perpetuate themselves.
>
> (*M* 1: 217)

Just as De Quincey's own sympathies are rewritten from a Wordsworthian point of view, so also it may be seen Lord Altamont's and Westport's views are now aligned with a revolutionary sympathy quite at odds with Altamont's correspondence. Far from supporting Pitt's measures to repress revolutionary activities in any form, De Quincey is in fact offering a critique of that repression from the perspective of early-Wordsworthian republicanism. I would suggest that such a reinscription is itself some indication of the political significance De Quincey would associate in time with Wordsworth and *Lyrical Ballads.*

It is important to note however that at this stage there could have been no obvious disparity for the young De Quincey in the purposes of the two authors of *Lyrical Ballads.* Coleridge's private disagreements with "Wordsworth's" Preface begin to emerge only after 1802, while his public statement appeared only with the *Biographia* in 1817. To all appearances then, and in Coleridge's own words of 30 September 1800, the Preface to *Lyrical Ballads* represented the "joint opinions on Poetry" of Wordsworth and Coleridge (*CL* 1: 627). While, to avoid confusion, I shall follow the critical convention of referring to the Preface as the work of Wordsworth, it must be remembered that the critical differential now commonly accepted between the roles of Wordsworth and Coleridge simply cannot be accepted in terms of its early impact on a reader such as De Quincey. Though Wordsworth is prioritized by his own assumed authority in the second edition of *Lyrical Ballads,* Coleridge must be seen in a concerted and mutually supporting position with Wordsworth. We may now return to the politics of the revolutionary sympathy which De Quincey would recognize underlying *Lyrical Ballads* in examining the records, both contemporary and retrospective, of his escape from the Manchester Grammar School.

At least in retrospect, De Quincey's flight from the Manchester Grammar School was achieved with *Lyrical Ballads* strongly in mind. The centrality of *Lyrical Ballads* to this key event of De Quincey's youth may be gauged from his later assertion that the escapade was accomplished with a copy of *Lyrical Ballads* in his pocket, and that his first impulse was to head for the Lake District. Yet the "very motives of love and honour" attending such a "pilgrimage" as contemplated by De Quincey, drew him temporarily away from Wordsworth. Clearly it would not do for De Quincey to present himself to Wordsworth "in a hurried and thoughtless state of excitement." Attempting to explain his careless sense of freedom in the 1856 *Confessions,* De Quincey located the cause of his joy

> in what Wordsworth, when describing the festal state of France during the happy morning-tide of her First Revolution (1788-1790), calls *"the senselessness of joy"*: this it was, joy—headlong—frantic—irreflective—and (as Wordsworth truly calls it), for that very reason, *sublime*—which swallowed up all capacities of rankling care or heart-corroding doubt.
>
> (*M* 3: 279, 284)

De Quincey's transposition of Wordsworth's telling phrase to describe his sense of freedom in running away from the Manchester Grammar School figures his own reaction in the cast of Wordsworth's revolutionary joy. Again, it is important to remind ourselves of the retrospective nature of this interpretation; but as before it is worth asking why De Quincey was representing his experience in such a manner. It has been often noted that De Quincey's descriptions of his escapade from the Manchester Grammar School are clothed in a religious language reflecting a Miltonic fall from grace; less noticed has been the *political* language of rights and liberty in the terms of which the episode has also been presented in De Quincey's contemporary letters and retrospective descriptions. If one recalls the political importance of Milton's republicanism to the Lake school it is possible to see the connection between the two forms of discourse, at one level a Christian parable of man's disobedience, and at the other, a form of defeated, but not wholly suppressed, revolutionary aspiration.[29] In the following section, I will consider De Quincey's flight from Manchester Grammar School as a paradigm of the "revolutionary" aspect of *Lyrical Ballads.* This aspect of the work will also be seen to act as a counterweight to De Quincey's evangelical upbringing.

De Quincey's childhood politics have been somewhat uncritically branded as that of an "instinctual Tory" (Lindop,

Opium-Eater 53) on the basis of his mother's influence and the background of conservative evangelicalism that characterized the "Clapham" sect of which Mrs. Quincey was a member. While evangelicalism might indeed be recognized as an important influence on De Quincey, I would point here to a more ambivalent attitude to evangelicalism than one of mere acceptance or rejection. It must be remembered moreover that the evangelical ethos was more complicated than the blanket label "conservatism" would suggest, and was profoundly oppositional on some aspects of government, most notably the slave-trade. Lindop has usefully pointed to the "traditions [. . .] of earnest self-examination and apocalyptic fervour" to which Mrs. Quincey subscribed as an evangelical, and suggested their relevance to the "mystical" or "visionary" aspects of De Quincey's work.[30] I would like to take up from Lindop's reading of De Quincey's flight from the Manchester Grammar School as an evangelical, confessional narrative of De Quincey's fall from grace, to advance the case that De Quincey's school "rebellion" was simultaneously figured in political terms as well. I do not wish to imply of course that De Quincey's school revolt was performed as an act of consciously political significance—but then neither has it been claimed that De Quincey's supposed fall from grace was achieved as a consciously theological act of rebellion. The crucial recognition is of the interpretation that the act bears later, and of the kind of discourse that reportedly propels the action.

In his fine study of the social and political connotations of nineteenth-century evangelicalism, Boyd Hilton has written that "the moderate evangelicalism which developed after 1789 represented a shift in natural religion from *evidences* to *paradoxes,* that is, from examples of benign contrivance in the natural world to demonstrations of how superficial misery may work inner improvement."[31] Mrs. Quincey's brand of evangelicalism, which was of the rationalist and moderate kind like that of the other members of the Clapham Sect with whom she was associated, clearly fits Hilton's emphasis on a lapsarian theology as its determining *telos.* This emphasis on the acceptance of a fallen order may be seen to inform Mrs. Quincey's correspondence with Thomas, together with her insistence on her own right to assume a divinely dispensed jurisdiction over the lad. Mrs. Quincey's correspondence to Thomas at this time indicates her clear perception of the issue as essentially one of authority, with the yet legally bound lad displaying a premature desire for "liberty." Her immediate reaction to De Quincey's proposal was to remind him of his obligations to his father's will, and the fact that it would not be long before he was free to exercise his choice:

> I would urge you to consider that the language you use when you say "I must" or "I will" is absolute disobedience to your father's last and most solemn act, which

appoints you to submit to the direction of your guardians, to Mr. Hall and myself in particular, in what regards your education. I cannot think you believe a total revolt from our rule will make you in any sense great if you have not the constituents of greatness in you, or that waiting the common course of time and expediency will at all hinder the maturity of your powers, if you have them.

(Japp, Memorials 1: 71)

In keeping with her evangelical beliefs, Mrs. Quincey saw herself as divinely invested with the power and the wisdom to decide Thomas's best interests. She had "an awful account to give as a parent" and evidently saw that De Quincey's chastisement was her chief duty at this time (Japp, *Memorials* 1: 73). De Quincey's subjectively defined "misery" was ironically better calculated to confirm Mrs. Quincey's original decision than to change it.

De Quincey's decision to flee his school and to claim his paternally inherited rights certainly fell foul of Mrs. Quincey's conception of his filial duties. Crucially Mrs. Quincey saw Thomas' desire for "unnatural liberty" as influenced by his reading, which is "all of a sort to weaken your mental optics," so that she advises him to "let your daily reading be the works of men who were neither infidels nor Jacobins." Thomas' "revolt" is viewed as a potentially threatening act, undermining Mrs. Quincey's authority, and likely to prove contagious with the other children as well. In his subsequent recollection of the topics of discussion between his mother and himself at the familial establishment of the Priory, just before his admission to Oxford in 1803, De Quincey cites the issue of "*Government* in relation to the duties (but also, which females are far too apt to overlook, in relation to the rights) of us outside barbarians, the governed." Such a topic was clearly linked to De Quincey's recalcitrant behavior at this time. As Mrs. Quincey wrote angrily in response to De Quincey's proposal to leave the school forthwith, the issue at stake was "must you govern me or must I govern you?" The neat distinction here, recognized by the later De Quincey, between "rights" and "duties" reflects the terminology of the radical versus conservative ideologies that continued to set the agenda for political debate of the nineteenth century. De Quincey's reminiscence on the issue of government in relation to rights and duties thus points the political moral of his adolescent rebellion. Mrs. Quincey's assertion of her authority is clearly contested in a political context which is made clear by her defensive statement to Thomas that she was "not becoming a stickler for established systems as though they were perfect ones, but then good may and often has been obtained under them" (Japp, *Memorials* 1: 75, 78, 83-85, 100). It should be remembered here that the moderate evangelicals, particularly the "Clapham sect," were an important oppositional force on the issue of the slave-trade (here is where Mrs. Quincey might have found sympathy for the liberal Whigs, Roscoe, Currie and Clarke, who were notable opponents of the large Liverpool slave-trade); and interestingly Thomas' arguments against the Manchester Grammar School on the grounds of its severe and monotonous regimen without any scope for recreational activities, might be seen to parallel some of the material arguments against the conditions of slavery. For the evangelicals however, as Hilton has pointed out, it was not the material arguments that ultimately counted but their theological belief in redemption as a matter of free-will individualism (*Atonement* 98). Mrs. Quincey's seemingly surprising failure to stop De Quincey's flight from Manchester Grammar School by reporting his plans to the headmaster may be seen within this context of a rationalist free-will suasion to which her letters bear testimony. Yet Mrs. Quincey's emphasis on spiritual and moral rather than physical coercion was of course inadequate to the profoundly variant beliefs now raised by De Quincey.

A crucial aspect of the clearly-differentiated perspectives adopted by Mrs. Quincey and Thomas was her insistence on the necessity of an established and systematic form of education, as opposed to the self-reliant scheme proposed by the latter. Here it is that the emphasis of *Lyrical Ballads* on a "natural" education in the Rousseauvian, prelapsarian sense poses the ideological challenge to the evangelistic parental authority attemptedly exerted by Mrs. Quincey. Although there are no direct references in the contemporary letters between Mrs. Quincey and Thomas to *Lyrical Ballads* as a motivating factor in the latter's decision to run away from the Manchester Grammar School, it may now be clear why Mrs. Quincey saw the boy's reading as so important to his rebellious outlook, and why De Quincey later figured *Lyrical Ballads* as central to his decision. Mrs. Quincey was a shrewd if rather authoritarian mother, and her warning to Thomas not to exalt "the most dangerous faculty of the mind, the imagination, over all the rest; but it will desolate your life and hopes, if it be not restrained and brought under religious government" (Japp, *Memorials* 1: 75) reads prophetically in the light of his career, as does his brilliantly subversive configuration of opium in relation to the Wordsworth-Coleridgean brand of romantic imagination. De Quincey's early letters to Wordsworth indicate his perception of Wordsworth as spiritual guide and teacher, an ironically displaced recognition of the role claimed ineffectually by his mother. Wordsworth's difference lay certainly in the fact that his authority was presented as a "natural" function, rather than in the impositional style assumed by Mrs. Quincey. Such an impression is conveyed by De Quincey when he writes to Wordsworth, "that your name is with me for ever linked to the lovely scenes of nature;—and that not yourself only but that each place and object you have mentioned . . . and all the souls in that delightful community of yours—to me "are dearer than the sun!" Of course, this is what Wordsworth, who had sought in the Preface to appeal to the untutored taste in poetry, would have wished to hear, and De Quincey is suppressing the implications of his apparently spontaneous love for Wordsworth. The spontaneity of De Quincey's recognition is seen to be a function of his ostensibly uncorrupted nature, a (mis)-representation that is reiterated in his claim later in the letter that "my life has been passed chiefly in the contemplation and altogether in the worship of nature—that I am but a boy and have therefore formed no connection which could draw you one step farther from the sweet retreats of poetry to the detested haunts of men" (*D* 185-86).

While such a claim is patently untrue for the well-connected Thomas, whose acquaintances included Lord Altamont and Lady Carbery, De Quincey's representation of himself indicates in no uncertain terms the new direction that his thinking had taken. Although such a movement appears to detach itself from political considerations, it may be seen that De Quincey's reading of *Lyrical Ballads* is set in an ideological context that is profoundly challenging to his evangelical background. De Quincey himself retrospectively attempts to figure the formative moment of his reading of *Lyrical Ballads* in explicitly "revolutionary" terms, but though these are not strictly accurate descriptions of his youthful politics, they yet point to an emerging outlook at this time. De Quincey's early reading of *Lyrical Ballads* indicates however a strong sense of its contextual significance, drawn from sources which he later attempts to suppress, such as the redoubtable Liverpool literary circle disparaged in his 1837 article in *Tait's*. So also De Quincey's later representations of his Irish political sympathies, and his own flight from the Manchester Grammar School, are reinscribed by political sympathies which are the result of his later experiences in political journalism, but at the same time may be read together with his contemporary records to suggest a seminal ideological influence involving his reading of *Lyrical Ballads*.

Notes

1. See the major biographies by Grevel Lindop, *The Opium-Eater: A Life of Thomas De Quincey* (London: J. M. Dent, 1981) 31-32, 49, and Horace Eaton, *Thomas De Quincey: A Biography* (London: Oxford UP, 1936) 94-97, 114, as well as the more specialized work by John Jordan, *De Quincey to Wordsworth: A Biography of a Relationship* (Berkeley and Los Angeles: U of California P, 1962) and numerous critical works such as D. D. Devlin, *De Quincey, Wordsworth and the Art of Prose* (London: Macmillan, 1983) 15-20; 22-24 and *passim;* John Beer, "De Quincey and the Dark Sublime: The Wordsworth-Coleridge Ethos," in

Thomas De Quincey: Bicentenary Studies, ed. R. L. Snyder (Norman: U of Oklahoma P, 1985) 164-98 and Margaret Russett, "Wordsworth's Gothic Interpreter: De Quincey Personifies 'We are Seven,'" *SiR* 30 (1991): 345-66.

2. Jordan, *De Quincey to Wordsworth* 30; Thomas De Quincey, *Recollections of the Lakes and the Lake Poets,* ed. David Wright (Harmondsworth: Penguin, 1970) 33 (hereafter cited as *R*).

   Though critics have disagreed on the date and edition of De Quincey's reading of *Lyrical Ballads* (Jordan suggests 1799 [7-8] whereas Lindop considers 1801 more probable [*Opium-Eater* 49]), it is clear from his 1803 *Diary* that he had read both the anonymous one-volume first edition and the two-volume second edition under Wordsworth's name alone. In his *Diary,* apart from referring to the two volumes of the second edition, he quotes a phrase from the 1798 text of "The Rime of the Ancyent Marinere," "Like God's own head," which Coleridge altered to "Like an Angel's head" in the second and subsequent editions until 1817, when he returned to the original. The *Diary* also reprints a facsimile of De Quincey's letter dated 13 May [1803] which includes a sentence originally beginning, "I read the 'Lyrical Ballads' soon after their first appearance [. . .]" but was later altered to read "From the strike though time when I first saw the 'Lyrical Ballads' [. . .]." See Horace Eaton, ed. *A Diary of Thomas De Quincey, 1803* (London: Noel Douglas, [1927]) [119], 155 (hereafter cited as *D*) and S. T. Coleridge, *Poetical-Works,* ed. E. H. Coleridge (1912; Oxford: Oxford UP, 1969) 190 (hereafter cited as *PW*). On this evidence, Jordan's estimate of 1799 appears more likely.

3. Lindop has interestingly suggested an evangelical source for De Quincey's acquaintance with "We are Seven" (*Opium-Eater* 31) but by and large there has been little speculation on the channels through which *Lyrical Ballads* might have become known to De Quincey.

4. Jerome McGann, *The Romantic Ideology* (Chicago: U of Chicago P, 1983).

5. David Masson, ed., *The Collected Writings of Thomas De Quincey,* 14 vols. (Edinburgh: Adam and Charles Black, 1889-90) 3: 302. Hereafter cited as *M*.

6. See especially Nigel Leask, *The Politics of Imagination in Coleridge's Critical Thought* (London: Macmillan, 1988) 46-55.

7. E. L. Griggs, ed. *The Collected Letters of Samuel Taylor Coleridge,* 6 vols. (Oxford: Oxford UP, 1956-71) 1: 607. Hereafter cited as *CL*.

8. For a good account of the political importance of the Liverpool group, see J. E. Cookson, *The Friends of Peace: Anti-war Liberalism in England, 1793-1815* (Cambridge: Cambridge UP, 1982).

9. A. H. Japp, ed. *De Quincey Memorials,* 2 vols. (London, 1891) 1: 60-62.

10. The catalogue of the Athenaeum shows that they purchased the first edition of *Lyrical Ballads,* but not the second or subsequent editions, despite the substantial new material in the later editions. Coleridge's unfair treatment by Wordsworth in the second edition of *Lyrical Ballads* would have been obvious to the likes of Currie and Roscoe, so perhaps the decision not to acquire the second edition was prompted by their support for Coleridge. On the impact of Wordsworth's suppression of Coleridge's name from the second edition of *Lyrical Ballads,* see Richard Holmes, *Coleridge: The Early Years* (London: Hodder and Stoughton, 1989) 283-90 and Stephen Gill, *William Wordsworth: A Life* (Oxford: Oxford UP, 1989) 184-87.

11. Henry Roscoe, *The Life of William Roscoe,* vol. 1 (London: Cadell and Blackwood, 1833) 231-33.

12. J. Currie, ed., *The Works of Robert Burns; with an account of his Life, and [. . .] some observations on the character and condition of the Scottish Peasantry,* 4 vols. (Liverpool, 1800). Regarding modern controversy surrounding Currie's editorship, see R. D. Thornton, *James Currie the Entire Stranger and Robert Burns* (Edinburgh: Oliver & Boyd, 1963); Donald Low, *Robert Burns: The Critical Heritage* (London: Routledge and Kegan Paul, 1974) 23-25 and *passim;* James Mackay, *R. B.: A Biography of Robert Burns* (1992; rpt. Edinburgh: Mainstream Publishing, 1993) 647-62; as well as Leith Davis, "James Currie's *Works of Robert Burns:* The Politics of Hypochondriasis" *SiR* 36 (1997): 43-60.

13. Robert Mayo, "The Contemporaneity of *Lyrical Ballads,*" *PMLA* 69 (1954): 486-522.

14. Duncan Wu, *Wordsworth's Reading 1800-1815* (Cambridge: Cambridge UP, 1995) 35.

15. W. J. B. Owen and J. W. Smyser, ed. *The Prose Works of William Wordsworth,* vol. 3 (Oxford: Oxford UP, 1974) 118.

16. *Tait's Edinburgh Magazine,* ns 4 (1837): 340.

17. Brett, R. L. and A. R. Jones, ed. *Lyrical Ballads: The text of the 1798 edition with the additional 1800 poems and the Prefaces* (1963; London: Methuen, 1965) 245. Hereafter cited as *LB.* I have used this edition rather than the more recent Cornell edition since the latter favors a manuscript source over the printed version for its reading text, whereas my emphasis on reception requires the printed version to be held primary.

18. E. P. Thompson, *The Making of the English Working-Class* (1963; Harmondsworth: Penguin, 1968).

19. S. T. Coleridge, *Biographia Literaria,* vol 2, ed., James Engell and W. Jackson Bate (Princeton: Princeton UP, 1983) 45.

20. It must be noted that De Quincey chose not to republish his reminiscences of the "Liverpool Coterie" in putting together his "Autobiographic Sketches" for his collected edition of his own writings, the *Selections Grave and Gay,* 14 vols. (Edinburgh: James Hogg, 1853-60). In an unpublished letter, 5 March 1840, De Quincey warned Thomas Talford that if he did ever read his "Autob. sketches in Tait, bear in mind that I disown them" (De Quincey, *Letters,* Carl H. Pforzheimer Library, New York, Misc MS 104) I am indebted to Dr. Barry Symonds for the transcript of this and other letters of De Quincey which deserve to be published.

21. Apart from Jeffrey however, De Quincey may have learnt of the association between the three poets from the Liverpool literatures, Roscoe and others. Significantly he does not apparently renew his acquaintance with the Liverpool circle this time round at Everton judging by the absence of any reference to them in his *Diary.*

22. *Edinburgh Review* 1 (1802): 64.

23. See also his complaints regarding "the wretched drivellings of that old dotard *Homer*" (*D* 176) and his "great contempt for *Porson* as an editor" (*D* 206). (Porson's negative attitude to modern [English] poetry may here be seen to be instrumental to De Quincey's contempt for him.)

24. Marilyn Butler, ed., *Burke, Paine, Godwin and the Revolution Controversy* (Cambridge: Cambridge UP, 1984) 19. John Horne Tooke, ΕΠΕΑ ΠΤΕΡΟΕΝΤΑ or *The Diversions of Purley,* vol. 1 (1786; 2nd ed, London: J. Johnson, 1798). For a discussion of Tooke's significance to Wordsworth and *Lyrical Ballads,* see Olivia Smith, *The Politics of Language* (Oxford: Clarendon, 1984) 202-52.

25. *Edinburgh Review* 1 (1802): 63-66, 71. Incidentally, Jeffrey's strictures on the false aims in poetic language propounded by Wordsworth were to be the point of his later comparison of the Lake poets with Burns in 1809 (*Edinburgh Review* 13 [1809]: 249-76). Wordsworth's later desire for identification with Burns which as we have seen De Quincey was to recover through his own "Jacobinical" support for the Scottish poet is thus integral to Wordsworth's literary warfare with the *Edinburgh Review.*

26. See J. R. Ebbatson, "Coleridge's Ancient Mariner and the Rights of Man," *SiR* 11 (1972): 171-206; as well as Peter Kitson, "Coleridge, the French Revolution and 'The Ancient Mariner': Collective Guilt and Individual Salvation," *The Yearbook of English Studies* 19 (1989): 192-207.

27. See Iain McCalman, *Radical Underworld: Prophets, Revolutionaries and Pornographers in London, 1795-1840* (Cambridge: Cambridge UP, 1988) 11-15, 23-24.

28. Japp, *Thomas De Quincey: His Life and Writings* (1877; London, 1890) 37-38.

29. See David Erdman, "Milton! Thou Shouldst be Living," *The Wordsworth Circle* 19 (1988): 2-9.

30. "Pursuing the Throne of God," *Charles Lamb Bulletin* ns 52 (1985): 97-111.

31. *The Age of Atonement* (Oxford: Clarendon, 1988) 20.

Charles J. Rzepka (essay date 1998)

SOURCE: "The 'Dark Problem' of Greek Tragedy: Sublimated Violence in De Quincey," in *The Wordsworth Circle,* Vol. 29, No. 2, Spring, 1998, pp. 114-20.

[*In the following essay, Rzepka contends that De Quincey's portraits of violence are deeply influenced by his reading of Greek and Shakespearean tragedy.*]

"The Greek Tragedy is a dark problem," announces Thomas De Quincey at the beginning of his essay, **"Theory of Greek Tragedy"** (X, 342),[1] the problem being, first, how to distinguish between Greek and Modern, or "Shakespearean," tragedy, and secondly, how to make this distinction intelligible to the un-Greeked, middle-class audience of *Blackwood's Edinburgh Magazine* in February, 1840. De Quincey, an adept popularizer, solves both problems by nesting Greek Tragedy within the framework of a Shakespearean example universally familiar to the literate classes of England: the "play within a play" of *Hamlet,* which he likens, in turn, to a painting within a painting:

> We see a chamber, suppose, exhibited by the artist, on the walls of which . . . hangs a picture. And, as this picture again might represent a room furnished with pictures, in the mere logical possibility of the case we might imagine this descent into a life below a life going on *ad infinitum.* . . . The original picture is a mimic, an unreal, life. But this unreal life is itself a real life with respect to the secondary picture; which again must be supposed realized with relation to the tertiary picture, if such a thing were attempted. Consequently, at every step of the *involution* . . . each term in the descending series, being first of all a mode of non-reality to the spectator, is next to assume the functions of a real life in its relations to the next lower or interior term of the series.
>
> (X, 344)

By means of such "involutions," De Quincey says, Shakespeare insured "that the secondary or inner drama should be non-realized upon a scale that would throw, by comparison, a reflex colouring of reality upon the principal drama" (344-45). For De Quincey, Greek Tragedy "stands in the very same circumstances" as the play within the play of *Hamlet,* a derealized "life within a life which the painter sometimes exhibits to the eye, and which the Hamlet of Shakespeare exhibits to the mind."

De Quincey's structural analogy between Greek and Shakespearean tragedy is founded upon an essential, and revealing, elision, which emerges only as he proceeds: Ancient tragedy, he reiterates, is "what the inner life of the mimetic play in Hamlet is to the outer life of the Hamlet itself. It is a life below a life" (347). But then, the question almost seems to form itself in De Quincey's mind as it must have in the minds of his readers, *what is it to our life?* That, after all, is the original "dark problem": How does one relate the ancient tragedy to oneself, to the modern, middle-class spectator of modern, Shakespearean tragedies like *Hamlet?*

Specifically, if the play within *Hamlet* "realizes" the "life" of *Hamlet* for its spectators, then what gets "realized" when we view directly, and without the mediation of another "picture," the "derealized" "life within a life" framed by Greek tragedy? De Quincey's answer is, *our own life:* "The Greek tragic life presupposed another life" *like* the play within *Hamlet,* but this life is actually "the spectator's, *thrown into relief before it*" (347). In the median place of that material signifier of our life occupied, in modern practice, by a play called *Hamlet,* we find only what De Quincey calls "an immeasurable gulf of shadows" that are, it turns out, nothing less than our own shadows, dematerialized phantasms that seem to inhabit the very mind beholding them.

The phrase "immeasurable gulf of shadows" recalls De Quincey's earliest published essay on Shakespearean tragedy, **"On the Knocking at the Gate in *Macbeth*."** There, the knocking at the gate immediately following the murder of Duncan interrupts the frantic exchanges of Macbeth and Lady Macbeth, reminding us, "by reaction" and the sudden "reflux" of "ordinary life," that we have for a time been suspended in a nightmare from which we are about to awaken. Macbeth and his wife have been "conformed to the image of devils; and the world of devils is suddenly revealed":

> The murderers, and the murder, must be insulated—*cut off by an immeasurable gulph* from the ordinary tide and succession of human affairs—locked up and sequestered in some deep recess . . . time must be annihilated; relation to things without abolished; and all must pass self-withdrawn into a deep syncope and suspension of earthly passion.
>
> (Lindop, 84; italics added)

The knocking at the gate "first makes us profoundly sensible of the awful parenthesis that had suspended" ordinary life (85).

This scene from the second act of *Macbeth* clearly assumed for De Quincey, as early as 1823, something of the same dreamlike status that Greek tragedy was to assume in his essay for *Blackwood's* seventeen years later—

sequestered, recessed, insulated, self-withdrawn, slumbering, inhuman, this Shakespearean moment strikes him almost as though it were itself "a play within the play" we call *Macbeth*. That the Macbeths are "devils," that we are indeed looking, as De Quincey puts it, "into . . . hell" (83), was probably suggested to him by the Porter's lines immediately following, which open scene three: "Here's a knocking indeed! If a man were porter of Hell gate, he should have [grown] old turning the key. Knock, knock, knock! Who's there, i' the name of Beelzebub?" (1-4). In the later essay on Greek tragedy, De Quincey likens its "life within a life," its "life sequestrated into some far-off slumbering state," to "Hades" (359).

Accordingly, says De Quincey, compared to the "painting" that is magically brought to life by that "Cornelius Agrippa" of the stage, Shakespeare, as "a thing now passing" (350) before our eyes, the "Tragedy of Greece is always held up as a thing long past": "We are invited by Sophocles or Euripides, as by some great necromancer, to see long-buried forms standing in solemn groups upon the stage—phantoms from Thebes or from Cyclopian cities" (350). The Greek tragedians enable us to stand in the presence of the "long past" dead, like Odysseus on the far shores of Oceanus (*Odyssey,* Book 11), and listen to their tale of suffering. In an otherwise irreverent and facetious essay on Greek literature predating **"Theory of Greek Tragedy"** by two years, De Quincey even goes so far as to say, in one of his few serious moments, that the presiding power of ancient tragedy is Death: "That sort of death, or of life locked up and frozen into everlasting slumber, which we see in sculpture" (X, 315).

If life of the spectator "presupposed" by Greek tragedy is indeed "thrown into relief before it," then this is not so much a life represented in present time across the *limen* of proscenium or orchestra, as in modern tragedy, as it is merged with the "immeasurable gulf" inhabited by the "long past" "shadows" of the dead we see before us. Theatrical spectacle has become a species of hallucination, and the symbolic space of modern tragedy has collapsed into the unmediated, pure Imaginary.

The state of mind in which, according to De Quincey, we view Greek tragedy resembles hypnogogic states of dreaming-waking that are typical of the opium hallucinations described in the *Confessions of an English Opium-Eater,* where, "as the creative state of the eye increased, a sympathy seemed to arise between the waking and the dreaming states of the brain" (Lindop, 68). In an unpublished fragment of the 1845 *Suspiria de Profundus* De Quincey described such experiences in terms more closely linked to his idea of Greek tragedy. Here he recalls his power as a child to "project a vast theatre of phantasmagorical figures moving forwards or backwards between [the]

bed-curtains and the chamber walls," and adds that similar "powers of self-projection lurk in the dark places of the human spirit—in grief, in fear, in vindictive wrath" (Japp, I, 7-8)—in short, in the pity and terror that Aristotle makes central to Greek tragedy.

As Nigel Leask puts it in a recent and important essay, "The deep 'recess' and 'life of shadows' that for De Quincey characterize the Greek tragic stage and the opium dream alike is evidently a psychic space, a site where the 'deep deep tragedies of childhood' are metamorphosed into a 'literature of power' (109).[2] Indeed, since De Quincey's only access to Greek tragedy (until 1846, when he reviewed a performance of *Antigone* on the Edinburgh stage) would have been through texts, the physical play-space of Greek theatre would have necessarily been introjected *as* "psychic space," a waking-dream or hallucination, a "vast theatre of phantasmagorical figures" unfolding *in* the mind, rather than *before* the eyes. The words "project" and "projection" in De Quincey's reminiscences of hypnogogic power not only resemble the idea of "another life, the spectator's, thrown into relief before" the spectacle itself, but are exactly echoed, in cryptic fashion, by what De Quincey adds next in **"Theory of Greek Tragedy"**: "The tragedy was *projected* upon the eye from a vast profundity in the rear" (347).

De Quincey never tells us, in "the rear" of what? In the rear of the spectator's eye? or in the rear of the tragedy itself? I believe the ambiguity is deliberate. On the one hand, De Quincey means "from a vast profundity in the rear" of the eye, where, as he writes in the "Introductory Notice" to the *Suspiria,* "the machinery for dreaming" is located.

> That faculty, in alliance with the mystery of darkness, is the one great tube through which man communicates with the shadowy. And the dreaming organ, in connexion with the heart, the eye, and the ear, compose the magnificent apparatus which forces the infinite into the chambers of the human brain, and throws dark reflections from eternities below all life upon the mirrors of the sleeping mind
>
> (Lindop, 88).

"In the rear" of the spectator's eye lies the "vast profundity" leading, through the "one great tube" of the "dreaming organ," to the very "life below a life" that Greek tragedy represents on stage before the spectator's eye.

On the other hand, however, De Quincey also seems to be referring to "a vast profundity in the rear" of the visible stage itself, a site that had a precise dramaturgical counterpart in ancient Greek stage practice: the *skene* or stage house set in back of the public *orchestra* space where the chorus sang and danced. With its doors located in the center of the stage, the *skene* represented palace, house, temple, or hut, as the demands of the play required. It was also, typically, the site of any bloody acts of off-stage violence understood to be performed indoors.[3]

"The vast profundity in the rear" of the Greek stage, then, would refer to what went on behind the closed doors of the *skene*. The ambiguity of De Quincey's phrasing, like so much else that is ambiguous in his writings, points to a hidden identity: the "chambers of the brain" at the rear of the spector's eye lead obliquely, via the "machinery of dreaming," down, under, and away—literally, according to one etymological derivation in the OED, in a *sublime* direction—toward that realm of death-like, superhuman, dreamlike stasis, that "life within" or "below a life" projected before the eye from the "vast profundity in the rear" of the stage itself, from beyond the "limen" or sacred threshold of the *oikos*.[4] Household violence, the recurrent and obsessive sado-masochistic fantasy that informs so much of De Quincey's autobiographical writings, fiction, and "impassioned prose"—including the Macbeth essay, the notorious three-part essay, **"Murder Considered as One of the Fine Arts,"** the novel, *Klosterheim,* and the story **"The Avenger"**—lies at the hidden heart of his theorization of ancient Greek tragedy as well.[5]

Violence, for De Quincey as for the Greek tragedians, achieves its sublime power by remaining hidden from the public eye, which is to say, out of the eye of public spectators or the "mob." Its power derives from its occlusion precisely because relegating violence to the realm of the "shadowy" forces it to express itself, almost literally, according to De Quincey's hydraulic metaphor, through the "one great tube" of the dreaming machinery, in the form of a hallucination that seems to envelope the spectator himself. The point of occlusion in this circuit of tragic sublimation is the point of empowerment: the *limen,* the threshold between public and private spheres.

De Quincey's understanding of the sub-liminal or sublime power of hidden violence depends on patriarchal cultural assumptions endemic to classical Greece. As Hannah Arendt argues, in *The Human Condition* (22-68), the public sphere of the Greek *polis* rested, ultimately, on each male citizen's power to exclude from public view all events and processes that could be understood as revealing his subjection to natural forces beyond his control: birth, death, illness, hunger—in general, all events endemic to the life of the body. Such events were relegated to the private, domestic sphere that lay beyond the threshold of the *oikos,* where female citizens were sequestered.

Of course, the male citizen's absolute—if nominal—authority over that domestic sphere could not encompass a corresponding power to control the dark forces circumscribed within it. Children were born, parents died. But the fiction of absolute patriarchal power over the *oikos* was essential to maintaining the fiction of the male citizen's absolute autonomy as a participant in the deliberations of the *polis*. This is why an outsider crossing the threshold of the *oikos* without permission, let alone doing violence to its inhabitants, was considered a crime second only in magnitude to the intramural defiance of the authority of the patriarch, or *kyrios,* by wife, children, or slaves. At the same time, however, the *hubris* displayed in such acts of violence—Oedipus's patricide, Clytemnestra's murder of her spouse—laid claim, as in a sublime orator's violations of the standard rules of rhetoric in Longinus's *Peri Hypsous,* to superhuman prerogatives in defiance of the laws of gods and men, with commensurate risks of violent punishment. The result, on the Greek stage, was to make the criminal both reprehensible and sublime.

Like the Greek tragedians, De Quincey understood that hubristic violence derived its imaginative power from its public occlusion. Relegated to the realm of the "shadowy," violence is forced to exert its power—almost palpably, according to De Quincey's hydraulic metaphor, through the "one great tube" of the dreaming machinery, in the displaced form of a hallucination that seems to envelope the spectator himself. The point of occlusion in this circuit of tragic sublimation is the point of imaginative empowerment: the *limen,* the threshold between public and private spheres.

In the highly sensational 1854 **"Postscript"** to his first two essays **"On Murder Considered as a Fine Art"** which were published separately in 1827 and 1839, De Quincey "sublimates" this threshold, traces this subterranean circuit, by pointedly shifting our imaginary point of view away from the murderer John Williams' imminent "extermination" of the Marr household at 29 Radcliffe Highway and then, only after the mayhem has ceased, bringing us back to the scene of the crime by means of an imaginative recreation pieced together from the "hieroglyphics" this "artist" left behind, as deciphered by the crowds who discovered them upon crossing the threshold themselves. Between the moment when Williams enters the house and the moment his "masterpiece" is discovered, however, we take up the point of view of a servant, Mary, who had been sent on an errand just prior to Williams' arrival and has returned just at the moment the bloody business is completed, but before Williams has left the house (XIII, 85).

What follows is a *tour de force*. We observe Mary arriving at the door and, finding it locked, knocking softly to be admitted. Receiving no answer from the inmates, who she assumes must still be awake, she begins to suspect that some disaster must have overtaken them. At that moment, she hears the stealthy footsteps of the murder[er] himself approaching the opposite side of the door. The two of them can hear each other breathing across the threshold. Suddenly, the horror of realization comes over her, and Mary starts "to ring the bell and to ply the knocker with unintermitting violence" (89). Williams flees, the crowd gathers, and the scene of carnage, like the corpses piled on the Greek *cycclema,* are displayed in all their gory splendor.

Mary's knocking had already, in the 1823 *Macbeth* essay, served to link Williams' 1811 "debut on the stage of Radcliffe Highway" with the murder of Duncan, to the delight of every "connoisseur in murder" (82). Leask offers a developmental reading of De Quincey's aesthetics of murder, moving from the **"Knocking"** essay of 1823 and the first two **"Murder"** essays of 1827 and 1839 through the period of De Quincey's writings on Greek tragedy (1838-1846) to the final **"Postscript"** to the **"Murder"** essays of 1854. Leask believes that De Quincey's shift to Mary's point of view in the more circumstantial **"Postscript"** marks an important departure from his earlier treatment of the Williams murders, insofar as, in the earlier **"Knocking"** and first two **"Murder"** essays, De Quincey professes the interest of murder to inhere primarily in our identification or "empathy" with the murderer, while in the **"Postscript"** that focus of empathy is centered on a potential victim, Mary. Leask attributes this "shift of narrative focus" to the "influence of the choric perspective of Greek tragedy" (114) resulting from the fact that in the years intervening between the second, **"Murder"** essay and the 1854 **"Postscript"** "De Quincey sought to elaborate and deepen his earlier *satirical* aesthetics of murder [in the first two **"Murder"** essays] by means of a study of Greek tragedy" (106).

The influence of Greek tragedy on this shift cannot, I believe, be denied, but Leask's developmental theory may be too neat to fit all the facts of the case. First, it is fiendishly difficult to determine the dates of composition for most of De Quincey's published writings. His work habits were, to say the least, untidy, and he often wrote MS drafts for articles that were never published, or were published as parts of later works, or were rescued from the bathtub that served as his *escritoire* and revised much later for publication. Masson notes that De Quincey's curious reference in the 1854 **"Postscript"** to his two previous essays as one "paper" in the singular suggests that the Postscript *may* have been in manuscript shortly after the publication of the **"First Paper"** [in 1827] and before the **"Second"** had been written [in 1839]" (XIII, 70n). To which one might add the fact that De Quincey continues to use the singular thereafter: "this *bagatelle*" (70), "this lecture on the aesthetics of murder" (71), "my own little paper" (72). In addition, De Quincey's first essay on Greek tragedy, **"A Brief Appraisal of the Greek Literature,"** predates by a year the publication of the second of the **"Murder"** es-

says, which shows no sign of what Leask contends is so important an influence on De Quincey's later aesthetic of murder. In the **"Postscript"** itself, moreover, the agenda of empathy is not as cleanly reversed as Leask would have it: for instance, we are never invited to identify with the actual victims of Williams' depredations, which is consistent with De Quincey's insistence, in the **"Knocking"** essay, that the feelings of victims are not aesthetically or psychologically interesting, while we are invited, several times, to look into the "wolfish" mind of Williams himself, who kills both for the aesthetic excitement of it and, more vulgarly, for money.

Most importantly, De Quincey had been since childhood an outstanding student of classical languages, especially Greek, in which, one of his teachers once declared, "he could harangue an Athenian mob, better than you or I could address an English one" (Lindop, 7). Thus, his acquaintance with Greek tragedy long predated even the earliest of his published writings, and famously left its mark on that earliest piece as well. At the beginning of the second installment of the *Confessions* in the *London Magazine* for October 1821, De Quincey likens himself in the throes of opium withdrawal to Orestes suffering the wrath of the Eumenides after having killed Clytemnestra. De Quincey calls his ministering young wife, Margaret, his "Elektra!" who "neither in nobility of mind nor in long-suffering affection, wouldst permit that a Grecian sister should excel an English wife" (Lindop, 36). Here, two years before the **"Knocking"** essay, De Quincey mingles citations on the "blessed balm" of sleep (35) from the opening scene of Euripides' *Orestes* with Macbeth's famous line, "sleep no more!" We need not postulate a developmental scheme for De Quincey's apparently "choric" shift in point of view in the **"Postscript"** of 1854: Greek tragedy was never very far from De Quincey's thoughts when they turned to murder.

Nor do I accept Leask's contention that De Quincey's shift to an extramural vantage in the **"Postscript"** marks the adoption of a "choric" point of view. If anything, it is the London crowd, the "mob," as De Quincey calls it (borrowing a common Euripidean epithet) that most clearly represents the "group think" De Quincey associates with the Greek chorus, whose function, as he indicates in the 1845 *Suspiria,* is "not to tell you anything absolutely new, *that* was done by the actors in the drama; but to recall you to your own lurking thoughts." In addition, the chorus is "to place before you . . . such commentaries, prophetic or looking back, pointing the moral or deciphering the mystery" (Lindop, 156), much as the crowds rushing into No. 29 Radcliffe Highway are said to have deciphered Williams' bloody "hieroglyphics" and to have voiced, collectively, our own thirst for vengeance. The point of view De Quincey adopts at the crucial moment of truth is, indeed, exterior to the *limen* or threshold, but it is centered in a single young female, and a potential victim of the murderer, at that. Let me offer, then, a much more specific model for De Quincey's empathic regard, drawn from his favorite play and playwright: the character of Hermione, daughter of Helen, from Euripides' *Orestes,* the play that figured so prominently at the structural center of the original ***Confessions.***

Leaving aside De Quincey's devoting an entire review to the Edinburgh *Antigone*—a choice of play dictated by circumstances—Euripides receives more citations (and more laudatory citations) than any other ancient playwright in the complete works, and *Orestes* receives more of these than any other Euripidean play. This should not surprise us: when he ran off from Manchester Grammar School at the age of 17 to seek his fortune in Wales and London, De Quincey took with him only two books: Wordsworth's *Lyrical Ballads* in one pocket, and "an odd volume, containing about one-half of Canter's 'Euripides' in the other" (III, 299).

William Canter's two-volume edition of Euripides (1602) is not exactly a pocket-sized affair by modern standards, and if De Quincey decided to take but one of the two volumes, it was most likely the first, weighing in at 757 pages, rather than the second, which, including Index and Annotations for the set, runs to 1248. The first volume contains *Orestes,* as well as two other plays featuring indoor violence—*Medea* and *Hecuba.* (*Elektra* is contained in the second volume.)

In **"Theory of Greek Tragedy,"** De Quincey praises Euripides as "the most Wordsworthian of the Athenian poets in the circumstance of having a peculiar theory of poetic diction, which lowered its tone of separation . . . These innovations ran in the very same direction as those of Wordsworth in our own times" (357n). Euripides' diction was designed to "impress pity," making it "less grand (it is true) and stately" than that of his predecessors, but "with far greater power of pure (sometimes, we may say, of holy) household pathos. Such also was the change wrought by Wordsworth" (357n). There is some truth to this. Euripides was cited by Longinus for his use of colloquial diction, a tendency most pronounced in *Andromache,* and his innovations in monody and strophic form were groundbreaking. He also shares with Wordsworth a sympathy for the virtuous lower classes and an interest in the deranging effects of powerful emotions. In his review of *Antigone,* De Quincey defends Euripides' emotional range against the relatively cold "artistry" of Sophocles by stating, "He was able to sweep *all* the chords of the impassioned spirit" (X, 371).

De Quincey's admiration for Euripides' way with "household pathos" corresponds to his praise, in a footnote to the

Orestes passage in the ***Confessions,*** for "the early scenes of the Orestes; one of the most beautiful exhibitions of the domestic affections which even the dramas of Euripides can furnish" (Lindop, 36n). This assessment leans uneasily against one translator's more recent, and more characteristic, description of the play: "howling spiritual lunacy," "an image of heroic action seen as botched, disfigured, and sick" (Grene, 186). William Arrowsmith continues: "the unifying motif of the play is the gradual exposure of the real criminal depravity of Orestes and his accomplices," his sister Elektra and his fast friend, Pylades—a motif, in short, entirely congruent with De Quincey's taste for household violence.

The action of the play is set in the interval between Orestes' murder of his mother, Clytemnestra, and her lover, Aegisthus, for *their* murder of his father, Agamemnon, and the son's journey to Athens where, according to legend, he will be released from the punishing torments of the Eumenides by the combined judgment of the Athenian assembly and the deciding vote of Athena herself, who thereby exonerates him. As the play opens, Elektra is watching by the side of Orestes' bed, where he has finally been able to fall asleep after six days of relentless mental torture by the Furies. Menalaus (Agamemnon's brother), Helen (his wife), and Hermione (their daughter), have come to pay their respects to the dead Clytemnestra, Helen's sister. The three are staying at the palace of Argos, with Orestes, Elektra, and Pylades. While Menalaus is abroad and Helen is within, Hermione has been sent to pour the libations at her aunt's grave. At the same moment, the townspeople of Argos are meeting to decide the fate of the matricide, his sister, and their friend. The decision comes back: the three are found guilty, but are allowed to take their own lives rather than be stoned to death.

Orestes, whose plea for help has been rejected by his uncle, decides to take the life of Helen in revenge, with the help of Pylades. Helen is within the palace, represented by the *skene.* Elektra adds to the plot—they shall seize Hermione upon her return from the grave and hold her hostage: "If, Helen slain, Menelaus seek to harm / Thee, him, or me," she tells Orestes, "Cry, thou wilt slay Hermione: the sword / Drawn must thou hold hard at the maiden's neck, / Then, if Menelaus, lest his daughter die, / Will save thee . . . Yield to her sire's embrace the maiden's form. / But if, controlling not his furious mood, / He seek to slay thee, pierce the maid's neck through" (1191-99; all citations to trans. by Way).

Williams' characteristic method of murder was bludgeoning followed by the cutting of his victim's throats. In both of the mass murders for which he was famous, Williams was feared to have had an accomplice, the vestigial "Pylades" figure. In the Marr case, the crime is committed while Mary is away from the house, just as Helen is dispatched (actually, as we later discover, she is whisked away by Apollo at the very last instant and apotheosized) while Hermione is on her errand of piety. At the approach of any passer-by, Elektra is to "give token," to "smite on the door, or send a cry within" (1221-22)—a "knocking at the gate" that never occurs. As the murder of Helen proceeds, Elektra and the chorus keep anxious watch, shying at shadows and chiding each other for their overactive imaginations. When Hermione arrives at the door, she is concerned and suspicious at having heard a cry within. Elektra tells her it is only the cry of Orestes, bewailing his and his sister's fate at the hands of Argos' citizenry. Then Elektra persuades Hermione to enter the house—a moment corresponding to the moment at which, as De Quincey imagines it, Mary was to be "inveigled" into entering the house by the insidious Williams (89). Unlike the valiant Mary, however, Hermione succumbs to Elektra's blandishments.

There is still another female figure from the saga of Orestes that informs the figure of Mary, however, and in some ways, even more precisely. In the *Agamemnon* of Aeschylus's trilogy, the *Oresteia,* it is Cassandra, the ever-unheeded prophetess of doom claimed by Agamemnon from the sack of Troy, who stands outside the palace while, within, the man who brought her back to Argos is ambushed by his wife in his bath. Having been invited by Clytemnestra just moments before to join Agamemnon inside, Cassandra hesitates, astonished at the visions of atrocity running through her mind. The chorus remains oblivious:

Cassandra:

What house is this?

Chorus:

The house of the Atreidae. If you understand not that, I can tell you; and so much at least is true.

Cassandra:

No, but a house that God hates, guilty within of kindred blood shed, torture of its own, the shambles for men's butchery, the dripping floor.

(1087-1092; all citations to Lattimore, trans.)

In what follows, Cassandra envisions both the violence that has led up to the slaying of Agamemnon—Atreus's murder of the children of his brother, Thyestes, and his serving them to their father to eat—and the slaying of Agamemnon that is now transpiring just beyond the doorsill: "That room reeks with blood like a slaughter house" (1309). Like Mary, Cassandra is suddenly overwhelmed by a realization of the violence taking place just across the *limen.* Unlike Mary, and again, like her Greek counterpart,

Hermione, she bends to her fate: "So I am going in, and mourning as I go/ my death and Agamemnon's" (1313-14).

The point of De Quincey's focusing on the Mary/ Hermione/Cassandra figure in his 1854 **"Postscript"** is not, as Leask would have it, to accentuate the "choric" perspective, but to enhance the spectator's sense of sublime terror by decreasing the distance between private violence and a potential victim who is protected by nothing more than her publicity, by her remaining in sight, on the near side of the sacred *limen* of the *oikos.*

There is no need to belabor Euripides' denouement: Menelaus returns, Orestes and Pylades appear on the roof of the *skene* with Orestes holding his sword to Hermione's throat, and Elektra follows, having just set fire to the palace. In Arrowsmith's words, "the quality of nightmare [is] pervasive" (188), and "all moral terms are either inverted or emptied of their meaning" (189), a judgment corresponding to De Quincey's characterizations in Act 2, scene 2 of *Macbeth.* At this point, the standard Euripidean *deus ex machina* intervenes, with ludicrous results: Apollo placates Menelaus by telling him that Helen is now living with the gods; he orders Pylades to marry Elektra; and (most fantastic!) he tells Orestes to drop his sword, marry Hermione, and set off immediately for Athens, where his fate is to be decided. In this melee of vengeance, betrayal, cowardice, and cold-blooded violence it is hard to remember the "household pathos" of the opening scene that De Quincey so much admired.

What remains constant, however, from the *Oresteia* of Aeschylus through the *Elektra* of Sophocles to the *Elektra* and *Orestes* of Euripides is the accentuated occlusion of violent household death, the hiding away from public view of "family extermination" unfolding behind the closed door of the *skene.*[6] The impact of the Greek example, and of Euripides' *Orestes* in particular, appears not just in **"Murder Considered,"** but throughout De Quincey's writings: in **Klosterheim,** for instance, where the apparent victims of the avenging "Masque" turn out, like Helen, to be alive after all, and the Masque himself turns out to be motivated in his violence, like Euripides' Orestes, by the political betrayal of a usurping uncle. Other students of De Quincey can no doubt cite their own examples. In nearly every case, the sublime of De Quinceyan terror is charged, as it were, like an electrical capacitor, by the thin but impermeable barrier erected and maintained at the *limen* or threshold between the private and the public spheres, the closed doorway at the back of the stage that imaginatively empowers the hallucinatory violence at the back of the mind.

Notes

1. All citations from De Quincey's works are taken from the edition of Masson, except for those marked

"Lindop," which are from the Lindop edition of *Confessions of an English Opium-Eater and Other Writings*.

2. The influence of Greek tragedy on De Quincey's writings had not received much attention before Leask's article appeared. Bilsland examines several allusions to classical drama in an unsystematic way, while O'Quinn focuses more on Plato's influence on Kant and De Quincey than on Greek tragedy itself.

3. I have been unable to determine precisely how much De Quincey would have known concerning the actual details of Greek staging, or exactly how much was knowable during this lifetime. As early as 1835, G. C. W. Schneider published a comprehensive list of ancient references to theatre performance, but it was not until the advent of Albert Muller's and Wilhelm Dorpfeld's more comprehensive and archaeologically informed studies near the end of the century that an accurate picture of the ancient Greek stage began to emerge. De Quincey was aware, like most of the classicists of his day, of the general dimensions of the Greek amphitheaters, of the Greeks' use of the *cothurnus* or high boots to elevate the actor, of the mask and its mysterious devices for amplifying the voice, and of the voluminous robes meant to lend proportional amplitude to the figure on stage. Regardless of his acquaintance with the *skene* itself, however, or with the *cycclema* on which freshly dispatched corpses were wheeled out for display to the audience, it would have been impossible for him to miss signs in the speeches of the characters themselves, or in the stage directions inserted by Latin translators, indicating that a particular act of violence—the murder of Agamemnon or Clytemnestra, for instance, or the self-blinding of Oedipus or the suicide of Jocasta—was to be performed "within doors."

4. The line of "vision" described by De Quincey seems to correspond to that of another "visionary" "tube," a reflecting telescope constructed at the Glasgow Observatory in 1841, which the writer had occasion to see and use during a brief stay in Glasgow in 1841-42. An observer using the reflecting telescope would stand with his or her back to the object being observed, in effect seeing in "before" him the "shadows" of an "immeasureable gulf" "projected upon the eye from a vast profundity in the rear" of the eye itself. These experiences, and his acquaintance with the astronomer John Pringle Nichol, provided the basis for De Quincey's dream-like prose poem on the "Nebular Hypothesis" of the Earl of Rosse, which appeared in *Tait's Magazine* in September 1846. (I am indebted to Grevel Lindop for this observation.)

5. The most important work on De Quincey and violence has been that of Robert M. Maniquis and, more recently, Joel Black. For Maniquis, De Quincey's fascination with violence is inseparable from his ideological commitments to imperial domination and labor exploitation as a Tory conservative. For Black, it represents the first flowering of a modern, mass-mediated taste for violence. See also, in response to Black's reading, Fred Burwick, and for another reading, similar to Leask's, of De Quincey's views of tragedy in relation to Kant, see O'Quinn.

6. Aeschylus's *Oresteia,* in fact, is the first extant drama for which a large building like the *skene* would have been necessary at the theater of Dionysus (Bieber, 57), and the violence hidden in the house of Atreus predominates over all other classic examples of domestic violence in the Greek tragedies that have survived antiquity.

Works Cited

Arendt, Hannah. *The Human Condition.* 1958.

Bieber, Margarete. *The History of Greek and Roman Theater.* 1961.

Bilsland, John W. "De Quincey's Critical Dilations," *U. of Toronto Quarterly* 52 (1982): 79-93.

Black, Joel. *The Aesthetics of Murder: A Study in Romantic Literature and Contemporary Culture.* 1991.

Grene, David, and Richmond Lattimore. *The Complete Greek Tragedies.* Volume 4. 1992.

Japp, Alexander H., ed. *The Posthumous Works of Thomas De Quincey.* 2 vols. 1891.

Leask, Nigel. "Toward a Universal Aesthetic: De Quincey on Murder as Carnival and Tragedy," In *Questioning Romanticism.* Ed. John Beer. 1995. Pp. 92-120

Lindop, Grevel, ed. *Confessions of an English Opium-Eater and Other Writings.* 1985.

Maniquis, Robert M. "The Dark Interpreter and the Palimpsest of Violence: De Quincey and the Unconscious." In *Thomas De Quincey: Bicentenary Studies.* Ed. Robert Lane Snyder. 1985. Pp. 109-39.

Maniquis, Robert M. *Lonely Empires: Personal and Public Visions of Thomas De Quincey.* 1976.

Masson, David, ed. *Collected Writings of Thomas De Quincey.* 14 vols. 1890.

O'Quinn, Daniel. "The Evil Theatrocracy: De Quincey, Kant and the Normative Laws of Tragedy," *European Romantic Review* 5:1 (1994): 32-48.

FURTHER READING

Criticism

Bate, Jonathan. "The Literature of Power: Coleridge and De Quincey." In *Coleridge's Visionary Languages: Essays*

in Honour of J. B. Beer, edited by Tim Fulford and Morton D. Paley, pp. 137-50. Cambridge: D. S. Brewer, 1993.
Traces Coleridge's influence on De Quincey.

Baxter, Edmund. *De Quincey's Art of Autobiography.* Edinburgh: Edinburgh University Press, 1990, 218 p.
Considers De Quincey's autobiographical writings as literature, rather than as direct representations of his life.

Cafarelli, Annette Wheeler. "Thomas De Quincey: The Allegory of Everyday Life." In *Prose in the Age of Poets: Romanticism and Biographical Narrative from Johnson to De Quincey,* pp. 151-91. Philadelphia: University of Pennsylvania Press, 1990.
Examines De Quincey's reminiscences of Wordsworth and Coleridge.

Groves, David. "Climbing the *Post:* Thomas De Quincey as a Newspaper Editor, 1827-28." *The Wordsworth Circle,* 29, No. 2 (Spring 1998): 126-31.
Discusses De Quincey's anonymous writings for the Edinburgh *Saturday Post* and Edinburgh *Evening Post.*

Levin, Susan M. "Thomas De Quincey: *Confessions of an Opium-Eater.*" In *The Romantic Art of Confession: De Quincey, Musset, Sand, Lamb, Hogg, Frémy, Soulié, Janin,* pp. 18-41. Columbia: Camden House, 1998.
Argues that De Quincey's autobiographical *Opium-Eater* is his most successful literary character.

McDonagh, Josephine. *De Quincey's Disciplines.* Oxford: Clarendon Press, 1994, 209 p.
Traces De Quincey's formulation of the disciplines of political economy, literary criticism, linguistics, and aesthetics, and their interrelationships.

McFarland, Thomas. "De Quincey's Journey to the End of the Night." In *Romantic Cruxes: The English Essayists and the Spirit of the Age,* pp. 90-122. Oxford: Clarendon Press, 1987.
Identifies the tropes of addiction and introspective fantasy which animate De Quincey's writing as paradigmatically Romantic.

Morrisson, Robert. "'I hereby present you, courteous reader': The Literary Presence of Thomas De Quincey." *The Charles Lamb Bulletin,* New Series No. 90 (April 1995): 68-72.

A general introduction to the critical reception of De Quincey's work.

North, Julian. *De Quincey Reviewed: Thomas De Quincey's Critical Reception, 1821-1994.* Columbia: Camden House, 1997, 179 p.
Surveys the diverse reviews and literary criticism of De Quincey.

Plumtree, A. S. "The Artist as Murderer: De Quincey's 'Essay On Murder Considered as One of the Fine Arts'." *Thomas De Quincey: Bicentenary Studies,* edited by Robert Lance Snyder, pp. 140-63. Norman: University of Oklahoma Press, 1985.
Contends that De Quincey's essay on murder reflects his elaboration of Romantic tropes, and establishes him as a precursor of modern crime literature.

Roberts, Daniel Sanjiv. "Exorcising the Malay: Dreams and the Unconscious in Coleridge and De Quincey." *The Wordsworth Circle* 29, No. 2 (Spring 1998): 91-96.
Explores the relation between opium use and creative vision for Coleridge and De Quincey.

Rzepka, Charles J. *Sacramental Commodities: Gift, Text, and the Sublime in De Quincey.* Amherst: University of Massachusetts Press, 1995, 340 p.
Examines the variety of figures—books, money, opium, and authorship—that occupy much of De Quincey's work.

Schmitt, Cannon. "De Quincey's Gothic Autobiography and the Opium Wars." In *Alien Nation: Nineteenth-Century Gothic Fictions and English Nationality,* pp. 46-75. Philadelphia: University of Pennsylvania Press, 1997.
Analyzes the complex connection between De Quincey's nationalism and his addiction to opium.

Smith, Jonathan. "De Quincey's Revisions to 'The System of the Heavens'." *Victorian Periodicals Review* 26, No. 4 (Winter 1993): 203-12.
Traces De Quincey's interest in astronomy and its possible relation to his literary corpus.

Additional coverage of Thomas De Quincey's life and career is contained in the following sources published by the Gale Group: *The Concise Dictionary of British Literary Biography* **1789–1832, and** *The Dictionary of Literary Biography,* **Vols. 110 and 144.**

George Moses Horton
1797?-1883?

American poet.

INTRODUCTION

Referred to by some critics as "the slave bard of North Carolina," Horton is generally praised for his poetic achievements, and his name is usually associated with several "firsts" in American literature. He was the first black southerner to have a book of poetry published; he was the only slave to derive a substantial income from selling his poems; he was the first American slave to write antislavery poems; and he was the only poet ever to publish a book of poetry before being able to write. His poems cover a wide variety of subjects, including freedom, antislavery, love, religion, and death, and although critics, in general, do not equate his talent with that of major nineteenth-century poets, they do find his achievements remarkable in light of the circumstances of his life as a slave.

BIOGRAPHICAL INFORMATION

Horton was born into slavery in North Carolina, probably in 1797, under the ownership of William Horton, a small landowner. Horton's mother and siblings were all slaves of the same owner, according to his autobiographical writings. He does not mention a great deal about his father except to say that he was his mother's second husband and apparently did not live with them. When Horton was very young, William Horton took his slaves and moved to a new farm near the town of Chapel Hill. George Moses Horton, of course, had no formal schooling, but with the help of his mother and her Wesley hymnal, which the slaves used at religious camp meetings, he did learn to read (before he could write). When Horton was about nineteen or twenty, he started making weekly treks from the farm into Chapel Hill on weekends to sell his master's fruit. Chapel Hill was the site of the state university, and it was on these weekend visits that Horton came into contact with university students and faculty. His literary "career" began when the students hired him to compose poetry, usually in the form of love poems or acrostics using their sweethearts' names. He would take "orders" on these weekends and create verse while working on the farm during the week. He would memorize the poems and later dictate them to one of the students, who would copy them.

Horton made a tidy sum from this business venture, charging a minimum of twenty-five cents per poem. He became so popular with the students that he earned enough money to pay his owner, James Horton (son of William, to whom ownership of George had passed), to allow him to stay in Chapel Hill all week long for a fee of twenty-five cents per day, an unheard-of arrangement in those days. Some critics argue that Horton was such a poor farmhand that it was more lucrative for James Horton to take the fee than to have him in the fields. It was also during his time in Chapel Hill that Horton met the poet and writer Caroline Lee Hentz, wife of a university faculty member. She advised him on his writing technique and helped him get some of his poetry into print. One of Horton's poems was published in abolitionist William Lloyd Garrison's popular *Liberator.*

Two efforts were made by northern and southern abolitionists on Horton's behalf to secure his freedom, one of which involved the publication of Horton's first book of poetry, *The Hope of Liberty* (1829). His supporters hoped that the proceeds from this book would be great enough to pay off Horton's owner and gain his freedom. Although the desired result did not occur, the book was noteworthy for several reasons, not the least of which was that it was the first book ever published by a slave in a slaveholding state. Horton later published two more books of poetry, *The Poetical Works of George M. Horton* (1845) and *Naked Genius* (1865). Horton returned to the farm with the outbreak of the Civil War, as many of his clients had left to enlist in the war and he could no longer earn enough money to stay in Chapel Hill. After the war, as a free man, he went to Philadelphia, and little is known about his activities there and until his death. Some critics suggest that he might have returned to North Carolina and died there; others believe he died in Philadelphia. At some point, perhaps around the late 1830s, Horton had married a slave woman from another farm and had two children with her, but since he never mentioned his family overtly in any of his writing, little is known about them.

MAJOR WORKS

Critics focus most of their commentary on Horton's first book, *The Hope of Liberty,* a collection of more than twenty poems about love, death, religion, and slavery, themes that Horton would revisit in his two other books.

John L. Cobbs argues that all of the poems have the underlying theme of flight—in essence, freedom—binding them together, and most critics agree that Horton's verse is influenced by biblical writings and hymns, as well as by British poets, especially Lord Byron, one of Horton's favorites. *The Hope of Liberty* was republished as *Poems by a Slave* in 1937 in Philadelphia by abolitionist Lewis Gunn. Horton's second book, *Poetical Works,* was published after the North Carolina state legislature had passed a law banning all slaves from learning how to read and write, it is therefore noteworthy that the book was published at all. Although the editors would have had to have been careful not to include poems about slavery and liberty, a few of the poems contain Horton's antislavery views. The poems in this volume also address the themes of religion, patriotism, drinking, scholarship, fame, and love. Horton's third poetry collection, *Naked Genius,* resulted from Horton's collaboration with a Civil War officer from Michigan named William Banks. This is by far the largest of the three volumes, containing over 130 poems. While many of these poems are on themes Horton had addressed previously, those on slavery are angrier and more strident than in earlier efforts. The volume also contains humorous and misogynistic poems. Some critics have speculated on whether the negative comments on women were directed at Horton's wife.

CRITICAL RECEPTION

Although Horton did well for himself financially and socially with his poems for the students at the university, he did not enjoy the same success with his three volumes of poetry. None of the three books brought him any significant financial gain nor any critical commentary; he was largely ignored. The latter is also largely true for the first half of the twentieth century; his work received some attention from critics, but most of it was dismissive or at best, mixed. Since then, however, Horton's poetry has gained a greater audience from those who recognize his talent and achievements despite the fact that his poetry is not considered among the best in American literature. Instead of dismissing Horton's poetry outright, these critics look at his entire life and career and find him quite unusual and extraordinary.

PRINCIPAL WORKS

The Hope of Liberty (poetry) 1829; revised as *Poems by a Slave* 1937
The Poetical Works of George M. Horton, The Colored Bard of North Carolina to Which is Prefixed the Life of the Author Written by Himself (poetry) 1845

Naked Genius (poetry) 1865

CRITICISM

Stephen B. Weeks (essay date 1914)

SOURCE: "George Moses Horton: Slave Poet," in *The Southern Workman,* Vol. XLIII, No. 10, October, 1914, pp. 571-77.

[*In the following essay, Weeks offers a brief overview of Horton's life and literary works.*]

> "Honor and shame from no condition rise;
> Act well your part, there all the honor lies."

Thus wrote Alexander Pope, and his lines had a unique fulfillment in the life of George Moses Horton, a slave of Chatham County, N.C., who has been recently characterized by a modern North Carolina scholar as "a slave who owned his master; a poet ignorant of the rules of prosody; a man of letters before he learned to read; a writer of short stories who published in several papers simultaneously before the day of newspaper syndicates; an author who supported himself and his family in an intellectual center before authorship had attained the dignity of a profession in America."

The documentary evidence on the life of George Moses Horton is small and the traditional accounts are more or less conflicting, but it is believed that the following is substantially correct. According to the preface to **"The Hope of Liberty"** George was born a slave in 1797. Professor George S. Willis, a careful and enthusiastic scholar who has gone into the matter of George's history at some length, says that George was born the slave of Mr. William Horton on Roanoke River in Northampton County, N.C.; that when he was about six years old his master removed to Chatham County, N.C., where he died in 1815. George then came into the possession of Mr. James Horton, son of William, with whom he remained until his death in 1832. It was necessary to sell Mr. Horton's property to settle his estate and George was bought by Mr. Hall Horton, son of James. This third owner is said to have been a hard master, but he allowed George to go to Chapel Hill, the seat of the University in the adjoining county of Orange, and later permitted him to hire his time at twenty-five, or, as others say, at fifty cents per day.

George is described by the old people around Chapel Hill who knew him as a full-blooded Negro who boasted of the purity of his black blood. He was of the type know today as negroid; was more Aryan than Semitic in features, and more like the natives of India and North America than those of the Sahara. On the other hand Negroes who knew him in Philadelphia report that he was of mixed blood.

As a slave George was usually employed on the farm, but besides some personal service to his master it is said that his main occupations in winter were hunting and fishing, and in summer attending protracted meetings, or, as they were then called, camp meetings. Like all of his race George was fond of melody and these meetings gave him an opportunity to cultivate his budding poetic temperament. At these services, like Cædmon, the earliest of the English poets, he became familiar with the Bible story by hearing it read. He also made completely his own the melodies and the words of the Methodist hymnal then in use. The melodies were in his heart and the forms of the corresponding words became fixed in his brain. These furnished him the first elements of a literary education. He begged a blue-backed spelling book from somewhere and from this learned his letters. After learning the letters he learned to spell by matching the words in his hymnal which he already knew by sight and by heart with the words in the spelling book—a practical evolution of the word-method by a man who was innocent of pedagogy. In this way he learned to read the Bible. From that he learned grammar and prosody and above all acquired a simple, straight-forward style and wrote good idiomatic English. It is said also that he became quite a voracious reader of books that were loaned him by Dr. Caldwell and other friends at the University. There is even a legend that James K. Polk, of the class of 1818, first started him in the art of writing, and that this was perfected by Professor Manuel Fetter; that Mrs. Caroline Lee Hentz, novelist and poet and wife of Professor Nicholas M. Hentz, gave him instruction in versification and corrected his work. It seems to be certain that he was ambitious to learn, with a good memory and power of imitation, and that he was fond of the poetry of Byron and Moore.

He published his first poems in 1829. The volume was issued by Joseph Gales and Son and was entitled **"The Hope of Liberty."** The preface, dated at Raleigh, July 2, 1829, was probably written by Mr. Weston R. Gale, the junior member of the publishing firm, and may be taken as the final authority in the matters of his life so far as it goes. It says:

"George, who is the author of the following poetical effusions, is a slave, the property of Mr. James Horton, of Chatham County, North Carolina. He has been in the habit, for some years past, of producing poetical pieces, sometimes on suggested subjects, to such persons as would write them while he dictated. Several compositions of his have already appeared in the Raleigh *Register.* Some have made their way into the Boston newspapers and have

evoked expressions of approbation and surprise. Many persons, some of whom are elevated in office and literary attainments, have now become interested in the promotion of his prospects. They are solicitious that efforts at length be made to obtain by subscription a sum for his emancipation, upon the condition of his going in the vessel which shall first afterwards sail for Liberia."

The author of the preface then continues: "To put to trial the plan here urged in his behalf, the paper now exhibited is published. Several of his productions are contained in the succeeding pages. Many more might have been added, which would have swelled it to a larger size. They would doubtless be interesting to many, but it is hoped that the specimens here inserted will be sufficient to accomplish the object of the publication. . . . It is proposed, that in every town or vicinity where contributions are made, they may be put into the hands of some person who will humanely consent to receive them. . . . As soon as it is ascertained that the collections will accomplish their object, it is expected that they will be transmitted without delay to Mr. Weston R. Gales.

"None will imagine that pieces produced as these have been should be free from blemish in composition and taste. The author is thirty-two years old and has always labored in the field on his master's farm, promiscuously with the few others whom Mr. Horton owns, in circumstances of the greatest possible simplicity. His master says he knew nothing of his poetry, but as he heard it from others. George knows how to read and is now learning to write. All his pieces are written down by others; and his reading, which is at night and at the usual intervals allowed to slaves, has been much employed on poetry, such as he could procure, this being the species of composition most interesting to him. It is thought best to print his productions without corrections, that the mind of the reader may be in no uncertainty as to the originality and genuineness of every part. We shall conclude this account of George with an assurance that he has been ever a faithful, honest, and industrious slave. That his heart has felt deeply and sensitively . . . is impressively confirmed by one of his stanzas:

> Come, melting Pity, from afar,
> And break this vast, enormous bar
>   Between a wretch and thee;
> Purchase a few short days of time
> And bid a vassal soar sublime,
>   On wings of Liberty.

It is of interest to call attention to the title of this little pamphlet for the important light it throws upon the condition of slaves in North Carolina at the date of its publication. It is usually said that all higher aspiration in the slave was crushed and that those individuals who were intelligent enough to desire freedom were ruthlessly suppressed, but in North Carolina Horton was not only allowed to express his feelings privately on the subject, but even to print and openly publish his desires, and in doing this he was aided and abetted by some of the best men in the state. Not only was Horton allowed to do this in 1829, but he continued to enjoy the same liberty after the enactment of the harder laws that were passed as a result of the Nat Turner insurrection of 1831.

The persons who were interested along with Dr. Caldwell and Mr. Gales in the purchase and manumission of Horton are said to have been Governor Owen and a Dr. Henderson, probably Dr. Pleasant Henderson of Chapel Hill. The matter of manumission was laid before his master, but the valuation placed on the slave poet was so great that the project was necessarily abandoned. It is probable that these gentlemen were in his mind when George wrote his "Lines on hearing of the intention of a gentlemen to purchase the poet's freedom;"

> Some philanthropic souls as from afar,
>> With pity strove to break the slavish bar;
> To whom my floods of gratitude shall roll,
>> And yield with pleasure to their soft control.

Although the plan for manumission failed, it is more than probable that it was as a result of this discussion that George was allowed to leave the farm and go to Chapel Hill about 1834 for, notwithstanding the printed recommendation in the preface to **"The Hope of Liberty,"** it was currently reported that, George was worthless as a farm hand, since his Pegasus resolutely refused to be harnessed to a plow. In and about Chapel Hill George spent most of his time for the next thirty years, waiting in the University itself, or on the students individually, or serving in the hotel kept by Miss Nancy Hilliard, and in this university town, the center of literary life and learning for the state, George's gift for versification secured him ready employment and produced for him considerable revenue.

During this University period of his literary career, George's work consisted mainly in writing, to supply orders from members of the student body, acrostics on ladies' names, and in the composition of love songs and amorous verses for ladies' albums. His scale of prices was modest enough: twenty-five cents for an ordinary effort and fifty cents when an extra amount of warmth and passion was demanded. The following specimen on "Love" is one of his earlier efforts and was dictated before he had learned to write, but it is of the type of those poems by which he earned his fame and money at the University:

> Whilst tracing thy visage, I sink in emotion,
>> For no other damsel so wond'rous I see;
> Thy looks are so pleasing, thy charms so amazing,
>> I think of no other, my true love, but thee.

> With heart-burning rapture I gaze on thy beauty,
>> And fly like a bird to the boughs of a tree;
> Thy looks are so pleasing, thy charms so amazing,
>> I fancy no other, my true-love, but thee.

> Thus oft in the valley I think, and I wonder
>> Why cannot a maid with her lover agree?
> Thy looks are so pleasing, thy charms so amazing,
>> I pine for no other, my true-love, but thee.

> I'd fly from thy frowns with a heart full of sorrow—
>> Return, pretty damsel, and smile thou on me;
> By every endeavor, I'll try thee forever,
>> And languish until I am fancied by thee.

The fortunes of the poet seem to have declined after the death of Dr. Caldwell, his patron, in 1838. The publication of **"The Hope of Liberty"** had not been a financial success and the idea of purchasing his freedom and going to Liberia was abandoned. He remained in and about Chapel Hill, but all the savings that he had accumulated for the Liberian voyage now went for drink, as did all that he could earn or beg. A favorite scheme to raise money was to write verses setting forth the sickness and distress of his family, and close with an appeal to the students to "lend a helping hand to the old, unfortunate bard." This he would take from room to room and read to the students, and these patrons of literature usually responded liberally. Dr. Battle tells us in his "History of the University of North Carolina," from which some of these facts are drawn, that George's manner was courteous and his moral character good.

In the meantime the fame of George's poetry had reached as far as Warrentown, N.C., where Miss Cheney, of Connecticut, who afterwards married Horace Greeley, was teaching school. Through her influence Greeley became interested in the poet, who addressed him the following, "Poet's Petition," which appeared in the *Tribune:*

> Bewailing mid the ruthless wave
>> I lift my feeble hand to thee;
> Let me no longer be a slave;
>> But drop the fetters and be free.

> Why will regardless Fortune sleep
>> Deaf to my penitential prayer
> Or leave the struggling bard to weep,
>> Alas, and languish in despair?

> He is an eagle void of wings,
>> Aspiring to the mountain height,
> Yet in the vale aloud he sings,
>> For Pity's aid to give him flight.

> Then listen, all who never felt
>> For fettered genius heretofore,
> Let hearts of petrifaction melt,
>> And bid the gifted Negro soar.

George remained in and around Chapel Hill till the end of the civil war. In 1865 he accompanied a U.S. cavalry officer, presumably Captain Will H. S. Banks, to Philadelphia. He was there in 1866, for the following extract from the published minutes of the Banneker Institute is furnished me by Mr. Daniel Murray of the Library of Congress, along with much other material on the career of the poet, as follows: "A special meeting of the institution was held on the evening of August 31, 1866, the object being to receive Mr. George Horton of North Carolina, a poet of considerable genius, it was claimed. The feasibility of publishing his book was submitted to Mr. John H. Smythe, but found too expensive."

Professor Collier Cobb, of the University of North Carolina, is authority for the further statement that after going to Philadelphia Horton wrote a number of poems in imitation of the "Passionate Shepherd to his Love" of Marlowe and "The Nymph's Reply" of Sir Walter Raleigh. He developed also while living there some talent as a story teller. Like Cædmon again his prose tales were based on the stories he had learned from the Bible in earlier days. This was always the source of his inspiration. It furnished him the themes and he decked them out in modern garb in such a way as to suit the immediate demands of the occasion. Professor Cobb also points out the curious facts that little of Horton's poetic work was done before he was forty; that the most productive period of his life began when he was sixty-seven and extended to his death, which is believed in North Carolina to have occurred about 1883. Others place it about 1880.

Horton was about five feet, eight inches in height, of medium build, quick in his movements, of pleasing address, and popular with the students whom he served. He married a slave of Mr. Franklin Snipes and had two children, a son who was known as Free Snipes, and a daughter Rhody who married Van Buren Byrum. The son died in Durham, N.C., in 1896. The daughter was still living in Raleigh, N.C., in 1897.

A second edition of **"The Hope of Liberty"** was published by L. C. G. in Philadelphia in 1837 under the title **"Poems by a Slave."** A third edition appeared in Boston in 1838 as a supplement to the "Memoir and Poems of Phillis Wheatley." Both of these editions were issued as a part of the anti-slavery propaganda and add nothing to our knowledge of the poet.

In 1845 there was published a volume of his miscellaneous poems. It was issued at Hillsboro by Dennis Heartt, editor of the Hillsboro *Recorder*. No copy has been seen.

Other editions of his poems are said to have been issued in 1850 and 1854. It is possible that such was the case and that they were published throughout the interest of his student friends in the University of North Carolina, but no copies have been seen. It is also said that a small duodecimo volume of his Poems was published in Boston early in the fifties, with his autobiography, but this is possibly a mistaken reference to the edition of 1838. It is also said that short stories and essays were published by him at this time, but I have seen none of them.

There is an interesting reference to Horton in a letter dated at Chapel Hill, N.C., February 27, 1843, addressed to the *Southern Literary Messenger* and signed "G"—possibly Professor William Mercer Green. The letter says:

> "Mr. Editor:
>
> "A volume of manuscript poems was lately placed in my hands by their author George Horton, a Negro belonging to a respectable farmer residing a few miles from Chapel Hill, from which I extract the following: [here a sample was inserted.] I have no doubt but that they will prove interesting to the readers of the *Messenger*. Should they meet with a suitable reception, I will continue them for several numbers, together with some sketches of the life, genius, and writings of their author."

It does not appear that this offer was accepted.

The last known edition of his poems contains the following:

> "**'Naked Genius'** by George Moses Horton. The Colored Bard of North Carolina. Author of 'The Black Poet,' a work being now compiled and revised by Captain Will. H. S. Banks, 9th Michigan Cavalry Volunteers, and which will be ready for publication about the 1st of October, 1865. This work will contain a concise history of the life of the author, written by the compiler, and will be offered to the public as one of many proofs that God in his infinite wisdom and mercy created the black man for a higher purpose than to toil his life away under the galling yoke of slavery. Revised and compiled by Will. H. S. Banks, Captain 9th Mich. Cav., Wm. B. Smith & Co., Southern Field and Fireside Book Publishing House, Raleigh, N.C., 1865."

The accuracy of the above title is not vouched for, but the book was a duodecimo of 100 pages and there is said to be a copy in the library of the Boston Athenaeum. It was the last contribution of the slave poet to the literature of his native state.

Richard Walser (essay date 1966)

SOURCE: "Prodigy at the University," in *The Black Poet*, Philosophical Library, 1966, pp. 18-51.

[*In the following essay, from the first and only biography of Horton, Walser details Horton's years as a poet-for-hire among the students at the University of North Carolina.*]

When he was nineteen or twenty, George Moses began his regular visits to Chapel Hill, seat of the University of North Carolina then only a quarter of a century old. He had heard that the young students cared for poetry as did he, and he was secretly eager to form their acquaintance. Though not apprised of the real reasons, James Horton was agreeable to his request to go there, provided the trips were made on free time and he would take along plantation products to sell.

For the next fifty years, Chapel Hill was to George Moses a place where he caroused in poetry and notoriety, delighting collegians and astounding the skeptics. He was first and foremost of a long line of campus curiosities.

The Chapel Hill of the late 1810s was still the primeval grove so appealing to the founding fathers of the university. As George Moses trudged up the hill on that last mile into the village, he passed through scrub and high oaks. Intersected by the Raleigh-Hillsborough road was the one street, called Franklin, which jutted along the hillside and provided frontage for a blacksmith's shop, a hotel, two stores, two boarding houses, and some dozen residences. The forest was everywhere, chinquapin bushes crowding each other underneath the giant trees. Cows and pigs wandered through the woods, crossed the road, rested on the paths, and, when so disposed, ambled into the campus to the south of Franklin Street.

Except for the trees, the campus was unimpressive. Two plain brick buildings, named East and South, crowned the hill at right angles. On their left, toward Franklin Street, was the tiny one floor of Person Hall, used as a chapel. Steward's Hall, an ugly two-storied wooden structure painted white with green blinds, faced East and South buildings from the other direction. Not far away was the simple house of President Joseph Caldwell, and across Franklin Street from the campus stood the Grammar School for boys not yet ready to enroll in the college courses.

In 1817 the student body numbered only a few over a hundred. Though loudly proclaiming their loyalty to democratic ideas, the young men were basically aristocratic in their outlooks and personal lives. What studying was done—and there was precious little of it—was an uninspired effort resorted to among the more pleasant pursuits of eating, sleeping, reading, card-playing, drinking, and performing tricks on each other, the faculty, and innocent intruders within their domain. They were sportsmen nearly all, finding great pleasure in draughts and chess, in bandy and cockfighting and horse-racing, in hunting the quail, rabbit, and opossum so abundant in surrounding woods. Dashing young gentlemen though they were, they aspired to one accomplishment: oratory. Studies were merely

means to that end, and their high regard for poetry stemmed from the practical use of it in the stentorian speeches they were constantly at work on. It was as orator that George Moses Horton first appeared before them.

> Having got in the way of carrying fruit to the college at Chapel Hill on the Sabbath *(he continued in his autobiography)*, the collegians who, for their diversion, were fond of pranking with the country servants who resorted there for the same purpose that I did, began also to prank with me. But somehow or other they discovered a spark of genius in me, either by discourse or other means, which excited their curiosity, and they often eagerly insisted on me to spout, as they called it. This inspired in me a kind of enthusiastic pride. I was indeed too full of vain egotism, which always discovers the gloom of ignorance or dims the lustre of popular distinction. I would stand forth and address myself extempore before them, as an orator of inspired promptitude. But I soon found it an object of aversion, and considered myself nothing but a public ignoramus.

For the students, Sunday was a dreary day at the college. Except for attendance at chapel, there was little for the high-spirited boys to do. Visiting along Franklin Street was discouraged, and afternoons were usually spent in rambling the woods behind East and South buildings. Those who remained on campus were grateful when country servants appeared. There was, it seemed to them, something odd about the Horton slave. For one thing, though he could not write, he could already read. Quickly the students singled him out for special attention. There is a tradition that James K. Polk, class of 1818 and later President of the United States, was the first student to encourage him toward improvement. If it is only a legend, at least it is a pleasant one.

George Moses' humiliation as an orator led him to seek some other way to impress the students. If given a subject, he could soon embellish it into poetic lines.

> Hence I abandoned my foolish harangues and began to speak of poetry, which lifted them still higher on the wing of astonishment; all eyes were on me, and all ears were open. Many were at first incredulous; but the experiment of acrostics established it as an incontestable fact. Hence my fame soon circulated like a stream throughout the college.

It was with acrostics, then, that the poet made his way in the world of letters. As a result of those first-letter spelling poems which the romantic young swains sent to their loved ones far from Chapel Hill, George Moses was welcomed on the campus with the deference due an artist. One student wrote of the "great kindness" with which the slave was treated, of how he "was considered an honest humble fellow." While George Moses was pleased with his newly acquired status, the most important thing was that at last he was busy in his chosen profession.

> Many of those acrostics I composed at the handle of the plough and retained them in my head (being unable

to write) until an opportunity offered, when I dictated whilst one of the gentlemen would serve as my amanuensis. I have composed love pieces in verse for courtiers from all parts of the state, and acrostics on the names of many of the tip-top belles of Virginia, South Carolina, and Georgia.

For George Moses it was an exciting time. He had an indulgent audience, he had friends, and he had work to do. Each Sunday now, equipped with both agricultural and literary products, he stepped along the eight miles to Chapel Hill, his head high, his heart singing. Once he was on the campus, students gathered around, bought his wares, listened to his latest compositions, and suggested "new topics upon which to exercise his poetic muse." Even when there were many different poems to be made up, he always managed during the following week to imprint them in his mind so firmly that they could be promptly copied down as he recited. Not only had he no difficulty in keeping the various poems separated; he was even able to designate where an abbreviation was necessary to preserve the meter.

Understandably, the acrostics of this period are lost, dispatched as they were to distant points in the handwriting of an impish sophomore who pretended to be the author himself. An example of a decade later will indicate the kind of poem of which he was capable. . . . Who is Julia Shepard? What is she that a slave poet, even on commission, commend her?

> Joy, like the morning, breaks from one divine—
> Unveiling streams which cannot fail to shine.
> Long have I strove to magnify her name
> Imperial, floating on the breeze of fame.
>
> Attracting beauty must delight afford,
> Sought of the world and of the Bards adored;
> Her grace of form and heart-alluring powers
> Express her more than fair, the queen of flowers.
>
> Pleasure, fond nature's stream, from beauty sprung,
> And was the softest strain the Muses sung,
> Reverting sorrows into speechless Joys,
> Dispelling gloom which human peace destroys.

One must not quarrel with George Moses about his sentences or even about their meaning. The poem would be difficult to defend on those scores. What is more important is the phrasing—the disciplined words of love's language. George Moses was not writing from his heart. He was doing a job. His pride demanded friends among the aristocratic gentlemen, and composing poems was a way to patronage. Rather than quarrel with him, one must imagine his standing straight and comely, his face beaming with self-assurance, the lines moving smoothly from confident lips. Before him at a desk, an entranced student copied the verses as the slave spoke.

This was the high moment. A pause of admiration, a suggestion for rewording, a final reading to be sure that all

was right, and then the student's comment: "Well done. Now next week have me an acrostic on Sallie—and one on Katharine—. That second one will be difficult." On the long walk home and during the week of work on the farm, George Moses would labor with Katharine, secure in the knowledge that when he faltered, his friends would help him out.

> But those criticizing gentlemen saw plainly what I lacked, and many of them very generously gave me such books as they considered useful in my case, which I received with much gratitude, and improved according to my limited opportunities. Among these gentlemen the following names occur to me: Mr. Robert Gilliam, Mr. Augustus Washington, Mr. Cornelius Roberson [*Robison*], Mr. Augustus Alston, Mr. Benjamin Long, Mr. William Harden [*Hardin*], Mr. Merryfort, Mr. Augustus Moore, Mr. Thomas Pipkin, Mr. A. Rencher, Mr. Ellerbee, Mr. Gilmer, Mr. William Pickett, Mr. Leonidas Polk, Mr. Samuel Hinton, Mr. Pain, Mr. Steward, Mr. Gatlin, Mr. J. Hogan, Mr. John Pew [*Pugh*], Messrs. W. and J. Haywood, and several more whose names have slipped my memory, all of whom were equally liberal to me, and to them I ascribe my lean grammatical studies.

Most of the twenty-two students whom George Moses mentioned can be identified with some accuracy. They span a ten-year period of university residence beginning in 1817. In the memory of a grateful slave they carved their names during Sunday hours. They brought presents.

> Among the books given me (*George Moses wrote of his young gentlemen*) were Murray's English Grammar and its accordant branches; Johnson's Dictionary in miniature, also Walker's and Sheridan's, and parts of others. And other books of use they gave me, which I had no chance to peruse minutely. Milton's Paradise Lost, Thomson's Seasons, parts of Homer's Iliad and Vergil's Aeneid, Beauties of Shakespeare, Beauties of Byron, part of Plutarch, Morse's Geography, the Columbian Orator, Snowden's History of the Revolution, Young's Night Thoughts, and some others, which my concentration of business did not suffer me to pursue with any scientific regularity.

These books, common titles of the day, reflect more the tastes of the students than forecast an influence on George Moses' subsequent style. Always the ding-dong of Wesley's hymns had more fascination for him than the blank verse of Shakespeare, Thomson, or Young, though the stilted measures and pompous epithets of the last two he frequently echoed. After all, he studied them but little, blaming rather his "business" for the negligence. Of Byron he became fondest. More helpful than the poets, he found, were the geography and the dictionaries. In them he could locate the fine words he loved to roll on his tongue, to say nothing of glorious names from mythology. Except for that awkward matter of handwriting, the poet's workshop was complete. He was ready for customers—paying customers.

Mr. Augustus Alston first laid (as he said) the low price of twenty-five cents on my compositions each, which was unanimously established and has been kept up ever since; but some gentlemen, extremely generous, have given me from fifty to seventy-five cents, besides many decent and respectable suits of clothes, professing that they would not suffer me to pass otherwise and write for them.

Augustus Alston, the "onlie begetter" of the slave's progress, was a university student from Georgia in the early 1820s. With twenty-five cents, he delivered the coup de grâce for the black man's adventure. Never again would George Moses be amateur. Thus did the slave become the first Negro professional man of letters in America and one of the first professional writers of any race in the South. For the rest of his life he supported himself, partially and at times wholly, from the fees he collected.

It must not be supposed that Alston or the classmates who followed his example were merely indulgent. If indulgence was indeed somewhat responsible for their generosity, it must be stressed that the young gentlemen had practical use for poems. Back home, Sallie and Katharine responded with rapture to both the verses which ingeniously employed their names and those which did not. In any age, a lover will use the means at his disposal. A poem purchased from George Moses was a poem owned with all its rights and privileges, including authorship. Yet the bard saw no need of waste, and if he slyly sold a particularly apt composition over and over again, he cannot be blamed. A particularly apt one was **"Love"**:

> While tracing thy visage I sink in emotion,
>   For no other damsel so wondrous I see:
> Thy looks are so pleasing, thy charms so amazing,
>   I think of no other, my true-love, but thee,
>
> With heart-burning rapture I gaze on thy beauty
>   And fly like a bird to the boughs of a tree;
> Thy looks are so pleasing, thy charms so amazing,
>   I fancy no other, my true-love, but thee.
>
> Thus oft in the valley I think and I wonder:
>   Why cannot a maid with her lover agree?
> Thy looks are so pleasing, thy charms so amazing,
>   I pine for no other, my true-love, but thee.
>
> I'd fly from thy frowns with a heart full of sorrow—
>   Return, pretty damsel, and smile thou on me.
> By every endeavor, I'll try thee forever
>   And languish until I am fancied by thee.

"Love" was at least a 50¢ poem. In 1825, when a student often was permitted only a dollar a month for pocket money, many a college lad spent his full allowance on such gems. With coins in his purse George Moses, dressed almost as well as the students themselves, strutted proudly on Sundays among the blue-clad gentlemen. They were his friends, but he looked forward to the time when an amanuensis was no longer required.

Even with so much about which to be thankful, all was not well with the poet and his collegians. A familiar demon stalked the shady paths of Chapel Hill just as it did the furrows of a Chatham plantation.

> But there is one thing with which I am sorry to charge many of these gentlemen. Before the moral evil of excessive drinking had been impressed upon my mind, they flattered me into the belief that it would hang me on the wings of new inspiration, which would waft me into the regions of poetical perfection. And I am not a little astonished that nature and reason had not taught me better before, after having walked so long on a line which plainly dictated and read to me, though young, the lesson of human destruction.
>
> This realizes the truth of the sentiment in the address of the Earl of Chatham, in which he spoke of "the wretch who, after having seen the difficulties of a thousand errors, continues still to blunder." And I have now [*in 1845*] experienced the destructive consequences of walking in such a devious line from the true center to which I was so early attracted by the magnet of genius. But I have discovered the beneficial effects of temperance and regularity, and fly as a penitent suppliant to the cell of private reflection, sorrowing that I ever had driven my boat of life so near the wrecking shoals of death, or that I was allured by the music of sirens that sing to ensnare the lovers of vanity.

During the 1820s, drinking among the students was so common that the faculty took little notice of it. Only intoxication was really condemned. Local rulings to control whiskey traffic were ineffective, for raw booze of nearby manufacture easily found its way to the campus, usually hidden in the clothing of Negroes frequenting the place. There is no reason to think that George Moses was one to enhance his poetry market with a sideline of illicit spirits. Merely he partook of the liquid when it was offered him. In **"The Tippler to His Bottle"** he wept:

> Often have I thy stream admired;
>   Thou nothing has availed me ever;
> Vain have I thought myself inspired.
> Say, have I else but pain acquired?
>   Not ever, no never! . . .

This is the sort of thing any man would write when firmly determined to give up a bad habit, but George Moses makes no promise here. For this man of pride, drinking—whether heavily indulged in or not—was a scapegoat to support his self-conscious imperfections.

His faults, his literary weaknesses, were never overcome. The young gentlemen helped when they could, and the professors, too, taught the black poet. But she who was to have the greatest influence on his life now arrived in Chapel Hill—an intelligent New England woman of twenty-six, only a few years younger than the bard.

In the fall of 1826, Caroline Lee Hentz settled in the village where her husband, Nicholas Marcellus Hentz, had come to teach modern languages. A native of France, Hentz had emigrated to America in 1816. In Massachusetts he met the poet Caroline Lee Whiting, whom he married in 1824. Hentz was an accomplished man. For one thing, he was author of a historical novel of Indian massacre, *Tadeuskund, the Last King of the Lenape* (1825). In Chapel Hill he was noted as an entomologist, and his monograph on spiders, when later published, was an authoritative work. Several days a week he rambled through the fringes of Orange County forests, collecting specimens for his glass cases.

From the first, both husband and wife felt cramped in the small university community. The village professors, staunch Calvinists all, were suspicious of Hentz's foreign birth and religious views; faculty wives, affable enough in domestic affairs, were unsympathetic companions for a talented and liberal woman from the North. During their five years in Chapel Hill, the couple more and more turned to inner resources. From the surrounding countryside and not-too-distant hamlets, they managed to draw to their fireside those who shared their literary and scientific interests. George Moses Horton was an early caller.

At that time the university was somewhat physically enlarged from the institution so happily discovered by a younger George Moses. With the addition of Old West and Gerrard Hall, the campus buildings formed a neat court, attractive and symmetrical. By 1824 the student body had increased to 157, but the financial panic of the next year caused a plunge in numbers. Soon there were only five members of the faculty, and not always could their salaries be met. During the late 1820s fewer than a hundred students were in residence.

Life in the village was simple, almost rural. University teachers had their own gardens where they raised produce for their kitchens. Town government was confined to the patrol system, men in their turn walking the streets at night. Though unaccompanied slaves were liable for a fine of a dollar or a whipping of ten lashes if caught without their owners' written permits allowing absence from home, George Moses was surely never challenged.

He was friendly with all—students, townspeople, even occasionally with Negro servants like Dave Barham and Doctor November, who made fires in the dormitories and classrooms. To President Caldwell he was particularly loyal. But it was Caroline Lee Hentz who won his deepest affection.

> To the much distinguished Mrs. Hentz of Boston [*actually of Lancaster, Massachusetts*], I owe much for the correction of many poetical errors. Being a professional poetess herself and a lover of genius, she discovered my little uncultivated talent and was moved to uncover

to me the beauties of correctness, together with the true importance of the object to which I aspired.

The young matron was impelled to help the struggler not only because he, like herself, was a composer of verse in a region substantially devoid of creative poets: he was ample illustration to the Northerner that slavery did not blot out intelligence and a sense of art, that human chattels were capable of more than physical drudgery. George Moses disproved the contention of Southern slaveholders that the blacks were subhuman, little more than foolish children.

Finally, when their friendship had developed and when the occasion seemed right, she spoke to him of his condition, remarking with surprise that he could court the Muse while bound in slavery. Poetry demanded freedom of the body as well as of the mind and spirit. It was natural, of course, that such a sentiment should appeal to George Moses, but not so much because emancipation was a possibility as because it offered him new material for rhyming.

His lessons continued. Mrs. Hentz wrote that she "often transcribed stanzas which he would dictate with quite an air of inspiration." She admitted her wonder "at the readiness with which he would change a verse or sentiment which was objected to as erroneous in expression or deficient in poetical harmony." She thought it awkward that though he was "familiar with the best classic works belonging to the fine libraries of the university, he had not been taught to write a legible hand, and was obliged to be indebted to others for embodying the dreams of his muse."

In the summer of 1827 a tragic accident in the Hentz household bound teacher and student even closer together. The older Hentz child, short of his second birthday, fell from a chair. A fracture of a bone in the neck brought instant death. He was buried in the garden of a professor's residence. George Moses shared the sorrow of his friends and expressed himself in the most suitable way he knew.

> She was extremely pleased with the dirge which I wrote on the death of her much lamented primogenial infant (*he boasted*) and for which she gave me much credit and a handsome reward. Not being able to write myself, I dictated while she wrote; and while thus engaged she strove in vain to avert the inevitable tear slow trickling down her ringlet-shaded cheek.

Neither the dirge nor the nature of the "handsome reward" is recorded, but a more tangible evidence still of Mrs. Hentz's gratitude was soon apparent. George Moses was not to be permitted, she decided, to blush unseen and waste his sweetness within the constricted university confines.

> She was indeed unequivocally anxious to announce the birth of my recent and astonishing fame, and sent its blast on the gale of passage back to the frozen plains of Massachusetts.

In her little home town, the *Lancaster Gazette* had initiated its weekly issues in March, 1828. The editors, old friends of the young woman, shortly received from her a communication relating a few details about her Negro friend and enclosing two slavery poems. When her letter with the selections appeared in the *Gazette* on April 8, it was evident that, under Mrs. Hentz's tutelage, the poet's improvement in prosody had been accompanied by a capacity for personal recognition which expressed itself in disillusionment. He looked upon himself and cursed his fate.

> Alas! and am I born for this,
>   To wear this slavish chain?
> Deprived of all creative bliss,
>   Condemned to toil and pain.
>
> How long have I in bondage lain
>   And languished to be free!
> Alas! and must I still complain,
>   Deprived of Liberty . . .
>
> Bid slavery hide her meager face
>   And barbarism fly.
> I scorn to see the sad disgrace
>   In which enslaved I lie.
>
> Dear Liberty! upon thy breast
>   I languished to respire;
> And like the swan unto her nest
>   I'd to thy smiles retire.

A second poem pursued this theme with such lachrymal tension that one suspects Mrs. Hentz of having turned the poor fellow's head with her sympathy. Matters were not so bad as the headlong rush of extravagant lines would indicate. For the moment, though, they suited his purpose and hers, to say nothing of the antislavery readers of the *Lancaster Gazette* in Massachusetts.

But George Moses, uncomplicated fellow, was not one to dwell lengthily on the sadder side of life. On June 24 appeared a placid lyric **"On Poetry and Music,"** in which he paid tribute to Nature, who had taught him to "sail upon the muse's wing."

From these poetic announcements of the birth of a recent and astonishing fame, sent northward by Mrs. Hentz to the insignificant *Gazette,* no immediate results were apparent; the slave's reputation in those icy parts came later. Yet the young woman's concern for her prodigy would not allow her to despair. Calmly she waited for a more propitious opportunity to help her friend.

During the first decade of Sundays in the college town—up to the time of his meeting with Mrs. Hentz—the poet's life was reasonably simple. A man in his prime, he worked in James Horton's fields on weekdays, waiting patiently to hike over the hills to be among educated friends on his time off. The condition of servitude was easily borne; it presented few problems. James Horton valued his chattel, but he made no harsh demands. For George Moses, life was hardly more confining than for any man free to act but held to the exigencies of providing for himself and others.

Occasionally he considered that affairs might have been arranged differently. He was indeed in slavery, a status unacceptable to any human being of intelligence; but the admission of bondage was more fearful than its actualities. More concerned about his plight than he, frankly, were his friends. What could they do? At one time there was a limp chance that the Manumission Society would provide for his purchase. When nothing came of it, George Moses did not worry. After all, he was happy enough and far more fortunate than his fellow laborers. Always proud, he was sufficiently wise to realize the difference of his status, and he gloried in it.

Then, like lightning on a sunny day, a real possibility struck. Suddenly it seemed that freedom was now to be his—not only freedom from legal bondage, which had never cramped him, but more deliciously, freedom from the fields, freedom to compose poems seven days a week.

In general, North Carolina policy was opposed to emancipation, but in Chatham County emancipation was nothing new. Generously sprinkled with slavery-hating Quakers, the county was an active area for operations of both the Manumission Society and the Colonization Society. Frequently slaves were purchased from their masters and freed, the Colonization Society further arranging transportation to Liberia. Aware of all this, gentle but property-minded James Horton had nevertheless no intention of disposing of his servants without full return.

In the university village across the county line, faculty and students for the most part held the traditional, aristocratic Southern view on the institution of slavery, but they were not enthusiastic proponents. In undergraduate literary halls, debaters argued whether slavery was advantageous to the United States, whether the importation of Africans was a good thing, and even whether slavery should be abolished. The mere wording of the queries implied some doubt. The community was liberal. In 1819 a small chapter of the American Colonization Society was briefly active in Chapel Hill.

In both Chatham and Orange counties, climate for the emancipation of a worthy individual was wholesome. It is no wonder that an unusual slave like George Moses attracted attention not only from the Hentz family, but from others. President Joseph D. Caldwell lent books to the university's protégé and otherwise encouraged him. A

Chapel Hill physician, Dr. James Henderson, was an admirer and agitator in his behalf.

But the first person to map out actual plans for the purchase of George Moses was an unidentified "philanthropic gentleman." In the summer of 1828 this mysterious benefactor made a trip to the village as a member of the annual visitation committee. He saw some of the slave's verses and was amazed.

One suspects that a faculty wife, with serious eyes above ringlet-shaded cheeks, hopefully observed the visitor, invited him to her cottage, handed him a sheaf of poems, and noted his delight as she told him the wondrous story of their author. As a Northern woman only two years a resident in the South, she dared not campaign actively for a slave. But there were newspaper friends, the Gales family of Raleigh, who would, she believed, welcome an account of the slave if communicated by a Southerner "proverbial for his philanthropic feelings." Would he be willing to meet the poet and talk with him? If so, Mrs. Hentz would be pleased to make the introduction.

While such a scene is conjectural, not so the result.

The first step of the "philanthropic gentleman" was to write the required news story of the "extraordinary young slave" for the influential Raleigh *Register* and its liberal English-born editor, Joseph Gales. Already Gales and his novel-writing wife, Winifred Marshall Gales, were friends of the Hentzes. On the meeting of the two families, there had been a recognition of mutual interests, including a curiosity about slavery. Gales, in favor of gradual emancipation, was secretary of the Raleigh auxiliary of the American Colonization Society. A son, Weston Raleigh Gales, supported his father's views.

If Mrs. Hentz had proposed to Gales that she write the account herself, she was surely dissuaded. How fortunate, then, was the appearance on the scene of the "philanthropic gentleman." His brief sketch, appearing in the *Register* on July 18, gave a few biographical facts about the poet, mentioned that he had "no pleasure in associating with any but those of intelligence," and demonstrated his craft with eight unobjectionable stanzas **"On the Evening and Morning"** beginning

> When Evening bids the sun to rest retire,
> Unwearied Ether sets her lamps on fire;
> Lit by one torch, each is supplied in turn
> Till all the candles in the concave burn.

Nowhere did the account reveal that there were schemes afoot to free the author.

Later issues of the *Register* printed other selections from a number which had been sent in. Thereafter, newspapers near and far copied both the sketch and the poems. Everywhere readers were delighted. One subscriber of the *Free Press* in Tarborough, seventy miles to the east of Raleigh, composed a panegyric "To George M. Horton, the Sable Poet of Chatham, N. C." Wonder of wonders! Rarely had any bard been poetically eulogized only a few months after his first appearance in print. The correspondent, who signed himself Pigmy Homer, wrote:

> Hail! wondrous George, thou flower of thy race,
> One gives thee joy who never saw thy face . . .
> "The Evening and the Morning, by George M. Horton" sung,
> Is pronounced "well done" by every critic's tongue.
> Six thousand years or more have past away
> Since earth commenced her rotary course, they say . . .
> But ne'er beneath yon Prince of Light before
> Sprung, methinks, a poet blackamoor . . .

The amiable feelings of such admirers as Pigmy Homer, to say nothing of the wide publicity, were all well enough, but there was more serious work to be done. The "philanthropic gentleman" wasted no time. Immediately he set about to determine if George Moses could be freed. A letter was posted to his master. James Horton replied that he was not in a position to do without the manual labor of the young man who, to be truthful, was "no less a farmer than a poet," but he added that toward the close of the farming season he might be induced to take a fair price for him.

With such a possibility, funds were solicited. In North Carolina, a small but insufficient amount was pledged. *Freedom's Journal,* an antislavery publication in New York, began fanning the effort in August, moaning that in George Moses' own state four or five hundred dollars could easily be gathered "for any other purpose sooner than the emancipation of a fellow being." From the North, the newspaper proclaimed, help was needed—help from benevolent societies and voluntary contributors to swell the sum already promised by a few North Carolina philanthropists whose "hands act with their hearts."

The passive figure in the crusade was not idle. If dollars could produce liberty, perhaps poems could incite the donation of dollars. The "poet blackamoor" set to the task. He wrote two poems to the nameless gentleman who allegedly intended purchasing and educating him. In **"Gratitude"** he invoked celestial benediction:

> May Providence reward each man
>   Who feels such safe regard for me,
> And in his breast enroll a plan
>   Devised for liberty.

With this acknowledgment of the poet's emotion *Freedom's Journal* beat the drums louder. *"Something must be done,"* it shouted in italics; *"George M. Horton must be liberated from a state of bondage."* If each Negro in New York were to donate but one penny, his freedom would be assured and his talents not buried in vile servitude. The *Journal* opined that its readers could raise one or two hundred dollars towards the purchase. On October 3 the *Journal* announced that a Bostonian had subscribed to the fund and that it hoped other New England friends would come forward. The time was drawing near for the "philanthropic gentleman" to act. As for the newspaper itself, "We would manifest to our Southern brethren that were our means equal to our wishes, the footsteps of a slave should not pollute the soil of our common country."

The Bostonian who allowed his name to be used had special sympathy for George Moses. Both were natives of North Carolina. Born in Wilmington of a bound father and a free Negro mother, David C. Walker had never known slavery. But he wrote that he could not live in the "bloody land" of his birth and would have rebelled if he had not left it. In Boston, where he prospered from the sale of old clothes, he became a violent abolitionist.

As the weeks passed, the *Journal's* crusade lagged from insufficient support. At least, no other subscribers were announced, and apparently Walker was never called on to redeem his pledge to help his fellow Carolinian. His gesture was futile. In the absence of additional response, the *Journal* ceased its editorial battle for the bard's purchase and went on to more immediate forays. Yet, Walker was still to enact a significant role in the Horton drama. He, too, was a writer, already formulating notions about how to bring an end to slavery. Unintentionally, a famous pamphlet which he issued two years later wrought a change from the liberal climate of that early autumn in 1828.

It is not possible to know how deeply George Moses was affected by the failure of the New York campaign in his behalf. If his poems are an indication of his feelings during those months, he was more pleased with the idea of freedom than with its possible reality. His slavery verses pulsate with no inner yearning. They sound as if he were writing what was expected of him, just as he produced the neat and trim acrostics commissioned by the students. George Moses Horton always delivered what was ordered. At any rate, the New York failure was echoed back home. Whether it was the slave's indifference or some insurmountable obstruction, the "philanthropic gentleman," too, was soon heard of no more. His plan also was without success. The money was not raised. One unreliable account has it that "Mr. Horton saw a fortune in dat niggah, and wouldn't sell unless he could get enough to buy four good field hands." Even a gentleman of undeniable philanthropic feelings was unwilling to be basely robbed; so he quietly suspended his project.

Some little credence in the exaggerated story of the four field hands is provided by the experience of George Moses' most powerful friend at this time—the Governor of North Carolina himself, John Owen. Though a politician in a slave-holding state, Governor Owen was known to be interested in manumission. When he was informed by Dr. James Henderson of efforts to free George Moses, the governor "made an extraordinary proposition which was refused with a frown of disdain," the slave later said. "The proposition was to pay $100 more than any person of sound judgment should say that I was worth. To this, my master would not accede. Such was the miscarriage of the proposition from the feeling Governor to a man who had no regard for liberty, science, or Genius. A smile of generosity from a few seldom prevails amidst the envious frown of thousands who point at the slightest faults in genius as an enormous crime."

Strong healthy males were selling for good prices, but clearly James Horton did not want to part with his dithyrambic plough-boy, even to the Governor. The Horton tradition was to keep slaves within the family. At the hour of cold decision the blacks were not for sale, either down the river at a fancy sum or in the cause of liberty, science, and genius.

Though for the moment all plans to free the poet were thwarted, George Moses' friends would not admit defeat. A year later, one final assault in the battle of emancipation was organized. To pile up an amount which James Horton could not refuse, they prepared once again to solicit contributions and, this time, to market a book of the slave's poems. In the summer of 1829 the printing office of Joseph Gales in Raleigh was set up as the center of operations.

The unofficial committee was composed of those "elevated in office and literary attainment" (Governor Owen? Caroline Lee Hentz?). Designated to receive contributions was Weston Raleigh Gales, who promised to return any donation if the collection proved insufficient to effect the poet's release. Keying the campaign, the edition of poems would purposely be kept small in order to cut expenses. The few selections, it was thought, would be "sufficient to accomplish the object of the publication." The verses were to appear "without correction, that the mind of the reader may be in no uncertainty as to the originality and genuineness of every part."

The sponsors made clear that all help to the slave was conditioned on "his going in the vessel which shall first afterwards sail for Liberia," for it was said that George Moses Horton had affirmed his wish "to become a member of that Colony, to enjoy its privileges, and apply his industry and mental abilities to the promotion of its prospects and his own." It has been suggested that possibly he had his eyes on the poet laureateship.

Though any great eagerness to emigrate was somewhat less than burning, George Moses was swept along in the hubbub. If he preferred more to remain a freeman among his congenial surroundings than to be rushed to foreign jungles, he nevertheless kept his mouth shut and faced up to the importunity of his sponsors. With them he was forced to believe in his degrading status. In that old copy of *The Columbian Orator,* one of the first gifts from his beloved boys, he had read of the slave who said to his master, "Look at these limbs. Are they not those of a man? . . . I have the spirit of a man too." George Moses' spirit was equal to the occasion. Excitedly he wrote for the new book one of his best poems, **"The Slave's Complaint."**

> Am I sadly cast aside
> On misfortune's rugged tide?
> Will the world my pains deride
>   Forever?
>
> Must I dwell in Slavery's night
> And all pleasure take its flight
> Far beyond my feeble sight
>   Forever?
>
> Worst of all, must Hope grow dim
> And withhold her cheering beam?
> Rather let me sleep and dream
>   Forever!
>
> Something still my heart surveys,
> Groping through this dreary maze,
> It is Hope?—then burn and blaze
>   Forever!
>
> Leave me not a wretch confined,
> Altogether lame and blind—
> Unto gross despair consigned
>   Forever!
>
> Heaven! in whom can I confide?
> Canst thou not for all provide?
> Condescend to be my guide
>   Forever?
>
> And when this transient life shall end,
> Oh, may some kind eternal friend
> Bid me from servitude ascend
>   Forever!

The Hope of Liberty, making its bow in July, belied the notion that slaves who spoke out for freedom were summarily throttled. George Moses' prayer for liberation, published in the capital of a Southern state by a leading editor, was supported by those of influence and position. A little book of twenty-two closely printed pages, it was the first poetic protest by any slave anywhere of his status and the first book by a Negro in the South. It was the third book of American Negro poetry, preceded only by the work of Jupiter Hammon and Phillis Wheatley, both of whom lived in the North more than a half century before.

With such honors as literary history would give it, the book should have been better than it was. **"On the Poetic Muse"** declares that the bard has been wafted "through the mental skies . . . on mystic fire," but truthfully he remains pretty much on the ground. There, in all frankness, he is happiest. His imitations of Gray, Scott, and Byron do not lift him high, nor does his fascination with the Graveyard School. Mrs. Hentz thought that **"On the Death of Rebecca"**—suggested by the tragedy of a female slave to whom he was much attached—had a "native feeling in the lines," but actually the stanzas are humdrum. The religious poems are inspired more by a confusion of deistic and Wesleyan concepts than by any transports at a country camp meeting.

Regardless of its shortcomings, surely to be expected, *The Hope of Liberty* was an ambitious effort to come from unpoetic North Carolina in the summer of 1829—ambitious in its mere publication, ambitious more in what it was trying to do. It would be gratifying to report that its reception was immediate, it sale wide, and its purpose accomplished. But whether from inadequate distribution, unsuitable promotion, public indifference, or racial opposition, the little booklet was ignored. The publisher later reported that not much profit was derived from it.

George Moses Horton was back where he started, not desperately unhappy, but considerably deflated. There would always be a next time, with no Liberian jungles in the offing. He continued to work in the corn fields of his master, anticipating Sunday jaunts to Chapel Hill where now more than ever he was a celebrity, an author with a published work to his credit. How many university professors could boast as much?

Until 1830 the lenient attitudes toward slavery worked well for George Moses. Compared with conditions in neighboring Virginia and South Carolina, those throughout North Carolina were lax. The black poet's liberation had been a near miss. Then in that year, a vast change took place. Two of the very men who had tried to help the slave, slammed the door of freedom in his face. They were conspirators in no combined effort to hurt him whose well-wishers they were. On the contrary, their actions were poles apart ethically. In what they did, neither had a thought of George Moses. But no two extremes ever worked so effectively toward the undoing of a mutual protégé's hopes.

In 1830, David C. Walker, the poet's erstwhile patron, issued his famous *Appeal in Four Articles,* in which he urged slaves to revolt and murder. A Wilmington Negro, whom Walker secured for his agent in distributing the pamphlet in North Carolina, was arrested with the vile goods upon him. The state was shaken with horror. Eastern towns near Wilmington doubled the watch and revamped the patrol system. Governor John Owen, shocked and alarmed, sent copies of the incendiary *Appeal* to the members of the Legislature, saying he was convinced it was part of a giant scheme in the minds of Northern abolitionists. Prodded by the Governor, the Legislature took prompt action. In a state which had suffered from almost no slavery agitation, a price was put on Walker's head: $1,000 dead, $10,000 alive. Persons found guilty of writing or circulating any publication exciting "insurrection, conspiracy, or resistance in the slaves or free Negroes" were to be imprisoned, whipped, or put in the pillory. For a second offense, it was death. In December, 1830, a law was passed forbidding the education of slaves to read and write, the use of figures excepted. The work of the Manumission Society was feared. Anyone with abolitionist sentiment was suspect. Even the Quakers, who had always been tolerated, were distrusted. Except among the Quakers, interest in colonization dropped. Joseph Gales, lonely within the ranks of newspaper editors, wrote sympathetically in behalf of the Negroes.

Walker and Owen had done their work.

Hardly had the furor lessened before the eruption, in 1831, of the Southampton plots led by Nat Turner, just across the state line in Virginia. The news that fifty-four white persons had been killed by Negroes aroused once more the already fearful planters in North Carolina. An insurrection, modeled after Nat Turner's, was uncovered in Sampson County down between Chatham and the coast. Two Negro leaders were executed. Panic spread to the West.

Of the prohibitive laws of 1830-1831, the one most affecting George Moses was that which required a slave, on being freed, to leave the state within ninety days, never to return. Manumission was thus made more painful than ever. An indulgent owner like James Horton found this obstruction and others so restraining that he shut his ears to pleas for the poet's legal enfranchisement. In compensation, the master allowed his slave more and more physical freedom. Aware of his owner's forbearance, local denizens never questioned George Moses' absence from the plantation, new legislative regulations notwithstanding. It was a hackneyed admission in Chapel Hill that Poet Horton owned Mr. Horton and all but owned President Caldwell.

Under these conditions, George Moses settled not too unpleasantly into the Sunday life of the rustic college town. Though emancipation was a dead issue, Mrs. Hentz was still there, soothing his ruffled interior with words of encouragement. President Caldwell spoke to him as one educated man to another. And devil-may-care young gentlemen welcomed him with smiles as he stepped toward them along the pathway almost hidden beneath tall oaks. There were poems ready to recite, poems ready to be sold.

The hundred-plus students were little changed from those affable book-givers of a decade before. They were just as fond of playing tricks as ever, just as fond of hunting, of pursuing the 'possums and 'coons in the woodlands nearby, just as eager to sip a drink of raw corn liquor, just as disinterested in scholarship. These were the men George Moses courted. He felt uncomfortable in the presence of serious square-tail-coat boys from the backwoods, hovering in their rooms over a meal of molasses and cold cornbread, shiveringly preparing their goose quills and homemade dip-candles for the evening study hour. Such churls were too close to George Moses' weekdays. He preferred those in tailored clothes, with money to spend, with a propensity for knowledge gained without dip-candles. It was they who inspired him in 1831 to write **"The Pleasures of a College Life,"** a lengthy nine-page hosanna. In the guise of a student, the poet praised the study of geography, botany, zoology, theology, and astronomy. Yet,

> Ancient and modern authors we may read:
> The soul must starve or on thy pleasures feed. . . .

The "pleasures" came mainly in the recitation of the names of Plato, Demosthenes, Cicero, Horace, Vergil, Ovid, the names of Shakespeare, Raleigh, Milton, Addison, Pope, Scott, Campbell, the names of Locke, Newton, Franklin, of others known to him and the students. Apparently the soul's hunger was for the square-tail-coat boys. Life at Chapel Hill was infinitely preferable to life in the jungles.

Vexations, however, began to mar Arcadia. In June, 1831, the Hentzes with their three children left for Kentucky after five disconsolate years at the university. So far as Calvinist faculty members were concerned, Professor Hentz was still a heretic; and Mrs. Hentz had found no congenial friends among their wives. To George Moses, the flight of his patron was severe.

> This celebrated lady, however, did not continue long at Chapel Hill *(he later wrote in his autobiography, skipping over the abortive attempts at manumission)* and I had to regret the loss of her aid, which I shall never forget in life. At her departure from Chapel Hill, she left behind her the laurel of Thalia blooming on my mind, and went with all the spotless gaiety of Euphrosyne with regard to the signal services which she had done me. In gratitude for all these favors, by which she attempted to supply and augment the stock of servile genius, I inscribe to her the following:
>
> #### "Eulogy"
>
> Deep on thy pillar, thou immortal dame,
> Trace the inscription of eternal fame;
> For bards unborn must yet thy works adore
> And bid thee live when others are no more.
> When other names are lost among the dead,
> Some genius yet may live thy fame to spread;
> Memory's fair bush shall not decline to bloom

But flourish fresh upon thy sacred tomb.
When nature's crown refuses to be gay
And ceaseless streams have worn their rocks away,
When age's vail shall beauty's visage mask
And bid oblivion blot the poet's task,
Time's final shock shall elevate thy name
And lift thee smiling to eternal fame.

Well might George Moses praise the lady. It was she who snapped the springs to his fame years before she achieved approval for herself. In *Lovell's Folly* (1833), the first of her many popular novels, she injected into her story of New England life several cordial pages about the slave bard, carefully explaining in a footnote that he was "not an imaginary character."

Even after her exodus from Chapel Hill, the seeds of her efforts in the slave's behalf continued to sprout. William Lloyd Garrison, Boston's fire-eating abolitionist, came across the poem **"Slavery"** which she had sent to the *Lancaster Gazette.* On March 29, 1834, he reprinted it in his *Liberator,* of all newspapers the most despised by Southerners. George Moses' words were enough to drive the abolitionist readers into frenzy. At "melting pity" he screamed:

> Is it because my skin is black
> That thou shouldst be so dull and slack
> 　　And scorn to set me free?
> Then let me hasten to the grave,
> The only refuge for the slave
> 　　Who mourns for Liberty.

Meanwhile, besides the absence of the Hentzes, another vexation marred the poet's peaceful days in the early 1830s. This second one was both a vigorous reminder to him of his bondage and of the futile hope, he knew, for release. In 1832 William Gaston, North Carolina's most distinguished man of the day, was invited to address the two literary societies at the university commencement. "Disguise the truth as we may, and throw the blame where we will," he proclaimed, "it is Slavery which, more than any other cause, keeps us back in the career of improvement." He asked the seniors to work "for the mitigation and (is it too much to hope for in North Carolina?) for the ultimate extirpation of the worst evil that afflicts the Southern part of our Confederacy." His hearers cheered, not so much for the statement of their convictions as for Gaston's powerful oratory. Nothing would be done. Nat Turner's murderers were fresh in everyone's mind. The slave groaned.

But there were happier hours. His struggles with penmanship had brought success. He could now write a legible hand, though hardly a Spencerian one. He could read the great poets and he could put his own poems on paper. On Saturdays as well as Sundays, his time was his own. If he was not to be freed, he was content to reign in the sphere where wayward fortune had placed him. The students, among whom he was of course a favorite, thought him deferential, respectful, polite.

With their assured approbation, he developed toward the other campus Negroes a superciliousness and taciturnity which they found difficult to stomach. The lowly servants who brought water, made fires, and cleaned shoes were beneath him. As time went on, the only servant deserving emulation was Sam Morphis, who "hired out his time" from his absentee master and had a lucrative business transporting townspeople and college men to and from the village in his hack.

That the George Moses Horton of this period was prosperous is attested by Richard Benbury Creecy, class of 1835: "On Saturday evening he came up to college from the country with his week's poetical work in manuscript which was ordered by the boys on the Saturday before. When he came, he was a lion. . . . His average budget of lyrics was about a dozen in number. They were mostly in the love line, and addressed to the girl at home. We usually invested a quarter a week, and generally to the tune of the girl we left behind us." Twenty-five cents a week was a noble sum in days when a year's expenses at the university were $138.

Occasionally, George Moses had verses of his own inspiration which he offered for sale, but these lured few customers. Christopher Columbus Battle, a classmate of Creecy's, rougishly commissioned a poem based on the Greek phrase *Gar nux erchetai,* expounding in erudite solemnity that it meant "For the night cometh in which no man can work." The slave neither faltered nor batted an eye. He brought in a stately composition on "industry," with its ringing refrain,

> For the yoke of industry is wealth,
> And the yoke of industry is health.

He ventured into prose. It was never his forte, yet he could, when urged, turn out a love letter not only grandiloquent but capable of ensnaring the proud beauty for whom it was intended. The only surviving example of this profitable commodity is **"A Billet Doux"**:

> Dear Miss: Notwithstanding the cloud of doubts which overshadows the mind of adoring fancy, when I trace that vermillion cheek, that sapphire eye of expressive softness, and that symmetrical form of grace, I am constrained to sink into a flood of admiration beneath those heavenly charms. Though, dear Miss, it may be useless to introduce a multiplicity of blandishments, which might either lead you into a field of confusion, or absorb the truth of affection in the gloom of doubts; but the bell of adulation may be told from the distance of its echo, and cannot be heard farther than seen. Dear Miss, whatever may be the final result of my adventur-

ous progress, I now feel a propensity to embark on the ocean of chance, and expand the sail of resolution in quest of the distant shore of connubial happiness with one so truly lovely. Though, my dearest, the thunders of parental aversion may inflect the guardian index of affection from its favorite star, the deviated needle recovers its course, and still points onwards to its native pole. Though the waves of calumny may reverberate the persevering mind of the sailing lover, the morning star of hope directs him through the gloom of trial to the object of his choice.

> My brightest hopes are mixed with tears,
>   Like hues of light and gloom;
> As when mid sunshine rain appears,
> Love rises with a thousand fears
>   To pine and still to bloom.
>
> When I have told my last fond tale
>   In lines of song to thee,
> And for departure spread my sail,
> Say, lovely princess, wilt thou fail
>   To drop a tear for me?
>
> O princess, should my votive strain
>   Salute thy ear no more,
> Like one deserted on the main,
> I still shall gaze, alas! but vain,
>   On wedlock's flowery shore.

Love letters like this with verses attached did not displace the popular acrostics, but they commanded a tantalizing price—50c or more. As possessor of a steady income of at least three dollars a week from his poetry, George Moses had a plan. He was in a position to "hire out his time," as the expression went, to leave the plantation and set up in Chapel Hill a shop devoted to the Muse. James Horton was approached: the slave would pay his master 25c a day for the privilege of not working in the fields. Master Horton gave it considerable thought, then agreed. Among his half dozen workers, George Moses was the least energetic on the place. The sweat of poetic frenzy left little sweat for hoeing corn. Month by month he had become less assiduous in the furrows. His Pegasus disdained dragging a plough. Though Master Horton was fond of his slave he had to admit that the proposition would benefit the economy of the small plantation. The deal was set.

Hiring time was prohibited by legislative decree, for it was thought that slaves used their semifreedom to plan insurrections. Moreover, such an arrangement was usually a first step toward emancipation, on which after 1831 the state frowned more than ever. But violations were numerous, particularly among slaves with special skills. And who could deny George Moses his distinctive craft? The main thing was not to attract attention.

At last, George Moses sank into the life he had dreamed of. He loafed, he talked, he took a dram every now and then, he fished in Morgan's Creek while the students went to classes. He dictated several poems a day and put by a quarter to pay his master. When student orders slacked off, he did odd jobs about the village for a consideration. Especially was he delighted when asked to help at President Caldwell's home on Franklin Street. President Caldwell was now his greatest friend.

George Moses was older and wiser, living within his means. He was, no hedging about it anymore, the completely professional man of letters. In that summer of 1838, even in slavery, he looked forward to days long, prosperous, and pleasant. Only occasionally did he let Time concern him, thinking that on the morrow he would improve it, for did it not pass quickly like a flash away?

W. Edward Farrison (essay date 1971)

SOURCE: "George Moses Horton: Poet for Freedom," in *CLA Journal,* Vol. XIV, No. 3, March, 1971, pp. 227-41.

[*In the following essay, Farrison intersperses biographical information about Horton with commentary on his poems about antislavery and freedom.*]

During his sixty-eight years in slavery in North Carolina, a mode of existence by no means conducive to an interest in literature, George Moses Horton managed to study poets and the art of poetry and to publish three remarkable collections of original verse. Of pure African parentage, it has been said, he was born on the plantation of William Horton in Northampton County, North Carolina, in 1797. When Horton was about six years old, William Horton moved his family and slaves to a new farm in Chatham County, about ten miles southwest of Chapel Hill. From that time until the end of the Civil War, Horton's home—as far as a slave could be said to have a home—was on that farm.

Horton's interest in learning to read, rhyme, and write was stimulated by the hymns which he heard at revival meetings, by the songs he saw in a hymnal his mother owned, and by his hearing the Bible read. In spite of a want of opportunities, not to speak of conveniences, for study, and although discouraged by his fellow-slaves who said "I was a vain fool to attempt learning to read with as little chance as I had," Horton persevered and "entered into reading lessons with triumph."[1] He read understandingly as well as enjoyably parts of the King James Version of the Bible and found in them the inspiration for verses which he composed before he began frequenting Chapel Hill and before he had learned to write. Having read the story of Christ's awaking and calming the tempest at sea, he began a paraphrase of it as follows:

> Master, we perish if thou sleep,
> We know not where to fly;

The thunder seems to rock the deep,
Death frowns from all the sky.

He rose, he ran, and looking out,
He said, ye seas, be still;
What art thou, cruel storm, about?
All silenced at his will.[2]

Horton said that he composed "many other pieces" based on the Bible—pieces which "slipped from my recollection" because it was a long time before he could get them written down. By way of comparison, one is reminded of the "two to three hundred lines" of *Kubla Khan* which an interruption prevented Samuel Taylor Coleridge from writing down, and which seem to have slipped forever from his recollection. If Horton's account of the beginning of his career as a poet is taken at face value—and there seems to be no reason why it should not be taken thus—Horton began his career as a poet by composing, not facile love poetry, but serious, religious poetry. This fact has been rather generally overlooked by those who have written about him.

Not only did Horton become "early fond of music, with an extraordinary appetite for singing lively times [tunes], for which I was a little remarkable," but also ere long he found himself more fond of reading poetry than the prose of the Bible. For a long time, until after he began spending most of his time in Chapel Hill, the only poetry available to him was hymns, especially those of Charles Wesley. Thus the common meter of the hymns became his first models for verse, as is evidenced by his biblical poems.

About 1817 Horton began to visit Chapel Hill to peddle fruit and farm products. There he soon aroused the interest of students at the University of North Carolina and also others in the University community in his genius for versifying and his desire for learning. At once, it has been repeatedly said, he began turning his talents to account by composing, for fees ranging from twenty-five cents upwards, love poems which the purchasing students themselves wrote down, before he himself learned to write. When students dispatched these poems to their ladyloves, they doubtless did not disclaim, if they did not claim, authorship; nor did they see any need, one may be sure, to mention Horton as the principal participant in these communal literary efforts. Accordingly some of Horton's best verses might have been left for posterity without their being known to be his work. For it stands to reason that the better a poem was, the more likely was he who had commissioned the writing of it to let the impression prevail that he was its author.

Whether because of a desire to enable Horton the better to play the slave poet for them, or because of their conviction that his was a mind worthy of development, some of the students at the University contributed directly to his

efforts to educate himself by giving him books of various kinds. Incidentally one of the beneficent students was Leonidas Polk, a brother of him who became the eleventh president of the United States. Among the books given to Horton were Lindley Murray's *English Grammar,* a small edition of Samuel Johnson's *Dictionary,* copies of John Walker's and Thomas Sheridan's dictionaries, Richard Snowden's *The American Revolution,* and *The Columbian Orator.* There were also John Milton's *Paradise Lost,* James Thomson's *The Seasons,* Edward Young's *Night Thoughts,* selections from Homer's *The Iliad,* Virgil's *The Aeneid,* and Plutarch's *Lives,* and some of the "Beauties" of Shakespeare and Lord Byron.[3]

Assuming that the donor of *The Columbian Orator* had read this book, one may find it remarkable that he gave a copy of it to Horton, for it contained antislavery sentiments sufficiently strong to prompt Horton to write his poem entitled **"The Slave's Complaint."** Said he in part in this poem,

> Am I sadly cast aside,
> On misfortune's rugged tide?
> Will the world my pains deride
> Forever?
>
> Must I dwell in Slavery's night
> And all pleasure take its flight,
> Far beyond my feeble sight,
> Forever?[4]

At the time, however, some of the students at the University harbored antislavery sentiments, and the donor of *The Columbian Orator* might have been one of them. As may be noted in passing, Frederick Douglass read this book while he was still a boy and was inspired with antislavery sentiments by it.

Horton's contact with the students at the University was not an unmixed blessing for him. There was evil as well as good in it. In addition to giving him books and clothes, some of the students gave him whiskey and flattered him into believing "that it would hang me on the wings of new inspiration, which would waft me into regions of poetical perfection," as he said in phraseology exemplary of his penchant for rhetorical flourishes.[5] Sooner or later, withal, he found that he had been misled, and he reformed, although it is doubtful that he became a total abstainer.

In 1816 Nicholas Marcellus Hentz (1797-1856) emigrated from his native France to the United States, and some time afterwards he became a schoolteacher in Northampton, Massachusetts. In 1824 he married Caroline Lee Whiting (1800-1856) of Lancaster, Massachusetts. Two years later the Hentzes settled in Chapel Hill, where Hentz had been appointed professor of modern languages and belles lettres at the University. Mrs. Hentz was already a minor poet, and later she became a novelist and playwright.[6]

One of the persons other than students in the University community who took an interest in Horton was Mrs. Hentz. She taught him to write, encouraged him to continue to write poetry, and helped him to improve his versification and his use of words. Moreover, abolitionist that she then was, she was instrumental in getting some of his poetry into print as evidence of the triumph of his mind "over the bonds of slavery, and the darkness and corruption which seem their inseparable attendants." Early in 1828 she sent two of his poems, namely, **"Liberty and Slavery"** and **"Slavery,"** to the *Lancaster Gazette,* her home-town newspaper. These poems were published in the newspaper for April 8, where they were prefaced by an introductory note of Mrs. Hentz's, from which I have just quoted.

The first and seventh of the ten stanzas in **"Liberty and Slavery"** as it is in the *Lancaster Gazette* are as follows:

> Alas! and am I born for this,
> To wear this slavish chain?
> Deprived of all created bliss,
> Condemned to toil and pain.
>
> Oh, Liberty! thou golden prize,
> So often sought by blood;
> I crave thy sacred sun to rise,
> The gift of nature's God.

The stanza last quoted leaves one wondering whether Horton had read The Declaration of Independence, since the stanza shares ideas and an important phrase with the opening sentences of that document.

Here follow the first and third of the six stanzas in the *Lancaster Gazette* version of **"Slavery,"** which is written in tail-rime:

> When first my bosom glow'd with hope,
> I gaz'd as from a mountain top
> On some delightful plain;
> But oh! how transient was the scene—
> It fled as though it had not been,
> And all my hopes were vain.
>
> Why was the dawning of my birth
> Upon this vile, accursed earth,
> Which is but pain to me?
> Oh! that my soul had wing'd its flight,
> When first I saw the morning light,
> To worlds of liberty!

The ideas in the third stanza were common in the thinking of many slaves, namely, that it was better not to have been born at all than to have been born a slave, and that it was better to be a dead freeman than a live slave.

Another of Horton's poems which Mrs. Hentz sent to the *Lancaster Gazette* was one entitled **"On Poetry and Musick,"** which was published in the newspaper for June 24,

1828. In her introductory note to this poem, Mrs. Hentz said that it was short. It consists, however, of four eight-line stanzas and four four-line choruses, all of which are iambic tetrameters. The lines in the long stanzas rhyme alternately, and those in the choruses rhyme in couplets. In the last chorus Horton said autobiographically.

> Regardless of the sound of fame,
> In early youth I caught the flame;
> And strove, unpolished, void of fear,
> To breathe a song in every ear.

In other words, unlike Macduff and Lennox in Shakespear's *The Tragedy of Macbeth,* who could not wake Duncan with their knocking, Horton thrilled (etymologically speaking) with his singing all neighboring ears which could not choose but hear. Although its subject was dear to Horton's heart, this poem is without the fervor of the two poems on slavery.

Like some of Horton's later verse, all three of these poems are characterized by the poetic diction which is one with much of that of eighteenth-century British poetry—a fact which does not necessarily amount to adverse criticism of that diction. Nor need William Wordsworth's dislike of it be considered an indisputable argument against it. As Sir Roger de Coverley said, although in a different context, "much might [still] be said on both sides." These early verses of Horton's cannot be considered great or even exceptionally good poetry, but they are obviously the product of genius—if genius not yet refined by much learning.

The first of these three poems was reprinted under the title **"On Liberty and Slavery"** with minor changes in Horton's *The Hope of Liberty. Containing a Number of Poetical Pieces.* The other two seem not to have been included in any of his collections of his poetry. The fourth stanza of **"Slavery,"** however, was quoted at the end of the introductory "Explanation" in *The Hope of Liberty,* and the whole poem was reprinted in *The Liberator* for March 29, 1834. Therein it was presented as an example in disproof of the doctrine of Negro inferiority, by which proslavery leaders tried to justify slavery.

After four years in Chapel Hill, the Hentzes moved away, and between 1830 and 1849 they lived during various periods in Covington, Kentucky; Cincinnati, Ohio; Florence, Tuscaloosa, and Tuskegee, Alabama; and Columbus, Georgia, keeping a school for some time in each of those places. Meanwhile, Mrs. Hentz continued her literary efforts, writing both novels and dramas.[7] In her novel entitled *Lovell's Folly* (Cincinnati, Ohio, 1833), she referred briefly to Horton. The Hentzes moved to Marianna, Florida, in 1851 for the sake of their health and spent their last years there.

Horton deeply regretted the Hentzes' removal from Chapel Hill, because thereby he lost his best teacher in the person of Mrs. Hentz. But he remembered her long afterwards; and she having "left behind her the laurel of Thalia blooming on my mind," he commemorated her in a **"Eulogy"** in verse. In this he predicted that

> When age's vail [veil] shall beauty's visage mask,
> And bid oblivion blot the poet's task,
> Time's final shock shall elevate thy name,
> And lift thee smiling to eternal fame.

Horton probably never knew that in her later years, Mrs. Hentz became an apologist for slavery if not a firm believer in it.[8] If he had known about this, he probably would have ceased regarding her so highly.

From much that has been published about Horton, principally in North Carolina newspapers and periodicals, it appears that he was a contented, carefree slave poetaster who flourished at the University of North Carolina, trading rhymes for subsistence and intoxicants, without taking either himself or his writing seriously. Early in the present century, Collier S. Cobb, for instance, said the following, among other things, about him:

> George never really cared for more liberty than he had, but he was fond of playing to the grandstand. It was a common saying in Chapel Hill that poet Horton owned Mr. Horton and all but owned the president of the University.[9]

Cobb's remarks are not consistent with the pertinent facts. As Horton was passed from the ownership of William Horton to that of William Horton's son James in 1814 and to that of James's son Hall in 1843, there was no confusion in his mind as to who claimed him as property at any time. While Horton was owned by James Horton, he found life as a versifier for students at the University and as a factotum there preferable to farm labor. Accordingly, in order to stay away from the farm, he bargained with James Horton to hire his time for twenty-five cents a day. The slaveholder agreed to the bargain, not because of consideration for Horton, but simply because he found it profitable. Now if Horton was inclined to doubt even momentarily who owned whom according to the legal dialectics of slavery, he was promptly relieved of his doubt by the daily necessity of earning money with which to pay the fee promised to James Horton. When Hall Horton became the slave poet's owner, still more exacting, he doubled the hiring price—an act which doubtless reemphasized for Horton the fact concerning who owned him.

As to Horton's all but owning the president of the University, the facts leave one no reason to take that even for a good joke. During Horton's sojourn of about forty-eight years in Chapel Hill, the University had only two different presidents. The first of these was Joseph D. Caldwell, who was perhaps as much of an abolitionist as one in his position could have been. He died in 1835 and was succeeded by David L. Swain, an ex-governor of North Carolina, who was still president when the Civil War ended and Horton left Chapel Hill. As will be seen further on in this essay, Swain proved to be the kind of person whom it was hardly worthwhile for Horton to own knowing.

In his two earliest published poems, it should be remembered, Horton frankly expressed his dissatisfaction with being a slave and his earnest desire to be free. Some time after the publication of those poems, he wrote a poem which he entitled **"Gratitude"** and dedicated to a gentleman who had become interested in helping him to get his freedom. The poem was published in *Freedom's Journal,* New York, for September 5, 1828.[10] At the time the editors of this, the first newspaper published by American Negroes, were heading a campaign to raise funds for the purchase of Horton's freedom. The campaign proved unsuccessful, but its failure did not discourage Horton. In fact he seems to have been challenged by the possibilities it suggested; and from 1829 until April, 1865, when he took refuge with a detachment of Sherman's army, he was busy with one unsuccessful scheme after another by which he hoped to achieve his freedom.

Probably Horton could have gained his freedom by means of the Underground Railroad, but apparently he never tried to liberate himself by that means. The fact that he did not, however, is no proof that he did not want his freedom. It might well have been simply that he preferred to bear the known ills to which he was then heir rather than fly to others unknown. Furthermore he was constantly nursing the hope that he would soon gain his freedom by legal means.

During his many years as a poet, Horton wrote verses on a variety of subjects—slavery, himself, religion, love, nature, death, learning, women, heroism, etc. Sometimes he dealt lightly or even frivolously with his subjects, as if the mere *joie de vivre* was his chief concern. Mainly because of this fact, many of those who have written about him have portrayed him as a black Pierrot and have ignored the fact that he was always serious when he wrote about slavery, and that he wrote a great deal against it.

The Hope of Liberty was the first of the three collections of Horton's poetry to appear during his life. This pamphlet consisting of twenty-two pages and twenty-one poems was published in Raleigh, North Carolina, in July, 1829. As its title indicated, Horton and his well-wishers, including Weston R. Gales, one of the publishers of the pamphlet, hoped that it would be the means of producing "by subscription, a sum sufficient for his emancipation, upon the condition of his going in the vessel which shall first afterwards sail for Liberia."[11] The pamphlet did not produce enough income to pay for Horton's freedom, but it brought attention to him as a poet and as another example of the Negro's genius. It was reentitled *Poems by a Slave* and reprinted in Philadelphia in 1837, and the reprint was attached to an edition of the *Memoir and Poems of Phillis Wheatley, a Native African and a Slave* which was published in Boston the next year.

Two of the poems in *The Hope of Liberty* are directly antislavery. These are **"On Liberty and Slavery"** and **"The Slave's Complaint,"** from both of which I have previously quoted. Two other poems in the collection are indirectly but clearly antislavery. One of these, **"On the Death of Rebecca,"** is an elegy on a slave girl whom Horton presumably knew. It consists of seven quatrains of anapestic tetrameters with alternate rhymes. Its theme is summarized in a line in its fifth stanza: "Oh, death is a song to the poor ransom'd slave." In substance this is a repetition of the idea that it was better to be free in death than alive in slavery. The other poem, **"On hearing of the intention of a gentleman to purchase the Poet's freedom,"** is a series of heroic couplets grouped into thirteen quatrains. Its subject matter is essentially the same as that of **"Gratitude."** It pays a tribute to the poet's would-be benefactor and dwells on the relief and joy which freedom would bring.

Still hoping to earn enough money by writing to purchase his freedom, Horton planned to publish a second collection of his poems entitled *The Museum*. This volume seems never to have been published, but in 1845, in at least one instance known to Horton, it was referred to as if it had been.[12] Meanwhile, in a letter dated at Chapel Hill, February 27, 1843, a correspondent who signed himself "G." informed the editor of *The Southern Literary Messenger* that a volume of manuscript poems had been recently put into the correspondent's hands by their author, "George Horton, a negro boy, belonging to a respectable farmer, residing a few miles from Chapel Hill." Horton was then about forty-six years old, but in the usage of slaveholders male slaves were commonly called "boys" until they were old enough to be called "uncle." The correspondent accompanied his letter with two poems from the manuscript and promised that if these met the editor's approval, he would send additional poems "together with some sketch of the life, genius and writings of their author." The correspondent has been identified as Professor William Mercer Green of the University of North Carolina, and most probably the manuscript he referred to was that of *The Museum*. The two poems Green submitted were **"Ode to Liberty"** and **"Lines to My—"** The latter is an ingeniously written love lyric and is beyond the scope of this essay. The two poems were published in *The Southern Literary Messenger*

for the following April.[13] I have found no other poems by Horton in that periodical.

The pattern of **"Ode to Liberty"** is basically the common-meter stanza. Every two lines of the tetrameters rhyme, but all of the trimeters have the same rhyme. The general theme of the poem is that all nations should be free. Horton was intelligent enough to know, of course, that a nation could be truly free only if all of its people were free, as was not then true of the United States, to which he referred as "Columbia." Accordingly, in a metaphor in the first four lines of the poem, he appealed for complete freedom within the nation:

> O, Liberty, thou dove of peace,
> We must aspire to thee,
> Whose wing thy pris'ners must release,
> And fan Columbia free.

The words "wing" and "pris'ners" were replaced with "wings" and "pinions" respectively in the version of the poem later included under the title **"Liberty"** in Horton's *Naked Genius*. These changes help to clarify the metaphor. Pinions, the end joints, the lowest parts, of wings, symbolized the slaves, the lowest class in America; and the dove, which symbolized the peace that only liberty could bring, would be free only when its entire wings were free. Herein, then, was an indirect and lofty antislavery argument which only the thoughtful would discern.

Horton's second printed collection of verse was his *Poetical Works,* a small volume of ninety-six pages, which was published in Hillsborough, North Carolina, in 1845, and which contains forty-five poems. There are no directly antislavery poems in this volume, not because Horton had become contented with his lot and was no longer inspired to write against slavery, but for another reason. In 1829 when **The Hope of Liberty** was published, there was considerable antislavery sentiment in North Carolina, but it did not continue very long after that time. By the 1840's proslavery leaders in the state, with those in other slave states, were not only defending slavery but also doing their best to prohibit public expressions against it. If, therefore, Horton had included such poems in his collection, most probably he could not have got it published in North Carolina; and he had no connections by which he might have got it published elsewhere. No publisher in the state, however liberal he might have been, would have risked publishing a book containing such poems—unless he had forgot what had happened to the Reverend Elijah P. Lovejoy and his printing press only eight years earlier in a supposedly free state. For Horton it must have been a simple choice between including such poems and not getting his book published and leaving them out and getting the book published, with the revival of the hope of earning from its sale money with which to purchase his freedom.

There are, nevertheless, two indirectly antislavery poems in the volume, namely, **"Farewell to Frances"** and **"Division of an Estate."** These portray one of the worst and most common evils of slavery—the forced separation by sales of loved ones and members of families.

Apart from his ventures into publication, Horton tried by at least two other means to achieve his freedom. In September, 1844, he wrote an oddly worded letter to William Lloyd Garrison soliciting that abolitionist's aid in his efforts to purchase his freedom. Eight years later, apparently upon Swain's suggestion, Horton wrote similarly to Horace Greeley, the editor of the *New York Daily Tribune*. In his letter to Greeley, he included **"The Poet's Feeble Petition,"** a short poem in which he expressed his longing for freedom.[14] Presuming too much upon the integrity and kindness of those in high places, Horton entrusted these letters to Swain for forwarding to their addressees. Swain, however, was not at all disposed to be the slave poet's Maecenas; and without telling Horton what he had done with the letters, he simply filed them among his papers, leaving their author to wonder why he never received any replies to them—and leaving for posterity additional proof, if any more was needed, that proslavery ethics was not necessarily the same as ethics.

Horton's third and last printed collection of poems was *Naked Genius,* which was published in Raleigh in the summer of 1865. This volume of 160 pages contains 132 poems. Forty-two of these were reprinted from the *Poetical Works.* Coming as it did after the Civil War had ended slavery, it was not intended to produce funds for the purchase of Horton's freedom, but to win distinction for him as a poet as well as to serve as "one of the many proofs that God, in His infinite wisdom and mercy, created the black man for a higher and nobler purpose than to toil his life away under the galling yoke of slavery."[15]

In addition to three previously published indirectly antislavery pieces—**"Farewell to Frances," "Division of an Estate,"** and **"Liberty"**—there are four directly antislavery poems in this volume. Horton probably wrote all four of these poems late in the 1850's when the conflict over slavery reached its climax, and the spirit of the time was rendering slave-holding less and less defensible. In **"The Slave,"** a poem of ten iambic quatrains with alternate rhymes, he condemned slavery as a gross violation of divine law, especially of the Golden Rule. **"A Slave's Reflections the Eve Before His Sale"** consists of three quatrains alternating with three six-line stanzas, all in varying meters and rhymes. In this poem Horton dwelt on the cruel uncertainties with which slaves were constantly threatened by the prospects of being sold. In **"Slavery,"** a poem of eight quatrains of iambic tetrameters with alternate rhymes, he argued that slavery was inconsistent with the doctrine of natural rights. In **"Negro Speculation"** there are four stanzas each of which is composed mainly of four anapestic trimeters rhyming alternately plus the fifth-line refrain "Weep [,] humanity weep!" As this refrain indicates, the theme of this poem is the various kinds of inhumanity—the cruelties and tyrannies—to which slaves were subjected, and especially the long days of hard work exacted from them—by all of which "nature is turned into hell!" Horton observed.

One cannot read Horton's writings without being impressed by the fact that he took himself seriously as a poet—that he diligently studied the art of poetry, as is evidenced by his experiments with various verse forms and his endeavors—admittedly not always successful—to appeal to the reader's imagination. He was determined to be a poet in spite of the handicap of slavery, the worst of possible handicaps. He was aware that slavery had kept him from getting the education he longed for and knew he needed. He was often discouraged by the fact that in other ways slavery frustrated his genius and his interest in the life of the mind. He himself took note of all of this in a poem entitled **"The Obstructions of Genius,"** which is the last poem in *Naked Genius.* In the second and third of the seven quatrains of this poem he said,

> Throughout my life I've tried the path,
> Which seemed as leading out of gloom,
> Beneath my feet still kindled wrath,
> Genius seemed leading to a tomb.
>
> No cultivating hand was found,
> To urge the night improving slave,
> Never by freedom's laurel crowned,
> But pushed through hardship to the grave.

Now that slavery had been abolished, however, he was no longer embittered by his experience as a slave. Rather, with malice toward none and with charity for all, he said in the last stanza of the poem,

> Let us the evil now forget,
> Which darkened the Columbian shore,
> Till sun shall fail to rise and set,
> And slavery's cries are heard no more.

At last freedom for the poet for freedom had become more than a word; it had become a reality. But alas the twilight, if not the night, of his career as a writer had come. Horton died either in Philadelphia or somewhere in North Carolina probably in 1883.

Notes

1. *The Poetical Works of George M. Horton, the Colored Bard of North Carolina, to Which Is Prefixed the Life* of the *Author, Written by Himself,* Hillsborough, North Carolina, 1845, pp. vi. and vii. Hereinafter cited as *Poetical Works.*

2. *Ibid.,* p. ix.

3. *Ibid.,* pp. xv and xvi.

4. Richard Walser, *The Black Poet . . . George Moses Horton,* New York, 1966, p. 40. George M. Horton, *The Hope of Liberty. Containing a Number of Poetical Pieces,* Raleigh, North Carolina, 1829, pp. 10-11.

5. *Poetical Works,* p. xvi.

6. *Appleton's Cyclopedia of American Biography,* New York, III (1900), 178-179. *Dictionary of American Biography,* New York, VIII (1932), 565-566.

7. *Appleton's Cyclopedia of American Biography,* New York, III (1900), 178-179. *Dictionary of American Biography,* New York, VIII (1932), 565-566. Arthur Hobson Quinn, *A History of American Drama from the Beginning to the Civil War,* New York, 1923, pp. 264-265.

8. *Poetical Works,* pp. xviii-xix. *Dictionary of American Biography,* New York, VIII (1932), 566.

9. Collier S. Cobb, "An American Man of Letters: George Horton, the Negro Poet," *The University of North Carolina Magazine,* October, 1909.

10. Horton did not include this poem in any of his collections of his poetry.

11. George M. Horton, *The Hope of Liberty,* Raleigh, North Carolina, 1829, "Explanation," p. 3.

12. *Poetical Works,* "Introduction," p. xxi.

13. Richard Walser, *op. cit.,* pp. 60-61. *The Southern Literary Messenger,* IX (April, 1843), 237-238.

14. For this poem see Richard Walser, *op. cit.,* pp. 79-80.

15. *Naked Genius By George Moses Horton, the Colored Bard of North Carolina, Author of "The Black Poet,"* Raleigh, North Carolina, 1865, Will. H. S. Banks's announcement on the title page.

Sondra O'Neale (essay date 1981)

SOURCE: "Roots of Our Literary Culture: George Moses Horton and Biblical Protest," in *Obsidian,* Vol. 7, Nos. 2 and 3, Summer/Winter, 1981, pp. 18-28.

[*In the following essay, O'Neale analyzes Horton's poem "The Slave" to argue that Horton used biblical symbolism to voice his antislavery sentiments.*]

George Moses Horton, the Nineteenth Century Slave poet who is known as the antebellum Black bard of the University of North Carolina at Chapel Hill, had the most romantic style among the three Early Black American poets—Horton, Jupiter Hammon and Phillis Wheatley—who published before the Civil War while they were still in slavery. That is ironic when one considers that unlike those two elder poets, Horton did not have the comparatively easier life of a Northern house servant or administrative slave worker. No, Horton's creative drive was marred by rough agrarian tasks and unrelenting Southern servitude. Of all the poets in the cannon of African-American literature, if any had the right not to sing, not to be filled with hope, not to be a romantic, it was Horton. Instead, as a slave he outpublished both Hammon and Wheatley while maintaining his romantic vision and the same devotion to egalitarian principles of Christianity which they also held.

Horton was owned by a middle-class farmer who cared nothing for education, who scoffed at Horton's reputed genius and who required a full return of physical labor for his investment.[1] In his autobiography, the beleaguered poet says of his owner, William Horton, Sr.:

> My old master, being an eminent farmer, who had acquired a competent stock of living through his own prudence and industry, did not descend to the particularity of schooling his children at any high rate; hence it is clear that he cared less for the improvement of the mind of his servants. In fact, he was a man who aspired to a great deal of elaborate business, and carried me into measures almost beyond my physical ability.[2]

In fact, most of the residents of Chatham and Northampton—the two North Carolina counties where Horton spent the first seventy years of his life—never deemed to consider him as an accomplished poet of intellectual worth.[3] To have done so would have been to deny the "righteousness" of a slave system based on the assumed mental incapacity of all Africans. Only a small circle of abolitionist readers in the North recognized his talent[4] and he wrote to these few sympathizers deploring the conditions of bondage and environment that inhibited his craft.[5] He taught himself to read, much in the manner of his contemporary, Frederick Douglass,[6] by bribing school boys, tricking slave-owners and sharing knowledge with other slaves.[7] Had it not been that his master sent him to husk vegetables at the University of North Carolina in Chapel Hill,[8] and had it not been for two or three townspeople of literary interest who published his work ostensibly to help him earn his passage to Liberia,[9] and had it not been for the Civil War[10]—the country may never have heard the cries of this most prophetic slave-poet of antebellum America.

A lyricist, whose works would demand attention even if he were not the only slave in Southern bondage to publish volumes of poetry, self-taught Horton had a command of Biblical and Classical allusion that is astounding when one considers the implications of the slave experience. But when the theme of a Horton poem was his hatred of slavery, he usually chose direct statement over allusion. Close examination of Horton's volumes reveals the use of Christian allusion to get his message above the heads of pro-slavery advocates who may not have known Scripture well enough to accept the indictment, and into the hearts of those who did. While Horton is known today as one of the forerunners of protest poetry, critics have not yet acknowledged his adroit statements on slavery made through the use of veiled Biblical symbol. Obviously written before his emancipation but published afterwards, as it was too stinging to be included in volumes "approved" by his masters (*Hope of Liberty* and *Poetic Works*), his poem "The Slave" is an outstanding example of Horton's use of Christian themes to plead for the right to Black equality:

"The Slave"

What right divine has mortal man received,
    To domineer with uncontroll'd command?
What philosophic wight has thus believed
    That Heaven entailed on him the weaker band?

If African was fraught with weaker light,
    Whilst to the tribes of Europe more was given,
Does this impart to them a lawful right
    To counterfeit the golden rule of Heaven?
Did sovereign justice give to robbery birth,
    And bid the fools to theft their rights betray,
To spread the seeds of slavery o'er the earth,
    That you should hold them as your lawful prey?

Why did the Almighty God the land divide,
    And bid each nation to maintain her own,
Rolling between the deep, the wind and tide,
    With all their rage to make his order known?

The sad phylactory bound on rebel Cain,
    For killing Abel is in blood reveal'd,
For which the soldier falls among the slain,
    A victim on the sanguinary field.

Thus, in the cause of vile and sordid gain;
    To gratify their lust is all the plea;
Like Cain you've your consanguine brother slain,
    And robbed him of his birthright—Liberty.

Why do ye not the Ishmaelites enslave,
    Or artful red man in his rude attire,
As well as with the Black man, split the wave,
    And to his progeny with rage aspire.

Because the brood-sow's left side pigs were black,
    Whose sable tincture was by nature struck,
Are you by justice bound to pull them back
    And leave the sandy colored pigs to suck?

Or can you deem that God does not intend
    His kingdom through creation to display,
The sacred right of nature to defend,
    And show to mortals who shall bear the sway?

Then suffer Heaven to vindicate the cause;
    The wrong abolish and the right restore;
To make a sacrifice of cruel laws,
    And slavish murmurs will be heard no more.[11]

Horton's autobiographical reference to imitating meter and form from his "old Wesley hymnbook"[12] indicates that he was a Methodist. Historians also confirm that this denomination was even more successful than the Baptist in converting North Carolina slaves during the first half of the nineteenth century.[13] This evidence makes it likely that his introduction denying "right divine" to "domineer with uncontrolled command" is a position against Calvinist tendencies to justify slavery on the basis of a predestined right to rule. Methodism proved throughout antebellum history to be a great equalizer by tearing down Calvinistic class distinctions which were more suitable to the British royalist colonialism.[14] In line three of the first stanzas, Horton labels these doctrines "philosophic." That term was understood to be an insult in evangelical circles, since Christian doctrine is not supposed to be equated to secular philosophy. The latter is considered unenlightened speculation by "infidel" intellectuals while the former is held to be the "inspired" Word of God.[15]

However, in the next stanza Horton concedes that God did seem to direct the gospel toward Europe to the "deprivement" of Africa. Here he is introducing a dichotomy that will continue throughout the poem. Although Methodist Arminianism does insist that the Bible offers salvation equally and freely to all, it concedes that God had to single out certain individuals and nations for specific work in accordance with His permitted will (for instance, even John Wesley, the founder of the Methodist Church, would be considered "called of God" for that purpose). But Horton develops this poem to prove that although Europe may have been thusly selected, it had no corresponding divinely sanctioned right to dominate the nation given the "weaker light." In "to counterfeit the golden rule," Horton refers to Christ's commandment in Matt. 5: "to do unto others what you would have them do unto you."

The first two lines of the third stanza, "Did sovereign justice give to robbery birth, And Bid the fools to theft their rights betray," establishes the theme of "chosen" and "rejected" brothers that recurs both in Horton's poem and the book of Genesis. The Cain and Abel archetype from Genesis chapter four appears in stanza six. The historically tragic tension between Ishmael and Isaac, the "bastard" slave son and legitimate heir of patriarch Abraham, is referred to in stanza seven and eight. And the story of the twins Esau and Jacob, found in Genesis 25 through 33, is alluded to in stanzas three, seven and eight.

In each of these three cases God chose, either through election or circumstance or because of the individual failures of the "rejected" sons, one son to be spiritual and earthly heir in deference to the other. But in making these ancient situations analogous to the white man's reception of the gospel before "rejected" Africans, Horton simultaneously points out that the "rejected" sons were never punished nor enslaved but that God blessed and prospered each of them to father and command nations. Thus to any defense of slavery based on the book of Genesis, Abraham's slave empire being a case in point, Horton's retort is that preordained election on the one hand does not mean preordained damnable enslavement on the other.

Theologians explain the divine choice of Abel over Cain in terms of the "favored" son's choosing to obey God's direction for sacrificial worship and Cain's refusal to do so:

> And in process of time it came to pass, that Cain brought of the fruit of the ground an offering unto the Lord. And Abel, he also brought of the firstlings of his flock and of the fat thereof. And the Lord had respect unto Abel and to his offering: but unto Cain and to his offering he had not respect. And Cain was very wroth, and his countenance fell.[16]

While God's sentence of Cain following the resultant revenge murder was severe, He did nonetheless protect Cain so that he could "build a city named Enoch,"[17] and live to see his lineage prosper through to the sixth generation.[18] Thus, although Cain may have exercised free choice in disdaining the spiritual aspirations of Abel and introducing the violence of which Horton speaks in the fifth stanza, he was still allowed to inherit the spiritual blessings of a prince. This was his birthright just as Horton felt that physical freedom to reach his potential within the bounds of his native Africa was the Black man's birthright.

But the irony in Horton's symbolism is that he positioned the white slave master as the rejected murderer Cain and the Black slave as the righteous, selected, true son who was denied his true birthright, **"Liberty"**:

> Like Cain you've your consanguine brother slain,
> And robbed him of his birthright—Liberty.

He is simultaneously attributing Cain's violent attributes to the slave master and inferring that any material blessings received after such willful destruction of one's blood relation is not because of the master's righteousness but because of the merciful will of God. Evangelicals would have known very well the extent to which Horton's use of the Cain myth ascribes to them an innate tendency to murder, theft and violence. These were the attributes with which Scripture described Cain and his descendants.[19]

The class distinction between the slave "bastard" Ishmael and his legitimate half-brother, Isaac, is next in the chronological history and is even more pertinent to the slavery debate. If it were so divinely ordained that a man enslave his brother humans, then he asks why whites did not likewise enslave descendants of Ishmael and Esau, as they were no less than the African inheritors of the splendid spiritual and material wealth of the true son:

> Why do ye not the Ishmaelites enslave,
>   Or artful red man in his rude attire,
> As well as with the Black man, split the wave,
>   And to his progeny with rage aspire.

Ishmael himself was a slave, born to the Egyptian slave girl Hagar and Abraham, the rich father of the Jewish faith:

> Now Sarai, Abram's wife, bore him no children; and she had a handmaid, an Egyptian, whose name was Hagar. And Sarai said unto Abram, Behold now, the Lord hath restrained me from bearing: I pray thee, go in unto my maid; it may be that I may obtain children by her. And Abram hearkened to the voice of Sarai . . . And Sarai said unto Abram, My wrong be upon thee: I have given my maid into thy bosom; and when she saw that she had conceived, I was despised in her eyes: the Lord judge between me and thee. But Abram said unto Sarai, Behold, thy maid is in thy hand; do to her as it pleaseth thee. And when Sarai dealt hardly with her, she fled from her face. And the angel of the Lord found her by a fountain of water in the wilderness, by the fountain in the way to Shur. And he said, Hagar, Sarai's maid, whence camest thou? and whither wilt thou go? And she said, I flee from the face of my mistress Sarai. And the angel of the Lord said unto her, Return to thy mistress, and submit thyself under her hand.[20]

It seemed that Ishmael, though a slave, would be accepted as legal heir since there was no other offspring to receive the inheritance. Abraham even prayed that God would consider this "makeshift" substitute.[21] But when Ishmael was fourteen years old a legitimate son was born to Abraham and Sarah and in due time Hagar and Ishmael were expelled again. Yet god promised both Abraham and Hagar that he would make a "great nation" from the "seed of Ishmael":

> And as for Ishmael, I have heard thee: Behold, I have blessed him, and will make him fruitful, and will multiply him exceedingly; twelve princes shall he beget, and I will make him a great nation. But my covenant will I establish with Isaac, . . . And God said unto Abraham, Let it not be grievous in thy sight because of the lad, and because of thy bondwoman; in all that Sarah hath said unto thee, hearken unto her voice; for in Isaac shall thy seed be called. And also of the son of the bondwoman will I make a nation, because he is thy seed.[22]

Scriptural evidence seems to prove that God kept his word. Ishmael had no less than twelve sons "and these are their names, by their towns, and by their castles; twelve princes according to their nations."[23] Again Horton's analogy is poignant. If free Christian America considers itself as the chosen "Isaac" then it must follow his example and allow God to prosper, not sinfully enslave, the "rejected" Ishmael.

Most preachers advocating slavery relied heavily upon the Scriptural record of Abraham's slave household to vindicate the system and some even traced the analogy to the New Testament where Paul was stressing that the new heir in Jesus Christ was freed from the "bondage" of sin. However, nineteenth century theologians such as Rev. W. T. Hamilton in his famous tract, *The Duties of Masters and Slaves Respectively* . . . chose to interpret the New Testament passage as a justification for slavery:

> Certain it is that long before the time of Moses, slavery existed. Abraham had slaves, and many of them. There are of this class, born in his house, no less than 300 capable of bearing arms, Gen. 14:14. Hagar, the maid of Sarah, whom her mistress surrendered to Abraham in hope of an heir, was an Egyptian slave, Gen. 16:3; and Ishmael, her son, was by birth a slave also, in contradistinction from Isaac, who was born free, being the son of a free mother. This admitted fact, "Hagar gendereth to bondage—she is in bondage with her children," is the basis of the Apostle's comparison, between the law and the gospel, Gal. 14:24-26.[24]

Such logic ignores the fact that Isaac and Ishmael are nonetheless brothers and that Ishmael did not remain a slave all of his life but was the prosperous founder of a new nation. Horton was refuting the Biblical background used by proslavers and even as an uneducated slave himself, he was evidently well-read enough to enforce his point with Scriptural data.

Horton's phrases "robbed him of his birthright" and "artful red man in his rude attire" allude to the last great "elected-rejected" brother cycle in the Genesis record—that of the twins Esau and Jacob. Again God's apparently arbitrary predestinated choice, "Jacob have I loved, but Esau have I hated,"[25] was based on decisions Esau made of his own free will. Thus Horton continues to rely on tensions between Calvinistic election and Arminianism free will set up in the earlier part of the poem. The twins were sons of Isaac and the third generation in the lineage of Abraham. As in the case of Isaac and Ishmael, a decision would have to be made as to the primary heir of the spiritual and material riches of Abraham's legacy. God told Rebecca, Isaac's wife and the boys' mother, that one boy would prevail over the other:

> And the Lord said unto her, Two nations are in thy womb, and two manner of people shall be separated from thy bowels; and the one people shall be stronger than the other people; and the elder shall serve the younger.[26]

Again the Apostle Paul used this reference to explain election:

> and not only this; but when Rebecca also had conceived by one, even by our father Isaac, (for the children being not yet born, neither having done any good or evil,

that the purpose of God according to election might stand, not of works but of him that calleth;) . . .[27]

Horton's referral to Esau as a "red man" was a description given to the patriarch from birth:

> And the first came out red, all over like a hairy garment; and they called his name Esau. And After that came his brother out, and his hand took hold on Esau's heel; and his name was called Jacob; and Isaac was threescore years old when she [Rebecca] bore them.[28]

Isaac, however, following regional tradition and ignoring any "visions" his wife may have had about Jacob's "election," favored Esau. Jacob and Rebecca, knowing full well that God had promised them that *He* would give Jacob the inheritance, conspired to take the birthright from Esau by force and deception:

> And the boys grew: and Esau was a cunning hunter, a man of the field; and Jacob was a plain man, dwelling in tents. And Isaac loved Esau, because he did eat of his venison: but Rebekah loved Jacob.
>
> And Jacob sod pottage: and Esau came from the field, and he was faint: and Esau said to Jacob, Feed me, I pray thee, with that same red pottage; for I am faint; therefore was his name called Edom. And Jacob said, Sell me this day thy birthright. And Esau said, Behold, I am at the point to die: and what profit shall this birthright do to me? And Jacob said, Swear to me this day; and he sware unto him: and he sold his birthright unto Jacob. Then Jacob gave Esau bread and pottage of lentils; and he did eat and drink, and rose up, and went his way. Thus Esau despised his birthright.[29]

Later, to confirm Esau's pledge, Jacob, disguised as his "hairy" brother, tricked aged, blind Isaac into giving him the inheritance of birthright due the eldest son.[30] Hence Horton's use of the term "robbed him of his birthright." If slavemasters were indeed, like Jacob, "elected" to receive God's graces to the deprivement of the "African of weaker light" there was no need to force God's will through robbery and subterfuge. "Election" did not give "right divine . . . to domineer with uncontroll'd command."

As in the metaphor of Cain, Horton used an image which ultimately reverts against the pro-slavery logic of election. It was Jacob and not Esau who left his father's house in shame and had to grovel like a slave in exile and it was Esau, the "rejected" son, who stayed home to enjoy all the family's riches.[31] Again Esau prospered. As in the case of Cain and Ishmael, there was no need for the "rejected" brother to "serve"[32] the other in slavery.

The poem's fourth stanza leads one to conclude that Horton wished to extend the "brother" metaphor to international proportions:

> Why did the Almighty God the land divide,
>   And bid each nation to maintain her own,

Rolling between the deep, the wind and tide,
  With all their rage to make his order known?

Here his source is Acts 17:26:

> . . . and hath made of one blood all nations of men for
> to dwell on all the face of the earth, and hath determined
> the times before appointed, and the bounds of their
> habitation; . . .[33]

Not only is Horton arguing that all men are brothers
because they are of one blood, he is also reminding proslavers that each of the "rejected" brothers went on to
establish nations in their own right—African nations.
Scofield points out that although Cain's descendants
perished in the Flood, "every element of material civilization is mentioned in (their Biblical history:) city and
pastoral life, and the development of arts and manufac-
tures."[34] Genesis reports their civilization to be in "the land
of Nod, on the east of Eden. . . ."[35] an area even in Horton's time thought to be in the Mesopotamian basin at the
gateway to Africa.[36]

Scripture also says that Ishmael established the nations of
his twelve sons "from Hamlah unto Shur, that is before
Egypt, as thou goest toward Assyria."[37] Horton, as an avid
Bible reader, would have been aware of that reference and
would have known that Egypt was a term contemporarily
synonymous with Africa. Similarly, Esau settled in a region
of northern Africa. Horton was obviously aware of the
Scriptural reference that *both* of the brothers were so rich
by the time of their tearful reunion after Jacob's repentance
for the evil he had done[38] that one region literally could
not hold them:

> And Esau took his wives, and his sons, and his
> daughters, and all the persons of his house, and his
> cattle, and all his beasts, and all his substance, which
> he had got in the land of Canaan; and went into the
> country from the face of his brother Jacob. For their
> riches were more than that they might dwell together;
> and the land wherein they were strangers could not
> bear them because of their cattle. Thus dwelt Esau in
> mount Seir: Esau is Edom.[39]

Scofield describes Edom as being a part of northern Africa,
"the country lying south of the ancient kingdom of Judah,
and extending from the Dead Sea to the Gulf of Akaba."
Thus Horton's final ironic statement to pro-slavery
advocates who would think through his symbolism with
him is that they could very well be enslaving African
descendants of Ishmael and Esau, heirs of their revered
patriarch Abraham. A true Methodist, Horton intends to
make his position clear: while God may select a few
individual men or nations in order to deliver His gospel
message to all mankind, He still intends that message, and
the political ramifications of its reforms, be extended to all
men equally and freely.

Notes

1. George Moses Horton, *The Poetical Works of George Moses Horton, The Colored Bard of North-Carolina, to Which is prefixed the Life of the Authour Written by Himself* (Hillsborough: D. Heartt, 1845), p. xi.

2. Horton, *The Poetical Works,* pp. xi-xii.

3. Vernon Loggins, *The Negro Author: His Development in America to 1900* (Port Washington, New York: Kennikat Press, Inc., 1959), p. 108.

4. Loggins, p. 108.

5. George Moses Horton, "Letters of George Moses Horton," *Slave Testimony,* ed. John W. Blassingame (Baton Rouge: Louisiana State University Press, 1977), p. 59.

6. Frederick Douglass, *Narrative of the Life of Frederick Douglass, an American Slave, Written by Himself* (Boston: Anti-Slavery Office, 1846), p. 38.

7. Horton, *The Poetical Works,* p. iv.

8. Horton, *The Poetical Works,* p. xiii.

9. Merle A. Richmond, *Bid the Vassal Soar* (Washington, D.C.: Howard University Press, 1974), pp. 105-108.

10. Richmond, pp. 157-62.

11. Horton, *The Poetical Works,* pp. iii-iv.

12. Horton, *The Poetical Works,* p. iv.

13. John Spencer Bassett, *Slavery in the State of North Carolina,* vol. XVII, *Johns Hopkins University Studies in Historical and Political Science,* ed. Herbert B. Adams (Baltimore: The Johns Hopkins Press, 1899), p. 9.

14. Richmond, p. 101.

15. The Bible, KJV, Colossions 2:8.

16. The Bible, KJV, Genesis 4:3-5.

17. The Bible, KJV, Genesis 4:17-23.

18. The Bible, KMV, Genesis 4:8-24. See also Scofield, p. 10 ff 3. (C.I. Scofield, The Scofield Reference Bible (New York: Oxford University Press, 1945)).

19. The Bible, KJV, Genesis 16:1-2, 5-9.

20. The Bible, KJV, Genesis 17:15-19.

21. The Bible, KJV, Genesis 17:20-21, 21:12-13.

22. The Bible, KJV, Genesis 25:13-17.

23. W. T. Hamilton, *Duties of Masters and Slaves Respectively: or Domestic Servitude as Sanctioned by the Bible* (Mobile: Wholesale Bookseller, 1845), p. 9.

24. The Bible, KJV, Romans 9:13.

25. The Bible, KJV, Genesis 25:23.

26. The Bible, KJV, Romans 9:10-11.

27. The Bible, KJV, Genesis 25:25-26.

28. The Bible, KJV, Genesis 25:27-34.

29. The Bible, KJV, Genesis 27.

30. The Bible, KJV, Genesis 27:38-40, 33:7-15.

31. The Bible, KJV, Genesis 27:40.

32. The Bible, KJV, Acts 17:26.

33. Scofield, p. 11, ff 2.

34. The Bible, KJV, Genesis 4:16.

35. The Bible, KJV, Genesis 2:10-13. See also Bush's discussions of rivers "eastward in Eden," one of which ended in Ethiopia, George Bust, *Notes Critical and Practical on the Book of Genesis* (New York: Ivison & Phinney, 1857), p. 55.

36. The Bible, KJV, Genesis 25:18.

37. The Bible, KJV, Genesis 32 and 33.

38. The Bible, KJV, Genesis 36:6-8.

39. Scofield, p. 52, ff 1.

John L. Cobbs (essay date 1982)

SOURCE: "George Moses Horton's *Hope of Liberty:* Thematic Unity in Early American Black Poetry," in *CLA Journal*, Vol. XXIV, No. 4, June, 1982, pp. 441-50.

[*In the following essay, Cobbs argues that Horton's first published book of poetry has a common theme throughout what some critics have called a random assortment of poems—the motif of flight.*]

A hundred and fifty years after its publication in 1829 in Raleigh, North Carolina, George Moses Horton's *Hope of Liberty*[1] is a little-read landmark in the development of black American poetry. There is no point in claiming for this slim volume of twenty-two poems either great intrinsic literary worth or lasting influence on the progress of either white or black literature. We don't know how many copies of the first edition were published, but literary historians are unanimous in claiming that sales were disappointing. None of the poems contained more than a few short stanzas, and all were representative of the florid rhetoric and derivative style that characterizes most—one is tempted to say all—early American poetry. Still, *Hope of Liberty* is a remarkable document, and one which deserves more than the passing reference it receives in even the most distinguished surveys of black literature.

To appreciate *Hope of Liberty* we must first understand the context within which it appeared. The Colonies and the early Republic were hardly a congenial climate for the production of great poetry. The works of Bradstreet, Freneau, Taylor, and Bryant are competent and occasionally moving, but only the most chauvinist of readers will call their poetry great. The literary cradles of New England, New York, and Philadelphia rocked out little of real worth in the first two hundred years of American history, and what seems most lasting is philosophical and historical prose. At the time George Moses Horton and his sponsors brought out *Hope of Liberty,*[2] only one truly major American poet had published, Poe with his slender and unacclaimed *Tammerlane* in 1827. The accomplishments of Emerson, Longfellow, Whitman, and Dickinson lay in the future.

Furthermore, poetry, even more than prose, through the first quarter of the nineteenth century, had been the product of the Northeast. The agrarian South was poor enough soil for intellectual development of any kind, but it was particularly hostile to the rarified flights of poetic fancy. Significantly, the first two black poets to publish in America, Jupiter Hammon and Phillis Wheatley, came respectively from New York and New England.

George Moses Horton, however, came from the rural part of a slave state. True, he was exposed from his late teens to the limited intellectual stimulation of the University of North Carolina at Chapel Hill, but we know from the memoirs of one of his mentors, Caroline Lee Hentz, that Chapel Hill in the 1820s could be pretty stultifying, even for the wife of a faculty member. How much more so for a slave who could only get to town on occasional trips, who worked the fields of his master James Horton in another country. It was remarkable, then, that *Hope of Liberty* appeared in 1829, when Horton was about thirty-two, the first book by a black poet in America in fifty years.

If literary scholarship has slighted *Hope of Liberty,* and it has, it has not entirely neglected it, and the volume has received passing mention in virtually every historical study of black poetry in America. Frequently, Horton is lumped with Jupiter Hammon and Phillis Wheatley as a "pioneer" or a "ground-breaker," a euphemism that implies, like Dr. Johnson's comment on women preachers, that it is quaint that such a freak should exist at all. *Hope of Liberty* is noted for its historical value, but seldom does a critic claim poetic merit for the work or find in the collection any thematic integrity. All critics, of course, are not as condemnatory as Vernon Loggins, who flatly says of *Hope of Liberty* that Horton's poems, ". . . are certainly not of a merit to be considered suitable for publication in a magazine of artistic standards."[3] Still, even the kindest critics usually deprecate the poetic quality of the book, even though they acknowledge its historical importance. The attitude of M. A. Richmond, one of the most perceptive commentators on Horton, is representative:

> Modest as the volume was, it was the first by an Afro-American poet to be published since Phillis Wheatley's had appeared fifty-six years earlier. It was the first

poetic volume ever by a black man in the South, slave or free. And it was the first, of course, by a black slave to cry out against his enslavement.[4]

Some of the critical disinclination to take the poetry of *Hope of Liberty* seriously may derive from popular conceptions about the character and life of Horton himself. His very existence as a black poet in the South made him an oddity in an age and place which stereotyped blacks as illiterate and prosaic. A widely circulated 1909 pamphlet by Chapel Hill amateur historian Collier Cobb portrayed Horton just this way, as a comic peculiarity.[5] This image of Horton as a kind of black court jester to the students of antebellum Chapel Hill has haunted the poet's literary reputation and inclined later critics to search in Horton's works for reflections of the popular image, that of a casual and shallow writer, almost a grotesque. Thus, Sterling Brown's feeling that, "In the main, however, Horton's works remain the hodge-podge of a clever slave with a turn for rhyming and a love of rolling words."[6]

Read superficially, Horton's poems support taking him lightly. Most of his poems lack the stolid, plodding piety of Phillis Wheatley or Jupiter Hammon, and even his protest poetry is "much milder than that found in the most bitter of the nineteenth-century protest poets, James M. Whitfield."[7] Horton tends to write of love and nature as much as religion and death. Richard Walser is being patronizing when he says, ". . . George Moses, uncomplicated fellow, was not one to dwell lengthily on the sadder side of life,"[8] but Saunders Redding is not when he claims that, "He never lost his naive conceit. His poems are concerned with love and nature, heavenly grace and divine miracles,"[9] or when he analyzes Horton at greater length:

> Beside the gray-mantled figures of Hammon and Phillis Wheatley, Horton appears dressed in motley. His humor, his audacious and homely wit, his lack of dignity give him important historical place as a forerunner of the minstrel poets, and this consideration outweighs whatever of intrinsic poetical value his poems possess.[10]

It is almost as if the variety of Horton's subjects seems to disturb his critics, as if they feel that he would be a better poet if his scope were narrower. His range is considerable, from pure pious moralizing to humorous anecdote, and his wit, in an almost neoclassical sense, produced a poetry full of word games—of acrostics, off rimes, and twists and turns of colloquialism. He was, in the words of two distinguished critics, ". . . a prolific and facile versifier, one who was willing to write about anything—no matter how sublime or trivial—that touched him."[11] It was perhaps this love of variety coupled with Horton's penchant for humor that has led to the poet's being taken less seriously than he might have been. As to the humor, he was, as Gerald Haslam says, ". . . the first Negro American writer to

present something of the unique humor that was so evident in Negro folk literature,"[12] and there is in much of his poetry a light touch that sets him apart from the more ponderous moralizers, both black and white, among the poets of early nineteenth-century America. It is this quality of which Addison Gayle, Jr., speaks when he says of Horton, "Throughout . . . he shows a consistently good and original nature, dwelling much on religion, nature and love. . . ."[13]

The problem of Horton's literary reputation is most thoroughly dealt with by W. Edward Farrison:

> During his many years as a poet, Horton wrote verses on a variety of subjects—slavery, himself, religion, love, nature, death, learning, women, heroism, etc. Sometimes he dealt lightly or even frivolously with his subjects, as if the mere *joie de vivre* was his chief concern. Mainly because of this fact, many of those who have written about him have portrayed him as a black Pierrot. . . .[14]

Whatever the reasons—the slimness of the volume, the variety of the subjects, or the reputation of the poet— *Hope of Liberty* has been generally written off as a random collection of poems, interesting and historically significant perhaps, but with little thematic unity and integrity of vision. Certainly it is true that the poems represented in the 1829 collection cover a variety of themes, and it is pointless to expect of Horton's work at this early period that it exhibit the polish and sophistication that black poetry was later to achieve. Still, there is in *Hope of Liberty* a fundamental thematic unity that seems to have escaped many readers, and which gives the work an artistic coherence that has been generally unrecognized.

At first glance *Hope of Liberty* is indeed a random collection of twenty-two poems on a variety of subjects. In addition to the three celebrated poems of slave protest, **"On Liberty and Slavery," "Slave's Complaint,"** and **"Lines"** (**"On learning of the intention of a gentleman to purchase the Poet's freedom"**), there are five poems on death, four on nature and pastoral life, four on love, three on God and his might, and one each on poetry and loss of innocence. In addition, the book opens with an invocation, which bears quoting in full; like the other poems, it is short:

> Come, melting pity, from afar
> And break this vast enormous bar
> Between a wretch and thee;
> Purchase a few short days of time,
> And bid a vassal soar sublime,
> On wings of liberty.[15]

This invocation is the key to the thematic unity of the poems which follow. The theme here is obvious enough— flight, escape, soaring "afar" from the problems of a world that keeps man in general and the slave in particular, "a wretch." We might simply read the invocation as a protest poem, and add it to the three slave protests which have been most noted and quoted from *Hope of Liberty.* Yet it is this very theme of flight which links the invocation to all the other poetry of the volume, not just the slave poems. It is Horton's preoccupation with and development of the motif of flight that provides *Hope of Liberty* with a cohesive quality.

The idea of flight in the slave protest poems themselves is too evident to be belabored. Practically by definition, a true slave poem[16] is a plea for escape and an expression of a desire to flee. In a more profound sense, of course, the very condition of slavery is literally and symbolically one of fettering—one in which man is unable to "soar," to use one of Horton's favorite words. Horton always thinks of poetry in terms of soaring, and had he written Countee Cullen's famous lines, he would doubtless have questioned God's making a poet black and bidding him fly, rather than sing. Freedom from slavery for Horton is the freedom to soar, to ascend, and thus in **"Lines"** [on the prospect of freedom] he sees the muse:

> like a proselyte, allied to Heaven—
> Of rising spirits . . .

In **"The Slave's Complaint,"** Horton reverses the metaphor of flight, seeing the condition of bondage as one in which pleasure is fled:

> Must I dwell in Slavery's night
> And all pleasure take its flight,
> Far beyond my feeble sigh,
> Forever?

If the flight motif is implicit in the slave poems, it is explicit in the five poems on death in *Hope of Liberty.* Conventionally perhaps, Horton thought of death as an escape from the trials of life and an ascent to God. In **"On the Death of an Infant,"** the soul "soars from the ocean of pain," and "mounts with delight at the call." In **"On Death,"** "some parting spirit bids the world farewell." **"Consequences of Happy Marriages"** shows an almost metaphysical vision of the reincarnation of love in death:

> Incinerated to revive again;
> From whose exalted urn young love shall rise,
> Exulting from a funeral sacrifice.

One of Horton's best poems, **"On the Death of Rebecca,"** melds the themes of death and slave protest, for death frees the dead woman from slavery, and her soul takes flight:

> Oh, death is a song to the poor ransom'd slave;
> Away with bright visions the spirit goes sailing.

Four of the poems in *Hope of Liberty* are on unrequited or lost love, a theme which was to concern much of Horton's

later poetry. Horton usually saw love as a trial—perhaps subliminally he thought of it as a subtle version of slavery—for although he bemoans the pangs of love, he speaks hopefully of the process of escaping those pangs, of taking flight from love. Horton opens **"To Eliza"** with the lines:

> Fare thee well—away I fly.
> I shun the lass who thus will grieve me,

and **"Love"** opens with the image of the lover who will "fly like a bird to the boughs of a tree," and closes with the line, "I'd fly from thy frowns with a heart full of sorrow." **"The Lover's Farewell"** is equally illustrative of the flight motif: "I steal on tiptoe from these bowers," and "I sigh, yet leave them all behind," and at last, "Farewell—I'm gone with love away."

In the nature poetry of *Hope of Liberty* the idea of flight is, understandably, less integral to the subject of the poems themselves, and it tends to manifest itself in terms of descriptive language rather than overt theme. In **"On Spring,"** for example, Horton imagines the land freed from the lock of winter and evokes again one of his favorite images, that of birds mounting:

> . . . rise
> And thus salute the fragrant skies.
> Let music rise from every tongue,
> Whilst winter flies before the song.

In **"On Summer,"** timid creatures strive with awe to fly," but are "unable to rise," because of the heat. In **"On Winter,"** "larks forbear to soar," and "youthful charms have fled."

In the religious poems of *Hope of Liberty* it is hardest to discern the flight motif. The **"Praise of Creation,"** which opens the mean body of *Hope of Liberty,* is a vigorous description of God's wonders, and **"On the Truth of the Savior"** is simply a catalogue of Christ's miracles. But in **"Praise of Creation,"** the final image of floating is certainly analogous to Horton's ubiquitous conception of soaring:

> But, oh my soul, still float along
> Upon the flood of praise.

And the poem **"Heavenly Love"** is actually more about the escape of the soul than about God, and virtually every line contains flight images:

> The mystic sound of sins forgiven
> Can waft the soul away . . .
> The pilgrims' spirits show this love,
> They often soar on high;
> Languish from this dim earth to move,
> And leave the flesh to die.

Nearly every poem in *Hope of Liberty* fits the pattern. Either in terms of immediate theme, or in terms of imagery and language, the idea of flight is central to all the poetry in this volume. As William Carroll says, "The idea of flight—or soaring, as he frequently expresses it—is central to much, perhaps most, of Horton's poetry."[17] Horton uses the concept in a variety of ways. In one sense the motif denotes flight from slavery, or love, or the sorrows of earthly life. In a more positive sense it expresses "soaring"—release, ecstasy, creation, and freedom. It is this second type of flight—the flight of the imagination—that is the subject of the single poem in *Hope of Liberty* on poetry itself, **"On the Poetic Muse."** This poem, of all George Moses Horton's works, presents flight in its most positive aspects:

> Far, far above this world I soar,
> Wafting through the skies . . .
> And when the vain, tumultuous crowd
> Shakes comfort from my mind,
> My muse ascends above the cloud
> And leaves the noise behind.

It is fascinating to find that a volume so frequently maligned for the lack of connection of its parts is so thoroughly unified by a single *leitmotif*. In this slender collection, George Moses Horton presents a diversity of major poetic subjects—nature, death, God, love—in addition to the celebrated subject of slave protest that made him "the first Black to employ protest themes in a volume of verse."[18] But each subject is interpreted by a poet whose poetic vision is filtered through the consciousness of his own bondage. And implicit in that bondage was the desire for freedom, for escape—for flight. It was a desire that Horton expressed in almost every poem of *Hope of Liberty* through the continual projection of a vision of flight, both of flight as escape from pain, and also of flight as exercise of the spirit, the chance to "soar."

Hope of Liberty is a more appropriately titled volume than is at first evident. Far from being a random collection of verses on a variety of unconnected subjects, it is informed by a thematic integrity. Each poem shows an ongoing poetic concern with the projection of this single image. George Moses Horton's "hope of liberty" was a hope of the liberty to flee and the liberty to fly. This twofold sense of the meaning of flight is expressed throughout the poems of this pioneer volume by an American black poet, and the consistency of that expression gives *Hope of Liberty* a unity that makes it a worthy and distinguished work to stand at the gateway of American black poetry.

Notes

1. George Moses Horton, *Hope of Liberty* (Raleigh, N.C.: Joseph Gales and Sons, 1829). All quotations from *Hope of Liberty* are from this edition, a copy of which is available from the Rare Books Room of the University of North Carolina at Chapel Hill's Wilson Library.

2. The 1829 edition of *Hope of Liberty* is prefaced by a note by Weston R. Gales explaining that Horton's poems were collected and published through the efforts of sponsors. Gales indicates that *Hope of Liberty* was published to raise money for Horton's emancipation and passage to Liberia, and Gales claims, "It is his [Horton's] ernest and only wish to become a member of that Colony. . . ." The suggestion is that *Hope of Liberty* was titled to reflect the purpose for which the volume was to be sold. Careful reading of the poems, however, indicates that the title is an organic function of the leitmoif of the poetry therein.

3. Vernon Loggins, *The Negro Author: His Development in America* (Port Washington, N.Y.: Kennikat Press, 1931), p. 117. In weighing Loggins' judgment on Horton, or any other black writer, we may recall that this is the critic who expressed the opinion, in the Introduction to *The Negro Author*, that the field of black literature is "productive of little that is truly artistic" (p. vii).

4. M. A. Richmond, *Bid the Vassal Soar: Interpretive Essays on the Life and Poetry of Phillis Wheatley (c. 1753-1784) and G. M. Horton (c. 1797-1883)* (Washington, D. C.: Howard University Press, 1974), p. 113.

5. Collier Cobb, "An American Man of Letters: George Moses Horton, the Negro Poet," *North Carolina Review* (Oct. 3, 1909), frequently reprinted as a pamphlet.

6. Sterling Brown, *Negro Poetry and Drama* (Washington, D.C.: The Associates in Negro Folk Education, 1937), p. 7.

7. Roger Whitlow, *Black American Literature* (Chicago: Nelson Hall, 1973), p. 30.

8. Richard Walser, *The Black Poet* (New York: Philosophical Library, 1967), p. 32.

9. J. Saunders Redding, *To Make a Poet Black* (Chapel Hill: University of North Carolina Press, 1939), p. 17.

10. Ibid.

11. Arthur P. Davis and Saunders Redding, "George Moses Horton," *Cavalcade: Negro American Writing from 1760 to the Present* (Boston: Houghton Mifflin, 1971), p. 41.

12. Gerald Haslam, "The Awakening of American Negro Literature, 1619-1900," in *The Black American Writer, Vol. II,* ed. C. W. E. Bigsby (Deland, Fla: Everett/Edwards, 1969), p. 44.

13. Addison Gayle, Jr., *Black Expression: Essays by and about Black Americans in the Creative Arts* (New York: Weybright and Talley, 1969), p. 67.

14. W. Edward Farrison, "George Moses: Hope for Freedom," *CLA Journal,* 14, No. 3 (March, 1971), 236.

15. Horton, *Hope of Liberty,* p. 1.

16. The question of what is a "true" slave poem is obviously open to debate. I am thinking here of poetry written about the condition of slavery from the point of view of the slave.

17. Dr. William Carroll, of the Department of English, Norfolk State University, who is currently completing a book-length study of the life and poetry of George Moses Horton, maintains that the motif of flight persists in Horton's works, particularly in the sense of the flight of the imagination. Thus, *Hope of Liberty* initiated a theme which the poet was to expand and develop throughout his life. Dr. Carroll says, "The idea of flight—or soaring, as he frequently expresses it—is central to much, perhaps most, of Horton's poetry." Personal interview with Dr. William Carroll, March 29, 1978.

18. Eugene B. Redmond, *Drumvoices: The Mission of Afro-American Poetry* (Garden City: Doubleday, 1976), p. 61.

FURTHER READING

Biography

Sherman, Joan R. "Introduction" to *The Black Bard of North Carolina: George Moses Horton and His Poetry,* edited by Joan R. Sherman, pp. 1-44. Chapel Hill: University of North Carolina Press, 1997,

A lengthy biographical sketch on Horton and a summary of the criticism of his work.

Criticism

Brabham, Robin. "To the Tip-Top Belles' of Mecklenburg County: Two Acrostics by George Moses Horton." *CLA Journal* XXX, No. 4 (June 1987): 454-60.

Discusses two acrostics by Horton recovered from the Torrance and Banks family papers in North Carolina.

Brawley, Benjamin. "Three Negro Poets: Horton, Mrs. Harper, and Whitman." *The Journal of Negro History* 2, No. 4 (October 1917): 384-92.

Very brief review of the work of three black poets.

Jackson, Blyden. "George Moses Horton, North Carolinian." *The North Carolina Historical Review* LIII, No. 2 (April 1976): 140-47.

Brief biography of Horton with some critical commentary on his poetry.

Reeves, William J. "The Significance of Audience in Black Poetry." *Negro American Literature Forum* 9, No. 1 (Spring 1975): 30-32.

Uses three examples of black poetry—including "On Liberty and Slavery" by Horton—to consider what influence audience has in interpreting the poems.

M. A. Richmond. "The Slave and the Citadel," in *Bid the Vassal Soar: Interpretive Essays on the Life and Poetry of Phillis Wheatley (ca. 1753-1784) and George Moses Horton (ca. 1797-1883),* pp. 84–96. Washington D.C.:Howard University Press, 1974.

Details the beginnings of Horton's literary career and the influences on his work, drawing on Horton's autobiographical writings.

Walser, Richard. "Newly Discovered Acrostic by George Moses Horton." *CLA Journal* XIX, No. 2 (December 1975): 258-60.

Briefly discusses two poems by Horton found in family papers in North Carolina.

Additional coverage of George Moses Horton's life and career is contained in the following source published by the Gale Group: *Dictionary of Literary Biography,* **Vol. 50.**

John Keble
1792-1866

English poet, priest, critic, essayist, and biographer.

INTRODUCTION

Keble was a principal advocate of the Tractarian, or Oxford, Movement in England of the 1830s—the leaders of which argued that the Anglican Church was one of three valid branches of the Catholic Church, the other two being the Roman Catholic and Greek Orthodox. As a poet, Keble is regarded for *The Christian Year* (1827), a collection of Victorian devotional verse which proposes that God is revealed analogically through nature. The work is counted among the most popular poetic collections in English of the nineteenth century. A noted clergyman, Keble produced a number of sermons on politico-religious themes, and also wrote critical essays and literary theory, a biography, and several more collections of religious poetry, including *Lyra Innocentium* (1846). While a decline in esteem for Keble's verse has occurred since his death, he is generally regarded as an influential figure of nineteenth-century Anglicanism and an important devotional poet.

BIOGRAPHICAL INFORMATION

Keble was born near Fairford in Gloustershire, England. His father John Keble, Sr. was the vicar of Coln St. Aldwyn's, and had graduated from Corpus Christi, Oxford, a school both John and his younger brother Thomas attended. Following his distinguished years at Oxford, which brought him in contact with many of the leading intellectual figures of the England of his day, Keble was ordained a deacon in 1815, and a priest the following year. He embarked on the career of a clergyman by serving as a curate in Gloustershire, and later, following his mother's death in 1823, in Southrop. By this time Keble had begun to write the poems of *The Christian Year.* In 1825, Keble moved to Hampshire after accepting a position at Hursley. His first departure from Hursley was swift; in response to the death of his youngest sister he returned to Fairford, eventually taking his father's place as vicar of Coln St. Aldwyn. A year after his father had died in 1835, Keble renewed his vicarship at Hursley, where he would reside for the remainder of his life. In addition to his priestly vocation, Keble continued writing poetry and prose until his death on 29 March 1866 in Bournemouth.

MAJOR WORKS

The Christian Year, which features numerous structural parallels to the *Anglican Book of Common Prayer,* contains a verse for every Sunday and holy day of the year, and offers a Wordsworthian view of nature as a revelation of God. In *National Apostasy Considered in a Sermon* (1833), Keble reviled the British government for its encroachment on the decision-making power of the Church of England, specifically in regard to the distribution of bishoprics in Ireland. *Primitive Tradition Recognized in Holy Scripture* (1836) illustrates the essential conservatism of Keble's religious thought. Though somewhat labored and verbose, Keble's eight-volume biography of a seventeenth-century Anglican bishop, *The Life and Work of the Right Reverend Father in God, Thomas Wilson,* nevertheless exhibits Keble's devoutness and dedication to detail in ecclesiastical matters. Among the eight pieces Keble contributed to *Tracts for the Times,* a collection of essays elucidating the views associated with the Oxford Movement, "On the

Mysticism Attributed to the Early Church Fathers" (1841) reveals the Tractarian notion of Analogy—the belief that God is revealed in the Bible and in nature analogically. Keble's critical work is exemplified in his 1844 *De Poeticae vi Medica: Praelectiones Academicae (Lectures on Poetry)*. In this work, Keble lays out his aesthetic theory, which hinges on a religious interpretation of poetry as a spiritual catharsis necessary to calm the soul.

CRITICAL RECEPTION

While Keble's works of prose and priestly sermons brought him early notoriety, his first nationwide recognition came with the publication of his poetry, notably the verses of *The Christian Year,* which became enormously popular. Later esteem came with Keble's involvement in the Oxford Movement, anticipated by the poems of this collection and by his sermons. As Keble's contemporary and fellow Tractarian John Henry Newman claimed, the Tractarian Movement was inaugurated with the delivery of Keble's 1833 *Assize Sermon,* a piece later published as *National Apostasy Considered in a Sermon.* Modern critics have since frequently compared his sermons to those of Newman, whose ideas and expression are thought to compliment Keble's own. Overall, commentators generally perceive Keble's lasting contribution in terms of his prose writings on Tractarian aesthetics and influence as a seminal member of the Oxford Movement. He is additionally regarded for the devotional verse of *The Christian Year*—a work principally viewed as an enduring statement of Victorian piety.

PRINCIPAL WORKS

On Translation from Dead Languages: A Prize Essay (essay) 1812

The Christian Year: Thoughts in Verse for the Sundays and Holydays throughout the Year. 2 vols. (poetry) 1827

National Apostasy Considered in a Sermon (speech) 1833

*Tracts for the Times by Members of the University of Oxford. 6 vols. (essays) 1833-1841

Ode for the Encaenia at Oxford [published anonymously] (poetry) 1834

Lyra Apostolica [by Keble and others; published anonymously] (poetry) 1836

Primitive Tradition Recognized in Holy Scripture: A Sermon (speech) 1836

The Psalter, or Psalms of David in English Verse; by a Member of the University of Oxford [published anonymously] (poetry) 1839

The Case of Catholic Subscription to the Thirty-nine Articles Considered (essay) 1841

De Poeticae vi Medica: Praelectiones Academicae [Lectures on Poetry 1832-1841] (poetry) 1844

Lyra Innocentium: Thoughts in Verse on Christian Children, Their Ways, and Their Privileges [published anonymously] (poetry) 1846

Sermons, Academical and Occasional (speeches) 1847

On Eucharistical Adoration (speech) 1857

The Life of the Right Reverend Father in God, Thomas Wilson. 8 vols. (biography) 1863

Sermons, Occasional and Parochial (speeches) 1868

Village Sermons on the Baptismal Service (speeches) 1868

Miscellaneous Poems (poetry) 1869

Letters of Spiritual Counsel and Guidance (letters) 1870

Sermons for the Christian Year. 11 vols. (speeches) 1875-1880

Occasional Papers and Reviews (essays and criticism) 1877

Studia Sacra (essays) 1877

*Keble contributed eight of the ninety pieces to this publication.

CRITICISM

Sir J. T. Coleridge (essay date 1869)

SOURCE: *A Memoir of the Rev. John Keble, M. A., Late Vicar of Hursley,* James Parker and Co., 1869, 620 p.

[*In the following excerpt, Coleridge recounts the early publication history of Keble's* The Christian Year.]

Keble returned to a home sadly changed by the death of his sister. I do not think that in the course of his life he sustained any loss which he felt more acutely; beyond the privation to himself in the death of a sister so loved, a companion at once so bright and lively, so sensible and good, he could not but be affected by the blow to his father, and even more his invalid and suffering sister, now left alone. Dyson, who visited at Fairford more often than I did, and knew Mary Anne more familiarly, wrote to me at the time, and I transcribe a part of his letter, as in a few words he does her so much more justice than I have been able to do in many:—

> Oh, Coleridge, what a sad blow to her family, the loss of Mary Anne Keble; poor I must not call her after the common usage, since she has so infinitely the advantage of all left behind. John Keble sent me word of her loss soon after it happened, and gave, as far as could be given so early after the blow, a comfortable account of his father and sister; and to be sure, if the truest piety, and most practical submission can give any comfort under such a loss, they will have it, and I dare to say, will perhaps at first feel it less, than their immediate friends will for them. But when I think what a loveable being she was in herself, what an affectionate, gentle, guileless, and truly simple heart she had, and how little the cares and affection of the best and tenderest men can supply the unwearying, assiduous, self-denying, attachment of a daughter and sister, I must be ap-

prehensive of the effect upon her father and Elizabeth from such a loss, a loss to be perceived not in one stunning blow, and all is over, but to be felt daily and hourly; I hope, however, and I pray for the best for them.

This was written early in October, 1826. The letters which both Dyson and I received in the following months shew that any apprehension of permanent depression of spirits would have been groundless; all three of the survivors were strong in their common faith, and the picture which Keble draws of his aged father and sister, and unconsciously of himself, under this visitation is most cheering and instructive.

He says to Dyson early in November:—

Amongst all the friendly letters we received, your's seemed one of the most valuable, because you both of you understood dearest Mary Anne so well, and loved her so truly. Whenever we meet or hear from you, it will seem something of an approach to her, and do not fear but by the blessing of God our meetings may be cheerful and happy enough. I am sure you would think so, if you could see how *very* comfortable both my father and Elizabeth are, and how unaffectedly they enter into the spirit of everything that is going on around them. Indeed, I don't think you would see any difference in my father, and I am not sure that you would in Elizabeth.

It was an additional trial to the former during this winter, that his increasing weakness prevented him from discharging his duties at Coln personally, to which Keble alludes in writing to me on the 22nd of January, 1827:—

You would like to see my father, how very quietly he takes his suspension from clerical duties, which I used always to fear would be too sharp a trial for him whenever it took place. But it really does not seem to vex him at all. He stays at home, and is quite contented and cheerful, in the office, as he says, of Chaplain to Elizabeth. And Elizabeth's great delight is to do all the things that Mary Anne used to do, and fancy her only gone away for a short visit to a place where she is very happy, and soon to shew herself again; if one may call it fancy, which one verily believes to be the real truth.

He speaks of himself as—

. . . Having swung comfortably back to his old moorings, and certainly," says he, "it is more comfortable to have some one to say 'good bye' to every night, and not to have to eat and drink, and talk by oneself, only it remains to be proved whether one who has been usually very idle, when he had a good deal to do, will suddenly turn industrious, when his sphere of action is so much diminished. Certainly the days do not seem long, or irksome, but I am afraid that is a very equivocal sign of industry. . . .

But he was not idle; he was now supplying his father's place at Coln entirely, and as Coln was three miles off, it occupied more of his time than if he had been strictly resident. Moreover, that tax was now beginning to be imposed upon him, which in after life became very burthensome, the answering the letters of those who consulted him in their religious doubts and difficulties. This, it is well known, is the lot of many distinguished persons; but it is remarkable that it should have commenced with him at a time when he would have seemed to be so little known.

In the same letter, from which my last extract was made, he tells me that he had gone "through every word of an immense bundle of papers," the remains of a deceased convert from Quakerism, with a view to advising whether they should be published or not. He asks for information on the question whether the present Quakers maintained the opinions of George Fox and Co.; on which the answer in that case seemed to him to turn. Again, and about the same time, Cornish had consulted him on the conscientious difficulties of a young lady; and his answer is so sensible, that I cannot forbear transcribing it; many persons, I believe, are occasionally in the condition of the young lady; who may perhaps profit by the advice:—

I am clearly of opinion the young lady should discontinue these observances which seem to fret and distract her so much. It seems like Fasting, which no one is tied to, even by the laws of the Church, when it is *bonâ fide* against their health: much less by any rule they can set themselves. Clearly this is a case of melancholy from bodily constitution, and the person should be recommended to avoid all vows and singularities of every kind, as mere snares. I seem to be speaking so positively about what I must be ignorant of, that I am afraid my opinion is worth even less than usual: but supposing the representation in your friend's letter to be correct, and Jeremy Taylor right in his *Ductor Dubitantium,* touching the management of a scrupulous conscience, (p. 158 et seqq.,) I don't think I can be very wide of the mark; besides you have given me a pretty broad hint in what way you mean to proceed, and wish to be advised. At any rate a person of this temperament should be cautioned, as matter of *duty,* to refrain from binding herself by anything like voluntary vows in future; it is a mere snare, and should be repressed like any other temptation. If she cannot be quite satisfied, (as at times I suppose she will not,) with having broken through her own rule in this instance, why cannot she add one sentence to her morning or evening devotions, relating to this particular subject; this, if made habitual, would, as it seems to me, answer all purposes; but she must not be fanciful, and imagine one's prayers do no good if one is uncomfortable all the time. I am sure it would be bad enough with some of us, if we let present comfort come into our calculations on that matter.

"*Fairford, April* 28, 1827."

These are but instances; he was busy too in his theological reading, and acquiring that intimate knowledge of the Fathers, which had such a marked influence on his theological feeling, if I may use that term, and the habitual train of his thoughts on any religious question. He was examining too, with an interest awakened by the times, the foundation and the limits of the alliance of Church and State, specially of the right of the latter to interfere with the former in matters purely ecclesiastical. In the letter dated June 22, 1827, in which he mentions the publication of *The Christian Year,* he goes on to a consideration which seems to me very interesting, and which I know not whether any other writer has ever noticed or enlarged on. It was clearly an original thought to Keble:—

> "The speculation," says he, "I referred to in a former letter, and on which you desired more explanation, was this. It seems clear to me, on reading over the Old Testament, that the example of the Jews *as a nation,* is there held out in such a way as to regulate and correct the religious conduct of us Christians *as individuals.* The covenant with them collectively was a type of that made with us separately; and the faults into which they fell analogous to what may be expected, and to what we really experience, in our own private dealings with the Almighty; this, I suppose, is what makes the Old Testament, as a whole, so useful to be considered by every Christian; and in this I persuade myself that I see a strong auxiliary evidence of the truth of both dispensations, as well as divers other useful corollaries, if I could but develope them; but it will take a great deal of reading, thinking, and writing, to make out the matter properly and usefully, and I have only, as it were, begun to think about it. I mention it to you, that you may tell me if it seems absurd at first sight, or sufficiently done already. I should like, if I could, to turn my hours to some account; but long habits of idleness are not got over in a moment. I have been to Oxford once or twice lately, and it makes one quite fidgetty to see what a bustle and business every one is always in. I had half a mind to go to Bishop Lloyd and ask him to set me some task."

He had a great regard and respect for that good, and able, and original man, and he thought his services as Divinity Professor, especially the private Lectures which he instituted, extremely valuable. The Bishop also was very fond of him.

Although Keble speaks of his idleness, which indeed he was fond of doing, the preceding months of the year had brought about the completion, and finished the printing of *The Christian Year.* Pursuing my plan of giving all details which seem to me at all interesting in respect of this great work, I must go back a little in my narrative and my extracts from his letters. In the beginning of February he acknowledges to me the return of some part of the manuscript which had been under my hands; he does this with his usual overflowing kindness, and I could hardly transcribe the passage, if I had not to qualify it by adding, that I believe after all he rejected, and with good reason, a very large proportion of my suggestions. The passage, moreover, adds a fact worth preserving as to the adviser to whom we owe the beautiful Verses on the *Occasional Services,* which, curiously enough, seem not to have formed part of his original plan:—

> Now I must thank you with all my might for the very kind trouble you have taken about my concerns; you have set to work like a true friend, and I shall always love you the better for it, only I am afraid you have been taking a good deal more trouble than the affair was worth. I have set myself at work rather hardish to revise the MS., and have made a good many corrections, one or two I hope to re-write entirely; and I also want to add something on each of the *Occasional Services,* in pursuance of a hint I had from Davison. I have done a few stanzas for the Communion, and if I have a good spring-flow of rhyme, I hope to be ready with the others, as far as the Commination, in a month or six weeks, and then I purpose to go up to Oxford, and print without delay. I had wished to put it off for a year for the sake of the vignettes, but my father seems really anxious to have it done without loss of time, and I think one should be uncomfortable, if one did not try one's best to meet his wishes; at the same time, I am quite aware of the defects you mention, and will do my best to mend them. I shall, however, be the more easy in not sending the rest of the MS. to you, as most of the passages you have marked were places which I was before dissatisfied with, and wished to alter; in some few you have not caught my meaning, as I believe, through hurry, and in some I differ in grammar or taste; but on the whole, I am exactly of your mind, and I hope to be a tolerable substitute for you in the office of criticising the rest. My theological plans, about which you enquire, are hardly plans enough to be stated on paper; they are mere schemes floating loosely in my head. But when I have done this job, and read one or two more of the Father, I hope to tell myself something more clearly about it. Farewell, my most dear friend.
>
> *"Fairford, Feby 9, 1827."*

The natural wish of his aged father to see the work published before he died, made it now to him an imperative duty to delay no longer; from this time he neither hesitated nor flagged in the prosecution of the work. His mention of vignettes had reference to a scheme, which he rather favoured at this time, of illustrating the book, with the help of some accomplished lady friends. Several vignettes, as he calls them, were indeed drawn; but he abandoned this idea, which Cornish dissuaded him from; and thenceforward he always opposed anything of the kind, though it was more than once pressed on him. I rather think he did not abide by the prudent resolution he announces of sending no more of the MS. to me for my criticism, for I possess a later and detailed acknowledgment, in which I was more surprised than pleased, to find that I had actually recommended the suppression entirely of the verses on the Tenth Sunday after Trinity. He meets this very simply with the remark, that it was a special favourite with some others of his critics.

On the 22nd of June, 1827, he announced to me that my copy of *The Christian Year* was on the road from Oxford, and on the next day I received it. His announcement was short and simple, and without comment, and then he passed on, as he said, "to more interesting affairs." I am certain that he had not the slightest idea at the time how important was the gift he had made to the world, nor how decisive a step he had taken in respect of his own character and reputation. We who had watched the work from the beginning were somewhat more enlightened, perhaps; but we had not, I think, fully comprehended the importance of the volume; we had, indeed, a very high opinion of it; we thought it would gradually win its way, and would exercise a great influence on its readers, but we were none of us prepared for its immediate success, still less for such a success as befel it. I have lying before me Mr. J. H. Parker's summary of the account from the beginning to January, 1854; in this period of less than twenty-six years I find 108,000 copies were issued in forty-three editions. The sale of the work never flagged through the remainder of his life; and in the Memoir of Mr. Moor, to which I have so often referred, a statement is made (especially remarkable considering a circumstance to which I must advert presently), that in the nine months immediately following his death seven editions were issued of 11,000 copies.

After what I have said above of my critical success in regard to this work in the prime of my life, I should be very unwise if in advanced old age I were to venture on an elaborate criticism of it here. Indeed, it seems to me hardly the fit subject for mere literary criticism as a volume of poetry. Whatever can be desired of that kind, however, has been admirably done already by Professor Shairp, of St. Andrews, in an "Essay on the Author of the Christian Year," published at Edinburgh in 1866, and those of my readers who shall be induced by this notice to read that masterly little book, will thank me, I am sure, for having referred them to it.

Yet the publication of **The Christian Year** was such an event in Keble's life, and the work itself so interesting and important, that I venture to set down, not with any system or order, what are rather my personal experiences in the reading it, than anything like regular criticism upon it. This may, perhaps, be the way in which my remarks may be most useful, especially to young persons. I will say, then, that it is one of those volumes of poetry which no one should take up to read through at once, or as a continued study; few volumes even of miscellaneous poetry will bear this; but the very design of **The Christian Year** protests against it; it was meant, and should be taken, as an accompaniment to the services of the Prayer-book. It will be found to have a special significance, if read as such; and for this mode of study and meditation, it is particularly fitted by two among other qualities. The first that it is so wonderfully Scriptural. Keble's mind was by long, and patient, and affectionate study of Scripture, so

imbued with it, that its language, its train of thought, its mode of reasoning, seem to flow out into his poetry, almost, one should think, unconsciously to himself. They are always there, yet never intruded. Many times, I may say for myself, the meaning of what had been an obscure passage in Holy Writ, or the true character and teaching of an incident, has flashed on me in reading the verses, of which it has been made the text for the day's meditation. I have heard of a clergyman in a rural parish in Worcestershire who was in the habit of reading, and explaining from the pulpit, in lieu of an afternoon sermon, the poem for the Sunday; and I have no doubt such a practice, with proper comments, might be pursued with very good effect. It has often struck me, what an excellent skeleton of a sermon this or that poem suggests. The second quality I would notice, is its almost inexhaustible novelty; whether this be owing to the depth of the thought, the pregnancy of the language, or, as severer critics have said, to the imperfect expression of the thought, or to all combined, I will not undertake to decide; but speaking generally, I should say, read it as often as you will, you will find it on each perusal to contain or to suggest some new matter for reflection. Take it up when you will, you are never likely to skim through a poem, as one sometimes does with what is familiar, however one may admire it; some thought seemingly new will arrest your attention, make you pause, and set you upon consideration. This is surely a great merit in a volume of poems intended to serve in the way of a manual.

I would further suggest to a new reader of the book, to remark on the vivid accuracy of Keble's descriptions of natural incidents or objects. I think Dr. Stanley has somewhere observed on this merit in Keble's poetry in regard to what he had never seen, the scenery of the East, and specially of the Holy Land; but we may all of us judge of it generally in regard to our own country. He was short-sighted, and though he was fond of simple music, he had not a keen or accurate ear for it. He complains in a well-known passage of the dulness of his hearing to apprehend the full beauty of harmonious sounds; yet whether as to objects of sight or sound, his numberless descriptions are accurate, not only in the general, but in the slightest and most delicate features: he seems to have observed them all, as true poets are sure to do, with a lover-like, and yet a discriminating interest; and his language is never more definite and distinct than in these passages. It is hard to forbear, but I must not indulge myself in citations. There is still another circumstance, which I have always been struck with, the happiness with which he spiritualizes all that he describes of natural scenery, and how constantly he deals with it in this way; one stanza I cite, not so much as an instance, but as illustrating my meaning:—

> He whose heart will bound to mark
>   The full bright burst of summer morn,

Loves too each little dewy spark
    By leaf or flow'ret worn:
Cheap forms, and common hues, 'tis true,
Through the bright shower-drop meet his view;
The colouring may be of this earth;
The lustre comes of heavenly birth.

"Second Sunday after Trinity."

I am not now unfolding the beauties, or passing judgment on the faults, of this wonderful book; its great, and rapid, and not less its enduring success, it is not at first sight easy to account for; it certainly cannot be ascribed to its addressing especially any one party in the Church; although the opinions of the author, whoever he might be, were declared throughout with sufficient distinctness, yet the book found favour equally with all; it did not rest in the beginning on the great name of its author; for some time its author was not known, and had it been, he had earned no reputation in the world at large which could have procured him such a host of readers. When it ceased to be anonymous in substance, party heat in the Church, and the very distinction he had earned, might, one would have thought, have diminished its general acceptance. I have no reason to believe that it has, even to the present time.

It is natural to ask to what cause especially is this exceptional success to be attributed, and will it still continue? I trust that an affirmative answer to the latter question may be given, founded on what I believe to be the true answer to the first. Of course the general success must be in a great measure attributed to the general merits of the execution; without the intrinsic beauty of the poetry, no success, or a very incomplete one, could have been obtained by the greatest excellence in the design; and, again, but for this last, the mere beauty of the poetry would, I think, after a while, have only placed the book on the library shelf with other volumes of beautiful poems in the language, a classic acknowledged and little read, exercising no daily and permanent influence. Now, as we know, a library book, or a book of the house, is just what it is not; it is rather a book of each person, and each room in the house. The design of it is very simply stated in the Preface. Keble wished to help towards the establishment of "a sober standard of feeling in matters of practical religion," and this by a work in close harmony with, and constant reference to, our Liturgy. In his title-page his motto is, "In quietness and in confidence shall be your strength." But this object, and this mode of obtaining it, both imply an appeal to a feeling, I believe, the most common and abiding in the heart of man, wherever absorbing worldliness or inveterate habits of vice have not overpowered it; I mean the religious and devotional sentiment. This may seem too flattering an estimate of the human heart, but it must be remembered, I do not speak of practice; I do not speak even of sentiment, that necessarily

results in a good life; but of sentiment and feeling merely. So limited, I believe the proposition to be true. How much of the pleasure we all take in works of fiction is owing to the existence of this feeling in our hearts. Those who shrink from the trials which religion may impose, and those who feel willing to undergo them, equally find their hearts excited by the lively picture of suffering, or triumphant virtue, though with regard to the former some bitterness may mingle with the sweet; and these two classes make up the bulk of those who read. On the other hand, speaking generally, how cold are we in comparison to the story which tells us of the labours of intellect, the perseverance or ingenuity of the discoverer, the intrigues of the politician. And is not this because the former takes us more out of what is purely selfish, and brings us more close to what is religious in our nature? Now to this feeling in the human heart *The Christian Year* makes unceasing appeal, with a voice so earnest, so manifestly sincere, so sad in its hopefulness, so unpretending as to the speaker, yet so authoritative and confident as to the cause and the subject, that for the time it is commonly irresistible; and to be so moved, as it is among the purest, so unquestionably it is among the highest of the pleasures which we are capable of enjoying.

This is an argument which I know must depend for its acceptance mainly on the inward consciousness and feelings of those to whom it may be addressed. And therefore I would ask any reader gifted with an ordinary degree of poetical feeling, what has been the effect of reading the verses for the day in *The Christian Year* under favourable circumstances of quiet and leisure? I apprehend that although immediately on the perusal, the thoughts which it occasions will vary much with the past conduct of the individual, in the end he will find he has passed very much into that state of feeling in regard to himself, which his conscience approves, and towards his fellow-creatures and his Maker that in which he would desire to be; he will feel soberly hopeful as to himself; loving, grateful, and reverential towards his Maker. And is not this the greatest happiness we can expect in this life. On these grounds I explain the Volume's exceptional and continued success, and I hope with great confidence for its indefinite enduring. It would lead me too far afield, if I compared its prospects on these grounds with Herbert's poems, which, however justly admired, and still studied by some, have certainly lost much of their general popularity. In truth the two men were more alike than their works, and what I have said may be true of *The Christian Year,* and yet could not be truly said of "The Church."

Keble would not have assented to these conclusions: as Wilkes is reported to have said he was no Wilkite, so Keble certainly was not a "Christian Year" man. Of course I do not suppose that he could think, or would profess, that it had no merits; like other modest men in regard to their own compositions, he thought these over-rated; and his taste and judgment made him very conscious of its faults in execution and finish; but this does not adequately explain the position of his mind with regard to it; it is strange, but it is certain that he always spoke of it, and that was seldom, with something of sadness and dissatisfaction. I do not think he often read it. There were reasons for this deeper than causes merely critical, and they are worth considering; the poems unavoidably paint Keble's own heart; they flowed out from it upon subjects which lay deepest and nearest to it, and no one can read them without believing all things good of the author. Keble felt this; he knew what the picture displayed; he knew it would be taken for a faithful likeness; he did not indeed fear the charge of self-display, but he thought the picture not true; he asked himself, was he then right in exhibiting it? and the good opinion of the world, on which he knew a woe had been pronounced, was to him with this impression a cause of real sorrow. In his poem on the **"Danger of Praise,"** in the *Lyra Innocentium,* he says:—

> And ah! to him what tenfold woe,
>   Who hides so well his sin,
> Through earth he seems a saint to go,
>   Yet dies impure within.

I have no doubt he had reference here to himself. Praise was at all times really painful to him. In writing to him on his mother's death I had used language, the particulars of which I do not recollect—but I spoke of him and his discharge of filial duties as I sincerely felt. Dyson, it appears, and some others in their letters of consolation, had written in the same strain—in his answer to me, he says:—

> I am afraid I shall be able only to send you an unsatisfactory hurried sort of letter, but I would rather do so, than let time run on, as I have done so often before, without thanking you as I do from my heart for your kind consoling letter; kind in all respects except some partial expressions, such as I would beg it of you as a kindness to forbear; they please me so well at first, that I am quite sure they are best not thrown in my way; and when I come to look at them or think of them afterwards, they seem, as it were, to spoil the rest of the letter: *if you please, therefore,* do not send me any more of them.

To Dyson he says—

> Your kind letter came to me at Oxford at a moment when I needed it, and proved, I assure you, a real comfort to me; indeed, I fear I was more delighted than I ought, both with your letter and 2 or 3 others which I received at the same time; for it is humiliating to see, on reading them over, how much undeserved credit one's friends give one. But this will not bear talking about.

It was the one subject on which ever after I was obliged in writing to him to be very guarded in my language, even when I wrote on occasions which had excited my feelings of admiration strongly; for though he could not write otherwise than gently and affectionately, I felt sure I had given him pain.

I have already printed an extract from his letter to Mr. Pruen respecting the Dedication. That is now very properly printed, I believe, in the Editions which have issued since his death, but he never would print it during his life. I remember when, in 1858, he allowed Mr. Parker to publish a handsome Edition in small folio, I suggested, or, rather, asked his permission for the printing it; he would not absolutely deny me, but he yielded in language manifesting so clearly his unwillingness, that it would have been unkind to act on it, and I forbore.

In all this he was perfectly sincere, nor can I think his feeling morbid, or unreasonable, though it may have been, indeed was in my judgment, exaggerated. The more pure and holy a man is, the more odious will sin be to him; and beside this, the more entirely will he refer every successful resistance to temptation, every good thought, all continuance in purity to the special favour of God, and feel that it calls on him for a more lively gratitude than common; so that every declension, through human infirmity unavoidable, will come to his conscience embittered with the sense of special ingratitude; sin in one who feels himself so favoured will seem double sin. This, I think, is the explanation of the declaration of St. Paul respecting himself, which I have always looked on as perfectly sincere. I am not comparing Keble, of course, with the great Apostle, but the same principle of judgment applies to both, indeed, to all good men; and when they say such things of themselves, though we may think them too severe in their judgments, we should acquit them of insincerity, and the miserable weakness of seeking for compliments.

Keble always published *The Christian Year* anonymously: at first the secret of authorship was tolerably well kept, but it was a prisoner committed to the custody of too many not to escape soon; however he availed himself always of the masque as he pleased, and sometimes he played with it amusingly enough. Not long after the publication, an old pupil, Mr. Bliss, in writing to him, mentioned the work, with some speculation as to the author; it might be, intending only to sound him; he answers, however:—

> I have seen the little book you mention, and I think I have heard it was written by an Oriel man. I have no wish to detract from its merit, but I can't say I am much in expectation of its cutting out our friend George Herbert.

I add, mainly for another reason, two notes written to a dignitary of the Church long after, who had questioned him as to the use of the word "wildering" in the verses on the Fifth Sunday in Lent:—

Ye, too, who tend Christ's *wildering* flock.

He says in answer:—

"My Dear——,

"It is very little use being anonymous, if one is to answer for the sense, or nonsense of all one writes just the same.

"But do you not think that such a passage as Ezekiel xxxiv. 12, in the Bible, and the mention of 'Christ's sheep that are scattered abroad' in the Ordination Service, joined with the present state of Christendom, is enough to justify and explain the word?

"You know the 'C. Y.' (as far as I remember it) every where supposes the Church to be in a state of decay.

  "Ever my dear friend,
  "affect^ly yours,
  "J. Keble."

To this there was a reply which I have not seen, and to that this rejoinder:—

"Brooking near Totness,

"*April* 15, 1858.

"My Dear——,

"As a proof that my conscience is not quite gone, I had really put your letter up to be answered among others when I left home for this place, and I now return its in-closures with many thanks. It is very pleasant to find so much sympathy with one's own travelling thoughts, such as they were in times past, or rather such as one wished them to be.

"With respect to the word which gave occasion to our little correspondence, I find that according to Johnson there is or was such word as 'wildering' or 'to wilder'—only unluckily for me it is a verb active—the same as to 'bewilder.' So it must be considered an er-ror, and 'wandering' or some such word must be kindly substituted for it. I find it unluckily in the Oxford 'Psalter' also.

  "I am always,
  "My dear——,
  "Affect^ly your's,
  "J. Keble."

It occurs in other parts of the book.

In spite of his concluding sentence it will be found, I believe, that the word "wildering" remained in all the edi-tions published in his lifetime, and the line remains unaltered still. It happened to me more than once to point out some inaccuracy of language, or metre, admitting eas-ily of correction; he used to answer not unkindly, but coldly, and intimated in effect that it was not worth while to alter it. This was the result, in great measure, of the feeling which he had grown to entertain towards the book, as well as of his constant occupation and the habit of

procrastination, which, of course, did not decrease with years. He seemed to me not unconscious of the merits of the book, or of its probable usefulness; but as if he half wished to disconnect himself from it, and as if he would rather it had been the work of some one else than himself. I have accounted for this, which seems so strange, as well as I can.

In the first two editions, there were no verses on what are called the State Services; he did not regard them as an integral part of the Common Prayer-book, and I cannot now recall why he was induced to write upon them. In the verses on the "Gunpowder Treason" he wrote a stanza, which on the first reading might certainly lead one to sup-pose that he denied the Presence of our Lord's Body in the Elements after consecration. Nobody, however, who knew his opinions on this subject, (and they were expressed openly again and again in public, and in private, and in print, with earnestness and uniformity,) could believe that he intended to be so understood; and when challenged on the subject, he always maintained that his language was misunderstood, and that any writer whose sentiments were unquestionably known should in justice have his language interpreted according to those senti-ments, where the meaning was not necessarily opposed to them. He pointed out that the omission of the word "only" after the expression "not in the hands," raised the whole difficulty, and for that short way of speaking he referred to passages in Scripture, which are numerous, as authority. The matter was mentioned to him several times, but he declined to make any alteration. Some weeks before his death, however, a member of the Upper House of Convo-cation, addressing it, quoted the lines with approbation in the sense most commonly attributed to them; this he thought entirely altered the case, and ought to prevent him from any longer overlooking or acquiescing in the misinterpretation, and he determined therefore to accept an alteration which had been before suggested by a friend; he at once directed that when a new edition should be called for, this should be substituted for the old reading, with a note, the substance of which he dictated. At the time he did this, there was no illness upon him which apparently threatened his life; a fortnight later, in a note to me about Mrs. Keble's state, he says, "As for myself, I eat, drink, and sleep heartily, so you need be in no care about me so far." His anxiety was entirely about her, and both contemplated that he would be the survivor. It pleased God that he should die first. She to whom he bequeathed the copyright, naturally felt bound by the injunction; and when she bequeathed the copyright to her nephew, she imposed it on him,—this direction he of course obeyed.

It cannot be doubted, on these facts, that the alteration was Keble's own as much as if he had written it himself years before, and that neither Mrs. Keble, or her nephew, could properly exercise any discretion in the matter. It would have seemed a matter of course for the latter to make it; and indeed, when thus explained, to be of little importance in itself. Keble's belief, it must be remembered, had been long and generally known; no one could have cited him as an authority for the doctrine which the words were supposed to convey; and it is difficult to understand how any one, knowing his belief, could desire to circulate as his any verses, with the intention thereby of conveying something entirely contrary to it, and acquiring thereby his authority for that which he neither thought nor believed. I must not be understood as making any insinuation of this kind in regard to the Right Reverend Bishop, who, citing the verse to grace the peroration of a speech, certainly was, in fact, the immediate occasion of the alteration. Nor, indeed, do I make any imputation against any individual, or any Body; what was said and done in consequence—though I cannot approve it—was, I doubt not, done upon grounds which seemed justifiable to the doers.

To one who is familiar with Keble's diction in *The Christian Year,* there is no difficulty in understanding how an ambiguity of expression might occur; and to one who knew him long and well, there is equally no difficulty in understanding either why the alteration was not made before, or why it was directed to be made at the time it was made. I do not think it was a happy one; but that the direction was given under improper pressure at a time when his judgment was obscured, or his power of maintaining his own opinion enfeebled (and both have been insinuated,) I am concerned strongly to deny; and those who impute that, I hope have not considered how grave an imputation they cast on his widow and her nephew, who must have known if such had taken place. But there is the most abundant evidence that this subject was perfectly familiar to Keble, and had been on his mind for years. By the kindness of a neighbouring clergyman, the Rev. Samuel Walker, who had written to him in February, 1863, I am able to print the material part of a letter, which sets this at rest:—

> "My dear Sir,

> "I am obliged by your kind suggestion regarding the passage in the 'Christian Year.' For many years it has been a matter which I have thought of at odd times, and you will find in my dear friend Hurrell Froude's 'Remains' that complaints were made of it near thirty years ago. I thought of an alteration, but other friends over-ruled it. Nor am I at present disposed to make any. Your's, I fear, would hardly come up to what is wanted in the way of doctrine. In a Note to the Preface of the Second Edition of a book of mine, which nobody reads, on 'Eucharistical Adoration,' I have given my own commentary on it: that it is to be understood, "Not in the hands *only,*" as against a carnal presence—vide S. John vi. 63; and the same idiom recurs elsewhere.

> "I have been shewn a passage in St. Bernard, but cannot now recall it, which seemed to me to justify the expression.

> "Do you not think that if it *can* be justified, it had best be retained, were it only to help in shewing, that such sayings do not necessarily bear such a meaning, and must be interpreted consistently with the writer's sentiments known unquestionably in other ways?"

Thus he wrote more than three years before his death, and thus he could not have written, had he intended to teach what those, who quarrelled with the alteration, desired he should be understood to have taught.

There is a story recorded by Isaac Walton, regarding George Herbert's "Temple," which is very apposite, and I will close what I have felt compelled to say on this painful matter, with repeating it. It is well known that in his last illness George Herbert committed the manuscript to the care of his friend Nicholas Ferrar, desiring him to publish it or burn it, according as he should think "it might turn to the advantage of any dejected poor soul," or not.

Mr. Ferrar, it is said, found that "there was in it the picture of a divine soul in every page, and that the whole book was such a harmony of holy passions, as would enrich the world with pleasure and piety:" he proceeded accordingly to publish.

"And this," says Walton, "ought to be noted, that when Mr. Ferrar sent this book to Cambridge to be licensed for the press, the Vice-Chancellor would by no means allow of the two so much noted verses—

> Religion stands a tip-toe in our land,
> Ready to pass to the American strand,

to be printed.

No doubt the Vice-Chancellor thought them untrue in fact, and likely to be injurious to the Church; which at that time many might see reason for believing. Nicholas Ferrar, however, felt that he had no power to enter into such considerations, and the controversy finally ended thus: "The Vice-Chancellor said, I knew Mr. Herbert well, and know that he had many heavenly speculations, and was a divine poet; but I hope the world will not take him to be an inspired prophet, and *therefore* I license the *whole* book."

Nicholas Ferrar discharged a plain duty conscientiously, and the Vice-Chancellor acted with great good sense.

J. C. Shairp (essay date 1872)

SOURCE: "Keble," in *Studies in Poetry and Philosophy,* Hurd and Houghton, 1872, pp. 204–68.

[*In the following essay, Shairp provides a summary of Keble's participation in the Oxford Movement and a critical analysis of* The Christian Year.]

The closing chapter of Lockhart's "Life of Scott" begins with these words: "We read in Solomon, 'The heart knoweth his own bitterness, and a stranger doth not intermeddle with his joy;' and a wise poet of our own time thus beautifully expands the saying—

> "'Why should we faint and fear to live alone,
>   Since all alone, so Heaven has willed, we die,
> Nor even the tenderest heart, and next our own,
>   Knows half the reasons why we smile or sigh?'"

On glancing to the footnote to see who the wise poet of our own time might be, the reader saw, for the first might be, the reader saw, for the first time perhaps, the name of KEBLE and **"The Christian Year."** To many, in Scotland at least, this was the earliest announcement of the existence of the poet, and the work which has immortalized him. If some friend soon afterwards happened to bring from England a copy of **"The Christian Year,"** and make a present of it, the young reader could not but be struck by a lyric here and there, which opened a new vein, and struck a note of meditative feeling, not exactly like anything he had heard before. But the little book contained much that was strange and unintelligible, some things even startling. Very vague were the rumors which at that time reached Scotland of the author. Men said he belonged to a party of Churchmen who were making a great stir in Oxford, and leavening the University with a kind of thought which was novel, and supposed to be dangerous. The most definite thing said was that the new school had a general Romanizing tendency. But this must be a mistake or strange exaggeration. Folly and sentimentalism might no doubt go far enough at Oxford. But as for Romanism, the revival of such antiquated nonsense was simply impossible in this enlightened nineteenth century. If such an absurdity were to show itself openly, was there not still extant the "Edinburgh Review" ready to crush it? To many a like folly ere now it had administered the quietus. Would it not deal as summarily with this one too? Such was the kind of talk that was heard when Scott's "Life" appeared in 1838. For more exact information, young men who were inquisitive had to wait, till a few years later gave them opportunities of seeing for themselves, and coming up into personal contact with what was actually going on in Oxford.

It was a strange experience for a young man trained anywhere, much more for one born and bred in Scotland, and brought up a Presbyterian, to enter Oxford when the religious movement was at its height. He found himself all at once in the midst of a system of teaching which unchurched himself and all whom he had hitherto known. In his simplicity he had believed that spiritual religion was a thing of the heart, and that neither Episcopacy nor Presbytery availeth anything. But here were men—able, learned, devout-minded men—maintaining that outward rites and ceremonies were of the very essence, and that where these were not, there was no true Christianity. How could men, such as these were reported to be, really go back themselves and try to lead others back to what were but the beggarly elements? It was all very perplexing, not to say irritating. However, there might be something more behind, which a young man could not understand. So he would wait and see what he should see.

Soon he came to know that the only portions of Oxford society unaffected by the new influence, were the two extremes. The older dons, that is, the heads of houses and the senior tutors, were unmoved by it, except to opposition. The whole younger half of the undergraduates generally took no part in it. But the great body that lay between these extremes, that is, most of the younger fellows of colleges, and most of the scholars and elder undergraduates, at least those of them who read or thought at all, were in some way or other busy with the new questions. When in time the new comer began to know some of the men who sympathized with the movement, his first impression was of something constrained and reserved in their manners and deportment. High character and ability many of them were said to have; but to a chance observer it seemed that, in as far as their system had moulded them, it had made them the opposite of natural in their views of things, and in their whole mental attitude. You longed for some free breath of mountain air to sweep away the stifling atmosphere that was about you. This might come partly, no doubt, from the feeling with which you knew that these men must from their system regard you, and all who had the misfortune to be born outside of their sacred pale. Not that they ever expressed such views in your hearing. Good manners, as well as their habitual reserve, forbade this. But, though they did not say it, you knew quite well that they felt it. And if at any time the "young barbarian" put a direct question, or made a remark which went straight at these opinions, they would only look at him, astonished at his rudeness and profanity, and shrink into themselves.

Now and then, however, it would happen that some adherent, or even leading man of the movement, more frank and outspoken than the rest, would deign to speak out his principles, and even to discuss them with undergraduates and controversial Scots. To him urging the necessity of Apostolical Succession, and the sacerdotal view of the Sacraments, some young man might venture to reply, "Well! If all you say be true, then I never can have known a Christian. For up to this time I have lived among people who were strangers to all these things, which, you tell me, are essentials of Christianity. And I am quite sure that, if I have never known a Christian till now, I shall never know one." The answer to this would probably be, "There is much in what you say. No doubt high virtues, very like the Christian graces, are to be found outside of the Christian Church. But it is a remarkable thing, those best acquainted with Church history tell me, that outside of the pale of the Church the saintly character is never found." This *naïf* reply was not likely to have much weight with the young listener. It would have taken something stronger to make him break faith with all that was most sacred in his early recollections. Beautiful examples of Presbyterian piety had stamped impressions on his memory not to be effaced by sacerdotal theories or subtleties of the schools. And the Church system which began by disowning these examples placed a barrier to its acceptance at the very outset.

But however unbelievable their theory, further acquaintance with the younger men of the new school, whether junior fellows or undergraduate scholars, disclosed many traits of character that could not but awaken respect or something more. If there was about many of them a constraint and reserve which seemed unnatural, there was also in many an unworldliness and self-denial, a purity of life and elevation of aim, in some a generosity of purpose and depth of devotion, not to be gainsaid. Could the movement which produced these qualities, or even attracted them to itself, be wholly false and bad? This movement, moreover, when at its height, extended its influence far beyond the circle of those who directly adopted its views. There was not, in Oxford at least, a reading man who was not more or less indirectly influenced by it. Only the very idle or the very frivolous were wholly proof against it. On all others it impressed a sobriety of conduct and a seriousness not usually found among large bodies of young men. It raised the tone of average morality in Oxford to a level which perhaps it had never before reached. You may call it over-wrought and too highly strung. Perhaps it was. It was better, however, for young men to be so, than to be doubters or cynics.

If such was the general aspect of Oxford society at that time, where was the centre and soul from which so mighty a power emanated? It lay, and had for some years lain, mainly in one man—a man in many ways the most remarkable that England has seen during this century, perhaps the most remarkable whom the English Church has produced in any century,—John Henry Newman.

The influence he had gained, apparently without setting himself to seek it, was something altogether unlike anything else in our time. A mysterious veneration had by degrees gathered round him, till now it was almost as though some Ambrose or Augustine of elder ages had reappeared. He himself tells how one day, when he was an undergraduate, a friend with whom he was walking in the Oxford street cried out eagerly, "There's Keble!" and with what awe he looked at him! A few years, and the same took place with regard to himself. In Oriel Lane light-hearted undergraduates would drop their voices and

whisper, "There's Newman!" when, head thrust forward, and gaze fixed as though on some vision seen only by himself, with swift, noiseless step he glided by. Awe fell on them for a moment, almost as if it had been some apparition that had passed. For his inner circle of friends, many of them younger men, he was said to have a quite romantic affection, which they returned with the most ardent devotion and the intensest faith in him. But to the outer world he was a mystery. What were the qualities that inspired these feelings? There was of course learning and refinement, there was genius, not indeed of a philosopher, but of a subtle and original thinker, an unequaled edge of dialectic, and these all glorified by the imagination of a poet. Then there was the utter unworldliness, the setting at naught of all things which men most prize, the tamelessness of soul, which was ready to essay the impossible. Men felt that here was—

> "One of that small transfigured band
> Which the world cannot tame."

It was this mysteriousness which, beyond all his gifts of head and heart, so strangely fascinated and overawed,—that something about him which made it impossible to reckon his course and take his bearings, that soul-hunger and quenchless yearning which nothing short of the eternal could satisfy. This deep and resolute ardor, this tenderness yet severity of soul, were no doubt an offense not to be forgiven by older men, especially by the wary and wordly-wise; but in these lay the very spell which drew to him the hearts of all the younger and the more enthusiastic. Such was the impression he had made in Oxford just before he relinquished his hold on it. And if at that time it seemed to persons at a distance extravagant and absurd, they may since have learnt that there was in him who was the object of this reverence enough to justify it.

But it may be asked, What actions or definite results were there to account for so deep and wide-spread a veneration? There were no doubt the numerous products of his prolific pen, his works, controversial, theological, religious. But none of these were so deep in learning as some of Dr. Pusey's writings, nor so widely popular as **"The Christian Year;"** and yet both Dr. Pusey and Mr. Keble were at that time quite second in importance to Mr. Newman. The centre from which his power went forth was the pulpit of St. Mary's, with those wonderful afternoon sermons. Sunday after Sunday, month by month, year by year, they went on, each continuing and deepening the impression the last had made. As the afternoon service at St. Mary's interfered with the dinner-hour of the colleges, most men preferred a warm dinner without Newman's sermon to a cold one with it, so the audience was not crowded—the large church little more than half filled. The service was very simple,—no pomp, no ritualism; for it was characteristic of the leading men of the movement that they left these things to the weaker brethren. Their thoughts, at all events, were set on great questions which touched the heart of unseen things. About the service, the most remarkable thing was the beauty, the silver intonation, of Mr. Newman's voice, as he read the Lessons. It seemed to bring new meaning out of the familiar words. Still lingers in memory the tone with which he read, "But Jerusalem which is above is free, which is the mother of us all." When he began to preach, a stranger was not likely to be much struck, especially if he had been accustomed to pulpit oratory of the Boanerges sort. Here was no vehemence, no declamation, no show of elaborated argument, so that one who came prepared to hear a "great intellectual effort" was almost sure to go away disappointed. Indeed, I believe that if he had preached one of his St. Mary's sermons before a Scotch town congregation, they would have thought the preacher a "silly body." The delivery had a peculiarity which it took a new hearer some time to get over. Each separate sentence, or at least each short paragraph, was spoken rapidly, but with great clearness of intonation; and then at its close there was a pause, lasting for nearly half a minute; then another rapidly but clearly spoken sentence, followed by another pause. It took some time to get over this, but, that once done, the wonderful charm began to dawn on you. The look and bearing of the preacher were as of one who dwelt apart, who, though he knew his age well, did not live in it. From his seclusion of study, and abstinence, and prayer, from habitual dwelling in the unseen, he seemed to come forth that one day of the week to speak to others of the things he had seen and known. Those who never heard him might fancy that his sermons would generally be about apostolical succession or rights of the Church, or against Dissenters. Nothing of the kind. You might hear him preach for weeks without an allusion to these things. What there was of High Church teaching was implied rather than enforced. The local, the temporary, and the modern were ennobled by the presence of the catholic truth belonging to all ages that pervaded the whole. His power showed itself chiefly in the new and unlooked-for way in which he touched into life old truths, moral or spiritual, which all Christians acknowledge, but most have ceased to feel—when he spoke of "Unreal Words," of "The Individuality of the Soul," of "The Invisible World," of a "Particular Providence;" or again, of "The Ventures of Faith," "Warfare the condition of Victory," "The Cross of Christ the Measure of the World," "The Church a Home for the Lonely." As he spoke, how the old truth became new! how it came home with a meaning never felt before! He laid his finger—how gently, yet how powerfully!—on some inner place in the hearer's heart, and told him things about himself he had never known till then. Subtlest truths, which it would have taken philosophers pages of circumlocution and big words to state, were dropt out by the way in a sentence or two of the most transparent Saxon. What delicacy of style, yet what calm power! how gentle, yet how strong! how simple, yet how suggestive! how homely, yet how refined! how penetrating, yet how tender-hearted! If now and then there was a forlorn undertone which at the time seemed inexplicable, if he spoke of "many a sad secret which a man dare not tell lest he find no sympathy," of "secrets lying like cold ice upon the heart," of "some solitary incommunicable grief," you might be perplexed at the drift of what he spoke, but you felt all the more drawn to the speaker. To call these sermons eloquent would be no word for them; high poems they rather were, as of an inspired singer, or the outpourings as a prophet, rapt yet self-possessed. And the tone of voice in which they were spoken, once you grew accustomed to it, sounded like a fine strain of unearthly music. Through the stillness of that high Gothic building the words fell on the ear like the measured drippings of water in some vast dim cave. After hearing these sermons you might come away still not believing the tenets peculiar to the High Church system; but you would be harder than most men, if you did not feel more than ever ashamed of coarseness, selfishness, worldliness, if you did not feel the things of faith brought closer to the soul

There was one occasion of a different kind, when he spoke from St. Mary's pulpit for the last time, not as Parish minister, but as University preacher. It was the crisis of the movement. On the 2d of February, 1843, the Feast of the Purification, all Oxford assembled to hear what Newman had to say, and St. Mary's was crowded to the door. The subject he spoke of was "The theory of Development in Christian Doctrine," a subject which since then has become common property, but which at that time was new even to the ablest men in Oxford. For an hour and a half he drew out the argument, and perhaps the acutest there did not quite follow the entire line of thought, or felt wearied by the length of it, lightened though it was by some startling illustrations. Such was the famous "Protestantism has at various times developed into Polygamy," or the still more famous "Scripture says the sun moves around the earth, Science that the earth moves, and the sun is comparatively at rest. How can we determine which of these opposite statements is true, till we know what motion is?" Few probably who heard it have forgot the tone of voice with which he uttered the beautiful passage about music as the audible embodiment of some unknown reality behind, itself sweeping like a strain of splendid music out of the heart of a subtle argument:—

"Take another instance of an outward and earthly form, or economy, under which great wonders unknown seem to be typified; I mean musical sounds, as they are exhibited most perfectly in instrumental harmony. There are seven notes in the scale; make them fourteen; yet what a slender outfit for so vast an enterprise! What science brings so much out of so little? Out of what poor elements does some master create his new world! Shall we say that all this exuberant inventiveness is a mere ingenuity or trick of art, like some game or fashion of the day, without reality, without meaning? We may do so; and then, perhaps, we shall also account the science of theology to be a matter of words; yet, as there is a divinity in the theology of the Church, which those who feel cannot communicate, so there is also in the wonderful creation of sublimity and beauty of which I am speaking. To many men the very names which the science employs are utterly incomprehensible. To speak of an idea or a subject seems to be fanciful or trifling, and of the views which it opens us to be childish extravagance; yet is it possible that that inexhaustible evolution and disposition of notes, so rich yet so simple, so intricate yet so regulated, so various yet so majestic, should be a mere sound which is gone and perishes? Can it be that those mysterious stirrings of heart, and keen emotions, and strange yearnings after we know not what, and awful impressions from we know not whence, should be wrought in us by what is unsubstantial, and comes and goes, and begins and ends in itself? It is not so! it cannot be. No; they have escaped from some higher sphere; they are the outpourings of eternal harmony in the medium of created sound; they are echoes from our Home; they are the voices of Angels, or the *Magnificat* of Saints, or the living laws of Divine governance, or the Divine attributes; something are they besides themselves, which we cannot compass, which we cannot utter, though mortal man, and he perhaps not otherwise distinguished above his fellows, has the power of eliciting them."

This was preached in the winter of 1843, the last time he appeared in the University pulpit. His parochial sermons had by this time assumed an uneasy tone which perplexed his followers with fear of change. That summer solved their doubt. In the quiet chapel of Littlemore, which he himself had built, when all Oxford was absent during the long vacation, he preached his last Anglican sermon to the country people and only a few friends, and poured forth that mournful and thrilling farewell to the Church of England. The sermon is entitled **"The Parting of Friends."** The text was "Man goeth forth to this work and his labor until the evening." He went through all the instances which Scripture records of human affection sorely tried, reproducing the incidents almost in the very words of Scripture,— Jacob, Hagar, Naomi, Jonathan and David, St. Paul and elders of Ephesus, and last, the weeping over Jerusalem, and the "Behold, your house is left unto you desolate,"— and then he bursts forth—

"A lesson, surely, and a warning to us all, in every place where He puts his name, to the end of time, lest we be cold towards his gifts, or unbelieving towards his word, or jealous of his workings, or heartless towards his mercies. . . . O mother of saints! O school of the wise! O nurse of the heroic! of whom went forth, in whom have dwelt

memorable names of old, to spread the truth abroad, or to cherish and illustrate it at home! O thou, from whom surrounding nations lit their lamps! O virgin of Israel! wherefore dost thou now sit on the ground and keep silence, like one of the foolish women who were without oil on the coming of the Bridegroom? Where is now the ruler in Sion, and the doctor in the Temple, and the ascetic on Carmel, and the herald in the wilderness, and the preacher in the market-place? Where are thy 'effectual fervent prayers' offered in secret, and thy alms and good works coming up as a memorial before God? How is it, O once holy place, that "the land mourneth, for the corn is wasted, the new wine is dried up, the oil languisheth, because joy is withered away from the sons of men'? 'Alas for the day! how do the beasts groan! the herds of cattle are perplexed, because they have no pasture; yea, the flocks are made desolate.' 'Lebanon is ashamed and hewn down; Sharon is like a wilderness, and Bashan and Carmel shake off their fruits.' O my mother, whence is this unto thee, that thou hast good things poured upon thee and canst not keep them, and bearest children, yet darest not own them? Why has thou not the skill to use their services, nor the heart to rejoice in their love? How is it that whatever is generous in purpose, and tender or deep in devotion, thy flower and thy promise falls from thy bosom, and finds no home within thine arms? Who hath put this note upon thee, to have 'a miscarrying womb and dry breasts,' to be strange to thine own flesh, and thine eye cruel to thy little ones? Thine own offspring, the fruit of thy womb, who would love thee and would toil for thee, thou dost gaze upon with fear as though a portent, or thou dost loathe as an offense; at best thou dost but endure, as if they had no claim but on thy patience, self-possession, and vigilance, to be rid of them as easily as thou mayest. Thou makest them 'stand all the day idle' as the very condition of thy bearing with them; or thou biddest them begone where they will be more welcome; or thou sellest them for naught to the stranger that passes by. And what wilt thou do in the end thereof?

"Scripture is a refuge in any trouble; only let us be on our guard against seeming to use it further than is fitting, or doing more than sheltering ourselves under its shadow. Let us use it according to our measure. It is far higher and wider than our need, and it conceals our feelings while it gives expression to them. It is sacred and heavenly; and it restrains and purifies, while it sanctions them. . . . And O my brethren, O kind and affectionate hearts, O loving friends, should you know any one whose lot it has been, by writing or by word of mouth, in some degree to help you thus to act; if he has ever told you what you knew about yourselves, or what you did not know; has read to you your wants and feelings, and comforted you by the very reading; has made you feel that there was a higher life than this daily one, and a brighter world than that you see; or encouraged you, or sobered you, or opened a way to the inquiring, or soothed the perplexed, if what he has said or done has ever made you take interest in him, and feel well-inclined towards him, remember such a one in time to come, though you hear him not, and pray for him, that in all things he may know God's will, and at all times he may be ready to fulfill it."

Then followed the resignation of his fellowship, the retirement to Littlemore, the withdrawal even from the intercourse of his friends, the unloosing of all the ties that bound him to Oxford, the two years' pondering of the step he was about to take. And at last, when in 1845 he went away to the Church of Rome, he did it by himself, making himself as much as possible responsible only for his own act, and followed by but one or two young friends who would not be kept back. Those who witnessed these things, and knew that, if a large following had been his object, he might, by leaving the Church of England three years earlier, in the plenitude of his power, have taken almost all the flower of young Oxford with him, needed no "Apologia," to convince them of his honesty of purpose.

On these things, looking over an interval of five and twenty years, how vividly comes back the remembrance of the aching blank, the awful pause, which fell on Oxford when that voice had ceased, and we knew that we should hear it no more. It was as when, to one kneeling by night, in the silence of some vast cathedral, the great bell tolling solemnly overhead has suddenly gone still. To many, no doubt, the pause was not of long continuance. Soon they began to look this way and that for new teachers, and to rush vehemently to the opposite extreme of thought. But there were those who could not so lightly forget. All the more these withdrew into themselves. On Sunday forenoons and evenings, in the retirement of their rooms, the printed words of those marvelous sermons would thrill them till they wept "abundant and most sweet tears." Since then many voices of powerful teachers they may have heard, but none that ever penetrated the soul like his.

Such was the impression made by the eventful time on impartial but not uninterested spectators—on those who by early education and conviction were kept quite aloof from the peculiar tenets of High Churchmen, but who could not acknowledge the moral quickening which resulted from the movement, and the marvelous character of him who was the soul of it.

Dr. Newman himself tells us that all the while the true and primary author of that movement was out of sight. The Rev. John Keble was at a distance from Oxford, in his vicarage at Hursley, there living in his own life, and carrying out in his daily services and parish ministry, those truths which he had first brought forward, and Newman

had carried out, in Oxford. But though out of sight, he was not out of mind. **"The Christian Year"** was in the hands of every one, even the youngest undergraduate. Besides its more intrinsic qualities, the tone of it blended well with the sentiment which the venerable aspect of the old city awakened. It used to be pleasing to try and identify amid the scenery around Oxford some of the spots from which were drawn those descriptions of nature with which the poems are inlaid. During these years the poet-priest's figure was but seldom seen in streets of Oxford,—only when some great question affecting the Church, some discussion of No. 90, or trial of Mr. Ward, had summoned Convocation together. Once, if my memory serves, I remember to have seen him in the University pulpit at St. Mary's, but his voice was not strong, and did not reach many of the audience. His service to his party had lain in another direction. It was he who, by his character, had first awakened a new tone of sentiment in Oxford, and attracted to himself whatever else was like-minded. He had sounded the first note which woke that sentiment into action, and embodied it in a party. He had kept up, though from a distance, sympathetic intercourse with the chief actors, counseled and encouraged them. Above all, he gave poetry to the movement, and a poetic aspect. Polemics by themselves are dreary work. They do not touch the springs of young hearts. But he who, in the midst of any line of thought, unlocks a fountain of genuine poetry, does more to humanize it and win for it a way to men's affections, than he who writes a hundred volumes, however able, of controversy. Without disparagement to the patristic and other learning of the party, the two permanent monuments of genius which it has bequeathed to England may be said to be Newman's "Parochial Sermons," and Keble's **"Christian Year."**

All that was known of Keble at that time to the outer world of Oxford was vague and scanty. The few facts here added are taken from what has since been made public by two of his most attached friends, Sir John Coleridge and Dr. Newman, the former in his beautiful letters, memorial of Keble, the latter in his "Apologia." Yet these facts, though few, are well worthy of attention, both because Keble's character is more than his poetry, and because his poetry can only be rightly understood in the light of his character. For there is no poet whose poetry is more truly an image of the man himself, both in his inner nature and in his outward circumstances.

His father, whose name the poet bore, was a country clergyman, vicar of Coln St. Aldwyns, in Gloucestershire, but the house in which he lived, and in which the poet was born, was at Fairford, three miles distant from the cure. John was the second child and elder son of a family which consisted of two sons and two daughters. His mother, Sarah Maule, was, as I have heard, of Scottish extraction. The father, who lived till his ninetieth year, was a man of no common ability. Of him his son, we are told, "always spoke not only with the love of a son, but with the profoundest reverence for his goodness and wisdom." It would seem that this was one of the few clerical homes in England in which the opinions, traditions, and peculiar piety of the Nonjurors lived on into the present century. Unlike most sons distinguished for ability, John Keble never outgrew the period of absolute filial reverence, never questioned a single opinion or prepossession which he had imbibed from his father. Some of his less reverential companions used to think that this was an intellectual loss to him.

The father's ability and scholarship are proved by his having himself educated his son, and sent him up to Oxford so well prepared, that at the age of fifteen he gained a Corpus scholarship, an honor which seems to have then held the same place in University estimation that Balliol scholarships have long held and still hold. This strictly home training, in the quiet of a Gloucestershire parsonage, placed in the very heart of rural England, under a roof where the old High Church tradition lived on, blending with what was best in modern piety, makes itself felt in every line the poet wrote. On all hands one hears it said that there is no education like that of one of the old English public schools. For the great run of ordinary boys, whether quick-witted and competitive, or lazy and self-indulgent, it may be so; but for natures of finer texture, for all boys who have a decided and original bias, how much is there that the rough handling of a public school would ruthlessly crush? From all the better public schools coarse bullying, I know, has disappeared; but for peculiarity of any kind, for whatever does not conform itself to the "tyrant tradition"—a manly and straightforward one, I admit—they have still but little tolerance. If Keble had once imbibed the public school spirit, **"The Christian Year"** would either never have been written at all, or it would have been written otherwise than it is.

If he was fortunate in having his boy-education at home, he was not less happy in the college which he entered and the companions he met there. It is the happiness of college life that a young man can command just as much retirement, and as much society as he pleases, and of the kind that he pleases. All readers of Arnold's life will remember the picture there drawn of the Scholars' Common Room at Corpus, by one of the last survivors, the venerable Sir J. Coleridge. He tells us that, when Keble came into residence, early in 1807, it was but a small society, numbering only about twenty undergraduate scholars, and these rather under the usual age, who lived on the most familiar terms with each other. The Bachelor scholars resided and lived entirely with the undergraduates. Two of Keble's chief friends among the Corpus scholars, though younger in academic standing than himself, were Coleridge (afterwards Judge Coleridge) and Arnold. Keble

indeed must have already graduated before Arnold came into residence. Besides these were many other men distinguished in their day in the University, but less known to the outer world. It was a stirring time when Keble was an undergraduate. Within the University the first awakening after long slumber had begun, and competitions for honors had been just established. From without news of the great Peninsular battles was from time to time arriving. Scott's trumpet-blasts of poetry were stirring young hearts. In Corpus Common Room, as elsewhere, the Peninsular battles were fought over again, and the classical and romantic schools of poetry were vehemently discussed. And among these more exciting subjects, the young scholar Coleridge would insinuate the stiller and deeper tones of Wordsworth's lyrical ballads, which, then but little known, he had heard of from his uncle the poet. These two, Scott and Wordsworth, were to the end Keble's first favorites of contemporary poets, and chiefly moulded his taste and style. Most of the scholars were high Tories in Church and State, great respecters of things as they are: none, no doubt, more so than Keble. The great questioner of the prevailing creed was Arnold, who often brought down on his own head the concentrated arguments of the whole Common Room. But youth's genial warmth healed these undergraduate disputes, as, alas! the same controversies could not be healed when taken up by the same combatants at a later day. In that kindly atmosphere Keble's affectionate nature expanded as a flower in the sun. His was a temperament to drink in deeply whatever there was of finest influence in Oxford. No doubt the learning he there gained was something to him, but far more was the vision of the fair city herself, "with high aisle, and solemn cloister, seated among groves, green meadows, and calm streams." These, and the young friendships which they for a few years embosom, are what made Oxford then, and make it even now, the one spot in England wherein "the curlèd darlings of the nation" find romance still realized. Keble seems to have been much the same in character then as in after years. His affection towards the friends he made at Oxford was warm and deep, and lasted in most instances with his life. With what feelings they regarded him be gathered from the words of his brother scholar at Corpus, who, when their fifty-five years' friendship had come to its earthly close, could say of him, "It was the singular happiness of his nature, remarkable even in his undergraduate days, that love for him was always sanctified, as it were, by reverence—reverence that did not make the love less tender, and love that did but add intensity to the reverence."

In Easter term, 1810, Keble obtained double first class honors, and this success was soon afterwards followed by another still greater—his election to an Oriel fellowship. The Oriel Common Room numbered among its Fellows, then and for some time afterwards, all that was most distinguished in Oxford for mental power and originality. Copleston, Davidson, Whately, then belonged to it, and were among Keble's electors. Arnold, Newman, Pusey, soon afterwards followed as Fellows of the same college. "Round the fire of the Oriel Common Room," we are told, "there were learned and able, not rarely subtle and disputatious conversations, in which this lad of nineteen was called to take his part. Amid these he sometimes yearned for the more easy, yet not unintellectual society of his old friends at Corpus." He found, no doubt, that undergraduate days are more congenial to warm friendships than the highly rarefied atmosphere of an intellectual Common Room. Where men touch chiefly by the head, they find that this is the seat as frequently of a repulsive as of an attractive force. While he was an undergraduate, and during the early days of his fellowship, he wrote a good many beautiful little poems, which surviving friends still possess, and the year after his election to Oriel he gained the University prizes for the English and Latin essay.

The interval from 1810 to 1815 he spent in Oriel, taking part in college tuition, and acting as an examiner in the Degree Schools. Was it some time during these years, or at a later date, that the incident recorded by Dr. Newman took place? "When one day I was walking in High Street, with my dear earliest friend, with what eagerness did he cry out, 'There's Keble!' and with what awe did I look at him! Then at another time I heard a Master of Arts of my college give an account, how he had just then had occasion to introduce himself on some business to Keble, and how gentle, courteous, and unaffected Keble had been, so as almost to put him out of countenance. Then, too, it was reported, truly or falsely, how a rising man of brilliant reputation, the present Dean of St. Paul's, Dr. Milman, admired and loved him, adding that somehow he was strangely unlike any one else."

In 1815 he was ordained Deacon, the following year Priest; soon afterwards he left the University, and never again permanently resided there. He had chosen the calling of a clergyman, and though within that field other paths more gratifying to ambition lay open to him, he turned aside from them, and gave himself to parochial work as the serious employment of his life. He became his father's curate, and lived with him at Fairford, engaged in this duty for twenty years, more or less. This rare absence or restraint of ambition, where it might have seemed natural or even right to have gratified it, was quite in keeping with Keble's whole character. "The Church," says Sir J. Coleridge, "he had deliberately chosen to be his profession, and he desired to follow out that in a country cure. With this he associated, and scarcely placed on a lower level, the affectionate discharge of his duties as a son and brother. Calls, temporary calls of duty to his college and University, for a time and at intervals diverted him (he was again Public Examiner from 1821 to 1823); but he always kept

these outlines in view, and as the occasion passed away, reverted to them with the permanent devotion of his heart. Traces of this feeling may be found again and again in **'The Christian Year.'"**

This book was first given to the world on the 23d of June, 1827, when Keble was in his thirty-fifth year. This, the great work of his life, which will keep his name fresh in men's memory when all else that he has done shall be forgotten, had been the silent gathering of years. Single poems had been in his friends' hands at least as early as 1819. They had urged him to complete the series, and by 1827 this was done. No record of the exact time when each poem was written has yet appeared. I should imagine that more of them were composed at Fairford than at Oxford. The discussion and criticism natural to a University are not generally favorable to poetic creation of any kind, least of all to so meditative a strain as that of Keble. But it may have been that in this, as in other things, he was "unlike any one else." It was only at the urgent entreaty of his friends that he published the little book. He was not anxious about poetic fame, and never thought that these poems would secure it. His own plan was "to go on improving the series all his life, and leave it to come out, if judged useful, only when he should be fairly out of the way." Had this plan been acted on, how many thousands would have been defrauded of the soothing delight these poems have ministered to them! But even those who most strongly counseled the publication, little dreamt what a destiny was in store for that little book. Of course, if the author had kept it by him he might have smoothed away some of its defects, but who knows how much it might have lost too in the process? "No one," we are told, "knew its literary shortcomings better than the author himself. Wisely, and not in pride, or through indolence, he abandoned the attempt at second-hand to amend this inharmonious line, or that imperfect rhyme, or the instances here and there in which his idea may be somewhat obscurely expressed. Wordsworth's acute poetical sense recognized such faults; yet the book was his delight." Probably it was a wise resolve. All emendation of poetry long after its first composition runs the risk of spoiling it. The author has to take up in one mood what was originally conceived in another. His first warm feeling of sentiment has gone cold, and he cannot at a later time revive it. This is true of all poetry, more especially of that which deals with subtle and evanescent emotions which can never perhaps recur exactly in the same form. Once only in a lifetime may he succeed in catching—

> "Those brief unisons which on the brain
> One tone that never can recur has cast,
> One accent never to return again."

In 1833 Keble was appointed Professor of Poetry at Oxford. The Statutes then required the Professor to give two or three lectures a year in Latin. The ancient language was required to be spoken from this chair longer than from any other, probably from fear of the trash men might talk if fairly unmuzzled. However prudent this may have been when a merely average functionary held the chair, it is greatly to be regretted that when it was filled by a true poet, who was intent on speaking the secret of his own art, he should have been so formidably weighted. The present gifted[1] occupant of that chair has fortunately been set free, and has vindicated the newly acquired freedom by enriching our literature with the finest poetical criticism it has received since the days of Coleridge. But Keble had to work in trammels. He was the last man to rebel against any limitations imposed by the wisdom or unwisdom of our ancestors. Faithfully he buckled himself to the task of translating into well-rounded Latin periods his cherished thoughts on his own favorite subject. Of the theory of poetry embodied in the two volumes of his published lectures, something may yet be said. The Latin is easy and unconstrained, the thought original and suggestive—a great contrast to the more than Ciceronian paragraphs of his predecessor Copleston, bristling as they do to a marvel with epigrammatic Latinity, but underneath that containing little that is not commonplace.

There was another duty which fell to Keble as Professor of Poetry,—to choose the subject for the annual Prize Poem at Oxford, to adjudicate along with others the prize to the best of the poems given in, and to look over and suggest corrections in the verses of the successful competitor. Of all these winners of the Newdigate Prize one only has described his interview with Keble, but he one of the most distinguished. Dean Stanley, who gained the Newdigate Prize in, I think, 1837, with his beautiful poem on "The Gypsies," thus describes his first meeting with Keble. By the Dean's kind leave I give it in his own words, taken from his paper on Keble, now published in "Essays on Church and State:" "There are still living those with whom his discharge of one of his duties left a far livelier recollection than his Latin lectures. It was part of his office to correct the poems which during his tenure of it obtained the Newdigate Prize. One of these young authors still retains so fresh and so characteristic a remembrance of his intercourse with the Professor, even then venerable in his eyes, that it may be worth recording. He recalls, after the lapse of more than thirty years, the quiet kindness of manner, the bright twinkling eye illuminating that otherwise inexpressive countenance, which greeted the bashful student on his entrance into the Professor's presence. One touch after another was given to the juvenile verses, substituting for this or that awkward phrase graceful turns of expression all his own:—

"'Is there a spot where earth's *dim daylight* falls,'"

has the delicate color of **'The Christian Year'** all over. In adding the expression—

"'Where shade, air, *waters'*—

he dwelt with all the ardor of the keenest critic on the curious subtlety of language, by which 'water' suggests all that is prosaic, and 'waters' all that is poetical.

"'The heavens all gloom, the *wearied earth* all crime;'

how powerfully does this embody the exhaustion of Europe in the fifteenth century! 'The *storied* Sphinx,' 'India's *ocean-floods;*' how vivid are these glances at the phenomena of the East!

'The wandering Israelite, from year to year,
Sees the Redeemer's conquering wheels draw near;"

how thoroughly here is Southey's language caught from the 'Curse of Kehama;' how thoroughly, too, the Judaic as contrasted with the Christian Advent! And it may be added, though not directly bearing on the present topic, how delighted was his youthful hearer to perceive the sympathetic warmth with which, at a certain point in the poem, he said, 'Ah, surely this was suggested by Dr. Arnold's sermon on "The Egyptians whom ye have seen to-day, ye shall see no more again forever."' This allusion was the more felt as showing his recollection of the friend from whom at that time he was so strangely alienated."

In a foot-note Dean Stanley adds that "on glancing at a note to this poem, which cited from Tennyson's 'Palace of Art,' but without naming the poet, the line

"'Who shuts love out shall be shut out from love,'

Keble remarked 'Shakespeare.' The Laureate will forgive this ignorance of his early fame in consideration of the grandeur of the comparison."

In this vivid description one thing Dean Stanley has refrained from giving, the "certain point in his poem" which Keble recognized as suggested by Dr. Arnold's sermon. But the lines are too good to be thus passed over. Taking the view of the Gypsies, as having had their original home in Egypt, the thought occurs to the young poet, that they and the Jews during their Egyptian sojourn must have met. And then he bursts into these fine lines, full of his own pictorial genius:—

"Long since ye parted by the Red Sea strand,
Now face to face ye meet in every land,
Aliens amidst a new-born world to dwell,
Egypt's lorn people, outcast Israel."

With slight interruptions Keble continued to live with his father at Fairford, and to assist him as his curate till 1835.

"In that year this tie was broken. At the very commencement of it the venerable old man, who to the last retained the full use of his faculties, was taken to his rest; and before the end of it Keble became the Vicar of Hursley, and the husband of Miss Charlotte Clarke, second daughter of an old college friend of his father's, who was incumbent of a parish in the neighborhood of Fairford. This was the happy settlement of his life. For himself he had now no ungratified wish, and the bonds then tied were loosened only by death."

Only two years before Keble left Fairford, and at the very time when he entered on his Poetry Professorship, began what is called the Oxford Movement. Of this, Dr. Newman tells us, Keble was the real author. Let us cast a glance back, and see how it arose, and what it aimed at. With what feelings Newman, when an undergraduate, looked at Keble, we have seen. Some years afterwards, it must have been in 1819 or 1820, Newman was elected to the Oriel Fellowship which Arnold vacated. Of that time he thus writes: "I had to hasten to the Tower to receive the congratulations of all the Fellows. I bore it till Keble took my hand, and then felt so abashed and unworthy of the honor done me, that I seemed quite desirous of sinking into the ground. His had been the first name I had heard spoken of with reverence rather than admiration when I came up to Oxford." This was probably the first meeting of these two. "When I was elected Fellow of Oriel," Dr. Newman continues, "Keble was not in residence, and he was shy of me for years, in consequence of the marks I bore upon me of the evangelical and liberal schools. Hurrell Froude brought us together about 1828. It is one of his sayings preserved in his Remains: 'If I was ever asked what good deed I had ever done, I should say that I had brought Keble and Newman to understand each other.'" The friendship thus cemented was to be fruitful of results for England.

It naturally occurs to ask, How far is **"The Christian Year"** identified with the principles of the Tractarian movement? On the one hand, **"The Christian Year"** was published in 1827; the movement did not begin till 1833. The former, therefore, cannot be regarded as in any way a child of the latter. And this accounts for what has often been remarked, how little of peculiar Tractarian teaching appears in these poems. On the other hand, it is easy to see how the same nature which, in a season of quiet, when controversy was at a lull, shaped out of its own musings **"The Christian Year,"** would, when confronted with opposing tendencies, and forced into a dogmatic attitude, find its true expression in the Tractarian theory. Keble was by nature a poet, living by intuition, not by reasoning; intuition born of, fed by, home affection, tradition, devout religion. His whole being leaned on authority. "Keble was a man who guided himself," says Dr. Newman, "and formed his judgments, not by processes of reason, by inquiry or argument, but, to use the word in a broad sense, by authority." And by authority in its broad sense he means conscience, the Bible, the Church, antiquity, words of the wise, hereditary lessons, ethical truths, historical memories. "It seemed to me as if he felt ever happier when he could speak and act under some such primary and external sanction; and could use argument mainly as a means of recommending or explaining what had claims on his reception prior to proof. What he hated instinctively was heresy, insubordination, resistance to things established, claims of independence, disloyalty, innovation, a critical or censorious spirit." Keble then lived by authority, and hated the dispositions that oppose it. There is a temper of mind which lives by denying authority—a temper whose essence, or at least whose bad side, is to foster these very dispositions which he hated. With that tone of mind, and the men possessed by it, sooner or later he must needs have come into collision. For such a collision, Oxford did not want materials.

During Keble's time of residence, and after he went down, the University had been awakening from a long torpor, and entering on a new era. "The march of the mind," as it was called, was led by a number of active-minded and able men, whose chief rallying point was Oriel Common Room, whose best representative was Whately. These men had set themselves to raise the standard of teaching and discipline in the Colleges and in the University. They were the University Reformers of their day, and to them Oxford, when first arousing itself from long intellectual slumber, owed much. As they had a common aim, to raise the intellectual standard, they were naturally much thrown together, and became the celebrities of the place. Those who did not belong to their party thought them not free from "pride of reason," an expression then, as now, derided by those who think themselves intellectual, but not the less on that account covering a real meaning. It is, as it has been called, "the moral malady" which besets those who live mainly by intellect. Men who could not in heart go along with them thought they carried liberty of thought into presumption and rationalism. They seemed to submit the things of faith too much to human judgment, and to seek to limit their religious belief by their own powers of understanding. They seemed then, as now, "to halve the gospel of God's grace," accepting the morality, and, if not rejecting, yet making little of the supernatural truths out of which that morality springs. Such at least was the judgment of their opponents. In the presence of men of this stamp, energetic but hard, upright but not over humble or reverent, a man of deep religious seriousness, like Keble, instinctively "shrank into himself." "He was young in years when he became a University celebrity, and younger in mind. He had the purity and simplicity of a child. He had few sympathies with the intellectual party, who sincerely welcomed him as a brilliant specimen of young

Oxford. He instinctively shut up before literary display, and pomp, and donnishness, faults which will always beset academical notabilities. He did not respond to their advances. 'Poor Keble,' Hurrell Froude used gravely to say, 'he was asked to join the aristocracy of talent, but he soon found his own level.' He went into the country, but he did not lose his place in the minds of men because he was out of sight." It could not be that Keble and these men could really be in harmony,—they, "sons of Aufklärung," men of mere understanding, bringing all things to the one touchstone of logic and common sense, and content with this; he, a child of faith, with more than half his nature in the unseen, and looking at things visible mainly as they shadow forth and reveal the invisible. They represented two opposite sides of human nature, sides in all but some rare instances antagonistic, and never seemingly more antagonistic than now. Dr. Arnold, indeed, though belonging in the main to the school of liberalism, combined with it more religious warmth than was common in his own party. It is this union of qualities, generally thought incompatible, which perhaps was the main secret of his great influence. But the combination which was almost unique in himself, he can hardly be said, by his example, to have rendered more easy for his followers in the present day.

The Catholic Emancipation was a trying and perplexing time for Keble. With the opponents of the measure in Oxford, the old Tory party of Church and State, he had no sympathy. He saw that they had no principle of growth in them, that their only aim was to keep things as they were. His sympathy for the old Catholic religion, that feeling which had made him say in **"The Christian Year,"**

> "Speak gently of our sister's fall,"

would naturally make him wish to see Catholic disabilities removed. But then he disliked both the men by whom, and the arguments by which, Emancipation was supported. He would rather have not seen the thing done at all, than done by the hands of Whiggery. A few years more brought on the crisis, the inevitable collision. The Earl Grey Administration, flushed with their great Reform victory, went on to lay hands on the English Church, that Church which for centuries had withstood the Whigs. They made their attack on the weakest point, the Irish Church, and suppressed ten of its bishoprics. This might seem to be but a small matter in itself, but it was an indication of more behind. Lord Grey had told the Bishops to set their house in order, and his party generally spoke of the Church as the mere creature of the State, which they might do with as they pleased. The Church must be liberalized, those last fangs must be pulled which had so often proved troublesome to Whiggery. This was too much for Keble. It touched him to the quick, and made him feel that now the time was come when he must speak and act. By nature he was no politi-

cian nor controversialist. He disliked the strife of tongues. But he was a man; he had deep religious convictions; and to change what was ancient and catholic in the Church was to touch the apple of his eye. When he looked to the Old Tory party he saw no help in them. To the aggressive spirit they had nothing to oppose but outworn Church and State theories. The Bishops too were helpless, and spoke slightingly of apostolic succession and the Nonjurors. Was the Establishment principle, then, the only rock on which the Church was built? Keble and his young friends thought scorn of that. This feeling first found utterance in the assize sermon which Keble preached from the University pulpit, on Sunday the 14th of July, 1833, and afterwards published under the title of **"National Apostasy."** "I have ever considered and kept the day," says Dr. Newman, "as the start of the religious movement of 1833." That sermon itself I have not seen, but the tone of it may be gathered from those lines in the **"Lyra Apostolica,"** in which Keble thus brands the spoliators:—

> "Is there no sound about our altars heard
> Of gliding forms that long have watched in vain
> For slumbering discipline to break her chain
> And aim the bolt by Theodosius feared?
> 'Let us depart;' these English souls are seared,
> Who for one grasp of perishable gold,
> Would brave the curse by holy men of old
> Laid on the robbers of the shrines they reared;
> Who shout for joy to see the ruffian band
> Come to reform, where ne'er they came to pray
> E'en where, unbidden, seraphs never trod.
> Let us depart, and leave the apostate land
> To meet the rising whirlwind as she may,
> Without her guardian Angels and her God."

"Robbers of the shrines," "the ruffian band, come to reform, where ne'er they came to pray," that was the trumpet-note which rallied to the standard of the Church whatever of ardor and devotion young Oxford then contained. These virtues had never been greatly countenanced in the Church of England. To staid respectability it has always been, and still is, one of the chief recommendations of that Church, that it is an embodied protest against what one of its own Bishops is said to have denounced as "that most dangerous of all errors—enthusiasm." In the last century she had cast out enthusiasm in the person of Wesley; at the beginning of this, she had barely tolerated it in the Newtons and Cecils, and other fathers of evangelicism. But here was a fresh attempt to reintroduce it in a new form. The young men who were roused by Keble's note of warning—able, zealous, resolute—flung aside with disdain timid arguments from expediency. They longed to do battle with that most prosaic of all political theories, Whiggery, and to smite to the ground the spirit of compromise which had so long paralyzed the Church of England. They set themselves to defend the Church with weapons of ethereal temper, and they found them, as they believed, in reviving her claims to a heavenly origin and a divine prerogative. That these claims sounded strange to the ears even of Churchmen at that time was to these men no stumbling-block—rather an incentive to more fearless action. True, such a course shut them out from preferment, hitherto the one recognized aim of the abler English Churchmen. But these younger men were content to do without preferment. They had at least got beyond that kind of worldliness. If self still clung to them in any shape, it was in that enlarged and nobler form in which it is one with the glory of the Church Catholic in all ages. The views and aims of the new party soon took shape, in the **"Tracts for the Times."** If Keble was the starter of the movement, John Henry Newman soon became its leader. In all his conduct of it, one of his great aims was to give to the sentiments and views which had originated with Keble a consistent logical basis. The sequel all men know. The inner working of the movement may be read in the "Apologia."

But deeply as Keble's heart was in the Oxford movement, his place of work was a quiet Hampshire parish. When, in 1835, he left the home of his childhood for the vicarage of Hursley, he found a church there not at all to his mind. It seems to have been a plain, not beautiful, building of flint and rubble. He determined to have a new one built—new all but the tower—and on this object he employed the profits of the many editions of **"The Christian Year;"** and when the building was finished, his friends, in token of their regard for him, filled all the windows with stained glass. In the words of Sir J. P. Coleridge, "Here daily for the residue of his life, until interrupted by the failing health of Mrs. Keble and his own, did he minister. . . . He had not, in the popular sense, great gifts of delivery; his voice was not powerful, nor was his ear perfect for harmony of sound; but I think it was difficult not to be impressed deeply both by his reading and his preaching; when he read, you saw that he felt, and he made you feel, that he was the servant of God, delivering his words; or leading you, as one of like infirmities and sins with your own, in your prayer. When he preached it was with an affectionate simplicity and hearty earnestness which were very moving; and the sermons themselves were at all times full of that abundant Scriptural knowledge which was the most remarkable quality in him as a divine; it has always seemed to me among the most striking characteristics of **"The Christian Year."** It is well known what his belief and feelings were in regard to the Sacraments. I remember on one occasion when I was present at a christening as godfather, how much he affected me, when a consciousness of his sense of the grace conferred became present to me. As he kept the newly-baptized infant for some moments in his arms, he gazed on it intently and lovingly with a tear in his eye, and apparently absorbed in the thought of the child of wrath become the child of grace. Here his natural affections gave clearness and intensity to

his belief; the fondest mother never loved children more dearly than this childless man."

During the eventful years that followed the Assize sermon, though his place was still in his country cure, his sympathies and coöperation were with Newman and other friends in Oxford. He contributed some of the more important Tracts; poems of his embodying the sentiments of the party appeared from time to time, and were republished in the **"Lyra Apostolica."** In 1841, when the famous No. 90 was published, to the scandal of the whole religious world, Keble was one of the few who stood by Newman. What then must his feelings have been when that younger friend, by whom he had so stood, with whom he had so often taken counsel, abandoned the Church of England, and sought refuge in that of Rome? As late as 1863, a friend of his, when walking with him near Hursley, drew his attention to a broken piece of ground—a chalk-pit, as it turned out—hard by. "'Ah!' he said, 'that is a sad place, connected with the most painful event of my life.' I began to fear that it had been the scene of some terrible accident which I had unwittingly recalled to his mind. 'It was there,' he went on, 'that I first knew for certain that J. H. N. had left us. We had made up our mind that such an event was all but inevitable; and one day I received a letter in his handwriting. I felt sure of what it contained, and I carried it about with me through the day, afraid to open it. At last I got away to that chalk-pit, and there, forcing myself to read the letter, I found that my forebodings had been too true; it was the announcement that he was gone.'"

It seems natural to ask how it came that, when Newman left, Keble adhered to the Church of England. They were at one in their fundamental principles. What, then, determined them to go different ways? Of many reasons that occur this one may be given. The two friends, though agreeing in their principles, differed widely in mental structure and in natural temperament. They differed scarcely less in training and circumstances. Keble, as we have seen, cared little for reasoning, and rested mainly on feeling and intuition. Newman, on the other hand, though fully alive to these, added an unresting intellectual instinct which could not be satisfied without a defined logical foundation for what it instinctively held. Not that Keble was without a theory. Taking from Butler the principle that probability is the guide of life, he applied it to theological truth. Butler, by a very questionable process, had employed the maxim of worldly prudence, that probability is the guide of life, as an argument for religion, but mainly in the natural sphere. Keble tried to carry it on into the sphere of revealed truth. The arguments which support religious doctrine, he said, may be only probable arguments judged intellectually; but faith and love, being directed towards their divine Object, and living in the contemplation of that Object, convert these probable arguments into certainties.

In fact, the inward assurance, which devout faith has of the reality of its Object, makes doctrines practically certain which may not be intellectually demonstrable. Newman tells us that he accepted this view so far, but, not being fully satisfied with it, tried, in his University sermons and other works, to supplement it with considerations of his own. In time, however, he felt it give way in his hands, and either abandoned it, or allowed it to carry him elsewhere.

But besides difference of mental structure, there were other causes which perhaps determined the divergent courses of the two friends. In the case of Keble, whatever is most sacred and endearing in the English Church had surrounded his infancy and boyhood, and gone with him into full manhood. With him loyalty to Home was hardly less sacred than loyalty to the Faith. These two influences were so intertwined in the inner fibres of his nature that it would have been to him very death to separate them. Of Dr. Newman's early associations I know no more than the little he has himself disclosed. It would appear, however, that the Anglican Church never had so invincible a hold on him as it had on Keble. By few perhaps has it been seen in so winning an aspect as it wore in the rural quiet of that Gloucestershire parsonage which was his early home.

When Newman was gone, on Keble, along with Dr. Pusey, was thrown the chief burden of the toil and responsibility arising out of his position in the Church. Naturally there was great searching of hearts amongst all the followers of the Oxford theology. Keble had to give himself to counsel the perplexed, to strengthen the wavering, and, as far as might be, to heal the breaches that had been made. Throughout the ecclesiastical contests of the last twenty years, though never loud or obtrusive, he yet took a resolute part in maintaining the principles with which his life had been identified. One last extract from Sir J. T. Coleridge's beautiful sketch of his friend, will give all that need here be said of this portion of Keble's life: "Circumstances had now placed him in a position which he would never have desired for himself, but from which a sense of duty compelled him not to shrink. Questions one after another arose touching the faith or the discipline of the Church, and affecting, as he believed, the morals and religion of the people. I need not specify the decisions of courts or the proceedings in Parliament to which I allude; those whose consciences were disturbed, but who shrank from public discussion, and those who stirred themselves in canvassing their propriety, or in counteracting their consequences, equally turned to him as a comforter and adviser in private and in public, and he could not turn a deaf ear to such applications. It is difficult to say with what affectionate zeal and industry he devoted himself to such cares, how much, and at length it is to be feared how injuriously to his health, he spent his time and strength in the labor these brought on him. Many of these involved, of course, questions of law, and it was not seldom that he applied to me—and thus I can testify with what care and learning and acuteness he wrote upon them. Many of his fugitive pieces were thus occasioned; and should these be, as they ought to be, collected, they will be found to possess even more than temporary interest. I had occasion but lately to refer to his tract on 'Marriage with the Wife's Sister,' and I can only hope that the question will soon be argued in Parliament with the soundness and clearness which are there employed. But even all this does not represent the calls made on his time by private correspondence, by personal visits, or, where it was necessary, by frequent, sometimes by long journeys, taken for the support of religion. I need hardly say that his manner of doing all this concurred in raising up for him that immense personal influence which he possessed; people found in their best adviser the most umpresuming, unwearied, affectionate friend, and they loved as well as venerated him."

The appearance of Dr. Newman's "Apologia" in 1864 was to Keble a great joy. Not that he had ever ceased to love Dr. Newman with his old affection, but the separation of now nearly twenty years, and the cause of it, had been to Keble the sorest trial of his life. If the book contained some things regarding the Church of England which must have pained Keble, there was much more in it to gladden him; not only the entire human-heartedness of its tone, which made its way to the hearts even of strangers, but the deep and tender affection which it breathes to Dr. Newman's early friends, and the proof it gave that Rome had made no change either in his heart or head which could hinder their real sympathy. The result was that in September, 1865, these three, Dr. Newman, Dr. Pusey, and Mr. Keble, met under the roof of Hursley vicarage, and after an interval of twenty years looked on each others' altered faces. One evening they passed together, no more. It happened, however, that at the very time of this meeting, Mrs. Keble had an alarming attack of illness. Keble writes: "He (Dr. Pusey) and J. H. N. met here the very day after my wife's attack. Pusey indeed was present when the attack began. Trying as it all was, I was very glad to have them here, and to sit by them and listen."

Soon after this, in October, Mr. and Mrs. Keble left Hursley for Bournemouth, not to return. Since the close of 1864, symptoms of declining health had shown themselves in him also. The long strain of the duties that accumulated on him in his later years, with the additional anxiety caused by Mrs. Keble's precarious health, had been gradually wearing him. After only a few days' illness he was taken to his rest on the day before Good Friday, 1866. In a few weeks Mrs. Keble followed, and now they are laid side by side in Hursley churchyard.

The picture of this saintly life will of course in time be given to the world. It is much to be hoped that the task will be intrusted in some one able to do justice to it. There are two kinds of biographies, and of each kind we have seen examples in our own time. One is as a golden chalice, held up by some wise hand, to gather the earthly memory ere it is split on the ground. The other kind is as a millstone, hung by a partial, yet ill-judging friend, round the hero's neck, to plunge him as deep as possible in oblivion. In looking back on the eminent men of last generation, we have seen one or two lives of the former stamp, many more of the latter. Let us indulge the hope that he who writes of Keble will take for his model the one or two nearly faultless biographies we possess, and above all that he will condense his work within such limits as shall commend it not only to partial friends, but also to all thoughtful readers.

By his character and influence, Keble did more than perhaps any other man to bring about the most widespread quickening of religious life which has taken place within the English Church during the present century. To him, and the party to which his very name was a tower of strength, England owes two great services. First, they, and they preëminently, have turned, and are still turning, a resolute front against the rationalizing spirit, which would pare down revelation to the measure of the human understanding—cut away its foundation in the supernatural, and virtually reduce it to a moral system, encased perhaps in a few historic facts. Secondly, they have introduced into the English Church a higher order of character, and taught it, one might almost say, new virtues. They have diffused widely through the clergy the contagion of their own zeal and resoluteness, their self-devotion and Christian chivalry. These are high services to have rendered to any country in any age. But with these acknowledgments two regrets must mingle: one, that with their defense of Christian truth they should have mixed up positions which are untenable, identifying with the simple faith doctrines which are no part of it, but rather alien accretions gathered by the Church in its progress down the ages. The result of this intermingling with Christianity things that seem superstitious, has been to drive many back into dislike and denial of that which is truly supernatural. The other cause of regret is, that they should have impaired the practical power of their example by the exclusive and unsympathetic side they have turned towards their fellow-Christians in other Reformed communions. This exclusiveness kept back from the Oxford theologians the sympathies of many, who, but for this, would have been strongly drawn to them by their unworldliness, fervor, and self-devotion. Both errors have one source, the confounding the Church with the clergy, or rather, perhaps I should say, the attempt to place the essence of the Church in a priestly organization. But though these things must be said, it is not as of a partisan

that one would like most to think of Keble. The circumstances of his time forced him to take a side, but his nature was too pure and holy to find fit expression in polemics; and the memory of his rare and saintly character will long survive in the hearts of his countrymen the party strifes in which it was his lot to mingle.

Of his two prose books, his edition of Hooker's works, which has, I believe, superseded every other, and his Life of the good Bishop Wilson of Sodor and Man, the author of the "Sacra Privata," this is not the place to speak. But before turning to **"The Christian Year,"** one word must be said about his later book of poetry, the **"Lyra Innocentium."** It appeared in 1846, at an interval of nearly twenty years after **"The Christian Year."** This collection of poems he speaks of in May, 1845, as "a set of things which have been accumulating on me for the last three or four years. It has been a great comfort to me in the desolating anxiety of the last two years, and I wish I could settle at once on some other such work." Children, as we have seen, had always been peculiarly dear to this childless man, and he had at first wished to have made these poems a Christian Year for teachers and nurses, and others much employed about children. In time it took a different shape, and it is perhaps to be regretted that he had not made it what he first intended. Children, their thoughts and ways, and the feelings which they awaken in their elders, are themes of quite exhaustless interest. And yet how seldom has any poet of adequate tenderness and depth approached that mysterious world of childhood! Wordsworth, indeed, has felt it deeply, and expressed it in some of his most exquisite poems:—

> "O dearest, dearest boy, my heart
>   For better lore would seldom yearn,
> Could I but teach the hundredth part
>   Of what from thee I learn."

This verse from Wordsworth is indeed the motto chosen by Keble for his **"Lyra Innocentium."**

Of the poems on children which the **"Lyra"** contains, I am free to confess that they approach their subject too exclusively from the Church side for general interest. **"Looking Westward," "The Bird's Nest," "Bereavement," "The Manna Gatherers,"** are fine lyrics, equal perhaps to most in **"The Christian Year."** But there is no thought in the **"Lyra Innocentium"** about childhood that comes near that earlier strain in which the poet, as he looks on children ranged to receive their first lessons in religion, bursts forth—

> "O! say not, dream not, heavenly notes
>   To childish ears are vain,
> That the young mind at random floats,
>   And cannot reach the strain.
> "Dim or unheard, the words may fall,
>   And yet the heaven-taught mind

May learn the sacred air, and all
    The harmony unwind.

"Was not our Lord a little child,
    Taught by degrees to pray,
By father dear and mother mild
    Instructed day by day?"

Then, after an interval, he goes on—

    "Each little voice in turn
Some glorious truth proclaims,
What sages would have died to learn,
    Now taught by cottage dames.

"And if some tones be false or low,
    What are all prayers beneath
But cries of babes that cannot know
    Half the deep thought they breathe?"

Whatever the reason may be, certainly the later book does not strike home to the universal heart as **"The Christian Year"** did, and it never has attained anything like the same popularity.

The reference to ecclesiastical usages, not known to the many, and the more pronounced High Church feeling which it embodies, will partly account for this. It is certainly much more restricted and less catholic in its range. Partly also it may be that the fountain of inspiration did not flow so fully as in earlier years. It may not have been that time had chilled it; but other duties and cares had come thick upon him since his poetic spring-time. Especially the polemical stir in which his share in the Oxford movement had involved him, and the anxiety in the midst of which the **"Lyra Innocentium"** was composed, must have left little of what leisure either of time or heart which is necessary for a free-flowing minstrelsy.

It may help to the fuller understanding of **"The Christian Year,"** if we turn for a moment to Keble's theory of poetry. He has set it forth at large in **"Prælections on Poetry,"** more shortly in his review of the **"Life of Scott,"** which, once famous in Oxford, is almost unknown to the present generation. That review, which first appeared in the "British Critic," is well worthy of being republished, both from the insight it gives into Keble's character, and views on poetry, and also as a study of Scott by a reverential admirer, in many things very unlike himself. The theory is that poetry is the natural relief of minds burdened by some engrossing idea, or strong emotion, or ruling taste, or imaginative regret, which from some cause or other they are kept from directly indulging. Rhythm and metrical form serve to regulate and restrain, while they express those strong or deep emotions, "which need relief, but cannot endure publicity." They are at once "vent for eager feelings and a veil to draw over them. For the utterance of high or tender feeling controlled and modified by a certain reserve is the very soul of poetry."

On this principle Keble founds what he regards as an essential distinction between primary and secondary poets. Primary poets are they who are driven by some overmastering enthusiasm, by passionate devotion to some range of objects, or line of thought, or aspect of life or nature, to utter their feelings in song. They sing, because they cannot help it. There is a melody within them which will out, a fire in their blood which cannot be suppressed. This is the true poetic [*mania;* madness, frenzy] of which Plato speaks. Secondary poets are not urged to poetry by any such overflowing sentiment; but learning, admiration of great masters, choice, and certain literary turn, have made them poetic artists. They were not born, but being possessed of a certain [*euphuia;* goodness of shape and of disposition], have made themselves poets. Of the former kind are Homer, Lucretius, Shakespeare, Burns, Scott; of the latter, Euripides, Dryden, Milton. This view, if it be somewhat too narrow a basis on which to found a comprehensive theory of poetry, certainly does lay hold of one side of the truth generally overlooked. In our own day, how many are there! possessed of a large measure of artistic faculty, able to treat poetically anything they take up, wanting only in one thing,—a subject which absorbs their interest. There is nothing in human life, or history, or nature, which they have made peculiarly their own, nothing about which they know more intimately, than the host of educated men. And so, though with a "skill in composition and felicity of language" greater than many poets possesses, they are still felt to be literary men rather than poets, because they have no overmastering impulse, no divine enthusiasm, driving them to seek relief in song.

If we apply to himself the author's own canon, **"The Christian Year"** would place him in the rank of primary poets. Not that it displays anything like the highest artistic faculty, but because it evidently flows from a native spring of inspiration. As far as it goes, it is genuine poetry. The author sings, in a strain of his own, of the things he has known and felt and loved. Beneath all the layers that early education and Oxford training have superimposed, there is felt to be a glow of internal heat not derived from these.

To English Church people without number **"The Christian Year"** has long been not only a cherished classic, but a sacred book, which they place beside their Bible and their Prayer-Book. On the other hand, a generation of literary young men has grown up, who, having had their tastes formed on a newer, more highly spiced style of poetry, scarcely know **"The Christian Year,"** and, if they knew it, would turn away from what seemed to them its meagre literary merit. It would be impossible to say anything regarding it which would not seem faint praise to the one class, and exaggeration to the other. But without trying to meet the views of either, it is worth while to study the poem for ourselves.

It cannot be too clearly kept in view that Keble is not a hymn writer, and that **"The Christian Year"** is not a collection of hymns. Those who have come to it expecting to find genuine hymns, will turn away in disappointment. They will seek in vain for anything of the directness, the fervor, the simplicity, the buoyancy of devotion which have delighted them in Charles Wesley. But to demand this is to mistake the nature and form of Keble's poems. There is all the difference between them and Charles Wesley's, that there is between meditation on the one hand, and prayer, or thanksgiving, or praise on the other. Indeed, so little did Keble's genius fit him for hymn writing, that in his two poems which are intended to be hymns—those for the morning and the evening—the opening in either case is a description of natural facts, wholly unsuited to hymn purposes. And so when these two poems are adopted into hymn collections, as they often are, a mere selection of certain stanzas from each is all that has been found possible. Besides these two, there is no other poem in the book, any large part of which can be used as a hymn. For they are all lyrical religious meditations, not hymns at all. Yet true though this is, every here and there, out of the midst of the reflections, there does flash a verse of fervid emotion and direct heart-appeal to God, which is quite hymnal in character. These occasional bursts are among the highest beauties of **"The Christian Year."** Yet they are neither so frequent nor so long-sustained as to change the prevailingly meditative cast of the whole book. It is owing perhaps to this prevalence of meditation, and that often of a refined and subtle kind, that **"The Christian Year"** is not, as we have often heard said, so well adapted as some simpler, less poetical collections, to be read by the sick-bed to the faint and weak. Unless long familiarity has made it easy, it requires more thought and mental elasticity to follow it, than the sick for the most part can supply. Yet it contains single verses, many, though not whole poems, which will come home full of consolation to any, even the weakest spirit. On the whole, however, it is not with Charles Wesley, or any of the hymn writers of this or the past century, nor even with Cowper in his hymns or his larger poems, that Keble should be compared. In outward form, and not a little in inward spirit, the religious poets to whom he bears the strongest likeness are Henry Vaughan and George Herbert, both of the seventeenth century. A comparison with these would be interesting, were this the place for it, but at present I must confine myself to the consideration of the special characteristics of **"The Christian Year."**

These seem to be, *first,* a tone of religious feeling, fresh, deep, and tender, beyond what was common even among religious men in the author's day, perhaps in any day; *secondly,* great intensity and tenderness of home affection; *thirdly,* a shy and delicate reserve, which loved quiet paths and shunned publicity; *fourthly,* a pure love of nature, and a spiritual eye to read nature's symbolism.

> "He sang of love, with quiet blending,
> Slow to begin, and never ending,
> Of serious faith, and inward glee."

1. ITS PECULIAR TONE OF RELIGIOUS FEELING

It embodies deep and tender religious sentiment in a form which is old, and yet new. Our best critic has lately told us that "the inevitable business for the modern poet, as it was for the Greek poet in the days of Pericles, is to interpret human life afresh, and find a new spiritual basis for it." Keble did not think so. He was content with the interpretation which Christianity has put on human life, and wished only to read man and nature as far as he might, in this light. Goethe, I suppose, is the great modern instance of a poet who has tried "to give a moral interpretation of man and the world from an independent point of view." Of course it would be simply ridiculous for a moment to place Keble for poetic power in comparison with such an one as Goethe. But, disparate as their powers are, Keble with limited faculty, just by virtue of his having accepted the Christian interpretation, while the other rejected it, has spoken, if one may venture to say so, more words that satisfy man's deepest yearnings, that sink into those simple places of the heart which lie beneath all culture, than Goethe with all his world-width has done. The religion which Keble laid to heart, and lived by, would not seem to have come to him through prolonged spiritual conflicts, as did that of the great Puritans; neither had he reached it by laborious critical processes, as modern philosophers would have us do. He had learned it first at his mother's knee. Then it was confirmed and systematized by the daily teaching of the Church he so devoutly loved. Time brought to it additions from various quarters, but no break. The powerful influences of his University, direct and indirect, chivalry reawakening in Scott's poetry, meditative depth in Wordsworth, these all melted naturally into his primal faith, and combined with the general tendencies of the time to carry him in spirit back to those older ages where his imagination found ampler range, his devotion severer, more self-denying virtues than modern life engenders. Out of that great past he brought some of the sterner stuff of which the martyrs were made, and introduced it like iron into the blood of modern religious feeling. A poet who received all these influences into himself, and vitalized them, could not but make the old new. For not till the authoritative had been inwardly transfused into the moral and spiritual did it for the most part find vent in his poetry. There are exceptions to this, which form what may be set down as the shortcomings of **"The Christian Year."** But in all its finer, more vital poems, the catholic faith has become personal, rests frankly on intuition and experience, as frankly as the vaguer, more impersonal meditations of greater poets.

"The eye in smiles may wander round,
    Caught by earth's shadows as they fleet,
But for the soul no home is found,
    Save Him who made it, meet."

Or again, the well-known—

"Abide with me from morn till eve,
For without Thee I cannot live;
Abide with me when night is nigh,
For without Thee I dare not die."

Or again—

"Who loves the Lord aright,
    No soul of man can worthless find;
All will be precious in his sight,
    Since Christ on all hath shined."

It is the many words, simple yet deep, devoutly Christian yet intensely human, like these, scattered throughout its pages, that have endeared **"The Christian Year"** to countless hearts within the English Church, and to many a heart beyond it. The new elements in the book are perhaps these—first, it translates religious sentiment out of the ancient and exclusively Hebrew dialect into the language of modern feeling. Hitherto English devotional poets, with the exception perhaps of Cowper, in some passages, had adhered rigorously to the Scriptural imagery and phraseology. This, besides immensely limiting their range, made their words often fall wide of modern experience. Keble took the thoughts and sentiments of which men at the present day are conscious, expressed them in fitting modern words, and transfused into them the Christian spirit. Secondly, there is visible in him, first perhaps of his contemporaries,—that which seems the best characteristic of modern religion,—combined with devout reverence for the person of our Lord, a closer, more personal love to Him as to a living friend. There were no doubt rare exceptions here and there, but, generally speaking, religious men before spoke of our Lord in a more distant way, as one holding the central place rather in a dogmatic system than in the devout affections. The best men of our own time have gone beyond this. The Lord of the Gospels, in his Divine humanity, has come closer to their hearts, and made Himself known in a more intimate and endearing way. In none perhaps was this change of feeling earlier seen, or more strongly marked, than in Keble. Thirdly, there is the close and abundant knowledge of Scripture, with a fine and delicate feeling for the beauty of its language. Without confining himself to the imagery or language of the Bible, he everywhere shows his intimacy with it, and interweaves its words and half sentences, its scenes and imagery naturally and gracefully with his own.

These are some of the more catholic notes of the book which have won for it a place in the affections of Christians of every communion. This depth of catholic religious sentiment, it is, no doubt, which is its chief and most valuable characteristic. From this some may be ready to draw an argument for Christian morality disjoined from Christian doctrine, or for some all-embracing religion which would comprehend whatever the various churches agree in, discarding all in which they differ. What that residuum exactly is, no one has yet stated. But before drawing such an argument from **"The Christian Year,"** it may be as well to ask whether that book would have been so charged with devout Christian sentiment if its author had not held with all his heart those doctrinal truths which were in him the roots out of which that sentiment grew, but which may now wish to get rid of? If we love the consummate flower, it might be as well not to begin by cutting away the root.

There is, however, another side on which **"The Christian Year"** is less catholic in its character. This, which may be called its ecclesiastical side, is inherent in the very form of the book. A poem for each Sunday in the year would be welcome to very many, but then what is to determine the subject of each Sunday's poem? A chance verse or phrase in the Gospel for the day, as this is given in the Prayer-Book, is hardly a catholic or universal ground for fixing the subject. Again, Christmas, Good Friday, Easter-day, Whitsunday, have of course a catholic meaning, because these days, though not observed by all churches, are yet memorials of the sacred facts by which all Christians live. But the lesser Saints' days, Circumcision, Purification, as well as the occasional services, have a local and temporary, not a universal import. Accordingly, a perusal of the poems suggests what the preface to them confirms, that they did not all flow off from a free spontaneous inspiration, awakened by the thought natural to each day, but that a good number were either poems previously composed and afterwards adapted to some particular Sunday, or written as it were to order after the thought of rounding **"The Christian Year"** had arisen. So clear does this seem that it would not be hard to go through the several poems and lay finger here on the spontaneous effusions, there on those of more labored manufacture. The former flow from the first verse to the last lucid in thought, simple and most faultless in diction; no break in the sense, no obscurity; seldom any harshness or poverty in the diction. The others are imperfect in rhythm and language, defaced by the conventionalities of poetic diction, frequently obscure or artificial, the thread of thought broken or hard to catch. The one set are like mountain streams, that run down the hillside in sunshine, clear and bright from end to end, the other are like streams that find their way through difficult places, often hidden underground or buried in heaps or stones. Yet even the most defective of them come forth to light in some single verse of profound thought or tender feeling, so well expressed as to make the reader willingly forgive for that one gleam the imperfection of the rest.

2. HOME-FEELING

The next quality I would notice is the deep tone of home affection which pervades these poems. This, perhaps as much as anything, has endeared them to his home-loving countrymen. Such is that feeling for an ancient home breathed in—

> "Since all that is not Heaven must fade,
> Light be the hand of Ruin laid
>   Upon the home I love:
> With lulling spell let soft Decay
> Steal on, and spare the giant sway
>   The crash of tower and grove.
>
> "Far opening down some woodland deep
> In their own quiet glade should sleep
>   The relics dear to thought,
> And wild-flower wreaths from side to side
> Their waving tracery hang, to hide
>   What ruthless Time has wrought."

Again, the hymn for St. Andrew's Day is so well known and loved as hardly to need quoting. Every line of it is instinct with simple pure affection, yet never, one might think, so deeply felt or so well expressed as here:—

> "When brothers part for manhood's race,
>   What gift may most endearing prove
> To keep fond memory in her place,
>   And certify a brother's love?
>   . . . . .
> "No fading frail memorial give
>   To soothe his soul when thou art gone,
> But wreaths of hope for aye to live,
>   And thoughts of good together done."

Besides the more obvious allusions to the household charities, there are many delicate, more reserved touches on the same chord. Such is the—

> "I cannot paint to Memory's eye
>   The scene, the glance, I dearest love—
> Unchanged themselves, in me they die,
>   Or faint, or false, their shadows prove.
>   . . . . .
> "Meanwhile, if over sea or sky
>   Some tender lights unnoticed fleet,
> Or, on loved features dawn and die,
>   Unread, to us, their lesson sweet;
>
> Yet are there saddening sights around,
>   Which heaven, in mercy, spares us too."

But there is no need to go on with quotations. Many more such passages will occur to every reader. High education and refined thought in him had not weakened, but only made more pure and intense, natural affection. Yet in all the tenderness there is no trace of effeminacy. True, the woman's heart everywhere shows itself. But as it has been said that in the countenance of most men of genius there is something of a womanly expression not seen in the faces of other men, so it is distinctive of true poetic temper that it ever carries the woman's heart within the man's. And certainly, of no poet's heart does this hold more truly than Keble's. They, however, must be but blind critics, insensible to the finer pathos of human life, who have on this account called Keble's poetry "effeminate." The woman's heart in him is blended with the martyr's courage. Hardly any modern poetry breathes so firm self-control, so fixed yet calm resolve, so stern self-denial. If these be qualities that can consist with effeminacy, then Keble's poetry may be allowed to pass for effeminate. But those who bring this charge against it, misled, it may be, by the loud bluster that passes with many for manliness, seem to forget that the bravest and most high-souled manhood is also the gentlest and most tender hearted; that, according to the saying, "A man is never so much a man as when he becomes most in heart a child."

3. RESERVE

This naturally leads on to the notice of another characteristic of his poetry—the fine reserve, which does not publish aloud, but only delicately hints, its deeper feelings. It was an intrinsic part of Keble's nature to shrink from obtruding himself, to dislike display,—

> "To love the sober shade
> More than the laughing light."

And one object he had in publishing **"The Christian Year"** was the hope that it might supply a sober standard of devotional feeling, in unison with that presented by the Prayer-Book. The time, he thought, was one of unbounded curiosity and morbid craving for excitement, symptoms which have not abated during the forty years since Keble so wrote. He wished, as far as might be, to supply some antidote to these tendencies. Again, modern thought has, as all know, turned in upon itself, and discovered a whole internal world of reflections and sensibilities hardly expressed in the older literature. Keble so far shared this tendency with his contemporaries. But he set himself not to feed and pamper it, but to direct, to sober, and to brace it, by bringing it into the presence of realities higher than itself.

This feeling of delicate reserve, sobered and strengthened by Christian thought, comes out in many of the poems, in none perhaps more than in the one which contains these stanzas:—

> "E'en human Love will shrink from sight
>   Here in the coarse rude earth:
> How then should rash intruding glance
> Break in upon *her* sacred trance
>   Who boasts a heavenly birth?

"So still and secret is her growth,
    Ever the truest heart,
Where deepest strikes her kindly root
For hope or joy, for flower or fruit,
    Least knows its happy part.

"God only, and good angels, look
    Behind the blissful screen—
As when, triumphant o'er his woes,
The Son of God by moonlight rose,
    By all but Heaven unseen."

I would not pause on verbal criticisms,—only the last line of the second stanza here is one of many instances in which the beauty of the finest thoughts is marred by the admission of some hackneyed conventional phrase. Otherwise, these stanzas, as well as the whole poem in which they occur, are in Keble's finest and most native vein. In keeping with the feeling breathed by these lines is another which should be noted. As he keeps his own deepest feelings under a close veil of reserve, so he loves best the virtues and the characters which are least obtrusive, and generally get least praise. Things which the world least recognizes, for these he reserves his heart's best sympathy. For the loud, the successful, the caressed, he has no word but perhaps one of admonition. It is the poor, the bowed down, the lonely, the forsaken, who draw out his deepest tenderness. And what makes this the nobler in Keble is, that it does not seem to come from the principle of *haud ignarus mali,* but rather from pure strength of Christian sympathy. The traits of character for which he has the keenest eye, the virtues on which he dwells most lovingly, are those which men in general take least note of. Those who belong to "the nameless family of God" kindle in him a deep enthusiasm, such as most poets have reserved for the earth's great heroes. Thus, in one of his finest passages, after contrasting those Christians who live in the "green earth" and under the "open sky" of the country, with those whose lot is cast in the streets and stifling alleys of the crowded city, he bursts forth—

"But Love's a flower that will not die
    For lack of leafy screen,
And Christian hope can cheer the eye
    That ne'er saw vernal green;
Then be ye sure that Love can bless
E'en in this crowded loneliness,
Where ever-moving myriads seem to say,
Go—thou art nought to us, nor we to thee—away!

"There are in this loud stunning tide
    Of human care and crime,
With whom the melodies abide
    Of th' everlasting chime;
Who carry music in their heart
Through dusty lane and wrangling mart,
Plying their daily task with busier feet,
Because their secret souls a holy strain repeat."

And as is the inward tone of feeling, so is its outward expression, chastened and subdued. There is no gorgeousness of coloring, no stunning sound, no highly spiced phrase or metaphor. From what have been the chief attractions of much poetry popular since his day,—scarlet hues and blare of trumpets, staring metaphors and metaphysical enigmas, he turned instinctively. He seemed to say these,—

"Farewell: for one short life we part:
I rather woo the soothing art,
Which only souls in sufferings tried
Bear to their suffering brethren's side."

Those who have called other parts of Keble effeminate, might perhaps call this ascetic. If it is so, it is an asceticism in harmony with true Christianity, and with the sober wisdom that comes from life's experience.

4. DESCRIPTION OF NATURE

Much has been said of Keble's eye for nature. His admirers perhaps exaggerate it, his depreciators as much underrate it. He certainly shared largely in that feeling about the visible world, so identified with Wordsworth that is now called Wordsworthian,—that feeling which more than any other marks the direction in which modern imagination has enlarged and deepened. The appearances of nature furnish Keble with the framework in which most of his lyrics are set, the mould in which they are cast. Some whole poems, as the one beginning—

"Lessons sweet of spring returning,"

are little more than descriptions of some scene in nature. Many more take some natural appearance and make it the symbol of a spiritual truth. Two small rills, born apart and afterwards blending in one large stream, are likened to two separate prayers uniting to bring about some great result. The autumn clouds, mantling round the sun for love, suggest that love is life's only sign. The robin singing unweariedly in the bleak November wind, suggests a lesson of content—

"Rather in all to be resigned than blest."

These and many more are the natural appearances which, some by resemblance, some by contrast, furnish him with key-notes to religious meditation. In many you feel at once that the poet has struck a true note, one which will be owned by the universal imagination, wherever that faculty is sufficiently cultivated to be alive to it. In some you feel more doubtful,—the analogy appears to be somewhat more faint or far-fetched. In others you seem to see clearly that the resemblance is arbitrary and capricious, a work of the mere fancy, not of the genuine imagination. An instance of the last kind has been severely commented on by a contemporary critic who, on the strength of some doubtful analogies which occur in Keble's poems, has voted him no poet. This critic specially comments on one poem, in which the moon is made a symbol of the Church, the stars are made symbols of saints in heaven, and the trees in Eden of saints on earth. This, if it be not some remote allusion to passages of Scripture, must be allowed to be a mere ecclesiastical reading of nature's symbols, repudiated by the universal heart of man, and therefore by true poetry. But if this and some other instances, pitched on a false key, can be pointed out, how many more are there where the chord struck answers with a genuine tone? Even in the very poem which contains the symbolism condemned, is there not the following:—

> "The glorious sky embracing all
>   Is like the Maker's love,
> Wherewith encompassed great and small
>   In peace and order move."

Here Keble has christianized an analogy, acknowledged not only by the Greek conception of Zeus, but more or less, we believe, by the primeval faith of the whole Aryan race.

Of the many instances that might easily be gathered from these poems, in which that mysterious chord of analogy that binds together human feeling and the outward world is truly touched, one more must be given. It is from the poem on All Saints' Day. As that day falls on the 1st of November, a time so often beautiful with the bright calm of St. Luke's summer, the following lines serve well to harmonize the feeling of the season with the thoughts which the Church festival is meant to awaken:—

> "How quiet shows the woodland scene!
>   Each flower and tree, its duty done,
> Reposing in decay serene,
>   Like weary men when age is won,
> Such calm old age as conscience pure
> And self-commanding hearts insure,
> Waiting their summons to the sky,
> Content to live, but not afraid to die.

As might be looked for in a real lover of nature, Keble's imagery is that which he had lived in the midst of, and knew. The shady lanes, the more open hursts and downs, such as may be seen near Oxford, and further west and south, "England's primrose meadow paths," the styles worn by generations, and the gray church-tower embowered in elm-trees,—with these his habitual thoughts and sentiments suit well. Even in this familiar landscape his eye and ear have caught facts and aspects of nature, which, as far as I know, have never before been put down in books. Take that instance from the poem on the Fifth Sunday after Easter—

> "Deep is the silence of the summer noon,
>   When a soft shower

> Will trickle soon,
> A gracious rain, freshening the weary bower—
>   O sweetly then far off is heard
>   The clear note of some lonely bird."

Many an ear before Keble's must have heard a solitary thrush singing in the distant fields amid the deep hush that preludes the thunder-storm; but no poet before Keble, as far as I know, had seized that impressive image and embalmed it in verse. Not a few such images or aspects of the quiet English landscape will be found reclaimed from the fields for the first time in **"The Christian Year."** With this kind of scenery, which was familiar to him all his life, he is for the most part content, and seldom travels beyond it. Indeed, a very true test of the genuineness of a poet's inspiration would seem to be, whether his imagery is mainly gathered from the scenes amidst which he has lived, or is borrowed from the writings of former poets or other artificial sources. Seldom does Keble visit mountain lands, only once or twice in **"The Christian Year."** But the poem for the 20th Sunday after Trinity, though good, might have been written by one who had never seen mountains, if only he had read descriptions of them.

Besides the English there is another kind of landscape in which Keble has shown himself at home. Dean Stanley has noted the fidelity with which he has pictured scenes in the Holy Land. This shows not only a close study of the hints that are to be found in the Bible and in the modern books about Palestine,—it proves how quick must have been the insight into nature of one who, though he had never himself beheld that country, could from such materials call up pictures true enough to satisfy the eye of the most graphic of modern travellers even while he gazed on those very scenes.

There are two sides which nature turns towards the imagination. One is that which the poet can read figuratively, in which he can see symbols and analogies of the spiritual world. This side Keble, as we have seen, felt and read, in the main I think truly, though sometimes he may have missed it. What the true reading is, and how it is to be discerned, is a weighty matter to be entered on here. One thing, however, is certain, that the correspondency between the natural object and the spiritual, between nature and the soul, is there existing independently of the individual man. He did not make the correspondency; his part is to see and interpret truly what was there beforehand, not to read into nature his own views and moods waywardly and capriciously. The truest poet is he who reads nature's hieroglyphics most truly and most widely; and the test of the true reading is that it is at once welcomed by the universal imagination of man. This universal or catholic imagination of man is far different from the universal suffrage of men. It means the imagination of those in whom that faculty exits in the highest degree, cultivated to the finest sensibility. The imagination is the faculty which reads truly, the fancy that which reads capriciously, and so falsely. The former seizes true and really existing analogies between nature and spirit; the latter makes arbitrary and fictitious ones. In the school of imagination, as opposed to fancy, Keble was a faithful and devout student. It was the music of his pious spirit to read aright the symbolical side which nature turns towards man.

But nature has another side, of which there is no indication in Keble's poetry. I mean her infinite and unhuman side, which yields no symbols to soothe man's yearnings. Outside of and far beyond man, his hopes and fears, his strivings and aspirations, there lies the vast immensity of nature's forces, which pays him no homage, and yields him no sympathy. This aspect of nature may be seen even amid the tamest landscape, if we look to the clouds or the stars above us, or to the ocean roaring around our shores. But nowhere is it borne in on man as in the midst of the vast deserts of the earth, or in the presence of the mountains, which seem so impressive and unchangeable. Their strength and permanence so contrast with man—of few years and full of trouble; they are so indifferent to his feelings or his destiny. He may smile or weep, he may live or die; they care not. They are the same in all their ongoings, happen what will to him. They respond to the sunrises and the sunsets, but not to his sympathies. All the same they fulfill their mighty functions careless though no human eye should ever look on them. So it is all the great movements of nature. Man holds his festal days, and nature frowns; he goes forth from the death-chamber, and nature affronts him with sunshine and the song of birds. Evidently, it seems, she marches on, having a purpose of her own inaccessible to man; she keeps her own secret, and drops no hint to him. This mysterious silence, this inhuman indifference, this inexorable deafness, has impressed the imagination of the greatest poets with a vague yet sublime awe. The sense of it lay heavy on Lucretius, Shelley, Wordsworth, and drew out of their soul's profoundest music. This side of things, whether philosophically or imaginatively regarded, seems to justify the saying, that "the visible world still remains without its divine interpretation." But it was not on thoughts of this kind that Keble loved to dwell. If they ever occurred to him, he has nowhere expressed them. He was content with that other side of nature, of which I spoke first, the side which allows itself to be humanized, that is, to be interpreted by man's faith and devout aspirations. This was the side that suited his religious purpose, and to this he limited himself. Within this range few have ever interpreted nature more soothingly and beautifully.

These are a few of the qualities that would strike any one on first opening **"The Christian Year."** They are not, however, enough to account for its unparalleled popularity. Indeed, popularity is no word to express the fact, that this

book has been for years the cherished companion of numbers of the best men, in their best moods—men too of the most diverse characters and schools—who have lived in our time. The secret of this power is a compound of many influences hard to state or explain. It has not been hindered by the blemishes obvious on the surface to every one, inharmonious rhythms, frequent obscurity, here and there poverty and conventionality of diction. In spite of these it has won its way to the hearts of the highly educated and refined, as no book of poetry, sacred or secular, in our time has done. Will it continue to do so? Will its own imperfections, and the changing currents of men's feelings not alienate from it a generation rendered fastidious by poetry of more artistic perfection, more highly colored, more richly flavored? Without speaking too confidently, it may be expected to live on, if not in so wonderful esteem, yet widely read and deeply felt; for it makes its appeal to no temporary or accidental feelings, but mainly to that which is permanent in man. It can hardly be that it should lose its hold on the affections of English-speaking men as long as Christianity retains it. For if we may judge from the past, it will be long ere another character of the same rare and saintly beauty shall again concur with a poetic gift and power of poetic expression, which, if not of the highest, are still of a very high order. Broader and bolder imagination, greater artistic faculty, many poets who were his contemporaries possessed. But in none of them did there burn a spiritual light so pure and heavenly, to transfigure these gifts from within. It is because **"The Christian Year"** has succeeded in conveying to the outer world some effluence of that character which his intimate friends loved and revered in Keble, that, as I believe, it will not cease to hold a quite peculiar place in the affections of posterity.

Notes

1. This ought now to be "the late gifted occupant," as it refers to Mr. Matthew Arnold.

Alba H. Warren, Jr. (essay date 1950)

SOURCE: *"Praelectiones Academicae. 1844,"* in *English Poetic Theory 1825-1865,* Princeton University Press, 1950, pp. 46-65.

[*In the following essay, Warren studies Keble's poetic theory as explicated in his* Praelectiones Academicae. *Warren observes that for Keble the basic function of poetry is as a psychological and spiritual catharsis.*]

As Professor of Poetry at Oxford over a period of ten years from 1831 to 1841, John Keble, priest, poet, and Tractarian, delivered a remarkable series of Latin lectures on the nature of poetry and the poetic practice of the major Greek and Roman poets. Collected and printed in 1844 under the general heading, *Praelectiones Academicae Oxonii Habitae, Annis* MDCCCXXXII . . . MDCCCXLI, with the subtitle, *De Poeticae Vi Medica,* the lectures were praised at the time by Newman and others of Keble's Oxford friends; George Saintsbury in 1904 noticed them briefly but appreciatively—had literary criticism been more than a pastime with Keble, "he would, I think, twenty years before Arnold, have given us the results of a more thorough scholarship, a reading certainly not less wide, a taste nearly as delicate and catholic, a broader theory, and a much greater freedom from mere crochet and caprice";[1] and in 1912 the lectures were made available in English in a translation by Edward Kershaw Francis.[2]

The *Praelectiones* are really essays in Christian criticism. Open war is declared on secularism, materialism, utilitarianism, and liberalism. God, the sacramental universe, analogy, are working concepts; order, tradition, and decorum are pervasive ideals. Poetry is prayer, contemplation, a means of grace, the predisposition to piety. Unhappily, and in spite of many good things by the way, Keble's position is defensive and radically conservative. Not only is orthodoxy, especially in the matter of morals, the ultimate standard of literary value, but in politics and in the social and economic order orthodoxy is interpreted to mean conformity to Tory and High Church principles. The humanistic studies are defended against both pietist and utilitarian rather as effective conditioning of the feelings than of the intellect; and of the Christian virtues exemplified in the creative act and the artistic product, it is to the shyer, the more sentimental, the less virile, that Keble seems to be temperamentally committed.

Plato is perhaps the strongest single influence on Keble's poetic theory. The epigraph to the printed lectures is the figure of the rhapsode and the ring from the *Ion,* "Through them God moves men's souls in the way he pleases, and suspends one man from another." The intimate correspondence of the visible universe with the human mind, the symbolic nature of objects and events, divine inspiration in a literal sense, possession, the profound and disturbing emotional power of poetry, the necessity of moral censorship, are all Platonic ideas central to Keble's argument. Keble's "seminal principle" of poetry from which he deduces all the rest owes much to Aristotle's concept of *catharsis,* but in general, like Newman, Keble finds Aristotle too narrow, too intellectual, too formalistic. Among other predecessors Longinus and Cicero are quoted with approval, and Reynolds supplies the point of departure for more than one discussion. Modern poetry, and with it modern criticism, are in a period of decadence, irresponsible and pretentious in their straining for original effect, lacking in clarity and repose. Exception is made, however, for Scott and Southey, and particularly for Wordsworth, to whom the lectures are dedicated, "true philosopher and inspired poet who by the special gift and calling of Almighty God whether he sang of man or of nature failed not to lift up men's hearts to holy things nor ever ceased to champion the cause of the poor and simple and so in perilous times was raised up to be a chief minister not only of sweetest poetry but also of high and sacred truth." Wordsworth's characteristic ideas and beliefs turn up everywhere in the text with little modification. Coleridge, on the other hand, probably for theological reasons, is never mentioned by name, although Keble had certainly read him, and in some important respects Keble's theory is closer to Coleridge than it is to the Wordsworth of the early preface with its prevailing tendency towards "realism."

Keble's definition of poetry is by confession unsystematic, the elaboration of a single root metaphor: poetry is "a kind of medicine divinely bestowed upon men: which gives healing relief to secret mental emotion, yet without detriment to modest reserve: and, while giving scope to enthusiasm, yet rules it with order and due control."[3] In terms of the metaphor the poetic sensibility is "diseased," and there is evidence that at times Keble so considered it in fact. Poets are "sufferers" and their condition often approaches insanity. Poetry, then, is the release, the expression of emotion—as Keble calls it, a safety-valve; but it is the expression of emotion under peculiar and characteristic conditions, "without detriment to modest reserve." Poetic expression is never open or direct, but consists, as it were, of "certain veils and disguises" which yet "reveal the fervent emotions of the mind."[4] Aristotle's *catharsis,* romantic expressionism, and the Christian virtue of modesty come together here in an odd simulacrum of the Freudian theory of art as the means by which the neurotic introvert sublimates his libido.

The basic function of poetry is *catharsis.* All men, according to Keble's psychology, naturally find relief for strong emotion in expression. In primitive and uncultivated societies the expression of emotion is direct and uninhibited, but generally and almost invariably an innate reticence, a sense of "shame," enforces the repression of personal feeling. To the sensitive, tortured by emotion and yet restrained by this "noble and natural" shame, and to some obsessed with vague aspirations to greatness or with "the vicissitudes of human affairs," with "the marvellous ordered symmetry of the universe," or with "the holy vision of true and divine goodness," and for whom therefore the language of daily life as well is utterly inadequate, to these "sufferers," unwilling, or unwilling and unable, to declare openly their inmost feelings, God in the gift of poetry has furnished the comfort which tears give to the harassed body. "It is the function of Poetry to facilitate, yet without prejudice to modest reserve, the expression of glowing emotion."[5]

By this account there is in some sense a poetry of life in those characters and incidents which carry with them "evidence of some hidden emotion," some refined consolation which appeases a yearning desire for the moment denied satisfaction. The play-acting of children and the inarticulate expression of the rural classes of their affection for particular places, their regard for the dead and for religion, are "incipient poetry." In Wordsworthian vein Keble maintains that countryfolk have more in common with poetry than townspeople, but his reasons are his own:

> Townsmen have less becoming reserve; they are more habituated to daily avocations in the full light of publicity: and so waste no time in search for expedients and indirect methods, but give full vent to their feeling.[6]

The idea of "publicity," it should be apparent, is always painful to Keble; so much so, in fact, that in its extreme statement his theory rejects the element of communication in art altogether, and approaches Crocean expressionism. He speaks, for instance, of "those who are made poets by Nature and true feeling before they occupy themselves with literary style and metrical form";[7] and in another place he is quite explicit, "For in the present discussion we do not give the title of poet to him who publishes his verse with great popular acclaim, but rather to the man who meditates the Muse at home for his own delectation and solace."[8] Again in the extreme statement of the theory, and as the natural corollary, there is a sharp break between "nature" and "art," expression and technique, content and form. In general the second term of each pair is a pejorative. The entire process of externalization is, at best, suspect and strictly secondary. It also follows that the essential characteristic of poetic expression according to this theory is spontaneity (Wordsworth?). That is "not poetry at all" which is not "obviously the spontaneous outburst of the poet's inmost feeling."[9] The concept of spontaneity brings up at once the familiar romantic difficulty with determinism, a difficulty of particular danger to Keble as a Christian critic, and a difficulty which he does not always succeed in avoiding. "Indeed," he writes, "there is nothing for which this human lot of ours is more wont to be deplored than the fact that we cannot ourselves command our feelings or solace them by expression."[10] And he frequently uses the words blind impulse, instinctive, unconscious, unintentional, necessity, inevitable fate, in connection with the poetic process in a sense which can only be interpreted as deterministic. In all fairness, however, it must be said that, when he is aware of the issue, he is unequivocal, "It has indeed always been God's method not to override the free-will of men, even of His prophets when most strongly moved by the fervour of inspiration."[11] He emphatically rejects historical literary determinism, the "too clever speculation of certain contemporary would-be critics, whose constant theme is that the age, not the writer, is the real author of all that is written: and that results both of talent and of literary achievement are produced by a kind of fatalistic destiny."[12]

Keble takes notice of the classical doctrine of *mimesis* only to bend it to his own theory. He points out that Plato, who considered imitation the very essence of poetry, applied the term to all the arts, treating them under the general heading of music. This suggests that "each several one of the so-called liberal arts contains a certain poetic quality of its own, and that this lies in its power to heal and relieve the human mind when agitated by care, passion, or ambition," and that poetry, of all the arts, is best fitted for this office because it makes use of rhythmical language.[13] Keble, like Newman, is pursuing "the poetical," an essence or spirit of poetry which can be expressed in terms of feeling. He clinches his argument by observing that poets have always been considered a little mad, but that artistic imitation is hardly characteristic of the mentally deranged; therefore it is obvious that imitation "does not carry the whole power" of poetry. It is the man who can use imitation to give relief who is the true poet. This, says Keble, is essentially Aristotle's position in his remarks on poetic enthusiasm and versatility.

> "We share," he says, "the agitation of those who appear to be truly agitated—the anger of those who appear to be truly angry. Hence it is that Poetry demands, either great natural quickness of parts, or an enthusiasm allied to madness. By the first of these we mould ourselves with facility to the imitation of every form; by the other, transported out of ourselves we become what we imagine." For what else do these phrases, "enthusiasm allied to madness," "transported out of ourselves," imply, but that images of distant objects have sunk deeply into the poet's mind and that he fixes his gaze upon, or reaches out towards them with an almost morbid longing, utterly oblivious of present realities.[14]

Keble here seems to be somewhat closer to Freud than to Aristotle.

What is expressed, the matter of poetry, is emotion, "some hidden emotion," some "yearning desire which for the present is denied satisfaction."[15] The richest of these emotions for poetry is "the unquenchable longing for some object which is absent."[16] We may "infer," for instance, that Homer "betook himself to composition in order to appease in some measure his restless, burning passion for bygone days and departed heroes."[17] If the matter of poetry is powerful emotion, however, and its mode of expression spontaneous, the form of poetry would necessarily seem to be confined to the lyric. To meet this objection Keble goes to Quintilian for a classification of the emotions into *pathos* and *ethos*, feeling and character, or more broadly, passionate feelings and mild and gentle feelings. The longer forms are produced by *ethos*.

> Now, strong passion visits us but rarely: we ordinarily follow the natural bent of our temperament and character; no wonder, then, that far the greater number of poetic productions strike the gentler note. Indeed, except some lyrics and elegies, and a few satires, I

hardly recall one famous poem which is a pure and simple outcome of passion. All other poems reflect the character of a lifetime, and tastes which have become familiar to the mind by long association. Yet none the less, they must be acknowledged to spring from the inmost heart: you might indeed say that really and truly they are framed after and accord with the man's secret nature even more faithfully. Other remedies are at hand to allay or distract sudden access of anger or grief. Swift emotion both dies away spontaneously, and, moreover, is wont to arouse and stimulate genuine and stable strength of spirit. But what remedy is to be found for troubles which have clearly grown up with the character, silent and unnoticed, interpenetrating a man's whole life? Certainly, it will be a most effective solace if a man can, in some sort, enshrine in verse something of the form and feature of that which is closest to his heart.[18]

At this point Keble reinforces his theory by introducing his version of the eighteenth century concept of "the ruling passion": "I am inclined to believe that no poet, indeed no human being, is without some master feeling which focuses and binds together into somewhat of a unity the fluctuating and many varying distractions of the mind."[19] It is the presence and especially the quality of the master passion that distinguishes the "Primary" poet, and it is the critic's task (which, by the way, is mainly instinctive)[20] precisely to discover and lay bare this central feeling. It is also characteristic that the poet is "for the most part unaware"[21] of his obsession. Virgil's master passion, for instance, is the desire for the joy and beauty of natural objects; his interest in the epic machinery of the *Aeneid* is purely accidental and perfunctory; and Sophocles is denied Primary rank altogether largely because Keble can find no single emotional source for all of the plays. In the end Keble's theory puts a premium (a clear index of his moralistic bias) on the self-consistency of the poet's emotion with the result, curious in the light of his basic principles, that he has to defend the lyric poet against charges of "inconstancy," and therefore of insincerity. There is a strong resemblance, it will be noted, between Keble's *ethos* and Newman's "moral centers."

The definition of poetry as "the index to men's cares and the interpreter of their fancies"[22] leads to a preoccupation with the poet's biography, real or imagined. "Indeed, the special hope which stimulates us to devote ourselves to these studies is the hope that we may in time become familiarly acquainted with great men and penetrate into their most intimate counsels: whence it follows that there is always something for us to learn."[23] Interestingly enough, in the case of Homer this preoccupation suggests an analysis in some detail of Homeric imagery along lines rather similar to those developed later by Miss Caroline Spurgeon. Keble observes that his theory runs counter to the critical temper of the times; readers "will be repelled completely by this view, and will not, without reluctance, suffer themselves to be drawn away from the charms of

language and imagery, and the outward show and ornament of Poetry, in order to pry into the secrets of the poet's mind. How, they demand, does it concern us, in what spirit and with what disposition the poet wrote, so long as his writings are such as delight and stimulate men's thought and feelings?" Allegory is rejected by modern taste on the same grounds; but in any case, whether the effect of poetry is achieved "by allegorical symbolism or by the transference of the poet's own passion and disposition to actual characters," the reader "who once surrenders himself heartily to the poet's real meaning, will have little leisure for mere ornament and prettiness." Keble is here insisting on the primacy of theme and subordination of artistic means, and at the same time he attempts to reconcile the rival claims of representation and expression:

> Whether, therefore, throughout the whole course of a poem one story is really told in fact and substance, another outwardly in words—which is the characteristic of Allegory: or whether we make the true tenor of a poem to depend not so much upon the things described as upon the spirit and temper of the poet, in either case it is clear that the force and beauty of true poetry is twofold. For not only are the direct themes of the poem themselves expressed with lucidity and beauty, but the whole work is tinctured with the character and leanings of the poet as by some mysterious aroma: and in such wise, indeed, that all recognize that he burst forth into such expression naturally, and not for artistic effect. Should either of these two qualities be lacking, the poetry will be maimed and defective, or absolutely not poetry at all: maimed, unless the subject be faithfully and finely treated; not poetry at all, should it not be obviously the spontaneous outburst of the poet's inmost feeling.[24]

This is a balanced statement, reminiscent of Wordsworth and pointing towards Arnold, but it does not excuse Keble from the "intentional fallacy." For the most part, his attempts at biographical reconstruction and ventriloquism (like those of other nineteenth century critics) are practically worthless and almost invariably diversionary. Often, as with Sophocles,[25] one has the uncomfortable suspicion that moral prejudice against known or imputed biographical detail prevents Keble from really looking at the poetry. The "poetry" of Milton, Burns, Byron, and Shelley, seems to be vitiated in this way.

Although he uses both of the terms original and genius, and although he undoubtedly admired great men, Keble was too much of a traditionalist to come under the influence of the concept of original genius. His understanding of originality is rather classical or neoclassical than romantic. The Primary poet will be indifferent to novelty and untouched by ambition; he will repeat the old familiar themes; he will even plagiarize when he pleases.[26] By the same token, and in keeping with the moral reticence of his basic theory, self-expression is summarily ruled out. He will allow that "it is the prerogative of Homer, and of such as stand forth commandingly like Homer, to impress their own personality and standpoint upon their contemporaries";[27] but he says that Byron, "one who should have been a minister and interpreter of the mysteries that lie hid in Nature, has, in spite of all the vehement passion and variety of his poetry, in the main given us nothing but the picture of his own mind and personality, excited now by an almost savage bitterness, and now by voluptuous exaltation."[28]

Keble's "seminal principle" acts to separate all poets into two classes: "on the one hand, we have those who, spontaneously moved by impulse, resort to composition for relief and solace of a burdened or over-wrought mind; on the other, those who, for one reason or another, imitate the ideas, the expression, and the measures of the former." The first he calls "Primary Poets"; the second are poets only by courtesy title. The classification has old roots as Keble points out, the inspired rhapsodes of Plato and Democritus, Aristotle's versatile poet, the poet born-not-made of Horace.[29] In another form the distinction is that between "poets by Nature and necessity" and poets of "consummate skill and culture." The Primary poets are again subdivided into poets of *pathos* and *ethos* (lyric and elegiac, and tragic, epic, and didactic); and poets who derive their basic impulse from *ethos* are further distinguished by their temperamental preoccupation with human action or with nature into active and contemplative. Homer and Virgil represent these two great types. Keble finds in the historical order of the appearance of active and contemplative poetry an index of Divine Benevolence revealing the two great sources of hidden solace to suffering mortals.[30]

The characteristic marks of Primary poets are four, all of them, incidentally, moral. First, consistency; this is the evidence of truth of character and sincerity which can be observed in the poet's tastes and particularly in his choice of themes. Shakespeare, for instance, was always "heartily on the side of virtue" (his looser scenes are mere concessions to the spirit of the times). Second, the genuine poet will be indifferent to the desire for originality, and third, he will always show a modest reserve in expressing his profound emotions. The last of these has interesting consequences for the poet's technique. The parallel of the *arcana disciplinae* in the Early Christian Church will justify a certain obscurity in his poetry. Generally, fear of ridicule imposes the principle of indirection: the poet will avoid the real object of his enthusiasm; he will rather hint and suggest by subtlety of detail than describe fully or flatly; and he will frequently resort to understatement and "innocent" irony.[31] These devices, it will be noted, prefigure the early Eliotine theory of the impersonality of art. One passage is particularly clear: according to the theory the poet's intimate feelings do not lie "wholly hidden," but take "refuge as it were in a kind of sanctuary."

Now, in the case of those who set themselves to weave a regular plot, I mean dramatic and epic poets, it is obvious that the composer's personality naturally holds itself apart and retires into the background. Opinions are expressed, judgments passed, praise and blame are meted out, not however as the utterances of Homer or Aeschylus, but as those of an Achilles or a Prometheus.[32]

It is also characteristic "that those suffering most keenly through real, perhaps irreparable affliction, are the very men who most lightly trifle and play with words"[33] (George Herbert hid "the deep love of God which consumed him behind a cloud of precious conceits," and Shakespeare jested in his scenes of grief).[34] Keble does not develop any of these points, but the mere recognition of the poetic function of irony and word-play is surprising in the theory of the period.

The critic who is primarily interested in emotion and moral ideas is unlikely to spend much time over questions of the medium or of form. Keble's attitude towards the medium is Hegelian with perhaps a suggestion of early Christian iconoclasm. Sensuous and material, the medium is conceived as an impediment to the expression of the artist's spiritual intuition. An art is more "poetical" as it succeeds in effecting expression by subordinating the medium. "Conception" (in eighteenth century terms) is all important; "execution," particularly when it calls attention to itself, is the clear sign of artificiality. "The poetry of painting simply consists in the apt expression of the artist's own feeling." Raphael, who embodies "in beautiful form the inner conception of the mind," is poetical in contrast to Rubens, who "seizes those unlooked-for combinations of colour, light, and form which endlessly present themselves to the artist's mind and eye at the very moment of painting." Raphael's weakness is really his strength, for

> it is said that Raffaelle, while possessing a noble and lofty though perhaps somewhat unelastic genius, was somewhat careless and has left some works too crudely executed: as one who would indeed far rather violate the rules of art than not satisfy the inner vision, which he had conceived with marvellous beauty.[35]

Sir Joshua Reynolds, by the way, is cited as the authority for Keble's argument. Sculpture, architecture, and music, in rising scale of perfection according to the transparency of the medium, approach poetry "on that side of its effect which is concerned in piercing into, and drawing out to the light, the secrets of the soul."[36] By the same standard of expressiveness applied to the distinction between poetical prose and rhetoric, Plato is more poetical than Homer himself, while Cicero never rises to poetry. This is because Cicero always has his audience in mind; he is interested in producing a moving effect. Plato on the other hand, "seems absorbed in his own delightful themes; he writes to please himself, not to win over others; he generally hints at rather than speaks out his deeper truths; rich as he is in most beautiful thoughts, he seems to leave even more unsaid."[37]

There is no general discussion of the problems of form in the lectures. The weight of the theory bears heavily on "Nature," expression, inner spirit, away from art (by which Keble usually means artifice), form or formalism, structure, framework, plot, "machinery." If it is true that "a poet's fine frenzy is subject to law or control,"[38] according to Keble's principles the law or form ought to be organic. He seems to recognize this, but at the same time he also thinks of form in eighteenth century terms, even when, in keeping with the basic metaphor of the theory, he ascribes to it a medicinal function. The use of "those indirect methods best known to poets" already mentioned is part of this function.[39] At its best, Keble's argument calls for the due artistic subordination of all the formal elements of poetry to the presentation of theme. His position is roughly that of Newman, but there are anticipations of Arnold's Preface of 1853.

The attack on Aristotle follows the lines laid down by Newman and is plainest perhaps in the lectures on Sophocles. Sophocles is generally praised by Aristotelian critics for the finish and subtlety of his diction and for his skill in plot construction. But it is a question whether either of these grounds "necessarily touch the real art and poetic gift, or may not merely be viewed as their formal part and machinery."[40] Words and meters, however, are "mere instruments" of "the heavenly flame," and praise for these qualities raises the suspicion that the poet has nothing in common with "those who are made poets by Nature and true feeling before they occupy themselves with literary style and metrical form."[41] In the matter of plot construction, Keble finds Aristotle and the critics pandering to popular taste for exciting incident. There is, indeed, a legitimate use of plot by the poet, "not with intent that his books may be devoured by boys and girls for mere amusement, but that he himself may enjoy a profounder sense of the laws which silently control and govern all things."[42]

The "seminal principle" carries with it the implication "that there are plainly as many kinds of Poetry as of opinions and of men (for Poetry, native and true Poetry, is nothing else than each poet's innermost feeling issuing in rhythmic language."[43] But if the "seminal principle" can give rise to expressionistic form, it also gives rise, apparently, to its opposite. In the case of the sonnet with all of its formal difficulties as practiced by genuine poets Keble is persuaded that "it was by no mere chance, but by a deeply-rooted instinct, that such men as these adopted this form, because the fact that it is unusually stringent enabled it to soothe and compose their deepest emotions and long-

ings without violating a true reserve."[44] Lyric poets in the same way deliberately choose to work with elaborate meters, so that with "marvellous skill, art of the most exquisite kind is made to minister its healing touch to disordered Nature."[45] Keble's conclusion seems to be that, rightly understood, form is the principle of indirection in poetry, cleanly separable from its essence, which is emotion, and strictly subordinate to expression.

> Indeed, on the same principle on which we have before declared that verse has more power to soothe than prose, we may, I think, plainly perceive why it is, that in composing a poem too, it is better to have some story or settled plan before us, than to utter the changing impulse of the moment. The very fact of orderly and methodized progress may not a little conduce to settlement of mind. . . . [46]

Poets, particularly young poets, are wrong in condemning skill and plan. "They think they have indeed written something great if by lucky chance they have stitched in, here and there, some striking and clever patches; caring nothing whether they are appropriate or inappropriate, since they deny that a poet's fine frenzy is subject to law or control."[47] The subject must be faithfully treated *and* the poem must show evidence of spontaneous emotion. Keble would force classical and romantic elements together into an organic unity of which the integrating principle is theme. Of Aeschylus he writes,

> All these descriptions are so splendid, if we only judge them by the test of poetic "vividness," that it should surprise no one if most men, while duly honouring the philosophy of Aeschylus, yet at the same time contend that he was not seriously concerned about anything, except those artistic beauties which, as they insist, are the peculiar glory of Poetry. But if they once read with more kindly eyes even the *Eumenides* alone, willing to credit the poem with an aim a little more sacred and the possession of an under-meaning, it is almost impossible to say how greatly their delight would be increased even in that one pleasure, which they praise at the expense of all others; and how much more deeply skilful narration, or smooth sweetness of the verse, or charm of the imagery, would penetrate and permeate the inmost recesses of their hearts, when bathed and illuminated in a kind of heavenly light, glorifying a picture already beautiful in itself.[48]

Matters of style, diction, imagery, and versification are all subordinate to expression. Keble disposes of the general problems of meter and imagery quite simply by making it axiomatic "that Poetry, of whatever kind, is in one way or another, closely associated with measure and a definite rhythm of sound," and "that its chief aim is to recall, to renew, and bring vividly before us pictures of absent objects"; "it is the handmaid to Imagination and Fancy." Meter and imagery both subserve the remedial function of poetry "in soothing men's emotions and steadying the balance of their mind."[49] Like Newman the Platonist, however,

Keble will call attention to the power of single words, "Truly, it is past belief how powerfully single words or phrases, even perhaps the cadences of syllables falling on the ear in a happy hour, call forth the hidden fire."[50] This sort of statement surely holds the seeds of a theory of "pure poetry."

Keble has little to say about the imagination. At least once in the course of the lectures it is given Coleridgean function along with Keble's own psychotherapeutic one.

> Forthwith the fevered anxieties and ponderings which were spreading hither and thither like a flood, are now controlled and confined to a single channel: thither are directed or naturally flow all that crowds into the mind from all sides: and as Imagination strives to draw them together, while consciously or unconsciously she gives them outline and ornament, men gradually become their own physicians and do not resent the change that comes over them.[51]

At other times, however, Keble thinks of it in eighteenth century terms as a mode of memory, the image-making faculty, an associative power of the mind. When he says of it that "it paints all things in the hues which the mind itself desires," he seems to place himself with Newman squarely in the category of the Baconian idealist. But in his analysis of the two-fold nature of poetry he claims that it is immaterial whether the imagination projects its own values into nature or whether it finds them already there.[52] There is, in fact, some evidence in the lectures, especially in the passages dealing with nature poetry, that Keble also recognized the "naturalism" of Wordsworth and Ruskin. Homer, for instance, is praised for his "realistic power, and simple, direct clearness," and Virgil is "the most delightful priest and interpreter of Nature."[53]

Keble's psychological analysis of Homer's imagery has been mentioned earlier. The view of imagery as the key to the poet's subconscious interests is a basic principle of Keble's theory, and his application of it is an interesting pointer towards modern critical method. Compare, he says, the lines, "in which Virgil treats, as I said, of his own favorite delights, with such lines as his description of Fame, or the picture of Mount Etna, or of the night vision of the fury Alecto. We shall infallibly find that these, which it is more than likely he introduced through poetic convention, not through any feeling of his own, are elaborated with a wealth of language and an ordered sequence of metaphor, whereas those springing from his own feeling are merely touched by the way, as it were, and incidentally."[54] Keble goes on to define the emotional and moral centers, and the dominant and subordinate themes of his subjects very largely through examination of dominant and recurrent imagery.

On meter Keble has very little to add to what has already been said. By definition poetry is "nothing else than each poet's innermost feeling issuing in rhythmic language." Verse has more "power to soothe" than prose; as a means of control, a principle of indirection, of escape from personality into form, poets, particularly lyric poets, voluntarily commit themselves to elaborate verse forms in the working out of which "art of the most exquisite kind is made to minister its healing touch to disordered Nature."

The end of poetry in its psychological aspect is *catharsis,* which means relief and delight, perhaps delight in relief, at any rate delight. But poetry also has its moral aspect in which the end of poetry is truth, and especially Christian truth:

> . . . in reading the Scriptures, we assuredly know that we are in presence of truth itself, and that not even the smallest detail need be withdrawn from their full story. Consequently it is by their standard, when we have once ascertained and tested it, that Homer and his fellows must be judged.[55]

Ultimately, then, the function of poetry is moral and religious, "to lift to a higher plane all the emotions of our minds, and to make them take their part in a diviner philosophy,"[56] and Keble is on the horns of the familiar dilemma. He is not unaware of his problem, however, and while there is at times a crude moralistic bias in both the theory and the individual critical judgments, he does to some extent attempt to escape his own limitations. He recognizes the validity of "natural truths";[57] he leans heavily on symbolic interpretation which he calls analogy or platonizing:

> In fact, in modern times, good and pious men take pleasure in the study of the ancient poets largely for this simple reason, that they can tacitly transfer to the Great and Good God that which is said in Homer (it may be) or in Pindar, in honour of the fabled Jove, regarding them as dimly feeling after Him and foreshadowing the true Revelation and Sacrifice.[58]

Surprisingly enough, he fights stubbornly through a whole series of ingenious and sometimes amusing manoeuvres for Lucretius' right to rank as a Primary poet in spite of his atheism. He was probably afflicted with insanity (which "for a time, holds us like a tragedy, rapt with a kind of pleasing horror"!); he may have been suffering from possession by evil spirits; in any case, we must not suppose "that nothing but what is base and impious could issue from such a source: for it seems with the Great and Good Ruler of us all to have been almost a law, to emphasize and declare his own decrees by the testimony, willing or unwilling, of his enemies, whether men or evil spirits."[59] Finally, one can resort to "parody" in dealing with the parts of his poem.

> And, in truth, you will not easily find any one among the poets who lacked the enlightenment of revealed Truth, who affords so many splendid lines which, as it

were spontaneously, cast their testimony in favour of sound and sincere piety. Not one of them has left more numerous passages which any one, perhaps changing here and there a word or two, but yet maintaining the general tenor of the whole, can quote on the side of goodness and righteousness. Such a method of quotation is technically called a "parody" [*paroidia*].[60]

Keble does not really develop an adequate answer to his problem, however, unless it is implicit in the idea of "the unwilling witness," and his own judgments often seem to be arbitrary.

The final lecture in the long series stresses the interrelationship between poetry and religion, the true remedy for human ills. They are alike in their powers of healing. Both approach "each stage of beauty by a quiet and well-ordered movement." Truth for both is difficult and will yield only to devotion. Poetry and religion are equally subject to "the vision of something more beautiful, greater and more lovable, than all that mortal eye can see";[61] and they make common use of the external world: poetry leads men "to the secret sources of Nature" for images and symbols which it lends to religion; religion clothes them with its splendor and returns them to poetry as sacraments.[62] Poetry is the prelude to piety. All the great religious revivals of history have been prepared for by great poets, Plato and Virgil in antiquity, Spenser and Shakespeare in the Renaissance. Acknowledging the decline of religion and poetry in modern times, Keble sees no reason why men should not be raised gradually to a better life, "by a new order of Poetry."[63]

Keble's theory of poetry is strongest in its statement of value, weakest in its handling of form, and most interesting in its psychological basis. The *malaise* of the nineteenth century discovered in poetry a consolation, and consolation was justified times over in theory, by Keble, by Newman, by Mill and Arnold. Keble stands with Wordsworth and the romantics in their emphasis on the emotions and faithful expression (not self-expression, for there are always the methods of indirection), with Arnold and the neoclassics in their recognition of the importance of subject and the subordination of parts to whole. Although he tends to think of imagery and verse in theoretical contexts as decorative, he gives a psychological function to both, and in the case of imagery develops a strikingly modern technique of analysis. The theory is confused and often mistaken, but it offers its anticipations, it insists on the human values of poetry, and it tries to reconcile the best of old and new.

Notes

1. George Saintsbury, *A History of English Criticism,* New York, n.d., p. 535.

2. *Keble's Lectures on Poetry 1832-1841,* translated by E. K. Francis, 2 vols., Oxford, 1912. Quotations are from this text.

3. *Ibid.,* I, 22.

4. *Ibid.,* I, 47.

5. *Ibid.,* I, 19-24, 36.

6. *Ibid.,* I, 24-37.

7. *Ibid.,* II, 218.

8. *Ibid.,* I, 317.

9. *Ibid.,* II, 37.

10. *Ibid.,* II, 276.

11. *Ibid.,* I, 61.

12. *Ibid.,* I, 99. Does Keble mean Carlyle?

13. *Ibid.,* I, 53.

14. *Ibid.,* I, 56.

15. *Ibid.,* I, 25-26.

16. *Ibid.,* II, 262. One of the characteristics of Wordsworth's Poet is "a disposition to be affected more than other men by absent things as if they were present." *Wordsworth's Literary Criticism,* edited by N. C. Smith, London, 1905, p. 23.

17. *Ibid.,* I, 100.

18. *Ibid.,* I, 86-91.

19. *Ibid.,* II, 96.

20. *Ibid.,* I, 67-68.

21. *Ibid.,* II, 397.

22. *Ibid.,* I, 44.

23. *Ibid.,* II, 225. Sophocles' interest in stagecraft is scored against him: "All such things have to do with the stage effect, not with the author." *Ibid.,* II, 221.

24. *Ibid.,* II, 35-37.

25. *Ibid.,* II, 222.

26. *Ibid.,* I, 71-72.

27. *Ibid.,* I, 167.

28. *Ibid.,* II, 339 and 398.

29. *Ibid.,* I, 53ff.

30. *Ibid.,* I, 86ff.; II, 202-3 (Mill, Browning, Ruskin, and Arnold were all interested in the classification of poets); II, 274ff.

31. *Ibid.,* I, 82-83. Spenser "betrays to us what was really ever in his thought, even when writing his *Faerie Queene.* Being, as he was, the most loyal and devoted of lovers, he has in many passages cleverly worked in allusions to his own love amid the praises of his Queen, and thus, without alienating the sympathy of his readers, or betraying his secret passion, he could ease his own love troubles through poetic expression."

32. *Ibid.,* II, 97.

33. *Ibid.,* I, 82-83.

34. *Ibid.,* II, 99; I, 83.

35. *Ibid.,* I, 39-42.

36. *Ibid.,* I, 48.

37. *Ibid.,* I, 49.

38. *Ibid.,* I, 91.

39. *Ibid.,* I, 22.

40. *Ibid.,* II, 217. Aristotle "nowhere even hints at his feeling any delight in the charms of Nature and all the beauty of earth and sky." *Ibid.,* II, 264.

41. *Ibid.,* II, 218.

42. *Ibid.,* II, 219.

43. *Ibid.,* II, 35.

44. *Ibid.,* II, 102.

45. *Ibid.,* II, 100.

46. *Ibid.,* I, 90-91.

47. *Ibid.,* I, 91.

48. *Ibid.,* II, 41-42.

49. *Ibid.,* I, 21.

50. *Ibid.,* I, 322.

51. *Ibid.,* I, 59.

52. *Ibid.,* II, 36.

53. *Ibid.,* I, 168; II, 375; also I, 163, 173; II, 229, 244, 429.

54. *Ibid.,* I, 78.

55. *Ibid.,* I, 174.

56. *Ibid.,* II, 157; also II, 272-73.

57. *Ibid.,* II, 471; also II, 464.

58. *Ibid.,* II, 314; also II, 199.

59. *Ibid.,* II, 331ff.; also II, 442.

60. *Ibid.,* II, 350.

61. *Ibid.,* II, 480.

62. *Ibid.,* II, 481.

63. *Ibid.,* II, 478.

Brian W. Martin (essay date 1976)

SOURCE: "Keble and Wordsworth," in *John Keble: Priest, Professor and Poet,* Croom Helm, 1976, pp. 73-89.

[*In the following essay, Martin probes William Wordsworth's impact on Keble's poetry.*]

Keble had been introduced to Wordsworth's poetry, when he was a young undergraduate at Corpus Cristi College, Oxford. Keble was there in 1806; and in 1809, John Taylor Coleridge, later a prominent High Court judge arrived there. He was the son of Samuel Taylor Coleridge's brother James, and he took to Corpus with him copies of *The Lyrical Ballads* and Wordsworth's *Poems in Two Volumes.*

Apart from John Coleridge, it does not seem probable that any, of the Corpus undergraduates had known Wordsworth's poetry before going up to the University. Later, John Coleridge, who was to become the first biographer of John Keble, wrote that the influence of Wordsworth's poetry undoubtedly played upon Arnold, one of the Corpus group, bringing out in him his great, lofty and imaginative ideas. No doubt it was Wordsworth's inspiration that drove him, when the headmaster of Rugby School, to take reading parties of senior boys to the Lake District, in order to seek spiritual refreshment away from the industrial towns during the vacations.

Keble became a great admirer of Wordsworth as his poetry clearly shows. It is interesting that Wordsworth's *Ecclesiastical Sketches* were published in 1822. He was not concerned with writing about the doctrines of the Christian faith. As Wordsworth wrote to Henry Alford on 21 February 1840, talking about the discussion of religious doctrine in poetry as a whole, he felt 'far too deeply to venture on handling the subject as familiarly as many scruple not to do'.[1]

It is impossible to believe that Wordsworth was in any way adversely criticising Keble for the publication of **The Christian Year.** It is more likely that Wordsworth was aware that Keble was competent in dealing with doctrine and liturgy in poems while others were not. It was always the rhythm, metre and language that Wordsworth condemned: never the content. Indeed Wordsworth admired **The Christian Year** so much that he declared, 'It is very good; so good, that if it were mine, I would write it all over again'; and it was Pusey's opinion that Wordsworth and Keble should jointly recast the poetry.

Two other sources support the view that Wordsworth admired the content of Keble's poetry. Henry Crabb Robinson wrote that Sara Coleridge had noted in her copy of the *Memoir* of Wordsworth that she herself 'heard Wordsworth declare that there is better poetry in Watts than in Keble'. Crabb Robinson also stated that he had heard Wordsworth 'speak slightingly of the mechanical talents of Keble, but he esteemed the tendency of his poems'. And Wordsworth himself wrote to his nephew Christopher in 1836 saying that he had analysed Keble's 'verses on baptism' and had proved the style: '. . . how vicious it was in diction, though the thoughts and feelings were quite suitable for the occasion. Keble has been seduced into many faults by his immoderate admiration of the ancient classics.'[2]

As it happens, although Keble owed much to Wordsworth in the composition of **The Christian Year,** it is undoubtedly true that Wordsworth himself owed something to Keble in his later work concerned with devotional and religious themes.

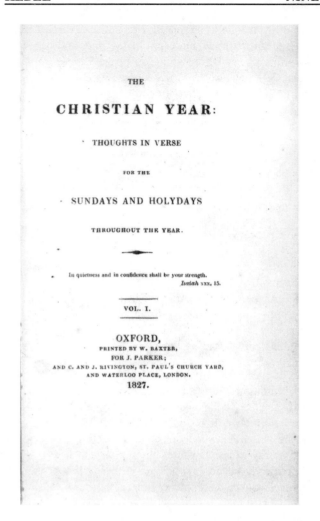

At no time was the relationship between Keble and Wordsworth close or intimate. There are references to Wordsworth in Keble's letters to Thomas, but they are mostly passing ones, or trivial. On 3 June 1815, he mentioned to Thomas, in a letter mainly concerned with telling about the manufacture of a wooden leg for their sister Elizabeth: 'Wordsworth is here [Oxford] and I am to go with Coleridge some day to see him. My review I see is out, and Coleridge has told him of it: which I had rather he had not, being as how I talk about his being childish etc.'[3] In 1825 Keble wrote to Thomas about a friend of theirs called Jack Menzies who had just sent a letter to John. Menzies was 'in as much of a passion as ever I knew him cause why he has not been writ to so long'. Keble reported that Menzies '. . . has been touring in the Lakes, and saw Wordsworth in a plaid jacket which was very surprising'.[4] Much later, in 1842, Keble wrote to Thomas from Low Wood, near Ambleside, on 25 July: 'I suppose I shall call on Wordsworth tomorrow: we are not 3 miles from him I believe.'[5]

However, while the relationship was not intimate, Keble's great respect for Wordsworth's poetry is evident throughout his work, and throughout his life. There was one period of brief correspondence between the two at the time when Keble was a tutor of Oriel College and Wordsworth was seeking admission for his son John at Oxford. Wordsworth's letters to Keble are in Keble College Library; and Keble's are in the collection of Dove Cottage Papers. It may be true, however, that one reason for Keble's reluctance to publish *The Christian Year* in 1827 was partly due to Wordsworth's indirect influence. In Wordsworth's poem 'The Liturgy' he denied having the power or the possibility of writing on the basic precepts of the Christian faith. The 'stupendous mysteries' were not within the bounds of his poetic gifts:

> Upon that circle traced from sacred story
> We only dare to cast a transient glance,
> Trusting in hope that Others may advance
> With mind intent upon the King of Glory,
> From his mild advent till his countenance
> Shall dissipate the seas and mountains hoary.

Mary Moorman, Wordsworth's biographer, writes that: '. . . the answer to this challenge came in 1827, in the publication of Keble's *Christian Year*—which for the next half-century was unrivalled as a book of devotion in Anglican households'. It is more likely though that Keble was put off publishing his poems by what Wordsworth had written; by all accounts he was a modest, and retiring man, and he took much persuading by his friends, especially Davison, and by his father, before he would publish—and even then he did so anonymously. The book was not only popular in Anglican households, but elsewhere as well: Newman's 'fons et origo mali' had a universal appeal, for dissenters as well as High Churchmen.

While the cause for Wordsworth's complaints against Keble's poetry can easily be recognised in Keble's archaic diction and often tortured syntax, it can also be appreciated both from Keble's poetry and his lectures that Keble thought much the same as Wordsworth over poetic inspiration. Indeed, much of what Keble wrote is a restatement of Wordsworth's Preface to the second edition of *The Lyrical Ballads,* published in 1800.[6]

Wordsworth's famous passage

> I have said that poetry is the spontaneous overflow of powerful feelings: it takes its origin from emotion recollected in tranquillity: the emotion is contemplated till, by a species of reaction, the tranquillity gradually disappears, and an emotion, kindred to that which was before the subject of contemplation, is gradually produced, and does itself actually exist in the mind.

accords with Keble's stipulation in **'Lecture xxii'** that poetry must be the 'spontaneous outburst of the poet's inmost feeling', though tempered by a due reserve and recourse to rhyme and metre; and in '**Lecture IV**' Keble had already made his distinction between poets of primary rank, and poets of secondary rank, in which primary poets are 'spontaneously moved by impulse' and 'resort to composition for relief and solace of a burdened or overwrought mind'.[7]

It is clear enough, however, that Wordsworth's influence must have been strong on Keble in the years before 1832 when he was elected to the Chair of Poetry. Then, despite his views on poetry obvious from his occasional reviews, and what was apparent from his own poetry, Keble found it necessary to think deeply about the nature of poetry and to write down his opinions in lecture form. As previously mentioned he did not find it a particularly easy task.

Sir John Coleridge records how Keble saw his way with difficulty into the term of office.[8] He quoted from a letter sent to him by Keble:

> I am not particularly sanguine about this Professorship, to which my friends have been so kind as to nominate me; I feel as if the Latin wouldn't come; and what is worse, I have not come to any resolution on the subject to lecture on; if anything occurs to you, the smallest donation will be thankfully received.

It was not long before he had decided on his theme for the lectures, and, as John Coleridge pointed out, he had touched on it in a letter to Froude as early as September, 1825, when writing of *The Christian Year.* Keble wrote with his usual modesty:[9]

> It would be a great delight to do something, which might be of use to the sort of persons you mention: but that must be left for someone who *can* do it—and probably whenever it is done, it will be done, it will be done by somebody who never thought of it himself, but merely wrote to relieve his own mind. Indeed, that was the original purpose of what you have seen, and so far it has proved very useful; but there is no making a silk purse out of a sow's ear—a foolish figure, but farewell that.[10]

So he showed that the poet wrote from a full heart which overflowed in order to relieve itself, much in accord with Wordsworth's ideas about the origin of poetry.

Even so, when it came to rationalising what he thought about poetry the task looked formidable, and the preparation was hard work. Keble wrote to Sir John Coleridge on 13 February 1832: 'I was at Oxford the beginning of this week "reading in",—it is uphill work to me, and you never said a much truer thing than when you told Tom I was ten years too old for the task.' In a similar vein, Keble wrote to his brother Tom in what must have been early 1832. The letter is undated:

> I have writ 1/3 or more of the first lecture, but can hardly tell how it may do. I mean to consider [*Poi-etike*][11] as affording relief to a full mind, in which single point of view I apprehend there is enough *sayable* on it to fill 20 lectures easily if one had the sense to find it out, and also the Latin to say it in.

And again to Tom, he remarked: 'N.B. The smallest donations either of sense or Latin will be thankfully received.'[12]

The business of composing and delivering the lectures in Latin was not a prospect which Keble relished: this is clear from his letters, too.

To Sir John Coleridge he wrote (in a letter already quoted):

> . . . and as to the Latin it will be, it will be [*agapeton*],[13] if I do not disgrace myself. However, I do not like the notion of making it English, even if the Doctors would allow it; because of the moral certainty of a large importation of trash, which ought not to be on the University account; and also because I think Latin would suffer more than Poetry would gain.

No doubt, too, the idea of keeping the lectures in Latin had much to do with the doctrine of Reserve which was very important in Keble's theory of poetry. The use of Latin meant that the ideas he was putting forward were not available to the vulgar and the uninitiated: there was no reason for the lectures to be popular: after all, they were about poetry, closely allied to religion, and therefore demanded reverence and a due amount of reserve. When occasion demanded, Keble was well aware of the disadvantage of using Latin as a means of communication. When he had composed the Protest over Peter Young's rejection, he sent a copy to Thomas, and wrote on 23 December 1841: 'I am afraid Charlotte's notion about doing it in Latin, though very nice in many respects, would have the effect of putting the thing on the shelf.'[14] With the lectures, it was not a case of putting them 'on the shelf', but of reserving what was said for those who were able to appreciate it, and for the *cognoscenti*. It was left to Matthew Arnold, when he filled the Chair later, to throw over the Latin traces and deliver his famous lectures, for the first time, in English. And so, bound up with Keble's commitment to lecturing in Latin was his recognition and acceptance of the doctrine of Reserve, not only in its relation to religion but also in relation to poetry, which, in any case, he regarded as allied to religion, if not indeed an integral part of it. In '**Lecture XL**', Keble wrote '. . . real Religion is in striking accord with true poetry', and later, in the same lecture, he saw it as 'a high-born handmaid' that 'may wait upon and minister to true Religion'.[15] He thought that if the lectures were given in English, the sacred subject of poetry might have been infected by a popular and vulgar interest. To maintain Latin was to keep the subject properly esoteric: subsequently it might be judged what should be communicated to the people in general. Keble saw in Latin the means of curbing popular extravagance. He considered that there were many men in the field of literary criticism who were pretentious, and that many of them were responsible for troublesomely insistent publications: some of these publications were even weekly. He regarded Latin as being the medium of good taste, which provided a kind of veil against the intrusions of pernicious opinion.

Nevertheless, the composition of Latin made his task difficult, and as is seen from his letters, he valued any help which might have been offered from his friends. The result was successful and his forebodings short-lived. Newman praised the *Lectures*: 'As coming from a person of high reputation[16] for Latinity they were displays of art.'[17] and: 'His greatest literary work, his *Lectures on Poetry* so full of acute remark and so beautiful in language, is in Latin.'[18]

However, having resigned himself to Latin, and briefly outlined the theme of his lectures to Thomas Keble in early 1832, he was much fuller in explanation when he wrote to Sir John Coleridge in February 1832. Keble gave his inaugural lecture towards the end of that month, but even so his ideas and theme expanded as time went on, as the lectures show, and led Keble into a second term of the Professorship. To Coleridge, on 13 February Keble wrote:

> My notion is, to consider Poetry as a vent for overcharged feelings, or a full imagination, and so account for the various classes into which poets naturally fall, by reference to the various objects which are apt to fill and overpower the mind, so as to require a sort of relief. Then there will come in a grand distinction between what I call Primary and Secondary Poets; the first poetising for their own relief, the second for any other reason. Then I should [*basanizein*][19] one after another each of the great Ancients, whom in my Royal Authority I think worthy of the name of a Primary Poet, and show what class he belongs to, and what sort of person I take him to have been. From which will arise certain conclusions as to the degree in which the interest of poetry depends on the character of the writer, as shewn in his works; and again, as to the relation between this art, and practical goodness, moral and religious.[20]

The similarity between the views on poetry of Wordsworth and Keble has already been stated, but here again the idea of poetry being the means of relief for overcharged feelings is consistent with Wordsworth's theories. Keble's reverence towards Wordsworth, though rarely expressed as such, is perfectly obvious. The *Lectures on Poetry* were dedicated to him:

> To William Wordsworth, true philosopher and inspired poet who by the special gift and calling of Almighty God whether he sang of man or of Nature failed not to lift up men's hearts to holy things nor ever ceased to champion the cause of the poor and simple and so in perilous times was raised up to be a chief minister not only of sweetest poetry but also of high and sacred truth. This tribute slight though it be, is offered by one

of the multitude who feel ever indebted for the immortal treasure of his splendid poems in testimony of respect, affection, and gratitude.

After such a dedication, it is not surprising that Keble's lectures bear the mark of Wordsworth's poetic theories.

Later in 1839, when Wordsworth was received by the University in Oxford, Keble as Professor of Poetry was called on to give the Creweian Oration. When Wordsworth arrived for the conferment of his honorary degree, he listened to Keble's praises:

> But I judged, Gentlemen of the University, that I should satisfy, and more than satisfy, what this topic demands if only I should recall to your recollection him (specially now as in this honourable circle which surrounds me he is himself present,) who of all poets, and above all has exhibited the manners, the pursuits, and the feelings, religious and traditional, of the poor,—I will not say in a favourable light merely, but in a light which glows with the rays of heaven. To his poetry, therefore, they should, I think, be now referred, who sincerely desire to understand and feel that secret and harmonious intimacy which exists between honourable Poverty, and the severer Muses, sublime Philosophy, yea, even, our most holy Religion.[21]

Though Wordsworth was gratified by this tribute at the end of Keble's oration, it seems curious that Keble should identify Wordsworth particularly as the poet of the poor. It is true that he had been a radical, which led to some second thoughts on the Kebles' part when the *Lectures* were about to be published. Keble wrote to his brother on 23 January 1844:

> You see the *Praelectiones* are now all in print and they are waiting only for the Index, Title and Preface. Now I have always intended to write a few lines of dedication to old Mr. Wordsworth: but Mrs. J.K. has started a doubt on account of his having begun life as a Radical. You must give me your unbiased opinion soon, for I want with all speed to write it and send it to C. Wordsworth to be criticized, unless someone dissuades me.[22]

So far as Wordsworth's youthful poverty was concerned, it might have been honourable, but it was not the sort of poverty which afflicted and oppressed Goody Blake. In the sense that Wordsworth was the poet of such characters as Goody Blake, and the Female Vagrant, Keble's statement was true; but perhaps the oration was one occasion when Keble was being over sententious and moralistic. Yet it still showed his great respect for Wordsworth.

Still more important in showing the consistent influence which Wordsworth's thoughts and poems had on Keble, is the motto chosen for *Lyra Innocentium* published in 1846, and subtitled *Thoughts in verse on Christian Children; their ways and their privileges*. The motto was the last stanza of Wordsworth's 'Anecdote for Fathers':

O dearest, dearest boy! my heart
For better lore would seldom yearn,
Could I but teach the hundredth part
Of what from thee I learn.

This poem, of course, is very appropriate and important in understanding Keble's theory of poetry; and it agrees very much with what Keble wrote elsewhere. In Wordsworth's poem, the adult tries to force the boy to rationalise his preference for Kilve rather than Liswyn Farm. The boy is unable, or unwilling, to do this, and finally, in order to satisfy the adult, casts around for some explanation that will stand as a reason for the insistent adult. He sees the weather-vane on Liswyn Farm and gives it as a negative reason for preferring Kilve by the seashore. The point, however, that Wordsworth was making, was that the boy's feelings for a place should have been sufficient for the adult: there was no need for reasons. What the poem states takes us back to Keble's review of Copleston's *Praelectiones,* already quoted, in which he stated that poetic criticism's 'axioms are drawn from the feelings, not the reason'.

In a number of other places, too, Keble referred directly to poems of Wordsworth. In his review of Lockhart's *Life of Sir Walter Scott,*[23] which is particularly interesting for showing more of what Keble thought about other contemporary poets, Keble reinforced his theory that ordinary and uneducated people were capable of poetical experience. He wrote:

> The quiet and domestic character will be recognized as poetical, when, being cast upon the turmoil of busy life, it betrays itself to be forever contriving imaginary escapes and little images of the repose for which it longs: the animated and soaring temper in like manner, when untoward circumstances keep it still in the shade and it manages to relieve itself by the same sort of indirect exercise.

Keble then went on to quote from 'The Reverie of Poor Susan', Wordsworth's poem about a girl from the country disorientated from her proper surroundings, isolated and alienated in London:

> The former will sympathise with those who in a great city cherish in secret the remembrance of their native mountains:—
>
> Bright volumes of vapour through Lothbury glide,
> And a river flows on down the vale of Cheapside.

Keble concluded that it was the difficulty, and the way, of overcoming the person's desperate longing for the old, habitual scenes, which marked such a character as Susan as poetical. It will be seen later, in Part III, that similar sentiments are echoed in Keble's own poetry, for example in the **'Morning Hymn'**, and the poem for St Matthew.

Later, in the same review Keble wrote of Scott's childhood, and showed how Lockhart described Scott's boy-hood and youth having a great influence on his writings. Keble noted: 'Nowhere, probably, in biography can be found a completer illustration of Wordsworth's sentiment. 'The child is father of the man'. Wordsworth wrote about the sentiment in the lines beginning 'My heart leaps up when I behold . . .', but the last three lines of that poem were used as a sort of introduction to his great Immortality Ode. This ode Keble indirectly referred to in '**Lecture XXXIX**' when he was discussing the ancient, Pythagorean theory of souls coming from an unknown region before birth and the Platonic theory of recollection. Without naming Wordsworth or the ode, Keble wrote:

> The finest poem of the greatest poet within our times is mainly based on this belief: namely, that our recollections of childhood are touched with their peculiarly exquisite and far-reaching charm, simply because of its dim feeling of a former existence and of a life closer to divine influence.

There could hardly have been better praise for a poem, or a poet: not even Walter Scott, before he gave up poetry because of Byron's competition,[24] earned that admiration.

Keble himself took childhood as a theme for *Lyra Innocentium: Thoughts in verse on Christian children, their ways and their privileges* (1846), in which a poem such as **'Children like Parents'** reflects a combined Wordsworthian and analogical view of babies:

> And even as loving nurses here
>   Joy in the babe to find
> The likeness true of kinsmen dear
>   Or brother good or kind,
> So in each budding inward grace
>   The Seraphs' searching ken
> The memory haply may retrace
>   Of ancient, holy men.

And the theme occurs often in *The Christian Year,* for example, in the poem for the Sixth Sunday after Epiphany, and **'Holy Baptism'**.

Wordsworth was looked to in **'Sacred Poetry'**, when Keble wanted to substantiate his claim that sacred poetry must reflect a poet's sustained general tone of thought. It was part of what Keble held to be the quality of a primary poet: the primary poet had to be consistent and sustained. If a poet in his own life was fickle and his temperament continually changing, if he had flashes of brilliance only on occasions, and if his thoughts constantly fluctuated, then he did not belong to the first order. Even such a poet as Dryden was denied the first rank (see p. 92). Keble quoted 'Wordsworth's beautiful description of the Stock-dove':

> He should sing 'of love with silence blending,
> Slow to begin, yet never ending
> Of serious faith and inward glee'.[25]

Certainly, it seems, Wordsworth as poet was always in Keble's mind. In **'Lecture xvi'** Keble remarked that as fire is kindled by fire 'so a poet's mind is kindled by contact with a brother poet'; and this must have been the case for Keble, judging by the pervasive, obvious influence of Wordsworth in his poetry and his writings about poetry. As remarked before, the *Lectures* echo the sounds of Wordsworth's poetic philosophy: in **'Lecture xxii'** Keble stated that poetry must be 'the spontaneous outburst of the poet's inmost feelings',[26] and in xxiv Keble added that, 'The essential requirement is that everything should flow from a full heart'.[27] In **'Lecture xxx'** Keble referred to 'The Excursion', book IV, lines 717-44, and 851-87, where Wordsworth talked of the Greeks, and said that in Greece:

> . . . emanations were perceived; and acts
> Of immortality, in Nature's course,
> Exemplified by mysteries . . .

Yet this was one of the areas where Keble and Wordsworth began to differ. In view of Wordsworth's declared opinion that Keble had been seduced by the classics, it is difficult to see the brother poets observing the ancient authors in the same light. Keble's emphasis lay very much on the Classics as the lectures on poetry show: he saw in the work of the great classical poets the promise of what was to come in English poetry, at the same time as interpreting them, together with the Hebrew authors, in the role of primitive priests of true religion which was later to be revealed to men by the coming of Christ. As a classical scholar, therefore, it was only natural that Keble should concentrate on the poets of Greece and Rome.

The other area where there was serious disagreement between the 'brother poets' was over the matter of diction. Wordsworth's opinion of *The Christian Year* has already been noted: he felt there was much room for improvement in the modes of Keble's expression. Certainly Keble was not bothered to use 'a selection of language really used by men'.[28] Keble's language rather belonged to the stock of poetic words whose repository lay in the eighteenth century; and, beyond that, much of Keble's diction was similar to that of Milton's minor poems. It was not so grand as that of 'Paradise Lost', but it bore remarkable resemblance to that of the shorter poems. To quote Wordsworth, in another context, he no doubt thought that Keble was one of those who 'From generation to generation . . . are the dupes of words';[29] but Keble would have seen in his recourse to an esoteric form of vocabulary yet another way of giving his poetry a due reserve and modesty which he believed was proper.

Where the poets did agree was in the field of rhythm and metre. In his review of Lockhart's *Life of Sir Walter Scott* Keble wrote that rhyme and metre in poetry are the necessary controls on the violent passion for expression.[30] Yet,

as usual with Keble, there was another purpose, that of investing the feelings seeking expression with a due sense of reserve:

> . . . the conventional rules of metre and rhythm may evidently have the effect of determining in some one direction, the overflow of sentiment and expression, where with the mind might otherwise be fairly oppressed. On the other hand, the like rules may be no less useful, in throwing a kind of veil over those strong or deep emotions, which need relief, but cannot endure publicity.

It is interesting that a little before in this review Keble stated that: 'Poetry is the indirect expression in words, most appropriately in metrical words, of some overpowering emotion, or ruling taste, or feeling, the direct indulgence whereof is somehow repressed.'[31]

This sentiment, so much in accord with what Wordsworth thought about poetry, was followed by the assertion 'that mountainous districts are more favourable to the poetical temper than unvaried plains, the habits of the country than those of the town, of an agricultural than of a commercial population'.[32] It is possible to see in this part of the review a direct reference to Wordsworth, and a plain statement about the sort of poetry Keble composed.

Elsewhere Keble wrote about the discipline of poetic form. In **'Lecture i',** he defined poetry as being associated with measure and a definite rhythm of sound, at the same time as declaring that it was the means of relief for sufferers with oppressed hearts: poetry's chief aim was to recall or renew, and 'bring vividly before us pictures of absent objects'.[33] And in **'Lecture xxviii'** Keble made sure that his listeners did not take his stress on poetic form with the wrong emphasis. Metre and rhythm were secondary: true feelings were most important. Keble made it clear that poetry:

> . . . uses both words and metres as mere instruments, just like a queen employing her messengers: they are not dominant, not of first importance. . . . Hence it follows, with regard to any poet who by general consent is mainly praised for the richness and beauty of his diction, that we may fairly question if he has anything in common with those who are made poets by Nature and true feeling before they occupy themselves with literary style and metrical form.[34]

The difference between Keble and Wordsworth on this ground was that Wordsworth made a distinction between prose, metrical composition, and poetry, and it was unnecessary for poetry to have the bounds of metre, whereas Keble regarded metre as an integral part of poetry. Wordsworth's views were expressed in the Preface to the Second Edition of *Lyrical Ballads* 1800, where he analysed Gray's sonnet 'In vain to me the smiling mornings shine'. Exactingly, and, perhaps, somewhat pedantically, Wordsworth noted: '. . . it is equally obvious, that, except for rhyme, and in the use of the single word "fruitless" for fruitlessly, which is so far a defect, the language of these lines does in no respect differ from that of prose'.

However, for his own part, Wordsworth went on to state that he thought metre and rhyme were an admirable means of restraining excitement and over balanced pleasure in poetry:

> If the words, however, by which this excitement is produced, be in themselves powerful, or the images and feelings have an undue proportion of pain connected with them, there is some danger that the excitement may be carried beyond its proper bounds. How the co-presence of something regular, something to which the mind has been accustomed in various moods and in a less exciting state, cannot but have great efficacy in tempering and restraining the passion by an inter-texture of ordinary feeling, and of feeling not strictly and necessarily connected with the passion.

It cannot be denied that there were differences between Wordsworth's and Keble's theories of poetry; but the main difference for Keble was implicit in a dilemma he found himself in which concerned privacy and publicity. For Keble poetry was a private affair, a form of catharsis if you wrote it, a source of possible catharsis in a vicarious way if you read it and a source of meditation and reflection. This view of poetry was too narrow for Wordsworth: poetry for him had a public duty and was not only concerned with the private, contemplative moods of Religion. A sense of social responsibility, and of man's place philosophically in his public world, occupied Wordsworth's mind more than Keble's. Both Wordsworth's poems and his various prefaces show this well enough. Keble's poetry was essentially private, narrower in theme than Wordsworth's; and, what is more important, Keble's theory of poetry was more extreme.

Notes

1. Quoted by Mary Moorman in *William Wordsworth: A Biography,* Oxford, 1965, Vol. II, p.394.

2. Moorman, Vol. II, p.480.

3. Correspondence, C13.

4. Correspondence, C13.

5. Correspondence, C15.

6. It does not seem that Keble paid much regard to Wordsworth's ideas on poetic diction, laid out in the appendix to the Preface in the third edition, 1802.

7. John Keble's lectures on poetry—*Praelectiones Academicae*—were in Latin. E. K. Francis translated them into English and the lectures were published in that form in 1912. Quotations from the lectures will be from his translation: John Keble, *Lectures on Poetry,* tr. E. K. Francis, Oxford, 1912.

8. Coleridge, *Memoir,* Vol. I, p.207.

9. See Appendix B.

10. Coleridge, Vol. I, p.121.

11. 'poetics'.

12. Correspondence, C14.

13. 'satisfactory'.

14. Correspondence, C15.

15. J. Keble, *Lectures on Poetry,* tr. E. K. Francis, Oxford, 1912, Vol. II, p.484.

16. Keble was the second person at Oxford to take a double first, that is a first class degree in both Mathematics and Classics. The first had been Robert Peel: Keble was thought to have out-Peeled Peel.

17. J. H. Newman, *Idea of a University:* Elementary Studies, Sect. 3(2).

18. J. H. Newman in John Keble, *Occ. Papers and Reviews,* Oxford, 1877, preface, p.xii.

19. 'put to the test'.

20. Coleridge, *Memoir,* Vol. I, p.208.

21. Coleridge, *Memoir,* Vol. I, p.260. Coleridge apologises for his translation of the original Latin.

22. Correspondence, C15.

23. *Occ. Papers and Reviews,* p.10. Originally published in 'British Critic', 1838.

24. Review of *Life of Sir W. Scott, Occ. Papers and Reviews,* Oxford, 1877. p.73. Keble wrote that Scott left off writing in poetry because he thought Byron was better.

25. *Occ. Papers and Reviews,* 'Sacred Poetry', p.90.

26. *Lectures,* Vol. II, p.37.

27. *Lectures,* Vol. II, p.96.

28. W. Wordsworth, Preface to 2nd Edition of *Lyrical Ballads,* 1800.

29. W. Wordsworth in his *Postscript* to the poems of 1835: he was discussing Poor Law amendment, and, later, Church reform.

30. *Occ. Papers and Reviews,* p.17.

31. *Occ. Papers and Reviews,* p.6.

32. *Occ. Papers and Reviews,* p.7.

33. *Lectures,* Vol. I, p.21.

34. *Lectures,* Vol. II, p.218.

G. B. Tennyson (essay date 1977)

SOURCE: "The Sacramental Imagination," in *Nature and the Victorian Imagination,* edited by U. C. Knoepflmacher and G. B. Tennyson, University of California Press, 1977, pp. 370-90.

[*In the following essay, Tennyson discusses the influence of Keble's* The Christian Year *and* Lectures on Poetry *in Victorian England.*]

> Every season Nature converts me from some unloving heresy, and will make a Catholic of me at last.
>
> Coleridge *Anima Poetae*

Even before the Victorian period was properly under way, poets of a religious cast of mind had abandoned an unqualified belief in the kind of pantheism of Nature that characterized Wordsworth's youthful Nature poetry. Not the least of such poets was Wordsworth himself, who introduced his *Ecclesiastical Sonnets* (1822) by describing himself as one who had formerly sung of "mountain-quiet and boon nature's grace," and now who was about to "seek upon the heights of Time the source / Of A HOLY RIVER, on whose banks are found / Sweet pastoral flowers."[1]

The sweet pastoral flowers of the Ecclesiastical sonnets are perhaps not their most outstanding feature, but there are certainly frequent Nature images and Nature references in these poems that trace the course of Christianity in Britain from the beginnings to "present times," along with a scattering of poems on certain sacraments, church practices, and miscellaneous ecclesiastical matters that interested Wordsworth. What is arresting about the Nature references, however, is the degree to which they have been subordinated to the demands of history and theological orthodoxy, the degree indeed to which they seem no longer Wordsworthian. Thus the opening lines of the sonnet on baptism read (p. 320):

> Dear be the Church that, watching o'er the needs
> Of Infancy, provides a timely shower
> Whose virtue changes to a christian Flower
> A Growth from sinful Nature's bed of weeds!

"Sinful Nature" here may be intended simply as sinful human nature suffering from the curse of Adam, but it seems rather more likely that it is the same personified Nature that Wordsworth once believed would never betray the heart that loved her.

The *Ecclesiastical Sonnets* were mostly composed in 1821, though additions, including "Baptism," were published in 1827, and again in 1842 and 1845. During the same decade, and indeed overlapping in composition some of the *Ecclesiastical Sonnets,* was published the most popular and influential volume of religious poetry that the Victorian age would know, a volume that helped to shape and define the age it preceded. The work was of course John Keble's *The Christian Year* (1827). Although Keble's subsequent leadership of the Tractarian movement helped make the volume a sacred one in High Anglican households, it had already become a favorite before Keble's 1833 sermon launched the movement, and it enjoyed an enormous popularity for the remainder of the century in Christian households of all levels of churchmanship, even including non-Anglican households. A large part of the reason for the popularity of *The Christian Year* was its blend of Nature and piety, a blend not nearly so frequent or so successful in the *Ecclesiastical Sonnets.*

To modern readers Keble's poetry seems little more than Wordsworth and water, chiefly because modern readers see only the Nature imagery and fail to respond to the purpose to which Keble directed his observations of Nature, a purpose that Victorians readily recognized and largely applauded. That purpose was, like that of the *Ecclesiastical Sonnets,* in the first instance didactic and indeed theologically didactic, but it was something else as well, something more imaginative and far-reaching than mere didacticism suggests. A part of Keble's purpose in *The Christian Year* was to show forth Nature as more than a Wordsworthian moral teacher instructing by vernal impulse; it was to show Nature as the hand-maiden of theology and at times the vehicle of a sacramental grace that brought man into contact with the divine.

Keble would have been the first to let such a purpose as that of establishing the right attitude toward Nature pass a reader by if he could still realize his larger aim of inculcating right religious feeling. In the **"Advertisement"** he appended to the first edition of *The Christian Year* he claims his aim is only that of assisting the reader "in bringing his own thoughts and feelings into more entire unison with those recommended and exemplified in the Prayer Book."[2] Keble would never have exalted Nature, or aesthetics for that matter, over a "sound rule of faith," the quality he placed even above a "sober standard of feeling in matters of practical religion" (p. xix). But the fact is that Keble did not perceive these matters to be in opposition. Like many of the Romantics Keble believed that a feeling for Nature was a positive good, but he believed that it was good not so much in itself as for the lessons it embodied, and these lessons were not merely generally moral: they were supernatural, theological, and Christian. It is indeed precisely in his subordination of Nature (and aesthetics) to overriding religious considerations that Keble shows himself more Victorian than Romantic, more Tractarian than Evangelical.

The poetry of *The Christian Year* shows Keble's principles in action, but in the following decades of Tractarianism proper Keble provided an explicit rationale for his treatment of Nature in poetry and a rationale for much of the treatment of Nature by religious minds for the rest of the century. The document in question is Keble's *Lectures on Poetry,*[3] available to his contemporaries only in their original Latin as *Praelectiones Academicae* under the title *De poetica vi medica.* The forty lectures that make up the two volumes were delivered between 1832 and 1841 when Keble served two terms as professor of Poetry at Oxford. The Latin edition was published in 1844, the translation not until 1912. Although the *Lectures on Poetry* had contemporary impact on those who heard them delivered (which would have included all the major Tractarians resident at Oxford) and those who could read the original volumes, it is certainly the case that Keble's influence as a theorist and aesthetician was less profound than his influence as a poet. But, since the lectures so often merely make explicit what was in fact Keble's practice in *The Christian Year* and elsewhere, they offer an instructive commentary on that practice and on what was to become a widespread Victorian adaptation of the legacy of Romantic Nature.

The few modern commentators who have looked into Keble's lectures have stressed the affinities of Keble's aesthetics with affective theories and with Wordsworthian notions of poetry as the overflow of emotion. The most perceptive of modern critics of Keble, M. H. Abrams, has also pointed to the somewhat surprising connection between Keble's poetics and that of Mill (which was in turn surprisingly Wordsworthian) and also to the extent to which Keble anticipates Freudian aesthetics. The basis for these judgments lies in Keble's definition of poetry as a kind of safety valve for intense emotion, poetry as catharsis—for the poet. Certainly this is Keble's position, but Abrams also rightly notes that in Keble, unlike Freud, the emotion and the catharsis, that is, the feeling and the poetry it produces, are always and everywhere subordinated to theology. In fact, Keble believes that poetry was given to man as a "divine medicine" by God as a means of easing spiritual torments. Abrams also remarks, although he does not develop the notion, that Keble has a view of poetry "as something near allied to religion, almost a sacrament."[4]

It is the theological and sacramental element in Keble's conception and practice of poetry, coupled as it is with his view of Nature, that sets his work apart from the Romantic Nature worshippers on whom he builds and the purely psychological critics who come after. It is, moreover, the theological and sacramental character of Keble's theory and practice that mark his work as the proximate source of a notable strain in the Victorian literary imagination that comprehends a host of other poets, some novelists, and even some naturalists.

Throughout the *Lectures on Poetry* Keble constantly repeats his assertion that poetry is catharsis for the emotionally surcharged spirit, a catharsis provided by Providence or perhaps even made available (to the first poets) by "express revelation of the Deity" (I:59). He finds, further, that the best poetry is marked by the same characteristic that the Tractarians prized in religious teaching—the quality of reserve, frequently called by Keble "due religious reserve."[5] This reserve, Keble finds, often accounts for the indirection, particularly on religious matters, of much pagan poetry, especially the work of the Greek and Latin poets that Keble turns to throughout his lectures to illustrate most of his contentions about poetry. Nevertheless, the reserve of pagan poetry was not such as to prevent pagan poets from all knowledge of those higher truths of Christianity that were to come. Keble finds indeed that poetry was "providentially ordered to prepare the way for Revealed Truth" (II:478). As he wrote of pre-Christian poets in one of the most popular sentiments in *The Christian Year:* "So thoughts beyond their thought to those high Bards were given" (**"Third Sunday in Lent"**).

Less explicit but ultimately inescapable is the implication in Keble's theory that the emotion that poetry releases is a religious emotion and, further, that the poetry that issues from the release of this religious emotion is itself a religious or quasi-religious activity. Nowhere does Keble come closer to stating such a concept than in his treatment of Nature poetry, a treatment that is also something like an apologia for the poetic practices of Keble himself, although he never cites his own poetry in illustration.

Nature poetry, as Keble approaches it chiefly through the works of Lucretius and Virgil, is a species of lyric poetry; and lyric poetry because of its intensity must preserve the reserve necessary in Keble's view to all good poetry by being indirect. But since the lyric is a short form, the indirection does not take the form of allegory but rather the form of analogy. To be sure, some indirection is attained through unusual and complex metrical schemes (in which Keble himself delighted), but the chief source of indirection in lyric poetry is also the source that most lends itself to analogy, namely Nature, and Nature is itself an analogue for God. It is in his treatment of Nature poetry that Keble calls poetry alternately the handmaid of theology and the handmaid of Nature. Nature poetry is therefore a kind of double instance of religious poetry: all poetry is in origin religious, but Nature poetry treats as subject that which also shows God by analogy.

Keble on analogy is consistently Tractarian. On this topic the Tractarians took their lead from Bishop Butler's *Analogy of Religion* (1736). Thus Newman cited the reading of Butler as a turning point in his intellectual development and attributed to Butler his own first awareness of the idea of analogy and the concept of probability in belief. Significantly, these same two principles, Newman said, came fully alive to him in reading Keble's *Christian Year.* It is in his discussion of Keble's volume that Newman defines what he means by the principle of analogy:

> The first of these [principles] was what may be called, in a large sense of the word, the Sacramental system;

that is, the doctrine that material phenomena are both the types and the instruments of real things unseen,—a doctrine, which embraces in its fulness, not only what Anglicans, as well as Catholics, believe about Sacraments properly so called; but also the article of "the Communion of Saints"; and likewise the Mysteries of the faith.[6]

Newman had earlier pointed out that the doctrine of analogy and the sacramental system extend throughout Church history and that Butler had prefaced his work with a quotation from Origen, known for his belief in the permeation of the universe with symbols and signs of the invisible world. Keble for his part developed the sacramental idea of Nature in his tract "On the Mysticism Attributed to the early Fathers of the Church," number 89 of the *Tracts for the Times.* There he lauds the Fathers for exhibiting "not a merely *poetical,* or a merely *moral,* but a *mystical* use of things visible." Keble extends St. Irenaeus's maxim about the Old Testament that there is with God nothing useless nor any empty sign to apply to "the whole creation."[7] As early as 1825 Keble had cited Nature by way of rebutting Dr. Johnson's complaint against religious poetry that the topics of devotion are too few: "How can the topics of devotion be few," Keble asked, "when we are taught to make every part of life, every scene in nature an occasion—in other words, a topic—of devotion?"[8] We are taught to make every scene in Nature a topic of devotion by the analogical or sacramental system that the Tractarians sought to revive. The more or less independent exaltation of Nature by the Romantics could only reinforce the Tractarian faith in the sacramental system.

The "sacraments properly so called" in Newman's definition are of course the seven sacraments of historic Catholicism. Newman and the Tractarians adhered to the Prayer Book definition of a sacrament: "An outward and visible sign of an inward and spiritual grace." The sacramental system, however, is larger than the seven sacraments, larger indeed than the "sacramentals," or additional sacraments, of medieval definition; it embraces the multitude of objects of the visible world which are symbols and signs of the invisible one. It sees Nature as one of the primary ways in which God reveals Himself to men. Keble cited Nature and human history as the two sources, apart from revelation, in which God reveals Himself. These are the two available to natural theology, and of the two Nature is obviously the one most suitable for lyric poetry. Keble even evolved a theory of history to account for the presence and absence at particular times of Nature poetry. The ancient Hebrews had little or no Nature poetry, Keble maintains, because they had God direct. The same was true in the Middle Ages. In other times, however, Nature or pastoral poetry is in evidence precisely because faith is weak. Therefore in Roman times Providence provided, first, Lucretius, who was in Keble's judgment religious *malgré lui* and was used by God to be a witness to how

much we should reverence the beauties of the world. Later Providence sent Virgil, whom Keble sees in the medieval way as a herald of the revelation to come. Through Virgil's English imitators Keble discerns a religious reverence for Nature flowing down to the present age, an age that, in Keble's view, is also weak in faith; it is therefore an age eminently suited to and in need of Nature poetry. There are some, he notes, so whole in faith that they do not require the medicine of divine poetry, but there are multitudes of the sick who do:

> May it not be by the special guidance of Providence that a love of country and Nature, and of the poetry which deals with them, should be strong, just at the time when the aids which led our forefathers willingly to forgo any claim to poetic taste are far removed from the habits of our daily life? (II:272)

Keble's aesthetics, then, posit poetry as a divine medicine for the overburdened spirit, a spirit that is longing to know God; thus poetry itself is a religious activity and partakes by analogy of the creative act, as Coleridge had affirmed. Nature poetry is an especially suitable mode for the impassioned utterances of poetry, for it enables a poet to give vent to religious feelings (even when the poet does not consciously know them to be religious) while preserving the due reserve appropriate to the treatment of sacred matters. In Nature poetry, that reserve operates not only by the very indirection of speaking about Nature as a way of speaking about theology, but also through a preference for lowly and humble domestic Nature, not the peaks and valleys of Romantic view-hunting, which Keble deplored as fully as did Carlyle. Since Nature teaches us of God by analogy, Nature poetry is inevitably theologically didactic. It is also especially needful in the present age because it is an age weak in faith.

All of this is fairly explicit, though scattered, in Keble's lectures on poetry. All of it constitutes grounds for moralizing and theologizing Romantic Nature. And despite the medieval and earlier echoes, it is also something other than simply a return to medievalism, for Keble goes, albeit cautiously, even further. Nature offers not merely signs and types but what can only be likened to a grace akin to that of the sacraments. Keble approaches this idea at various times in the lectures, but in keeping with the doctrine of reserve (and perhaps concerned too lest he appear to offend against orthodoxy), he holds any very explicit utterance of it until the end. Then he states:

> For once let that magic wand [i.e., religion] . . . touch any region of Nature, forthwith all that before seemed secular and profane is illumined with a new and celestial light: men come to realize that the various images and similes of things, and all other poetic charms, are not merely the play of a keen and clever mind, nor to be put down as empty fancies: but rather they guide us by gentle hints and no uncertain signs, to the very

utterances of Nature, or we may more truly say, of the Author of Nature. And thus it has come to pass, that great and pre-eminent poets have almost been ranked as the representatives of religion, and their sphere has been treated with religious reverence. In short, Poetry lends Religion her wealth of symbols and similes: Religion restores these again to Poetry, clothed with so splendid a radiance that they appear to be no longer merely symbols, but to partake (I might almost say) of the nature of sacraments. (II:481)

By harmonizing a Romantic love of Nature with orthodox theology Keble has adapted and updated for the literature of his age the sacramental system of historic Catholicism.

Much of the foregoing was absorbed by Victorians not so much through the agency of Keble's lectures as through the poetry of *The Christian Year*. That volume is instinct with the practice that Keble adumbrated later in the *Lectures on Poetry*. One can open it almost at random to find instances of Nature as a teacher, indeed as theologian. Less frequent but still much in evidence are passages indicating Nature as a vehicle of sacramental grace. The poem for Septuagesima Sunday, for example, is a lengthy illustration of Keble's belief in the analogy of Nature. The text for the poem is the Pauline one: "The invisible things of Him from the creation of the world are clearly seen, being understood by the things that are made." The first two stanzas set the stage for what will be a sustained comparison of the works of Nature with their author:

> There is a Book, who runs may read,
>> Which heavenly Truth imparts
> And all the lore its scholars need,
>> Pure eyes and Christian hearts.
> The works of God above, below,
>> Within us and around,
> Are pages in that Book, to show
>> How God Himself is found.

After nine more stanzas expanding on this principle Keble concludes with a direct address to the Deity, asking for the ability to read the book of Nature aright:

> Thou, Who hast given me eyes to see
>> And love this sight so fair.
> Give me a heart to find out Thee,
>> And read Thee everywhere.

Throughout Nature Keble finds repeated evidences of God and constant reminders of one's Christian duty:

> Every leaf in every nook,
>> Every wave in every brook,
> Chanting with a solemn voice,
>> Minds us of our better choice.

("First Sunday after Epiphany")

He also finds that refreshment he associated with the reflective pastoral poetry of Virgil, but for Keble the refreshment is explicitly religious and sacramental—but reserved, more often than not disclosing sacramental grace through the homely things of Nature. Such is his treatment, for example, of the dew on flowers of a summer morning, which he likens to the freshness of the baptised soul:

> But he, whose heart will bound to mark
>> The full bright burst of summer morn,
> Loves too each little dewy spark,
>> By leaf or flow'ret worn:
> Cheap forms, and common hues, 'tis true,
> Through the bright shower-drop meet his view;
> The colouring may be of this earth;
> The lustre comes of heavenly birth.
>
> E'en so, who loves the Lord aright,
>> No soul of man can worthless find;
> All will be precious in his sight,
>> Since Christ on all hath shin'd:
> But chiefly Christian souls; for they,
> Though worn and soil'd with sinful clay,
> Are yet, to eyes that see them true,
> All glistening with baptismal dew.

("Second Sunday after Trinity")

Baptism of course is one of the two chief sacraments (the other is the Eucharist) and was especially dear to the Tractarians. As Wordsworth in the *Ecclesiastical Sonnets* had likened it to a "timely shower," the Tractarians likened it often to the fall of fresh morning dew, both images having less originality than familiarity to commend them. In his poem on baptism in *The Christian Year* Keble refers to the water of baptism as "holy dew," and in the series of poems on baptism in his later *Lyra Innocentium* (1846) Keble uses similar imagery, in one almost Herbert-like instance comparing the death of a newly baptised infant to the evaporation of a dew drop in the light of the sun (Christ).[9] Keble and other Tractarians see in dew a kind of perpetual baptism of the earth, and they draw from the experience the sustaining grace of a sacramental communion with the divine.

Likewise the rainbow, beloved of those who would read typology in external Nature, is a favorite with Keble. In an almost clever comparison, verging on a metaphysical conceit, in the poem for Quinquagesima Sunday Keble likens the rainbow to Christ, carrying the traditional image beyond the Old Testament notion of the Covenant:

> The Son of God in radiance beam'd
>> Too bright for us to scan,
> But we may face the rays that stream'd
>> From the mild Son of Man.
>
> There, parted into rainbow hues,
>> In sweet harmonious strife,
> We see celestial love diffuse
>> Its light o'er Jesus' life.

Keble's Nature views in *The Christian Year* are not of course all of a piece. At times he notes the difficulty of reading from "Nature's beauteous book":

> It lies before me, fair outspread—
> I only cast a wishful look.
>
> **("Fourth Sunday in Advent")**

At other times Keble notes that Nature is not always gentle. To God rather than man is reserved the thunder and the storm, for even Nature's harsher manifestations carry a lesson. It is either that of God's power or of his efforts to reach down to human beings:

> Thy sunshine smiles beneath the gloom
> Thou seek'st to warn us, not confound,
> Thy Showers would pierce the harden'd ground,
> And win it to give out its brightness and perfume.
>
> **("First Sunday after Christmas")**

At times too Keble finds Nature not always equally lavish with her signs. Certain spots are more favored than others. This idea is both classical and Christian. Keble seems to incline toward illustration of it more in his later poetry than in *The Christian Year.* One of his most telling illustrations is the poem he wrote for the rustic fountain at Ampfield in his own parish of Hursley. In part Keble was motivated by admiration for the Continental practice of honoring wayside shrines and sacred spots.

> While cooling waters here you drink
> Rest not your thoughts below,
> Look to the sacred sign and think
> Whence living waters flow,
> Then fearlessly advance by night or day
> The holy Cross stands guardian of your way.[10]

The Ampfield fountain verse notwithstanding, Keble never surpassed his success with *The Christian Year,* largely because he scarcely altered or developed his poetic gifts beyond what was evident in that collection. His later poems, especially the section "Lessons of Nature" from the *Lyra Innocentium,* read very like the poems in the early volume, although the personal element is somewhat stronger. But the merit or variety of Keble's poetry is of less moment than its symptomatic and influential character. The pervasive appeal of *The Christian Year* disposed many Victorian minds to view Nature as Keble and the Tractarians viewed it, as God's book which he who runs might read as a means, for the rightly disposed Christian soul, of experiencing through the visible world that contact with the invisible one that is normally effected through the sacraments.

The sons and daughters of Keble the Nature poet and sacramentalist have never been numbered, yet they include most of the writers of Catholic sentiment for the rest of the age. His immediate impact fell, of course, on the Trac-

tarians. A glance at two conscious followers of Keble will show the range of the Tractarian response to Nature and at the same time point to the direction the religious response to Nature was to take in the middle and later years of the century.

Isaac Williams (1802-65), as the author of the tract on Reserve and as a contributor, along with Newman, Keble, and others, to the *Lyra Apostolica,* was one of the earliest Tractarians, albeit today one of the less celebrated. His home, and the setting for much of his Nature poetry, was Wales. At the same time he is counted as a member of the Bisley School, so-called after the Gloucestershire parish served by Keble's brother Thomas. It was to Bisley and later to nearby Stinchcome that Williams repaired after his defeat (on anti-Tractarian, not poetic, grounds) in his candidacy for the chair of poetry at Oxford vacated by Keble in 1842. Williams had by that time already established a considerable reputation as a poet through the publication of *Thoughts in Past Years* (1838), *The Cathedral* (1838), and *The Baptistery* (1842). In these and in other volumes Williams shows himself ever the complete Tractarian student of Nature as one who, in the words of a friend, "sees meaning in everything, the mystical within the material world."[11]

The differences between Keble's and Williams's Nature poetry are not especially pronounced, although those there are sometimes work in Williams's favor. Williams tends to exhibit more frequently a melancholy strain (a characteristic that one of his critics sees as linking him to the eighteenth-century graveyard school). His melancholy and the rather wilder character of the Welsh landscape are often deployed so as to give Williams's poems greater intensity than Keble's. In one of the poems from "The Mountain Home" section of *Thoughts in Past Years* Williams's sorrowful disposition finds only the following comfort in Nature:

> Though pain and grief prevail, that God is good,
> That nothing can be evil on this earth,
> Wherein His sacred Spirit hath abode,
> Save what from man and evil will hath birth.[12]

In another instance, however, Williams responds with passion to the spectacle of the night sky (p. 65):

> The stars of night
> Were mingling with my dreams, and where e'en now
> The purple imagery of eve, there glowed
> Thro' the deep vault, what seem's the silvery track
> Of some ethereal visitant;—a cloud
> Of living lustre;—or, as deem'd of old,
> An isle Elysian mid the seas of light,
> Sailing among the eternal lamps of Heav'n:
> Solemn assemblage of mysterious worlds,
> Speaking of immortality to man,
> Of houses in Eternity!

When Williams takes a walk to the sea he finds the same evidence in shells and rocks that he found in flowers and woodland (p. 113):

> There came in these a healing sense,
>   To thoughts of my despair;
> A living and felt evidence
>   Of sweet protecting care.
>
> If thus His presence stands confest
>   In shell, and flower, and stone,
> To Him each want within my breast,
>   And every pain is known.

Williams had an especial fondness for book-length poems and collections constructed on analogy with Catholic ecclesiastical buildings and ornaments; such are *The Cathedral, The Baptistery,* and *The Altar.* He provided *The Altar* (1847) with numerous illustrations that constitute a kind of Victorian religious iconography. In *The Baptistery* he also added illustrations, but these were taken from a fifteenth-century Dutch book by Gerald de Bosverts. Although the style of illustration clearly betrays its non-Victorian origin, Williams found it congenial enough to his own Tractarian thinking to let the illustrations reinforce his poetry. The volume is thus filled with "images" with corresponding explanations for the various figures and events labeled in the pictures, almost all of them showing a rain of sacramental grace falling on men or a path to a sunlit heaven open to him who follows virtue. It is an instance of Tractarian analogical thinking carried to the point of allegory, and an instance of the tendency in Williams to express himself with more fervor than Keble, a tendency that was to become more pronounced in later religious Nature poetry.

No such allegorical mode was possible in the novels of manners and domestic life that occupied the inexhaustible energies of Charlotte Mary Yonge, but neither was Miss Yonge insensitive to the learning she imbibed from Keble at Hursley. Like Keble's poetry, her novels received a warm welcome in households ranging from Tractarian to Evangelical. Charlotte Mary Yonge wove religious elements of various kinds into her novels, including elements that showed how thoroughly she had incorporated Keble's teaching on Nature into her own thought.

In the wildly successful *Heir of Redclyffe* (1852) Charlotte Mary Yonge takes a more severe view of Byronic Nature than even Keble had in the **Lectures on Poetry,** where he had pronounced Byron and Shelley as "rather unhappy than impious" (II:339).[13] Of misapplied Nature poetry, however, Miss Yonge has the hero Guy say:

> There is a danger in listening to a man who is sure to misunderstand the voice of nature—danger, lest by filling our ears with the wrong voice we should close them to the true one. I should think there was a great

chance of being led to stop short at the material beauty, or worse, to link human passions with the glories of nature, and so distort, defile, profane them.[14]

Interestingly, Guy's outburst against Byronic Nature comes in the same chapter in which he earlier had rescued Amabel from a dangerous descent of the Beatenberg where she had gone to sketch the Jungfrau. Being attracted by a "tuft of deep purple, the beautiful Alpine saxifrage," she attempted to pluck it and found herself sliding down the mountainside, much as Coleridge had descended Scafell. Guy pulls her to safety as she clings to a low bush. When the adventure is over, Amabel exclaims: "Oh, I am sure it was Providence that made those bushes grow just there!"[15]

Providence for Miss Yonge also made domestic British Nature the kind of teacher that Keble showed her to be, for in *Heartsease* she has John read from the diary of the dead Helen Fotheringham whom he loved:

> "This morning was a pattern one for February, and I went out before the brightness was passed, and had several turns in the walled garden. I am afraid you will never be able to understand the pleasantness of such a morning. Perhaps you will say the very description makes you shiver, but I must tell you how beautiful it was. The frost last night was not sharp, but just sufficient to detain the dew till the sun could turn it to diamonds. There were some so brilliant, glancing green or red in difference lights, they were quite a study. It is pleasant to think that this pretty frost is not adorning the plants with unwholesome beauty, though the poor little green buds of currant and gooseberry don't like it, and the pairs of woodbine leaves turn in their edges. It is doing them good against their will, keeping them from spreading too soon. I fancied it like early trouble keeping baptismal dew fresh and bright; and those jewels of living light went on to connect themselves with the radiant coronets of some whom the world might call blighted in—"

The emotion aroused by the passage causes John to break off in a fit of coughing, but eventually he recovers and proceeds:

> "The world might call them blighted in their early bloom and deprived of all that life was bestowed for; but how different is the inner view, and how glorious the thought of the numbers of quiet, common-place sufferers in homely life, like my currant and gooseberry bushes, who have found their frost has preserved their dew-drops to be diamonds for ever."[16]

It is perhaps fanciful to see in so steadfast a student of the original Tractarian principles as Charlotte Mary Yonge signs of the tendency to abandon the reserve that Tractarians always advocated in religious matters and therefore in Nature description; but frost sparkling like diamonds, flashing green and red, and baptismal dews becoming radiant coronets incline toward a fervency not wholly consonant with the severer forms of reserve. Of course

Miss Yonge makes plain that the real comparison is with that of the commonplace person and the gooseberry bush, which is reserved enough; and she has Helen go on to apologize for the extravagance of her musings. Thus the passage is perhaps best cited as an instance of the way the Tractarian mind sought, successfully for the most part, to balance passion with reserve in responding to Nature and only incidentally as an instance of passion overpowering reserve.

But if Keble and his immediate followers were able to temper emotion with reserve, such was not always the case or even the intention of other Victorian Nature sacramentalists from Faber to Dolben to Hopkins to Patmore. For just as the sober character of Tractarian worship gave way to the sumptuosities of the Ritualist movement, so too Tractarian reserve in the imaginative response to Nature sometimes gave way to more exuberant expression in writers of later generations. Reserve was in any case implicitly at variance with the intense emotion Keble held to be the cause of poetry. But the Tractarian effort to accommodate the two probably made possible the transition from Romantic Nature worship to an appreciation of Nature subordinated to religion, even as it has tended to obscure the lines of descent from Keble to later Victorian sacramentalists. By incorporating the Romantic love of Nature into the historic sacramental system, the Tractarians preserved for many a Nature that might otherwise have been jettisoned as incompatible with Christianity, and at the same time preserved for others a Christianity that might otherwise have been jettisoned as incompatible with Nature. It is moreover likely that the reverence Keble and his school cultivated towards Nature disposed many Victorians to read Nature poetry and Nature description of whatever stripe in a moral and theological context.

In the 1870s when the great age of amateur naturalists was entering its St. Martin's Summer, one can still hear the echo of the Tractarian response to Nature in the reflections of the clergyman and naturalist Francis Kilver on a March afternoon in country close to that native to Isaac Williams:

> The afternoon had been stormy but it cleared towards sunset.

> Gradually the heavy rain clouds rolled across the valley to the foot of the opposite mountains and began climbing up their sides wreathing in rolling masses of vapour. One solitary cloud still hung over the brilliant sunlit town, and that whole cloud was a rainbow. Gradually it lost its bright prismatic hues and moved away up the Cusop Dingle in the shape of a pillar and of the colour of golden dark smoke. The Black Mountains were invisible, being wrapped in clouds, and I saw one very white brilliant dazzling cloud where the mountains ought to have been. This cloud grew more white and dazzling every moment, till a clear burst of sunlight scattered the mists and revealed the

truth. This brilliant white cloud that I had been looking and wondering at was the mountain in snow. The last cloud and mist rolled away over the mountain tops and the mountains stood up in the clear blue heaven, a long rampart line of dazzling glittering snow such as no fuller on earth can white them. I stood rooted to the ground, struck with amazement and over-whelmed at the extraordinary splendour of this marvellous spectacle. I never saw anything to equal it I think, even among the high Alps. One's first involuntary thought in the presence of these magnificent sights is to lift up the heart to God and humbly thank Him for having made the earth so beautiful.[17]

Writing to Richard Watson Dixon a full decade after Kilvert recorded his observations of the pillar of the cloud, Gerard Manley Hopkins dismissed the Tractarian Nature poets by saying: "The Lake School expires in Keble and Faber and Cardinal Newman."[18] In one sense it does, but only to be reborn into a sacramentalism of Nature that had its repercussions even down to Hopkins himself. Keble in his poem "Holy Baptism" had found that the "eternal Dove / Hovers on softest wings" over the baptismal font. For Hopkins that same dove, the Holy Ghost,

> over the bent
> World broods with warm breast and with ah! bright wings.

Notes

1. William Wordsworth, *The Poetical Works of Wordsworth,* ed. Thomas Hutchinson and Ernest de Selincourt (London, 1936), p. 329. Subsequent references will be incorporated into the text.

2. John Keble, *The Christian Year, Lyra Innocentium, and Other Poems* (London, 1914), p. xix. The text for all citations is taken from this edition, but because *The Christian Year* exists in so many editions, subsequent references will be made to the poems by name and will be incorporated into the text.

3. John Keble, *Lectures on Poetry, 1832-1841,* trans. Edward Kershaw Francis, 2 vols. (Oxford, 1912). Subsequent references will be incorporated into the text by volume and page number.

4. M. H. Abrams, *The Mirror and the Lamp: Romantic Theory and the Critical Tradition* (New York, 1958), p. 147.

5. Tractarian reserve became a byword of the early phase of the Movement. In defense of it Isaac Williams wrote Tract 80, "On Reserve in Communicating Religious Knowledge," which provoked criticism of the Tractarians as devious.

6. John Henry Newman, *Apologia pro Vita Sua,* ed. Martin Svaglic (Oxford, 1967), p. 29.

7. *Tracts for the Times,* no. 89 (London, 1841), pp. 144, 149. Keble translated St. Irenaeus's work for the Tractarian "Library of the Fathers." It was not published until 1872.

8. John Keble, *Occasional Papers and Reviews* (Oxford, 1877), p. 82.

9. Keble, *The Christian Year,* p. 223 ("Death of the New-Baptized").

10. The lines are reprinted only in Charlotte Mary Yonge, *John Keble's Parishes* (London, 1898), p. 113.

11. O. W. Jones, *Isaac Williams and His Circle* (London, 1971), p. 120.

12. Isaac Williams, *Thoughts in Past Years* (3d ed., London, 1843), p. 88. Subsequent references incorporated into the text.

13. Earlier in his lectures, however, Keble had attacked Byron for sullying his powers by "many serious vices" and for his "want of true modesty" (I:258-59).

14. Charlotte Mary Yonge, *The Heir of Redclyffe* (London, 1853), II:125-27 (chap. viii; chap. xxx in later one-volume editions).

15. *Ibid.,* p. 306. Charlotte Mary Yonge seems here to share the general preference of Victorian novelists for the lowlands over the mountains, as discussed by George Levine in Chapter Seven.

16. Charlotte Mary Yonge, *Heartsease, or The Brother's Wife* (London, 1854), I:206-7 (chap. vii).

17. E. D. H. Johnson, ed., *The Poetry of Earth* (New York, 1974), p. 361.

18. Claude Colleer Abbott, ed., *The Correspondence of Gerard Manley Hopkins and Richard Watson Dixon* (London, 1935), p. 99.

G. B. Tennyson (essay date 1979)

SOURCE: "Tractarian Aesthetics: Analogy and Reserve in Keble and Newman," in *The Victorian Newsletter,* No. 55, Spring, 1979, pp. 8-10.

[*In the following essay, Tennyson summarizes Tractarian aesthetics and its emphasis on "the religious character of poetry" as exemplified in Keble's verse.*]

Among the many aspects of the Oxford or Tractarian Movement that have captured the attention of subsequent students of the subject the matter of aesthetics has until recently been one of the least thoroughly explored. To be sure, theology, politics, social events, ecclesiastical developments, and even personal experience all played their part in the emergence and course of what the participants thought of as a campaign to redeem the Church of England. Recently, however, there has emerged an awareness that an approach through aesthetics casts a good deal of light on the deepest nature of Tractarianism, not in opposition to any of the previously cited aspects but rather complementary to them, especially to the most important of all—Tractarian theology. I propose today to summarize the findings on Tractarian aesthetics,[1] and then to do what has still hitherto been very little done—to apply a few of the important aspects of Tractarian aesthetics to some of the literary works written in the spirit of that aesthetic position to see what kind of practical critical insights flow from the recently won understanding of the theoretical critical principles. It is, to adopt and modify Matthew Arnold's phrase for his effort in *God and the Bible,* an "attempt literary, and an attempt religious,"[2] for, as we shall see, it is imprudent to approach the Tractarians exclusively from one or the other perspective. They best come alive through an approach from both.

The Tractarian aesthetic insists above all on the religious character of poetry and by extension of all art. Poetry is the result of a welling-up and expression of an intense emotion, which in turn is the desire of the soul to know God. Poetry is thus the outward expression of a powerful inward, even subconscious, religious feeling. This is the fundamental principle of Tractarian aesthetics, perhaps indeed of the Tractarian worldview, and it represents the ultimate subordination of poetry, and art, to theology. For, if art is in origin religious, it can best be judged, pursued, and evaluated from a theological standpoint. And the Tractarians did just that, which accounts for the religious character of all of their literary works.

In addition to the fundamental Tractarian principle of arts as religious self-expression, we should note also the importance for the Tractarians of what one may call the two essential Tractarian corollaries. These are the Doctrine of Analogy and the Doctrine of Reserve. Briefly stated, the Doctrine of Analogy or Correspondences is the application to art of the text from St. Paul: "The invisible things of [God] from the creation of the world are clearly seen, being understood by the things that are made" (Romans, i. 20). That is, the visible world is a world full of correspondences with the invisible world; physical things are signs and symbols of spiritual things. The doctrine of Reserve held by the Tractarians was that in communicating religious knowledge (which would, of course, in their view include also poetry and art) the communicator (including of course the poet) should exercise "due religious reserve,"[3] a kind of restraint and even indirection in expression appropriate to the sacredness of the subject being discussed.

Recent commentators on Tractarian aesthetics point out also the importance of the following emphases in Tractarian theory which I can no more than cite in passing. They are: the use of the terms "poetry" and "poetic" in Tractarian discourse as equivalents to "imagination" and "aesthetic"; the tendency of the Tractarians to speak of religion itself as a work of art; and the inclination of the Tractarian aesthetic position to issue in a theologized and sacramentalized view of Nature.[4]

The relation of theology and aesthetics in Tractarianism, then, is one of a mutually stimulating and modifying union of the two disciplines. This may best be grasped by considering Newman's assertion that poetry is for those who do not have the benefit of the Catholic Church. His statement becomes two-edged: that is, poetry is inferior to the Church and to her theology, but only because the Church and her theology are the greater poem.[5]

II

Now, having arrived at this understanding of Tractarian aesthetics, we should, I believe, raise what has hitherto been a quite secondary or wholly ignored consideration. It is: what, if anything, were the actual literary consequences of the Tractarian aesthetic position? That is, are there notable literary works that illustrate Tractarian aesthetics in action? Can we better grasp them as a result of our understanding of Tractarian aesthetics? To each of these questions I would answer, Yes, and in the remaining time I shall endeavor to justify those affirmative answers.

First of all, it is important to note that all of our sources on Tractarian aesthetics come from men who were, not only theologians and Tractarians, but literary artists as well. The two most prominent of these are of course Keble and Newman. Writing on the death of Keble, J. C. Shairp claimed that the two "permanent monuments of genius" left by the Oxford Movement were Keble's *The Christian Year* and Newman's parochial sermons.[6] Taking these two as the pre-eminent Tractarian works, let us apply Tractarian critical precepts to them.

First, *The Christian Year.* If a canvass were taken here as to whether that volume had poetic merit, I think the most common responses would be No, Undecided, and No Opinion—especially No Opinion. But that it exemplifies Tractarian aesthetics can hardly be disputed. Virtually all students of the subject have turned at once to Keble's poem for Septuagesima Sunday to illustrate the Doctrine of Analogy in practice. That is the poem that begins, "There is a Book, who runs may read. . . ."[7] That "Book," I need hardly tell you, is the Book of Nature. Since the remainder of the poem illustrates the doctrine of Analogy more successfully than it does anything else, I will not dwell on it further here. Rather more subtly and, I think, more poetically a similar Tractarian vision of a sacramentalized Romantic nature is captured in the poem for the Fourth Sunday in Advent.

In the poem for Advent IV, Keble unites several favorite Tractarian ideas about poetry in a way that seems to me to exhibit considerably greater poetic vigor than in the more doctrinaire poem for Septuagesima. We have here above all the sense of the surcharged spirit, the overburdened soul, seeking release for the tensions within. We have too the action of a nature filled with correspondences. We have, further, the sense of restraint or reserve in expressing both the emotion and the recognition of the correspondences. For it is all rendered as an inward struggle, not as a simple matter of applying the theological textbook to nature. It begins with the Romantic dream world through which the speaker struggles to discern the analogical relationships. But Keble's orthodoxy pulls the poem away from merely echoing Coleridge. In stanza six he asserts that with patience the time will come when eye and ear will see and hear aright. With the "blissful vision" one will "deeper and deeper plunge in light." This is, I believe, an effort to supplant, or complete the Romantic vision with the beatific one.

Keble goes on in the poem to instruct the reader that the soul itself—"if duly purged our mental view"—will approach ever nearer that goal of light, till it will "with that inward Music fraught, / For ever rise, and sing, and shine." The ultimate aim of the Tractarian aesthetic vision is also the ultimate aim of the Tractarian religious vision. The soul of the poet, or of the simple believer, fraught with the inward music of divine love, will one day "for ever rise, and sing and shine."

Virtually all of the poems of *The Christian Year* offer examples of Tractarian aesthetic-theological ideas, especially of the idea of Analogy. Perhaps more of these poems have literary merit than is commonly supposed. The curious should look especially at Keble's poems for the Second Sunday after Easter and the Fourth Sunday after Trinity for successful illustrations of Tractarian aesthetics in action. As understanding of Tractarian aesthetics grows, appreciation of Keble as a poet is likely to grow with it.

When we come to the other of the enduring monuments of the Oxford Movement, Newman's parochial sermons, the issue of merit is not a disputed one, and I will accordingly take it for granted that we all recognize Newman's mastery as a prose writer. One cause for this, I believe, is that Newman's writing has not generally been approached through Tractarian theory. But I think we can profitably do so as a means of understanding one of the most commonly remarked aspects of Newman's prose—its intensity in the face of its apparent objectivity and rationality.

The matter of the emotional appeal of what by most analyses seems unemotional prose is one of the continuing themes or puzzlements in Newman studies. Let me suggest that we consider the peculiar power of Newman's writing in terms of some of the leading ideas of Tractarian aesthetics and especially in terms of the doctrine of Reserve.

We must remember that the Doctrine of Reserve was not only theological; it was also aesthetic and, as I have argued, it was a corollary to the fundamental principle that artistic creation was the personal outpouring of an overwhelmingly religious impulse. Reserve comes into play as the means whereby such an outpouring is prevented from becoming vulgar and profane and merely emotional. One might say that Reserve was the means of insuring that what would come forth from the artist would be Tractarian rather than merely Romantic or, worse, Evangelical.

When we think of Newman's motto—"Cor ad cor loquitur"—Heart speaking to Heart—we should have no trouble linking that with the Tractarian first principle of the deep emotion lying behind artistic utterance. And when we try to understand how Newman managed to convey such intensity without the verbal pyrotechnics of, say, Thomas Carlyle, we would do well to bring into play the doctrine of Reserve. Hear him, for example, concluding a sermon of 1832 titled, after a common Tractarian conviction, "On Personal Influence, the Means of Propagating the Truth":

> Let all those, then, who acknowledge the voice of God speaking within them, and urging them heavenward, wait patiently for the End, exercising themselves, and diligently working, with a view to that day when the books shall be opened, and all the disorder of human affairs reviewed and set right; when "the last shall be first, and the first last"; when "all things that offend and they which do iniquity," shall be gathered out and removed; when "the righteous shall shine forth as the sun," and Faith shall see her God; when "they that be wise shall shine as the brightness of the firmament, and they that turn many to righteousness as the stars, for ever and ever.[8]

The reference to God speaking and urging within calls to mind the Tractarian view of the interior power of the religious-poetic impulse. In keeping with the doctrine of Reserve, however, it is linked to the idea of patience and diligence. And the highly Tractarian stringing together of Biblical passages leads finally to the emergence of the righteous to shine like those visible analogues of the invisible world, the sun and the stars of the heavens. "For ever rise, and sing, and shine," as Keble had it.

Even on the matter of Newman's personal style in preaching we may see the effects of Tractarian aesthetic doctrine. David DeLaura has ably traced the abundant references throughout the Victorian age to Newman's personal preaching style and provided us with a rich picture of the effect of that "unforgotten voice" as it echoed down the decades of the nineteenth century.[9] Anyone who has read his account must be struck by the frequency with which Newman's auditors, among them Matthew Arnold, remember his delivery as having been "soft," "sweet," "mournful," "subduing," yet withal "thrilling," "magnetic," "entrancing," and—the one that struck DeLaura so force-

fully—"silvery" like the cool radiance of the Church as Keble described it in the Septuagesima Sunday poem, basking in the glow of the moon, which in turn derives its light from the sun that is also the Son of God. This subtle, sweet, restrained, and silvery eloquence that haunted the memories of Oxonians for the rest of their lives is, I believe, an eloquence wholly consonant with the precepts of Tractarian aesthetics and even dictated by those precepts. It is the eloquence of an irresistible religious emotion tempered by a humbling and self-effacing religious reserve.

We can still hear the pathos that such a combination elicits from Newman well after the time of the University sermons. And perhaps in "The Parting of Friends," in 1843, his great sermon of leavetaking from the Church of England, we can see Reserve almost giving way before the intensity of the emotion, which is surely religious as well as personal, that provoked this particular jewel of Newman literary art:

> And, O my brethren, O kind and affectionate hearts, O loving friends, should you know any one whose lot it has been, by writing or by word of mouth, in some degree to help you thus to act; if he has ever told you what you knew about yourself, or what you did not know; has read to you your wants or feelings, and comforted you by the very reading; has made you feel that there was a higher life than this daily one, and a brighter world than that you see; or encouraged you, or sobered you, or opened a way to the inquiring, or soothed the perplexed; if what he has said or done has ever made you feel well inclined towards him; remember such a one in time to come, though you hear him not, and pray for him, that in all things he may know God's will, and at all times he may be ready to fulfill it.[10]

J. C. Shairp called Newman's sermons "high poems . . . as of an inspired singer, or the outpourings as of a prophet, rapt yet self-possessed."[11] "Rapt yet self-possessed"—the exact combination propounded by Tractarian aesthetics of an overwhelming religious emotion conveyed with due religious reserve. Newman may have subsequently enjoyed the benefits of what he viewed as in itself the greatest of poems, the Catholic Church, but that he was able to see it in such a light was possible only because of the Tractarian aesthetic he took with him when he parted from his friends.

Notes

1. Modern study of Tractarian aesthetics begins in the 1950's with Alba H. Warren, Jr., *English Poetic Theory 1825-1865* (Princeton: Princeton University Press, 1950); and M. H. Abrams, *The Mirror and the Lamp: Romantic Theory and the Critical Tradition* (1953) (rpt. New York: W. W. Norton, 1958). Recent studies include Stephen Prickett, *Romanticism and Religion: The Tradition of Coleridge and Wordsworth in the Victorian Church*

(Cambridge: Cambridge University Press, 1976); Lawrence G. Starzyk, *The Imprisoned Splendor: A Study of Early Victorian Critical Theory* (Port Washington, N. Y.: Kennikat Press, 1977); and G. B. Tennyson, "The Sacramental Imagination" in U. C. Knoepflmacher and G. B. Tennyson, eds., *Nature and the Victorian Imagination* (Berkeley and Los Angeles: University of California Press, 1977), pp. 370-390.

Among the Tractarians a primary source is Keble's Latin *Lectures on Poetry,* delivered between 1831 and 1841, but not translated into English until 1912. His other essays are collected in his *Occasional Papers and Reviews* (1877). Newman's critical views are found chiefly in his essays, "Poetry, with Reference to Aristotle's *Poetics,*" and "Literature," and scattered throughout his works. The most important of the *Tracts for the Times* for critical theory are No. 80, "On Reserve in Communicating Religious Knowledge," by Isaac Williams, and No. 89, "On the Mysticism Attributed to the Early Fathers of the Church," by John Keble.

2. *Complete Prose Works of Matthew Arnold,* ed. R. H. Super (Ann Arbor: University of Michigan Press, 1960-77), 7:398. Arnold's phrase was "an attempt conservative, and an attempt religious."

3. Keble uses this and similar expressions throughout the *Lectures on Poetry.* The most celebrated formulation of the idea occurs in Isaac Williams' Tract 80, cited above, note 1.

4. See especially Prickett, pp. 105-107; Starzyk, pp. 160-161; and Tennyson, p. 374.

5. Prickett, pp. 172-173; Starzyk, pp. 157-162.

6. John Campbell Shairp, *Studies in Poetry and Philosophy,* 2nd. Am. ed. (Boston, 1887), p. 219. The essay was originally published in the *North British Review* in 1866, the year of Keble's death.

7. John Keble, *The Christian Year, Lyra Innocentium, and Other Poems* (London: Oxford University Press, 1914). The texts from Keble are taken from this edition, but for ease in using any of the many editions of *The Christian Year* reference is made only to the title of the poem.

8. *Newman's University Sermons,* ed. D. M. MacKinnon and J. D. Holmes (London: SPCK, 1970), p. 98.

9. David J. DeLaura, "'O Unforgotten Voice': The Memory of Newman in the Nineteenth Century," in *The Uses of Nineteenth-Century Documents: Essays in Honor of C.L. Cline* (Austin: Department of English and Humanities Research Center, The University of Texas at Austin, 1975), pp. 23-55. Quoted words in this paragraph are from this article, *passim.* See also DeLaura's "Some Victorian Experiments in Closure," and Benjamin Dunlap's "Newman in the Pulpit: The Power of Simplicity," both in *Studies in the Literary Imagination,* 7 (1975), 19-35, 63-75.

10. *Sermons Bearing on Subjects of the Day* (London, 1869), p. 409.

11. Shairp, p. 212. See also DeLaura, "'O Unforgotten Voice,'" pp. 41-42.

G. B. Tennyson (essay date 1981)

SOURCE: "Keble and *The Christian Year,*" in *Victorian Devotional Poetry: The Tractarian Mode,* Harvard University Press, 1981, pp. 72-113.

[*In the following essay, Tennyson evaluates the structure and poetic style of* The Christian Year, *a work he regards as a "practical application of Tractarian poetics."*]

> Now through her round of holy thought
> The Church our annual steps has brought
>
> —*The Christian Year,* "Sunday Next before Advent"

Keble's modern biographer, Georgina Battiscombe, uttering a general sentiment, has observed that **The Christian Year** has become for twentieth-century readers the obstacle rather than the avenue to an understanding of Keble.[1] One could add that **The Christian Year** has become for twentieth-century readers the obstacle to an understanding of **The Christian Year.** Few volumes of poetry so influential in their own day can have fallen into such obscurity and even disrepute in aftertimes as the volume that helped launch the Oxford Movement and profoundly colored a large body of poetry for more than two generations. Today it exists only in the spectral half-life of footnotes, along with Marmontel's *Mémoires* and Senancour's *Obermann,* except that too frequently the footnotes identifying **The Christian Year** are in error.[2] Recent scholarship has gone some way toward rehabilitating Keble, especially in his role as shaper of and spokesman for Tractarian critical principles.[3] But recent scholarship has treated gingerly or not at all Keble's chief claim to fame in his own day and his chief contribution to the practical application of Tractarian poetics—**The Christian Year.**

Victorian laudations of **The Christian Year** are legion and come from all levels of society and churchmanship, but such modern assessments as exist have generally relegated the volume to a low place on the scale of poetic excellence. Critics find apparent support from Wordsworth, who praised the work backhandedly by remarking that it was so good he only wished he could have written it himself to make it better.[4] Likewise, A. E. Housman's praise for the volume seems to us appropriately tempered by his conviction that what "devout women" admirers of it really like is not its poetry but its piety and that "good religious poetry, whether in Keble or Dante or Job, is likely to be most justly appreciated and most discriminatingly relished by the undevout."[5] The not infrequent acerbity of Hoxie Neale Fairchild seems to the modern mind for once justly evoked when he writes of *The Christian Year,* "Let no critic accuse me of praising Keble's pious nature-poetry because it is so unromantic: I think it is rubbish."[6] Modern critics are convinced that the Victorians were responding to the "sweetly pretty,"[7] pious sentiments of a volume that extolled the conventional beauties of nature and the primacy of domestic virtues. Modern readers conceive of a mentality rather like that ridiculed by Matthew Arnold in speaking of the Victorian idea of heaven as "a kind of perfected middle-class home, with labour ended, the table spread, goodness all around, the lost ones restored, hymnody incessant." It comes, then, as a surprise to find Arnold immediately thereafter quoting Keble as an apparent ally in opposition to such sentiments: "'*Poor fragments all of this low earth!*' Keble might well say."[8] Arnold is citing a line from *The Christian Year* to ridicule what twentieth-century critics take to be the essential appeal of the work itself.

Arnold's invocation of Keble to censure the middle-class vision is not a sign of Arnold's misapprehension of Keble's position; rather, it is a sign that Arnold understood Keble's uncompromising orthodoxy better than modern critics and that Arnold understood the point and purpose of *The Christian Year* better than those who take their cue solely from the conventional Victorian middle-class image of the work. Keble, of course, would not have rejected the gushing Victorian response that comes across to us as a kind of condemnation, nor would he have taken issue with Housman's "devout women" responding to the pious sentiments rather than to the poetry, but even more certainly Keble would have been pleased to find his godson Arnold quoting *The Christian Year* in a way that uses it to direct the mind to eternal things rather than things of this world. For Keble wrote *The Christian Year* from an aesthetic quite at variance with our own exaltation of the literary artifact as an autonomous world of its own; he wrote *The Christian Year* as an act of religious devotion rather than as an act of literary self-sufficiency.

Donald Davie[9] has rightly chastised modern readers for a disinclination to entertain religious poetry unless it is very far removed in time, generally as far as the seventeenth century or earlier. If, as he argues, this militates against serious reading of Watts and other eighteenth-century poets, it does so even more strongly against Keble and the Victorians. I hope the previous chapter has provided the necessary background against which to view Keble and his fellows, for in order to understand the appeal of *The Christian Year,* what it was to its more thoughtful admirers, and how it exercised its extraordinary literary, religious, and social influence, we must consider it, not in the light of its later status as the standard confirmation gift or Sunday School attendance prize (these are, after all, the

proof of that influence), but in the light of the poetic principles that govern its poetry and its form. Then we can see how it exerted its impact on the Tractarians and their successors.

THE FORM OF *THE CHRISTIAN YEAR*

The Christian Year is, first of all, a work of devotional poetry, that is, a literary work designed to enhance devotion, to advance Christian truth in a form appropriate to its august character. It is the work of the quintessential Tractarian poet-priest "seeking the Deity in poetry or prayer." The best way to understand *The Christian Year* as a Tractarian work is to see it in relation to the worship it was designed to enhance, and that requires an understanding of its most visible, and most overlooked, feature—its subordination to the liturgical year generally and to the Book of Common Prayer specifically. The linkage of poetry to the annual cycle of worship is the premier achievement of *The Christian Year.* Today this linkage can scarcely be sufficiently emphasized, so far are modern readers from familiarity with the Prayer Book. Yet in a very real sense *The Christian Year* is its form; without it, it is simply an uneven collection of poems, all of them religious, many on nature, but only a few rising to a high level of poetic distinction. Seen in terms of its form, however, *The Christian Year* is a highly original poetic document that caused a quiet revolution in prayer and poetry in the Victorian age.

The outward shape and form of *The Christian Year* came to be taken for granted by mid- and late-Victorian readers, but it will strike most modern readers with even greater novelty than it presented to readers of the earliest editions. That outward form is wholly dependent on the Book of Common Prayer. The Book of Common Prayer in turn is the specifically Anglican formulation of Christian worship based on ancient and medieval practice and organized chiefly around the liturgical year developed over the Christian centuries. In a time of widespread liturgical experiment coupled with even more widespread liturgical ignorance like the present, it is well to remind ourselves of the main outlines of the historical liturgical year and also to look at its presentation in the Book of Common Prayer as received by Keble and others in the nineteenth century.[10]

The most accessible points of contact with the liturgical year for the contemporary mind are the organization of the year into weeks and the two great festivals of Christmas and Easter. These three features are still generally familiar and are the irreducible elements in the elaborate structure of the annual sequence of Christian worship. Of the three, the most central, indeed, the anchor of the church year, is the annual recurrence of Easter. This has been so since the very beginnings of Christian worship. Because Easter is linked to the Jewish Passover and hence to the lunar calendar, it is a movable feast, and the changes in its date cause some variation annually in the number of Sundays in other seasons before and after Easter. Moreover, it is the Easter events that constitute the essence of the Sunday eucharistic worship, so that the week itself is seen in terms of a re-enactment every seven days of the central event of Christian history. As Keble wrote in his poem for Easter: "Sundays by thee [that is, Easter] more glorious break / An Easter Day in every week." The very existence of the seven-day week, although of great antiquity in the east, was in the west a product of Christianity and did not become universal until the late fourth century. It was in the fourth century too that the fixing of the date of Christmas gave the liturgical year its other anchor. From that period on, the weeks of the church year have been disposed and often named in terms of their relationship to one or the other of these two festivals. In time, other festivals also gave their names to liturgical seasons, but their division and occurrence are dependent upon the fixed date of Christmas and the movable date of Easter.

Since the early middle ages, it has been customary to divide the church year into six main seasons, the first two related to the date of Christmas, the other four to the date of Easter. The six seasons are: Advent, Christmastide, Septuagesima, Lent, Eastertide, and Trinity season. The year begins with the Advent season, which in turn begins on Advent Sunday, the Sunday closest to St. Andrew's Day, November 30. Advent is a season of four Sundays of preparation for the celebration of the birth of Christ. That event in turn ushers in Christmastide, with its well-known twelve days beginning December 25 and culminating in the visit of the Magi, the Feast of the Epiphany on January 6, but containing also the following period of two to six Sundays (depending on the date of Easter in any given year), which are reckoned as Sundays after Epiphany. The calendar then moves to the pre-lenten period of Septuagesima, Sexagesima, and Quinquagesima, three Sundays named in terms of the approximate number of days before Easter (seventy, sixty, and fifty, respectively).[11] The lenten season proper begins with the Wednesday after Quinquagesima, Ash Wednesday, forty days before Easter, and moves through six Sundays in Lent to Easter, some of these Sundays bearing their own special names, such as Passion Sunday and Palm Sunday, but all part of the lenten season. Easter is followed by five Sundays called Sundays after Easter, and then by Ascension Day, the Thursday falling forty days after Easter. The following Sunday is called the Sunday after Ascension Day. All of the period from Easter day through the Octave of the Ascension is Eastertide or Paschaltide. The next Sunday is Pentecost, or Whitsunday, fifty days after Easter, the day commemorating the founding of the visible Church. In the Roman Church (and increasingly today in the Anglican) all following Sundays up to Advent are reckoned as Sundays after Pentecost, but historically in the Church of England, following medieval Sarum use (that is, the pattern followed at Salisbury), the Sunday after Pentecost is known as Trinity Sunday and all Sundays following it up to Advent are reckoned as Sundays after Trinity. The maximum possible number of such Sundays after Trinity is twenty-six (twenty-seven if reckoned after Pentecost), but again the date of Easter will determine just how many such Sundays actually are observed in any given year. In Anglican use the final Sunday in Trinity (or Pentecost) season is called The Sunday next before Advent. Then the year begins anew.

The foregoing is the main outline of the church year, but there are also other special feasts and observances commemorated on particular, usually fixed, days in the church year. In the Church of England there are relatively more such days than in dissenting churches, but relatively fewer than in Roman or Orthodox churches; in all Christian churches some elements of the liturgical year are observed, at a minimum Christmas, Easter, and the division into weeks. It is an obvious rule of thumb that the "higher" the denomination, the more extensive and elaborated the liturgical year, not only in terms of specific seasons, saints' days, festivals, and other commemorations, but also in terms of the appropriate vestments, colors, and prescribed prayers and procedures for seasons and days within the liturgical year.

In Anglican usage the liturgical year finds its expression in the Book of Common Prayer. From its earliest form as the First Prayer Book of Edward VI in 1549, to the 1559 Elizabethan Prayer Book, through the 1662 revision that held sway to our own times, the Book of Common Prayer adhered more rather than less to the fully elaborated year. In addition to provision for all the main seasons and festivals cited above, the Prayer Book provides also for thirty-two other named saints' days, holy days, and festivals: such days as the feasts of St. Stephen, St. John, and the Holy Innocents, which fall in immediate three-day succession after Christmas day; or the days in Holy Week preceding Easter; and such long-established feasts as the Purification or Candlemas (February 2), the Annunciation or Ladyday (March 25), All Saints (November 1), and the like. In keeping with the historic practice of the Church, the Book of Common Prayer provides for each of these named Sundays, festivals, or saints' days specific readings, normally a collect, epistle, and gospel, to be read at the appointed place in the communion service on the Sunday or holy day in question. These are known as the proper prefaces, or propers, for the day, being the readings proper or appropriate to the particular named celebration. Also in keeping with the medieval missals, breviaries, and service books from which it was derived, the Book of Common Prayer provides forms of worship and orders of procedure for various other sacraments and aspects of Church life.

For example, at the beginning, the Prayer Book offers forms for Morning and Evening Prayer (or Evensong), which are Anglican adaptations of medieval matins and vespers, with additions from the other canonical hours. Following the cycle of the Church year and of named feasts and saints' days, the Prayer Book provides forms and prayers for the sacraments of Baptism, Matrimony, Ordination, Burial of the Dead, and then some distinctively Anglican prayers, such as those for the deliverance from the Gunpowder Plot, the martyrdom of Charles I, the Restoration, and so on, for a total of sixteen such forms. Keble included poems for all special services and procedures in the Prayer Book, omitting only poems on purely utilitarian and undevotional Prayer Book inclusions like the Lectionary, the Thirty-nine Articles, and the Tables of Kindred.[12] The result is a series of poems that matches in exact order the sequence of worship in the Book of Common Prayer and that was designed to be read in the light of that book.

The liturgical pattern of the Prayer Book not only dictates the sequence of poems in *The Christian Year* but in fact gives the volume a coherence and purpose that it would otherwise lack. So overriding is the importance of this shaping element that one can understand why the volume is sometimes referred to as a single poem, though it is in fact a collection of 109 poems, for in one sense the collection is a single poem, a poem on the Book of Common Prayer. Much of the modern misunderstanding of what the volume is stems from the unwillingness or inability to approach it in relation to its model. It is as though the reader came to *Paradise Lost* without any awareness of its relation to the Bible, or to the *Divine Comedy* without an understanding of the concepts of Hell, Purgatory, and Heaven, though such parallels are inexact, for Dante and Milton draw on multiple sources and they structure their poems independently of any single source. *The Christian Year* not only refers to something outside itself; it exists and is shaped by virtue of the prior existence and form of that outside work. Without it, *The Christian Year* would not be.

The dependence of *The Christian Year* on the form of the Prayer Book could be called slavish were it not for the fact that Keble aspired to no originality in the matter. "Don't be original," was a Keble watchword often quoted by the young Tractarians with something like approving awe. Yet that same avoidance of originality became in itself a kind of originality; by making it old, Keble made it new. The few anticipations of Keble's pattern that exist in seventeenth-century poetry or among the small number of eighteenth-century collections of hymns must be considered no more than suggestive to Keble, even allowing for the unlikely assumption that he knew of the hymn collections in the first place.[13] The idea of a collection of poems organized in exact sequence of the order of worship in the Prayer Book turns out to be a strikingly original concept in devotional poetry. But it was an idea whose time had come. Keble, perhaps without fully realizing it, catalyzed a latent sensibility. He was to do something of the same kind in 1833 with the Assize Sermon. Twentieth-century readers view the Assize Sermon with some perplexity, seeing in it the very modest expression of ideas put more vigorously by Newman and others. They are likely to do the same with *The Christian Year* and to puzzle over its enormous popularity and influence. In both cases the quiet activation of something just below the surface sparked the imagination of the Tractarians and eventually of the population at large. It was Keble's capacity for calling attention to those "long-neglected truths" of Leslie and Sikes that made his Assize Sermon electrifying, and his capacity for looking afresh at so familiar a document as the Prayer Book that made *The Christian Year* a new departure in poetry.

As has been noted, *The Christian Year* parallels the Book of Common Prayer throughout, from the opening poems "Morning" and "Evening" (corresponding to the offices for Morning and Evening Prayer at the beginning of the book), through the year and the holy days, to the special offices and provisions of the Prayer Book, and ending with the Ordination Service. This organization is vital to the character and effects of *The Christian Year* overall, but another formal element in *The Christian Year* that reflects the shaping influence of the Prayer Book is the structure of the poems themselves as prayers. Perhaps the most common, certainly the most memorable, phrase in the Prayer Book orders for worship is "Let us pray." Keble's frequent pattern in the poetry of *The Christian Year* follows this recurring Prayer Book injunction, and it would be possible to specify in the poems the various recognized types of prayer—petitionary, intercessory, prayers of thanksgiving and praise, and the like; Charlotte Mary Yonge has virtually done so in her study of *The Christian Year*.[14] The most characteristic form for a poem in the collection is a meditation or reflection on nature or daily life seen from a Christian perspective, or a retelling of a Christian story (normally one appointed for the day), both generally concluding with an explicit prayer. The final stanzas of **"Morning"** and **"Evening"** illustrate the practice in its simplest form:

> Only, O Lord, in Thy dear love
> Fit us for perfect Rest above;
> And help us, this and every day,
> To live more nearly as we pray.

> ("Morning")

and

> Come near and bless us when we wake,
> Ere through the world our way we take;

Till in the ocean of Thy love
We lose ourselves in Heaven above.

("Evening")

The frequency of prayers within and at the end of poems reinforces the Prayer Book identification of the volume and invites the reader to link his own prayerful reflections to the liturgical pattern provided by the Prayer Book.

The structural linkage of *The Christian Year* with the Book of Common Prayer had several obvious practical consequences. It made possible the use of the volume as a companion to the Book of Common Prayer. Countless Victorian families came to use it in that way, reading aloud the appropriate Keble poem along with family Bible verses throughout the year. These readings tended to reinforce each other, making *The Christian Year* a kind of extension of the Prayer Book and probably in many minds intermingling the two, transferring even some of the sanctity of the Book of Common Prayer onto Keble's volume. The organization of Keble's collection also served to renew attention to the Prayer Book itself and to the liturgical year, both of which became hallmarks of the Oxford Movement and eventually spread beyond the confines of the Movement. Thus while Keble may have been the recipient of some of the piety and devotion directed to the Prayer Book, he was also the cause of renewed interest in that book and therefore of renewed interest in an ordered, liturgical system of worship. *The Christian Year* also directed attention to the Church itself as a visible body, for it was the Church that was the source and keeper of the ecclesiastical year and of its observance through the Prayer Book. *The Christian Year* thus exercised a gentle polemic in favor of the visible Church and her formularies. One of the points on which the Tractarians insisted in all of their arguments and "innovations" was that they were doing nothing more than what was enjoined by the Prayer Book itself. By creating a mirror-effect of influence on and subordination to the Prayer Book, *The Christian Year* benefited from the authority of the Prayer Book while also reinforcing that authority.

Much has been made in earlier criticism of the fact that the poems in *The Christian Year* were not originally composed in the sequence they occupy in the volume and that many are not uniquely appropriate to the Sunday or holy day to which they are ostensibly directed. In truth, the period of composition of the poems ranged from 1819 to 1827, and later editions carrying the date of composition next to the poem (these did not appear in the first edition) show clearly how Keble rearranged a gathering of poems written over a long period to correspond to the Church year. Likewise, there are poems attached to a particular Sunday or holy day referring to some other season of the year than the one in which the day falls (an April poem in Epiphany season, for example[15]). But these

aspects of Keble's arrangement only make the more clear his liturgical and devotional purpose when he collected his poems, and they have the same value (and no more) as the examination of the order (where it can be known) of Tennyson's stanzas in the poem some Victorians held to be a kind of secular *Christian Year—In Memoriam*.[16] Keble's final arrangement of his poems shows that the idea informing *The Christian Year* grew on him throughout the 1820s, when he was composing the poems, much as *In Memoriam* grew on Tennyson. And the arrangement also shows that the final form in which he presented his poems to the public is one in which the sequence is a fundamental part of the presentation and that *The Christian Year* is what it is because of that sequence.

Yet a further link between Keble's volume and the Prayer Book comes through his prefacing each poem with a biblical epigraph, in most cases a passage from the proper readings for the day from the Prayer Book. Thus the poem for Christmas Day is preceded by the passage from Luke, "And suddenly there was with the Angel, a multitude of the heavenly host, praising God"; the poem for Whitsunday or Pentecost is preceded by the passage from Acts telling of the cloven tongues of fire. And so on. These passages of course appear in the readings for the day appointed in the Prayer Book. One can move from the Prayer Book readings to the corresponding day in *The Christian Year* with a sense of passing to an elaboration of or commentary on the reading in the Prayer Book.[17]

Largely as a consequence of his High Church background and his own clerical experience (Keble was serving as his father's curate during the time of the composition of most of these poems), Keble's mind moved naturally in terms of the Church year, and most of the poems, whenever composed, turn on events commemorated in the ecclesiastical year. Poem after poem in the collection offers reflections on (and therefore reinforcement of) the events of the Christian story and their liturgical commemoration.

With the sequence of the poems, the epigraphs from the propers, and the subjects of the poems themselves directing the reader ever and again to the Prayer Book and to the cycle of worship throughout the year, there would appear to be no further way to emphasize the Prayer Book affinities of *The Christian Year.* Yet it proved possible to make the Prayer Book connection and the devotional character of the volume even more evident in succeeding editions. The course of this development is extremely revealing of the way in which the collection was received and the way in which its potential was realized, even beyond the presentation of the first edition. It makes us realize how much *The Christian Year* developed in concert with the Oxford Movement. Margaret Oliphant gives us the flavor of these later editions in *Salem Chapel* (1863) when the dissenting minister Mr. Vincent ventures into the Anglican bookshop and bends over "the much-multiplied volume . . . poising in one hand a tiny miniature copy just made to slip within the pocket of an Anglican waistcoat, and in the other the big red-leaved and morocco-bound edition, as if weighing their respective merits." Shortly afterwards she refers to it as "the Anglican lyre." She has Lady Western order two gift copies. "I know they are all on the side table, and I shall go and look at them," says Lady Western. "Not the very smallest copy, Mr. Masters, and not that solemn one with the red edges; something pretty, with a little ornament and gilding: they are for two little *protégées* of mine. Oh, here is exactly what I want! another one like this please."[18]

What had happened in these succeeding editions of *The Christian Year* offers the ultimate proof of its symbiosis with the Prayer Book. It offers as well an illustration in miniature of the course of the Anglo-Catholic movement in the Church of England and of the way in which Keble and the Tractarians opened new avenues for religious expression. *The Christian Year* became in itself a kind of Prayer Book, an Anglican devotional manual complete in physical detail with the features characteristic of devotional publications.

Keble had early toyed with the idea of illustrations to accompany the collection but abandoned the notion before publication. Later editions, especially after the book went out of copyright, put the idea into practice, sometimes with a vengeance. Illustrations ranged from vague pastoral scenes of the sort the Victorians used for editions of Wordsworth, to the sentimental Sunday School style pictures of biblical events, to vivid and very Continental religious iconography of the Crucifixion, the Crown of Thorns, the Sacred Heart, and the like. That is, they range from Evangelical to Catholic. And while the illustrations were growing in frequency and intensity, the physical format of the volume was changing. Increasingly, later editions appeared with gilt edges in the manner of Prayer Books, Bibles, and missals. Colored streamer bookmarks were added; margins were marked in black or red ruled lines, frequently with religious devices at the corners or elsewhere on the page. Bindings went to soft white, red, or black stippled leather with gold crosses on them. The volume was issued, as Mrs. Oliphant makes clear, in a multitude of sizes, from the tiny vest-pocket size to large, almost lecternsized editions. There even appeared individual editions of separate poems from the volume, normally the poems for Morning and Evening, the two from the collection that had the greatest currency as hymns. The great bulk of these decorated editions aimed at the market for religious gifts, and, like the Prayer Book itself, were probably thought of far more in religious than in literary terms.

It is almost impossible today to trace in detail the exact dates of the changes in format of these editions, but from an examination of many library and private copies, I find that the movement toward what we may call the "missalization" of *The Christian Year* began fairly early in the course of its publication history, was well established before Keble's death, and must therefore have had his approval. By the 1870s, when the volume could be freely reprinted, the decorated style had reached flood tide, rather like the Gothic Revival. Cause and effect cannot be disentangled here to say with confidence that either the Prayer Book or *The Christian Year* led the way. Both were subject to an increasingly Catholic visual presentation as the Tractarian Movement became more ritualistic. The increasing elaboration of the physical format of *The Christian Year* must be seen as the bibliographic counterpart to priestly vestments and altar decorations, which are the outward and visible signs of an inward and spiritual conviction about the nature of worship. The Book of Common Prayer itself appeared in more obviously religious formats throughout the age, in contrast to the publication style of eighteenth-century Prayer Books, which was indistinguishable from that of any other kind of book. That *The Christian Year* lent itself to ever more Catholic treatment illustrates one of the inherent characteristics of the Tractarian position. The volume was from the start an incitement to devotion; it was inevitable that this quality would find expression in the physical presentation of the book.

None of these developments appears to have dismayed the Tractarians. Nor could they have, given the aesthetic position the Tractarians held. Poetry was the handmaiden of religion, and religious handmaidens were rightly vested in garments suited to their office.

THE POETRY OF THE CHRISTIAN YEAR

Once we recognize that the form of *The Christian Year* is both its most distinctive feature and an exemplification of the Tractarian poetic, which construed literature as a mode of "seeking the Diety in prayer"—once, that is, we recognize the work as a devotional manual—we are able to take an equally Tractarian approach to the poetry in the volume. Such an approach reminds us that, however necessary it is for critical purposes to isolate a given poem or portion of it for examination, the poem still functions as part of the larger construct of a sequence of poetic devotions keyed to the Church year. The poem takes much of its coloration and force from its setting and from the devotional attitude of the rightly disposed reader. A Tractarian approach offers other pointers to the character of the poetry in *The Christian Year,* for like the structure of the volume, the poetry also grows out of Tractarian poetics. The poetry exemplifies the two leading Tractarian concepts of Analogy and Reserve; Analogy governs the subject matter of the poetry, Reserve the style.

We have seen that the doctrine of Analogy in Tractarian eyes is more than a kind of nature typology whereby certain objects in nature symbolize and point to truths of both natural and revealed religion, though it is of course at least that. At most, however, Analogy is the doctrine of the sacramental system. Newman put it well in speaking of *The Christian Year* as one of the main avenues by which he came to understand the meaning of that system:

> yet I think I am not wrong in saying, that the two main intellectual truths which [*The Christian Year*] brought home to me, were the same two, which I had learned from Butler, though recast in the creative mind of my new master. The first of these was what may be called, in a large sense of the word, the Sacramental system; that is, the doctrine that material phenomena are both the types and the instruments of real things unseen,—a doctrine, which embraces, not only what Anglicans, as well as Catholics, believe about Sacraments properly so called; but also the article of "the Communion of Saints" in its fulness; and likewise the Mysteries of the faith. (A, p. 29)[19]

It is the sacramental system, Tractarian Analogy, that comprehends the overall subject matter of the poems of *The Christian Year.* Walter Lock recognized this element in his edition of the volume, though Lock did not specifically link it to Tractarian Analogy. He wrote: "The most striking feature [of *The Christian Year*] is its width of sympathy, its sense of the consecration of all life" (*CY,* p. xii). And later he wrote of its "large-hearted sympathy which includes all creation within its embrace, and sees the consecration of God's presence on every side" (*CY,* p. xiii).[20]

If the subject matter of the poetry of *The Christian Year* generally is the sacramental system, specifically that system is most often illustrated through external nature. Nature is the single most visible topic of the poems and the one most likely to be interpreted as a kind of defused Wordsworthianism. Accordingly, we must consider Keble's use of nature, the subject of so many of his poems, in the light of both Wordsworth's work and of Tractarian Analogy.

In 1832 Wordsworth wrote a poem called "Devotional Incitements" that reads almost like a poem from *The Christian Year.*[21] One is tempted to speculate that it may have been an instance of Wordsworth's improving upon or even answering Keble. In the poem, Wordsworth urges man to aspire heavenward just as all things in Nature do—the spirits of the flowers, fragrances, the songs of birds and brooks, and so on. He regrets that religious practices that also teach man to aspire—the use of hymns, incense, pictures—have decayed or been spurned. But Nature, he assures the reader, unchangingly teaches, providing in all seasons "divine monition" that we do not live by bread alone and that "Every day should leave some part / For a sabbath of the heart."

Keble would surely have agreed that nature regularly yields divine monition, and he would have agreed that church forms have been permitted in some quarters to "decay and languish" or to be spurned. But Keble, whose motto was "in medio Ecclesiae,"[22] would certainly not have accepted nature as sufficient substitute for the Church, as Wordsworth appears to do in "Devotional Incitements." It is precisely the willingness to accept nature as sole teacher that renders Wordsworth's poem not quite Tractarian and that points to the peculiar quality Keble brought to nature poetry in *The Christian Year.*

The locus classicus for Keble's view of nature lies in the poem for **"Septuagesima Sunday,"** which begins:

> There is a Book, who runs may read,
>   Which heavenly Truth imparts,
> And all the lore its scholars need,
>   Pure eyes and Christian hearts.
>
> The works of God above, below,
>   Within us and around,
> Are pages in that Book to shew
>   How God Himself is found.

These first two stanzas are Wordsworthian and something more. Like Wordsworth, Keble is asserting that nature offers "divine monition," but Keble makes plain that the lessons of nature require "pure eyes and Christian hearts" for correct understanding. The rest of the poem provides a capsule version of Tractarian Analogy: the sky is like the love of the Maker, for it embraces all; the Church on earth is an analogue of the moon in heaven, for each borrows its radiance from its "sun," which is both the heavenly body and the Son of God; the saints in heaven are stars; the saints on earth are like trees, having for their root, flower, and fruits, the virtues of Faith, Hope, and Charity; dew that falls is like heavenly grace; storms and tempests are analogues of God's power; and the gentle breeze is like the activity of the Holy Spirit.[23]

All of this analogizing marks the poem as something more than Wordsworthian, as indeed distinctly Tractarian. And what is done so transparently in the poem for Septuagesima is done with greater or lesser explicitness in the treatment of nature (and other topics) throughout the volume, beginning even with the opening poems corresponding to Morning and Evening Prayer. In the latter, for example, Keble shows the way a Christian heart sees Analogy in nature:

> When round Thy wondrous works below
> My searching rapturous glance I throw,
> Tracing out Wisdom, Power, and Love,
> In earth or sky, in stream or grove.

And in the former he assures his readers that they will know the "bliss of souls serene" when they have sworn to see God in everything. Also very much to this point is the poem for the **"Fourth Sunday after Advent,"** which begins with the assertion that it is not an idle "poet's dream" that we should see messages in nature, that we should hear

> In the low chant of wakeful birds,
>   In the deep weltering flood,
> In whispering leaves, these solemn words—
>   "God made us all for good."
>
> All true, all faultless, all in tune,
>   Creation's wondrous choir
> Opened in mystic unison
>   To last till time expire.

Numerous other poems in the volume give varied expression to Keble's conviction that "the low sweet tones of Nature's lyre" are meant to instruct us about God's works and ways. For all the love of nature readers discern in *The Christian Year,* they do not come away from Keble's volume with the same sense of nature as herself a deity that readers of Wordsworth can well take away from his poetry. They see nature rather as a system offering a series of correspondences with qualities of her creator.

Readers come away from Keble not only with a sense of nature offering correspondences but also with an awareness of the Tractarian sense of sin touching even nature. In the recital of the analogy of nature in the poem for Septuagesima, Keble concludes:

> Two worlds are ours: 'tis only Sin
>   Forbids us to descry
> The mystic heaven and earth within,
>   Plain as the sea and sky.
>
> Thou who hast given me eyes to see
>   And love this sight so fair,
> Give me a heart to find out Thee,
>   And read Thee everywhere,

In the poem for the **"Fourth Sunday after Trinity,"** Keble dwells at greater length on the way sin beclouds perception of the two worlds:

> Sin is with man at morning break,
>   And through the live-long day
> Deafens the ear that fain would wake
>   To Nature's simple lay.

The solution he offers is twofold. First, it is Wordsworthian: to hear nature's lay one must remove oneself from the sound of man, from the din of human cities;

> When one by one each human sound
>   Dies on the awful ear,
> Then Nature's voice no more is drowned,
>   She speaks and we must hear.

But Keble does not stop there:

> Then pours she on the Christian heart
>   That warning still and deep,
> At which high spirits of old would start
>   E'en from their Pagan sleep.

The "warning" is that behind the appearances of nature stands the creator of nature: "Streaks of brightest heaven behind / Cloudless depths of light."

Keble's implied reader is thus always a Christian reader. It is not enough to be responsive to nature's beauties as things in themselves, or even as vague pointers to a higher power. One must have a Christian understanding of nature as an analogue of God and a Christian understanding of sin as an impediment to seeing God clearly through nature:

> Mine eye unworthy seems to read
>   One page of Nature's beauteous book;
> It lies before me, fair outspread—
>   I only cast a wishful look.
>
>   **("Fourth Sunday in Advent")**[24]

The corrective to such a condition is Christian patience and humility:

> But patience! there may come a time
>   When these dull ears shall scan aright
> Strains that outring Earth's drowsy chime,
>   As Heaven outshines the taper's light.
>
> These eyes, that dazzled now and weak,
>   At glancing motes in sunshine wink,
> Shall see the King's full glory break,
>   Nor from the blissful vision shrink:
>
> In fearless love and hope uncloyed
>   For ever on that ocean bright
> Empowered to gaze; and undestroyed,
>   Deeper and deeper plunge in light.
>
>   **("Fourth Sunday in Advent")**

The insistent theological reminders of human sin and the imperfections of nature give a mournful cast to Keble's nature poetry, but at the same time they give it a peculiar tension quite different from the tension in Wordsworth's poetry, though Keble rarely knows how to exploit it for the best poetic effect. Where Wordsworth, even in a late poem like "Devotional Incitements," finds a pure delight in nature ("where birds and brooks from leafy dells. / Chime forth unwearied canticles"), Keble's joy in nature usually draws forth somber reflections on the imperfections of this world as a consequence of original sin:

> Hence all thy groans and travail pains,
>   Hence, till thy God return,
> In wisdom's ear thy blithest strains,
>   O Nature, seem to mourn.

This mournful element on the one hand harks back to the eighteenth-century graveyard school (though Cowper is an even more likely source) and on the other anticipates the sadder and more elegiac character of so much Victorian nature poetry as compared with Romantic. Keble's poetry may have been a contributing factor to the subtle but unmistakable difference between Victorian and Romantic response to nature; and in many an inward ear, when a Victorian contemplated nature, may have been sounding (as it did for Pendennis) the "solemn church music" of *The Christian Year.* One rather thinks it was in Arnold's ear when he wrote on the occasion of Wordsworth's death of Wordsworth's "healing power."

Even when Keble and Wordsworth agree in finding epiphanies in nature, they part company in attribution of the source. Wordsworth, especially in his early poetry, is far less specific than Keble in attributing the transcendent experiences of nature to the traditional Christian God. By not doing so Wordsworth lays himself open to charges of pantheism, but perhaps he also commends himself to less theologically inclined readers then and now. Keble insistently relates the glories of nature to a right understanding of Christian truth:

> Till thou art duly trained, and taught
>   The concord sweet of Love divine:
> Then with that inward Music fraught,
>   For ever rise, and sing, and shine.
>
>   (**"Fourth Sunday in Advent"**)

Nature for Keble is sacramental in the sense that, like a sacrament, it is an "outward and visible sign of an inward and spiritual truth."[25] The key words in the poetry, however, are not "sacrament" or "sacramental" (neither of which appears in *The Christian Year;* nor does any form of the word "analogy"), but words like "dew," "divine," "light," "radiance," "rapture," "sweet," and above all "love" (this latter the most frequent word in the volume).[26] While he can be overly didactic about the function of nature in a poem like that for Septuagesima, the doctrine of Reserve prevents him from speaking as openly and directly of something as holy as a sacrament. Yet the atmosphere breathed by the volume is precisely that of "consecration of all life," as Lock put it, or the sacramental system, as Newman recognized. Nature occupies center stage in this system, but it is the system, not nature itself, that the poetry is designed to illuminate. Nature to the Tractarian mind is, like poetry, a handmaiden to divine truth. No wonder that the lines Newman found himself thinking his own were Keble's:[27]

> Every leaf in every nook,
> Every wave in every brook,
> Chanting with a solemn voice
> Minds us of our better choice.
>
>   (**"First Sunday after Epiphany"**)

Nature, like poetry, serves to reinforce Christian truth, not to originate her own. Nature and the analogical system also reinforce the characteristic structure of the poems that moves from contemplation to prayer, for nature leads the Christian mind from observation of physical beauty to reflection on what lies behind the appearances to worship of the creator of all things.

Thus the widespread belief that Keble's poetry is Wordsworth and water is really off the mark, as far as concerns its intellectual content. Keble's nature poetry is rather Wordsworth *moralisé* or Wordsworth plus theology. If it is less effective than Wordsworth's nature poetry, this has more to do with Keble's gifts as a poet than with the intellectual assumptions behind the poetry, for those same assumptions—nature as God's creation and sign, nature as fallen with man and yet redeemed through Christ—when exploited so brilliantly by Hopkins, become a basis for transcending Wordsworth and reinvigorating a faded Romantic nature, moving it to something far more deeply interfused with a philosophy and a theology.[28] Keble's strong sense of the sacramental system must be counted a bridge between the two. In Keble's case the theological dimension—nature as part of the analogy of creation—is always dominant.

It is mainly as a reflection of the sacramental or analogical system that Keble approaches the other topics of his poetry in *The Christian Year.* The treatment of nature can stand as a paradigm for Keble's treatment of these other topics: daily life, the home, family relations, work, rural scenes, and, of course, biblical and Christian story in conjunction with saints' days and Church feasts. Like nature, all of these are regularly related to traditional moral and theological teaching, with perhaps an especially Tractarian stress on humility and self-denial:

> The trivial round, the common task,
> Would furnish all we ought to ask;
> Room to deny ourselves; a road
> To bring us daily, nearer God.
>
>   (**"Morning"**)

Also especially Tractarian is the emphasis on the role of the Church, though this aspect is less pronounced in the poetry (as opposed to the organization) of *The Christian Year* than it would come to be in later Tractarian verse.[29] Perhaps this is why only the most severe dissenters found the volume too Catholic. The poem for the First Sunday in Lent links both Church and home as forms of God's blessings to humankind. **"The Church, our Zoar,"**[30] Keble calls it. In the poem for Whitsunday (Penetecost) he recalls the founding of the visible Church by the tongues of fire. For Tuesday in Whitsun-week he speaks of the function of the Church to remind one of God: "And yet of Thee from year to year / The Church's solemn chant we hear." Most arresting in this connection is his poem for Trinity Sunday in which he very modestly anticipates what will provide

Isaac Williams with the subject of most of his devotional poetry—the physical structure of the Church as a means of teaching about God:

> Along the Church's central space
> The sacred weeks with unfelt pace
> Have borne us on from grace to grace.
>
> From each carved nook and fretted bend
> Cornice and gallery seem to send
> Tones that with seraph hymns might blend.
>
> Three solemn parts together twine
> In harmony's mysterious line;
> Three solemn aisles approach the shrine.[31]

The seven sacraments also appear, but chiefly in the poems especially appointed for them in correspondence with the Prayer Book. The sacramental element is thus conveyed as much through references to nature, daily life, and Christian story as through specific actions of the Church, striking that balance between personal feeling and formal ritual that the Tractarians tried to maintain.

Finally, among topics of poems in the volume, the reader cannot but be struck by the intense Christology of Keble's views. The words "Christ," "Jesus," and "Saviour" appear far more often than the word "Church." Keble's Christ has not the valor and act of a windhover, but neither is he exclusively the gentle Jesus, meek and mild, of so much Evangelical hymnody. He is shown often in suffering and in triumph, while the poems retrace the events in Christ's life that are commemorated throughout the year, and he is especially compared to light and radiance and glory in nature, and, with almost medieval consistency, to the sun. Keble's "Sun of my soul! Thou Saviour dear" from **"Evening"** is but the best known example of a persistent imagery of light and dazzling radiance associated with Christ in the poems. But Keble's position is encompassing enough to allow for the subsequent illustrations of the text that could be tailored to Protestant or Catholic views.

There are some more or less polemic pieces in the volume, but these are very much in the minority. Discussion of poems like that for Gunpowder Treason, with its jibe at Rome and its much agitated doctrinal change in its lines on the Eucharist,[32] should not be allowed to obscure the fact that, for the most part, the volume found favor for its absence of polemics and its capturing of the "soothing tendency" of the Prayer Book that Keble claimed was his purpose in the introduction. The real "polemic," as I have argued, is far subtler; it comes through the adaptation of the form of **The Christian Year** to the Prayer Book, providing continual reinforcement of the idea of formal worship through the visible Church. The cumulative effect of the poetry itself is to offer guidance and reassurance to the reader as he goes through the Church year that there is

possible in the world about him holiness, devotion, and consecration of life—in other words, Tractarian Analogy made accessible to everyday experience. It is the atmosphere, the ethos, of Keble's own circle, of the so-called Bisley School, and of Tractarianism itself. As Keble remarked, "we are taught to make every scene in nature a topic of devotion."

THE STYLE OF *THE CHRISTIAN YEAR*

The Tractarian ethos shapes also those aspects of the poetry of **The Christian Year** that come under the general heading of style, by which I mean such technical matters as language, diction, imagery, and metrics, as well as such elusive qualities as verbal complexity, ingenuity, ambiguity, irony, and the like. Most modern critics place a higher value on these aspects of poetry than on any others, certainly a higher value than did Tractarian poetic theory, which is notably silent on technical questions. Accordingly, Keble does not fare well when attention is directed exclusively to stylistic issues. Using these criteria alone we cannot but find Keble's poetic achievement a rather modest one, and I have no intention of making extravagant claims for him on purely verbal grounds. But I do believe that even on purely verbal grounds much of what Keble does can be better understood if it is related to Tractarian poetic theory and to the personal ethos that in Keble so thoroughly complements it.

The meditative and contemplative character of the typical poem and pattern of poems in **The Christian Year** is a consequence of the shaping power of the Book of Common Prayer and a complement to the doctrine of Analogy. The meditative character is also a consequence of another aspect of Tractarian, and especially Keblian, poetic theory. In the **Lectures on Poetry,** Keble distinguishes between poetry of action and poetry of contemplation, clearly preferring the latter. Contemplative poetry, as Keble sees it, reminds us of our human limitations; in his view, such poetry nicely coincides with Tractarian ideas of humility and holiness: "The vein of poetry that seeks a life of quiet and tender feelings, that loves to hide in sheltered nooks, may stand as eternal proof how little mortal minds are self-sufficing, whether they betake themselves to worldly business or philosophic contemplation. It might reprove the folly of those who, when the certainties of heaven are offered them, prefer to cling to the uncertainties of earth" (**LP,** II, 280-281).

Keble's contemplative poetry lends itself to the use of nature as subject, which in turn means a preference for the country over the city, as in Wordsworth, a preference for Keble's own "trivial round, the common task." Nature inevitably involves the poet, especially the Christian poet, in Analogy and the Sacramental system. And the obverse of the Tractarian coin of Analogy is the concept of

Reserve, for Nature both proclaims and conceals her message in something of the manner of Carlyle's Open Secret, that is, the secret of the goodness of the universe, hidden from the vulgar but visible to the poet. Just as Analogy prompts a certain kind of subject matter (and is itself prompted by that subject, hence the inadvertent virtues of pagan nature poetry), so Reserve inclines the poet to a certain kind of style, one that is subdued and humble, both as a means of showing reverence for the sacred truths with which he is dealing and as a discipline for denying the self. Reserve determines what, or how much, the poet will say and how he will say it. Reserve also inclines the poet to be a poet of contemplation rather than action. Once again we can see how remarkably self-consistent and self-contained the Tractarian position is, to say nothing of how much it is a codification of Keble's own methods as a poet and of Keble's own personal style, which by the late 1820s had been stamped on the other Tractarians-to-be.

Reserve, then, dictates that the poet will be guarded and gradual in revealing sacred truth, hence in writing verse at all. While poetry serves as a safety-valve for the expression of intense religious emotion, Analogy and Reserve see to it that the expression will be veiled, indirect, subdued, and self-effacing. Keble versified the concept of Reserve in his poem for the "Fourth Sunday in Lent," a poem titled **"The Rosebud."** In it he notes how one can never actually capture the exact moment when a flower opens:

> Fondly we seek the dawning bloom
>   On features wan and fair,—
> The gazing eye no change can trace,
> But look away a little space,
>   Then turn, and, lo! 'tis there.

The rose is a type of heavenly and human love; these things hide themselves from sight. And it is meet and right that they do:

> No—let the dainty rose a while
>   Her bashful fragrance hide—
> Rend not her silken veil too soon,
> But leave her, in her own soft noon,
>   To flourish and abide.

There can be no question that Reserve is the problematic element in Tractarian poetics, one that will later come to be mainly honored in the breach, but for Keble it was as firm a ruling principle as any in Tractarian poetics. His poetry accordingly is a poetry that hides itself in sheltered nooks, that has as its "chief purpose" to exhibit the "soothing tendency of the Prayer Book." By design it does not overpower the reader by force of language or compel him by the ingenuity of its technical devices. Rather it stands almost as an antitype to the poetry of the figure with whom Keble was most often compared in his own day, George

Herbert.[33] Since it is the devotional poetry of Herbert and Donne that for modern readers provides the paradigm of what devotional poetry is supposed to be, Keble's poetry by comparison seems plain, flaccid, and sedate. One is reminded of the remark about the difference between a biblical angel and a Victorian one. The former strikes terror and appropriately says to the beholder, "Fear not"; the latter seems to say to the observer, "There, there."

Yet underneath its plain and modest vesture, Keble's poetry contains some elements of novelty and vigor that help explain its appeal and that give it more staying power than one would expect of poems governed by a principle like Tractarian Reserve, especially when Reserve is construed, as by Keble, to require extreme reticence. The chief element of novelty in the poetry is the surprising metrical and stanzaic variety of the verses, surprising because somehow this diversity does not stand out in the reading. Partly, it escapes notice because the stanzaic patterns are not reinforced by physical devices in the manner of emblem verse or by wordplay in the manner of metaphysical verse. Moreover, the metrical and stanzaically varied forms coexist with a good deal of quite conventional verse forms and throughout, use of language avoids calling attention to itself and hence to the form. Like the intellectual virtues of *The Christian Year,* the technical ones emerge only after repeated and reflective reading, and they are oddly more effective for it, being like the discovery of new facets of something familiar and well known.

B. M. Lott has catalogued the technical data for the poems in *The Christian Year.*[34] Seen against a background of Reserve as a stylistic concept, the data are extremely revealing. On the one hand the most common metrical and stanzaic forms in *The Christian Year* are long meter and long meter doubled, and ballad or common meter, that is, forms best known through their use in hymns and ballads. On the other hand, these frequent forms, accounting for forty-one, or slightly over a third, of the poems in the collection, are more than balanced by thirty-eight other, different stanzaic patterns in the remaining two-thirds of the poems, for a final total of forty-two stanzaic patterns among the 109 poems in the collection. The thirty-eight other stanzaic forms do not derive from the hymn tradition, nor are they suitable for adaptation as hymns, being usually too complicated for such use. Some of Keble's forms come from the album verse popular in the period, that is, verse in miscellaneous literary collections, usually annuals (*The Keepsake* is a well-known example), designed especially for female readers. Other of Keble's forms are evidently his own creations. The result in any case is an abundance of stanzaic variety and experimentation, yet its effect is not haphazard because it is cemented by intermixture with hymn and ballad forms and by recurrence of the conventional metrical feet. Here Keble abides very largely with the usual iamb, his most notable departures being extra syllables at the beginnings and ends of lines, and these are not always happy additions. His consistent use of three-, four-, or five-beat iambic lines and of rhyme (there is only one unrhymed poem in the collection) makes his poetry seem immediately easy and familiar and lacking in surprises. The novelty comes only in the rhyme *scheme* and could pass unnoticed, especially when Keble relies, as he does excessively, on sight rhymes. Yet the variety of rhyme schemes has moved Lott to call Keble the chief stanzaic experimenter in the age until the appearance of Christina Rossetti.

Keble's poetic diction is also a function of Reserve and is as easily misunderstood as his metrics. His language is marked by conventional word choice, by traditional eighteenth-century poetic locutions—"fain," "vernal," "lo," "'tis," "ere," and the like, and a heavy use of the biblical "ye" and the second-person familiar, with corresponding archaic verb endings. Such language is designed not to call attention to itself (if it does so today, it is by historical accident), but to blend on the one hand with conventional poetic language and on the other with the language of the Prayer Book and the Bible. This is not to say that Keble was a great lyric poet who denied himself his gifts, but it is to argue that he was not simply faltering or verbally inept and that he designed his language for particular effects. The Victorian concordance to *The Christian Year* is a substantial volume displaying a large vocabulary. What it contains little of is word coinages or verbal oddities, for these were consciously eschewed by a poet intent on exercising Reserve in his poetry.

To move beyond rhyme and diction to the texture of the poetry itself is to move into the atmosphere that these technical practices undergird. Apart from the novelty of the stanzaic variety and a tendency towards syntactic that Keble's Victorian admirers felt obliged to apologize for because it diminishes his directness and clarity, the texture of the poetry itself is intentionally low-key and subdued. Keble does not aim for the tight expression, the compacted utterance, the surprising verbal turn. From time to time, of course, he attains these, but almost always he fails to stop, pressing on with yet a further elaboration of what seems a point fully made. His aim is not so much to make neat points as to dispose the reader to reflect on certain truths. Some of Keble's most telling lines are embedded within a poem. His sense of an ending is that of bringing the reader gently to a state of mind or condition of prayer that takes him outside of and beyond the limits of the poem. Sometimes, by virtue of his prayer structure, he does end with forceful expressions that are also pointers beyond: "To live more nearly as we pray," for example, or "For ever rise and sing, and shine," where each word seems to count, or his particularly telling conclusion to the idea of Nature as God's book: "Give me a heart to find out Thee, / And read Thee everywhere." But these occasions are outnumbered by those in which the language and sequence are designed to bring the reader to rest rather than to revelation.

None of the foregoing is to say that there are no poems of singular merit in the collection. More than one reader has fixed upon a particular poem as especially beautiful or memorable; Saintsbury on the **"Third Sunday in Advent"** and **"Second Sunday in Lent,"** A. E. Housman on the **"Second Sunday after Easter,"** David Cecil on the **"Tuesday before Easter"** and the **"Twenty-third Sunday after Trinity"** are some modern instances.[35] Victorian readers too had favorite poems, although more often they seem to have had favorite lines and passages.[36] But to join this process of singling out individual poems is to abandon the aid of the aesthetic by which *The Christian Year* was composed. It is not that here and there the volume throws up an individually good line or even entire poems; it is that the whole work breathes an atmosphere appropriate to its subject. The style of *The Christian Year* is always at the service of something other than itself. Keble's poetry is not meant to be but to mean, and not to mean in an original and arresting way but in an oddly translucent way. He would have considered his poetry to have performed its service if it succeeded in pointing the reader to something beyond itself; he would have considered it to have performed a disservice if it caused the reader (or the author) to think too much of style and method and too little of what it was designed to do.

In the poems for **"Palm Sunday"** and the **"Sixth Sunday after Trinity"** Keble considers the role of the poet in terms of the poet's mission, which is to open the hearts of his readers to eternal truth. Poets, whom he calls "Sovereign masters of all hearts," should be mindful of the source of their gifts, of who set them "God's own work to do on earth." And if they fail in their calling, or "in idol-hymns profane / The sacred soul-enthralling strain," the poet prays that God will show His power and mercy by infusing "noble breath" into these "vile things," until the poets give back His due to God.

> Childlike though the voices be,
>   And untunable the parts,
> Thou wilt own the minstrelsy,
>   If it flow from childlike hearts.

> **("Palm Sunday")**

In the poem for the **"Sixth Sunday after Trinity"** Keble admonished poets not to become so concerned with form as to remain poets only. The lines are based on David's repentance, hence the title of the poem **"The Psalmist's Repenting,"** and the entire poem exhibits most of the characteristics of Keble's style—an eight-line stanza of alternating tetrameter and pentameter couplets with eye and slant rhymes, concluding with a prayerful request.

Near the end he entreats those who have been moved to spiritual things by poetry to pray for the poet:

> If ever, floating from faint earthly lyre,
> Was wafted to your soul one high desire,
>   By all the trembling hope ye feel,
>   Think on the minstrel as ye kneel:

Keble is concerned above all that the singer may work his magic only on others and be himself indifferent to his own music:

> Think on the shame, that dreadful hour
>   When tears shall have no power,
> Should his own lay the accuser prove,
> Cold while he kindled others' love:
> And let your prayer for charity arise,
> That his own heart may hear his melodies,
>   And a true voice to him may cry,
>   "Thy God forgives—thou shalt not die."

The self-effacing style of Keble's verse is finally the appropriate complement to his organization and intention in **The Christian Year.** Like the landscape of Gloucester and the west country which is the source for most of the nature description, the poetry of **The Christian Year** is gentle and initially unremarkable. It grows on the reader by association with the Prayer Book and the Bible, by repetition and reflection; it induces in the reader the very contemplative cast of mind that produced the poetry in the first place. That it was astonishingly effective in touching Victorian readers is testified to by the reverence in which it was held in the age and by the way in which its peculiar music stole upon readers in Wordsworthian quiet or pensive moods. That a taste for such poetry has largely evanesced no one would deny, but something of that taste can be recaptured by an effort of historical imagination. As a historical phenomenon alone, the poetry deserves a permanent if modest place in literary history.

As always in matters relating to Tractarianism, Newman has the last word. His assessment, two decades after the first appearance of **The Christian Year,** fixes for posterity the high-water mark of that volume and can stand as its epitaph:

> Much certainly came of the **Christian Year:** it was the most soothing, tranquilizing, subduing work of the day; if poems can be found to enliven in dejection, and to comfort in anxiety; to cool the over-sanguine, to refresh the weary, and to awe the worldly; to instil resignation into the impatient, and calmness into the fearful and agitated—they are these (N, *Essays,* I, 441).

Notes

1. Georgina Battiscombe, *John Keble* (London, 1964), p. 104.

2. To cite but two examples, *Bartlett's Familiar Quotations* (14th ed., Boston, 1968), p. 567, gives four passages from *The Christian Year,* but one of them is the first stanza of "Abide with Me," which was written by Henry Francis Lyte; Michael Hardwick, *A Literary Atlas and Gazetteer of the British Isles* (Detroit, 1973), p. 70, lists Keble under Gloucestershire with the notice: "His principal work apart from hymns was *The Christian Year,* a briefly successful collection of sacred poems."

3. In addition to works on Keble and the Movement already cited, see Brian W. Martin, *John Keble: Priest, Professor and Poet* (London, 1976). Martin also considers Keble's poetry in relation to his theory and is especially strong on Keble's reflections of earlier poets like Milton; see pp. 119-167. Keble in relation to specifically Anglican devotional attitudes is treated by C. J. Stranks, *Anglican Devotion* (London, 1961), esp. pp. 236-266.

4. This remark is quoted extensively and in various formulations in the literature. See Battiscombe, p. 104. Mary Moorman, *William Wordsworth: The Later Years, 1808-1850* (Oxford, 1965), pp. 479-480, also records that Wordsworth thought Keble's verse "vicious in diction." For the general Victorian response, see Appendix C, below.

5. A. E. Housman, *The Name and Nature of Poetry* (New York, 1933), pp. 32-33.

6. Hoxie Neale Fairchild, *Religious Trends in English Poetry,* 4 (New York, 1957), 251. This massive survey contains a wealth of information and has observations on almost all the poets treated in the present study, but Fairchild's critical judgments are marred by an unrelenting hostility to Romanticism that renders him incapable of understanding the Tractarian enterprise.

7. Amy Cruse's term in *The Victorians and Their Reading* (Boston, 1935), p. 19.

8. Matthew Arnold, *Literature and Dogma,* in *Prose Works of Matthew Arnold,* ed. R. H. Super, 6 (Ann Arbor, Mich., 1968), 403. The Keble line that Arnold italicized appears in the poem for the "Sixth Sunday after Epiphany" (*CY,* p. 60).

9. Donald Davie, *A Gathered Church: The Literature of the English Dissenting Interest, 1700-1930* (New York, 1978), pp. 15-16.

10. For a contemporary illustrated guide to the Church year, see L. W. Cowie and John Selwyn Gummer, *The Christian Calendar* (Springfield, Mass., 1974).

11. In most modern usage Epiphany is counted as the season after Christmas, and Sundays up to Lent are now numbered in terms of their distance from Epiphany, thus absorbing the old pre-Lenten period of Septuagesima.

12. The poems for "Gunpowder Treason," "King Charles the Martyr," and "The Restoration of the Royal Family" were added to the third and

subsequent editions to round out the sequence in the Prayer Book. They were not provided initially because they are not part of the universal Christian calendar. In the Victorian age the commemoration of the martyrdom of Charles I on January 30 was dropped from the Prayer Book to the considerable annoyance of Anglo-Catholics, who, however, continued to keep the day. The Lectionary is the table of Bible readings for the entire year; the Thirty-nine Articles are the Calvinist-inspired statement of principles and beliefs that generated Newman's Tract 90; the Tables of Kindred list family relations among whom marriage is forbidden.

13. See Appendix B on the antecedents of *The Christian Year.*

14. Charlotte Mary Yonge, *Musings over "The Christian Year," and "Lyra Innocentium"* (Oxford, 1871). This now scarce volume contains Yonge's own reminiscences of Keble, contributions from others related to his life and times, and Yonge's extensive individual commentaries on every poem in *The Christian Year.* It is thus a companion to a companion to the Book of Common Prayer. Charlotte Mary Yonge was Keble's catechumen at Hursley, and her thinking on religious matters was always very close to Keble's own.

15. The First Sunday in Epiphany can never fall later than January 13.

16. James Anthony Froude, the younger brother of Hurrell Froude and himself a quondam Tractarian, made the comparison between Tennyson's poems and *The Christian Year.* See A. Dwight Culler, *The Poetry of Tennyson* (New Haven, 1977), p. 156.

17. B. M. Lott, "The Poetry of John Keble, with Special Reference to *The Christian Year* and His Contribution to *Lyra Apostolica*" (diss., London University, 1960), p. 210, notes that the Lectionary was changed in the nineteenth century, so that some of the correspondences are not so clear today as they once were in those poems where the readings for the day come from the Lectionary rather than from printed readings in the Prayer Book propers.

18. Margaret Oliphant, *Salem Chapel* (1863; London, 1907), pp. 53-54. Mrs. Oliphant is here certainly playing on the language of the Book of Common Prayer in the prayer for acceptance of the offering following the consecration of bread and wine: "We beseech Thee to accept this our bounden duty and service, not weighing our merits, but pardoning our offences." In the subsequent reference to the "Anglican lyre" she links *The Christian Year* to the other great Tractarian devotional collection, *Lyra Apostolica,* and in effect notes the frequency with which the idea of the lyre occurs in Tractarian poetry.

19. The other truth that Keble's poetry brought home to Newman was the doctrine of probability, which, as Newman himself notes in this passage, "runs through very much that I have written."

20. Similar points are made in other sympathetic Victorian commentaries, a good example of which is the Preface to Keble's *Miscellaneous Poems* (Oxford, 1869), pp. v-xxv, by G[eorge] M[oberly].

21. *Poetical Works of Wordsworth,* ed. Thomas Hutchinson and Ernest DeSelincourt (London, 1950), pp. 181-182.

22. Used as the motto for Keble's *Occasional Papers and Reviews.* The full passage reads: "In medio Ecclesiae aperuit os ejus, et implevit eum Dominus Spiritu sapientiae et intellectus" (In the middle of the Church he opened his mouth, and the Lord filled him with the Spirit of wisdom and understanding). I have not been able to trace the source. Keble's motto for *The Christian Year* was: "In quietness and confidence shall be your strength" (Isaiah, 30:15).

23. The only natural phenomenon missing from this catalogue is the rainbow, but Keble frequently refers to it in other poems. See George Landow, "The Rainbow: A Problematic Image," in U. C. Knoepflmacher and G. B. Tennyson, eds., *Nature and the Victorian Imagination* (Berkeley, 1977), pp. 347-348. Keble's analogues are more or less consistent in *The Christian Year* but not so rigorously applied as to make possible any kind of allegory.

24. In the original manuscript "wishful" reads "wistful." Lock in *CY* records all such changes and variants from the manuscripts at Keble College. There was also a facsimile publication in 1878 of Keble's 1822 manuscript of most of the poems in *The Christian Year* and many sonnets dating from as early as 1810. The facsimile was titled after Keble's notation on the first page of the manuscript *Manuscript Verses, Chiefly on Sacred Subjects.* The facsimile was unauthorized and soon suppressed. Copies are now rare.

25. This is the phrasing from "A Catechism" in the Book of Common Prayer defining a sacrament.

26. The ten most frequent words in *The Christian Year,* with number of times they appear following each in parentheses, are: Love (227), Heart (182), Heaven (180), God (149), Earth (119), Lord (117), Light (98), World (95), Eye (92), High (89). Computed from the entries in *A Concordance to The Christian Year* (1871; rpt., New York, 1968).

27. Battiscombe, p. 113, quotes Newman: "'In riding out today I have been impressed more powerfully than before I had an idea was possible with the two lines "Chanting with a solemn voice / Minds us of our better choice." I could hardly believe the lines were not my own and that Keble had not taken them from me. I wish it were possible for words to put down the indefinable vague and withal subtle feelings with which God pierces the soul and makes

it sick.'" The original source is a letter from Newman to his sister Jemima in 1828; see *Letters and Correspondence of John Henry Newman,* ed. Anne Mozley (London, 1891), I, 183.

28. Wordsworth himself tried to do something of the same sort in the later "Ecclesiastical Sonnets," especially those that abandon the historical format of the "Ecclesiastical Sketches" to concentrate on Church rites and offices. It is noteworthy that the great bulk of these appeared after the publication of *The Christian Year* in 1827. See Appendix B.

29. Keble's remark that in *The Christian Year* he assumed the Church to be in "a state of decay" has been much quoted. See *CY,* p. xvii. One of his aims was to arrest this decay by revitalizing Church practices.

30. Zoar was Lot's city of refuge when God destroyed Sodom and Gomorrah.

31. Late Victorian Keble hagiographic works make much of the impact of Fairford Church on Keble's imagination, and in truth the church is an impressive late Gothic structure justly famed for its stained glass windows once believed to be by Dürer. See Yonge, *Musings,* pp. cxxxviii-cxlvii; J. G. Joyce, *The Fairford Windows* (London, 1872); W. T. Warren, *Kebleland* (Winchester, 1900); Oscar G. Farmer, *Fairford Church and Its Stained Glass Windows* (Fairford, n.d.).

32. The thirteenth stanza of this poem originally read: "O come to our Communion Feast: / There present, in the heart / Not in the hands, the eternal Priest / Will His true self impart." After repeated requests, Keble changed the third line just before his death to read: "As in the hands . . . " in order to make clear that he was not denying the doctrine of the Real Presence. See *CY,* p. 297, and J. T. Coleridge, *Memoir of the Rev. John Keble* (London, 1869), p. 163. The anti-Roman lines are actually very mild: "Speak gently of our sister's fall: / Who knows but gentle love / May win her at our patient call / The surer way to prove?"

33. Despite frequent Victorian comparisons of the two poets, modern critics have not found the subject rewarding, but see Elbert N. S. Thompson, "*The Temple* and *The Christian Year,*" PMLA, 54 (1939), 1018-1025; and Jean Wilkinson, "Three Sets of Religious Poems," *Huntington Library Quarterly,* 36 (1972-73), 203-226.

34. Lott, pp. 66-71. I have taken the statistical data from Lott but not the linkage of it with the stylistic imperatives of Reserve, which is my own interpretation.

35. George Saintsbury in the *Cambridge History of English Literature,* ed. A. W. Ward and A. R. Waller, 12, pt. 2 (Cambridge, 1917), p. 189; Housman, p. 33; David Cecil includes the two Keble poems I have mentioned in *The Oxford Book of Christian Verse* (Oxford, 1940).

36. Pusey was especially given to citing passages and lines in letters, and he testified that "scraps of *The Christian Year,* as they have occurred to me, have been a great comfort, and will be amid whatever He sees best to send" (quoted by Battiscombe, p. 113).

Sheridan Gilley (essay date 1983)

SOURCE: "John Keble and the Victorian Churching of Romanticism," in *An Infinite Complexity: Essays in Romanticism,* edited by J. R. Watson, Edinburgh University Press, 1983, pp. 226-239.

[*In the following essay, Gilley considers Keble's place as the leading poet of the Victorian High Church revival.*]

Among the more attractive figures from the English past are the clergy scholars and poets who have served and loved the Church of England. Richard Hooker, chased by his wife from his books to mind the sheep; George Herbert and Robert Herrick; John Ray, with scientific eye discerning the glory of God in all creation; Gilbert White of Selborne, whose parish was universe enough. On a still humbler level, but evocative of the tradition, are the annals of Cole and Kilvert and Woodforde who have left remarkable diaries. A secure place in this gallery of English worthies is held by John Keble, Victorian Vicar of the parish of Hursley near Winchester. His ministry was peaceful, dedicated and devout, the qualities which reappear in his poetry; and to his contemporaries, he was a worthy successor to Hooker and Herbert as well as the very model of the rural parish priest, the pastor and shepherd of his people. For pious Anglicans, his name still evokes that romantic ecclesiastical Arcadia and heaven on earth recalled by another Victorian High Churchman in a letter from Rome: 'the hill-side, and the Spring evenings, the dusk and the stillness, the Evening Lecture . . . the world of inner thoughts, hopes, faith and happiness without a doubt or cloud . . . alms and kindliness, bright hearths and loving faces, and the homely plain open Xtmas joy of the Church of England'.[1] This vision of Christianity was Keble's, one intrinsically rustic and English. There was more about him, however, than the peace and plenty of the rural parsonage. Keble was also a national figure as one of the best-loved of English poets and a leader of the High Church revival. To his own generation he was a prophet in Israel, and for many Victorians, *the* poet of the religious world.

John Keble was born in 1792, the son of a country priest, also named John Keble, and never thought of any calling but the ministry. He went up to Oxford in 1807, proved himself the most brilliant student of his generation, took double first class honours in 1810, and was elected a Fellow of Oriel in 1811. Oriel was the centre of the Oxford renaissance of classical and philosophical studies, under the leadership of the overpowering so-called 'Noetics'—Whately, Copleston, and Hawkins.[2] The dialectical brilliance of the Oriel common-room—which it was said, 'stank of Logic'[3]—made it a nursery of genius; and the leaders of the High Church revival—Newman, Pusey, Keble, Robert Wilberforce and Froude—had all been Fellows of Oriel. Keble resigned his Oriel tutorship in 1823 and became his father's curate, and it was only in 1836 that we became Vicar of Hursley where he lived for thirty years until his death. He achieved national fame in 1827 with a volume of poems called *The Christian Year,* and after 1833, was a leading light of the Oxford Movement for the renewal of the Church of England. He held, however, no high ecclesiastical or academic office, except the Oxford Professorship of Poetry. Otherwise he was buried for forty years as curate and vicar of country parishes, in a life well-hidden from the world.

Why was the most brilliant student of his generation, the leader of a national religious movement, so unrewarded by his Church? The answer lies partly in the controversial character of his religious opinions, but more in his acute sense of his own 'limitations'.[4] These were partly imposed by his shyness and reserve: a personal reserve which he was to turn into a principle of aesthetic theory, and a dogma in theology. At a simpler level he had no wish to shine. He deliberately made his university teaching dull—something most of us achieve without effort—lest others should wrongly praise him. He took as a motto the injunction 'Don't be original', and he was ideally placed to transform his tradition because his role aim was to keep it as it was. His early manhood was dominated by his love for his father, and his highest ideal was to perpetuate his father's kind of rural ministry. Thus his loyalty to his Church was too strong to be broken, so that unlike Newman, he felt no temptation to join the Church of Rome because of the sins of the Church of England. The Church might apostasise almost everywhere, he thought, but it would still survive whole within his own parish. His father gave him the old fashioned High Church loyalty to the religious establishment and its parochial system and what went with them, strong Tory politics, and a love for England and her king.

These formidable convictions might have seemed a ruinous legacy. In the eighteenth century, High Churchmanship fell on evil days, often declining into pure politics. Many so-called High Churchmen were simply Church-and-King Tories, blind zealots for the Tory party and the traditional connection between Church and State, 'Erastians' in fact if not in theory, acquiescing in a Babylonian captivity wherein the Church was state-controlled. Their fiercest passions were hating Methodists and loving tithes; they were untheological, sometimes irreligious. Among the notorious 'two-bottle orthodox'[5] fellows of Oxford, High Churchmanship meant a taste for port and claret. At best, the Church-and-King Tory was a stout-hearted English gentleman, at worst, he was doubtfully a gentleman, let alone a Christian.

Moreover even devout High Churchmen were affected by a rationalism which made them proverbially 'High and Dry' to the point of lifelessness. In their worship, they kept to the letter of the Prayer Book, in their cold repudiation of Dissenting irregularity. Their sermons were cautious and elegant statements of beliefs too ingrained for emotional expression; there was no appeal to the imagination and the senses, and only the most formal poetry. Despite their high doctrine of Church and Sacrament, there was no ritualist nonsense about them. Indeed as High Churchmen most of them were proud to be Protestant, among the strongest anti-papists in England. Their characteristics, therefore, were a strong Protestantism, a pronounced formalism, a rational 'High and Dryness'; and a loyalty to Church, King and Prayerbook which was at root religious, but which sometimes smacked of tribal prejudice.

This was only one side of the picture, and the tradition was not dead which could claim Dr Johnson. High Churchmanship, however, was the very reverse of 'romantic', appearing at its most defensive in its hatred of emotional excess and enthusiasm, especially in religion, that 'pretending to extraordinary revelations and gifts of the Holy Ghost' which Bishop Joseph Butler told John Wesley was 'a very horrid thing'.[6] The Evangelical appeal to immediate experience of God, of a bloody Christ dying for human sin, was regarded as a kind of madness revolting every canon of Augustan good taste as well as the churchman's insistence on settled ministry and church order. Evangelical enthusiasm was also lower class and vulgar. The devout Anglican—Joshua Watson, Jones of Nayland—was a gentleman of breeding and culture; his fastidiousness was a badge of social caste, a mark of refinement and good manners. He knew that he belonged to polite society, in this world, and in another.

These qualities were strengthened after 1790, in the face of an outpouring of 'enthusiasm' quite horrifying to High Churchmen. They were stunned by the raw energy of the secular apocalyptic of the French Revolution, and by the destruction of aristocracy, king and church in France, which they could only ascribe to Satan. Even in England, democratic radicals, allegedly French spies and sympathisers, appealed by wild oratory to the lower passions of the lower orders; but other signs of the times were as unsettling. There was the sinister spread of Evangelical enthusiasm in the Church Establishment; there was the mushroom growth outside it of Methodism and Evangelical Dissent; there were the stirrings of popish enthusiasm in Ireland. Even in literature, there was the dissolving of form and rule in the romantic revival.[7] The young Wordsworth, Southey, Coleridge, were Unitarians or revolutionaries; and even after their return to the bosom of Mother Church, worse examples were set by Byron and Shelley. Shelley indeed was a notorious atheist, a virulent anticlerical, and ardent republican. The

> Anarchs and priests, who feed on gold and blood
> Till with the stain their inmost souls are dyed,[8]

had every reason to dislike him. High Churchmen were therefore suspicious of every new appeal to imaginative experience; such experience was dangerous and destructive. Perhaps, on the basis of his new defence of experience, Shelley as an aristocrat could do what he liked in the old eighteenth-century manner; but the cost was paid by the first Mrs Shelley, as also by Lady Byron. The outburst against Byron, like Bowdler's Shakespeare, was part of a growing if spasmodic reaction against everything 'romantic' that threatened religion and the family;[9] such notions were as unsettling as the expression of raw emotion in the new democratic politics, the mass conversions achieved by Primitive Methodist hedge preachers, the rebellion preached by O'Connell's Catholic Association in Ireland.[10] This seething mass of unrests and discontents could only heighten the High Churchman's emotional reserve, his insistence upon formal control.

Part of his problem was one of worldly success. High Churchmen were often given preferment after 1760; they dominated the Church after 1793, when a Tory government went to war with revolutionary France, and only lost office once in nearly forty years. A gaggle of High and Dry churchmen, the 'Hackney Phalanx', controlled episcopal appointments during the fifteen-year prime ministership of the Tory Lord Liverpool;[11] and the High Churchmen found themselves as unpopular as their Tory allies in the 1820s, when radicals, nonconformists, and Roman Catholics demanded reforms in Church and State together, notably a drastic reduction in the privileges, possessions and powers of the Church of England. It was this attack on the Church, and Church fears of the new Whig administration after 1830, which resulted in the foundation of the University of Durham; and no less importantly, in a High Church reaction, the Oxford Movement of the 1830s (inaugurated for the young John Henry Newman by a sermon from Keble in 1833, on the sin of National Apostasy from Anglican Christianity). Thus in Keble's **Christian Year,** the established Church is assumed to be in decay: like the dry bones in Ezekiel's vision, at first sight with no hope of resurrection.

Keble's response was to seek out a new source of spiritual life for the Church in romantic poetry and in aesthetic theory, in a partial reversal of his inherited tradition.

Though the Hutchinsonian philosophers of the High Church movement rejected the notion of subjecting revelation to rational criticism,[12] the Anglican reaction to the French Revolution and its radical sympathisers in England had been orthodox rationalist apologetic in the best eighteenth-century manner: the clearest, most perfect of Augustan polemic appeared as late as 1794 and 1802, William Paley's *Evidences of Christianity* and *Natural Theology.* The younger Oriel Fellows encountered this rationalism in their Noetic teachers, and they rejected it and the Noetics together. For rationalism had also hatched Tom Paine's *Age of Reason;* and it was not by Paley's path that the Lake Poets returned to the Church of England.

One approach was mapped out by Wordsworth in his *Ecclesiastical Sketches* of 1822, a history in sonnets of the English Church, saturated with reference to older Anglican historians and divines, suffused with a new kind of feeling for the national religious past, a new sympathy for monasticism and the middle ages, a new depth of devotion to the Blessed Virgin Mary, even to her Immaculate Conception.[13] Faith was no longer a matter of mere rational conviction, but of a sense of awe and wonder before mystery, in the spirit of the famous lines from an earlier Wordsworth sonnet collection,

> The holy time is quiet as a Nun
> Breathless with adoration . . .[14]

More explicitly political was Robert Southey's prose history of the Church of England, *The Book of the Church,* of 1824: splendid with denunciations of papists and puritans, vindicating the Church's power and privileges as the guarantors of her central role in the nation's life, as the guardian of English culture and English freedom.[15] Coleridge's *Aids to Reflection* of 1825 announced a new romantic idealist Anglican theology, his *On the Constitution of the Church and State* of 1830 extended Anglican apologetic into an ideal sociology, and attempted to combine the supernatural good of the Catholic Church of Christ with the secular and national good of Church Establishment.[16] This was the background for Keble's *Christian Year:* of the quest for a religious apologetic wholly different from Paley's, one open to new imaginative ideals.

This religious mood was most evident in the *Ecclesiastical Sketches,* which stressed the more tender, loving, sentimental aspects of Christianity against the eighteenth-century 'usurpations of reason'.[17] In this Wordsworth came to assign a central imaginative role to the rural parish church. In a more industrial world it suggested peace, in a more complex world, simplicity, in a more sophisticated world, the innocence, the unsophistication, of the rustic poor and their gentle pastor. The ideal only dimly reflected the brutality of much of English rural life, and that widespread resentment of church and parson, which helped to make the half-century from 1790 a boom time for rural Non-comformity. To many agricultural labourers the parish priest was the absentee beneficiary of church rate and tithe, and priests were the objects of many popular demonstrations in the Swing Riots of 1830.[18] Yet even Shelley, astonishingly, could think of becoming a rural clergyman, on the ground that in no other sphere could a man do so much good.[19] A vicar like Keble made the ideal live, and it was the unruffled world of English groves and streams, of a humble Gothic building in a mossy church-yard, the parish of Wordsworth's honest peasant and pas-tor, which inspired Keble's poetry, as it sustained his Christian life.

But Keble's approach to nature came only partly from Wordsworth, for the Tractarians found in Wordsworth a sacramentalism of nature which was more deeply rooted in their Catholic theology. One set of sources was Irenaeus, whom Keble translated, and the Alexandrian Fathers, Clement and Origen, in whom Keble saw the principle that natural phenomena are the types and instruments of things unseen, a supernaturally ordained 'economy' of im-ages and symbols, pointing men by analogy to God.[20] Nature was also a sacrament of a divine indwelling: a view he encountered in the *Analogy of Religion* of Bishop Joseph Butler.[21] Keble was still more deeply read in the writings of the sixteenth-century Richard Hooker, which he edited, and in the tradition of Anglican natural theology extending from Hooker to Butler, with its teleological view of nature as a purposive revelation of divine good-ness, disclosing a moral law to man. The didactic implica-tions of the ideals of nature as symbol, sacrament and source of moral order, were therefore only reinforced for Keble by the imaginative illustrations of romantic poetry. On a natural level,

> . . . the dead leaves of the woodland are symbols of resignation; the strong clear note of the blackbird recalls all the words of friends that 'brace and cheer' us in times of sadness and depression; the glories of the autumn sunset are like the promise of the good man's joy in heaven; the flowers in their carelessness of fear, growing beneath our very foot-tread, are types of in-nocence.[22]

On a sublimer plane,

> . . . the sky is like the love of the Maker, for it embraces all; the Church on earth is an analogue of the moon in heaven, for each borrows its radiance from its 'sun', which is both the heavenly body and the Son of God; the saints in heaven are stars; the saints on earth are like trees, having for their root, flower and fruits, the virtues of Faith, Hope and Charity; dew that falls is like heavenly grace; storms and tempests are analogues of God's power; and the gentle breeze is like the activ-ity of the Holy Spirit.[23]

Thus the perfect beauty of sun and stars, tree and leaf, awakens the soul to the perfect goodness of their author, who inspires men to poetry and religion through nature, giving them new and loving hearts.

The curious implication of this argument is the characteris-tic Victorian conviction that if through nature men are inspired to be poets, they ought also be inspired to be good. Nature, in giving us great poets, must make them good men.[24] Keble does not overcome the problem in his forty ***Praelectiones,*** his ***Lectures on Poetry,*** which he delivered as Professor of Poetry at Oxford between 1832 and 1841.[25] Byron and Shelley, by Keble's standards bad men, were better poets than Keble; and critics declare that Wordsworth's poetry was not improved by returning to the Church of England. Yet Keble had this excuse, that he was assuring his High Churchmen that poetry was safe; nay, more, that it was the handmaid of religion, the inspiration of the same nature and the creation of the same God. The example of the later, more moral and conservative Word-sworth was also, thank God, a reassurance: and Keble's lectures were dedicated to him:

> To William Wordsworth
> True Philosopher and Inspired Poet
> Who By The Special Gift and Calling of Almighty God
> Whether He Sang of Man or of Nature
> Failed Not To Lift Up Men's Hearts To Holy Things
> nor Ever Ceased To Champion the Cause
> of the Poor and Simple.
> and So in Perilous Times was Raised Up
> to be a Chief Minister
> Not Only of Sweetest Poetry
> but Also of High and Sacred Truth[26]

Much heart-searching went into this dedication: even in the 1840s, Keble could not quite forgive Wordsworth the sins of his radical youth. But all the right references are here: the happy union of poetic inspiration and religion, of 'sweetest poetry' and 'high and sacred truth', the 'poor and simple' peasantry, the 'perilous times' through which Church and State had passed, the reassurance that the romantic sensibility had been baptised into Anglo-Catholic Christianity, and that the High Churchmen were carrying its honey to their hive.

What then, of the old High Church fear of religious experi-ence and imagination, as a sort of mental disease? For this kind of sickness Keble had a cure in the ***Lectures on Poetry*** in his doctrine of inspiration, which abandoned the formal classical aesthetic of literary types, in the very act of for-malising the romantic aesthetic of impassioned self-expression. Keble's poets conquer their violent agitations of strong feeling by discharging them into poetry; and they recover health and wholeness and tranquillity by giv-ing their emotions poetic form, in a formal structure. Ke-ble's inspiration, then, is not a spontaneous overflow of feeling like a spring or fountain: it is more like 'a safety-valve of a steam boiler':[27] the blast of steam is tremendous, but is never uncontrolled. So the poet distances himself from the turmoil of the pleasures and pains of his imaginative experience with every sort of poetic device: by irony, by complex metrical schemes, by circumlocution and paraphrase; by learned allusions, elaborate patterns of image, metaphor and symbol; by the formal structures of rhythm and rhyme.[28] The experience, is, however, intensified in the act of hiding and subduing it, as a flame burns more steadily in a confined space. There are then two stages in poetic composition: the wild emotion of free inspiration, and then achieved control, in which the spirit is calmed and healed.

A distinguished literary critic has called Keble's **Lectures** 'the most sensationally radical criticism of their time', a 'radical, proto-Freudian theory, which conceives literature as disguised wish-fulfillment, serving the artist as a way back from incipient neurosis'.[29] This is not a description which Keble could have recognised himself, but it does point to the role of the High Church revival, as a sublimation of the dangers of romanticism under a discipline of religious self-control. This aesthetic doctrine of poetry as a cloak for inspiration, was, moreover, an undisguised theological High Church conviction: the principle of reserve. The notion of reserve was developed by seventeenth-century Roman Catholic theologians to explain the early Church's silence on some Catholic doctrines: as Christ had taught in parables, so the Church by her *disciplina arcani* had withheld her full teaching from her catechumens, until they could receive it in the fulness of faith.[30] To High Churchmen like Keble, reserve meant therefore that the deepest truths of Christianity were mysteries only penetrable by men of awakened spiritual insight and power; and that principle condemned mere rational proofs and the ignorant radical critics of the Church without more than rational insight, as well as the emotional enthusiasm of the Evangelicals.[31] As another Oxford High Churchman, Newman, said of Evangelical preaching of the Atonement, the most sacred doctrine of Christ's suffering was bandied about like a talisman or charm to convert men. His own preaching of the Passion was exactly the reverse. As a hearer recalled it, Newman paused in his recital:

> For a few moments there was a breathless silence. Then, in a low, clear voice, of which the faintest vibration was audible in the farthest corner of St. Mary's, he said, 'Now, I bid you recollect that He to whom these things were done was Almighty God.' It was as if an electric stroke had gone through the church, as if every person present understood for the first time the meaning of what he had all his life been saying.[32]

Treat the doctrine in tones of quiet, though it is tremendous; even hide it; then when you unveil it, strike, and strike to the heart.

This theological reserve was suspect to Protestants, who thought that High Churchmen were holding popish doctrine in reserve until their dupes could be trusted to receive it. The extra-theological dimension of reserve was, however, still more widely rooted in the old High Church culture; through reserve, Keble wished to preserve its refinement and good breeding, an ideal only possible to the educated. Such High Anglican snobbery carried weight with the young Sam Wilberforce, son of the most famous of Anglican Evangelicals, who discovered to his dismay at Oxford that Evangelicals were not considered gentlemen.[33] Thus the Oxford Movement's influence was restricted to the gentility until in trying to evangelise the urban poor, it slunk off to the slums to become ritualist and vulgar. Keble's teaching was not for them. As the statutes required, the **Lectures on Poetry** were delivered to the Oxford elect in ecclesiastical Latin, even a Burns stanza—'I look to the West when I gae to rest'—being rendered into Theocritan Greek. The lectures were not translated into English until 1912, and were directed to the few with the learning to understand them.

It was, however, exactly the sociological imprisonment in the pattern of ideas and emotions proper to gentlemen that exasperated some ex-Evangelicals turned High Churchmen; another minor religious poet, like Keble in the later Wordsworth's confidence, Frederick Faber, author of *The Prayer-Book, a safeguard against Religious Excitement*, turned to Rome for the vulgar enthusiasms which Keble denied him.[34] For the heart of Keble's teaching was this contrast, that false enthusiasm simply excited where true inspiration found an expression that soothed, in religion as in poetry. The poet offers us a cool distillation of experience, a refreshing draught with power to heal and calm. For poetry and religion alike are medicines given man to provide the heat of emotion with a safe release. The experience is the more intense for being so repressed—but as in the quiet of Wordsworth's nun, breathless with adoration, the heart is stilled in the holy silence, as the ardour and passion and wildness of naked feeling are refined and chastened and subdued.

It is the aim of worship to intensify experience by subduing it, containing it in a form, and thereby healing. The later Anglo-Catholic ritualist movement acted on Keble's principle, controlling emotion in a structure while giving it highly coloured expression through the senses; but Keble was no ritualist but a strictly reserved old-fashioned Prayer-Book Anglican, and his method of restoring religious experience to the liturgy was by writing poems on all the major Anglican services, and one for every feast and fast day and Sunday of the Christian Year, even unto the 25th Sunday after Trinity. This was a task which might have taxed any poet's powers—not Keble's. 'Next to a sound rule of faith', he wrote in his Advertisement to the poems, 'there is nothing of so much consequence as a sober standard of feeling in matters of practical religion'. This the Anglican liturgy happily possessed. 'But in times of much leisure and unbounded curiosity, when excitement of every kind is sought after with a morbid eagerness, this part of the merit of our Liturgy is likely in some measure to be lost'.[35] Poetic inspiration, religion's handmaid, could be called on to invest the old dry forms of the Prayer Book with a new romantic tenderness, the sense of awe and mystery and wonder, with a new exalted moral feeling and love of nature as symbol, sacrament and source of moral law. Englishmen were all too increasingly agitated by the anxious excitements of Evangelical enthusiasm and secular romanticism and popular politics: they needed to relearn the Prayer Book's power to soothe: to inspire, but to calm and heal.

Keble did not feel himself adequate to his task. By his own classification, he was a Secondary Poet, dependent on the revolutionary insight of the Primary Poets, who like the prophets of religion were directly inspired by God. His conception of 'imagination' comes from the later Wordsworth and is a lowly one, more like Coleridge's Fancy, as the power of Secondary Poets to deploy the metaphors which the Primary Poets provide.[36] Keble therefore did not consider *The Christian Year* great poetry; and though individual poems in the collection have been singled out for praise by George Saintsbury, A. E. Housman and David Cecil,[37] the work might be considered a failure to demonstrate his theory of reserve. Though many of the verses have a limpid simplicity, some of them are obscure by Keble's own deliberate choice, in their indirect formulations of sacred truth, especially their allusions to the classics and the appointed service for each Sunday. Only a mind saturated with the Prayer Book, the Bible, and the Anglican tradition will recognise all the references,[38] and there is so much learning in the poetry that a bishop called the work his Sunday puzzle. The rigidity of Keble's awkward rhythms lacks the true romantic freedom as completely as his stilted eighteenth-century diction, which Wordsworth called 'vicious', lacks the true romantic simplicity.[39] Keble was notoriously tone deaf, and his verses were no incitement to Wordsworth's communal ecstasy of song. Even Wordsworth's tribute to the book had a sting in its tail: that it was so good that he wanted to rewrite it. Later critics vary from Housman's slightly defensive— 'Keble is a poet';[40] some clearly doubted it—to a more recent claim that Keble's poetic skills had fallen off the back of a lorry.[41] *The Christian Year* is not much studied in academic schools of English literature, nor do most of these institutions sympathise with Keble's high moral and religious purpose, to edify, elevate and heal.

Our difficulty with Keble therefore lies in the fact that he owed his popularity not just to literary merit, but to his spiritual teaching. He was so widely read because he provided an historic resolution of the problem posed for Anglicanism by radical enthusiasm and romanticism. *The Christian Year* was important for its period, and its

enormous Victorian success is another barrier in the book for a modern audience.[42] Another High Church poet, Isaac Williams, produced a copy of *The Christian Year* for the entertainment of a not very pious party of holiday trippers who had spent a rainy morning listening to Byron's *Don Juan;* Williams was as astonished as a modern reader might be to find that his hearers preferred Keble.[43] Not Keble's most ardent efforts at reserve could prevent his book selling five hundred thousand copies in fifty years;[44] it formed Victorian religious taste, in Newman's words, 'waking up in the hearts of thousands a new music, the music of a school, long unknown in England'.[45]

This was not because its doctrine was abnormally 'High', for all its devotion to Our Lady, and Church and Prayerbook: indeed one of its verses seemed to deny Christ's Real Presence in the sacrament, and was only amended by Keble three weeks before his death. There is a story of Evangelicals thereafter buying up the earlier, less popish editions,[46] as both Evangelicals and Liberals had welcomed it. For the 'new music', according to an appreciative Presbyterian Scot, was simply that Keble had shown a gentle Christ as a kind and loving friend, with a stress on his humanity lacking in the severer popular soteriologies.[47] 'Sun of my soul! Thou Saviour dear' might seem a trite enough sentiment; but even as a non-doctrinal statement it penetrated the young D.H. Lawrence 'with wonder and the mystery of twilight',[48] and it was with a novel tenderness that Keble set forth the divine possession of the soul to whom Christ is as the sun. His best-known verses open with the beatitude 'Bless'd are the pure in heart', and his favourite adjectives are 'kind', 'gentle', 'humble', 'soft', 'meek', 'pure', and above all, 'loving': the virtues of self-control and of his own home circle, wife, father and sisters, whom Newman loved seeing *The Christian Year* written on their faces. Keble's kindness in the work extended even to controversy. In the heat of the conflict over Catholic Emancipation, he urged restraint in his verses on the Gunpowder Plot towards the Roman Catholics: 'Speak gently of our sister's fall': kindness might redeem even her.

To most moderns, however, these gentle virtues are a problem, in part because of a perverse preference for their ugly opposites, in part because they have been so vulgarised into the 'all things bright and beautiful' kind of children's corner piety which turns to St Francis, and never to St Dominic: so that *The Christian Year*'s influence was as a work of vulgarisation of neo-Wordsworthian sacramentalism in exactly the manner which Keble wanted to avoid. He therefore resented *The Christian Year* for its failure in reserve, for exhibiting in public sacred feelings which he ought to have kept to himself; and the vogue for the work taught him the ill-fortune of the writer of a successful book, 'the greatest trial of a life-time'[49] as he called it, violating the inner sanctuary of a faith best hidden from the world.

But vulgarised or not, the tender human Christ of Keble, speaking to the heart and affections, transformed the High Church tradition, which would henceforth deliberately seek to transmit the divine comfort and consolation through a more loving presentation of church and liturgy. Faith was no longer mere rational conviction or tribal duty to set forms, but the bond of worship and sacrament linking Christ and the soul. This devotional revolution underlay the High Church repudiation of much in its rationalist and Erastian and Protestant inheritance; for the new Anglo-Catholic teachings after 1830 were to speak to the heart and imagination, transforming the life of doctrine by the life of devotion, changing what Anglicans believed by changing the manner in which they said their prayers.[50]

It was Keble who gave the Greek word *ethos* its modern currency to mean the spirit or atmosphere of a time and place: and it was Keble who began the process in which the High Anglican *ethos* was transmuted into a Catholic devotional ethos which was made to seem safely Anglican, and which cornered the market in the safer romantic commodities for a new kind of Anglo-Catholicism. And so Keble's best loved verses describing Christ's consolation solaced sick beds and death beds, or were creamed off into hymnals, to find a still wider public than the Anglo-Catholic through congregational singing; and there its deepest influence becomes inaccessible to mere historians. To countless Victorians, **The Christian Year** was a holy book, the regular Sunday companion to Prayer Book and Bible, the poetic commentary on Collect, Epistle and Gospel, a support in struggle and sorrow, and a refuge in times of hope and fear. David Newsome records the sentimental ritual developed by 'Soapy Sam' Wilberforce, Bishop of Oxford and later Winchester, who as master of the lovely parsonage of Lavington would read **The Christian Year** to visitors in a garden summerhouse. In a rite of private sealing, 'He would then inscribe all their names on a piece of paper and place this in a bottle which was hidden there under a stone'.[51] The influence of **The Christian Year** was as Keble would have wished it, an unseen ministry to souls; and except from God, that unseen ministry was even better hidden than Sam Wilberforce's bottle.

Notes

1. David Newsome, *The Parting of Friends. A Study of the Wilberforces and Henry Manning* (London 1966) p.326.

2. A. Dwight Culler, *The Imperial Intellect. A Study of Newman's Educational Ideal* (New Haven, Connecticut 1955).

3. John Henry Newman, *Apologia Pro Vita Sua*, edited by Martin J. Svaglic (Oxford 1967) p.156.

4. Hence the subtitle of Georgina Battiscombe's *John Keble. A Study in Limitations* (London 1963).

5. 'though earnest, active Church workers were few and far between, the vast majority professed to be churchmen to the backbone. They were only too ready to fight for the Church, to shout for the Church, and above all to drink for the Church . . .' J. H. Overton and F. Relton, *The English Church from the Accession of George I to the end of the Eighteenth Century (1714-1800)* (London 1906) pp.279-80.

6. *The Journal of the Rev. John Wesley, A.M.,* edited by Nehemiah Curnock, 8 vols (London 1909-16) II, p.257.

7. On the political setting of romanticism, see Marilyn Butler, *Romantics, Rebels and Reactionaries: English Literature and its Background 1760-1830* (Oxford 1981).

8. 'Ode to Liberty', *The Complete Poetical Works of Percy Bysshe Shelley,* edited by Thomas Hutchinson (Oxford 1945) p.604.

9. Michael Hennell, 'Evangelicalism and Worldliness 1770-1870', in *Popular Belief and Practice Studies in Church History,* 8, edited by G. J. Cuming and Derek Baker (Cambridge 1972) pp.229-36.

10. The best survey of the religious turmoil of those years is W. R. Ward's *Religion and Society in England 1790-1850* (London and New York 1973).

11. There is no proper history of the Phalanx. But see A. Webster, *Joshua Watson. The Story of a Layman* (London 1954); and Francis Warre Cornish, *The English Church in the Nineteenth Century,* 2 parts (London 1910) part 1, pp.62-76.

12. C. B. Wilde, 'Hutchinsonianism, Natural Philosophy and Religious Controversy in 18th Century Britain', *History of Science* (1980) xviii, pp.1-24.

13. Renamed the *Ecclesiastical Sonnets* from the edition of 1837. *Ecclesiastical Sonnets. . . . A critical edition by Abbie Findlay Potts* (New Haven, Connecticut 1922). A. F. Potts provides a useful list of Wordsworth's theological and historical sources, and is a work overlooked in the essay by Kenneth J. Hughes, 'Troubled Tories: Theory of History and Didactic Function of Wordsworth's Ecclesiastical Sonnets', *Central Institute of English and Foreign Languages Bulletin* (1979) xv, pp.29-34. Hughes ignores these English influences in favour of a German influence on Wordsworth. He also overlooks the anti-Dissenting strand in the *Sonnets,* the parallel with Southey (see footnote 14), and the continuity with Wordsworth's earlier political opinions. He understates the 'Catholic' element in Wordsworth, which the Oxford Movement was to make more clear, in criticising the admirable

exposition of Mary Moorman's *William Wordsworth: A Biography* 2 vols (Oxford 1957, 1965) 2, pp.389-401.

14. 'Miscellaneous Sonnets', in *The Poetical Works of Wordsworth,* edited by Thomas Hutchinson (Oxford 1956) p.205.

15. See my article, 'Nationality and Liberty, Protestant and Catholic: Robert Southey's *Book of the Church*', in *Religion and Nationality Studies in Church History,* 18, edited by Stuart Mews (Oxford 1982) pp.409-32. See also footnote 19.

16. *The Collected Works of Samuel Taylor Coleridge,* general editor K. Colman, associate editor B. Winer, vol. 10, *On the Constitution of the Church and State,* edited by J. Colmer (Princeton and London 1976), from the improved second edition of 1830.

17. Newman's phrase: 'The Usurpations of Reason', in *Fifteen Sermons preached before the University of Oxford* (London 1871); reissued with introductory essays by D. M. MacKinnon and J. D. Holmes (London 1970).

18. E. J. Hobsbawn and George Rudé, *Captain Swing* (London 1969).

19. Geoffrey Carnall, *Robert Southey and his Age: The Development of a Conservative Mind* (Oxford 1980) p.218.

20. John Keble, 'On the Mysticism attributed to the Early Fathers of the Church', Tract 89, *Tracts for the Times* (Oxford 1833-41). See also *'The Alexandrian Fathers and "Economy"'*, in Alf Härdelin, *The Tractarian Understanding of the Eucharist* (Uppsala 1965) pp.69-71.

21. *'Butler and the Sacramental Principle',* ibid., pp.65-9.

22. C. Prince, *Leading Ideas of Keble's 'Christian Year'* (London 1900) p.17, cited Brian W. Martin, *John Keble: Priest, Professor and Poet* (London 1976) p.123.

23. G. B. Tennyson, *Victorian Devotional Poetry: The Tractarian Mode* (Cambridge, Massachusetts 1981) p.96.

24. For the equivalent doctrine in Victorian architecture, that 'Good men build good buildings', see Kenneth Clark, *The Gothic Revival: An Essay in the History of Taste* (London 1964) p.131.

25. *Keble's Lectures on Poetry 1832-1841,* translated by E. K. Francis, 2 vols (Oxford 1912). Originally published as *De poeticae vi Medica. Praelectiones Academicae Oxonii habitae, annis 1832-1841* 2 vols (Oxford 1844).

26. Cited Stephen Prickett, *Romanticism and Religion: The Tradition of Coleridge and Wordsworth in the Victorian Church* (Cambridge 1976) p.109.

27. ibid., p.110.

28. The standard analysis of the use of these devices in *The Christian Year* is B. M. Lott's unpublished Ph.D thesis, *The Poetry of John Keble, with special reference to* The Christian Year *and his contribution to* Lyra Apostolica (University of London 1960). See also footnote 38.

29. M. H. Abrams, *The Mirror and the Lamp: Romantic Theory and the Critical Tradition* (London 1953) pp.145, 147.

30. 'Disciplina Arcani' in *The Oxford Dictionary of the Christian Church,* edited by F. L. Cross (London 1958) pp.405-6.

31. The classic statement is Isaac Williams' 'On Reserve in Communicating Religious Knowledge', Tracts 80 and 87, *Tracts for the Times* (Oxford 1833-41). See also R. C. Selby, *The Principle of Reserve in the writings of John Henry Cardinal Newman* (London 1975).

32. James Anthony Froude, 'The Oxford Counter-Reformation', *Short Studies on Great Subjects,* 4 vols (London 1893) IV, p.286.

33. Newsome, p.56.

34. On Faber and enthusiasm, see my 'Catholic Faith of the Irish Slums. London 1840-70', in *The Victorian City: Images and Realities,* edited by H. J. Dyos and Michael Wolff, 2 vols (London 1973) 2, pp.837-53; also my article 'Vulgar Piety and the Brompton Oratory', in the *Durham University Journal* N.S.43 (1981) pp.15-21. Cf. Newman's 'Religious Worship, a Remedy for Excitements', in *Parochial Sermons* 6 vols (London 1835-42) III, pp.366-80; 'The Tractarian Attitude towards Enthusiasm', in Härdelin, pp.290-5.

35. John Keble, *The Christian Year,* edited by Walter Lock (London 1901) p.xxxv.

36. Prickett, p.117.

37. Tennyson, p.110, with supporting references.

38. These are fully set out in Lock's edition (see footnote 35). Lock was Warden of Keble College, and author of a life of Keble (eighth edition, London 1923).

There is also some exegetical material in the first American edition of *The Christian Year* (Philadelphia 1834). See also W. J. A. M. Beek, *John Keble's Literary and Religious Contribution to the Oxford Movement* (Nijmegen 1959).

39. Martin, pp.73-4.

40. Cited Battiscombe, p.105.

41. E. R. Norman, in the *Times Literary Supplement,* 25 February 1977. Cf. Sir Geoffrey Faber on Keble as 'the Ella Wheeler Wilcox of his time'. Cited C. J. Stranks, 'The Christian Year', in *Anglican Devotion* (London 1961) p.261.

42. For Mrs Battiscombe, *The Christian Year* is *the* barrier to understanding Keble. Battiscombe, p.104.

43. ibid., p.113.

44. Owen Chadwick, *The Victorian Church,* 2 Parts (London 1966-70) Part I, p.68, suggests 265,000 copies sold by April 1868. Brian Martin suggests half a million (p.110) by 1877.

45. Newman, p.29.

46. Battiscombe, p.111.

47. J. C. Shairp, *John Keble. An Essay on the Author of the 'Christian Year'* (Edinburgh 1866) p.89.

48. J. R. Watson, *The Victorian Hymn* (Durham 1981) p.5.

49. Battiscombe, p.114.

50. See Owen Chadwick, *The Mind of the Oxford Movement* (London 1963) pp.30-41.

51. Newsome, p. 123.

Gregory H. Goodwin (essay date 1987)

SOURCE: "Keble and Newman: Tractarian Aesthetics and the Romantic Tradition," in *Victorian Studies,* Vol. 30, No. 4, Summer, 1987, pp. 475-94.

[*In the following essay, Goodwin interprets Keble's aesthetic theory in relation to the Romantic Tradition, arguing that Keble's poetry is ignored by that tradition. Goodwin goes on to enumerate areas of divergence in the aesthetics of Keble and of his Tractarian contemporary John Henry Newman.*]

John Henry Newman was the theologian of the Tractarian Movement, but John Keble was its poet. Any inquiry into the thinking of the Tractarians on poetry and literature may end with Newman, but it should begin with Keble. Keble's greatest contribution to the Oxford movement and to English literature was **The Christian Year.** This book of devotional verse, first published in 1827, went through ninety-five editions during Keble's lifetime, and "at the end of the year following his death, the number had arisen to a hundred-and-nine."[1] The volume appealed not only to those sympathetic with the Anglo-Catholic movement, but also to a broader spectrum of Victorian readers who agreed with Newman's remark that "if poems can be found to enliven in dejection, and to comfort in anxiety, to cool the over-sanguine, and to refresh the weary, to awe the worldly, and to instill resignation into the impatient, and calmness into the fearful and agitated, they are these."[2]

The popularity of Keble's verse has not survived; instead, modern readers have been interested in the thinking of the leaders of the Oxford movement on the nature of poetry. Keble and Newman—pillars of Victorian religious orthodoxy—seem to have used poetry for the expression and even discovery of religious truth and perhaps anticipated the late-Romantic and modern tendency to view poetry as a "new spiritual mythus."[3] This approach to the Tractarians needs attention. M. H. Abrams found in Keble "a surprisingly modern view of poetry," elements of which were an equation of poetry and religion and a "radical proto-Freudian theory." More recently, connections between Romantic and Tractarian aesthetics have been studied by Stephen Prickett and G. B. Tennyson. Tennyson fully agrees with Prickett on the general equation of poetry and religion in Tractarian aesthetics, but he has less confidence than Prickett in the synthetic impulse to group Keble and Newman "with Romantic predecessors like Herder, and Victorian successors like Carlyle and Arnold."[4]

While connections between Tractarianism and the Romantic tradition exist, there is danger of over-emphasizing the extent to which Keble and Newman could feel comfortable with the tradition, or the tradition with them. As I will show, while both writers borrowed from the Romantics, Keble handled what he borrowed in so conservative a fashion that the tradition simply ignored him. Newman was admired by the tradition, not for a religio-aesthetic theory that he might have shared with it, but for quite another reason. As to a supposed unity between Keble and Newman on aesthetics, no such thing existed.

I

Before considering Keble's extensive comments on the relationship between poetry and religion, a short survey of his theory of poetry and its debt to Romanticism is in order. We encounter Keble's definition of poetry early in his review of J. G. Lockhart's *Memoirs of the Life of Sir Walter Scott* (1838): "Poetry is the indirect expression in words, most appropriately in metrical words, of some overpowering emotion, or ruling taste, or feeling, the direct indulgence whereof is somehow repressed" (*Occasional Papers,* p. 6). The striking thing about this definition is that it looks both backwards and forwards in the history of criticism. "Expression . . . of overpowering emotion" is suggestive of William Wordsworth's 1802 Preface to *Lyrical Ballads,* where he describes poetry as the "overflow of powerful feelings." Later in the essay, Keble says that "poetry is the overflow of sentiment and expression." Both statements are near paraphrases of Wordsworth, and in this Keble was no different from most other writers on poetry in the nineteenth century who found that, try as they might, their words always echoed Wordsworth's. The phrase "most appropriately in metrical words" takes us back even further than Wordsworth, to classical poetry and the *Poetics* of Aristotle, who valued meter as one of the elements of poetry but who insisted that "it is not metrical form that makes the poem."[5] But if the definition reminds us of much that had already been said about poetry, it also points ahead. Simplify Keble's definition and we have "expression . . . repressed," a troublesome and contradictory phrase that is central to Keble's thinking on poetry.

Keble explains that poetry involves a conflict between assertive and defensive tendencies within the individual mind. On the one hand, poetry proceeds from "wild and tumultuous feelings," feelings "whose very excess and violence would seem to make the utterance of them almost impossible." It "concerns certain longings of our nature after perfection." This is the strong assertive element of poetry, which, as Keble notes, makes the poet resemble the lunatic and the possessed. On the other hand, poetry is defensive; its ideas and feelings are presented indirectly and in veiled form. In the mind of the poet, "the direct enunciation of a fact or feeling is impeded, and the mind, full of that fact or feeling, finds out for itself indirect ways of conveying it to others." For Keble, poetry is always a conflict of expression and repression—a conflict that is originally in the mind of the poet but is also evident in the poem. In fact, Keble asserts, "the *difficulty,* and the way of overcoming it, . . . marks the poetical" (*Occasional Papers,* pp. 17, 14, 8, 11).

To resolve the antithetical impulses of expression and repression, the poet, Keble thought, typically turns to meter. While meter channels the poet's strongest feelings, it is "no less useful in throwing a kind of veil over those strong or deep emotions, which need relief, but cannot endure publicity." Meter is not the only channel and veil to which the poet may turn to resolve this difficulty. In poetic prose, something "will always be discoverable . . . which answers the purpose . . . assigned to numbers." In the prose romances of Walter Scott, the stories themselves serve this function. The poetry that emerges from this struggle between expression and repression will evince the writer's "ruling passion," but under a sort of "shading" which renders it "tolerable" and "interesting to us" (*Occasional Papers,* pp. 17, 18). Poetry represents at once difficulty and resolution—the struggle and its outcome.

Keble's contribution to aesthetics is not, as he would have us believe, a mere restatement of Aristotle's theories of imitation and catharsis. His several references to Aristotle—placed before, during, and after his own treatment of poetry—are instances of Keble's modesty. Aristotle is the veil or shading that Keble employs to disguise the radical nature of his aesthetics. Others, Wordsworth among them, had maintained that poetry was the reconciliation of opposite or discordant qualities, but Keble was among the first to insist that the discord be as much in evidence in the poem as the reconciliation, that the poem to be a poem must present us with difficulty.

Keble uses the concept of difficulty to distinguish primary from secondary poets. Dryden he judges to be "at the very head of the list of secondary poets." Dryden writes with the greatest balance and beauty, and, Keble admits, it would be a very "strange definition of poetry which should

exclude him." Yet, while there is the greatest control in Dryden, there was nothing in him in need of repression. He "seems to have written *con amore* on opposite sides of the same question: his thoughts breathe and his words burn as keenly for Cromwell as for Charles." He lacked "enthusiasm, the passionate devotion to some one class of objects or train of thought." Keble concludes that a "want of reality about his manner" hinders his admission into the higher class of poets (*Occasional Papers,* pp. 21-22).

If Dryden's poetry is secondary because it lacks difficulty, the work of the primary poets always contains it. Such poetry "does not always succeed in finding out, among existing moulds and forms, the most appropriate whereby to express itself." The primary poet may have to break with the form in order to find his or her own voice, and these breaks will be evident in the poetry. Keble's example is Virgil. By nature a "rural and melancholy poet" whose instinctive voice was heard in the *Georgics,* Virgil found "the professed character of a warlike Homeric tale" an incumbrance to his muse. As far as he kept to epic conventions in the *Aeneid,* "working evidently by rule and against the grain," he produced secondary poetry. Virgil wrote primary poetry when he departed from the convention and allowed for the "development of his true self"—the expression of his melancholia channeled and veiled by reference to "country sights and sounds" (*Occasional Papers,* pp. 23-24).

Though Keble's thinking on poetry owes much to Wordsworth, it anticipates developments in the Romantic tradition that had not yet taken place when Keble wrote in 1838. The idea that the best poetry is flawed would find its finest expression in John Ruskin and Robert Browning, Keble's younger contemporaries. Ruskin, in *The Stones of Venice* (1853), held that works that "are more perfect in their kind . . . are always inferior to those which are, in their nature, liable to more faults and shortcomings. . . . We are . . . not to set the meaner thing in its narrow accomplishment above shattered majesty."[6] Browning dramatized this theory in *Men and Women* (1855), particularly in the portrait of Andrea del Sarto who laments the vacuity of his own "faultless" painting and admires the flawed intensity of younger painters whose achievement stems from their confusion, from "their vexed beating stuffed and stopped-up brain."

But Keble's thinking goes beyond the Victorian age. It anticipates Freudian ideas of repression and the related theory of poetic precursors developed by Harold Bloom.[7] Keble's examples of repression are drawn from Walter Scott's attempts to express indirectly his boyhood affection for the life of the Scottish Border. Scott's tendency to romanticize childhood was due in part, Keble thought, to his lameness, which cut him off from the active life of the countryside. His failures in love led him to create ethereal enchantresses like the Lady of the Lake (*Occasional Papers,* pp. 50-51, 54-55). The idea of emotional displacement or psychic substitution vaguely expressed by Keble would not be developed fully until Freudian theories of psychoanalysis were taken up by modern poets and critics. Yet Bloom's theory of precursors is presaged in Keble's explanation of Virgil's breaking with Homeric conventions in the *Aeneid* in order to express his melancholia under the veil of the pastoral. Keble's primary poet expresses his own authentic voice despite the weight of the tradition.

While Keble owes much to the Romantic tradition and might have contributed much to it, his contributions went largely unnoticed until recently. Even those writers who because of shared interests were likely to know his work were not impressed by it. Gerard Manley Hopkins is a good instance. His letters contain many references to Newman but few to Keble, and in the most sustained of these he says that in Keble, Frederick Faber, and Cardinal Newman "the Lake School expires."[8] Hopkins was, I believe, wrong about Newman, and clearly wrong as well in thinking that the "Lake School" would entirely expire. He was, however, right in thinking that Keble had ended rather than begun or continued something. Not even those most excited about Newman's contributions to the Romantic movement—Walter Pater and the critics of the nineties—cared much about Keble or knew his writings. Pater at age fifteen visited Keble, but by 1860 had sold his copy of *The Christian Year* along with other "overtly Christian books." In a February 1886 letter to the editor of the *Pall Mall Gazette,* Oscar Wilde admitted that in *The Christian Year* there are "poetic qualities of a certain kind," but added that any large appreciation of Keble as a poet would require an "absolute catholicity of taste" that "is not without its dangers."[9] Matthew Arnold, Keble's godson, began to read John Taylor Coleridge's *Memoir* (1870) of Keble and put it down, impatient with Keble's "provinciality"; Arnold thought that Newman, alone among the Tractarians, might be exempted from this judgment.[10]

Despite his great popularity with the Victorian public, Keble was ignored by the Romantic tradition—not simply because he led a retired life and pursued antiquarian research in the Church Fathers and the Caroline divines, but rather because his mind was fundamentally conservative. He referred nearly everything he took from the Romantic tradition backwards to traditions in which he had more faith. This tendency in his thinking is evident in small matters—his lecturing at Oxford in Latin long after it was necessary to do so, and his reflexive references to Aristotle in the review of Lockhart's *Scott.*[11] But it can also be observed in larger matters—his life-long commitment to Tory politics, his devotion to his father, and his unshakable attachment to the communion of his birth. J. C. Shairp notes that Keble, even after his marriage, lived with his father, who did not die until age ninety. Keble "never outgrew the period of absolute filial reverence, never questioned a single opinion or prepossession which he had imbibed from his father."[12] To Newman's many arguments in support of conversion to Roman Catholicism, Keble replied that he felt safer in the position in which he had been placed.[13]

II

This same conservatism also governs Keble's thoughts about the connections between religion and poetry, the great question of the Romantic tradition. In his review of Lockhart's *Scott,* Keble draws parallels between poets and religious writers, but his treatment of the matter has a decidedly conservative tone and constitutes a strong argument against the Romantic tradition's tendency to see poetry and religion as equivalent. Early in the review, Keble hints at a hierarchical arrangement that should be kept in mind when religion and poetry are spoken of together. He hopes that his remarks on poetry will contribute to "higher interests" to which poetry, "to be worth cultivating at all, must eventually do suit and service" (*Occasional Papers,* p. 6). Having subordinated poetry to religion, Keble feels free to pursue parallels between the two.

The first of these parallels appears several paragraphs later, in Keble's account of the general use of the word "poetical." The term, Keble notes, is rightly used to describe not just a certain arrangement of words, but all modes of expression where "overpowering emotion" is presented indirectly or in veiled form. Such are the "expressions of uneducated men," which are "said to have more or less of unconscious 'poetry' in them." The "poetical" can also be found in arts kindred to poetry, so that we can speak of a "poetry of painting, of sculpture, of architecture, of music." There is even, Keble allows, a poetry of theology. The "orthodox and Catholic side in theological debate" argues "not by reason, but by feelings akin to poetical ones" (*Occasional Papers,* pp. 6-8). Although Keble's comments on a poetry of theology are sketchy, he suggests that the best religious thinking begins not with the "cold" argument of reasoning, but with the warm, intuitive vision of an imaginative mind, later confirmed by more "accurate examination" or rational inquiry.

This position is similar to Newman's in the *Grammar of Assent* (1870), where intuition is seen as an important aspect of any full act of reasoning. Newman's reference to "an unscientific reasoning" found in "rude as well as . . . gifted minds" and his comparison of this form of reasoning to poetry's "spontaneous outpouring of thought" may be marks of Keble's influence, though Newman might have drawn the same ideas from Wordsworth.[14] In his notes of 1860 on "Assent and Intuition," in part the basis for these remarks in the *Grammar*, Newman cites both Wordsworth and Keble as having supplied evidence for the role of intuition in reasoning.[15]

Neither Newman nor Keble insisted on a strict separation of poetical and theological ways of thinking, because neither thought the two were likely to be confused. Following his remarks on intuition in the *Grammar*, Newman goes on to explain that religious assent is a complex act involving intuition, logic, memory, and the conscience—the latter faculty providing the supernatural element always present in religious reasoning. Its parallel in formal theological reasoning is the voice of the Church: "theological reasoning professes to be sanctioned by a more than human power, and to be guaranteed by a more than human authority" (*Grammar*, p. 383). Newman and Keble would never have thought that poetry, however high it aimed, could partake of the same supernatural guarantee—unless of course it was religious poetry, a special case that Keble treats in his review of Lockhart's *Scott* and more fully in his tract "On the Mysticism Attributed to the Early Fathers of the Church."

In the review Keble's instances of religious poetry are the Psalmist and the Church Fathers, but he also considers the possibility of a Catholic poetry that might in some measure share the supernatural certainties available to inspired writers. In Keble's opinion, Scott's only deficiency was that he was not a Catholic poet. His positive attitude toward the supernatural, his careful preservation of "family relics," and his deep "natural piety" pointed towards a faith that Scott never possessed. "What if," Keble asks, "these generous feelings had been allowed to ripen into that of which undoubtedly they are the germ and rudiment?" The question tantalizes Keble, not only as it refers to the particular case of Walter Scott, but also as it applies to the larger issue of Catholic poetry. Such a poetry, Keble maintains, would not feel cramped by the discipline of the Church. Romantic poetry that depends on the "free exercise of sympathy and imagination" would in fact benefit from the restraining influence of the Church—the "severe calmness in her tone and sentiment." The Church would veil and channel the poet's tumultuous feelings, and this perfect balance would make the poet "sure he was telling substantial truth" (*Occasional Papers*, pp. 79-80).

The prospect of the Church giving her blessing to new voices that would interpret the divine in the spirit of the early Church is a question from which Keble turns aside in the final paragraph of the review, but takes up again in his later commentary on the Fathers and on poetry. But before examining this, we should consider just what kind of question Keble is asking. He is not asking whether poetry could by means of its own imaginative vision apprehend the divine—the question that intrigued Percy Bysshe Shelley in "The Skylark" and Wordsworth in "Tintern Abbey." This traditional Romantic question links Wordsworth with Pater, W. B. Yeats, and Wallace Stevens, and gives the Romantic tradition its special edge and urgency. Keble does not ask himself this question because he already knows the answer. The "free exercise of sympathy and imagination" would be unbalanced if it lacked the restraining influence of the Church. Such a poetry, no matter how intense and high-minded, would remain raw expression, without the blessing of veil or channel. The question that Keble does ask himself is whether the work of the Fathers could be extended, whether under the guidance of the Church a new set of signs and symbols could be found to augment those received from Scripture and elaborated on by the Fathers. The same question occupied Newman in the *Development of Christian Doctrine* (1845). It was the great question toward which all of the Tractarian movement tended and on which it finally split apart. Both Keble and Newman answered the question by reference to the Church Fathers, but their approaches were different. Keble looked for a developing symbolic tradition, an idea suggested to him by his study of poetry. Newman, as we shall see, refused to accept this literary approach.

Keble wrote Tract 89, **"On the Mysticism Attributed to the Early Fathers of the Church,"** shortly after the review of Lockhart's *Scott*. His object was to defend the Fathers against the Protestant tendency to discount them. Particularly, Keble defends their habit of allegorizing Scripture and the natural world. The numerologies of the *Epistle Attributed to St. Barnabas*, St. Cyprian's meditations on the wood of the Cross, St. Augustine's readings of the *Psalms*—all of this seemed to Protestants to be mere enthusiasm and fancy, if not rank superstition. Keble explains that the Fathers were doing no more than elaborating on the sacramental nature of the world, sanctioned by Christ's use of parables and by St. Paul in the letter to the Romans, who says "the invisible things of Him from the creation of the world are clearly seen, being understood by the things that are made."[16]

Poetry comes into Keble's defense of the Fathers since they employed poetry—a system of images and symbols—to embody their faith and to teach it. In fact, Keble ends the tract with a great tribute to poetry. Remarking on "the studied preference of *poetical* forms of thought and language, as the channel of supernatural knowledge to mankind," Keble continues,

> Poetry traced up as high as we can go, may almost seem to be God's gift from the beginning, vouchsafed to us for this very purpose; at any rate the very fact is unquestionable, that it was the ordained vehicle of revelation, until God himself was made manifest in the

flesh. And since the characteristic tendency of poetical minds is to make the world of sense, from the beginning to end, symbolical of the absent and unseen, any instance of divine favour shown to Poetry, any divine use of it in the training of God's people, would seem, as far as it goes, to warrant that tendency; to set God's seal upon it, and witness it as remarkable and true.

(*Tracts,* VI, 189-190).

These are nearly the last words of a 190-page tract (the *Tracts for the Times* were no three-page give-aways).[17]

The considerable eloquence of this passage is due to its careful blending of assertion and reservation. With the reservations extracted, we might conclude that Keble had in Tract 89 moved quite beyond the question he had asked himself in the essay on Lockhart's *Scott* and instead now asked himself the Romantic question of whether poetry could by its own unaided vision apprehend the divine. Without the qualifications, the passage seems to answer: "Poetical forms of thought and language" are "the channel of supernatural grace." But as soon as we restore the reservations the answer changes, as does the question the passage answers: poetry is a channel of supernatural grace when it enjoys "divine favour" and when "divine use" of it is made in "the training of God's people." The question answered when the whole of the passage is considered is the Tractarian question asked at the end of the essay on Lockhart's *Scott*—whether the work of the Fathers can be augmented under the guidance of the Church—and the answer seems to be a tentative "yes." The qualifications of the passage are as important as the assertions. To favor one to the exclusion of the other is to misinterpret Keble—to make him a Romantic instead of a Tractarian. The reservations are in this final passage of the tract not just for the sake of a modest, unassuming style; they reflect definite lines of argument pursued in the discussion that the passage is meant to end.

The poetry that Keble discusses in the tract is what he calls "mystical" poetry, a phrase whose meaning he tries to rescue from the reductionist versions employed by Protestant commentators on the Fathers. "Mystical" poetry was not, as the Protestants thought, something fanciful—something vague and indeterminate, whose source might be everywhere and nowhere—it originated with God and was expressed both in Scripture and in the created world. Scripture is, Keble tells us, poetical because it employs "symbolical language taken from natural objects." But this symbolic language is not at all ordinary. The Holy Ghost raises symbolic language in Scripture to "the rank of Divine Hieroglyphics." The hieroglyphs or types differ from mere illustrations or analogies in that the former are divine and certain, while the latter have about them "no particular certainty, much less any sacredness." The types are certain and unchanging because they come from God

and were "ordered . . . from the beginning, with reference to that meaning." The physical world was created to include a "fixed and regular" number of these hieroglyphs, and Scripture revealed them. Thereafter this system of symbols was the special study of God's people (*Tracts,* VI, 171, 170).

The "supposed mysticism" of the Fathers was no more than a meditation on this symbolic system. Although these symbols were limited in number and treasured for their scarcity, they were also, by means of divine dispensation, protean. From the sacred symbols of Scripture could be deduced a larger system of correspondences, which might seem to be equally holy. Meditation involved elaboration. From Scripture's use of "one such image taken from the works of nature . . . we might . . . begin to speculate on other possible associations" (*Tracts,* VI, 171). Keble was aware that he had reached the most difficult part of his argument. Here Keble's Protestant might put his finger down on what was most adventitious about the writing of the Fathers: they had pursued inference beyond what was reasonable, had departed from the simple words of Scripture, and had indulged in an unreal and fanciful mysticism. At the same time, Keble's thinking might seem to support the Romantic tradition that would make a religion out of poetry. Given that there is a set of sacred symbols to which we can add by inference, does it not follow that any poetic assessment of the world of correspondences would issue, if not in a new set of symbols, at least in an elaboration that might be consonant with the work of the Fathers and qualify as religious activity? To both his Protestant antagonist and the Romantic tradition, Keble answers no. He would have us conclude that Protestant attempts to minimize the deposit of faith and Romantic attempts to maximize it are both wrong in neglecting the manner in which the divine hieroglyphs of Scripture were pursued by the Fathers.

The Fathers were not afraid to follow inferences from the types of Scripture because they seemed "almost driven to such speculations." They were impelled by the force of logic and by Scripture itself, especially the "manner in which the Old Testament is commented on in the New" (*Tracts,* VI, 171). Their interpretations had the character of sacred criticism because they were both sanctioned and restricted by the system of correspondences and by the voice of the Church. Keble tells us that the Fathers were protected against the twin errors of the "minimum of the mystical sense" and the tendency "to extract as much as ever we can" by a reverential approach to the logic of the system in which they were working. They were conscious of degrees, as have been all those who have followed them (*Tracts,* VI, 176). There was, Keble thought, another and even more unimpeachable safeguard against the tendency to "unsettle foundations, making all doctrines subjective rather than objective." A faithful adherence to the limitations of the system of analogies was reinforced for the Fathers by the community of believers: "The Catholic Faith, the Mind of Christ testified by His universal Church, limits the range of symbolical interpretation both in Scripture and in nature" (**Tracts,** VI, 182).

From Keble's reference to a "universal Church" that acts as a judge of poetry that would hope to extend the work of the Fathers, we can assume that such a poetry might be possible, since the existence of a judge implies someone who might make a plea. But this is as close as we get in Tract 89 to an avowal of a developing symbolic tradition in the Church. This accounts, in part, for the general tentativeness of the concluding passage of the tract and for the reservations that accompany each of its assertions. In the final analysis, Keble could not get beyond the Fathers. There might be such a developing tradition; Keble was not sure. But he was sure that if there were such a developing tradition, it was not the contemporary tradition of private inquiry or what we have since learned to call the Romantic tradition. The making of religious symbols took place in the Church and only there, for only in the confines of the Church could one be sure of divine favor: "Let an uninspired poet or theologian be never so ingenious in his comparisons between earthly things and heavenly, we cannot build anything upon them; there is no particular certainty, much less any sacredness in them: but let the same words come out of the mouth of God, and we know the resemblance was intended from the beginning, and intended to be noticed and treasured up by us" (**Tracts,** VI, 170-171).

Tract 89 is the last time Keble gave direct attention to the question of a Christian symbolic tradition developing through time. He does, though, consider the subject indirectly in the last lectures given while he was professor of poetry at Oxford. In these his references are not to the Fathers, but to the classical tradition of poetry that preceded them. Standing for a moment with poets who had not been influenced by the Christian tradition, Keble can ask himself the Romantic question: whether the creative imagination of poetry can, without the aid of the teaching Church, apprehend the divine. He answers, though, as a Tractarian and as a student of the Fathers. Poets like Lucretius and Virgil are worthy of praise for having readied people's minds for revelation. Like the Hebrew prophets, there was in the work of these classical poets "a certain implicit suggestion of aims and aspirations unfulfilled."[18] This observation led Keble to a discussion of a "hidden kinship" between poetry and religion, the brief delineation of which he thought a fitting end to his whole course of lectures—a noble "crown upon our whole work." He ends by calling poetry the "high-born hand-maid" to religion, always its "minister" but never its equal (**Lectures,** II, 479-480, 484).

Here is the same clear subordination of poetry to religion with which Keble begins the essay on Lockhart's *Scott.* But the end of that earlier essay is also present in these last of the poetry lectures. The possibility of a Catholic poetry that had fascinated him in the earlier essay still interests him. His approach to it, though, is the same. The principle of balancing the creative mind of the poet with the restraining influence of the Church had allowed him in the essay on Lockhart's *Scott* to imagine a Catholic poetry that would refresh the Church with signs and symbols that reflected "substantial truth." As he closes his poetry lectures, he allows himself a last look at this, the greatest of his visions.

Although he is still tentative and hesitant, he imagines a reciprocity between poetry and religion, where "Poetry lends Religion her wealth of symbols and similes," and "Religion restores these again to Poetry, clothed with so splendid a radiance that they appear to be no longer merely symbols, but to partake (I might almost say) of the nature of sacraments" (**Lectures,** II, 481). As he conceives of them, poetry and religion are correspondent, though in no sense the same. Poetry gives its language to religion because without religion its language is merely aspiration, or, as Keble had said earlier about the poetry of Lucretius, a wandering "near the doors and thresholds with sadness and longing desire" (**Lectures,** II, 368). Once it has passed beyond the doorway and entered the "inmost shrine," poetry almost becomes religion, for its voice is no longer uncertain but spiritualized, so that it "partakes . . . almost . . . of the nature of sacraments." Such a voice Keble knew to be present in the Fathers; but nowhere else, except in his own imagination, was he so sure of its existence.

Although Keble's aesthetic theory owes much to the Romantic tradition, his special genius is manifested in the attempt to accommodate this new tradition with the older—and to his mind more reliable—one of Scripture and the Church Fathers. What emerges from this effort is not a spiritualized Romanticism, as some have imagined, but a deeper understanding of the Christian symbolic tradition most perfectly illustrated in the Church Fathers. The Romantic tradition as it developed in the Victorian and modern periods could make nothing of this; and so it simply bypassed Keble, preferring to draw its inspiration from less conservative thinkers than the Vicar of Hursley. One of these was John Henry, Cardinal Newman.

III

As I have indicated, there was no simple unanimity between Keble and Newman on the matter of aesthetics. In the first place, Newman takes much less delight in poetry than does Keble and holds a much lower opinion of it. One critic has said that Newman's references to poetry are always condescending (Starzyk, pp. 159-160), and when we look into *The Idea of a University* (1873) we find this to be the case. In the lecture on "Literature," Newman seems to have just put down Keble's essay on Lockhart's *Scott*. He expatiates on the connection between thought and speech and then turns to give some examples:

> But can they really think that Homer, or Pindar, or Shakespeare, or Dryden, or Walter Scott, was accustomed to aim at diction for its own sake, instead of being inspired by their subject, and pouring forth beautiful words because they had beautiful thoughts? . . . Rather it is the fire within the author's breast which overflows in the torrent of his burning, irresistible eloquence; it is the poetry of his inner soul, which relieves itself in the Ode or the Elegy; and his mental attitude and bearing, the beauty of his moral countenance, the force and keeness of his logic, are imagined in the tenderness, or energy, or richness of his language.[19]

The remarkable thing about this passage is not so much its close resemblance to Keble's essay on Lockhart's *Scott* as how little Newman seems to have entered into Keble's thinking. The examples are the same—Homer, Shakespeare, Dryden, and Walter Scott—and the definition is a neat paraphrase of Keble—poetry is "a fire within the author's breast which overflows . . . and relieves itself"—but what we have is merely the shell of Keble's thinking. The reference to Dryden signals this. Keble placed Dryden at the head of his list of secondary poets because his verse displayed none of that difficulty which Keble thought necessary to primary poetry. Newman either sees more in Dryden than Keble or did not entirely follow Keble's thinking on the place of difficulty in poetry. If we look more closely at Newman's statement, the second of these conclusions seems forced upon us. The poet, Newman tells us, pours forth "beautiful words" because he has "beautiful thoughts." Poetry is balanced, measured, harmonious. What is this but a pre-Romantic or even classical view of poetry onto which Keble's words have been grafted?

Not only does Newman not seem to follow Keble's modern views of poetry, he is much quicker than Keble to speak of poetry's limitations and especially to distinguish it from religion. In the ninth of the Dublin discourses, Newman is almost brutal in his denigration of literature to a place well below religion and theology in the hierarchy of subjects of which a liberal education is composed. Literature is not a science, Newman tells us. Rather, literature is an account of human history not as religion would have it be, but as humanity is without religion's illuminating aid. Newman allows that literature may be "tinctured by a religious spirit," and gives as his example Hebrew literature, as in the Old Testament. But this is not altogether literature, since it "certainly is simply theological, and has a character imprinted on it which is above nature." Ordinary literature is not at all innocent. Man is

"sure to sin, and his literature will be an expression of his sin, and this whether it be heathen or Christian" (*Idea*, p. 173).

While Keble was fascinated with the possibility of a Catholic poetry that would extend the symbolic tradition of the Fathers, Newman discounted all such theorizing. In "English Catholic Literature," a lecture included in the second part of *The Idea of a University*, Newman insists that in using the phrase "Catholic literature" one cannot mean more than the "works of Catholics" on all the subjects which literature ordinarily treats. The subject matter of religious literature would not be the world of men and things, but rather "Catholic doctrine, controversy, history, persons, or politics." This is the work not of the laity, but mainly of "ecclesiastics" in "a Seminary or a Theological School" (*Idea*, p. 222). Newman draws a stricter line than Keble between literature and religion because he is sure that they have different subject matters. As we have noted earlier in the case of the *Grammar of Assent*, theology, and by extension religion, have to do with what is "more than human." Literature addresses the world of the natural man, and, according to Newman, it will always find a mixture of good and bad, a world deeply flawed. Literature "will have the beauty and the fierceness, the sweetness and rankness of the natural man" (*Idea*, p. 237).

Such judgments are to be found throughout Newman's writings. Newman's general assessment of the natural world and its literature differs both from Keble's and from the Romantic tradition inherited from Wordsworth. When Keble speaks of a "system of correspondences," he is using the language of Bishop Butler, who saw everywhere in the natural world hints of a divine author. Butler's argument for the existence of God from design had a profound influence on eighteenth- and early nineteenth-century religious thinking. No doubt Wordsworth owes something at least indirectly to Butler when in "Tintern Abbey" he catches glimpses of "something far more deeply interfused." In the *Apologia* (1864), Newman tells us that he received the doctrine of the sacramental world from Butler, but more especially as it was recast by Keble in *The Christian Year,* and that thereafter it was a principle that was at the bottom of "a great portion" of his teaching.[20] Although Newman never entirely departed from this doctrine, he never relied on it as Keble did. He was suspicious of the argument from design when used as an exclusive proof for God's existence, mainly because he did not share Keble's or Butler's ready faith in a natural order that spoke of its divine authorship.

Almost all Newman's major works speak to this point. In the second of the *University Sermons* (1843), Newman explicitly accepts Butler's argument for correspondence between the natural and revealed systems, while at the same time he employs language that qualifies that acceptance. Revealed religion, Newman says, is "rooted" in nature. But how deeply? Nature's accents are "faint or broken," and only in Christ are they interpreted in a fashion that would make them clearly consonant with revelation. The doctrine of the Incarnation has "no parallel in this world," and without it the best of paganism had to be content with "laws of our being, which wander idle and forlorn over the surface of the moral world, and often appear to diverge from each other." Pre-Christian thinkers could, as a rule, make nothing of these "multiplied and inconsistent images"; hence, they shattered "the moral scheme of the world into partial and discordant systems, in which appetite and expedience received the sanction due only to virtue."[21] When, much later, Newman comes to this subject in the *Apologia,* he explains that while he is "far from denying" the argument from design and the doctrine of a sacramental world on which that argument rests, he could nevertheless say for himself that these "do not warm or enlighten me; they do not take away the winter of my desolation." The sight of this world is nothing else than "lamentations, and mourning, and woe" (*Apologia,* p. 217).

Unlike Keble or Butler or Wordsworth, Newman fully entered into the desolation of skepticism, and thus always said that there was no medium between Christianity and atheism. The natural world, when fully considered, did not provide enough to support a visionary apprehension of the divine. In fact, its unaided testimony went all the other way. In "Dejection: An Ode," Samuel Taylor Coleridge gives voice to a skepticism that destroys the poet's image-making capacity. It was a profound skepticism, but for Coleridge it was intermittent—a passing cloud over an otherwise more hopeful view of the world. For Newman it was an "encircling gloom" and a constant element in his thinking. This, more than anything else, marks his divergence from the Romantic tradition.

Newman's attitude towards the natural world and natural religion made it impossible for him to share the Romantic tradition's interests in connections between literature and religion, and it made him suspicious of Keble's inquiries into a developing Christian symbolic tradition. Newman's most sustained commentary on Keble's poetry comes in his 1846 review of Keble's *Lyra Innocentium* (*Essays,* II, 435-461). Among the first things that Newman wrote after becoming a Catholic, the essay is in part a defense of the step he had taken. His theme is that the Catholic sentiment present in Keble's poems is foreign to the Anglican Church and really only natural to Roman Catholics. Behind this general approach, though, lies Newman's conviction that Keble had made too much of poetry and that Keble's readers would be inclined to compound this error.

Newman's prose displays a double intent. He begins with generous praise for *The Christian Year* in the passage

quoted at the beginning of this paper. His praise seems so generous that Pusey, apparently unaware of the general direction of Newman's essay, placed the passage at the beginning of Keble's *Occasional Papers and Reviews* (p. vii). Out of its context the passage seems simply to bless Keble's verse, but Newman's intent was more complicated and ambivalent than Pusey and many subsequent readers have imagined.[22] Following close upon this passage is Newman's admission that the author of *The Christian Year* did much by his "happy magic" to make the Anglican Church "seem what Catholicism was and is." Keble found the Anglican system "all but destitute of [the] divine element," and "his poems became a sort of comment on its formularies and ordinances, and almost elevated them into the dignity of a religious system." Keble's poetry brought enthusiasm where before there had only been a dreary indifference, and it had given hope to "the gentle and forlorn" (*Essays,* II, 443-445). But after giving attention to all that is positive in Newman's statements, we are left with an overwhelming sense of how guarded he is in his praise. Keble had applied a "happy magic" to Anglicanism, a transforming power akin to Prospero's "rough magic," gentler but no more substantial than that "airy charm" that Prospero abjures at the end of *The Tempest.* His poems made the Anglican system "seem" Catholic and "almost elevated" it, giving a "something" to cling to. In Newman's estimation Keble's poetry did all that poetry could do to serve the cause of religion, but in the last analysis it could not, because of its nature, produce religion. Keble had called poets "high-born" handmaidens. Newman is less expansive. Poets live under the Church's "shadow" and are taken "into her service"; a few rise to the heights of Aquinas, while most go about rather ordinary business—they "embellish shrines, or . . . determine ceremonies, or . . . marshall processions" (*Essays,* II, 443).

Poetry, Newman says, is "the refuge of those who have not the Catholic Church to turn to" (*Essays,* II, 442). This refuge is comforting, but potentially deadly. In concluding the essay on Keble, Newman notes that "Anglo-Catholic writers may reduce the inquiring mind;—they may throw it, by a reaction, into rationalism." Newman hints at his meaning: if the refuge that poetry supplies is treated as a substitute for the faith that it merely serves, if it is treated as an end in itself and not some secondary and middle term, then it becomes false and the mind will be thrown back on itself. With reference to Keble and to all that poetry can do to serve religion, Newman observes: "When the opening heart and eager intellect find themselves led on by their teachers, as if by the hand, to the See of St. Peter, and then all of a sudden, without good reason assigned, are stopped in their course, bid stand still in some half position, on the middle of a steep, or in the depth of a forest, the natural reflection which such a command excites is, 'This is a mockery; I have come here for nothing; If I do not go on, I must go back'" (*Essays,* II, 451). The imagery of steep and forest is Dantesque. Is not Newman suggesting that Keble's situation and that of those who would make poetry their refuge is similar to what Dante's would have been had he stopped along the way, either at the entrance to Hell or somewhere on Mt. Purgatory, and refused to enter Paradise?

The connection between skepticism and a literature that is made to supplant religion is perhaps only hinted at in the 1846 essay partly in deference to Keble and partly because Newman had already given so much attention to it in his writings. The most recent instance had been his 1841 essays collected and published under the title *The Tamworth Reading Room.* Newman thought so much of the essays that he reprinted parts of them verbatim in the *Grammar of Assent.* There he tells us that the essays had been written in response to "a dangerous doctrine maintained . . . by Lord Brougham and Sir Robert Peel . . . to the effect that the claims of religion could be secured . . . by acquaintance with literature and physical science, and through the instrumentality of Mechanics Institutes and Reading Rooms, to the serious disparagement . . . of direct Christian instruction" (*Grammar,* p. 91).

In the 1841 essays Newman noted that Peel and Brougham intended to exclude religion from the reading rooms, since in their view it engendered "party feeling." To Newman this was tantamount to saying that for them religion was dead and fit only to be abandoned. In its place they would put knowledge. But knowledge, Newman argued, whether discovered and expressed by literature or by science, is no substitute for religion. Science proceeds by deductions and literature by conclusions and inferences, but neither has the power to display directly the concrete realities of supernatural religion. All human forms of knowledge are founded upon doubt, a fact that Newman believed was observable in the very nature of language, where every affirmation suggests its own negation: "To say that a thing *must* be, is to admit that it *may not* be." Religious knowledge does not admit of doubt because its foundations are not merely in language, but in the testimony of "facts and events, by history." It is not "a deduction from what we know"; it has "ever been synonymous with Revelation."[23] To attempt to build a religion upon inference—on science, literature, or art—is to invite skepticism: "We shall ever be laying our foundations; we shall turn theology into evidences, and divines into textuaries. We shall never get at our first principles. Resolve to believe nothing, and you must prove your proofs and analyze your elements, sinking further and further, and finding 'in the lower depth a lower deep,' till you come to the broad bosom of scepticism" (*Discussions,* p. 295).

Newman's distrust of natural religion, or a religion of inferences, had intensified during the Tractarian years. He had come to think of Anglicanism as little more than a "paper religion," at best a highly selective but inchoate grouping of doctrine and opinion gathered from the Church Fathers and from the Reformation. Keble's Christian symbolic tradition, had he been able to define it fully, would have been part and parcel of a religion of inferences. It would have been based in the Fathers, and hence on a more trustworthy foundation than the scientific religion of Brougham and Peel, but nevertheless it would have remained a religion of the intellect, prone to doubt. As Newman reread the Fathers in the late 1830s and early 1840s—reading them for the first time with his own eyes, rather than as the Caroline divines dictated that they should be read—he discovered that the Fathers appealed to more than a system of symbols or body of doctrine. Their appeal was to something broader than their own interpretations of Scripture and history. Such interpretations were ever, they thought, to be tested against the faith of revelation, the faith held by a living, infallible Church. Newman speaks most fully of this in the *Essay on the Development of Christian Doctrine* (1845), the work toward which all of his Tractarian writings point. There Newman explains that the Fathers supply us with "tokens of the multiplicity of openings which the mind of the Church was making into the treasure-house of Truth; real openings, but incomplete or irregular."[24] They do not provide, as Keble had argued, an unimpeachable meditation on a "fixed and regular" set of divine hieroglyphs. The Fathers, though closer to the truth than we, were still prone to error. In the startling language of the introduction to the essay, "St. Ignatius may be considered a Patripassian, St. Justin Arianizes, and St. Hippolytus is a Photinian" (*Development,* p. 80). The Fathers are not so much exponents of orthodox opinions as they are of an orthodox faith present in a community of believers. Against a religion of the intellect, Newman recommends a religion of history and of fact, defined by a "living and present guide," who is the "arbiter of all true doctrine and holy practice to her children" (*Development,* p. 175).

Keble, as I have said, referred the Romantic tradition to the Fathers and arrived at a fuller view of Patristics. His conservative response to the tradition went unnoticed. Newman drew from the Fathers and from a number of traditions but was mastered by none of them, save that universal tradition to which he believed all other traditions referred. As he could take from the Caroline divines a deep interest in the Fathers and yet part company with them over the way in which the Fathers were to be regarded as authorities, as he could credit Gibbon with having been the only English ecclesiastical writer worthy of the name and yet reverse Gibbon's interpretations, so too could Newman borrow Keble's enthusiasm for poetry and the Romantic tradition's emphasis on intuition and make them part of a system of his own that was larger than they were and, when contrasted with them, serve as a commentary on their deficiencies.

Newman's originality did not go unnoticed by the Romantic tradition. Despite his having judged the tradition and found it wanting, exponents of the tradition in the latter half of the nineteenth century were drawn to Newman's genius. Walter Pater, whom Harold Bloom has described as "a kind of hinge upon which turns the single gate, one side of which is Romantic and the other modern poetry,"[25] found in Newman's writings, particularly the *Grammar of Assent,* the perfect expression of a religion of aesthetics—a religion based on intuition and personal experience that tended toward the Catholic faith. As David DeLaura has explained, Pater exploited one element of Newman's thinking to the exclusion of the rest; he accepted Newman's emphasis on "inwardness" and spiritual individualism and discarded most of what Newman had said about a religion based on revelation (DeLaura, p. 314).

Pater and the critics of the nineties—particularly Oscar Wilde and Lionel Johnson—were intrigued with Newman for many reasons.[26] Who else had looked so steadily at skepticism and yet had triumphed over it by an act of faith? More importantly, who else had been able to rise above the Romantic tradition that had held the century in thrall? Newman, they knew, had put his finger on the tradition's greatest difficulty—its constant war with precursors, who, Newman had said, exercised an oppressive influence over the writing of the day, making the writing self-conscious and leaving it with the impression that in Shakespeare, Milton, and Pope "an existing want" had been supplied and there was "no need for further workmen" (*Idea,* p. 244). They realized that in his own field of theological inquiry, Newman had escaped the Romantic predicament. His mind, "unresting and powerful," had imposed its "own pattern" on all its material.[27] His was the very type of mind that Romantic poets and prose writers had always celebrated. He had written with the freshness of earlier times and had fearlessly bridged gaps between logic and intuition, religion and science, doubt and certainty—the great antitheses of nineteenth-century thought.

Despite his considerable modesty, Newman would not have disowned this influence. He would, though, have deeply regretted the tendency, observable first in Pater and then later in some modern criticism, to emphasize one portion of his teaching to the exclusion of others, to take him as a model for a synthetic approach to religion and human experience and yet to ignore the particular synthesis before which he humbled himself.

Notes

1. E. B. Pusey, "Preface," in John Keble, *Occasional Papers and Reviews,* ed. E. B. Pusey (Oxford: James Parker, 1877), p. viii.

2. John Henry Newman, "John Keble" (1846), in *Essays Critical and Historical,* 2 vols. (New York: Longmans, Green, 1897), II, 441.

3. The phrase comes from Lawrence J. Starzyk, *The Imprisoned Splendor: A Study of Victorian Critical Theory* (Port Washington, NY: Kennikat Press, 1977), p. 179. The tendency of the late Romantic tradition to make a religion out of poetry was observed much earlier in this century by T. S. Eliot in his essay "Arnold and Pater." Eliot notes that in the latter part of the nineteenth century "religious art" and in due course "aesthetic religion" developed (*Selected Essays* [New York: Harcourt Brace, 1964], p. 390).

4. M. H. Abrams, *The Mirror and the Lamp: Romantic Poetry and the Critical Tradition* (New York: Norton, 1958), pp. 147-148; G. B. Tennyson, *Victorian Devotional Poetry: The Tractarian Mode* (Cambridge: Harvard University Press, 1981), pp. 60-61, 69; Stephen Prickett, *Romanticism and Religion: The Tradition of Coleridge and Wordsworth in the Victorian Church* (Cambridge: Cambridge University Press, 1976).

5. S. H. Butcher, *Aristotle's Theory of Poetry and Fine Art* (1911; rpt. ed. New York: Dover, 1951), p. 141.

6. John Ruskin, *The Stones of Venice,* vol. II, chap. 6, quoted by Donald Smalley, ed. *Poems of Robert Browning* (Boston: Houghton Mifflin, 1956), p. 510 n. 233.

7. Harold Bloom, *The Anxiety of Influence: A Theory of Poetry* (New York: Oxford University Press, 1973).

8. Gerard Manley Hopkins, *Selected Prose,* ed. Gerald Roberts (Oxford: Oxford University Press, 1980), p. 107.

9. Thomas Wright, *The Life of Walter Pater* (London: Everett, 1907), p. 89; *Selected Letters of Oscar Wilde,* ed. Rupert Hart-Davis (Oxford: Oxford University Press, 1979), p. 66.

10. David J. DeLaura, *Hebrew and Hellene in Victorian England: Newman, Arnold, and Pater* (Austin: University of Texas Press, 1969), pp. 58-59.

11. Matthew Arnold was the first to dispense with Latin for the Oxford poetry lectures. Keble found writing in Latin difficult, but preferred to abide by the tradition; see J. T. Coleridge, *A Memoir of the Rev. John Keble* (1870; rpt. ed. Farnborough, England: Gregg International, 1969), pp. 207-213.

12. J. C. Shairp, *Studies in Poetry and Philosophy* (Boston: Houghton Mifflin, 1893), p. 220. Although this sounds exaggerated, I think it correct in its general assessment of Keble.

13. *Correspondence of John Henry Newman with John Keble and Others, 1839-1845,* ed. at the Birmingham Oratory (London: Longmans, Green, 1917), p. 319.

14. John Henry Newman, *An Essay in Aid of a Grammar of Assent* (1870; rpt. London: Longmans, 1892), p. 331.

15. *The Theological Papers of John Henry Newman on Faith and Certainty,* ed. Hugo M. de Achaval and J. Derek Holmes (Oxford: Clarendon Press, 1976), pp. 74-75.

16. Romans 1:20, quoted in John Keble, *On the Mysticism Attributed to the Early Fathers of the Church,* Tract 89 of *Tracts for the Times,* 6 vols. (Oxford: James Parker, 1868), VI, 189.

17. This well-known passage is reprinted in the standard modern source on the Tractarian movement, Owen Chadwick, *The Mind of the Oxford Movement* (Stanford: Stanford University Press, 1967), p. 68.

18. *Keble's Lectures on Poetry: 1832-1841,* trans. Edward Kershaw Francis, 2 vols. (Oxford: Clarendon Press, 1912), II, 474.

19. John Henry Newman, *The Idea of a University,* ed. Martin J. Svaglic (Notre Dame, IN: University of Notre Dame Press, 1982), p. 210.

20. John Henry Newman, *Apologia Pro Vita Sua,* ed. Martin J. Svaglic (Oxford: Clarendon Press, 1967), pp. 23, 29.

21. *Newman's University Sermons: Fifteen Sermons Preached Before the University of Oxford 1826-43,* ed. D. M. MacKinnon and J. D. Holmes (London: Society for the Promulgation of Christian Knowledge, 1970), pp. 31, 27, 24.

22. For instance, see G. B. Tennyson's use of the passage in *Victorian Devotional Poetry,* pp. 112-113.

23. John Henry Newman, "The Tamworth Reading Room," *Discussions and Arguments on Various Subjects* (London: Basil Montague, 1872), pp. 285-286, 293, 296.

24. John Henry Newman, *An Essay on the Development of Christian Doctrine: The Edition of 1845,* ed. J. M. Cameron (Harmondsworth: Penguin, 1974), p. 360.

25. Harold Bloom, *The Ringers in the Tower: Studies in Romantic Tradition* (Chicago: University of Chicago Press, 1971), pp. 186-187.

26. Lionel Johnson very nearly worshiped Newman and claimed to know his work from the most "splendid and familiar passages down to their slightest and most occasional note." Newman, Johnson says, "takes up the scattered and wayward influences of his day, and sifts them through his conscience" (*Post Liminium: Essays and Critical Papers of Lionel Johnson* [London: Elkin Mathews, 1911], pp. 303, 307). Oscar Wilde respected Newman because he was both a good Christian and a good philosopher. During his imprisonment, Wilde had sent to him—along with St. Augustine's *Confessions,* Pater's *Renaissance,* and Renan's *Vie de Jesus*—Newman's *Grammar of Assent, Apologia, Two Essays on Miracles,* and *The Idea of a University* (*Letters of Oscar Wilde,* ed. Rupert Hart-Davis [London: Hart-Davis, 1962], pp. 20, 399 n. 4, 405 n. 1). To these judgments of Newman might be added that of John Holloway, who accounts for the admiration of Newman among non-Catholics by saying that Newman "proves to have had perhaps the most comprehensive, detailed and integrated view of things—in the sage's sense—of any English writer of the century" (*The Victorian Sage: Studies in Argument* [New York: Norton, 1965], p. 158).

27. Owen Chadwick, *From Bossuet to Newman: The Idea of Doctrinal Development* (Cambridge: Cambridge University Press, 1957), p. 111.

John R. Griffin (essay date 1987)

SOURCE: "*The Christian Year,*" in *John Keble, Saint of Anglicanism,* Mercer University Press, 1987, pp. 57-76.

[*In the following essay, Griffin provides a thematic analysis of* The Christian Year, *explaining the purpose behind Keble's collection of religious poetry.*]

The Christian Year was first published anonymously in 1827. A complete edition was published the following year when Keble added a series of poems in honor of certain state "feast days." Most of his friends knew that Keble was the author of the book. Newman remarked briefly, "Keble's hymns are just out . . . they seem quite excellent."[1] As I have earlier remarked, sales of the volume came to be one of the great success stories of the nineteenth century. **The Christian Year** was certainly important to the reader of poetry in the Victorian age.[2] Yet no one wrote about Keble's poetry during his lifetime. It was only with the edition of 1866 (the year of his death) and later that reviewers began to discuss the significance of Keble's volume.

At the time of writing and publishing his first volume, Keble was not yet what might be called an Anglo-Catholic, and it is therefore questionable whether the work can be regarded as a "Tractarian" text. Throughout the poetry we find references to "principles" of religion that the Oxford Movement later opposed. Yet there is a link between the poetry and the ideology of 1833, for one of the ideas in **The Christian Year** is that the clergy of the Church of England should reform itself. Indeed, the reform motif of the poetry is one of its most interesting elements.

If Keble's poetry does not readily accommodate itself to the later ideals of **"National Apostasy"** or the *Tracts for the Times,* it is even more of a mistake to suggest that he was working under the influence of George Herbert or William Wordsworth. Keble denied that Herbert had been an influence on his poetry, and in various places apologized for the "quaint" imagery of his supposed mentor. The influence of Wordsworth is even more suspect if we remember Keble's earlier review of Wordsworth's first two volumes of poetry; but even at a much later date, when he was writing his **"Dedication"** of the lectures to Wordsworth, he expressed a concern to J. T. Coleridge that he did not wish to seem to give approval to the "pantheistic air" in Wordsworth.[3] Keble's approach to Nature, I will argue, is wholly different from that of his supposed mentor, and the phrase used to describe Keble's approach—"sacramental imagination"—is very different in the uses it makes of the created world.[4]

THE PURPOSE OF *THE CHRISTIAN YEAR*

In his **"Advertisement"** (actually a brief preface) to the volume, Keble declared that his purpose in writing and publishing *The Christian Year* was to promote a "sober standard of feeling in matters of practical religion" at a time when "excitement of every kind is sought after with a morbid eagerness." He concluded his brief preface by noting that his intention was to recommend the "soothing" tendency of the Anglican Prayer Book.

> The object of the present publication will be attained if any person finds assistance from it in bringing his own thoughts and feelings into more entire unison with those recommended and exemplified in the Prayer Book. . . . Something has been added at the end concerning the several Occasional Services: which constitute, from their personal and domestic nature, the most perfect instance of the *soothing* tendency in the Prayer Book, which it is the chief purpose of these pages to exhibit.

In these brief comments, we can understand why Keble's poetry has been so generally ignored by twentieth-century readers. The idea of poetry being used to soothe or quiet the emotions is completely alien to a modern reader's expectations of what poetry, including religious poetry, should do for the reader. Yet it was this quality that Keble admired most of all in the poetry of Wordsworth, and one of the feelings that Keble sought to promote was a proper attitude towards poverty.

> I have [he told Wordsworth] many thoughts in my mind of the desirableness of engaging all ranks of people more immediately in the service of the Church . . . nothing would lead more securely to such a purpose than enducing them [the poor] to feel rightly about poverty.[5]

Such was Wordsworth's great achievement. As Keble wrote in the dedication to his *Lectures on Poetry,* Words-worth was a poet who had described the "manners and religion of the poor . . . in an celestial light." While it is easy to dismiss such a tribute, Keble was in earnest in his praise of the quieting power of Wordsworth's poetry. The great lesson of the Prayer Book was "cheerful obedience"; Wordsworth, almost alone of the Romantic poets, had nurtured just that spirit in his descriptions of the country poor.

Yet *The Christian Year* is more than a complacent description of English rural society and religion. As we will see, the most important link between Keble's poetry and the Oxford Movement of 1833 is its quiet call for a reformation in the lives of the English rural clergy and in the poetry of his own age.

The major theme in *The Christian Year* is the love of God for the whole of the created world. That love created in man an obligation to reciprocate, either by a more zealous performance of his duties or a cheerful acceptance of his place in life. Nature is the best example of God's love for mankind, and in Keble's frequent poems about Nature we find a very different approach to his subject from that which is commonly called "Romantic." In Keble's poetry, the beauties and varieties of Nature provide the most striking proof for the existence of God. Keble's argument, so far as it may be called such, derives from Butler's *Analogy of Religion* and personal experience. Nature presented a link between God and Man, and Keble's poetic meditations of Nature always lead the reader upwards to a contemplation of God. The poet's method, however, is seldom direct, for it is the analogy between religion and Nature that Keble finds so instructive.

There are exceptions to this method, and the reader should not be misled by Keble's comments on the "soothing" tendency of either the Prayer Book or his own poetry. Several of the poems are concerned with the low spiritual state of the Anglican clergy and "the ruler of the Christian land"—the king or his representatives. In the poems about the clergy Keble sometimes sounds like a contributor to some of the "liberal" or radical journals of his day, for he witnessed the apparent laziness of his clerical brethren on a firsthand basis. In his frequent poems on poetry, Keble was severe with the egotism and sensuality of his fellow poets.

Yet the reforming motif in Keble's poetry is urged so gently that it does not take away from Keble's ideal as expressed in the Advertisement. Each of the poems sustains the major theme in *The Christian Year.* Keble, as a rule, followed the scriptural text of the service for the day, and the poems might be read as a meditation on the text. Occasionally, the poet did throw off some of his natural restraint, and it was no accident that one of his closest friends warned him of sounding very like a "methodist" in his response to scripture or Nature.⁶ Yet Keble was able to balance his own natural piety and simplicity by constantly appealing to the beauties of creation. As a recent scholar has noted, Nature in the eyes of Keble was the instrument by which we gained our knowledge of God; it was "the handmaiden to divine truth."⁷ It should be added that such a view was largely Keble's own and not that of Oxford or the Oxford Movement. Both of Keble's closest friends, Newman and Froude, were unmoved by Keble's proofs for the existence of a benevolent God.

THE POETRY

The Christian Year opens with a set of companion poems, **"Morning"** and **"Evening,"** an idea taken perhaps from the method of Bishop Ken's *Hymns for All the Festivals of the Year,* published after Ken's death in 1721. (Ken was a nonjuring bishop whom Keble referred to frequently in his letters and in several places throughout his sermons.) Both of Keble's poems set the tone for the volume as a whole in that each was to be read as a meditative prayer or hymn. Two lines from **"Morning"** serve to illustrate what Keble's critics and admirers believe is most attractive or sentimental in the poetry.

> And help us, this and every day,
> To live more nearly as we pray.

Simple, direct, and possibly banal—the lines and the sentiments conveyed in them are almost too much for a modern reader or critic. Of course, there is nothing startling or original in the idea, but it is the very opposite of "simplistic" or insipid. To follow the mandates of the Lord's Prayer is surely the most challenging task that a Christian can undertake.

The diction of **"Morning"** has its closest affinities with Neo-Classicism, especially, one might suggest, with the odes of Collins and shorter poetry of Samuel Johnson. And in its emphasis on the basics of the Christian life, the ideology is much closer to the eighteenth century. Keble directly advised against a life of excessive zeal. The Christian life was not to be found in "the cloistered cell."

> We need not bid, for cloistered cell
> Our neighbor and our work farewell,
> Nor strive to wind ourselves too high
> For sinful man beneath the sky . . .

Rather, Keble emphasized, the saintly life was to be found in "each returning day," in "the trivial round, the common task," and "in our daily course." The Christian spirit could adorn the most humble aspects of life.

> Old Friends, old scenes, will lovelier be,
> As more of Heaven in each we see:

> Some softening glean of love and prayer
> Shall dawn on every cross and care.

"Evening" uses the same verse form and stanzaic pattern, and its message is closely parallel to the above: the love of God can make the most prosaic activity into a religious exercise. But Keble introduced an idea into **"Evening"** that was one of the major themes in *The Christian Year*— the reform of the lower clergy. Such a theme in itself explicitly challenges the idea that Keble was an establishment man and indifferent to the highly visible problems in the Church of England. Towards the end of the poem, we read,

> Oh, by Thine own sad burthen borne
> So meekly up the hill of scorn,
> Teach Thou Thy Priests their daily cross
> To bear as Thine, nor count it loss!

Keble, in the above and in other poems, was encouraging the clergy to look more critically at itself and its performance of priestly duties. The concluding line, ". . . nor count it loss," served as a comment on the social climbing clergy who neglected humbler duties in pursuit of a better living or an episcopal see.

As in the opening poem, Keble argued that the real basis for the Christian life, and the standard by which each of us will be judged, is to be found in the performance of our daily duties.

There is another idea in **"Evening"** that is important because it marks the religious difference between the poems and the Oxford Movement (1833-1845). The idea was that the king, or his agents (Prime Minister and Parliament), was head of the Church of England.

> The Rulers of this Christian land,
> 'Twixt Thee and us ordained to stand,—
> Guide Thou their course, O Lord, aright
> Let all do all as in thy sight.

My reading of these lines, placed as they are between the comments on the Anglican clergy, suggests that in 1827 Keble upheld the traditional notion that the king (or his representatives) was the "head" of the English church and people an idea confirmed by Keble's later description of the English monarch as "nursing father" of the church (a metaphor taken from the Old Testament, and the topic of Keble's sermon of 5 November 1835). Based on these lines and the description of the king as a "nursing father" to the church, I would suggest that Keble was an upholder of the Erastianism that he and his colleagues in the Oxford Movement were to later challenge.

In the first poem of the text proper, **"The First Sunday after Advent,"** Keble returned to his comments on the lower clergy in the church. The poem opens,

Awake! again the Gospel-trump is blown

This almost stern note is reiterated in the body of the poem where we find the poet criticizing his colleagues for their lack of faith and charity.

Awake! why linger in the gorgeous town,
Sworn liegemen of the Cross and thorny crown?
Up from your beds of sloth for shame

Following this indictment of the clergy, Keble offered a long commentary on hypocrisy in the national church. Yet the poem is not an indictment of the clergy in the style of Milton. The church has always been a mixture of "the chosen few" and the hypocrites. In all likelihood Keble's poem was based on direct observation and, notwithstanding his complaints about an indolent clergy, the real thrust of the poem is against the political liberals of the day with "the changeful burden still of their rude lawless cry."

There is one more idea in this poem that might be noted. Having surveyed the disastrous episodes—"decaying ages"—of church history, Keble advised his readers to turn aside from the controversies of the moment in favor of waiting patiently for the final moment.

Thus bad and good their several warnings give
Of His approach, whom none may see and live:
    Faith's ear, with awful still delight
    Counts them like minute-bells at night,
Keeping the heart awake till dawn of morn,
While to her funeral pile this aged world is born.

The reforming impulse is throughout *The Christian Year.* For the most part it is directed against the clergy of the Church of England, but on one occasion (**"Thursday Before Easter""**) Keble seems to attack the king.

Oh! grief to think that grapes of gall
    Should cluster round thine healthiest shoot!
God's herald prove a heartless thrall,
    Who, if he dared, would fain be mute!
Even such in this bad world we see. . . .

The answer to the widespread corruptions in the government and in the church was not revolution. The lesson of bad clergy was that men should turn away from such problems, ". . . and trembling strive / To keep the lingering flame in thine own heart alive."

There are other themes in Keble's first volume that might be noted, for they also are quite peculiar to either the Church of England or Keble's ancestral background. The most striking of these is the recurrent praise of virginity as the highest state of the Christian life. In several poems Keble praised in an extraordinary way Mary, as the Virgin Mother of God, the supreme object of veneration in the Christian life. In the poem **"Wednesday Before Easter"** the praise of virginity is amplified to be slightly lower

than that of martyrdom in the kingdom of God. I quote from the fourth and following stanzas:

They say, who know the life divine,
And upward gaze with eagle eyne,
That by each golden crown on high,
Rich with celestial jewelry
Which for our Lord's redeemed is set,
There hangs a radiant coronet,
All gemmed with pure and living light,
Too dazzling for a sinner's sight,
Prepared for virgin souls, and they
Who seek the Martyr's diadem.
Nor deem, who to that bliss aspire,
Must win their way through blood and fire.
The writhings of a wounded heart
Are fiercer than a foeman's dart.
Oft in Life stillest shade reclining,
In Desolation unrepining,
Without a hope on earth to find
A mirror in an answering mind,
Meek souls there are, who little dream
Their daily strife an Angel's theme,
Or that the rod they take so calm
        . . . . .
Shall prove in Heaven a martyr's palm.
By purest pleasures unbeguiled
To idolise a wife or child;
Such wedded souls our God shall own
For faultless virgins round his throne.

The ideal of celebate priesthood was later posited during the Oxford Movement as one of the remedies for a lethargic, caste-conscious clergy—"pampered aristocrats," as Froude later put it—but the ideal survived only in the person of Newman.

Another important subject in *The Christian Year* was the state of poetry in the early nineteenth century. It is fairly obvious that Keble was unhappy with the work of most nineteenth-century poets. He may have been referring only to Byron and the "miserable school" of Mr. Leigh Hunt, but the indictment of Romantic poets sounds much more comprehensive.

In several of his poems Keble commented on what he thought was the essential task of a poet living in a Christian society. **"Palm Sunday"** is a fair example of Keble's theory. The poem resembles Gray's "Progress of Poesy" with its mixture of Hebrew and Greek influences, but Gray's poem of course celebrates the rise of poetry, while Keble's was an extended lament over the decline of poetry in his own time. Both poets were heavily indebted to the *Psalms* of David. Keble's argument, in part, was that the God who inspired David should inspire the modern poet. Both poets regarded poetry as a kind of sacred rite, yet Keble's comments on poetry transcend two ideas in Gray's "Progress." All that was necessary for the inspiration of the Christian poet was scripture and Nature.

The epigraph to the poem, "If these should hold their peace, the stones would immediately cry out," (Luke 19:

40) provides a clue to Keble's meaning and method. The relevant stanzas are:

> Ye whose hearts are beating high
> With the pulse of Poesy,
> Heirs of more than royal race,
> Framed by Heaven's peculiar grace,
> God's own work to do on earth,
> (If the word be not too bold,)
> Giving virtue a new birth,
> And a life that ne'er grows old—
>
> Sovereign masters of all hearts!
> Know ye, Who hath set your parts?
> He who gave you breath to sing,
> By whose strength ye sweep the string,
> He hath chosen you, to lead
> His Hosannas here below;—
> Mount, and claim your glorious meed;
> Linger not with sin and woe.
>
> Then waken into sound divine
> The very pavement of Thy shrine
> Till we, like Heaven's star-sprinkled floor,
> Faintly give back what we adore
> Childlike though the voices be,
> And untunable the parts,
> Thou wilt own the minstrelsy,
> If it flow from childlike hearts.

The poet was like a priest who was failing to perform his sacred task. The phrase, "Heaven's peculiar grace," suggests that Keble had come to accept the Romantic premise that the poet was different from the rest of humanity. Yet in Keble's insistence that the mission of the poet was religious we find a significant distance that separates him from most Romantic poets. In the comments, "Linger not with sin and woe," Keble expressed his concern for the subject matter of so many of his contemporaries, particularly the work of Lord Byron.

In another poem Keble raised the topic of the proper material for the poet in a Christian society. **"The Fourth Sunday after Trinity"** proposes the idea that all poems about Nature are religious poems. In a series of quatrains he celebrates the poetic impulse and its finest expression—the praise of God and the world that God created.

> It was not then a poet's dream,
> An idle vaunt of song,
> Such as beneath the moon's soft gleam
> On vacant fancies throng;
>
> Which bids us see in heaven and earth,
> In all fair things around,
> Strong yearnings for a blest new birth
> With sinless glories crown'd;
>
> Which bids us hear, at each sweet pause,
> From care and want and toil,
> When dewy eve her curtain draws
> Over the day's turmoil;

> In the low chant of wakeful birds,
> In the deep weltering flood,
> In the whispering leaves,
> these solemn words—
> "God made us all for good."

Keble's argument in brief was that Nature and the positive aspects of life were the essential materials for the poet. The theme of these poems, especially those on Nature, imply a criticism of nineteenth-century poets who concerned themselves with the darker aspects of Nature and life itself.

A final example of Keble's theory of poetry is **"The Sixth Sunday after Trinity,"** a poem about the repentance of David. Poetry was almost an instrument of grace for the poet because it inspired love and hope in the reader who might, being so inspired, pray for the poet.

> If ever, floating from faint earthly lyre,
> Was wafted to your soul one high desire,
>   By all the trembling hope ye feel,
>   Think on the minstrel as ye kneel.

The grace of contrition, in keeping with Keble's general appeal to the analogies of Nature, is likened to a "silent April rain," and the poetry of David was, in part, a means of his conversion.

The poems about Nature and the analogies of Nature to grace are throughout the whole of *The Christian Year,* but **"Septuagesima Sunday"** is a convenient starting point, in spite of its "piety." The theme of the poem is illustrated in its scriptural epigraph:

> The invisible things of Him from the creation
> of the world are clearly seen, being understood
> of things that are made. (Romans 1:20)

The poem has been described as Wordsworthian in its style, but its method is rather different. The opening stanzas emphasize Keble's theme.

> There is a book, who runs may read,
> Which heavenly truth imparts.
> And all the lore its scholars need,
> Pure eyes and Christian hearts.
>
> The works of God above, below,
>   Within us and around,
> Are pages in that book, to show
>   How God Himself is found.
>
> The glorious sky embracing all,
> Is like the Maker's love,
> Wherewith encompass'd, great and small,
> In peace and order move.
>
> The Moon above, the Church below,
> A wondrous race they run,

> But all their radiance, all their glow,
> Each borrows of its Sun.

In addition to the epigraph, which provides the theological basis for the poem, the use of the material of Nature suggests to me an essential difference from Wordsworth. All of created Nature—its beauties and its terrors—were analogues of God's power and mercy.

Keble's method was to approach God through the evidences of Nature with what he described as the "eye of faith," which enabled man to trace, in spite of human frailties, the hand of God. Keble seemed to urge that it was only through such a process that we could come to know God, Nature, and, by implication, true poetry. It was this method that enabled Keble to find out all that he wished to know about God in even the most prosaic subject matter.

From a naturalistic point of view Keble's approach or method might seem to be unsatisfactory. For Keble Nature, while beautiful in itself, is never viewed alone. Its function is to serve as a stepping stone to something higher.

Such an approach to God and Nature is not without its weaknesses. Keble was not what we would call an optimist about the human condition or even Nature itself, but the reader does get the impression that Keble was somewhat diffident about the painful episodes of the Christian life, in particular the crucifixion. The poems on the subject of Passion Week are among the least satisfying in the *The Christian Year.*

At the same time, however, I cannot deny the impression that Keble's shyness or reserve, from a religious point of view, is sometimes preferable to the direct approach of the Metaphysical poets of the seventeenth century. Dr. Johnson was far from being the only critic to complain of the ease and familiarity with God that the metaphysicals sometimes exhibit. The reader may not always think on the religious subject that was, ostensibly at least, the reason for the poem.

It would be wrong to assume that Keble's faith was complacent, as opposed to the complexities of belief in other religious poets. Several of the poems in the collection exhibit the dark side of human consciousness—the possibility that there may be no God and that faith is no more than a delusion.

"The Sixth Sunday after Epiphany" is one of the most perfect in *The Christian Year* to exhibit this problem. The poem presents no grave problems of interpretation, and a careful reader might trace out the influence of this poem on two more celebrated poets, Matthew Arnold ("Dover Beach") and Emily Dickinson ("Success is Counted Sweetest"). The poem addresses those who wished for an absolute knowledge of God or the knowledge that God does not exist. The middle state of obscure knowledge, "doubt's galling chain," was more oppressive than even a complete negation of God's existence.

Keble was sympathetic to the question and his poem provides his own method of answering that question.

> There are, who darkling and alone,
> Would wish the weary night were gone,
> Though dawning morn should only show
> The secret of their unknown woe:
>
> Who pray for sharpest throbs of pain
> To ease them of doubt's galling chain:
> Only disperse the cloud, they cry,
> And if our fate be death, give light and let us die.
>
> Unwise I deem them. Lord, unmeet
> To profit by Thy chastenings sweet,
> For Thou wouldst have us linger still
> Upon the verge of good or ill,
>
> That on Thy guiding hand unseen
> Our undivided hearts may lean,
> And this our frail and foundering bark
> Glides in the narrow wake of Thy beloved Ark.

Keble argues that the lack of direct evidence for the existence of God is not itself a mystery. Man knows of the existence of God through the exercise of conscience, "Thy guiding hand unseen." That the evidence of God's existence is so frail to "gross mortal" eyes (as he wrote in **"Baptism"**) makes faith a much greater possession. The Christian holds to his "dim" and limited vision through the power of love. Such a vision is worth more than empirical proof, which does not require love or faith.

The scarcity of doctrinal ideas in *The Christian Year* is one of the most significant clues to the work's popularity in the Victorian Age. Doctrine was the religious equivalent of a quality that Keble disliked in poetry—"metaphysics"; and we find him closely following his own precepts in his poetry. General readers did not read poetry for direct instruction in either religion or philosophy. The most notable exception to this rule is Keble's lovely poem on baptism, for the poem anticipates Keble's later activity on behalf of the Catholic principles of Anglicanism. A few of the relevant stanzas are:

> Where is it, mothers learn their love?—
> In every Church a fountain springs
> O'er which th' eternal Dove
> Hovers on softest wings.
>
> What sparkles in that lucid flood
> Is water, by gross mortals eyed;
>   But seen by Faith, 'tis blood
>   Out of a dear Friend's side
>
> A few calm words of faith and prayer,
>   A few bright drops of holy dew,

> Shall work a wonder there
> Earth's charmers never knew

So far as I have been able to discern, the doctrine of Baptismal Regeneration as suggested in the above is the only Catholic doctrine in the whole of *The Christian Year.* His version of the Eucharist was not.

There are several poems in *The Christian Year* that celebrate the Eucharistic service. None of these suggest a belief in the Real Presence; and in **"Gunpowder Treason,"** (one of the state feast-day poems), Keble offered a version of the Eucharist that seemed to deny such a belief. The critical lines occur towards the end of the poem:

> O come to our Communion Feast:
> There present in the heart,
> Not in the hands, th'eternal Priest
> Will His true self impart.

The controversy in the poem centers on Keble's apparent denial of the Real Presence in the above stanza. Keble's biographers and historians of the Oxford Movement have insisted that Keble really meant "Not only in the hands" instead of the apparent denial contained in the original.

In the first edition of *The Christian Year,* which was published after Keble's death in 1866, the lines were changed to read "as in the hands." A controversy greeted the changed version. In the *Quarterly Review,* the Bishop of Oxford (Samuel Wilberforce) published an essay on the poetry in which he denounced the change, while the *Guardian,* an Anglo-Catholic weekly, defended it. The question remains as to who made the change. The accepted version is that Keble approved of it on his deathbed, but there is no record of any significance to justify that explanation. The rest of the poem is filled with other forms of anti-Catholic statements. It therefore seems unlikely that Keble would have accepted anything like a "high position" on the Eucharist at that stage in his life. Even in his later years Keble was strong in his condemnation of Roman doctrines, including the Real Presence, and his readers were content with the idea that the Eucharistic ritual was only commemorative. Newman did not believe in the doctrine of the Real Presence until his conversion, and then only because the church taught such a doctrine. Further, he was severe in his criticisms of Pusey and the other Anglo-Catholics for their promoting of the doctrine since they violated the Anglican consensus on the subject.[8] It would have been most unlikely that Keble had come up with anything approaching a Catholic teaching on the subject of the Eucharist since he was prone to criticize the eucharistic views of one of his friends for his tendency to "turn good young Protestants into Papists."[9]

Pusey tried to defend the revised version of the lines in a letter to Newman.

What do you think was the original meaning of the Not in the hands. Do you think that it was really written under the influence of Hooker? . . . Dear J. K's leaving it for so many years is more accountable, if he always understood in the sense of I will have mercy and not sacrifice as he did in later years.[10]

Newman answered Pusey's letter:

Certainly I have always thought dear Keble meant that verse in an anti-catholic sense, when he wrote it. First, the *draft* of that poem shows it—Next, Hurrell Froude always thought so, and expressly attacks Keble for it in one of the Letters in his Remains. Thirdly, Hooker, though tolerant of the Catholic view does surely himself take the Calvinistic; and Keble was especially a disciple of Hooker. According to my own idea, it was Jewel . . . whose writings first opened Keble's eyes to the unsatisfactory doctrine of the Reformers as such, in contradistinction to the high Anglican school; and from that time Keble took a much higher line of theology. . . .[11]

Froude (a younger pupil of John Keble and one of the first members of the Oxford Movement) had complained bitterly about the "Protestantism" of the stanza,[12] but Keble had not responded to the criticism and had left the lines unchanged. He was apparently content with the obvious meaning of the lines and the poem as a whole until some period beyond 1854. There are many other reasons to suggest that Keble was content with the literal meaning of the early editions. The later correspondence with John Taylor Coleridge is filled with references to *The Christian Year*— certain lines, words, the copyrights, illustrations, and so forth—but there is no mention of these lines or any change. If Keble were unhappy with the stanza or with the poem as a whole, he did not tell Coleridge.[13]

However, what Keble did mention about the poetry in his letters to Coleridge is interesting and perhaps relevant to this discussion. Pusey, it appears, had twice offered Keble a thousand pounds for the copyright to the volume; Keble had remarked that he did not trust Pusey on this matter.[14]

It would not be a complete surprise, therefore, if Pusey had obtained the copyright through some agreement with Parker (Keble's publisher) and made the change to suit himself and what he believed would have suited Keble. The letter to Newman, cited above, seems to seek approval for the changed version. Moreover, Pusey's silence, when the controversy was going on in the press is striking if we remember that Pusey's method was usually just the opposite: his published letters to the Anglo-Catholic and secular press would easily fill a volume.

The suggestion that Keble approved of the change on his deathbed comes from Dr. Pusey, who did profess a belief in the Real Presence (though never in the Roman sense of the word). In 1879 Pusey wrote and published a small "letter" (actually a pamphlet) to H. P. Liddon on the subject of the revised version. In his letter Pusey admitted that the idea for the changed lines was originally his own.

> I remember saying strongly, "Explanations are useless: they have been made over and over again, and are ignored." [Then, Keble wrote to Liddon] "I have made up my mind, that it will be best when a reprint is called for, to adopt E. B. P's emendation and note with a few words pointing out that it does but express the true meaning of the printed text." The line then, after all, is neither yours nor mine [i.e., neither Pusey's nor Liddon's but Keble's].[15]

Following this, an extract from the *Journal of the Rev. Thomas Keble* (Keble's younger brother) is cited, in which Pusey is told by Thomas Keble's wife to make the change right away.

I have never heard of the journal mentioned by Pusey, and there is reason to suggest that the changed lines and the defense of the change is pretty much of an invention. One of the later Tractarians, who did profess a belief in the principle of the Real Presence (G. A. Denison) and whose interpretation of the Eucharist was rejected by the Privy Council in 1854, noted a difference between himself and Keble on this subject.[16] Certainly the other poetry in *The Christian Year* derives from a generally Protestant view of the English church and its teachings.

Quite apart from the many questions about Keble's personal faith or his relationship to either the Neo-Classic or Romantic theory of literature, there is a larger context in which *The Christian Year* ought to be read. The poems, taken as a whole, represent one of the last major, or "widely-read," expressions of a philosophic and religious system once known as "cosmic toryism." This system has been interpreted as a form of complacent conservatism for its resistance to change in the political and social spheres. Keble was deeply embued with that kind of conservatism, but it was not primarily a matter of "looking out for number one." He was a conservative in the sense that St. Paul was a conservative: the established order was the best instrument for promoting the common good.

A second aspect of this "philosophy" is to be found in the domain of mysticism, and it is ultimately beyond human description. It predicates a belief that all human enterprises, including evil itself, tend towards a final good; and it includes an "extinction of one's separate individuality" and "an acceptance of all existence as a part of the divine pattern."[17] The alleged simplicity of *The Christian Year* is most certainly scriptural in its essential premise that, in spite of evil and the general decay of the world, there is a provident God who rules the world.

There is scarcely an item in this system that has not been challenged in our own time. Even in the latter half of the nineteenth century, the various forms of "cosmic toryism" were rejected in favor of an often extreme form of pessimism. It is no accident, as one scholar has pointed out, that three of the major Victorian poems are apocalyptic. In each instance the validity of the Christian promise is directly questioned.[18]

The enduring popularity of Keble's first volume is especially significant, for it represents a continuous reminder that, with all of the many evils of the nineteenth century, there were still reasons for hope. Such a "solution" must always appear complacent. Even so great a man as Cardinal Newman remarked that the *data* of human experience tended to deny rather than confirm the existence of God. Yet Newman would have been the first to insist that the theological virtue of hope was also a Christian duty. It is the virtue of hope that is written so large in Keble's poetry.

Every reader must decide for himself about the merits of *The Christian Year;* but the relevance of Keble's poetry to our own time is especially intense if we remember that many theologians and writers have insisted that the one virtue so lacking in modern man is hope.

CONCLUSION

In this [essay] I have suggested a series of reasons why Keble's first volume is at once good and important. The value of the poems, as in the case of all poetry, is the most difficult part of my argument. The very merits of clarity and simplicity would tend to cause a modern reader to be suspicious, if not contemptuous, of their content. *The Christian Year* was based on a system of belief not so far removed from our time as to attract the antiquarian; but it is based on one that is clearly dated in its essential optimism. It would require a major revolution in theology and philosophy to bring back that belief in a providential Creator who controlled the world and punished evil. For this reason, future students of nineteenth century poetry may find Keble to be the most complex and strange of the Victorian poets.

What might be noted, however, is that Keble was almost a "pure" original in his composition of *The Christian Year.* His limited borrowings were based on a desire to complement those from whom he had learned; but he was always independent and, while such a remark tends to turn us away from the idea that he was a saint, it might help us appreciate the poetry more. *The Christian Year* was not a high-church collection of hymns. It was a collection of the most elevated sentiments belonging to the common experience of Christians.

Notes

1. *Letters and Diaries of John Henry Newman,* ed. Gerald Tracey (Oxford: Clarendon Press, 1979) 2:20.

2. Thomas Mozley, *Reminiscences Chiefly of Oriel College and the Oxford Movement,* 2 vols. (Boston: Houghton Mifflin Co., 1882) 1:219.

3. Keble to Coleridge, April 1844, CC.

4. Cf. George B. Tennyson, "The Sacramental Imagination," in *Nature and the Victorian Imagination,* ed. George B. Tennyson and U. C. Knoepfimacher (Berkeley CA: University of California Press, 1977) 370-75; also, Gerald Tennyson, *Victorian Devotional Poetry: The Tractarian Mode* (Berkeley CA: University of California Press, 1981) 72.

5. Mary Moorman, *William Wordsworth,* 2 vols. (Oxford: Oxford University Press, 1965) 2:542-43.

6. *Remains of Richard Hurrell Froude,* ed. John Henry Newman and John Keble, 4 vols. (Oxford: James Parker, 1838-1839) 1:232.

7. Tennyson, *Victorian Devotional Poetry,* 96.

8. John Henry Newman, *Difficulties Felt by Anglicans,* 2 vols. (Westminster MD: Christian Classics, ed. 1969) vol. 1, ch. 4.

9. Keble to Arthur Perceval, June 1832, Keble-Perceval Correspondence, Pusey House, Oxford.

10. *Letters and Diaries of John Henry Newman,* ed. Charles Dessain, (Oxford: Oxford University Press, 1973) 23:43.

11. Ibid., 43-44.

12. *Remains of Richard Hurrell Froude,* 1:403.

13. For example, Keble wrote to James Parker in 1847 to express his satisfaction with the latest edition of *The Christian Year:* "I am *extremely well satisfied* with the style of the book." Keble to James Parker, 28 October 1847, in Lewis Collection, Yale University.

14. Keble to Coleridge, 19 June 1854, CC.

15. *Postscript on the Alteration of a Line in* The Christian Year (Oxford: James Parker, 1878) 2; see also Liddon Diaries, 5 September 1856: "A great deal of conversation with Keble. He told me that he had frequently wished to withdraw the words 'Not in the hand but in the heart': but that his friends had prevented him." Liddon House, London.

16. George A. Denison, *Notes of My Life* (London: Macmillan, 1878) 254.

17. Basil Willey, *Eighteenth-Century Background: Studies on the Idea of Nature in Thought of the Period* (Boston: Beacon Press, 1961) 43.

18. John Rosenberg, *The Fall of Camelot* (Cambridge: Harvard University Press, 1973) 36.

FURTHER READING

Biography

Battiscombe, Georgina. *John Keble: A Study in Limitations.* London: Constable and Co., 1963, 395 p.
    Critical biography of Keble that explores his influence on the Oxford Movement and Anglicanism.

Criticism

Edgecombe, Rodney Stenning. "Keble's *Christian Year* Surveyed." In *Two Poets of the Oxford Movement: John Keble and John Henry Newman,* pp. 35-167. Cranbury, N. J.: Associated University Presses, 1996.
    Extensive stylistic analysis of *The Christian Year,* in which Edgecombe minimizes Keble's poetic debt to William Wordsworth.

Griffin, John. "John Keble and *The Quarterly Review.*" In *Review of English Studies* XXIX, No. 116 (November 1978): 452-56.
    Discusses a neglected review essay of Keble's "as a masterpiece of early Wordsworthian criticism" and considers Keble's early liberalism.

Hale, John K. "'Hail! Gladdening Light': A Note on John Keble's Verse Translations." *Victorian Poetry* 24, No. 1 (Spring 1986): 92-95.
    Probes Keble's changes to the Christian Hymn "Hail! Gladdening Light" in his translation from the original Greek.

Martin, B. W. "Wordsworth, Faber, and Keble: Commentary on a Triangular Relationship." In *Review of English Studies* XXVI, No. 104 (November 1975): 436-42.
    Studies the mutual influence of Keble, William Wordsworth, and Frederick William Faber using epistolary evidence.

Additional coverage of Keble's life and career is contained in the following sources published by the Gale Group: *Dictionary of Literary Biography,* Vols. 32 and 55.

Les Liaisons dangereuses

Pierre Ambroise François Choderlos de Laclos

The following entry presents criticism of Laclos's eighteenth-century French epistolary novel, *Les Liaisons dangereuses* (1782). For information on Laclos's complete career, see *NCLC,* Volume 4.

INTRODUCTION

Scholars consider *Les Liaisons dangereuses,* or *Dangerous Liaisons,* as it is known in English, to be the greatest epistolary novel ever written, as well as an important contribution to the canon of world literature. Published in 1782, the novel consists of a series of letters exchanged between a cast of characters which reveal the tangled web of sexual liaisons between members of the French noble class. Laclos's representation of libertine philosophy and the ambiguous moral tone of the novel reflect the mood of France at the time and foreshadow the French Revolution, which occurred in opposition to the corruption of the French upper class. At one time considered scandalous, *Dangerous Liaisons* is now admired by critics as a masterpiece of subtlety that reveals the full potential of the epistolary form.

BIOGRAPHICAL INFORMATION

Pierre Choderlos de Laclos was born in 1741, the son of a newly ennobled family of Spanish origin. His low social position prevented Laclos from progressing as an officer in the French military. To relieve boredom, the young soldier wrote *Les Liaisons dangereuses,* basing the novel on libertine attitudes common at the time. While his motivations for writing the novel remain unclear, in part because of his conflicting explanations and rationalizations, most scholars posit that the novel's focus on the moral decay of the upper classes was tied to Laclos's political reform position. Though a monarchist, Laclos supported the removal of King Louis XVI, in favor of his cousin the Duc d'Orléans, for whom Laclos served as secretary prior to the French Revolution. However, Orléans was never able to seize power and, when the French Revolution occurred, he was beheaded. Although Laclos was jailed numerous times during the Revolution, his life was spared. Under the political leadership of Napoleon, Laclos

achieved greater success as a military officer, serving out the rest of his career in Italy. He died in 1803.

PLOT AND MAJOR CHARACTERS

Les Liaisons dangereuses consists of numerous letters sent between characters revealing an intricate pattern of affairs, infidelity, and power struggles within the French noble class. As the novel opens, Cécile de Volanges has departed from the convent where she was educated in preparation for her marriage to the older nobleman, Comte de Gercourt. Cécile's mother, Madame de Volanges, has arranged the marriage without informing her daughter, although her daughter suspects marriage is imminent. The Marquise de Merteuil, the jilted lover of the Comte de Gercourt, is determined to ruin the match, thus taking revenge on her former lover. She attempts to enlist the aid of another former lover, a libertine named the Vicomte de Valmont.

However, he is focused on his own conquest, the challenge of seducing Madame de Tourvel, a virtuous woman known for her piety. A competition ensues between the Marquise and Valmont over who can exercise the greater control over others; this fierce battle, which imitates a military campaign, is the focus of the novel. The pair orchestrate a love affair between Cécile and her admirer, the Chevalier Danceny. In addition, Valmont himself seduces Cécile. After much persuasion, Valmont is successful in his conquest of Madame de Tourvel. However, when the Marquise deduces that Valmont has fallen in love with his conquest, she resolves to destroy the love affair and, as a result, Madame de Tourvel. Learning of Valmont's seduction of Cécile, Danceny challenges Valmont to a duel in which the libertine is mortally wounded. On his deathbed, Valmont befriends Danceny, entrusting him to make public the letters between Valmont and the Marquise, letters that will prove her deceptive and destructive nature. The Marquise is publicly ruined, falls ill to smallpox, which ravages her beauty, and is forced to flee Paris in disgrace. Cécile enters a convent, while Danceny pledges himself as a celibate among the Knights of Malta.

MAJOR THEMES

In *Les Liaisons dangereuses* Laclos reveals the world of wealthy French noble families and the attitudes of the libertines. At the center of his novel is an egotistical battle between two immoral, ruthless, and cunning adversaries—Valmont and the Marquise. Although critics have long been divided over Laclos's intentions in writing the novel, in part because he offered various conflicting explanations during his life, most agree that the novel is linked to his views on the political and social conditions of France in the late eighteenth century and, specifically, to his concerns about the education of women. The juxtaposition of the naive, if not innocent, Cécile, whose convent education has sheltered her from society, and the evil and intelligent Marquise who destroys the lives of others out of retaliation for her own lack of freedom, reflects themes that Laclos developed in a series of essays on the education of women. Laclos argued that women were not and could not be equal to men as long as they were kept ignorant. They could only compliment man when they understood their world and were allowed choices. In addition, most critics today believe that Laclos was challenging his readers to reject the decadent lifestyle of the characters in the novel and to understand the limitations of such a life.

CRITICAL RECEPTION

Critics have long been troubled by Laclos's ambivalent tone in *Les Liaisons dangereuses*. As Sandra Camargo notes, the novel has been interpreted in countless contradictory ways since its publication. Some scholars claim that the novel voices Laclos's objection to the immorality of the age; others argue that Laclos exhibited a cynical attitude, or that his sole aim was to entertain his audience rather than to moralize. Refuting the claim that the characters are destroyed by their decadence, critics note that while Valmont dies, the Marquise survives, and they argue that her disfigurement empowers her rather than destroys her. However, Susan Dunn warns that "description should not be confused with prescription." Valerie Minogue suggests that Laclos's intent was for the reader to identify with Valmont and the Marquise only to question their own morality as they discover the shamefulness of these characters' acts. Some scholars celebrate Laclos's liberal ideas on empowering women, arguing that he was an early feminist. Others state that the author was a misogynist, citing the inherent strength of man's temperament in the novel as compared to woman's. Many scholars are in agreement that Laclos exhibited a fine mastery of the epistolary form, developing Samuel Richardson's early attempt in *Clarissa* to much greater skill. Scholars note Laclos's use of language in the novel and point out that his employment of editorial footnotes lends credence to the letters. Reviewers argue that Laclos was one of the most subtle and skillful novelists of his era. Renee Winegarten states that "(b)y concentrating only upon what would advance the drama, Laclos produced a book that has been called the first well-made French novel."

PRINCIPAL WORKS

Les liaisons dangereuses; ou, Lettres recueillies dans une société et publiées pour l'instruction de quelques autres (epistolary novel) 1782 [*Dangerous Connections; or, Letters Collected in a Society, and Published for the Instruction of Other Societies,* 1784; also published as *Dangerous Acquaintances,* 1924]

Lettre à Messieurs de l'Académie française sur l'éloge de M le Maréchal de Vauban, proposé pour sujet du prix d'éloquence de l'année 1787 (essay) 1786

De l'éducation des femmes (essays) 1903

Lettres inédites de Choderlos de Laclos (letters) 1904

Oeuvres Complètes (epistolary novel, essays, and poetry) 1951

CRITICISM

C. J. Greshoff (essay date 1964)

SOURCE: "The Moral Structure of *Les Liaisons Dangereuses,*" *The French Review,* Vol. XXXVII, No. 3, February, 1964, pp. 383-99.

[*In the following essay, Greshoff clarifies the fundamental intellectual, psychological, and moral content of* Les Liaisons dangereuses.]

Les Liaisons dangereuses is an accident both in the life of literature and in the life of Laclos. It is the only novel and the only valid piece of literature he ever wrote. The rest of his work is curious merely because it was written by the author of *Les Liaisons dangereuses.* Giraudoux describes him in his other works as "déclamatoire, maladroitement badin, terriblement plat et sensible. . . ."[1] As a novel *Les Liaisons dangereuses* is unique. Superficially it is part of the XVIIIth century tradition of erotic literature; it has also no doubt been influenced by *Clarissa Harlowe* and *La Nouvelle Héloïse.* Nevertheless *Les Liaisons dangereuses* stands alone and Laclos with greater justice than Rousseau could have taken for himself the famous opening sentence of *Les Confessions:* "Je forme une entreprise qui n'eût jamais d'exemple et dont l'exécution n'aura point d'imitateur." Laclos however made his own rather bombastic declaration. In London he said to his friend Tilly: ". . . je résolus de faire un ouvrage qui sortit de la route ordinaire, qui fît du bruit, *et qui rententît encore sur terre quand j'y aurai passé.*"[2] In this Laclos succeeded.

Let us first take *Les Liaisons dangereuses* at its most superficial level. It is a novel in letter form dealing with a number of cold-blooded seductions: the Vicomte de Valmont wants to seduce Mme de Tourvel (also known as La Présidente); in passing, and on the suggestion of Mme de Merteuil, he seduces a young girl, Cécile Volanges; Mme de Merteuil in her turn seduces a young man, the Chevalier Danceny. Yet, even when looking at the novel from this simple point of view, one is struck by the extreme intricacy of the plot: all the actions are interrelated so that each move by each character echoes in the mind or in the actions of the other characters. At the same time the various movements of the plot have a certain formal quality which is equally striking. The reader has the impression of becoming the spectator of a number of highly skilful manoeuvres and counter-manoeuvres, which for all their apparent complication seem nevertheless to obey some rule or law. In fact, he is looking at a highly organised and formalised game which is being played by Valmont and Mme de Merteuil with deadly earnestness, but which does not thereby lose any of its playfulness.

The amorous game played before us in *Les Liaisons* bears a striking and significant resemblance to the formal wars of the XVIIth and XVIIIth centuries:

> "C'est alors que la guerre ressemble vraiment à une partie d'échecs. Lorsque après des manoeuvres compliquées, un des adversaires a perdu ou gagné plusieurs pièces—villes ou places fortes—alors vient la grande bataille: du sommet de quelque coteau, où lui apparaît tout le terrain du combat, tout l'échiquier, le maréchal fait avancer ou reculer habilement ses beaux régiments. . . . Échec et mat, le perdant range son jeu: on remet les pions dans leur boîte ou les régiments dans leurs quartiers d'hiver, et chacun va à ses petites affaires en attendant la partie ou la campagne suivante."[3]

This description of war in the XVIIth century could just as well serve as a description of the actions shown in *Les Liaisons dangereuses.* For what Laclos deals with in his novel is a war, and it is not merely because Laclos was an artillery officer that he uses the vocabulary of war. The use of such a vocabulary when talking about love goes back to the days of courtly love.

> "L'amant *fait le siège* de sa Dame. Il livre *d'amoureux assauts* à sa vertu. Il la *serre de près*, il la *poursuit*, il cherche à *vaincre* les dernières *défenses* de sa pudeur, et à les *tourner par surprise;* enfin la dame *se rend à merci.* Mais alors, par une curieuse inversion bien typique de la courtoisie, c'est l'amant qui sera son *prisonnier* en même temps que son *vainqueur.* Il deviendra le vassal de cette *suzeraine,* selon la règle des guerres féodales, tout comme si c'était lui qui avait subi la *défaite.*"[4]

Here we have, with very few differences, the very vocabulary of Laclos' novel. The originality of Laclos, however, is to use this conventional metaphorical vocabulary almost in its literal sense and thus to make us realise that what we see in this novel is not a sham battle, but a war fought with relentless ferocity and in which people die and get maimed. But it is also a game and a brief glance at its origin will be enlightening.

Like the vocabulary, the game itself goes back to the Middle-Ages and to the beginnings of Courtly Love.[5] It is the courtly tradition which gives love its style (or a style); and in France the mode was continued, with Petrarchian and Neo-Platonic accretions, into the XVIIth century by *l'amour précieux* and its playing at passion, its toying with feelings in the framework of a series of conventions. But this stylisation of love in the XIIIth century had grown out of the necessity to curb the primitive ferocity of lust and passion. "To formalize love is the supreme aspiration of the life beautiful . . . to formalize love is, moreover, a social necessity, a need that is the more imperious as life is more ferocious. Love was to be elevated to the height of a rite. The overflowing of passion demands it. Only by constructing a system of forms and rules for the vehement emotions can barbarity be escaped."[6]

It is only when one sees the actions of Valmont and Mme de Merteuil against this background that one of the innumerable ironies of Laclos' novel comes to light. For what is happening in *Les Liaisons* is that Valmont and Mme de Merteuil have brought back in this formal stylized game of love the very cruelty and violence and barbarity which courtly love tried to oust. And in this way the very nature of the game, its innocence, is being negated and betrayed, while at the same time it still retains its external façade of playfulness. Here lies one of the fascinations of the novel and also one of the sources of its tension. The game played by Valmont and Mme de Merteuil is not devoid of risk, neither for them nor for their victims. It is not merely a ballet or a parlour game but it becomes "une tauromachie". On the surface, however, it retains all the lightness and gaiety of a game. It is here that Laclos uses his language so admirably. Valmont and Mme de Merteuil and, for that matter, all the characters write in the conventional epistolary style of the XVIIIth century. They could not possibly write in any other way. But Laclos uses this gay, sophisticated, elegantly light but conventional language in order to underline, by ironic contrast, the profoundly sinister nature of Valmont's and Mme de Merteuil's activities.

The psychological aspect of *Les Liaisons dangereuses* is perhaps not the most important but it is certainly the one which attracts the reader's attention most immediately. And, of course, the reality and "vraisemblance" of the relationships between the characters gives substance and body to the novel. But in discussing this psychological side of the novel we come across a very peculiar confusion. Since both the writer and his characters display a considerable amount of psychological insight—but of an entirely different kind—Laclos, by showing us the kind of psychological intelligence Valmont and Mme de Merteuil possess, reveals to us at the same time their limitations.

The action of the novel is based on the psychological perspicacity of its protagonists. It is this perspicacity which, because of its surface brilliance, tends to dazzle us and to hide from us the very much deeper insight which Laclos displays through his heroes into the workings of pride and evil.

The psychological insight of Valmont and Mme de Merteuil, although sharply intelligent, is strictly limited. There comes a point in any game—and let us not forget that it is a game they are playing—when its rules become so sophisticated and so intricate that the knowledge of these rules seems to replace intelligence and insight, and the full exploitation of the possibilities of a game becomes a work of art. Hence the aesthetic satisfaction which Valmont and Mme de Merteuil derive from their activities. But although they display a considerable amount of intelligence, this intelligence remains on the surface: they have only such insight as is immediately useful to them. They are political or diplomatic manoeuverers, no more. When Valmont writes to Mme de Merteuil: "On ne peut que s'humilier devant la profondeur de vos vues, si on en juge par le succès de vos démarches", he writes, in fact, the very language of the *chancelleries* and he reveals at the same

time ironically that these views are not genuinely profound but superficial since they are directed towards the attainment of an immediate aim which itself is superficial. There is one other obvious factor which limits Valmont's and Mme de Merteuil's psychological insight: their complete lack of sympathy and understanding. They are therefore essentially "intellectuals"; they do have a real intelligence of the game they are playing, and it is characteristic that this intelligence is applied not to life or people but to an abstraction: the game.

Laclos, on the other hand, has both a very real insight into the living psychological mechanism of his characters and, what is more important, a profound knowledge of the moral forces which are revealed through their actions. It is this which gives *Les Liaisons Dangereuses* its other dimension. For it is, no doubt, a psychological novel, but it is not only that, hence its greatness.

There are three groups of people in Laclos' novel: The victims: Mme de Tourvel, Cécile Volanges and Danceny; the executioners: Mme de Merteuil and Valmont; and finally Mme de Rosemonde and Mme Volanges who, for want of a better word, "represent" society.

Let us look at the victims first. Danceny is, no doubt, important for the working out of the plot, but has otherwise little stature and remains throughout the novel no more than a shadow. The real victims, then, are Cécile and La Présidente. But they are not victims in the same degree. Laclos is careful to establish a hierarchy: they are not equally innocent. The innocence of Mme de Tourvel is a function of her being, she *is* innocent. But Cécile is innocent only because of her age. If Mme de Tourvel is naturally good, Cécile is naturally debauched. This is how Mme de Merteuil describes her in a letter to Valmont:

> "Savez-vous que vous avez perdu plus que vous ne croyez, à ne pas vous charger de cet enfant? elle est vraiment délicieuse! cela n'a ni caractère ni principes; jugez combien sa société sera douce et facile. Je ne crois pas qu'elle brille jamais par le sentiment; mais tout annonce en elle les sensations les plus vives. Sans esprit et sans finesse, elle a pourtant une certaine fausseté naturelle, si l'on peut parler ainsi, qui quelquefois m'étonne moi-même, et qui réussira d'autant mieux, que sa figure offre l'image de la candeur et de l'ingénuité."

The passage reveals not only her natural corruptness ("ni caractère, ni principes", "fausseté naturelle") but also the fact that she is incapable of any feeling ("je ne crois pas qu'elle brille jamais par le sentiment"), which in the novel is shown by her ability to divorce her "sentiments" for Danceny from the pleasure she takes with Valmont. This is where Gide sees quite correctly the root of her debauched nature: "Au demeurant elle (la débauche) n'est pas du côté de la Merteuil et de Valmont, mais bien de Danceny et de la petite Volange; la débauche commence où commence à se dissocier de l'amour le plaisir."[7]

In order to underline Cécile's real nature Laclos links her closely with Mme de Merteuil. There is little doubt that there exists between these two characters a real affinity. Cécile feels naturally attracted to Mme de Merteuil, who, in turn, recognises in the young girl someone of her own kind. She is as yet young and unformed but she has the vacuous sensuality combined with a lack of feeling which might turn her into a second Mme de Merteuil. What she lacks, however, is intelligence and it is for this reason alone that Mme de Merteuil rejects her:

> "Je me désintéresse entièrement sur son compte. J'avais eu quelque envie d'en faire au moins une intrigante subalterne, et de la prendre pour jouer *les seconds* sous moi: mais je vois qu'il n'y a pas d'étoffe; elle a une sotte ingénuité qui n'a pas cédé même au spécifique que vous avez employé, lequel pourtant n'en manque guère; et c'est selon moi, la maladie la plus dangereuse que femme puisse avoir. Elle dénote, surtout, une faiblesse de caractère presque toujours incurable et qui s'oppose à tout de sorte que, tandis que nous nous occuperions à former cette petite fille pour l'intrigue, nous n'en ferions qu'une femme facile. Or, je ne connais rien de si plat que cette facilité de bêtise, qui se rend sans savoir ni comment ni pourquoi, uniquement parce qu'on l'attaque et qu'elle ne sait pas résister. Ces sortes de femmes ne sont absolument que des machines à plaisir."

Although the cold-blooded death sentence which Mme de Merteuil passes on her ". . . pour se servir de celle-ci sans danger, il faut se dépêcher, s'arrêter de bonne heure, et la briser ensuite . . ." fills us with horror, her eventual destruction does not move us and we are clearly, at no stage, intended to be moved by her fate. For she was, in fact, neither seduced nor corrupted but merely yielded to her real nature.

Mme de Tourvel is different. She is, as we have seen, truly innocent and virtuous; it is this which puts her outside the reach of Valmont, just as the absence of true virtue puts Cécile inside Valmont's easy reach. She is also natural and not, like Cécile, superficially spontaneous. This naturalness of Mme de Tourvel is important. It is revealed to us not only by the direct tone of her letters but indirectly by two descriptions of her, one by Mme de Merteuil the other by Valmont. On hearing of the quarry Valmont has chosen to pursue Mme de Merteuil writes:

> "Qu'est-ce donc que cette femme? des traits réguliers si vous voulez, mais nulle expression: passablement faite, mais sans grâces: toujours mise à faire rire! avec ses paquets de fichus sur la gorge, et son corps qui remote au menton! Je vous le dis en amie, il ne vous faudrait pas deux femmes comme celle-là, pour vous faire perdre toute votre considération. Rappelez-vous donc ce jour où elle quêtait à Saint-Roch, et où vous

> me remerciâtes tant de vous avoir procuré ce cpectacle. Je crois la voir encore, donnant la main à ce grand échalas en cheveux longs, prête à tomber à chaque pas, ayant toujours son panier de quatre aunes sur la tête de quelqu'un, et rougissant à chaque révérence."

The description is obviously coloured by envy or jealousy but what it shows is a person who cannot "dress up" and who is ill at ease in the artificial society in which she moves. In his reply to Mme de Merteuil, Valmont writes:

> "Mais que dis-je? Madame de Tourvel a-t-elle besoin d'illusion? non; pour être adorable il lui suffit d'être elle-même. Vous lui reprochez de se mettre mal; je le crois bien: toute parure lui nuit; tout ce qui la cache la dépare: c'est dans l'abandon du négligé qu'elle est vraiment ravissante. Grâce aux chaleurs accablantes que nous éprouvons, un déshabillé de simple toile me laisse voir sa taille ronde et souple. Une seule mousseline couvre sa gorge; et mes regards furtifs, mais pénétrants, en ont déjà saisi les formes enchanteresses. Sa figure, dites-vous, n'a nulle expression. Et qu'exprimerait-elle, dans les moments où rien ne parle à son coeur? Non, sans doute, elle n'a point, comme nos femmes coquettes, ce regard menteur qui séduit quelquefois et nous trompe toujours."

Leaving aside the erotic innuendoes, Valmont speaks the exact truth and Mme de Tourvel does not need to "dress up", "il lui suffit d'être elle-même". It is this directness, this naturalness which brings her so close to Corneille's heroines, or to Mme de Clèves: like Pauline she speaks "à coeur ouvert", like her she is suddenly assailed by "les suprises des sens" and like Mme de Clèves she fights with all her strength against them, but only, unlike Mme de la Fayette's heroine, to succumb and to be destroyed.

In this context it might be useful to note that Valmont and Mme de Merteuil are also akin to the Cornelian heroes: they are of the race of men and women of action, of the conquerors ("Conquérir est notre destin" writes Valmont). If they seduce it is partly "pour la gloire", and Mme de Tourvel is sacrificed by Valmont so that he can show himself "worthy" of Mme de Merteuil, in the same way that Rodrigue kills the Count so that he shall remain worthy of Chimène. And at times they talk like characters of Corneille. But they are corrupted Cornelian heroes. The same thing happens here as happened with the game of courtly love. The Cornelian actions and attitudes remain but they are emptied of all content and only serve to conceal a stinking reality.

One other factor makes Mme de Tourvel different: she belongs to an orderly world. She is the only character who is married, and the fact that she is a genuinely devout person is by no means accidental. It all contributes to build up the image of a person who is part of a real and solid world and whose entire life is framed by equally real and solid values.

Mme de Tourvel remains outside Parisian society and her physical remoteness from it, the fact that she lives together with Mme de Rosemonde in an isolated *Château,* is not solely dictated by the necessities of the form in which the novel is written. A considerable part of the correspondence between *La Présidente* and Valmont takes place inside Mme de Rosemonde's castle and when Valmont is in Paris he continues nevertheless to correspond with Mme de Merteuil. The real purpose of the physical *éloignement* of Mme de Tourvel is to emphasise her moral separateness from her society. It goes without saying that she does not belong to the world of Valmont and Mme de Merteuil. But at the same time it would be a mistake to believe that she is part of Mme Volanges' society. The stiff formality with which she writes to Cécile's mother indicates the distance that separates them.

Mme Volanges, in spite of her shadowy appearance, is by no means unimportant in the moral structure of the novel. She represents, in Gide's words, "le parti des bonnes moeurs", that is, public morality and convention, which is shown here as double faced. For Mme Volanges at one and the same time knows Valmont and condemns him, and yet receives him as a guest, an equal in her drawing room. The distance which separates Valmont from Mme Volanges is far less great than the one which separates him from *La Présidente.*

Society, then, is a force which is present in *Les Liaisons dangereuses.* It is not merely represented by Mme Volanges, but it can be said that the whole book is directed against the moral corruption of a society. Giraudoux thinks that the real reason why the publication of Laclos' novel created such a scandal lies in the fact that it was a betrayal of the secret workings of a society.[8]

Now the society which is indirectly shown in *Les Liaisons* is first of all one where no permanent human relationships seem to exist, but only passing social contacts. It creates the impression of being a society without centre, without order and without authority: it is significant that *La Présidente* is the sole character who has a husband and that Cécile's father does not exist.

It is also a society which seems to be obsessed by *amour propre,* intrigue and eroticism. But it is important to see that all three of these obsessions depend for their existence on appearance. The *intrigant* plays a part and hides his true motives behind a mask. The vain man and the eroticist must make their action public, they must be shown to and shared by a public. Hence, as Seylaz points out, the necessity for Valmont and Mme de Merteuil to write letters.[9] A society preoccupied by such interests transforms itself into a theatre and its members become actors. Valmont, writing about Prévan, a fellow-intrigant and seducer,

says: "En effet, je l'ai empêché longtemps, par ce moyen, de paraître sur ce que nous appelons le grand théâtre"; Mme de Merteuil writes about herself: "Alors je commençai à déployer sur le grand théâtre les talents que je m'étais donnés"; Valmont says of himself and of his activities:

> "Au fait, n'y ai-je jouissances, privations, espoir, incertitude? Qu'a-t-on de plus sur un plus grand théâtre? des spectateurs? Hé! laissez faire, ils ne me manqueront pas. S'ils ne me voient pas à l'ouvrage, je leur montererai ma besogne faite; ils n'auront plus qu'à admirer et applaudir. Oui, ils applaudiront; car je puis enfin prédire, avec certitude, le moment de la chute de mon austère Dévote."

And one could easily find many more such examples.

Perhaps the nature of the society which Laclos shows, and to which Mme de Tourvel is so foreign, might be made clearer by a comparison. It is the exact opposite of the society which Jane Austen shows us in *Mansfield Park.* Or rather, and the reference to the theatre is apposite, the world of *Les Liaisons dangereuses* is that of *Mansfield Park* had Mary Crawford and her brother succeeded with their plans and turned Mansfield Park into a theatre. In Jane Austen's novel the father returns and puts things back into order. But there is no father and no authority in *Les Liaisons dangereuses* and it is this absence of natural authority which enables the Valmonts and the Merteuils to rule and to dominate.[10]

Valmont is, beyond doubt, Laclos' greatest and also his most puzzling creation. For while it is certainly clear what Valmont wants to be, what image of himself he projects before himself, partly to satisfy his vanity, partly for the benefit of Mme de Merteuil, it is much less clear what kind of person he is in actual fact. On the surface this seems simple enough and Laclos multiplies the examples of his needless cruelty, his gratuitous nastiness and the dark corruption of his mind. Yet he is not only and wholly that. He stands in contrast to Mme de Tourvel who is wholly good but also to Mme de Merteuil who is wholly bad. Valmont is not made of one piece, and physically as well as morally he stands between the two.[11] One must proceed here with the greatest care. It is not for one moment being suggested that Valmont is not evil, but merely that he is not wholly evil. The ambiguous nature of his feelings for Mme de Tourvel, the ambiguous relationship which exists between him and Mme de Merteuil, finally the fact that he is divided between these two imply Valmont's own ambiguous nature. And this ineradicable question mark placed right in the very heart of the novel is one of its greatest glories.

There is no doubt however that Valmont is the cold-blooded seducer and corrupter of *La Présidente.* And a passage such as this one shows the sadistic turn of his mind.

"Mon projet, au contraire, est qu'elle sente, qu'elle sente bien la valeur et l'étendue de chacun des sacrifices qu'elle me fera; de ne pas la conduire si vite, que le remords ne puisse la suivre; de faire expirer sa vertu dans une lente agonie; de la fixer sans cesse sur ce désolant spectacle; et de ne lui accorder le bonheur de m'avoir dans ses bras, qu'après l'avoir forcée à n'en plus dissimuler le désir."

The passage brings immediately to mind the sadistic order of Camus' Caligula to his executioner: "Strike him so that he feels himself die". Yet he is, however slightly, involved with Mme de Tourvel. He himself right at the beginning of the book says: "J'ai besoin d'avoir cette femme, pour me sauver du ridicule d'en être amoureux . . ." And although the word "amoureux" when written by Valmont should be considered with great suspicion, there is other evidence that he is in love with Mme de Tourvel, that he is, as it were tempted by love:

Je suis encore trop plein de mon bonheur, pour pouvoir l'apprécier, mais je m'étonne du charme inconnu que j'ai ressenti. Serait-il donc vrai que la vertu augmentât le prix d'une femme, jusque dans le moment même de sa faiblesse? Mais reléguons cette idée puérile avec les contes de bonnes femmes. Ne recontret-on pas presque partout, une résistance plus ou moins bien feinte au premier triomphe? et ai-je trouvé nulle part le charme dont je parle? ce n'est pourtant pas non plus celui de l'amour; car enfin, si j'ai eu quelquefois, auprès de cette femme étonnante, des moments de faiblesse qui ressemblaient à cette passion pusillanime, j'ai toujours su les vaincre et revenir à mes principes.

And the intensity of this involvement is betrayed when he writes:

Il n'est plus pour moi de bonheur, de repos, que par la possession de cette femme que je hais et que j'aime avec une égale fureur. Je ne supporterai mon sort que du moment où je disposerai du sien. Alors tranquille et satisfait, je la verrai, à son tour, livrée aux orages que j'éprouve en ce moment; j'en exciterai mille autres encore. L'espoir et la crainte, la méfiance et la sécurité, tous les maux inventés par la haine, tous les biens accordés par l'amour, je veux qu'ils remplissent son coeur, qu'ils s'y succèdent à ma volonté.

Now we have here the very language of passion with all its tension. And although immediately after "que j'aime avec fureur" Valmont returns to his sadistic self, love, nevertheless, for a minute showed "le bout de l'oreille". And finally Mme de Merteuil makes no mistake about the nature of Valmont's involvement with Mme de Tourvel: "Oui, Vicomte, vous aimiez beaucoup Mme de Tourvel, et même vous l'aimez encore, vous l'aimez comme un fou. . . ."

Valmont then is not completely insensitive and above all he is not totally insensitive to virtue. He is moved by the natural gratefulness of the people he rescues from a "saisie":

J'examinais ce spectacle! lorsqu'un autre paysan, plus jeune, conduisant par la main une femme et deux enfants, et s'avançant vers moi à pas précipités, leur dit: "Tombons tous aux pieds de cette image de Dieu"; et dans le même instant, j'ai été entouré de cette famille, prosternée à mes genoux. J'avouerai ma faiblesse; mes yeux se sont mouillés de larmes, et j'ai senti en moi un mouvement involontaire, mais délicieux. J'ai été étonné du plaisir qu'on éprouve en faisant le bien; et je serais tenté de croire que ce que nous appelons les gens vertueux, n'ont pas tant de mérite qu'on se plaît à nous dire.

The little pirouette at the end should not take us in as it is meant to do and hide from us the importance of this "movement involontaire mais délicieux". Moreover part of the attraction Valmont feels for Mme de Tourvel lies in her virtues: "De la vertu c'est bien à elle (Cécile) d'en avoir! Ah! qu'elle la laisse à une femme véritablement née pour elle. La seule qui sache l'embellir, qui la ferait aimer". It is true that Valmont, like Néron faced with Junie, wants to destroy and outrage this virtue. It is equally true that its sight vaguely stirs in him atrophied and dulled feelings.

The drawing of Valmont is wonderfully balanced, for Laclos is not only careful to enrobe Valmont's velleities towards love and virtue in irony so that we never know how real and serious they are, but he also surrounds them, drowns them in examples of Valmont's corruption and sadism so that they are barely recognisable. But however infinitesimal they are, these stirrings do exist. And it is they which help to make Valmont the profoundly disturbing character he is. "Tout dans ce livre me déconcerte", writes Gide, but it is Valmont who is the most disconcerting character of all.

Mme de Merteuil is obviously the central figure; it is she who holds in her hands all the strings of the intrigue; it is she who dominates not only the novel but also the society in which she lives. Moreover the story of her relationship with Valmont is one of the important strands of the plot. The exact nature of this relationship remains unsolved and will always remain so, therefore a detailed analysis of it is of little real use. However a few things must be said about it.

It is obvious that Mme de Merteuil dominates Valmont: she is clearly his superior in intelligence, enterprise and immorality, and this forms part of her attraction for him; for in Mme de Merteuil he sees an image of himself, the embodiment of what he wants to be, and it is partly to prove himself her equal that he sacrifices Mme de Tourvel. It is equally obvious that Mme de Merteuil "feels" nothing for Valmont, but at the same time she is jealous of Mme de Tourvel; it is she who kills her (". . . quand une femme frappe dans le coeur d'une autre, elle manque rarement de trouver l'endroit sensible, et la blessure est incurable").

The real source of Mme de Merteuil's jealousy and the cause of her action is the fear that Mme de Tourvel is gaining a hold on Valmont, that she is for him something more than merely one of his innumerable victims. Mme de Merteuil is jealous, rather like Agrippine in *Britannicus,* of her loss of power.

Finally there exists between the two protagonists, right from the start of the novel, a tension which grows into a sort of covert smouldering war and eventually burst into the open with Mme de Merteuil's ominous answer to Valmont's ultimatum: "Eh bien! la guerre". But while this tension is born from a conflict between two people, it has, at the same time, a curious impersonality which the formal quality of the epistolary style tends to enhance. This impersonality comes from the fact that the conflict which opposes Valmont and Mme de Merteuil transcends their personalities. In her autobiographical letter Mme de Merteuil makes it quite clear that she looks upon man as an enemy. Her "règles" and "principes" are arms used in her fight against man in order to gain her freedom from his domination. She is therefore not only at war with Valmont but he is, as man, her natural enemy. And one of the themes of *Les Liaisons dangereuses,* although admittedly a minor one, is the clash between the sexes.

Mme de Merteuil, unlike Valmont, is a wholly monstrous character. Morally she is totally deformed. She tells the story of her own wilful distortion in a famous letter (LXXXI) which is a brief spiritual autobiography. What we see here is a woman who through willpower forces her intellect to control her natural being, once again not unlike a corrupted Cornelian character. The corruption comes from the fact that it is not reason, but its disincarnated, cerebral form, intellect, which controls her. She submits and dominates her feelings and their outward signs, she studies love like a science ("Cette première nuit, dont on se fait pour l'ordinaire une idée si cruelle ou si douce, ne me présentait qu'une occasion d'expérience . . .") and works out the rules and principles which will guide her every action and her entire life. Mme de Merteuil's actions then are born not from thoughts or feelings but from abstract principles. Because of this *Les Liaisons dangereuses* is in the world of fiction, the farthest and coldest promontory of rationalism.

It is in this famous letter that we come across one phrase which illuminates so vividly the true implication of Mme de Merteuil's "work":[12] "Je puis dire que je suis mon ouvrage". In other words she is an artificial creation and has replaced what is natural by what is unnatural. And the power that has corrupted her is the same one which she in turn will use to corrupt others: intellect. But this intellect, this disembodied form of reason is antithetical to life[13] that is why it corrupts and kills.

At this point of our analysis we find ourselves in the world of Rousseauistic and romantic values. The point which Laclos makes in his novel is simply this: the further one is removed from Nature, the more corrupt one is. Mme de Tourvel, as we have seen, is natural and therefore she is naturally virtuous; Mme de Merteuil, on the other hand is completely corrupted because she has uprooted everything that was natural in her. But the Rousseauistic, typical XVIIIth century sentimentality about Nature is ironically corrected in *Les Liaisons dangereuses* by the presence of Cécile Volange who is both natural and corrupt.

With Mme de Merteuil and Valmont in the centre of the action it is natural that we should find the element which defines them, their intellect, in the centre of the novel. It is through their intellect and through their intellect alone that they act. Seduction becomes an intellectual activity. Rarely if ever does Valmont try to move Mme de Tourvel, but he tries to prove to her that the friendship she offers is unreal and a mask for her real feelings, he tries to prove that she should give herself to him. The fact that the novel is written in letter-form is partly linked to this predominant role intellect plays in the novel. (Seylaz has pointed out the organic nature of the letters in this novel). For letters are above all a medium of exposition or a means of exchanging ideas. When they are used to express feelings—and the love letters of Mme de Tourvel are an example of this—they lose their life and become an insanely monotonous repetition of the same sentiment. Malraux, describing Mme de Tourvel's later letters to Valmont, talks aptly of "le langage opiniâtre et maniaque de la passion véritable".[14]

More important, however, is the fact that the particular horror of *Les Liaisons dangereuses* is also a function of this domination of the intellect, and more especially of the ends towards which this intellect is directed. For what Valmont and Mme de Merteuil seek, eventually, is death and destruction. When intelligence and reason are diverted from their proper end, which is to order and preserve the continuance of human life, and are used to disrupt order and to destroy life, than a state of terror exists. And it is precisely such a state which Laclos describes. Part of the horror of the Concentration Camps comes from this: what inspires terror is not death or torture but the organised way in which they are meted out. And in *Les Liaisons dangereuses* it is not the fact of seduction which is horrifying but the manner in which Valmont seduces and then destroys Mme de Tourvel.

This is what creates the great difference between Valmont and Don Juan. Don Juan is a professional seducer, he is a hard-hearted *Libertin,* but he retains nevertheless some human qualities: he has a certain lighthearted gaiety, and a great deal of courage which we cannot but admire: he remains, however corrupted he might be, *un grand seig-*

neur. But not so Valmont who is a Don Juan but shorn of those qualities which linked Don Juan to our world. Don Juan, when he seduces, uses his charm, and the fact that he has charm is in itself a proof of his humanity. But Valmont, as we have seen, uses his intelligence, and this dehumanises him.

The diversion of intelligence from its proper ends also affects language. For when intelligence and reason cease to fulfill their right function, language, through which they express themselves, also becomes corrupted. Words are emptied of their content and meaning. The fact that the Nazis put over the entrance gate of one of their Concentration Camps the motto *Arbeit adelt den Menschen* indicates neither an ironic intent nor cynicism but is merely an example of this linguistic corruption: it means strictly nothing. In *Les Liaisons dangereuses* we see a very similar phenomenon. Words and notions are emptied of their meaning, turned inside out and upside down. Thus when Mme de Merteuil, writes to Valmont about Cécile: ". . . si une fois vous formez cette petite . . ." or about Mme de Tourvel: "peut-être si vous eussiez connu cette femme plus tôt en eussiezvous pu faire quelque chose", she means exactly the opposite: *former* becomes *déformer; faire, défaire.* We find then, especially centering around Valmont, a deep linguistic uncertainty in Laclos' novel. The words Valmont uses when he writes to Mme de Tourvel or when he writes about her,—have they meaning? are they empty words? We find hanging above *Les Liaisons dangereuses* the same unanswerable question which hangs over Diderot's *Neveu de Rameau* (the Neveu and the protagonists of Laclos' novel certainly have something in common): *Est-ce ironie ou vérité?*

Intellect, thus corrupted and distorted, is nevertheless the force through which Valmont and Mme de Merteuil act. But this intellect is put into the service of higher interests. Valmont and Mme de Merteuil are moved by deeper and darker powers, which use intellect, and of which sex and seduction are but the superficial expression. Here we reach what is in fact the core of this novel. In seeking to seduce, Valmont and Mme de Merteuil do not seek to satisfy a desire, nor is vanity primarily involved. In this sense they go beyond Don Juan. What they seek is to conquer: "Conquérir est notre destin" writes Valmont and it is not by mere chance that this sentence, which illuminates the entire novel, is found in the very first letter Valmont writes to Mme de Merteuil. It is through this sentence that we enter the novel. They seek to conquer, to dominate, and ultimately they seek Power. (It is a great pity the English language does not make the fine and necessary distinction which exists in French between *le pouvoir* and *la puissance*). It is because the novel is really about power that sex, which superficially seems to be the central theme, is, in fact, but a marginal one. This might perhaps explain, at least in part, the strange, abstract quality sex has in this

novel. But, it seems, the rest of the answer to this question must be sought elsewhere. In *Les Liaisons dangereuses* sex is literally disembodied by intellect.[15] The profoundly ironic paradox of this novel is that a disincarnated intellect lives, acts and corrupts through the body. It is because of this that both Valmont and Mme de Merteuil are truly satanic forces.[16] Pride and lust for power are Satan's and their driving force. What the hero and heroine of *Les Liaisons* seek through power is an extension of the self which is, in fact, a desire for spiritual possession of others. Here the role of sex becomes again important: it might be a marginal theme of the novel, but it is the only way by which the possession of one person by another can be directly and concretely expressed.

What Valmont wants is to destroy Mme de Tourvel's will and to replace it by his own; it is in this way too that Mme de Merteuil wants to possess Cécile.

> Quant à Gercourt, premier objet de mes soins, je serais bien malheureuse ou bien maladroite, si, maîtresse de l'esprit de sa femme, comme je le suis et vais l'être plus encore, je ne trouvais pas mille moyens d'en faire ce que je veux qu'il soit.

And she sneers at Valmont for not possessing Cécile in this same manner:

> Ce n'est même pas à vrai dire, une entière jouissance: vous ne possédez absolument que sa personne! je ne parle pas de son coeur, dont je me doute bien que vous ne vous souciez guère: mais vous n'occupez seulement pas sa tête.

But they want to go further. The possession of people is but a means to control events.

> Sans doute, vous ne nierez pas ces vérités que leur évidence a rendues triviales. Si cependant vous m'avez vue, disposant des événements et des opinions, faire de ces hommes si redoutables le jouet de mes caprices ou de mes fantaisies; ôter aux uns la volonté, aux autres la puissance de me nuire.

But in turn this desire to control events is born from the desire to rule out chance, to eradicate contingency, to become destiny. They want, in other words, to become God and the sentence from Mme de Merteuil's autobiographical letter which I quoted earlier ("Je puis dire que je suis mon propre ouvrage") acquires now an even deeper significance. For what creature is self-created and self-generated but God? Laclos is careful to make clear this parallel between Valmont, Mme de Merteuil and God— hence the profoundly blasphemous nature of these two characters. Valmont writes to Mme de Merteuil:

> J'eus l'heureuse et simple idée de tenter de voir à travers la serrure, et je vis en effet cette femme adorable à genoux, baignée de larmes, et priant avec ferveur. Quel Dieu allait-elle invoquer? en est-il d'assez

puissant contre l'amour? En vain cherche-t-elle à présent des secours étrangers: c'est moi qui réglerai son sort.

And even more striking still:

> Oui, j'aime à voir, à considérer cette femme prudente, engagée, sans s'en être aperçue, dans un sentier qui ne permet plus de retour, et dont la pente rapide et dangereuse l'entraîne malgré elle, et la force à me suivre. Là, effrayée du péril qu'elle court, elle voudrait s'arrêter et ne peut se retenir. Ses soins et son adresse peuvent bien rendre ses pas moins grands; mais il faut qu'ils se succèdent. Quelquefois, n'osant fixer le danger, elle ferme les yeux, et se laissant aller, s'abandonne à mes soins. Plus souvent, une nouvelle crainte ranime ses efforts: dans son effroi mortel, elle veut tenter encore de retourner en arrière; elle épuise ses forces pour gravir péniblement un court espace; et bientôt un magique pouvoir la replace plus près de ce danger, que vainement elle avait voulu fuir. Alors n'ayant plus que moi pour guide et pour appui, sans songer à me reprocher davantage une chute inévitable, elle m'implore pour la retarder. Les ferventes prières, les humbles supplications, tout ce que les mortels, dans leur crainte, offrent à la Divinité, c'est moi qui le reçois d'elle; et vous voulez que, sourd à ses voeux, et détruisant moi-même le culte qu'elle me rend, j'emploie à la précipiter, la puissance qu'elle invoque pour la soutenir![17]

Ultimately then, and at its deepest level *Les Liaisons dangereuses* deals with Luciferian evil. It is only when this is clearly seen that the end and the "punishment" of Mme de Merteuil becomes understandable. After the death of Valmont, the machinations of Mme de Merteuil become known, she is ruined by losing her *procès* and, finally disfigured by smallpox, she flees from Paris.

But, and this is of the greatest importance and throws the most revealing light not merely on the end but on the entire novel, Mme de Merteuil does not die. Now, Mme de Merteuil did not, for her evil actions, depend on either her wealth or her looks, but solely on her mind. But this truly satanic mind, now housed in a disfigured body, remains untouched. The real Mme de Merteuil continues to live. She cannot die. She is immortal and indestructible in the same way that evil is immortal and indestructible.

Notes

1. J. Giraudoux, *Littérature,* Paris, Grasset, n.d., p. 63.

2. *Mémoires du Comte de Tilly pour servir à l'histoire des moeurs de la fin du XVIIIᵉ siècle,* quoted in Choderlos de Laclos, *Oeuvres Complètes.* Paris, Bibliothèque de la Pléiade, n.d., p. 733. The italics are in the text and indicate that these were the actual words spoken by Laclos.

3. J. Boulenger, *Le Grand siècle,* quoted by Denis de Rougemont, *L'Amour et l'Occident,* Paris, Plon, n.d., p. 255.

4. Denis de Rougemont, op. cit., p. 21

5. Valmont and Mme de Merteuil are not unaware of this link with a far removed past, as this passage, in which Mme de Merteuil uses ironically the language of courtly love, clearly shows (p. 37): "Je veux donc bien vous instruire de mes projets: mais jurez-moi qu'en fidèle Chevalier, vous ne courrez aucune aventure que vous n'ayez mis celle-ci à fin. Elle est digne d'un Héros: vous servirez l'amour et la vengeance."

6. J. Huizinga, *The Waning of the Middle-Ages,* London, Edward Arnold, p. 96.

7. A. Gide, *Oeuvres Complètes,* Paris Gallimard, n.d. vol. VII, p. 453.

8. See J. Giraudoux, *Littérature,* Paris, Grasset, pp. 57-75.

9. I would like to record here my indebtedness to Seylaz's remarkable book, *La Création romanesque chez Laclos,* Paris, Lib. Michard, 1958.

10. Writing about Balzac, William Troy also gives a clear description of the type of society we find in Laclos' novel: "Even in *Antigone,* in which the claims of society are held in uncertain balance with more ancient pieties, society stands for order—an objective authoritative norm by which individual conduct can be measured. But the society that Balzac describes is itself given over to unregenerate expression of 'Will'; it is simply an aggregation of predatory individuals." ("On re-reading Balzac", *Kenyon Review,* summer 1940).

11. It is in this sense that one could speak of *Les Liaisons* as a manichean novel.

12. "Le travail sur moi-même," "Je me suis travaillée avec le même soin. . . ."

13. Writing about the prejudice existing against intellect Jacques Barzun says: "Indeed if we look further into this primal anti-intellectualism, we find it enshrines a true perception and an impulse of respect. The perception is that, like all artifacts, Intellect is the enemy of life." *The House of Intellect,* London, Secker and Warburg, 1959, p. 8.

14. A. Malraux, "Choderlos de Laclos", in *Tableau de la littérature française.* Paris, Gallimard, n.d., p. 419.

15. It is this which transforms the sexual act into an erotic one, eroticism being essentially an intellectualisation of sex. The French prostitutes call their clients with peculiar tastes *des Cérébraux.*

16. The corruptible flesh made not the soul to sin, but the sinning soul made the flesh corruptible. From which corruption although there arise some incitements unto sin, and some vicious desires, yet are not all the sins of an evil life to be laid upon the flesh; otherwise we shall make *the devil, that has no flesh,* sinless: for though we cannot call him a fornicator, a drunkard, or by any one of those carnally vicious names (though he be a secret

provoker of man unto all those), yet is he truly styled most proud and envious, which vices have possessed him so far, that on account of them he is destined unto eternal torment in the prisons of this obscure air. Now those vices that domineer in him the apostle calls the works of the flesh, though certain it is that he has no flesh. For he says that enmity, contention, emulation, wrath, and envy are the works of the flesh; to all which pride gives being, yet rules pride in *the fleshless devil.* (My italics. C. J. G.) St. Augustin, *The City of God,* Bk. XIV, ch. III.

17. Would it be far fetched to see in this paragraph a parody of Bossuet's famous passage from his *Sermon pour le jour de Pâques:*

"Je voudrais retourner en arrière: Marche! marche! Un poids invincible, une force irrésistible nous entraînent; il faut sans cesse avancer vers le précipice. Mille traverses, mille peines nous fatiguent et nous inquiètent dans la route. Encore si je pouvais éviter ce précipice affreux! Non, non; il faut marcher, il faut courir: telle est la rapidité des années. On se console pourtant, parce que de temps en temps on rencontre des objets qui nous divertissent, des eaux courantes, des fleurs qui passent. On voudrait s'arrêter: Marche! marche! Et cependant on voit tomber derrière soi tout ce qu'on avait passé: fracas effroyable! inévitable ruine!"

Susan Dunn (essay date 1980)

SOURCE: "Education and Seduction in *Les Liaisons Dangereuses,*" *Symposium,* Vol. 24, No. 2, Summer, 1980, pp. 125-37.

[*In the essay below, Dunn links Laclos's ideas about morality and equality in* Les Liaisons dangereuses *to his later writing on the education of women.*]

The problem of education is central to *Les Liaisons dangereuses* and is part of its thematics of power and sexuality. In addition, Laclos's attitude toward education may provide a way to view the question of the morality or immorality of the novel. In the *Préface du Rédacteur,* Laclos agrees with the mother who told him that she read the manuscript of *Les Liaisons dangereuses* and found it an ideal pre-nuptial education for a young woman: "Je croirais . . . rendre un vrai service à ma fille, en lui donnant ce Livre le jour de son mariage."[1] The *Préface,* then, already anticipates the question of women's education and the relation between education and sexuality. The novel itself begins under the sign of education. Cécile, still something of a Lockean *tabula rasa* after her convent education, is unprepared for life and society. Will she be seduced by Valmont or married to Gercourt? It might seem as if the pretext or even the motor of the plot is the educa-

tion of Gercourt. Madame de Merteuil seeks to expose his hypocritical illusions and his faith in a convent education as a guarantee of a wife's fidelity. However, Laclos is interested not in the education of Gercourt, but rather in the problem of education for women in a society where women are neither free nor equal.

In 1783, the year after the publication of *Les Liaisons dangereuses,* Laclos began composing three essays on women's education which remained unpublished until 1904.[2] In the first essay, Laclos discusses the meaning of the word "education." Although he does not specifically mention its Latin root, he does insist, in his definition, upon the two concepts of development (*ducere*) and direction (*ex*): "Ou le mot éducation ne présente aucun sens, ou l'on ne peut l'entendre que du développement des facultés vers l'utilité sociale."[3] Laclos then describes two distortions of education, two ways in which education can be perverted: "si au lieu d'étendre les facultés on les restreint, . . . ce n'est plus éducation, c'est dépravation; si au lieu de les diriger vers l'utilité sociale on les replie sur l'individu, c'est seulement alors instinct perfectionné" (p. 404). One cannot say that an individual is educated if his faculties are restrained: this is "dépravation" for Laclos, an unusual sense of the word, but I shall adopt it here. If, on the other hand, the individual's faculties are indeed developed but for his benefit only and not for the social good, Laclos calls this "instinct perfectionné."

The most perverse form of education, which goes unmentioned in this essay and yet plays the greatest role in *Les Liaisons dangereuses,* is seduction. The words "seduction" and "education" share the same Latin root, but whereas education leads the student forth, seduction (*seducere*) leads the student astray. In *Les Liaisons dangereuses,* seduction, corruption, and education are virtually inseparable.

The educator and the seducer are one and the same person. Valmont and Madame de Merteuil do not dissociate their interest in education from their devotion to seduction. And pupils like Cécile and Danceny discover sooner or later that they have been not only educated but also seduced. Being a pupil and being the victim of a seduction seem to be equally demeaning conditions. Even Valmont will discover himself in the double situation of pupil and victim of seduction.

Madame de Merteuil understands clearly the interrelationship between education and seduction and uses this knowledge to ensure her own freedom and control over others. She is certainly never seduced, and she is educated by no one but herself. She refuses to yield to the will of another, whether educator or seducer. She will make others be object to her subject: she herself will never be object. There is no Other in her education of herself: no one else will touch her mind or her heart. She is her own "ouvrage": "Je n'avais à moi que ma pensée, et je m'indignais qu'on pût me la ravir ou me la surprendre contre ma volonté . . . non contente de ne plus me laisser pénétrer, je m'amusais à me montrer sous des formes différentes" (pp. 176-77). The sexual resonances of words like "ravir" and "pénétrer" reveal the parallels between seduction and education. Yielding the autonomy and integrity of her mind to another would be the intellectual equivalent of seduction or rape; indeed, in this case, the teacher is considered perhaps even more dangerous than the seducer.

For the Marquise, education is a way to gain mastery over herself and control over others. Such education is completely self-contained. This special kind of narcissism seems to be what Laclos called "instinct perfectionné." The individual's faculties are not directed toward a social good. Rather, "on les replie sur l'individu." Indeed, the knowledge Madame de Merteuil seeks to gain from her education has no social function whatsoever. Her desire for knowledge is inseparable from her desire to understand pleasure. For her, understanding sexuality all but replaces enjoying its physicality: "Ma tête seule fermentait; je ne désirais pas de jouir, je voulais savoir; le désir de m'instruire m'en suggéra les moyens" (p. 177). The locus of this education is not the classroom but the bed, and her own initiation into sexuality is an initiation of the mind far more than of the body: "Cette première nuit, dont on se fait pour l'ordinaire une idée si cruelle ou si douce, ne me présentait qu'une occasion d'expérience: douleur et plaisir, j'observai tout exactement, et ne voyais dans ces diverses sensations, que des faits à recueillir et à méditer" (p. 178). Since she has banished all others from participation in her education, even in bed she makes no mention of the Other.

Education, inseparable from Eros, is also inseparable, for the Marquise, from theatre: "Cette utile curiosité, en servant à m'instruire, m'apprit encore à dissimuler" (p. 176). She studies the art of the mask: "Ressentais-je quelque chagrin, je m'étudiais à prendre l'air de la sérénité, même celui de la joie" (p. 176). She uses the works of novelists, philosophers, and strict moralists in order to understand how, respectively, one *could* behave, how one *should* think, and how one *must* appear: "J'etudiai nos murs dans les romans; nos opinions dans les philosophes; je cherchai même dans les moralistes les plus sévères ce qu'ils exigeaient de nous, et je m'assurai ainsi de ce qu'on pouvait faire, de ce qu'on devait penser, et de ce qu'il fallait paraître" (p. 178-79). Education, sexuality, and role-playing all converge when Madame de Merteuil prepares a seduction. She then turns to books to help her play her sexual role: "je lis un chapitre du *Sopha,* une lettre d'*Héloïse* et deux Contes de La Fontaine, pour recorder les différents tons que je voulais prendre" (p. 30).

However, Madame de Merteuil also recognizes that education and sexuality are not always interrelated. In fact, the very process of aging ultimately obliges women to reconsider their education seriously, in a new and different, non-sexual, light. As her sexual attractiveness diminishes, the intelligent older woman will appreciate the importance of the life of the mind:

> C'est de quarante à cinquante ans que le désespoir de voir leur figure se flétrir, la rage de se sentir obligées d'abandonner des prétentions et des plaisirs auxquels elles tiennent encore, rendent presque toutes les femmes bégueules et acariâtres. Il leur faut ce long intervalle pour faire en entier ce grand sacrifice: mais dès qu'il est consommé, toutes se partagent en deux classes.
>
> La plus nombreuse, celle des femmes qui n'ont eu pour elles que leur figure et leur jeunesse, tombe dans une imbécile apathie. . . .
>
> L'autre classe, beaucoup plus rare, mais véritablement précieuse, est celle des femmes qui, ayant eu un caractère et n'ayant pas négligé de nourrir leur raison, savent se créer une existence, quand celle de la nature leur manque; et prennent le parti de mettre à leur esprit, les parures qu'elles employaient avant pour leur figure. (pp. 268-69)

Madame de Merteuil's stance is usually rigorously individualistic. She writes to Valmont: "ne me confondez plus avec les autres femmes" (p. 190). However, in this discourse, she perceives aging primarily as a social problem and realizes that, at least in this regard, her destiny is inevitably similar to that of other women and that there is nothing she can do to control or alter this situation. In her analysis, Madame de Merteuil unexpectedly separates education and sexuality, indeed opposes one to the other. But this is, of course, precisely a function of the nature of the problem of aging for women.[4]

In addition, although the Marquise makes a point of refusing all affective bonds with men, she seems to have genuine affection for certain older women and to enjoy their company: "ayant toujours recherché les vieilles femmes, dont j'ai reconnu de bonne heure l'utilité des suffrages, j'ai rencontré plusieurs d'entre elles auprès de qui l'inclination me ramenait autant que l'intérêt" (p. 269). Madame de Merteuil is thus not without female role models: there are women whose judgment, goodness, intelligence, and understanding she admires. And yet, her own attempt to be the role model of another woman, to educate Cécile, and make of her a free woman, becomes a purely destructive enterprise.

Madame de Merteuil seems interested in having Cécile as her student and disciple: "je m'attache sincèrement à elle. Je lui ai promis de la former et je crois que je lui tiendrai parole" (p. 114). There is nevertheless confusion between the education of Cécile and her seduction. Madame de

Merteuil's own sexual ambivalence makes it unclear, even to her, whether she is educator or seducer (or seduced): "elle me prie de l'instruire avec une bonne foi réellement séduisante. En vérité, je suis presque jalouse de celui à qui ce plaisir est réservé" (p. 81). Madame de Merteuil, in this case, makes no clear distinction between education and sexuality. She views sexual knowledge as a prerequisite for all other knowledge. If Cécile is to be her pupil and to have a relationship of mutual trust with her, the Marquise insists that Cécile first be seduced and corrupted: "Je me suis souvent aperçue du besoin d'avoir une femme dans ma confidence, et j'aimerais mieux celle-là qu'une autre; mais je ne puis en rien faire, tant qu'elle ne sera pas . . . ce qu'il faut qu'elle soit" (p. 114). Madame de Merteuil sees no contradiction in helping Valmont plan his seduction of Cécile and, at the same time, in regarding Cécile as a pupil whom she likes and even trusts: "Si la petite fille en revient telle qu'elle y aura été, je m'en prendrai à vous. Si vous jugez qu'elle ait besoin de quelque encouragement de ma part, mandez-le-moi. Je crois lui avoir donné une assez bonne leçon sur le danger de garder des Lettres, pour oser lui écrire à présent; et je suis toujours dans le dessein d'en faire mon élève" (p. 131).

For Madame de Merteuil, seduction is either an essential part of education or is in itself an education. But if a calculated sexual initiation is indeed a mode of education, Cécile must be made aware, not of her victimization, but of her own freedom. In Letter CV, Madame de Merteuil in effect communicates her own principles to Cécile, once again linking sexuality, education, and role playing. She explains to Cécile the primacy of pleasure and the need for dealing with the hypocrisy of society in order to ensure one's pleasure, telling her how to maintain an appearance of purity with one lover in order to enjoy clandestine pleasure with another. She demonstrates how marriage, correctly understood and exploited, can be liberating: "Une fois plus contente de vous, votre Maman vous mariera enfin; et alors, plus libre dans vos démarches, vous pourrez, à votre choix, quitter Valmont pour prendre Danceny, ou même les garder tous deux" (pp. 248-49). Madame de Merteuil's didactic letter ends with a postscript on the art of letter writing, a lesson in the stylistics of hypocrisy: "quand vous écrivez à quelqu'un, c'est pour lui et non pas pour vous: vous devez donc moins chercher à lui dire ce que vous pensez, que ce qui lui plaît davantage" (p. 249).[5] Madame de Merteuil models Cécile's education after her own, in as much as Cécile's intellectual initiation consists of instruction in theatre and Eros. The Marquise had even hoped to make a fellow actress of Cécile: "j'avais eu quelque envie d'en faire au moins une intrigante subalterne, et de la prendre pour jouer les seconds sous moi" (p. 251).

But although Madame de Merteuil begins, in Letter CV, to communicate precious knowledge to Cécile, on the very same day she writes to Valmont that she is abandoning Cécile as her pupil: "Je me désintéresse entièrement sur son compte . . . je vois qu'il n'y a pas d'étoffe" (p. 251). She says that Cécile is nothing more than a "machine à plaisir" and that her "sotte ingénuité" is incurable. The seduction that might have been a form of education or a first step to freedom, now means only corruption. Cécile will ultimately be aware, not of her potential freedom, but only of her victimization and "dépravation."

Valmont's attitude toward Cécile's "education" is more perfidious than Madame de Merteuil's, for he considers all education a form of corruption: "Je regrette de n'avoir pas le talent des filous. Ne devrait-il pas, en effet, entrer dans l'éducation d'un homme qui se mêle d'intrigues? . . . Mais nos parents ne songent à rien" (p. 90). Valmont establishes a curriculum of sexual and intellectual corruption, rather than seeing Cécile's education/seduction as a prelude to her independence and freedom: his intentions are exclusively destructive. In order to ensure that Cécile's "dépravation" would be irremediable, he plotted a way to destroy her self-respect: "je lui inspirais . . . le plus profond mépris pour sa mère. J'ai remarqué depuis longtemps, que si ce moyen n'est pas toujours nécessaire à employer pour séduire une jeune fille, il est indispensable . . . quand on veut la dépraver; car celle qui ne respecte pas sa mère, ne se respectera pas elle-même" (p. 263). Valmont seeks a corruption of the mind as well as of the body. He is delighted that "l'écolière est devenue presque aussi savante que le maître" (p. 263), but he is interested in controlling her mind perhaps even more than her body. Like Madame de Merteuil, who ends her lesson for Cécile in sexual amorality with advice on hypocrisy in letter-writing and who begins her seduction of Danceny with opposite advice on sincerity in letter-writing (Letter CXXI), Valmont is also compelled to exercise his power over his pupil's sense of language: "j'occupe mon loisir . . . à composer une espèce de catéchisme de débauche, à l'usage de mon écolière. Je m'amuse à n'y rien nommer que par le mot technique; et je ris d'avance de l'intéressante conversation que cela doit fournir entre elle et Gercourt la première nuit de leur mariage" (p. 264). Between them, Madame de Merteuil and Valmont make sure that Cécile's language, written and spoken, reflects hypocrisy and corruption. Losing control over one's use of language is perhaps the ultimate symbol of servitude and humiliation, especially in a society where one exists in as much as one writes and receives letters.

There are, then, two models of seduction: it can be an initiation into and a prerequisite of education; or it can be merely corruption and "dépravation." But not only is seduction, when disguised as education, a form of "dépravation"; Cécile's other education, her convent education, is also "dépravation," according to the definition Laclos gave in his first essay on women's education. The convent education, forbidding autonomy and preventing a young woman's intellectual and sexual development, as well as the sexual victimization that is seduction, are both forms of "dépravation." One denies the flesh, the other exploits it: both deprive women of consciousness and freedom.

The power relationship between student and teacher, which to such a great extent characterizes education, is typical, for Laclos, of all social and affective relationships. In his second essay on women's education, he describes society as the battlefield in the war between the sexes. Contrasting the state of nature with his own highly developed society, he finds that "la nature ne crée que des êtres libres; la société ne fait que des tyrans et des esclaves. Parcourez l'univers connu, vous trouverez l'homme fort et tyran, la femme faible et esclave" (p. 433). Laclos does not discuss at length the origin of this universal inequality; he says only that women "ont étè primitivement subjuguées, et que l'homme a sur elles un droit de conquête dont il use rigoureusement" (p. 434). His real interest lies in analyzing the institutions and the behavior that are the product of the war between the sexes. A complex system of values (ideological, social, affective, esthetic) owes its existence to the imbalance of power between men and women. And perhaps the most important of these values is love. For Laclos, love, as we know it in society, is not primarily a natural or authentic emotion; it is a reaction, emanating from resentment (re-sentiment) and not from spontaneous feeling (sentiment). He argues that love is the invention and strategem of women in their struggle to regain lost power:

> Elles sentirent enfin que, puisqu'elles étaient plus faibles, leur unique ressource était de séduire; elles connurent que si elles étaient dépendantes de ces hommes par la force, ils pouvaient le devenir á elles par le plaisir . . . elles pratiquèrent l'art pénible de refuser lors même qu'elles désiraient de consentir; de ce moment elles surent allumer l'imagination des hommes, elles surent à leur gré faire naître et diriger les désirs: ainsi naquirent la beauté et l'amour. (pp. 434-36)

Therefore, in a society in which men and women are unequal, a love relationship cannot reestablish equality. Love is not the solution to the problem of the war between the sexes; to the contrary, it is a product of that war. On this issue, Madame de Merteuil's position seems close to Laclos's. She writes to Valmont: "Jamais vous n'êtes ni l'amant ni l'ami d'une femme; mais toujours son tyran ou son esclave" (p. 337). And, of course, no happy or even satisfactory love relationship is anywhere to be seen in the novel, nor could it be. Power and inequality corrupt love as they corrupt education. Just as love, in a society where women are unequal and inferior, is not love but seduction, education in that same society is also a form of seduction. Neither the real love nor the real education we may assume to be possible in the state of nature can occur in

society: "Partout où il y a esclavage, il ne peut y avoir éducation; dans toute société, les femmes sont esclaves; donc la femme sociale n'est pas susceptible d'éducation . . . c'est le propre de l'éducation de développer les facultés, le propre de l'esclavage c'est de les étouffer" (p. 405).

In *Les Liaisons dangereuses* tyrants educate slaves. The young woman is totally dependent upon the teacher or authority figure and has no resources of her own: "Madame de Merteuil me prêterait des Livres qui parlaient de tout cela, et qui m'apprendraient bien à me conduire, et aussi à mieux écrire que je ne fais" (p. 64). And the guardian— here Valmont—insists on the passivity of his ward: "Adieu, ma belle pupille: car vous êtes ma pupille. Aimez un peu votre tuteru, et surtout ayez avec lui de la docilité" (p. 189). In Laclos's first essay on women's education, he despairs of the possibility of educating women in a society so profoundly rooted in the inequality of the sexes: "il n'est aucun moyen de perfectionner l'éducation des femmes . . . l'éducation prétendue, donnée aux femmes jusqu'à ce jour, ne mérite pas en effet le nom d'éducation" (p. 403). However, in his third essay on education, he offers concrete suggestions for educating a young woman who would not be subordinate to an authority figure. In this essay, he speaks not once of a student or of a teacher, but only of the young woman and her "guide." In describing this guide, Laclos emphasizes equality, understanding, and sharing rather than authority; the guide should be "quelqu'un d'éclairé et d'adroit qui fit dans le même temps les mêmes lectures, avec qui on pût causer chaque jour, et qui sût diriger l'opinion sans la dicter" (p. 457). Stressing the absolute primacy of the young woman's personal judgment, Laclos suggests an alternative way for the student to form her own opinions without a guide: "Il est un moyen peut-être plus utile, mais aussi plus sévère; c'est de faire de chaque ouvrage, à mesure qu'on l'a lu, un extrait dans le genre de ceux qu'on met dans les journaux: contenant un compte rendu de l'ouvrage suffisant pour en donner une idée, et un jugement motivé du même ouvrage" (p. 457). Like Montaigne, Laclos also believes that the young woman's capacity for independent judgment and not her acceptance of authority should be both the means and the end of education.

The consequences of power and inequality in education concern men as well as women. Valmont, as much as Cécile, falls victim in the power struggle that is education. It is symptomatic of Madame de Merteuil's ascendancy in her relationship with Valmont that she begins to treat him as schoolboy: "vous restez court comme un Ecolier" (p. 251). "Je m'étonne, je l'avoue, que ce soit moi que vous ayez entrepris de traiter comme un écolier" (p. 357). Although he is confused by his double role as Madame de Merteuil's rival and her *chevalier,* Valmont finally submits to her authority and accepts the role of pupil and slave.

Madame de Merteuil chides Valmont, as she chided Cécile and Danceny, about his letter-writing: "Relisez votre Lettre: il y règne un ordre qui vous décèle à chaque phrase" (p. 70). But she truly humiliates and destroys him when he agrees, without reflection or understanding, to copy a letter she composed and to send it as his own. He places himself in the same degrading role of *écolier* that he imposed upon Cécile when he dictated to her a letter (CXVII) for Danceny. Revolted by the reality of his *esclavage,* Valmont tries, in a last vain effort, to reestablish some semblance of equality with Madame de Merteuil and to reconquer the role of teacher by placing her in the subordinate role of student. He gropes ineffectually, grasping portentously at trivial straws, for proof that she is an inadequate educator:

> Puisque vous commencez à faire des éducations, apprenez à vos élèves à ne pas rougir et se déconcerter à la moindre plaisanterie: à ne pas nier si vivement, pour une seule femme, les mêmes choses dont ils se défendent avec tant de mollesse pour toutes les autres. Apprenezleur encore à savoir entendre l'éloge de leur Maîtresse, sans se croire obligés d'en faire les honneurs. . . . Albors vous pourrez les faire paraître dans vos exercices publics, sans que leur conduite fasse tort à leur sage institutrice; et moi-même, trop heureux de concourir à votre célébrité, je vous promets de faire et de publier les programmes de ce nouveau collège. (p. 357)

Power and authority, however, elude Valmont and finally, unable to mask his weakness, he can only issue a self-destructive ultimatum: "je serai ou votre Amant ou votre ennemi" (p. 361).

At the same time Valmont is becoming the unwitting pupil of Madame de Merteuil, he pretends to be the pupil of Madame de Tourvel, convinced of his ability to exploit the student-teacher power relationship for his own advantage. He first claims to be seduced by Madame de Tourvel's virtue: "séduit . . . ici par l'exemple des vertus, sans espérer de vous atteindre, j'ai au moins essayé de vous suivre" (p. 52). Valmont then moves from the language of seduction to the language of education. He feigns abdication of his autonomy by promising to be her obedient student, eager for knowledge and enlightenment: "Prêtezmoi votre raison, puisque vous avez ravi la mienne; après m'avoir corrigé, éclairez-moi pour finir mon ouvrage . . . vous m'apprendrez à . . . régler [l'amour]: en guidant mes démarches, en dictant mes discours, vous me sauverez au moins du malheur affreux de vous déplaire" (p. 56).

Although Valmont intended to be master by playing the role of slave and student, after he had succeeded in seducing Madame de Tourvel, he was forced to wonder whether indeed there had been a role and power reversal: "Je chéris cette façon de voir, qui me sauve l'humiliation de penser que je puisse dépendre en quelque manière de l'esclave même que je me serais asservie" (p. 297). He understands that the role has become reality. Valmont, seducer, believing that he has been seduced, expresses his sense of bewilderment and powerlessness by returning once again to the language of education. He wonders whether he has truly become a pupil: "Serai-je, à mon âge, mâitrisé comme un écolier?" (p. 296). Valmont, student in spite of himself, may also receive an education in spite of himself, a heretofore refused or repressed understanding of emotion. For the first time, he is overwhelmed by his feelings: "l'ivresse fut complète et réciproque" (p. 304). He seems to glimpse the possibility of a love that is based not on power but on mutual feeling and sharing. We may believe him when he says: "je regrette Madame de Tourvel . . . je suis au désespoir d'être séparé d'elle . . . je paierais de la moitié de ma vie, le bonheur de lui consacrer l'autre" (p. 366). The seducer, Valmont, has not been seduced by Madame de Tourvel, for we must not confuse the love she inspired with artifice. It is because Valmont's love for Madame de Tourvel may be authentic and not the result of seduction that education is possible. Any meaningful education must issue from equality and reciprocity and not from servitude or power.

In his relationships with both Madame de Merteuil and Madame de Tourvel, Valmont loses the advantage, and in both cases Laclos expresses his fall through the image of the pupil. In their war with men, women will occasionally seize the advantage and defeat their enemy: "dans l'état de guerre perpétuelle qui subsiste entre elles et les hommes, on les a vues, à l'aide des caresses qu'elles ont su se créer, combattre sans cesse, vaincre quelquefois, et souvent, plus adroites, tirer avantage des forces mêmes dirigées contre elles" (p. 436). Both men and women, forced by centuries of tradition into mistaking seduction and "dépravation" for education and into confusing seduction and love, suffer from the consequences of man's tyranny over woman.

Does this novel about education and seduction educate or seduce its reader? In the *Préface du Rédacteur,* Laclos presents himself as a moralist who is writing this novel to counteract the corrupting influence of certain people: "Il me semble au moins que c'est rendre un service aux murs, que de dévoiler les moyens qu'emploient ceux qui en ont de mauvaises pour corrompre ceux qui en ont de bonnes" (p. 8). The novel may then be thought of as an educational experience for the reader who will be taught to understand and to resist corruption and seduction. Laclos tells us that his novel reveals two truths, both of which protect against the danger of seduction: "l'une, que toute femme qui consent à recevoir dans sa sociéte un homme sans murs, finit par en devenir la victime; l'autre, que toute mère est au moins imprudente, qui souffre qu'un autre qu'elle ait la confiance de sa fille" (p. 8). These two "truths" do, in fact, correspond to the structure of the novel: the first refers to Madame de Tourvel's problematic situation, the second to

Cécile's. Although one tends to discount statements authors make about their books, especially moral statements made by eighteenth-century novelists, we cannot always dismiss an author's conscious intentions. Nor can we always consider unconscious motivation more important than conscious thought. Thody's judgment that Laclos is sincere in his *Préface* and that his advice to women is indeed sound seems judicious.[6]

In the *Préface,* Laclos also raises the problem of censorship and education, implying that, under certain conditions, the novel itself may seduce rather than educate its reader. Laclos agrees with the mother who would not let her daughter read *Les Liaisons dangereuses* until the day of her wedding. It is not immediately clear why this novel—which, after all, contains not one happily united couple, which undermines and mocks marriage, which exposes a cruel but triumphant double standard—would constitute an ideal nuptial education for a woman, or why the wedding day is the most propitious moment for this education. And it is not clear why Laclos believes that his own novel, although dealing with the problem of women's education, should be the object of censorship.

In his third essay on women's education, concerned specifically with the role of reading in a woman's education, Laclos speaks of the problem of choice and guidance in what one reads. He offers the example of a novel about seduction, *Clarissa,* and shows how guidance, not censorship, will help the young woman: "On peut donc craindre qu'une jeune personne ne soit rassurée par cet exemple et . . . cette lecture peut lui être dangereuse. Mais si, au contraire, on fait observer à la jeune personne que Clarisse . . . a été nécessairement entraînée dans tous les malheurs dont elle finit par être la victime, alors il y aura peu de lectures plus utiles" (p. 455). A novel about seduction, such as *Clarissa* or *Les Liaisons dangereuses,* can be a means of education, but the same novel, read without discernment, can be seduction and corruption.

When reading Laclos's *Préface du Rédacteur,* it is important to realize that he is talking about his novel both as a tool of education ("l'utilité de l'ouvrage") and as a potential instrument of seduction ("loin de conseiller cette lecture à la jeunesse, il me paraît très important d'éloigner d'elle toutes celles de ce genre" [p. 8]). Whether *Les Liaisons dangereuses* educates or seduces its reader will depend on his or (particularly) her level of awareness and discernment. Will the reader be seduced by the charismatic and cruel Madame de Merteuil and Valmont? Will the reader identify with these fascinating characters and become, in his or her turn, seducer? If the reader is not seduced and is educated instead, he or she may then become more critical of the hypocrisy of society and more sensitive to the problems encountered by women. Above

all, he may come to see the need to educate young women in order to prevent their seduction.[7] The reader may find *Les Liaisons dangereuses* a highly moral novel: "*Les Liaisons dangereuses* is a moral book because it shows very clearly what happens to people when they are immoral in the deepest and most dangerous way possible: by treating others as if they were objects to be manipulated and not as individuals to be respected" (Thody, p. 67). Alternatively, he might wonder about the impact of Laclos's artistic creation on his moral intentions: "Laclos voulait démontrer le 'danger des liaisons' et il a écrit le roman séduisant de la séduction. Le moraliste en lui a été vaincu par le romancier."[8] Or, finally, the reader might simply be seduced and captivated by cruelty, intelligence, and egoism: "The downfall of Merteuil concerns only a superficial loss of fortune and beauty, leaving her great mind untouched."[9] The ambiguous relationship between education and seduction is ultimately not only the problem of a pupil and victim such as Cécile; it is also the problem of each one of the readers of *Les Liaisons dangereuses.*

The wide spectrum of views held by intelligent critics concerning the morality or immorality of *Les Liaisons dangereuses* suggests the great amount of freedom Laclos grants his readers. In his second essay on women's education, in which he studies the effects of society and social institutions on women and presents an ahistorical model of the condition of women in a state of nature, Laclos's bias is clear; he describes the woman of the eighteenth century as "défigurée par nos institutions" (p. 406). In spite of this, he nevertheless specifically states that he will attempt to withhold judgment so that his reader can evaluate for himself the material and hypotheses presented in the essay: "Ont-elles gagné ou perdu à ces institutions? Nous prétendons moins décider cette question que mettre nos lecteurs en état de le faire" (p. 406). In both *Les Liaisons dangereuses* and the second essay on women's education, Laclos poses the problem of the condition of women and places his reader in the problematical situation of deciding what is corruption and what is morality.

However, the moral judgment ultimately made by the reader will be an indication of his freedom from or involvement in a corrupt and unequal society, for Laclos holds strongly that social and intellectual freedom is and must be the guarantee of morality, without which there can be no education: "on ne peut sortir de ce principe général que sans liberté point de moralité et sans moralité point d'éducation" (p. 405). In a society where men and women are free and equal, education goes hand in hand with morality. But in a society founded on principles of inequality between the sexes and in which social and sexual relationships take on the characteristics of a power struggle, education, as we have seen, comes to be confused with seduction and corruption. Laclos's descriptions of sexual and moral corruption are indeed seductive—

purposely and necessarily seductive. However, description should not be confused with prescription: Laclos clearly believes in education and morality, freedom and equality. As a response to the reader who is convinced of the immorality of the novel, Laclos might have called to his attention the words of Seneca used as the epigraph in his first essay on women's education: "Le mal est sans remèdes quand les vices se sont changés en murs" (p. 403).

Notes

1. Choderlos de Laclos, *Les Liaisons dangereuses in uvres complètes* (Paris: Gallimard, 1951), pp. 8-9. All parenthetical page references are to this edition.

2. For a discussion of the place of Laclos among eighteenth-century theoreticians of women's education, see Laurent Versini, *Laclos et la tradition* (Paris: Klincksiek, 1968), pp. 521-79.

3. Choderlos de Laclos, *De l'éducation des femmes in Oeuvres*, p. 404. Parenthetical page references are to this edition.

4. In his chapter "De la vieillesse et de la mort" in the second essay on women's education, Laclos goes to some length to deny sexual satisfaction to the aging woman and man:

   O! quel spectacle hideux présente cette femme effrénée, dont l'âge n'a pu modérer les désirs, et qui recherche encore un plaisir qu'elle ne peut plus faire partager! Que de peines lui sont préparées! A combien d'humiliations elle doit s'attendre! L'homme, dans ce même cas, n'est pas moins ridicule, mais il peut être moins malheureux; s'il possède un reste de puissance, le vil intérêt lui fera trouver une fille complaisante . . . La femme n'a pas même cette ressource douteuse; en vain, a-t-elle employé les mêmes moyens pour s'attacher un homme; il perd, entre ses bras, la force qu'il avait promise; il reste mort, entre elle et sa fortune (p. 419).

5. Laclos also believes that learning to write well is essential to a woman's education: "il n'est plus permis à une femme qui prétend à quelque éducation personnelle d'écrire sans pureté et même sans élégance" (p. 450).

6. P. M. W. Thody, "*Manon Lescaut* and *Les Liaisons dangereuses:* The Problems of Morality in Literature," *Modern Languages,* 56 (1975), p. 63.

7. In the next to last letter of the novel, Danceny blames the seduction of Cécile on her convent education: "Quelle jeune personne, sortant de même du couvent, sans experience et presque sans idees, et ne portant dans le monde . . . qu'une egale ignorance du bien et du mal; quelle jeune personne, dis-je, aurait pu résister davantage à de si coupables artifices" (pp. 396-97).

8. René Pomeau, "D'*Ernestine* aux *Liaisons dangereuses:* le dessein de Laclos," *Revue d'Histoire Littéraire de la France,* 68 (1968), p. 631.

9. Dianne Alstad, "*Les Liaisons dangereuses:* Hustlers and Hypocrites," *Yale French Studies,* 40 (1968), p. 166.

Susan Dunn (essay date 1984)

SOURCE: "Valmont, Actor and Spectator," *The French Review,* Vol. LVIII, No. 1, October, 1984, pp. 41-7.

[*In the essay below, Dunn analyzes Valmont's role as an actor and an observer in the novel, arguing that his inability to understand himself ultimately destroys him.*]

Madame de Merteuil and the Vicomte de Valmont are essentially theatrical beings, brilliant and entertaining performers who weave webs of illusion and deception in which they trap their victims, exploiting the gullibility of others while assuring their own power and freedom. Their acting ability is a function not of talent, emotion, or sincerity, but rather of intelligence and will: to perform is to be in possession of oneself and of one's role.

Students of *Les Liaisons dangereuses* have often seen Valmont and Madame de Merteuil as actors ("Ce sont des protagonistes libertins, toujours masqués, toujours acteurs"[1]), realizing that although both are ultimately victims of their own belief in theater, Madame de Merteuil is a totally successful actress, whereas Valmont can only be characterized as an *acteur manqué.*[2]

Les Liaisons dangereuses, however, is concerned with the spectators of the performance almost as much as it is concerned with those who perform. Jean Rousset demonstrates that the reader of *Les Liaisons dangereuses,* "observateur d'intimités," occupies the special position of knowing not only what each correspondent is thinking but also what they are all thinking simultaneously and unbeknownst to each other. Because Merteuil and Valmont read letters not destined for them, they share the privileged situation of the reader. Rousset suggests that an equality and a complicity are thereby established between the reader and the *couple libertin (Forme et signification,* p. 99). Seen in this light, the observer is a person of intelligence, lucidity, comprehension, and power.

Other critics, too, assimilate the powerful actor with the intelligent, and therefore powerful, observer and spectator: "[Madame de Merteuil] will act on them and make them act, while she remains free, the unmoved spectator of them all."[3] Valmont is also seen as a masterful spectator at his own performance: "Valmont sait aussi se mettre à la place du spectateur de la pièce qu'il joue, et par un dédoublement curieux devient lui-même ce spectateur, prenant un plaisir de connaissance à sa propre pièce."[4] The spectator is thus a privileged being in no way inferior to the actor: his intelligent observation is as active and as effective as the actor's *jeu*.

Valmont, however, is not only the lucid, intelligent, powerful spectator, discerned by previous critics; I should like to suggest that he is also passive and inactive, credulous and uncomprehending. He waits, watches, and listens while others act and direct. He is as gullible as the actor is lucid, as emotionally vulnerable as the actor is intellectually controlled.

Both Madame de Merteuil and Valmont are seduced by theater; however, their "theatrical" failures are different. Madame de Merteuil falls victim to her own ideology of theater, her banishment of emotion, and her assimilation of life and play-acting. Valmont owes his destruction to his ambivalent attitude towards theater; unable to sustain the mastery required of the actor, he identifies with—and takes pleasure in—the passive role of spectator, the last refuge of the failed actor.

Valmont, of course, considers himself an inventive, talented actor.[5] Unlike Madame de Merteuil, whose masks are rather guarantors of privacy, he craves celebrity and constantly seeks the glory of applause: "Je leur montrerai ma besogne faite; ils n'auront plus qu'à admirer et applaudir" (Letter 99, p. 220[6]). He would have us believe that his behavior is always a premeditated performance, but it becomes apparent that he is not the lucid, rational, and emotionally uninvolved actor that he would wish to be. Constantly confusing himself with his role,[7] he is a poor disciple of the Marquise.

Madame de Merteuil's model of the polymorphous actor (a model similar to that of Diderot) explicity excludes genuine emotion from the actor's performance. The actor who is moved by his role loses intellectual and physical control. Yet, the ability to portray genuine emotion and to move one's audience is the touchstone of the great actor. As Jean Rousset phrases it, "les larmes véritables du spectateur sont provoquées par les fausses larmes de l'acteur."[8] Madame de Merteuil's mastery over her tears is proof that she is indeed an accomplished actress: "Mais voulant frapper le coup décisif, j'appelai les larmes à mon secours" (Letter 85, p. 189).

Baudelaire is no doubt correct in remarking that Valmont possesses "un reste de sensibilité par quoi il est inférieur à la Merteuil, chez qui tout ce qui est humain est calciné."[9] Valmont's sensibility makes his system—or lack of system—of acting more complicated and contradictory

than hers. The intrusion of emotion into Valmont's performances confuses, in his own mind, theater and self-identity.

Valmont's uncertainty about the nature of theatrical illusion is apparent in Letter 21, which describes his contrived act of beneficence and charity toward a destitute family. He begins the scene as actor. His use of the present tense—"j'arrive au Village; je vois de la rumeur; je m'avance: j'interroge; on me raconte le fait"—creates a sense of the immediacy of his actions. Self-conscious and ironic, he takes control of the situation and acts out his part according to his own script. The dynamics of the passage and of Valmont's role change, however, as he witnesses the highly emotional reaction of the father of the family who weeps because he accepts Valmont's pretended generosity as reality. The passing nobleman is readily perceived as an intermediary of divine charity, "une image de Dieu," a natural event in a world in which the sacred is an everyday presence. But for Valmont, reality consists of nothing but appearance, and here he finds himself involved in a new theatrical experience. He focuses his attention on the family patriarch: he is fascinated by his face and entirely absorbed as he witnesses the transformation of previously hideous features into handsome ones. The man briefly becomes for Valmont an actor whose tears, performance, and mobile, expressive physiognomy mesmerize him. This is the turning point in the passage. The family now consists of actors; Valmont, no longer a performer, has become a spectator: "J'examinais ce spectacle." Moreover, he abandons the present tense and adopts past tenses as he moves from the role of performer to the role of observer and commentator: description replaces action. In a perfectly symmetrical reversal of roles, it is now Valmont who is moved to tears by what he himself describes as "spectacle": "J'avouerai ma faiblesse; mes yeux se sont mouillés de larmes, et j'ai senti en moi un mouvement involontaire, mais délicieux." His genuine tears are those of a spectator, proof that he is no longer the cool and rational performer, master of masks and of the stage.

Twice Valmont gives money to the poor family: the first time as performer, the second as spectator. He is quite explicit about this: "j'ai trouvé juste de payer à ces pauvres gens le plaisir qu'ils venaient de me faire." He buys his ticket, the price one gladly pays for a moving and unforgettable theatrical experience, for the pleasure of weeping. But like most theater-goers, Valmont is somewhat critical of the performance; he is mildly disappointed by the second act: "Ici ont recommencé les remerciements, mais ils n'avaient plus ce même degré de pathétique" (p. 47).

Valmont has been taken in by his own performance in particular and by theatrical illusion in general. Don Juan,

Valmont's ancestor, was also a master of appearance, ultimately seduced by his belief in false appearances. Although Don Juan believes in nothing, the Statue, that which by definition can only be illusion, is the one thing to which he gives credence, and this belief in illusion destroys him. In a not dissimilar way, Valmont is also duped by theater; he weeps like a spectator at a "spectacle" and in so doing he is destroyed as an actor. He is not cast down to Hell but is placed in Limbo.

Whereas the distance between the Marquise, the consummate actress, and Valmont, an *acteur manqué,* is now great, this scene has created a certain equality between Valmont and Madame de Tourvel, for they are both spectators, moved to tears. When Madame de Tourvel hears the story, she too weeps: "le seul récit m'a attendrie jusqu'aux larmes" (Letter 22, p. 48).

The touchstone of an actor's tears continually reveals a Valmont confused about the nature of acting. In a scene with Madame de Tourvel, he is unclear about the source of his tears:

> Ah! malheureuse! s'écria-t-elle; puis elle fondit en larmes. Par bonheur je m'étais livré à tel point, que je pleurais aussi; et, reprenant ses mains, je les baignais de pleurs. Cette précaution etait bien nécessaire; car elle était si occupée de sa douleur, qu'elle ne se serait pas aperçue de la mienne, si je n'avais pas trouvé ce moyen de l'en avertir. . . . Ma tête s'échauffait, et j'étais si peu maître de moi, que je fus tenté de profiter de ce moment. (Letter 23, pp. 51-52)

Valmont's tears seem to be a reaction to the tears of Madame de Tourvel; he admits that fortuitous circumstance and his emotional state cause him to weep. However, in the next sentence, he claims that his tears were part of his method, a "précaution." He is pretending—to Madame de Merteuil, to whom his letter is addressed—that he is pretending emotion, when, in reality, his feelings are genuine. But he is incapable of sustaining even the vocabulary or the illusion of mastery and control, and he once again admits that he was overcome with emotion.

Valmont's inability to control his tears or shed them at will for theatrical effect is also apparent in his seduction of Madame de Tourvel: "J'avoue qu'en me livrant à ce point j'avais beaucoup compté sur le secours des larmes: mais . . . il me fut impossible de pleurer" (Letter 125, p. 291).

It is far from clear to Valmont whether or not he loves Madame de Tourvel; his letters contain innumerable confessions as well as denials of love for her. He justifies these contradictions by claiming that he is acting. However, this explanation is also a strangely argued abdication of responsibility: "Non, je ne suis point amoureux, et ce n'est pas ma faute si les circonstances me forcent d'en jouer le rôle" (Letter 138, p. 320). He portrays acting, not as a creative and willful activity, not as action, but rather as reaction; and he portrays himself as an actor who is a victim rather than a master of circumstance. His expression, "ce n'est pas ma faute," will be the refrain in his letter of rupture, written by the Marquise and copied by him, to Madame de Tourvel. In both cases, his "ce n'est pas ma faute" is a sign not only of his abdication of free will and personal responsibility, but also of the ultimately self-destructive consequences of his addiction to performance.

Valmont's contradictory statements and lack of sincerity are not the lucidly and willfully feigned behavior of the actor; they are rather a function of his own lack of self-understanding. He is confused by his various roles and is unable to fathom his true feelings. He refuses responsibility for his contradictions and ambivalence and assumes, more and more, a passive and humble position that is reflected in his sense of himself as an actor subservient to the director, Madame de Merteuil: "Instruisez-moi donc de ce qui est et de ce que je dois faire, . . . donnez-moi les réclames de mon rôle" (Letter 59, p. 118).

When he does invent roles for himself, they seem passive, even feminine: "J'eus soin d'avoir toute la soirée une douceur mélancolique" (Letter 44, p. 92). His strategy of seduction includes pretending weakness and illness. A "feinte indisposition" due to certain "violentes agitations" and "un saignement de nez" (*Suite de la Lettre* 40, p. 87) are part of his repertory. He is comfortable in the mask of physical illness and suffering:

> J'ai déclaré que j'étais *perdu de vapeurs;* j'ai annoncé aussi un peu de fièvre. Il ne m'en coûte que de parler d'une voix lente et éteinte. . . . Je réglerai l'état de ma santé sur l'impression qu'il fera sur [Madame de Tourvel]. (Letter 110, pp. 256-57)

Madame de Rosemonde's description of Valmont, caught by surprise, does suggest physical disarray as well as psychological distress: "Il était . . . sans toilette et sans poudre; mais je l'ai trouvé pâle et défait, et ayant surtout la physionomie altérée. Son regard que nous avons vu si vif et si gai, était triste et abattu" (Letter 122, p. 280). But since he speaks to her in melodramatic allusions to suicide, it is impossible to know whether he is acting, and hence calculating his behavior and appearance, or whether intensity of emotion has indeed changed his health. In any case, his feigned indispositions, his threats of suicide, and his ultimate death suggest, not heroes of will and energy, but past and future passionate, suffering, and dying heroines—Julie, Amélie, Ellénore.

The change from passive actor to passive spectator seems a natural transition. Week after week, immobile in the château of his aunt, Valmont is subject to boredom: "Je comptais aller à la chasse ce matin: mais il fait un temps détestable. Je n'ai pour toute lecture qu'un Roman nouveau, qui ennuierait même une Pensionnaire" (Letter 79, p. 159). But the negative state of boredom becomes the positive state of waiting, as Valmont relaxes into enjoying the pleasure of being a passive member of a theater audience:

> Véritablement je m'accoutume fort bien à mon séjour ici; et je puis dire que dans le triste Château de ma vieille tante, je n'ai pas éprouvé un moment d'ennui. Au fait, n'y ai-je pas jouissances, privations, espoir, incertitude? Qu'a-t-on de plus sur un plus grand théâtre? (Letter 99, p. 220)

Valmont now identifies not with the actor but with the spectator whose role is to observe. The "jouissance" that he associates here with theater is precisely the pleasure the spectator experiences in observing and listening:

> Oui, j'aime à *voir,* à *considérer* cette femme prudente, engagée sans s'en être aperçue, dans un sentier qui ne permet plus de retour. . . . Ah! laissez-moi du moins le temps d'*observer* ces touchants combats entre l'amour et la vertu. Eh quoi! ce même *spectacle* qui vous fait courir au *Théâtre* . . . le croyez-vous moins attachant dans la réalité? Ces sentiments d'une âme pure et tendre . . . vous les *écoutez* avec enthousiasme. . . . Voilà pourtant, voilà les délicieuses *jouissances* que cette femme céleste m'offre chaque jour. (Letter 96, pp. 209-10, *italics added*)

Waiting and watching become Valmont's occupations. Whereas Don Juan's perpetual travels are stopped only by the Statue's command, "Arrêtez, Dom Juan," Valmont chooses to inhabit a world in which both time and movement are arrested: "Jamais je n'avais goûté le plaisir que j'éprouve dans ces lenteurs prétendues" (Letter 96, p. 209). He lingers for three months, waiting for a seduction to take place. When Madame de Tourvel abruptly leaves the château without warning, Valmont's inclination is to remain: "Je n'ose tenter aucune démarche . . . je crois que je resterai ici quelque temps . . . J'aime mieux . . . annoncer . . . que je reste ici" (Letter 100, p. 227). Preferring to stay in one place, he calls into question the essence of Don Juan, "le plus grand coureur du monde": "Pourquoi courir apres le plaisir qui nous fuit, et negliger ceux qui se présentent?" (Letter 100, p. 226).

When Valmont decides to reaffirm himself both as actor and as Don Juan, he performs Don Juan's archetypal deed, the destruction of a happy couple. Valmont realizes, only when it is too late, that his act was completely self-destructive, for he was part of the couple he destroys. He accomplishes this irreversible and deadly act when he copies verbatim and sends to Madame de Tourvel a letter written by Madame de Merteuil. He does not comprehend the nature of his act or the meaning of the letter. His only comment on this grotesque epistle is that it is "original et propre à faire de l'effet." Other than that, he confesses to a

general lack of understanding: "ma foi, ma belle amie, je ne sais si j'ai mal lu ou mal entendu, et votre lettre, et l'histoire que vous m'y faites, et le petit modèle épistolaire qui y était compris" (Letter 142, p. 329). He nevertheless copies the letter, "tout simplement," submissively performing the role assigned to him, without feeling, without understanding, virtually insuring the terrible consequences of his action.

Finally jarred into an awareness of the meaning and the irreversibility of his act, Valmont understands that his deed, "le grand événement," as he calls it, does not belong to the abstract, atemporal, and immobile world which he has come to associate with theater and performance. The reality of the consequences of his letter has forced his entrance into a world in which words and acts are not mere performances but communicate meaning and feelings. Time, which had been an abstract function of theater, the duration of a prolonged performance of a seduction, is now a real and acutely felt presence. The following day, in a letter to Madame de Merteuil, he notes time with unusual precision:

> J'espérais pouvoir vous renvoyer ce matin la réponse de ma bien-aimée: mais il est près de *midi,* et je n'ai encore rien reçu. J'attendrai jusqu'à *cinq heures.* . . . Adieu, ma charmante amie, je ne fermerai cette Lettre qu'à *deux heures.* (Letter 142, p. 329, *italics added*)

The next day, too, he is again painfully conscious of time:

> Hier, à *trois heures du soir* . . . je me suis présenté chez la belle délaissée; on m'a dit qu'elle était sortie. . . . L'envie que j'avais de . . . recevoir [un mot de réponse] m'a fait passer exprès chez moi *vers les neuf heures.* . . . [Mon chasseur] m'a appris que madame de Tourvel était sortie en effet à *onze heures du matin,* . . . qu'elle s'était fait conduire au Couvent de . . . , et qu'à *sept heures du soir,* elle avait renvoyé sa voiture et ses gens. (Letter 144, p. 331, *italics added*)

Acting and deception have not produced the desired freedom and power. As an actor and illusionist, Valmont ultimately deludes himself and becomes his own victim, unsure of his true feelings, desires, and intentions. His addiction to performance results in a paralyzing alienation from his own self.

Valmont does not exactly present the case of an actor transformed or "taken in" by his role; he is not like Rotrou's Saint-Genest, "le comédien converti par son 'personnage.'"[10] The two roles that Valmont chooses to play, that of Don Juan and that of the tender, ardent, and obsessed lover, both correspond to real aspects of his personality—his cynicism, his cruelty, his megalomania, his sensibility—that antecede his decision to play these parts. When Valmont becomes the tender lover, succumbing to his feelings and to Madame de Tourvel, he is not merely taken in by his role, since the similarity between himself and the theatrical persona had always existed. Although Valmont would not admit that he was limited to playing roles that corresponded to his true feelings, this nevertheless seems to be his situation. Jean Rousset, in his analysis of Romantic attitudes toward the relationship between the actor and his role, comments that "la similitude des sentiments joués et des sentiments vécus autorise des structures où les deux plans de l'existence se reflètent, s'interpénètrent, et finissent par se fondre l'un dans l'autre, mais toujours aux dépens du jeu et de la scène qui se subordonnent à la réalité" (*L'Intérieur et l'extérieur,* p. 156).

Valmont's emotional identification with his role makes him a precursor of the Romantic actor; his acting, by giving expression to his deepest feelings, leads him, albeit unsuccessfully, in the direction of self-discovery rather than of self-mastery. We are far from Diderot's conception of the emotionally distanced and intellectually controlled actor. But Valmont's Romantic emotional involvement in his role, antithetical to both his own and Madame de Merteuil's notion of acting, echoes Laclos' preference for *sensibilité* over emotional distance in the creation of art.[11] Although Valmont's identification with his role ultimately dooms him to be a weak actor, it is also a sign of a certain capacity for emotion and empathy: redemption and salvation, completely out of the range of Madame de Merteuil, are at least a possibility for Valmont.

Notes

1. Jean Rousset, *Forme et signification* (Paris: Corti, 1962), p. 95.

2. See Peter Brooks, *The Novel of Worldliness* (Princeton: Princeton University Press, 1969), p. 191.

3. Emita B. Hill, "Man and Mask: The Art of the Actor in the *Liaisons dangereuses,*" *Romantic Review,* 63 (1972), 115.

4. Laurent Versini, *Laclos et la tradition* (Paris: Klincksieck, 1968), p. 93.

5. In his seduction of Madame de Tourvel, Valmont describes himself as adopting "le ton le plus tendre," "le ton de reproche," "le ton dramatique," "un ton bas et sinistre," "une voix plus faible," "un air composé mais contraint," "un air égaré," "l'air du dépit," and "des regards farouches" (Letter 125, pp. 290-92). For a discussion of Valmont as actor, see Versini, *Laclos et la tradition,* pp. 90-95.

6. Choderlos de Laclos, *Les Liaisons dangereuses* in *uvres complètes,* Bibliothèque de la Pléiade (Paris: Gallimard, 1979). Subsequent parenthetical page numbers refer to this edition.

7. "J'ai tant dit [à Danceny] que l'amour honnête était le bien suprême . . . que j'étais moi-même, dans ce moment, amoureux et timide" (Letter 57, p. 115).

8. Jean Rousset, "Le Jeu de l'acteur," in *Le Jeu au XVIIIe siècle,* Colloque d'Aix-en-Provence (Aix-en-Provence: Edisud, 1976), p. 237.

9. Baudelaire, "Notes sur *Les Liaisons dangereuses,*" *uvres complètes,* Bibliothèque de la Pléiade (Paris: Gallimard, 1961), p. 645.

10. Jean Rousset, *L'Intérieur et l'extérieur,* (Paris: Corti, 1968), p. 156.

11. In his article "Cecilia ou les Mémoires d'une héritière," Laclos discusses the essential qualities of a novelist and emphasizes both the verb *sentir* and the noun *sensibilité:* "Observer, sentir et peindre, sont les trois qualités nécessaires à tout Auteur de Romans. Qu'il ait donc à la fois de la finesse et de la profondeur, du tact et de la délicatesse, de la grâce et de la vérité; mais que surtout il possède cette sensibilité précieuse, sans laquelle il n'existe point de talent, et qui elle seule peut les remplacer tous" (Laclos, *uvres complètes,* p. 449).

Peter V. Conroy, Jr. (essay date 1987)

SOURCE: "Split Personalities: Characterizing Writers and Readers" in *Intimate, Intrusive, and Triumphant: Readers in the* Liaisons Dangereuses, John Benjamins Publishing Company, 1987, pp. 81-96.

[*In the excerpt below, Conroy analyzes the characters in the novel as both readers and writers of letters.*]

. . . [Each] of the novel's characters has a double function, first that of writing letters or of being a narrator, and second, that of receiving another's letters or of being a reader. This dual function in the structure of the novel corresponds to a double personality profile at the psychological level of characterization, since each personage displays a different aspect of his or her personality according to his or her role as either narrator or reader. Consequently, we can analyze each character in terms of this narrator/reader distinction. In such successful and well-rounded figures as we find in the **Liaisons dangereuses,** this distinction might at first seem arbitrary. Nonetheless, the value of the distinction and of the consequent analysis is real. As subtle as the two faces of each character are, and as difficult as it may be to differentiate precisely between them, the contrast between the very same character as writer and as reader reveals accurately the secret workings of their personalties and demonstrates another subtle element of Laclos's artistry.

Cécile Volanges

Cécile Volanges changes drastically when we compare her personality as narrator to her character as reader. Cécile opens the novel, and her frequent letters at the outset carry a heavy burden of exposition. Of the first twenty letters, she contributes eight, while the remaining twelve are distributed among Valmont, Merteuil, Danceny, Mme de Tourvel, and Mme de Volanges. Critics have commented upon the particular tone of voice[1] that Laclos has given to Cécile's letters and consequently to her personality as narrator: juvenile, ingenuous, garrulous, credulous, disorganized, overly enthusiastic, and easily moved from one emotional height to another. Even her grammatical faults are indications of her unformed intelligence and lack of sophistication. They point up the gap, even if it is for the moment merely linguistic, that separates her from such adepts of word and deed as Valmont and Merteuil. For an admittedly secondary character, Cécile does write a large number of letters, a number that is perhaps disproportionate to her importance in the intrigue, since she writes more than Mme de Tourvel (twenty-five versus twenty-four). Like the latter, Cécile is important as a victim, the prey of Valmont and Merteuil. Nevertheless, she does not capture our interest as a human being as much or as intensely as the Présidente, who is so much more mature and intelligent. Mme de Tourvel is a moving and fascinating woman who rewards our interest with the complexity of her own personality. Cécile is neither as rich nor as deep a character as the Présidente, and consequently she attracts our attention less.

Still, Mlle de Volanges's seduction and fall remain key structural elements, indispensable for the full impact of this depiction of libertine behavior and betrayed innocence. As regards the psychology of the characters, however, Cécile is but a minor figure, filling out the cast but not really permitted to linger in the spotlight. This brief personality sketch, which could be expanded without changing anything essential, is based on Cécile's role as narrator. We have judged her upon what she has written, we have evaluated her in terms of her presence as a producer of letters.

Let us complete our personality sketch by looking now at Cécile as a reader and assessing her as a receiver of letters. Immediately we notice how reduced a character she becomes. While writing twenty-five letters, she receives only eleven. Furthermore, her principal epistolary exchange with Sophie Carnay is severely truncated, cut in half by the elimination of all of Sophie's letters. What Cécile reads and what inspires her to write in her turn do not exist in the novel. Alone of all the personages, Cécile is deprived of the motivations that would be apparent in a two-sided correspondence. She loses the richness of human interest that a written dialogue would supply. Without Sophie and the writer/reader balance she would provide, Cécile remains quite literally without texture. Of course, this reduction is a necessary artistic economy, eliminating a possible diversion and concentrating our attention on the principal characters and the main intrigue. Sophie's letters would add nothing to the thrust of the plot and would

needlessly encumber the forward impulsion of the action. Despite these self-evident reasons, the editors do feel obliged to explain this omission and in a sense to defend it:

> Pour ne pas abuser de la patience du lecteur, on supprime beaucoup de lettres de cette correspondance journalière, qui à elle seule comprendrait plusieurs volumes, on ne donne que celles qui ont paru nécessaires à l'intelligence des événements de cette société. C'est par le même motif qu'on supprime aussi toutes les lettres de Sophie Carnay et plusieurs de celles des autres acteurs de ces aventures. (Letter 7, note, p. 20)

Cécile has the misfortune to be the victim of this editorial policy on more than one occasion. In a footnote to a reference made by Danceny in one of his letters to Cécile, the editors intervene and explain once again:

> Cette lettre est celle dont Cécile Volanges envoie copie à Madame de Merteuil. Comme elle redit en partie les mêmes choses que les deux précédentes on a cru qu'elle suffisait pour ne pas grossir inutilement ce recueil. (Letter 28, note, p. 59)

And finally, one last deletion:

> On continue de supprimer les lettres de Cécile Volanges et du chevalier Danceny, qui sont peu intéressantes et n'annoncent aucun événement. (Letter 39, note, p. 81)

We have already discussed how these editors belong to the twilight fringe of this fictional universe. They separate or perhaps they connect the fictive world of the novel and the real, eighteenth-century society in which this novel is inscribed and upon which it depends for authenticating support and for a referential background. Laclos's decision to suppress Sophie is artistically correct and the reasons for diminishing Cécile are perfectly sound, since her letters are "not very interesting" and therefore not "necessary." However correct in artistic terms, these suppressions nevertheless do violate the logic of the epistolary genre, which is premised on two-sided exchanges, and the example of the *Liaisons* itself, which grants its other characters this privilege of give-and-take correspondences. This detail does then belong to our consideration of the fictional reader even though it might at first appear meaningless. Not only has the author de-created a fictional reader, but he chooses precisely those ironic, contradictory, and problematic figures, the two editors, to perform this deletion and to justify it.

Because her letters are not reproduced, Sophie does not exist within the text. If Sophie does not exist as a narrator, then Cécile is rendered moot as a reader. Furthermore, Cécile's writerly impact is seriously reduced because as an addresser she is deprived of her addressee, Sophie. Cécile's rank as a secondary or minor character is not therefore a subjective value judgment that compares her unfavorably with the Présidente or that is based on a literary convention concerning the psychology of fictional characters. It is rather a structural fact and the simple consequence of the written record, or rather of the gaps in that written record. Cécile barely exists as a reader while the other characters display a balance or at least a justifiable proportion between their writing and reading functions.

Because of this reduced presence, Cécile reveals most clearly the frontier or boundary where fiction starts and ends. Finding herself in the abnormal position of a writer who has no reader, Cécile defines the point of incision, that cut in the otherwise seamless fabric where the novel's first threads begin. Her deficit as a personality is redeemed by the structural importance she has in the novel's incipit. Her diminished role as a reader (it is principally the non-existent Sophie who writes to her) allows the fiction to slip into an apparently real world of letters. Reduced to the bare minimum, honed to a razor's edge, Cécile's textual presence/absence, her appearance as narrator juxtaposed to her disappearance as a reader, mark that vanishing point where Laclos hopes to create the illusion of fiction blending into reality, of the fictional world disappearing into the real society which inspired it.

Armed with this analysis, we can now return to our discussion of Cécile's personality and complete the thumbnail sketch that we made of her character based on her activity as a narrator. Psychologically, Mlle de Volanges is the ideal candidate for the structural reduction that losing one's existence as a reader supposes. To refuse her the normal condition of a complete epistolary character, both writer and reader, created in a regular two-way exchange of letters, emphasizes her half-developed intelligence, her inability to adjust successfully to her mother's social milieu, and her own catastrophic efforts to shift for herself and to behave like an adult. Her special vulnerability is prepared by her incompleteness as an addressee and by her unfilled textual relationship with Sophie. Once the novel is beyond its exposition phase, the editors announce that they will even omit the letters Cécile writes to Sophie:

> Mlle de Volanges ayant peu de temps après de confidente, comme on le verra par la suite de ces lettres, on ne trouvera plus dans ce recueil aucune de celles qu'elle a continué d'écrire à son amie du couvent: elles n'apprendraient rien au lecteur. (Letter 75, note, p. 153)

Form mirrors content here; the pattern set in the infrastructure parallels that in the plot. Cécile's social and moral naiveté stems from the absence of any sure criteria for making sane judgments as well as from the textual absence that surrounds her and isolates her from any possibility of rescue. She is cut adrift from her addressee, and ignored by her mother. Deprived of Sophie's replies and of her

mother's attention, Cécile cannot resist the presence of Mme de Merteuil and the response the latter gives her. As her very name indicates, Mlle de Volanges is *volage,* light and flighty because, in part, she lacks the weight and seriousness that being a complete reader would confer upon her. To make a pun which should not however obscure the gravity of this situation, we can go so far as to say that Cécile's textual insufficiency explains her sexual immaturity. Furthermore, since we are dealing here with a novel and not with life, that is to say with a reality that exists only in letters, we can claim that her textual deficiency is in large part responsible for her sexual difficulties.

Mme de Volanges

Mme de Volanges, Cécile's mother, also reveals two distinct personalities according to her activity either as narrator or reader. As a writer of letters, Mme de Volanges presents herself as a relatively sophisticated, intelligent, and typically correct example of a certain eighteenth-century social class under the *ancien régime.* Her letters to the Présidente de Tourvel exhibit a polish and *savoir-faire* as well as a discerning grasp on the libertine realities of the world she lives in:

> Je n'ai jamais douté, ma jeune et belle amie, ni de l'amitié que vous avez pour moi, ni de l'intérêt sincère que vous prenez à tout ce qui me regarde. . . . Mais Valmont n'est pas cela. Sa conduite est le résultat de ses principes. Il sait calculer tout ce qu'un homme peut se permettre d'horreurs sans se compromettre; et pour être cruel et méchant sans danger, il a choisi les femmes pour victimes. (Letter 9, pp. 22-23)

Her haughty letter to Danceny, which attempts to thwart his incipient romance with Cécile, is eloquent. Its carefully worded demands and threats, its barely disguised outrage, and its willful suppression of personal emotion in favor of a socially acceptable solution indicate that Mme de Volanges is indeed a woman of sense and intelligence, and one who thoroughly comprehends the need for decorum and the respect due to appearances:

> Après avoir abusé, Monsieur, de la confiance d'un mère et de l'innocence d'un enfant, vous ne serez pas surpris, sans doute, de ne plus être reçu dans une maison où vous n'avez répondu aux preuves de l'amitié la plus sincère que par l'oubli de tous les procédés. . . . Je vous préviens aussi que si vous faites à l'avenir la moindre tentative pour entretenir ma fille dans l'égarement où vous l'avez plongée, une retraite austère et éternelle la soustraira à vos poursuites. (Letter 62, p. 123)

Her single letter to the Marquise de Merteuil touches on the pathetic as Mme de Volanges plaintively demands how to react to her daughter's sudden change in demeanor and behavior:

Quel parti prendre pourtant, si cela dure? ferai-je le malheur de ma fille? tournerai-je contre elle les qualités les plus précieuses de l'âme, la sensibilité et la constance? est-ce pour cela que je suis sa mère? . . . si je force son choix, n'aurai-je pas à répondre des suites funestes qu'il peut avoir? Quel usage à faire de l'autorité maternelle, que de placer sa fille entre le crime et le malheur! (Letter 98, pp. 221-22)

These searching questions ring true. Mme de Volanges is perfectly sincere in trying to resolve this dilemma even though she is addressing the person least apt to help her or her daughter. Finally, Mme de Volanges insists upon remaining faithful to those she considers friends even when the latter fall on hard times. This noble and courageous gesture is somewhat tarnished since the friend in question is none other than the Marquise who has just been shunned by everyone she meets at the theater. Despite our awareness that the Marquise's disgrace is justified, that she has been rightfully unmasked, and that she will now be punished for her immoral conduct, Mme de Volanges's report of Merteuil's fall and Prévan's triumph displays an admirable skepticism about the still unproven rumors circulating in the salons and an acute consciousness of how fickle the public's applause can really be:

Il se répand ici, ma chère et digne amie, sur le compte de Mme de Merteuil, des bruits bien étonnants et bien fâcheux. Assurément je suis loin d'y croire, et je parierais bien que ce n'est qu'une affreuse calomnie; mais je sais trop combien les méchancetés, même les moins vraisemblables, prennent aisément consistance, et combien l'impression qu'elles laissent s'efface difficilement. . . . J'ai heureusement les plus fortes raisons de croire que ces imputations sont aussi fausses qu'odieuses. . . . Ces réflexions me porteraient à le [i.e., Prévan] soupçonner l'auteur des bruits qui courent aujourd'hui, et à regarder ces noirceurs comme l'ouvrage de sa haine et de sa vengeance, fait dans l'espoir de répandre au moins des doutes, et de causer peut-être une diversion utile. (Letter 168, pp. 378, 379, 380)

Eventually Mme de Volanges sees the truth and understands that the Marquise never deserved her support and fidelity. Nonetheless, in defense of Mme de Volanges, we must admit that she does display here some noble qualities even if they are directed towards an unworthy object in Merteuil. In addition, she takes her responsibility towards Cécile most solemnly, although once again she is sorely deceived about her true interest. If Mme de Volanges is duped and betrayed by her ostensible friends, she is herself not an evil individual, but rather a misguided one who tries her best to do what is right even when her best is far from sufficient.

And yet Mme de Volanges leaves the distinct impression of being a sinner as well as one sinned against. Such a strong negative judgment comes almost entirely from her presentation as a reader. Her most grievous fault is that she never listens to her daughter. The absence of any valid communication between mother and daughter is the most damning evidence we have against Mme de Volanges. Even if a written exchange would have been difficult to motivate or justify in terms of epistolary logic, the plain fact that they do not communicate in any fashion is indisputable since Cécile herself complains of not being able to talk with her mother. Not surprisingly, she quickly finds that Mme de Merteuil pays more attention to her than her own flesh and blood:

C'est pourtant bien extraordinaire qu'une femme qui ne m'est presque pas parente, prenne plus de soin de moi que ma mère! (Letter 29, p. 61)

It is precisely this lack of a sympathetic listener or reader that defines the relationship between Cécile and Mme de Volanges. Indeed, all by itself, this noncommunication explains the inevitable tragedy that will send Cécile to a convent and leave her mother alone, shaken, and unable to fathom how and why this catastrophe took place.

Only on one occasion is Mme de Volanges her daughter's reader. Tipped off by the Marquise de Merteuil, she surprises Cécile in her room and confiscates her entire correspondence with Danceny, which up until then had been a well-kept secret. Mme de Volanges therefore becomes her daughter's reader only through force, and furthermore, through unlawful force since on this occasion her authority oversteps its bounds. Such use of force of course negates the true meaning of being a reader, which usually supposes a great deal of intimacy. There is no shared confidence, no mutual respect, no willing exchange of thoughts and feelings between them. It is ironic but entirely fitting in terms of the plot that Mme de Volanges be an intrusive, spying, and dishonest reader for her own daughter. The positive aspect of the readerly relationship which implies friendship, openness, and sharing is denied her. Cécile confides in the Marquise because she cannot speak to her own mother. In usurping Mme de Volanges's rightful place as confidante and confessor, even as mother, Merteuil perverts the true spirit of reading. But it is always Cécile who suffers, and doubly, from these two distortions of the reader's potential. Cécile's seduction and victimization by both Valmont and Merteuil derive ultimately from this same fact, namely that the normal and healthy relationship of confiding and exchanging, of having and of being a reader, was impossible for Mme de Volanges and her daughter. The maternal inability to act as a receiver and reader not only foreshadows the filial abandonment but actually causes it. As a failed reader, Mme de Volanges is responsible for her daughter's downfall; she causes Cécile's immoral conduct to the extent that she turned a deaf ear to her. Because she refuses to become her own daughter's confidante and friend, Mme de Volanges earns our negative assessment as insensitive, blind, and too wrapped up in herself. Had she been able to listen and to hear, she could have avoided for her own daughter the terrible fate that she sees so clearly as threatening the Présidente. In both of her letters to Mme de Tourvel, Mme de Volanges accurately identifies the danger that the Présidente is running:

> La seule chose que j'aie à vous dire, c'est que, de toutes les femmes auxquelles il [Valmont] a rendu des soins, succès ou non, il n'en est point qui n'aient eu à s'en plaindre. (Letter 9, p. 23)

Ironically for herself, she pleads with the Présidente to accept her warnings with the confidence and the sureness that characterize any true communication of mind and heart:

> Ah! revenez, revenez, je vous en conjure. Si mes raisons ne suffisent pas pour vous persuader, cédez à mon amitié; c'est elle qui me fait renouveler mes instances, c'est à elle à les justifier. (Letter 32, p. 66)

In all that concerns the Présidente, Mme de Volanges is attentive, her judgments are perceptive, and her warnings infallible, whereas she is totally mistaken about the dangers that threaten her own Cécile. For Mme de Tourvel, she remains a most perspicacious writer, while she can only be considered a criminally ineffectual reader for Cécile.

THE CHEVALIER DANCENY

The third personage who benefits from the distinction between writer and reader is the Chevalier Danceny. He is very much a fragmented figure who is only seen at certain points within the novel. He undergoes changes outside our view, beyond the ken of the fiction itself. In Danceny we see the product of a transformation rather than the process itself. An epistolary novel can reinforce the effect of such a disjointed characterization. By its very nature, the epistolary format is composed of discrete and discontinuous letters, of various narrators who take turns as the single voice and perspective through which the novel is presented, and of several plot lines followed simultaneously even when they do not intertwine. Thus the letter-novel is particularly well adapted to the type of sudden metamorphosis that Danceny experiences. The Chevalier can be successfully depicted as subject to these sudden modifications because he does not fix our attention with the same intensity as do main figures like Valmont, Merteuil, or Tourvel. He cannot support the same kind of close and relentless analysis as they do. Nonetheless, as a peripheral character, useful for reinforcing the symmetry of the seduction of the Présidente and Cécile, and as a foil for Valmont, Danceny profits from the distance that this discontinuous characterization allows. What interests us most here is that the Chevalier's fragmented character is revealed in several distinct stages not so much by what he himself says but rather by whom he listens to and reads.

Danceny's discontinuous characterization is most effectively analyzed by reference to his role as a reader.

There are three distinct stages or periods of Danceny's personality. The first comprises his relationship to Cécile, and consequently his activity as writer and reader with her. In both functions, he is naive, unresourceful, and passive. He courts Mlle de Volanges by sending letters (in rather unusual if not entirely original fashion, it is true, by hiding them in her harp as mentioned in letter 16), but undertakes nothing more positive or daring until Valmont decides to assist him. As Cécile's reader, he is even more helpless. Each one of her letters to him provokes a different emotion. Several of Cécile's letters to her other correspondents contain a series of static views or snapshots of the Chevalier in his various moods and reactions. At first, only his pretty face and musical talent distinguish him from the rest of the crowd in the salon or drawing room:

> M. le chevalier Danceny, ce monsieur dont je t'ai parlé, et avec qui j'ai chanté chez Mme de Merteuil, a la complaisance de venir ici tous les jours, et de chanter avec moi des heures entières. Il est extrêmement aimable. Il chante comme un ange, et compose de très jolies airs dont il fait aussi les paroles. C'est bien dommage qu'il soit chevalier de Malte! (Letter 7, p. 20)

As he falls in love with Cécile, he displays the marks of an all-consuming passion, a romantic agony:

> Depuis il était devenu triste, mais si triste, si triste que ça me faisait de la peine; et quand je lui demandais pourquoi, il me disait que non; mais je voyais bien que si. Enfin hier il l'était encore plus que de coutume. (Letter 16, pp. 35-36)

When he does not receive a letter from Cécile, he is depressed:

> Je ne le regardai qu'un petit moment. Il ne me regardait pas, lui: mais il avait un air, qu'on aurait dit qu'il était malade. . . . Je rencontrai ses yeux, et il me fut impossible de détourner les miens. Un moment après je vis ses larmes couler. (Letter 18, p. 39)

But when he does receive one, his joy knows no bounds:

> Mais au retour, oh! comme il était content! En posant ma harpe vis-à-vis de moi, il se plaça de façon que Maman ne pouvait voir, et il prit ma main qu'il serra . . . mais d'une façon! (Letter 18, p. 40, ellipsis in original)

Despite his frequent outbursts of passionate words and expressions, Danceny seems incapable of realizing anything more audacious than holding hands. Never does he take any other liberties with Cécile. Only under Valmont's protection and guidance does he finally aspire to really enterprising behavior. When Mme de Volanges discovers his secret correspondence with Cécile, she firmly and irrevocably dismisses him from her salon. He does not dare to return.

During the second stage of his personal development, he is the Marquise de Merteuil's reader. Although there are but five letters corresponding to this period (three from Danceny, numbers 118, 148, and 150, and two from the Marquise, 121 and 146), this phase of Danceny's emotional and social evolution is a critical one. During this period he becomes more self-confident, more capable, more enterprising. In a word, the same Chevalier who was so ingenuous and respectful with Cécile has become a gallant companion and successful suitor of the Marquise. Since it is surely the Marquise who leads in this dance of mutual seduction, we can rightfully claim that Danceny, a nascent rake on the threshold of a libertine career of sexual triumphs, is indeed her product. He is learning from Merteuil's letters, just as Valmont once did, and he is being led by the nose just like Prévan, who suffered a resounding defeat at her hands. For Danceny to be the Marquise's reader implies equally that he is her pupil, her creature, and inevitably her victim: we have observed throughout this novel the wiles and skill of the Marquise enough not to doubt the outcome of this encounter. Whatever may be the eventual fate that Merteuil is preparing for him (but which never comes to fruition since the novel ends before that scheme matures), Danceny is a markedly different man when he reads the Marquise from the gauche young boy he was in his letters with Cécile. Mme de Merteuil herself points this out when remarking on the language that the Chevalier has just recently learned:

> Quittez donc, si vous m'en croyez, ce ton de cajolerie, qui n'est plus que du jargon, dès qu'il n'est pas l'expression de l'amour. Est-ce donc là le style de l'amitié? non, mon ami. (Letter 121, p. 283)

In any epistolary novel, characters are presented through the letters they write; they are created by their own words. Merteuil's comment is to be taken most seriously. The fact that his style has been corrupted by jargon is a critical and accurate reflection of his character.

Later, the Marquise invites him to pay her a secret visit on the eve of her departure from Paris, a visit that should remain secret even from Valmont whom Danceny still considers his true friend and confidant. Confidence is the ostensible topic of Merteuil's words, but her phrases betray a sentiment that is quite different as she attempts to provoke an entirely different kind of reaction in the Chevalier:

> Qui m'aurait dit, il y a quelque temps, que bientôt vous auriez ainsi ma confiance exclusive, je ne l'aurais pas cru. Mais la vôtre a entraîné la mienne. Je serais tentée de croire que vous y avez mis de l'adresse, peut-être même de la séduction. (Letter 146, pp. 341-42)

The Marquise is exaggerating Danceny's skill as a seducer, of course. Nevertheless, he does attempt to play this libertine role with her, even if she remains always in control of the situation and of her lover-pupil. This Chevalier talking love to the Marquise and initiating some sexual advances, even if she always calls the tune, is miles from the Danceny who could barely hold Cécile's hand.

The partial nature of Danceny's presentation and the unseen elements of his personal development (that is, unrecorded in the text that we are reading) are most apparent here. The progress of Merteuil and Danceny's relationship is clearly suggested, but even its main outlines are barely sketched. Moreover, we must beware the Marquise's own seductive technique. She is flattering Danceny and most probably giving him more credit than he deserves for winning and seducing her. Still, the end result is unmistakable. Danceny achieves with Mme de Merteuil the ultimate sexual communication which he could only dream of in his courtship of Cécile:

> O vous que j'aime! ô toi que j'adore! ô vous qui avez commencé mon bonheur! ô toi qui l'as comblé! Amie sensible, tendre amante. . . . Ainsi que moi, ma tendre amie, tu éprouvais, sans le connaître, ce charme impérieux qui livrait nos âmes aux douces impressions de la tendresse; et tous deux n'avons reconnu l'amour qu'en sortant de l'ivresse où ce dieu nous avait plongés. (Letter 148, pp. 346-47)

The rare use of the intimate *tu*-form suffices to explain the new relationship that now binds the Chevalier to the Marquise. It also emphasizes the raw power and the intensity of the emotion that Danceny is experiencing. Closing this hymn to their lovemaking, Danceny pretends to believe that he and Merteuil were inspired by their friendship alone and that they have not betrayed Cécile in giving expression to their passion:

> Hé! quels reproches avez-vous donc à vous faire? croyez-moi, votre délicatesse vous abuse. Les regrets qu'elle vous cause, les torts dont elle m'accuse, sont également illusoires. . . . Non, tu n'as pas trahi l'amitié, et je n'ai pas davantage abusé de ta confiance. (Letter 148, pp. 346-47)

Mme de Merteuil was not wrong, nor did she exaggerate in saying that Danceny had acquired a new language and all that new language implied. Danceny displays a total lack of moral principles to accompany his linguistic affectations. The jargon of the *petits maîtres* who seduced women with their deceptive words is rife in every one of his phrases and even more so in the obfuscating logic and tendentious rationale behind them.

Only because he enters into this epistolary contact with the Marquise de Merteuil does Danceny undergo this change in character. His transformation is due entirely to the Marquise. However, because a full presentation of this subplot is missing from the text, we have only a few traces of this period left in the five letters between Danceny and Merteuil. Rather than wishing there had been more development of this episode, we maintain that this partial presentation is sufficient as it stands. As brief as it is, it nonetheless suggests possible connections and symmetries with other actions in other plot lines of the novel. Most important, it is anchored in the concept of the reader. The reading connection between the Chevalier and the Marquise is indeed the only trace that even hints at Danceny's transformation. Merteuil's power over her reader is real, while Danceny's less active role as receiver of her message is underscored by his subordinate and even passive status as he is manipulated and seduced by her. Sexually and psychologically, Danceny exists in the shadow of Merteuil: the Marquise bends him to her will in terms both of personality and of text. For as long as he remains the Marquise de Merteuil's intended addressee (and we emphasize that term "intended" because it defines the precise nature of Merteuil's domination over Danceny while it also delimits the chronological duration of this relationship), he is also her plaything, her product, and her conquest.

The third and last of Danceny's faces derives once again from reading. His final experience as a reader in the novel changes him definitively. Afterwards, he recoils from the pretenses of society, he renounces the social whirl and all its attractions, and he flees Paris to embrace his once despised but original calling as a Knight of Malta. Reading Valmont's *cassette,* which contains his *Compte ouvert entre la marquise de Merteuil et le vicomte de Valmont,* is the event that provokes this drastic transformation. Now an avenger of iniquity and eager to compensate somehow for having killed Valmont in their duel, Danceny destroys the Marquise with the very papers and letters he has read. This third Danceny is markedly different from the other two personas and especially from the immediately preceding one. No longer Merteuil's intended reader, he escapes from her domination because she is not addressing him directly. In letters 121 and 146, she knew he was reading her and she wrote accordingly, with the intention of seducing him. Once he is no longer her intended reader, she loses her power over him.

Delivered after Valmont's death, these written revelations concerning Merteuil transform Danceny, their first outside reader, into a new man. Armed with this evidence which he owes to the reading half of his character, the Chevalier pursues the Marquise and avenges the Vicomte. Thanks to the knowledge he gains as a reader, as a writer he publishes Merteuil's own letter which details how she entrapped Prévan and exposed him to public ridicule and censure. Written in Merteuil's own hand, this letter is the Waterloo of that superb woman who compared herself to the Maréchal de Saxe as well as to God Himself. In his third and final incarnation, Danceny appears as an avenging angel who reestablishes the moral code and rights wrongs:

> J'ai cru, de plus, que c'était rendre un véritable service à la société que de démasquer une femme aussi réellement dangereuse que l'est Mme de Merteuil, et qui, comme vous pourriez le voir, est la seule, la véritable cause de tout ce qui s'est passé entre M. de Valmont et moi. (Letter 169, p. 382)

Thus, the reading process is itself critical in undoing Merteuil. More pointedly, we could say that Danceny destroys Merteuil because of what he has read as well as through what he has read. In a world of false appearances and deceptions of all sorts, reading alone can pass for an authentic activity which inspires confidence and guarantees veracity. By inviting Mme de Rosemonde to become, in her turn, another reader of Valmont's secret papers, Danceny shows to what extent he believes that the act of reading leads to the truth:

> N'en croyez pas mes discours; mais lisez, si vous en avez le courage, la correspondance que je dépose entre vos mains. (Letter 169, p. 382)

Danceny's belief in the positive power of the reading process transcends the limits of the novel itself. As the editors report in their footnote, the letters deposited by Danceny with Mme de Rosemonde will become the basis for the novel which they have edited and which we are reading. Laclos is cleverly prolonging his novel beyond its fictional space and into the real world that it mirrors. This is more than a simple game of illusions, however. Danceny's assurance that subsequent readers will react correctly, that is to say, that they will agree with him and approve his actions, is critical to the denouement of the novel and the punishment of the Marquise. Through Mme de Rosemonde, Danceny is reaching out to the other fictional readers, to all those in Merteuil's Paris, but also to the real reader in our world. More than any other character, Danceny is speaking out in the name of honesty and social morality in order to condemn vice and recommend virtue. He has not always been heard, since other times have found this novel either inaccurate in its depiction of society or immoral in its glorification of vice. Nonetheless, Danceny's injunction is to *read* and not to judge on any other criteria. A correct reading, we believe along with the Chevalier, would lead to an appropriately moral conclusion. But even more than that, Laclos is inviting us, through Danceny, to a literary event that precedes any consideration of morality: *lisez.*

Danceny's own story and the development of his personality can therefore best be understood as the result of his activity as a reader. Fresh, ineffectual, and unsure how to interpret the signs around him, he at first writes to Cécile and receives from her letters that are marked by their youth and inexperience. Reading the Marquise de Merteuil makes a different man out of him. He acquires a thin veneer of sophistication, joins the ranks of rakes and *petits maîtres,* and learns to speak a language debased by jargon. Reading Valmont posthumously transforms Danceny again. It gives him a mission to perform and opens new depths of knowledge both about himself and about the world surrounding him.

MME DE ROSEMONDE

Although we have already discussed Mme de Rosemonde both as the last fictional reader inside the novel and as the first real reader outside it, she can bear further comment here as we separate her character as addresser from that as addressee.

Whenever she writes letters, Mme de Rosemonde seems to be singularly misinformed about the true nature of her nephew. Perhaps she is simply blind to his shortcomings, perhaps she has decided not to recognize him for the rogue that he is. Her early letters to Mme de Tourvel are full of his praises even though she is forced on occasion to admit his all too obvious faults. Her loving interest in Valmont is combined with an almost comic inability to discover what is really happening and what the Vicomte is actually doing. For example, she completely misinterprets Valmont's shock and disappointment at the Présidente's early morning departure from the château as the effects of a mild cold:

> Mon neveu est aussi un peu indisposé, mais sans aucun danger, et sans qu'il faille en prendre aucune inquiétude; c'est une incommodité légère, qui, à ce qu'il me semble, affecte plus son humeur que sa santé. Nous ne le voyons presque plus. (Letter 112, p. 263)

She also misconstrues Cécile's tiredness, and fails even to suspect those nocturnal meetings which have caused such obvious fatigue:

> La petite Volanges, surtout, vous trouve furieusement à dire, et bâille, tant que la journée dure, à avaler ses poings. (Letter 112, p. 263)

We can smile at Mme de Rosemonde's observation since we know that Valmont and Cécile are spending their nights in bed together, he giving a course in libertinage, she becoming a star pupil.

By the end of the novel, her opinion has not changed substantially. Even though she has learned all the details of the Vicomte's seduction and betrayal of both the Présidente and Cécile, and of his ongoing libertine pact with the Marquise de Merteuil, she cannot bring herself to judge him harshly. In fact, she appears to blame only the Marquise for their joint conduct:

> Après ce que vous m'avez fait connaître, Monsieur [Danceny], il ne reste qu'à pleurer et se taire. On regrette de vivre encore, quand on apprend de pareilles horreurs; on rougit d'être femme, quand on en voit une capable de semblables excès. (Letter 171, p. 386)

She is honest enough, however, to recognize her weakness for her nephew and her unshakable attachment to him:

> Malgré ses torts, que je suis forcée de reconnaître, je sens que je ne me consolerai jamais de sa perte. (Letter 171, p. 386)

"Forced to recognize" his wrongs is not an exaggeration. Until she received Danceny's unimpeachable evidence against the Vicomte, Mme de Rosemonde was prepared to go to the limit of the law in favor of her nephew:

> mon intention est que vous en rendiez plainte sur-le-champ, et en mon nom. En pardonnant à son ennemi, à son meurtrier, mon neveu a pu satisfaire à sa générosité naturelle; mais moi, je dois venger à la fois sa mort, l'humanité et la religion. (Letter 164, p. 373)

Even though she is aware of the Présidente's ordeal at Valmont's hands, Mme de Rosemonde can without sarcasm or irony still speak of his "generosity" (which doubtless retains part of its etymological sense of one who acts nobly so as to win honor for himself and his family), accuse Danceny of being a murderer (both adversaries were willing and fairly matched even if dueling was illegal), and invoke principles like humanity and religion even though in his life Valmont respected neither.

However commendable Mme de Rosemonde's attachment to the Vicomte might be under normal circumstances, it certainly does not do justice to his many victims nor can it claim any logical or justifiable origin in his own conduct and attitude towards others. On this score Mme de Rosemonde disappoints us, since she chooses to ignore the question of whether Valmont really deserves her uncritical affection.

As a reader, however, Mme de Rosemonde is quite different from what she is as a narrator and as a third party described by other correspondents. As a reader, she is particularly aware of Valmont's faults and remains acutely attentive to the best ways of resisting him and his charms. The letters which Mme de Tourvel addresses to her, especially after the Présidente's flight from the château to Paris, document the Vicomte's unconscionable behavior as well as the terrible dilemma that loving him poses for the Présidente. It is remarkable that, given her usual defensive and protective attitude about Valmont, Mme de Rosemonde listens so sympathetically to all that the Présidente reports about the moral difficulties that Valmont's aggressive conduct has caused. Then she encourages the Présidente to confide in her even more! As a writer she may be Valmont's aunt, but as a reader, she becomes Mme de Tourvel's mother:

Regardez-moi comme votre enfant. Ayez pour moi les bontés maternelles; je les implore. . . . O vous, que je choisis pour ma mère, recevez-en le serment. (Letter 102, pp. 235-36)

In the world of the *Liaisons dangereuses,* however, a mother is neither a powerful nor an efficacious figure. Mme de Volanges was incapable of protecting her daughter, and Mme de Rosemonde is guarded in estimating the value of the succor she can offer to the Présidente:

En laissant à la Providence le soin de vous secourir dans un danger contre lequel je ne peux rien, je me réserve de vous soutenir et vous consoler autant qu'il sera en moi. (Letter 103, p. 238)

Unable either to save the Présidente or to stop loving her nephew, powerless to act as a protective mother or a disciplining aunt, Mme de Rosemonde is split by her affections and the two distinct mental states they imply. Like the other personages examined in this chapter, her double character is best illustrated by separating the two strands of her fictional nature and by studying her both as a writer and as a reader.

Notes

1. See Yves Le Hir, "La Langue et le style," in his introduction to *Les Liaisons dangereuses* (Paris: Garnier Frères, 1961), pp. xxi-l.

References

Choderlos de Laclos, Pierre-Ambroise-François. *Les Liaisons dangereuses.* Edition de Y. Le Hir. Paris: Garnier Frères, 1961.

—. *uvres complètes.* Texte établi et annoté par Maurice Allem. Bibliothèque de la Pléiade. Paris: Gallimard, 1951.

—. *uvres complètes.* Texte établi, présenté et annoté par Laurent Versini. Bibliothèque de la Pléiade. Paris: Gallimard, 1979.

Susan Rosa (essay date 1988)

SOURCE: "The Anonymous Public in *Les Liaisons dangereuses,*" *Studies in Eighteenth-Century Culture,* Vol. 18, 1988, pp. 479-87.

[*In the essay below, Rosa claims that Laclos raises questions about his intended moral objective in writing* Les Liaisons dangereuses *in order to more fully engage the reader.*]

Throughout the eighteenth century in France, novelists insisted that their works were morally useful. In countless *préfaces, avertissements,* and *avis au lecteur,* they reiterated their aims of pleasing and moving readers in order to instruct and improve them in an agreeable way. Though

adherence to this view of the novel may have been for many novelists only nominal—a defensive maneuver designed to placate right-thinking critics and gain a modicum of respectability for a genre considered disreputable—its repeated expression nevertheless reflects the accepted view of literary production in a society which increasingly valued art for its usefulness, and in which literary works were thought of, not as "self-affirming objects,"[1] but as instruments for provoking some sort of change—preferably a moral one—in audience or reader.

Among novelists, Rousseau is perhaps the most cogent, conscientious, and effective exponent of this view. In the prefaces to *La Nouvelle Héloïse,* he insists that in a corrupt society the novel is the only means of reform, and that therefore novelists must attempt to change not only the values but the behavior of their readers. While Rousseau often presents himself as a voice crying in the wilderness, his very insistence on the power of the novel to affect the moral behavior of his audience indicates his belief that at least some readers will read him as he wants to be read. Despite his melancholy portrayal of life in society, Rousseau betrays a certain optimism; he is convinced that his readers, once alerted, will hear and understand his message, that they will recognize its truth and apply it to themselves, and finally, that they will transform their lives accordingly.

The presence of Rousseau is evident on virtually every page of *Les Liaisons dangereuses,* and Laclos engages in an intertextual dialogue with the *maître* on a variety of subjects, including the question of how readers read. While one might easily argue that reading and interpretation in general are important concerns of *Les Liaisons dangereuses* as a whole, I shall concentrate here on the opening and closing pages of the novel where, in broad outline, Laclos depicts a fictional reading public which includes both critics—the *éditeur* of the first preface, and nonprofessional readers—the "bonne mère" of the second preface, and the men and women of society to whom the letters of Valmont and Merteuil are revealed at the end of the novel. Based on misunderstandings or partial readings, and singularly at odds with the moral intentions stated by the *rédacteur* in the second preface, the reactions of this public to the intrigue unveiled in the correspondence show Laclos to be far less sanguine than Rousseau about the docility of the public to the reforming efforts of the novelist, and indicate that, in his view, there is no guarantee that the reactions of readers will correspond to the intentions of authors. Framing the narrative, this portrait of the novel's first readers, who show neither the ability nor the inclination to be morally improved by the exposure of the crimes of Valmont and Merteuil, challenges all claims on behalf of the didactic and improving function of the novel, and through its implications about the nature of audience response, necessitates the rethinking of a view of literary production which, despite an injection of new life by Rousseau, had hardened into conventionality.

In typical eighteenth-century fashion, **Les Liaisons dangereuses** is presented to readers under the aegis of instruction. Arguing in the second preface that the moral usefulness of the work is easy to establish, the *rédacteur,* or supposed editor of the correspondence, insists that the publication of these scandalous letters will render an important service to public morals by unveiling the strategies of those who would corrupt the innocent. More specifically, he adds, it will provide proof and example of some important truths that too often go unrecognized by an unwary public:

> . . . l'une, que toute femme qui consent à recevoir dans sa société un homme sans moeurs, finit par en devenir la victime; l'autre, que toute mère est au moins imprudente, qui souffre qu'un autre qu'elle ait la confiance de sa fille. Les jeunes gens de l'un et de l'autre sexe, pourraient encore y apprendre que l'amitié que les personnes de mauvaises moeurs paraîssent leur accorder si facilement, n'est jamais qu'un piège dangereux, et aussi fatale à leur bonheur qu'à leur vertu.[2]

Accompanying these righteous assertions of moral utility on the part of the *rédacteur* are the reactions of two readers which, in different ways, seem designed to challenge them. The first occurs in a *caveat* to future readers from the supposed *éditeur,* a rather pompous and complacent individual who, taking pride of place as publisher, and speaking with the carping voice of traditional criticism, insists in the first preface that it is his duty to warn the public, despite the protest of the *rédacteur,* that this collection of letters is only a novel. His reason for coming to this conclusion, he argues, is that the work lacks verisimilitude, a contention based in turn on the scandalous behavior of the characters. Betraying a rather anodyne faith in progress, he maintains that such evil persons can only have been the products of other places and other times:

> En effet, plusieurs des personnages qu'il met en scène ont de si mauvaises moeurs, qu'il est impossible de supposer qu'ils aient vécu dans notre siècle; dans ce siècle de philosophie, où les lumières, répandues de toutes parts, ont rendu, comme chacun sait, tous les hommes si honnêtes et toutes les femmes si réservées. (29)

Here the willful blindness of the *éditeur,* accentuated by the ironic reference to "lumières," calls into serious question the possible effectiveness of the lessons the *rédacteur* proposes to impress on the public. Confronted on the one hand with the desire on the part of the *rédacteur* to unveil the strategies of those who would corrupt the innocent, and so improve public morals, and on the other with the refusal of the *éditeur* to recognize the reality of these same strategies, as well as with his stubborn absolutism ("*toutes*

parts," "*tous* les hommes," "*toutes* les femmes"), we may very well wonder about the moral usefulness of unveiling something to an audience that is unwilling to see what is being unveiled.

The hard-headed complacency of the *éditeur* is not the only evidence which suggests that the moral instruction of readers may be difficult to achieve. Concluding his defense of the usefulness of the correspondence with the usual warning that such works may nevertheless be dangerous to youth, the *rédacteur* presents the reaction of a respectable woman to whom he has shown the work in manuscript. Her wise intention to give this correspondence to her daughter on the day of her marriage, he argues, attests the success of his project:

> L'époque, où [cette lecture] peut cesser d'être dangereuse et devenir utile, me paraît avoir été très bien saisie, pour son sexe, par une bonne mère qui non seulement a de l'esprit, mais qui a du bon esprit. "Je croirais," me disait-elle, après avoir lu le manuscrit de cette correspondance, "rendre un vrai service à ma fille, en lui donnant le livre le jour de son mariage." Si toutes les mères de famille en pensent ainsi, je me féliciterai eternellement de l'avoir publié. (32-33)

The response of this "bonne mère" is based on a laughable misunderstanding of the intrigue unveiled in the correspondence. The whole point of Merteuil's suggestion in Letter 2 that Valmont seduce Cécile, whose sad story supposedly provides a warning to other innocent daughters, is to corrupt her *before* her marriage and so to humiliate her future husband, Gercourt. Obviously, one does not have to read very far to realize that if the purpose of this collection of letters is to warn innocent young girls to beware the machinations of corrupt seducers, it should be made available to them well before their wedding day. Seen in this light, the decision of the "bonne mère" to give the correspondence to her daughter after her marriage is but a futile gesture. Her "wise intentions," therefore, do not provide evidence for the utility of the work, but further undermine the claims of the *rédacteur* on behalf of its instructional value. By mustering her questionable testimony in his defense and blindly associating her acceptance of the proposed moral lessons with so blatant a misreading of the work, the *rédacteur* reveals his own obtuseness, and implicitly, the inadequacy of the moralistic reading he demands.

When we come to the ending of **Les Liaisons dangereuses,** we face a similar juxtaposition: while the narrative itself lays claim to moral utility through the account of the death and disgrace of the villains Valmont and Merteuil, the reactions of another group of fictional readers to the "secret correspondence" demonstrate, in various ways, the hollowness of this very claim. In accordance with the desire of the *rédacteur* to unveil the strategies of the wicked, the final scenes of the novel regale us with the exposure of Valmont and Merteuil. Their secret correspondence is revealed, and their letters circulate in society. As a result, they are punished, and in a manner appropriate to the most moralizing of novels. With the publication of their crimes, these masters of rhetoric are forced into silence. Valmont is killed in a duel by the young and inexperienced Danceny—a perfect punishment for this Don Juan, who has spent more time in the bedroom than in the lists. Merteuil is ostracized by society and attacked by smallpox; previously so adept at self-disguise, she is left hideously disfigured, so that, as a rather catty Marquis remarks, ". . . à présent son âme [est] sur sa figure" (Letter CLXXV, 422). As a result of the exposure of her crimes, the eloquence of her attorneys proves insufficient to defend her claims to her dead husband's estate. Ill and virtually penniless, she flees to Holland.

Much ink has been spilled on the subject of this denouement, whose perfect symmetry between punishment and crime offends contemporary aesthetic sensibilities. In the past, critics argued that the punishment and exposure of Valmont and Merteuil provided evidence that Laclos had fallen victim to his own apparent protestations of moral utility. Georges May, for example, remarked that:

> . . . le ton . . . de ce dénouement incriminé . . . nous [paraît] si conforme . . . à ce qui était alors l'idée qu'on se faisait de la nature et de la fonction du roman, qu'on se demande si Laclos n'a pas été à quelque degré victime lui-même de sa propre comédie; et s'il n'a pas cru . . . qu'il avait, lui aussi, . . . fait une oeuvre riche en leçons morales.[3]

For various reasons, more recent Laclos scholars have been less inclined to find this ending quite so arbitrary, and, as D. A. Coward has pointed out, "it is now generally held . . . to be a logical development of the nature of the unholy alliance between Valmont and Merteuil, of the essentially doomed future of their impossible enterprise, of their psychology, or of the theatricality or overall structure of the novel."[4] Despite this change of opinion all attempts to explain the much criticized denouement concentrate exclusively on the exposure and punishment of Valmont and Merteuil and neglect the equally detailed response of Laclos's fictional public to the revelation of their crimes.

If we examine the various readings of the scandalous correspondence which occur at the end of the novel, we encounter responses which, like those of the *éditeur* and the "bonne mère," either thwart or undermine the moral intentions of the *rédacteur* and render the perfect punishment of Valmont and Merteuil superfluous. The most dramatic of these is the righteous indignation against Merteuil on the part of the men and women of society who have been shown her letters by a vengeful Danceny. This indignation takes the form of the social rehabilitation of a certain Prévan, whose reputation Merteuil has ruined, and its moral quality will perhaps best be made clear by a brief examination of his character. Like Valmont, Prévan is renowned for his sexual exploits. So skilled is he at the art of seduction, in fact, that Valmont regards him as a dangerous competitor: "Il me reste à vous dire," he writes to Merteuil, "que ce Prévan que vous ne connaissez pas, est infiniment aimable et encore plus adroit. Que si quelquefois vous m'avez entendu le contraire, c'est seulement que je ne l'aime pas, que je me plais à contrarier ses succès. . . ." (Letter LXX, 167). His life, like Valmont's, consists of an endless series of sexual conquests, and his power is measured by the number of women whose reputations are in his hands. Indeed, it is his desire to destroy Merteuil's virtuous reputation which leads him in pursuit of her and provokes her revenge. While plotting his downfall, however, she doesn't fail to appreciate his technique, which she describes in detail to Valmont, teasingly suggesting that Prévan can perhaps beat him at his own game:

> J'avais l'air de pressentir ma défaite, et de redouter mon vainqueur. Il le remarqua à merveille; aussi le traître changea-t-il sur le champ de ton et de maintien. Il était galant, il devint tendre. Ce n'est pas que les propos ne fussent à peu près les mêmes; la circonstance y forçait: mais son regard, devenu moins vif, était plus caressant; l'inflexion de sa voix plus douce; son sourire n'etait plus celui de la finesse, mais du contentement. Enfin dans ses discours, éteignant peu à peu le feu de la saillie, l'esprit fit place à la délicatesse. Je vous le demande, qu'eussiez-vous fait de mieux? (Letter LXXXV, 216)

Like Valmont, then, Prévan is skilled at suiting his style, subject matter, and presentation of self to the victim and to the occasion. As would be expected, he is also a master manipulator of language, adept, like Valmont, at *double entendre* (Letter LXXXV) and able to defeat his victims rhetorically as well as sexually.

Defending himself against the attacks of Madame Riccoboni on the immorality of *Les Liaisons dangereuses,* Laclos insisted that his purpose in writing was to arouse public indignation, which, he argued, is an effective weapon against the power of vice. In the novel itself, however, he expresses less confidence in the high moral quality of this indignation. Identified with the rehabilitation of Prévan, who is, after all, merely another Valmont, the angry response of the public to the exposure of Merteuil's crimes is less an indication of moral renewal than a mere transfer of allegiance from one scoundrel to another. An author, Laclos seems to imply here, may punish vice to his heart's content, but there is no guarantee that such moralizing will have any real effect on the deep-rooted attitudes, values, or assumptions of the public.

To complete the portrait of Laclos's fictional reading public, I would like to turn briefly to two readers, whose responses to the scandalous correspondence, while not anonymous, also work to undermine the moral claims of the *rédacteur*. The first of these is the wise and humane Madame de Rosemonde, Valmont's aged aunt, who, with his death, reassumes her position as head of his family and so speaks with the voice of authority in the final pages of the novel. Unlike the *éditeur*, Rosemonde cannot be accused of complacency. Profoundly affected by the events of the correspondence, which she has read in its entirety, and sadly convinced that they are true, she writes to Danceny: "Après ce que vous m'avez fait connaître, Monsieur, il ne reste qu'à pleurer et qu'à se taire. On regrette de vivre encore, quand on apprend de pareilles horreurs. . . ." (Letter CLXX, 414). Nevertheless, her repeated demands that the entire affair be committed to silence and oblivion, and that it remain shrouded in obscurity (Letter CLXXI), present a challenge to the stated moral intentions of the *rédacteur* which is at least equal to that contained in the remarks of the *éditeur*. When we remember that the *rédacteur's* purpose in publishing the correspondence was to improve public morals by unveiling the strategies of those who would corrupt the innocent, it is difficult not to conclude from Rosemonde's repeated and insistent requests for silence and obscurity that even the best and most conscientious of readers may not be amenable to the moral lessons of authors, or that at the very least, they may be resistant to the manner in which these lessons are conveyed. Like the complacency of the *éditeur*, Rosemonde's demands for silence are emblematic of the failure of the stated moral intentions of the *rédacteur*.

Equally subversive of these intentions is the response of Madame de Volanges, who, throughout the text, has spoken for right-thinking morality. Like the "bonne mère," Volanges is a dutiful reader, who not only accepts the proposed moral lessons of the *rédacteur*, but repeats them in the final letter of the novel:

> Qui pourrait ne pas frémir en songeant aux malheurs que peut causer une seule liaison dangereuse? et quelles peines ne s'éviterait-on point en y réfléchissant davantage! Quelle femme ne fuirait pas au premier propos d'un séducteur? Quelle mère pourrait, sans trembler, voir une autre personne qu'elle parler à sa fille? (Letter CLXXV, 423)

Unfortunately, like the response of the "bonne mère," her words have a sadly after-the-fact quality about them since Madame de Tourvel is already dead, and Volanges's own daughter, Cécile, whom she had hoped to marry so gloriously, has been ignominiously seduced and has retired in disgrace to a convent. Moreover, her response is coupled with an extreme intellectual obtuseness and a complete lack of true moral sensibility. Having read the correspondence only in part, she knows nothing of the letters which relate to her daughter and remains in blind ignorance of the scandal which touches her most closely. When confronted with Merteuil's connivance at the seduction and abandonment of Tourvel by Valmont, she does not question the morality or immorality of Merteuil's actions, but worries only about how those actions may affect her own as yet untarnished reputation: "Il est affreux de se trouver parente de cette femme," she complains righteously to Rosemonde (Letter CLXXIII, 412). Like the "bonne mère," Volanges is a poor reader; her reading of the correspondence has been only partial, and her futile acceptance of the moral lessons supposedly embodied there is contaminated by her ignorance and narrow-mindedness, once again an indication that a moralistic reading of the work is perhaps the most inadequate.

In conclusion, the responses of Laclos's fictional readers suggest that, in his opinion, the accepted view of the novel as a means of moral instruction is at once too ambitious and too restrictive. To expect novels to change behavior, he implies, is to ask too much. As the indignation of the public against Merteuil, the recalcitrance of the *éditeur*, and the demands of Rosemonde for silence all show, readers approach a work, not *tabula rasa*-like, but imbued with values, priorities, and assumptions which may not necessarily be those of the author, and which, more often than not, will nullify his desired effects. To use current terminology, readers are "interpreting entities, endowed with purposes and concerns,"[5] whose readings may not correspond to the author's reading of his own text.

At the same time, and somewhat paradoxically, to insist that novelists write merely to inculcate lessons in a docile public, is to fail to do justice to the complex activities of reading and writing. As the responses of the "bonne mère" and Madame de Volanges make clear, readers who read "for the lessons" are poor readers, whose misreadings or partial readings provide evidence of their inadequate reception of the work. Equally at fault are writers who envision their work as mere instruction; they are pilloried in the figure of the foolish *rédacteur*, who relies on a blatant misreading to support his claims for the moral utility of his work, and whose very existence implies that of an author who takes a less reductive view of his text.

Since Laclos's attack on the didactic conception of the novel is virtually unique, any attempt to explain it can only be conjectural. However, I would suggest that his ironic stance, with its implied movement toward a less audience-centered view of the writer's role, is evidence of his sensitivity to the increasing diversity of the late-eighteenth-century novel-reading public, whose relative heterogeneity made it impossible to solicit from them specific actions, emotions, or convictions on the basis of shared moral norms. For Laclos, the consequences of this perceived gap between author and audience are liberating indeed. Recognizing the independence of readers, he demands from them a new activity; profoundly uneasy in the role of moral guide, he refuses to provide directions for the evaluation of his work; and readers, whose necessary docility to the lessons of the novelist is no longer taken for granted, are left to decide the merits of the novel on their own. At this point, I hasten to add that in rejecting the view of the novel as a means of moral instruction, Laclos does not challenge its capacity to deal with moral issues; indeed, it is impossible to imagine a novel which forces readers to ponder moral questions in more detail or in greater depth than does *Les Liaisons dangereuses.* In abandoning the aim of instruction, however, Laclos demands that readers ask questions rather than accept answers, and it is this insistence which explains much of the power of his remarkable work.

Notes

1. Hugh M. Davidson, *Audience, Words, and Art: Studies in Seventeenth-Century French Rhetoric* (Columbus, Ohio: Ohio State University Press, 1965), 174.

2. Pierre Ambroise François Choderlos de Laclos, *Les Liaisons dangereuses, Oeuvres complètes,* ed. Maurice Allem (Paris: Gallimard, 1951), 32. All further references to the text of *Les Liaisons dangereuses* will be from this edition.

3. Quoted in Jean A. Perkins, "Irony and Candour in Certain *Libertin* Novels," *Studies on Voltaire and the Eighteenth Century* 60 (1968): 245.

4. D. A. Coward, "Laclos Studies, 1968-1982," *Studies on Voltaire and the Eighteenth Century* 219 (1983): 324.

5. Stanley Fish, *Is There a Text in This Class?* (Cambridge, Mass.: Harvard University Press, 1980), 8.

Suellen Diaconoff (essay date 1989)

SOURCE: "Resistance and Retreat: A Laclosian Primer for Women," *The University of Toronto Quarterly,* Vol. 58, No. 3, Spring, 1989, pp. 391-408.

[*In the following essay, Diaconoff compares Laclos's essays with* Les Liaisons dangereuses, *arguing that his views on feminism lacked vision and did not call for fundamental change.*]

In the past ten or fifteen years the assessment of Choderlos de Laclos's treatment of women has undergone significant revision. For if during decades he was celebrated as the first feminist writer and continues to be so called by some critics, male especially,[1] in recent years an increasing number of others have asserted new judgments. Various critics now suggest that, far from being feminist, Laclos's work *in toto* reveals a misogynist mentality (arising out of

the *imaginaire viril,*[2] a sort of ambivalence towards women best defined as 'reductive misogyny,)'[3] the kind of writing that poses as femino-centric but whose ideological subscript is really that of female vulnerability and the re-establishment and ratification of the male order.[4]

The lack of agreement among critics indicates not only changing currents in criticism and differing ideological stands, but also, and most important, the recognition that Laclos delivers to women a mixed message of resistance and retreat. Author of *Les Liaisons dangereuses* (1782), arguably the century's finest novel and often considered the first genuinely feminist novel in French literature, Laclos followed that *succès de scandale* with a foray into non-fiction when in 1783 he took up the competition essay question proposed by the Académie de Châlons-sur-Marne, 'Quels seraient les meilleurs moyens de perfectionner l'éducation des femmes?' The question is characteristic of the intellectual debate sponsored by various regional *académies* in France during the century of Enlightenment, and also illustrates the typical formulation of the 'woman question' in the eighteenth century—that is, almost strictly in terms of education.[5] Indeed, by 1783 hundreds of essays had already been devoted to the issue, and the chances of the competition's eliciting much originality were fairly slight. Laclos's approach was, however, striking because from the beginning he boldly asserted that it was not a different education that would improve conditions for women, but a different society. He caught his reader's attention by declaring, in the first pages of an essay on improving women's education, that in fact it could *not* be improved. In the three essays he eventually produced on the topic, he would show why this was so and how women could accommodate themselves to this knowledge, but he would never return to argue the case for the radical overthrow of society, something he had seemed to promise to women in that tantalizing phrase on the third page: 'Apprenez qu'on ne sort de l'esclavage que par une grande révolution.'

Disappointing as this must be for us today, it is, nonetheless, wholly consistent with who Laclos was and particularly who he was in March 1783, when he decided to try his hand at essay-writing. Indeed, in his biography of Laclos, Georges Poisson offers a chronology of the essays' genesis that, if correct, is highly suggestive for the correlation between events in Laclos's life and the evolution of his notions about women. Following the publication of his novel in early April 1782, Laclos, a career military man stationed at La Rochelle, made the acquaintance of Marie-Solange Duperre, a young woman half his age with whose family he was billeted. It was the next March (1783) that he began writing the first of the three essays to which posterity has given the collective title **'De l'Education des femmes,'** the one which gives greatest import to the necessity of freedom. However, he wrote only three pages before concluding that the subject required greater amplitude, and it was not until later that summer, at age forty-one and for the first time in his life in love, that he would make a second attempt to deal with the subject. His approach was now to consider the development of women's sensual, social, and moral dimensions and to seek to protect rather than to free them. This development, which is expressed implicitly in the second essay, is understandable, Poisson suggests, because his young mistress was pregnant with his child, and the feelings he had towards her were naturally extended to all women. (On 1 May 1784 their son was born, and the parents were married two years later almost to the day.) As for the third essay, the most conformist and the least original, some critics suggest that it probably was completed soon after the second, and others believe that it may have been written much later than the other two, perhaps in the period 1795-9, or even in 1802, largely after Revolutionary events and when Laclos was a happily married man.[6]

Today what makes Laclos's essays on the question of women's education worthy of sustained examination is, first, that while they do not contain much of interest about pedagogy, they have a great deal to say about women's condition in the eighteenth century; and, second, that if they lack the elegant ironies of his novel, they reveal in almost exemplary fashion the paradoxes of a type of Enlightenment thinking, born in passionate commitment to liberty and justice and ending in the bankrupt arguments of reformism. Nowhere is this clearer than in Enlightenment discourse on women with its characteristic and continual movement between promise and retraction, advocacy and containment. The paradox is repeatedly illustrated in these essays, in which Laclos's thinking about women can be characterized as feministic but not feminist. Thus, though he will bear accurate testimony to woman's condition and deplore her lack of freedom in the social contract with its patriarchal assumptions, he will not genuinely seek to free or empower her. Though he will lament the systematic underdevelopment and underuse of her faculties and will indict men for keeping her dependent, irresponsible, and unfree, he will not propose an educational program of substantial and thoroughgoing innovation that could lead to real change for her. And though he believes that social conditioning and not physical predisposition constitutes the real problem for women, he will not, because of conservatism or perhaps male pessimism, take a radical stand for the programmatic advancement of women, or even in *Les Liaisons dangereuses* posit a fictional world without sexual privilege or exploitation. Indeed, though he infuses his novel with the controlling consciousness of a woman, a character who dominates men and is superior to them in the execution of a libertine philosophy, he does not permit her to vanquish definitively any of her rivals, either male or female. Rather, he sets up such a system of social and psychological checks and bal-ances that in the end the same result is obtained in the novel as in the essays: that is, a re-enactment of the status quo. Hence he undermines what he argues for, revealing in so doing the impotence of reformism and a lack of belief in real change. The history of the women's movement is littered with broken promises and disillusionment, and Laclos's essays demonstrate that this is not always because of the ill will or misogyny of men, but because of a lack of vision and of the daring to contemplate a truly new society.

Because his position, like that of many of his countrymen on the question of women's role in society, remains resolutely wedded to a notion of equality based on *complementarity* (the sexes should complete one another) rather than *sameness* (the sexes should have the right to the same privileges and responsibilities), and despite his arguments in favour of justice and liberty for all, he repeatedly shows in the elaboration of his thoughts on woman a reversionary predilection to re-enslave her. Indeed, in **'De l'Education'** Laclos moves backwards in his commitment to woman, making in the first essay the strongest case for her, but weakening it in the second when he shows her as the victim of a tripartite machine—nature, sex, and society—and finally in the third backing himself into a corner, implicitly pleading not so much for equality and empowerment of woman as for accommodation to the status quo.

I propose to study this phenomenon by reading each of the three essays under a separate heading—freedom, sexuality, and education, respectively—in order to show that the movement in each, after some initial expansiveness, becomes narrow and restrictive, 'naturalizing' woman's condition and reconciling and rationalizing inequalities, not because Laclos is a closet misogynist but because he is deeply sceptical about freedom, sexuality, education, and the viability of real change. By narrowing his vision, by reducing the scope and space of his inquiry and proposals in these essays, he becomes caught in a backward and downward spiral of thinking and writing. In this vortex of negative and restrictive rhetoric he is led repeatedly to counsel resistance and then retreat. This mechanism of *feministic* thinking within the essays bears study, for it is this kind of analysis, widespread in the age of freedom, that, ironically, perpetuates the very paradigm of slavery it intended to destroy.

FREEDOM AND REVOLUTION: A CONSERVATIVE ESTIMATE

If we cannot exactly reconstruct Laclos's intentions in 1783 when he turned to address the question set forth by the Académie de Châlons-sur-Marne on the best ways to improve women's education, we can at least uncover his mode of thinking through examining his treatment of the subject—the ambiguities and contradictions, in particular. The essays demonstrate how an argument starting in paradox and a pessimistic appraisal of mankind's potential will necessarily and futilely circle back upon itself. Examination of the essays contradicts the notion that Laclos is an outspoken feminist who preaches revolution.

In this first essay his primary concern is to reveal to woman herself that the essence of the problem is her lack of freedom, as established by the social contract, to which she has merely acceded and not consented.[7] Addressing himself to women, he says:

> Venez apprendre comment, nées compagnes de l'homme, vous êtes devenues son esclave; comment, tombées dans cet état abject, vous êtes parvenues à vous y plaire, à le regarder comme votre état naturel; comment enfin, dégradées de plus en plus par votre longue habitude de l'esclavage, vous en avez préféré les vices avilissants, mais commodes, aux vertus plus pénibles d'un être libre et respectable. (404)

For it is that lack of freedom, Laclos argues, that deprives a woman, first of her morality, and secondly of her capacity to be educated, a judgment which leads him to declare that 'On ne peut sortir de ce principe général que sans liberté point de moralité et sans moralité point d'éducation' (405). His initial approach, then, is, as Madelyn Gutwirth has said, to deconstruct the Académie's proposition and to argue, even from the first pages, that there is no hope of improving either women's education or their condition—until or unless there is a revolution, whose feasibility he immediately casts into doubt by asking his female reader:

> Cette révolution est-elle possible? C'est à vous seules à le dire puisqu'elle dépend de votre courage. Est-elle vraisemblable? Je me tais sur cette question; mais jusqu'à ce qu'elle soit arrivée, et tant que les hommes règleront votre sort, je serai autorisé à dire, et il me sera facile de prouver qu'il n'est aucun moyen de perfectionner l'éducation des femmes. (405)

The problem in improving women's lot is, as he sees it, men, for as arbiters of women's fate they will not or cannot accept women's accession to full and equal rights. Speaking to his female readership, he reminds them:

> Ne vous laissez plus abuser par de trompeuses promesses, n'attendez point les secours des hommes auteurs de vos maux: ils n'ont ni la volonté, ni la puissance de les finir, et comment pourroient-ils vouloir former des femmes devant lesquelles ils seraient forcés de rougir? (405)

It is for this very reason that he remains so ambivalent about not only the probability but also the advisability of women's being better educated. Indeed, one of the questions he is to set for himself in this essay is whether

> dans l'état actuel de la société une femme telle qu'on peut la concevoir formée par une bonne éducation ne

serait pas très malheureuse en se tenant à sa place et très dangereuse si elle tentait d'en sortir. (404)

The answer, as it turns out, will be in the affirmative to both questions, specifically because Laclos, the pragmatic military man, is entrenched in what is—'l'état actuel de la société'—rather than drawn to working on the actualization of what he might be able to visualize. However, it is because of his bifurcated view of the real and the ideal that his argument and logic become murky, compromised, contradictory. For instance, the notion of freedom that might be achieved if she could break the chains of her slavery, but rather merely the relative freedom that he invokes repeatedly is sometimes used in its most complete sense, as relating to the moral, social, and political, and sometimes in only a partial sense; at times Laclos appears to be talking about all women and at other times only about some; he will describe women as having no choice and yet at other times implore them to act and take the initiative. Torn between what is and what he thinks ought to be, he finds that the only solution is to blur distinctions and to establish two tiers, freedom and slavery, the public and the private. By doing so, he can suggest that women are enslaved in a public sector controlled by an immutable social contract, but capable, if removed from that arena, of creating a kind of internal freedom for themselves in the private sphere—and hence of becoming educable.

The freedom he holds out for woman the slave, however, is not the absolute freedom that could be had by loosening the chains through awareness of the possibility of internal freedom. For Laclos, the slave does have a measure of freedom and can, within her slavery, profit from it. Hence he says, 'On ne niera pas . . . que [la liberté] soit une des facultés de la femme et [cela] implique que la liberté puisse se développer dans l'esclavage' (405). To be sure, that freedom will have no effect except on the self, because it cannot be directed 'vers l'utilité sociale puisque la liberté d'un esclave serait une atteinte portée au pacte social *fondé sur l'esclavagé* (my italics).

What seems obvious, then, is that by emphasizing the existence of an inner realm which can be in opposition to outer reality, Laclos is in effect accommodating himself to the immutability of woman's inequality and oppression in the public sphere and consigning her hopes for improvement and justice to the exclusively personal realm. Though ostensibly this first essay was to sketch out why woman's education could not be improved as long as she was unfree and hence immoral, Laclos is also constricted by his own feelings about the unchangeability of the social contract. But he seems to want to suggest that if women are enlightened as to the real and unadulterated nature of their condition, they will be able within their fetters and within the private sphere to create a kind of freedom through awareness. In view of this, he will encourage women to envision freedom as that which they can create for themselves by disposing of the slavelike mentality which prevents them from valuing what is 'in their own real best interests.' Clearly, what he is asking is that women create their own internal, *moral* freedom through an effort of will, and that they accept the social contract and its injustices not because women are an inferior gender but because, he fears, the social contract which binds society cannot be changed: the only possible revolution is small and personal. To modern eyes, his advice suspiciously suggests a revolution in the sense of revolving backward rather than going forward. Hence, he counsels that women seek to free themselves from a state of *moral* degradation and *moral* servitude while remaining unfree in a social or civil sense.[8]

Though he challenges women, as would Simone be Beauvoir in *Le Deuxième Sexe,* to reseize control of their destiny, to recognize the part they have played in their own slavery (using female sexuality as instrumentality, preferring easy vice to difficult virtue, defining freedom as licence or luxury), these challenges are no more than rhetoric, for the so-called revolution he evokes as necessary for change is, in the final analysis, merely that which each individual herself can achieve *internally.* The freedom which Laclos ultimately seems to grant woman is what the prisoner invents for herself, what woman discovers *within* her servitude. It is what Montesquieu's Roxane found within the confines of the seraglio and to which she testifies when she tells Usbek, 'J'ai pu vivre dans la servitude, mais j'ai toujours été libré (*Les Lettres persanes,* letter CLXI). For Laclos, this may not be an ideal solution, but, given his pessimism about real change and his discipline as a defence strategist, it is reasonable to speculate that he may have considered it to be the wisest if not most just course for women.[9]

Taken in its brief, three-page entirety, then, this first essay, while radical in its recognition of the magnitude of the tyranny perpetrated against women, is also inherently contradictory and conservative, a fact made particularly clear in the last paragraph, which functions primarily to imprison woman in a web of negatives. Despite some suggestive but misleading language, this first essay is not at all the feminist—let alone *militantly* feminist—call to arms that many have sought to make it.[10] Though it ostensibly commits itself to helping women achieve the fullest social and civil rights possible and although it is imbued with sympathy for women, it will ultimately and ironically counsel only passive resistance and moral renewal because Laclos does not believe in or is too apprehensive about the possibility of real revolution. It is his inability to return woman to any but a slightly different status quo which causes him during the course of his deliberations on women twice to suspend his writing and twice to make a new attempt in yet another essay to create a different reality and a new and improved future for women.

FEMALE SEXUALITY AND THE SOCIAL CONTRACT

The second essay, a forty-two-page account of Laclos's interpretation of the 'passage' of woman from nature to society, is in many ways pedestrian, but within its seemingly naïve and simplistic discourse is another very important and exceedingly interesting discussion of female sexuality. Unlike Diderot in 'Sur les Femmes' (1772), Laclos does not establish a pathology of femininity or consider, as did his compatriot, the phases of a woman's life starting from puberty and going through menopause as one continuous cycle of illness. Though he does, indeed, idealize the natural woman's sexuality, he does so primarily in order to contrast natural sexuality—sex in nature—with the artificiality and calculation that have invaded the expression and exploitation of woman's sexuality in society. He does not believe that female libido or passion is harmful in itself, but rather that sex has become an instrument that ultimately debases and distances the female from what ought to be the real core of her happiness: that is, her virtue. In consonance, then, with the theme that is being established of discovery and withdrawal, Laclos in this second essay recognizes and celebrates female sexuality, but concludes simultaneously that while it is pleasure in Nature, it is danger in Society, and so must be repressed and redirected, in order to ensure, if not woman's freedom, then her happiness—defined, of course, by him.

What is especially interesting and what, indeed, gives the essay a certain modernity or progressive spirit is the extent to which Laclos shows that he understands sexual difference as a *social* construction, and culture or society as having had an inimical effect on the relations between the sexes. After a long exposé encompassing several chapters, Laclos turns to summing up, and in a section entitled 'Des Premiers Effets de la société' he states clearly his belief that 'la nature ne crée que des êtres libres; la société ne fait que des tyrans et des esclaves' (453). Furthermore, he advances the idea that women, 'manquant de forces ne purent défendre et conserver leur existence civile,' with the result that 'compagnes de nom, elles devinrent bientôt esclaves de fait.' In his interpretation, then, women's lot would be little more than oppression and scorn, if it were not that

> dans l'état de guerre perpétuelle qui subsiste entre elles et les hommes, on les a vues, à l'aide des caresses qu'elles ont su se créer, combattre sans cesse, vaincre quelquefois, et souvent, plus adroites, tirer avantage des forces même dirigées contre elles . . . (436)

In what amounts to a rather conventional reading of the issue, then, Laclos considers that female sexuality has become a tool used by women to redress the unequal balance of power between the sexes in this, a man's world, ruled by a social contract which has posited the fundamental hostility underlying sexual relations and which was *his* invention and not hers. For it was the social contract that condemned the sexes to live in a state of ongoing war just as it condemned women to the role of 'esclaves malheureuses,' whose destiny, said Laclos, was scarcely 'meilleur que celui des noirs de nos colonies' (434). Given this situation, the single hope for women was that since the contract had posited only female vulnerability and not female inadequacy, women could seek restitution by substituting 'l'adresse à la force': they could make men, on whom they were dependent economically and in terms of physical strength, depend on them for physical pleasure:

> Elles sentirent enfin que, puisqu'elles étaient plus faibles, leur unique ressource état de séduire; elles connurent que si elles étaient dépendantes de ces hommes par la force, ils pouvaient le devenir à elles par le plaisir. (435)

Woman, then, according to Laclos, learned to appeal to and manipulate man's imagination ('facile à séduire'), beguiling him into concentrating on the *promise* of unknown pleasure, rather than the pleasure itself. For, he argues, women (like modern sexologists who emphasize the importance of the imagination and mental activity in enhancing the sexual experience) knew that if the pleasure was essentially always the same, the promise of it could be made to be infinitely different and the key to their manipulation of men. Madame de Merteuil's use of this psychological mechanism is made amply clear in letter x of *Les Liaisons dangereuses,* in which she describes for Valmont how, in order to inflame the Chevalier's passions, she had, with panache and mystification, staged an erotic encounter with him at her *petite maison.* And how, once he arrived, she adopted a variety of attitudes, 'tour à tour enfant et raisonnable, folâtre et sensible, quelquefois même libertine,' and treated him as 'un Sultan au milieu de son Sérail, dont j'étais tour à tour les Favorites différentes.' Mad with pleasure, he paid her repeated hommage which, she boasts, was received by 'la même femme,' who was, however, also always 'une Maîtresse nouvelle' (31). Hence, she schemed, beguiled, and conquered. And she now sought, through her narration and its word picture of erotic promise and pleasure, to reduplicate both the scene and her power over the man by arousing in Valmont an overwhelming desire for her.

In Laclos's interpretation, then, woman's power arises directly out of her sexuality and is totally dependent upon her ability to create in man a continually new desire for her. But he also sees that her sexuality can be a source of danger for her, because it can entrap even while it gratifies her physically. Neither in the novel nor in the essays does Laclos deny women's capacity for sexual pleasure. In fact,

he celebrates her latent erotic power and sensuality and shows her not as a passive partner, not a victim, forced to submit to the male's 'brute needs,' but often an active and enjoying participant in sex. But he still feels that it is equally possible that her sexuality will enslave her if she falls into promiscuity or permits love to become the very pivot of her oppression, as does, for instance, Madame de Tourvel. Or, on the other hand, if she chooses to reject the notion that she is merely chattel, with no control over her own destiny, and attempts to shake the chain and create for herself some type of freedom, she may be involved in an ultimately destructive form of self-deception. Such is the case with Madame de Merteuil, who wanted to throw out the entire subtext with regard to gender ideology, but ends up trapping herself in a behaviour—libertinage—of limited value, patterned as it is on that of the 'enemy' and imitating his model rather than being a creation of her own principles, as she alleges. We might judge that what she does not see is that her acceptance of eroticism or libertinage as the only means to power does little more than re-establish the male prerogative she is ostensibly attacking, by once again limiting the domain of female action to a total dependence on male pleasure. Of course, it is largely her sense of outrage that women must play the game as set forth by men that constitutes the basis of her fury against Valmont and leads to the exposition in letter LXXXI of what she erroneously believes is her own unique philosophy.

One might read in the destiny of Madame de Merteuil an indictment of the feminist demand to be treated the same way and to have the same rights and privileges as men. For we might well conclude that her experience demonstrates that this stance of 'sameness' is tantamount to arguing for what Elizabeth Meese has called 'an unending regression within an oppressive and phallocentric economy.'[11] Sadly, it appears, Madame de Merteuil's attack is on the exclusivity of male privilege, not on the nature or quality of the privilege itself, so that while she adopts the feminist posture of defiance and challenges the phallocentric economy, all she does is destroy some individual predators, not the system itself, which protects the tyrant and oppresses women.

As he draws towards the end of this essay, Laclos shows that he wishes both to protect women from the predators/tyrants (men who would turn against women 'ces armes qu'elles avaient forgées pour . . . les combattre' and who would make their slavery yet worse [435]), and from her own misuse of her sexuality. He accuses women, for instance, of contributing to their own enslavement by devising notions of beauty that do little more than accentuate both their dependency on men and men's definition of them as primarily sexual and sensual beings. He claims that it is women who have fabricated what today we would call an essentially self-defeating notion of beauty, for they have declared that 'la beauté n'est . . . que l'apparence la plus favorable à la jouissance, la manière d'être qui fait espérer la jouissance la plus délicieuse' (437). Thus, he reveals, they define their central concern as sexual in nature and reduce themselves to creatures who compete with one another to serve men better. For the 'jouissance' referred to is man's, which means that even while women are attempting to assert themselves, they do so by embracing rules set forth by men and by seeking to please men.

In a final chapter on 'De la Parure' he adopts a new tone and takes a prescriptive approach, as though he were writing a conduct book for women, counselling what could be called a virtuous 'economy of voluptuousness,' offering advice on how to accommodate oneself to the unchangeable social contract and how to find some modicum of happiness within it. He admonishes women to be healthy, to avoid excess in everything, whether it be alcohol, sun, or exercise; he tells them to moderate their emotions, not to be evil-tempered, and to avoid envy and ambition; he counsels cleanliness (including, even, a daily bath), and gives beauty hints on cleansers and perfumes. Warning women away from artificial stimulants, he says 'Vous êtes jeunes et belles: qu'avez-vous besoin de liqueurs fortes? C'est d'amour qu'il faut vous enivrer.' What more conventional advice to women could he give? And what, indeed, has happened to any notion of revolution and to equality and female rights?

Clearly, they have receded far back in his mind, as he now contemplates female sexuality and accepts both the status quo and the cultural fabrication of woman. But if she cannot be made free, he would like at least to ensure some happiness for her in her reduced space, and in accordance with his basically bourgeois instincts he decides that only in marriage can she be protected from society and have much chance for happiness. Obviously he is compromising, for earlier he had portrayed marriage too as an institution of confinement when, in lauding the intensely erotic nature of natural woman's sexual encounters, he had asked the married woman:

> En est-il une, parmi vous, qui ait joui constamment sans crainte, sans jalousie, sans remords, ou sans l'ennui pénible du devoir ou de l'uniformité? . . . ayez le courage de scruter vos coeurs et jugez par vous-mêmes. (417-18)

Now, however, because of the dangers that he concludes society holds for her, he encourages her to seek happiness and protection in marriage. Consequently we must judge that Laclos has treated the question of woman's sexuality as he did her freedom—finding it desirable, justifiable, positive, but also dangerous to her in the imperfect society in which she lives. As he has advanced in his deliberations

and become more and more sensitive to female vulnerability, he has opted increasingly to see danger in the social contract and to want to defend woman from it, at the same time, however, limiting her growth—clearly a case of what Pierre Darnon has called paternalistic feminism.[12] Again, as in the first essay, Laclos has taken stock of the situation and has tightened the yoke, despite his original idea of loosening it, because he has entrapped himself, as much as woman, in a rhetoric of reflection rather than in one of visionary promise.

EDUCATION, THE FINAL DISILLUSION

Having now so curbed or recurbed woman, as he reinvented her natural history and traced her unfortunate passage into the state of society, Laclos will attempt at last in the third and final essay of not quite nine pages to focus on the specific details—subject matter, books, instructors—of the education he proposes for women. However, an examination of its contents, objectives, and what would have to be called a very modest, limited, and unoriginal program leads the reader to conclude not only that, when he was writing this essay, Laclos was in the rearguard when it came to progressive thinking about woman's education but also—surprisingly in an essay on this subject in the eighteenth century—that he appears deeply doubtful about the power of education to generate significant change. To understand this position one must recall that by the third essay Laclos has slipped into complicity with the status quo and its ideology, having 'naturalized' the social reality of women's condition, with the effect of making it seem, if not as value-free, at least as unchangeable as Nature itself.

Women's education, Laclos believes, must necessarily be a reflection of their role in society, and indeed for their own happiness, he judges, it should be consistent with that role. This position, which seems to arise less from an appreciation of any heritage or tradition than from a desire not to take risks, to respect certain prejudices, if to do so is less harmful than to revolt against them, is very much like the claustrophobic though pragmatic conservatism of a Montaigne or a Pascal, in that it has little to do with justice, but possibly a great deal to do with social order and with personal happiness. Dismissing or forgetting the importance that he had once attributed to freedom in improving women's conditions, Laclos now gives the appearance of arguing that happiness is a more appropriate goal for women because they should seek to create the most perfect relationship possible between the self and the ideas of virtue, modesty, and morality. It can be argued that these are qualities that in the eighteenth century were in direct opposition to the reigning code of sociability. In other words, what Laclos is pressing for is the rejection of this code, which has always kept woman enslaved, and the adoption of another standard of personal and moral fortification whose ostensible purpose will be greater happiness than she has henceforth enjoyed. On the final page of the essay he says:

> Si la jeune personne qui nous occupe en ce moment a le courage de se livrer au travail que nous lui proposons, nous croyons pouvoir l'assurer qu'elle sera non seulement plus instruite, mais aussi plus heureuse que la plupart des autres femmes. (458)

Thus, Laclos advocates an education that would help woman cope with her individual life rather than encourage her to see herself as part of a collective whose aspirations have been held in check. Significantly, he also tells her, in the second most memorable sentence of the work, that whatever knowledge she obtains should remain largely private: 'Nous espérons,' he says, on the last page, 'qu'elle y gagnera un assez bon esprit pour ne jamais montrer ses connaissances qu'à des amis les plus intimes et, pour ainsi dire, comme confidences' (458). Any education will hence be strictly for private and domestic consumption; it will not be the means of changing one's public lot.

Laclos begins this essay by asserting that 'la lecture est réellement une seconde éducation qui supplée à l'insuffisance de la première.' Though he believes that experience is the greatest teacher, he realizes that it may come too late and be too fraught with risk to provide real aid, and so he counsels women to turn to books as they cultivate their reason, hearts, and minds. One should read books, he believes, primarily to gain knowledge about the self and others, and secondarily to learn about the world through study of the sciences. Laclos advises reading moralists (to learn 'ce qui doit être'), historians (who teach 'ce qui est'), and 'littérateurs,' including poets, orators, historians, and bellettrists, though he gives some conventional warnings concerning the potential danger of novels. The objective of this proposed reading of moralists will be to develop in 'un sujet bien né' a love of virtue, an appreciation for 'le beau, le juste et l'honnête,' and the development of an attitude of compassion and tolerance for others but severity towards the self, along with stoical courage or resignation in the face of pain; it will also teach 'ce qu' on doit à soi-même et ce qu'on doit aux autres' (450).

He provides a few specific suggestions, giving customary accolades to Greek and Roman writers and the value of reading about 'les principes des grandes et belles actions'; he tells women that they should learn something about the history of the various European nations, but that their sex frees them from having to know the details; he disparages the usefulness both of the contemporary morality of 'nos philosophes' who 'n'ont rien ajouté à la morale des anciens' and of preachers who have not improved upon the Bible. He counsels the aid of a good guide in the choice of novels ('Presque tout dépend . . . en ce genre, ou de l'addresse du guide, ou du bon esprit de la personne qui lit'); he proposes that the female student learn Latin, largely because it is a language whose knowledge is for oneself rather than to show off to others, but he accepts that if she finds it too difficult, she should learn either Italian or English; he advises some knowledge of astronomy, physics, chemistry, natural history, and botany; he shows that he values both oral and written expression, and believes that one must develop adequately those skills for successful personal relations. Finally, he says, taking a cue from Montaigne (and many others):

> Ce n'est pas ce qu'on mange qui nourrit, mais seulement ce qu'on digère. Il ne suffit donc pas de lire beaucoup, ni même de lire avec méthode, il faut encore lire avec fruit, de manière à retenir et à s'approprier en quelque sorte, ce qu'on a lu. (457)

It is not unreasonable to conclude from the extreme moderation and lack of verve in this section that, as Laclos reaches the end of his meditations on women, he is not really convinced that education is, in the final analysis, the central issue in the problem of woman's condition. After all, it is not because Cécile has not read enough that she is corrupted by Valmont, or because Madame de Tourvel is undereducated that she is led to become an adultress. And for Madame de Merteuil, who reads Crébillon and Rousseau and La Fontaine 'pour recorder les différents tons que je voulais prendre' (letter x), education is merely a means to an end—her own angry one. Indeed, she seems to pride herself on her classical education, but even more on the uses to which she has put it in the development of her philosophy of personal advancement. As she explains to Valmont:

> Je . . . fortifiai [mes observations sur la société] par le secours de la lecture: mais ne croyez pas qu'elle fût toute du genre que vous la supposez. J'étudiai nos moeurs dans les Romans; nos opinions dans les Philosophes; je cherchai même dans les Moralistes les plus sévères ce qu'ils exigeaient de nous, et je m'assurai ainsi de ce qu'on pouvait faire, de ce qu'on devait penser et de ce qu'il fallait paraître. (Letter LXXXI)

Hence, in the society such as it is established (the one Laclos does not believe can be changed), her education has served only her selfish ends. In the war with men, it has permitted her at times to best them at their own games, but in the final analysis it wins her no permanent gains.

Indeed, Laclos does not seem to believe that education can change much at all, either for the individual woman (who must hide her knowledge, so as to preserve her modesty) or for society as a whole. Nowhere does he assert that education is the necessary first step in bringing about positive change in the relations between the sexes, nor does he even take up again the idea, presented in the first essay, of the positive role of education with regard to 'l'utilité sociale.' The idealistic though empty rhetoric of the first pages is not repeated here; rather Laclos retreats to the language of accommodation and constraint, which is mirrored in the reduced educational objectives he sets forth for women. Education is not presented as capable of opening an improved civil existence for women; it does not seriously address the issues of justice and equality; and there can never be one standard of education for all women. In fact, Laclos is not even talking about women as a group, for the optic has been significantly narrowed since the first essay, which he addressed to all women, and the second, in which he described the passage of most into chattels. Now he is concerned only with the few or privileged ones, those who have an obligation to become 'properly' educated.

It is no surprise, then, to learn that he, unlike Condorcet, is no proponent of the same education presented in the same way for all individuals. What books are chosen by the student's guide becomes a matter that depends, he says, on age, sex, condition, intelligence, and taste for a subject. Several times he specifically mentions that he has in mind the 'sujet bien né,' 'une personne qui a de l'esprit et de la figure, et que son rang et sa fortune mettent dans le cas de vivre dans la compagnie la plus distinguée et même d'y avoir de l'influence' (450). To so limit his audience of pupils is to suggest not only an élitist attitude, but perhaps also some deep-seated doubt about both the appeal and efficacy of mass education—disturbingly anti-democratic ideas in an essay which ostensibly deals with equality. Reading this essay, we are aware that while its spirit is that of egalitarianism, there are few specific points made that would support the implementation of equality. There is no egalitarian argument made here for giving women the same education as men or giving it for the same reasons. Nor does Laclos take the argument for women's education and against women's oppression very far: he is not advancing the idea that all women have a right to education; he is not proposing the establishment of schools for women, subsidized by the state and committed to teaching a specific curriculum; he is not even asserting that women should be educated so as to provide the state with more responsible citizens and properly brought up children—an argument many female feminists advanced in support of their demands for better education.[13] He seems to believe that the best education is that which the woman will receive at home in the company of a tutor who will guide her into making correct and moral applications of her reading. The education he is advancing is 'safe,' useful, and appropriate, offering the right moral lessons. The philosophy Laclos embraces is one that limits choice. It suggests a view of humanity—not just of women, perhaps—that is excessively reserved if not deeply pessimistic

and certainly at great variance with his reputation as a liberator or feminist.

But Laclos's paternalism in wishing to protect women from having to live in the maelstrom of society's conflicts may exist, not because of any hidden disdain for females on his part, but rather because of deep conservatism and weighty reservations about humankind and society. For the social scene both referred to in the essays and painted in *Les Liaisons dangereuses* is one rife with rivalries and ambitions, competitions and clashes from which a participant rarely emerges the victor and never with virtue intact; and Laclos, with chivalrous concern, seems to wish to protect women from such harsh realities. Moreover, in view of his implied pessimism about humanity, it is difficult to accuse him of misogyny or of having broken faith with women by failing to present a program of education that will prepare them for new roles of social power. The object of **'De l'Education des femmes'** is not in the end to offer strategies for subverting the social contract; the most Laclos may have had in mind was to serve up some defensive strategies to be used by women in a politics of moral fortification. In other words, we misread him when we wish to read him as an early committed feminist.

Close study of the essays leads us to conclude that Laclos has systematically, if without malice, reduced woman's space in the course of these three essays. While granting her freedom *from* past enslavement, he has not granted her the freedom *to* develop to the fullest extent her own abilities and humanity. Ultimately, his position is that of a reformist, though one who recognizes the falseness of reformism, its broken promises and tarnished ideals. Hence the double view and contradictory message of this work: that is, of resistance and retreat. In **'De l'Education des femmes'** we have a text which pulls against itself, which is ambivalent in its relation to women, representing both an attack on the sexual politics of the social contract and a redemonstration through example of those same politics. Laclos's relationship to feminism, like his relationship to the pedagogical act, is ambivalent: while expressing belief in women's rights and in education, he undermines those beliefs by casting doubts, drawing such narrow limits that in the end both his target and his commitment appear uncertain and begin to recede from view. Curiously, then, the essay begun in paradox also ends in paradox—hardly a clear pedagogical device—and, while condemning the lesson of futility taught to women in the constrictive social contract, Laclos is caught up in his own constrictive tendencies and comes close to propagating the very lessons he has sought to discredit. Ultimately, the primer he offers women is not only disappointing but also destructive and debilitating, for it re-enacts the very paradigm of slavery it set out to destroy.

Notes

1. For instance, Georges Poisson, in a 1985 biography of Laclos (the first since Emile Dard's 1936 version and based on new archival materials Poisson uncovered), calls him 'le premier écrivain féministe de notre littérature,' saying *Les Liaisons dangereuses* represents a 'roman féministe, et même d'un féminisme agressif.' *Choderlos de Laclos ou l'obstination* (Paris: Grasset 1985), 131.

2. Jean-Marie Goulemot speaks of a misogynist mentality underlying *Les Liaisons dangereuses* which he sees as defining the basic ethic of social and sexual interactions in the novel. 'Le lecteur-voyeur et la mise en scène de l'imaginaire viril,' *Laclos et le libertinage, 1782-1982* (Paris: Presses Universitaires 1983), 163-75.

3. Using Madame Riccoboni's correspondence with Laclos, in which she protests against the image of womanhood presented in his novel, Madelyn Gutwirth writes that Laclos's sympathy for females, even in *Les Liaisons dangereuses,* is mottled with ambivalence and that the final effect of the novel is belittling to women. Gutwirth asserts that the emotional *Tendenz,* if not the intent, of Laclos's novel is to lament women's sexual fate, but to put her 'back in her proper sphere.' 'Laclos and Le Sexe: The Rack of Ambivalence,' *Studies on Voltaire and the Eighteenth Century* (189), 247-96.

4. In *The Heroine's Text: Readings in the French and English Novel, 1722-1782* (New York: Columbia University Press 1980), Nancy K. Miller deals with female characters created by male writers whom she accuses of inscribing female destiny exclusively as sexual vulnerability. In what she calls the heroine's text, written by men, the rule of the female experience is the drama of a single misstep. In her reading of male writing, all female characters—Madame de Merteuil no less than Madame de Tourvel—will go from 'all' in this world to 'nothing,' sacrificed to a masculine idea and ideal. Miller's final assessment is that the commonplaces of culture do not provide women with any plots other than those that arise from the erotic or the familial. Taking an opposite stand is Geoffrey Wagner, who wishes to show that imagination can rise above sex and that the male writer can bear true testimony to the feminine experience. In support of this view he asks if one has to have murdered to be able to imagine what the experience might be like. *Five for Freedom: A Study of Feminism in Fiction* (Rutherford, NJ: Fairleigh Dickinson University Press 1973).

5. For a recent history of the education of females in the eighteenth century see Martine Sonnet, *L'Education des filles au temps des Lumières* (Paris: Editions du CERF 1987).

6. Laurent Versini, *Laclos et la tradition: Essai sur les sources et la technique des 'Liaisons dangereuses'* (Paris: Klincksieck 1968), 202.

7. He says this specifically in an important chapter, 'Des Premier Effets de la société,' in the second essay, when he observes, 'on est tenté de croire qu'elles n'ont que cédé, et non pas consenti au contrat social, qu'elles ont été primitivement subjuguées, et que l'homme a sur elles un droit de conquête dont il use rigoureusement' (434). All references to Laclos's writings are from *Oeuvres complètes* (Paris: Gallimard 1951).

8. Paul Hoffmann has described the type of revolt found in the eighteenth-century novel as a sort of moral and 'spiritual feminism,' in which there is a filiation between feminism and stoicism, and woman becomes 'l'unique témoin de sa propre excellence' ('Sur le thème de la révolte dans quelques romans du XVIIIe siècle français,' *Romanische Forschungen,* 99 [1987], 19-34). It would appear that this is the character of Laclosian feminism as well.

9. Since Laclos's military career was as a defence strategist, it is natural that critics should seek to uncover the presence of such a dimension in his other writing. Joan De Jean, for instance, deals with what has been called 'fortress logic' as it is manifested in both the novel and the essays, and suggests that Laclos believed military strategy could be reduced to defensive strategy (*Literary Fortifications: Rousseau, Laclos, Sade* [Princeton: Princeton University Press 1984], 201). There is, moreover, she feels, a defensive strategy that permeates Laclos's thinking and that posits an essential collusion between pedagogy and defensiveness. I would like to suggest that this is particularly true and appropriate with regard to his thinking about women, to whom the lessons of 'De l'Education' are destined.

10. For instance, in a recent book, *Sex and the Enlightenment: Women in Richardson and Diderot* (Cambridge University Press 1984), Rita Goldberg describes the essays as 'a passionate treatise . . . urging women to take up the struggle for their own equality and freedom' (5). This is a conclusion, I submit, that can be reached only if one takes Laclos's line about revolution out of context and does not consider the extent to which his thinking remains fundamentally ambivalent.

11. *Crossing the Double-Cross: The Practice of Feminist Criticism* (Chapel Hill: University of North Carolina Press 1986), 17. Meese recognizes as valid the argument of those who believe that equality is situated in sameness, but also observes that newer critical approaches have caused many feminists to rethink the question of sameness and difference, realizing that valuing *difference* has the additional benefit of bringing the feminist critic closer to the mainstream of critical debate. While eschewing such a politically opportunistic stance herself, Meese argues for a new politics of positive deconstruction and reconstruction of women, one which emphasizes

meaning, difference, and identity, and the valuation of a standard other than that of phallocentrism. Laclos's failure to establish another standard and his acceptance of what is (that is, the phallocentric economy) would disqualify him as a feminist in Meese's eyes.

12. *Mythologie de la femme dans l'ancienne France* (Paris: Editions du Seuil 1983). See especially the chapter 'Les Mythes dépoussiérés des Lumières,' 148-73. Darnon judges harshly Laclos's essays, about which he says, 'l'ennui se substitue au génie . . . et l'opposition manichéenne entre la "femme sociale" qui porte le germe de la perversion, et la "femme naturelle," qui inspire à l'auteur une succession d'envolées apologétiques, n'emporte guère les convictions' (157).

13. The *Journal des dames,* for instance, published in June 1774 a speech given to the Académie de Dijon the preceding summer, entitled 'L'Admission de quelques femmes lettrées dans les Académies, proposée comme un moyen d'étendre et de rendre plus utiles les Influences de l'Esprit philosophique,' in which a Monsieur Saizi of the Académie des Sciences de Dijon underscored the advantages that would accrue to society by improving women's education: 'L'étude, en élevant leur esprit aux vues de la Philosophie règlera leurs affections, les éclairera sur *leurs devoirs de mères & de citoyennes* [my italics], leur fera connoître l'importance & les suites effrayantes de leur négligence à les remplir.' Mention even is made of revolution: 'Qui pourroit douter que l'admission de quelques femmes lettrées dans les Académies ne soit un moyen de hâter cette révolution qui sera le plus beau des trophées de la Philosophie?'

Peter V. Conroy, Jr. (essay date 1989)

SOURCE: "Male Bonding and Female Isolation in Laclos's *Les Liaisons dangereuses*," *Studies on Voltaire and The Eighteenth Century,* No. 267, 1989, pp. 253-71.

[*In the essay below, Conroy argues that Laclos champions the power of male friendship over the lesser power of the female acting alone.*]

Near the end of Choderlos de Laclos's libertine masterpiece, *Les Liaisons dangereuses* (1782), the Chevalier Danceny challenges the Vicomte de Valmont to a duel. Danceny has just discovered that Valmont has been seducing the woman he loves, Cécile Volanges, while pretending to be his friend and confidant. Naively, Danceny had thought that Valmont was helping to further his amorous intentions towards Cécile. Enraged, the Chevalier demands satisfaction for this spot on his manly honour, for this mockery made of friendship. The two men cross swords and Danceny obtains his revenge by wounding Valmont

fatally. At this point in the novel, a momentous event takes place, one that has been duly noted by critics but also one that has never been fully analysed for its deepest, secret meaning.[1] As he dies of his wounds, Valmont makes a noble, an heroic, a most manly gesture: he forgives his murderer. To demonstrate the sincerity of this pardon and the depth of this newly forged friendship between the erstwhile adversaries, the Vicomte gives Danceny his most precious and secret possession: to the man who has mortally wounded him, he confides his entire libertine correspondence, the intimate record of his private soul. This gesture on Valmont's part is described in suitably moving terms by the Vicomte's longtime acquaintance, the family lawyer, Maître Bertrand:[2]

> Mais c'est là que M. le vicomte s'est montré bien véritablement grand. Il m'a ordonné de me taire; et celui-là même, qui était son meurtrier, il lui a pris la main, l'a appelé son ami, l'a embrassé devant nous tous [. . .] Il lui a, de plus, fait remettre, devant moi, des papiers fort volumineux, que je ne connais pas, mais auxquels je sais bien qu'il attachait beaucoup d'importance. Ensuite, il a voulu qu'on les laissât seuls ensemble pendant un moment.

This reconciliation between two foes who only moments before were trying to kill each other is a powerful depiction of male bonding, of men who in a moment of ultimate stress and antagonism can put aside their differences and establish a real intimacy. In Laclos's fictional universe of dangerous relationships the implications of this bonding as well as its corollary, female isolation, are enormous.

Les Liaisons dangereuses is not only about seductions and deceptions, it also incorporates mendacity and hypocrisy into its very narrative fabric. At its libertine centre lies a monumental struggle, not only of the good (Mme de Tourvel, Cécile) against the bad (Valmont and Merteuil), but also of the bad against each other. To determine who will be the champion libertine and the supreme rake, Valmont and Merteuil finally attempt to destroy each other just as they have already ruined those weaker than themselves. The complementary phenomena of male bonding and female isolation emphasise the sexual subtext of this libertine Armageddon which pits a masculine force, the audacious and adventurous Valmont, against a feminine principle, the clever and wily Merteuil.

Returning now to the duel between Valmont and Danceny and the subsequent act of bonding, we can begin to understand one critical aspect of the libertine code and of the 'war between the sexes' which was so much a part of the eighteenth-century *roman libertin et licentieux.* It is thanks to man's ability to bond, to form friendships with his fellow man, that men (plural) triumph over woman (singular). In the sexual war that opposes the Vicomte and the Marquise, Valmont cannot win a decisive victory alone.

With Danceny's assistance, however, he is able to implement the strategy that will defeat Merteuil definitively. By giving Danceny Merteuil's own secret and intimate letters, which she had written to him in confidence, Valmont provides the weapons and the ammunition for the Marquise's defeat. Danceny makes these secret letters public, thereby destroying Merteuil's reputation and causing her ultimate moral ruin: 'J'ai cru, de plus, que c'était rendre un véritable service à la société que de démasquer une femme aussi réellement dangereuse que l'est Mme de Merteuil' (letter 169, p.382). On her own, Merteuil is more than capable of outsmarting Danceny and of tricking Valmont into betraying and abandoning Mme de Tourvel. She can outmanuvre and beat either of them in a one-to-one confrontation. When they join forces, however, in that mysterious and exclusively male act of bonding, they acquire as a pair sufficient strength to defeat her: 'Au reste, j'ai reçu ces papiers, tels que j'ai l'honneur de vous les adresser, de M. de Valmont luimême. Je n'y ai rien ajouté, et je n'en ai distrait que deux Lettres que je me suis permis de publier' (letter 169, p.382). The Marquise suffers a number of tremendous blows as the novel closes: smallpox disfigures her hideously; her virtuous reputation is exposed as a fraud and her licentiousness made known to all; she loses a court case that she was confident she would win; she is ostracised at the theatre by her former friends; finally, in the dark of night, she flees from Paris into exile. All these separate items combine to make up Merteuil's irrevocable defeat. Some critics have argued that these incidents are cosmetic and that in fact the Marquise escapes to become an even more powerful embodiment of evil.[3] In such a view, the disfiguring attack of smallpox, for example, is seen not as a devastating punishment but rather as a form of liberation which frees Merteuil from the limitations that the physicality of her body places on her capacity to wreak havoc. When we see each of these incidents in isolation, we might find such an interpretation plausible. When we view these incidents together and from the perspective of male bonding, however, we understand how interrelated they are and how closely they depend upon this voluntary cooperation among men directed against women. Only the smallpox stands outside this causal chain. Even then it complements and accentuates the defeated, downward thrust of the other events. Each step in Merteuil's downfall can be traced, however indirectly, to those letters that Danceny made public after Valmont handed them over to him. It is the cooperation and collaboration of Danceny and Valmont that defeat the isolated and solitary Marquise. Because they know how to bond and to cooperate, the men win this licentious struggle; because, as a woman, she remains alone and solitary, Merteuil suffers defeat. This striking instance of men's friendship overcoming a single woman is only one example of this typically male behaviour which contrasts so sharply with normal female conduct even as it contributes to the subjugation of women. Bonding and isolation are typical actions that define male and female behaviour in Laclos's fictional world. In this novel, men triumph because they know how to bond, while women become the victims of masculine aggression precisely because they fail to do likewise and thus remain alone and isolated.

In the world depicted in *Les Liaisons dangereuses,* men participate in a free-flowing circuit of friendship. A man can be a rival and then a friend, as was the case of Valmont and Danceny. A woman, as we shall see later, can be only one or the other. Valmont, for example, seduces the Vicomtesse de M*** who is at a country estate with both her current lover, Pressac, and her husband. The latter two men are obviously rivals because they both covet the same woman and vie over spending their nights with her and sharing her sexual favours. But they also try to be friends. Thus Pressac passes the (day)time with the husband hunting 'malgré son peu de goût pour la chasse' (letter 71, p.144). Valmont enters the circuit and becomes the lover's rival. After having evicted him from his accustomed or expected place in the lady's bed, Valmont proceeds on the morning after to repair the damage he did the night before. The preceding evening he was Pressac's rival; the next morning he is his friend, trying to patch up the quarrel that he himself provoked in order to hide his own sexual escapade. In the end, he is more proud of this work of reconciliation and the mark of male friendship which seals it, than he is of his sexual conquest of a woman: 'je plaidai la cause de Pressac, et j'amenai le raccommodement. Les deux amants s'embrassèrent, et je fus à mon tour embrassé par tous deux. Je ne me souciais plus des baisers de la Vicomtesse: mais j'avoue que celui de Pressac me fit plaisir' (letter 71, p.146). Even for a rogue like Valmont, there is a hierarchy of values that he respects. Intimacy, even if temporary, with another man scores highest on this scale, while any obligation or honour due a woman ranks close to the bottom.

As strange as it may seem, this kind of male friendship allows rapid changes of direction. Without feeling any guilt or inconsistency Valmont can provoke a quarrel between the Vicomtesse and Pressac while maintaining his amicable status with both of them: 'car vous saurez que comme ami de tous deux, j'étais en tiers dans cette conversation' (letter 71, p.145). That term 'ami' is vague but also rich in its multiple connotations, indicating simultaneously Valmont's sexual desire for the Vicomtesse as well as his male bonding with Pressac. A man can become another man's friend even as he remains the seducer of that same man's, or any other man's woman. Male bonding does not replace the seduction of females; it takes priority over it. Nonetheless, male friendship, defined by the act of bonding, is comprised of ebbs and flows: it is alternating and apparently contradictory. Valmont picks up on the inconsistency inherent in male bonding and reflected in this term 'ami' when, again writing to the Marquise, he congratulates himself on his double accomplishment of dictating a letter to Cécile that encourages Danceny to love her and of loving her himself. Referring to the Chevalier, he says: 'J'aurai été à la fois son ami, son confident, son rival et sa maîtresse! (letter 115, p.275). The concepts of 'rival' and 'friend' are not exclusive for Valmont. Neither is a permanent state, so he can float between these seemingly contradictory positions without any apprehension. As both the Vicomte's words and actions demonstrate so clearly, a man can always be different and changing. He can be both friend and adversary to his fellow man, moving from ally to enemy and back to ally again.

We have already quoted M. Bertrand's description of the bonding that takes place between Danceny and Valmont. A subsequent letter (no. 164) from Mme de Rosemonde, Valmont's aunt, asks him to initiate legal procedures against Danceny, although she later renounces this course of action. In the meantime, the Chevalier receives an anonymous letter (no. 167) which warns him of the imminent legal proceedings and advises him to go into hiding before he is arrested. Who is the author of this 'tip off? Since the letter is not signed, there is no clear-cut evidence in the novel about its author. However, based on internal and stylistic evidence, several critics have identified Bertrand as the author of this letter to Danceny.[4] If this is true, we have here a key example of male complicity in opposition to female intentions. As the family lawyer, Bertrand should obey Mme de Rosemonde's instructions scrupulously; however, as a male and a witness and therefore a partial participant in Valmont and Danceny's bonding, Bertrand finds that his first loyalty is to his fellow men. Thus, he subverts a woman's intention in order to protect a man: he thwarts Rosemonde's legal pursuit of the Chevalier by warning him of this danger. Even if Bertrand is not the author of this letter, our conclusion about the force and extent of male complicity is still valid. Some other man has violated the trust of his profession by writing this warning since this letter can have been written only by some (male) member of the legal profession involved in carrying out Mme de Rosemonde's wishes. What is most significant here is the solidarity of the men who protect each other against the outsider's, the woman's, desire for retribution: 'Des raisons particulières m'empêchent de signer cette lettre. Mais je compte que, pour ne pas savoir de qui elle vous vient, vous n'en rendrez pas moins de justice au *sentiment* qui l'a dictée' (letter 167, p.378, my italics). Such complicity running deep throughout the male sphere of society is a necessary and enabling condition that prepares men for bonding. We can further document the extent of this pervasive and unspoken bond among men by looking at Prévan and his relationship to Valmont.

The Vicomte's account of Prévan's adventure with 'les trois inséparables' has often been considered an *hors d'œuvre,* a poorly motivated set-piece (how could Merteuil not have heard about this?) that is awkwardly integrated into the narrative.[5] Seen from our present perspective, these criticisms miss a central fact about this letter. Its purpose is to demonstrate Valmont's respect for Prévan and to establish the high degree of male complicity that exists even between those ostensible rivals. Merteuil immediately recognises the hidden emotion, this latent appreciation in the Vicomte's narrative even as she misinterprets its positive and cohesive force: 'Vous-même, vous êtes forcé de lui rendre justice; vous faites plus que le louer, vous en êtes jaloux' (letter 74, p.150). These men are adversaries only in the sense that they both aspire to the elevated rank of master rogue and seducer, an exclusive title that permits only one champion. Despite this rivalry, Valmont displays a real respect and almost a certain affection for Prévan, which Merteuil misconstrues as jealousy. On the contrary, the Vicomte is impressed by Prévan's accomplishment which he recounts with pride. Furthermore, even though he knows the Marquise's skill and intelligence, he does not for a moment imagine that she can resist a man like Prévan . . . who is, in fact, so much like himself: 'J'ai donc pu croire cet homme dangereux pour tout le monde: mais pour vous, Marquise, ne suffisait-il pas qu'il fût *joli, très joli,* comme vous le dites vous-même?' (letter 76, p.154, italics in the text). In his rival and adversary, the Vicomte recognises himself. Beyond his present affection and past love for the Marquise, Valmont acknowledges the bond which links him to Prévan, and which takes precedence over any attachment to Merteuil. Male complicity and its immediate sequel, male bonding, are more powerful than the hetero-sexual urges that provoke the predatory behaviour of a rogue like Valmont.

One further episode underlines the extent of this male complicity, this web of cooperation which ties men together in opposition to women. At the end of his triple seduction, Prévan brings the three women together so that they may realise how thoroughly he has deceived each one of them. After having seduced these women in turn and secretly, he has each of them send 'à l'amant disgracié, une lettre éclatante de rupture'. At first the three lovers are angry and ready to challenge him to a duel (letter 79, p.166, my italics):

> chacun d'eux ne pouvait douter qu'il n'eût été sacrifié à Prévan; et le dépit d'avoir été joué, se joignant à l'humeur que donne presque toujours la petite humiliation d'être quitté, tous trois, *sans se communiquer, mais comme de concert,* avaient résolu d'en avoir raison, et pris le parti de la demander à leur fortuné rival.

Prévan gives to all three the same time and place for the duel. Each one is, of course, astonished to see the other two victims and thus to learn that he shares a common fate with them. However mean-spirited they might be individually, Laclos's fictional men behave well in a group because there masculine complicity can come into play. Prévan's 'air affable et cavalier' produces a good effect which is amplified when he invites them to eat with him as friends: 'J'ai donné mes ordres pour qu'on tînt ici un déjeuner prêt; faites-moi l'honneur de l'accepter. Déjeûnons ensemble, et surtout déjeûnons gaiement. On peut se battre pour de semblables bagatelles, mais elles ne doivent pas, je crois, altérer notre humeur' (letter 79, p.167). Thus does male conviviality triumph over temporary rivalries and relegate women to the decidedly minor status of 'bagatelles'. Like Danceny and Valmont after their duel, Prévan and the three lovers bond before their scheduled combat. Male solidarity triumphs over their concern with women: 'tout s'arrangeait de soi-même [. . .] on y avait déjà répété dix fois que de pareilles femmes ne méritaient pas que d'honnêtes gens se battissent pour elles [. . .] on se jura amitié sans réserve' (letter 79, p.167). One consequence of this new friendship is that the men's conflict is forgotten and their duel cancelled; the other is that they all agree to humiliate the women. For a fillip, they even thank Prévan for revealing their mistresses' hidden perversity. As initiator of this whole adventure, Prévan should be deemed guilty of having found and exploited the weakness of the 'trois inséparables'. But blame is not shared. The women receive all of it, the man none: 'les femmes durent se croire pardonnées: mais les hommes, qui avaient conservé leur ressentiment, firent dès le lendemain une rupture qui n'eut point de retour; et non contents de quitter leurs infidèles maîtresses, ils achevèrent leur vengeance, en publiant leur aventure' (letter 79, p.169). These unhappy rivals do not resent the male's victory even though they punish the female's defeat. This is exactly the same conduct we have observed in the episode of the Vicomtesse de M***. There Valmont seduced a woman without raising the ire of her husband or her lover; here Prévan wins the affection of the lovers and turns them against their mistresses. It is as much for this ability to maintain the respect and affection of his fellow men as for his skill in seducing women that Valmont admires Prévan. Both are master seducers of women while able to remain friends with their fellow men.

Whereas men can reach a point at which they will cooperate with each other even though they may have been recent rivals, women never do. Women do not possess men's talent to create new friends out of old enemies. As Merteuil clearly states, a woman does not enjoy a man's luxury of modifying words and actions, friends and rivals at will. A woman is definitive in what she does as in what she says: 'Prenez-y garde, Vicomte! si une fois je réponds, ma réponse sera irrévocable' (letter 141, p.333). A woman is a prisoner of her words and deeds and even of her previous relationships. A man, as our examples show, always keeps

his freedom to change his adversaries into friends. If women are victims, defeated at the (collective) hands of men, like Merteuil and the 'inséparables', it is due in great part to their inability to find new allies in old adversaries. Man's capacity to bond even with his former enemy makes him formidable in the war between the sexes, just as woman's failure to strike such alliances marks her as vulnerable.

Lacking the masculine reflex to bond, the women in this novel remain isolated. This female isolation, squarely juxtaposed to male complicity and friendship, can take two principal forms. Either women remain 'loners', alienated and sharing no honest intimacy with other women, and/or they become excessively critical, almost stridently anti-female, and judge their fellow women harshly, never seeking the high ground of compassion and indulgence.

Both the Marquise de Merteuil and Mme de Tourvel illustrate the dilemma of the isolated female alienated from emotional intimacy with her own sex. The former is evil and machiavellian, the latter good and candid; both suffer eventual defeat at the hands of men because they fail to bond with other women. Mme de Tourvel is vulnerable to Valmont's seduction because she is alone and unprotected. Abandoned even if only symbolically by her husband who tends to his legal duties in Burgundy, she isolates herself in the country at Mme de Rosemonde's lonely château. She has no female friends of her own age, and writes only to two older women, Mmes de Rosemonde and de Volanges, both of whom she calls 'mother'. She entirely ignores Cécile who is so much closer to her in age and who should have so much in common with her. The daughter of one of her best friends, Cécile is preparing for marriage and for her social début. These same events in her own life have deeply affected the Présidente. We naturally expect then that she would communicate with someone going through these experiences and for whom she is almost a 'big sister'. Mme de Tourvel's last desperate attempt to escape from Valmont only echoes her previous acts of isolation: fleeing the adult world of her peers, she returns to her convent school, locks herself in her former room, and accepts no visitors. In very few of her actions does Mme de Tourvel behave intelligently or effectively. She completely fails to establish contact with women of her own age and situation. In part she causes her own downfall by conduct that cuts her off from communion and cooperation with those women who would be able to help her.

For an even more powerful and thorough indictment of female alienation, we can point to the Marquise who seems to be so self-reliant and successful. However, she suffers seriously both from being unjustly critical of other women and preferring solitude to complicity. In letter 133, Merteuil attempts to refute Valmont's suggestion that as women age they slowly become 'rêches et sévères'. For the Marquise, this change in temperament takes place quickly and at a specific chronological point: 'C'est de quarante à cinquante ans que le désespoir de voir leur figure se flétrir, la rage de se sentir obligées d'abandonner des prétentions et des plaisirs auxquels elles tiennent encore, rendent presque toutes les femmes bégueules et acariâtres' (letter 113, p.265-66). Women suffer a physical transformation which alters their moral character; men do not. One consequence of becoming 'bégueules et acariâtres', which is no great improvement over the Vicomte's terms, 'rêches et sévères', is that women are most harsh in their judgement of other women, as Merteuil is of Tourvel. Lest we believe that this tendency to judge their fellow women harshly is restricted to libertines like Merteuil, let us look quickly at a rather sympathetic character, Mme de Rosemonde. She too suffers from the same hypercritical mentality as does the Marquise, albeit to a much lesser extent. At the very end of the novel, she is slowly informed of all the tragic events that have taken place: Valmont's seductions of the Présidente and Cécile as well as his libertine pact with Merteuil. Whom does she blame for all this sorrow? Not Valmont, her nephew, the male; only the female perpetrator of this evil, the Marquise: 'On regrette de vivre encore, quand, on apprend de pareilles horreurs; on rougit d'être femme, quand on en voit une capable de semblables excès' (letter 171, p.386). Mme de Rosemonde reserves her womanly scorn for another woman. For the man, she expresses a much more moving compassion and forgiveness: 'Malgré ses torts, que je suis forcée de reconnaître, je sens que je ne me consolerai jamais de sa perte' (letter 171, p.386). Even the mild-mannered and indulgent Rosemonde does not escape this rage to criticise which isolates women and which then makes them incapable of forming effective and affective bonds with each other. In a similar vein, Mme de Volanges warns the Présidente that as a woman, she will be the object of careful scrutiny in all her actions: 'Songez donc que vous aurez pour juges, d'une part, des gens frivoles, qui ne croiront pas à une vertu dont ils ne trouvent pas le modèle chez eux; et de l'autre, des méchants qui feindront de n'y pas croire, pour vous punir de l'avoir eue' (letter 32, p.66). She will find herself then in a classic double bind, damned if she does and damned if she doesn't. The most difficult of these *juges* are other women, like the Marquise de Merteuil who never relents in her dogged criticisms of the Présidente. These two women have never really met face to face. Yet the Marquise vents her anger upon Tourvel in her letters to Valmont. The depth of her animosity can be felt in those continual sarcastic references to the 'céleste Présidente' and the 'prude' or in gratuitous insults like this mocking description (letter 5, p.15):

> Vous, avoir la présidente Tourvel! mais quel ridicule caprice! Je reconnais bien là votre mauvaise tête [. . .] Qu'est-ce donc que cette femme? des traits réguliers si vous voulez, mais nulle expression: passablement faite, mais sans grâce: toujours mise à faire rire! avec ses paquets de fichus sur la gorge, et son corps qui remonte au menton!

Without knowing Mme de Tourvel at all, the Marquise persists in denigrating the woman even on the most personal and intimate of topics: 'Sérieusement, je suis curieuse de voir ce que peut écrire une prude après un tel moment [after the physical act of love], et quel voile elle met sur ses actions, après n'en avoir plus laissé sur sa personne' (letter 20, p.42). Merteuil's deep hostility towards the Présidente is far from the male complicity which allowed Valmont and Danceny to form an intense although short-lived friendship or even that which Prévan enjoyed with his three rivals.

More than any other female character in this novel, the Marquise lives the dilemma of the woman who cannot bond and who therefore remains isolated, alienated, and vulnerable. Merteuil is the most virile and masculine of the females in *Les Liaisons dangereuses* even though she always remains thoroughly a woman.[6] By aspiring to be a libertine like Valmont and Prévan, she takes on certain masculine characteristics. Nonetheless, she remains unmistakably female in that she never bonds with any fellow woman; indeed, the only individual who inspires her trust is Valmont. But even that relationship, as confidential and as loving as it does at times appear, is tragically flawed. Under the surface of their intimate exchanges, Valmont and Merteuil are bitter rivals who will fight to the death in the closing pages of the novel. What stands out in the Marquise's personality, her distinctive characteristic as a woman, is her stubborn independence, her adamant refusal to confide fully and absolutely in another woman.[7] In this context, however, these characteristics are not positive because they lead inevitably to isolation and alienation from fellow women and ultimately to defeat at the hands of men.

Never does the Marquise confess her secret longings to another woman, as Mme de Tourvel does to Mme de Rosemonde; never does she seek advice as Mme de Volanges does about the wisdom of continuing Cécile's engagement to Gercourt. Furthermore, Merteuil cannot accept at face value the honest emotions that other women, e.g., Cécile and Mme de Volanges, attempt to confide in her. Rather she chooses to pervert the friendship these women offer her by transforming their personal and intimate confessions into the stuff of mockery and derision (letter 63, p.126, italics in the text):

> A mon réveil, je trouvai deux billets, un de la mère et un de la fille; et je ne pus m'empêcher de rire, en trou-

vant dans tous deux littéralement cette même phrase: *C'est de vous seule que j'attends quelque consolation.* N'est-il pas plaisant, en effet, de consoler pour et contre, et d'être seul agent de deux intérêts directement contraires?

The intimacy sought for in these letters, which could eventually lead to something similar to male bonding, is lost on the Marquise. She thinks only of the opportunities these letters provide to cause harm, and never of the chance they offer to bond or to create some kind of feminine solidarity.

Since she does not even attempt to establish some shared confidentiality, the Marquise appears to be cold and calculating, a *femme de tête* but never *de cur.* When we compare her to Valmont, the difference in personalities produced by the ability or the refusal to bond is striking. Many readers of this novel have reacted to this factor since they claim to *like* Valmont, as does Mme de Rosemonde in the quote above, because he is so sociable, so 'warm' and 'human'. Merteuil strikes those same readers as distant and disagreeable; they grudgingly recognise her intelligence but never feel close to her. The equality that balances the Vicomte and the Marquise as libertines and rakes then is offset by this complementary imbalance which emphasises Valmont's human touch and Merteuil's unsociable aloofness. Without realising precisely why, literary critics have fallen neatly into a trap when they speak of Valmont's final repentance and his deep and true love for Mme de Tourvel. Laclos and his novel are purposely taciturn here. The critic supplies what he or she would like to believe by filling in the silence.[8] Valmont touches our hearts and so, we feel, he *must* have loved the Présidente. On the other hand, Merteuil strikes no such responsive chord. Critics have therefore called her 'satanic', 'diabolical', and 'evil incarnate' because she seems to deny in herself (and therefore in us) affection and emotion. It is difficult, nonetheless, to pretend that Merteuil is a woman without feelings. She has loved Valmont deeply and sincerely, before the novel began, and perhaps has never recovered from this love; her jealousy of the Présidente surely springs as much from her love for Valmont as from her own pride as a woman and lover; her hatred for Gercourt bears witness to a depth of powerful emotion, even if it is negative. What Valmont does have, however, and what Merteuil lacks, is precisely that ability to bond with another. The Marquise appears cold and inhuman because she proves incapable of intimacy with another woman, unable to form bonds as men like Valmont and Prévan so easily do.

The ultimate consequence of this failure to bond is not just the loss of literary critics' affection. There is a much more serious effect. Because she remains isolated and solitary, denied a partner in bonding, the resourceful and intelligent Marquise will be defeated by the males just like the weak, gullible figures, Mme de Tourvel and Cécile. Although she is more intelligent and clever than any other single man (she succeeds in disgracing Prévan just as she manuvres Valmont into betraying the Présidente), she is undone in the end. Valmont and Danceny combine forces to overcome her in that act of bonding and complicity which we described at the beginning of this essay. In one sense, Merteuil is the greatest libertine and the undisputed master-rogue in the novel since she achieves her victories on her own. She is defeated only when several men band (or rather bond) against her. The glory of her achievement is that it is solitary, but that very same isolation is her Achilles' heel. Merteuil wins her great victories when she plays singles, but she cannot avoid becoming in the end another victim of male bonding because they are playing doubles.

Since we as readers know what her inevitable fate will be, Merteuil's autobiographical letter, in which she reveals her own education and her formation as a woman, contains a most chilling depiction of female isolation. At no point in her life does she confide in another woman. From her earliest years onwards, Merteuil was and always remains the quintessential loner, 'n'ayant jamais été au couvent, n'ayant point de bonne amie, et surveillée par une mère vigilante' (letter 81, p.176). The Marquise sees social relations as surfaces, as masks, as occasions for hiding her true feelings. Lacking any feminine models to imitate, she never learned how to express her deepest emotions. Thus she has developed only partially. Her intelligence has been honed to a fine edge, but her ability to interact emotively with other human beings has been severely stunted. In this Merteuil exemplifies perfectly the libertine spirit which debases the most human and emotional act, sexuality, and makes of it a will to triumph over others and to dehumanise them.[9]

Only on one occasion does Merteuil seem to want to establish some kind of intimate bond with another woman. While she is using Cécile as a pawn in her gambit of revenge against Gercourt, the Marquise suddenly exposes this emotional lacuna in her life: 'Je me suis souvent aperçue du besoin d'avoir une femme dans ma confidence, et j'aimerais mieux celle-là [Cécile] qu'une autre; mais je ne puis en rien faire, tant qu'elle ne sera pas . . . ce qu'il faut qu'elle soit' (letter 54, p.112, ellipsis in the text). Her own ellipsis betrays the Marquise's quandary. She can not even express what another woman should be so as to qualify as a friend and intimate. In the gap signified by those points of suspension lies the female dilemma, her inability to bond like a man. Merteuil's failure to relate emotionally to another woman and her consequent lack of personal fulfilment define her as the most perverse and the most perverted character in this novel whose libertine storyline offers numerous variations on the feminine inability to form intimate emotional bonds with others of the same sex.

The major result of such emotional isolation and the chief danger latent in such female alienation is that Merteuil literally (in the sense of 'word for word', i.e. through her letters, and thus letter-ally) kills Mme de Tourvel. Knowing full well the impact it will have, the Marquise writes out for Valmont the letter that reads 'Adieu mon ange . . .' and that knocks the Présidente into a fatal coma. Indeed, Merteuil demands that Valmont recognise her hand as the hand that delivered the deadly blow to the Présidente: 'quand une femme frappe dans le coeur d'une autre, elle manque rarement de trouver l'endroit sensible, et la blessure est incurable. Tandis que je frappais celle-ci, ou plutôt que je dirigeais vos coùps . . .' (letter 145, p.340). Female isolation and the inability to establish the kind of friendship that the men enjoy leads finally to this tragic dénouement, one woman killing another without regret and without even a second thought.

The Marquise's affective alienation from others of her sex is paradigmatic of the female condition throughout this novel. Other characters echo this solitude, albeit in less monstrous but equally telling terms. The women victimised by Prévan are known as the 'inséparables'. Such intimacy among women seems so improbable that they have become famous solely because of it. Their fame is not a noble achievement but rather the result of envy and malicious gossip initiated by 'des femmes jalouses': 'la scandaleuse constance fut soumise à la censure publique' (letter 79, p.164). Indeed Prévan is inspired to undertake their seduction so as to prove that women cannot be inseparable. Since he does succeed and thus shows the jealous gossip to be correct, he demonstrates both that such intimacy is uniquely male and that men will jealously guard their exclusive right to bond.

Cécile Volanges offers an instructive example of female solitude that is very different from the Marquise's. Cécile's isolation is marked in the narrative fabric itself. In this epistolary novel whose nature and format are predicated upon the reciprocal, two-way exchange of letters, Cécile suffers the ironic and illogical fate of having a correspondent who never writes![10] Her convent friend, Sophie Carnay, 'exists' in a shadowy manner only because Cécile writes to her. However, Sophie's replies are never reproduced. They are simply eliminated. This deletion is brought to our attention on several occasions by the notes of the *rédacteur* who unsuccessfully justifies the omission: 'Pour ne pas abuser de la patience du lecteur, on supprime beaucoup de lettres de cette correspondance journalière' (letter 7, note, p.20). By not giving us Sophie's letters, the novel deprives us of the opportunity to know better the

friendship between these two young girls and the confidences they share. More significantly, the novel thereby strips Cécile of her only legitimate friend and of her only opportunity to bond like men. The few other female candidates for intimacy with Cécile are her mother, who never listens to her, and the Marquise, who is using her to avenge herself against Gercourt. It is possible, as the *rédacteur* claims, that the Cécile-Sophie letters would have slowed down the plot line. On the other hand, they might have provided an important instance of a genuinely intimate exchange between equals which would have resembled the numerous examples of male bonding and complicity.

Other bits of plot line and characterisation fill in this vision of pervasive female isolation. Cécile, for example, seems totally incapable of understanding her mother; Mme de Volanges, for her part, is equally at fault because she cannot establish any lines of communication to her daughter. Mme de Tourvel abandons the one woman who gave her good advice and who warned her precisely and cogently against Valmont's schemes. She refuses to recognise that Mme de Volanges supplies exactly the kind of advice, support, and encouragement that she needs to resist Valmont. Instead, she turns to the Vicomte's aunt, Mme de Rosemonde, and seeks her friendship. Although willing, Rosemonde is thoroughly unable to provide what is required, as she herself admits: 'En laissant à la Providence le soin de vous secourir dans un danger contre lequel je ne peux rien, je me réserve de vous soutenir et vous consoler autant qu'il sera en moi. Je ne soulagerai pas vos peines, mais je les partagerai' (letter 103, p.238). The sentiment expressed here is noble indeed, but it is totally ineffective in saving the Présidente from Valmont. As this last example shows, on those rare occasions when women do seek intimacy and advice from other females, they are notably unsuccessful. Either they chose an ineffectual friend (Mme de Rosemonde), or they mistake the other woman's true intentions (Mme de Volanges asking for Merteuil's advice). Unpractised in the art of bonding, women do not know their own best interests and make choices that serve them poorly.

Even at the secondary level of the domestics, this contrast between a masculine complicity and a feminine solitude continues to hold true. When Valmont wants to read Mme de Tourvel's letters, he blackmails the Présidente's chambermaid into stealing them for him. He does this by catching her *in flagrante* with his own valet, and then threatening to reveal this indiscretion if she does not cooperate: the price of his silence is that she 'livrât les poches de sa maîtresse' (letter 44, p.92). The girl capitulates and steals the letters in question. But does she have to? Might she not have remained faithful to her mistress, admitting her fault and hoping for her indulgence? Is the Présidente so prudish and unbending that this young servant cannot count on her understanding and compassion? Does the girl really expect better treatment at Valmont's hands than at the Présidente's? All these questions are difficult to answer except in the context of women's profound insecurity and inability to confide fully in each other.

In contrast to the Présidente's chambermaid stands Valmont's valet, Azolan. His fidelity to his master is beyond question, even though it remains inexplicable in light of Valmont's poor treatment of him. The Vicomte's letter to Azolan (no. 101) is haughty and condescending; he blames the valet for his own failure to foresee Mme de Tourvel's flight to Paris and berates his domestic's lack of intelligence. Nonetheless Azolan is always ready to help his master. His participation in the famous scene of *bienfaisance* (letter 21) is critical to its success, while his interception of Mme de Tourvel's letters is also important. Despite the Vicomte's mercurial moods and the quickness with which he turns on his valet, Azolan serves him much more loyally than the Présidente's lady serves her.

A third domestic completes this pattern of behaviour. At first glance, we might think that Victoire, the Marquise's trusted servant, offers an example of female friendship and bonding even though these two women belong to very different social spheres. A certain equality in age, social rank, and character is after all necessary for the bonding we are talking about. Nonetheless, Merteuil mentions on one occasion that she has Victoire's complete confidence because they were raised together and thus share a longstanding intimacy: 'cette fille est ma soeur de lait' (letter 81, p.180). If this were all, we might have a legitimate although minor example of female bonding. But even that is not so. Merteuil goes on to advance the main reason for Victoire's faithfulness. She alone possesses information which would ruin the girl if it were known and which she is always ready to divulge at the slightest provocation (letter 81, p.180-81):

> de plus, j'ai son secret, et mieux encore; victime d'une folie de l'amour, elle était perdue si je ne l'eusse sauvée. Ses parents, tout hérissés d'honneur, ne voulaient pas moins que la faire enfermer [. . .] je les fis tous consentir à me laisser dépositaire de cet ordre, et maîtresse d'en arrêter ou demander l'éxecution, suivant que je jugerais du mérite de la conduite future de cette fille. Elle sait donc que j'ai son sort entre les mains.

In short, the Marquise is blackmailing her servant. Obviously the intimate friendship that results from bonding is incompatible with such base motives. Let it be remembered that Valmont's power over the Présidente's servant was also the consequence of blackmail.

Our analysis of Laclos's depiction of male bonding and female isolation would not be complete if we did not attempt to place them in their larger fictional context, against the background of the novel's vision of society. Laclos has not depicted these sexually characteristic patterns of behaviour in a vacuum; on the contrary, he clearly integrates them into the social fabric.

After Merteuil has been unmasked by Danceny, Prévan and the Marquise meet at the Comédie Italienne. According to Merteuil's own autobiographical letter, the theatre is the symbolic realm of her power, the area of her great strength in creating illusions. Doubtless she is a regular theatre-goer and has many friends and acquaintances here. But suddenly all these former friends, especially the women, desert her: 'elle alla s'y asseoir; mais aussitôt toutes les femmes qui y étaient déjà se levèrent comme de concert, et l'y laissèrent absolument seule. Ce mouvement marqué d'indignation générale fut applaudi de tous les hommes' (letter 173, p.390). Significantly, the women initiate this process of shunning the Marquise while the men stand back like spectators (we are at the theatre!) and applaud. Here again each sex obeys its characteristic logic: the women attack another woman while the men band together. A few minutes later, everyone gathers around Prévan and congratulates him. The crowd is reacting to the revelations about Merteuil's character brought to light by Danceny and Valmont's collusion. At this point, we should ask ourselves why Prévan is exalted and Mme de Merteuil ostracised. True, he was the Marquise's victim, disgraced in public, and here he regains his former prestige through this general and collective expression of the public's esteem. Although justice is in fact served, public opinion is not really as upright or as moral as it might appear either from the punishment meted out to the Marquise or from righting the wrong done to Prévan. The same public which rejects Merteuil at the theatre obliges Mme de Volanges to receive Valmont in her salon even though she disapproves of him. When she warns Mme de Tourvel about Valmont, Mme de Volanges attempts to explain this inconsistency. She cannot refuse Valmont entry because public opinion would not permit it (letter 32, p.65)

> vous me demanderez pourquoi je le reçois chez moi: vous me direz que, loin d'être rejeté par les gens honnêtes, il est admis, recherché même dans ce qu'on appelle la bonne compagnie [. . .] Sans doute je reçois M. de Valmont, et il est reçu partout; c'est une inconséquence de plus à ajouter à mille autres qui gouvernent la société.

We must then keep in mind that the moral and social consciousness which ostracises the Marquise when her vice is revealed is the same social pressure that procures the Valmonts and Prévans entry everywhere even though their equally sordid behaviour is widely known. Such inconsistency can better be described by its true name: the double standard. Prévan is a well-known rake whose heartless seductions of women have doubtless been legion.

Nonetheless, society condones this behaviour in a man while it reproves similar conduct in a woman. Prévan and Merteuil are both libertines. Society accepts a male rogue however while it punishes a female rake. In the warped scales of a hypocritical double standard, Prévan's apotheosis balances Merteuil's disgrace.[11]

One very pertinent comment by the Marquise highlights this double standard and the hypocrisy of the society that accepts it. Criticising the Vicomte for what she considers his insufficiently rakish attack on the Présidente, Merteuil warns him that any failure in his libertine projects would grievously harm his reputation (letter 113, p.264):

> Songez que si une fois vous laissez perdre l'idée qu'on ne vous résiste pas, vous éprouverez bientôt qu'on vous résistera en effet plus facilement; que vos rivaux vont perdre leur respect pour vous, et oser vous combattre [. . .] Songez surtout que dans la multitude des femmes que vous avez affichées, toutes celles que vous n'avez pas eues vont tenter de détromper le public, tandis que les autres s'efforceront de l'abuser.

Such carefully chosen words show to what extreme point this society is riddled with mendacity. Telling the truth is a variant of deception (literally 'détromper' means to 'undeceive'), while illusion is the basic reality (Valmont's reputation is based not on fact but on the 'idée' that he is irresistible). The woman whom Valmont claims to have seduced ('affichées' focusses on the ostentatious and illusory elements in the Vicomte's gesture) will now try either to 'détromper le public [ou] de l'abuser'. Merteuil's cleverly parallel verbs accuse the widening gap between truth and reality in this realm of false appearances. Thus, in a world where the normal expectations about veracity and morality have been turned topsy-turvy, Valmont would lose the public's esteem only if he failed as a rogue! Through this kind of public opinion and the heroes it creates, society is sending out a strong signal that libertine behaviour in an man is not only tolerated but it is positively prized. In the public's eye, Valmont and Prévan belong to a social élite thanks to their gallant adventures, not despite them.[12] In contrast, a woman can only lose her reputation and the public's esteem should she be associated with such behaviour. A woman does not actually have to be a libertine to suffer such a loss. A hint or even a suspicion of guilt suffices to tarnish a lady's honour. At one point Valmont explains to Merteuil how the letters written by Cécile to Danceny could be manipulated to damage her reputation. Clever editing could make Cécile appear to be a wanton who has thrown herself at a man. Obviously, society must have some unquestioned notions about 'proper' sexual behaviour which permit such easily fabricated illusions to pass for truth. The shadow that even the suggestion of scandal throws across a woman does not end there, by any means. Valmont goes on to declare that,

under the proper circumstances, the public's censure could even reach Mme de Volanges! (letter 66, p.135, italics in the text):

> Alors, en choisissant bien dans cette correspondance, et n'en produisant qu'une partie, la petite Volanges paraîtrait avoir fait toutes les premières démarches, et s'être absolument jetée à la tête. Quelques-unes des lettres pourraient même compromettre la mère, et *l'entacheraient* au moins d'une négligence impardonnable.

Mme de Volanges is not an entirely sympathetic character. However, merely to suggest that she could be compromised by the Cécile-Danceny correspondence, which she has tried to break up, indicates the scope of the public's gullibility . . . or its perversity. Just as in the case of Prévan's seduction of the 'inséparables', public opinion prefers to not find fault with a man while it is always ready to credit some evil about a woman.

There is no simple conclusion that can be drawn from our discussion of bonding, isolation, and society's double standard in matters sexual. With its plethora of equal and competing voices, the polyphonic epistolary format itself offers no single privileged viewpoint. Indeed, the author's refusal to pronounce more definitively seems a conscious attempt to keep his novel mysterious and ambiguous in this as in so many other matters.[13] What we can say, however, is that *Les Liaisons dangereuses* presents a very disturbing vision of late eighteenth-century French society. Its depiction of male bonding and female isolation results in a problematic view of women, even a negative depiction of them, since they are responsible for their own seduction and sexual defeat by not seeking emotional intimacy with each other. Although triumphant in the end, men are not superior to their female victims, merely luckier in that they know how to cooperate in their libidinous enterprises. Confused in its own moral standards, society as a whole is both corrupt and corrupting as it vacillates between the contradictory extremes of its double standard, punishing women for the same conduct it rewards in men. When it was first published in 1782, this novel provoked in Martin Turnell's phrase 'an immense *trahison*' because it revealed the secret inner workings of a social class corrupted by its lack of morals and perverse in its dehumanization of love and sexuality.[14] More than two centuries later, this same novel has lost none of its power, none of its ability to shock and to scandalise. The solitary and isolated women of Laclos's world are not simply the victims of unconscionable male libertines who know how to network. More important, they are both the producers and the products of a specifically feminine pattern of behaviour which proves terribly detrimental to women themselves.

Bonding is a powerful weapon in the male arsenal which men use ruthlessly in the libertine war between the sexes.

Its point of attack is woman's weakest defensive position, her emotional isolation and indeed her affective alienation from her fellow women. In this novel there is no possibility of genuine female intimacy which can be compared to this pervasive male complicity. Women remain incapable of forming any legitimate or helpful connections among themselves; the only *liaisons* we find are those formed by men, and invariably these are *dangereuses* to woman.

Notes

1. Usually this episode is seen as another example of the manipulative strategies constantly at work in this novel. Since this duel results in an exchange of letters which in turn leads directly to the publication of the incriminating letter 81, the Vicomte's gesture can be seen as a last vengeful manipulation, a parting shot that will prove fatal to the Marquise. To be effective, however, such a posthumous manœuvre depends on Valmont's absolute certainty that Danceny will cooperate. Only the male bonding which we are analysing here provides an adequate explanation for such a scheme of revenge.

2. Choderlos de Laclos, *Les Liaisons dangereuses* (Paris 1961), édition de Y. Le Hir, letter 163, p.371-72. All subsequent references will be made to this edition, and the letter and page number will be indicated in the text parenthetically.

3. See Elizabeth Douvan and Lloyd Free, '*Les Liaisons dangereuses* and contemporary consciousness', in *Laclos: critical approaches to 'Les Liaisons dangereuses'* (Madrid 1978), Studia Humanitatis, p.279: Merteuil 'is not defeated. She escapes with some resources and, though physically disfigured, she will, one feels, survive.' C.J. Greshoff, 'The moral structure of *Les Liaisons dangereuses*', *French review* 37 (1964), p.399: 'This truly satanic mind, now housed in a disfigured body, remains untouched. The real Mme de Merteuil [. . .] is immortal and indestructible.' Geoffrey Wagner, *Five for freedom: a study of feminism in fiction* (London 1972), p.64: 'Laclos afflicts her with smallpox in a highly factitious retribution', and p.90: 'She is finally free. Her end is purely spurious.' Pierre Fauchery, in *La Destinée féminine dans le roman européen du dixhuitième siècle* (Paris 1972), p.674-75, considers Merteuil a 'reine en exil' and her final departure a victory: 'Pourtant cette fuite est aussi une espèce de triomphe [. . .] Elle gagne un univers où la vengeance de ce monde, et jusqu'à celle des morts, ne la peut atteindre [. . .] Aucune *fin* de roman n'est à cet égard plus valorisante, aucune femme imaginaire du XVIIIe siècle ne disparaît dans une plus irritante "majesté".'

4. Dorothy Thelander, *Laclos and the epistolary novel* (Geneva 1963), p.124: 'Bertrand is the author of the anonymous letter which warns Danceny to go into hiding.' Also Laurent Versini, *Laclos et la tradition: essai sur les sources et la technique des 'Liaisons dangereuses'* (Paris 1968), p.314; and Sylvie Witkin, 'Laclos and Stendhal' (Ph.D. thesis, University of Wisconsin, 1982), p.89.

5. Such criticisms are quite similar to those levelled against Merteuil's autobiographical letter (no. 81). The structural symmetry and consequently the possible parallel meanings of these two letters, one Merteuil's direct self-analysis, the other Valmont's indirect portrayal of himself through Prévan, will become apparent later when we examine the Marquise's epistle for its depiction of female isolation.

6. On this question of Merteuil's virility or femininity, see Aram Vartanian, 'The Marquise de Merteuil: a case of mistaken identity', *L'Esprit créateur* 3 (1963), p.172-80, and Nancy Miller, *The Heroine's text* (New York 1980), ch.8 and 9.

7. In the context of male bonding and female alienation, I see this independence as having a negative impact. Paradoxically, Merteuil's great strength, her fierce independence, contributes to her downfall because at the end she is defeated when she struggles alone against several male adversaries. For the other side of this question, the positive side of her self-reliance, see Paul Hoffmann, 'Aspects de la condition féminine dans les *Liaisons dangereuses* de Choderlos de Laclos', *L'Information littéraire* 15 (mars-avril 1963), p.51: 'il n'y a de véritable liberté de la femme que dans une indépendance qui soit solitude et refus de tout lien durable'.

8. The gender component among readers themselves is surely at work here. The older, more traditional view, which favours Valmont, was largely formulated by a male-dominated consensus; feminist readings have led the more recent reevaluation and appreciation of Merteuil. Notice, by the way, the long-established convention of referring to Mme de Merteuil as 'la Merteuil', a derogatory use of the definite article, or just 'Merteuil', like Valmont, while the other female characters always have 'Mme' in front of their names: Mme de Tourvel, Mme de Volanges, Mme de Rosemonde. Cécile alone is affectionately called by her given name.

9. Such a harsh analysis of Merteuil might seem antifeminist to some. Let us remember, however, that Laclos himself had to defend his novel against similar charges. In his letters to Mme Riccoboni, he declares that he was not vilifying all Frenchwomen in Mme de Merteuil. Nonetheless, he does maintain that he did intend to condemn a certain type of woman who really existed and whom he considered depraved and monstrous: 'Que si j'en ai rencontré quelques-unes, jetées en quelque sorte hors de leur sexe par la dépravation et la méchanceté; si frappé du mal qu'elles faisaient, des maux qu'elles pouvaient faire, j'ai répandu l'alarme et dévoilé leurs coupables artifices; qu'ai-je fait en cela, que servir les femmes honnêtes, et pourquoi me

reprocheraient-elles d'avoir combattu l'ennemi qui faisait leur honte, et pouvait faire leur malheur?', Laclos, *œuvres complètes,* éd. Laurent Versini, Bibliothèque de la Pléiade (Paris 1979), p.760-61.

10. For an analysis of the entire novel from the perspective of exchange and the role of the reader, see my *Intimate, intrusive and triumphant: readers in the 'Liaisons dangereuses'* (Philadelphia 1987), Purdue University monographs in Romance languages 23.

11. This is of course a point that feminists have continually denounced. See Kate Millet, *Sexual politics* (New York 1978), p.174: 'The degradation in which the prostitute is held and holds herself, the punitive attitude society adopts toward her, are but the reflections of a culture whose general attitudes toward sexuality are negative and which attaches great penalties to a promiscuity in woman it does not think to punish in men.'

12. See H. T. Mason, 'Women in Marivaux', in Jacobs, Barber, *et al.* (ed.), *Woman and society in 18th-century France* (London 1979), p.48: Marivaux 'is exercised by the double standard which prevails concerning conjugal infidelity. A man, far from suffering any punishment, does not even need to conceal his libertinage. Indeed, his "galanterie" makes him a hero: "on se le montre au spectacle" . . .; one thinks of Prévan at the end of *Les Liaisons dangereuses*'.

13. Given the author's intentional reticence, we would be rash to seek an answer to these questions in texts outside the novel itself. Nonetheless we are aware how tempting that possibility is. Sensitive to the inferior status accorded women, Laclos wrote a treatise (there are several versions) on woman's education and its relation to her social condition. See Madeleine Raaphorst, 'Choderlos de Laclos et l'éducation des femmes au XVIIIe siècle', *Rice University Studies* 53 (1967), p.33-41; and Jean Bloch, 'Laclos and women's education', *French Studies* 38 (1984), p.144-58.

14. Martin Turnell, *The Novel in France* (New York 1951), p.51.

Elizabeth J. MacArthur (essay date 1989)

SOURCE: "Trading Genres: Epistolarity and Theatricality in *Britannicus* and *Les Liaisons dangereuses*," *Yale French Studies,* No. 76, 1989, pp. 243-64.

[*In the essay below, MacArthur explores the ways in which* Les Liaisons dangereuses *and Jean Racine's* Britannicus *are transformed through shared text.*]

It is a critical commonplace to compare Racine and Laclos, for their rigorous textual construction, their creation of stiflingly closed worlds, or their culminating positions in two related genres, classical tragedy and the epistolary novel.[1] In such comparisons, of course, Laclos is usually seen as very much the follower, "a little Racine"[2] borrowing belatedly his illustrious model's words and adapting them as well as possible to a new context. Rather than describing the intertextual relations between Racine and Laclos in any more precise way, critics have tended to reiterate claims of influence based on resemblances between the two authors' themes or vocabulary, claims which are moreover somewhat unconvincing because many of the passages cited suggest merely that both writers belonged to the same literary tradition.[3] Instead of pursuing such generalizations, this essay will approach the relation between Racine and Laclos through one particular passage, the one-and-a-half lines that the Vicomte de Valmont quotes from Néron's description of his first encounter with Junie in *Britannicus.*

Conceptions of intertextuality vary enormously, from Bloom's discussions of the agonistic relation between great writers and their precursors, to Riffaterre's descriptions of how a given work is overdetermined by its use of a matrix borrowed from an earlier work or tradition, to literary-historical summaries of a writer's "sources." I will not be concerned with the psychoanalytic or historical connections between Racine and Laclos, but with the way *Britannicus* and ***Les Liaisons dangereuses*** transform each other when read together. I will consider a very specific type of intertextuality, the dialogue set up between texts when the second one quotes from the first, and in some way acknowledges the quotation.[4] When Valmont borrows a passage from *Britannicus,* he creates a bridge between the two works, making each in some sense a part of the other, and in the process enriching both. The shared passage links the two texts as a kind of channel through which characteristics can be transferred. It also sets up a provisional parallel, like the word "like." If two texts touch at one point, perhaps, by extension, they touch in other ways as well. As Borges has taught us, such intertextual transformations do not work in only one direction: "The fact is that every writer creates his own precursors. His work modifies our conception of the past, as it will modify the future."[5] ***Les Liaisons dangereuses*** thus transforms *Britannicus* just as surely as *Britannicus* helps to "form" the ***Liaisons.***

In a letter to the Marquise de Merteuil (71), Valmont quotes from the central scene of *Britannicus,* in which Néron recounts to Narcisse his first sight of Junie (II, ii). The one-and-a-half lines Valmont quotes come from Néron's description of Junie: "[Belle, sans ornement,] dans le simple appareil / D'une beauté qu'on vient d'arracher au sommeil" [(Beautiful, without ornament,) in the simple attire / Of a beauty who has just been dragged from sleep] (389-90). This sole reference to Racine thus invokes the relationship between Néron and Junie, a relationship that is played out again in Laclos's novel, between Valmont and the Présidente de Tourvel. In both works a cruel and scheming man seeks to win the heart of an innocent, unscheming, and ultimately heroic woman. At first glance it would seem that Laclos is rewriting the plot and themes of a classical drama as classical epistolary novel, but in fact Laclos's reference to Racine exposes the *epistolarity* of *Britannicus,* and rewrites it as *theatricality* in the *Liaisons dangereuses.*

I. THEATRICAL EPISTOLARITY

To readers familiar with Laclos, Néron's speech describing his first meeting with Junie seems to contain a quotation from *Les Liaisons dangereuses.* It is appropriate that Racine should invoke his epistolary successor in this particular scene of this particular play, for Néron's story is epistolary, and this scene a central revelation of its epistolarity. Of course I am not claiming that *Britannicus* is an epistolary novel, but its hero, Néron, refuses theatricality in favor of epistolarity, and the whole play is about closing the gap between the "writing" and the "reading" of his true character.

Néron might at first appear to be the ultimate theatrical figure, a character whose power lies in masking his own true self and in directing the behavior of others. The entire action of the play in fact results from his having successfully hidden his cruel nature, played the role of just leader. Junie realizes fairly quickly that Néron's palace is a theatre where no one's words can be taken at face value, but she never succeeds in convincing Britannicus, who goes to his death believing Néron has pardoned him. "[D]ans cette cour," Junie explains urgently, "Combien tout ce qu'on dit est loin de ce qu'on pense! / Que la bouche et le coeur sont peu d'intelligence!" [In this court, how far is what people say from what they think! / How little are lips and heart in agreement!].[6] She herself is forced to act on this dangerous stage by Néron, who perhaps realizes that making her act is the cruelest torture he can inflict on the "simple" (unduplicitous) Junie. When Néron tells her to deceive Britannicus, to make him believe she no longer loves him, while he himself watches her performance from the wings, she protests that she won't be capable of it:

> Moi! Que je lui prononce un arrêt si sévère!
> Ma bouche mille fois lui jura le contraire.
> Quand même jusque-là je pourrais me trahir,
> Mes yeux lui défendront, Seigneur, de m'obéir.
>
> I? I must announce to him such a cruel sentence!
> My lips a thousand times have sworn the opposite.
> Even if I could betray myself to that extent,
> My eyes will forbid him, My Lord, from obeying me.
>
> [675-78]

Néron's only response is to tell Junie that Britannicus's life depends on her deception, and to reiterate his com-

mand: "Renfermez votre amour dans le fond de votre âme" [Confine your love in the depths of your soul] (680). He then slips out of sight, with a final reminder to Junie that he will be audience to her acting: "Madame, en le voyant, songez que je vous voi" [In seeing him, Madame, remember that I see you] (690).

But in spite of Néron's previous success at staging his own appearance of virtue, the scene he stages between Junie and Britannicus ultimately demonstrates that one can as easily be manipulated by theatricality as one manipulates others. For one thing, although Junie appears to follow Néron's instructions in her icy reception of her lover, her words do contain hidden messages. If she tells Britannicus that "Ces murs mêmes . . . peuvent avoir des yeux" [These walls themselves . . . might have eyes] (713), the figure is to be taken literally: Néron is watching. Then she interrupts Britannicus's discussion of the plot against Néron, protesting that his criticisms hide his true admiration for Néron. While Britannicus reads Junie's ambiguous statements as signs of a surprising new affection for Néron, the statements are double-edged, as Néron, listening in, must recognize. Even though the untheatrical Britannicus doesn't understand the ambiguities of his scene with Junie—indeed, doesn't realize that what he and Junie are involved in is not a rendez-vous but a scene—Néron does perceive these ambiguities. What is worse, even if Junie had said nothing ambiguous to Britannicus, the look in her eyes and her very silences would have betrayed her passion; as Néron, alone with Narcisse afterwards, exclaims: "Hé bien! de leur amour tu vois la violence, / Narcisse: elle a paru jusque dans son silence" [Well! You see the violence of their love, / Narcisse: it appeared even in her silence] (747). Néron gives Junie her script, and watches her act, but the performance still gets beyond his control. The presence of one person to another required by theatricality brings with it the risk of unexpected outcomes.

It is not only other people's performances that risk escaping Néron's control, but even his own performance. Later in the play Narcisse succeeds in convincing Néron to go ahead with their plans for poisoning Britannicus by suggesting that Néron's staged virtue is being misinterpreted by the Roman people. Néron's meeting with Burrhus has persuaded him to save Britannicus, but Narcisse uses the insinuation of ineffectual theatrical gesturing to provoke Néron's anger. He represents to Néron what the Romans supposedly say about him:

> Il ne dit, il ne fait que ce qu'on lui prescrit:
> . . . . .
> Pour toute ambition, pour vertu singulière,
> Il excelle à conduire un char dans la carrière,
> . . . . .
>
> A se donner lui-même en spectacle aux Romains,
> A venir prodiguer sa voix sur un théâtre,
> . . . . .

Tandis que des soldats, de moments en moments,
Vont arracher pour lui les applaudissements
He says and does only what is prescribed to him:

. . . . .

His sole ambition, his particular talent,
Is to excel at racing a chariot,

. . . . .

To make himself a spectacle to the Romans,
To pour out his voice upon a stage,

. . . . .

While soldiers, at every moment,
Drag out applause for him.

[1459-68]

In order to stop (alleged) rumors that his words are dictated by others, that he is merely a theatrical diversion, a spectacle to his people who are forced to clap for him, Néron once again agrees to murder Britannicus—and now puts the plan into action. Narcisse forces him to realize that theatricality implies not only the possibility of deceiving others and controlling their actions, but also the risk of coming under someone else's power, or of having one's own artifices interpreted in the wrong ways.

The greatest danger of theatricality for Néron resides in its potential for exchange, the impossibility of foreseeing fully what will be said by those who share the stage, or by those who watch one perform. Even pre-scripted speeches may mean different things depending on how they are spoken, or what is left unsaid. In Racine's play, this treacherous potential of theatricality is countered by what could be called a kind of theatrical epistolarity. This epistolarity signifies not so much writing, as a spatial and temporal gap between the enunciation of a message and its reception. If theatre brings speaker and listener together, letters suppose absence, that is, both distance and delay.

Given the danger of theatrical presence, we can begin to understand why Néron seems to favor epistolary absence. As I hinted earlier, Néron's first meeting with Junie reveals a subconscious preference for epistolarity. When he sees Junie, surrounded by the shadows of night and the flames of torches, he tries to speak to her but is unable to do so. His words come only later, when he is alone in his room. "J'ai voulu lui parler, et ma voix s'est perdue," [I tried to speak to her, and I lost my voice] (396) Néron explains to Narcisse, but later, in his chamber,

. . . C'est là que solitaire,
De son image en vain j'ai voulu me distraire.
Trop présente à mes yeux, je croyais lui parler.

. . . It's there that solitary,
I tried in vain to distract myself from her image.
Too present to my eyes, I thought I was speaking to her.

[399-401]

Néron cannot speak while Junie is there to hear him; as in a letter, the sender of the message is separated in time and space from its intended recipient. His first encounter with Junie is thus more epistolary than theatrical.

Néron's inability, or perhaps unconscious unwillingness, to express himself in the presence of an interlocutor extends beyond this scene as well, characterizing his relations with both his mother and Junie. Later in the scene in which he describes his first sight of Junie, Néron tells Narcisse that he has avoided meeting with Agrippine because her presence would prevent him from saying what he intends:

Eloigné de ses yeux, j'ordonne, je menace,

. . . . .

Je m'excite contre elle, et tâche à la braver.
Mais (je t'expose ici mon âme toute nue)
Sitôt que mon malheur me ramène à sa vue,

. . . . .

. . . mes efforts ne me servent de rien.

Distant from her eyes, I command, I threaten,

. . . . .

I work myself up against her, and try to defy her.
But (here I am laying bare my soul to you)
As soon as my bad luck brings me back into her sight

. . . . .

. . . my efforts do me no good.

[496-505]

Néron's threats and orders come to nothing when he is actually faced with his mother. Like his love for Junie, his authority over Agrippine can only be expressed in her absence. His "secret soul" manifests itself only across a kind of epistolary gap, never in a theatrical confrontation: he needs the control that epistolary distance allows him. Even at the end of the play Néron remains silent while the people escort Junie to the temple, then repeats her name hopelessly after she has disappeared ("Le seul nom de Junie échappe de sa bouche" [Only the name of Junie escapes from his lips] [1746]). Now that she has sequestered herself their relationship will be permanently epistolary; perhaps he will write to her.[7]

Not only do Néron's "conversations" with Junie, and to some extent with his mother, require a spatial and temporal gap characteristic of epistolarity, but Néron himself is also implicitly compared to a letter. In the play's first scene Agrippine tells Albine that she knows how to read him: "Il se déguise en vain: je lis sur son visage / Des fiers Domitius l'humeur triste et sauvage" [He disguises himself in vain: I read on his face / The wild and unhappy character of the proud Domitius family] (35-36). Néron is like a letter that only Agrippine is able to read. Agrippine also protests to Burrhus her own erasure from the written pages of her son's mind ("Entre Sénèque et vous disputez-vous la gloire / A qui m'effacera plutôt de sa mémoire?" [Are you and Sénèque fighting for the glory / Of erasing me more quickly from his memory?] [147-48]). Appropriately enough, then, in his first words to Junie Néron refers to himself as a text: "Lisez-vous dans mes yeux quelque triste présage?" [Do you read some unhappy presage in my eyes?] (528). After a night spent speaking to her in her absence, in a sense writing a letter to her, the first thing he does when he sees her is ask her to read the letter. Shortly after "quoting" his epistolary successor Valmont, Néron himself becomes a letter.

The language of Agrippine's and Néron's references to him as a written text suggests both that not everyone knows how to read him (yet), and that if read properly he is a frightening document ("triste et sauvage", "triste présage"). Néron thus resembles a letter that has been written but not yet received: his evil character *has already been determined* but has not yet manifested itself. The play is about the moment when he sends the letter that is himself, that is, when he begins to reveal his character, to close the gap between the heretofore private enunciation of his evil words (love for Junie, power over his mother, and by extension willingness to murder) and their reception. As Racine writes in his second preface to the play, "c'est ici un monstre naissant, mais qui n'ose encore *se déclarer*" [he is here a budding monster, but who does not yet dare *declare himself*] (258, my emphasis). During the course of the play not only Agrippine but Junie, Britannicus and Burrhus, as well as the Roman people, will hear him declare himself, learn to read him correctly.

At the start of *Britannicus* only Agrippine realizes that Néron's apparent kindness hides a cruel nature, and that this hidden nature is about to become manifest. From the start of the play she refers to sinister predictions for Néron's future; by the end his deeds have come to match these predictions. In the opening scene, Agrippine announces to Albine that what she has foretold is about to be realized:

> Tout ce que j'ai prédit n'est que trop assuré
> . . . . .
> L'impatient Néron cesse de se contraindre
> . . . . .
> Britannicus le gêne, Albine; et chaque jour
> Je sens que je deviens importune à mon tour.
> All that I have foretold is but too sure to happen
> . . . . .
> The impatient Néron can hardly hold himself back
> . . . . .
>
> Britannicus is in his way, Albine, and every day
> I feel that I in turn am becoming importunate.
>
> [9-14]

At this point Agrippine's sinister predictions have not come to pass. She fears that they are "assured," but

presumably she hopes to intervene in time to save herself. After Néron has murdered Britannicus, though, Agrippine outlines explicitly, and without any mitigating doubts, the bloody course of his future:

> Ta main a commencé par le sang de ton frère;
> Je prévois que tes coups viendront jusqu'à ta mère
> . . . . .
>
> Ta fureur, s'irritant soi-même dans son cours,
> D'un sang toujours nouveau marquera tous tes jours
> . . . . .
>
> Et ton nom paraîtra dans la race future,
> Aux plus cruels tyrans une cruelle injure.
>
> Your hand has begun with the blood of your brother;
> I foresee that your blows will reach your mother
> . . . . .
>
> Your furor, aggravating itself in its course,
> Will mark all your days with renewed blood . . .
> . . . . .
>
> And your name will appear, to future generations,
> A cruel insult to the cruelest of tyrants.
>
> [1665-82, see also 1689-90]

Agrippine correctly predicts that Néron's fratricide will lead to matricide, and that posterity will consider him the most barbarous of tyrants. Néron has been born.[8]

One of Agrippine's functions in the play is to remind readers and spectators of what they in fact already know: that Néron is to murder his mother and become a cruel tyrant. The play depends on our knowledge of his future, which for us, of course, is past. As Picard points out, "the interest [of the play] is summed up quite well in the question: will Néron become *Néron?*"[9] In other words, will the seemingly innocent and just Néron of the play's opening become the Nero of history, whose cruelty spectators and readers are familiar with? By the end of the play, "the Néron of the tragedy and the historical Néron have become identified: they are now indistinguishable" (Picard, 380). Agrippine's dark hints scattered throughout the play help keep us from forgetting to identify Racine's Néron with the historical one. Racine makes it clear in his prefaces to *Britannicus* that he expected his audience to remember Néron: "I believed that the mere name of Néron meant something worse than cruel . . . it seems to me that he reveals enough cruelty to prevent anyone from *mistaking* him" (254, my emphasis). And of course the prefaces also serve to remind readers of Néron's predetermined future, in case they have forgotten his story.

At the start of the play Néron knows what he wants to say but doesn't yet dare say it publicly. His future has been determined but not yet revealed. To return to the epistolary image, he is like a letter that has been written by history but not yet deciphered by his contemporaries. Paradoxically, it is Néron's future that "writes" him as a letter: we feel that Néron's story has been predetermined because we know its outcome in history. It is not so much that he has some essential nature that must come to light (although that may also be the case), but that his tyrannical life has already happened historically by the time we meet the young Néron in Racine's play. Néron can only become Néron. He resembles a letter sent by the future to the past, which we reread over the shoulders of his contemporaries.

Néron might be said to choose epistolarity not only in order to avoid the danger of presence, but also, in a larger sense, in order to try to open up a temporal space in which to act freely. For until Néron has committed fratricide, the audience, Agrippine, and even Néron himself cling to the hope that he might ultimately choose good over evil. In other words, before the murder Néron appears to have the freedom to make choices, and thus to have some control over his destiny. Néron delays in exposing his true nature in order to give himself the illusion that that nature has not yet been determined. He transforms himself into a letter in an attempt to create a temporal gap, and with it the possibility of free will.

Rather than liberating Néron from a preordained future, though, epistolarity becomes the very sign of an entrapping destiny. No matter how long Néron waits to reveal the "letter" of his true character, that letter has already been written, and present action is imprisoned by past and future. Georges Poulet argues that in *Britannicus,* as in all but the last three of Racine's plays, the present is fatally, painfully determined by the past and/or the future:

> The Racinian movement thus becomes the slave of an interior or posterior duration which draws it in and fixes it at its extremity. Extreme point of a past coming to an end, of a future, of a monster "being born," it is as if it were smothered between two walls of events which are coming together, which are already touching.[10]

The space of *Britannicus* is the space of the inexorably closing gap between Néron's heredity (Agrippine's murder of Claudius, the savage Domitius character, etc.) and his already-written future. The epistolary gap is only a mockery of temporality, for the past and the future touch already. Néron's story has been written (and in fact even read by the audience) before the play opens, and his present actions can only uncover or make legible a predetermined future. Néron chooses the epistolary for control (over the unexpected and the emotional) and for freedom (the space to choose his own future), but in fact epistolarity uncovers the absence of both control and freedom. Néron's fate is predetermined, time but an illusory gap before the letter of his destiny is read.

This smothering inevitability is reflected in the images of being born and of awakening which frame the play. Ra-

cine compares Néron's passage from silence to speech with birth: in *Britannicus* he is a monster in the process of being born. This transition is also represented by the image of the sun rising, and an awakening from sleep.[11] The play opens with Agrippine waiting, symbolically, for her son to awaken. The first words of the play are Albine's surprised query, "Quoi! tandis que Néron s'abandonne au sommeil, / Faut-il que vous veniez attendre son réveil?" [What! While Néron abandons himself to sleep, / Must you come and wait for his awakening?] (1-2). Unlike Albine, who considers Néron a kind and just ruler, Agrippine suspects that Néron is about to "awaken" to an evil nature. When Britannicus exclaims later "Quelle nuit! Quel réveil!" [What a night! What an awakening!] (699), he is referring to Junie's abduction and his own discovery of it upon waking, but the words reveal also the horror of Néron's metaphoric awakening. The natural, cyclical images of birth and awakening suggest the predetermined inevitability of Néron's development. Just as the sun rises inexorably each day, so the shadowed, hidden Néron inexorably comes to light. Néron has no more freedom of choice than the sun has the power not to rise, or a letter the power to rewrite itself before it is read.

Racine envisions his play too as a kind of letter to the past. If Néron can speak his love for Junie only before or after seeing her, and if his whole story is about bridging the gap between present and future Néron, likewise the work must cross a temporal gap to reach its true public, Antiquity. The "grands hommes de l'antiquité" [great men of Antiquity] are, according to the first preface, "les véritables spectateurs que nous devons nous proposer" [the true spectators that we should imagine for ourselves] (256). Only a public not present to him, (and thus perhaps more docile, more subject to his control, than his contemporaries?) can properly interpret Racine's text. Racine also could be said to "send" *Britannicus* along with the play's dedicatory epistle to the Duc de Chevreuse, so that the play becomes a letter, or an enclosure to a letter. It is appropriate that this epistle to the past, this story of epistolary gaps between writing and reception, should have been staged for the first time in 1669, the year of the publication of the *Lettres portugaises,* the year that marks the start of the explosion of the epistolary form.

II. Epistolary Theatricality

As we have seen, Néron's first meeting with Junie is more epistolary than theatrical. Struck by the sight of Junie, Néron is unable to speak to her and regains his speech only later, alone in his room. He can only "converse" with her across a spatial and temporal gap. One hundred and thirteen years later, at the peak of the popularity of the epistolary form, Laclos's Vicomte de Valmont appropriates an excerpt from this epistolary scene for his description of a thoroughly theatrical one. Valmont and the Vicomtesse de M***, both guests of the Comtesse de ***, agree on a nighttime rendez-vous, and she arrives in his room "dans le simple appareil / D'une beauté qu'on vient d'arracher au sommeil."[12] The encounter is staged, with both actors playing pre-determined roles and perfectly aware of each other's artifice. The scene also gains an audience, though belatedly, since Valmont recounts it to the Marquise de Merteuil with instructions to spread it to the wider public of society ("il est juste que le Public ait son tour" [it is fair that the public have its turn] [2:71; 143]). Unlike Junie, who has been unexpectedly awakened and thus wears her nightclothes, the Vicomtesse chooses this "simple appareil" as a costume, feigning innocence. In a sense she acts the part of Junie (the pure, unduplicitous woman) to Valmont's Néron (the sadistic tyrant). And given the resemblance between Junie and the Présidente de Tourvel, and the parallels between the Néron-Junie and Valmont-Tourvel relationships, the Vicomtesse might also be said to play the part of Tourvel. The Vicomtesse de M*** is anonymous, interchangeable, the ultimate actress. Valmont's encounter with her is probably the most theatrical scene in *Les Liaisons dangereuses.*

In a larger sense, however, this scene is characteristic of the self-conscious theatricality of much of the *Liaisons,* including the scene between Valmont and Tourvel which it anticipates. Throughout the novel Valmont and Merteuil regularly use theatrical vocabulary and extended theatrical metaphors to describe their actions.[13] They refer to themselves and others as "acteurs" playing "rôles" in "le grand théâtre," in "scènes" from "Comédies" with "entr'actes" and above all "dénouements," and so forth. Theatrical language is never used by any of the other characters, except in passing references to a "scène" or "spectacle," and Merteuil and Valmont use it almost exclusively in writing to each other. The most important extended staged scenes are Merteuil's seduction and exposure of Prévan (2: 82, 85, 86, 87), Prévan's own separation of the three "inseparable" couples (recounted by Valmont, 2:79), and Valmont's victorious attack on Tourvel (4:125). The functioning of these scenes, and their exclusive association with the novel's libertine heroes, reveal that acting and stage-directing are meant to guarantee control over one's own life and the lives of others. Prévan poses a real threat to Merteuil because of his mastery over the actions of the three "inséparables" and their lovers, whose seduction and reunion he directs and which culminate on a stage of his choosing. Each of the women in succession, expecting her recent seducer Prévan, discovers her lover instead, and each couple retires to an adjoining room to "ratify the peace": "et la scène, restée vide, fut alternativement remplie par les autres Acteurs, à peu près de la même manière, et surtout avec le même dénouement" [and the stage, left empty, was occupied

alternately by the other Actors, more or less in the same way, and above all with the same ending] (2:79; 164).

These explicitly theatrical scenes embody that which is implicit in virtually all of Merteuil and Valmont's actions. Society really is a theatre for Laclos's protagonists, and one that must be taken seriously; all that remains to be determined is what roles people will play, and who will direct them. "The so-called liberated hero is merely one who plays more roles than his victims,"[14] remarks Jennifer Birkett, but one might add that such heroes are also those who can force others to play particular roles, and who can assure a favorable reception of their work by the public.

Probably the most important theatrical scene in the novel, and the one which Valmont's rendez-vous with the Vicomtesse rehearses, is the meeting between Tourvel and Valmont in which they finally become lovers. Valmont recounts the episode at great length to Merteuil, using theatrical vocabulary to transform their encounter into a drama for which he is both director and leading man. When he arrives at Tourvel's house, ostensibly to return her letters and break off his attachment to her for good, he carefully chooses "le théâtre de ma victoire" [the theatre of my victory] (4:125; 289). He then stages a strategic series of scenes that weaken her resolve and cause her to faint in his arms, giving herself up to him (at least in Valmont's interpretation). "[C]ette manière brusque" [this brusque manner] (290) is followed by "[le] ton le plus tendre" [the tenderest of tones] (290); "cette scène languissante" [this langorous scene] (290) gives way to a "scène de désespoir" [scene of despair] (291). Valmont reports the episode in detail, including the two players' movements and their entire dialogue. Vivienne Mylne has pointed out that Laclos's characters rarely report dialogues in direct discourse, perhaps in the interest of *vraisemblance.* She counts forty-seven scenes (in twenty-nine letters) that contain direct discourse; in thirty-two of the forty-seven, only one comment is reproduced directly, nine of the remaining examples contain only two or three remarks exchanged, and five contain four to seven.[15] The one scene that breaks this pattern is Valmont's seduction of Tourvel, containing thirty-four responses reported in direct discourse. Valmont's narration of the scene is exceptionally theatrical, then, not only in its continual references to "scenes," "tones," and carefully staged movements, but also in its direct reporting of a lengthy dialogue.[16]

I have already suggested that the Vicomtesse de M*** plays the part of Junie or Tourvel in her rendez-vous with Valmont. This scene can be viewed as a rehearsal for Valmont's culminating scene with Tourvel, and more generally for all his meetings with her. For in fact Valmont and Tourvel's relationship is the most theatrical one in the novel, to judge by the percentage of direct discourse associated with their conversations. Mylne observes that "almost all the scenes that include several lines, or quite extended segments, of direct discourse are exchanges between Valmont and the Présidente" (586). Valmont's invocation of *Britannicus* in his encounter with the Vicomtesse thus sets up a parallel between his theatrical relationship with Tourvel, and Néron's epistolary relationship with Junie. In both cases a duplicitous strategist falls in love with a woman who refuses to play roles, but the hero of Racine's classical drama chooses to maintain his control by making his relationship with Junie epistolary, while the hero of Laclos's letter-novel loses control when he allows his relationship with Tourvel to become theatrical.

Theatricality has two important values in *Les Liaisons dangereuses,* as it does in *Britannicus.* First and foremost, the theatrical represents an attempt at control, manipulation, and mastery. Valmont does not quote Racine simply in order to create an interesting parallel between his love for Tourvel and Néron's for Junie; rather, his quotation, one of fourteen italicized borrowings from literary texts in *Les Liaisons dangereuses,* is part of a larger strategy of appropriating the language of others to one's own ends. Of the fourteen italicized literary references, nine are in Valmont's letters, five in Merteuil's.[17] Ten of the quotations come from plays, suggesting once again that Merteuil and Valmont conceive of themselves as dramatists, writing the scripts for other people's actions. The passages quoted function less as acknowledgments of these theatrical models, however, than as attempts to demonstrate their own control over all discourse. Valmont and Merteuil quote to show off their knowledge of literature to each other, but above all to subordinate the language of well-known authors to their own. As Michel Delon remarks, "One must, on the other hand, ascribe the perversion of texts to the wishes of Laclos and his heroes. . . . Disrespect towards the classics is a school where handling language and taking possession of others are learned."[18] Valmont and Merteuil's manipulation of literary quotations thus merges with their use of theatrical vocabulary; both are part of the overall project of writing and staging a drama through which they control their lives and the lives of the people around them.

This project may help explain why Valmont quotes Racine in a remarkably tangential episode of *Les Liaisons dangereuses.* The quotation is part of his narration of an amusing but insignificant encounter with a virtually unnamed woman, that occurs while he is en route from Paris to Mme de Rosemonde's château: in other words, in a marginal episode with a marginal character at a marginal location. What is more, the letter describing the episode owes its existence to the fluke of Valmont's valet having inadvertently left Valmont's *portefeuille* in Paris. "Il va partir pour réparer sa sottise," explains Valmont, "et tandis qu'il selle son cheval, je vous raconterai mon histoire de cette nuit" [He is going to depart to repair his stupidity, and while he saddles his horse, I will tell you my story of last night] (2:71; 140). The entire episode could easily be removed from the work without affecting the plot or the character of the protagonists. By quoting from *Britannicus* in this context, Valmont (and Laclos) reduces Racine's stature. Junie is transformed into a shallow, duplicitous Vicomtesse, interchangeable with other women, and her crucial first meeting with Néron, which awakens his passion and leads him to murder Britannicus, becomes an insignificant frolic. Valmont displaces his reference to Racine from the scene with Tourvel, which it more faithfully describes, to a kind of warped, ironized precursor of that scene. Valmont's one-and-a-half line excerpt also deliberately breaks up Racine's alexandrine. The placement of the quotation and its abridgment reveal Valmont's irreverent attitude towards the celebrated classical dramatist, while still suggesting resemblances between Valmont and Néron, Tourvel and Junie.

In spite of Valmont's (and Laclos's) attempt to diminish and subordinate Racine, the ambivalence of the theatricality which he represents comes back to haunt Valmont, just as epistolarity ends up being not an escape, but rather a trap, for Néron. Theatricality may start out being a desire to manipulate and control, but it never rids itself of the danger of the unexpected, of tragic *peripeteia* or reversal, and this is precisely the value which theatricality ultimately takes on for Valmont. For although Valmont presents his "victory" over Tourvel in theatrical terms which suggest a masterful and ironic detachment from their relationship, other passages in his letter already hint at real emotional involvement and loss of mastery.[19] Before beginning his play-by-play account of the seduction, Valmont reflects on the difference between his feelings for Tourvel and what he has felt for other women. He seems to be trying to reassure himself that it can't be love, despite the fact that even a day later the "unknown charm" created by the encounter "subsists" (4:125; 287). "J'aurais même," admits Valmont, "un plaisir assez doux à m'y livrer, s'il ne me causait quelque inquiétude. Serai-je donc, à mon âge, maîtrisé comme un écolier par un sentiment involontaire et inconnu?" [I would even feel rather a sweet pleasure in abandoning myself to it, if it didn't cause me some anxiety. Will I, at my age, be mastered like a schoolboy by an involuntary and unknown sentiment?] (287-88). At the end of their meeting, Valmont tells Merteuil, "Je ne sortis de ses bras que pour tomber à ses genoux, pour lui jurer un amour éternel; et, il faut tout avouer, *je pensais ce que je disais*" [I left her arms only to fall at her knees, to swear eternal love to her; and, to be honest, *I believed what I was saying*] (295, my emphasis). The lines Valmont invented in order to seduce Tourvel have ceased to be duplicitous: they now represent his true feelings.

Ironically, Valmont himself had pointed out the power of words to remake feelings and actions in their own mold, in an earlier letter to Merteuil: "vous savez assez que femme qui consent à parler d'amour, finit bientôt par en prendre, ou au moins par se conduire comme si elle en avait" [You know well enough that a woman who consents to speak of love, soon ends up feeling it, or at least behaving as if she did] (2:76; 150). Valmont, a victim of his own theatre, is the embodiment of what Atalide fears will happen to Bajazet, in Racine's later play. Bajazet must persuade Roxane, the Sultana, who controls both his and Atalide's lives, that he loves her, despite the fact that he and Atalide are secret lovers. Atalide wants him to play his part convincingly, yet at the same time she fears that acting as if he were in love might lead him really to fall in love. When she hears that Roxane believes in Bajazet's love, Atalide worries that "Tout ce qu'il a pu dire, il a pu le penser" [All that he was able to say, he could have thought as well] (*Bajazet,* l. 916). Although for Bajazet word and thought never come together, for Valmont, in his theatrical meeting with Tourvel, they do.

Having just experienced the frightening power of theatricality, Valmont uses his letter to Merteuil to regain control. He devotes several paragraphs to trying to persuade himself (and certainly his correspondent as well) that the unknown feeling produced by his meeting with Tourvel hasn't mastered him, and that it results simply from his perfectly executed victory. "Je chéris cette façon de voir," he concludes, "qui me sauve l'humiliation de penser que . . . je n'aie pas en moi seul la plénitude de mon bonheur" [I cherish this way of seeing things, which saves me from the humiliation of thinking . . . that I don't have in myself the fullness of my happiness] (288). As Peter Brooks observes,

> Clearly, Valmont senses that what has happened to him is in some way unique, and he can only explain this sensation—to himself as much as to the Marquise—by transforming it into the effect of a glorious victory won by knowing maneuvers.[20]

Valmont's self-consciously theatrical account is thus a more retrospective attempt to gain control of his frightening feelings for Tourvel, than an "accurate" representation of how he felt during the encounter. He hopes to substitute epistolary distance and control for the peripatetic theatricality of his passionate evening with Tourvel. Valmont and Merteuil's retellings of events in their letters are motivated partly by the desire for an appreciative audience for exploits that must be hidden from the public, but also, perhaps especially for Valmont, by the need to bring potentially wayward events and emotions under rational control. Valmont and Merteuil's theatrical metaphors both show off their detached mastery and help produce it. Their entire correspondence, in fact, is an attempt at mastering the risks of presence, of theatricality, through writing.

Valmont and Merteuil both espouse theatricality in the sense of a self-conscious acting and staging of life. In his affair with Tourvel, though, Valmont comes under the sway of theatricality in the second sense, the one that directly threatens epistolarity: presence. If Néron's relationship with Junie is characterized by absence (the absence that is supposed to allow him to maintain control), Valmont's relationship with Tourvel is characterized, at least for a time, by presence (presence which subverts his control). I have mentioned already that the majority of the scenes that include direct discourse, as well as by far the longest such scene, are conversations between Tourvel and Valmont. More than any other characters in the novel, they are portrayed as present to each other. Valmont ultimately succeeds in seducing Tourvel not through letters, though these do perhaps bring her to love him, but through a visit to her house. (Perhaps this is because she can only admit to her love for him when she senses that he has begun to love her?)[21] And it is significant that at this point in the novel, when he moves away from epistolarity towards interactive theatricality, he brings with him Tourvel's letters, as a symbol of his rejection of epistolarity. Valmont's explanation of his gradual movement towards Tourvel during the seduction scene suggests the larger importance of presence for love: "comme en amour rien ne se finit que de très près, et que nous étions alors assez loin l'un de l'autre, il fallait avant tout se rapprocher" [since in love nothing is accomplished except from very close, and we were at that point quite far apart, it was above all necessary to get closer] (4:125; 291-92). Of course all the sexual encounters in the novel require that the couple be together, but Valmont and Tourvel's presence to each other is "represented" to the reader.

By the end of the novel the epistolarity that was Valmont and Merteuil's ethic has, for Valmont, become almost subservient to presence. After Tourvel sees him with Emilie, and writes a letter ending their affair, Valmont has to "present himself" in order to preserve the relationship:

> dans un moment, j'irai moi-même faire signer mon pardon; car dans les torts de cette espèce, il n'y a qu'une seule formule qui porte absolution générale, et celle-là ne s'expédie qu'en présence.

> in a moment, I will go myself to have my pardon signed: for in wrongs of this type, there is only one formula that brings complete absolution, and that one can be dispatched only in person [presence]. [4:138, 322]

Valmont's use of an epistolary metaphor, "faire signer mon pardon," for an actual encounter suggests a subordination of writing to presence. Valmont's love for Tourvel subverts both epistolarity and the theatricality of manipulation and control.

From the beginning of the novel Valmont's unpredictable encounters with Tourvel threaten his ironic detachment and mastery. He attempts to mask and control this emotional involvement with detailed and self-congratulatory accounts of escapades with Emilie or the Vicomtesse de M***, as well as through the almost perpetually amused tone of his letters. As Brooks argues,

> Valmont's repeated insistence on the grandiose significance of his coming victory over the Présidente, his detailing of diversionary tactics—the night with the Vicomtesse de M***, the seduction of Cécile—are designed to direct the Marquise's and his own attention away from the question of his relations with the Présidente. [192-93]

Merteuil may or may not be taken in by Valmont's mask initially, but after she reads the account of his triumph over Tourvel her letters make it clear that she is no longer deceived. Although Valmont himself may not realize he loves Tourvel, Merteuil knows it, and her subsequent letters are devoted to destroying this love and bringing Valmont under her epistolary control. Her devastating culminating move in this deadly game is the letter of rupture she sends Valmont to use on Tourvel. Merteuil sees that she has lost Valmont to Tourvel through the power of presence, of theatrical unexpectedness, and she responds by bringing him back to the realm of epistolarity. The letter of rupture terminates Valmont's affair with Tourvel more definitively than any meeting could, and subordinates Valmont's language to Merteuil's. The celebrated refrain, "ce n'est pas ma faute" [it's not my fault] (404), perfectly expresses Valmont's loss of autonomy in copying and sending it. Most of all the letter returns Valmont's relationship with Tourvel to the epistolary, and thus to Merteuil's control.

In setting up the rupture between Valmont and Tourvel, Merteuil replays the famous scene of rupture Néron staged between Britannicus and Junie. Merteuil thus puts herself in Néron's controlling position, and thrusts Valmont into the naïve, albeit virtuous, role of Britannicus. What is more, having recognized the danger of theatrical presence, of peripeteia, which subverted Néron's attempt to separate Junie and Britannicus, and brought Valmont to love Tourvel in the first place, Merteuil forces Valmont to end his affair in a *letter*. The failed theatrical breakup becomes an eminently successful epistolary one. Since theatrical encounters can backfire, Merteuil carefully orchestrates the entire episode in letters: she writes to Valmont, sending him the model letter; he mails the letter to Tourvel; he is never allowed to see Tourvel again. Merteuil seems to have brought everyone's lives under her control through her consummate epistolary manoeuvering. She appears to have succeeded where even Néron failed.

What the events of the end of the novel violently bring home to Merteuil, however, is that epistolarity too can back-fire. Throughout the novel Merteuil has consistently used letters as instruments of mastery and manipulation. The rupture episode epitomizes her faith in epistolarity as a means of control, a way of dominating the unexpected or the emotional. But letters too are dangerous, as Merteuil herself clearly recognizes: the very distance between sender and recipient that allows for control also implies that the sender can never be sure just who will receive the message.[22] Valmont's indirect response to Merteuil's termination of his love affair with Tourvel is thus the distribution of her letters to a wider, hostile audience. When the letters are read by the wrong recipients, Merteuil loses her trial, is disfigured by smallpox, and is forced to flee the country. Popular opinion in Paris has it that the disease has brought her evil character to the surface: "Le Marquis de *** . . . disait hier . . . que la maladie l'avait retournée, et qu'à présent son âme était sur sa figure" [The Marquis de *** . . . was saying yesterday . . . that the disease had turned her inside out, and that now her soul was on her face] (4:175; 385). It is as if she were an opened letter. Perhaps one could say that Merteuil, like Néron, is a monster who declares herself, whose true character comes to light at the work's end. Néron and Merteuil resemble letters that are deciphered by those around them, and both are ultimately trapped by the epistolarity that seemed to promise freedom and control.

Merteuil's final exposure is not, however, solely epistolary, but becomes theatrical as well. When she first appears in society after Danceny has publicized her letters, it is at the Comédie Italienne, where she is received with "general indignation" (4:173; 382). She learns of her disgrace not through letters, or even a private conversation, but through the reaction of her audience in this "cruel scene" at the theatre. If letters reveal her crimes, then, theatre punishes her for them. Her ultimate choice in favor of epistolarity (with the letter of rupture for Tourvel) both destroys her and tosses her back on the cruel stage of theatricality. In contrast, Valmont renounces epistolarity, not only in his affair with Tourvel, but also in his final encounter with Danceny. After a physical (not linguistic) duel, Valmont turns over his letters to Danceny, just as he had earlier to Tourvel. His choice in favor of theatricality subverts his perfect control and causes his death, but also brings him love (however brief) and a semblance of honor.

Valmont and Merteuil could be said to represent two possible attitudes towards intertextuality. Valmont quotes more often than Merteuil, and at least in the case of Racine, the passage borrowed comes to dominate and shape his entire life. He succumbs to the unpredictable risks of an intertextual dialogue, just as he does to the destabilizing interpersonal dialogue with Tourvel. Merteuil, on the other hand, never allows dialogues with texts or with other people to threaten her perfect mastery. But because she has based her survival on subordinating any voice that enters her closed system, she is destroyed by the one true dialogue she has permitted: her correspondence with Valmont. While Valmont enters into dialogue with others and lets himself be transformed by them, Merteuil refuses such transformations in her obsession with utter control.

It might seem initially that Laclos's attitude towards Racine, and towards intertextuality in general, resembles Merteuil's rather than Valmont's. The passages Laclos quotes from other literary works are thoroughly subordinate to his own tight textual organization; words used sincerely to describe the virtuous Junie, for example, are applied to an ironic description of the duplicitous and insignificant Vicomtesse. Laclos's disruption of Racine's alexandrine epitomizes his desire to appropriate the language of others for his own purposes, to force others' words to convey his own meanings and to fit his own forms. Like Valmont, however, Laclos, or at least his novel, ends up in dialogue with the voices he had attempted to master. As we have seen, the brief reference to *Britannicus* draws with it the rest of the play, infecting other scenes of the *Liaisons* with theatricality and with Racinian characters and situations. Laclos's novel does transform *Britannicus*, but in the process it is also transformed by it. The intertextual dialogue, once begun, leaves neither text unchanged.

Notes

1. See, for example, Jean Rousset, "Le Roman par lettres," *Forme et signification* (Paris: Corti, 1962), 96, and Peter Brooks, *The Novel of Worldliness* (Princeton: Princeton University Press, 1969), 187, 194.

2. Jean Giraudoux, "Choderlos de Laclos," *Littérature* (Paris: Grasset, 1941), 67. Translations from the French, here and elsewhere, are mine.

3. In "Racine et *Les Liaisons dangereuses*," *French Review* 23, no. 6 (1950): 452-61, Georges May discusses similarities in esthetic between Racine and Laclos (spatial and temporal concentration, etc.). See also Laurent Versini, *Laclos et la tradition. Essai sur les sources et la technique des 'Liaisons dangereuses'* (Paris: Klincksieck, 1968), 87-95, 327-29, for a thorough summary of Laclos's borrowings from and resemblances to Racine.

4. See Antoine Compagon, *La Seconde main* (Paris: Seuil, 1979) for a discussion of the structural and historical functioning of quotations.

5. Jorge Luis Borges, "Kafka and his Precursors," in *Labyrinths: Selected Stories and Other Writings* (New York: New Directions, 1962), 201.

6. Racine, *Théâtre complet* (Paris: Garnier Frères, 1980), ll. 1512-14. All further references to Racine will be to this edition and will appear parenthetically in the text (by line number, except in the case of Racine's prefaces to the play).

7. I would like to thank Richard Goodkin for this suggestion, as well as for his generous collaboration at various stages in the writing of this article.

8. Néron himself suggests the connection between his fratricide and matricide: "il faut que sa ruine / Me délivre à jamais des fureurs d'Agrippine" [it is necessary that his ruin / Deliver me forever from the furies of Agrippine] (1305-06).

9. Raymond Picard, "Présentation" to *Britannicus,* in Pléiade edition of Racine's *Oeuvres complètes* (Paris: Gallimard, 1950), vol. 1: 378.

10. George Poulet, "Notes sur le temps racinien," in *Racine,* ed. Wolfgang Theile (Darmstadt: Wissenschaftliche Buchgesellschaft, 1976), 104.

11. For discussions of the image of the sun in Racine, see Roland Barthes, *Sur Racine* (Paris: Seuil, 1963), 30-33, and Poulet, "Notes sur le temps racinien."

12. The quotation is footnoted by the novel's fictional editor: "Racine, Tragédie de *Britannicus.*" Choderlos de Laclos, *Oeuvres complètes* (Paris: Gallimard, 1979), part 2, letter 71, page 142. Further references to the *Liaisons* will be to this edition. References in the text are to part, letter, and page.

13. For discussions of theatricality in *Les Liaisons dangereuses,* see Philip Stewart and Madeleine Therrien, "Aspects de texture verbale dans 'Les Liaisons dangereuses,'" *Revue d'Histoire Littèraire de la France (RHLF)* 82, no. 4 (1982): 547-58; also Emita B. Hill, "Man and Mask: the Art of the Actor in the *Liaisons dangereuses,*" *Romanic Review* 63, no. 2 (1972): 111-24.

14. Jennifer Birkett, "Dangerous Liaisons: Literary and Political Form in Choderlos de Laclos," *Literature and History,* 8, no. 1 (1982): 88.

15. Vivienne Mylne, "Le Parler des personnages dans 'Les Liaisons dangereuses,'" *RHLF* 82, no. 4 (1982): 581.

16. It is interesting to note that this is the only scene which undergoes almost no alteration in Christopher Hampton's adaptation of *Les Liaisons dangereuses* for the stage (performed in London, and on Broadway, 1985 and 1986; published by London: Faber & Faber, 1985). Laclos (in the voice of Valmont) has already given the scene a theatrical form, and Hampton merely abridges it.

17. There are, however, many other borrowings, notably from Rousseau, integrated silently into the text.

18. Michel Delon, "Le Discours italique dans 'Les Liaisons dangereuses,'" *Laclos et le libertinage* (Paris: Presses Universitaires de France, 1983), 144-45. These pages also contain a brief discussion of how the passages cited are transformed by their new contexts. See also the Notes to the Pléiade edition.

19. Earlier scenes too reveal Valmont's tendency to be moved by his own theatrical artifices. Several critics have noted, for example, that he is affected by the charity scene staged for Tourvel's benefit (see Hill, 120; Stewart, 550).

20. Brooks, *The Novel of Worldliness,* 197.

21. Emita Hill argues that during the seduction Tourvel "gives herself freely" (122) only when Valmont has ceased to act and begun to love her.

22. In her long autobiographical letter, for example, Merteuil refers to the various "precautions" she takes in order to avoid having her love affairs exposed, including "celle de ne jamais écrire" [that of never writing] (2:81; 175).

Susan K. Jackson (essay date 1989)

SOURCE: "In Search of a Female Voice: *Les Liaisons dangereuses,*" in *Writing the Female Voice: Essays on Epistolary Literature,* edited by Elizabeth C. Goldsmith, Northeastern University Press, 1989, pp. 154-71.

[*In the essay below, Jackson analyzes the attributes of female voices in the letters that comprise* Les Liaisons dangereuses.]

> *Women of sincerity, it is you whom we are questioning. . . . You will not answer us; but dare to examine your hearts and judge for yourselves.*
>
> Choderlos de Laclos, *On the Education of Women*[1]

Countless analyses of *Les Liaisons dangereuses* originate in the statement or assumption that they are dealing with a "masterpiece." If the exceptional paucity of Laclos's *oeuvres complètes* allows his only novel to be read, as if by default, as his *chef d'oeuvre,* the metaphorical possibilities of this biographical phenomenon have not been lost on literary historians who single out the *Liaisons* as a masterpiece unrivaled in the lifetime of epistolary fiction. Christopher Hampton puts it wittily in "A Note on Laclos," which prefaces his recent adaptation of the novel for the commercial stage: "In many respects, Pierre-A.-F. Choderlos de Laclos (1741-1803) is the perfect author: he wrote, at around the age of forty, one piece of fiction, which was not merely a masterpiece, but the supreme example of its genre, the epistolary novel; and then troubled the public no further."[2] Whatever the competition, the *Liaisons* can be said to dwarf it. Likewise, in a further extension of the metaphor, Merteuil and Valmont, the novel's own two "masters" of deceit, are credited with reducing their victims (and their own avatars in French letters) to the status of more or less insipid secondary characters. The word would seem to have gone out that any writing relative to the *Liaisons* had better produce yet another successful exercise of *libido dominandi*—a cover blurb does not fail to herald Hampton's adaptation as "masterful"—or else. Irving Wohlfarth's deconstructive survey of Laclos criticism details this obsession with what he calls "control," and uses the critics' own favorite term, "irony," to condemn it to futility; but he leaves unexplored some of its dangerous implications.[3]

For one thing, a tradition of celebrating and striving after mastery, of canonizing masters and masterpieces, necessarily complicates discussion of the *Liaisons* in terms of the female voice. Where the stakes are literary stature, dwarfing is a matter of drowning out. By the term "masterpiece," we designate, as Nancy J. Vickers reminds us, "the single part of a whole (a genre, an author's *corpus*) that silences, by the strength of its voice, all other parts."[4] In the case of the epistolary genre, the parts which the *Liaisons* as masterpiece would silence are in a disproportionately high number of instances novels written for, about, and by women. A certain view of literary history thus confirms the gender specificity of a certain model of literary achievement. Even as he gives a hearing to many women's letter novels previously consigned to oblivion, even as he makes a refrain of insistence on "the feminine vocation of the genre," Laurent Versini prepares to champion more fervently than any other critic I have read the *Liaisons*'s privileged status as the genre's *terminus ad quem*. More compelling than any single argument is the reenactment of an implicit teleology by which all roads lead to the *Liaisons* not only in the monumental *Laclos et la tradition* but in Versini's general study *Le Roman épistolaire*. It is as though the *Liaisons* accomplished, with respect to women's letter novels, what the Présidente de Tourvel at one point in the novel contemplates doing to her own letters: rereading them and, in the process, erasing them (with her tears). In the aftermath of what Versini calls the "crowning" and "liquidation" of a genre by its masterpiece, the female voice must to some extent strain to be heard, and readers strain once again to hear it.[5]

The several essays in this volume devoted to female practitioners of epistolary fiction address that challenge more straightforwardly than can this one, since I have chosen to attend primarily to authorial voices (and only in passing to those of fictional characters like Merteuil and Tourvel), and to label as "female" only voices emanating from biological women. I do not mean to suggest that accidents of birth exclude anyone a priori from "feminine" or "feminist" discourse; depending on one's understanding of those two terms, a case can be made that Laclos engages in both. But to the extent that his text yields evidence of dissatisfaction with those possibilities, the most narrowly defined female voice becomes important in absentia. Laclos had no way of foreseeing that posterity would give him credit for besting women at their own game of epistolarity, or for collaborating with gentlemen-in-waiting like Richardson and Rousseau to make the game worth playing, and watching. And yet, the nearly unanimous adulation that his contemporary public accorded Laclos on other grounds already deflected attention from what the chorus of post-Romantic criticism has all but suppressed: a certain uneasiness in and about the author's voice, a sense that she or he who speaks as the other may not be playing fair.

Expressions of this uneasiness frame the novel, surfacing noticeably at the outset and at the opposite extreme. In anticipation of reading the postface provided by Laclos's correspondence on the *Liaisons* with Mme Riccoboni, I would look first to the liminal letter addressed by young Cécile Volanges to Sophie Carnay, a fellow pensioner and best chum recently left behind in the convent. An informal survey has confirmed my suspicion that readers tend to remember this letter for two reasons: as the locus of an amusing *quiproquo* (Cécile recounts having mistaken her mother's shoemaker for her own partner in an arranged marriage, the presumed pretext of her leaving the convent), and as an exemplum of Laclos's consummate ventriloquism; within the context of a closed aristocratic society, schoolgirlish babbling stands at the furthest imaginable remove from the "personal" style of a savvy general and man of the world. In fact, what will in hindsight have rendered these features salient is the shocking contrast in style and substance provided by the immediately ensuing letter, from Merteuil to Valmont. Well-wrought phrases running the gamut of tones from command to cajolery and calculated by the marquise to win the vicomte's support for her diabolical plot to cuckold a former lover—and, incidentally, to deflower "the Volanges girl" (6)—have the honor of underwriting a binarism essential to the thematics of mastery. The apparent closure of Cécile's letter, which resolves its own problem of mistaken identity, is exposed as illusory by the creation of much graver problems of which she has no inkling. Rather than for their own sake, her error must be remembered as foreshadowing the fatal misprision to come, her "discovery" that the shoemaker is not her intended as a sign of Merteuil's immense epistemological advantage. Merteuil possesses knowledge of vital interest to Cécile, Cécile knowledge of no interest whatsoever to Merteuil.

There would seem to be no resisting a coupling that victimizes, overpowers, indeed masters both the character of Cécile and her letter, silencing as eminently forgettable whatever parts of that letter the *telos* of mastery does not absolutely need to appropriate. That which will only have forestalled letter 2's confrontation between the queen (Merteuil) and king (Valmont) of the gods is tantamount to the prattle of Echo and, so, punishable by forfeiture of the right to an autonomous voice. Inevitably caught in the cross fire, letter 1 becomes the first civilian casualty in a war of words between the sexes. In the face of such unmistakable rewards for reading the situation right as the putative editor's thoughtful suppression of later scribbling from and to Cécile, it will take an almost perverse counterreading, if not an outright reversal of figure and ground, to dissociate ourselves from the enterprise of mastery, uncouple letters 1 and 2, and begin again at the beginning.

"You see, my dear, that I have kept my word and that bonnets and pom-poms do not take up all my time—there will always be some left over for you" (3). The initial sentence of letter 1 uses grammatical (*ma bonne amie*) and cultural ("bonnets and pom-poms") codes to overdetermine the mutual femaleness of correspondents already named as Cécile Volanges and Sophie Carnay. Beyond that, it serves primarily to fill the pair's time—past, present, and future—with instances of linguistic exchange. The first clause declares the double present of Sophie's reading ("You see") and Cécile's writing ("I keep my word"), the latter depicted as fulfilling a past promise to write, which the rest of the sentence implicitly renews and extends into the future. What the letter puts, redundantly, into words is an assurance of its own existence and a presumption of safe arrival at its destination. The missive is the message, the minimal epistolary gesture that establishes as more important than anything else Cécile and Sophie might say or hear the fact of their being in relation to language.

It requires no foreknowledge of the many uses to which Merteuil and Valmont will put the epistolary act to imagine that the present letter will somehow move beyond this linking of female correspondents to their correspondence. In fact, halfway through her first paragraph, Cécile interjects a further reminder that she is writing into a sentence whose accent nevertheless falls on extralinguistic acts of acquisition: "I have my own maid; I have a room and a study at my disposal and I am writing to you at a very pretty writing-table whose key was given to me so that I can shut up anything I want in it" (3). By the same paragraph's end, however, Cécile complains of having run out of things to say: "It is not yet five o'clock; I do not see Mamma until seven; plenty of time, if I had anything to say to you!" (3). Lest we leap too hastily to solemn conclusions about the "utter bankruptcy of spiritual existence in the waning hours of the Ancien Régime," Cécile does manage to pen another paragraph *before* the shoemaker's unexpected arrival provides genuinely new material.

In the interval, letter 1 carries on with none other than the two activities launched by what comes to look more and more like a topic sentence: naming females, naming them in such a way that there can be no doubt as to their sex; and matching them with verbs of speech, animating them almost exclusively as supports for language. This all-female cast comprises, in order of appearance: the haughty (*la superbe*) Tanville, identified by an editor's note as "pupil in the same convent"; the afore-mentioned maid or *femme de chambre;* Mamma, named four times and referred to by numerous subject and object pronouns; Mother Perpetue; numbers of sewing women; and the good (*la bonne*) Josephine, "attendant of the convent turning-box," according to a second note (3-4). As practiced here, name-dropping can easily be explained as feeding the illusion of an authentic correspondence oblivious to the ignorance of third-party readers. (The *incidence* of name-dropping is abnormally high only in light of as yet unestablished norms of masterful plotting, including the economical deployment of limited personnel and the elimination of extras.) Nor, given prevailing mores, does the cast's uniform femaleness, whatever pains are taken to proclaim and preserve it, come as any surprise. A series of implicit pairings (Mother Perpetue/Mamma, the good Josephine/ the maid, and so forth) continually tests the difference between one interior, the convent, from which males were excluded by law, and another, the aristocratic drawing room, where idled warriors were increasingly welcomed but still viewed to some extent as foreign invaders. Limited to the womanly ritual of assembling a trousseau, wedding preparations apparently in progress function to perpetuate the conventual order, to suspend "real" difference indefinitely, in favor of such relative differences as Cécile is positioned to perceive. "I have seen more clothes in this single day than in the four years we spent together" (3).

Neither literary nor sociological conventions account, however, for the systematic way in which letter 1 goes about assigning speaking parts to its incidental females. Cécile anticipates showing off her finery to Tanville ("I intend to ask for her"); weighs the pros and cons of her new life ("Mamma asks my opinion in everything. . . . Mother Perpetue is not here to scold me . . . my Sophie is not here to talk and laugh with me"); and wonders whether rumors of her engagement can be chalked up to further drivel (*un radotage de plus*) on the part of the good Josephine (3-4). Amidst this flurry of asking, consulting, scolding, chatting, laughing, and rambling, only the voices of the sewing women who parade through the Volanges's household in silence go unrecorded. Not that the others are charged with delivering anything much in the way of specific lines; on the contrary, if Madame de Volanges's utterances to her daughter consist essentially of telling her that she will tell her later when they will talk, this potentially infinite deferral of content recalls promises to write made in the absence of anything to write about. Intransitive verbs (chat, laugh, ramble), verbs that take interlocutors rather than locutions as their objects (ask for, consult, scold), make for a high volume of female voices, but tend toward dissociating the faculty of speech from the production of meaning.

Even Cécile seems inclined to dismiss the female voices she faithfully records as so much background noise. When it comes to something as important as her long-term future, it is no longer "she," her mother, who is accused of keeping Cécile in the dark, but the neuter *on* (one). Rendered by the passive voice in Aldington's translation, the pronoun occurs twice in the original. "So far nothing has been said [*on ne m'a encore parlé de rien*] and except for the preparations I see being made and the numbers of sewing-women who all come for me I should think there is no intention of marrying me [*je croirais qu'on ne songe pas à me marier*] and that it was one more delusion [*un radot-*

age de plus] on the part of the good Josephine" (3-4). Not only is the feminine pronoun precluded from standing in for the voice of truth and authority, but pronouncements withheld by *on* derive value from explicit contrast with feminine drivel, such that *on* becomes a barely disguised synonym for *il* (he). The voice of authority must be *his*. But whose? For want of an available male referent, for want of an *il/on* to tell her the truth in no uncertain terms, Cécile can only piece together syllogisms out of the repetitive, inconclusive propositions of her female entourage. "Mamma has told me so often that a young lady should remain at the convent until she is married that Josephine must be right, since Mamma has taken me away" (4).

It is at this juncture, the absence of male voices having been rendered conspicuous and problematical, that the chance arrival of a carriage interrupts the letter-writing process. Needless to say, ensuing developments carry to parodic extremes the sexual naïveté of a stock literary figure, the conventionally educated ingénue. But Cécile's progress from hypothesis to belief to certainty that the carriage has delivered none other than her fiancé can also be read as confirming our own hypotheses about male and female voices. "Suppose it were *he [le Monsieur]*?" (4)—any man could be *the* man, the deus ex machina equipped by nature to rescue language from the impasse of inconclusiveness. What matters is maleness; whatever his proper name, the visitor announced as Mr. C. fulfills the essential criterion for belief that "it *is* he [*c'est lui*]," he who will declare (himself). The belief needs verifying, however, insofar as the maid's announcement terminates, not in a positive identification, but in appropriately ambiguous laughter (4). What clinches the case, inspiring Cécile to such heretofore unscaled heights of inarticulateness as "a piercing cry," is the verbal and body language emitted by "the gentleman" himself. No "remark" could be more "plain" than his compliment: "'Madame,' said he to my mother, as he bowed to me, 'This is a charming young lady and I feel more than ever the value of your favour'"—unless, of course, he should subsequently assume the unmistakable posture of a smitten supplicant: "I had scarcely sat down when this man was at my knees!" As though to underscore the fact that at long last the bass rumblings of a male voice have made themselves heard, Cécile's search for a situation of comparable horror leads her back to "the day of the thunderstorm" (4).

Jupiter has spoken, or would have if he did not turn out to be a shoemaker speaking only in the discharge of his duties, leaving Cécile as ignorant as had the silence of his fellow tradespeople the sewing women. Not that Mamma seizes this golden opportunity to appropriate the voice of truth; she responds typically to Cécile's predicament with a burst of laughter and an order: "Sit down and give Monsieur your foot," which stops short of revealing the truth even of the present situation. The matter of fact that

"'Monsieur' was a shoemaker" is reported without attribution to any speaker, male or female. *On* has yet to be heard from; the letter's complimentary closing repairs the rift between past and present and makes it clear that nothing has changed. "Good-bye, dear Sophie. I love you as if I were still at the convent" (4).

As for the future. Cécile ventures only to say: "I think that when I am married I shall never employ this shoemaker" (4). His impeccable conduct notwithstanding, the shoemaker has been scapegoated. Mister has become Mister Wrong, victimized by the inescapable fact of his maleness, put out of a job for the unforgivable impropriety of speaking with a bass voice (and thus leading Cécile down the primrose path through sexual to intellectual shame). Poor fellow! What *was* his name anyway, or, more puzzling still, what possible reason could there be for referring to Cécile's mysterious visitor only as *M. C ****? It makes no sense to ascribe the suppression by asterisks to Cécile: though she may not have caught the name on first hearing, a point is made of the fact that she got a second chance. Willful suppression on her part would be more unlikely still: C.'s anonymity hardly needs protecting from the likes of Sophie, with whom Cécile obviously shares everything, including an ignorance of men, which makes Sophie a poor candidate for guessing games. In fact, the longstanding conventions of protective anonymity and guessing games (*romans à clé*) frame a message—these unnamed individuals are/were real—belonging primarily not to the discourse between characters, but to that between novelists and their external readers. Readers like us, novelists like the one we have come to call "Laclos," but whose initials appear on the original title page of the *Liaisons* as "M. C. . . . de L. . . .," and who, until late in his life, "was referred to and referred to himself as Choderlos or Choderlos de Laclos."[6] What if the mysterious recurrence of the initial "C" so few pages later were charged with writing a cameo part for the novelist qua novelist in and out of his novel? The possibility of such a provisional incarnation of the authorial voice would be less appealing if we felt obliged to silence all possible objections with a masterful proof of conscious intentions, less intriguing if the letter in which M. C*** makes his lone appearance did not so consistently and coherently problematize the issue of voice and sensitize the unhurried exegete to the questions of who is speaking and how.

Read as an aside to the external reader, the shoemaker's dismissal as persona non grata formalizes the implications for the novelist of his decision to write an epistolary novel: exclusion from speaking in his own name either as a character or as a global narrator, self-conscious retreat into marginal craftsmanship (the editor as shoemaker). The basis for his dismissal, Cécile's error, in turn warns us readers against mistaking the voice of any character, no matter how eloquent the speaker or how desperate our

need, for the authorial *on,* which the entirety of letter 1 solicits in vain. The joke of the author's plight is on us: *on* will, for the duration of this or any epistolary novel, remain elusive, resisting all attempts at localizing in this or that scriptor's body what emanates instead from an overall corpus. Even the authorial voice that we might claim to read between the lines (of a double entendre like C.'s compliment, for example) does not really speak for itself; it depends, for the production of meaning, on the sometimes unwitting collusion of a reader's (in)experience, expectations, and values. Like C.'s, Laclos's power to disconcert resides, paradoxically, in the alienation of his discourse, in the act of speaking, never in his own name, but always through roles *and* through his readers. "The very nature of epistolary fiction supposes the novelist's protean talent to transmute his voice into that of another."[7]

But what are we to make, for purposes of our analogy, of the fact that C. wields his power inadvertently and derives from its exercise not exultation but acute embarrassment? Why does this version of mastery look so much like misery? The cameo does more than provide an occasion for rehearsing generalities about the authorial voice in epistolary fiction; it *particularizes* the voice at work everywhere and nowhere in *this* novel and, in so doing, reminds us that no voice can avoid forever being traced to a particular individual. Whether that individual has the right or responsibility to claim it as his or her own remains a question for philosophers and moralists. It is a matter of common sense that some*body* wrote, published, and made his reputation from *Les Liaisons dangereuses,* that somebody being not some asexual, perfectly protean God, but Choderlos de Laclos, "Monsieur . . . he . . . a gentleman in black . . . this man" (4).

The limits of biology are most succinctly rendered by C.'s compliment: "'Madame, . . . This is a charming young lady and I feel more than ever the value of your favour.'" The male author can speak in terms of utmost respect *to* women and *about* them; he can prostrate himself, literally and metaphorically, at their knees. Like shoemaking, novel making provides him access to the secret gyneceum or no man's land from which those of his sex are normally banned; he can make his life's work of pleasing his female clientele and setting them off to their best advantage. What more eloquent gesture of good faith than that his liminal letter should make a mockery, at the novelist's own expense, of the authority too automatically and universally ascribed to the male voice? A show of embarrassment at the interchangeability of *il* and *on* does not, of course, explain away the unproductive noisiness of the letter's various *elles.* But the argument could be made—and Laclos will make it in the fragments on the education of women—that the fault lies with the phallologocentric social order, which encourages women to buy into this mystique of the male voice (417-18). What more is Laclos to do in the present context than to validate the female voice in its virtuality, even as he hesitates, however briefly, to put words into *her* mouth? And yet, even in the guise of self-appointed spokesman *for* women, even through his many experiments in speaking as women might, Laclos cannot, short and simple, speak as a woman. Neither abdicating the authority of *on* nor appropriating it with the best of intentions brings him all the way out of himself. Letter 1 stages the cruel joke played by nature on whoever knows sexual difference to make a difference. However tenuous in the writing of a letter novel—as Merteuil reminds Valmont, letters are read where the writer's body is not (59)—the inescapable liaison of voice and body gives rise to a certain anxiety of authorship.

Symbolic compensation for this anxiety takes many forms in *Les Liaisons dangereuses,* among them the quantitative and qualitative advantages enjoyed by the novel's female correspondents. Not only do their voices continue to outnumber those of their male counterparts, but they have a virtual monopoly, for example, on thoughtful discussion of sexual difference. (This unequal distribution of the best lines and tirades becomes all the more striking when they are spoken aloud in the theater.) Truths told at length by Merteuil and Rosemonde sustain the illusion of a female presence where none exists behind the scenes. In his final curtain call as editor, M. C. . . . de L. . . . does more than a little to dispel that illusion. The sequel he has in mind for the *Liaisons* would necessarily be scripted or at least received as a pair of discrete third-person narratives *about* the novel's two surviving heroines: "For the moment, we cannot give the reader the continuation of Mademoiselle de Volanges's adventures nor inform him of the sinister events which completed the misfortunes or the punishment of Madame de Merteuil" (368). With this bracketing of epistolarity, a monopoly on discourse reverts to the male editor and his generic *lecteur.* And rightly so: no Mademoiselle or Madame, neither Juno nor Echo, will really have spoken anywhere in the *Liaisons.* Of course, the possibility that letters have been arbitrarily withheld from us perpetuates the fantasy of *libido dominandi.* But the more likely possibility, that no further letters exist (to whom could either Cécile or Merteuil have written? Surely not to each other) would, if admitted directly, put too emphatic an end to the concurrent fantasy of coauthorship, of authentically polyphonic composition. What the editor says and fails to say at the last begs the question: Could Laclos have a personal investment not only in Merteuil's plot to master her male rival but in her earlier dream gone astray of collaborating with a member of the opposite sex in the writing of a novel?

A sequel of sorts does exist, which testifies better than anything Laclos himself could have written to the survival of his preoccupation with the female voice. To the 1787 edition of the novel, the last Laclos supervised personally

and the one he claimed to prefer,[8] was appended an exchange of eight letters between Laclos and the popular novelist Madame Marie-Jeanne Riccoboni. A bookseller's foreword facetiously advertises these letters as neatly summarizing for readers too lazy or unsure of themselves to form their own opinions all possible arguments for and against the *Liaisons,* and opines that this authentic correspondence might have ranked among the all-time great literary polemics had the correspondents not refrained from trading insults (730).

Indeed, what is disappointing about the exchange as literary criticism—aside from the fact that the theoretical assumptions jointly espoused seem so far in arrears of Laclos's practice—is the amount of space reserved, especially by him, for the formulation of elaborate, even extravagant compliments. At one point, Riccoboni bids him back off from what is verging on gallantry, with a reminder of her advanced age: How can someone who first talked about her with his grandmother expect her to take seriously claims that he would experience the termination of their correspondence as "deprivation" (692)? His hastening to endorse and justify the wording stands as only one example among many of what our reading makes understandable as delight at having been addressed by a living, breathing female (694). Riccoboni's first sally having arrived as much by chance, from as far out of the blue as C.'s carriage, Laclos seems to relish his lack of authorial control over the correspondence as such, to thrill in the tenuousness of the liaison that connects his with this other autonomous voice. Will Riccoboni write back even after, putting that tenuousness to the test, he gratuitously "confesses" that she has every right not to continue (690)? When she catches him in the contradiction of attaching his address (692), as when mere politeness dictates that she thank him for enclosing a copy of *Les Liaisons* (689), he is happy enough to admit to the transparency of subterfuges which, in each instance, guarantee him at least one more reply (694). How palpably different from the absence of real female voices in the *Liaisons* is that silence rendered eloquent by his "threat" to send along another installment unless he hears from her forthwith (696).

However much they must have unnerved an addressee more or less fated to read the possibility of Valmont's mocking overtones into the discourse of his creator, we third-party readers have the luxury of appreciating that these otherwise banal and suspect compliments also bespeak a certain gratitude for making the dream of epistolarity come true. In combination with repeated direct assurances of the high value he attaches to Riccoboni's approval or *suffrage* (692, 696, 697)—the French term also translates as "vote," as does *voix,* the term for "voice"— peripheral expressions of thanks for her expressions of thanks (689), for her very willingness to engage in debate (697), draw attention to a truly honest difference (of opinion). Whereas Riccoboni starts out by referring to herself in the first person singular and to Laclos in the third person respectful as "the son of M. de Chauderlos" (686), his response uses a pair of third persons not only to redress tactfully the implied inequality of extralinguistic stature but to linger over the realization that discourse is really in progress between a male and a female of equal status *in* that discourse. "M. Laclos sincerely thanks Mme Riccoboni . . . M. Laclos begins by congratulating Mme Riccoboni," and so forth (687). Even *after* the correspondence has been appended to *his **Liaisons***, Laclos nurtures an illusion of perfect parity by placing responsibility for what looks suspiciously like reappropriation of the female voice squarely on the shoulders of *on,* some other authority (***Lettres inédites,*** 295).

A hidden agenda incompatible with master planning on Laclos's part is further served by Riccoboni's spontaneously setting an agenda for debate which centers on the character of Merteuil. To be sure, the presence of a female interlocutor who happens to be a widely respected author and former collaborator provides grounds enough for Laclos's assuming in his own name and with all due seriousness C.'s reverential (if seductive) posture before this particularly prized client.[9] But deflection of his compliments onto a wider public requires Riccoboni's easily won admission that the portrayal of the she-devil Merteuil offends her personally *as a woman*. It is she whose hints that others of her sex are similarly offended give way to warnings about incurring the wrath of women without exception, she who goes so far as to put herself at risk of having her eyes scratched out for her relative indulgence (689, 693). Laclos thus finds himself "forced" to rehearse, in the face of seemingly insurmountable evidence to the contrary, his impeccable credentials as a man who loves and respects the other as other. He manifests a desire to do just that by declaring Merteuil's nationality to be contingent to her essential character (691), thereby dismissing as equally contingent Riccoboni's further claims to have responded viscerally as a "Frenchwoman" and "zealous patriot" (689). Nor does he pay more than lip service to the easy but unconvincing argument according to which Merteuil's demonic version of womanhood would be offset by the positive images projected by, for example, Tourvel and Rosemonde (687-88). He must already have sensed that Riccoboni would refuse to honor the argument with a single word of rebuttal when he referred her for "proof" to one in particular (130) of Rosemonde's letters. By contrast, his reader's memory required no such refreshing about the otherwise memorable marquise. In fact, his reference to the Rosemonde letter remains the only specific allusion in this correspondence between connoisseurs to the text of the novel—and, remarkable as it may seem, given our present-day fascination with form—the only clue as to the novel's epistolarity. Laclos's half-hearted attempt to locate

and amplify artificially the voice of female virtue attests to the virtually unlimited silencing powers of what was already presumed to be a unique masterpiece of characterization, Merteuil.

It is in the guise of yet another victim, as the master ironically silenced by his own masterpiece, that Laclos now dusts off C.'s black suit. Painstakingly, ingeniously, exhaustively, even defensively, as Ronald Rosbottom has suggested (*Choderlos de Laclos,* 48), he sets about answering the eighteenth century's favorite charges of untruth and immoralism in characterization, as Riccoboni has made them pertain to his own attitudes toward women. In no way the projection of some vengeful misogynist, the character of Merteuil has its source in external, observable, everyday reality (687, 691). Were it less true to life, it would scarcely have touched a collective nerve or created such a furor; who, after all, thought to attack poor Don Quixote for tilting at windmills, or leapt to the defense of the windmills themselves (690)? On the other hand, though the models are many and the character a composite, it represents not the essence of womanhood as Laclos himself understands it, but rather a deplorable perversion of that essence by a seditious fringe element. The virtuous majority should applaud rather than lambaste him for exposing and combatting the traitress in their midst (690-91). And so forth.

Much more could be written about and against these arguments than Riccoboni, with a much smaller stake than Laclos's in "winning" a debate that she could only assume to be private, chose to write. Rather than abandon so early on the issue or Merteuil's troubling attractiveness as a role model, she might, for example, have demanded to know where exactly in the novel Laclos "combats" vice and makes its "horror" so unmistakably repugnant as to discourage all thoughts of imitation (687-88, 690). By way of contrast, another contemporary female reader, Isabelle de Charrière, scoffs at the inconsequentiality of whatever punishments the novel's dénouement metes out, and reads the "moral" of the story as follows: give me the pleasures and power of a Merteuil, and I'll know enough not to write incriminating letters or catch smallpox, which I've already had.[10]

In the course of the correspondence, Riccoboni's role is thus gradually reduced to that of prompter for the long-winded laments of one who fancies himself to be womankind's misunderstood lover. Louder and more plaintive still, and more germane to our discussion of the female voice, are those passages where Laclos blames the characterization of Merteuil on what once again emerges as a crucial limitation, his very biological maleness. How unfair that women in society should heap further abuse on those whom nature has already "condemned," leaving them no choice but to write as men (688). This claim begs to be buttressed and it is, however sketchily, by an explanation of what Laclos perceives to be the fundamental difference between characteristically male or masculine writing and that feminine writing declared off limits to those of his sex. The former is or would be, at its best, essentially voiceless. Perfectly analogous with the plastic arts—the metaphor recurs ad nauseum—masculine writing can aspire to no other perfection than adequate representation of external models. Far from coming naturally to its practitioners, this version of mimesis demands harder, less pleasant work (*un travail plus sévère*) than feminine writing, and brings few rewards. Failure to let the facts, all the facts, speak for themselves means falling short of masculine writing's only accessible goal, "rendering nature exactly and faithfully" (688). Hard-won artistic success in turn means falling victim to the kind of misunderstanding that would not have arisen had Laclos spoken for himself in the only way available to him as a male artist, by "silencing at least a part of what he has seen" (687). Limited in this enterprise of unrelieved grimness to approaching psychological realism as a limit from the underside of less than full disclosure of perceived reality, the male novelist can set his sights only on the Pyrrhic victories of characters like Merteuil. He stands to be damned by his female readership if he tells all he knows, damned as an artist if he holds anything back.

The eye is indeed covetous which looks up to "feminine" writing—and here the novels of Laclos's correspondent provide an exemplary case in point—as uniquely "charming" and charmed (688). What makes the difference is women's exclusive birthright to a faculty that Laclos—after Valmont (66)!—calls "precious sensibility" (688). Supplementing or even replacing "observation" and "painting," this sensibility corresponds in its functioning to our notion of voice. By "embellishing" and "adding to," the increment of voice propels female writing beyond the austere masculine ideal of voicelessness into the far side of more than external reality, the "real" ideal. Unlike eyes, which must be trained to see clearly, and hands disciplined to paint without trembling, voice emanates spontaneously, as is, "smiling" and "facile," from within the female body (695, 688). Considerations of technique have nothing at all to do with the designation of the best female writers as those "born" to the greatest quantity of sensibility (695). To compliment a woman's work thus amounts to congratulating the woman herself on the extent of her femaleness. As if on cue, Riccoboni takes personally the praise that Laclos showers on her novels and takes *them* not at all seriously; "trifles emitted by my pen," she calls them (689).

But the liaison between the female writer and her writing turns out to be more complex and more consubstantial still. Invoking the painting metaphor in what looks like a desperate attempt at reestablishing some common ground, lest his two poles spin off wildly in opposite directions, Laclos locates the "models" for Riccoboni's characters "in the heart of the painter" (688). That female voice credited with embellishing "everything it touches" would thus touch nothing beyond the speaker herself, except that even "she" must inevitably be lost in the very process of embellishing, which yields no other truth than that of its own inexhaustible energy. The best woman writer "pours out" only a portion of her innate sensibility onto the self-"portrait she traces" (695). Tending always towards auto-referentiality, the female voice thus constitutes itself as the unique, forever elusive object of female discourse. Echoes of Echo, shades of Cécile's vociferous coterie: their having "nothing to say" renders more faithfully and fundamentally even than Tourvel's characteristic solipsism or Merteuil's fatal attraction to autobiography an essential conflation of means and ends into the single self-sustaining, self-proclaiming entity of voice. For all the limitless possibilities held out by Laclos's positively charged rhetoric and by an enabling pseudologic of supplementarity, serious limits are being placed on the domain of women's letters.

Laclos's rhetoric further dissimulates the obvious proximity of embellishment to willful dissimulation. His implicit model of feminine writing is borrowed, not from any fine art, but from the everyday art of cosmetology, a subject discussed at some length in two chapters of *De l'éducation des femmes* (436-48). The woman who paints herself with words has everything in common with the seductress who uses cosmetics to "make herself up," including ready means to the end of pleasing men. How much more transparent is the motive when courtship of the opposite sex entails simply letting one's own voice be heard, rather than, as he has had to do, allowing a Merteuil to speak for herself. Laclos thus makes it against women's best interests to challenge his version of the female voice, and makes virtually irresistible the temptation to venture self-consciously even further into the realm of the ideal, of "objects as they should be," than the untrained voice—if indeed it exists—would naturally lead (688).

Riccoboni's tacit compliance with this theoretical demonstration also leaves unchallenged the fundamental inequality for which, try as he might, Laclos's effusions cannot overcompensate. Just as predictably as he (and Riccoboni) come back time and again to the painting metaphor, that metaphor breaks down when asked to perform the literally inappropriate task of rendering the operations of the female voice. For it is masculine, voiceless writing à la Laclos that conforms on every count to the literary values of the mainstream moralist tradition in French letters, feminine writing that derives and differs from that which controls the difference. More is less, voice the sign and the stigma of failure to conform. The so-called "son of M. Chauderlos" can lay claim as well to an impeccable literary bloodline passing from the illustrious Molière through Crébillon fils and Richardson (687, 690-91) and get no argument or alternative genealogy from a woman as imbued as he with the prescriptions of the patriarchy. How telling that, in his article on Fanny Burney's *Cecilia,* Laclos should linger admiringly over the circumstances of Burney's coming to writing out of a desire to please not some lover of her own generation, as might have been feared, but rather her adored and adoring father. Laclos's further recollection that Burney revealed to no one the secret of work on her first novel until it was fully finished remystifies the *process* of female writing more honestly than do the forced metaphors of his letters to Riccoboni (502). So too does a latent analogy between Burney's clandestine operations and those of the solitary natural childbirth exalted in the essay on female education (408).

There is another reason for reading, as a companion piece to the Riccoboni letters, the essay on *Cecilia,* which, in its theoretical introduction, attenuates to the point of blurring distinctions between the writings of the two sexes. Successful novels, his *and* hers, depend, according to the essayist, on the novelist's possessing a threshold level of talent whose three component parts—the familiar observation, sensibility, and painting—may coexist in varying proportions. Women tend toward sensibility but have no corner on this precious commodity (501); nor are women in general and Burney in particular precluded from the accurate depiction of mores (521).[11] It would appear, then, that we have Riccoboni's intervention to thank for transforming this relative difference into an absolute one. A hardening of the lines that works, at least rhetorically, to the advantage of women, giving them a voice of their own, even voice itself, pays homage to that intervention; Laclos seeks to reproduce, in the arena of public letters, the rhetorical frame of separate but equal participation in epistolary exchange.

To be sure, the male novelist has everything to gain from a separation that effectively eliminates the possibility of "bisexual" women writers. Aram Vartanian has convincingly read the demise of Merteuil as Laclos's way of dealing with the threat of female bisexuality.[12] I would only add to his arguments the reminder that Merteuil, she who would be king *and* queen, is paired at both extremes of the novel with Cécile, whose attraction to and for members of both sexes places her sexual preference literally in doubt. Assuming control over the future adventures of both heroines may well be the response of the "editor" to the specter of Jupiter's absence from the decisive confrontation where Juno and Echo manage to settle the question of voice between themselves.

Nor does the expenditure of energy involved in masterminding (a semblance of) parity by overvaluing the

feminine go unrewarded. If Laclos backs Riccoboni into a corner of silence from which only an ingrate would come out swinging, he also gets a chance to wallow in that victim's role whose persistent attractiveness to him I hope to have suggested. However patronizing (and unconvincing) the appropriation of that role by one of the really empowered, it places into question the more or less universal assumption of Laclos's exclusive identification with the dominant protagonists of the *Liaisons.* I would argue that the novel's virtuosity depends less on superficial ventriloquism than on the wide-ranging possibilities of the novelist's own inner voice, on his feeling equally at home in the three registers of mastery, co-mastery, *and* victimization. What passes for the unremitting practice of mastery might more inclusively be rethought as a preoccupation with mastery as a problematics.

Sensitivity to that problematics, the ability to consider it from vantage points other than that of the master, would seem to account for Laclos's intuition of the threat posed to Riccoboni's novels by a masterpiece such as his own. His rhetorical question, posed by way of reassurance— "What could one write that could ever destroy the charm of those delicious works which you alone call trifles?" (690)—admits of a three-word response, *Les Liaisons dangereuses,* which appears already obvious to him. So too the prophecy in his declaration that a posterity with no taste for Riccoboni's novels would forfeit his esteem can be read as betraying a vague awareness of the sexual politics of canon formation (690). It would be going way too far to fantasize a Laclos indifferent to his own present "glory" (698) or to the prospect of being installed, at whatever cost to others, in a central niche of the canon. He would no doubt have been horrified to learn that the public's attention could be so really "fickle" (697) as to delay the proceedings for more than a century.

Indeed, he has it both ways, controlling and publishing in his own name a correspondence that reveals him to be always in control of everything *except* Riccoboni's vote of approval, which her terminal letter refuses in the name of personal integrity to surrender: "To say what I do not think seems to me a betrayal" (698). Co-opting at the stage of publication a voice that he will earlier have failed to co-opt, Laclos commemorates and undermines whatever need for equality the correspondence may temporarily have served. Still, however much he uses and abuses Riccoboni's letters for his own purposes, he does rescue them from silence; he makes a public spectacle of pursuing earnest exchange, of turning a deaf ear on the self-deprecation of a would-be "unknown cenobite" who, in an uncanny coincidence, relegates her own voice to (Cécile's) convent and (Echo's) cave (698, 692). Most invitingly, in his several incarnations, Laclos—alias C***, alias M. C. . . . de L. . . ., alias son of Chauderlos—never fails to remind us that, when he speaks, (only) a man will have spoken. We could do worse than accept his open invitation to read "*Ernestine, Fanny, Catesby,* etc., etc., etc." (688), there to learn what Echo has to say, and with what unexpected force, otherwise than in the service of Jupiter, even as we continue to listen for regions of silence *in* the masterpiece.[13] On two separate occasions, Laclos proposes to Riccoboni a model of right reading that would consist in seeing the body or essential through the drapery or contingent (688, 691). In writing back, we continue to wonder aloud how bodies make a difference, and whether that difference might have something to do with disagreement as to where the drapery leaves off and the body begins.

Notes

1. In citing *De l'éducation des femmes,* the correspondence with Riccoboni, and the essay on *Cecilia,* I have used the text of Laclos's *Oeuvres complètes* edited for the Bibliothèque de la Pléiade by Maurice Allem (Paris: Gallimard, 1951); English translations are mine. In the case of *Les Liaisons dangereuses,* I cite (and page numbers refer to) Richard Aldington's English translation, *Dangerous Acquaintances* (New York: New Directions, 1957). The original French wording is given wherever essential to my reading.

2. *Les Liaisons dangereuses, from the Novel by Pierre-Ambroise-François Choderlos de Laclos* (London: Faber and Faber, 1985), 7.

3. Irving Wohlfarth, "The Irony of Criticism and the Criticism of Irony: A Study of Laclos Criticism," *Studies in Voltaire and the Eighteenth Century* 120 (1974): 269-317.

4. In Nancy J. Vickers, "The Mistress in the Masterpiece," in *The Poetics of Gender,* ed. Nancy K. Miller (New York: Columbia University Press, 1986), 19.

5. *Laclos et la tradition: Essai sur les sources et la technique des "Liaisons dangereuses"* (Paris: Klincksieck, 1968); *Le Roman épistolaire* (Paris: Presses Universitaires de France, 1979), 11, 60, 182, 149-67; *Dangerous Acquaintances,* 271.

6. Ronald C. Rosbottom, *Choderlos de Laclos* (Boston: Twayne Publishers, 1978), 18.

7. Lloyd R. Free, ed., *Laclos: Critical Approaches to "Les Liaisons dangereuses"* (Madrid: Porrúa, 1978), 42.

8. In a letter to his son, See Louis de Chauvigny, ed., *Lettres inédites de Choderlos de Laclos* (Paris: Mercure de France, 1904), 295.

9. Laclos had penned the libretto for a disastrous operatic adaptation of Riccoboni's novel *Ernestine.*

10. Isabelle de Charrière, *Suite des Trois Femmes,* in her *Oeuvres complètes,* 9 (Amsterdam: G. A. van Oorschot, 1981), 135.

11. Since completing this essay, I have read what Nancy K. Miller writes along similar lines about Laclos's piece on *Cecilia:* "Although we find here the classic move of putting the woman in her place that Delon et al. repeat, what interests me in Laclos's poetics of the novel is its explicitly bi-sexual approach to comparative literature." See Nancy K. Miller, "Authorized Versions," *French Review* 61:3 (1988): 411.

12. In Aram Vartanian, "The Marquise de Merteuil: A Case of Mistaken Identity," *L'Esprit créateur* 3 (1963): 172-80.

13. How much we would miss were we to take Laclos's word alone for the uniform essence of Riccoboni's corpus is already implicit in their contemporary Mme de Genlis's reading of Fanni Butlerd as "a vehement, passionate woman" who "utterly lacks decency and charm." See Joan Hinde Stewart, intro. to *Lettres de Mistriss Fanni Butlerd,* by Madame Riccoboni (Geneva: Droz, 1979), xix.

Anne Deneys (essay date 1991)

SOURCE: "The Political Economy of the Body in the *Liaisons dangereuses* of Choderlos de Laclos" in *Eroticism and the Body Politic,* edited by Lynn Hunt, The Johns Hopkins University Press, 1991, pp. 41-62.

[*In the following essay, Deneys explores the tenets of libertinism as expressed in* Les Liaisons dangereuses, *arguing that an exchange system operates at the linguistic, economic, and ethical level.*]

Why speak of "economy" in the *Liaisons dangereuses*? Because in this novel interpersonal relationships are organized like a system of exchange: letters, promises, libertine accounts, agreements, and challenges are exchanged; also women.[1] As I shall attempt to show, every one of these exchanges assumes above all that women are exchanged, that women circulate among a number of men.

Among libertines, women, goods, and words (in letters) are exchanged, which Lévi-Strauss has shown to have been the general rule of the basic structure of human societies even before they engaged in material production or in political discourse. Does this tell us that, by its system of exchange, the elitist and refined society of the *Liaisons* subconsciously attempts to constitute a vast family clan, where women tend to be the common property of the masters and where a strict division of functions governs the respective functions of men and of women?

Libertinism in the *Liaisons* controls all forms of exchange, from its most primitive forms—barter, potlatch, the exchange of goods in trade, services, or women—to its highly sophisticated and, in a way, abstract forms: those that concern signs of value and of "conquests" and that no longer aim at any kind of exchange, even epistolary exchange. I shall thus try to describe the libertinism of *Les Liaisons dangereuses* as a system of exchange defined at three levels: economic, ethical, and linguistic.[2]

A number of ideas about libertinism are often repeated and presented as self-evident truths, and they are certainly not without their share of validity. The first is that eighteenth-century French libertinism can only be thought of sociologically, as a symptom of the historical decline of a class or "order" (the aristocracy) that was to play its last influential role on the stage of the erotic.[3] The second commonly accepted idea is that libertinism more than anything else constitutes a quest—a sometimes frustrated, but nevertheless positive, search for pleasure.[4] The third idea—even more attractive than the previous two for those who exalt transgression in contemporary culture—is that libertinism is the perfect model of transgression (be it moral or immoral) of existing sexual law, because it benefits from the uses and abuses of liberty or of license.[5] In analyzing *Les Liaisons* under the aegis of the supreme law of exchange, I hope to show that libertinism can, on the contrary, be interpreted, not in the preceding ways, but rather as a structure that reinforces law at every level on which law prevails, as economic law, as ethical law, and as the law of the signifier.

LIBERTINISM AS ECONOMIC SYSTEM, OR, THE RULES OF THE EXCHANGE OF WOMEN

First I want to show how libertinism, in *Les Liaisons dangereuses,* by establishing an administrative system that regulates relationships between men and women, is organized along the lines of a market economy. Woman is defined from the outset as capital. The novel begins with a letter from Cécile Volanges about her upcoming marriage, which the marquise de Merteuil discusses in her following letters in terms of a financial transaction, referring, for example, to "an income of sixty thousand livres" (letter 2, p. 14). Other economic metaphors may be found throughout the novel. For example, when the marquise proposes the famous pact with Valmont under which she must give herself to him once again in exchange for written proof that he has incontrovertibly "had" the Présidente de Tourvel, the supposedly courtly and heroic vocabulary (speaking of "noble knights who would come and place the dazzling fruits of victory at the feet of their lady") is finally transformed into a mercantile metaphor: "It is up to you to see whether I have set too high a price, but I warn you that there can be no bargaining" (20, p. 44). It is also a financial transaction. The "fifty-six livre and twenty-six louis" entrusted to his servant Azolan allow Valmont to win the Présidente de Tourvel. As he says, "having essentially paid for her in advance, I had the right to make use of her at my will" (21, p. 47).

By use of words such as *price* and *paid,* the woman in the libertine discourse is always put in the position of something bought—that is, in the position of merchandise that can be bought, traded, or even destroyed, as in the case of potlatch, but, in any case, always in the position of that which circulates. I shall take the story of the "three inseparables" told by Valmont to the marquise de Merteuil (letter 79) as an example of this circulation of the woman within a system put in place and set in motion by men. To summarize, Prévan, an infamous lady-killer, introduces himself into the company of three women and seduces them one by one, in each case without the knowledge of the other two. The night of his victory is described thus: "The night was granted by the one whose husband was absent; and daybreak, the moment of this third spouse's departure, was appointed by her during the morning twilight" (79, p. 162). Libertine sexuality operates on the model of division of labor and of repetition, as in assembly-line production. In the second part of the story, the disgraced lovers challenge Prévan to a duel, but during the meal that precedes the duel an odd reversal takes place: "The breakfast was not even finished before they started repeating again and again that such women were not worth fighting over," and the duel is transformed into merrymaking, "This idea brought cordiality along with it; it was further fortified by wine to the point where it was no longer enough to dispense with ill-will: they swore an unreserved friendship" (79, p. 163). The third part of the story tells of the vengeance taken upon the women: Prévan secretly summons each of the women to his "little house" on the pretext of a romantic dinner (p. 164). Eventually an orgy reconciles the three women, the three men, and Prévan. The story is finally made public, and the three women go into seclusion in a convent—their destiny therefore prefiguring that of Cécile and the Présidente de Trouvel.

This story allows us to lay bare the structure of the erotic system in *Les Liaisons dangereuses* as a system of exchange and to specify the respective place occupied by men and women within this system with great precision. The system can be formalized according to the following schema: (1) a seducer steals away the woman of another, (2) he uses her up, (3) he returns her. This movement is not circular; it does not involve a simple return to the point of departure. Moreover, as I shall show, this circulation of women yields a "profit."

This very simple schema is taken up again in the story of the vicomtesse. The vicomtesse circulates among three men (her husband, Vressac, Valmont), and the outcome replays the scenario of the masculine pact as in the story of the "three inseparables." In this story, one sees Valmont return the vicomtesse to her titular lover, Vressac: "The two lovers kissed, and I, in turn, was kissed by both of them. I was no longer interested in the kisses of the vicomtesse, but I must admit that those of Vressac were quite pleasurable" (71, p. 143). Once the woman is obtained, she is put back in circulation, and in each scenario, the exchange and circulation of women leads to the establishment of sociability among men, with all of the symbolic attributes of celebration (wine, high spirits, embraces, and so forth).

It is at this moment that the near-total lack of epistolary relationships between men finds all its meaning. There is no private relationship between Valmont and the other men in the novel exactly because the relationship between men unfolds in public and because that relationship requires women to be put into a common pool of circulation in order to manifest itself. In the relationships between men and women, there is therefore a primacy of the masculine contract. The exercise of virility among men in fact allows a rewriting of the social contract in an erotic mode.[6] This raises the problem of the social status of women treated as mere objects of transaction. This in fact holds masculine society together. It is for this reason that there is such a contrast within the novel between the plurality and diversity of women (Merteuil, Cécile, Emilie, the vicomtesse, Mme de Rosemonde, Mme de Volanges, Tourvel), which stands for the indefinite series of seduceable women, and the singular figure of Valmont, with his double Prévan and his inferior Danceny. The primacy of masculine sociability over erotic relationships with women is inscribed within the structure of every relationship, since rivalry between men always ends with a pact of friendship. Thus Valmont and Danceny finally reconcile before Valmont dies (163, p. 364). It is perhaps of this polarity between exchangers that Marx speaks in an enigmatic sentence quoted by Gilles Deleuze and Félix Guattari in *The Anti-Oedipus:* "The relation of man and woman is the immediate, natural, and necessary relation between man and man; that is, the relation between the two sexes (of man with woman) is only the measure of the sexual relation in general."[7] This statement can be interpreted as either ethnological or ethical: (1) either Marx is declaring, by means of a paradox, that sexuality is a system of exchange within which woman necessarily occupies the position of merchandise, or of the token of exchange in general, in a society thus constituted as an ethnological system, (2) or he is saying that, in an ethical rather than ethnological system, woman is included in the universal category of "man."

Marx defines merchandise in the first chapters of the first book of *Capital* with reference to a general theory of value.[8] According to Marx, each piece of merchandise, each good, is endowed with a double value within any economy: use value and exchange value. These two aspects of value are complementary rather than contradictory.[9] For example, fruits are purchased because they can either be used (eaten) or exchanged or sold. But the revolutionary aspect of capitalist society, as Marx says, lies precisely in its emancipation of exchange value from use value. Marx speaks of the "mystery of the genesis of exchange value" in its ever-greater divergence from use and consumption.

This liberation of exchange value from use value that is characteristic of the capitalist economy allows us to account for a particularly troubling recurrent detail in the "erotic" scenes of *Les Liaisons*—namely, the disappearance, within the story, of the moment of "consumption," the erotic act itself. For example, in the episode of the vicomtesse, told by Valmont to the marquise in letter 71, the entire story is devoted to the "circumstances" of the night, "[t]he circumstances [which] were not favorable" (p. 140). He speaks only of the elaboration of the plan against Vressac and the husband, then proceeds to describe the setting and the movements of the various characters between the bedrooms and the hallway. And the long-awaited erotic scene is excised by Valmont himself: "Since I am not vain, I will not dwell on the details of the night, but you know me, and I was satisfied with my performance" (p. 142). Whereas at the beginning of his letter Valmont announces that the affair with the vicomtesse "interested me in its details" (p. 140), one must conclude from it that in the libertine tale certain "details" are worth more than others, or rather, that the erotic act amounts to a mise-en-scène or to a place, in which, as Mallarmé puts it, in an image that laconically condenses temporality and phantasm into place, "nothing will have taken place but the place."

Even though it is never described, the erotic act nevertheless "inhabits" the text through the obscure presence of a metaphor. The scene is always sexualized indirectly, but even so insistently, since it is constant and persistent: as a formal mark, as a transformation of the story, as a brutal appearance (significant therefore by its very brutality) of direct discourse. Whereas free indirect discourse is the usual narrative form in *Les Liaisons dangereuses,* the change to direct discourse always points out an entry into "the other scene," that of desire and sex, of which it in some ways constitutes a metonymy. For example, in the Belleroche tale, a rakish episode the marquise de Merteuil offers to Valmont as a model, the only moment in the whole story that is told through direct discourse announces and prepares a move to the act that it at the same time excises. "There, half by design and half sentimentally, I embraced him and fell to my knees. 'O my friend, I said, I reproach myself for having troubled you with my pretence of ill-humor, which came only from a wish to keep the surprise of this moment from you; I regret that I was able, even for a mere moment, to hide the true feelings of my heart from you. Please forgive my wrongs: I will expiate them with the strength of my love.' You may guess the effect of this sentimental pronouncement. The happy Chevalier lifted me from the floor and my pardon was ratified on the very ottoman where once you and I so joyfully sealed our eternal rupture" (10, p. 31). The erotic act is therefore dissolved in this double reference to the furniture in the scene and to Valmont; it is reduced, so to speak, to the discursive act itself. This centrality of language within the erotic act is symbolized in other places within the novel by the "catechism of debauchery" that Valmont inculcates upon Cécile "to speed up her education" (110, p. 255).

The woman is not seduced to be consumed but rather to be exchanged. This domination of exchange over consumption allows us to account for another striking feature in the novel—namely, the total disappearance of bodies in the course of the erotic scenes. In no episode—except for that of the Présidente—is the woman's body described at the moment of the act, because the woman's body exists only as an abstract exchange value.[10]

The incessant movement of libertine desire, which reproduces the incessant circulation of capital, is not the result of purchase for purposes of consumption but is instead for exchange. As described in Jean François Lyotard's discussion of capital in *L'Economie libidinale,*[11] libertine desire privileges circulation over merchandise, prefers movement to product; the product in both is only a means for further production. The establishment of the pact of exchange—the contract for the barter of Tourvel for Mertueil—expresses the essence of libertine desire: "Once you have had your beautiful devotee and you can give me proof of it, come to me and I am yours" (20, p. 43). It is a migratory, nomadic desire, which lays siege to entire groups by moving from individual to individual, which always desires the rarest thing on the market, therefore preferring the virtuous Tourvel to the youthful Cécile.[12] This introduces its insatiability: a trait common to libertinism and capitalism. "For the most obvious thing is that desire does not have the people or groups that it traverses."[13] In mercantile capitalist economy, wealth is generated from this incessant movement, this redoubling of exchange, this famous "spiral of increasing value."

In *Les Liaisons dangereuses* what is described is the front line, the moment of production, the moment of the seductive or maneuvering "work." (I am using the term *work* to pursue the economic metaphor and at the same time because seduction is always alluded to as work, and even as arduous work [81, p. 171] by Valmont and the marquise.) Valmont ironically comments on the Belleroche episode in these terms: "You are giving yourself the trouble to deceive him and he is happier than you . . . he sleeps peacefully while you keep watch for his pleasures. Would his slave do any more?" (15, p. 36). It is thus the amount of accumulated work in a seduction that is described, and then the moment after, the always sudden moment of breaking off, the moment of the woman's reintegration into the open system of exchange, and the subsequent

transformation of the affair into a "tale," a story. And such a story is only valuable if it is told, diffused, made public, "I rather like your affair with the vicomtesse," writes Merteuil, "but it needs to be made public, as you say" (74, p. 147).

It is this diffusion that allows the generation of an increase in value, a "reputation" for the man. Such a story is valuable in proportion to the amount of renown it brings to the seducer. This ebb and flow of desires is no longer, as in *Don Juan,* bound to an economy of expense and of metaphysical challenge to higher powers. The libertine in *Les Liaisons* is a hoarder, and even if he does not keep an exact account of the women he has seduced as does Molière's libertine (who counts "1,003"), he does capitalize on his good stories.[14] It is not merchandise that is fetishized in this economy, but rather the renown acquired through conquests. A sort of enormous fund of phallic values, renown is both the end and the means of seduction. Hegel, quick to schematize the spirit of historical periods in *The Phenomenology of Spirit,* writes: "The Enlightenment reduced all values to their utilitarian value."[15] Eros is set up as a "utilitarian value" in *Les Liaisons,* becoming the means to the attainment of renown, a bastard version of glory. Conversely, renown allows one to attain Eros. We see, therefore, a dematerialization of Eros; by means of a default of the moment of the act and of its consummation, Eros becomes pure sign, a fable, a tale, or letters.

In fact, it is never the man who seduces by means of his own qualities and talents, it is his reputation. Thus, the marquise de Merteuil no longer resists the idea of an affair with Prévan once Valmont tells her the story of the "three inseparables": "this Prévan is so very formidable . . . and you're saying that he wants me, that he wants to have me. Surely it will be my honor and my pleasure" (74, p. 146). Similarly, the Présidente de Tourvel acknowledges in all innocence to Mme de Volanges: "I only know him [Valmont] by his reputation." This confirms the closeness of the ties maintained between desire and the social in this novel. It is always conclusively from others—that is, from the "audience"—that the desirability of object choice comes.

It is also for the sake of his reputation that Merteuil warns Valmont about the slow progress of his designs on Tourvel: "Right now, I am tempted to believe that you do not merit your reputation" (5, p. 20). Valmont is only desirable for the marquise if he is recognized, by public renown, as invincible. Reputation, defined by these libertines as both end and means, defines a sort of transcendent law for the libertine economy itself, a law incarnated by the "audience," which appears within the novel as the fiction of its own exteriority.[16]

This allows us to think of the system of libertine economy not as one that transgresses social law, but instead as the maximal expression of conformity to that law. Whereas Don Juan constantly curses and blasphemes in the name of every devil, exposing himself to damnation, Laclos's libertine has access to everyone. "Of course I receive M de Valmont and he is received everywhere," Madame de Volanges writes to Tourvel (32, p. 66). Furthermore, for Sade, there is no exteriority with respect to the libertine law; the places of debauchery are always closed places, protected from the rest of the world, they are always institutional (isolated estates, fortresses, monasteries), emblems of debauchery made law. In **Les Liaisons,** however, the places of debauchery (suites, "little houses," boudoirs) are always included in the space of the most official, most entrenched social law. In addition, every erotic scene has value according to a generalized theatricality, in proportion to the spectacle it provides for an audience that Merteuil, and we as readers, represent. In the novel, within the discourse itself, this "Audience," with a capital *A,* institutes the fiction of an exteriority that combines the social horizon and the theatrical horizon, or the addressee and the law, within one word.

Given the above analysis, the place occupied by Merteuil within this economy must now be specified. The ironically courtly relationship she has established with Valmont, in which she maintains the position of the master or tyrant, as Valmont notes gallantly by saying, "Your orders are charming; your way of conveying them is more charming still; you will soon have us cherish despotism" (4, p. 16), is reversed by the logic of the system of exchange, as it is defined by an exclusively masculine contract.

Even if she manages to subvert the division of the masculine and feminine positions in the system of exchange and to put the man (Prévan, for example) in the position of merchandise, consumed and abandoned, she can never go so far as to put herself in an exchange or barter situation with respect to Tourvel and Valmont.[17] Her only resource, to maintain herself in a position other than that of merchandise, is to remain outside of the system of exchange—that is, to exclude herself from an erotic relationship with Valmont. Her only way of maintaining herself at the summit of the system of value is to postpone indefinitely the renewal of her *liaison dangereuse* with Valmont, to renounce the real relationship and to put in place a narrative relationship, based on a metonymic economy; in other words, the erotic relationships they have with others take the place of their own erotic relationship. Seduction, as a war of the sexes, far from being a war of the aristocratic rearguard, far from being transgressive, is revealed instead to be a metaphor for a bourgeois economy of exchange. Moreover, libertinism as an economy of exchange is aligned along an ethics of auster-

ity and asceticism, and not of fulfilment, as the following section will demonstrate.

LIBERTINISM AS ETHICAL SYSTEM: THE CONFIRMATION OF THE LAW

Libertinism is often defined as an exaggerated search for pleasure. The libertinism specific to Valmont and the marquise, which takes the form of jousting matches of pride and honor—typically aristocratic games—is also presented as an ethical system. The place reserved for fulfillment within this ethics remains to be specified.

One could begin by pointing out the ambiguous status of the term *fulfillment* itself in the libertine discourse. In a letter to Valmont, Merteuil defines what true fulfillment is, as opposed to the partial fulfillments prudes obtain: "Don't hope for any pleasure from it. Is there ever pleasure with prudes? At least, with those who are in good faith reserved even at the height of pleasure, you are only offered a partial fulfillment. The total self-abandon and the delirium of pleasure in which pleasure is purified through excess itself, these benefits of love are unknown to them" (5, p. 19). Even if the marquise defines the concept, which would lead one to suppose that she knows what it is, the term of *fulfillment* itself never appears in the stories of gallant episodes in her little house told to Valmont. In the discourse of the marquise, fulfillment is always the fulfillment of the other. To finish the story of the Belleroche episode, she says, "I made him happy" (10, p. 29).

There is the same ambiguity in the status of the term in the discourse of Valmont. For example, Valmont opposes—is it a slip?—happiness and fulfillment in the matter of the Présidente de Tourvel. "With her, I don't need fulfillment to be happy" (6, p. 22). In other places, when it is mentioned, fulfillment is never desired as the end of the erotic act, but instead always as a means of disengaging oneself from another, as a means, for the man, of freeing himself from desire, while also keeping open that system of interchangeability within which one woman is always equivalent to another. "Oh, sweet fulfillment! I implore you for my happiness and for my repose. How lucky we are that women defend themselves so badly! Otherwise we would be no more than their timid slaves" (4, p. 18).

The goal here is both rest and mastery, according to a sort of stoic or skeptic ideal; it is apathy or the complete absence of desire that allows the man to reconstitute himself as a free subject and master. Libertinism is thus in no way a quest for fulfillment or, in Merteuil's terms, for a "complete abandoning of oneself"; it is not defined as a quest for fusion with the other, but rather as a search for the division between self and others, as well as within oneself. In this quest, the gravest danger, as Valmont anxiously discovers after his "success" with Tourvel, is abandon or "laxity": "I believe that is all that can be done, but I am afraid that I have become soft like Hannibal amid the pleasures of Capua" (125, p. 293).

Libertinism is thus not a quest for pleasure, but, paradoxically, an asceticism that attempts to deflect the dangers of fulfillment—excess of sensation, disappearance into the other, lack of distinction.[18] As Joan De Jean has demonstrated, it incorporates the strategies of the hunt and of war: "The insipid honor of having one more woman. Let her give herself up, but not without a struggle. Let her, without having the strength to conquer, have enough to resist. Let her relish the feeling of weakness at leisure and be constrained to admit her defeat. Only a miserable poacher would lie in wait and kill the stag he has surprised; a true hunter should enjoy the hunt" (23, p. 52).

Libertinism attempts to attenuate the dangers of the flesh by establishing a "method" based on principles and rules, the definition of which is provided by Merteuil. Of the two libertines, it is she who fills the role of guardian or judge whose duties are imposed by the law. The vocabulary of the libertine method—as, for example, in the marquise's reproach to Valmont, "There you are moving along without principles and leaving everything to chance, or rather to caprice" (10, p. 28)—is oddly Cartesian. "Method," "principle," "order," "observation," "reflection," this is its rhetoric, which is quite logically articulated upon an ethics whose basis is precisely dualistic, upon the maintenance, even at the moment of the erotic act, of self-control and of control of the other.[19] This self-control is attained by means of a long labor of disengagement from affect and from the body. It is this sort of disengagement that allows the attainment of "head libertinism," obtained by dividing the "head" from the "body," a labor the epic struggle of which the marquise relates in letter 81. It is a labor comparable to that to which the Comedian in Diderot's *Paradoxe sur le Comédien* submits his body in order to dissociate it from affect.

This long apprenticeship of the division of the head from the body and this asceticism that allows one to attain a total instrumentalization of the body and its total submission to the direction of "the head" both come out of pain and "labor," just as in the *Paradoxe*. Merteuil explains: "I carried this zeal so far as voluntarily to inflict pains upon myself while looking for a pleased expression on my face. I worked on myself with the same care to repress the symptoms of an unexpected joy" (81, p. 171).

The definition of the moral as a voluntary ethics of self-mastery proposed by Descartes in *Les Passions de l'âme*, article 211—"The labors that can correct the falsities of one's nature as we attempt to separate the movements of our blood and our spirit from the thoughts to which they are customarily joined"—provides a perfect definition of the libertine method, a labor of division, of separation of the subject from his affections and passions.[20]

Even if the Cartesian project of substituting the authority of science for that of the church is an entirely different project from that of the marquise, one can, nevertheless, make out so many similarities between these two discourses that one is led to wonder whether the *Discours de la méthode* does not constitute a central "intertext" for letter 81.[21]

The theme of letter 81, "I can say that I am a product of my own work," expresses the essence of the Cartesian project of positing the subject as foundation of the criterion for truth. Similarly, the marquise affirms the primacy of the desire for knowledge over the desire for fulfillment: "I did not wish to be fulfilled, I wanted to know; the desire to instruct myself suggested the means to do so" (81, p. 172), recalling the beginning of the *Discours de la méthode:* "I have always felt an extreme desire to learn how to distinguish true and false, to see my actions clearly and to walk in this life with assurance."[22] The whole letter, an autobiographical tale of self-creation, is thus given as an ironic rewriting of the first parts of the *Discours de la méthode.* The opposition between "first training" through education and "second training," which is perhaps an apprenticeship through a conscious and progressive method based, as in Descartes, on the criterion of "conspicuousness"—"undoubtedly you will not deny these truths, which are so obvious as to be trivial" (81, p. 169)—only makes sense if it is related to the Cartesian discourse of which it is a parody down to its smallest details.

This education that the marquise methodically imposes upon herself is carried out in four phases: mastery of the body, mastery of discourse, mastery of love (first in the form of knowledge extorted from a confessor, then as praxis, through marriage), and, finally, widowhood, which allows completion of the education through reading. What is most notable about it is the central role played by observation and experience in the establishment of method. "I still had many observations to make," the marquise asserts (pp. 172-73), paraphrasing, so to speak, the following passage of the *Discours de la méthode:* "I made many observations and gained much experience, giving particular reflexion in each matter."[23] It is by a similar declaration of will, "I resolved" (p. 174), that the marquise decides to form the libertine method and Descartes the philosophical: "One day, I resolved to study within myself as well."[24] This resolution in both cases transforms the subject into an object of introspection: "I studied myself . . . pain and pleasure, I observed everything exactly and I only saw within these different sensations facts to gather and to meditate over," as the marquise says (p. 172). The movement is similar to the conversion of sensation into an object of study that one can see at work in the fourth part of the *Discours de la méthode*. This resolution at the same time either makes a vast theater of the world ("Then I began to exert the talents I had given myself in the grand theater," declaims the marquise [pp. 174-75]) or, as in Descartes's resolve to "try to be a spectator rather than a participant in every comedy that plays,"[25] makes a vast comedy of life.

This relationship between the two texts could be pursued, especially as we develop a method to progress from "a penetrating glance" to the "rudiments of the science I wished to acquire" (p. 171), from the mask of a provisional morality to a true science, movement libertinism derives from its philosophical ancestor (Descartes). For our purposes, however, it suffices to keep in mind that this letter on method is considered by Madame de Volanges, in a letter to Madame de Rosemonde, as "the height of horror":

> It is also said that Danceny, while still in the throes of his outrage, showed these letters to all who wished to see them and that they are at present circulating through all of Paris. Two of them are cited especially frequently: in the first of them she tells the whole story of her life and of her principles, and it is this one which is said to be the height of horror. (168, p. 371)

It is especially interesting to note that Laclos, who usually does not intervene in the text, takes the trouble at this point to insert a note specifying that Mme de Volanges refers here to letters 81 and 85. The scandal of letter 81 is the scandal of a libertinism—until now purely a practical matter—suddenly raised, through the aberrant female *cogito,* to the status of theory. The marquise de Merteuil is something like a bad dream of Cartesianism, a Cartesianism that turns into a nightmare since, for libertines, the goal of method is no longer detached from the social, no longer identified, as in Descartes, as a "search for the truth," but is instead identified as the only means of survival in the context of a generalized social war, in a universe in which, according to Merteuil, "one must win or perish" (p. 177).

The libertine method therefore appears as a method of adaptation for the purposes of a social war, and not as the negation of social law. In fact, although the entire story of letter 81 consists in opposing the sovereign law of the subject to the law of the world, and although the marquise presents herself as self-created, the whole process of the acquisition of method is really a way of adaptation to the law of the world, even through masquerade, in order to transgress certain rules. In the letter Merteuil really sets out a new theory of social ties based on a double contract between being and appearance; it is a theory of a contract that is no longer collective but is instead between individuals.

Identifying himself with the fantasm of absolute knowledge, of a sovereign subjectivity that becomes law, the

libertine is really a completely repressed subject, a sort of upside-down Don Juan, symbolizing sensuality, desire made law, the very figure of immediacy whose only "task," to take up the expression of André Malraux in his description of the characters in *Les Liaisons,* consists in the revelation that in the social world truth lies only in farce, lies, and hypocrisy.[26]

In the course of this revelation, method becomes a substitute for the object of desire. Fulfillment in *Les Liaisons dangereuses* is, to use an expression used by Marcel Hénaff on Sade, "the fulfillment of method."[27] The marquise de Merteuil's fulfillment is her incarnation of the law, and her identification of herself to it: "When have you ever seen me stray from the rules I have given myself or be lax in my own principles?" (81, p. 170). The erotic activity between the marquise and the vicomte becomes the exercise of, and repetitive commentary upon, method. The marquise spends her time judging, comparing, and evaluating the purity of method implemented by Valmont in his seduction of the Présidente de Tourvel. It is precisely within this notion of fulfillment that method becomes a substitute for the object of desire. Fulfillment in *Les Liaisons dangereuses* is finally the fulfillment of the "Merteuil method." The final punishment of Merteuil, the loss of an eye and disfiguration by smallpox, is quite significant in its ironic negation of this methodological negation of the body, this monstrous, unheard-of attempt to be always superior to one's desire. The disfiguration of Merteuil is simultaneously a return to the repressed body and, through this corporeity, a return to morality. It is the overturning of the scandal of a female *cogito;* the woman who wished to be "head," law, and method is revealed to be only a body, a sex organ, a woman. The paradox of libertinism is that, while practicing a cult of inconstancy and cynicism, while positing itself as the reversal of traditional morality, it reveals the hollow, false quality of the morality it reverses. Its rejection of the morality of sincerity and sentimentality, its rejection of abandonment to pleasure and amorous fusion in fact betrays a nostalgic quest of that lost sincerity and authenticity both moral and erotic. Libertinism is thus a kind of asceticism; it is a protest against the absence of an authentic morality and eroticism, dramatizing this absence by representing it. The systematic challenge to morality and the outbidding of worldly conventions express the desire for a morality, the desire for something or someone in the absence of morality.[28] By creating a metamorality—that is, an even more severe system of laws and principles—libertinism comes to replace the missing law exactly at the point where it is flawed.

The libertines in *Les Liaisons* punish themselves and others to protest the absence of a real morality. In so doing they become representatives of law. This comes close to Sade. For Lacan, the Sadean torturer is the true representation of the superego in literature, the representative of pure morality.[29] Lacan can say this about Sade because, in fact, the Sadean torturer has no subjectivity; he is there only for the other, the one whom he tortures; he is no longer an individual but instead completely assumes the role of the law. For Laclos, things are different; one does not find this extreme specialization of function that one finds in the universe of Sade's black novels. For in Laclos, the characters play the roles of executioner and victim at the same time. Merteuil tries to punish others in the name of the absent law, to punish them for pretending to believe in morality and love while looking only for pleasure. At the same time, she does not herself in any way escape from law, in the form of smallpox or natural law; she is thus also a victim. The same holds for Valmont: the executioner of Tourvel, he forces himself to be his own executioner by sending her the insulting letter of dismissal written by the marquise (145, p. 333).

The transgression of sentimentality is a representation of law, a way to search for a deeper and truer law. It is perhaps for these obscure reasons that Valmont punishes Tourvel, because she gives in and precisely by her "fall" reveals the absence of authentic moral law. The aim of the libertine within the social space, as Jean Marie Goulemot has noted, is to prove that "within every woman [is hidden] a prostitute, passionate or guilty, modest or seductive, but always there,"[30] from Cécile, of whom the marquise says that she is "absolutely nothing but a pleasure-machine," to Tourvel. Valmont's page boy sums it up: "'Monsieur surely knows better than I do,' he told me, 'that to sleep with a girl is only to make her do what pleases her.'" ("Sometimes the good sense of the rascal astonishes me," adds Valmont.) It is striking that not a single woman escapes this law of desire in the novel:

> All are implicated in it, young and old, prostitutes and innocents, like Cécile who yields "everything that one does not even dare to expect from girls whose career is to do such things." Cécile's destiny is in this respect especially significant. Barely out of convent school, attracted to the first man who comes along, a shoemaker, seduced by Danceny, taken by Valmont, she is the very sketch of femininity. She goes as far as to write love letters to Danceny from the arms of Valmont.[31]

Libertines therefore expose these desiring women to infamy and to public reproof, and by so doing, far from contradicting the moral law, they are trying desperately to reconstitute it. Ultimately, libertinism, despite the sophistication of its motives, through its trivial critique of what Baudelaire called "universal *fouterie*,"[32] is a desperate attempt to find a certain lacking transcendence again. This is what the marquise de Merteuil says in her own way:

> Women of this sort are nothing more than pleasure-machines. You will tell me that all there is to do is that, and that that's enough, for our plans. Very well! But let

us not forget that with such machines, anybody can quickly get to know their springs and motors. So, in order to use this one without danger, you must hurry, stop at just the right time and then break it. (106, p. 244)

This is an old dream of metaphysicians; they have a grudge against machines and against what in man is mechanical and therefore reveals desire. "But your measured pace is so easily guessed! The arrival, the aspect, the tone, the language: I knew all that the day before" (85, p. 188).

Thus libertinism, as exacerbated protest against, and punishment of, desiring women, is a protest against the absence of spirituality and of transcendence in the machine of desire, an absence whose entirely profane mechanism is laid bare by their "machinations":

> Once the structural unity of the machine is undone, once the personal and specific unity of the living being is overthrown, a direct link appears between the machine and desire, the machine passes to the center of desire, the machine desires and desire is machined. It is not desire that is in the subject but the machine that is in desire, and the residual subject is on the other side, beside the machine, at the perimeter, a parasite of machines and an accessory of the vertebro-mechanic desire.[33]

LIBERTINISM AS A SYSTEM OF SUBVERSION OF SIGNS, OR, THE TRIUMPH OF THE LAW OF THE SIGNIFIER

Given the above, I would like to attempt now to show how libertinism attempts to subvert the system of signs, the code of decency and propriety of language according to which one says what one feels and does what one says, and also, finally, how the novel undoes and condemns this subversion of the signs of natural language, so that it is the law of the signifier that wins out.

Within the novel two uses of language can be distinguished: a "naive" use, which is proper to victims and dupes, and a tactical, "political," use, which is proper to libertines and non-dupes. Victims possess only an unconscious use of language, and therefore their language, which expresses the voice of nature and sentiment at the same time as the voice of morality, does not vary. Libertines, however, change styles the way they change their socks, borrowing from every possible tone (the virtuous style of the prude, the "stupid" style of Cécile, the cynical style, and so on).[34] The discourse of libertines attempts to establish an economy of the sign dominated by a generalized exchange similar to that of their erotic system. They attempt to elaborate a particular economy of signs in which a "sign" or "signifier" no longer corresponds to a true "sentiment" or to any moral "signified," in opposition to what happens in natural language. In this economy, the sign becomes a mask, a false pretense whose only finality is to mystify the other. Libertine discourse is no longer "expressive"; it is a discourse of exchange. It is always as a function of the addressee that discourse is organized. The goal consists of certain effects to be produced within the other, rather than of "communication" with the other.[35] It is this strategy that the marquise de Merteuil explains in a postscript to Cécile that defines the rule of the libertine epistolary genre: "Be sure that, when you write to someone, it is for him and not for you; you must look to telling him not so much what you think but instead what pleases him" (105, p. 242).

The libertine discourse is, then, a strategic discourse that tries to make an instrument of language as well as of the body, to make of it a simple tool, which the marquise and Valmont think of as both docile and resistant. It is of this particular resistance of writing, which in a way renders it less susceptible to plagiarism than speech, that Merteuil speaks when she says: "An observation it surprises me that you have not made already is that there is nothing so difficult in matters of love as to write what one does not feel. I mean write in a convincing manner, of course: it is not that you do not employ the same words, but you do not arrange them in the same way, or, rather, you arrange them thinking that that is enough" (33, p. 68).

Libertine discourse thus implements a theory and a classification of the forms that "naive" discourse takes, all the while trying to imitate it, to appropriate it, not only in its utterances but also in the properties of its uttering. In the same way that the rhetorician is in fact he who calls attention to the traces that the passions leave in language, libertines establish tables of equivalencies that enable the orator to express a passion he does not feel. Thus the equivalency between tenderness and "disorder," virtue and simplicity, or, even further, between love and languor, allows Valmont to speak of a passion that he does not feel: "I reread my letter. I discovered that I had not been sufficiently watchful and that I conveyed more ardor than love, more ill-humor than sadness. I'll have to redo it" (23, p. 53).

The opposition between libertine discourse and the discourse of the Présidente de Tourvel is not a simple opposition of true and false or lie and sincerity, but is rather one of conscious and unconscious lies. In fact, the discourse of the Présidente is riddled with slips, denials, and arguments in bad faith, as Valmont points out to Merteuil: "Read and judge; see with what evident falsity she swears that she feels no love when I am sure of the contrary" (25, p. 55). By pointing this out, libertine discourse lays bare all of the "insincerity" contained in the "sincerity" of the Présidente; it is a sincere insincerity, which Valmont turns into an insincere sincerity: "How can I answer your last letter, Madame? How can I dare to

speak the truth when my sincerity will ruin me in your eyes? No matter, I must; I will have the courage" (68, p. 135). Valmont does not stop telling Tourvel that he refuses to lie; in so doing he brutally exposes her to the discourse of desire and of love. Since denial is the dominant rhetorical figure in Tourvel's discourse, Valmont keeps telling her that he denies denial, and that that is the proof of his sincerity. In so doing, he exposes Tourvel to the truth of her own lie, he backs her up against the bad conscience of her language, all the while using this bad conscience to his own best advantage, as a guarantee of his credibility.

The game of signs becomes complicated by one more degree if one remembers that Valmont spends his time telling the Présidente that he loves her and all the while explaining to the marquise that, when he tells the Présidente that he loves her, it proves that he does not love her and that his declarations of love are purely tactical. The novel completely reverses the structure of the relationships between truth and lies, between hypocrisy and denial. In fact, by telling Tourvel that he loves her—declarations that are, moreover, only tactical—Valmont nevertheless falls in love with her by accident, which is exactly what Merteuil keeps telling him: "Now it is true, vicomte, that you are under an illusion as to the sentiment that attaches you to Mme de Tourvel. Either it is love or love has never existed" (134, p. 312).

This turn of the screw thus totally reverses the relationship between hypocrisy and denial. What was given as false, as hypocrisy, as pure masquerade—the correspondence between Valmont and Tourvel—becomes true; what was given as the real truth—the cynicism behind the correspondence between Valmont and Merteuil, becomes pure denial. Denial changes sides; it was on the side of the dupe—Tourvel—but it goes over to the side of the non-dupes—Valmont, Merteuil.

Libertinism that attempts to make a pure artefact, a pure (and impure) instrument of the linguistic sign, is therefore finally caught in the trap of words. The moral of the novel is perhaps that in playing at saying that one loves so as to say that one does not, one ends by loving; that no one, man or woman, is master over the signifier, that words hold us and implicate us, especially words of love, because there is no pure word. This is exactly what Valmont says—he is taken who thought himself to take!—about Tourvel: "Well, you know that a woman who consents to speak of love ends up falling in love or at least acts as if she had" (76, p. 150). To speak with military metaphors, as libertines do, the words of war end up turning into a real war, as the marquise declares so succinctly, "Well, then, it is war!" (153, p. 350). The meaning of these successive reversals, then, is that one cannot play with the law of the signifier with impunity (any more than with moral or natural law).

We might well finish by wondering what the place of the reader is within this narrative economy. The reader enjoys the deconstruction of Tourvel's denial by the libertines; he is at first on the side of Valmont and Merteuil, thereby believing himself to be in the position of mastery. Then he witnesses the turning of libertinism against itself. His absolute knowledge is deconstructed by the novel, since the dupers reveal themselves to be duped. The final fulfillment is that of the reader of the stolen letters, of the indiscreet third party: it is found in the recognition of the law that is superior to all others, because of the reversals it provokes, the law of the novel.[36] It is from having systematically and loyally served this supreme law of the novel, whatever his intentions may have been, that Laclos does indeed merit being judged "the honest man par excellence" and not by reason of any overly edifying final morality.[37]

Notes

1. The complexity of epistolary exchange in *Les Liaisons dangereuses* has been admirably analyzed by Tzvetan Todorov in *Littérature et signification* (Paris: Larousse, 1967). All references to *Les Liaisons* are taken and translated from *Laclos: Oeuvres complètes,* ed. Laurent Versini (Paris: Gallimard, La Pléiade, 1979).

2. The notion of "system" applied to *Les Liaisons* comes from Peter Brooks's *The Novel of Worldliness* (Princeton: Princeton University Press, 1959), p. 177: "*Les Liaisons dangereuses* is profoundly a novel about system, processes of systematization, man as creature of system."

3. An example is Baudelaire's commentary on *Les Liaisons,* "How love was made under the ancien régime," from "Notes analytiques et critiques sur *Les Liaisons dangereuses,*" in *Oeuvres* (Paris: Club Francais du Livre, 1955), p. 1229. See also Joan De Jean's *Literary Fortifications: Rousseau, Laclos, Sade* (Princeton: Princeton University Press, 1984), ch. 5, "The Attack on the Vaubanian Fortress," pp. 191ff.

4. Nancy Miller implicitly associates Valmont with pleasure in his opposition to Tourvel: "Opposed to that is Valmont's conception of happiness, posited on the existence of pleasures unknown to her" (*The Heroine's Text* [New York: Columbia University Press, 1980], p. 124).

5. See, e.g., Anne Marie Jaton, "Libertinage féminin, libertinage dangereux," in *Laclos et le libertinage, 1782-1982: Actes du Colloque du bicentenaire des Liaisons dangereuses* (Paris: Presses Universitaires de France, 1983), pp. 151-62.

6. On the relation between Laclos and Rousseau in *Les Liaisons,* see De Jean's analysis in *Literary Fortifications*.

7. Gilles Deleuze and Félix Guattari, *L'Anti-Oedipe: Capitalisme et schizophrénie* (Paris: Editions de Minuit, 1972), p. 350. Text from Marx's *Critique* of Hegel's *Philosophy of Right*.

8. Karl Marx, *Capital: A Critique of Political Economy,* book 1, trans. Ben Fowkes, vol. 1, sec. 1, ch. 1, "The Commodity" (New York: Vintage Books, Marx Library, 1976), pp. 125ff.

9. "He who satisfies his own need with the product of his own labor admittedly creates use-value, but not commodities. In order to produce the latter, he must not only produce use-values, but use-values for others, social use-values . . . Finally, nothing can be a value without being an object of utility" (ibid., p. 131). This principle of Marx's theory of value is discussed in detail in *La Logique de Marx* (Paris: Presses Universitaires de France, 1974), specifically in F. Ricci's chapter, "Structure logique du 1 paragraphe du *Capital,*" pp. 105ff.

10. See *Les Liaisons dangereuses,* letter 71, p. 142.

11. "Movement will be good, investment, bad; action as far as innovation and power of events will be good, reaction reintegrating identity, bad," says J. F. Lyotard in *L'Economie libidinale* (Paris: Editions de Minuit, 1974), p. 123.

12. Marx considers the concept of scarcity especially in the *Introduction to the Critique of Political Economy* in *Grundrisse* (New York: Vintage Books, Marx Library, 1973).

13. Deleuze and Guattari, *L'Anti-Oedipe,* p. 348.

14. "He [the capitalist] is fanatically intent on the valorization of value. . . . Only as a personification of capital is the capitalist respectable. As such, he shares with the miser an absolute drive towards self-enrichment," Marx says (*Capital,* book 1, sec. 7, ch. 24, p. 739).

15. G. W. F. Hegel, *The Phenomenology of Spirit,* trans. A. V. Miller (Oxford: Clarendon Press, 1977), sec. 2, "Culture," "The Enlightenment," p. 354.

16. *Les Liaisons,* letter 71, Valmont to Merteuil: "If you find this story amusing, I do not ask you to keep it secret. Now that I have amused myself with it, it is only right that the public should have its turn" (p. 143).

17. *Les Liaisons,* letter 81: "Born to avenge my sex and to master yours, I knew enough to create means known only to me" (p. 170).

18. André Malraux has perceptively analyzed the mixture of sexuality and will in this novel in *Le Triangle noir* (Paris: Gallimard, 1970): "*Les Liaisons dangereuses* is a mythology of will, and its permanent mixture of will and sexuality is its most powerful means of action" (p. 47).

19. Jean Luc Seylaz very accurately characterizes *Les Liaisons* as "the novel of pure intelligence" in *Les Liaisons dangereuses et la création romanesque chez Laclos* (Geneva: Droz, 1958), p. 151.

20. René Descartes, *Les Passions de l'âme,* part 3, article 211, "Un remède général contre les passions," in *Oeuvres complètes,* ed. A. Bridoux (Paris: Gallimard, La Pléiade, 1953), p. 794.

21. Colette Verger Michael interprets this similarly, but with respect to the Spinozism of Laclos's novel, in *Laclos: Les Milieux philosophiques et le mal* (Nîmes: Ed. Akpagnon, 1985), pp. 65ff. and 133ff.

22. Descartes, *Le Discours de la méthode,* in *Oeuvres,* p. 131.

23. Ibid., p. 145.

24. Ibid., p. 132.

25. Ibid., pp. 144-45.

26. Malraux, *Le Triangle noir,* p. 47.

27. Marcel Hénaff, *Sade: l'Invention du corps libertin* (Paris: Presses Universitaires de France, 1978), esp. ch. 3, "Les Jouissances de la méthode," pp. 99-117.

28. Baudelaire understood the aspiration to a higher morality of the cynical libertines in *Les Liaisons,* "the work of a moralist as moral as the most moral, as deep as the deepest" ("Notes analytiques et critiques sur *Les Liaisons dangereuses,*" *Oeuvres,* p. 1228).

29. Jacques Lacan, "Kant avec Sade," in *Ecrits* (Paris: Editions du Seuil, 1966), pp. 765-90.

30. J. M. Goulemot, "Le Lecteur voyeur et la mise en scène de l'imaginare viril dans *Les Liaisons dangereuses,*" in *Laclos et le libertinage, 1782-1982: Actes du Colloque du bi-centenaire des Liaisons Dangereuses* (Paris: Presses Universitaires de France, 1983), pp. 168-69.

31. Ibid., p. 169.

32. Baudelaire: "*Fouterie* and the glory of *fouterie,* were they any more immoral than our modern fashion of adoring and mixing the holy and the profane?" ("Notes analytiques et critiques sur *Les Liaisons dangereuses,*" *Oeuvres,* p. 1228).

33. Gilles Deleuze and Félix Guattari, *Mille Plateaux: Capitalisme et schizophrénie II* (Paris: Editions de Minuit, 1980), p. 339.

34. On the function of italics in libertine discourse, see Michel Delon, *Choderlos de Laclos: Les Liaisons dangereuses* (Paris: Presses Universitaires de France, Etudes littéraires, 1986), p. 87.

35. See Janet Gurkin Altman, "Addressed and Undressed Language in *Les Liaisons dangereuses,*" in *Laclos: Critical Approaches to Les Liaisons dangereuses,* ed. Lloyd R. Free (Madrid: Studia Humanitatis, 1978).

36. Joan De Jean perceptively remarks on "the relationship to authority [that] fuels Laclos's devious masterpiece" (*Literary Fortifications,* p. 193).

37. Marcel Proust, *A la recherche du temps perdu,* vol. 3, *La Prisonnière* (Paris: Gallimard, La Pléiade, 1958), p. 379.

Alan J. Singerman (essay date 1993)

SOURCE: "Merteuil and Mirrors: Stephen Frears's Freudian Reading of *Les Liaisons dangereuses,*" in *Eighteenth-Century Fiction,* Vol. 5, No. 3, April, 1993, pp. 269-81.

[*In the following essay, Singerman applies Sigmund Freud's concepts of psychoanalysis to Stephen Frears's and Christopher Hampton's 1988 film adaptation of* Les Liaisons dangereuses.]

Choderlos de Laclos's notorious epistolary novel, ***Les Liaisons dangereuses*** (1782), portrays the agonistic relationship between two master libertines, the Vicomte de Valmont and the Marquise de Merteuil, and the catastrophic consequences of their efforts to dominate each other while pursuing their sadistic games of seduction and humiliation against lesser opponents. The libertine character, as mythically incarnated by Don Juan, has been subjected to extensive psychoanalytical study, including well-known analyses by Jean-Pierre Jouve and Otto Rank, as well as the more recent "Oedipal reading" by Peter Gay.[1] Don Juan's comportment has been cited, for instance, as a striking example of the unconscious workings of a repressed, unresolved "Oedipal fixation" (Gay, p. 76); that is, his repeated seductions of women are interpreted as phantasmal "repetitions" of the child's primal wish, buried deep in the psyche, to possess again the Mother from whom he was traumatically separated as a child. In the same Freudian context, Don Juan has been described variously as an impotent, a homosexual, and a narcissist.[2] Surprisingly, very little reflection of this kind has been accorded Laclos's libertine protagonists, despite the obvious identification of the Don Juan and Valmont characters, widely recognized by readers from Baudelaire to Malraux and, more recently, by Peter Brooks, Henri Blanc, Bernard Bray, and Marina Warner.[3] While occasional passing references to Merteuil's narcissism and her homosexual tendencies have surfaced, the psychoanalytical perspective has been generally neglected in discussions of the ***Liaisons dangereuses.***[4]

Stephen Frears and Christopher Hampton's recent screen adaptation of Laclos's novel, *Dangerous Liaisons* (1988), seems, however, to bring emphasis to bear precisely on the psychoanalytical dimensions of the Valmont and Merteuil characters in their relations with each other and with their victims. In addition to the preponderance of close-up shots, traditional signifiers of psychological analysis in the cinema, the mode of the film is established from the opening shot, in which we see the Marquise preening self-complacently before her vanity, a smug smile caressing her image in the mirror. Were this the only mirror scene in the film, we might be inclined to dismiss it as incidental. Mirrors are, to the contrary, seemingly omnipresent in the body of the film, whether it be in the intimate discussions

Michelle Pfeiffer and John Malkovich in a scene from the 1988 film Dangerous Liaisons.

between Merteuil and Valmont, the seduction of Tourvel, or the violent rupture scene between the Vicomte and the Présidente, to mention just the major examples. Moreover, the film comes full circle, closing with a final mirror scene in which a defeated, humiliated Marquise rubs off her cosmetic "mask" before the very same vanity at which she sat at the beginning of the film. Such obvious emphasis on the mirror motif prompts the spectator, necessarily, to speculate on its function within the film.

From a purely trans-semiotic viewpoint, the mirror, as a locus of images, can be perceived as a filmic metaphor, or corollary, for the novel's letters, which also "reflect" the image the sender wishes to convey. Merteuil's "corridor of mirrors," with its multiple reflections of the two libertines, is the most striking illustration of this function of the mirror in the film, which alludes to the Protean character they display in their correspondence, changing their image at will according to the addressee of each letter. As Christopher Hampton writes in his screenplay, when we first see Valmont and Merteuil in the gallery: "She and Valmont pass down the corridor, their images shifting and multiplying in the candlelight."[5] By the same token, the multitude of mirrors evokes a central theme of Laclos's work: the

dominance of appearance over reality (underlined by the mirror which, in reality, dissimulates a door to the Marquise's private chambers), of *paraître* over *être*, of image over substance, in the debauched Parisian aristocracy at the end of the Old Regime. But beyond this admittedly facile symbolism, one is struck by Merteuil's blatantly narcissistic behaviour in the opening shot, as well as by the implications of the final shot, in which a hitherto unsuspected psychological fragility is intimated beneath the consummately composed façade she habitually maintains. In its psychoanalytical acceptation, the narcissism exhibited by Merteuil in Frears's film may well be a critical key to the understanding of her character as depicted in the novel.

In his "On Narcissism: An Introduction" (1914), Freud hypothesizes that the "primary narcissism" he attributes to every infant—that is, that very early state in which the child takes himself as a love-object before he directs his libido towards the outside—"may in some cases manifest itself in a dominating fashion in his object-choice" as an adult.[6] It is perhaps well at this point to recall a basic tenet of psychoanalytical theory, formulated clearly by the British psychoanalyst Melanie Klein when she recalls that "we find in the adult all the stages of his early childish develop- ment. We find them in the unconscious which contains all repressed phantasies and tendencies."[7] When a child undergoes "normal" development, according to Freud's theory, he or she will, as an adult, unconsciously choose a love-object modelled on the parent of the opposite sex. On the other hand, Freud discovered that in the case of some males, for instance, "whose libidinal development has suf- fered some disturbance . . . they have taken as a model not their mother but their own selves. They are plainly seeking *themselves* as a love-object, and are exhibiting a type of object-choice which must be termed 'narcissistic.'"[8] While either sex may effect a narcissistic object-choice, Freud finds the tendency particularly prevalent among at- tractive females. In addition to the normal "intensification of the original narcissism" triggered by the onset of puberty in females, the particularly attractive woman, as she develops, compensates narcissistically for *social restrictions on her own choice of object:* "Strictly speak- ing," Freud continues, "it is only themselves that such women love with an intensity comparable to that of the man's love for them. Nor does their need lie in the direc- tion of loving, but of being loved."[9] Freud thus establishes an interesting relationship between narcissism and the reaction of certain women to the repressiveness of the society in which they live. It is not difficult to apply Freud's profile to the Marquise de Merteuil. An exception- ally attractive woman, or so we assume, she is, on the one hand, generally devoid of love for men (with the possible exception of Valmont); she does, however, enjoy attracting and manipulating lovers. In short, in a typically narcis- sistic fashion, she prefers being loved to loving. On the other hand, her exacerbated narcissism produces a rather violent revolt against the male-dominated society into which she is born. As she declares to Valmont in her celebrated autobiographical letter, her goal in life is to "venger mon sexe et maîtriser le vôtre" in response to the indignity women have always suffered by being subjected to male tyranny.[10]

Freud further speculates that narcissism is also at the basis of the phenomenon of homosexuality, maintaining that homosexuals are driven by narcissistic tendencies to seek out object-choices which resemble themselves.[11] Whether or not we agree with this hypothesis today, Freud's analysis seems particularly germane to the narcissistic Merteuil character, whose homosexual proclivities are clearly revealed in her relationship with Cécile de Vol- anges, in whom she perceives, at first, a budding libertine on her own model (nos. 20, 38, 63). Although Frears curi- ously skirts this theme in his film,[12] Merteuil's obvious physical attraction to Cécile may be attributed in large part to her narcissistic perception of the girl as a reflection of her younger self, all the more so since her interest in Cécile rapidly wanes as she realizes how little Cécile resembles

her in reality.[13] It is noteworthy, moreover, that Freud, in his essay on "Female Sexuality" (1931), also links the female homosexual object-choice to the so-called "mascu- linity complex," which, he theorizes, grows out of the castration complex in girls and is a form of rebellion against the assertion of male superiority.[14] Nothing could be more evocative of the Marquise de Merteuil, whose masculine character is obvious and whose rejection of male superiority resounds throughout Laclos's novel. It is scarcely an exaggeration to observe, in this context, a distinct intimation in the Merteuil character of the "penis envy" which, Freud tells us, motivates the development of the female castration complex. In relating to Valmont her lesbian games with Cécile, who begs her to teach her more, she comments, tellingly: "En vérité, je suis presque jal- ouse de celui à qui ce plaisir est réservé" (no. 38). We recall that Merteuil's principal project is to *deflower* Cécile in order to humiliate the young virgin's husband-to-be. To that end, after Valmont's initial refusal, she tries to enlist the unwitting help of the Chevalier Danceny, Cécile's music teacher. In Frears's film, she remarks about the timid Chevalier that it will be necessary to "stiffen his resolve, if that's the phrase" (p. 25) to achieve the seduc- tion of Cécile. We realize, of course, that that is not precisely the right phrase, and we see that Danceny is only meant to serve as a phallic proxy for the Marquise, a role which Valmont will later, in fact, capably fulfil.

Merteuil's overt masculinity, combined with her constant denigration of Valmont, her attempts—quite successful at- tempts—to humiliate him, identifies the Merteuil figure with the concept of the "phallic woman," in both the popular and psychoanalytical senses.[15] In this reference, it is most interesting to note the importance of *le regard,* the act of being seen and of seeing others, for Madame de Merteuil. In letter 81, she describes, in strikingly equivo- cal terms, how she learned the art of dissimulation to prevent others from violating her thoughts. One would think she was speaking of her virginity when she states: "je n'avais à moi que ma pensée, et je m'indignais qu'on pût me la ravir ou me la surprendre contre ma volonté: . . . non contente de ne plus me laisser pénétrer, je m'amusais à me montrer sous des formes différentes." As a result of her rigorous training, she gains what she refers to as "ce coup d'il pénétrant" ("this penetrating glance") which permits her, in effect, to penetrate rapidly the defences of her opponents. In other words, the Marquise has turned the tables on her male counterparts: she is the one who does the "penetrating." The sexual connotations of Merteuil's language in relation to the importance of the act of looking evoke Jacques Lacan's analysis of the *regard,* the gaze, as "object petit *a*" in the well-known book 11 of his *Séminaire.*[16] Lacan maintains that the gaze is naturally both deceptive and delusive, since the subject never presents itself as it is, and never sees in the other what it wants to see. Consequently, the function of the eye is related to what Lacan calls, enigmatically, the "object little *a*," an algebraic representation of the psychical *manque* in whatever form it takes, upon which desire is founded.[17] The symbolic "lack" to which Lacan refers specifically is the absence of the phallus, or the fantasized lack thereof, in the unconscious, stemming from the infantile castration complex. The "look" and the "lack" are further linked psychoanalytically when Lacan contends that "c'est en tant que tout désir humain est basé sur la castration que l'il prend sa fonction virulente, agressive."[18] The aggressiveness of Merteuil's "eye," her dominating subjectivity which transforms all others into objects,[19] may thus be related to the "masculinity complex" discussed above, to the extent that both phenomena are products of the castration complex, that is, the fear of the lack of the phallus, taken symbolically or literally, imbedded in the unconscious mind. Merteuil's "penetrating glance" may be taken as a metaphor for the assertion of her own fantasized virility, expressed in her desire to play an active masculine role in society rather than accept the passive *femme-objet* role prescribed for women by the society of her time. It is tempting to understand in this context the violent reaction of the Marquise at the end of Frears's film. Unmasked when her letters to Valmont are publicly circulated, she flies into a rage and ransacks her dressing room, destroying literally the artificial means by which she had maintained her personal appearance, her duplicitous public face. Later, after her public humiliation at the theatre, where multiple shots reiterate her reduction to an object—of the spectators' (theatre public's) collective eye—her new status is emphatically asserted in the closing shot of the film in which she is again seated before her vanity mirror. Mercilessly exposed to the spectators' (moviegoers') gaze as the camera relentlessly tracks in closer and closer, cutting out the mirror completely, Merteuil slowly rubs off her make-up as tears well up in her eyes, revealing a shattered, frightened being beneath the social mask. The Marquise's violent reaction to her unmasking, her transformation from subject to object, may be perceived as an example of what Lacan refers to as "la rencontre du réel," "the encounter with the real,"[20] wherein the adult individual undergoes an experience which momentarily puts him or her in jarring contact, subliminally, with an infantile experience long repressed in the unconscious mind. Merteuil's public chastisement and concomitant reduction to object status may be seen as the psychical equivalent of castration, the loss of the virility identified with her dominance over others. The castration motif is further sustained when we reflect that in Laclos's novel Merteuil's ultimate punishment is the loss of an eye through smallpox. Recalling that her power over others, her virility, was founded to a large extent on her "penetrating glance," her loss of an eye may well be interpreted as a form of symbolic emasculation.[21] Although Frears and

Hampton do not retain the smallpox incident in *Dangerous Liaisons,* their depiction of her reaction to what may be perceived as a symbolic castration, her transformation from subject to object, is consistent with the implications of her optical diminishment.

At the risk of provoking a collective rise of eyebrows, I would like to point out that the name "Merteuil" is composed of two words: *mère* and *il,* "mother" and "eye," joined by the phonetic hyphen, "t." While this may appear to be a simple play on words, Freud has amply demonstrated that plays on words are often far from simple, and rarely innocent. Moreover, there is ample evidence that Laclos did not coin his characters' names arbitrarily: Cécile "Volanges" calls to mind the notion of "stolen from the angels," as "Tourvel" evokes a "tower" (of virtue?); "Danceny" seems to suggest someone "lead around by the nose," "Valmont" the "ups and downs" of the vicomte, and "Rosemonde" the remarkable indulgence of Valmont's elderly aunt. We have seen above the undeniable importance of the eye for the Merteuil character, whether or not we accept the psychoanalytical implications of the motif. How may we understand the *mère,* the "mother," in Merteuil? The maternal position of the Marquise is quite evident in Laclos's novel: she blatantly supplants Cécile's own mother, Mme de Volanges, as the young girl's principal counsellor and confidante. Her relationship with Danceny is scarcely different, creating a somewhat incestuous situation when she finally takes the Chevalier as a lover. In Frears's film this aspect of Merteuil's liaison with Danceny is emphasized in the scene in which Valmont intrudes upon their intimacy. Using a mirror, once again, Frears places Merteuil's reflection between Valmont and the much younger Danceny. While the mirror image may be seen to evoke the contrasting images of the Marquise in the minds of Danceny and Valmont, it is also an obvious reference to the Oedipal triangle in which the father, incarnated here by Valmont, opposes an "incestuous" desire binding "mother" and "son."[22] This particular triangular figure is not, however, the main focus of Frears's film. It is the maternal dimensions of Merteuil's relationship with Valmont himself which come to the fore—with a decidedly Freudian flavour. Merteuil, as played by Glenn Close, is portrayed as a self-composed, rather matronly personage, while John Malkovitch's Valmont is boyish and somewhat adolescent in demeanour. As in the novel, which the film follows quite closely, Valmont is positioned between the Marquise, with whom he shares the nostalgia of a prior intimate relationship, a prior "union," and Mme de Tourvel, with whom he has fallen in love while plotting her seduction, despite a direct prohibition by the libertine code. At one point in the film, as in the novel (cf. no. 100), Valmont wonders aloud before Merteuil, "Why do you suppose we only feel compelled to chase the ones who run away?" (p. 51), which prompts, *in the film* (and not in the novel), Merteuil's cryptic rejoinder: "Immaturity?" By relating Valmont's womanizing to emotional immaturity, the film invites a psychoanalytical deciphering of the Vicomte's behaviour much like that accorded the Don Juan figure: the woman that men are always chasing, the one they eternally desire and can never have, is, of course, the absent Mother. If desire, as Lacan suggests, can always be traced back to the castration complex, it is because the child's desire for the mother will remain eternally unsatisfied—that is, it will remain desire—by virtue of the child's acceptance of their definitive separation, his submission to the Law of the Father—which is the sense that Lacan gives to the symbolic, and ultimately positive, notion of "castration." Desire repressed but not eradicated, "original" desire to which all subsequent desire is related.[23]

Immediately following Merteuil's "Immaturity?" barb in the film, Valmont expresses a painful ambivalence about the object of his desire (Tourvel): "I love her, I hate her, my life's a misery" (p. 51), an ambivalence which appears in the novel as well.[24] Both Freud and Melanie Klein emphasize the ambivalence which characterizes the male infant's relationship to the mother, an ambivalence which may resonate in his feelings towards her long into adulthood and which may be displaced onto other love objects. Klein finds the source of this love-hate ambivalence in the oral frustration suffered by the infant when denied the maternal breast, resulting in the infant's division of his perception of the maternal figure into a "good mother" who gives the breast and a "bad mother" who refuses it.[25] It may be significant to recall, in this context, Valmont's obvious obsession with breasts in Frears's film, in all of his relationships with women, whether it be Merteuil, Cécile, the prostitute Emilie, or even Tourvel (albeit discreetly). In a particularly significant early scene, Valmont plants a pair of kisses on Merteuil's prominently exposed bosom and solicits an "advance" on the sexual favours she has promised him as a reward for the seduction of Tourvel. Merteuil refuses, clearly frustrating Valmont's desire. The film emphasizes, in fact, up to the very end, the frustration of desire in Valmont's relationship with the Marquise, a frustration which will drive him to commit physical aggression against her—a slap—and to issue the fatal ultimatum. His "amorous desire," at this point, is scarcely distinguishable from hate. The violence of Valmont's reaction may be attributed to his subconscious association of Merteuil and a long-repressed image of the "bad mother," the hated and feared "genital mother" who, according to Klein, is one of the sources of the infant's fear of castration.[26] And Merteuil is, if anything, a castrating mother.

It is most interesting to consider, in this general context, that the reward for Valmont's possession of Mme de Tour-

vel is the possession of the Marquise herself, a fact that is repeatedly drawn to our attention in the novel (for example, nos. 20, 100, 106, 110, 125, 131, 144). The dominant mother figure is the prize, the ultimate goal of his seductive enterprise—the ultimate goal, so to speak, of his desire. To Valmont's request for sexual favours, she responds, in the film: "Come back when you've succeeded with Mme de Tourvel . . . and I will offer you . . . a reward" (p. 9; cf. no. 20). This triangulation of desire (in the Girardian sense) involving a maternal character is mirrored, moreover, in the parallel plot to seduce Cécile de Volanges. Who, after all, is the real target of Valmont's rape and subsequent depravation of Cécile? Her mother, who has been a hindrance in the Vicomte's enterprise against Tourvel's virtue. As he tells Merteuil in the novel, when he discovers the role of Cécile's mother: "Ah! sans doute il faut séduire sa fille: mais ce n'est pas assez, il faut la perdre; et puisque l'âge de cette maudite femme la met à l'abri de mes coups, il faut la frapper dans l'objet de ses affections" (no. 44). As part of Cécile's moral corruption, Valmont denigrates Mme de Volanges, telling the girl, as she says, "de drôles de choses" about her mother's conduct (no. 109). Hampton's scenario, however, is much more explicit: Valmont informs Cécile that her mother had been "one of the most notorious young women in Paris" and that he had himself enjoyed her favours, before her daughter's birth (p. 41). In effect, the Frears film again links a prior relationship of sexual desire with a maternal figure to a current female object of desire, adding a suggestion of incest by implying that Valmont *could* have been her father. But the corruption of Cécile is primarily a reflection of—and commentary on—Valmont's seduction of Tourvel, and the inextricably interwoven relationships—between Valmont and Merteuil on the one hand, and between Valmont and Tourvel on the other—may also be explained through reference to the classical Oedipus complex: Valmont's desire is simultaneously directed towards Tourvel and to a maternal figure, incarnated by Merteuil, which is at the very source of his desire. At the height of his exhilaration, after his seduction of Tourvel, Valmont rushes to Merteuil's residence and continues his efforts to persuade her to reunite with him, insisting, "We just united the knot, it was never broken," and adding, a moment later, "I want to come home" (p. 56; cf. no. 133).[27] With this in mind, we recall the earlier scene in Frears's film—non-existent in the novel—where Valmont sits between Merteuil and Tourvel at Rosemonde's musical *soirée,* alternately gazing intently at Tourvel and kissing Merteuil's hand as a *castrato* entertains the company with a Handel aria (p. 40). The castration motif, which is underlined in this scene, is doubly important here, evoking both the unresolved Oedipus complex governing the apparent ambivalence of Valmont's desire and the "castrating" nature of Merteuil's action as a phallic mother figure.

We remember, with regard to the phallic mother theme, that throughout the film and the novel Merteuil consistently attempts to deflate Valmont's ego, to humiliate him—to emasculate him, figuratively speaking. But she is particularly antagonistic towards Valmont's desire to possess Tourvel and regularly taunts him with the accusation that he is in love, the worst possible infraction of the libertine code to which they proudly adhere. The Marquise uses the code to enable her to assume the masculine role of lawgiver, that is, paradoxically, to assume the role of the Father, whose Law is the basis of the castration complex. Merteuil's censuring of Valmont's love for Tourvel, perceived as a taboo in the libertine code, thus seems homologous to the Father's censuring of the Child's love for the Mother—she acts as the libertine conscience or "superego." And when the Vicomte pursues the object of his desire despite her admonitions, the Marquise punishes him, applies the Law, by forcing him to break with Tourvel.[28]

It is, in fact, the *mère-il*, the maternal eye, replacing the paternal eye as the source of the Law, which drives Valmont to his violent rupture with Tourvel, one of the most psychoanalytically significant scenes of the film. Responding to Merteuil's mocking denigration of his love, the Vicomte brutally and sadistically terminates his relationship with Tourvel, declaring throughout the encounter that "it's beyond my control" (pp. 65-66). He begins his recitation as he stares at his reflection in a large mirror on the wall, obviously torn between the cynical image he is trying to project and his love for Tourvel. The schizophrenic reference, in conjunction with the repeated assertion that his conduct is "beyond his control," evokes the psychical origin of the Vicomte's action, the traumatic event that the "compulsion to repeat" drives him to re-enact. If Valmont is himself so devastated by his rupture with Tourvel, as is apparent in the film, we may conjecture that he too has experienced the shock of contact with "the real" by repeating the long-repressed and very painful separation from the Mother, the symbolic castration which propels the male child towards adulthood. The sadistic nature of Valmont's action at this point in the film, emphasized explicitly by the physical abuse he adds to his emotional torture of Merteuil, recalls Melanie Klein's insistence on the sadistic tendencies of the infant during both the narcissistic and Oedipal stages of its development, in reaction to oral frustration by the mother.[29] Valmont's sadism, which figures prominently in the novel as well, where he titillates himself at the thought of Tourvel's "lente agonie"—the "slow death" of her virtue (no. 70)—may thus also be perceived as a compulsive repetition of a tendency characteristic of infantile sexuality. The traumatic effect, on himself, of Valmont's separation from Tourvel will be magnified by the subsequent refusal by Merteuil to grant Valmont the long-hoped-for sexual possession, forcing the

Vicomte to relive, once again, the frustration of original desire, the separation from the maternal figure, the "éternelle rupture" against which he so vigorously protested at the beginning of the novel (no. 15).[30]

Valmont's Oedipal dilemma, finally, is again thrust into the foreground in the duel scene at the end of Frears's film. In a sequence informed by Valmont's flashbacks of lovemaking with Tourvel, "imaginary" scenes evoking sexual desire, the Vicomte symbolically submits to castration, allowing his own sword, an obvious phallic symbol, to drop to the ground as he lets himself be fatally wounded—that is, emasculated—by Danceny's weapon. Danceny is, here again, only a proxy for Merteuil, however, as we are reminded by Valmont as he warns the Chevalier to beware of the Marquise: "I must tell you: in this affair, we are both her creatures" (p. 73). The son is, literally, the creature of the mother and, in this case, the victim as well. Valmont's symbolic acceptance of castration, his definitive separation from the Mother, is accompanied, significantly, by a realization of the authenticity of his love for Tourvel, who is dying in the convent: "I'm glad not to have to live without her. Tell her her love was the only real happiness I've ever known," he instructs Danceny as he draws his final breath (p. 73). Valmont's story ends, as the Oedipus complex ends, when he finally enters manhood and is able to love a woman for herself, and not as a proxy for his mother. Too late, of course, to do him much good.

The purpose of this study has been to re-examine the Merteuil and Valmont characters in the light of psychoanalytical clues provided by the Frears-Hampton film, *Dangerous Liaisons,* which offers, in this respect, an original and thought-provoking reading of Laclos's novel. The complexity of the Merteuil character, which has long fascinated and sometimes consternated readers of Laclos, may be attributed, as we have attempted to demonstrate, to her multiple functions as narcissistic female, phallic Mother, and even, in a certain sense, as a symbolic Father figure. As for Valmont, the film encourages us to read the novel, like the Don Juan myth, as a Freudian parable on sexual immaturity, a symbolic discourse portraying the libertine as an infantilized male compulsively repeating the pleasurable and painful stages of the Oedipus complex and its sequels.

Notes

1. Otto Rank summarizes the standard Freudian interpretation of the Don Juan character as follows: "D'après la psychanalyse les nombreuses femmes que Don Juan doit conquérir constamment représenteraient l'unique mère irremplaçable. Les concurrents et adversaires trompés, bafoués, combattus et finalement tués, représenteraient l'unique ennemi mortel invincible, le père" (*Don*

Juan et le double [Paris: Payot, 1973], p. 124). Rank himself takes a somewhat different psychoanalytical view (see pp. 133-39), concentrating on the double symbolism of the secondary characters in relation to the libertine hero, that is, guilty conscience (Leporello) and the fear of death (the Commander); Jean-Pierre Jouve, *Le Don Juan de Mozart* (Fribourg: Librairie de l'Université, 1942), pp. 61, 105-6; Peter Gay, "The Father's Revenge," in *Don Giovanni: Myths of Seduction and Betrayal,* ed. Jonathan Miller (Baltimore: Johns Hopkins University Press, 1990), pp. 70-80.

2. See, respectively, François-Régis Bastide, "La Peur d'aimer," *Psyché* 16 (1948), 188; Jouve, p. 61; and Rank, p. 86.

3. See Baudelaire's notes in Choderlos de Laclos, *uvres complètes* (Paris: Gallimard, 1951), pp. 712-21; André Malraux, *Le Triangle noir: Laclos, Goya, Saint-Just* (Paris: Gallimard, 1970), p. 31; Peter Brooks, *The Novel of Worldliness* (Princeton: Princeton University Press, 1969), p. 182; Henri Blanc, *Les Liaisons dangereuses de Choderlos de Laclos* (Paris: Hachette, 1972), p. 82; Bernard Bray, "L'Hypocrisie du libertin," in *Laclos et le libertinage. Actes du Colloque du bicentenaire des "Liaisons dangereuses"* (Paris: Presses Universitaires de France, 1983), pp. 97-109; Marina Warner, "Valmont—or the Marquise Unmasked," in *Don Giovanni: Myths of Seduction and Betrayal,* pp. 93-107.

4. While Elizabeth Douvan and Lloyd Free evoke the workings of the unconscious in Laclos's novel, their examples are related rather to what Freud calls the "preconscious" ("*Les Liaisons dangereuses* and Contemporary Consciousness," in *Laclos: Critical Approaches to Les Liaisons dangereuses,* ed. Lloyd R. Free (Madrid: Studia Humanitatis, 1978), pp. 288-91.

5. See Christopher Hampton's screenplay, *Dangerous Liaisons: The Film* (London: Faber and Faber, 1989), p. 8. References to dialogue in the film are from this edition. The Hampton screenplay is based on both his own play and Laclos's novel, of which the play is an adaptation. The play itself has been published under the title *Les Liaisons dangereuses: A Play* (London: Samuel French, 1985).

6. See *The Standard Edition of the Complete Psychological Works of Sigmund Freud,* 14 vols, trans. James Strachey (London: Hogarth Press, 1953), 14:88.

7. *Love, Guilt and Reparation and Other Works* (New York: Delacorte Press, 1975), p. 170.

8. *Standard Edition,* 14:88.

9. *Standard Edition,* 14:89.

10. *Les Liaisons dangereuses* (Paris: Garnier Frères, 1961), no. 81. References are to the letters by number in this edition.

11. See J. Laplanche and J.B. Pontalis, *Vocabulaire de la psychanalyse* (Paris: Presses Universitaires de France, 1967), p. 261.

12. I say "curiously" because homosexuality plays a prominent role in Frears's best-known previous films, *My Beautiful Laundrette* and *Sammy and Rosie Get Laid.* The theme is featured prominently, moreover, in Charles Brabant's 1979 television adaptation of the *Liaisons* and is clearly suggested in Milos Forman's *Valmont* (1989).

13. "Je me désintéresse entièrement sur son compte . . . Ces sortes de femmes ne sont absolument que des machines à plaisir" (no. 106). In Milos Forman and Jean-Claude Carrière's adaptation, *Valmont,* Merteuil states unequivocally, with regard to Cécile: "She reminds me so much of myself."

14. *Sexuality and the Psychology of Love* (New York: Collier, 1963), p. 198.

15. Psychoanalytical sense: a woman who fantasizes possession of a phallus; popular sense: a domineering, "masculine" woman (Laplanche and Pontalis, p. 310).

16. *Le Séminaire,* livre 11 (Paris: Seuil, 1964), pp. 65-109.

17. Lacan, pp. 96, 97.

18. Lacan, pp. 73, 95, 108.

19. A facet of the Marquise's character emphasized by a number of modern readers, such as Anne-Marie Jaton: "Laclos crée une subjectivité féminine lucide qui revendique et exerce son droit de regard et . . . fait de l'homme un object non seulement comme instrument de plaisir, mais comme être humain" ("Libertinage féminin, libertinage dangereux," in *Laclos et le libertinage. Actes du Colloque du Bicentenaire des "Liaisons dangereuses,"* p. 160); cf. Susan Dunn: "She will make others be object to her subject; she herself will never be object" ("Education and Seduction in *Les Liaisons dangereuses,*" *Symposium* 34:1 (1980), 126.

20. Lacan, p. 53.

21. Cf. Didier Masseau, who comments that the Merteuil figure "assimile l'exercice du pouvoir à la manifestation d'un regard omniprésent et invisible" ("Le Narrataire des *Liaisons dangereuses,*" in *Laclos et le libertinage. Actes du Colloque du Bicentenaire des "Liaisons dangereuses,"* p. 126). Merteuil's fate, in the Freudian context, may evoke the blinding of Oedipus, his symbolic castration before entering voluntary exile—an exile which Merteuil will "emulate" as well.

22. The incestuous overtones of the Merteuil-Danceny liaison have not been overlooked by previous readers (see, for example, Douvan and Free, p. 299). When viewed in the context of Valmont's death in the duel with Danceny, the Merteuil-Danceny-Valmont triangle yields all the

essential motifs, somewhat displaced to be sure, of the Oedipal situation: incestuous desire, jealousy over the possession of the Mother, disapproval and threat of punishment by the Father, and the Son's desire to kill the father who has, in his mind, injured the object of his affections (Cécile).

23. For a brief but clear discussion of this fundamental Lacanian thesis, see Anika Lemaire, *Jacques Lacan* (Brussels: Pierre Mardaga, 1977), pp. 249-52.

24. "Il n'est plus pour moi de bonheur, de repos, que par la possession de cette femme que je hais et que j'aime avec une égale fureur" (no. 100).

25. Klein, p. 377.

26. Klein, pp. 395-96.

27. Cf. Laclos: "Ai-je donc jamais cessé d'être constant pour vous? Nos liens ont été dénoués, et non pas rompus; notre prétendue rupture ne fut qu'une erreur de notre imagination" (no. 133). In a very recent study of Frears's *Dangerous Liaisons* in the context of the Don Juan myth (discovered, most gratefully, after the writing of this study), Marina Warner remarks that "in the late 1980s, when the rake asks to come home, he is not talking to a beloved mistress or a forsaken wife, but rather to another woman in his life—his mother" ("Valmont—or the Marquise Unmasked," in *Don Giovanni: Myths of Seduction and Betrayal,* pp. 99-100). Warner adds, in further support of the notion of Merteuil's maternal relationship to Valmont: "Laclos shadows forth another kind of mothering in the famous seducer's life [Don Juan's] when he creates his monstrous Marquise, and Hampton caught his drift and rendered visible the invisible mother of Don Juan in the form of Mme de Merteuil" (p. 100).

28. Cf. Warner: "Just as the law is embodied by the Commendatore [in *Don Giovanni*], so Valmont's law is laid down by the Marquise" (p. 102).

29. Klein, p. 214.

30. The nostalgia of a happiness irrevocably lost, evocative of the Oedipal stage, is stressed by the Marquise near the end of the novel, after she wistfully recalls the love and happiness she and Valmont once shared: "Mais pourquoi s'occuper encore d'un bonheur qui ne peut revenir? Non, quoi que vous en disiez, c'est un retour impossible" (no. 131). The archetypal "retour impossible" is the adult male's reunion with the Mother.

Renee Winegarten (essay date 1994)

SOURCE: "Seductive Monsters: Laclos's *Liaisons dangereuses*," *The New Criterion,* Vol. 12, No. 7, March, 1994, pp. 24-30.

[*In the essay below, Winegarten links Laclos's political ideology with the themes developed in* Les Liaisons dangereuses.]

I believe that the sect of Epicurus, introduced into Rome at the end of the republic, contributed greatly to produce a harmful effect on the heart and mind of the Romans.

　　　　　　　　　　　　　—Montesquieu

Sometime during the winter of 1789-90, Pierre-Ambroise Choderlos de Laclos, notorious author of *Les Liaisons dangereuses,* was impatiently cooling his heels in a London antechamber, because that paragon of dandies, George Prince of Wales, had not yet finished his toilette. So bored was Laclos at this princely levee that, although reputedly a figure of glacial reserve, he unburdened himself to Comte Alexandre de Tilly, no mean roué in his day. The dubious Tilly reported the novelist's words in memoirs published many years later. "I decided to write a work that should depart from the trodden path, make a stir, and reverberate on this earth after my demise," confided Laclos, adding for good measure that certain characters and events in his novel were based on actual persons (indicated with tantalizing discretion), and on circumstances with which he himself was directly or indirectly acquainted. Tilly, surprised by his companion's unaccustomed eloquence, added a footnote to stress that he remembered what Laclos had said as if it were yesterday.

Deliberate, lucid, far-seeing, Laclos (as reported by Tilly) sounds as if working in fulfillment of a plan of campaign. He certainly achieved all three of the declared aims. While adopting the form of the story-in-letters employed by writers he most admired—Samuel Richardson in *Clarissa* and Richardson's disciple Jean-Jacques Rousseau in *Julie ou la Nouvelle Héloïse*—he subverted with wit and irony these lengthy moralizing works of seduction. By concentrating only upon what would advance the drama, Laclos produced a book that has been called the first well-made French novel. Drama indeed: Laclos favored the theater and theatrical metaphor. He wrote a play and the libretto for an *opéra comique*—both lost.

When it was published in 1782, *Les Liaisons dangereuses* caused a veritable sensation. Along with Tilly, the novelist's contemporaries looked for real persons behind the Vicomte de Valmont, the Marquise de Merteuil, and Cécile Volanges. Queen Marie-Antoinette had her copy bound without title or name of author. The famous actress and novelist Marie-Jeanne Riccoboni wrote to Laclos to defend French womanhood against aspersions that she felt were cast upon it by the portrayal of Mme de Merteuil and her monstrous machinations. Comtesse Félicité de Genlis, a prolific and celebrated novelist, claimed in her memoirs that no woman could publicly admit to having read so infamous a work. There would be no love lost between Laclos and Félicité de Genlis. Yet if the novel made Laclos famous, it also blackened his reputation. His contemporaries would persist in seeing Laclos—who was to prove a most devoted husband and father, of solidly conventional family views—as Valmont, the machiavellian libertine. When Laclos became secretary to the Duc d'Orléans in January 1789, a few months before the fall of the Bastille, ousting from political influence that prince's former mistress, Félicité de Genlis, he was widely conceived as a man of darkness, a conspirator capable of anything.

Are readers to take *Les Liaisons dangereuses* simply as a salacious work whose "moral" is tacked on for convention's sake, or does the book pursue a deeper intention? Fascination with the enigma of *Les Liaisons dangereuses* has endured down to our own day. The dramatized English version by Christopher Hampton, which most skillfully fillets the novel, was originally staged in 1985 by the Royal Shakespeare Company at Stratford-upon-Avon on the intimate stage of The Other Place, with the egregious Alan Rickman as Valmont. It transferred to London, to the Barbican Pit, and then to the West End, survived various changes of cast, toured the provinces, and evolved into a popular American film. Another movie based on the novel appeared at about the same time. Hampton's stage version has often been revived, and the Royal Shakespeare Company alludes to the piece as one of its major successes of the last decade. Now an opera based on the novel is announced for the San Francisco Opera House. What is there in this tale of pleasure-loving, perverse French aristocrats on the eve of the French Revolution, to capture a modern British and American audience? The answer may well lie in its treatment of sexual warfare and of woman's fate, and in the hidden agenda suggested by its author's political and social views.

The resentment that inspired *Les Liaisons dangereuses* still burns through this singular work, the only novel produced by Laclos, a deeply ambitious soldier, inventor, politician, journalist, and wit. Born in 1741, Laclos came of a family only recently ennobled, and he thus remained on the lower rungs of the nobility. He entered the army at a time when advancement and the most prominent posts went to those of high birth, often regardless of merit. Despite various attempts that were made to reform this unjust system, Laclos never seemed to benefit from them. He was esteemed an exemplary officer, but for many years he did not rise above the rank of artillery captain, nor did he see active service in the American War of Independence and elsewhere, as he ardently desired.

Extremely well read, he passed his time in various garrisons, like the one at Grenoble (scene of the exploits of a possible model for Mme de Merteuil), composing mostly undistinguished light, satirical, or libertine verse. Some youthful adventures of his own and his sharp observation of the conduct of friends, and of the social mores of the privileged, provided him with material for his novel. His

powers were reflective rather than imaginative. As he said in his long, admiring essay on Fanny Burney's *Cecilia, or the Memoirs of an Heiress,* he counted the essential qualities for a novelist to be observation, sensibility, and the ability to depict life truthfully. He left sweetness and light to the novels of Mme Riccoboni. The scandal of *Les Liaisons dangereuses* blotted his copybook in the eyes of his military superiors. So did his attack on Vauban, the great military engineer who had built fortifications under Louis XIV and who was commonly regarded as above criticism. Mere artillery captains were not expected to publish their critical views on such matters. Moreover, the experiments that Laclos undertook to develop a new kind of bullet were not pursued. In short, Laclos was a man of talent, energy, and independent mind, who was being constantly frustrated in his chosen profession.

The opportunity for Laclos to try to change the existing unfair order of things came when an aristocratic protector introduced him into the household of Louis-Philippe-Joseph, Duc d'Orléans. This liberal, pleasure-loving, irresponsible prince, regular thorn in the flesh of his distant cousin Louis XVI, would later become notorious as Philippe Egalité. Historians differ as to how far the activities of the Anglophile Duc d'Orléans in the early months of the Revolution were influential. What matters here is that contemporaries firmly believed that there existed an Orléanist conspiracy and that Laclos, his new secretary, on leave from the army, was its moving spirit. The wealthy Duc d'Orléans then had on his payroll many of those who were to be leading actors in the revolutionary period, including Mirabeau, Danton, and Brissot, future luminary of the Girondins. It was Laclos, however, who is thought to have composed the famous *Instructions,* an influential and much imitated document sent out by the Duc d'Orléans to his bailiwicks in the period leading up to the Estates-General of 1789. This document demanded guarantees of personal liberty and freedom of expression, and even advocated divorce.

Rightly or wrongly, Laclos was believed to be responsible for distributing "Orléans gold" to win popularity for his master. Consequently, he was accused of suborning not only the rioters at the Réveillon wallpaper factory in April 1789 but also the working women of Paris who marched to Versailles in October of that year, an upheaval which resulted in the humiliating forced return of Louis XVI and his family to the capital. Much to Mirabeau's disgust, that weak reed the Duc d'Orléans failed to seize the opportunity to become Regent, and found himself dispatched on a "diplomatic mission" (virtual exile) to the Court of St. James, where we first met Laclos. It was Laclos who penned the correspondence of the Duc d'Orléans with the French Court, including that prince's long letter of self-justification requesting permission to return to Paris (a letter scorned by Félicité de Genlis, who was convinced that she could have done better).

Once back in Paris, the Duc d'Orléans and his secretary became active in the Jacobin Club. Laclos took part in debates as well as busying himself with the creation, editing, and publication of its journal. The flight of Louis XVI and his family, their recapture at Varennes, renewed the question of the King's abdication, and once more opened the path to the Regency of the Duc d'Orléans. Again he declined to seize the opportunity. Laclos, apparently unable to abandon the hopes he had pinned to this wavering star, wanted to make his master Regent in spite of himself. He keenly favored a national petition in which everyone, "all good citizens"—a category that significantly included women—would be able to express their opinion. Privily, to favor the Orléans cause, Laclos even made an alteration to Brissot's text of the petition, which led Brissot to say that all unknowingly he had been party to yet another *liaison dangereuse.* Laclos was foiled—by his old enemy, Félicité de Genlis. He retired from politics and returned to the army. The Duc d'Orléans went on as Philippe Egalité to vote for the death of the king and to die like his cousin by the guillotine.

During the Terror, Laclos was imprisoned on three occasions but, possibly owing to some powerful protector, he was eventually released. Laclos was not a republican like Brissot: he was a monarchist who had wanted a change of dynasty to bring about "a regenerative revolution." He was among the few prominent revolutionaries to have the good fortune to survive the Terror. He could not, though, escape the odium that attached to all those who had served Philippe Egalité.

Laclos said once that he wanted a monarchy "so as not to have to decide one day, perhaps very soon, between Caesar and Pompey." Soon enough, after the coup d'état of 18 Brumaire (November 9) 1799, he would be enjoying the favor of Napoleon Bonaparte, a fellow artillery officer, some twenty-eight years his junior. As General Laclos, his experiments with the bullet were now welcomed. Promoted to commander of the artillery reserve, he served under Marmont during Bonaparte's Italian campaign. Stendhal (who said that as a boy in Grenoble he had been given sweetmeats by the original of Mme de Merteuil) later claimed to have met the elderly General Laclos in Milan in a box at La Scala in 1800, and to have courted him as the author of *Les Liaisons dangereuses.* On hearing that Stendhal (then, as Henri Beyle, a sublieutenant of dragoons aged seventeen) was a native of Grenoble, Laclos showed that he was moved. It seems less likely, however, that on another occasion in Naples, Laclos gave him a list of "great lords of 1778" with notes on morality. Laclos fell gravely ill and died in Taranto in 1803. No trace remains of his tomb, which was destroyed at the Bourbon Restoration in 1815.

Such was the author of *Les Liaisons dangereuses, or Letters collected in a certain Society, and published for the instruction of others,* to give the book its full title of 1782. The enigmatic epigraph, taken from the Preface to Rousseau's *Julie ou la Nouvelle Héloïse,* ran: "I have seen the manners of my day, and I have published these letters." The so-called "Publisher's Foreword" observed with biting sarcasm: "Indeed, several of the characters he [the Author] places upon the stage, are so immoral that it is impossible to imagine that they could have lived in our age; in this age of philosophy where the universal spread of enlightenment has, as everyone knows, made all men so virtuous and all women so modest and retiring." The "Editor's Preface" laid the claim to a moral intent, as was then *de rigueur.* The ending of the novel, with the exemplary death of Valmont in a duel (after the style of Richardson's Lovelace), and the social and financial ruin of Mme de Merteuil and her disfigurement by smallpox, are clearly intended to convey the salutary message that the evil-doers have been punished. Yet eighteenth-century critics, to be followed by their heirs, could not help noticing that the depiction of the seducers and their wiles is adorned with every attraction, including charm, intelligence, and wit.

Laclos would not be the only writer to intend to write one kind of book and to appear to produce another. If taken as the portrayal of the manners of a certain privileged class in general, the book could be seen as "one of the revolutionary flood waters which poured into the ocean that submerged the Court," wrote Tilly, long after the event. (In this sense Christopher Hampton would not be far off the mark in suggesting that Mme de Merteuil was going to be punished not by smallpox but by the guillotine). There were those who thought that what they called "the moral degradation of the aristocracy" was a major cause of the Revolution. Doubtless, the contempt that the sexual license of the privileged engendered, especially as rudely targeted in satirical underground scandal sheets, contributed to undermine respect for the society and institutions of the *ancien régime.*

Laclos himself was to perceive that this total absorption in sexual pleasure was harmful to society and to the body politic. In a memoir on foreign policy addressed to Committee of Public Safety in 1795, he listed among the causes of the Revolution not only financial mismanagement but also something from which he himself had suffered, "the scandalous abuse of favor and intrigue which allowed only incapable persons or those of ill repute to attain position," together with "a profound immorality which the Court no longer even took the trouble to conceal." There is no doubt about the existence of debauched eighteenth-century rulers and monarchs, like the Regent Philippe III d'Orléans (great-grandfather of Philippe Egalité) or Louis XV, and libertine aristocrats of both sexes, from Mme de Tencin to the Maréchal de Richelieu. The Marquis de Sade himself (born 1740), so astonishingly and consistently rehabilitated by writers in our own day, was a close contemporary of Laclos: *Les 120 Journées de Sodome ou l'Ecole du Libertinage* was written in 1785, three years after *Les Liaisons dangereuses* appeared. Baron Grimm had declared in 1782 in his *Correspondance littéraire,* addressed to subscribers among the crowned heads of Europe, that people mentioned more than one society that could have given Laclos the idea for his seductive monsters.

The ambiguity inseparable from *Les Liaisons dangereuses,* one aspect of its perennial fascination, is linked to the legend of Don Juan from which the novel can scarcely be disassociated. Laclos mentioned Molière's Tartuffe when discussing the hypocrisy of his characters with fellow novelist Mme Riccoboni, but it was above all another of Molière's hypocrites, his Don Juan, that Laclos could not have overlooked. Valmont, after Molière's libertine anti-hero, places noble birth above virtue and piety; he also sees his pursuit of women in terms of military heroism, *gloire,* and conquest; he, too, makes use of religion in his desire to overcome the scruples of the devout Mme de Tourvel.

The Don Juan legend, from Tirso de Molina's *El Burlador de Sevilla* to Mozart's *Don Giovanni,* can scarcely be separated from religion and repentance; it moves from the seducer who constantly postpones the day of reckoning to the Don who defies the repeated warning to repent: "Pentiti, scellerato!"—both of whom are swept down to hell. Valmont is not a Satanist, as Baudelaire suggested, because that would imply belief in Satan, and he has no belief at all. Rather Valmont appears as an overreacher, a blasphemer who needs a divinity to defy. He does not want Mme de Tourvel to abandon religion; on the contrary, he cruelly wants her to suffer all the more through her faith and her torments of conscience. He cries: "I shall have this woman; . . . I shall dare to ravish her from the very God she worships." And he adds that in the moment of success, "I shall really be the God she will have preferred." The frisson that such a horrid boast provokes has less to do with faith than with something deeply primitive and contrary to reason and order. There needs no Statue come from beyond the grave to punish such hubris. We are in the world of human beings abandoned to themselves and their own instincts, their own destructive and self-destructive urges—the world we know.

Yet as if the masculine Don Juan were not enough, Laclos presents us with a singular feminine version of Don Juan ("a real female Lovelace," according to Grimm) in Mme de Merteuil. Like Valmont, her former lover and her co-conspirator, she too cares nothing for religion, and she lives only for power and sexual gratification in numerous amours. However, as a woman she is obliged to hide behind a mask of social respectability. Whereas Valmont is received in high society despite his reputation as a seducer, she would not be received there if her mask of virtue were to slip for a moment. In the famous Letter 81, Mme de Merteuil gives an account of her upbringing, her loveless marriage, her realization that only by ruse, by secretly pursuing cold policy, could she achieve her aims. "Not yet fifteen, I already had all the talents to which the majority of our politicians owe their reputation," she owns. It is this startling observation that makes us realize to the full the deviation of her gifts.

All her fine skills of study and intellect are now devoted to punishing her faithless lover, the Comte de Gercourt, by having him (so to speak) made a cuckold before his marriage to young Cécile Volanges. Similarly, Valmont, with his great name, wealth, position, and all the brilliant attractions of youth and wit, can believe that his conquest of women is equal to the heroic exploits of famous military commanders. The scene of the perverse and pernicious activity of Valmont and Mme de Merteuil seems far too small for them. As Baudelaire remarked, their "strategy is devoted to winning a very frivolous prize." With so many gifts and so much energy they should surely be able to do something more significant. Instead, they occupy their time in intrigue, in manipulating other people in order to "fill the emptiness of their hearts, the futility of their existence," as Grimm expressed it. It is here, perhaps, that we may sense the gist of the novelist's social, moral, and political criticism.

Proud, cold, vengeful, Mme de Merteuil is fully conscious of her superiority over Valmont—indeed, over all men and women. Gradually, we are drawn to see how she has made him her instrument, although he is far too vain to realize this. She quickly perceives that he has really fallen in love with Mme de Tourvel without knowing it. In his rapture he can tell Mme de Merteuil, his former lover, that he has never experienced such bliss; to her, this avowal cannot but appear as an outrage to herself. She plays on his vanity to have him send the cruel letter of dismissal that will destroy the life of his devoted victim. In the warfare that follows, both Valmont and Mme de Merteuil are also destroyed. Yet there remains a vital distinction. We are told by a witness that in the moment of his death Valmont revealed himself to be "truly great," as he sought reconciliation with his opponent, young Danceny, whom he had wronged. As for M. de Prévan, the vicious rake whom Mme de Merteuil had exposed to ridicule and obloquy, he is restored to favor in society. In contrast, Mme de Merteuil herself is reduced to public disgrace and ostracism.

Laclos has Mme de Merteuil say to Valmont that "I was born to avenge my sex and to master yours," through means original to herself. Oddly enough, Laclos—with Condorcet—was a feminist. His three writings on the education of women (1783 and after), a question which had long been a theme for impassioned discussion, adapt the ideas of Rousseau. According to Laclos, all women were free in a state of nature but in society they are now in chains. For Laclos, where there is slavery—and, he insists, women are "slaves" in society—there can be no education. Society reduces women to exercise seduction and guile since they lack the physical force to overcome men. In the perennial sex war that rages, women can rarely win, and when they lose, their enslavement only becomes more bitter.

These acute views illuminate retrospectively not only the depiction of Mme de Tourvel and Cécile Volanges as pawns in the sex game but also the treatment of the conduct and destiny of Mme de Merteuil as scourge and avenger. Laclos began his reflections on perfecting women's education with a paradox: there is no way to perfect the education of women in the present state of affairs. The supposed education hitherto given to women does not merit the name. Indeed, the very laws and manners are opposed to providing them with a better education, in his opinion.

After his grim analysis of existing conditions, Laclos went on to propose a surprising solution: he advised women not to wait for men, tyrants and "authors of your ills," to come to their rescue, but to realize that the only way out of slavery was through "a great revolution." And he added: "Is this revolution possible? It is for you alone to say so since it depends on your courage." Laclos puts the ball in women's court—perhaps the easiest thing for him to do in the circumstances, in these pre-Revolution writings that remained unfinished and were never published in his lifetime. A strong hint of his feminist stance, however, does percolate through the portrayal of Mme de Merteuil to startle the modern reader or spectator.

Laclos, then, is at once traditional in his depiction of dangerous female power and highly original in his challenge to women themselves to seek to right the wrongs that he feels are done to them. A number of women would attempt to do so during the French Revolution—in vain. His attitude may be seen as optimistic and utopian in its urge to change society ("a great revolution") and pessimistic in its analysis, thus remaining in accord with eighteenth-century ambivalence. Mme de Rosemonde, Valmont's aunt and a compassionate friend to Mme de Tourvel, maintains that the sexes are never truly at one: above all, the perfect happiness in love that women dream about is an illusion, a trick of the imagination, a "deceptive hope." It is with these dour notions that Mme de Rosemonde tries to console her friend—Job's comforter indeed. Yet this disillusion harmonizes with the author's profound pessimism.

The novel as a whole leaves the impression that his decent characters, or those who are trying to be decent, are blind fools. Mme de Volanges is deceived by Mme de Merteuil's mask of virtue; she fails to keep a keen maternal eye on her young daughter, Cécile, who is all too easily corrupted and debauched by Valmont. As for Mme de Tourvel, she is tricked by her pride into believing that she has wrought Valmont's conversion, and worn down by his passionate pursuit. Brutally cast aside, Mme de Tourvel withdraws to the convent in shame and agony, and she virtually wills her own death. In this respect she resembles Richardson's Clarissa, but without the odor of sanctity. In the world of Laclos, the decent are defeated, the innocent maimed. As a good husband and father, Laclos fully intended to write a second novel to embody the notion that "there is no happiness outside the family": he spent many years thinking about it, but he could not do it.

This is a world where those with the means and urge to do so can freely enjoy manipulating and destroying others. The sheer intelligence of Valmont and Mme de Merteuil, and their insight into the minds and hearts, the weaknesses of their victims, are nothing less than stunning. One might at first be inclined to speak of motiveless evil on the lines of Iago, were it not that these supreme egoists do have the motive of selfish pleasure and the superior satisfaction of exercising deceit and power. Moreover, there is often a kind of black humor in their deleterious activity that recalls the tone of Richard III rather than of Iago. The supreme example of this is the brilliant letter of *double entendre,* addressed to Mme de Tourvel, that Valmont pens in bed with a courtesan while using her back as a desk. There is here a blending of cynicism and wit to which one responds with a certain revulsion, astonishment at the skill with the words—and, it must be owned, rather ashamed amusement at the black comedy.

In his telling 1939 essay on Laclos, André Malraux said that the book presented more than the application of the will to sexual ends: rather it revealed what he called "the eroticization of the will," the transformation of something without an explicit sexual meaning into the motive for erotic pleasure, the intermingling of will and sexuality until they formed a single realm. All that separates the novel from the mores of today is the presence of social constraints that were ineluctable in the eighteenth century and that added to the savor of the dangerous game.

In the novel everything has moved into the sphere of sexuality and power. The word "heart" is employed to mean sexual pleasure. Only Mme de Tourvel sacrifices herself for love and finds her self-sacrifice mocked. Significantly, she is the one major character that Laclos had totally invented, if the avowals to Tilly are to be believed. Here are careless fools, blind instruments, along with clever knaves who might be better employed—a privileged society that does not realize it is on the brink of ruin. With its ruthless probing of the interplay of egoism, sexual gratification, domination, and power politics, the theme of *Les Liaisons dangereuses* chimes with one of the most all-embracing and so far apparently ineradicable preoccupations of present-day culture, as expressed through many of its leading and lesser pundits and its artistic products. Even the undercurrent of danger and threat, adumbrated by Laclos, is not entirely missing.

Sandra Camargo (essay date 1996)

SOURCE: "Face Value and the Value of Face in *Les Liaisons dangereuses:* The Rhetoric of Form and the Critic's Seduction," *The Journal of Narrative Technique,* Vol. 26, No. 3, Fall, 1996, pp. 228-48.

[*In the following essay, Camargo provides an overview of recent scholarly reaction to* Les Liaisons dangereuses, *outlining distinctions between different critical interpretations of the novel.*]

Written by Choderlos de Laclos to pass the time when he was stationed at a boring outpost on the western coast of France, *Les Liaisons dangereuses* has been the subject of intense debate since its publication in 1782 and has been variously described as both cynical and moralizing, as feminist and misogynist, as counseling hypocrisy and as attacking it, as a textbook of seduction techniques and as a warning not to use them. In a review of the literature on the occasion of the two-hundredth anniversary of the novel's publication, David Coward noted that "*Les Liaisons dangereuses* has been scrutinized in a bewildering variety of ways. Traditionalists, structuralists, feminists, and others besides have investigated its themes and tensions, analyzed its language and form and set it in contexts both ancient and modern. *Les Liaisons dangereuses* lends itself admirably to elucidation by virtue of its elusive, ambiguous and ultimately mysterious clarity and it has proved a super malleable material from which to shape theories, angles, and convictions" (1982, 291). Despite the wide range of critical approaches that have been brought to bear on Choderlos de Laclos's novel, the majority of studies seem to take one of two positions: either they foreground the form of the work and thus empty it of content (see, for example, the structural analyses of Todorov 1966, 1967; or the historical-traditional work of Versini 1962), or they focus on content, appropriating the characters for psychoanalysis, politics, or sociology, taking the form for granted and analyzing the behavior of the characters as if they were personages in a modern novel instead of in an epistolary novel of the eighteenth century (see, for example, Barny 1883; Byrne 1989; Jaton 1983a, 1983b; and Miller 1980). However, we only experience these characters through their letters, and gaps in our knowledge are an inevitable consequence of the epistolary form. In the long run, what we do *not* know about the characters in the novel proves to be more valuable in determining the motives for their behavior than what we do know.

The novel's main characters—the Vicomte de Valmont and the Marquise de Merteuil—are active participants in the libertine tradition, are supremely experienced, and present themselves as masters of their craft. The rest of the characters are their prey, particularly Cécile de Volanges, the young convent girl seduced by Valmont at Merteuil's request, and Madame de Tourvel, a virtuous married woman whom Valmont also seduces, whether as a challenge, out of boredom, or from sincere attraction. As the novel proceeds, the tension between the Vicomte and the Marquise increases to the point where they begin to prey on each other as well. It is this shift in their affections—and the viciousness with which their war is carried out—that has most intrigued critics of this work. Establishing the motives for their behavior is problematized by the epistolary structure of the narrative, and critics have been at pains to fill in the blanks in the psychological portraits drawn by Laclos. Most critics have nominated the Marquise as the linchpin of the novel and the majority of readings of the novel have concentrated on her.

The central narrative conflict is a relatively simple one: Madame de Merteuil wants the Vicomte to return to Paris from the country where he is staying with his old aunt. The first word of the first letter that Merteuil writes to Valmont is *revenez* ("come back"). He drags his feet because he is involved in his own affairs, specifically his pursuit of Tourvel. As Merteuil becomes increasingly impatient, her letters generally have two tones: the majority of her letters tease, chide, and berate the Vicomte, but there are others, particularly toward the end of the novel, that express affection for the Vicomte and nostalgia for their past closeness. Critics have always recognized this two-faced quality in Merteuil; where they differ is in their views on which of the two tones is more sincere (or less insincere). In other words, does Merteuil hide her love behind witty banter, or are the loving passages a mask for her deep-seated resentment of the Vicomte?

Readings of Merteuil's character and motivation take mainly two forms. One group of critics suggests that Merteuil regrets the end of her affair with Valmont, and that she is jealous of Tourvel because she loves Valmont and wants him back. She is content to tease Valmont about his pursuit of Tourvel, as long as she sees it as just another sexual conquest. Then, however, in Letter 125, Valmont insults her—he overpraises Tourvel, and speaks of his pleasure outlasting the act of love "for the first time," words no discarded lover would hear gladly, particularly not one whose *amour-propre* is as large as the Marquise's. Valmont has got her where it hurts, and she declares war on him and on her rival, Tourvel. Despite Merteuil's boldness, sharp wit, and preternatural self-consciousness, this reading suggests that she is as ruled by her emotions as any heroine of soap opera. Critics who take this approach interpret Valmont's feelings for Tourvel as love and accept Merteuil's punishment as just deserts for the destruction of their relationship and the deaths of the lovers.

The second group of critics sees the Marquise as "not having a heart for love," as Laclos describes her in a letter to his friend Madame Riccoboni. These critics see Merteuil's conflict with Valmont in terms of competition rather than desire. Their relationship is configured as a rivalry in a sort of libertine's sweepstakes rather than as a shared love that is unrequited from Merteuil's perspective and unrealized from Valmont's. As a fellow libertine, Merteuil seems to have taken it on herself to uphold the rules of the order. Valmont's falling so desperately in love with Tourvel is, in this latter interpretation, treated with contempt by Merteuil rather than with jealousy. Valmont is undone by his own fear for his reputation rather than by the machinations of a woman scorned. The fact that Merteuil presents herself as an equal to Valmont in this reading has made her an attractive model for feminist critics who see her exercising her great power skillfully in a man's world.

This group of critics reads the end of the novel as representing Merteuil's downfall due to her failure to recognize the true strength of male power in her world (see, for example, Byrne 1989). Nancy Miller (1980) describes the male bond as powerful enough to control even the most powerful of women. In fact, Miller suggests that, in acting as if she were powerful, Merteuil is only deluding herself, by accepting as real what Valmont calls "the illusory authority that we [males] appear to let women take" (L. 40).[1] In this reading, Merteuil's arrogant exercise of power is only tolerated for a time by the males in her society. However, Valmont also says that this illusion of power is meant to entrap women by giving them the illusion of freedom, and it is "one of the snares they avoid with the most difficulty," probably because it is an illusion in which they want most fervently to believe. Inevitably, the trap is sprung, and the men finally decide that they have had enough and turn on her. Merteuil's punishment is based on her having broken the "laws of an economy of circulation intended to protect phallic identity" (Miller 1980, 69-70). Merteuil breaks this law when she attempts to seize the male prerogative of managing her own social and sexual roles.

According to Anne Marie Jaton, since libertinage may be seen as subversive to social mores, rather than simply as decadent and sinful, Merteuil as a female libertine embodies an even more "virulent attack on the integrity of the social order" than that represented by males like Valmont (1983b, 153; my translation). Viewed in political rather than in moral terms, Merteuil's behavior is socially disruptive and justifies her exclusion from society at the end of the novel. As Jaton describes it, the male must publish his exploits, and he arranges to do this by seducing his victim and then, coming to his senses, as it were, by renouncing her. This public renunciation is his entrée back into polite society. Thus the male libertine has his cake and is forgiven for eating it. The female libertine, on the other hand, must remain always discreet. Perhaps we sympathize with Merteuil's desire for appreciation and praise to the extent that we do not question the danger she is in when she writes her sexual exploits down for Valmont.

Regardless of their view of Merteuil's motives, critics of the novel emphasize these exploits—the seduction scenes with Belleroche and Prévan described in Merteuil's letters to Valmont—interpreting those episodes as having a role in Merteuil's master plan, whether that is to make Valmont jealous and thus win him back, or to establish her bona fides as a libertine so convincingly and unequivocally that Valmont will take her contempt of him seriously enough to come to heel. In either case, both groups of critics assume that Merteuil is writing the truth to Valmont about these episodes. I suggest, however, that when lying is a central motif in a novel, as it is in *Les Liaisons dangereuses,* we can never be certain where the truth is, that there is no point at which we are justified in assuming that a character is not lying, and that the epistolary nature of *Les Liaisons dangereuses* has seduced the critics into neglecting that possibility. The use of the letters in the novel to deceive the other characters has, of course, long been noted; that the letters also deceive the critics simply adds another layer of irony to a work already bathed in it.

The formal nature of the work certainly creates snares for the unwary. *Les Liaisons dangereuses* is based on a form, the letter, that has such a quotidian reality for us that its transparency may be taken for granted. In tracing the history of the epistolary novel, Laurent Versini notes the irony that a genre that today seems so artificial was once considered the height of realism. He describes the genre as especially attractive to writers who wanted a more realistic medium: "The epistolary genre suited some writers who were looking for a certificate of authenticity, who had in addition discovered a formula that concerned and was well adapted to the culture of sociability" (1968, 251; my translation). That this greater sense of verisimilitude was enthusiastically desired by the public is also noted by Versini: "The reader of novels in the eighteenth century, distrusting fantasies and other works without verisimilitude, finds in the epistolary novel a quantity of truth and nourishment for his feelings" (252; my translation). The memoir, a genre in which fictional autobiographies were presented as history, was also highly popular in the eighteenth century; and letters were found to be equally convincing of authenticity. Versini also relates the genre's success to its ability to convey emotion with immediacy and believability. The epistolary novel "will find perhaps its triumph in rendering the lie as believable as the truth" (Versini 1968, 263; my translation). In other words, the epistolary form itself creates effects of verisimilitude and authenticity on which the illusion of truth as well as the reality of the lie depend.

The representation of a narrative through letters affects the ways that the events are experienced, the characters are analyzed, and truth value is assigned. Tzvetan Todorov (1967) has listed qualities related to letter-writing that encourage critical trust: their self-reflexive character; direct style; first-person narration; the writer's signature attesting to the truth of the contents; the letter's own physicality, which thus becomes a publishable form of proof; the present tense; and the connection between letter-writing and performative speech acts. The writing of a letter creates an intimate bond between the sender and the receiver. The letters in *Les Liaisons dangereuses* are not business letters, but letters written from one close friend or confidant to another, an apparently open and frank communication between kindred souls on which the reader is blatantly eavesdropping. Valmont seems to lie to everyone but Merteuil, and his patience with her overbearingness and his respect for her intelligence suggest to the reader that they are a matched pair with a long history of intimacy. One jumps to the assumption that, if *he* would not lie to *her*—he says to her, "You have shared all the secrets of my heart" (L. 4)—then she would not lie to him. But why wouldn't she? Although Valmont says in the fourth letter that he has long confided in Merteuil, Merteuil apparently waits until Letter 81 to reveal her heart to him. Perhaps the candidness of their relationship has not been as reciprocal as Valmont and most critics have supposed.

Letters clearly permit the strategic withholding of information, which not only points up the limitations in a particular character's view of his or her circumstances, but also flatters the reader by implying that the reader occupies a position of omniscience relative to any single character. Thus, we know long before Valmont does that Mme de Volanges is his secret enemy because we have already read the letter in which she warns Tourvel against him. Even after Valmont discovers his accuser's identity, we are still superior in knowledge to him because we know something that he does not: that Mme de Volanges wrote to Mme de Tourvel on the hint of Mme de Merteuil.

Since the withholding of information from one character by another is a basic stratagem of the book, why should

the reader be exempt? Why should secrets not be kept from us as well? As Todorov says:

> The reader finds himself therefore here superior to the characters, and he is the only one who is all-powerful and omniscient, the characters are only the little pieces on the chessboard of intrigue. . . . But the same process [of exploiting the possibilities of the epistolary to withhold information] also permits the inverse effect: at certain moments, the reader is plunged into mystery, while the characters know perfectly well what's going on. (1966, 21; my translation)

In fairness, although the effects of those elements of epistolarity noted by Todorov can be suggestively undermined, their presence generally works to support truth. But the contradictions, reticence, and psychological opacity embodied in the letters in *Les Liaisons dangereuses* make our usual practice of analyzing texts on the basis of what is present within them an extraordinarily complex and problematic operation. Critics who grapple with this protean text and attempt to assert their dominance over it trust the characters at their own risk, largely because the epistolary form also motivates the *absence* of elements that are considered basic to the establishment of truth in other sorts of narratives.

First, the epistolary form tends to efface the author, either as creator of the text or as the omniscient narrator whose commentary might be used to guide the reader through it. Since the verisimilitude of the epistolary form depends on an effaced authorial presence, any intrusions that the author does make must be especially marked. Laclos's presence in *Les Liaisons dangereuses* is limited to the two prefaces, to his footnotes, to the narrative ruptures that he achieves through the order in which the letters are presented, to information that he "neglects" to tell us, and, most tellingly, through those letters that he chooses *not* to present.

The two prefaces have been commented on by many critics. The "publisher's note," which is called "L'Avertissement de L'Editeur" in the French, undermines the self-effacing editor's preface and clearly alerts us to the fact that things may not be what they seem: "The Public is notified that despite the title of this work and what is said by the editor in his preface, we do not guarantee the authenticity of the collection and we have good reason to believe it is only a novel" (xv). The French word Avertissement has the sense of "warning" as well as the more common sense of "notice" or "advertisement." Laclos seems to be warning us not to be naive in linking the letters we are about to read with truth, but the textual marginality of prefaces often leads to their being ignored.

The Editor's Preface foregrounds the editor's power of selection: "this collection . . . contains only a very small number of the letters composing the whole correspondence from which it is taken. When I was requested to put in order this correspondence, . . . I have tried to preserve only those letters which seemed to me needed for the understanding of events or to reveal character" (xvii). In assessing the book's chances of success, the editor worries that the book's multiple protagonists will weaken audience identification and involvement and lead readers to pay more attention to the book's faults than they might otherwise. This alienating effect on the reader might have been ameliorated if the book were able to represent sincere feeling, but "since almost all the sentiments here expressed are feigned or dissimulated they can only arouse the interest of curiosity which is always far below the interest of sentiment" (xix). While Laclos, in his personae as publisher and as editor, clearly alerts the reader to expect mis-representation, insincerity, and hypocrisy within the novel, the majority of critics seem to accept as lies only those statements that are explicitly labeled as such.

But the main type of authorial intrusion that provides the basis for my argument is found in the editor's footnotes to the text. One of the most telling examples of the author's explicit manipulation of the knowledge available to the reader occurs in Letter 81, Merteuil's famous self-justification, when she refers obliquely to secrets that she and Valmont share and asks, "whether, of us two, it is I who should be charged with imprudence." The reader might think little of this remark or might simply relate it to the characters' present situation if not for an "editorial" footnote that says, "It will be seen later, in *Letter 152,* not what M. de Valmont's secret was, but practically of what kind it was; and the reader will understand that further enlightenment on this subject could not be given" (p. 183). While, as Ronald C. Rosbottom (1982) has argued, secrecy is an aesthetic, social, and cognitive strategy in **Les Liaisons dangereuses** and the fundamental role in the narrative structure of the book is played by the secret, in this case the reader's desire for information is only partially satisfied. This gesture, so apparently marginal, reminds the reader of the presence of the author behind the text and of that author's absolute power to tantalize and frustrate the reader as well as cater to his or her illusions of omnipotence. More important, the footnote acts as a red flag that marks Merteuil's secret as critical to our understanding of the text. Without that footnote, her comment would likely have little claim on our attention.

The footnote's deferring the revelation of the secret to Letter 152 also foregrounds that letter, which occurs at a key point in the narrative, just after the Marquise and the Vicomte finally meet. One of the novel's ironies is that, although Merteuil seems to have an urgent desire to see Valmont, the two only meet face-to-face once. They miss each other when he returns to Paris; in Letter 59, he writes to her: "Where were you yesterday? I never succeed in seeing you now. Really, it was not worth keeping me in

Paris in September. Make up your mind, for I have just received a very pressing invitation from the Comtesse de B . . . to go and see her in the country." Finally, they meet at her house, where Valmont barges in on a tête-à-tête between Merteuil and Danceny, the young suitor of Cécile de Volanges. The actual meeting is, of course, *not* recorded in a letter, and we only have their subsequent responses to it. Valmont's letter expresses offense and anger at Merteuil's not telling him that she was in Paris for four days rather than jealousy about her involvement with Danceny:

> You have been four days in Paris; and each day you have seen Danceny and you have seen him alone. To-day even, your door was still shut; and to prevent my coming in upon you, your porter only lacked an assurance equal to your own. But you wrote me that I should be the first to be informed of your arrival, of this arrival whose date you could not tell me, though you wrote to me on the eve of your departure. Will you deny these facts or will you try to excuse yourself? (Letter 151).

Merteuil's response follows immediately in Letter 152, where she accuses Valmont of acting like a husband and reminds him obliquely of that great secret:

> Pray be careful, Vicomte, and treat my extreme timidity with more caution! How do you expect me to endure the crushing idea of incurring your indignation and, especially, not to succumb to the fear of your vengeance? The more so since, as you know, if you do anything cruel to me it would be impossible for me to revenge it! Whatever I said, your existence would not be less brilliant or less peaceful. After all, what would you have to fear? To be obliged to leave the country—if you were given time to do so! But do not people live abroad as they do here? After all, provided the Court of France left you in peace at the foreign court you resided at, it would only mean for you that you had changed the scene of your triumphs. After this attempt to make you cool again with these moral considerations, let me come back to our affairs.

Since the topic comes up at about the same time as Valmont's boasting of having impregnated Cécile, and since Merteuil hints that the Court of France would have an interest in Valmont should the secret come out, Henri Coulet (1982) suggests that the secret might impact the legitimacy of the royal line. Like Laclos, I shall ask the reader to be patient, as I must defer the explanation of this secret's importance until later.

Just as a secret depends on the absence of information, the "editor" also asserts in a footnote appended to Letter 7 that he has chosen to delete whole letters that are of little interest because they add no information to the central intrigue or because they repeat events already described in another letter. Since that sort of repetition might provide independent verification of a character's testimony, its absence is an important clue to the letter writer's veracity. The calculated absence of exactly this sort of outside confirmation is a primary invitation to doubt that Merteuil's libertine escapades really happened.

This decision on the part of the editor to eliminate confirmation through repetition is particularly striking because, despite his flagging the practice through several footnotes, he does not always do it. Valmont's charity to the poor family is described by him as well as by Tourvel (Letters 21 and 22). Likewise, Valmont and Cécile both describe their playing post office at Mme de Rosamonde's house (Letters 76 and 77) and their first night of love (Letters 96 and 97), and Mme de Tourvel's seeing Emilie with Valmont at the Opéra is discussed in several letters (Letters 135, 136, 137, and 138) written by Tourvel and the Vicomte. While these repetitions are designed to foreground Valmont's hypocrisy, on the one hand, and the women's naiveté, on the other, and make the discovery of truth truly a subjective issue, these repeated letters are still simple confirmation that the events that the writers describe actually occurred, and thus establish their veracity as reporters.

We do not have this type of "stereoscopic vision," to use Todorov's term, in the case of Merteuil's love affairs with Belleroche and Prévan. While Belleroche is mentioned briefly in several of Merteuil's letters to Valmont, it is the story that she tells in Letter 10 that serves as a snare to catch Valmont. In that letter, she rehearses a night of love in her *petite maison d'amour* with the Chevalier, whom she describes as a friend of Valmont. The story is told in immense detail: the elaborate plans, the circuitous route that Belleroche follows to find her, the costume that she wears "of my own invention; it lets nothing be seen and yet allows everything to be guessed at":

> He arrives at last; and surprise and love positively enchant him. To give him time to recover we take a turn in the shrubbery; then I bring him back to the house. He sees a table laid for two and a bed made up: we then go to the boudoir, which has all its decorations displayed. There, half out of premeditation, half from sentiment, I threw my arms around him and fell at his knees. "To prepare you the surprise of this moment," I said, "I reproach myself for having troubled you with an appearance of ill-humour, with having veiled for an instant my heart from your gaze. Forgive these faults, I will expiate them by my love." You may imagine the effect of that sentimental discourse. The happy Chevalier raised me and my pardon was sealed on the same ottoman upon which you and I so gaily and in the same way sealed our eternal separation.

Here a key quality of Merteuil's style can be seen: she appeals to the reader's (Valmont's) previous knowledge of her behavior as a point of verification. She insists that her reader fill in the blanks in her description from his own

experience, not only of her but of the proper conduct of a seduction. Since Valmont does not question her, we do not either.

She uses the same tactic in Letter 85, which describes her seduction of Prévan:

> How convenient it is to have to deal with you "men of principles"! Sometimes a bungling lover disconcerts one by his timidity or embarrasses one by his passionate raptures; it is a fever which, like others, has its cold shiverings and its burning, and sometimes varies in its symptoms. But it is so easy to guess your prearranged advance! The arrival, the bearing, the tone, the remarks—I knew what they would all be the evening before. I shall therefore not tell you our conversation which you will easily supply.

By this tactic she also accomplishes another goal: by linking her supposedly successful seduction of Prévan to Valmont's not-so-successful pursuit of Tourvel, Merteuil can present herself as an object lesson for the recalcitrant Vicomte. But this grounding of a present narration on a previous experience, while apparently conforming to scientific procedures, implies a stability of circumstances and variables that may not indeed apply.

The bare facts of the encounter with Prévan may be deduced by comparing the contents of Letter 85, which Merteuil writes to Valmont, and Letter 87, which she writes to Mme de Volanges: as she says at the end of Letter 85, "You owe this long letter to my solitude. I shall write one to Madame de Volanges [Letter 87], who will surely read it in public, and you will see how the story ought to be told." In its published form the story is that Prévan secreted himself in the Marquise's boudoir and revealed himself only after her servants had departed for the night. They returned at her outcry and captured Prévan, who was arrested. The story that she tells Valmont in Letter 85 is much more elaborate: how she arranges to sit near him at dinner and at the theatre, how she invites him to her house for dinner and tells him how to enter her room secretly, all without ever being alone with him. Finally,

> Can you see me, Vicomte, in my light toilette, walking timidly and carefully, and opening the door to my conqueror with trembling hand? He saw me—a flash is not quicker. How shall I tell you? I was overcome, completely overcome, before I could say a word to stop him or to defend myself. He then wished to put himself into a more comfortable situation, more suitable to the circumstances. He cursed his clothes which, he said, kept him at a distance from me; he wished to combat me with equal weapons, but my extreme timidity opposed this plan and my tender caresses did not leave him time for it. He busied himself with other matters. (L. 85)

The wealth of details that she uses to embroider her story should not blind us to the possibility that she is writing a fiction. While waiting for Belleroche's arrival, as she describes in Letter 10, Merteuil "read a chapter of the *Sopha,* a letter of *Héloïse* and two tales of *La Fontaine,* to rehearse the different tones I desired to take." In other words, Merteuil is a reader of novels and is self-consciously preoccupied with her own creation and self-presentation, aware of the power of the detail to create a response in her readers. Moreover, as she makes clear, there are no witnesses.

Merteuil's manipulation of the letter's power to persuade may be one reason why she herself is so unconvinced by what she reads. Versini notes that "in the period of Laclos, the epistolary novel enters an 'era of suspicion.' Laclos himself installs in the interior of his novel a debate between the partisans of letters, Danceny and Valmont, and their adversary, Mme de Merteuil" (1962, 266; my translation). Danceny and Valmont view the letter as a vehicle for the effective conveyance of feelings, real or counterfeit. Merteuil, on the other hand, has a more skeptical relationship to language than they do. She notes that the major fault of novels is that "the author lashes his sides to warm himself up, but the reader remains cold" (L. 33). This limitation on language's ability to achieve an emotional response from its reader leads Merteuil to assert several times that she does not believe in the letter's powers to seduce. "It is not only out of prudence that the marquise never writes," as she says in Letter 81, "it is because she does not have confidence in such an indirect method" (Versini 1962, 265; my translation). Her reservations may also be founded on her own experience of how easy it is to lie through letters.

Most important, despite the apparent verisimilitude of Merteuil's account, the key confirmative strategy used in the novel is lacking in both the Belleroche and Prévan episodes: while Valmont's activities are independently confirmed by other letter-writers, Merteuil's are not. Neither of her putative lovers writes to his mistress (or anyone else). Letter 86, the odd enclosure from the Maréchale de **** that Merteuil sends to Valmont along with her Letter 85, describing her entrapment of Prévan, seems at first to confirm the events that Merteuil describes, but it contains the telling phrase, "if what I am told is true." In the absence of a confirming letter from another source, Letter 85 might be reread as a tale of Potiphar's wife in which the younger man is surprised by the appearance of an older woman in a "light toilette" and incurs her wrath by attempting to flee.

Merteuil's relationship with Danceny needs special treatment since we learn of it through Valmont as well as from the letters exchanged by the Marquise and the young Chevalier. While clearly not created out of whole cloth, as the earlier episodes with Belleroche and Prévan may be,

the nature of Merteuil and Danceny's relationship is still open to question. Once Merteuil's earlier affairs with Belleroche and Prévan are cast into doubt, the letters that Merteuil receives from Danceny may be reread as a case of less there than meets the eye. Friendship, not love, is the theme in the majority of them. Merteuil even waits over a month between letters to him (Letters 121 and 146), and the tone of Letter 146 is somewhat sulky and insecure: "When the heroine [Cécile] is on the stage nobody cares about the confidante . . . Good-bye, Chevalier; it will be a great delight to me to see you again; will you come?" The circumspection with which Merteuil makes her arrangements with Prévan, as described in Letter 85 ("Notice that the affair had been arranged and that nobody had yet seen Prévan alone with me"), makes her explicit invitation to Danceny unlikely to be a seducer's gambit. Danceny responds with the excessive enthusiasm of youth in Letter 148—"O you whom I love! you whom I adore!"—apparently frightening Merteuil so badly that, as he says in Letter 150, she breaks off the correspondence. Merteuil literally disappears from the novel, in the sense that she stops writing letters, after Valmont has ruined her affair with Danceny, not, as one might expect, by revealing her duplicity, but by teasing Danceny, by making fun of Merteuil, and by reminding him of his love for Cécile: "You have a rendezvous for tonight, have you not? With a charming woman whom you adore? For at your age, what woman does one not adore, at least for the first week! The setting of the scene will add even more to your pleasures. A 'delicious little house,' 'which has only been taken for you,' will embellish the pleasure with the charms of liberty and of mystery" (Letter 155; note that Valmont is rather cattily quoting from Letter 10 in which Merteuil's night with Belleroche is described). By Letter 157, Danceny is writing to Valmont that he has only loved Cécile and will break off his relationship with Merteuil, about which Valmont has teased him.

Once the possibility is admitted that Merteuil has lied to Valmont about her amorous conquests, or has at least recast them in a golden glow of rococo embellishment, one becomes curious to know why lying is necessary. Is Merteuil simply a pathological liar to whom mendacity is as mother's milk? What does she have to gain by lying to Valmont?

Patrick Byrne (1989) has suggested that in Letter 131 above all, where she confesses that she once loved Valmont and was truly happy, but in other places as well, Merteuil is lying, and Valmont's Achilles heel—his vanity—keeps him from seeing it. According to Byrne, Valmont's mistake was in imagining that she did indeed still love him, and that her jealousy of Tourvel was personal and therefore amenable to cajolery and flattery. Byrne argues, however, that Merteuil's motive for lying is her obsession with Gercourt, the absent fiancé of Cécile, who broke off with her a long time ago, and who Byrne contends remains the true object of her love.

I suggest, on the other hand, that Merteuil lies to Valmont for reasons that have more to do with herself than with him or any other man. My argument is again based on the *absence* of information within the text. I suggest that Merteuil has to lie about her powers of seduction because they are in the process of waning. She is, in fact, at that transition point in her life that every attractive woman dreads, at that point which Merteuil herself describes so bitterly, when a woman's beauty has faded but her sexual desires have not: as she says in Letter 113, "It is not true that 'the older women are, the more harsh and severe they become.' It is between forty and fifty that the despair of seeing their beauty fade, the rage of feeling themselves obliged to abandon the pretensions and the pleasures to which they still cling, make almost all women disdainfully prudish and crabbed." While Merteuil goes on to describe the two possible results of "that great sacrifice"—a Mme de Volanges-like "imbecile apathy," on the one hand, versus becoming a woman of real character who shifts her attentions from her body to her mind and who is likely to represent Merteuil's own ideal for a postmenopausal self—it is nonetheless likely that, forced to face this transition herself, she is unwilling to admit that she is becoming too old to play the game for real. She is jealous of Tourvel and Cécile, not because they are loved—she wants Valmont as little as she wants Danceny—but because they are young.

The relative absence in the epistolary novel of passages that describe the characters for the reader opens the door for speculation about their appearance. What references do we find to the characters' ages in *Les Liaisons dangereuses*? In Letter 2, Merteuil asks Valmont irritably, "What can you be doing with an old aunt whose property is entailed on you?," a comment that seems to indicate a belief that older women have nothing to offer a man besides wealth and, since Valmont is already assured of that, there is no reason for him to seek Mme de Rosamonde's society. In Letter 2, Merteuil also describes Cécile as "only fifteen; a rosebud." In Letter 5 to Valmont, Merteuil explicitly gives Tourvel's age as well: "Perhaps if you had known this woman sooner you might have made something of her; but she is twenty-two and has been married nearly two years." Although age is not solely Merteuil's obsession—in Letter 8, for example, Tourvel gives Mme de Rosamonde's age as eighty-eight, and in Letter 39, Cécile says that Gercourt is old, "at least thirty-six"—it is striking that, when ages for the other women in Valmont's circle are given in such precise detail, Merteuil's age is not mentioned at all. The only reference to her appearance (until the denouement) that is not made by a man is made in Letter 14—"I can see that all the men think that she is prettier than I am"—but that is in a letter by Cécile, a naive young girl who thought that her shoemaker was a suitor. Although a minor detail, the explicit absence of description turns into a major question when one decides not to take the text at "face value." In fact, as Henri Coulet (1982) has pointed out, the primary emotion represented by the letters of *Les Liaisons dangereuses* may be narcissism rather than hypocrisy, since eighty of the 166 letters in the collection go unanswered.

The engines of Merteuil's vengeance begin grinding when Valmont refuses to come running when she whistles. It must be especially grating for her when he writes, in Letter 6, "I thought my heart withered up and, . . . I pitied myself for a premature old age. Madame de Tourvel has given me back the charming illusions of youth." Denied such consolations herself, since society always equates December with the man and May with the woman, Merteuil repeats the phrase "illusions of youth" in Letter 10, italicizing it for emphasis and in scornful recognition of the ease with which men manage to secure for themselves the comforts of love regardless of their actual age. It cannot be an accident that her first great fiction, the night with Belleroche in her *petite maison d'amour* is appended to that very letter.

Valmont responds to her description of her seduction of Belleroche in Letter 15:

> Come, my fair friend, as long as you share yourself between several, I am not in the least jealous; I simply see your lovers as the successors of Alexander, incapable of holding among them all that empire where I reigned alone. But that you should give yourself entirely to one of them! That there should exist another man as happy as I! I will not endure it; do not think that I will endure it. Either take me back or at least take someone else as well; and do not let an exclusive caprice betray the inviolable friendship we have sworn each other.

Merteuil responds to his apparent desire for her by proposing the famous wager in Letter 20: "As soon as you have had your fair devotée [Tourvel], and can furnish me with a proof, come, and I am yours."

The wager that she makes with Valmont in Letter 20 depends on her desirability. Since it has been a long time since they were lovers (the editor's footnote to Letter 2 tells us that Merteuil and Valmont's affair occurred "*much earlier* than the events dealt with in these letters" [my italics]), and since Merteuil takes great pains to keep from meeting Valmont when he does return to Paris, a suspicious mind might wonder what she has to hide. If what she is hiding are the early ravages of age, her wager would be an empty one unless she believes that the Belleroche and Prévan episodes could convince Valmont that she was still a worthy trophy for him. The only time when they do meet, however, when Valmont discovers Danceny at the

Marquise's house, Valmont hardly acts like a jealous lover and is more interested in embarrassing Danceny than in laying claim to Merteuil as his trophy.

The importance of this "reward" to Valmont has been overstated by many critics. In fact, he does not mention it again until Letter 57, and then not in the context of his winning of Tourvel, or of his desire for Merteuil, but in the context of Merteuil's being unfaithful to Belleroche. Clearly, far from being overcome with desire, he resists her attempt to appropriate his project, to transform him from actor to agent. The contract comes up again in Letter 99, written at the moment of his greatest confidence of success—the night before Tourvel absconds from Mme de Rosamonde's estate—and again the "reward" is phrased in terms of "this infidelity to your chevalier."

Valmont apparently is willing to go along with Merteuil's increasingly fictional self-presentation, up to a certain point. He flatters her and, possibly with his tongue in his cheek, warns her about Prévan, perhaps to distract her from his attachment to Tourvel. Why, then, does possession of her become such a desperate thing after the breakup with Tourvel? The traditional interpretation is the psychological reading of Valmont's behavior: his guilt about breaking Tourvel's heart requires the legitimation of Merteuil as a reward. Merteuil's refusal of that reward motivates Valmont's betrayal of Merteuil and allows us to see it as justified.

There are two other possible explanations for this change in Valmont's attitude toward Merteuil. First, the great secret referred to in Letter 81 and again in Letter 152 may be motive enough to keep on Merteuil's good side, since its revelation would lead to Valmont's imprisonment or exile. The editor's footnote to Letter 81 seems to underscore this option. Another possibility is offered by Peggy Kamuf. She describes the meeting between Merteuil and Valmont, as expressed in Letter 151, as "an interim between two points of arrival, two projects of seduction, two women" (1982, 128). Since Valmont has broken with Tourvel, but has not yet received his reward from Merteuil, he is apparently in some sort of social limbo. Valmont's desperation to receive this reward even though he, more than anyone, knows how shopworn the goods are, brings up the interesting possibility that, in this society, *both* men and women needed attachments to be socially valuable. Without an active relationship, a male is highly vulnerable since his exploits must be publicized in order to be credited in the sexual economy governing this society.

To look for Merteuil's motives, one needs to return to Letter 81, that anomalous confessional whose danger to Merteuil is realized in its eventual publication by Danceny.

Letter 81 is Merteuil's look back at her conscious self-creation. It is a gesture much more appropriate as a retrospective, made by a woman looking back on her career at the end of her active life. Merteuil has become frustrated at her inability to control Valmont, which has forced her to admit to herself the truth about her fading powers. She now faces an arena in the salon rather than in the boudoir. While power may still be exercised in the salon, it is of a different order, and the satisfactions less personal and immediate, than those obtainable through active sexuality. As Madelyn Gutwirth has said,

> Voltaire could speak with malignity of "the societies where some woman always presides who, in the decline of her beauty, makes the halo of her spirit shine instead." . . . A salon in the eighteenth century is a little court presided over by a woman at least a little mature. . . . She can reign with a strict discipline, showing to her familiars the affectionate and tyrannical solicitude of a mother. (1980, 258; my translation)

At the time when Merteuil writes letter 81, being a *salonière* is the best that she can hope for. She will be able to observe the intrigues of others and gossip about them, but participate in none on her own behalf. Since she already behaves throughout the novel as an observer rather than as a participant, there is a certain irony in her struggle to resist her fate. Instead of accepting the fact that she will be trusted by her society because her appearance and her reality are finally about to match, Merteuil denies that her beauty has been dimmed by her years. Her disfigurement in the denouement, which has been described as simply egregious moralizing, may thus be read as the body's forceful return to her consciousness, from whence she has tried so hard to repress it.

In this reading of the novel, then, Mme de Volanges and Mme de Rosamonde have the last word, not because they are the blind eye of conventional society or the moral center of the novel, but because they have graciously made the transition to asexuality. The younger generation of sexually active women—Cécile, Tourvel, and Merteuil—are unable to do this and return to childhood, die, or live on in a hideously disfigured state neither in society nor out of it. Merteuil does not represent a proto-feminist ideal who struggles against the narrow confines that male power places on her activities, though she does do that; nor is she essentially a victim of male cruelty and selfishness, though she does suffer on that account; nor is she a sentimental romantic, pining away for her one true love, though she may do that, too. She represents instead a more universal female dilemma: every woman's inevitable confrontation with her own body, the final battle to stop time and age that no woman can win.

Notes

1. All quotes from *Les Liaisons dangereuses* have been taken from the translation by Richard Aldington (New York: Signet, 1962).

Works Cited

Altman, Janet Gurkin. *Epistolarity: Approaches to a Form.* Columbus: Ohio State University Press, 1982.

Barny, Roger. "Madame de Merteuil et la critique du libertinage." In *Dix-huitième Siècle: Revue annuelle,* vol. 15. Paris: Editions Garnier Frères, 1983.

Bloch, Jean. "Laclos and Women's Education." *French Studies* 38:2 (April 1984): 144-58.

Byrne, Patrick. "The Valmont-Merteuil Relationship: Coming to Terms with the Ambiguities of Laclos's Text." *Studies on Voltaire and the Eighteenth Century* 266 (1989): 373-409.

———. "The Moral of *Les Liaisons dangereuses:* A Review of the Arguments." *Essays in French Literature* 23 (November 1986): 1-18.

Conroy, Peter V., Jr. "Male Bonding and Female Isolation in Laclos's *Les Liaisons dangereuses.*" *Studies on Voltaire and the Eighteenth Century* 267 (1989): 253-71.

Coulet, Henri. "L'espace et le temps du libertinage dans *Les Liaisons dangereuses.*" In René Pomeau and Laurent Versini, eds., *Laclos et le libertinage.* Paris: Presses Universitaires de France, 1983. Pp. 177-89.

———. "Les lettres occultées des *Liaisons dangereuses.*" *Revue d'Histoire Littéraire de la France* 82:4 (July-August 1982): 600-14.

Coward, David. "Laclos Studies, 1968-1982." *Studies on Voltaire and the Eighteenth Century* 219 (1983): 289-330.

Diaconoff, Suellen. "Resistance and Retreat: A Laclosian Primer for Women." *University of Toronto Quarterly* 58:3 (Spring 1989): 391-408.

Duyfhuizen, Bernard. "Epistolary Narratives of Transmission and Transgression." *Comparative Literature* 37:1 (Winter 1985): 1-26.

Goulemot, Jean-Marie. "Le lecteur-voyeur et la mise en scène de l'imaginaire viril dans *Les Liaisons dangereuses.*" In René Pomeau and Laurent Versini, eds., *Laclos et le libertinage.* Paris: Presses Universitaires de France, 1983. Pp. 163-75.

Gutwirth, Madelyn. "Laclos and 'Le sexe': The Rack of Ambivalence." *Studies on Voltaire and the Eighteenth Century* 189 (1980): 247-96.

Jackson, Susan. "In Search of a Female Voice: *Les Liaisons dangereuses.*" In Elizabeth C. Goldsmith, ed., *Writing the Female Voice: Essays on Epistolary Literature.* Boston: Northeastern University Press, 1989. Pp. 154-71.

Jaton, Anne-Marie. *Le Corps de la liberté: Lecture de Laclos.* Vienna: Age d'Homme Karolinger, 1983a.

———."Libertinage féminin, libertinage dangereux." In René Pomeau and Laurent Versini, eds., *Laclos et le libertinage.* Paris: Presses Universitaires de France, 1983b. Pp. 151-62.

Jones, Shirley. "Literary and Philosophical Elements in *Les Liaisons dangereuses:* The Case of Merteuil." *French Studies* 38:2 (April 1984): 159-69.

Kamuf, Peggy. *Fictions of Feminine Desire: Disclosures of Heloise.* Lincoln: University of Nebraska Press, 1982.

Kavanagh, Thomas M. "Educating Women: Laclos and the Conduct of Sexuality." In Nancy Armstrong and Leonard Tennenhouse, eds., *The Ideology of Conduct: Essays on Literature and the History of Sexuality.* New York and London: Methuen, 1987. Pp. 142-59.

Laclos, Pierre Choderlos de. *Les Liaisons dangereuses, ou Lettres recueillies dans une Societé, et publiées pour l'instruction de quelques autres.* Paris: Flammarion, 1981.

———. *Les Liaisons dangereuses.* Trans. Richard Aldington. New York: Signet, 1962.

Meltzer, Françoise. "Laclos' Purloined Letters." *Critical Inquiry* 8:3 (Spring 1982): 515-30.

Miller, Nancy K. *The Heroine's Text: Readings in the French and English Novel, 1722-1782.* New York: Columbia University Press, 1980.

———. "Rereading as a Woman: The Body in Practice." *Poetics Today* 6:1-2 (1985): 291-99.

Mylne, Vivienne. "Le parler des personnages dans *Les Liaisons dangereuses.*" *Revue d'Histoire Littéraire de la France* 82:4 (July-August 1982): 575-87.

Rogers, Katharine M. "Creative Variation: *Clarissa* and *Les Liaisons dangereuses.*" *Comparative Literature* 38:1 (Winter 1986): 36-52.

Rosbottom. Ronald C. "Roman et secret: le cas des *Liaisons dangereuses.*" *Revue d'Histoire Littéraire de la France* 82:4 (July-August 1982): 588-99.

Roussel, Roy. *The Conversation of the Sexes: Seduction and Equality in Selected Seventeenth- and Eighteenth-Century Texts.* New York: Oxford University Press, 1986.

Rousset, Jean. *Forme et signification: Essais sur les structures littéraires de Corneille à Claudel.* Paris: Librairie José Corti, 1962.

Sedgwick, Eve Kosofsky. *Between Men: English Literature and Male Homosocial Desire.* New York: Columbia University Press, 1985.

Seylaz, Jean-Luc. "Les mots et la chose: sur l'emploi des mots 'amour' et 'aimer' chez Mme de Merteuil et Valmont." *Revue d'Histoire Littéraire de la France* 82:4 (July-August 1982): 559-74.

Stewart, Philip, and Therrien, Madeleine. "Aspects de texture verbale dans *Les Liaisons dangereuses.*" *Revue d'Histoire Littéraire de la France* 82:4 (July-August 1982): 547-58.

Todorov, Tzvetan. "Choderlos de Laclos et la théorie du récit." *Tel Quel* 27: (Autumn 1966): 17-28.

———. "The Discovery of Language: *Les Liaisons dangereuses* and *Adolphe*." Trans. Frances Chew. *Yale French Studies* 45 (1970): 113-26.

———. *Littérature et signification*. Paris: Librairie Larousse, 1967.

Versini, Laurent. *Laclos et la tradition: Essai sur les sources et la technique des* Liaisons dangereuses. Paris: Klincksieck, 1968.

Armine Kotin Mortimer (essay date 1996)

SOURCE: "Dialogues of the Deaf: The Failure of Consolation in *Les Liaisons dangereuses*," *MLN*, Vol. 111, No. 4, September, 1996, pp. 671-87.

[*In the essay below, Mortimer contends that Laclos's characters are denied consolation through misunderstandings that result from their communication by letter.*]

Auditory Voyeurs

Jacques the fatalist, lying with wounded knee on a poor peasant's bed, overhears his host and hostess in amorous embrace, then in testy disagreement over the charity she has shown him in spite of their poverty. All the more reason, protests the wife, not to produce a new child—and she is sure to become pregnant because "cela n'a jamais manqué quand l'oreille me démange après, et j'y sens une démangeaison comme jamais . . ." (*Jacques le fataliste*, 26). "Ton oreille ne sait ce qu'elle dit," says he—but in spite of his objection the metaphor lending speech to the ear eroticizes it, as she fully realizes: "Ne me touche pas! Laisse là mon oreille!" If, as the editors gravely note, the erotic connotations of the ear are a constant of libertine fictions, I think we have here one of the most inventive and beguiling versions of the sexual ear. The language itself conveys, by its rhythms and its strategies, the action it purports to hide in words that go on "behind" the paper, just as Jacques lies on the other side of a wall of paper. For we can easily read in the text how the couple take their pleasure three times, in Jacques's hearing. The first has already happened during "une assez courte pause" (25), before the dispute.[1] The second (after a short moralizing digression whose purpose is to tease the reader) doubles Jacques's cries of pain: "je m'écriai: Ah! le genou! . . . Et le mari s'écria: Ah! ma femme! . . . Et la femme s'écria: Ah! mon homme!" (27)—in all, rather noisier than the first (all ellipses are in the text). The third occurs when the woman protests that her ear is worse than ever because "cet homme qui est là" will have heard them: "Ah! L'oreille! Ah! L'oreille!" she cries, and her husband replies, again irrationally linking speech to the ear:

"L'oreille, l'oreille, cela est bien aisé à dire. . . ." Here the writing pretends still to hide what is happening:

> Je ne vous dirai point ce qui se passait entre eux, mais la femme après avoir répété l'oreille, l'oreille plusieurs fois de suite à voix basse et précipitée, finit par balbutier à syllabes interrompues l'or . . . eil . . . le, et à la suite de cette or . . . eil . . . le, je ne sais quoi qui joint au silence qui succéda, me fit imaginer que son mal d'oreille s'était appaisé d'une ou d'autre façon; il n'importe, cela me fit plaisir, et à elle donc? (27-28)

We receive this mediated communication via Jacques's praeteritio ("je ne vous dirai point," "je ne sais quoi") and feigned indifference ("d'une ou d'autre façon; il n'importe"): we would not be in a position to overhear this couple making love without Jacques's voluntary or involuntary listening. With his help, we become auditory *voyeurs*,[2] just as the husband and wife are (as Diderot's rhetoric takes pains to suggest) auditory *exhibitionists*, whose pleasure is augmented because somebody is listening.[3] In this article, I am looking at a text in which the reader is placed, like Jacques, in the position of the auditory voyeur and gets pleasure and meaning from an indirect listening.

Listening and hearing are not identical, but complementary. Yet these two activities are often confused and hence the verbs misused—they are loosely taken as synonymous, and they are sometimes spoken interchangeably with no serious loss to understanding. It will be crucial to keep in mind that to listen is not always to hear, and that hearing does not necessarily imply listening. It would further be a mistake to assume that hearing is a passive activity, and that only listening is active; on the contrary, a subject who hears may define himself as active, precisely because he hears, and the presumably active subject who listens may be doing so distractedly, not willfully. In sum, to listen is not necessarily to hear, and there is such a thing as hearing without listening. So much is fairly obvious, and hardly needs defending. What does stand to be developed, however, is the interpretation we may give to this complementary relationship of listening to hearing as literary functions.

I have in mind a most unusual affirmation of indirect listening, in which the duad listening/hearing reaches us via a charming comparison. Let us listen to Roland Barthes in a fragment called "Écoute" from his extended discourse on intertextuality, *Le Plaisir du texte*:

> Être avec qui on aime et penser à autre chose: c'est ainsi que j'ai les meilleures pensées, que j'invente le mieux ce qui est nécessaire à mon travail. De même pour le texte: il produit en moi le meilleur plaisir s'il parvient à se faire écouter indirectement; si, le lisant, je suis entraîné à souvent lever la tête, à entendre autre chose. Je ne suis pas nécessairement captivé par le

texte de plaisir; ce peut être un acte léger, complexe, ténu, presque étourdi: mouvement brusque de la tête, tel celui d'un oiseau qui n'entend rien de ce que nous écoutons, qui écoute ce que nous n'entendons pas. (*Le Plaisir du texte,* 41-42)

The bird—the text—may be listening to something we are unable to hear: a text we do not know, for instance. But the text, on the other hand, cannot possibly hear everything we are listening to as we read; in reading, we listen to something the text does not hear or understand—perhaps a later text. I have claimed that the terms in this fragment of *Le Plaisir du texte* pose the conditions of intertextuality, for I consider this passage a compelling though idiosyncratic definition. With the indirection of rhetoric, a double mediation of reading pleasure through listening and the movement of the bird's head, Barthes *performs* the pleasure he describes; his definition is "presque étourdi," and we are obliged to listen to it indirectly—perhaps incompletely, or even wrongly. In just such a way does the text have intertexts we may not have access to. At the same time, we bring our intertexts to the text, and the text cannot know of them—some of them.

Now what this has to do with how literary texts reach us in general lies in our acceptance of the generality of intertextuality (and thus, in part, the pertinence and usefulness of distinguishing this term from allusion, reference, sources, and the many other narrower entities or procedures that contribute to its qualities). Intertextuality understood at its broadest concerns the very conditions of the existence of texts; all texts exist in the textual universe, to which they contribute stars and galaxies, and from which they draw their spatial and temporal definition. Texts are made of other texts, are themselves the "entre-textes" of other texts.[4] Writing itself depends on and produces intertextuality. It follows that messages the text contains may or may not be heard. We can see that writing may seek to transmit a certain knowledge, but nothing insures that the writing will be received with the same meaning. This risk is inherent in referential writing. When in *Les Liaisons dangereuses* the two libertines are in agreement, we understand as well: "au moins, je parle à quelqu'un qui m'entend," says the vicomte to the marquise (227, letter 100).[5] Later Valmont will object, "vous avez pris le parti de ne pas entendre" (343, letter 153); the war that separates them only confirms how ill-founded their "entente" was, and how much our own understanding depends on an uncertain mediation.

This uncertain mediation of events by writing is the focus of this reading. When letters are misaddressed, received by the wrong person, written by someone other than the subject who says "I," we may speak of dialogues of the deaf and the role of the *accidental* in the narrative plot. The reader's understanding, in *Les Liaisons dangereuses,*

is mediated by this mis-understanding or "malentendu," this bad hearing. What I am looking at here, then, is properly scandalous: obstacles or stumbling blocks to direct communication. My purpose is to show that, although for the characters writing stumbles, for the reader the writing as event forces our attention onto the semiotic level at which realism occurs—and there it never stumbles.

IMPOSSIBLE CONSOLATION

The last word of *Les Liaisons dangereuses* is the verb "consoler": "Adieu, ma chère et digne amie; j'éprouve en ce moment que notre raison, déjà si insuffisante pour prévenir nos malheurs, l'est encore davantage pour nous en consoler" (379, letter 175). This last word belongs to Mme de Volanges, conforming to her structural role as worldly—if obtuse—observer of, rather than intimate actor in, the events that have been recounted in the letters, in spite of her daughter's significant part in them.[6] With such an assessment as a suitably strong, final guide, we may well ask why consolation is impossible for all who desire it, for all the letter-writing characters seek consolation, except Mme de Merteuil.[7] It is as if to write is to console oneself, to seek a reply that would console, to recount one's own consolations, or to propose one to another. Like the letters themselves, consolation is given and taken by writing, much the way the "voice" is given and taken in the *Heptaméron*. But the project of obtaining consolation is bound to fail, not only because different ears hear the word differently, or because their writing falls on deaf ears, or because the characters do not "hear ear to ear," as it were. The impossibility of consolation is also inscribed in the defective, limping network of letters that, in narrating experience, do so only imperfectly: always too much or too little, and always after the fact. As Henri Coulet concludes his fine account of occulted letters, "Tout ce qui est refusé au lecteur l'oblige à une lecture soupçonneuse, d'autant plus attentive que l'occultation est moins soulignée" (614). So extensive and numerous are the *faults* in the network that to tell them all would be to retell the entire tale, inventorying its scandals. One might call it convenient that on the mimetic level *Les Liaisons dangereuses* tells *scandalous* tales, the better to induce the reader into an awareness of the scandals of its semiosis: the *scandalon* that raises obstacles to smooth progress. While the letter-writers tell mimetic stories like analogues of the author, their writing radically subverts the relation between the thing told and writing. Hence, with the characters, we stumble over the impediments to consolation inscribed in the fact that the correspondence does not correspond to experience.

Yet the characters apparently write in the belief that their writing will take over from a defective reality. A striking and famous illustration of this belief, which has the merit of concision as well, can be found in Rousseau's *Confes-*

sions, in the concert recounted in Book IV in which his music is performed to the unrestrained derision of all present, including the musicians. This nevertheless evokes a consolation: "Les musiciens étouffaient de rire; les auditeurs ouvraient de grands yeux, et auraient bien voulu fermer les oreilles. . . . Pour ma consolation, j'entendais autour de moi les assistants se dire à leur oreille, ou plutôt à la mienne, l'un: Il n'y a rien là de supportable; un autre: Quelle musique enragée?" (165-66). The example interests me not only for Rousseau's bemusement but also for the insistence on ears, particularly the rhetorical device (what has been called "attelage" in French) that focalizes the impossible desire to close them and the indirection by which words reach Rousseau's ears, the "unintended, intended" hearer. We will see these very forces at play in the representations of letter-writing in *Les Liaisons dangereuses.* But if Rousseau *writes* this debacle, it is because a real consolation, not imaginary or rhetorical (in this case, ironic), flows from writing it, one that in fact mirrors the consolation of Rousseau's entire autobiographical project. For it is only at the moment that he realizes this project—that is, in this same passage from the *Confessions,* where we now hear the instance of composition—that he can write: "Pauvre Jean-Jacques, dans ce cruel moment tu n'espérais guère qu'un jour devant le Roi de France et toute sa cour tes sons exciteraient des murmures de surprise et d'applaudissement" (166). In the space of a few lines, a written consolation supplements the humiliation he had suffered in his youth, and it does so by invoking the future anterior of "un jour," a manipulation of time made possible only by writing. Both replacing (substituting for) the time of derision, or ironic consolation, and adding to (filling in) a lack of success, or real consolation, the writing wipes out the bad sounds: it closes our ears to the mimesis of humiliation and opens them to the semiosis of consolation. I take this writing as emblematic of what I wish to develop here.

Rousseau's writing does what the writer wants it to do—it is not defective. That would be the correspondents' consolation in *Les Liaisons dangereuses.* To be sure, "consoler" means to alleviate suffering (see for instance the article "Pain béni" in the *Encyclopédie,* written by Voltaire [138]), but by a deflection of language that is characteristic of libertine discourse, the "sufferings" to be alleviated, in this novel, are often sexual. Valmont, playing on the ambivalence of the word, imposes this second meaning; the sexual act is a consolation, and the "consolateurs" are the lovers taken by forsaken women (265, letter 115; 325, letter 144). It is a measure of his influence on Mme de Tourvel that she writes to Mme de Rosemonde, at the moment she escapes from Valmont's company at his aunt's country estate: "Condamnée . . . à n'oser ni me plaindre, ni le consoler" (230, letter 102), a usage in which we must read the sexual sense. It is further a measure of misunder-

standings in this novel that Mme de Rosemonde replies offering moral consolations: "réservez-vous au moins la consolation d'avoir combattu"; "je me réserve de vous soutenir et vous consoler autant qu'il sera en moi. Je ne soulagerai pas vos peines, mais je les partagerai" (232, letter 103). So much for her experience in love; Laclos no doubt sacrifices to the commonplace that an old woman no longer knows desire, in spite of her rose-colored worldliness. The marquise for her part finds it pleasing and amusing to "consoler pour et contre" (127)—both the apparently moral "ange consolateur" (128) of Mme de Volanges in her distress and the sexual seductress of her daughter, according to the scandalous letter 63: "je ne lui donnai d'abord que ces consolations gauches, qui augmentent plus les peines qu'elles ne les soulagent"; "Quand la belle désolée fut au lit, je me mis à la consoler de bonne foi" (128). Apparently "consoler pour" is meant to suggest the alleviation of moral suffering, while "consoler contre" would define the libertine's stance against society. Writing to Mme de Volanges, however, the marquise forbids herself the sexual sense of the word, and the vicomte de Valmont for his part knows how to lie adroitly to the présidente de Tourvel by feigning the moral register with which he is familiar: "Vous vous occupez de punir! et moi, je vous demande des consolations: non que je les mérite; mais parce qu'elles me sont nécessaires, et qu'elles ne peuvent me venir que de vous" (314). No surprise that moral consolation is not the same as the physical; in the enlightened context of "Reason," the sexual "suffering" to be alleviated can imitate moral ills, as it does in this sentence, only via duplicity or irony, and the letter full of double entendres that Valmont writes to the présidente while using the body of the courtisane Émilie as a desk (103-104, letter 48) is the striking emblem of this ironic doubling, typical of Valmont's prose.[8] Finally, in this hasty review of consolation's senses, the topos of the scoundrel punished, illustrated in eighteenth-century theater, would allow one man's suffering to bring consolation to others, but this effect, evoked in the last uses of the word, is exactly what is missing: "Je vois bien dans tout cela les méchants punis; mais je n'y trouve nulle consolation pour leurs malheureuses victimes" (376, letter 173).[9] Cécile, Danceny, Mme de Volanges, Mme de Rosemonde find no consolation in the chastisement of the rakes—on the contrary. Taken all together, these simple differences of definition indicate deeper ones, for which they prepare the terrain.

I propose, then, a principal motif: consolation sought for in the writing but rendered inaccessible by the misunderstandings of this same writing. In truth, so little one lends it an ear, this motif will hammer at our eardrums. Misunderstanding is everywhere; discord reigns. Absence being the condition of correspondence, we are well warned by this sentence of Valmont's: "C'est une chose inconcevable . . . comme aussitôt qu'on s'éloigne, on cesse facilement de s'entendre" (264). Since a letter must bridge a distance, which is measured by time, it happens that the temporal separation between the writing of one letter and the reception of its reply reproduces the disagreement between the values of the word consolation or of its application. Thus, as we saw, Mme de Rosemonde thinks she is consoling Mme de Tourvel by exposing Valmont as a libertine, hoping to apply the specific to her malady. She speaks of consolation in the moral sense, as that which promises her friend the "repos de votre conscience," which stems from her "courageuse résistance" and from her virtue (292). But Mme de Rosemonde does not know yet that Mme de Tourvel has just obtained a sexual consolation, and that she is perfectly lucid about the happiness that it brings her. To these letters that cross each other, to which answers are beside the point because they arrive after the reply, we can add those that are missing (indicated in a note by the "rédacteur"), or those that arrive at their destination by indirect routes.

Misunderstanding stems also from the particular status of the epistolary narrative. The multiplicity of writers proposes impediments; it is difficult to distinguish the lies from the truths because the actors who write and the events they describe are not translated before our eyes and ears by a narrative authority as in a non-epistolary narrative. The fragmentation of point of view generates the fragmentation of values. There is a kind of stereophony: two or several writings recount the same event, partially and usually with partiality; none of the characters knows everything. The written presents itself as a record of the spoken, or the mediation of the voice; but who is speaking, and who is listening? The letter is a written speaking, whose status as *graphie* or *phoné* is not certain. Dialogism cuts the voice from its origin. For the event to reach us, another writing has to take charge: a third party then recounts what happened, and this filling in of lacks is interposed between the fact and the receiver of the letter. The third tone is Laclos's; the voices one hears are always doubled by the author's, which often says what the writer of the letter does not hear or understand.

To illustrate, let me first consider what Ross Chambers called the "ingérence" of Valmont between Cécile and Danceny, then the letter of rupture that kills the présidente—which is a different kind of interference.[10]

Consolation, in Cécile's candid writing, connotes a charitable goodness that she seeks in Mme de Merteuil and that she would like to offer to Danceny. Reading Cécile's letters to Danceny, Valmont scolds that "ce n'était pas ainsi qu'elle consolerait son amant" (267, letter 115). Cécile will have understood "to relieve from suffering"; her guileless use of the word invokes only the idea of warm-heartedness toward one's neighbor: "Je voudrais

bien le consoler; mais je ne voudrais rien faire qui fût mal," she says, after receiving Danceny's first letter (45, letter 16). To inflect her toward a sexual understanding, which we may also call an "entente," Valmont dictates letter 117 hoping to "nourrir l'amour du jeune homme, par un espoir plus certain" (267). In this last use of the word "consoler" by Cécile, a voice speaks for her—but it is misheard. The tactic consists in suggesting to Danceny that the consolation he hopes for can be more than an alleviation of moral ills; Valmont insinuates a sexual act. Here is how this sounds, with the voice of Valmont speaking in Cécile's tongue: "Croyez-vous que je ne sache pas que ce que vous voulez est bien mal? Et pourtant, si j'ai déjà tant de peine à vous refuser de loin, que serait-ce donc si vous étiez là? Et puis, pour avoir voulu vous consoler un moment, je resterais affligée toute ma vie" (269).[11] In spite of the hand that holds the pen, the word takes on its sexual connotation. Furthermore, this reply that Valmont formulates for Cécile appears to correspond to Danceny's sexual desire, whereas the young man's language is in fact entirely conventional, and the consolation he speaks of is never sexual: "L'espoir que vous m'aviez donné de vous voir à cette campagne, je m'aperçois bien qu'il faut y renoncer. Je n'ai plus de consolation que celle de me persuader qu'en effet cela ne vous est pas possible" (268, letter 116). Cécile thinks to repel Danceny's insistent demands through her virtuous refusals ("ne me demandez plus une chose que j'ai de bonnes raisons pour ne pas faire" [270]). The "chose" insinuates itself into these very refusals.

Receiving this doubly focused letter, Danceny still refuses to hear a sexual consolation. He listens only to the protestations of honor and honesty that Valmont dictated for plausibility's sake, and he fails to hear the Valmont behind Cécile. The text written to transmit a message is belied by the receipt of this text with another message. The correspondence limps because there is, precisely, no correspondence between the request and the reply. Danceny follows Cécile's request to the letter—that is, exactly—and asks for nothing more in writing. He is, one could say, hearing something other than what he is listening to. When, at the end of the novel, Mme de Rosemonde advises Mme de Volanges to leave Cécile in her convent, she suggests that far from being the passive victim of a mundane seduction by Danceny, Cécile had made advances.

This dictated letter is the material trace of Valmont's entire sexual activity with Cécile: in it, he leaves, as it were, his semiotic seed, encoded in the double entendres. His interference in the writing of Cécile and Danceny, obviously emblematic of his replacing Danceny in love, will end with his death, with Cécile's and Danceny's deaths to the world, as they take their respective orders, and with the vanishing of any consolation.

When Valmont's seed flourishes, and Cécile becomes pregnant, she knows as little about it as she knows what consolations she was writing to Danceny. What informs her is an event the text calls an "accident" and an "événement imprévu": "Des maux de reins, de violentes coliques, des symptômes moins équivoques encore, m'ont eu bientôt éclairé sur son état: mais, pour le lui apprendre, il a fallu lui dire d'abord celui où elle était auparavant; car elle ne s'en doutait pas" (319, letter 140). Such an accident would not have occurred with Danceny, so that what is significant—the information in this noisy channel—is Valmont's mediation. By metonymy, the miscarriage stands for Cécile's loss of virginity. As an element of the plot, it appears as an accident, while the loss of virginity is the outcome of scheming and planning and so could not be called accidental *in the mimetic realm.* As an element of the writing, however, in the semiotic realm, the loss of virginity appears as an obstacle to consolation. This case of mishearing the nature of the consolation requested or denied shows Cécile entrapped in the semiotic web.

Unique among all is the letter the marquise writes to the vicomte transmitting, by a doubly or triply mediated route, a letter of death. This embedded letter is the one with the refrain "Ce n'est pas ma faute" (321-22, letter 141). Feigning to bury her jealous anger against Valmont ("Aussi je n'en veux absolument plus parler"), Merteuil invents a story in which the letter takes its place as a quotation. It is a fiction perhaps prompted by a sentence in a letter just received from Valmont: "non, je ne suis point amoureux; et ce n'est pas ma faute si les circonstances me forcent d'en jouer le rôle" (315, letter 138). In this fiction told by the marquise, "un homme de sa connaissance . . . passait ainsi sa vie, ne cessant de faire des sottises, et ne cessant de dire après: *Ce n'est pas ma faute*" (321); his "belle amie" sees that he gets a copy of a letter signifying the end of a relationship. Valmont understands perfectly that the marquise intends him to rewrite it for Mme de Tourvel, but this understanding or intelligence arrives by an indirect listening: "Ma foi, ma belle amie, je ne sais si j'ai mal lu ou mal entendu, et votre lettre, et l'histoire que vous m'y faites, et le petit modèle épistolaire qui y était compris" (323, letter 142). In spite of its drifting presentation, which Valmont underscores in his reply, the inserted letter is heard accurately because it is part of another narration that takes charge of the story. In this, it contradicts the general rule: nothing limps here. The narrative function guarantees a sure delivery and good reception.

Faithful to an ethic of understanding ("entente")—for Valmont better sustains agreement and understanding than the marquise, who refuses to hear and provokes the war—he pays enough attention to it "pour la bien entendre" (321). As a letter that seems to interpose itself between the event and writing, Valmont has only to copy it . . . to the letter, in order to understand it.[12] His reading of it would match

what Barthes called "une troisième aventure de la lecture," which is the adventure of writing, where reading is "conductrice du Désir d'écrire" ("Sur la lecture," 44-45). Since rewriting the letter sends the destinatee to her death (rather than to the impossible "consolateur" Valmont callously suggests), this is the only letter that is fully an act, the only one where the language is exactly the same thing as experience, where "la chose" and writing correspond perfectly.

The effect of this letter that kills, and of the correspondence in general, nevertheless cannot arrive to our hearing except by a mediation whose characteristics and consequences remain to be explained. Cécile speaks of a consolation that she does not recognize through the writing that Valmont lends her; Valmont borrows a writing whose origin is suspect and whose status is singular to telegraph death to the présidente. Never do we see the text of the letter of rupture addressed to Tourvel; it appears only in the marquise's letter in which it is inserted. The interference of Valmont between Cécile and Danceny and of the marquise between Valmont and the présidente has the same effect; in both cases, the source of the letter is not its apparent emitter, and its destinatee is double or more than double. The message only transits the letter-writer, whose listening is defective: Cécile cannot see her letter's hidden sense, and Valmont rewrites his letter with only a part of himself, the rake's copy. While he dreams of rekindling the présidente's love, the marquise is boasting of directing his blows against her: "quand une femme frappe dans le cur d'une autre, elle manque rarement de trouver l'endroit sensible, et la blessure est incurable" (328, letter 145). These effects of writing institute an inevitable dialogue of the deaf between the emitter of the text and its reader. But "dialogue of the deaf" does not mean that no one hears. The last letter by Mme de Tourvel fails to obtain the consolation it demands because it is without destinatee: "Toute consolation m'est refusée," she writes, in which the passive construction underscores the absence of address (354, letter 161). Aimed toward whoever receives it, this writing does not reach its goal, for who would reply? But it reaches the reader, ultimate destinatee, through the flux of its possible multiple receivers. Valmont copies the epistolary model in Merteuil's letter because he is listening to *another story* and hears his own: he wasn't listening, but he heard perfectly. Our hearing is analogous to his: we do just what causes Mme de Tourvel's downfall, when she admits: "je passe mon temps à *écouter* ce que je ne devrais pas *entendre*" (199, letter 90, emphasis added). Accepting the impossibility of consolation, we have to want to *listen badly* in order to *hear everything.* The text pushes us toward this bad listening, forcing us to engage in listening elsewhere, if we are to hear well.

When the author himself addresses the reader, through the address to the correspondent, what assures that we will lend an ear? What are the stakes of our listening, and what have we heard? Paul de Man formerly used the visual metaphor opposing "Blindness and Insight"; lucidity is the fruit of our sightlessness, for where we see not do we find knowledge. The auditory correspondent of this opposition, in French, is "le malentendu" and "l'entendement." That is to say, understanding comes to the reader precisely through the misunderstandings and accidents of the correspondents' writing, mishearings that trouble our listening. By this means does the reader hear well, on the condition of listening elsewhere, of accepting a drifting listening, of listening to disorder. For if "l'entendement," which is allied with Reason, is defective or insufficient among the correspondents, on the level of mimesis, it is assumed complete for the reader, on the level of semiosis. Perpetual misunderstanding, then, for the characters, but, through it, understanding for the readers.

The putative gathering of the entire correspondence in Mme de Rosemonde's hands figures this knowledge or insight, in the end. With an exemplary concern for verisimilitude, Laclos has his characters describe exactly, in their letters, the transmission routes by which each letter arrives there. I find an interesting parallel, in this painstaking effort to insure the letters reach the next level of hearing, with Marguerite de Navarre's insistence on the gift of the voice and the taking of "place" in the *Heptaméron*. Both are phatic strategies concerned to ensure the life of the narrative as well as its realism; that is, the care taken to maintain the channel of communication functions on the mimetic level for the characters in situation, and on the semiotic level for the reader. On the mimetic level, only Rosemonde might enjoy the possibility of knowing what everybody has written; to entomb the secret is then the only consolation that remains available to her. In asking Danceny for Cécile Volanges's letters, she begs him to concur in "la sûreté d'un secret, dont la publicité vous ferait tort à vous-même, et porterait la mort dans un cur maternel. . . . Enfin, Monsieur, . . . si je pouvais craindre que vous me refusassiez cette consolation, je vous demanderais de songer auparavant que c'est la seule que vous m'ayez laissée" (372). A page later she will say to Mme de Volanges that, "dans l'impuissance où je suis d'y joindre aucune consolation, la grâce qui me reste à vous demander, ma chère amie, est de ne plus m'interroger sur rien qui ait rapport à ces tristes événements; laissons-les dans l'oubli qui leur convient" (373), in which the impossibility of consolation is expressed by silence. From these papers piled high at Rosemonde's chateau, the real emitter, Laclos, posing as the "rédacteur," can now "extract" a novel, for our hearing. The novel we hear *includes* the gaps and other disturbances to completion and order. Our profit, as readers, is to receive a forfeit paid by the correspondents, who lost the game—a forfeit one could well call the payment of a consolation.

The "éditeur," who is not the "rédacteur," had projected another consolation for his readers—and it would perhaps be well to admit here that it is he who had the last word, in an appended note, and that Mme de Volanges's summative "adieu" is last only within the fiction of the letters. It is a constant in the eighteenth-century novel that the last words promise to continue it—the text leaves an open door, lays a stepping stone, figures a raised foot. Professing that "[d]es raisons particulières et des considérations que nous nous ferons toujours un devoir de respecter nous forcent de nous arrêter ici" (379), the editor thus provides a gloss on the word "consoler."[13] The note appears motivated by the need to explain the stopping point to which the letters have come—and to console the reader for the absent future. In postponing to an uncertain future time "la suite des aventures de mademoiselle de Volanges" and "les sinistres événements qui ont comblé les malheurs ou achevé la punition de madame de Merteuil," the editor terminates the tragedy "dans ce moment." Joan DeJean believes the note was written by the real *éditeur*, or publisher of the novel, Durand (255); as such, it would clearly mark an intention that the real author may not have been responsible for. Indeed, whatever the editor may have claimed, Laclos knew full well that the events of his novel come to a stop because there is no moral or physical consolation. There remains only a coffer enclosing the letters that we read, and in which we hear absent voices bequeathing to us this warning, "A bon entendeur, salut!"

And what exactly do we hear? In the story told by these letters, Reason fails, consolation is impossible, mishearings proliferate, but it would have been better for the characters if Reason reigned, if consolation were provided, if understanding were at hand—if, in sum, writing letters arranged the world properly. Such a desire for order, translated to the semiotic level, is the familiar task of the "rédacteur," to the extent that his claim to a work of Reason would consist in putting the heap of letters into logical and chronological order, making judicious selections, arraying them according to criteria of readability, adding necessary explanations in the notes—the tasks he outlines in the "Préface du rédacteur." A novel containing an intrigue, suspense, motivations, ironies, destinies can claim the generic status of an "ouvrage" or even a "roman," as the editor asserts in contrast to the repeated denials by the "rédacteur," who insists rather on the collection of the letters themselves (14-18). From the moment one takes up the pen, the marquise reminds us, one "arranges" words to make an "order" reign in writing that cannot plausibly imitate feelings; "le discours [parlé] moins suivi amène plus aisément cet air de trouble et de désordre qui est la véritable éloquence de l'amour" (73-74, letter 33). But letters in *Les Liaisons dangereuses* that pass to secondary or tertiary destinatees vehiculate messages that the writers did not put in them.[14] Accidental meanings are thereby available to the reader. Just as Reason is defective, and disorder and mishearing prevent the characters' understanding, our ears are forcibly tuned to how the writing invents disorder: anachronisms, holes, undeliverable letters, letters without destinatees, second, third, or other destinatees, secrets, jolts, mysteries, suppressed letters, interruptions, diversity of styles, abrupt cuts. It is precisely these limpings in the semiotic order that make the correspondence into a novel and that constitute its eloquence and even elegance, not the fashioning of an orderly world. Writing thus fulfills a lack or fault for us, when we recognize it as novel; it replaces experience, on condition we accept that semiotic practice or *significance,* the textual play by which a story reaches the reader, has meaning as much as the story does. Then writing is neither too much, nor too little, but just right, and that may well be a consolation.

LENDING AN EAR

"Lorsqu'on fait un conte, à quelqu'un qui l'écoute, et pour peu que le conte dure, il est rare que le conteur ne soit pas interrompu quelquefois par son auditeur."—*Ceci n'est pas un conte*

The crossing interferences of the messages contained in the letters of *Les Liaisons dangereuses* contribute to the disorder stemming from the failure of Reason. Yet in spite of disturbances to narrative authority and point of view, it remains largely a classical novel, unlike *Jacques le fataliste.* This is because it reserves a role for the real reader that is entirely compatible with the authors' role, that is parallel with it. (I say *authors* in the plural to accommodate Laclos, the "éditeur" and the "rédacteur.") For both roles, Reason's failure is necessary to writing. Laclos's strategy is to "entendre mal," so we may hear well by listening to the "malentendus." On our side, it is listening, whether indirect or mediated, that is "bad," but productive of good hearing. We are then like Diderot at the theater blocking his ears to "hear" via the gestures of the actors: "je répondis que chacun avoit sa façon d'écouter, & que la mienne étoit de me boucher les oreilles pour mieux entendre" (*Lettre sur les sourds et muets,* 53). Or we are in the listening utopia Barthes describes, the distracted psychoanalytic listening in its "lay" form, in the mediated communications of literature:

l'écoute inclut dans son champ, non seulement l'inconscient, au sens topique du terme, mais aussi, si l'on peut dire, ses formes laïques: *l'implicite, l'indirect, le supplémentaire, le retardé:* il y a ouverture de l'écoute à toutes les formes de polysémie, de surdéterminations, de superpositions, il y a effritement de la Loi qui prescrit l'écoute droite, unique . . . ("Écoute," 228-29; my emphasis)

Limping, stumbling dialogues make us listen "badly," in contravention to the law of direct listening, but it is at this price *to the characters* that we obtain our pleasure as readers. "Se faire écouter indirectement," Barthes had said in *Le plaisir du texte,* is how the text best procures the reader's pleasure. "Ton oreille ne sait ce qu'elle dit," Jacques's host had said. However:

JACQUES.—Vous croyez apparemment que les femmes qui ont une oreille comme la sienne écoutent volontiers?

LE MAITRE.—Je crois que cela est écrit là-haut.

JACQUES.—Je crois qu'il est écrit à la suite qu'elles n'écoutent pas longtemps le même, et qu'elles sont tant soit peu sujettes à prêter l'oreille à un autre. (28)

At the risk of refiring the smoldering *querelle des femmes,* I would suggest that although it is written up above that we may listen voluntarily, we are happy to lend an ear to another; we are hearing something else. Our eroticized ear seeks pleasure in unruly listening. Within its fictional, mimetic frames, *Les Liaisons dangereuses* figures this dynamic, which underlies all our reading of fiction, and so it puts forward for our attention and enjoyment the processes of its semiosis.

Notes

1. "Comment diable! vous qui êtes de la secte de Diderot et de la mienne, ne lisez-vous pas le blanc des ouvrages? Lisez le blanc, lisez ce que je n'ai pas écrit et qui y est pourtant." So said l'abbé Galiani to Suard, on September 8, 1770—sage advice for any reader of Diderot. The abbé is quoted by Eric Walter in *Colloque International Diderot (1713-1784),* 208.

2. Barthes wished for such a term: "on devrait pouvoir dire ici *écouteur* comme on dit voyeur"; see *S/Z,* 138. My student Charles Batson has astutely proposed *oyeur.*

3. A stimulating reading of this episode, and of listening in relation to *jouissance,* can be found in Jean Starobinski's contribution to the 1984 colloquium on Diderot, "Du pied de la favorite au genou de Jacques."

4. According to Barthes, in "De l'uvre au texte" (73), the text is "entièrement tissé de citations, de références, d'échos . . . qui le traversent de part en part dans une vaste stéréophonie. L'intertextuel dans lequel est pris tout texte, puisqu'il est lui-même l'entre-texte d'un autre texte, ne peut se confondre avec quelque origine du texte: rechercher les 'sources,' les 'influences' d'une uvre, c'est satisfaire au mythe de la filiation; les citations dont est fait un texte sont anonymes, irrepérables et cependant *déjà lues:* ce sont des citations sans guillemets."

5. I quote from the 1964 Garnier-Flammarion edition.

6. As Henri Coulet so deliciously puts it, "la sotte Mme de Volanges, seul personnage autorisé à conclure le roman" (610).

7. Only Prévan, who does not write, obtains a social consolation when the marquise's letters circulate in society. Joyce Lowrie has demonstrated the importance of Prévan as a mirror of Valmont, and of the Prévan episode as a reflection on the novel.

8. It is interesting that Valmont, in the midst of his sexual consolations during this brilliant act of writing deflected from experience, speaks no more of seeking consolation from Tourvel, but deplores instead her "rigueurs désolantes [qui] ne m'empêchent point de m'abandonner entièrement à l'amour et d'oublier, dans le délire qu'il me cause, le désespoir auquel vous me livrez" (103).

9. See for instance Jean-Baptiste Louis Gresset's play *Le Méchant* (1747); Mme de Merteuil quotes an alexandrine from this play in letter 63.

10. I am borrowing the term "ingérence" from Ross Chambers, who uses the French word (410). Like Chambers, I think that it leads necessarily to death.

11. Compare to this pretty little maxim couched in Valmont's own style: "car vous posséder et vous perdre, c'est acheter un moment de bonheur par une éternité de regrets" (267, letter 115). Laclos's stylistic mastery shows in the way the same sentiment can be expressed in these different tones, precisely in the context of the letter where Valmont explains that he dictated the letter to Danceny to console him.

12. As Jean Rousset (94) appropriately describes it, the rewriting is a real quotation of a fictive quotation.

13. According to Laurent Versini, the editor's note is not in Laclos's hand. See his edition of Laclos's *uvres complètes* (1411).

14. Peter V. Conroy groups these readers among the "hidden readers" (49-50).

Works Cited

Barthes, Roland. "Écoute." *L'Obvie et l'obtus.* Paris: Seuil, 1982. 217-30.

——. "De l'uvre au texte." *Le Bruissement de la langue.* Paris: Seuil 1984. 69-77.

——. *Le Plaisir du texte.* Paris: Seuil, 1973.

——. "Sur la lecture." *Le Bruissement de la langue.* Paris: Seuil, 1984. 37-47.

——. *S/Z.* Paris: Seuil, 1970.

Chambers, Ross. "Reading and the Voice of Death: Balzac's 'Le Message.'" *Nineteenth-Century French Studies* 18 (1990): 408-423.

Colloque International Diderot (1713-1784). Ed. Anne-Marie Chouillet. Paris: Aux Amateurs de Livres, 1985.

Conroy, Peter V. *Intimate, Intrusive and Triumphant: Readers in the* Liaisons Dangereuses. Amsterdam: John Benjamins, 1987.

Coulet, Henri. "Les Lettres occultées des 'Liaisons dangereuses.'" *Revue d'Histoire Littéraire de la France* 82 (1982): 600-614.

DeJean, Joan. *Literary Fortifications: Rousseau, Laclos, Sade.* Princeton: Princeton UP, 1984.

Diderot, Denis. *Jacques le fataliste et son maître.* TLF 230. Ed. Simone Lecointre and Jean Le Galliot. Genève: Droz, 1976.

——. *Lettre sur les sourds et muets. Diderot Studies* 7 (1965): 1-232.

——. *L'Encyclopédie.* Paris: Bordas, 1967.

Laclos, Choderlos de. *Les Liaisons dangereuses.* Paris: Garnier-Flammarion, 1964.

——. uvres complètes. Ed. Laurent Versini. Paris: Gallimard [Pléiade], 1979.

Lowrie, Joyce O. "Pretexts and Reflections: A Reflection upon Pre-Texts in *Les Liaisons dangereuses.*" *Modern Language Studies* 18 (1988): 150-64.

Mortimer, Armine Kotin. *The Gentlest Law: Roland Barthes's* The Pleasure of the Text. New York: Peter Lang, 1989.

Rousseau, Jean-Jacques. *Les Confessions.* Ed. Jacques Voisine. Paris: Garnier, 1964.

Rousset, Jean. "Les Lecteurs indiscrets." *Laclos et le libertinage. 1782-1982. Actes du Colloque du bicentenaire des Liaisons dangereuses.* Paris: PUF, 1983. 89-96.

Starobinski, Jean. "Du pied de la favorite au genou de Jacques." *Colloque International Diderot (1713-1784).* Ed. Anne-Marie Chouillet. Paris: Aux Amateurs de Livres, 1985. 359-80.

FURTHER READING

Criticism

Birkett, Jennifer. "*Dangereuses liaisons:* Literary and Political Form in Choderlos de Laclos." *Literature and History* 8, No. 1 (Spring 1982): 82-94.

    Examines the political and social conflict found both in Laclos's fiction and his political activities.

Byrne, Patrick. "The Valmont-Merteuil Relationship: Coming to Terms with the Ambiguities of Laclos's Text." *Studies on Voltaire and the Eighteenth Century,* No. 266 (1989): 373-409.

    Proposes an interpretation of the relationship between Valmont and Merteuil.

Coward, D. A. "Laclos and the Dénouement of the *Liaisons dangereuses.*" *Eighteenth-Century Studies* 5, No. 3 (Spring 1972): 431-49.

> Discusses the novel's literary importance relative to other French novels of the period and remarks on the thematic meaning of the final letters.

———. "Laclos Studies, 1968-82." *Studies on Voltaire and the Eighteenth Century,* No. 219 (1983): 289-328.

> Provides an overview of scholarship on *Les Liaisons dangereuses.*

Jones, Shirley. "Literary and Philosophical Elements in *Les Liaisons dangereuses:* The Case of Merteuil." *French Studies* XXXVIII, No. 2 (April 1984): 159-69.

> Argues that while there is a strong link between *Les Liaisons dangereuses* and Laclos's earlier philosophical writings, the novel differs in that it is a piece of literature.

Lowrie, Joyce O. "Pretexts and Reflections: A Reflection upon Pre-Texts in *Les Liaisons dangereuses.*" *Modern Language Studies* XVIII, No. 1 (Winter 1988): 150-64.

> Analyzes the novel's structure, arguing that its self-referential symmetry is negated by the plot.

Minogue, Valerie. "*Les Liaisons dangereuses:* A Practical Lesson in the Art of Seduction." *The Modern Language Review* 67, No. 4 (October 1972): 775-86.

> Argues that the impact of the novel lies in the reader's identification with the seducers and their sense of shame at the novel's end.

Palka, Keith A. "The Workings of Chance in *Les Liaisons dangereuses.*" *Rackham Literary Studies,* No. 5 (1974): 47-71.

> Examines Laclos's use of chance events and their meaning in the novel.

Preston, John. "*Les Liaisons dangereuses:* Epistolary Narrative and Moral Discovery." *French Studies* XXIV, No. 1 (January 1970): 23-36.

> Analyzes Laclos's use of the epistolary form to convey his moral message.

Roussel, Roy. "The Project of Seduction and the Equality of the Sexes in *Les Liaisons dangereuses.*" *MLN* 96, No. 4 (May 1981): 725-45.

> Explores the relationship between seduction and notions of convention in *Les Liaisons dangereuses.*

Lydia (Howard Huntley) Sigourney
1791-1865

American poet, sketch writer, essayist, novelist, and travel writer. For additional information on Sigourney's life and works, see *NCLC,* Volume 21.

INTRODUCTION

Known as "the sweet singer of Hartford," Sigourney was one of America's most popular poets during the first half of the nineteenth century. Her celebration of religious and patriotic values, talent for writing commemorative poetry, and reputation for moral integrity strongly appealed to her contemporary public. A prolific author, Sigourney contributed widely to magazines and published numerous volumes of her work, becoming one of the first women in the United States to establish a successful and remunerative career as a writer.

BIOGRAPHICAL INFORMATION

Sigourney was born in Norwich, Connecticut, the only daughter of Sophia Wentworth Huntley and Ezekiel Huntley, a gardener in the employ of a wealthy matron, Mrs. Daniel Lathrop. Encouraged by both her mother and Mrs. Lathrop to read and write at an early age, Sigourney received her primary education from local schools. She later paid tribute to the influential guidance of her father's employer in her fictional *Sketch of Connecticut, Forty Years Since* (1824) and in her autobiography, *Letters of Life* (1866). Determined to become a teacher and aid her parents financially, Sigourney went on to supplement her early education by studying at a Hartford school. Subsequently, she opened schools for young ladies in Norwich and Hartford; after the failure of the school in Norwich, Sigourney established the Hartford school, in which, instead of teaching such traditionally "feminine" subjects as art and needlework, she instructed young women in reading, arithmetic, rhetoric, natural and moral philosophy, and history.

In 1815, she published her first book, *Moral Pieces, in Prose and Verse,* to critical acclaim. Encouraged by this positive reception, Sigourney continued to write. However, when in 1819 she married Charles Sigourney, a Hartford hardware merchant who disapproved of her writing career, she modified her literary aspirations by publishing anonymously and under pseudonyms. During the early

years of their marriage, she not only published books but also contributed poems and prose pieces to over twenty periodicals, using the proceeds to aid her parents and support such charities as war relief, temperance movements, and missionary work. In 1833, Sigourney published *Letters to Young Ladies,* one of her most popular works. Prompted by its success and an increasing need for money, Sigourney allowed her name to be placed on later editions of the book, despite her husband's objections. The popularity of this volume created new demand for her work, and, by 1839, she was able to support her household by writings published under her own name.

As her reputation grew, Sigourney was able to sustain the family with her writing and editorial work. She edited the annual *Religious Souvenir* in 1838 and 1839, and from 1839 to 1842 she is listed as an editor of *Godey's Lady's Book,* primarily for the prestige her name conferred on the journal. A prolific contributor to periodicals as well as to annuals and gift books, Sigourney became familiar to a broad range of the reading public, reissuing much of her magazine verse in numerous collections and editions. By the early 1840s, her popularity was so great that magazine editors vied for her contributions. In 1841, Edgar Allan Poe, then editor of *Graham's Magazine,* requested material for the journal, and the editor of the competing *Godey's Lady's Book* paid her—purportedly five hundred dollars a year—for exclusive use of her name on the title page. Her prestige as a writer was established, and on a tour of England she visited such figures as William Wordsworth, Joanna Baillie, Samuel Rogers, Thomas Carlyle, and Maria Edgeworth; Sigourney would later recount these travels in *Pleasant Memories of Pleasant Lands* (1842). Sigourney reached the height of her popularity in the late 1840s with the publication of *Illustrated Poems* (1849), a lavish edition issued in a series that included the works of William Cullen Bryant and Henry Wadsworth Longfellow. A national figure, she was often courted by dignitaries and literary celebrities, and her works were anthologized in many collections of American prose and poetry. During the last years of her life, Sigourney composed few new writings, choosing instead to reissue retitled versions of earlier volumes. She died at her Hartford home in 1865, after having prepared her autobiography, which was published the following year.

MAJOR WORKS

A prolific author, Sigourney produced more than sixty-five books and several thousand articles that appeared in such periodicals as the *North American Review, Graham's Magazine,* and the *Southern Literary Messenger.* Although Sigourney also produced a number of prose works, including writings on history, biography, a novel, sketches, essays, and an autobiography, she was primarily recognized for her poetry, most of which was first introduced to the public in periodicals, then collected in her books. Her first published volume, *Moral Pieces, in Prose and Verse,* was drawn from the poems and prose that she composed for her students and was, by and large, received enthusiastically by her contemporaries. The book is filled with the sentimental verse, moralistic tone, and fondness for the so-called graveyard school of poetry that characterize most of her writings; many critics contend that the subjects of her verse—death, religion, and history—never changed. In this and later works such as *Poems* (1827), *Pocahontas, and Other Poems* (1841), and *Poetry for Seamen* (1845), her best-loved poems commemorated the deaths of both famous and unknown persons, especially young children; indeed, the three-hundred-page *Zinzendorff, and Other Poems* (1835) consists almost entirely of funereal verse. Such eulogistic poems as "'Twas but a Babe" and "The Faithful Editor" were admired for their sentimentality and elaborate, euphemistic language, but also their honesty in coming to terms with personal tragedy.

CRITICAL RECEPTION

Despite Sigourney's widespread popularity, critical reception of her works has often been unfavorable. During her lifetime, reviewers acknowledged her skill with blank verse and language, but found little original thought in her writing. For example, in a review of her *Zinzendorff, and Other Poems,* Poe labeled her work imitative of the work of Felicia Hemans; he did concede that "many passages are very noble and breathe the truest spirit of the Muse," however, and, bending to the force of her popularity, Poe would later retract the charge and solicit work from her for *Graham's Magazine.* At the height of her popularity in June, 1850, the *Western Literary Messenger* declared: "[Her poems are] laid on a million of memory's shelves. Children in our infant schools lisp her mellow canzonets; older youths recite her poems for riper minds in our grammar schools and academies; mothers pore over her pages of prose for counsel, and the aged of either sex draw consolation from the inspirations of her sanctified muse in their declining years." And, while many critics accused Sigourney of publishing too much unpolished material, contemporary criticism was never completely derogatory, since few magazine editors competing for her poetry and prose wished to offend her.

After Sigourney's death the popularity of her writings waned as the heyday of sentimental writing passed. In *The Poetry of American Women from 1632 to 1945,* Emily Stipes Watts describes Sigourney's mature work as "padded, pedantic, and prudish," and the characteristics of her works that captured nineteenth-century audiences—sentimentality and didacticism—seem to have rendered Sigourney little more than a historical curiosity through much of the twentieth century. Recently, however, there has been a renewed interest in Sigourney, particularly among feminist literary scholars. Critics such as Annie Finch, Nina Baym, and Dorothy Z. Baker have studied Sigourney's successful attempt to establish herself as a distinctly American and distinctly female poet. Critics are divided, however, on whether Sigourney's writing represents a feminist empowerment or, as Ann Douglas Wood claims, "a means for a kind of militant sublimation." In contrast to both the popular adulation of her contemporaries and the indifference of early twentieth-century critics, modern literary scholars have come to recognize the importance of studying Sigourney's position in American letters, both for her limitations and her transgression of limits.

PRINCIPAL WORKS

Moral Pieces, in Prose and Verse (poetry and essays) 1815
Traits of the Aborigines of America (poetry) 1822

Sketch of Connecticut, Forty Years Since (sketch) 1824
Poems (poetry) 1827
Female Biography: Containing Sketches of the Life and Character of Twelve American Women (sketches) 1829
Evening Readings in History: Comprising Portions of the History of Assyria, Egypt, Tyre, Syria, Persia, and the Sacred Scriptures (history) 1833
Letters to Young Ladies (letters) 1833
Poems (poetry) 1834; also published as *Selected Poems,* 1838
Poetry for Children (poetry) 1834
Sketches (sketches) 1834
Zinzendorff, and Other Poems (poetry) 1835
History of Marcus Aurelius, Emperor of Rome (biography) 1836
Pocahontas, and Other Poems (poetry) 1841
Pleasant Memories of Pleasant Lands (sketches) 1842
Poetry for Seamen (poetry) 1845
Myrtis, with Other Etchings and Sketchings (sketches) 1846
Illustrated Poems (poetry) 1849
The Faded Hope (memoir) 1853
Lucy Howard's Journal (novel) 1858
The Man of Uz, and Other Poems (poetry) 1862
Letters of Life (autobiography) 1866

CRITICISM

John S. Hart (essay date 1852)

SOURCE: "Lydia H. Sigourney," in *The Female Prose Writers of America with Portraits, Biographical Notices, and Specimens of Their Writings,* E. H. Butler & Co., 1852, pp. 76–92.

[*In the following essay, Hart presents a study of Sigourney's life and works with excerpts from her prose.*]

Justice has hardly been done to Mrs. Sigourney as a prose writer. She has been so long, and is so familiarly, quoted as a poet, that the public has in a measure forgotten that her indefatigable pen has sent forth almost a volume of prose yearly for more than a quarter of a century—that her prose works already issued number, in fact, twenty-five volumes, averaging more than two hundred pages each, and some of them having gone through not less than twenty editions. She has indeed produced no one work of a thrilling or startling character, wherewith to electrify the public mind. Her writings have been more like the dew than the lightning. Yet the dew, it is well to remember, is not only one of the most beneficent, but one of the most powerful of nature's agents—far more potential in grand results than its brilliant rival. When account shall be made of the various agencies, moral and intellectual, that have moulded the American mind and heart during the first half

of the nineteenth century, few names will be honoured with a larger credit than that of Lydia H. Sigourney.

The maiden name of this most excellent woman was Lydia Howard Huntley. She was born in Norwich, Connecticut, September 1st, 1791, of Ezekiel and Sophia Huntley. Being an only child, she was nurtured with special care and tenderness. But besides the ordinary parental influences, there was in her early history one circumstance of a peculiar character, which, according to the testimony of those who have known her best, contributed largely and most happily to the moulding of her mind and heart. I refer to the remarkable intimacy that existed between the gifted and brilliant young girl and an aged lady that lived for many years in the same house. Madam Jerusha Lathrop, the lady referred to was the relict of Dr. Daniel Lathrop, and daughter of Joseph Talcot, one of the Provincial Governors of Connecticut.

Madam Lathrop is reported to have been gifted by nature with strong powers of mind, and a dignity of person and manners that commanded universal respect. Her character had been matured by intercourse with men of powerful intellect, and by participation in great and trying scenes. The parents of Mrs. Sigourney resided under the roof of Madam Lathrop, who had been bereft of her husband and children, and though the household was separate, the latter manifested from the first a tender solicitude for their infant daughter. As the mind of the child began to unfold itself, and to give promise of future richness and depth, the attachment became mutual, and in a few years an enduring confidence, an almost inseparable companionship, was established between the little maiden of six and the venerable woman of eighty.

The following glimpse into the chamber of Madam Lathrop is from one entirely conversant with the subject. For its substantial correctness as to fact, we are permitted to quote the authority of Mrs. Sigourney herself. It is quoted, not only as a beautiful episode in human life, but also as affording a key to some of the most charming peculiarities of Mrs. Sigourney's writings.

> Methinks we stand upon that ancient threshold; we enter those low-browed, but ample rooms; we mark the wood-fire gleaming upon crimson moreen curtains, gilded clock, ebony-framed mirror, and polished wainscot; but what engages our attention, is the venerable occupant and her youthful companion. There sits the lady in her large arm-chair, and the young friend beside her, with face upturned, and loving eyes fixed on that beaming countenance. We can imagine that we hear, in alternate notes, the quick, gushing voice of childhood, and the tremulous tones of age, as question and reply are freely interchanged. And now we are startled, as the tremulous voice unexpectedly recovers strength and fulness, and breaks forth into some wild or pathetic melody—the ballad or patriotic stanza of

former days. The young auditor listens with rapt delight, and now, as the scene changes, with light breath and glowing aspect, she sits attentive to the minute and lively details of some domestic tale of truth, or striking episode of our national history—treasuring up the diamond-dust, to be fused hereafter, by her genius, into pellucid gems. As night closes round, and the light from the two stately candlesticks glimmers through the room, the lady takes the cushioned seat in the corner, and the young inmate spreads out upon the table some well-kept, ancient book, often perused, yet never found wearisome; and beguiles, with incessant reading, all too mature for her years, the long and lonely knitting hours of her aged friend.

This glimpse into the parlor of Madam Lathrop is no fancy sketch. The evening was usually closed by the singing of devotional hymns, and the reception, from memory, of favourite psalms, or choice specimens of serious verse. The readings were mostly of devotional works. Young's Night Thoughts stood highest upon the list, and had several times been read aloud, from the beginning to end, by the young student, at an age in which most children can scarcely read, intelligibly, the simplest verse. Other tomes, and some heavy and sombrous, were also made familiar to her young mind, by repeated perusal; but as the upper shelves of the lady's library contained some volumes of a lighter character, the curiosity of childhood would render it pardonable, if now and then those shelves were furtively explored, or some old play or romance withdrawn, to be read by stealth in the solitary chamber.

The chamber, to the young student, is a sacred precinct. There, not only is the evening problem and the morning recitation faithfully prepared for the school, and the borrowed book pored over in delightful secrecy, with no intrusive eye to note the smiles and tears and unconscious gesticulation, that respond to the moving incidents of the tale—but there, too, in silent and solitary hours, the light-footed muse slips in, and makes her earliest visits, leaving behind those first faintly dotted notes of music, which are for a long time bashfully kept concealed from every eye.

Madam Lathrop watched with entire complacency the dawning genius of her young favourite. The simple, poetic effusion occasionally brought from that solitary chamber and timidly submitted to her inspection, was sure to be received with encouraging praise, and to kindle in the face of her aged friend that glow of approbation which was the highest reward that the imagination of the young aspirant had then conceived.

The death of her venerable benefactress, which took place when she was fourteen years of age, was the first deep sorrow which her young heart had known. It was a disruption of very tender ties—the breaking up of a peculiar intimacy between youth and age, and she could not be easily solaced for the bereavement. Nor has her mind ever lost the influence of this early association. It has kept with her through life, and runs like a fine vein through all her writings. The memory, the image, the teachings of this sainted friend, seem to accompany her like an invisible presence, and wherever the scene may be, she turns aside to commune with her spirit, or to cast a fresh flower upon her grave.

Mrs. Sigourney has been remarkable through life for the steadfastness of her friendships. Besides the venerable companion already commemorated, she became early in life very tenderly attached to one of her own age, whose history has become identified with her own. This was Anna Maria Hyde; a young lady whose sterling worth and fine mental powers were graced and rendered winning by uncommon vivacity and sweetness of disposition, unaffected modesty, and varied acquirements. The friendship of these two young persons for each other was intimate and endearing. They were companions in long rural walks, they sat side by side at their studies, visited each other's dwellings, read together, wrought the same needle-work pattern, or, with paint and pencil, shaded the same flower. The neighbours regarded them as inseparable; the names of Hyde and Huntley were wreathed together, and one was seldom mentioned without the other. Youthful friendships are, however, so common, and usually so transient, that this would scarcely demand notice, but for the strength of its foundation. It appeared to be based upon a mutual, strong desire to do good to others; a fixed purpose to employ the talents which God had given them, for the benefit of the world upon which they had entered. In pursuance of this object, they not only addressed themselves to the assiduous cultivation of their mental powers, but they engaged with alacrity in domestic affairs and household duties; and they found time, also, to make garments for the poor, to instruct indigent children, to visit the old and infirm, read with them, and administer to their temporal comfort, and to watch with the sick and dying.

Among the plans for future usefulness which these young friends revolved, none seem so feasible, or so congenial to their tastes, as that of devoting themselves to the office of instruction. This, therefore, they adopted as their province, their chosen sphere of action, and they resolutely kept this object in view, through the course of their education. The books they read, the studies they pursued, the accomplishments they sought, all had a reference to this main design. After qualifying themselves to teach those English sciences which were considered necessary to the education of young females, together with the elements of the Latin tongue, they went to Hartford and spent the winter of 1810–11 principally in attention to the ornamental branches, which were then in vogue. Returning from thence, they entered at once, at the age of nineteen, upon their grand pursuit. A class of young ladies in their native town gathered joyfully around them, and into this circle they cast not only the affluence of their well stored minds, and the cheering inspiration of youthful zeal, but all the strength of their best and holiest principles. Animated, blooming, happy, linked affectionately arm in arm, they daily came in among their pupils, diffusing love and cheerfulness, as well as knowledge, and commanding the most grateful attention and respect.

The cordial affection between these interesting young teachers was itself a most important lesson to their pupils. One of the privileged few, writing after a lapse of forty years, thus testifies to the lasting impression it produced upon their young hearts. "Pleasant it is to review those dove-like days—to recall the lineaments of that diligent, earnest, mind-expanding group; and to note again the dissimilarity so beautifully harmonious, between those whom we delighted to call our sweet *sister-teachers—the two inseparables, inimitables*. It was a matter of admiration to the pupils, that such oneness of sentiment, opinion, and affection, should co-exist with such a diversity in feature, voice, eyes, expression, manner, and movement, as the two friends exhibited."

After a pleasing association of two years, the young teachers parted, each to pursue the same line of occupation in a different sphere. But another separation, fatal and afflictive, soon took place. The interesting and accomplished Miss Hyde was taken away in the midst of usefulness and promise—mowed down like a rose-tree in bloom, March 26th, 1816, at the age of twenty-four. Of this beloved companion of her youth, Mrs. Sigourney wrote an interesting memoir, soon after her decease; and she again recurs to her with gushing tenderness, in the piece entitled **"Home of an Early Friend,"** written nearly thirty years after the scene of bereavement. In flowing verse, and prose almost as harmonious as music, she has twined a lasting memorial of the worth of the departed, and of that tender friendship which was a marked incident in her own young life.

Before the death of her friend, she had transferred her residence to Hartford, and again entered, with fresh enthusiasm, upon the task of instruction. In this path she was happy and successful; it was regarded as a privilege to be received into her circle, and many of her pupils became life-long friends, strewing her subsequent pathways with flowers.

In Hartford, she was at once received as a welcome and cherished inmate of the family of Madam Wadsworth, relict of Col. Jeremiah Wadsworth, whose mother was a Talcot, and nearly connected with the revered Madam Lathrop. The mansion-house in which Madam Wadsworth and the aged sisters of her husband dwelt, stood upon the spot now occupied by the Wadsworth Athenaeum. It was a spacious structure; unadorned, but deeply interesting in its historic associations. To the young guest it seemed a consecrated roof, whose every room was peopled with images of the past; nor was her ear ever inattentive to those descriptive sketches of the heroic age of our country, with which its venerable inhabitants enlivened the evening hours. The poem, **"On the Removal of an Ancient Mansion,"** is a graphic delineation of the impressions made on her mind by her acquaintance with the threshold and hearth-stone of this fine old house, and her communication with its excellent inmates.

Another member of the same family, Daniel Wadsworth, Esq., had always manifested a lively interest in her mental cultivation. He had known her in childhood, under the roof of Madam Lathrop, and had there seen some of her early effusions, both in prose and verse. At his earnest solicitation, she made a collection of her fugitive pieces, and under his patronage, and with his influence and liberality cast around her as a shield, she first ventured to appear before the public as an author. Mr. Wadsworth's regard for her suffered no diminution till his death, which took place in 1848. Few authors have found a friend so kind and so true. Of her affection for him and his amiable wife, her writings contain many proofs. Her Monody on the death of Mr. Wadsworth has the following noble stanza:—

> "Oh, friend! thou didst o'ermaster well
> The pride of wealth, and multiply
> Good deeds not alone for the good word of men,
> But for Heaven's judging ken,
> And clear, omniscient eye,
> And surely where the 'just made perfect' dwell,
> Earth's voice of highest eulogy
> Is like the bubble of the far-off sea;
> A sigh upon the grave
> Scarce moving the frail flowers that o'er its surface wave."

We have thus far glanced at the principal scenes and circumstances, which appear to have had an influence in forming the character of Mrs. Sigourney, and preparing her genius for flight. As Miss Huntley, she gave no works to the press except those to which allusion has been made, viz: **"Moral Pieces in Prose and Verse,"** and a memoir of her friend, Miss Hyde. The **"Sketch of Connecticut, forty years since,"** was, however, one of her earliest productions, though not published until 1824. It is honorable to her sensibilities, that so large a portion of these works was prompted by the grateful feelings of the heart. Her later emanations are enriched with deeper trains of thought, and melodies of higher and more varied power, but these are the genuine outpourings of affection—the first fruits of mind, bathed in the dew of life's morning, and laid upon the altar of gratitude.

The marriage of Miss Huntley with Charles Sigourney, Esq., merchant of Hartford, took place at Norwich, June 16th, 1819.

Mrs. Sigourney's domestic life has been varied with frequent excursions and tours, which have rendered her familiar with the scenery and society of most parts of her own country, and in 1840, she went to Europe, and remained there nearly a year, visiting England, Scotland, and France. **"Pleasant Memories of Pleasant Lands,"** published in 1843, and **"Scenes in my Native Land,"** published in 1845, afford sufficient evidence that travelling had a conspicuous agency in giving richness and variety to her productions.

A personal stranger to Mrs. Sigourney, acquainted only with her varied literary pursuits and numerous writings, might be disposed to think that they occupied her whole time, and that she had accomplished little else in life. Such an assumption would be entirely at variance with the truth. The popular, but now somewhat stale notion, that female writers are, of course, negligent in personal costume, domestic thrift, and all those social offices which are woman's appropriate and beautiful sphere of action, can never prop its baseless and falling fabric with her example. She has sacrificed no womanly or household duty, no office of friendship or benevolence for the society of the muses. That she is able to perform so much in so many varied departments of literature and social obligation, is owing to her diligence. She acquired in early life that lesson—simple, homely, but invaluable—to make the most of passing time. Hours are seeds of gold; she has not sewn them on the wind, but planted them in good ground, and the harvest is consequently a hundred fold.

Authentic report informs us that no one better fills the arduous station of a New England housekeeper, in all its various and complicated departments. Nor are the calls of benevolence unheeded. Like that distinguished philanthropist, from whom she derives her intermediate name, she is said to go about doing good. Much of her time is devoted to the practical silent, unambitious duties of charity. Nor must we omit the crowning praise of all—the report of her humble, unceasing, unpretending, untiring devotion.

We may not conclude this brief review of Mrs. Sigourney, without allusion to a recent afflictive stroke of Providence, which has overshadowed her path with a dark cloud, and almost bowed her spirit to the earth with its weight. She was the mother of two children; the youngest, an only son, had just arrived at the verge of manhood, when he was selected by the Destroying Angel as his own, and veiled from her sight.[1] A sorrow like this, she had never before known. Such a bereavement cannot take place and not leave desolation behind. Around this early-smitten one, the fond hopes of a mother's heart had clustered; all those hopes are extinguished; innumerable, tender sympathies are cut away; the glowing expectations, nurtured for many years, are destroyed, and the cold urn left in their place.

But the Divine Hand knows how to remove branches from the tree without blighting it; and though crushed and wounded, the faith of the Christian sustains the bereaved parent. Her reply to a friend who sympathized in her affliction, will show both the depth of her sorrow, and the source of her consolation—"God's time and will are beautiful, and through bursts of blinding tears I give him thanks."

The amount of Mrs. Sigourney's literary labours may be estimated from the following list of her publications, which is believed to be nearly complete. The works are all prose, and all 12mo., unless otherwise expressly stated: **"Moral Pieces in Prose and Verse,"** 267 pages, 1815; **"Biography and Writings of A. M. Hyde,"** 241 pp., 1816; **"Traits of the Aborigines,"** a poem, 284 pp., 1822; **"Sketch of Connecticut, forty years since,"** 280 pp., 1824; **"Poems,"** 228 pp., 1827; **"Biography of Females,"** 112 pp., small size, 1829; **"Biography of Pious Persons,"** 338 pp., 1832, two editions the first year, now out of print, as are all the preceding volumes; **"Evening Readings in History,"** 128 pp., 1833; **"Letters to Young Ladies,"** 295 pp., 1833, twenty editions; **"Memoirs of Phebe Hammond,"** 30 pp., 1833; **"How to be Happy,"** 126 pp., 1833, two editions first year, and several in London; **"Sketches,"** 216 pp., 1834; **"Poetry for Children,"** 102 pp., small size, 1834; **"Select Poems,"** 338 pp., 1834, eleven editions; **"Tales and Essays for Children,"** 128 pp., 1834; **"Zinzendorff and other Poems,"** 300 pp., 1834; **"History of Marcus Aurelius,"** 122 pp., 1835; **"Olive Buds,"** 136 pp., 1836; **"Girls' Reading Book,"** prose and poetry, 243 pp., 1838, between twenty and thirty editions; **"Boys' Reading Book,"** prose and poetry, 247 pp., 1839, many editions; **"Letters to Mothers,"** 296 pp., 1838, eight editions; **"Pocahontas and other Poems,"** 283 pp., 1841, reprinted in London; **"Poems,"** 255 pp., small size, 1842; **"Pleasant Memoirs of Pleasant Lands,"** 368 pp., prose and poetry, 1842; **"Child's Book,"** prose and poetry, 150 pp., small size, 1844; **"Scenes in my Native Land,"** prose and poetry, 319 pp., 1844; **"Poems for the Sea,"** 152 pp., 1845; **"Voice of Flowers,"** prose and poetry, 123 pp., small size, 1845, eight editions in five years; **"The Lovely Sisters,"** 100 pp., small size, 1845; **"Myrtis and other Etchings,"** 292 pp., 1846; **"Weeping Willow,"** poetry, 128 pp., small size, 1846, six editions in four years; **"Water Drops,"** prose and poetry, 275 pp., 1847; **"Illustrated Poems,"** 408 pp., 8vo., 1848; **"Whisper to a Bride,"** prose and poetry, 80 pp., small size, 1849; **"Letters to my Pupils,"** 320 pp., 1851.

Besides these volumes, thirty-five in number, she has produced several pamphlets, and almost innumerable contributions to current periodical literature. She has moreover maintained a very extensive literary correspondence, amounting in some years to an exchange of thirteen or fourteen hundred letters.

Perhaps no one, who has written so much as Mrs. Sigourney, has written so little to cause self-regret in the review. The secret of this lies in that paramount sense of duty which is the obvious spring of her writings, as of all her conduct. If it has not led her to the highest regions of fancy, it has saved her from all those disgraceful falls that too often mark the track of genius. Along the calm, sequestered vale of duty and usefulness, her writings, like a gentle river fresh from its mountain springs, have gladdened many a quiet home, have stimulated into fertility many a generous heart. Some of her small volumes, like the **"Whisper to a Bride,"** are unpretending in character as they are diminutive in appearance, but they contain a wealth of beauty and goodness that few would believe that have not examined them. Of her larger volumes, none are more widely known than the **"Letters to Young Ladies,"** and **"Letters to Mothers." "Letters to my Pupils,"** just published, will probably be equally popular, as they are equally beautiful. The scraps of autobiography, so gracefully mixed up with her reminiscences of others, will add a special charm to this volume for the thousands who have felt the genial influence of her teachings and writings.

Notes

1. Andrew M. Sigourney died in Hartford, June, 1850, aged nineteen years.

E. B. Huntington (essay date 1869)

SOURCE: "Lydia H. Sigourney," in *Eminent Women of the Age; Being Narratives of the Lives and Deeds of the Most Prominent Women of the Present Generation,* by James Parton et al., S. M. Betts & Company, 1869, pp. 85-101.

[*In the following essay, Huntington briefly sketches Sigourney's life in an effort to account for her widespread popularity.*]

Were any intelligent American citizen now asked to name the American woman, who, for a quarter of a century before 1855, held a higher place in the respect and affections of the American people than any other woman of the times had secured, it can hardly be questioned that the prompt reply would be, Mrs. LYDIA HUNTLEY SIGOURNEY.

And this would be the answer, not simply on the ground of her varied and extensive learning; nor on that of her acknowledged poetic gifts; nor on that of her voluminous contributions to our current literature, both in prose and verse; but rather, because with these gifts and this success, she had with singular kindliness of heart made her very life-work itself a constant source of blessing and joy to others. Her very goodness had made her great. Her genial goodwill had given her power. Her loving friendliness had

made herself and her name everywhere a charm. So that, granted that other women could be named, more gifted in some endowments, more learned in certain branches, and even more ably represented in the literature of the times; still, no one of them, by universal consent, had succeeded in winning so largely the esteem and admiration of her age.

It is of this woman that we need not hesitate to write, when we would make up our list of the representative women of our times. She was a woman so rare, we need not hesitate to claim it, for her native gifts, and still more, so genial and lovable, in deed and spirit, that her very life seemed a sort of divine benediction upon our age. And who, more worthily than she, can represent to us the best and highest type of cultivated womanhood?

LYDIA HOWARD HUNTLEY, the only child of Ezekiel and Sophia (Wentworth) Huntley, was born in Norwich, Connecticut, Sept. 1, 1791. In her parentage and birthplace we have no indistinct prophecy of her future life. Their lessons, wrought into the very texture of her sensitive soul, served as the good genius of her long and bright career. She could never forget or deny them. Their precious memory was to her a perpetual and exceeding joy.

Witness this sweet picture of her early home, drawn by her own child-hand, yet, even so early, foreshowing the lifelong brightness of her loving spirit:—

> My gentle kitten at my footstool sings
> Her song, monotonous and full of joy.
> Close by my side, my tender mother sits,
> Industriously bent—her brow still bright
> With beams of lingering youth, while he, the sire,
> The faithful guide, indulgently doth smile.

What but a blessed influence over her could such a home have had? And we shall not wonder, when, fifty years later, we find her filial hand sketching, so exquisitely, the "beaming smile," and "the love and patience sweet," with which those dear names were embalmed. Few, very few, have borne with them through life, so freshly and so lovingly, the forms and the affections of their home-friends. The impression they made upon her must have been exceedingly precious to her heart; and so her affectionate love kept faithful vigil over these dearest treasures of her memory.

Hardly less forceful than these home-influences, must have been the beautiful and romantic sceneries, and the genial social life of her native town. It could but have stirred and educated such a soul as hers to have spent her childhood amid such scenes:—

> Rocks, gray rocks, with their caverns dark,
> Leaping rills, like the diamond spark,

Torrent voices, thundering by,
Where the pride of the vernal floods swelled high.

It is her own testimony which reveals to us the power of these home-charms over her life,—a testimony given, when, to use her own felicitous figure, she was now "journeying towards the gates of the West":—

"Yet came there forth from its beauty a silent, secret influence, moulding the heart to happiness, and love of the beneficent Creator."

And still again she records their power:—

We have garnered those charms and attractions that bring
A spell o'er our souls when existence was young.

So nurtured, we can understand the secret of that love for Norwich and its scenery which she never failed to show to her latest day. It only needed an invitation to her to revisit the "dear old places" of her childhood, to kindle anew the fervors of more than her childhood joy:—

We accept, we will come, wheresoever we rove,
And wreathe round thy birthday our honor and love.
We love thee, we love thee; thy smile, like a star,
Hath gleamed in our skies, though our homes were afar.

Added to the affection of her parents, and to these sweet charms of her native town, was still another, and a very marked home-influence, which was destined to prove educational to her. Madame Lathrop, one of the noblest of the many worthy Norwich matrons of that day, a daughter of Governor Talcott, of Hartford, and widow of Daniel Lathrop, a wealthy and accomplished citizen of Norwich, had made her own elegant and hospitable home that also of the Huntley family. She took great interest in Lydia, and drew strongly to her own the heart of the sensitive girl. And did she not, in the daily communing of their souls, leave somewhat of her own noble spirit of self-denial and rich charity as fruitful seed in that young heart? What other proof do we need than that which comes from the oft-repeated testimony of the child herself, even down to her latest years? Let her sketch for us, in her own sweet way, the record of this blessed influence over her character and life:—

A fair countenance, a clear blue eye, and a voice of music return to me as I recall the image of that venerated lady over whom more than threescore and ten years had passed ere I saw the light. Her tall, graceful form, moving with elastic step through the parterres whose numerous flowers she superintended, and her brow raised in calm meditation from the sacred volume she was reading, were to me beautiful. The sorrowful came to be enlightened by the sunbeam that dwelt in her spirit, and the children of want to find bread and a garment. The beauty of the soul was hers that waxeth

not old. Love was in her heart to all whom God had made. At her grave I learned my first lesson of a bursting grief that has never been forgotten. Let none say that the aged die unloved or unmourned by the young.

It must have been an influence of great power which such a character wielded over such a nature; and we cannot wonder that, long years after that hallowed intimacy, we find the grateful child thus recording her remembrance of it: "The cream of all my happiness was a loving intercourse with venerable old age." Nor can we deny her the dutiful joy of dedicating one of her earliest publications, as "an offering of gratitude to her whose influence, like a golden thread, had run through the whole woof of my life."

It was under influences like these that her life had its dawning. Exceedingly sensitive and impressible, she readily responded to their power. They found her a keen observer, and a very rapid learner. Her infancy seems to have been like the later childhood of most girls, and her girlhood wore the thoughtfulness and reached the attainments of ordinary womanhood.

The insight into this earliest period of her life, which her *Letters of Life* so artlessly give us, is one of the most curious pages in our autobiographic literature. We have here, perhaps, the most unaffected and childlike prattle about child-life, in the language of doting old age. Possibly there may be something excessive in the coloring given to the whole picture; but surely we can afford to let the pen of old age use the freedom which a warm heart, warming anew amid the scenes and play-places of its young life, might dictate. Let the venerated authoress, if in her deep joy she recalls the events which seemed so important to her young fancy, tell the whole story, which once she might have hesitated to do, and which other authors, more careful to prune their thoughts to the accepted proprieties, would not assuredly have done. It certainly cannot harm us to be made, once in our lives, familiar in letters with the very precocities, if you will, which are so often seen in bright children, yet which we do not usually elevate to the dignity of the printed page.

If she speaks of the little attempts at conversation made in the first year of her life, have we not all heard and been charmed with hearing the same thing in our own little ones? If she details even the prattle, and the occasional wise and over-scholarly sayings or fancies of her third summer among the flowers, why not give her credit for what, though perhaps not very common, is still plainly possible to a child of gifts, especially if she has spent her first three years under the most helpful of influences? It need not be counted an offence if she tell us over what nobody else will be likely to tell us,—the whole story of her doll-teaching and training. It is a pretty picture which that same scene makes when acted in all of our homes, and why should not its sketch, whether by the pencil of the artist or the pen of the writer, charm us too?

But is there not, also, in this the very best of sense? How it aids us to understand the woman, to see the little one with her dolls around her, and hear her begin there her work of persuasion and authority! It instructs as well as charms us to visit the artless child in her "spacious garret;" to note her curious search among its gathered household treasures; to find her settling herself down like the bee to its flower-food, as she finds an old hymn-book there; to see her hearty love for the "large black horse," "the red-coat cows," "the crowing, brooding, and peeping poultry," and the "pliant pussy" which sat in her lap or sported by her side, and which was "as a sister" to her. It will instruct us, where we shall need light, to roam awhile with the laughing babe and child, "from garden to garden;" to run with her "at full speed through the alleys;" to recline by her side, "when wearied, in some shaded recess," or even on the "mow of hay in the large, lofty barn," where we can together "watch the quiet cows over their fragrant food;" and then to sit down with her at the family table, and taste with her of the bread so sweet, "made in capacious iron basins." Suppose, in this way, we learn how early and how regular her meals were; how uniform and simple the diet on which she was reared; and how exact and respectful and decorous the behavior of that hour. Do not all of these lessons explain the character which they so certainly help to form? And so we may well thank the authoress of seventy years that she allowed herself to recall, for our delight and instruction, those germinal forces of her favored childhood.

Let us now follow this child, as she prepares herself for the life-work before her. At four years of age we find her in the school nearest to the house of her parents; and we only learn of that first school, that its "spelling-classes" were the chief delight of the child. Trivial as this fact is, it gives us no unmeaning hint. Her second teacher, a gentleman, perhaps the teacher of the winter school, won the child to the use of the pen, and laid the foundation of that distinct, printlike chirography which was so serviceable to her whole future career. Next, the teacher of needle-work does her good service by starting her well in this feminine art, of which she made later the best of use. And now comes the young ladies' school, under an English lady of varied accomplishment; and here she makes a good beginning in music and painting and embroidery. And here, too, we get valuable hints, and it would well repay us, had we time, to watch the child in the beginning of her art-life. It was full of meaning,—that extemporized studio at home, that "piece of gamboge," that "fragment of indigo, begged of the washerwoman," those coffee-grounds to give the ambered brown, and those child-experiments, again and again repeated, to secure desired tints. We may note, too, about this time, how the literary taste and enthusiasm of

the child was aroused. How life-like was its beginning! She started a story, which the record does not finish; for they all said it was too much for her. She was "only just eight years old."

Next we find her in the school of a graduate of Dublin, and here she makes rapid progress in mathematics. Her next step forward, in the school on the Green, under an educated and veteran teacher, places her at the head of the reading-classes. Then, under the training of Mr. Pelatiah Perit, who became so eminent among the business men of the country, she spent another year of successful study. Pursuing still the English classics and Latin, she finished in her fourteenth year her school-life at home. Then followed a course of domestic training in the duties of housekeeping, yet not so pressingly as to hinder the private study of the Latin. For the higher ornamental branches she spent parts of two years in Hartford; and, with more than ordinary mental activity and attainment, she takes leave of her school-life. Yet, such was her thirst for learning, that nothing could hinder her studies; and we find her, with the enthusiasm of a scholar, devoting her later girlhood to the study of even the original Hebrew of the Christian Scriptures.

And now begins her career as teacher, a life which she seems to have chosen scarcely more for want of something to do than from love of teaching itself. Her first experiment had been made in her father's house, and the result confirmed her purpose to make it her life-work. In her nineteenth year, in company with Miss Nancy M. Hyde, a very intimate friend, she opened a select school for girls in Chelsea, now Norwich City. Her interest in the work was very great, and her success no less so. We can readily accept her later testimony that she found her daily employment "less a toil than privilege." But, through the influence of Mr. Daniel Wadsworth, of Hartford, she was induced to establish for herself a private school for girls in that city; and, in 1814, she entered upon its duties.

During the five years she remained in this school she won a twofold reputation. Her success as teacher was well-nigh unparalleled for the times, and deservedly so; while her influence over the social circles of the city had become no less marked. Her influence over her pupils was something wonderful. They loved her with a love which nothing could repress; and their devotion was as true and lasting as their love. What testimony to the strength of her hold upon them those annual reunions on their commencement day furnishes! Even long years after they had become scattered over the land, those days were held sacred in their hearts. And when their little ones began to gather about them, they, too, were taken to the hallowed place, that on them also might fall the sweet influence which had so long blessed their mothers.

But, from the very beginning of her life in Hartford, she made for herself a place in the confidence and affections of the people, which every successive year only served to confirm. She became, in the just language of as high authority as the venerable S. G. Goodrich, "the presiding genius of its young social circle," and she was never called in her long career to vacate that post of honor.

It was while thus winning her way as teacher that she also began her public literary life. At the urgent request of her friend, Mr. Wadsworth, she consented to issue her first volume, entitled, *Pieces in Prose and Verse.* This work was printed in 1815, at the expense of Mr. Wadsworth. And the list of subscribers, which was also printed, indicates thus early the reputation which newspaper publicity had given her.

But another event soon interrupts her career as teacher. Charles Sigourney, a merchant of the city, a gentleman of wealth and literary culture and high social position, solicits and wins her hand. Their marriage was celebrated in the Episcopal church of her native town, in the early summer of 1819. Mr. Sigourney, of Huguenot descent, was already a communicant in the Episcopal church; and, on her marriage, Mrs. Sigourney, who, since 1809, had been a devoted Christian and a member of the Congregational church, felt it to be her privilege and duty to transfer her membership to the church to which her husband belonged.

This marriage threw upon Mrs. Sigourney the care of the three children of her husband by a former wife; and that care was assumed with a singular devotion to their comfort and welfare; and in this field only did she find room henceforth for her gifts as teacher. But both her position at the head of the first circle in the leading metropolis of the State, and her means, and the culture of her husband, conspired to encourage her in the literary field in which she was now winning such a triumph. Besides the volume printed in 1815, in 1816 she had published her *Life and Writings of Nancy Maria Hyde,* an interesting tribute to the memory of her most intimate friend and fellow-teacher; and during the year of her marriage appeared, also, *The Square Table,* a pamphlet designed as a corrective of what were deemed the harmful tendencies of "Arthur's Round Table," which was then exciting considerable attention in the community.

From this date to that of her death our record must be that of an earnest woman, filling up every hour of her day with its allotted duty, cheerfully and nobly done. Few women have been so diligent workers, few have maintained such fervency of spirit, and few have, in all their working, so faithfully served the Lord.

Her position, that of second wife and step-mother, has not always been found an easy one to fill; yet, even with the temptations which her literary tastes might be supposed to offer, she could never be justly reproached for neglecting any home-duty. Bound to her friends with no ordinary ties of affection, she lived, first of all, for them. Even her literary life is most crowded with its witnesses to her home-love, and indeed was largely its result. She worked, and wrote, and prayed, that she might faithfully meet this prime claim upon her heart and life.

We cannot follow, in detail this busy and painstaking career. We find her at the head of her household, which at times was large, shrinking from no burden or self-denial needed in her work, living to see her two step-daughters educated and settled in life, and their brother, at the age of forty-five, consigned to a consumptive's grave; to educate her own daughter and son, and then, just on the verge of a promising manhood, to follow him, too, to his grave; to care for both her own parents, until, in a good old age, she might tenderly hand them down to their last rest; to follow her beloved and honored husband to his grave; to give her own only daughter away in acceptable marriage; and then to settle herself down, joyful and trustful yet, in her own home, vacated indeed of her loved ones, but filled still with precious mementos of their love, until her own change should come. These forty-six years, between her marriage and her death, were mainly spent at her home in Hartford. Her travels were chiefly those of brief journeys through the Eastern and Middle States. Once she visited Virginia, and once crossed the Atlantic, visiting within the year the chief points of attraction in England, Scotland, and France. The rest of those forty-six years were most industriously employed in her own loved home, filled up with domestic duties or with literary and benevolent work; and it is safe to say that few women have ever worked to better account. She won universal respect and love. The poor and the rich, the ignorant and the educated, alike found in her that which delighted and charmed them; and so she came to occupy a place in their affections which they accorded to no other.

But, doubtless, it will be as a literary woman that she will be most widely known. And no estimate of her career which leaves out of the account the character and value of her writings can do justice to her memory. Beginning in 1815, and closing with her posthumous *Letters of Life* in 1866, her published writings numbered fifty-seven volumes. Besides these, our newspaper and magazine literature must have furnished nearly as much more. Her correspondence, not published, amounting to nearly one thousand seven hundred letters annually for several years, must have exceeded largely these printed writings; so that she must have been one of the most voluminous writers of her age.

We have not space for a critical analysis of her writings. We would simply indicate their aim and success. Whatever may be said of their artistic execution, of one thing we are sure, that their spirit and aim are as noble as ever inspired human literature; and the world has already accepted them as a worthy offering. A sharp critical judgment must agree with Mrs. Sigourney's own decision, that she wrote too much for highest success, both in invention and style. But when we stop to ask why she wrote so much, we shall find our answer in the very elements of her character, which contributed most to her eminence. Her first published volume reveals with great clearness at least these two qualities of the writer: the strength of her affections, and her equally strong sense of duty to others. We feel that she wrote what her kind heart prompted, that she might please or aid those who seemed to her to have just claims upon her. Instead of using the precious moments on the mere style of her expression, she was ever hurrying along on some urgent call of affection or duty. She could not stop to think of her literary reputation when some dear friend was pleading at her heart, or some sorrowing soul needed to be comforted. More than almost any other writer of the day, she wrote not for herself, but for others. And it is precisely here that we find the real key, both to whatever faults of style her writings may betray, and to the very best success of her life. For, while she greatly blessed the multitudes for whom she so rapidly wrote, we cannot but notice, also, how in her successive works, she is gaining both in the force and beauty of her style.

We see on almost every page of her writings how tender her spirit, how sensitive her sympathy was. From the beginning, her affections, sanctified by a Christian purpose, took the lead. We know that it was her greatest

> . . . joy to raise
> The trembler from the shade,
> To bind the broken, and to heal
> The wounds she never made.

But we must not dwell on these charming witnesses to the tenderness of her loving heart. It is easy to see that one so ruled, would not regard the mere style of her expression of highest value. And yet it would do injustice to Mrs. Sigourney, to leave out of the account the care and painstaking, with which she sought to make her writings most effective. We know she must have sought ease and fluency as well as exactness and vigor of expression. Her writings abound in witnesses innumerable to these graces. The call made upon her pen from the first magazines of the day, and from the more solid works issuing from our best publishing-houses, of itself testifies to the great merit even of her style.

No critic can read that beautiful poem on the **"Death of an Infant,"** commencing with

> Death found strange beauty on that polished brow,
> And dashed it out,

without feeling that none but a true poet, practised in the art, could have written it. We might instance her **"Scottish Weaver," "Breakfast," "Birthday of Longfellow," "My Stuffed Owl," "Niagara,"** and hundreds of other poems, in all of which may be found passages of great beauty and power. We are sure we cannot afford, these many years, to let those graceful, and at times exquisite, gems, drop out of our literature; nor can we doubt that their author will continue to rank high even among the poets of her age.

Without space for repeating the entire list, even of her poetic works, it is due to our readers to indicate those which shall best exhibit the merits and the extent of her poetic writings, and we believe we shall do this by naming the eight following volumes, with their dates:—

Her *Poems,* 1827, pp. 228; *Zinzendorff, and other Poems,* 1835, 2d edition, pp. 300; *Pocahontas, and other Poems,* 1841, pp. 284; London edition, 1841, pp. 348; *Select Poems,* 1842, pp. 324, fourth edition, of which eight thousand copies had been already sold; Illustrated edition, 1848, pp. 408; *Western Home, and other Poems,* 1854, pp. 360; and *Gleanings,* 1860, pp. 264.

Of her prose works we can only indicate that which most clearly establishes the writer's rank among our very best prose-writers of the age. Her *Past Meridian,* given to the world in her sixty-fifth year, which has now reached its fourth edition, is one of our most charming classics. One cannot read those delightful pages, without gratitude that the gifted author was spared to give us such a coronal of her useful authorship. It were easy to collect quite a volume of the most enthusiastic commendations of this charming work; but we must leave it, with the assurance that it gives a new title to its beloved author to a perpetual fame in English literature.

And what a testimony we also have in the reception our authoress has received among even our best critics! It certainly was no mean praise, which Hart, in his selections from the *Female Prose Writers* gives us, when he so graphically and truthfully says of her writings, that they "are more like the dew than the lightning." Peter Parley pronounced her, "next to Willis, the most successful and liberal contributor to the Token." Professor Cleveland, in his Compend of English Literature, could not more truthfully have characterized her writings than he did, as "pure, lofty, and holy in tendency and influence." C. W. Everest, in his Connecticut Poets, only repeats the common judgment in his decision, "Love and religion are the unvarying elements of her song." E. P. Whipple, the very Nestor of our critics, was obliged to bear testimony to the popularity of her works. He speaks of her facility in versification, and her fluency both in thought and language; and only claims, what all critics will easily allow, that from the very quantity of her writing, she "hardly does justice to her real powers."

But we need not pursue our citations of critical approval further.

We acknowledge the skill with which Mrs. Sigourney used our flexible English tongue; but we still more admire, and would never fail to honor, the deep undertone of "the still, sad music of humanity," which hallowed all her song. We will let her, though unwittingly, while describing the noble devotion of the pleading Queen Philippa, sketch herself:—

> THE ADVOCATE OF SORROW, AND THE FRIEND
> OF THOSE WHOM ALL FORSAKE.

We cannot but return to this ruling spirit of her life, equally unaffected and controlling in her girlhood and her latest years. Her gifts of charity and love often exceeded the allowance of her income which she saved for herself.

What monuments she thus built for herself in grateful hearts! Witness her frequent visits to the Reform School in Meriden. Those delighted boys cannot soon forget that beautiful orchard, whose thrifty trees she gave as her blessing to them; nor that last gift, the generous Easter cake, which made that festival so joyous to them; nor, most of all, that beautiful smile of hers, always so radiant with her hearty good-will and hope. Oh, there was a blessing in that presence, even for young lives that have been tempted down into the dark shadows of a premature disgrace!

Or who shall make her presence good to the pupils of the Deaf and Dumb Asylum in her own city, on whose mute joy her very looks beamed a more eloquent sympathy than our best words can express? Or when will the poor orphans of the asylums she so loved to visit forget her tenderness and love?

Hear this good woman, even amid the pain and exhaustion of her last sickness, thoughtful still of the suffering ones who might miss her timely charity, tenderly asking, morning after morning, "Is there any gift for me to send today?" More touchingly still, as you stand over her on the very last night of her stay on earth, you will hear this faintly, yet clearly uttered wish of the dying woman, "I would that I might live until morning, that I may, with my own hand, do up that little lace cap for that dear little babe." And so she left us, with her thought of love still on those whom she was to leave behind. Blessed departure, that! And did she not find how true her own sweet verse proved:—

> And thy good-morning shall be spoke
> By sweet-voiced angels, that shall bear thee home
> To the divine Redeemer?

And how appropriate the last lines of the last poem that she was permitted to write on earth,—the beautiful image of her soul to leave for us to look on forever:—

> Heaven's peace be with you all!
> Farewell! Farewell!

Saturday morning, June 10, 1866, was the date of her death. Her funeral was itself a witness to us of all that we have claimed for her in the city where she lived and died. Specially fitting was it, that those "children of silence" to whom she had loved to minister, and those now doubly orphaned little ones from the asylum, should have their place in that mourning throng.

And after the funeral, when the papers of the city attempted to sum up the city's loss, it was specially fitting that from the pen of a neighbor we should have this testimony: "For fifty years this good lady has blessed our city."

To these abundant witnesses to Mrs. Sigourney's noble goodness, we can only add that of her personal friend, S. G. Goodrich, who was, also, extensively acquainted with the best characters of the generation to which she belonged: "No one whom I know can look back upon a long and earnest career of such unblemished beneficence."

And how can we better close this too brief sketch of this honored woman, than in the words in which she so well has announced the imperishable fame of the gifted Mrs. Hemans:—

> Therefore, we will not say
> Farewell to thee; for every unborn age
> Shall mix thee with its household charities.
> The sage shall greet thee with his benison,
> And woman shrine thee as a vestal flame
> In all the temples of her sanctity;
> And the young child shall take thee by the hand
> And travel with a surer step to heaven.

Annie Finch (essay date 1988)

SOURCE: "The Sentimental Poetess in the World: Metaphor and Subjectivity in Lydia Sigourney's Nature Poetry," in *Legacy,* Vol. 5, No. 2, Fall, 1988, pp. 3-18.

[*In the following essay, Finch claims that Sigourney has been widely neglected recently because she fails to accommodate the predominant model of poetic subjectivity and instead describes nature poetically, but without using it as a means to her own self-expression.*]

In the revision of American women's literary history that has been taking place over the past few decades, one important area has remained almost completely untouched.[1] While novels, stories, and memoirs by eighteenth- and nineteenth-century American women are reissued and reappraised every year in mounting numbers, years after Cheryl Walker's *The Nightingale's Burden* and Emily Stipes

Watts's history of American women's poetry, virtually no new revisionist work has been done on American women poets. Apparently, most scholars feel that there was no American woman poet worth reading between Wheatley and Dickinson, or between Dickinson and H. D. The usual explanations offered for this situation do not account for such monolithic neglect of a major part of the American poetic tradition. The dedication with which these literary silences have been respected—even by committed feminist literary historians—suggests that the very existence of this poetry fundamentally opposes our accepted ideas of poetic value. Typically, readers simply dismiss this literature out of hand as "sentimental," as if the label were a self-evident justification for the treatment—and in fact, to most contemporary ears "sentimental poetry" forms a contradiction in terms, a horrifying oxymoron.

While sentimental American women novelists like Susan Warner, Harriet Beecher Stowe, Catharine Maria Sedgwick, and E. D. E. N. Southworth are finally receiving sympathetic and imaginative critical treatment, and work on Emily Dickinson burgeons as never before, "poetesses" like Lydia Sigourney, Alice Cary, Elizabeth Oakes Smith, and Frances Osgood remain unread. When feminist scholars do discuss the work of poets like Sigourney, they almost invariably say, like Walker, that it is "amateurish" and "defies reassessment"; for Catherine Sklar, it is "weak" (65); for Susan Conrad, it is "cloying" and "monotonous" and shows "minimal artistic ability" (26). Emily Dickinson's relation with the sentimental tradition is evoked only to show how far she is superior to it.[2]

Why should the sentimental poets receive a different critical reception than the sentimental novelists? The alleged aesthetic "inferiority" of sentimental poetry is not a complete explanation, nor is the major shift in poetic taste between the centuries. Scores of "minor" poets of all periods are still anthologized and read, and popular male nineteenth-century poets such as Longfellow, Bryant and Whittier, who write very differently from the typical twentieth-century poetic taste, have remained anthologized and have even found sufficient critical defenders to keep them more or less respectable, or, at least, in print.[3]

Nor can the sentimental poets' moral and religious didacticism, conventionality, and limited subject matter fully explain their neglect. Their piety is no more cloying than that of novels like *The Wide, Wide World* or *Uncle Tom's Cabin*. Recent critics, like Jane Tompkins, have been able to surpass culturally determined differences in literary taste in examining these novels.[4] Yet it is clear that even generally open-minded feminist critics, concerned with understanding rather than with ranking literature, feel perfectly free to pass sweepingly negative judgments on the poetesses. The usual rationales of cloying piety or conventional sentiments have little to do with the neglect of and contempt for these writers; their current reception stems instead from the unexamined assumption on the part of modern readers that all good or serious lyric poets maintain a subjective, self-centered poetic "authority" in their poems. Before the era of free verse, a reader could classify a poem as such on the basis of its form; today, if a text lacks the central authority of an apparent ego—sometimes referred to as a "strong voice"—many would hesitate to call it a poem at all.

This egocentric model of poetry is based on the male-defined poetic tradition of romanticism, within which many of the currently canonized female poets established themselves with great difficulty. Since the poetesses, for the most part, did not struggle with that tradition, they offer a gynocentric alternative model for critics of women's poetry. It is in recognition of this fact, as well as in an attempt to uncover the falsely universal aesthetic implied by the term "poet" in current usage, that I revive for the duration of this paper the discarded term "poetess." The study of poetesses—those writers whom even female poets themselves have hated and disowned—not only reveals an important and influential literary tradition, it helps us to rethink some of our most basic critical assumptions about the nature of poetry and the construction of the canon.[5]

Feminist criticism of the female poetic tradition has tended to focus on an inherent incompatibility between the concept of the "poetic self" and the reality of female identity, exploring the ways that poets such as Rossetti, Barrett Browning, and Dickinson struggled with the desire to express a subjective romantic lyric authority even though it was impossible for them to adopt that role consistently or unambivalently. In Gilbert and Gubar's words, poetry has been more forbidden to women than prose in our tradition because it is far less "selfless":

> the lyric poem acts as if it is an "effusion" . . . from a strong and assertive "I," a central self that is forcefully defined, whether real or imaginary. The novel, on the other hand, allows—even encourages—just the self-effacing withdrawal that society fosters in women. (*Madwoman* 547-48)

The female poets who have been accepted so far into both the mainstream and the feminist twentieth-century canons are taken seriously because their attempts to approach the world as poets are comprehensible within the definition of poetry we have inherited from the male lyric tradition: although they may subvert and contradict the subjective lyric "I," it remains crucial to their work. This is evident, for instance, in the studies by Dorothy Mermin on Barrett Browning, by Joanne Feit Diehl on Dickinson, and by Margaret Homans on Rossetti and Dickinson. Because contemporary mainstream women's poetry has reclaimed a central lyric "I" for women, furthermore, these canonical female poets continue to be read and understood. In spite of major differences in attitude and subject matter, they share with most contemporary female poets (even if unwillingly) the fundamental belief that lyric poems express a central self. This belief constitutes a definitional bias resulting in a canon of poetry that I will call "the subjective tradition." Typically in this tradition, a poet-speaker reads "meanings into the [literal or figurative] landscape" though always ultimately, to use Geoffrey Hartmann's phrase, "reaffirm[ing the mind's] autonomy vis-a-vis nature" (54). In the type of romantic lyric that might be called the subjective nature poem, for example, "Ode to a Nightingale" by Keats, Sigourney's contemporary, a central self presents aspects of the world as unchanging objects whose exploration and description can cast light on the speaker's own changing state of mind. The poet-speaker is always the true subject of such lyrics, in which, again to quote Hartmann, "Subjectivity—even solipsism—becomes the subject of poems which *qua* poetry seeks to transmute it" (53).

The sentimental American nineteenth-century poetesses did not as a rule struggle with this model of poetic subjectivity. Their poetry rarely projects the self into metaphorical readings of the world; it does not effuse from a "poet" in the traditional sense of a seer or "priest" for whom nature is important only insofar as it reflects the individual poetic soul (Gilbert and Gubar, *Madwoman* 546). Instead, it is structured to allow the natural world an independent identity no less privileged than the poetic self.[6] This lack of a privileged central self, in conjunction with the elevation of public, communally shared values such as religion and family love, is what gives their poetry that quality we have defined as "sentimental."

Sentimental art exists primarily to evoke emotion (Todd 3), and it seems to presuppose a public community of viewers who will feel what the artist has intended them to feel. The presumption that the audience will react as planned is probably a major reason that contemporary viewers typically dislike sentimental art. The fear of being violated, of being known so intimately by an artist that one can be too obviously manipulated (not in the subtle, secret way of high art, but in a way that is embarrassingly evident to, and easily shared by, any other person), ties in with our fears of uncontrolled intimacy and, perhaps particularly for Americans, with our fears of losing individual power. Worse, sentimental art accomplishes this aim by reversing the crucial hierarchy of reason over emotion. Art that manipulates rational power in the service of communally sanctioned emotions (i.e., naturalistic but sentimental art) can be even more threatening to our individualized personalities than art that chooses to do without rationality altogether (i.e., abstract art). Sentimental art takes our common sense, the weapon we most strongly control, and uses it to undermine our sense of individual

self. Such exploitation of reason for the sake of emotion may help to explain the violence with which educated people tend to discount sentimental art during periods when it is out of style, as well as the undercurrent of fear that often seems to accompany the aesthetic reaction, "Yuc-chk! That's corny!"

Numerous works of popular art, including the paintings of Norman Rockwell as well as a host of nineteenth-century painters, are sentimental by the above definition. But it is in poetry, of all art forms, that sentimentality is hardest to accept, because it is there that the post-romantic reader most expects to find the central self reinforced. In contrast to a still-recognized poet like Longfellow, who might be called "sentimentalistic" because his communal, conventional themes appear in poems in which metaphors and lyrical structures issue from a central poetic self, the nineteenth-century American poetesses wrote poems that are sentimental in structure as well as theme.

Lydia Sigourney was the most popular of the large number of popular women poets in the nineteenth century. In her lifetime Sigourney published 56 books, some of which went through as many as 20 editions, and 2000 articles. At one point she received $100 for the publication of four poems (Walker 79). As a more popular poet in their time than William Cullen Bryant, Sigourney preceded Longfellow as the unofficial poet laureate of the United States.[7] Now, however, her poetry is not considered seriously as poetry; she is known to most feminist scholars as the absurd and contemptible versifier described by Ann Douglas in her critique of American funereal poetry in *The Feminization of American Culture.*

In order to illustrate some fundamental strategies used by the poetess, I will examine several poems that Sigourney published in the 1830s and 1840s. Sigourney describes nature poetically, but without using it as mere raw material for her own central self-expression. Only when God plays an important role in Sigourney's poems do they approach the romantic lyric model of a poet-speaker exploiting the world through objectification; even in these poems, however, God can function as much to objectify the poetess as to help her objectify the world, thus preserving the poetess' sentimental self-effacement.

Since metaphor is an indicator of the subject/object relation within a poem, and hence a synechdoche for the way a poet positions her or his poetic self in relation to the world the poem describes, my reading of these poems will focus primarily on Sigourney's use of metaphor. I will discuss some of her nature poems, examples of a type of poem which, by the mid-nineteenth century, had largely replaced the love poem as the archetypal confrontation between the poetic self and the objectified world. In Sigourney's nature poems, the speaker frequently addresses, describes, or meditates alone on nature, thus providing the poetess ample opportunity to develop subjective romantic lyric "insight" and to describe nature's transformations in relation to a central poet-self.

But, in the vast majority of her poems, Sigourney avoids such self-oriented expressions, concerning herself instead with natural existence as something independent of the self. This fact is clearest on a structural level. While it is obvious that poems in the Western representational tradition almost inevitably "use" the world in the service of poetry, a typical Sigourney poem allows natural objects to speak in addition to the poetess. Though these other voices of course emanate from the poem's author, they function grammatically—and structurally, insofar as they interact with and affect the poetess' voice in the poem—as if they were independent of the poetess. If a subjective romantic lyric can be diagrammed as a wheel radiating from one central point—one subject to whom all the perceptions occur and from whom all the language issues—, the structure of a Sigourney poem can be imagined as an interaction of lines emanating from two or more subjects. In Sigourney's **"The Butterfly"** (*PO* 143), for instance, two natural "objects" hold a conversation:[8]

> A butterfly bask'd on a baby's grave,
>   Where a lily had chanced to grow:
> "Why art thou here, with thy gaudy die,
>   When she of the blue and sparkling eye,
> Must sleep in the churchyard low?"
>
> Then it lightly soar'd through the sunny air,
>   And spoke from its shining track:
> "I was a worm till I won my wings,
> And she whom thou mourn'st like a seraph sings:
>   Wouldst thou call the bless'd one back?"

Structurally, because of its lack of a central poet-speaker, **"The Butterfly"** is a self-defining, self-objectifying artifact, the poetic symbols of which objectify themselves in their own voices; it does not have the form of self-expression. The butterfly's voice carries the most authority here, not the poetess'; the butterfly even imposes its own metaphorical meaning onto the child, the only human in the poem. While it is obvious that the views expressed here are Sigourney's, structurally there is no *self* in this poem with whom the reader can identify at the expense of everything else in the poem. This poem does not provide a reader's ego with the vicarious emotional experiences of "To a Skylark" or "Ode to a Nightingale." Where the romantic poetic tradition leads readers to expect a poem to be an object passed between an authoritative subject-author and an authoritative subject-reader, such a communicative model is disrupted by the dialogic pattern of a sentimental poem like "The Butterfly." Rather than any characteristic of diction or theme, this is probably the major issue

confronting those critics who find the poetess' work, to quote Susan Conrad, "lack[ing in] *authority*" [emphasis mine] (222).

Not only does **"The Butterfly"** replace the poetic authority of the poet as "divine ruler" (Gilbert and Gubar, *Madwoman* 212) by an encounter with the poet in the root sense—as a "maker"; it also replaces the inherent poetic "authority" of culturally sanctioned meanings with its own internal meanings, seeming to suggest that the symbolism created within its two stanzas is truer, within the poem, than any inherited symbolism. This approach is consistent with Sigourney's artificiality. Paradoxically, Sigourney's conventional religious beliefs, as opposed to Shelley's atheism, for instance, allow her to present her poems and their various allegories and metaphors as imaginative creations rather than as privileged symbolic representations of ineffable personal experience. This freedom with symbolic structures extends even to a Christian symbol: in **"The Butterfly"** the lily, a traditional Christian symbol of rebirth which might be expected to be on the child's grave for a significant reason, is described as having just "chanced" to grow there; its conventional meaning is resisted. The importance of such created symbolism is emphasized when Sigourney justifies the use of the butterfly as a symbol of transcendence not on her authority as a member of her culture or on her poetic authority, but on the "authority" of the words she gives the butterfly *itself* to speak within the poem. The lily, perhaps because it has not helped to create its own significance within the poem but only inherited it, is ignorant, and the butterfly has the last word.

To make clearer the radical differences in orientation between Sigourney's sentimental poetics and those of the canonized romantic tradition in America, we can turn to a romantic poem, "Thanatopsis," by William Cullen Bryant. A poem that was published two years before Sigourney's first book, and the only poem by Bryant preserved in many American literature surveys today, it offers a good example of the subjective nature poem in America in the early nineteenth century. In this poem a feminized Nature directly solaces the speaker with her "voice of gladness," her "smile," and her "healing sympathy." The ocean is "melancholy," the vales "pensive," and the brooks "complaining." The poem's central conceit implies that all this is because the hills, woods, and waters are "but the solemn decorations all / of the great tomb of man." Nature seems equally available as a decoration for man's great poem. The appropriation of nature is subtler in Bryant's "To a Waterfowl": here the poet questions a waterfowl about its evening destination, allowing it some independent identity through the very fact of questioning it. In fact, however, the appropriation of the waterfowl into the poet's meaning-system remains the structuring force of the poem, as the questioning first section is resolved and balanced by the conclusion in which the poet finds out something about himself. At the end of the poem, after the poet has himself answered the questions that he asked the bird earlier, and has taken the liberty of informing the bird where it is going—to "scream among thy fellows"—, he makes the poem's ultimate point:

> He, who, from zone to zone,
> Guides through the boundless sky thy certain flight
> In the long way that I must tread alone
> Will lead my steps aright.

The waterfowl's status as a vehicle has been clear since the moment when the poet answered his own questions himself. Rather than a confrontation with an independent creature, the address to the waterfowl turns out to be a way for the poet to get in touch with his own internal knowledge.

Generally Sigourney does not transform nature, as Bryant does, into a book in which to read self-transforming meanings. On the other hand, neither does she disrupt referentiality altogether, as Margaret Homans has described Dickinson doing in order to avoid the patriarchal trap of romantic objectification ("Syllables" 583-86). Sigourney does use language referentially to talk about nature, but she accomplishes this without completely objectifying nature *vis-a-vis* the poetic self. Significantly, the few poems in which Sigourney does use nature as a device to describe a central human state are poems celebrating public institutions or involving male speakers, such as the patriotic poem **"Connecticut River"** (*P* 13) with its theme of "devotion" for the *"fatherland,"* or **"The Dying Philosopher"** (*SP* 245), in which she adopts the voice of a male persona.

Aside from these exceptions, none of Sigourney's nature poems transforms natural objects in the service of the poetess' own concerns unless they make it clear that that is what they are doing. Such clarity is often attained through the use of those exaggerated figures which have given her work the epithet "artificial."[9] The consciousness of artificiality is developed to great complexity near the end of **"Autumn"** (*P* 247), where several of the poem's symbols explicitly explain their own significance to the poetess (the complete texts of this and several other Sigourney poems discussed are appended below). Sigourney places the words spoken by the symbols in quotes:

> "We are symbols, ye say, of the hasting doom
> Of youth, and of health, and of beauty's bloom,
> When Disease, with a hectic flush doth glow,
> And Time steal on with his tress of snow."

Not only do the symbols describe their own meaning to the poetess; the phrase "ye say," which Sigourney has them address to her, indicates an additional level of self-

consciousness. The words emphasize that the symbolism occurs in the poetess' mind alone, and that the symbols do not seem to represent a truth outside the text of the poem. In other words, the poetess herself is aware that the meanings she sees in nature are constructed ones. This fact is not hidden in any way, but is one of the most apparent aspects of the poem. As a result, this poem cannot be deconstructed in the same terms as a romantic lyric; the reader in a sense has nothing at all to lose by seeing through the arbitrariness of the poem's imaginary meanings, since the arbitrariness is built into the poem's most accessible surface. This point is reinforced by the poet in the line, "Yet ye still have a voice *to the musing heart,* / Tree, Stream and Rose . . ." [emphasis mine]. When the symbols proceed to give a moral at the end of the poem, it is clear that this metaphorical moral,

> "The soul that admits in an evil hour,
> The breath of vice to its sacred bower,
> Will find its peace with its glory die,
> Like the fading hues of an autumn sky."

is not any extra-textual truth but only a further continuation of the poetess' very self-conscious musing. But, by putting the poem's meanings and morals into the voices of the natural objects rather than into her own voice, Sigourney has managed simultaneously to make it clear that all the meanings in the poem are obviously her own fictions *and* to avoid the subjective self that would be created if she were to draw these conclusions in a central human voice. By foregoing the illusion of unaffected communication about natural facts in favor of this extreme self-consciousness, Sigourney might be said to have avoided the kind of exploitation—of the poet, the natural world and the reader—which is built into the romantic lyric.[10]

Sigourney's preservation of nature's independence is clearly evident in the many instances when the poetic speaker in her poems questions natural objects directly and repeatedly about their motives and perceptions. In **"Autumn,"** for instance, almost every metaphor is embedded in direct questions such as, "Stream! why is thy rushing step delayed?" and, "Rose! why art thou drooping thy beautiful head?"—questions that Sigourney (unlike Bryant) never answers except with other questions. It is typical that in these examples, each appropriative act of personifying nature is in a sense counteracted by the unanswered question in which the metaphor appears. Nature is distanced and mystified as if in compensation for being poeticized.

At times Sigourney's refusal to metaphorize nature in relation to a subjective poetic self is pushed to the point where the poetess (structurally speaking, although of course she remains the "subject" of the poem's discourse), must cross the boundary of subjectivity altogether and share in the role of the metaphorized object. In **"Oak in Autumn"** (*PO* 71) the speaker, as a "poet," is a natural and self-evident object with predictable attributes as much as is the tree she writes about:

> Old oak! old oak! the chosen one,
>   Round which my poet's mesh I twine,
> When rosy wakes the joyous sun,
>   Or, wearied, sinks at day's decline,
> I see the frost-king here and there,
>   Claim some brown leaflet for his own,
> Or point in cold derision. . . .

Since poetic creation is a craft independent of the particular circumstances that inspired it, the poetess seems capable of casually entwining her "mesh" around any object without altering her own essential qualities. The other side of this naturalization and objectification of the speaker is that in **"Oak in Autumn,"** as in many poems by Sigourney and the other poetesses, metaphors are presented as something highly negative. Each metaphor is a defeat for someone. The reason for this attitude becomes clear when it becomes apparent that the metaphors threaten the speaker herself: the poetess tries to remain the subject rather than the object of her metaphors, only to lose the battle eventually as winter arrives.

The speaker describes the "frost-king," common enemy of both speaker and tree, with various personifications at the beginning of the poem, almost as if she thinks she can protect her chosen oak with this "mesh" of tropes. But when the frost wins, in spite of her poetic efforts, it becomes clear that metaphors are as deadly as frost in this poem. As the tree succumbs to frost it is metaphorized, for the first time, into a "banner-staff" marking the frost's victory. The poetess is next to fall: in the very next line, she herself is defeated by this aspect of the poetic process. Objectifying herself, the speaker describes herself with a single simile:

> I, too, old friend, when thou art gone,
>   Must pensive to my casement go,
> Or, like the shuddering Druid, moan
>   The withering of his mistletoe. . . .

The poetess and the ostensible object of her poem, the oak of the opening address, have become so identified with each other that the defeat of the one to frost coincides with the loss of poetic "power" on the part of the other. Now that the tree and the poetess who identifies with it have been objectified, metaphorical references to the frost by the poetess are no longer possible, and there are no more of them in the poem.

"The Dying Philosopher" is one of Sigourney's only nature poems in which a speaker *does* transform nature metaphorically throughout, according to subjective conventions. It is a rare male persona poem, and its speaker describes an intense romantic communion with nature:

> I have crept forth to die among the trees.
> They have sweet voices that I love to hear,
> Sweet, lute-like voices. . . . They sent down
> Soft summer breezes, fraught with pitying sighs,
> To fan my blanching cheek. Their lofty boughs
> Pointed with thousand fingers to the sky. . . .

The trees with their voices and fingers and the breeze that pities the philosopher-speaker could almost have come out of "Thanatopsis." **"The Dying Philosopher"** ends with a Shelleyan yearning as, in the final lines, the philosopher addresses to the stars his desire to transcend them:

> Hail, holy stars!
> . . . . What have I said?
> I will not learn of you, for ye shall fall.
> Lo! with swift wing I mount above your spheres,
> To see the Invisible, to know the Unknown,
> To love the Uncreated! Earth, farewell!

Sigourney's equivalent of the romantic epiphany is almost always a Christian meditation; this kind of explicit interest in sublime transcendence is very rare in her work. The fact that **"The Dying Philosopher"** does metaphorize nature unrestrainedly suggests not only that the male persona gives Sigourney greater access to romantic subjectivity, but also that her Christian orientation might help her, in the majority of her poems, to preserve nature's independence.[11]

In sharp contrast to the poetess, who hardly enters her poems as a subject at all, God in Sigourney's poems is simultaneously an overarching subjectivity like the self in subjective poetry and an ultimate mysterious object, structurally similar to nature, truth, beauty, or the beloved in subjective poetry. This aesthetic function of God may help to explain the vital importance of religion for nineteenth-century American women in general. As well as giving them social and psychological power, Christianity provided, in the form of God as ultimate object and subject, a concept against which to structure their own subjecthood or, paradoxically, to reclaim their own socially structured objecthood as a spiritually significant and ahistorical condition.

One function of the God that often appears in Sigourney's poems is to carry the objectification that the poetess might otherwise have to impose on the natural world. Because this frees the poetess from concern about objectifying nature, the poems with religious subtexts directly involving God are often among the most subjective of Sigourney's nature poems. **"The Deep,"** for instance, is one of the relatively few poems by Sigourney in which the poetess speaks in the first person as herself, using the pronoun "I." The poem is therefore structurally much closer to a romantic lyric than is a poem in her typical second- or third-person voice or even a persona poem like **"The Dying Philosopher."** The association of the sea with God in

"The Deep" also allows the poetess-speaker to sustain an unusually long and metaphorically loaded series of questions in which she compares the sea to God's weaving, sculpture and treasure without any of the usual compensations or qualifications for such metaphorization. Furthermore, although in a nature poem more typical of Sigourney the speaker would not answer her own questions, here the presence of God provides answers. The answers, which refer to God rather than to the poetess, do not seem to be projections of the poetic self as Bryant's answers do, however; they consist of the ambiguous phrase "One reply!" and other, loaded questions: ". . . but one answer? of that One Dread Name? . . ."

Paradoxically, the same God that allowed Sigourney to sustain such unusual subjectivity becomes an objectifying ultimate subject himself by the end of this poem. This question-poem's only statement after the opening occurs in its last stanza:

> Therefore I come, a listener to thy voice,
> And bow me at thy feet, and touch my lip
> To thy cool billow, if perchance my soul,
> That fleeting wanderer on these shores of time,
> May, by thy voice instructed, learn of God.

With the "of" of the poem's last line, the subject/object ambiguity becomes grammatically evident: the poetess at the same time desires to learn *about* God, thus preserving her subjective centrality, and *from* God, now become the poem's other subject, and, one may assume, a more powerful subject than the poetess. The relationship between God and the sea described in the latter reading is one of ventriloquism and manipulation. It suggests, by analogy, a still greater objectification of the poetess: it is as if even in the process of learning about God she will remain, when contrasted with God's greater subjectivity, only a part of nature.

In **"Niagara,"** probably the most anthologized and one of the most complex of Sigourney's poems, God's double role as both subject and object is more obvious and more extended than it is in **"The Deep."** **"Niagara"** highlights, and unwinds to their ultimate unresolvable conflicts, the difficulties faced by Sigourney's poetic persona in a highly "poetic" subjective situation: the poetess addresses, in the first person, the famous waterfall that was for her culture a widely appropriated symbol of nature's sublime power.

In the first stanza, confusion between the appropriate roles for the poetess and the waterfall in this poetic situation are already evident. Which is the subject and which is the object; who is in control of the meanings in this text? The waterfall is described as resistless; if this word is meant in the sense of "unresisting," then how does the water remain "unfathomed"? If it is resistless in the sense of "irresist-

ible," then how is the poetess able to command it? The next adjectives used to describe the waterfall, "terror and beauty," give a clue to this dilemma that underscores the compassion the poetess might feel for a natural object that shares the woman's role of fetishized icon as well as pointing out her participation in the opposing, subjective conventions of romantic nature poetry: the robe "of terror" could mean not only that the waterfall inspires terror but that as an object *it is terrified,* perhaps because of its very beauty, its objectifiable sublimity. Perhaps the speaker here leaves the waterfall unfathomed out of compassion for it.

As the poem proceeds, the sense of the waterfall's subjectivity increases until, like the frost in **"Autumn,"** it overtakes the poetess' own subjectivity. When God clothes the falls in a wreath and mantle in the first stanza—as if, one might think, to further objectify them—he counteracts this by giving them, at the same time, a subjective voice. The waterfall is able to speak one thing with this voice—a "hymn" of "him", with God being the ultimate object at this point in the poem. This makes the waterfall more subjective than either the earth or the ocean, both of which are feminized in comparison with it at this point: (the earth explicitly, the ocean implicitly as it shrinks from brotherhood and plays a parental role towards its billows).

But while the waterfall's subjectivity increases, the poetess' reaches a crisis and declines. The crucial moment occurs as her description of the environment around the falls reaches the birds. Unlike the earth, water and plants the poetess has described previously, the birds present themselves to her as clear subjects in relation to the waterfall: "bold they venture near, dipping their wing." The poetess at first objectifies the birds anyway, however, carried away by the momentum of her second-person address to the waterfall: she includes the birds in her description without any compensatory poetic devices such as unanswered questions or metaphorization of herself. The poetess' awareness that the act of objectifying the birds has situated her within the subjective poetic tradition is apparent in the phrases "for us" and "our pencil's point" (which replace the earlier "lip of man," a lip from which the poetess as a female might conceivably have disassociated herself, even in the nineteenth century). Just at this point in the poem, however, when the poetess' subjective authorial voice is strongest, her subjectivity begins to turn in on itself. The remarks about poetry's futility signal the beginning of a retreat. The sole God-given "voice" in this poem is, after all, not the poetess' but the waterfall's.

In the short last stanza, God and the waterfall begin to function in place of the poetic self and actually to objectify the poetess in a subtle way. The phrase "Thou doth speak alone of God" can be read to mean not only that the falls speak only of God but that only the waterfall is entitled to speak of God, so that the poetess should be silent, an object rather than a subject in her poem. At the same time, paradoxically, such objectification of herself from the waterfall's perspective gives the poetess a Godlike subjective authority in the poem: since the waterfall can only speak of God, the poetess, as an object of the waterfall's speech in the poem, must become God which, as the creator of this poem, she in fact is, inside the poem. The connection between the poetess and God is emphasized by the reference to God's right hand, evoking a writer's hand; it is possible to read the statement "Thou dost speak / Alone of God, who pour'd thee as a drop / From his right-hand" as a reference to the writer creating the waterfall within the poem.

As her double roles of object and subject develop simultaneously, the poetess' authority and her lack of it are conflated, at the end of the poem, into an internalized version of the transcendent, ineffable sublimity that she might, in a subjective poem, have been expected to project outwards onto the great waterfall. The subject of the verb "bidding" in the final sentence, "Thou dost speak / Alone of God . . . bidding the soul . . . be still" can be read as either "Thou" or "God." If the subject of the verb is "Thou," then the waterfall closes the poem by asking the poetess' soul, the soul that looks on its fearful majesty, to be still, to remember her own "nothingness," her own objectification, and to stop writing about the world. If the subject of the verb is "God," however, then the lines describe God telling both the poetess, as reader of the waterfall, and the reader of the poem to be still. The poetess implores the reader not to objectify her while reading her poem, begging that the reader be wrapped in her or his own nothingness and become one with the God that the poetess is able to objectify, and that is already contained within her poem. At the same time, the God in the poem also bids the poetess, "the soul that looks / Upon" the waterfall in the poem, to be still.

The poetess' fears of the assertions involved in nature poetry, both the fears of violating and exploiting nature and the apparently consequent fears of being violated and exploited by readers, have been activated during the poem. The sublime romantic epiphany here is not so much something that the reader watches the poetess experience as something that occurs in the lack of consistent distinctions between subjects and objects in the poem—a process in which the reader participates by simultaneously identifying with and objectifying the poetess, the waterfall and God.

Many of the exquisite difficulties with poetic objectification apparent in the above reading of **"Niagara"** are contingent, I think, on the poetess' project in this particular poem: to find meaning in an accepted, culturally acknowl-edged symbol of the sublime that was commonly supposed to inspire private epiphanies. To the extent that it communalized noncommunal emotion, the waterfall must have put the sentimental attitude to a severe test. The speaker in this poem, privileging a socially sanctioned feeling of awe in the face of natural power, finds that it does not bind her to her society in a nonindividuated, non-egotistical way like the emotions of Christian faith and parental or filial love usually expressed in sentimental poetry of the period; instead, she is thrown by the already existent structure of this awe into the middle of a current of romantic ego. As if in a gesture of defense, **"Niagara,"** unlike the majority of Sigourney's nature poems, introduces God blatantly at its beginning. The poetess' subsequent continued attempt at a grand manner in treating a natural object puts her into repeated and direct confrontation with the very poetic processes that she generally avoids. The tension in this poem already prefigures, at the beginning of the nineteenth century, the conflict between the sentimental and romantic attitudes that would later structure many of Dickinson's nature poems.

Perhaps because of its encounter with romanticism, **"Niagara"** is, as I have said, currently Sigourney's best-known poem in spite of the fact that it is quite uncharacteristic of her work. In other poems which are less concerned with the poetic process, like **"The Coral Insect"** (*P* 167), Sigourney's attitude toward nature is free of such concerns and, in turn, frees nature to be the subject, not the object, of her poem. This true nature poem addresses the mystery of the coral's independent existence—including its possible allegorical celebration of human persistence—without filtering the experience through the drama of an individual human "I." And, far from suffering triteness or amateurishness due to its lack of a central poetic self, **"The Coral Insect"** seems to be freed by its relinquishing of romantic conventions: the exultant rhymes and triple rhythms reveal a contagious delight in the poetic imagination.

In this article, the definition of the sentimental poetic tradition rests largely on negatives: the absence of a central poetic self and the avoidance of the unequivocal metaphorization of nature. The qualities in Sigourney's poems that do not "succeed" according to prevalent aesthetic standards have been defined in terms of those standards nonetheless, rather than in their own terms. Perhaps this procedure is unavoidable at a time when critical discussion of poetry is so dominated by the assumptions of the subjective tradition that it is difficult to perceive poems from any other perspective. But I hope that before too long it will be possible to see the sentimental tradition as a literary movement in its own right, as a movement having its own roots, its own aesthetics, its own world-view, and its own inheritors.

Notes

1. I would like to thank Joanne Dobson and Martha Ackmann for their careful reading of this essay and their helpful suggestions on all levels of revision, as well as Jay Fliegelman for his consistent encouragement.

2. During the first half of the twentieth century, the few critics who wrote about Sigourney were only slightly less condescending than contemporary critics. Even Haight's lengthy discussion of her work in the biography, while acknowledging her "sweetness of versification," spends most of its time analyzing the "absurdities" of her style (92). Also see Collin, Green, and Jordan. For scholarship connecting Dickinson with the poetesses, see Dobson and St. Armand.

3. See for example Hyatt J. Waggoner's introduction to Whittier and Gelpi on Bryant.

4. See Tompkins's chapters on *Uncle Tom's Cabin* and *The Wide, Wide World* and Douglas's introduction to *Uncle Tom's Cabin*.

5. For a recent discussion of female poets' hatred of the sentimental tradition, see Gilbert and Gubar's "Forward into the Past" (255-56).

6. Certain sentimental poems such as Frances Osgood's "Oh! Hasten to My Side!" or Alice Cary's "The Bridal of Woe" do seem "egocentric" in that they explicitly concern the self's moods and thoughts. These poems anticipate the later development of the poetess tradition as it became increasingly interiorized in the work of such writers as Ella Wheeler Wilcox and Sara Teasdale. To the extent that the religion of romantic love replaces that of Christianity in the poetess tradition, poetesses concentrate more on the individual self. Crucial differences, however, separate even their self-concerned love poems from poems in the subjective tradition. In the poetess tradition, the self tends to be perceived (and metaphorically described) in terms of the natural world rather than the natural world being perceived in terms of the self. The result is that the self and its moods are created and presented to the reader almost as a kind of natural object or landscape, in a movement very different from the encompassing of external reality typical of the subjective tradition.

7. To this statement Fetterley adds, "she made poetry an acceptable and profitable profession for women" (107).

8. Hereafter, *P* will refer to Sigourney's *Poems, PO* to *Pocahontas and Other Poems* and *SP* to *Select Poems.*

9. Two recent theories of feminist aesthetics illuminate Sigourney's recognition of nature's separateness and her conventionality. Schweickart has postulated a feminist model of reading which

> features an intersubjective construction. . . . The reader . . . comes into close contact with an interiority—a power, a creativity, a suffering, a vision—that is not identical with her own. . . . the subject of the literary work is its author, not the reader.
>
> (52)

Sigourney's attitude toward nature in those poems where she questions it can be compared to the attitude of the feminist reader in this model; nature preserves its interiority and difference, while the poetess as reader puts much more emphasis on the mysteries of nature than on her own response. Sigourney's "artificiality" is illuminated by Elaine Showalter's essay "Piecing and Writing." Showalter makes a connection between the "strongly marked American women's tradition of piecing, patchwork, and quilting" and the structures of contrast and repetition in some nineteenth-century women's texts (223). The patchwork quilt, which incorporates scraps of various already-woven fabrics into a new design, is a useful figure for Sigourney's artificial, conventional nature poems. In an aesthetic much like that of the patchwork quilt, the poems combine inherited idioms and cliches in new ways, not for the sake of realistic representation, but for function—financial, artistic and often moral—and for decorative abstraction.

10. Margaret Homans has pointed out that "the romantic lyric depends on an implicit plot, the plot of male heterosexual desire" ("Syllables" 583-86). Following Iragary, Homans sees the processes of both metaphorizing and linguistic representation itself as hierarchical and essentially masculine (I would say, patriarchal) while the referent and the vehicle of a metaphor are "categorically feminine" (572-73). Following Homans, we can postulate that the poetess' discomfort with metaphorizing nature is intimately connected with a consciousness that they, as women, are habitually metaphorized as part of nature and that, in the larger context, "appropriation is the relationship between the self-centred Romantic speaker or poet and the feminine objects about which he writes" (*Women Writers* 37).

11. The fact that other Christian poets, such as Rossetti (see "Amor Mundi" or "A Rose Plant in Jericho") and Hopkins (see "The Caged Skylark" or the figure of evening in "Spelt from Sibyl's Leaves"), found it possible to metaphorize nature in the service of Christianity leads me to believe that Christianity did not lead Sigourney not to metaphorize nature. Rather, it provided her with a means not to do so. (Even in poems by Sigourney that almost seem like religious metaphors, like "Midnight Thoughts at Sea" (*PO* 149) or "Hymn at Sea" (*PO* 119), the storms and waves are in fact literal.)

Works Cited

Bryant, William Cullen. *The Poetical Works of William Cullen Bryant.* Ed. H. C. Sturges. New York: D. Appleton, 1903.

Collin, Grace Lathrop. "Lydia Huntley Sigourney." *New England Magazine* 27 (1902): 15-20.

Conrad, Susan P. *Perish the Thought: Intellectual Women in Romantic America 1830-1860.* Secaucus: Citadel Press, 1978.

Dobson, Joanne. "'The Invisible Lady': Emily Dickinson and the Conventions of the Female Self." *Legacy* 3.1 (1986): 41-55.

Douglas, Ann. Introduction. "The Art of Controversy." *Uncle Tom's Cabin.* By Harriet Beecher Stowe. New York: Viking Penguin, 1981. 7-36.

Fetterley, Judith, ed. *Provisions: A Reader From 19th-Century American Women.* Bloomington: Indiana UP, 1985.

Gelpi, Albert. *The Tenth Muse: The Psyche of the American Poet.* Cambridge:.Harvard UP, 1975.

Gilbert, Sandra, and Susan Gubar. *The Madwoman in the Attic.* New Haven: Yale UP, 1979.

———. "Forward Into the Past." *Historical Studies and Literary Criticism.* Ed. Jerome McGann. Madison: U of Wisconsin P, 1985.

Green, David Bonnell. "William Wordsworth and Lydia Huntley Sigourney." *New England Quarterly* 37 (1964): 527-31.

Haight, Gordon S. "Longfellow and Mrs. Sigourney." *New England Quarterly* 3 (1930): 532-37.

———. *Mrs. Sigourney: Sweet Singer of Hartford.* New York: Yale UP, 1930.

Hartmann, Geoffrey. "Romanticism and 'Anti-Self-Consciousness'" *Romanticism and Consciousness.* Ed. Harold Bloom. New York: Norton, 1970.

Homans, Margaret. "'Syllables of Velvet': Dickinson, Rossetti, and the Rhetorics of Sexuality." *Feminist Studies* 11 (1985): 569-93.

———. *Women Writers and Poetic Identity.* Princeton: Princeton UP, 1980.

Jordan, Philip D. "The Source of Mrs. Sigourney's 'Indian Girl's Burial'." *American Literature* 4 (1932): 300-05.

Mermin, Dorothy. "The Female Poet and the Embarrassed Reader: Elizabeth Barrett Browning's *Sonnets From the Portuguese.*" *ELH* 48 (1981): 351-67.

St. Armand, Barton Levi. *Emily Dickinson and Her Culture: The Soul's Society..* Cambridge: Cambridge UP, 1984.

Schweikart, Patrocinio P. "Reading Ourselves: Toward a Feminist Theory of Reading." *Gender and Reading.* Ed. Elizabeth A. Flynn and Patrocinio P. Schweickart. Baltimore: Johns Hopkins UP, 1986, 31-62.

Showalter, Elaine. "Piecing and Writing." *The Poetics of Gender.* Ed. Nancy K. Miller. New York: Columbia UP, 1986.

Sigourney, Lydia H. *Pocahontas and Other Poems.* New York: Harper, 1841.

———. *Poems.* Philadelphia: Key & Biddle, 1834.

———. *Select Poems.* Philadelphia: John E. Potter, 1845.

Sklar, Kathryn Kish. *Catharine Beecher: A Study in American Domesticity.* New Haven: Yale UP, 1973.

Todd, Janet. *Sensibility: An Introduction.* London: Metheun, 1986.

Tompkins, Jane P. *Sensational Designs: The Cultural Work of American Fiction 1790-1860.* New York: Oxford UP, 1985.

Walker, Cheryl. *The Nightingale's Burden: Women Poets and American Culture Before 1900.* Bloomington: Indiana UP, 1982.

Watts, Emily Stipes. *The Poetry of American Women from 1932 to 1945.* Austin: U of Texas P, 1977.

Waggoner, Hyatt H. Introduction. *The Poetical Works of Whittier.* Boston: Houghton Mifflin, 1975, xv-xxv.

Wimsatt, William K. "The Structure of Romantic Nature Imagery." *Romanticism and Consciousness.* Ed. Harold Bloom. New York: Norton, 1970.

Wood, Ann Douglas. "Mrs. Sigourney and the Sensibility of the Inner Space." *New England Quarterly* 45 (1972): 165-81.

Nina Baym (essay date 1990)

SOURCE: "Reinventing Lydia Sigourney," in *American Literature,* Vol. 62, No. 3, September, 1990, pp. 385-404.

[*In the following essay, Baym claims that critics have failed to appreciate the extent to which Sigourney's writings express a very public (as opposed to domestic) program, which required Sigourney to assume particular social roles as a strategy to achieve a mass audience.*]

If Lydia Howard Huntley Sigourney had not existed, it would have been necessary to invent her. In fact, she was invented. As American women writers began to publish in numbers before the Civil War, one of their number would inevitably be construed as an epitome of the phenomenon of female authorship in its range of allowed achievements and required inadequacies. Now, here was a poor, virtuous, essentially self-educated woman whose writing was sponsored by one of the leading families in Hartford, Connecticut, with additional patronage from many other New England aristocrats.[1] She published pious poetry on domestic subjects in the major magazines and wrote for the Sunday School League. Having made a good marriage (from the social point of view), she faithfully performed her duties as wife, mother, and hostess; and she began to write for money only after financial reverses put the family under economic duress.

Here, in short, was a woman whose example could instruct all would-be literary women as to what they could do, what they should do, and also what they had better not do. Here also was a life in which a modern success story of upward mobility through hard work and self-sacrifice led to an affirmation of traditional class structure. The social construction of Lydia Sigourney began, then, in her own lifetime. And, with Sigourney's canny participation, it continued throughout her lifetime as well.

For example, the prefatory "advertisement" to the 1815 *Moral Pieces in Prose and Verse,* which was written by Daniel Wadsworth, stresses the necessary haste with which she wrote: for the most part her compositions "arose from the impulse of the moment, at intervals of relaxation from such domestic employments, as the circumstances of the writer, and her parents, rendered indispensable." Thirty-two years later, Sigourney's preface to the fifth (1847) edition of her *Select Poems* iterates the implications of that early notice; most of the poems in the book "were suggested by passing occasions, and partake of the nature of extemporaneous productions; all reveal by their brevity, the short periods of time allotted to their construction."[2] The poet encourages readers to think that she wrote only short poems, and wrote them quickly; one would never guess from this preface that by 1847 she had also written (among other things) a 4,000 line historical epic in five cantos and two other historical poems each over 500 lines long.[3] Haste, perhaps; extemporaneous brevity, no. But the poems in *Select Poems* are a selection from her work consisting mainly "of the more popular poems which had appeared during several years in various periodicals" (*Letters,* p. 337). In other words, this book was designed to recirculate such work as had already proved itself in the public arena, and thus was directed to audience rather than author preference. (Or the author preference that it was directed toward was money-making.) The incremental popularity of collections of the already-popular (*Select Poems*—called simply *Poems* in its first edition of 1834— went through more than twenty-five editions during Sigourney's life) further consolidated a representation of the author based on her best-loved, or most widely known, poetry. The reappearance of these poems in anthologies like Rufus Griswold's or Caroline May's added to the effect.

We conventionally lament the way in which careers of "major" nineteenth-century American authors were deformed by market pressures. "Dollars damn me," Herman Melville complained in a much quoted letter to Nathaniel Hawthorne. Dollars most certainly did *not* damn Sigourney; but the Lydia Sigourney who was so often albeit so ambiguously and ambivalently praised in her own lifetime, and has been so heartily calumniated subsequently, is a representation based on only some fraction of what she wrote and published. The Sigourney of the consolation elegy, the funerary poem, the Sigourney obsessed with dead children and dead mothers, has been constituted by a succession of audiences, each basing its commentary and opinion on an ever smaller portion of the original record. Even now, when writing by antebellum American women is more highly valued than it has been for a long time, the mere mention of Sigourney's name suffices to invoke a caricature: a mildly comical figure who exemplifies the worst aspects of domestic sentimentalism.[4]

It would of course be utterly perverse to argue that Sigourney did *not* write many poems about death, among which were poems about dead mothers and children.[5] Sigourney herself frequently called attention to her elegiac practice, as for example in her preface to *Zinzendorff,* which said among other things that "should it be objected that too great a proportion of [the poems] are elegiac, the required apology would fain clothe itself in the language of the gifted Lord Bacon:—If we listen to David's harp, we shall find as many hearse-like harmonies, as carols; and the pencil of Inspiration hath more labored to describe the afflictions of Job, than the felicities of Solomon" (p. 6). The category of elegy, or consolation poetry, or funerary verse is, however, quite general; and one may discern within the Sigourney elegiac corpus a variety of poetic subtypes. There are *memento mori* poems of a reflective cast deriving from some general observation on nature or the world; there are what I would want to call generic or situational elegies whose subject is denoted as a member of a class, rather than as an individual; and then there are elegies for named persons—memorial or obituary poems. One need go no further afield than the table of contents of *Zinzendorff* for examples of each type. **"Death among the Trees"** would appear to be (and is) a general reflection on the inevitability of death, as is **"Thoughts for Mourners."** **"Death of the Wife of a Clergyman, during the Sickness of Her Husband," "Death of a Young Wife," "Burial of Two Young Sisters," "Death of a Young Lady at the Retreat for the Insane," "Farewell of a Missionary to Africa, at the Grave of his Wife and Child,"** and **"Death of a Young Musician"** are situational elegies. **"Funeral of Dr. Mason F. Cogswell," "Death of the Rev. Gordon Hall," "Death of Mrs. Harriet W. L. Winslow," "Death of a Son of the Late Honorable Fisher Ames," "Death of the Rev. Alfred Mitchell,"** and **"Death of the Rev. W. C. Walton"** are some of the specific memorials.

My distinctions here are not merely formal; each of the three kinds of poem invokes a different sort of poetic occasion. (And, as the titles above show, the subjects are by no means exclusively women and/or children.) The *memento mori* poem, the type that Sigourney practices the least, is composed as an internal dialogue in which the persona attempts to come to terms with death in general, with the death of a loved one, or with one's own inevitable death. As a reflection, it is distanced from any immediate occasion of death. Thus, it bespeaks an interval of leisure, privacy, and solitude for the persona as well as any reader whose mental processes it may seek to guide and mime.

The generic and specific consolation poetry that Sigourney most often wrote, in contrast, is designed for immediate intervention at the moment of death or funeral. A generic elegy, like a greeting card, is available to the large number of people whose circumstances it suits at the moment; the memorial for a named person is designed to palliate the grief of a unique set of mourners. This set, however, can extend beyond close family to those who knew the dead individual by acquaintance or by name only. So newspaper obituaries serve us today. Thus, both the situational elegy and the obituary poem bespeak a public arena and a practical goal. They do not have time to expatiate on religious uncertainty, to exhibit the depth and extent of one's own grief, or to manage a personal catharsis; they aim to make suffering people feel better—and make them feel better fast. "Her muse has been a comforter to the mourner," Sarah Hale observed, and one necessary aspect of this comforting function is that the elegies are never about the speaker, always about others.[6]

Invariably, these useful poems designed specifically for Christians plug in a strong affirmation of the life to come. From the converging perspectives of High Victorianism and High Modernism, Sigourney's unsympathetic biographer Gordon Haight derides the intellectual simplicity of her religiosity; but *In Memoriam,* to which he invidiously compares Sigourney's elegiac corpus, was certainly not supposed to comfort any mourner besides its author.[7] Perhaps this other-directedness of Sigourney's elegiac voice also explains her minimal position in the narcissistic woman's poetic tradition developed by Cheryl Walker's *Nightingale's Burden,* a tradition centered on the topic of how hard it is to be a woman poet.[8] The activist and interventionist element in this elegiac poetry—an element that by all accounts succeeded in its intentions—would also seem to undermine Ann Douglas Wood's construal of Sigourney's death poetry: its "heroine was herself, but emptied of conflict, sublimated, and desexualized . . . a small figure . . . seemingly submissive, submerged, half-hypnotized and half automaton," and also to qualify Richard Brodhead's recent Foucauldian speculations on the "veiled ladies" who are supposed to comprise antebellum female authorship and readership.[9] In sum, even if we were to agree that Sigourney was a funerary poet and nothing but, we would need to develop a less homogeneous representation of her elegiac project.[10]

However, Sigourney wrote a great deal more than consolation verse. And she wrote a great deal that was not poetry; about two-thirds of her published books are prose. The range of her work inevitably allows for the construction of several Sigourneys who are unknown to modern criticism. One obvious such construction, which I will mention without developing, is the female of love and ritual, Sigourney the preceptress, author of books like *Letters to Young Ladies, Letters to Mothers,* and *Whispers to a Bride.*[11] In these conversational works she assumes the persona of trusted sisterly or motherly guide. This persona advocates a mix of republican and Victorian domestic ideologies that positions women in a home space at once within and apart from the larger social body.

But another, and to some degree opposed, Sigourney—whom I wish to elaborate on here—is Sigourney the history teacher and the historian. This Sigourney is much more directly related to the polity than the womanly preceptress, for through historical representations she constructs a view of the public sphere and aggressively comments on it.[12] For this Sigourney, history writing in various forms is a central and continuing literary endeavor. It would appear, in fact, that well over half of what she published in both prose *and* poetry was historical in content; and it was also political—in a fairly conventional sense of the term—in implication.[13] Through the learning, teaching, and writing of history, Sigourney (like several other literary women of the era) enacted womanly behavior that in many ways nullified the distinction between public and private that operated so crucially in other contexts.[14]

Only one work from this sizable and ignored segment of Sigourney's output has hitherto been excavated and analyzed. In an important essay, Sandra A. Zagarell makes the general claim that Sigourney's *Sketch of Connecticut, Forty Years Since* (Hartford: Oliver D. Cooke, 1824) is "quite directly concerned with the foundations and organization of public life" and offers a vision that "deliberately extended official definitions of the nation to imagine an America grounded in inclusiveness and communitarianism."[15] Since the sketch deals with real events from a past era, I consider it a work of history; and I strongly concur with Zagarell that it has public intentions. Many other works by Sigourney are similarly directed to the public sphere and attempt to bring a womanly perspective to national (and even transnational) historical issues.

But rather than psychologize that perspective, as Zagarell does, I would prefer to historicize it. When historicized, Sigourney's politics emerge as a self-conscious advocacy of the tenets of "classical" (i.e., conservative) republicanism in an age of increasing liberalism; as an urging of the merits of non-sectarian evangelical Christianity on an increasingly disputatious and fragmented religious scene;

and as an effort to reconcile the civic with the spiritual realms in an amalgam of Christianity and republicanism.[16] These historical writings are internally conflicted because their attempt to affirm the progress of history is continually frustrated by the evident failure of Christian-republican ethics to meet the single most important test of the moral caliber of the American nation—the obligation to preserve the continent's "aborigines" by Christianizing them and integrating them into American society.

Sigourney used historical material in short poems and long poems, in sketches of varying length, in free-standing and embedded fictional narratives, and in a variety of non-fictional modes including biography, narrative history, and lesson books. By "lesson book" I mean a work designed for home teaching, whether by parents instructing young children or by people teaching themselves. Two examples of this genre are Sigourney's 1833 *Evening Readings in History*—"written with a desire of aiding a laudable custom, established by some of my particular friends, of devoting an hour in the evening to a course of reading with the younger members of their families, and examinations into their proficiency in the general departments of Education"—and her 1835 *Marcus Aurelius*—"this book was commenced as an assistant to parents in domestic education. Its highest ambition is to be in the hand of the mother, who seeks to aid in that most delightful of all departments, the instruction of her little ones."[17]

The subject matter of all this writing falls into four major categories: ancient and Biblical history; the history of Connecticut (more specifically of her own locale comprising the region around Hartford, Norwich, and New London) from settlement through Revolution; the American Revolution; and the history of the American Indians after the European arrival on the continent.[18] This fourth category is the subject that most preoccupied her; the other three topics often merged with it. In particular, the history of her own region and Indian history were inextricably connected. The Pequod War had been fought there, the local Mohegan tribe had joined with English settlers in their wars against the Pequods and (later) the Naragansetts, and the Mohegan chief Uncas was supposed to have ceded the land around Norwich to the English in return for protection from King Philip and other enemies. This meant that the establishment of the Christian American community that Sigourney extolled in the *Sketch of Connecticut* and elsewhere depended directly on white access to Indian land.[19]

Sigourney was fully aware of this fact, and drew from it the conclusion that the Anglo-American national character was defined by how whites acquired the land they needed and what happened to the Indians afterwards. In writing about the Indians she confronted the insoluble narrative problem that while three of her subjects were representable as comedies (the pagan world gave way to the Christian; the American Revolution was won by the right side; the Connecticut Valley fostered the most moral society ever known on earth) the fourth was an unmitigated tragedy. Sigourney also faced the insoluble *political* and *moral* problem that the triumphs of Christianity and republicanism in America were achieved at the cost of their own basic tenets. In destroying the Indians rather than domesticating them, republicanism ignored its commitments to civic virtue and to the amelioration of the lot of the needy by the fortunate; Christianity neglected its imperatives of charity and of taking all souls as equals before God.

Sigourney's narratives of the Indian disaster lead to the culminating plea that her countrymen should return to the essence of republican and Christian doctrine and stop destroying the Indians by murder and relocation. But this plea undermines the affirmative dynamic of her other historical representations by substituting an implicit declension model of American and Christian history; and it does this without mitigating in the least the unrepublican and unchristian carnage that has already taken place. From her historical perspective, the cessation of Indian destruction in the future—though it is much to be hoped for and though her writings are designed in part to further that goal—could not justify the erasure of past massacre. Whatever happened in future, that is, it was necessary to remember what had happened in the past. Unwilling to adopt a tragic or ironic stance toward history (though she could not always avoid doing so), Sigourney could not accept the palliating conviction found in so many writings of the time that the destruction of the Indians is merely inevitable. And convinced that a Christian must see the Indians as human kin, however "other" they may be, she cannot write a history in which their obliteration could be frankly presented as a sign of historical progress.

There is no honest way to resolve her dilemma, so Sigourney's historical narratives typically end in an outright articulation of contradiction. "We are struck with the prominence and discordance of some of the features in the character of our ancestors," she writes in a prose sketch called **"The Fall of the Pequod."** Boldness, cruelty, and "the piety to which they turned for sanction, even when the deed and motive seemed at variance," make a strange combination:

> The unresting vigilance with which they blotted out the very name of Pequod . . . was not less arbitrary than the dismemberment of Poland, and savored more of the policy of heathen Rome than of Christ. Mason, in common with the historians of that age, bitterly blamed the Indians for stratagems in war, but chose to adopt the creed he had denounced, and to prove himself an adept in the theory that he condemned. . . . The once-

powerful aboriginal tribe . . . perished without a hand to write its epitaph: an emblem of the fate of that vanishing race to whom the brotherhood of the white man hath hitherto been as the kiss of Judas.[20]

No doubt, some might see prose like this as intellectually confused. But it could be equally described as intellectually honest in a political context where blunt hypocrisy and debonair obfuscation were the order of the day.

"Traits of the Aborigines of America" was Sigourney's first work about American Indians. Despite its bland title and its anonymous publication, this five-canto work of 4,000 blank verse lines, with extensive scholarly annotation, is her longest and most ambitious poem.[21] It is packed with classical references and historical allusion, and dense with information about Indian tribes. While it might be thought of as a belated entry in the competition for "the" American epic, it is uniquely structured from the Indian point of view and its narrative extends beyond the territorial United States to include the story of the continent from the Arctic circle to South America. This story, regardless of where it transpires, is always the same: the Indians welcome the newcomers and are exterminated. The core of this story is embodied in another poem, a short piece called **"The Indian's Welcome to the Pilgrim Fathers,"** which appeared in the *Zinzendorff* volume, and reads in part:

> When sudden from the forest wide,
>   A red-brow'd chieftain came,
> With towering form, and haughty stride,
>   And eye like kindling flame:
> No wrath he breath'd, no conflict sought,
>   To no dark ambush drew,
> But simply *to the Old World brought,*
>   *The welcome of the New.*
>
> That *welcome* was a blast and ban
>   Upon thy race unborn.
> Was there no seer, thou fated Man!
>   Thy lavish zeal to warn?
> Thou in thy fearless faith didst hail
>   A weak, invading band,
> But who shall heed thy children's wail,
>   Swept from their native land?
>
> (pp. 47-48)

"Traits of the Aborigines" calls on us to revise many of our conceptions of the literary aims, if not achievements, of American women before the Civil War. Here I want only to sketch the epic's organization and suggest the position it takes toward American history and contemporaneous American historiography. Canto I begins with the Indians in undisturbed possession of the continent and then introduces a chronicle of incursion: "First, to their northern coast / Wander'd the Scandinavian" (I, 253-54); after a while Columbus comes—the Indians thought he and his men were Gods, "nor dream'd their secret aim /

Was theft and cruelty, to snatch the gold / That sparkled in their streams, and bid their blood / Stain those pure waters" (I, 44-47); Portuguese, French, Irish, English—everybody comes. Christians come too, bringing the potential benefit of their religion to the Indians. But that benefit does not develop, because the Christians do not behave like Christians.

In Canto II, incursions become more extensive and frequent: "Almost it seemed / As if old Europe, weary of her load, / Pour'd on a younger world her thousand sons / In ceaseless deluge" (II, 8-11). The bulk of the canto narrates the life of John Smith, allowing the poet to provide a geography and history of most of the world through a chronicle of his travels. Pocahontas' rescue of him is compared to Pharoah's daughter rescuing Moses—and with the same ultimately disastrous effect on her people: "little thought / The Indian Monarch, that his child's weak arm / Fostered that colony, whose rising light / Should quench his own forever" (II, 1093-96). Sigourney vacillates between comic and tragic interpretations of the narrative, and simultaneously avoids and intensifies both readings by focusing on the conversion and early death of Pocahontas herself. There is some unspecified and contradictory connection between the conversion and the death—on the one hand it seems that Christianity itself is what kills Pocahontas, on the other that, thanks to her conversion, she dies regenerate. The canto ends with brief attention to the founding of Pennsylvania, Delaware, and Florida, always from the vantage point of those who are forced out by European settlement. "Pressing west / O'er the vain barrier, and retreating tide / Of Mississippi, spread our ancestors, / Taking a goodly portion, with the sword, / And with their bow" (II, 1186-90).

Canto III positions itself with the now outcast and understandably hostile Indians in their various forest refuges, describes many instances of savage warfare (some of which are described with classical allusions casting the Indians as heroes) with a ringing attack on white people for their own instigatory barbarism as well as the hypocrisy with which they fault the Indians. "Who are these, / Red from the bloody wine-press, with its stains / Dark'ning their raiment? Yet I dare not ask / Their clime and lineage, lest the accusing blasts, / Waking the angry echoes, should reply / 'Thy Countrymen!'" (III, 905-10).

Canto IV is the shortest in the poem, and in some sense is also its conceptual heart. It begins by praising those few—Eliot, Heckewelder—who went among the Indians to preach Christianity, but gives most of its lines to Tuscarora, who mocks those of his tribe who want to convert:

> Behold! what glorious gifts
> Ye owe to white men. What good-will and peace
> They shed upon you! Exile and the sword!

Poisons and rifled sepulchres! and see!
They fain would fill the measure of their guilt
With the dark cheat of that accursed faith
Whose precepts justify *their* nameless crimes,
Your countless woes.

(IV, 348-54)

The point that Sigourney is after here is that the whites have created not only justifiable Indian hostility to them as a group, but hostility as well to the Christianity that they claim to represent. The necessary task of joining with the Indians in brotherly love has been made infinitely more difficult by the white people's betrayal of their own religion.

Canto V then departs from the historical record to urge on Christian Americans the true obligations of their Christianity. "Make these foes your friends" (V, 546-47). The narrator acknowledges that most living Indians are already demoralized and degraded and sees the possibility—albeit at some horrendous bloody cost to themselves—of the whites completely exterminating the Indians. But it argues vehemently that "our God hath made / All of one blood, who dwell upon the earth" (V, 406-07); the only important difference between red and white people is that whites are (supposedly) Christian. Their very religion requires whites to Christianize the Indians. And when the Indians also become Christians, their justified desire for revenge will be set aside; they will then become an integral part of the American republic, and that republic, though no longer purely white, will be purely Christian.

Obviously this missionary perspective works from an idea of the Indians' likeness to whites rather than of their dignity in difference; it assumes that Indian culture is inferior and must give way to Christian culture. Even so, **"Traits of the Aborigines"** made public demands that at the time were thoroughly Utopian. In the memoir written some forty years later, Sigourney dryly observes that the poem "was singularly unpopular, there existing in the community no reciprocity with the subject." But her own views had not changed in the intervening years; "our injustice and hard-hearted policy with regard to the original owners of the soil has ever seemed to me one of our greatest national sins" (Letters, p. 327).

Two years after the publication of **"Traits of the Aborigines,"** a book on an ostensibly different subject reverted to the Indian theme; nine of the eighteen chapters of the ***Sketch of Connecticut, Forty Years Since*** are about the Mohegan remnant living on a reservation near Norwich, where the sketch is set. The work as a whole is designed around the central figure of Madam L———, a benevolent aristocratic widow whose charities and liberalities sustain a hierarchical community in productive harmony.[22] This conservative republican theme is sounded at the very start of the sketch with its evocation of the town of N——— (Norwich) as site of "the singular example of an aristocracy, less intent upon family aggrandizement, than upon becoming illustrious in virtue" (p. 4). Unlike other sections of the country in the years immediately following the Revolution, there was no "agitation" in Connecticut because "the body of the people trusted in the wisdom of those heroes and sages of whom they had furnished their proportion. They believed that the hands, which had been strengthened to lay the foundation of their liberty, amid the tempests of war, would be enabled to complete the fabric, beneath the smiles of peace" (p. 16). Madam L———'s contribution to the fabric, as a woman of social prominence and fortune, is to disburse appropriate charity and thereby maintain harmonious relations among the social classes. She gives out money, food, clothing, jobs, and advice to the deserving poor around her in return for their loyalty and subordination.

Madam L———'s beneficence usually succeeds in producing a peaceful and cohesive community, and is especially effective with marginalized women. As one impoverished woman is made to say, "what a blessed thing it is, when the hearts of the rich are turned to give work to the poor, and assist them to get the necessaries of life, for themselves and families" (p. 73). But with the Indians the story is different. In chapters 12 and 13, two tribal leaders—its chief and its Christian minister—inform her that most of their members have decided to leave Norwich and move to the interior where they will unite with another tribe. This decision shows that Madam L———'s charities are insufficient and beside the point where Indians are concerned. Individualistic Indians cannot accept a position at the bottom of a class hierarchy, which is where the community of N——— places them. Their distaste for settled agriculture makes it impossible for them to survive on their reservation, which "would have been more than adequate to their wants, had they been assiduous in its cultivation" (p. 31). Most of all, they believe—they know—that the whites are determined to exterminate them (always excepting Madam L——— herself), and after experiencing a century and a half of violence, they have given up all thought of resisting. Their move is only a stopgap. "Ere long, white men will cease to crush us, for we will cease to be" (p. 160). Occum, the minister, insists that Christianity holds promise for Indians, but Robert Ashbow, the chief, counters that "Christianity is for white men" (p. 161). As they depart, one young warrior asks despairingly, "Whither shall we go, and not hear the speech of the white man?" (p. 173).

The ***Sketch*** concludes with three chapters given over to the intriguing allegory of Oriana, a beautiful white woman whose life has been saved in war by a Mohegan warrior who adopts her to replace his own dead daughter. Indian adoption of whites was a well-documented historical phenomenon; in the *Sketch* the gesture also stands for the behavior of those many Indians who welcomed, fed, and protected the original white colonists, wherever they set foot on American soil. The reciprocal willingness of Oriana to become their daughter and help them become civilized Christians, however, does *not* conform to documented white behavior; it is a representation of what whites *should* have done. Oriana's lingering death during the narrative is an event susceptible of various interpretations and perhaps signifies the fantasy status of her behavior; the image in any case derives from a radical Christianity that leaves republican ideology, even as practiced by the exemplary Madam L———, completely out of the picture.[23]

This brings me to the *Zinzendorff* volume of 1835. The piece that gives its name to the title is a 584-line annotated poem in blank verse about Count Zinzendorff, founder of the radical Christian Moravian sect. It centers on Zinzendorff's mission to the Indians of the Wyoming Valley in 1742, and blends supposed historical fact with legend. The focus is on his bravery in going among Indians who deeply distrust his purposes. "Sought he to grasp their lands? / To search for gold? to found a mystic throne / Of dangerous power?" (lines 100-02). Zinzendorff's peaceful persistence and his appeal to the women, children, and old people of the tribe, as well as the evidence of his remarkable escapes from plots against his life, persuade the Indian rulers to take his message seriously.

Sigourney begins with a brief allusion to the Wyoming Valley massacre of 1778, when an alliance of Tory Pennsylvanians and Indians attacked emigrants from Connecticut who had settled in the Pennsylvania valley. She maintains that the aggressions of whites as they had appropriated Indian land in the decades before the massacre had created Indian hostility and thus were the actual historical cause of the massacre. Zinzendorff, in contrast, had gone among the Indians with truly Christian motives. When, toward the end of the poem, the Indians are made to lament Zinzendorff's return to Europe, their grief is interpreted by the poet as prophetic of their future at the hands of people who will settle with self-aggrandizing rather than self-effacing intentions (lines 495-505). In brief, Zinzendorff's was the road not taken, and so the poem closes with an appeal to Christians to desist from sectarian controversy and unite in peaceful missionary activities among the Indians. Maybe there is still time, the poem says, to reverse the historical process and bring Indians into the nation. If this were to happen, the nation would become the Christian entity that it only pretends to be now.

Sigourney also wrote a sensationalist sketch about the Wyoming massacre, **"Legend of Pennsylvania,"** collected in *Myrtis*. She begins with the history that led to carnage. "The Connecticut colonists evinced their national courage and tenacity in defence of their homes, and what they deemed their legal possessions. The Pennsylvanians were equally inflexible in what they considered their antecedent rights. The Aborigines contended for their favorite dominion with a lion-like despair" (p. 179). One disaster after another is represented in the destruction of families and registered in the responses of surviving women. At the story's end, the last member of a once-thriving family of Connecticut pioneers in the valley joins the Moravians at Nazareth, living out the rest of her life as a teacher in the girls' school there. (The Moravians had an interest in women's education and founded some of the earliest boarding schools for young women in the country.) Here again Sigourney typically invokes the pacific and womanly alternative to carnage.

The mood of **"Pocahontas,"** published in the 1841 volume *Pocahontas, and Other Poems,* is less hopeful. The 504-line poem, in fifty-six modified Spenserian stanzas, recounts the life of Pocahontas as a memorial to the Indian princess. Although by 1841 numerous tributes to her had appeared in American literature, Sigourney's stamp on the story material is recognizable. She begins as she had begun **"Aborigines,"** from an assumed Indian perspective in the New World before the Europeans arrive. Apostrophizing the "clime of the West," she asks whether it was not "sweet, in cradled rest to lie, / And 'scape the ills that older regions know?" An entrance into history, long deferred, begins when the "roving hordes of savage men" look up to "behold a sail! another, and another!" She sounds her motif of Christian brotherhood: "What were thy secret thoughts, oh red-brow'd brother, / As toward the shore those white-wing'd wanderers press'd?" And when Powhatan, moved by his daughter's intercession, spares John Smith's life, Sigourney notes the ironic outcome of that event with the same comparison to Pharoah's daughter that she had made in **"Traits"** (Stanza XX).

"Thou wert the saviour of the Saxon vine, / And for this deed alone our praise and love are thine" (Stanza XXI), Sigourney says, once again stressing the self-destructive, ironically Christian tendency of the Indians to nurture and protect white intruders. Then, moving forward in time to the era of Indian surprise attacks on white settlements, she challenges the historians' accounts: "ye, who hold of history's scroll the pen, / Blame not too much those erring, red-brow'd men, / Though nursed in wiles. Fear is the white-lipp'd sire / Of subterfuge and treachery. 'Twere in vain / To bid the soul be true, that writhes beneath his chain" (Stanza XXIV). In other words, the whites, answering Indian generosity with oppression and dislocation, created the vengeful Indians whose behavior they now slander and use as a pretext for further incursions against them.

The poem continues with a chronicle of Pocahontas' capture, conversion, marriage, journey to England, and early death; but it makes clear that this personal narrative screens another, larger narrative when it returns at the end to the long view with which it began and addresses the Indians en masse:

> I would ye were not, from your fathers' soil
>   Track'd like the dun wolf, ever in your breast
> The coal of vengeance and the curse of toil;
>   I would we had not to your mad lip prest
> The fiery poison-cup, nor on ye turn'd
>   The blood-tooth'd ban-dog, foaming, as he burn'd
> To tear your flesh; but thrown in kindness bless'd
>   The brother's arm around ye, as ye trod,
> And led ye, sad of heart, to the bless'd Lamb of God.
>
> (Stanza LIV)

I wish we hadn't, but we have—this is undoubtedly a weak, sentimental, acknowledgment of national crime; but at least it is an acknowledgment. Sigourney's conventional memorializing of Pocahontas, savior and servant of the whites, leads to an invocation of those nameless Indian dead who heroically *resisted* white incursion—"King, stately chief, and warrior-host are dead, / Nor remnant nor memorial left behind" (Stanza LVI). Sigourney's poem memorializes them as well as Pocahontas.

All history writing, in Sigourney's literary approach to it, is a memorial to the past—not the past made to live again, not even a representation of the past, but a memorial of it. (And this point allows us to think of her elegiac verse as another, individualized, form of history writing.) Her writing about Indians can be seen as an attempt to influence the present moment in three ways. First, it argued for a sense of white responsibility toward the surviving remnants of Indian tribes; second, it tried to ensure that the Indian story became a part of American history no matter how badly the story reflected on the white conquerors; third, it insisted that the Indians were Americans. Here, her schooling in ancient history, with its chronicle of aggressor empires culminating in the mighty, yet decadent Rome, served as a storehouse of parallels for interpreting and representing more recent history. The conventional classical references through which the Founders historicized their vision of a nation became, when Sigourney treated the Indians, references rather to empire than to republic.

Sigourney's Indian writings can be followed into the 1850s where another long poem (this one about a pioneer family from Connecticut settling in Ohio) features a stalwart Indian woman whose medicinal skills save the life of one of the settler children.[24] And the general historical strain in her writing continues to the very end of her life, as ***Letters of Life*** iterates the arcadian vision of early republican Connecticut that had animated the ***Sketch*** of 1822. Whether we should reinstall Sigourney as an important nineteenth-century American writer is a matter beyond the scope of this essay; but that she has been the victim of a social construction based on limited awareness of her own work cannot be doubted. That a writer with so obviously public a program should come down to us as the most private and domesticated of antebellum women authors suggests the need to look again at the scope of antebellum women's writing.

Notes

1. Sigourney's first book was *Moral Pieces, in Prose and Verse* (Hartford: Sheldon & Goodwin, 1815). Publication was arranged by Daniel Wadsworth of Hartford. The subscribers' list at the back of *Moral Pieces* comprises some 721 names that are a virtual roll-call of conservative first families from Hartford, Farmington, New Haven, New London, Norwich, Middletown, Fairfield, Litchfield, Boston, Salem, Cambridge, Charlestown, Marblehead, and other Connecticut and Massachusetts towns.

2. *Select Poems* (Philadelphia: E. B. and J. Biddle, 1847), p. vii.

3. Sigourney's memoir lists fifty-six different books published in her lifetime, a few of these edited; the posthumous memoir itself becomes the fifty-seventh. She asserted that uncollected material published in almost three hundred different periodicals would easily amount to several additional volumes, and Gordon Haight, her only biographer, accepts this claim. See her memoir, *Letters of Life* (New York: D. Appleton, 1866), p. 366 (hereafter cited as *Letters*). See also Haight, *Mrs. Sigourney: The Sweet Singer of Hartford* (New Haven: Yale Univ. Press, 1930), p. 173. There is no Sigourney bibliography; many of her published books are difficult to find, and much if not most of the uncollected periodical material is probably now unrecoverable.

4. E.g., Jane Tompkins, in "The Other American Renaissance," *Sensational Designs: The Cultural Work of American Fiction, 1790-1860* (New York: Oxford Univ. Press, 1985), refers in passing to "Mrs. Sigourney—who epitomizes the sentimental tradition for modern critics" (p. 160). In *Notable American Women*—whose purpose, one thought, was to overturn stereotypes—Gordon Haight says that "death was always her favorite theme—the death of infants, of consumptive children, of missionaries in Burma and Liberia, of poets and lunatics, of artists and sailors, of college students and deaf-dumb-and-blind girls. Her rhyming of pious truisms made a wide appeal and established a trade that newspaper poets have carried on prosperously"—*Notable American Women* (Cambridge: Harvard Univ. Press, 1971), III, 289.

5. In her 1827 *Poems,* I count 16 elegies out of 114 pieces in the volume; in the 1835 *Zinzendorff, and Other Poems,* 50 out of 172; in the 1841

Pocahontas, and Other Poems, 15 out of 115; and in the 1847 *Select Poems* already cited, 32 out of 126—Poems (Boston: S. G. Goodrich, 1827); *Zinzendorff, and Other Poems* (New York: Leavitt, Lord, 1835); *Pocahontas, and Other Poems* (New York: Harper, 1841). Ann Douglas Wood, "Mrs. Sigourney and the Sensibility of the Inner Space," *New England Quarterly,* 45 (1972), 163-87, says that Zinzendorff is "almost solidly funerary verse" (p. 177). Assuming that she was not exaggerating for effect, as so many scholars have done when confronted with Sigourney's work, the difference between her "almost solidly" and my twenty-nine percent for the same volume may result from different criteria for defining the funerary genre.

6. Sarah Hale, *Woman's Record,* 2nd ed. (New York: Harper, 1855), p. 783.

7. "There were plenty of strong souls in the Victorian age whose 'piping took a troubled sound' when they chose to struggle with their doubts rather than drown them out with the cymbals of conformity" (Haight, p. 160). What Griswold did to Poe is, for students of American literature, a national calamity; what biographers have done to women still passes for urbanity and even (heaven help us) gallantry.

8. *The Nightingale's Burden: Women Poets and American Culture Before 1900* (Bloomington: Indiana Univ. Press, 1982). Walker briefly cites three of Sigourney's poems—two elegies and a poem praising Felicia Hemans—but centers the antebellum women's poetic tradition on Frances Osgood and Elizabeth Oakes-Smith.

9. Wood, "Mrs. Sigourney and the Sensibility of the Inner Space," pp. 170-71. Douglas has since modified the severe judgment of sentimental writing expressed in this essay and also in her influential *Feminization of American Culture* (New York: Knopf, 1977). Brodhead, "Sparing the Rod: Discipline and Fiction in Antebellum America," *Representations,* 21 (1988), 67-96, and "Veiled Ladies: Toward a History of Antebellum Entertainment," *American Literary History,* 1 (1989), 273-94, argues for the increasing privatization of reading in the antebellum era (or, rather, for that era's invention of mass reading as a private activity), with individual readers constructed as isolated and passive consumers of mass-produced literary goods. Without denying that such a reading practice existed or might have existed, I see in the memorial poem that forms part of the public occasion of the funeral and is then used, re-used, and adapted by successive groups of mourners who find it pertinent a very different representation of antebellum reading. Sigourney's success in this endeavor may be partly measured by the fact that she was constantly asked to write obituary verse, frequently by people she did not know. *Letters* recounts some of the requests that she found particularly amusing; e.g., "the owner of a canary-bird, which had accidentally been starved to death, wishes some elegiac verses" (p. 373). What she did not find amusing, however, was the expectation of these supplicants that she would supply such poetry gratis.

10. Emily Stipes Watts, the most clear-headed commentator on Sigourney's obituary verse, thinks it confronts women's increasing isolation within the family as antebellum industrialization separated the worlds of men and women. See *The Poetry of American Women from 1632 to 1945* (Austin: Univ. of Texas Press, 1977), pp. 83-97. Watts's claim that the 1834 *Poems* contains Sigourney's best poetry and her decision to limit analysis to that volume seem to me problematic (p. 84).

11. I allude to Carroll Smith-Rosenberg's well-known essay, "The Female World of Love and Ritual: Relations between Women in Nineteenth-Century America," *Signs,* 1 (1975), 1-29. As a former schoolteacher who was probably never again as happy as she had been in the classroom, Sigourney took particular pleasure in this mother-sister-mentor persona. In *Letters* she says that "communion with those of my own sex in life's blossoming season has always been to me delightful" (p. 335). She recalls that her "earliest promptings of ambition" were "to keep a school," and that even as a child she "arranged my dolls in various classes, instructing them not only in the scanty knowledge I had myself attained, but boldly exhorting and lecturing them on the higher moral duties" (pp. 186-87).

12. Actually, the domestic preceptress was also a student of history and found history the most pleasant and important subject to teach her female charges: "How much did I enjoy unfolding with them the broad annals of History. Seated in a circle, like a band of sisters, we traced in the afternoon, by the guidance of Rollin, the progress of ancient times, or the fall of buried empires" (*Letters,* p. 203).

13. I generalize from a reading of eighteen of Sigourney's books and from her descriptive catalogue of all her books in *Letters,* pp. 324-65.

14. See Linda Kerber's "Separate Spheres, Female Worlds, Woman's Place: The Rhetoric of Women's History," *Journal of American History,* 75 (1988), 9-39, for an excellent discussion of the usefulness and limitation of the idea of the separate spheres as a tool of cultural analysis. At least one important element in our probable misunderstanding of the public sphere for women like Sigourney is our Catch-22 decision to treat religion as a private matter beginning with the very historical moment when women became religious activists. For another example of female Christian activism see my "Onward Christian Women: Sarah Hale's History of the World," *New England Quarterly,* 63 (June, 1990), 249-70.

15. "Expanding 'America': Lydia Sigourney's Sketch of Connecticut, Catharine Sedgwick's Hope Leslie," *Tulsa Studies in Women's Literature,* 6 (1987), 225-46. In her "Narrative of Community: The Identification of a Genre," *Signs,* 13 (1988), 498-527, Zagarell situates the Sketch of Connecticut in a specifically female genre conformable to the paradigm developed by Nancy Chodorow and Carol Gilligan in *The Reproduction of Mothering: Psychoanalysis and the Sociology of Gender* (Berkeley: Univ. of California Press, 1978) and *In a Different Voice: Psychological Theory and Women's Development* (Cambridge: Harvard Univ. Press, 1982), respectively. This paradigm supports a view of the male and female spheres as mutually exclusive. Aaron Kramer's *Prophetic Tradition in American Poetry* (Rutherford, N.J.: Farleigh Dickinson Univ. Press, 1968), p. 223, briefly notes the moral outrage expressed in "Pocahontas"; Joanne Dobson mentions "Pocahontas" and "Traits of the Aborigines" to contrast Sigourney's public themes with Emily Dickinson's aloof privatism in *Dickinson and the Strategies of Reticence: The Woman Writer in Nineteenth-Century America* (Bloomington: Indiana Univ. Press, 1989), p. 93. Annie Finch, in "The Sentimental Poetess in the World: Metaphor and Subjectivity in Lydia Sigourney's Nature Poetry," *Legacy,* 5 (1988), 3-18, considers Sigourney's nature poetry as public, but not political utterance. These are the only notices of Sigourney as a public writer.

16. For good succinct discussions of republican ideologies see Linda Kerber, "The Republican Ideology of the Revolutionary Generation," *American Quarterly,* 37 (1985), 474-95; and Joyce Appleby, "Republicanism in Old and New Contexts," *William and Mary Quarterly,* 43 (1986), 20-43. On the religiocentric strain in antebellum New England writing, see Lawrence Buell, *New England Literary Culture: From Revolution Through Renaissance* (New York: Cambridge Univ. Press, 1986). Jane Tompkins, in "The Other American Renaissance" (see n. 4), concisely describes a national movement participated in by writers, clergymen, and teachers, all striving "to educate their readers in Christian perfection and to move the nation as a whole closer to the city of God" (p. 149). Her stress on the tracts ignores, however, the social fact that tracts were written exclusively for the use of the lower classes, as a tool in their conversion. Tracts did not comprise the reading matter of a middle- or upper-class audience.

17. *Evening Readings in History: Comprising Portions of the History of Assyria, Egypt, Tyre, Syria, Persia, and the Sacred Scriptures; with Questions, Arranged for the Use of the Young, and of Family Circles* (Springfield: G. & C. Merriam, 1833), p. v; *History of Marcus Aurelius, Emperor of Rome* (Hartford: Belknap & Hamersley, 1835), p. iii.

18. Haight's bibliography lists an 1837 *History of the Condition of Women,* which he says he was unable to examine; this work is really by Lydia Maria Child, however. Women's history was not one of Sigourney's categories. She wrote numerous biographical sketches of exemplary women, but designed her historical writings not to construct a separate history of women but to give them significant roles within traditional Christian and republican narratives.

19. One of Sigourney's first pupils and close friends, Frances Manwaring Caulkins (whose name has disappeared completely from literary history) wrote two massive local histories of Norwich and New London and became the first (and for a long time the only) woman member of the Massachusetts Historical Society. Caulkins' chapters on the Indian history of the region offer a substantially different account from Sigourney's work because they concentrate on intertribal hostilities rather than warfare between whites and Indians. This difference is attributable to Caulkins' much greater filiopietism, and I mention it to make the point that the antebellum women who wrote history did so in various ways and for various purposes. But all their history writing, in my view, had a public intention and thus might have been seen as an incursion on the male sphere. That it was not so seen suggests a need for us to rethink the interrelation of the male and female spheres, at least in literature, in antebellum America.

20. *Myrtis, with Other Etchings and Sketchings* (New York: Harper, 1846), pp. 137-38.

21. "Traits of the Aborigines of America. A Poem" (Cambridge, Mass.: "from the University Press," 1822). Sigourney says that the poem was written two years before her marriage in 1819 (i.e., in 1817) but that its publication was delayed. Even the 1822 date makes this one of the earliest non-captivity publications on the Indian topic. Haight declares that it was Charles Sigourney's idea to annotate the poem, and that he wrote the notes as well (*Sweet Singer,* p. 25; *Notable American Women,* III, 289); Sigourney says only that her husband helped her revise the notes (*Letters,* p. 327).

22. The real-life model for this woman was Jerusha Talcot Lathrop, widow of Daniel Lathrop, a prosperous druggist. Until Madame Lathrop died in 1806, Sigourney's father, Ezekial Huntley, was employed as a gardener and general handyman on her estate. After her death the family of Daniel Wadsworth, a nephew, took an interest in the Huntleys and particularly in Lydia (see n. 1). In 1814 Daniel set Sigourney up as a schoolteacher in Hartford, assembling a group of elite students for her to instruct and setting aside a room in his house as the schoolroom. In 1815 he supervised the publication of *Moral Pieces.* Sigourney's own life story, then, would confirm to her the efficacy of a

moral republicanism in which the fortunate encouraged and supported the virtuous poor by giving them opportunities to support themselves. Thus, I interpret the social politics of the *Sketch* quite differently from Zagarell, who sees in it a vision of egalitarian community.

23. Sigourney saw enough potential in this segment of the *Sketch* to extract it and republish it as "Oriana" in her twice-reprinted collection *Sketches* (Philadelphia: Key and Biddle, 1834).

24. "The Western Home," in *The Western Home, and Other Poems* (Philadelphia: Parry and McMillan, 1854).

Dorothy Z. Baker (essay date 1997)

SOURCE: "*Ars Poetica/Ars Domestica:* The Self-Reflexive Poetry of Lydia Sigourney and Emily Dickinson," in *Poetics in the Poem: Critical Essays on American Self-Reflexive Poetry,* edited by Dorothy Z. Baker, Peter Lang, 1997, pp. 69-89.

[*In the following essay, Baker claims that both Sigourney and Dickinson use images of domesticity in attempts to forge an identity for the American woman poet.*]

> I'm plain at speech, direct in purpose: when
> I speak, you'll take the meaning as it is,
> And not allow for puckerings in the silks
> By clever stitches. I'm a woman, sir,
> And use the woman's figures naturally,
> As you, the male license.
>
> (Elizabeth Barrett Browning, *Aurora Leigh*)

When Aurora Leigh points out that she "uses the woman's figures," she is speaking of rhetorical tropes, in particular, of metaphor. In this conversation with Romney, who is also an artist, Aurora distinguishes between the range of her metaphorical language and his. Romney possesses "the male license" to poetic language that places him within the tradition of the poet as seer and shaman, prophet and priest. Yet, Aurora's use of feminine and domestic figures is linguistic evidence of her essential nature as a woman, and signals her identification with an alternate, female poetic voice. It is a commonplace that nineteenth-century American female authors often address their domestic roles and domestic concerns within their art. This essay argues that Lydia Sigourney and Emily Dickinson—like Browning's Aurora Leigh—foreground images of the *ars domestica* within their *ars poetica,* and they do so with an eye to securing the identity of the American woman poet.

Lydia Sigourney is most widely recognized as a singer of home and hearth. Although her poetic concerns are, in fact, much broader, Lydia Sigourney devoted much of her poetic career to celebration and examination of the woman's life—girlhood and education, marriage choice and maternity, religious life, and the joys and travails of the domestic sphere.[1] One can also look to her domestic lyrics for some of her most valuable discussions of poetics. Her domestic, self-reflexive lyrics put forth an aesthetic agenda that champions the role of *ars domestica* within literature. More precisely, within her poetry Sigourney fuses the poetic and domestic arts to assert the ability of the woman's sphere, the commonplaces of housewifery, to engender complex and compelling poetry. Common to these lyrics is the invocation of the *genius loci* that affirms the value of the feminine in her poetry.[2]

The invocation of the *genius loci* through the trope of apostrophe became a frequent literary convention in European Medieval and Renaissance poetry, and assumed great importance in British poetry of place.[3] Later, as a prominent feature of Romantic nature poetry, the creative fusion of the poet's genius with the *genius loci* often stimulates poetic invention.[4] Lydia Sigourney's domestic verse exhibits much the same phenomenon, and should be read within the context of this poetic tradition. In works such as **"To a Shred of Linen"** and **"To a Fragment of Cotton,"** Sigourney spotlights a modest, homely object for use not as a metaphor but as a vehicle for poetic expression in its own right. In each poem she invokes the domestic genius, and asks that it speak its own tale, that it exhibit its true value as distinct from its obvious utilitarian role. In doing so, she invests the object with dignity, and, what is more important, asserts the validity of the feminine and the domestic in the poetic arena. One need not invoke the genius of a Tintern Abbey in order to create rich, complex poetry. The womanly sphere of home and hearth, too, can engender lyric expression.

True, a rag worn thin does not draw attention to itself as an aesthetic object; it is not as traditionally poetic as a Grecian urn or a nightingale. Lydia Sigourney acknowledges as much in the opening lines of what has become the signature poem of her domestic literature, **"To a Shred of Linen."**[5] Spying a "littering shred" on the floor, the poet imagines the reproach of an older woman who would undoubtedly claim that this domestic lapse results from her reading books. Or worse yet, a potential suitor might shy from courting her under suspicion of greater misconduct, that of writing poetry. Sigourney reveals her ironic distance from these voices when she dismisses this misguided criticism with a quick, "Well—well—." To justify her literacy and artistry, Sigourney's saucy retort is to produce a poem, or rather to ask the linen to do so.

> Come forth—offender!—hast thou aught to say?
> Canst thou by merry thought, or quaint conceit,
> Repay this risk, that I have run for thee?
> —Begin at alpha, and resolve thyself
> Into thine elements . . .

Sigourney gives voice to the shred of linen, and in lines 18 through 40 spins the tale of its noble heritage. Through the poet, the linen can reveal its sacred origins as flax, growing on the banks of the Nile, and witnessing the miracles wrought by God through Moses. Later, the flax takes its place in a New England parlor where a young maid spins as her swain watches in admiration. The story of the scrap of linen is conflated with Biblical history and the history of the American nation such that the linen takes on mythopoetic significance, the recognition of which identifies the speaker as a poet. The genius of the linen effects the transformation of the cloth scrap in the inventive eyes of the poet; it allows the poet to witness these events, to hear their music, and ultimately to sing the history of the unassuming shred of linen.

The speaker then interrupts the history of her "littering scrap" for personal meditation on the importance of this domestic scene. She is taken with the industry of the "ruddy damsel" at her spinning wheel and is moved by her "voice of music." In lines 41-56, she ponders the values of a society centered on the hearthstone for both its work and play. The spinning wheel then becomes an "old Hygeian harp" that issues music to restore the soul. Just as the Aeolian harp traditionally creates music to fire the imagination, the Hygeian harp, the spinning wheel, creates the threads for linen that, in the context of this poem, fires woman's imagination.

The poet abruptly suspends her musing in line 53 when she recognizes that she has interrupted the primary discourse of the poem, the history of the linen. She physically drops the scrap, and simultaneously realizes that she has dropped the subject, and has lost her role as the voice of the linen. However, the interpolation of the poet's meditation in the center of the tale of the linen's origins is significant and ultimately central to the poem. Its insertion serves as a form of response to the "rustic lover" of our busy young spinner. As he looks upon the maiden, he does not contemplate her beauty, her virtue, or the joy in her song. He takes no aesthetic pleasure or emotional warmth from the domestic scene. Rather, he is already counting his proverbial chickens and selling them in the marketplace. He is "calculating what a thrifty wife / The maid will make" and eyeing with excessive, greedy pleasure the cheeses, butter, and skeins of wool this girl will produce for him. When sketching his thoughts, Sigourney notes ironically, *"For men have deeper minds than women— sure!"* This interjection is italicized as are the demeaning comments of the "neat lady" and "spruce beau" at the opening of the poem. Just as the speaker sought to refute the early charges with the creation of a lyric, so too the meditation in lines 41-56 becomes a refutation of the assumption that masculine intellect and enterprise are more potent or compelling than the feminine. The young man may lay claim to a "shrewd eye" as he calculates the

economic value of the spinning wheel and the girl who works the treadle. Nonetheless, Sigourney's philosophical interpolation indicates that he has no notion of the true value of either. That the swain puts his mind to affairs of the marketplace does not mean that his ideas are more valuable than aesthetic contemplations of domestic life. Although the speaker apologizes for dropping the "thread" of the discourse, this segment actually mirrors the primary statement of the poem. It serves as the spinner's *apologia* before the "rustic lover," just as the larger poem serves as a feminine self-reflexive response to the masculine poetic tradition.

A poem that opens with the "alpha" of a shred of linen would appropriately close with its omega. Indeed, the speaker sends her scrap with its "majesty and mystery" and "curious lore" to the paper mill. There it will be transformed from a shred, a frayed, wrinkled patch, into a pure sheet of paper awaiting the infinite possibilities of poetic creation. The shred of linen has already provided the poet with inventive material from which to create; its apotheosis will now offer the poet a physical substance on which to inscribe her artistic creation.

"To a Fragment of Cotton" (1841) offers additional insight into Sigourney's celebration of *ars domestica.*[6] In this poem, the speaker again spies a scrap of cloth littering the floorboards. Once a lovely cravat, the fragment has been kicking around the house for days, chewed by the dog, grabbed by the baby, swept up, and now it reappears. The speaker expects that a piece of fabric with such endurance must have wonderful tales to tell, and she strives to invoke its genius: "Hast e'er a tongue? / No doubt, The veriest triflers oft can boast / Great store of words."

As **"To a Shred of Linen,"** this poem takes shape in the distinguished and romantic history of the domestic object. This time, however, the speaker begins the tale neither in her own voice, nor in lending her voice to the cotton for the purpose of the poetry. The poet suggests that she is merely repeating the information whispered to her by the genius of the object: "So, thou wert known in history! and thy sire / The sounding name of Sir Gossypium bore." The cotton's history begins in the distinct conversational tone that indicates that the information being spoken is so interesting or surprising that it is now being repeated out of delight. The housewife soon drops this guise as if to signal that the genius of the cotton quickly merges with the genius of the poet. The speaker then recounts for herself/themselves the noble history of the personified image. The dirty scrap of cloth is far from what it may seem to be. This rag is brother to the golden fleece, another object with the capacity to inspire verse.

Sigourney's poet then recites the universal, utilitarian roles of cotton in this poem just as she does in **"To a Shred of**

Linen." Cotton figures in the life of man from his infant swaddling to his "snowy shroud;" it clothes man as he works and drapes him in his leisure. Yet, this litany is mere preparation for the central theme of the poem, a self-reflexive theme.

> But yet thou hast a higher ministry
> Of kindliness, and, when thou well hast served
> His body's need, dost turn thy hand and touch
> The ethereal mind. Yea, when thou seem'st to die,
> Thou only dropp'st thy grosser elements
> To commune with the soul.

The "higher ministry" of the fragment of cotton is that of kindling the poetic imagination of the housewife. The cloth comforted her body; now it communes with her spirit. It permits her a lyric moment. The significance of this passage is the transcendence afforded by the fragment of cotton. Misreadings of these lines often insist upon the work-a-day woman luxuriating in fantasies that allow her to escape household drudgery. Overlooked is Sigourney's obvious celebration of the scrap. *Ars domestica* is the inspiration of *ars poetica*. Domestic clutter provides the impetus for poetry, and then becomes the central theme and informing image of the poem.

In a self-reflexive exploration of the role of the cotton in her poetic creation, the poet ultimately expresses her gratitude to this icon of domesticity in religious terms. She refers to the scrap as a "Mysterious Guest" and offers a scriptural allusion to Christ as the stranger who appears unannounced.[7] The speaker confesses that the stranger's "ministry" has afforded her a spiritual experience, too. The domestic life that was all too familiar is now rich and inventive. As in religious ritual, she genuflects to this scrap, and "with reverent hand" picks it off the floor.

The reader cannot dismiss these poems as a sentimentalized depictions of housecleaning. Read as self-reflexive texts, **"To a Shred of Linen"** and **"To a Fragment of Cotton"** argue the ability of the traditionally feminine domain to engender poetry. When the male poet in Coleridge's "Apologia Pro Vita Sua" relaxes with his evening pipe, he perceives "phantoms of sublimity" in masculine images such as the smoke rising from the pipe. So too Sigourney asserts the ability of the woman as poet to discern the sublime in her feminine, indeed her domestic sphere.[8] Margaret Homans has observed that "where the major literary tradition normatively identifies the figure of the poet as masculine, and voice as a masculine property, women writers cannot see their minds as androgynous, or as sexless, but must take part in a self-definition by contraries" (3). When Lydia Sigourney enters into discussion of the creative process, she finds that her imagination is compelled not by pipe smoke, but rather by images that are closer to her experience as a nineteenth-century American woman.[9]

Moreover, by her deliberate choice of a feminine poetic persona invoking the genius of a domestic locus, Sigourney issues a vision of the role of the American woman as artist and her exacting choice of literary motifs. As a true literary artist, she seeks a manner of resolution in the tradition of poetry itself, and finds such in the *genius loci*. Jonathan Culler has argued that the use of apostrophe signals "the subject's claim that in his verse he is not merely an empirical poet, a writer of verse, but the embodiment of poetic tradition and of the spirit of poesy" (63).[10] Consequently, Sigourney's invocations of the otherwise ragged scraps implicitly assert that an icon of domestic life allows the woman as poet to lay claim to her heritage of spiritual, historical, and aesthetic treasures. Celebrating a domestic icon in this traditional, mannered fashion implies that she values this motif at the level of Hebrew, Greek, and Roman myths. Indeed, within the context of the poetry, she allies the remnants with potent tales from Biblical literature, Greek mythology, and the more modern scenes from colonial American history. For Sigourney, housewifery is thus worthy of aesthetic representation, and moreover serves as the genius of aesthetic experience.

. . . . .

That Emily Dickinson had domestic responsibilities is well established. That she relished her domestic role has been a matter for a considerable debate among Dickinson scholars.[11] Nonetheless, as many nineteenth-century women poets, Dickinson invokes images of domestic life to ground a full range of poetic expressions.

In her treatment of nature, Dickinson draws on the convention of earth as a feminine, and often maternal figure. Yet, her work does not merely echo that of many traditional romantic poets who confine their association of nature and the figure of mother to a contemplation of nature giving birth to man, nurturing man, amplifying his joys, and sympathizing with him in moments of grief. In contrast, Emily Dickinson frequently creates concrete images of nature as domestic woman. The poet depicts nature "in an Opal Apron, / Mixing fresher Air" (Poem 1397) or "sweep[ing] with many-colored Brooms" (Poem 219).[12] "In Ovens green our Mother bakes, / By Fires of the Sun" (Poem 1143). Her winter wind sweeps the streets with "Brooms of Steel" (Poem 1252), and the summer wind "knead[s] the Grass / As Women do a Dough" (Poem 824). Snow is described as flour that "sifts from Leaden Sieves— / It powders all the wood" (Poem 311). And, lightning is a yellow fork dropped from its placesetting in the sky (Poem 1173). Among Dickinson's flora and fauna, we see spiders who sew by night (Poem 1138), and trees who weave on a loom (Poem 18). In these poems, nature is not merely a female foil for male sentiment; neither is she a temptress, a sorceress, a consolatrice, or a muse; she is a woman doing the real work of real women in the nineteenth century—cooking, cleaning, and sewing.

Likewise, Dickinson draws on images of domestic life in her lyric expressions of emotional extremes. Mending and piecing provide the poet with a vehicle for metaphor in Poem 1442:

> To mend each tattered Faith
> There is a needle fair
> Though no appearance indicate—
> 'Tis threaded in the Air—

In an expression of profound grief, Dickinson finds that her accommodation with death mirrors an exercise in housekeeping:

> The Bustle in a House
> The Morning after Death
> Is solemnest of industries
> Enacted upon Earth—
>
> The Sweeping up the Heart
> And putting Love away
> We shall not want to use again
> Until Eternity.

(Poem 1078)

This poem relies on domestic metaphor to express the struggle to maintain emotional order after the death of someone much loved. Just as the housewife keeps everything in its place and stores unused items until they are again needed, so the grieving woman does the spring cleaning of the heart, storing all sentiments of warmth and intimacy that are not needed in the coming season of bereavement. But the wise housewife does not discard such items; she hopes that they will be useful to her in a new season. In poem 1743, the grave is a "little cottage" where the speaker, clearly a female voice, keeps house, makes the parlor orderly, and "lay[s] the marble tea" in anticipation of the death of another. Lastly, in the prayerful expression, "Ample make this Bed—," Dickinson delineates how she would like her funereal bed to be made, with sheets straight and pillow plump, in a quiet, dim room. Again, the domestic arts are used as a potent point of concrete reference.

Within her self-reflexive verse, Dickinson's poets wear the masks of carpenters, martyrs, and "little tipplers." But they also light lamps and trim wicks; they clean closets, make attar, pick berries, concoct recipes, and knit. Among Dickinson's many and varied poetic personae, the artist as domestic woman is central. Yet, in her *ars domestica/ars poetica,* one sees Dickinson's impetus to defy the order of housekeeping. Although domestic metaphors inform the poetry, Dickinson frequently challenges the activities relegated to woman to assert that poetic invention and artistic vision spring from domestic disorder.[13]

In Poem 1755, Dickinson looks to the kitchen and offers the reader a "recipe" for poetic creation.[14]

> To make a prairie it takes a clover and one bee,
> One clover, and a bee,
> And revery.
> The revery alone will do,
> If bees are few.

Like the housewife's recipe, this poem opens with a list of precise amounts of specific ingredients and would normally then offer a sequenced process to arrive at a finished product. However, Dickinson's ingredients are unlikely for cooking, and the product, a prairie, is not standard culinary fare. Furthermore, in the final two lines, the author retains the formulaic language of the cookbook genre, but ruptures the proscriptive cookbook formula. As in the typical recipe, the poem offers a substitution, for those out of stock of an item or two, but the substitution, too, is atypical and ironic. Instead of specifying exact quantities of numerous ingredients, the poet as housewife needs only an unspecified quantity of one ingredient—revery. Far from reinforcing the busyness of the domestic woman, Poem 1755 asserts the fruitfulness of imagination and leisured contemplation. The daydreaming housewife is far from idle.[15] Indeed, she can rescript the tightly conscripted home and homely duties to create a landscape, an entire world from a single ingredient, the artistic imagination.

The conflict between the *ars domestica* and the *ars poetica* is foremost in Poem 1273 which is informed by the metaphor of the poet's memory as a closet waiting to be cleaned. However, the speaker of the poem undermines the domestic task with a series of imperatives: "Select a reverential Broom—," "Do it silently," and, finally, "Let [the Dust] lie—." Generally, the object of cleaning closets is to jettison unnecessary items or to impose new order on material, whereas the activity described in this poem is decidedly different. The speaker asks us to use a broom that does not eliminate or purify, but one that honors the contents of our memory and does not challenge their right to be there. "August the Dust of that Domain," Dickinson tells us. The dust of the past is full of voices, ours and others; it is valuable and complex. Moreover, the voices of memory are powerful and take on a life of their own, which cannot and must not be modified. The chore of the poet *qua* housewife is to visit the closet with the goal of encountering the past, meeting its speakers, and attending to its many voices. Yet, the reader must remember that a closet is but a small cranny in the house; it is essential, but it is not where one lives. One visits the closet when necessary, then steps without, and closes the door. The speaker in Poem 1273 does not sequester herself in the dark, airless storage space. In fact, she alerts the reader of this danger: "it can silence you." The poet must take from the closet's treasures and leave to confront the larger room and the still larger house where the poet lives and speaks in the present.

An examination of the manuscript copy of Poem 1273—as opposed to the typeset version in the Johnson edition—offers additional insight. [. . .] In the first line of the manuscript, the line break after the word "sacred" offers greater prominence to the word, and asks the reader to anticipate the substantive that will follow in the next line. As such, the delay offered by the line break makes the language of the continuing line even more interesting and unsettling. Dickinson is not speaking of a sacred book or relic, as the reader might have speculated, but of a sacred closet, an uncommon pairing. In this same line, the word "when" has greater emphasis than in the Johnson version, where it is a mere connector between two more important words. In fact, in the longer, normalized typeset line, the word "when" is attached to the words that follow rather than to the preceding word "closet." The terse two-word line, "Closet when," draws attention to the curious use of the word "when." The sensible reader might have anticipated "where" in its place—that is, the closet where, not the closet when—because, logically, the closet is a place, and not a time. However, when this line is separated from the next, and the poem no longer reads "when you sweep," but "the closet when," the reader recognizes that something exceptional is happening in this poem. Dickinson is collapsing time and space in the process of exploring the memory in preparation for poetic creation.

Furthermore, the unconventional spatial arrangement of the fair copy mirrors the poet's rupture of the conventions of the informing metaphor of the poem, that of closet-cleaning. Just as Dickinson upsets our received notion of cleaning ("Let [the dust] lie—"), she upsets the format of the poem by printing the final two lines upside down at the top of the page. The words "sede" and "itself" trail from the antepenultimate line along the right hand margin to point us to the final lines. When Dickinson separates the final syllable from the first two in the word "supersede," she gives the syllable "sede" independence, and asks us to consider the obvious play on the word "seed." When the speaker of the poem understands that "You cannot super seed itself," she is mindful that to clean the closet of memory is to harvest a rich "August" crop, at which time sowing new seed is of no use; it is contrary to the agrarian cycle of New England. The speaker is in possession of a harvest of memory, which takes on a life of its own. Memory is identified as "itself," an independent entity. Spatially, it rises from the page to liberate itself from the poet. The poem takes the place of the poet, the act is complete, and the reader is led to the top of the page to begin the process yet again. Thus, the poem speaks to the reversal of aesthetics at every level of poetic construction.

In Poem 937, sewing and knitting, feminine, domestic artistry, are metaphors for poetic artistry.[16] Although in this poem Dickinson does not set the domestic and creative at odds with one another, she once again looks to an image of domesticity gone awry.

> I felt a Cleaving in my Mind—
> As if my Brain had split—
> I tried to match it—Seam by Seam—
> But could not make them fit
>
> The thought behind, I strove to join
> Unto the thought before—
> But Sequence ravelled out of Sound
> Like Balls—upon a Floor.

Poem 937 is a study of the difficulty of poetic creation, and, as such, emerges from a long tradition of self-reflexive explorations of poetic anxiety and authorial impotence. Dickinson, however, searches in her experience as a knitter and mender for a domestic analogue of her poetic challenges. The poem begins in confession; the speaker reveals that her thought processes are ruptured. She suspects that her brain, which is charged with ordering human perception, is actually "split." Her response is to mend her mind, to sew the fragments of her brain at the seam such that they work "normally," then to piece her disordered perceptions until they form a coherent whole. Yet, the first strophe ends in failure. The speaker cannot mend her disjoint brain.

Strophe two reveals the consequence of this malfunctioning for the poet. Just as the speaker could not seam her brain, she cannot knit together the ideas and images that emerge from that mind. She is unable to make normal connections between thoughts—temporal, causal, or otherwise associational. The final two lines reveal the significance of this disorder specifically for the poet and secure the identification of Poem 937 as a self-reflexive poem: "Sequence ravelled out of Sound / Like Balls—upon a Floor." The poet's thoughts have ravelled. They are strung out, kinked and crimped, apart from the body of a whole, strong piece of knitting. Moreover, the piece of knitting is identified as "Sound." The feature of sound is integral to language in general and of critical importance to poetry. With this image, the speaker specifies the nature of her difficulty: the poet's thoughts cannot be articulated. Her artistic desires cannot be "matched" with or "fit" into language. The poet's incoherent thoughts pull themselves loose from the body of common language. They ravel apart from sound, like balls of yarn, and defy attempts to control them, to integrate them, to delimit them.

Although the domestic sphere is the focus of Poem 1275, the poet depicted is not a housewife, but the natural enemy of the domestic woman. The artist is a spider who confounds the best efforts of the housekeeper and defies domestic order.

> The Spider as an Artist
> Has never been employed—
> Though his surpassing Merit
> Is freely certified

By every Broom and Bridget
Throughout a Christian Land—
Neglected Son of Genius
I take thee by the Hand—

The work of the spider is at odds with the domestic sphere; moreover he stands outside of the public domain, the marketplace, as well. The artist has never been employed, although he is "certified" and has recognized "merit." Furthermore, his accomplishments are recognized as superior to the efforts of domestic women, in this case, women who earn their living as domestics. Images of the private, public, and religious are fused in the second strophe, with the mission of a clean house and of wage-earning assuming spiritual significance. As such, Christian values in this Christian land are defied by the seemingly unproductive and disorderly activity of the spider as an artist. The singular pursuit of order, of the clean home, and its tidy moral strictures is not the vision of the poet. To reinforce this conflict, the speaker identifies the spider as the "Son of Genius," a prince of misrule, the profane, poetic counterpart to the sacred Son of God.[17]

When the speaker sets forth the contrary impulses of the spider and the domestic woman, she clearly distances herself from the only female figure in the poem. Bridget is introduced as the second party in the comic, alliterative pairing of "every Broom and Bridget," the generic identification of the prosaic domestic with the tool she most resembles. While the domestic woman is coupled with an inanimate object, the speaker elects to take the hand of a dark, curious animal, whose every instinct compels him to confound the obsessive order of the world's Bridgets.[18] In Dickinson's fair copy, the final line, "I take thee by the Hand—" is indented and set apart from the three previous lines to form a separate strophe of two lines divided after the word "thee." [. . .] Standing in relief from the body of the poem, these lines no longer describe the work of the spider as an artist. The speaker is instead describing herself and her actions. She allies herself with the spider, marries him, takes on his artistic goals, and assumes for herself the role of artist.

The goal of the speaker in Poem 1275, then, is to establish a space in which the poet can speak and to identify the artistic ethos. In the nineteenth-century debate between the public and the private, Dickinson discloses a third arena. Her speaker rejects her place in the domestic sphere and denies the values of the world of commerce. She takes on the role of poet, aware of the marginalized position of the artist. To do so, she disassociates herself from the traditional female model of zealous housekeeper and tidy Christian moralist. This is not to say that she assumes masculine codes and qualities. She rejects both to consort with the "Son of Genius," a dark seducer and an animal, and in doing so, she becomes a poet.[19]

Common to these and other domestic, self-reflexive poems of Dickinson is the alliance of the anti-domestic with the creative.[20] When Dickinson's lyric persona invokes a genius, it is the liberating force of disorder and misrule within the home. The spider—and not Orpheus—is her artistic prototype, while dust—and not a Grecian urn—emerges as a source of poetic invention. Yet, it would be unfair to insist that Dickinson foregrounds domesticity only for the purpose of ironic dismissal. The poet tests the highly codified domestic role that has been elevated in the nineteenth century to the level of religiosity, just as she challenges the poetic tradition, tests the limits of language, pushes the boundaries of every aspect of poetic device. Ultimately, when we consider the full range of Dickinson's self-reflexive statements, we note that she elevates no experience and no concern higher than that of poetic creation. With the exception of the poetic vocation, nothing is sacred. "I reckon when I count at all—/ First—Poets—Then the Sun—"(Poem 569).

. . . . .

In approaching nineteenth-century women's poetry, the reader must tune the ear to a new range of metaphor issued by the new range of experience that the female poet brings to a traditionally masculine enterprise. These metaphors include those of home and hearth, and the many glorious and inglorious aspects of the domestic sphere. The reader must also train the eye to recognize statements of self-reflexivity in lyric expressions whose metaphors may stand outside the tradition of the masculine poet as priest and prophet, seer and shaman. Surely, one of the most radical responses to the patriarchal topoi of lyric self-reflexivity is the portrait of the artist as domestic woman. Joanne Dobson notes that "'genius,' as literary talent was almost inevitably called, transgressed the codes and caused personal conflict for the woman writer, placing contradictory claims on her time and energy and jeopardizing her sense of identity" (41). The self-reflexive poetry of Lydia Sigourney and Emily Dickinson is expressive of the self-conscious and often conflicted response of the nineteenth-century woman to her double role as artist and "angel in the home," especially because these authors represent anomalies to both traditions. Situating their poetic genius in the domestic sphere, Sigourney and Dickinson redefine both roles.

In her study of women's domestic literature in nineteenth-century America, Ann Wood finds that "women in becoming writers were not leaving the home for the market place, . . . but bringing the home into the market" (6).[21] In doing so, women writers such as Lydia Sigourney and Emily Dickinson were compelled to reevaluate what constitutes appropriate and compelling literary material, poetic motifs, and themes. Sigourney's and Dickinson's self-reflexive poems, firmly grounded in *ars domestica,* issue an aesthetic agenda, a statement of *ars poetica.* The "littering shreds" under Sigourney's sofa and the "august Dust" of Dickinson's closets—much like the smoke from Coleridge's pipe—evoke the most genial of genii and engender the most sublime of poetic experiences.

Notes

1. See Nina Baym's provocative essay, "Reinventing Lydia Sigourney," for discussion of the full range of Sigourney's oeuvre.

2. The concept of genius issues from the ancient Romans who believe that every place, every thing, and, indeed, every man and woman has his or her own genius, a generative spirit that uniquely characterizes that place, object or person. Charles Estienne's 1596 *Dictionarium Historium, Geographium, Poeticum* observes that in Roman mythology the genius is a divine offspring, capable in his turn of creating man and nature ("Genius, dicebat a priscis deus naturae, & qui omnium rerum gignendarum vim haberet, unde cuiusque rei dicebatur suus Genius . . .") (229). It must be noted that the genius serves not only to create a specific place or object, but, once fashioned, the genius animates its creation, and thus informs its character. For a comprehensive treatment of the Latin origins of the genius, see Jane Chance Nitzsche, *The Genius Figure in Antiquity and the Middle Ages.*

3. Discussion of the genius figure in Medieval and Renaissance European literature can be found in E. C. Knowlton, "Genius as an Allegorical Figure," and in D. T. Starnes, "The Figure Genius in the Renaissance," as well as in Nitzsche, *The Genius Figure.*

4. Geoffrey H. Hartman's "Romantic Poetry and the Genius Loci" provides a thorough exploration of the role of the genius in British literature.

5. *Select Poems,* 50-53. All further reference to this poem are from this edition and will be cited in text.

6. *Poems,* 188-90. All further reference to this poem are from this edition and will be cited in text.

7. See, for example, Matthew 31:38-44.

8. In her *Letters to Young Ladies,* Sigourney celebrates "true womanhood" and insists that housework develops a woman's mind and sensibilities. "The science of housekeeping affords exercise for the judgment and energy, ready recollection, and patient self-possession, that are the characteristics of a superior mind" (27). Caroline May's introduction to her 1869 anthology, *The American Female Poets,* puts forth this very claim, emphasizing the relationship between domesticity and artistry: "It must be borne in mind that not many ladies in this country are permitted sufficient leisure from the cares and duties of home to devote themselves, either from choice, or as a means of living, to literary pursuits. Hence, the themes which have suggested the greater part of the following poems have been derived from the incidents and associations of every-day life. And home, with its quiet joys, its deep pure sympathies, and its secret sorrows, with which a stranger must not intermeddle, is a sphere by no means limited for woman, whose inspiration lies more in her heart than her head" (vi).

9. Domestic imagery and invocation of the similar to that of "To a Shred of Linen" and "To a Piece of Cotton" can be found in "To an Ancient Rocking Chair" (*Poems: by the Author of "Moral Pieces in Prose and Verse,"* 199-201), "The Broken Vase" (*Select Poems,* 43-5) and "The Ancient Family Clock" (*Select Poems,* 46-9).

10. In his seminal study of the *genius loci,* Geoffrey Hartman observes that "whenever the question of persona arises in a radical way, whenever self-choosing, self-identification, becomes a more than personal, indeed a prophetic, decision—which happens when the poet feels himself alien to the genius of country or age and destined to assume an adversary role—poetry renews itself by contact with what may seem to be archaic forces" (335). Thus, Sigourney's overt championing of the domestic genius responds to her role in American letters, and becomes a poetic manifesto.

11. For detailed commentary on Emily Dickinson's domestic role, see Joanne Dobson, *Strategies,* 40-55, and Elizabeth Phillips, 7-26. For arguments that she rejected the domestic sphere, see Betsy Erkilla, 20, Alicia Ostriker, 39. Issues of domesticity and self-reflexivity are addressed by Jane Donahue Eberwein, "Doing Without: Dickinson as Yankee Woman Poet" and Gertrude Reif Hughes, "Subverting the Cult of Domesticity: Dickinson's Critique of Women's Work." See also Barbara Mossberg who argues that Dickinson psychologically pairs domesticity with poetic impotence (42-45, 52-57).

12. All quotations from the poetry of Emily Dickinson are from *The Complete Poems of Emily Dickinson,* ed. Thomas H. Johnson, and will be identified by poem number within the text.

13. This aspect of Dickinson's domestic, self-reflexive poetry is consonant with her domestic, nature poetry in which nature is often at its most beautiful when it is disorderly. In Poem 219, the wind as a broom "litters" the landscape with colorful shreds and threads, does a poor job of sweeping, but creates a splendid landscape.

14. The identification of Poem 1755 as self-reflexive is not new to this essay; neither is the identification of the poem as a recipe. As Jane Donahue Eberwein puts it, "This, of course, is cookbook language: a recipe for the American sublime" (221).

15. This poem recalls Dickinson's "Indolent Housewife—in Daisies—lain!" whom Christanne

Miller has identified as a "prototype for the secret poet." See her insightful reading of Poem 187 in "How 'Low Feet' Stagger" (135). Poem 617, "Don't put up my Thread and Needle—" foregrounds a similar domestic situation in which the speaker protests that she will sew more finely in the morning when she is rested. But, the woman appears to protest too much. Her interest is not in sewing, but in sowing. Inspired by her domestic activity, she nonetheless needs to dream, and sow the seeds of poetic invention that will enable her to execute within her poetry finer knots and fancier stitches than are ever possible in physical reality. Thus, the figure of the "Indolent Housewife" once again illustrates the productivity of revery.

16. Elaine Showalter's important essay "Piecing and Writing" asks "whether the strongly marked American tradition of piecing, patchwork, and quilting has consequences for the structures, genres, themes, and meaning of American women's writing in the nineteenth and twentieth centuries" (223), and explores the idea of quilting as a metaphor for narrative technique in women's fiction as well as for the self-conception of American women authors.

17. My understanding of this poem is influenced by Barton Levi St. Armand's thorough and revealing commentary of the spider figure in Dickinson's poetry. St. Armand situates Dickinson's spiders in the context of those of Edward Taylor and Jonathan Edwards, and identifies the spider in Poem 1275 as "a pagan artificer in an orthodox Christian world, a primitive folk survival, so in tune with the *genius loci* that even the assiduity of new immigrants like Dickinson's own Irish maid, Maggie Maher, cannot completely eradicate its delicate craftsmanship" (33).

18. This poem, of course, recalls Poem 605, "The Spider holds a Silver Ball" in which the spider as artist is able to obscure full tapestries with his "Yarn of Pearl." Described as "unsubstantial" and measuring from "Nought to Nought," his web nonetheless forms entire "Continents of Light" until destroyed by domesticity.

19. Margaret Homans has identified the source of Dickinson's poetic language in the poet's taking on the language code of Eve, derived from the serpent. See 170-76 for a thorough, insightful treatment of Dickinson's voice as the tempter and the tempted, a study which underpins my understanding of the spider figure in her poetry.

20. See, for example, "Perhaps I asked too large—" (Poem 352), "I tie my Hat—I crease my Shawl—" (Poem 443), "This was a Poet—It is That" (Poem 448), "Don't put up my Thread and Needle—" (Poem 617), "The Poets light but Lamps—" (Poem 883), and "A Word dropped careless on a Page" (Poem 1261).

21. In *Private Woman, Public Stage: Literary Domesticity in Nineteenth-Century America,* Mary

Kelley, too, makes the point that nineteenth-century woman novelists attempt to unify their otherwise bifurcated private, domestic identity and public, authorial persona through the writing of domestic novels.

Works Cited

Baym, Nina. "Reinventing Lydia Sigourney." *American Literature* 62.3 (1990): 385-404.

Culler, Jonathan. "Apostrophe." *Diacritics* 7.4 (1974): 59-69.

Dickinson, Emily. *The Complete Poems of Emily Dickinson.* Ed. Thomas H. Johnson. Boston: Little, Brown, 1960.

———. *The Manuscript Books of Emily Dickinson.* Ed. R. W. Franklin. 2 vols. Cambridge: Belknap Press of Harvard UP, 1981.

Diehl, Joanne Feit. "'Come Slowly—Eden": An Exploration of Women Poets and Their Muse." *Signs: Journal of Women in Culture and Society* 3.3 (1978): 572-587.

———. *Dickinson and the Romantic Imagination.* Princeton: Princeton UP, 1981.

Dobson, Joanne. *Dickinson and the Strategies of Reticence: The Woman Writer in Nineteenth-Century America.* Bloomington: Indiana UP, 1989.

Eberwein, Jane Donahue. "Doing Without: Dickinson as Yankee Woman Poet." *Critical Essays on Emily Dickinson.* Ed. Paul J. Ferlazzo. Boston: G. K. Hall, 1984.

Erkkila, Betsy. "Emily Dickinson and Class." *American Literary History* 4.1 (1992): 1-27.

Estienne, Charles. *Dictionarium Historium, Georgraphicum, Poeticum.* Paris, 1596.

Farr, Judith. *The Passion of Emily Dickinson.* Cambridge: Harvard UP, 1992.

Finch, Annie. "The Sentimental Poetess in the World: Metaphor and Subjectivity in Lydia Sigourney's Nature Poetry." *Legacy* 5.2 (1988): 3-18.

Hartman, Geoffrey H. "Romantic Poetry and the *genius loci*." *Beyond Formalism: Literary Essays 1958-1970.* New Haven: Yale UP, 1970. 311-336.

Homans, Margaret. *Women Writers and Poetic Identity.* Princeton: Princeton UP, 1980.

Hughes, Gertrude Reif. "Subverting the Cult of Domesticity: Emily Dickinson's Critique of Women's Work." *Legacy* 3.1 (1986): 17-28.

Jacobus, Mary. "Apostrophe and Lyric Voice in The Prelude." *Lyric Poetry Beyond New Criticism.* Ed. Chaviva Hosek and Patricia Parker. Ithaca: Cornell UP, 1985. 167-82.

Kelley, Mary. *Private Woman, Public Stage: Literary Domesticity in Nineteenth-Century America.* New York: Oxford UP, 1984.

Knowlton, E. C. "Genius as an Allegorical Figure." *Modern Language Notes* 39.2 (1924): 89-95.

————. "The Genii of Spenser." *Studies in Philology* 25.4 (1928): 439-456.

May, Caroline, ed. *American Female Poets.* 1869. New York: Garret, 1969.

Miller, Cristanne. "How 'Low Feet' Stagger: Disruptions of Language in Dickinson's Poetry." *Feminist Critics Read Emily Dickinson.* Ed. Suzanne Juhasz. Bloomington: Indiana UP, 1983.

Mossberg, Barbara Antonina Clarke. *Emily Dickinson: When a Writer Is a Daughter.* Bloomington: Indiana UP, 1982.

Nitzsche, Jane Chance. *The Genius Figure in Antiquity and the Middle Ages.* New York: Columbia UP, 1975.

Ostriker, Alicia Suskin. *Stealing the Language: The Emergence of Women's Poetry in America.* Boston: Beacon, 1986.

Phillips, Elizabeth. *Emily Dickinson: Personae and Performance.* University Park: The Pennsylvania State UP, 1988.

————. *Writing Like a Woman.* Ann Arbor: U of Michigan P, 1983.

St. Armand, Barton Levi. *Emily Dickinson and Her Culture.* Cambridge: Cambridge UP, 1984.

Showalter, Elaine. "Piecing and Writing." *The Poetics of Gender.* Ed. Nancy K. Miller. New York: Columbia UP, 1986.

Sigourney, Mrs. L. H. *Letters to Young Ladies.* Hartford, 1835.

————. *Poems.* New York, 1875.

————. *Poems: by the Author of "Moral Pieces in Prose and Verse."* Boston, 1827.

————. *Scenes in My Native Land.* Boston, 1849.

————. *Select Poems.* Philadelphia, 1838.

Starnes, D. T. "The Figure Genius in the Renaissance." *Studies in the Renaissance* 11 (1964): 234-244.

Walker, Cheryl. *American Women Poets of the Nineteenth Century: An Anthology.* New Brunswick: Rutgers UP, 1992.

————. *The Nightingale's Burden: Women Poets and American Culture before 1900.* Bloomington: Indiana UP, 1982.

Watts, Emily Stipes. *The Poetry of American Women from 1632 to 1945.* Austin: U of Texas P, 1977.

Wood, Ann D. "The 'Scribbling Women' and Fanny Fern: Why Women Wrote." *American Quarterly* 23 (1971): 3-24.

Zagarell, Sandra A. "Expanding 'America': Lydia Sigourney's Sketch of Connecticut, Catharine Sedgwick's Hope Leslie." *Tulsa Studies in Women's Literature* 6 (1987): 225-46.

FURTHER READING

Biographies

Griswold, Rufus Wilmot, and Stoddard, R. H. "Lydia H. Sigourney." In *The Female Poets of America,* pp. 91-101. 1873. Reprint. New York: Garrett Press, 1969.

> A discussion of Sigourney's life and works prefixing a selection of her poetry.

Haight, Gordon S. *Mrs. Sigourney: The Sweet Singer of Hartford.* New Haven: Yale University Press, 1930, 201 p.

> Critical biography of Sigourney that seeks to explain both her reputation as "America's leading poetess" during her lifetime as well as the subsequent neglect of her work.

Hale, Sarah Josepha. "Sigourney, Lydia Huntley." In *Woman's Record; or, Sketches of All Distinguished Women from the Creation to A.D. 1854,* pp. 782-84. 1855. Reprint. New York: Source Book Press, 1970.

> A sketch of Sigourney's life and literary career followed by extracts from her work.

Kilcup, Karen L. "Lydia Howard Huntley Sigourney (1791-1865)." In *Nineteenth-Century American Women Writers: A Bio-Bibliographic Sourcebook,* edited by Denise D. Knight, pp. 361-67. Westport, Conn.: Greenwood Press, 1997.

> Brief biographical study of Sigourney, along with a review of her major works' themes and a bibliography of primary and secondary materials.

Criticism

Bode, Carl. "The Sentimental Muse." In his *The Anatomy of American Popular Culture: 1840-1861,* p. 188-200. Berkeley and Los Angeles: University of California Press, 1959.

> Examines the reasons for Sigourney's immense popularity in her day and offers a negative assessment of the lasting value of her work.

————, ed. "Document 34: Glorious Columbia." In *American Life in the 1840s,* pp. 279-82. Documents in American Civilization Series, edited by Hennig Cohen and John William Ward. Garden City, N.Y.: Doubleday and Co., 1967.

Discusses Sigourney's patriotic poem *"Our Country"* in its historical context.

De Jong, Mary G. "Lydia Howard Huntley Sigourney (1791-1865)." In *Legacy* 5, No. 1 (Spring 1988): 35-43.
Briefly discusses Sigourney's life and political and social commitments, and surveys Sigourney's critical reception in the twentieth century.

Fetterley, Judith. "Lydia Sigourney (1791-1865)." In *Provisions: A Reader from 19th-Century American Women,* edited by Judith Fetterley, pp. 105-16. Bloomington: Indiana University Press, 1985.
Prefaces Sigourney's short story *"The Father"* with a short analysis and biography.

Green, David Bonnell. "William Wordsworth and Lydia Huntley Sigourney." In *The New England Quarterly* XXXVII, No. 4 (December 1964): 527-31.
An account of Sigourney's acquaintance and correspondence with William Wordsworth.

Hogue, William M. "The Sweet Singer of Hartford." In *Historical Magazine of the Protestant Episcopal Church* XLV, No. 1 (March 1976): 57-77.
Explores Sigourney's evangelical Episcopalianism as evidenced in her poetry.

Jordan, Philip D. "The Source of Mrs. Sigourney's 'Indian Girl's Burial'." In *American Literature* 4, No. 3 (November 1932): 300-05.
Notes Sigourney's familiarity with journals published in the American West.

Kramer, Aaron. *The Prophetic Tradition in American Poetry: 1835-1900.* Rutherford, N.J.: Fairleigh Dickinson University Press, 1968, 416 p.
Contains references to Sigourney's positions on secession, the slavery question, and the plight of American Indians.

Okker, Patricia. "Sarah Josepha Hale, Lydia Sigourney, and the Poetic Tradition in Two Nineteenth-Century Women's Magazines." In *American Periodicals* 3 (1993): 32-42.
Contends that, contrary to general critical opinion, the poetry that Hale and Sigourney published during their time as editors of women's magazines reveals powerful feminine poetics that attempted to glorify rather than restrict women's poetic achievements.

Petrino, Elizabeth A. "'Feet so precious charged': Dickinson, Sigourney, and the Child Elegy." In *Tulsa Studies in Women's Literature* 13, No. 2 (Fall 1994): 317-38.
Sets Dickinson's child elegies against those of Sigourney and other sentimental writers, claiming that Dickinson rejected the sentimentality, materialism, and religiosity of her Victorian forebearers.

Watts, Emily Stipes. "Lydia Huntley Sigourney (1797-1865)." In *The Poetry of American Women from 1632 to 1945,* pp. 83-97. Austin: University of Texas Press, 1977.
Discusses Sigourney's writings in their historical context, particularly as they distinguish themselves in concept and theme from similar works written by contemporary male authors.

Additional coverage of Sigourney's life and career is contained in the following source published by the Gale Group: *Dictionary of Literary Biography,* **Vols. 1, 42, 73, 183.**

How to Use This Index

The main references

> **Calvino, Italo**
> 1923-1985 .... CLC **5, 8, 11, 22, 33, 39,**
> **73; SSC 3**

list all author entries in the following Gale Literary Criticism series:

BLC = *Black Literature Criticism*
CLC = *Contemporary Literary Criticism*
CLR = *Children's Literature Review*
CMLC = *Classical and Medieval Literature Criticism*
DA = *DISCovering Authors*
DAB = *DISCovering Authors: British*
DAC = *DISCovering Authors: Canadian*
DAM = *DISCovering Authors: Modules*
      DRAM: *Dramatists Module;* **MST:** *Most-Studied Authors Module;*
      MULT: *Multicultural Authors Module;* **NOV:** *Novelists Module;*
      POET: *Poets Module;* **POP:** *Popular Fiction and Genre Authors Module*
DC = *Drama Criticism*
HLC = *Hispanic Literature Criticism*
LC = *Literature Criticism from 1400 to 1800*
NNAL = *Native North American Literature*
NCLC = *Nineteenth-Century Literature Criticism*
PC = *Poetry Criticism*
SSC = *Short Story Criticism*
TCLC = *Twentieth-Century Literary Criticism*
WLC = *World Literature Criticism, 1500 to the Present*

The cross-references

> See also CANR 23; CA 85-88;
> obituary CA116

list all author entries in the following Gale biographical and literary sources:

AAYA = *Authors & Artists for Young Adults*
AITN = *Authors in the News*
BEST = *Bestsellers*
BW = *Black Writers*
CA = *Contemporary Authors*
CAAS = *Contemporary Authors Autobiography Series*
CABS = *Contemporary Authors Bibliographical Series*
CANR = *Contemporary Authors New Revision Series*
CAP = *Contemporary Authors Permanent Series*
CDALB = *Concise Dictionary of American Literary Biography*
CDBLB = *Concise Dictionary of British Literary Biography*
DLB = *Dictionary of Literary Biography*
DLBD = *Dictionary of Literary Biography Documentary Series*
DLBY = *Dictionary of Literary Biography Yearbook*
HW = *Hispanic Writers*
JRDA = *Junior DISCovering Authors*
MAICYA = *Major Authors and Illustrators for Children and Young Adults*
MTCW = *Major 20th-Century Writers*
SAAS = *Something about the Author Autobiography Series*
SATA = *Something about the Author*
YABC = *Yesterday's Authors of Books for Children*

Literary Criticism Series
Cumulative Author Index

20/1631
See Upward, Allen
A/C Cross
See Lawrence, T(homas) E(dward)
Abasiyanik, Sait Faik 1906-1954
See Sait Faik
See also CA 123
Abbey, Edward 1927-1989 **CLC 36, 59**
See also CA 45-48; 128; CANR 2, 41; DA3;
MTCW 2
Abbott, Lee K(ittredge) 1947- **CLC 48**
See also CA 124; CANR 51; DLB 130
Abe, Kobo 1924-1993 **CLC 8, 22, 53, 81;
DAM NOV**
See also CA 65-68; 140; CANR 24, 60;
DLB 182; MTCW 1, 2
Abelard, Peter c. 1079-c. 1142 **CMLC 11**
See also DLB 115, 208
Abell, Kjeld 1901-1961 **CLC 15**
See also CA 111
Abish, Walter 1931- **CLC 22**
See also CA 101; CANR 37; DLB 130
Abrahams, Peter (Henry) 1919- **CLC 4**
See also BW 1; CA 57-60; CANR 26; DLB
117; MTCW 1, 2
Abrams, M(eyer) H(oward) 1912- **CLC 24**
See also CA 57-60; CANR 13, 33; DLB 67
Abse, Dannie 1923- **CLC 7, 29; DAB; DAM
POET**
See also CA 53-56; CAAS 1; CANR 4, 46,
74; DLB 27; MTCW 1
Achebe, (Albert) Chinua(lumogu) 1930- **CLC
1, 3, 5, 7, 11, 26, 51, 75, 127; BLC 1;
DA; DAB; DAC; DAM MST, MULT,
NOV; WLC**
See also AAYA 15; BW 2, 3; CA 1-4R;
CANR 6, 26, 47; CLR 20; DA3; DLB
117; MAICYA; MTCW 1, 2; SATA 38,
40; SATA-Brief 38
Acker, Kathy 1948-1997 **CLC 45, 111**
See also CA 117; 122; 162; CANR 55
Ackroyd, Peter 1949- **CLC 34, 52**
See also CA 123; 127; CANR 51, 74; DLB
155; INT 127; MTCW 2
Acorn, Milton 1923- **CLC 15; DAC**
See also CA 103; DLB 53; INT 103
Adamov, Arthur 1908-1970 **CLC 4, 25; DAM
DRAM**
See also CA 17-18; 25-28R; CAP 2; MTCW
1
Adams, Alice (Boyd) 1926-1999 **CLC 6, 13,
46; SSC 24**
See also CA 81-84; 179; CANR 26, 53, 75,
88; DLBY 86; INT CANR-26; MTCW 1,
2
Adams, Andy 1859-1935 **TCLC 56**
See also YABC 1
Adams, Brooks 1848-1927 **TCLC 80**

See also CA 123; DLB 47
Adams, Douglas (Noel) 1952- **CLC 27, 60;
DAM POP**
See also AAYA 4, 33; BEST 89:3; CA 106;
CANR 34, 64; DA3; DLBY 83; JRDA;
MTCW 1; SATA 116
Adams, Francis 1862-1893 **NCLC 33**
Adams, Henry (Brooks) 1838-1918 **TCLC 4,
52; DA; DAB; DAC; DAM MST**
See also CA 104; 133; CANR 77; DLB 12,
47, 189; MTCW 1
Adams, Richard (George) 1920- **CLC 4, 5,
18; DAM NOV**
See also AAYA 16; AITN 1, 2; CA 49-52;
CANR 3, 35; CLR 20; JRDA; MAICYA;
MTCW 1, 2; SATA 7, 69
Adamson, Joy(-Friederike Victoria)
1910-1980 **CLC 17**
See also CA 69-72; 93-96; CANR 22;
MTCW 1; SATA 11; SATA-Obit 22
Adcock, Fleur 1934- **CLC 41**
See also CA 25-28R, 182; CAAE 182;
CAAS 23; CANR 11, 34, 69; DLB 40
Addams, Charles (Samuel) 1912-1988 **CLC
30**
See also CA 61-64; 126; CANR 12, 79
Addams, Jane 1860-1945 **TCLC 76**
Addison, Joseph 1672-1719 **LC 18**
See also CDBLB 1660-1789; DLB 101
Adler, Alfred (F.) 1870-1937 **TCLC 61**
See also CA 119; 159
Adler, C(arole) S(chwerdtfeger) 1932- **CLC
35**
See also AAYA 4; CA 89-92; CANR 19,
40; JRDA; MAICYA; SAAS 15; SATA
26, 63, 102
Adler, Renata 1938- **CLC 8, 31**
See also CA 49-52; CANR 5, 22, 52;
MTCW 1
Ady, Endre 1877-1919 **TCLC 11**
See also CA 107
A.E. 1867-1935 **TCLC 3, 10**
See also Russell, George William
Aeschylus 525B.C.-456B.C. **CMLC 11; DA;
DAB; DAC; DAM DRAM, MST; DC 8;
WLCS**
See also DLB 176
Aesop 620(?)B.C.-(?)B.C. **CMLC 24**
See also CLR 14; MAICYA; SATA 64
Affable Hawk
See MacCarthy, Sir(Charles Otto) Desmond
Africa, Ben
See Bosman, Herman Charles
Afton, Effie
See Harper, Frances Ellen Watkins
Agapida, Fray Antonio
See Irving, Washington

Agee, James (Rufus) 1909-1955 **TCLC 1, 19;
DAM NOV**
See also AITN 1; CA 108; 148; CDALB
1941-1968; DLB 2, 26, 152; MTCW 1
Aghill, Gordon
See Silverberg, Robert
Agnon, S(hmuel) Y(osef Halevi) 1888-1970
CLC 4, 8, 14; SSC 30
See also CA 17-18; 25-28R; CANR 60;
CAP 2; MTCW 1, 2
Agrippa von Nettesheim, Henry Cornelius
1486-1535 **LC 27**
Aguilera Malta, Demetrio 1909-1981
See also CA 111; 124; CANR 87; DAM
MULT, NOV; DLB 145; HLCS 1; HW 1
Agustini, Delmira 1886-1914
See also CA 166; HLCS 1; HW 1, 2
Aherne, Owen
See Cassill, R(onald) V(erlin)
Ai 1947- **CLC 4, 14, 69**
See also CA 85-88; CAAS 13; CANR 70;
DLB 120
Aickman, Robert (Fordyce) 1914-1981 **CLC
57**
See also CA 5-8R; CANR 3, 72
Aiken, Conrad (Potter) 1889-1973 **CLC 1, 3,
5, 10, 52; DAM NOV, POET; PC 26;
SSC 9**
See also CA 5-8R; 45-48; CANR 4, 60;
CDALB 1929-1941; DLB 9, 45, 102;
MTCW 1, 2; SATA 3, 30
Aiken, Joan (Delano) 1924- **CLC 35**
See also AAYA 1, 25; CA 9-12R, 182;
CAAE 182; CANR 4, 23, 34, 64; CLR 1,
19; DLB 161; JRDA; MAICYA; MTCW
1; SAAS 1; SATA 2, 30, 73; SATA-Essay
109
Ainsworth, William Harrison 1805-1882
NCLC 13
See also DLB 21; SATA 24
Aitmatov, Chingiz (Torekulovich) 1928- **CLC
71**
See also CA 103; CANR 38; MTCW 1;
SATA 56
Akers, Floyd
See Baum, L(yman) Frank
Akhmadulina, Bella Akhatovna 1937- **CLC
53; DAM POET**
See also CA 65-68
Akhmatova, Anna 1888-1966 **CLC 11, 25, 64,
126; DAM POET; PC 2**
See also CA 19-20; 25-28R; CANR 35;
CAP 1; DA3; MTCW 1, 2
Aksakov, Sergei Timofeyvich 1791-1859
NCLC 2
See also DLB 198

Aksenov, Vassily
　　See Aksyonov, Vassily (Pavlovich)
Akst, Daniel 1956- **CLC 109**
　　See also CA 161
Aksyonov, Vassily (Pavlovich) 1932- **CLC 22, 37, 101**
　　See also CA 53-56; CANR 12, 48, 77
Akutagawa, Ryunosuke 1892-1927 **TCLC 16**
　　See also CA 117; 154
Alain 1868-1951 **TCLC 41**
　　See also CA 163
Alain-Fournier TCLC 6
　　See also Fournier, Henri Alban
　　See also DLB 65
Alarcon, Pedro Antonio de 1833-1891 **NCLC 1**
Alas (y Urena), Leopoldo (Enrique Garcia) 1852-1901 **TCLC 29**
　　See also CA 113; 131; HW 1
Albee, Edward (Franklin III) 1928- **CLC 1, 2, 3, 5, 9, 11, 13, 25, 53, 86, 113; DA; DAB; DAC; DAM DRAM, MST; DC 11; WLC**
　　See also AITN 1; CA 5-8R; CABS 3; CANR 8, 54, 74; CDALB 1941-1968; DA3; DLB 7; INT CANR-8; MTCW 1, 2
Alberti, Rafael 1902-1999 **CLC 7**
　　See also CA 85-88; 185; CANR 81; DLB 108; HW 2
Albert the Great 1200(?)-1280 **CMLC 16**
　　See also DLB 115
Alcala-Galiano, Juan Valera y
　　See Valera y Alcala-Galiano, Juan
Alcott, Amos Bronson 1799-1888 **NCLC 1**
　　See also DLB 1, 223
Alcott, Louisa May 1832-1888 **NCLC 6, 58, 83; DA; DAB; DAC; DAM MST, NOV; SSC 27; WLC**
　　See also AAYA 20; CDALB 1865-1917; CLR 1, 38; DA3; DLB 1, 42, 79, 223; DLBD 14; JRDA; MAICYA; SATA 100; YABC 1
Aldanov, M. A.
　　See Aldanov, Mark (Alexandrovich)
Aldanov, Mark (Alexandrovich) 1886(?)-1957 **TCLC 23**
　　See also CA 118; 181
Aldington, Richard 1892-1962 **CLC 49**
　　See also CA 85-88; CANR 45; DLB 20, 36, 100, 149
Aldiss, Brian W(ilson) 1925- **CLC 5, 14, 40; DAM NOV; SSC 36**
　　See also CA 5-8R; CAAS 2; CANR 5, 28, 64; DLB 14; MTCW 1, 2; SATA 34
Alegria, Claribel 1924- **CLC 75; DAM MULT; HLCS 1; PC 26**
　　See also CA 131; CAAS 15; CANR 66; DLB 145; HW 1; MTCW 1
Alegria, Fernando 1918- **CLC 57**
　　See also CA 9-12R; CANR 5, 32, 72; HW 1, 2
Aleichem, Sholom TCLC 1, 35; SSC 33
　　See also Rabinovitch, Sholem
Aleixandre, Vicente 1898-1984
　　See also CANR 81; HLCS 1; HW 2
Alepoudelis, Odysseus
　　See Elytis, Odysseus
Aleshkovsky, Joseph 1929-
　　See Aleshkovsky, Yuz
　　See also CA 121; 128
Aleshkovsky, Yuz CLC 44
　　See also Aleshkovsky, Joseph
Alexander, Lloyd (Chudley) 1924- **CLC 35**
　　See also AAYA 1, 27; CA 1-4R; CANR 1, 24, 38, 55; CLR 1, 5, 48; DLB 52; JRDA; MAICYA; MTCW 1; SAAS 19; SATA 3, 49, 81
Alexander, Meena 1951- **CLC 121**
　　See also CA 115; CANR 38, 70

Alexander, Samuel 1859-1938 **TCLC 77**
Alexie, Sherman (Joseph, Jr.) 1966- **CLC 96; DAM MULT**
　　See also AAYA 28; CA 138; CANR 65; DA3; DLB 175, 206; MTCW 1; NNAL
Alfau, Felipe 1902- **CLC 66**
　　See also CA 137
Alfred, Jean Gaston
　　See Ponge, Francis
Alger, Horatio Jr., Jr. 1832-1899 **NCLC 8, 83**
　　See also DLB 42; SATA 16
Algren, Nelson 1909-1981 **CLC 4, 10, 33; SSC 33**
　　See also CA 13-16R; 103; CANR 20, 61; CDALB 1941-1968; DLB 9; DLBY 81, 82; MTCW 1, 2
Ali, Ahmed 1910- **CLC 69**
　　See also CA 25-28R; CANR 15, 34
Alighieri, Dante
　　See Dante
Allan, John B.
　　See Westlake, Donald E(dwin)
Allan, Sidney
　　See Hartmann, Sadakichi
Allan, Sydney
　　See Hartmann, Sadakichi
Allen, Edward 1948- **CLC 59**
Allen, Fred 1894-1956 **TCLC 87**
Allen, Paula Gunn 1939- **CLC 84; DAM MULT**
　　See also CA 112; 143; CANR 63; DA3; DLB 175; MTCW 1; NNAL
Allen, Roland
　　See Ayckbourn, Alan
Allen, Sarah A.
　　See Hopkins, Pauline Elizabeth
Allen, Sidney H.
　　See Hartmann, Sadakichi
Allen, Woody 1935- **CLC 16, 52; DAM POP**
　　See also AAYA 10; CA 33-36R; CANR 27, 38, 63; DLB 44; MTCW 1
Allende, Isabel 1942- **CLC 39, 57, 97; DAM MULT, NOV; HLC 1; WLCS**
　　See also AAYA 18; CA 125; 130; CANR 51, 74; DA3; DLB 145; HW 1, 2; INT 130; MTCW 1, 2
Alleyn, Ellen
　　See Rossetti, Christina (Georgina)
Allingham, Margery (Louise) 1904-1966 **CLC 19**
　　See also CA 5-8R; 25-28R; CANR 4, 58; DLB 77; MTCW 1, 2
Allingham, William 1824-1889 **NCLC 25**
　　See also DLB 35
Allison, Dorothy E. 1949- **CLC 78**
　　See also CA 140; CANR 66; DA3; MTCW 1
Allston, Washington 1779-1843 **NCLC 2**
　　See also DLB 1
Almedingen, E. M. CLC 12
　　See also Almedingen, Martha Edith von
　　See also SATA 3
Almedingen, Martha Edith von 1898-1971
　　See Almedingen, E. M.
　　See also CA 1-4R; CANR 1
Almodovar, Pedro 1949(?)- **CLC 114; HLCS 1**
　　See also CA 133; CANR 72; HW 2
Almqvist, Carl Jonas Love 1793-1866 **NCLC 42**
Alonso, Damaso 1898-1990 **CLC 14**
　　See also CA 110; 131; 130; CANR 72; DLB 108; HW 1, 2
Alov
　　See Gogol, Nikolai (Vasilyevich)
Alta 1942- **CLC 19**
　　See also CA 57-60
Alter, Robert B(ernard) 1935- **CLC 34**

　　See also CA 49-52; CANR 1, 47
Alther, Lisa 1944- **CLC 7, 41**
　　See also CA 65-68; CAAS 30; CANR 12, 30, 51; MTCW 1
Althusser, L.
　　See Althusser, Louis
Althusser, Louis 1918-1990 **CLC 106**
　　See also CA 131; 132
Altman, Robert 1925- **CLC 16, 116**
　　See also CA 73-76; CANR 43
Alurista 1949-
　　See Urista, Alberto H.
　　See also DLB 82; HLCS 1
Alvarez, A(lfred) 1929- **CLC 5, 13**
　　See also CA 1-4R; CANR 3, 33, 63; DLB 14, 40
Alvarez, Alejandro Rodriguez 1903-1965
　　See Casona, Alejandro
　　See also CA 131; 93-96; HW 1
Alvarez, Julia 1950- **CLC 93; HLCS 1**
　　See also AAYA 25; CA 147; CANR 69; DA3; MTCW 1
Alvaro, Corrado 1896-1956 **TCLC 60**
　　See also CA 163
Amado, Jorge 1912- **CLC 13, 40, 106; DAM MULT, NOV; HLC 1**
　　See also CA 77-80; CANR 35, 74; DLB 113; HW 2; MTCW 1, 2
Ambler, Eric 1909-1998 **CLC 4, 6, 9**
　　See also CA 9-12R; 171; CANR 7, 38, 74; DLB 77; MTCW 1, 2
Amichai, Yehuda 1924- **CLC 9, 22, 57, 116**
　　See also CA 85-88; CANR 46, 60; MTCW 1
Amichai, Yehudah
　　See Amichai, Yehuda
Amiel, Henri Frederic 1821-1881 **NCLC 4**
Amis, Kingsley (William) 1922-1995 **CLC 1, 2, 3, 5, 8, 13, 40, 44, 129; DA; DAB; DAC; DAM MST, NOV**
　　See also AITN 2; CA 9-12R; 150; CANR 8, 28, 54; CDBLB 1945-1960; DA3; DLB 15, 27, 100, 139; DLBY 96; INT CANR-8; MTCW 1, 2
Amis, Martin (Louis) 1949- **CLC 4, 9, 38, 62, 101**
　　See also BEST 90:3; CA 65-68; CANR 8, 27, 54, 73; DA3; DLB 14, 194; INT CANR-27; MTCW 1
Ammons, A(rchie) R(andolph) 1926- **CLC 2, 3, 5, 8, 9, 25, 57, 108; DAM POET; PC 16**
　　See also AITN 1; CA 9-12R; CANR 6, 36, 51, 73; DLB 5, 165; MTCW 1, 2
Amo, Tauraatua i
　　See Adams, Henry (Brooks)
Amory, Thomas 1691(?)-1788 **LC 48**
Anand, Mulk Raj 1905- **CLC 23, 93; DAM NOV**
　　See also CA 65-68; CANR 32, 64; MTCW 1, 2
Anatol
　　See Schnitzler, Arthur
Anaximander c. 610B.C.-c. 546B.C. **CMLC 22**
Anaya, Rudolfo A(lfonso) 1937- **CLC 23; DAM MULT, NOV; HLC 1**
　　See also AAYA 20; CA 45-48; CAAS 4; CANR 1, 32, 51; DLB 82, 206; HW 1; MTCW 1, 2
Andersen, Hans Christian 1805-1875 **NCLC 7, 79; DA; DAB; DAC; DAM MST, POP; SSC 6; WLC**
　　See also CLR 6; DA3; MAICYA; SATA 100; YABC 1
Anderson, C. Farley
　　See Mencken, H(enry) L(ouis); Nathan, George Jean

Anderson, Jessica (Margaret) Queale 1916-
CLC **37**
See also CA 9-12R; CANR 4, 62

Anderson, Jon (Victor) 1940- **CLC 9; DAM
POET**
See also CA 25-28R; CANR 20

Anderson, Lindsay (Gordon) 1923-1994 **CLC
20**
See also CA 125; 128; 146; CANR 77

Anderson, Maxwell 1888-1959 **TCLC 2;
DAM DRAM**
See also CA 105; 152; DLB 7; MTCW 2

Anderson, Poul (William) 1926- **CLC 15**
See also AAYA 5, 34; CA 1-4R, 181; CAAE
181; CAAS 2; CANR 2, 15, 34, 64; CLR
58; DLB 8; INT CANR-15; MTCW 1, 2;
SATA 90; SATA-Brief 39; SATA-Essay
106

Anderson, Robert (Woodruff) 1917- **CLC 23;
DAM DRAM**
See also AITN 1; CA 21-24R; CANR 32;
DLB 7

Anderson, Sherwood 1876-1941 **TCLC 1, 10,
24; DA; DAB; DAC; DAM MST, NOV;
SSC 1; WLC**
See also AAYA 30; CA 104; 121; CANR
61; CDALB 1917-1929; DA3; DLB 4, 9,
86; DLBD 1; MTCW 1, 2

Andier, Pierre
See Desnos, Robert

Andouard
See Giraudoux, (Hippolyte) Jean

Andrade, Carlos Drummond de CLC 18
See also Drummond de Andrade, Carlos

Andrade, Mario de 1893-1945 **TCLC 43**

Andreae, Johann V(alentin) 1586-1654 **LC
32**
See also DLB 164

Andreas-Salome, Lou 1861-1937 **TCLC 56**
See also CA 178; DLB 66

Andress, Lesley
See Sanders, Lawrence

Andrewes, Lancelot 1555-1626 **LC 5**
See also DLB 151, 172

Andrews, Cicily Fairfield
See West, Rebecca

Andrews, Elton V.
See Pohl, Frederik

Andreyev, Leonid (Nikolaevich) 1871-1919
TCLC 3
See also CA 104; 185

Andric, Ivo 1892-1975 **CLC 8; SSC 36**
See also CA 81-84; 57-60; CANR 43, 60;
DLB 147; MTCW 1

Androvar
See Prado (Calvo), Pedro

Angelique, Pierre
See Bataille, Georges

Angell, Roger 1920- **CLC 26**
See also CA 57-60; CANR 13, 44, 70; DLB
171, 185

Angelou, Maya 1928- **CLC 12, 35, 64, 77;
BLC 1; DA; DAB; DAC; DAM MST,
MULT, POET, POP; WLCS**
See also AAYA 7, 20; BW 2, 3; CA 65-68;
CANR 19, 42, 65; CDALBS; CLR 53;
DA3; DLB 38; MTCW 1, 2; SATA 49

Anna Comnena 1083-1153 **CMLC 25**

Annensky, Innokenty (Fyodorovich)
1856-1909 **TCLC 14**
See also CA 110; 155

Annunzio, Gabriele d'
See D'Annunzio, Gabriele

Anodos
See Coleridge, Mary E(lizabeth)

Anon, Charles Robert
See Pessoa, Fernando (Antonio Nogueira)

Anouilh, Jean (Marie Lucien Pierre)
1910-1987 **CLC 1, 3, 8, 13, 40, 50; DAM
DRAM; DC 8**
See also CA 17-20R; 123; CANR 32;
MTCW 1, 2

Anthony, Florence
See Ai

Anthony, John
See Ciardi, John (Anthony)

Anthony, Peter
See Shaffer, Anthony (Joshua); Shaffer,
Peter (Levin)

Anthony, Piers 1934- **CLC 35; DAM POP**
See also AAYA 11; CA 21-24R; CANR 28,
56, 73; DLB 8; MTCW 1, 2; SAAS 22;
SATA 84

Anthony, Susan B(rownell) 1916-1991 **TCLC
84**
See also CA 89-92; 134

Antoine, Marc
See Proust, (Valentin-Louis-George-
Eugene-) Marcel

Antoninus, Brother
See Everson, William (Oliver)

Antonioni, Michelangelo 1912- **CLC 20**
See also CA 73-76; CANR 45, 77

Antschel, Paul 1920-1970
See Celan, Paul
See also CA 85-88; CANR 33, 61; MTCW
1

Anwar, Chairil 1922-1949 **TCLC 22**
See also CA 121

Anzaldua, Gloria 1942-
See also CA 175; DLB 122; HLCS 1

Apess, William 1798-1839(?) **NCLC 73; DAM
MULT**
See also DLB 175; NNAL

Apollinaire, Guillaume 1880-1918 **TCLC 3,
8, 51; DAM POET; PC 7**
See also Kostrowitzki, Wilhelm Apollinaris
de
See also CA 152; MTCW 1

Appelfeld, Aharon 1932- **CLC 23, 47**
See also CA 112; 133; CANR 86

Apple, Max (Isaac) 1941- **CLC 9, 33**
See also CA 81-84; CANR 19, 54; DLB
130

Appleman, Philip (Dean) 1926- **CLC 51**
See also CA 13-16R; CAAS 18; CANR 6,
29, 56

Appleton, Lawrence
See Lovecraft, H(oward) P(hillips)

Apteryx
See Eliot, T(homas) S(tearns)

Apuleius, (Lucius Madaurensis)
125(?)-175(?) **CMLC 1**
See also DLB 211

Aquin, Hubert 1929-1977 **CLC 15**
See also CA 105; DLB 53

Aquinas, Thomas 1224(?)-1274 **CMLC 33**
See also DLB 115

Aragon, Louis 1897-1982 **CLC 3, 22; DAM
NOV, POET**
See also CA 69-72; 108; CANR 28, 71;
DLB 72; MTCW 1, 2

Arany, Janos 1817-1882 **NCLC 34**

Aranyos, Kakay
See Mikszath, Kalman

Arbuthnot, John 1667-1735 **LC 1**
See also DLB 101

Archer, Herbert Winslow
See Mencken, H(enry) L(ouis)

Archer, Jeffrey (Howard) 1940- **CLC 28;
DAM POP**
See also AAYA 16; BEST 89:3; CA 77-80;
CANR 22, 52; DA3; INT CANR-22

Archer, Jules 1915- **CLC 12**
See also CA 9-12R; CANR 6, 69; SAAS 5;
SATA 4, 85

Archer, Lee
See Ellison, Harlan (Jay)

Arden, John 1930- **CLC 6, 13, 15; DAM
DRAM**
See also CA 13-16R; CAAS 4; CANR 31,
65, 67; DLB 13; MTCW 1

Arenas, Reinaldo 1943-1990 **CLC 41; DAM
MULT; HLC 1**
See also CA 124; 128; 133; CANR 73; DLB
145; HW 1; MTCW 1

Arendt, Hannah 1906-1975 **CLC 66, 98**
See also CA 17-20R; 61-64; CANR 26, 60;
MTCW 1, 2

Aretino, Pietro 1492-1556 **LC 12**

Arghezi, Tudor 1880-1967 **CLC 80**
See also Theodorescu, Ion N.
See also CA 167

Arguedas, Jose Maria 1911-1969 **CLC 10,
18; HLCS 1**
See also CA 89-92; CANR 73; DLB 113;
HW 1

Argueta, Manlio 1936- **CLC 31**
See also CA 131; CANR 73; DLB 145; HW
1

Arias, Ron(ald Francis) 1941-
See also CA 131; CANR 81; DAM MULT;
DLB 82; HLC 1; HW 1, 2; MTCW 2

Ariosto, Ludovico 1474-1533 **LC 6**

Aristides
See Epstein, Joseph

Aristophanes 450B.C.-385B.C. **CMLC 4; DA;
DAB; DAC; DAM DRAM, MST; DC 2;
WLCS**
See also DA3; DLB 176

Aristotle 384B.C.-322B.C. **CMLC 31; DA;
DAB; DAC; DAM MST; WLCS**
See also DA3; DLB 176

Arlt, Roberto (Godofredo Christophersen)
1900-1942 **TCLC 29; DAM MULT;
HLC 1**
See also CA 123; 131; CANR 67; HW 1, 2

Armah, Ayi Kwei 1939- **CLC 5, 33; BLC 1;
DAM MULT, POET**
See also BW 1; CA 61-64; CANR 21, 64;
DLB 117; MTCW 1

Armatrading, Joan 1950- **CLC 17**
See also CA 114; 186

Arnette, Robert
See Silverberg, Robert

**Arnim, Achim von (Ludwig Joachim von
Arnim)** 1781-1831 **NCLC 5; SSC 29**
See also DLB 90

Arnim, Bettina von 1785-1859 **NCLC 38**
See also DLB 90

Arnold, Matthew 1822-1888 **NCLC 6, 29;
DA; DAB; DAC; DAM MST, POET;
PC 5; WLC**
See also CDBLB 1832-1890; DLB 32, 57

Arnold, Thomas 1795-1842 **NCLC 18**
See also DLB 55

Arnow, Harriette (Louisa) Simpson
1908-1986 **CLC 2, 7, 18**
See also CA 9-12R; 118; CANR 14; DLB
6; MTCW 1, 2; SATA 42; SATA-Obit 47

Arouet, Francois-Marie
See Voltaire

Arp, Hans
See Arp, Jean

Arp, Jean 1887-1966 **CLC 5**
See also CA 81-84; 25-28R; CANR 42, 77

Arrabal
See Arrabal, Fernando

Arrabal, Fernando 1932- **CLC 2, 9, 18, 58**
See also CA 9-12R; CANR 15

Arreola, Juan Jose 1918- **SSC 38; DAM
MULT; HLC 1**
See also CA 113; 131; CANR 81; DLB 113;
HW 1, 2

Arrick, Fran CLC 30

See also Gaberman, Judie Angell

Artaud, Antonin (Marie Joseph) 1896-1948 **TCLC 3, 36; DAM DRAM**
See also CA 104; 149; DA3; MTCW 1

Arthur, Ruth M(abel) 1905-1979 **CLC 12**
See also CA 9-12R; 85-88; CANR 4; SATA 7, 26

Artsybashev, Mikhail (Petrovich) 1878-1927 **TCLC 31**
See also CA 170

Arundel, Honor (Morfydd) 1919-1973 **CLC 17**
See also CA 21-22; 41-44R; CAP 2; CLR 35; SATA 4; SATA-Obit 24

Arzner, Dorothy 1897-1979 **CLC 98**

Asch, Sholem 1880-1957 **TCLC 3**
See also CA 105

Ash, Shalom
See Asch, Sholem

Ashbery, John (Lawrence) 1927- **CLC 2, 3, 4, 6, 9, 13, 15, 25, 41, 77, 125; DAM POET; PC 26**
See also CA 5-8R; CANR 9, 37, 66; DA3; DLB 5, 165; DLBY 81; INT CANR-9; MTCW 1, 2

Ashdown, Clifford
See Freeman, R(ichard) Austin

Ashe, Gordon
See Creasey, John

Ashton-Warner, Sylvia (Constance) 1908-1984 **CLC 19**
See also CA 69-72; 112; CANR 29; MTCW 1, 2

Asimov, Isaac 1920-1992 **CLC 1, 3, 9, 19, 26, 76, 92; DAM POP**
See also AAYA 13; BEST 90:2; CA 1-4R; 137; CANR 2, 19, 36, 60; CLR 12; DA3; DLB 8; DLBY 92; INT CANR-19; JRDA; MAICYA; MTCW 1, 2; SATA 1, 26, 74

Assis, Joaquim Maria Machado de
See Machado de Assis, Joaquim Maria

Astley, Thea (Beatrice May) 1925- **CLC 41**
See also CA 65-68; CANR 11, 43, 78

Aston, James
See White, T(erence) H(anbury)

Asturias, Miguel Angel 1899-1974 **CLC 3, 8, 13; DAM MULT, NOV; HLC 1**
See also CA 25-28; 49-52; CANR 32; CAP 2; DA3; DLB 113; HW 1; MTCW 1, 2

Atares, Carlos Saura
See Saura (Atares), Carlos

Atheling, William
See Pound, Ezra (Weston Loomis)

Atheling, William, Jr.
See Blish, James (Benjamin)

Atherton, Gertrude (Franklin Horn) 1857-1948 **TCLC 2**
See also CA 104; 155; DLB 9, 78, 186

Atherton, Lucius
See Masters, Edgar Lee

Atkins, Jack
See Harris, Mark

Atkinson, Kate CLC 99
See also CA 166

Attaway, William (Alexander) 1911-1986 **CLC 92; BLC 1; DAM MULT**
See also BW 2, 3; CA 143; CANR 82; DLB 76

Atticus
See Fleming, Ian (Lancaster); Wilson, (Thomas) Woodrow

Atwood, Margaret (Eleanor) 1939- **CLC 2, 3, 4, 8, 13, 15, 25, 44, 84; DA; DAB; DAC; DAM MST, NOV, POET; PC 8; SSC 2; WLC**
See also AAYA 12; BEST 89:2; CA 49-52; CANR 3, 24, 33, 59; DA3; DLB 53; INT CANR-24; MTCW 1, 2; SATA 50

Aubigny, Pierre d'
See Mencken, H(enry) L(ouis)

Aubin, Penelope 1685-1731(?) **LC 9**
See also DLB 39

Auchincloss, Louis (Stanton) 1917- **CLC 4, 6, 9, 18, 45; DAM NOV; SSC 22**
See also CA 1-4R; CANR 6, 29, 55, 87; DLB 2; DLBY 80; INT CANR-29; MTCW 1

Auden, W(ystan) H(ugh) 1907-1973 **CLC 1, 2, 3, 4, 6, 9, 11, 14, 43; DA; DAB; DAC; DAM DRAM, MST, POET; PC 1; WLC**
See also AAYA 18; CA 9-12R; 45-48; CANR 5, 61; CDBLB 1914-1945; DA3; DLB 10, 20; MTCW 1, 2

Audiberti, Jacques 1900-1965 **CLC 38; DAM DRAM**
See also CA 25-28R

Audubon, John James 1785-1851 **NCLC 47**

Auel, Jean M(arie) 1936- **CLC 31, 107; DAM POP**
See also AAYA 7; BEST 90:4; CA 103; CANR 21, 64; DA3; INT CANR-21; SATA 91

Auerbach, Erich 1892-1957 **TCLC 43**
See also CA 118; 155

Augier, Emile 1820-1889 **NCLC 31**
See also DLB 192

August, John
See De Voto, Bernard (Augustine)

Augustine 354-430 **CMLC 6; DA; DAB; DAC; DAM MST; WLCS**
See also DA3; DLB 115

Aurelius
See Bourne, Randolph S(illiman)

Aurobindo, Sri
See Ghose, Aurabinda

Austen, Jane 1775-1817 **NCLC 1, 13, 19, 33, 51, 81; DA; DAB; DAC; DAM MST, NOV; WLC**
See also AAYA 19; CDBLB 1789-1832; DA3; DLB 116

Auster, Paul 1947- **CLC 47, 131**
See also CA 69-72; CANR 23, 52, 75; DA3; MTCW 1

Austin, Frank
See Faust, Frederick (Schiller)

Austin, Mary (Hunter) 1868-1934 **TCLC 25**
See also CA 109; 178; DLB 9, 78, 206, 221

Averroes 1126-1198 **CMLC 7**
See also DLB 115

Avicenna 980-1037 **CMLC 16**
See also DLB 115

Avison, Margaret 1918- **CLC 2, 4, 97; DAC; DAM POET**
See also CA 17-20R; DLB 53; MTCW 1

Axton, David
See Koontz, Dean R(ay)

Ayckbourn, Alan 1939- **CLC 5, 8, 18, 33, 74; DAB; DAM DRAM**
See also CA 21-24R; CANR 31, 59; DLB 13; MTCW 1, 2

Aydy, Catherine
See Tennant, Emma (Christina)

Ayme, Marcel (Andre) 1902-1967 **CLC 11**
See also CA 89-92; CANR 67; CLR 25; DLB 72; SATA 91

Ayrton, Michael 1921-1975 **CLC 7**
See also CA 5-8R; 61-64; CANR 9, 21

Azorin CLC 11
See also Martinez Ruiz, Jose

Azuela, Mariano 1873-1952 **TCLC 3; DAM MULT; HLC 1**
See also CA 104; 131; CANR 81; HW 1, 2; MTCW 1, 2

Baastad, Babbis Friis
See Friis-Baastad, Babbis Ellinor

Bab
See Gilbert, W(illiam) S(chwenck)

Babbis, Eleanor
See Friis-Baastad, Babbis Ellinor

Babel, Isaac
See Babel, Isaak (Emmanuilovich)

Babel, Isaak (Emmanuilovich) 1894-1941(?) **TCLC 2, 13; SSC 16**
See also CA 104; 155; MTCW 1

Babits, Mihaly 1883-1941 **TCLC 14**
See also CA 114

Babur 1483-1530 **LC 18**

Baca, Jimmy Santiago 1952-
See also CA 131; CANR 81, 90; DAM MULT; DLB 122; HLC 1; HW 1, 2

Bacchelli, Riccardo 1891-1985 **CLC 19**
See also CA 29-32R; 117

Bach, Richard (David) 1936- **CLC 14; DAM NOV, POP**
See also AITN 1; BEST 89:2; CA 9-12R; CANR 18; MTCW 1; SATA 13

Bachman, Richard
See King, Stephen (Edwin)

Bachmann, Ingeborg 1926-1973 **CLC 69**
See also CA 93-96; 45-48; CANR 69; DLB 85

Bacon, Francis 1561-1626 **LC 18, 32**
See also CDBLB Before 1660; DLB 151

Bacon, Roger 1214(?)-1292 **CMLC 14**
See also DLB 115

Bacovia, George TCLC 24
See also Vasiliu, Gheorghe
See also DLB 220

Badanes, Jerome 1937- **CLC 59**

Bagehot, Walter 1826-1877 **NCLC 10**
See also DLB 55

Bagnold, Enid 1889-1981 **CLC 25; DAM DRAM**
See also CA 5-8R; 103; CANR 5, 40; DLB 13, 160, 191; MAICYA; SATA 1, 25

Bagritsky, Eduard 1895-1934 **TCLC 60**

Bagrjana, Elisaveta
See Belcheva, Elisaveta

Bagryana, Elisaveta 1893-1991 **CLC 10**
See also Belcheva, Elisaveta
See also CA 178; DLB 147

Bailey, Paul 1937- **CLC 45**
See also CA 21-24R; CANR 16, 62; DLB 14

Baillie, Joanna 1762-1851 **NCLC 71**
See also DLB 93

Bainbridge, Beryl (Margaret) 1934- **CLC 4, 5, 8, 10, 14, 18, 22, 62, 130; DAM NOV**
See also CA 21-24R; CANR 24, 55, 75, 88; DLB 14; MTCW 1, 2

Baker, Elliott 1922- **CLC 8**
See also CA 45-48; CANR 2, 63

Baker, Jean H. TCLC 3, 10
See also Russell, George William

Baker, Nicholson 1957- **CLC 61; DAM POP**
See also CA 135; CANR 63; DA3

Baker, Ray Stannard 1870-1946 **TCLC 47**
See also CA 118

Baker, Russell (Wayne) 1925- **CLC 31**
See also BEST 89:4; CA 57-60; CANR 11, 41, 59; MTCW 1, 2

Bakhtin, M.
See Bakhtin, Mikhail Mikhailovich

Bakhtin, M. M.
See Bakhtin, Mikhail Mikhailovich

Bakhtin, Mikhail
See Bakhtin, Mikhail Mikhailovich

Bakhtin, Mikhail Mikhailovich 1895-1975 **CLC 83**
See also CA 128; 113

Bakshi, Ralph 1938(?)- **CLC 26**
See also CA 112; 138

Bakunin, Mikhail (Alexandrovich) 1814-1876 **NCLC 25, 58**

Baldwin, James (Arthur) 1924-1987 **CLC 1,**

2, 3, 4, 5, 8, 13, 15, 17, 42, 50, 67, 90, 127; BLC 1; DA; DAB; DAC; DAM MST, MULT, NOV, POP; DC 1; SSC 10, 33; WLC
See also AAYA 4, 34; BW 1; CA 1-4R; 124; CABS 1; CANR 3, 24; CDALB 1941-1968; DA3; DLB 2, 7, 33; DLBY 87; MTCW 1, 2; SATA 9; SATA-Obit 54

Ballard, J(ames) G(raham) 1930- CLC 3, 6, 14, 36; DAM NOV, POP; SSC 1
See also AAYA 3; CA 5-8R; CANR 15, 39, 65; DA3; DLB 14, 207; MTCW 1, 2; SATA 93

Balmont, Konstantin (Dmitriyevich) 1867-1943 TCLC 11
See also CA 109; 155

Baltausis, Vincas
See Mikszath, Kalman

Balzac, Honore de 1799-1850 NCLC 5, 35, 53; DA; DAB; DAC; DAM MST, NOV; SSC 5; WLC
See also DA3; DLB 119

Bambara, Toni Cade 1939-1995 CLC 19, 88; BLC 1; DA; DAC; DAM MST, MULT; SSC 35; WLCS
See also AAYA 5; BW 2, 3; CA 29-32R; 150; CANR 24, 49, 81; CDALBS; DA3; DLB 38; MTCW 1, 2; SATA 112

Bamdad, A.
See Shamlu, Ahmad

Banat, D. R.
See Bradbury, Ray (Douglas)

Bancroft, Laura
See Baum, L(yman) Frank

Banim, John 1798-1842 NCLC 13
See also DLB 116, 158, 159

Banim, Michael 1796-1874 NCLC 13
See also DLB 158, 159

Banjo, The
See Paterson, A(ndrew) B(arton)

Banks, Iain
See Banks, Iain M(enzies)

Banks, Iain M(enzies) 1954- CLC 34
See also CA 123; 128; CANR 61; DLB 194; INT 128

Banks, Lynne Reid CLC 23
See also Reid Banks, Lynne
See also AAYA 6

Banks, Russell 1940- CLC 37, 72
See also CA 65-68; CAAS 15; CANR 19, 52, 73; DLB 130

Banville, John 1945- CLC 46, 118
See also CA 117; 128; DLB 14; INT 128

Banville, Theodore (Faullain) de 1832-1891 NCLC 9

Baraka, Amiri 1934- CLC 1, 2, 3, 5, 10, 14, 33, 115; BLC 1; DA; DAC; DAM MST, MULT, POET, POP; DC 6; PC 4; WLCS
See also Jones, LeRoi
See also BW 2, 3; CA 21-24R; CABS 3; CANR 27, 38, 61; CDALB 1941-1968; DA3; DLB 5, 7, 16, 38; DLBD 8; MTCW 1, 2

Barbauld, Anna Laetitia 1743-1825 NCLC 50
See also DLB 107, 109, 142, 158

Barbellion, W. N. P. TCLC 24
See also Cummings, Bruce F(rederick)

Barbera, Jack (Vincent) 1945- CLC 44
See also CA 110; CANR 45

Barbey d'Aurevilly, Jules Amedee 1808-1889 NCLC 1; SSC 17
See also DLB 119

Barbour, John c. 1316-1395 CMLC 33
See also DLB 146

Barbusse, Henri 1873-1935 TCLC 5
See also CA 105; 154; DLB 65

Barclay, Bill
See Moorcock, Michael (John)

Barclay, William Ewert
See Moorcock, Michael (John)

Barea, Arturo 1897-1957 TCLC 14
See also CA 111

Barfoot, Joan 1946- CLC 18
See also CA 105

Barham, Richard Harris 1788-1845 NCLC 77
See also DLB 159

Baring, Maurice 1874-1945 TCLC 8
See also CA 105; 168; DLB 34

Baring-Gould, Sabine 1834-1924 TCLC 88
See also DLB 156, 190

Barker, Clive 1952- CLC 52; DAM POP
See also AAYA 10; BEST 90:3; CA 121; 129; CANR 71; DA3; INT 129; MTCW 1, 2

Barker, George Granville 1913-1991 CLC 8, 48; DAM POET
See also CA 9-12R; 135; CANR 7, 38; DLB 20; MTCW 1

Barker, Harley Granville
See Granville-Barker, Harley
See also DLB 10

Barker, Howard 1946- CLC 37
See also CA 102; DLB 13

Barker, Jane 1652-1732 LC 42

Barker, Pat(ricia) 1943- CLC 32, 94
See also CA 117; 122; CANR 50; INT 122

Barlach, Ernst (Heinrich) 1870-1938 TCLC 84
See also CA 178; DLB 56, 118

Barlow, Joel 1754-1812 NCLC 23
See also DLB 37

Barnard, Mary (Ethel) 1909- CLC 48
See also CA 21-22; CAP 2

Barnes, Djuna 1892-1982 CLC 3, 4, 8, 11, 29, 127; SSC 3
See also CA 9-12R; 107; CANR 16, 55; DLB 4, 9, 45; MTCW 1, 2

Barnes, Julian (Patrick) 1946- CLC 42; DAB
See also CA 102; CANR 19, 54; DLB 194; DLBY 93; MTCW 1

Barnes, Peter 1931- CLC 5, 56
See also CA 65-68; CAAS 12; CANR 33, 34, 64; DLB 13; MTCW 1

Barnes, William 1801-1886 NCLC 75
See also DLB 32

Baroja (y Nessi), Pio 1872-1956 TCLC 8; HLC 1
See also CA 104

Baron, David
See Pinter, Harold

Baron Corvo
See Rolfe, Frederick (William Serafino Austin Lewis Mary)

Barondess, Sue K(aufman) 1926-1977 CLC 8
See also Kaufman, Sue
See also CA 1-4R; 69-72; CANR 1

Baron de Teive
See Pessoa, Fernando (Antonio Nogueira)

Baroness Von S.
See Zangwill, Israel

Barres, (Auguste-) Maurice 1862-1923 TCLC 47
See also CA 164; DLB 123

Barreto, Afonso Henrique de Lima
See Lima Barreto, Afonso Henrique de

Barrett, (Roger) Syd 1946- CLC 35

Barrett, William (Christopher) 1913-1992 CLC 27
See also CA 13-16R; 139; CANR 11, 67; INT CANR-11

Barrie, J(ames) M(atthew) 1860-1937 TCLC 2; DAB; DAM DRAM

See also CA 104; 136; CANR 77; CDBLB 1890-1914; CLR 16; DA3; DLB 10, 141, 156; MAICYA; MTCW 1; SATA 100; YABC 1

Barrington, Michael
See Moorcock, Michael (John)

Barrol, Grady
See Bograd, Larry

Barry, Mike
See Malzberg, Barry N(athaniel)

Barry, Philip 1896-1949 TCLC 11
See also CA 109; DLB 7

Bart, Andre Schwarz
See Schwarz-Bart, Andre

Barth, John (Simmons) 1930- CLC 1, 2, 3, 5, 7, 9, 10, 14, 27, 51, 89; DAM NOV; SSC 10
See also AITN 1, 2; CA 1-4R; CABS 1; CANR 5, 23, 49, 64; DLB 2; MTCW 1

Barthelme, Donald 1931-1989 CLC 1, 2, 3, 5, 6, 8, 13, 23, 46, 59, 115; DAM NOV; SSC 2
See also CA 21-24R; 129; CANR 20, 58; DA3; DLB 2; DLBY 80, 89; MTCW 1, 2; SATA 7; SATA-Obit 62

Barthelme, Frederick 1943- CLC 36, 117
See also CA 114; 122; CANR 77; DLBY 85; INT 122

Barthes, Roland (Gerard) 1915-1980 CLC 24, 83
See also CA 130; 97-100; CANR 66; MTCW 1, 2

Barzun, Jacques (Martin) 1907- CLC 51
See also CA 61-64; CANR 22

Bashevis, Isaac
See Singer, Isaac Bashevis

Bashkirtseff, Marie 1859-1884 NCLC 27

Basho
See Matsuo Basho

Basil of Caesaria c. 330-379 CMLC 35

Bass, Kingsley B., Jr.
See Bullins, Ed

Bass, Rick 1958- CLC 79
See also CA 126; CANR 53; DLB 212

Bassani, Giorgio 1916- CLC 9
See also CA 65-68; CANR 33; DLB 128, 177; MTCW 1

Bastos, Augusto (Antonio) Roa
See Roa Bastos, Augusto (Antonio)

Bataille, Georges 1897-1962 CLC 29
See also CA 101; 89-92

Bates, H(erbert) E(rnest) 1905-1974 CLC 46; DAB; DAM POP; SSC 10
See also CA 93-96; 45-48; CANR 34; DA3; DLB 162, 191; MTCW 1, 2

Bauchart
See Camus, Albert

Baudelaire, Charles 1821-1867 NCLC 6, 29, 55; DA; DAB; DAC; DAM MST, POET; PC 1; SSC 18; WLC
See also DA3

Baudrillard, Jean 1929- CLC 60

Baum, L(yman) Frank 1856-1919 TCLC 7
See also CA 108; 133; CLR 15; DLB 22; JRDA; MAICYA; MTCW 1, 2; SATA 18, 100

Baum, Louis F.
See Baum, L(yman) Frank

Baumbach, Jonathan 1933- CLC 6, 23
See also CA 13-16R; CAAS 5; CANR 12, 66; DLBY 80; INT CANR-12; MTCW 1

Bausch, Richard (Carl) 1945- CLC 51
See also CA 101; CAAS 14; CANR 43, 61, 87; DLB 130

Baxter, Charles (Morley) 1947- CLC 45, 78; DAM POP
See also CA 57-60; CANR 40, 64; DLB 130; MTCW 2

Blackwood, Caroline 1931-1996 **CLC 6, 9, 100**
See also CA 85-88; 151; CANR 32, 61, 65; DLB 14, 207; MTCW 1

Blade, Alexander
See Hamilton, Edmond; Silverberg, Robert

Blaga, Lucian 1895-1961 **CLC 75**
See also CA 157; DLB 220

Blair, Eric (Arthur) 1903-1950
See Orwell, George
See also CA 104; 132; DA; DAB; DAC; DAM MST, NOV; DA3; MTCW 1, 2; SATA 29

Blair, Hugh 1718-1800 **NCLC 75**

Blais, Marie-Claire 1939- **CLC 2, 4, 6, 13, 22; DAC; DAM MST**
See also CA 21-24R; CAAS 4; CANR 38, 75; DLB 53; MTCW 1, 2

Blaise, Clark 1940- **CLC 29**
See also AITN 2; CA 53-56; CAAS 3; CANR 5, 66; DLB 53

Blake, Fairley
See De Voto, Bernard (Augustine)

Blake, Nicholas
See Day Lewis, C(ecil)
See also DLB 77

Blake, William 1757-1827 **NCLC 13, 37, 57; DA; DAB; DAC; DAM MST, POET; PC 12; WLC**
See also CDBLB 1789-1832; CLR 52; DA3; DLB 93, 163; MAICYA; SATA 30

Blasco Ibanez, Vicente 1867-1928 **TCLC 12; DAM NOV**
See also CA 110; 131; CANR 81; DA3; HW 1, 2; MTCW 1

Blatty, William Peter 1928- **CLC 2; DAM POP**
See also CA 5-8R; CANR 9

Bleeck, Oliver
See Thomas, Ross (Elmore)

Blessing, Lee 1949- **CLC 54**

Blight, Rose
See Greer, Germaine

Blish, James (Benjamin) 1921-1975 **CLC 14**
See also CA 1-4R; 57-60; CANR 3; DLB 8; MTCW 1; SATA 66

Bliss, Reginald
See Wells, H(erbert) G(eorge)

Blixen, Karen (Christentze Dinesen) 1885-1962
See Dinesen, Isak
See also CA 25-28; CANR 22, 50; CAP 2; DA3; MTCW 1, 2; SATA 44

Bloch, Robert (Albert) 1917-1994 **CLC 33**
See also AAYA 29; CA 5-8R, 179; 146; CAAE 179; CAAS 20; CANR 5, 78; DA3; DLB 44; INT CANR-5; MTCW 1; SATA 12; SATA-Obit 82

Blok, Alexander (Alexandrovich) 1880-1921 **TCLC 5; PC 21**
See also CA 104; 183

Blom, Jan
See Breytenbach, Breyten

Bloom, Harold 1930- **CLC 24, 103**
See also CA 13-16R; CANR 39, 75; DLB 67; MTCW 1

Bloomfield, Aurelius
See Bourne, Randolph S(illiman)

Blount, Roy (Alton), Jr. 1941- **CLC 38**
See also CA 53-56; CANR 10, 28, 61; INT CANR-28; MTCW 1, 2

Bloy, Leon 1846-1917 **TCLC 22**
See also CA 121; 183; DLB 123

Blume, Judy (Sussman) 1938- **CLC 12, 30; DAM NOV, POP**
See also AAYA 3, 26; CA 29-32R; CANR 13, 37, 66; CLR 2, 15; DA3; DLB 52; JRDA; MAICYA; MTCW 1, 2; SATA 2, 31, 79

Blunden, Edmund (Charles) 1896-1974 **CLC 2, 56**
See also CA 17-18; 45-48; CANR 54; CAP 2; DLB 20, 100, 155; MTCW 1

Bly, Robert (Elwood) 1926- **CLC 1, 2, 5, 10, 15, 38, 128; DAM POET**
See also CA 5-8R; CANR 41, 73; DA3; DLB 5; MTCW 1, 2

Boas, Franz 1858-1942 **TCLC 56**
See also CA 115; 181

Bobette
See Simenon, Georges (Jacques Christian)

Boccaccio, Giovanni 1313-1375 **CMLC 13; SSC 10**

Bochco, Steven 1943- **CLC 35**
See also AAYA 11; CA 124; 138

Bodel, Jean 1167(?)-1210 **CMLC 28**

Bodenheim, Maxwell 1892-1954 **TCLC 44**
See also CA 110; DLB 9, 45

Bodker, Cecil 1927- **CLC 21**
See also CA 73-76; CANR 13, 44; CLR 23; MAICYA; SATA 14

Boell, Heinrich (Theodor) 1917-1985 **CLC 2, 3, 6, 9, 11, 15, 27, 32, 72; DA; DAB; DAC; DAM MST, NOV; SSC 23; WLC**
See also CA 21-24R; 116; CANR 24; DA3; DLB 69; DLBY 85; MTCW 1, 2

Boerne, Alfred
See Doeblin, Alfred

Boethius 480(?)-524(?) **CMLC 15**
See also DLB 115

Boff, Leonardo (Genezio Darci) 1938-
See also CA 150; DAM MULT; HLC 1; HW 2

Bogan, Louise 1897-1970 **CLC 4, 39, 46, 93; DAM POET; PC 12**
See also CA 73-76; 25-28R; CANR 33, 82; DLB 45, 169; MTCW 1, 2

Bogarde, Dirk 1921-1999
See Van Den Bogarde, Derek Jules Gaspard Ulric Niven

Bogosian, Eric 1953- **CLC 45**
See also CA 138

Bograd, Larry 1953- **CLC 35**
See also CA 93-96; CANR 57; SAAS 21; SATA 33, 89

Boiardo, Matteo Maria 1441-1494 **LC 6**

Boileau-Despreaux, Nicolas 1636-1711 **LC 3**

Bojer, Johan 1872-1959 **TCLC 64**

Boland, Eavan (Aisling) 1944- **CLC 40, 67, 113; DAM POET**
See also CA 143; CANR 61; DLB 40; MTCW 2

Boll, Heinrich
See Boell, Heinrich (Theodor)

Bolt, Lee
See Faust, Frederick (Schiller)

Bolt, Robert (Oxton) 1924-1995 **CLC 14; DAM DRAM**
See also CA 17-20R; 147; CANR 35, 67; DLB 13; MTCW 1

Bombal, Maria Luisa 1910-1980 **SSC 37; HLCS 1**
See also CA 127; CANR 72; HW 1

Bombet, Louis-Alexandre-Cesar
See Stendhal

Bomkauf
See Kaufman, Bob (Garnell)

Bonaventura NCLC 35
See also DLB 90

Bond, Edward 1934- **CLC 4, 6, 13, 23; DAM DRAM**
See also CA 25-28R; CANR 38, 67; DLB 13; MTCW 1

Bonham, Frank 1914-1989 **CLC 12**
See also AAYA 1; CA 9-12R; CANR 4, 36; JRDA; MAICYA; SAAS 3; SATA 1, 49; SATA-Obit 62

Bonnefoy, Yves 1923- **CLC 9, 15, 58; DAM MST, POET**
See also CA 85-88; CANR 33, 75; MTCW 1, 2

Bontemps, Arna(ud Wendell) 1902-1973 **CLC 1, 18; BLC 1; DAM MULT, NOV, POET**
See also BW 1; CA 1-4R; 41-44R; CANR 4, 35; CLR 6; DA3; DLB 48, 51; JRDA; MAICYA; MTCW 1, 2; SATA 2, 44; SATA-Obit 24

Booth, Martin 1944- **CLC 13**
See also CA 93-96; CAAS 2

Booth, Philip 1925- **CLC 23**
See also CA 5-8R; CANR 5, 88; DLBY 82

Booth, Wayne C(layson) 1921- **CLC 24**
See also CA 1-4R; CAAS 5; CANR 3, 43; DLB 67

Borchert, Wolfgang 1921-1947 **TCLC 5**
See also CA 104; DLB 69, 124

Borel, Petrus 1809-1859 **NCLC 41**

Borges, Jorge Luis 1899-1986 **CLC 1, 2, 3, 4, 6, 8, 9, 10, 13, 19, 44, 48, 83; DA; DAB; DAC; DAM MST, MULT; HLC 1; PC 22; SSC 4; WLC**
See also AAYA 26; CA 21-24R; CANR 19, 33, 75; DA3; DLB 113; DLBY 86; HW 1, 2; MTCW 1, 2

Borowski, Tadeusz 1922-1951 **TCLC 9**
See also CA 106; 154

Borrow, George (Henry) 1803-1881 **NCLC 9**
See also DLB 21, 55, 166

Bosch (Gavino), Juan 1909-
See also CA 151; DAM MST, MULT; DLB 145; HLCS 1; HW 1, 2

Bosman, Herman Charles 1905-1951 **TCLC 49**
See also Malan, Herman
See also CA 160

Bosschere, Jean de 1878(?)-1953 **TCLC 19**
See also CA 115; 186

Boswell, James 1740-1795 **LC 4, 50; DA; DAB; DAC; DAM MST; WLC**
See also CDBLB 1660-1789; DLB 104, 142

Bottoms, David 1949- **CLC 53**
See also CA 105; CANR 22; DLB 120; DLBY 83

Boucicault, Dion 1820-1890 **NCLC 41**

Bourget, Paul (Charles Joseph) 1852-1935 **TCLC 12**
See also CA 107; DLB 123

Bourjaily, Vance (Nye) 1922- **CLC 8, 62**
See also CA 1-4R; CAAS 1; CANR 2, 72; DLB 2, 143

Bourne, Randolph S(illiman) 1886-1918 **TCLC 16**
See also CA 117; 155; DLB 63

Bova, Ben(jamin William) 1932- **CLC 45**
See also AAYA 16; CA 5-8R; CAAS 18; CANR 11, 56; CLR 3; DLBY 81; INT CANR-11; MAICYA; MTCW 1; SATA 6, 68

Bowen, Elizabeth (Dorothea Cole) 1899-1973 **CLC 1, 3, 6, 11, 15, 22, 118; DAM NOV; SSC 3, 28**
See also CA 17-18; 41-44R; CANR 35; CAP 2; CDBLB 1945-1960; DA3; DLB 15, 162; MTCW 1, 2

Bowering, George 1935- **CLC 15, 47**
See also CA 21-24R; CAAS 16; CANR 10; DLB 53

Bowering, Marilyn R(uthe) 1949- **CLC 32**
See also CA 101; CANR 49

Bowers, Edgar 1924- **CLC 9**
See also CA 5-8R; CANR 24; DLB 5

Bowie, David CLC 17
See also Jones, David Robert

Bowles, Jane (Sydney) 1917-1973 **CLC 3, 68**
See also CA 19-20; 41-44R; CAP 2

Bowles, Paul (Frederick) 1910-1999 **CLC 1, 2, 19, 53; SSC 3**
See also CA 1-4R; 186; CAAS 1; CANR 1, 19, 50, 75; DA3; DLB 5, 6; MTCW 1, 2

Box, Edgar
See Vidal, Gore

Boyd, Nancy
See Millay, Edna St. Vincent

Boyd, William 1952- **CLC 28, 53, 70**
See also CA 114; 120; CANR 51, 71

Boyle, Kay 1902-1992 **CLC 1, 5, 19, 58, 121; SSC 5**
See also CA 13-16R; 140; CAAS 1; CANR 29, 61; DLB 4, 9, 48, 86; DLBY 93; MTCW 1, 2

Boyle, Mark
See Kienzle, William X(avier)

Boyle, Patrick 1905-1982 **CLC 19**
See also CA 127

Boyle, T. C. 1948-
See Boyle, T(homas) Coraghessan

Boyle, T(homas) Coraghessan 1948- **CLC 36, 55, 90; DAM POP; SSC 16**
See also BEST 90:4; CA 120; CANR 44, 76, 89; DA3; DLBY 86; MTCW 2

Boz
See Dickens, Charles (John Huffam)

Brackenridge, Hugh Henry 1748-1816 **NCLC 7**
See also DLB 11, 37

Bradbury, Edward P.
See Moorcock, Michael (John)
See also MTCW 2

Bradbury, Malcolm (Stanley) 1932- **CLC 32, 61; DAM NOV**
See also CA 1-4R; CANR 1, 33, 91; DA3; DLB 14, 207; MTCW 1, 2

Bradbury, Ray (Douglas) 1920- **CLC 1, 3, 10, 15, 42, 98; DA; DAB; DAC; DAM MST, NOV, POP; SSC 29; WLC**
See also AAYA 15; AITN 1, 2; CA 1-4R; CANR 2, 30, 75; CDALB 1968-1988; DA3; DLB 2, 8; MTCW 1, 2; SATA 11, 64

Bradford, Gamaliel 1863-1932 **TCLC 36**
See also CA 160; DLB 17

Bradley, David (Henry), Jr. 1950- **CLC 23, 118; BLC 1; DAM MULT**
See also BW 1, 3; CA 104; CANR 26, 81; DLB 33

Bradley, John Ed(mund, Jr.) 1958- **CLC 55**
See also CA 139

Bradley, Marion Zimmer 1930-1999 **CLC 30; DAM POP**
See also AAYA 9; CA 57-60; 185; CAAS 10; CANR 7, 31, 51, 75; DA3; DLB 8; MTCW 1, 2; SATA 90; SATA-Obit 116

Bradstreet, Anne 1612(?)-1672 **LC 4, 30; DA; DAC; DAM MST, POET; PC 10**
See also CDALB 1640-1865; DA3; DLB 24

Brady, Joan 1939- **CLC 86**
See also CA 141

Bragg, Melvyn 1939- **CLC 10**
See also BEST 89:3; CA 57-60; CANR 10, 48, 89; DLB 14

Brahe, Tycho 1546-1601 **LC 45**

Braine, John (Gerard) 1922-1986 **CLC 1, 3, 41**
See also CA 1-4R; 120; CANR 1, 33; CDBLB 1945-1960; DLB 15; DLBY 86; MTCW 1

Bramah, Ernest 1868-1942 **TCLC 72**
See also CA 156; DLB 70

Brammer, William 1930(?)-1978 **CLC 31**
See also CA 77-80

Brancati, Vitaliano 1907-1954 **TCLC 12**
See also CA 109

Brancato, Robin F(idler) 1936- **CLC 35**

See also AAYA 9; CA 69-72; CANR 11, 45; CLR 32; JRDA; SAAS 9; SATA 97

Brand, Max
See Faust, Frederick (Schiller)

Brand, Millen 1906-1980 **CLC 7**
See also CA 21-24R; 97-100; CANR 72

Branden, Barbara CLC 44
See also CA 148

Brandes, Georg (Morris Cohen) 1842-1927 **TCLC 10**
See also CA 105

Brandys, Kazimierz 1916- **CLC 62**

Branley, Franklyn M(ansfield) 1915- **CLC 21**
See also CA 33-36R; CANR 14, 39; CLR 13; MAICYA; SAAS 16; SATA 4, 68

Brathwaite, Edward (Kamau) 1930- **CLC 11; BLCS; DAM POET**
See also BW 2, 3; CA 25-28R; CANR 11, 26, 47; DLB 125

Brautigan, Richard (Gary) 1935-1984 **CLC 1, 3, 5, 9, 12, 34, 42; DAM NOV**
See also CA 53-56; 113; CANR 34; DA3; DLB 2, 5, 206; DLBY 80, 84; MTCW 1; SATA 56

Brave Bird, Mary 1953-
See Crow Dog, Mary (Ellen)
See also NNAL

Braverman, Kate 1950- **CLC 67**
See also CA 89-92

Brecht, (Eugen) Bertolt (Friedrich) 1898-1956 **TCLC 1, 6, 13, 35; DA; DAB; DAC; DAM DRAM, MST; DC 3; WLC**
See also CA 104; 133; CANR 62; DA3; DLB 56, 124; MTCW 1, 2

Brecht, Eugen Berthold Friedrich
See Brecht, (Eugen) Bertolt (Friedrich)

Bremer, Fredrika 1801-1865 **NCLC 11**

Brennan, Christopher John 1870-1932 **TCLC 17**
See also CA 117

Brennan, Maeve 1917-1993 **CLC 5**
See also CA 81-84; CANR 72

Brent, Linda
See Jacobs, Harriet A(nn)

Brentano, Clemens (Maria) 1778-1842 **NCLC 1**
See also DLB 90

Brent of Bin Bin
See Franklin, (Stella Maria Sarah) Miles (Lampe)

Brenton, Howard 1942- **CLC 31**
See also CA 69-72; CANR 33, 67; DLB 13; MTCW 1

Breslin, James 1930-1996
See Breslin, Jimmy
See also CA 73-76; CANR 31, 75; DAM NOV; MTCW 1, 2

Breslin, Jimmy CLC 4, 43
See also Breslin, James
See also AITN 1; DLB 185; MTCW 2

Bresson, Robert 1901- **CLC 16**
See also CA 110; CANR 49

Breton, Andre 1896-1966 **CLC 2, 9, 15, 54; PC 15**
See also CA 19-20; 25-28R; CANR 40, 60; CAP 2; DLB 65; MTCW 1, 2

Breytenbach, Breyten 1939(?)- **CLC 23, 37, 126; DAM POET**
See also CA 113; 129; CANR 61

Bridgers, Sue Ellen 1942- **CLC 26**
See also AAYA 8; CA 65-68; CANR 11, 36; CLR 18; DLB 52; JRDA; MAICYA; SAAS 1; SATA 22, 90; SATA-Essay 109

Bridges, Robert (Seymour) 1844-1930 **TCLC 1; DAM POET; PC 28**
See also CA 104; 152; CDBLB 1890-1914; DLB 19, 98

Bridie, James TCLC 3

See also Mavor, Osborne Henry
See also DLB 10

Brin, David 1950- **CLC 34**
See also AAYA 21; CA 102; CANR 24, 70; INT CANR-24; SATA 65

Brink, Andre (Philippus) 1935- **CLC 18, 36, 106**
See also CA 104; CANR 39, 62; INT 103; MTCW 1, 2

Brinsmead, H(esba) F(ay) 1922- **CLC 21**
See also CA 21-24R; CANR 10; CLR 47; MAICYA; SAAS 5; SATA 18, 78

Brittain, Vera (Mary) 1893(?)-1970 **CLC 23**
See also CA 13-16; 25-28R; CANR 58; CAP 1; DLB 191; MTCW 1, 2

Broch, Hermann 1886-1951 **TCLC 20**
See also CA 117; DLB 85, 124

Brock, Rose
See Hansen, Joseph

Brodkey, Harold (Roy) 1930-1996 **CLC 56**
See also CA 111; 151; CANR 71; DLB 130

Brodskii, Iosif
See Brodsky, Joseph

Brodsky, Iosif Alexandrovich 1940-1996
See Brodsky, Joseph
See also AITN 1; CA 41-44R; 151; CANR 37; DAM POET; DA3; MTCW 1, 2

Brodsky, Joseph 1940-1996 **CLC 4, 6, 13, 36, 100; PC 9**
See also Brodskii, Iosif; Brodsky, Iosif Alexandrovich
See also MTCW 1

Brodsky, Michael (Mark) 1948- **CLC 19**
See also CA 102; CANR 18, 41, 58

Bromell, Henry 1947- **CLC 5**
See also CA 53-56; CANR 9

Bromfield, Louis (Brucker) 1896-1956 **TCLC 11**
See also CA 107; 155; DLB 4, 9, 86

Broner, E(sther) M(asserman) 1930- **CLC 19**
See also CA 17-20R; CANR 8, 25, 72; DLB 28

Bronk, William (M.) 1918-1999 **CLC 10**
See also CA 89-92; 177; CANR 23; DLB 165

Bronstein, Lev Davidovich
See Trotsky, Leon

Bronte, Anne 1820-1849 **NCLC 4, 71**
See also DA3; DLB 21, 199

Bronte, Charlotte 1816-1855 **NCLC 3, 8, 33, 58; DA; DAB; DAC; DAM MST, NOV; WLC**
See also AAYA 17; CDBLB 1832-1890; DA3; DLB 21, 159, 199

Bronte, Emily (Jane) 1818-1848 **NCLC 16, 35; DA; DAB; DAC; DAM MST, NOV, POET; PC 8; WLC**
See also AAYA 17; CDBLB 1832-1890; DA3; DLB 21, 32, 199

Brooke, Frances 1724-1789 **LC 6, 48**
See also DLB 39, 99

Brooke, Henry 1703(?)-1783 **LC 1**
See also DLB 39

Brooke, Rupert (Chawner) 1887-1915 **TCLC 2, 7; DA; DAB; DAC; DAM MST, POET; PC 24; WLC**
See also CA 104; 132; CANR 61; CDBLB 1914-1945; DLB 19; MTCW 1, 2

Brooke-Haven, P.
See Wodehouse, P(elham) G(renville)

Brooke-Rose, Christine 1926(?)- **CLC 40**
See also CA 13-16R; CANR 58; DLB 14

Brookner, Anita 1928- **CLC 32, 34, 51; DAB; DAM POP**
See also CA 114; 120; CANR 37, 56, 87; DA3; DLB 194; DLBY 87; MTCW 1, 2

Brooks, Cleanth 1906-1994 **CLC 24, 86, 110**

See also CA 73-76; CANR 40

Caragiale, Ion Luca 1852-1912 **TCLC 76**
See also CA 157

Card, Orson Scott 1951- **CLC 44, 47, 50;**
DAM POP
See also AAYA 11; CA 102; CANR 27, 47,
73; DA3; INT CANR-27; MTCW 1, 2;
SATA 83

Cardenal, Ernesto 1925- **CLC 31; DAM**
MULT, POET; HLC 1; PC 22
See also CA 49-52; CANR 2, 32, 66; HW
1, 2; MTCW 1, 2

Cardozo, Benjamin N(athan) 1870-1938
TCLC 65
See also CA 117; 164

Carducci, Giosue (Alessandro Giuseppe)
1835-1907 **TCLC 32**
See also CA 163

Carew, Thomas 1595(?)-1640 **LC 13; PC 29**
See also DLB 126

Carey, Ernestine Gilbreth 1908- **CLC 17**
See also CA 5-8R; CANR 71; SATA 2

Carey, Peter 1943- **CLC 40, 55, 96**
See also CA 123; 127; CANR 53, 76; INT
127; MTCW 1, 2; SATA 94

Carleton, William 1794-1869 **NCLC 3**
See also DLB 159

Carlisle, Henry (Coffin) 1926- **CLC 33**
See also CA 13-16R; CANR 15, 85

Carlsen, Chris
See Holdstock, Robert P.

Carlson, Ron(ald F.) 1947- **CLC 54**
See also CA 105; CANR 27

Carlyle, Thomas 1795-1881 **NCLC 70; DA;**
DAB; DAC; DAM MST
See also CDBLB 1789-1832; DLB 55; 144

Carman, (William) Bliss 1861-1929 **TCLC 7;**
DAC
See also CA 104; 152; DLB 92

Carnegie, Dale 1888-1955 **TCLC 53**

Carossa, Hans 1878-1956 **TCLC 48**
See also CA 170; DLB 66

Carpenter, Don(ald Richard) 1931-1995 **CLC**
41
See also CA 45-48; 149; CANR 1, 71

Carpenter, Edward 1844-1929 **TCLC 88**
See also CA 163

Carpentier (y Valmont), Alejo 1904-1980
CLC 8, 11, 38, 110; DAM MULT; HLC
1; SSC 35
See also CA 65-68; 97-100; CANR 11, 70;
DLB 113; HW 1, 2

Carr, Caleb 1955(?)- **CLC 86**
See also CA 147; CANR 73; DA3

Carr, Emily 1871-1945 **TCLC 32**
See also CA 159; DLB 68

Carr, John Dickson 1906-1977 **CLC 3**
See also Fairbairn, Roger
See also CA 49-52; 69-72; CANR 3, 33,
60; MTCW 1, 2

Carr, Philippa
See Hibbert, Eleanor Alice Burford

Carr, Virginia Spencer 1929- **CLC 34**
See also CA 61-64; DLB 111

Carrere, Emmanuel 1957- **CLC 89**

Carrier, Roch 1937- **CLC 13, 78; DAC; DAM**
MST
See also CA 130; CANR 61; DLB 53;
SATA 105

Carroll, James P. 1943(?)- **CLC 38**
See also CA 81-84; CANR 73; MTCW 1

Carroll, Jim 1951- **CLC 35**
See also AAYA 17; CA 45-48; CANR 42

Carroll, Lewis NCLC 2, 53; PC 18; WLC
See also Dodgson, Charles Lutwidge
See also CDBLB 1832-1890; CLR 2, 18;
DLB 18, 163, 178; DLBY 98; JRDA

Carroll, Paul Vincent 1900-1968 **CLC 10**

See also CA 9-12R; 25-28R; DLB 10

Carruth, Hayden 1921- **CLC 4, 7, 10, 18, 84;**
PC 10
See also CA 9-12R; CANR 4, 38, 59; DLB
5, 165; INT CANR-4; MTCW 1, 2; SATA
47

Carson, Rachel Louise 1907-1964 **CLC 71;**
DAM POP
See also CA 77-80; CANR 35; DA3;
MTCW 1, 2; SATA 23

Carter, Angela (Olive) 1940-1992 **CLC 5, 41,**
76; SSC 13
See also CA 53-56; 136; CANR 12, 36, 61;
DA3; DLB 14, 207; MTCW 1, 2; SATA
66; SATA-Obit 70

Carter, Nick
See Smith, Martin Cruz

Carver, Raymond 1938-1988 **CLC 22, 36, 53,**
55, 126; DAM NOV; SSC 8
See also CA 33-36R; 126; CANR 17, 34,
61; DA3; DLB 130; DLBY 84, 88;
MTCW 1, 2

Cary, Elizabeth, Lady Falkland 1585-1639
LC 30

Cary, (Arthur) Joyce (Lunel) 1888-1957
TCLC 1, 29
See also CA 104; 164; CDBLB 1914-1945;
DLB 15, 100; MTCW 2

Casanova de Seingalt, Giovanni Jacopo
1725-1798 **LC 13**

Casares, Adolfo Bioy
See Bioy Casares, Adolfo

Casely-Hayford, J(oseph) E(phraim)
1866-1930 **TCLC 24; BLC 1; DAM**
MULT
See also BW 2; CA 123; 152

Casey, John (Dudley) 1939- **CLC 59**
See also BEST 90:2; CA 69-72; CANR 23

Casey, Michael 1947- **CLC 2**
See also CA 65-68; DLB 5

Casey, Patrick
See Thurman, Wallace (Henry)

Casey, Warren (Peter) 1935-1988 **CLC 12**
See also CA 101; 127; INT 101

Casona, Alejandro CLC 49
See also Alvarez, Alejandro Rodriguez

Cassavetes, John 1929-1989 **CLC 20**
See also CA 85-88; 127; CANR 82

Cassian, Nina 1924- **PC 17**

Cassill, R(onald) V(erlin) 1919- **CLC 4, 23**
See also CA 9-12R; CAAS 1; CANR 7, 45;
DLB 6

Cassirer, Ernst 1874-1945 **TCLC 61**
See also CA 157

Cassity, (Allen) Turner 1929- **CLC 6, 42**
See also CA 17-20R; CAAS 8; CANR 11;
DLB 105

Castaneda, Carlos (Cesar Aranha)
1931(?)-1998 **CLC 12, 119**
See also CA 25-28R; CANR 32, 66; HW 1;
MTCW 1

Castedo, Elena 1937- **CLC 65**
See also CA 132

Castedo-Ellerman, Elena
See Castedo, Elena

Castellanos, Rosario 1925-1974 **CLC 66;**
DAM MULT; HLC 1; SSC 39
See also CA 131; 53-56; CANR 58; DLB
113; HW 1; MTCW 1

Castelvetro, Lodovico 1505-1571 **LC 12**

Castiglione, Baldassare 1478-1529 **LC 12**

Castle, Robert
See Hamilton, Edmond

Castro (Ruz), Fidel 1926(?)-
See also CA 110; 129; CANR 81; DAM
MULT; HLC 1; HW 2

Castro, Guillen de 1569-1631 **LC 19**

Castro, Rosalia de 1837-1885 **NCLC 3, 78;**
DAM MULT

Cather, Willa
See Cather, Willa Sibert

Cather, Willa Sibert 1873-1947 **TCLC 1, 11,**
31; DA; DAB; DAC; DAM MST, NOV;
SSC 2; WLC
See also Cather, Willa
See also AAYA 24; CA 104; 128; CDALB
1865-1917; DA3; DLB 9, 54, 78; DLBD
1; MTCW 1, 2; SATA 30

Catherine, Saint 1347-1380 **CMLC 27**

Cato, Marcus Porcius 234B.C.-149B.C.
CMLC 21
See also DLB 211

Catton, (Charles) Bruce 1899-1978 **CLC 35**
See also AITN 1; CA 5-8R; 81-84; CANR
7, 74; DLB 17; SATA 2; SATA-Obit 24

Catullus c. 84B.C.-c. 54B.C. **CMLC 18**
See also DLB 211

Cauldwell, Frank
See King, Francis (Henry)

Caunitz, William J. 1933-1996 **CLC 34**
See also BEST 89:3; CA 125; 130; 152;
CANR 73; INT 130

Causley, Charles (Stanley) 1917- **CLC 7**
See also CA 9-12R; CANR 5, 35; CLR 30;
DLB 27; MTCW 1; SATA 3, 66

Caute, (John) David 1936- **CLC 29; DAM**
NOV
See also CA 1-4R; CAAS 4; CANR 1, 33,
64; DLB 14

Cavafy, C(onstantine) P(eter) 1863-1933
TCLC 2, 7; DAM POET
See also Kavafis, Konstantinos Petrou
See also CA 148; DA3; MTCW 1

Cavallo, Evelyn
See Spark, Muriel (Sarah)

Cavanna, Betty CLC 12
See also Harrison, Elizabeth Cavanna
See also JRDA; MAICYA; SAAS 4; SATA
1, 30

Cavendish, Margaret Lucas 1623-1673 **LC**
30
See also DLB 131

Caxton, William 1421(?)-1491(?) **LC 17**
See also DLB 170

Cayer, D. M.
See Duffy, Maureen

Cayrol, Jean 1911- **CLC 11**
See also CA 89-92; DLB 83

Cela, Camilo Jose 1916- **CLC 4, 13, 59, 122;**
DAM MULT; HLC 1
See also BEST 90:2; CA 21-24R; CAAS
10; CANR 21, 32, 76; DLBY 89; HW 1;
MTCW 1, 2

Celan, Paul CLC 10, 19, 53, 82; PC 10
See also Antschel, Paul
See also DLB 69

Celine, Louis-Ferdinand CLC 1, 3, 4, 7, 9,
15, 47, 124
See also Destouches, Louis-Ferdinand
See also DLB 72

Cellini, Benvenuto 1500-1571 **LC 7**

Cendrars, Blaise 1887-1961 **CLC 18, 106**
See also Sauser-Hall, Frederic

Cernuda (y Bidon), Luis 1902-1963 **CLC 54;**
DAM POET
See also CA 131; 89-92; DLB 134; HW 1

Cervantes, Lorna Dee 1954-
See also CA 131; CANR 80; DLB 82;
HLCS 1; HW 1

Cervantes (Saavedra), Miguel de 1547-1616
LC 6, 23; DA; DAB; DAC; DAM MST,
NOV; SSC 12; WLC

Cesaire, Aime (Fernand) 1913- **CLC 19, 32,**
112; BLC 1; DAM MULT, POET; PC
25

See also BW 2, 3; CA 65-68; CANR 24, 43, 81; DA3; MTCW 1, 2

Chabon, Michael 1963- **CLC 55**
See also CA 139; CANR 57

Chabrol, Claude 1930- **CLC 16**
See also CA 110

Challans, Mary 1905-1983
See Renault, Mary
See also CA 81-84; 111; CANR 74; DA3; MTCW 2; SATA 23; SATA-Obit 36

Challis, George
See Faust, Frederick (Schiller)

Chambers, Aidan 1934- **CLC 35**
See also AAYA 27; CA 25-28R; CANR 12, 31, 58; JRDA; MAICYA; SAAS 12; SATA 1, 69, 108

Chambers, James 1948-
See Cliff, Jimmy
See also CA 124

Chambers, Jessie
See Lawrence, D(avid) H(erbert Richards)

Chambers, Robert W(illiam) 1865-1933
TCLC 41
See also CA 165; DLB 202; SATA 107

Chamisso, Adelbert von 1781-1838 **NCLC 82**
See also DLB 90

Chandler, Raymond (Thornton) 1888-1959
TCLC 1, 7; SSC 23
See also AAYA 25; CA 104; 129; CANR 60; CDALB 1929-1941; DA3; DLBD 6; MTCW 1, 2

Chang, Eileen 1920-1995 **SSC 28**
See also CA 166

Chang, Jung 1952- **CLC 71**
See also CA 142

Chang Ai-Ling
See Chang, Eileen

Channing, William Ellery 1780-1842 **NCLC 17**
See also DLB 1, 59

Chao, Patricia 1955- **CLC 119**
See also CA 163

Chaplin, Charles Spencer 1889-1977 **CLC 16**
See also Chaplin, Charlie
See also CA 81-84; 73-76

Chaplin, Charlie
See Chaplin, Charles Spencer
See also DLB 44

Chapman, George 1559(?)-1634 **LC 22; DAM DRAM**
See also DLB 62, 121

Chapman, Graham 1941-1989 **CLC 21**
See also Monty Python
See also CA 116; 129; CANR 35

Chapman, John Jay 1862-1933 **TCLC 7**
See also CA 104

Chapman, Lee
See Bradley, Marion Zimmer

Chapman, Walker
See Silverberg, Robert

Chappell, Fred (Davis) 1936- **CLC 40, 78**
See also CA 5-8R; CAAS 4; CANR 8, 33, 67; DLB 6, 105

Char, Rene(-Emile) 1907-1988 **CLC 9, 11, 14, 55; DAM POET**
See also CA 13-16R; 124; CANR 32; MTCW 1, 2

Charby, Jay
See Ellison, Harlan (Jay)

Chardin, Pierre Teilhard de
See Teilhard de Chardin, (Marie Joseph) Pierre

Charlemagne 742-814 **CMLC 37**

Charles I 1600-1649 **LC 13**

Charriere, Isabelle de 1740-1805 **NCLC 66**

Charyn, Jerome 1937- **CLC 5, 8, 18**
See also CA 5-8R; CAAS 1; CANR 7, 61; DLBY 83; MTCW 1

Chase, Mary (Coyle) 1907-1981 **DC 1**
See also CA 77-80; 105; SATA 17; SATA-Obit 29

Chase, Mary Ellen 1887-1973 **CLC 2**
See also CA 13-16; 41-44R; CAP 1; SATA 10

Chase, Nicholas
See Hyde, Anthony

Chateaubriand, Francois Rene de 1768-1848
NCLC 3
See also DLB 119

Chatterje, Sarat Chandra 1876-1936(?)
See Chatterji, Saratchandra
See also CA 109

Chatterji, Bankim Chandra 1838-1894
NCLC 19

Chatterji, Saratchandra -1938 **TCLC 13**
See also Chatterje, Sarat Chandra
See also CA 186

Chatterton, Thomas 1752-1770 **LC 3, 54; DAM POET**
See also DLB 109

Chatwin, (Charles) Bruce 1940-1989 **CLC 28, 57, 59; DAM POP**
See also AAYA 4; BEST 90:1; CA 85-88; 127; DLB 194, 204

Chaucer, Daniel
See Ford, Ford Madox

Chaucer, Geoffrey 1340(?)-1400 **LC 17, 56; DA; DAB; DAC; DAM MST, POET; PC 19; WLCS**
See also CDBLB Before 1660; DA3; DLB 146

Chavez, Denise (Elia) 1948-
See also CA 131; CANR 56, 81; DAM MULT; DLB 122; HLC 1; HW 1, 2; MTCW 2

Chaviaras, Strates 1935-
See Haviaras, Stratis
See also CA 105

Chayefsky, Paddy CLC 23
See also Chayefsky, Sidney
See also DLB 7, 44; DLBY 81

Chayefsky, Sidney 1923-1981
See Chayefsky, Paddy
See also CA 9-12R; 104; CANR 18; DAM DRAM

Chedid, Andree 1920- **CLC 47**
See also CA 145

Cheever, John 1912-1982 **CLC 3, 7, 8, 11, 15, 25, 64; DA; DAB; DAC; DAM MST, NOV, POP; SSC 1, 38; WLC**
See also CA 5-8R; 106; CABS 1; CANR 5, 27, 76; CDALB 1941-1968; DA3; DLB 2, 102; DLBY 80, 82; INT CANR-5; MTCW 1, 2

Cheever, Susan 1943- **CLC 18, 48**
See also CA 103; CANR 27, 51; DLBY 82; INT CANR-27

Chekhonte, Antosha
See Chekhov, Anton (Pavlovich)

Chekhov, Anton (Pavlovich) 1860-1904
TCLC 3, 10, 31, 55, 96; DA; DAB; DAC; DAM DRAM, MST; DC 9; SSC 2, 28; WLC
See also CA 104; 124; DA3; SATA 90

Chernyshevsky, Nikolay Gavrilovich
1828-1889 **NCLC 1**

Cherry, Carolyn Janice 1942-
See Cherryh, C. J.
See also CA 65-68; CANR 10

Cherryh, C. J. CLC 35
See also Cherry, Carolyn Janice
See also AAYA 24; DLBY 80; SATA 93

Chesnutt, Charles W(addell) 1858-1932
TCLC 5, 39; BLC 1; DAM MULT; SSC 7
See also BW 1, 3; CA 106; 125; CANR 76; DLB 12, 50, 78; MTCW 1, 2

Chester, Alfred 1929(?)-1971 **CLC 49**
See also CA 33-36R; DLB 130

Chesterton, G(ilbert) K(eith) 1874-1936
TCLC 1, 6, 64; DAM NOV, POET; PC 28; SSC 1
See also CA 104; 132; CANR 73; CDBLB 1914-1945; DLB 10, 19, 34, 70, 98, 149, 178; MTCW 1, 2; SATA 27

Chiang, Pin-chin 1904-1986
See Ding Ling
See also CA 118

Ch'ien Chung-shu 1910- **CLC 22**
See also CA 130; CANR 73; MTCW 1, 2

Child, L. Maria
See Child, Lydia Maria

Child, Lydia Maria 1802-1880 **NCLC 6, 73**
See also DLB 1, 74; SATA 67

Child, Mrs.
See Child, Lydia Maria

Child, Philip 1898-1978 **CLC 19, 68**
See also CA 13-14; CAP 1; SATA 47

Childers, (Robert) Erskine 1870-1922 **TCLC 65**
See also CA 113; 153; DLB 70

Childress, Alice 1920-1994 **CLC 12, 15, 86, 96; BLC 1; DAM DRAM, MULT, NOV; DC 4**
See also AAYA 8; BW 2, 3; CA 45-48; 146; CANR 3, 27, 50, 74; CLR 14; DA3; DLB 7, 38; JRDA; MAICYA; MTCW 1, 2; SATA 7, 48, 81

Chin, Frank (Chew, Jr.) 1940- **DC 7**
See also CA 33-36R; CANR 71; DAM MULT; DLB 206

Chislett, (Margaret) Anne 1943- **CLC 34**
See also CA 151

Chitty, Thomas Willes 1926- **CLC 11**
See also Hinde, Thomas
See also CA 5-8R

Chivers, Thomas Holley 1809-1858 **NCLC 49**
See also DLB 3

Choi, Susan CLC 119

Chomette, Rene Lucien 1898-1981
See Clair, Rene
See also CA 103

Chomsky, (Avram) Noam 1928- **CLC 132**
See also CA 17-20R; CANR 28, 62; DA3; MTCW 1, 2

Chopin, Kate TCLC 5, 14; DA; DAB; SSC 8; WLCS
See also Chopin, Katherine
See also AAYA 33; CDALB 1865-1917; DLB 12, 78

Chopin, Katherine 1851-1904
See Chopin, Kate
See also CA 104; 122; DAC; DAM MST, NOV; DA3

Chretien de Troyes c. 12th cent. - **CMLC 10**
See also DLB 208

Christie
See Ichikawa, Kon

Christie, Agatha (Mary Clarissa) 1890-1976
CLC 1, 6, 8, 12, 39, 48, 110; DAB; DAC; DAM NOV
See also AAYA 9; AITN 1, 2; CA 17-20R; 61-64; CANR 10, 37; CDBLB 1914-1945; DA3; DLB 13, 77; MTCW 1, 2; SATA 36

Christie, (Ann) Philippa
See Pearce, Philippa
See also CA 5-8R; CANR 4

Christine de Pizan 1365(?)-1431(?) **LC 9**
See also DLB 208

Chubb, Elmer
See Masters, Edgar Lee

Chulkov, Mikhail Dmitrievich 1743-1792 **LC 2**
See also DLB 150

Churchill, Caryl 1938- **CLC 31, 55; DC 5**

29, 51; DAM DRAM
See also AITN 1; CA 17-18; 41-44R; CANR 35; CAP 2; CDBLB 1914-1945; DA3; DLB 10; MTCW 1, 2

Cowley, Abraham 1618-1667 **LC 43**
See also DLB 131, 151

Cowley, Malcolm 1898-1989 **CLC 39**
See also CA 5-8R; 128; CANR 3, 55; DLB 4, 48; DLBY 81, 89; MTCW 1, 2

Cowper, William 1731-1800 **NCLC 8; DAM POET**
See also DA3; DLB 104, 109

Cox, William Trevor 1928- **CLC 9, 14, 71; DAM NOV**
See Trevor, William
See also CA 9-12R; CANR 4, 37, 55, 76; DLB 14; INT CANR-37; MTCW 1, 2

Coyne, P. J.
See Masters, Hilary

Cozzens, James Gould 1903-1978 **CLC 1, 4, 11, 92**
See also CA 9-12R; 81-84; CANR 19; CDALB 1941-1968; DLB 9; DLBD 2; DLBY 84, 97; MTCW 1, 2

Crabbe, George 1754-1832 **NCLC 26**
See also DLB 93

Craddock, Charles Egbert
See Murfree, Mary Noailles

Craig, A. A.
See Anderson, Poul (William)

Craik, Dinah Maria (Mulock) 1826-1887 **NCLC 38**
See also DLB 35, 163; MAICYA; SATA 34

Cram, Ralph Adams 1863-1942 **TCLC 45**
See also CA 160

Crane, (Harold) Hart 1899-1932 **TCLC 2, 5, 80; DA; DAB; DAC; DAM MST, POET; PC 3; WLC**
See also CA 104; 127; CDALB 1917-1929; DA3; DLB 4, 48; MTCW 1, 2

Crane, R(onald) S(almon) 1886-1967 **CLC 27**
See also CA 85-88; DLB 63

Crane, Stephen (Townley) 1871-1900 **TCLC 11, 17, 32; DA; DAB; DAC; DAM MST, NOV, POET; SSC 7; WLC**
See also AAYA 21; CA 109; 140; CANR 84; CDALB 1865-1917; DA3; DLB 12, 54, 78; YABC 2

Cranshaw, Stanley
See Fisher, Dorothy (Frances) Canfield

Crase, Douglas 1944- **CLC 58**
See also CA 106

Crashaw, Richard 1612(?)-1649 **LC 24**
See also DLB 126

Craven, Margaret 1901-1980 **CLC 17; DAC**
See also CA 103

Crawford, F(rancis) Marion 1854-1909 **TCLC 10**
See also CA 107; 168; DLB 71

Crawford, Isabella Valancy 1850-1887 **NCLC 12**
See also DLB 92

Crayon, Geoffrey
See Irving, Washington

Creasey, John 1908-1973 **CLC 11**
See also CA 5-8R; 41-44R; CANR 8, 59; DLB 77; MTCW 1

Crebillon, Claude Prosper Jolyot de (fils) 1707-1777 **LC 1, 28**

Credo
See Creasey, John

Credo, Alvaro J. de
See Prado (Calvo), Pedro

Creeley, Robert (White) 1926- **CLC 1, 2, 4, 8, 11, 15, 36, 78; DAM POET**
See also CA 1-4R; CAAS 10; CANR 23, 43, 89; DA3; DLB 5, 16, 169; DLBD 17; MTCW 1, 2

Crews, Harry (Eugene) 1935- **CLC 6, 23, 49**
See also AITN 1; CA 25-28R; CANR 20, 57; DA3; DLB 6, 143, 185; MTCW 1, 2

Crichton, (John) Michael 1942- **CLC 2, 6, 54, 90; DAM NOV, POP**
See also AAYA 10; AITN 2; CA 25-28R; CANR 13, 40, 54, 76; DA3; DLBY 81; INT CANR-13; JRDA; MTCW 1, 2; SATA 9, 88

Crispin, Edmund CLC 22
See also Montgomery, (Robert) Bruce
See also DLB 87

Cristofer, Michael 1945(?)- **CLC 28; DAM DRAM**
See also CA 110; 152; DLB 7

Croce, Benedetto 1866-1952 **TCLC 37**
See also CA 120; 155

Crockett, David 1786-1836 **NCLC 8**
See also DLB 3, 11

Crockett, Davy
See Crockett, David

Crofts, Freeman Wills 1879-1957 **TCLC 55**
See also CA 115; DLB 77

Croker, John Wilson 1780-1857 **NCLC 10**
See also DLB 110

Crommelynck, Fernand 1885-1970 **CLC 75**
See also CA 89-92

Cromwell, Oliver 1599-1658 **LC 43**

Cronin, A(rchibald) J(oseph) 1896-1981 **CLC 32**
See also CA 1-4R; 102; CANR 5; DLB 191; SATA 47; SATA-Obit 25

Cross, Amanda
See Heilbrun, Carolyn G(old)

Crothers, Rachel 1878(?)-1958 **TCLC 19**
See also CA 113; DLB 7

Croves, Hal
See Traven, B.

Crow Dog, Mary (Ellen) (?)- **CLC 93**
See also Brave Bird, Mary
See also CA 154

Crowfield, Christopher
See Stowe, Harriet (Elizabeth) Beecher

Crowley, Aleister TCLC 7
See also Crowley, Edward Alexander

Crowley, Edward Alexander 1875-1947
See Crowley, Aleister
See also CA 104

Crowley, John 1942- **CLC 57**
See also CA 61-64; CANR 43; DLBY 82; SATA 65

Crud
See Crumb, R(obert)

Crumarums
See Crumb, R(obert)

Crumb, R(obert) 1943- **CLC 17**
See also CA 106

Crumbum
See Crumb, R(obert)

Crumski
See Crumb, R(obert)

Crum the Bum
See Crumb, R(obert)

Crunk
See Crumb, R(obert)

Crustt
See Crumb, R(obert)

Cruz, Victor Hernandez 1949-
See also BW 2; CA 65-68; CAAS 17; CANR 14, 32, 74; DAM MULT, POET; DLB 41; HLC 1; HW 1, 2; MTCW 1

Cryer, Gretchen (Kiger) 1935- **CLC 21**
See also CA 114; 123

Csath, Geza 1887-1919 **TCLC 13**
See also CA 111

Cudlip, David R(ockwell) 1933- **CLC 34**
See also CA 177

Cullen, Countee 1903-1946 **TCLC 4, 37; BLC**

1; DA; DAC; DAM MST, MULT, POET; PC 20; WLCS
See also BW 1; CA 108; 124; CDALB 1917-1929; DA3; DLB 4, 48, 51; MTCW 1, 2; SATA 18

Cum, R.
See Crumb, R(obert)

Cummings, Bruce F(rederick) 1889-1919
See Barbellion, W. N. P.
See also CA 123

Cummings, E(dward) E(stlin) 1894-1962 **CLC 1, 3, 8, 12, 15, 68; DA; DAB; DAC; DAM MST, POET; PC 5; WLC**
See also CA 73-76; CANR 31; CDALB 1929-1941; DA3; DLB 4, 48; MTCW 1, 2

Cunha, Euclides (Rodrigues Pimenta) da 1866-1909 **TCLC 24**
See also CA 123

Cunningham, E. V.
See Fast, Howard (Melvin)

Cunningham, J(ames) V(incent) 1911-1985 **CLC 3, 31**
See also CA 1-4R; 115; CANR 1, 72; DLB 5

Cunningham, Julia (Woolfolk) 1916- **CLC 12**
See also CA 9-12R; CANR 4, 19, 36; JRDA; MAICYA; SAAS 2; SATA 1, 26

Cunningham, Michael 1952- **CLC 34**
See also CA 136

Cunninghame Graham, R. B.
See Cunninghame Graham, Robert (Gallnigad) Bontine

Cunninghame Graham, Robert (Gallnigad) Bontine 1852-1936 **TCLC 19**
See also Graham, R(obert) B(ontine) Cunninghame
See also CA 119; 184; DLB 98

Currie, Ellen 19(?)- **CLC 44**

Curtin, Philip
See Lowndes, Marie Adelaide (Belloc)

Curtis, Price
See Ellison, Harlan (Jay)

Cutrate, Joe
See Spiegelman, Art

Cynewulf c. 770-c. 840 **CMLC 23**

Czaczkes, Shmuel Yosef
See Agnon, S(hmuel) Y(osef Halevi)

Dabrowska, Maria (Szumska) 1889-1965 **CLC 15**
See also CA 106

Dabydeen, David 1955- **CLC 34**
See also BW 1; CA 125; CANR 56

Dacey, Philip 1939- **CLC 51**
See also CA 37-40R; CAAS 17; CANR 14, 32, 64; DLB 105

Dagerman, Stig (Halvard) 1923-1954 **TCLC 17**
See also CA 117; 155

Dahl, Roald 1916-1990 **CLC 1, 6, 18, 79; DAB; DAC; DAM MST, NOV, POP**
See also AAYA 15; CA 1-4R; 133; CANR 6, 32, 37, 62; CLR 1, 7, 41; DA3; DLB 139; JRDA; MAICYA; MTCW 1, 2; SATA 1, 26, 73; SATA-Obit 65

Dahlberg, Edward 1900-1977 **CLC 1, 7, 14**
See also CA 9-12R; 69-72; CANR 31, 62; DLB 48; MTCW 1

Daitch, Susan 1954- **CLC 103**
See also CA 161

Dale, Colin TCLC 18
See also Lawrence, T(homas) E(dward)

Dale, George E.
See Asimov, Isaac

Dalton, Roque 1935-1975
See also HLCS 1; HW 2

Daly, Elizabeth 1878-1967 **CLC 52**
See also CA 23-24; 25-28R; CANR 60; CAP 2

Daly, Maureen 1921- **CLC 17**
See also AAYA 5; CANR 37, 83; JRDA;
MAICYA; SAAS 1; SATA 2

Damas, Leon-Gontran 1912-1978 **CLC 84**
See also BW 1; CA 125; 73-76

Dana, Richard Henry Sr. 1787-1879 **NCLC 53**

Daniel, Samuel 1562(?)-1619 **LC 24**
See also DLB 62

Daniels, Brett
See Adler, Renata

Dannay, Frederic 1905-1982 **CLC 11; DAM POP**
See also Queen, Ellery
See also CA 1-4R; 107; CANR 1, 39; DLB
137; MTCW 1

D'Annunzio, Gabriele 1863-1938 **TCLC 6, 40**
See also CA 104; 155

Danois, N. le
See Gourmont, Remy (-Marie-Charles) de

Dante 1265-1321 **CMLC 3, 18, 39; DA; DAB; DAC; DAM MST, POET; PC 21; WLCS**
See also Alighieri, Dante
See also DA3

d'Antibes, Germain
See Simenon, Georges (Jacques Christian)

Danticat, Edwidge 1969- **CLC 94**
See also AAYA 29; CA 152; CANR 73;
MTCW 1

Danvers, Dennis 1947- **CLC 70**

Danziger, Paula 1944- **CLC 21**
See also AAYA 4; CA 112; 115; CANR 37;
CLR 20; JRDA; MAICYA; SATA 36, 63,
102; SATA-Brief 30

Da Ponte, Lorenzo 1749-1838 **NCLC 50**

Dario, Ruben 1867-1916 **TCLC 4; DAM MULT; HLC 1; PC 15**
See also CA 131; CANR 81; HW 1, 2;
MTCW 1, 2

Darley, George 1795-1846 **NCLC 2**
See also DLB 96

Darrow, Clarence (Seward) 1857-1938 **TCLC 81**
See also CA 164

Darwin, Charles 1809-1882 **NCLC 57**
See also DLB 57, 166

Daryush, Elizabeth 1887-1977 **CLC 6, 19**
See also CA 49-52; CANR 3, 81; DLB 20

Dasgupta, Surendranath 1887-1952 **TCLC 81**
See also CA 157

Dashwood, Edmee Elizabeth Monica de la Pasture 1890-1943
See Delafield, E. M.
See also CA 119; 154

Daudet, (Louis Marie) Alphonse 1840-1897 **NCLC 1**
See also DLB 123

Daumal, Rene 1908-1944 **TCLC 14**
See also CA 114

Davenant, William 1606-1668 **LC 13**
See also DLB 58, 126

Davenport, Guy (Mattison, Jr.) 1927- **CLC 6, 14, 38; SSC 16**
See also CA 33-36R; CANR 23, 73; DLB
130

Davidson, Avram (James) 1923-1993
See Queen, Ellery
See also CA 101; 171; CANR 26; DLB 8

Davidson, Donald (Grady) 1893-1968 **CLC 2, 13, 19**
See also CA 5-8R; 25-28R; CANR 4, 84;
DLB 45

Davidson, Hugh
See Hamilton, Edmond

Davidson, John 1857-1909 **TCLC 24**
See also CA 118; DLB 19

Davidson, Sara 1943- **CLC 9**
See also CA 81-84; CANR 44, 68; DLB
185

Davie, Donald (Alfred) 1922-1995 **CLC 5, 8, 10, 31; PC 29**
See also CA 1-4R; 149; CAAS 3; CANR 1,
44; DLB 27; MTCW 1

Davies, Ray(mond Douglas) 1944- **CLC 21**
See also CA 116; 146

Davies, Rhys 1901-1978 **CLC 23**
See also CA 9-12R; 81-84; CANR 4; DLB
139, 191

Davies, (William) Robertson 1913-1995 **CLC 2, 7, 13, 25, 42, 75, 91; DA; DAB; DAC; DAM MST, NOV, POP; WLC**
See also BEST 89:2; CA 33-36R; 150;
CANR 17, 42; DA3; DLB 68; INT
CANR-17; MTCW 1, 2

Davies, Walter C.
See Kornbluth, C(yril) M.

Davies, William Henry 1871-1940 **TCLC 5**
See also CA 104; 179; DLB 19, 174

Da Vinci, Leonardo 1452-1519 **LC 12, 57**

Davis, Angela (Yvonne) 1944- **CLC 77; DAM MULT**
See also BW 2, 3; CA 57-60; CANR 10,
81; DA3

Davis, B. Lynch
See Bioy Casares, Adolfo; Borges, Jorge
Luis

Davis, B. Lynch
See Bioy Casares, Adolfo

Davis, H(arold) L(enoir) 1894-1960 **CLC 49**
See also CA 178; 89-92; DLB 9, 206; SATA
114

Davis, Rebecca (Blaine) Harding 1831-1910 **TCLC 6; SSC 38**
See also CA 104; 179; DLB 74

Davis, Richard Harding 1864-1916 **TCLC 24**
See also CA 114; 179; DLB 12, 23, 78, 79,
189; DLBD 13

Davison, Frank Dalby 1893-1970 **CLC 15**
See also CA 116

Davison, Lawrence H.
See Lawrence, D(avid) H(erbert Richards)

Davison, Peter (Hubert) 1928- **CLC 28**
See also CA 9-12R; CAAS 4; CANR 3, 43,
84; DLB 5

Davys, Mary 1674-1732 **LC 1, 46**
See also DLB 39

Dawson, Fielding 1930- **CLC 6**
See also CA 85-88; DLB 130

Dawson, Peter
See Faust, Frederick (Schiller)

Day, Clarence (Shepard, Jr.) 1874-1935 **TCLC 25**
See also CA 108; DLB 11

Day, Thomas 1748-1789 **LC 1**
See also DLB 39; YABC 1

Day Lewis, C(ecil) 1904-1972 **CLC 1, 6, 10; DAM POET; PC 11**
See also Blake, Nicholas
See also CA 13-16; 33-36R; CANR 34;
CAP 1; DLB 15, 20; MTCW 1, 2

Dazai Osamu 1909-1948 **TCLC 11**
See also Tsushima, Shuji
See also CA 164; DLB 182

de Andrade, Carlos Drummond 1892-1945
See Drummond de Andrade, Carlos

Deane, Norman
See Creasey, John

Deane, Seamus (Francis) 1940- **CLC 122**
See also CA 118; CANR 42

de Beauvoir, Simone (Lucie Ernestine Marie Bertrand)
See Beauvoir, Simone (Lucie Ernestine
Marie Bertrand) de

de Beer, P.
See Bosman, Herman Charles

de Brissac, Malcolm
See Dickinson, Peter (Malcolm)

de Campos, Alvaro
See Pessoa, Fernando (Antonio Nogueira)

de Chardin, Pierre Teilhard
See Teilhard de Chardin, (Marie Joseph)
Pierre

Dee, John 1527-1608 **LC 20**

Deer, Sandra 1940- **CLC 45**
See also CA 186

De Ferrari, Gabriella 1941- **CLC 65**
See also CA 146

Defoe, Daniel 1660(?)-1731 **LC 1, 42; DA; DAB; DAC; DAM MST, NOV; WLC**
See also AAYA 27; CDBLB 1660-1789;
CLR 61; DA3; DLB 39, 95, 101; JRDA;
MAICYA; SATA 22

de Gourmont, Remy(-Marie-Charles)
See Gourmont, Remy (-Marie-Charles) de

de Hartog, Jan 1914- **CLC 19**
See also CA 1-4R; CANR 1

de Hostos, E. M.
See Hostos (y Bonilla), Eugenio Maria de

de Hostos, Eugenio M.
See Hostos (y Bonilla), Eugenio Maria de

Deighton, Len CLC 4, 7, 22, 46
See also Deighton, Leonard Cyril
See also AAYA 6; BEST 89:2; CDBLB
1960 to Present; DLB 87

Deighton, Leonard Cyril 1929-
See Deighton, Len
See also CA 9-12R; CANR 19, 33, 68;
DAM NOV, POP; DA3; MTCW 1, 2

Dekker, Thomas 1572(?)-1632 **LC 22; DAM DRAM; DC 12**
See also CDBLB Before 1660; DLB 62, 172

Delafield, E. M. 1890-1943 **TCLC 61**
See also Dashwood, Edmee Elizabeth
Monica de la Pasture
See also DLB 34

de la Mare, Walter (John) 1873-1956 **TCLC 4, 53; DAB; DAC; DAM MST, POET; SSC 14; WLC**
See also CA 163; CDBLB 1914-1945; CLR
23; DA3; DLB 162; MTCW 1; SATA 16

Delaney, Franey
See O'Hara, John (Henry)

Delaney, Shelagh 1939- **CLC 29; DAM DRAM**
See also CA 17-20R; CANR 30, 67; CD-
BLB 1960 to Present; DLB 13; MTCW 1

Delany, Mary (Granville Pendarves) 1700-1788 **LC 12**

Delany, Samuel R(ay, Jr.) 1942- **CLC 8, 14, 38; BLC 1; DAM MULT**
See also AAYA 24; BW 2, 3; CA 81-84;
CANR 27, 43; DLB 8, 33; MTCW 1, 2

De La Ramee, (Marie) Louise 1839-1908
See Ouida
See also SATA 20

de la Roche, Mazo 1879-1961 **CLC 14**
See also CA 85-88; CANR 30; DLB 68;
SATA 64

De La Salle, Innocent
See Hartmann, Sadakichi

Delbanco, Nicholas (Franklin) 1942- **CLC 6, 13**
See also CA 17-20R; CAAS 2; CANR 29,
55; DLB 6

del Castillo, Michel 1933- **CLC 38**
See also CA 109; CANR 77

Deledda, Grazia (Cosima) 1875(?)-1936 **TCLC 23**
See also CA 123

Delgado, Abelardo (Lalo) B(arrientos) 1930-
See also CA 131; CAAS 15; CANR 90;
DAM MST, MULT; DLB 82; HLC 1; HW
1, 2

Delibes, Miguel CLC 8, 18

Dobrolyubov, Nikolai Alexandrovich 1836-1861 **NCLC 5**

Dobson, Austin 1840-1921 **TCLC 79**
See also DLB 35; 144

Dobyns, Stephen 1941- **CLC 37**
See also CA 45-48; CANR 2, 18

Doctorow, E(dgar) L(aurence) 1931- **CLC 6, 11, 15, 18, 37, 44, 65, 113; DAM NOV, POP**
See also AAYA 22; AITN 2; BEST 89:3; CA 45-48; CANR 2, 33, 51, 76; CDALB 1968-1988; DA3; DLB 2, 28, 173; DLBY 80; MTCW 1, 2

Dodgson, Charles Lutwidge 1832-1898
See Carroll, Lewis
See also CLR 2; DA; DAB; DAC; DAM MST, NOV, POET; DA3; MAICYA; SATA 100; YABC 2

Dodson, Owen (Vincent) 1914-1983 **CLC 79; BLC 1; DAM MULT**
See also BW 1; CA 65-68; 110; CANR 24; DLB 76

Doeblin, Alfred 1878-1957 **TCLC 13**
See also Doblin, Alfred
See also CA 110; 141; DLB 66

Doerr, Harriet 1910- **CLC 34**
See also CA 117; 122; CANR 47; INT 122

Domecq, H(onorio Bustos)
See Bioy Casares, Adolfo

Domecq, H(onorio) Bustos
See Bioy Casares, Adolfo; Borges, Jorge Luis

Domini, Rey
See Lorde, Audre (Geraldine)

Dominique
See Proust, (Valentin-Louis-George-Eugene-) Marcel

Don, A
See Stephen, SirLeslie

Donaldson, Stephen R. 1947- **CLC 46; DAM POP**
See also CA 89-92; CANR 13, 55; INT CANR-13

Donleavy, J(ames) P(atrick) 1926- **CLC 1, 4, 6, 10, 45**
See also AITN 2; CA 9-12R; CANR 24, 49, 62, 80; DLB 6, 173; INT CANR-24; MTCW 1, 2

Donne, John 1572-1631 **LC 10, 24; DA; DAB; DAC; DAM MST, POET; PC 1; WLC**
See also CDBLB Before 1660; DLB 121, 151

Donnell, David 1939(?)- **CLC 34**

Donoghue, P. S.
See Hunt, E(verette) Howard, (Jr.)

Donoso (Yanez), Jose 1924-1996 **CLC 4, 8, 11, 32, 99; DAM MULT; HLC 1; SSC 34**
See also CA 81-84; 155; CANR 32, 73; DLB 113; HW 1, 2; MTCW 1, 2

Donovan, John 1928-1992 **CLC 35**
See also AAYA 20; CA 97-100; 137; CLR 3; MAICYA; SATA 72; SATA-Brief 29

Don Roberto
See Cunninghame Graham, Robert (Gallnigad) Bontine

Doolittle, Hilda 1886-1961 **CLC 3, 8, 14, 31, 34, 73; DA; DAC; DAM MST, POET; PC 5; WLC**
See also H. D.
See also CA 97-100; CANR 35; DLB 4, 45; MTCW 1, 2

Dorfman, Ariel 1942- **CLC 48, 77; DAM MULT; HLC 1**
See also CA 124; 130; CANR 67, 70; HW 1, 2; INT 130

Dorn, Edward (Merton) 1929- **CLC 10, 18**

See also CA 93-96; CANR 42, 79; DLB 5; INT 93-96

Dorris, Michael (Anthony) 1945-1997 **CLC 109; DAM MULT, NOV**
See also AAYA 20; BEST 90:1; CA 102; 157; CANR 19, 46, 75; CLR 58; DA3; DLB 175; MTCW 2; NNAL; SATA 75; SATA-Obit 94

Dorris, Michael A.
See Dorris, Michael (Anthony)

Dorsan, Luc
See Simenon, Georges (Jacques Christian)

Dorsange, Jean
See Simenon, Georges (Jacques Christian)

Dos Passos, John (Roderigo) 1896-1970 **CLC 1, 4, 8, 11, 15, 25, 34, 82; DA; DAB; DAC; DAM MST, NOV; WLC**
See also CA 1-4R; 29-32R; CANR 3; CDALB 1929-1941; DA3; DLB 4, 9; DLBD 1, 15; DLBY 96; MTCW 1, 2

Dossage, Jean
See Simenon, Georges (Jacques Christian)

Dostoevsky, Fedor Mikhailovich 1821-1881 **NCLC 2, 7, 21, 33, 43; DA; DAB; DAC; DAM MST, NOV; SSC 2, 33; WLC**
See also DA3

Doughty, Charles M(ontagu) 1843-1926 **TCLC 27**
See also CA 115; 178; DLB 19, 57, 174

Douglas, Ellen CLC 73
See also Haxton, Josephine Ayres; Williamson, Ellen Douglas

Douglas, Gavin 1475(?)-1522 **LC 20**
See also DLB 132

Douglas, George
See Brown, George Douglas

Douglas, Keith (Castellain) 1920-1944 **TCLC 40**
See also CA 160; DLB 27

Douglas, Leonard
See Bradbury, Ray (Douglas)

Douglas, Michael
See Crichton, (John) Michael

Douglas, (George) Norman 1868-1952 **TCLC 68**
See also CA 119; 157; DLB 34, 195

Douglas, William
See Brown, George Douglas

Douglass, Frederick 1817(?)-1895 **NCLC 7, 55; BLC 1; DA; DAC; DAM MST, MULT; WLC**
See also CDALB 1640-1865; DA3; DLB 1, 43, 50, 79; SATA 29

Dourado, (Waldomiro Freitas) Autran 1926- **CLC 23, 60**
See also CA 25-28R; 179; CANR 34, 81; DLB 145; HW 2

Dourado, Waldomiro Autran 1926-
See Dourado, (Waldomiro Freitas) Autran
See also CA 179

Dove, Rita (Frances) 1952- **CLC 50, 81; BLCS; DAM MULT, POET; PC 6**
See also BW 2; CA 109; CAAS 19; CANR 27, 42, 68, 76; CDALBS; DA3; DLB 120; MTCW 1

Doveglion
See Villa, Jose Garcia

Dowell, Coleman 1925-1985 **CLC 60**
See also CA 25-28R; 117; CANR 10; DLB 130

Dowson, Ernest (Christopher) 1867-1900 **TCLC 4**
See also CA 105; 150; DLB 19, 135

Doyle, A. Conan
See Doyle, Arthur Conan

Doyle, Arthur Conan 1859-1930 **TCLC 7; DA; DAB; DAC; DAM MST, NOV; SSC 12; WLC**

See also AAYA 14; CA 104; 122; CDBLB 1890-1914; DA3; DLB 18, 70, 156, 178; MTCW 1, 2; SATA 24

Doyle, Conan
See Doyle, Arthur Conan

Doyle, John
See Graves, Robert (von Ranke)

Doyle, Roddy 1958(?)- **CLC 81**
See also AAYA 14; CA 143; CANR 73; DA3; DLB 194

Doyle, Sir A. Conan
See Doyle, Arthur Conan

Doyle, Sir Arthur Conan
See Doyle, Arthur Conan

Dr. A
See Asimov, Isaac; Silverstein, Alvin

Drabble, Margaret 1939- **CLC 2, 3, 5, 8, 10, 22, 53, 129; DAB; DAC; DAM MST, NOV, POP**
See also CA 13-16R; CANR 18, 35, 63; CDBLB 1960 to Present; DA3; DLB 14, 155; MTCW 1, 2; SATA 48

Drapier, M. B.
See Swift, Jonathan

Drayham, James
See Mencken, H(enry) L(ouis)

Drayton, Michael 1563-1631 **LC 8; DAM POET**
See also DLB 121

Dreadstone, Carl
See Campbell, (John) Ramsey

Dreiser, Theodore (Herman Albert) 1871-1945 **TCLC 10, 18, 35, 83; DA; DAC; DAM MST, NOV; SSC 30; WLC**
See also CA 106; 132; CDALB 1865-1917; DA3; DLB 9, 12, 102, 137; DLBD 1; MTCW 1, 2

Drexler, Rosalyn 1926- **CLC 2, 6**
See also CA 81-84; CANR 68

Dreyer, Carl Theodor 1889-1968 **CLC 16**
See also CA 116

Drieu la Rochelle, Pierre(-Eugene) 1893-1945 **TCLC 21**
See also CA 117; DLB 72

Drinkwater, John 1882-1937 **TCLC 57**
See also CA 109; 149; DLB 10, 19, 149

Drop Shot
See Cable, George Washington

Droste-Hulshoff, Annette Freiin von 1797-1848 **NCLC 3**
See also DLB 133

Drummond, Walter
See Silverberg, Robert

Drummond, William Henry 1854-1907 **TCLC 25**
See also CA 160; DLB 92

Drummond de Andrade, Carlos 1902-1987 **CLC 18**
See also Andrade, Carlos Drummond de
See also CA 132; 123

Drury, Allen (Stuart) 1918-1998 **CLC 37**
See also CA 57-60; 170; CANR 18, 52; INT CANR-18

Dryden, John 1631-1700 **LC 3, 21; DA; DAB; DAC; DAM DRAM, MST, POET; DC 3; PC 25; WLC**
See also CDBLB 1660-1789; DLB 80, 101, 131

Duberman, Martin (Bauml) 1930- **CLC 8**
See also CA 1-4R; CANR 2, 63

Dubie, Norman (Evans) 1945- **CLC 36**
See also CA 69-72; CANR 12; DLB 120

Du Bois, W(illiam) E(dward) B(urghardt) 1868-1963 **CLC 1, 2, 13, 64, 96; BLC 1; DA; DAC; DAM MST, MULT, NOV; WLC**
See also BW 1, 3; CA 85-88; CANR 34, 82; CDALB 1865-1917; DA3; DLB 47, 50, 91; MTCW 1, 2; SATA 42

Ehrenburg, Ilyo (Grigoryevich)
See Ehrenburg, Ilya (Grigoryevich)

Ehrenreich, Barbara 1941- **CLC 110**
See also BEST 90:4; CA 73-76; CANR 16, 37, 62; MTCW 1, 2

Eich, Guenter 1907-1972 **CLC 15**
See also CA 111; 93-96; DLB 69, 124

Eichendorff, Joseph Freiherr von 1788-1857 **NCLC 8**
See also DLB 90

Eigner, Larry CLC 9
See also Eigner, Laurence (Joel)
See also CAAS 23; DLB 5

Eigner, Laurence (Joel) 1927-1996
See Eigner, Larry
See also CA 9-12R; 151; CANR 6, 84; DLB 193

Einstein, Albert 1879-1955 **TCLC 65**
See also CA 121; 133; MTCW 1, 2

Eiseley, Loren Corey 1907-1977 **CLC 7**
See also AAYA 5; CA 1-4R; 73-76; CANR 6; DLBD 17

Eisenstadt, Jill 1963- **CLC 50**
See also CA 140

Eisenstein, Sergei (Mikhailovich) 1898-1948 **TCLC 57**
See also CA 114; 149

Eisner, Simon
See Kornbluth, C(yril) M.

Ekeloef, (Bengt) Gunnar 1907-1968 **CLC 27; DAM POET; PC 23**
See also CA 123; 25-28R

Ekelof, (Bengt) Gunnar
See Ekeloef, (Bengt) Gunnar

Ekelund, Vilhelm 1880-1949 **TCLC 75**

Ekwensi, C. O. D.
See Ekwensi, Cyprian (Odiatu Duaka)

Ekwensi, Cyprian (Odiatu Duaka) 1921-
CLC 4; BLC 1; DAM MULT
See also BW 2, 3; CA 29-32R; CANR 18, 42, 74; DLB 117; MTCW 1, 2; SATA 66

Elaine TCLC 18
See also Leverson, Ada

El Crummo
See Crumb, R(obert)

Elder, Lonne III 1931-1996 **DC 8**
See also BLC 1; BW 1, 3; CA 81-84; 152; CANR 25; DAM MULT; DLB 7, 38, 44

Eleanor of Aquitaine 1122-1204 **CMLC 39**

Elia
See Lamb, Charles

Eliade, Mircea 1907-1986 **CLC 19**
See also CA 65-68; 119; CANR 30, 62; DLB 220; MTCW 1

Eliot, A. D.
See Jewett, (Theodora) Sarah Orne

Eliot, Alice
See Jewett, (Theodora) Sarah Orne

Eliot, Dan
See Silverberg, Robert

Eliot, George 1819-1880 **NCLC 4, 13, 23, 41, 49; DA; DAB; DAC; DAM MST, NOV; PC 20; WLC**
See also CDBLB 1832-1890; DA3; DLB 21, 35, 55

Eliot, John 1604-1690 **LC 5**
See also DLB 24

Eliot, T(homas) S(tearns) 1888-1965 **CLC 1, 2, 3, 6, 9, 10, 13, 15, 24, 34, 41, 55, 57, 113; DA; DAB; DAC; DAM DRAM, MST, POET; PC 5; WLC**
See also AAYA 28; CA 5-8R; 25-28R; CANR 41; CDALB 1929-1941; DA3; DLB 7, 10, 45, 63; DLBY 88; MTCW 1, 2

Elizabeth 1866-1941 **TCLC 41**

Elkin, Stanley L(awrence) 1930-1995 **CLC 4,**
6, 9, 14, 27, 51, 91; DAM NOV, POP; SSC 12
See also CA 9-12R; 148; CANR 8, 46; DLB 2, 28; DLBY 80; INT CANR-8; MTCW 1, 2

Elledge, Scott CLC 34

Elliot, Don
See Silverberg, Robert

Elliott, Don
See Silverberg, Robert

Elliott, George P(aul) 1918-1980 **CLC 2**
See also CA 1-4R; 97-100; CANR 2

Elliott, Janice 1931- **CLC 47**
See also CA 13-16R; CANR 8, 29, 84; DLB 14

Elliott, Sumner Locke 1917-1991 **CLC 38**
See also CA 5-8R; 134; CANR 2, 21

Elliott, William
See Bradbury, Ray (Douglas)

Ellis, A. E. CLC 7

Ellis, Alice Thomas CLC 40
See also Haycraft, Anna (Margaret)
See also DLB 194; MTCW 1

Ellis, Bret Easton 1964- **CLC 39, 71, 117; DAM POP**
See also AAYA 2; CA 118; 123; CANR 51, 74; DA3; INT 123; MTCW 1

Ellis, (Henry) Havelock 1859-1939 **TCLC 14**
See also CA 109; 169; DLB 190

Ellis, Landon
See Ellison, Harlan (Jay)

Ellis, Trey 1962- **CLC 55**
See also CA 146

Ellison, Harlan (Jay) 1934- **CLC 1, 13, 42; DAM POP; SSC 14**
See also AAYA 29; CA 5-8R; CANR 5, 46; DLB 8; INT CANR-5; MTCW 1, 2

Ellison, Ralph (Waldo) 1914-1994 **CLC 1, 3, 11, 54, 86, 114; BLC 1; DA; DAB; DAC; DAM MST, MULT, NOV; SSC 26; WLC**
See also AAYA 19; BW 1, 3; CA 9-12R; 145; CANR 24, 53; CDALB 1941-1968; DA3; DLB 2, 76; DLBY 94; MTCW 1, 2

Ellmann, Lucy (Elizabeth) 1956- **CLC 61**
See also CA 128

Ellmann, Richard (David) 1918-1987 **CLC 50**
See also BEST 89:2; CA 1-4R; 122; CANR 2, 28, 61; DLB 103; DLBY 87; MTCW 1, 2

Elman, Richard (Martin) 1934-1997 **CLC 19**
See also CA 17-20R; 163; CAAS 3; CANR 47

Elron
See Hubbard, L(afayette) Ron(ald)

Eluard, Paul TCLC 7, 41
See also Grindel, Eugene

Elyot, Sir Thomas 1490(?)-1546 **LC 11**

Elytis, Odysseus 1911-1996 **CLC 15, 49, 100; DAM POET; PC 21**
See also CA 102; 151; MTCW 1, 2

Emecheta, (Florence Onye) Buchi 1944- **CLC 14, 48; BLC 2; DAM MULT**
See also BW 2, 3; CA 81-84; CANR 27, 81; DA3; DLB 117; MTCW 1, 2; SATA 66

Emerson, Mary Moody 1774-1863 **NCLC 66**

Emerson, Ralph Waldo 1803-1882 **NCLC 1, 38; DA; DAB; DAC; DAM MST, POET; PC 18; WLC**
See also CDALB 1640-1865; DA3; DLB 1, 59, 73, 223

Eminescu, Mihail 1850-1889 **NCLC 33**

Empson, William 1906-1984 **CLC 3, 8, 19, 33, 34**
See also CA 17-20R; 112; CANR 31, 61; DLB 20; MTCW 1, 2

Enchi, Fumiko (Ueda) 1905-1986 **CLC 31**

See also CA 129; 121; DLB 182

Ende, Michael (Andreas Helmuth) 1929-1995 **CLC 31**
See also CA 118; 124; 149; CANR 36; CLR 14; DLB 75; MAICYA; SATA 61; SATA-Brief 42; SATA-Obit 86

Endo, Shusaku 1923-1996 **CLC 7, 14, 19, 54, 99; DAM NOV**
See also CA 29-32R; 153; CANR 21, 54; DA3; DLB 182; MTCW 1, 2

Engel, Marian 1933-1985 **CLC 36**
See also CA 25-28R; CANR 12; DLB 53; INT CANR-12

Engelhardt, Frederick
See Hubbard, L(afayette) Ron(ald)

Engels, Friedrich 1820-1895 **NCLC 85**
See also DLB 129

Enright, D(ennis) J(oseph) 1920- **CLC 4, 8, 31**
See also CA 1-4R; CANR 1, 42, 83; DLB 27; SATA 25

Enzensberger, Hans Magnus 1929- **CLC 43; PC 28**
See also CA 116; 119

Ephron, Nora 1941- **CLC 17, 31**
See also AITN 2; CA 65-68; CANR 12, 39, 83

Epicurus 341B.C.-270B.C. **CMLC 21**
See also DLB 176

Epsilon
See Betjeman, John

Epstein, Daniel Mark 1948- **CLC 7**
See also CA 49-52; CANR 2, 53, 90

Epstein, Jacob 1956- **CLC 19**
See also CA 114

Epstein, Jean 1897-1953 **TCLC 92**

Epstein, Joseph 1937- **CLC 39**
See also CA 112; 119; CANR 50, 65

Epstein, Leslie 1938- **CLC 27**
See also CA 73-76; CAAS 12; CANR 23, 69

Equiano, Olaudah 1745(?)-1797 **LC 16; BLC 2; DAM MULT**
See also DLB 37, 50

ER TCLC 33
See also CA 160; DLB 85

Erasmus, Desiderius 1469(?)-1536 **LC 16**

Erdman, Paul E(mil) 1932- **CLC 25**
See also AITN 1; CA 61-64; CANR 13, 43, 84

Erdrich, Louise 1954- **CLC 39, 54, 120; DAM MULT, NOV, POP**
See also AAYA 10; BEST 89:1; CA 114; CANR 41, 62; CDALBS; DA3; DLB 152, 175, 206; MTCW 1; NNAL; SATA 94

Erenburg, Ilya (Grigoryevich)
See Ehrenburg, Ilya (Grigoryevich)

Erickson, Stephen Michael 1950-
See Erickson, Steve
See also CA 129

Erickson, Steve 1950- **CLC 64**
See also Erickson, Stephen Michael
See also CANR 60, 68

Ericson, Walter
See Fast, Howard (Melvin)

Eriksson, Buntel
See Bergman, (Ernst) Ingmar

Ernaux, Annie 1940- **CLC 88**
See also CA 147

Erskine, John 1879-1951 **TCLC 84**
See also CA 112; 159; DLB 9, 102

Eschenbach, Wolfram von
See Wolfram von Eschenbach

Eseki, Bruno
See Mphahlele, Ezekiel

Esenin, Sergei (Alexandrovich) 1895-1925 **TCLC 4**
See also CA 104

Eshleman, Clayton 1935- **CLC 7**
  See also CA 33-36R; CAAS 6; DLB 5
Espriella, Don Manuel Alvarez
  See Southey, Robert
Espriu, Salvador 1913-1985 **CLC 9**
  See also CA 154; 115; DLB 134
Espronceda, Jose de 1808-1842 **NCLC 39**
Esquivel, Laura 1951(?)-
  See also AAYA 29; CA 143; CANR 68;
    DA3; HLCS 1; MTCW 1
Esse, James
  See Stephens, James
Esterbrook, Tom
  See Hubbard, L(afayette) Ron(ald)
Estleman, Loren D. 1952- **CLC 48; DAM
    NOV, POP**
  See also AAYA 27; CA 85-88; CANR 27,
    74; DA3; INT CANR-27; MTCW 1, 2
Euclid 306B.C.-283B.C. **CMLC 25**
Eugenides, Jeffrey 1960(?)- **CLC 81**
  See also CA 144
Euripides c. 485B.C.-406B.C. **CMLC 23; DA;
    DAB; DAC; DAM DRAM, MST; DC 4;
    WLCS**
  See also DA3; DLB 176
Evan, Evin
  See Faust, Frederick (Schiller)
Evans, Caradoc 1878-1945 **TCLC 85**
Evans, Evan
  See Faust, Frederick (Schiller)
Evans, Marian
  See Eliot, George
Evans, Mary Ann
  See Eliot, George
Evarts, Esther
  See Benson, Sally
Everett, Percival L. 1956- **CLC 57**
  See also BW 2; CA 129
Everson, R(onald) G(ilmour) 1903- **CLC 27**
  See also CA 17-20R; DLB 88
Everson, William (Oliver) 1912-1994 **CLC 1,
    5, 14**
  See also CA 9-12R; 145; CANR 20; DLB
    212; MTCW 1
Evtushenko, Evgenii Aleksandrovich
  See Yevtushenko, Yevgeny (Alexandrovich)
Ewart, Gavin (Buchanan) 1916-1995 **CLC
    13, 46**
  See also CA 89-92; 150; CANR 17, 46;
    DLB 40; MTCW 1
Ewers, Hanns Heinz 1871-1943 **TCLC 12**
  See also CA 109; 149
Ewing, Frederick R.
  See Sturgeon, Theodore (Hamilton)
Exley, Frederick (Earl) 1929-1992 **CLC 6, 11**
  See also AITN 2; CA 81-84; 138; DLB 143;
    DLBY 81
Eynhardt, Guillermo
  See Quiroga, Horacio (Sylvestre)
Ezekiel, Nissim 1924- **CLC 61**
  See also CA 61-64
Ezekiel, Tish O'Dowd 1943- **CLC 34**
  See also CA 129
Fadeyev, A.
  See Bulgya, Alexander Alexandrovich
Fadeyev, Alexander TCLC 53
  See also Bulgya, Alexander Alexandrovich
Fagen, Donald 1948- **CLC 26**
Fainzilberg, Ilya Arnoldovich 1897-1937
  See Ilf, Ilya
  See also CA 120; 165
Fair, Ronald L. 1932- **CLC 18**
  See also BW 1; CA 69-72; CANR 25; DLB
    33
Fairbairn, Roger
  See Carr, John Dickson
Fairbairns, Zoe (Ann) 1948- **CLC 32**
  See also CA 103; CANR 21, 85

Falco, Gian
  See Papini, Giovanni
Falconer, James
  See Kirkup, James
Falconer, Kenneth
  See Kornbluth, C(yril) M.
Falkland, Samuel
  See Heijermans, Herman
Fallaci, Oriana 1930- **CLC 11, 110**
  See also CA 77-80; CANR 15, 58; MTCW
    1
Faludy, George 1913- **CLC 42**
  See also CA 21-24R
Faludy, Gyoergy
  See Faludy, George
Fanon, Frantz 1925-1961 **CLC 74; BLC 2;
    DAM MULT**
  See also BW 1; CA 116; 89-92
Fanshawe, Ann 1625-1680 **LC 11**
Fante, John (Thomas) 1911-1983 **CLC 60**
  See also CA 69-72; 109; CANR 23; DLB
    130; DLBY 83
Farah, Nuruddin 1945- **CLC 53; BLC 2;
    DAM MULT**
  See also BW 2, 3; CA 106; CANR 81; DLB
    125
Fargue, Leon-Paul 1876(?)-1947 **TCLC 11**
  See also CA 109
Farigoule, Louis
  See Romains, Jules
Farina, Richard 1936(?)-1966 **CLC 9**
  See also CA 81-84; 25-28R
Farley, Walter (Lorimer) 1915-1989 **CLC 17**
  See also CA 17-20R; CANR 8, 29, 84; DLB
    22; JRDA; MAICYA; SATA 2, 43
Farmer, Philip Jose 1918- **CLC 1, 19**
  See also AAYA 28; CA 1-4R; CANR 4, 35;
    DLB 8; MTCW 1; SATA 93
Farquhar, George 1677-1707 **LC 21; DAM
    DRAM**
  See also DLB 84
Farrell, J(ames) G(ordon) 1935-1979 **CLC 6**
  See also CA 73-76; 89-92; CANR 36; DLB
    14; MTCW 1
Farrell, James T(homas) 1904-1979 **CLC 1,
    4, 8, 11, 66; SSC 28**
  See also CA 5-8R; 89-92; CANR 9, 61;
    DLB 4, 9, 86; DLBD 2; MTCW 1, 2
Farren, Richard J.
  See Betjeman, John
Farren, Richard M.
  See Betjeman, John
Fassbinder, Rainer Werner 1946-1982 **CLC
    20**
  See also CA 93-96; 106; CANR 31
Fast, Howard (Melvin) 1914- **CLC 23, 131;
    DAM NOV**
  See also AAYA 16; CA 1-4R, 181; CAAE
    181; CAAS 18; CANR 1, 33, 54, 75; DLB
    9; INT CANR-33; MTCW 1; SATA 7;
    SATA-Essay 107
Faulcon, Robert
  See Holdstock, Robert P.
Faulkner, William (Cuthbert) 1897-1962
    **CLC 1, 3, 6, 8, 9, 11, 14, 18, 28, 52, 68;
    DA; DAB; DAC; DAM MST, NOV;
    SSC 1, 35; WLC**
  See also AAYA 7; CA 81-84; CANR 33;
    CDALB 1929-1941; DA3; DLB 9, 11, 44,
    102; DLBD 2; DLBY 86, 97; MTCW 1, 2
Fauset, Jessie Redmon 1884(?)-1961 **CLC 19,
    54; BLC 2; DAM MULT**
  See also BW 1; CA 109; CANR 83; DLB
    51
Faust, Frederick (Schiller) 1892-1944(?)
    TCLC 49; DAM POP
  See also CA 108; 152
Faust, Irvin 1924- **CLC 8**

  See also CA 33-36R; CANR 28, 67; DLB
    2, 28; DLBY 80
Fawkes, Guy
  See Benchley, Robert (Charles)
Fearing, Kenneth (Flexner) 1902-1961 **CLC
    51**
  See also CA 93-96; CANR 59; DLB 9
Fecamps, Elise
  See Creasey, John
Federman, Raymond 1928- **CLC 6, 47**
  See also CA 17-20R; CAAS 8; CANR 10,
    43, 83; DLBY 80
Federspiel, J(uerg) F. 1931- **CLC 42**
  See also CA 146
Feiffer, Jules (Ralph) 1929- **CLC 2, 8, 64;
    DAM DRAM**
  See also AAYA 3; CA 17-20R; CANR 30,
    59; DLB 7, 44; INT CANR-30; MTCW
    1; SATA 8, 61, 111
Feige, Hermann Albert Otto Maximilian
  See Traven, B.
Feinberg, David B. 1956-1994 **CLC 59**
  See also CA 135; 147
Feinstein, Elaine 1930- **CLC 36**
  See also CA 69-72; CAAS 1; CANR 31,
    68; DLB 14, 40; MTCW 1
Feldman, Irving (Mordecai) 1928- **CLC 7**
  See also CA 1-4R; CANR 1; DLB 169
Felix-Tchicaya, Gerald
  See Tchicaya, Gerald Felix
Fellini, Federico 1920-1993 **CLC 16, 85**
  See also CA 65-68; 143; CANR 33
Felsen, Henry Gregor 1916-1995 **CLC 17**
  See also CA 1-4R; 180; CANR 1; SAAS 2;
    SATA 1
Fenno, Jack
  See Calisher, Hortense
Fenollosa, Ernest (Francisco) 1853-1908
    TCLC 91
Fenton, James Martin 1949- **CLC 32**
  See also CA 102; DLB 40
Ferber, Edna 1887-1968 **CLC 18, 93**
  See also AITN 1; CA 5-8R; 25-28R; CANR
    68; DLB 9, 28, 86; MTCW 1, 2; SATA 7
Ferguson, Helen
  See Kavan, Anna
Ferguson, Samuel 1810-1886 **NCLC 33**
  See also DLB 32
Fergusson, Robert 1750-1774 **LC 29**
  See also DLB 109
Ferling, Lawrence
  See Ferlinghetti, Lawrence (Monsanto)
Ferlinghetti, Lawrence (Monsanto) 1919(?)-
    **CLC 2, 6, 10, 27, 111; DAM POET; PC
    1**
  See also CA 5-8R; CANR 3, 41, 73;
    CDALB 1941-1968; DA3; DLB 5, 16;
    MTCW 1, 2
Fern, Fanny 1811-1872
  See Parton, Sara Payson Willis
Fernandez, Vicente Garcia Huidobro
  See Huidobro Fernandez, Vicente Garcia
Ferre, Rosario 1942- **SSC 36; HLCS 1**
  See also CA 131; CANR 55, 81; DLB 145;
    HW 1, 2; MTCW 1
Ferrer, Gabriel (Francisco Victor) Miro
  See Miro (Ferrer), Gabriel (Francisco
    Victor)
Ferrier, Susan (Edmonstone) 1782-1854
    NCLC 8
  See also DLB 116
Ferrigno, Robert 1948(?)- **CLC 65**
  See also CA 140
Ferron, Jacques 1921-1985 **CLC 94; DAC**
  See also CA 117; 129; DLB 60
Feuchtwanger, Lion 1884-1958 **TCLC 3**
  See also CA 104; DLB 66
Feuillet, Octave 1821-1890 **NCLC 45**

See also DLB 192
Feydeau, Georges (Leon Jules Marie)
1862-1921 **TCLC 22; DAM DRAM**
See also CA 113; 152; CANR 84; DLB 192
Fichte, Johann Gottlieb 1762-1814 **NCLC 62**
See also DLB 90
Ficino, Marsilio 1433-1499 **LC 12**
Fiedeler, Hans
See Doeblin, Alfred
Fiedler, Leslie A(aron) 1917- **CLC 4, 13, 24**
See also CA 9-12R; CANR 7, 63; DLB 28, 67; MTCW 1, 2
Field, Andrew 1938- **CLC 44**
See also CA 97-100; CANR 25
Field, Eugene 1850-1895 **NCLC 3**
See also DLB 23, 42, 140; DLBD 13; MAI-CYA; SATA 16
Field, Gans T.
See Wellman, Manly Wade
Field, Michael 1915-1971 **TCLC 43**
See also CA 29-32R
Field, Peter
See Hobson, Laura Z(ametkin)
Fielding, Henry 1707-1754 **LC 1, 46; DA; DAB; DAC; DAM DRAM, MST, NOV; WLC**
See also CDBLB 1660-1789; DA3; DLB 39, 84, 101
Fielding, Sarah 1710-1768 **LC 1, 44**
See also DLB 39
Fields, W. C. 1880-1946 **TCLC 80**
See also DLB 44
Fierstein, Harvey (Forbes) 1954- **CLC 33; DAM DRAM, POP**
See also CA 123; 129; DA3
Figes, Eva 1932- **CLC 31**
See also CA 53-56; CANR 4, 44, 83; DLB 14
Finch, Anne 1661-1720 **LC 3; PC 21**
See also DLB 95
Finch, Robert (Duer Claydon) 1900- **CLC 18**
See also CA 57-60; CANR 9, 24, 49; DLB 88
Findley, Timothy 1930- **CLC 27, 102; DAC; DAM MST**
See also CA 25-28R; CANR 12, 42, 69; DLB 53
Fink, William
See Mencken, H(enry) L(ouis)
Firbank, Louis 1942-
See Reed, Lou
See also CA 117
Firbank, (Arthur Annesley) Ronald
1886-1926 **TCLC 1**
See also CA 104; 177; DLB 36
Fisher, Dorothy (Frances) Canfield
1879-1958 **TCLC 87**
See also CA 114; 136; CANR 80; DLB 9, 102; MAICYA; YABC 1
Fisher, M(ary) F(rances) K(ennedy)
1908-1992 **CLC 76, 87**
See also CA 77-80; 138; CANR 44; MTCW 1
Fisher, Roy 1930- **CLC 25**
See also CA 81-84; CAAS 10; CANR 16; DLB 40
Fisher, Rudolph 1897-1934 **TCLC 11; BLC 2; DAM MULT; SSC 25**
See also BW 1, 3; CA 107; 124; CANR 80; DLB 51, 102
Fisher, Vardis (Alvero) 1895-1968 **CLC 7**
See also CA 5-8R; 25-28R; CANR 68; DLB 9, 206
Fiske, Tarleton
See Bloch, Robert (Albert)
Fitch, Clarke
See Sinclair, Upton (Beall)

Fitch, John IV
See Cormier, Robert (Edmund)
Fitzgerald, Captain Hugh
See Baum, L(yman) Frank
FitzGerald, Edward 1809-1883 **NCLC 9**
See also DLB 32
Fitzgerald, F(rancis) Scott (Key) 1896-1940
TCLC 1, 6, 14, 28, 55; DA; DAB; DAC; DAM MST, NOV; SSC 6, 31; WLC
See also AAYA 24; AITN 1; CA 110; 123; CDALB 1917-1929; DA3; DLB 4, 9, 86; DLBD 1, 15, 16; DLBY 81, 96; MTCW 1, 2
Fitzgerald, Penelope 1916-2000 **CLC 19, 51, 61**
See also CA 85-88; CAAS 10; CANR 56, 86; DLB 14, 194; MTCW 2
Fitzgerald, Robert (Stuart) 1910-1985 **CLC 39**
See also CA 1-4R; 114; CANR 1; DLBY 80
FitzGerald, Robert D(avid) 1902-1987 **CLC 19**
See also CA 17-20R
Fitzgerald, Zelda (Sayre) 1900-1948 **TCLC 52**
See also CA 117; 126; DLBY 84
Flanagan, Thomas (James Bonner) 1923- **CLC 25, 52**
See also CA 108; CANR 55; DLBY 80; INT 108; MTCW 1
Flaubert, Gustave 1821-1880 **NCLC 2, 10, 19, 62, 66; DA; DAB; DAC; DAM MST, NOV; SSC 11; WLC**
See also DA3; DLB 119
Flecker, Herman Elroy
See Flecker, (Herman) James Elroy
Flecker, (Herman) James Elroy 1884-1915 **TCLC 43**
See also CA 109; 150; DLB 10, 19
Fleming, Ian (Lancaster) 1908-1964 **CLC 3, 30; DAM POP**
See also AAYA 26; CA 5-8R; CANR 59; CDBLB 1945-1960; DA3; DLB 87, 201; MTCW 1, 2; SATA 9
Fleming, Thomas (James) 1927- **CLC 37**
See also CA 5-8R; CANR 10; INT CANR-10; SATA 8
Fletcher, John 1579-1625 **LC 33; DC 6**
See also CDBLB Before 1660; DLB 58
Fletcher, John Gould 1886-1950 **TCLC 35**
See also CA 107; 167; DLB 4, 45
Fleur, Paul
See Pohl, Frederik
Flooglebuckle, Al
See Spiegelman, Art
Flying Officer X
See Bates, H(erbert) E(rnest)
Fo, Dario 1926- **CLC 32, 109; DAM DRAM; DC 10**
See also CA 116; 128; CANR 68; DA3; DLBY 97; MTCW 1, 2
Fogarty, Jonathan Titulescu Esq.
See Farrell, James T(homas)
Follett, Ken(neth Martin) 1949- **CLC 18; DAM NOV, POP**
See also AAYA 6; BEST 89:4; CA 81-84; CANR 13, 33, 54; DA3; DLB 87; DLBY 81; INT CANR-33; MTCW 1
Fontane, Theodor 1819-1898 **NCLC 26**
See also DLB 129
Foote, Horton 1916- **CLC 51, 91; DAM DRAM**
See also CA 73-76; CANR 34, 51; DA3; DLB 26; INT CANR-34
Foote, Shelby 1916- **CLC 75; DAM NOV, POP**
See also CA 5-8R; CANR 3, 45, 74; DA3; DLB 2, 17; MTCW 2

Forbes, Esther 1891-1967 **CLC 12**
See also AAYA 17; CA 13-14; 25-28R; CAP 1; CLR 27; DLB 22; JRDA; MAICYA; SATA 2, 100
Forche, Carolyn (Louise) 1950- **CLC 25, 83, 86; DAM POET; PC 10**
See also CA 109; 117; CANR 50, 74; DA3; DLB 5, 193; INT 117; MTCW 1
Ford, Elbur
See Hibbert, Eleanor Alice Burford
Ford, Ford Madox 1873-1939 **TCLC 1, 15, 39, 57; DAM NOV**
See also CA 104; 132; CANR 74; CDBLB 1914-1945; DA3; DLB 162; MTCW 1, 2
Ford, Henry 1863-1947 **TCLC 73**
See also CA 115; 148
Ford, John 1586-(?) **DC 8**
See also CDBLB Before 1660; DAM DRAM; DA3; DLB 58
Ford, John 1895-1973 **CLC 16**
See also CA 45-48
Ford, Richard 1944- **CLC 46, 99**
See also CA 69-72; CANR 11, 47, 86; MTCW 1
Ford, Webster
See Masters, Edgar Lee
Foreman, Richard 1937- **CLC 50**
See also CA 65-68; CANR 32, 63
Forester, C(ecil) S(cott) 1899-1966 **CLC 35**
See also CA 73-76; 25-28R; CANR 83; DLB 191; SATA 13
Forez
See Mauriac, Francois (Charles)
Forman, James Douglas 1932- **CLC 21**
See also AAYA 17; CA 9-12R; CANR 4, 19, 42; JRDA; MAICYA; SATA 8, 70
Fornes, Maria Irene 1930- **CLC 39, 61; DC 10; HLCS 1**
See also CA 25-28R; CANR 28, 81; DLB 7; HW 1, 2; INT CANR-28; MTCW 1
Forrest, Leon (Richard) 1937-1997 **CLC 4; BLCS**
See also BW 2; CA 89-92; 162; CAAS 7; CANR 25, 52, 87; DLB 33
Forster, E(dward) M(organ) 1879-1970 **CLC 1, 2, 3, 4, 9, 10, 13, 15, 22, 45, 77; DA; DAB; DAC; DAM MST, NOV; SSC 27; WLC**
See also AAYA 2; CA 13-14; 25-28R; CANR 45; CAP 1; CDBLB 1914-1945; DA3; DLB 34, 98, 162, 178, 195; DLBD 10; MTCW 1, 2; SATA 57
Forster, John 1812-1876 **NCLC 11**
See also DLB 144, 184
Forsyth, Frederick 1938- **CLC 2, 5, 36; DAM NOV, POP**
See also BEST 89:4; CA 85-88; CANR 38, 62; DLB 87; MTCW 1, 2
Forten, Charlotte L. TCLC 16; BLC 2
See also Grimke, Charlotte L(ottie) Forten
See also DLB 50
Foscolo, Ugo 1778-1827 **NCLC 8**
Fosse, Bob CLC 20
See also Fosse, Robert Louis
Fosse, Robert Louis 1927-1987
See Fosse, Bob
See also CA 110; 123
Foster, Stephen Collins 1826-1864 **NCLC 26**
Foucault, Michel 1926-1984 **CLC 31, 34, 69**
See also CA 105; 113; CANR 34; MTCW 1, 2
Fouque, Friedrich (Heinrich Karl) de la Motte 1777-1843 **NCLC 2**
See also DLB 90
Fourier, Charles 1772-1837 **NCLC 51**
Fournier, Pierre 1916- **CLC 11**
See also Gascar, Pierre
See also CA 89-92; CANR 16, 40
Fowles, John (Philip) 1926- **CLC 1, 2, 3, 4, 6,**

9, 10, 15, 33, 87; DAB; DAC; DAM MST; SSC 33
See also CA 5-8R; CANR 25, 71; CDBLB 1960 to Present; DA3; DLB 14, 139, 207; MTCW 1, 2; SATA 22

Fox, Paula 1923- **CLC 2, 8, 121**
See also AAYA 3; CA 73-76; CANR 20, 36, 62; CLR 1, 44; DLB 52; JRDA; MAICYA; MTCW 1; SATA 17, 60

Fox, William Price (Jr.) 1926- **CLC 22**
See also CA 17-20R; CAAS 19; CANR 11; DLB 2; DLBY 81

Foxe, John 1516(?)-1587 **LC 14**
See also DLB 132

Frame, Janet 1924- **CLC 2, 3, 6, 22, 66, 96; SSC 29**
See also Clutha, Janet Paterson Frame

France, Anatole TCLC 9
See also Thibault, Jacques Anatole Francois
See also DLB 123; MTCW 1

Francis, Claude 19(?)- **CLC 50**

Francis, Dick 1920- **CLC 2, 22, 42, 102; DAM POP**
See also AAYA 5, 21; BEST 89:3; CA 5-8R; CANR 9, 42, 68; CDBLB 1960 to Present; DA3; DLB 87; INT CANR-9; MTCW 1, 2

Francis, Robert (Churchill) 1901-1987 **CLC 15**
See also CA 1-4R; 123; CANR 1

Frank, Anne(lies Marie) 1929-1945 **TCLC 17; DA; DAB; DAC; DAM MST; WLC**
See also AAYA 12; CA 113; 133; CANR 68; DA3; MTCW 1, 2; SATA 87; SATABrief 42

Frank, Bruno 1887-1945 **TCLC 81**
See also DLB 118

Frank, Elizabeth 1945- **CLC 39**
See also CA 121; 126; CANR 78; INT 126

Frankl, Viktor E(mil) 1905-1997 **CLC 93**
See also CA 65-68; 161

Franklin, Benjamin
See Hasek, Jaroslav (Matej Frantisek)

Franklin, Benjamin 1706-1790 **LC 25; DA; DAB; DAC; DAM MST; WLCS**
See also CDALB 1640-1865; DA3; DLB 24, 43, 73

Franklin, (Stella Maria Sarah) Miles (Lampe) 1879-1954 **TCLC 7**
See also CA 104; 164

Fraser, (Lady) Antonia (Pakenham) 1932- **CLC 32, 107**
See also CA 85-88; CANR 44, 65; MTCW 1, 2; SATA-Brief 32

Fraser, George MacDonald 1925- **CLC 7**
See also CA 45-48, 180; CAAE 180; CANR 2, 48, 74; MTCW 1

Fraser, Sylvia 1935- **CLC 64**
See also CA 45-48; CANR 1, 16, 60

Frayn, Michael 1933- **CLC 3, 7, 31, 47; DAM DRAM, NOV**
See also CA 5-8R; CANR 30, 69; DLB 13, 14, 194; MTCW 1, 2

Fraze, Candida (Merrill) 1945- **CLC 50**
See also CA 126

Frazer, J(ames) G(eorge) 1854-1941 **TCLC 32**
See also CA 118

Frazer, Robert Caine
See Creasey, John

Frazer, Sir James George
See Frazer, J(ames) G(eorge)

Frazier, Charles 1950- **CLC 109**
See also AAYA 34; CA 161

Frazier, Ian 1951- **CLC 46**
See also CA 130; CANR 54

Frederic, Harold 1856-1898 **NCLC 10**
See also DLB 12, 23; DLBD 13

Frederick, John
See Faust, Frederick (Schiller)

Frederick the Great 1712-1786 **LC 14**

Fredro, Aleksander 1793-1876 **NCLC 8**

Freeling, Nicolas 1927- **CLC 38**
See also CA 49-52; CAAS 12; CANR 1, 17, 50, 84; DLB 87

Freeman, Douglas Southall 1886-1953 **TCLC 11**
See also CA 109; DLB 17; DLBD 17

Freeman, Judith 1946- **CLC 55**
See also CA 148

Freeman, Mary E(leanor) Wilkins 1852-1930 **TCLC 9; SSC 1**
See also CA 106; 177; DLB 12, 78, 221

Freeman, R(ichard) Austin 1862-1943 **TCLC 21**
See also CA 113; CANR 84; DLB 70

French, Albert 1943- **CLC 86**
See also BW 3; CA 167

French, Marilyn 1929- **CLC 10, 18, 60; DAM DRAM, NOV, POP**
See also CA 69-72; CANR 3, 31; INT CANR-31; MTCW 1, 2

French, Paul
See Asimov, Isaac

Freneau, Philip Morin 1752-1832 **NCLC 1**
See also DLB 37, 43

Freud, Sigmund 1856-1939 **TCLC 52**
See also CA 115; 133; CANR 69; MTCW 1, 2

Friedan, Betty (Naomi) 1921- **CLC 74**
See also CA 65-68; CANR 18, 45, 74; MTCW 1, 2

Friedlander, Saul 1932- **CLC 90**
See also CA 117; 130; CANR 72

Friedman, B(ernard) H(arper) 1926- **CLC 7**
See also CA 1-4R; CANR 3, 48

Friedman, Bruce Jay 1930- **CLC 3, 5, 56**
See also CA 9-12R; CANR 25, 52; DLB 2, 28; INT CANR-25

Friel, Brian 1929- **CLC 5, 42, 59, 115; DC 8**
See also CA 21-24R; CANR 33, 69; DLB 13; MTCW 1

Friis-Baastad, Babbis Ellinor 1921-1970 **CLC 12**
See also CA 17-20R; 134; SATA 7

Frisch, Max (Rudolf) 1911-1991 **CLC 3, 9, 14, 18, 32, 44; DAM DRAM, NOV**
See also CA 85-88; 134; CANR 32, 74; DLB 69, 124; MTCW 1, 2

Fromentin, Eugene (Samuel Auguste) 1820-1876 **NCLC 10**
See also DLB 123

Frost, Frederick
See Faust, Frederick (Schiller)

Frost, Robert (Lee) 1874-1963 **CLC 1, 3, 4, 9, 10, 13, 15, 26, 34, 44; DA; DAB; DAC; DAM MST, POET; PC 1; WLC**
See also AAYA 21; CA 89-92; CANR 33; CDALB 1917-1929; DA3; DLB 54; DLBD 7; MTCW 1, 2; SATA 14

Froude, James Anthony 1818-1894 **NCLC 43**
See also DLB 18, 57, 144

Froy, Herald
See Waterhouse, Keith (Spencer)

Fry, Christopher 1907- **CLC 2, 10, 14; DAM DRAM**
See also CA 17-20R; CAAS 23; CANR 9, 30, 74; DLB 13; MTCW 1, 2; SATA 66

Frye, (Herman) Northrop 1912-1991 **CLC 24, 70**
See also CA 5-8R; 133; CANR 8, 37; DLB 67, 68; MTCW 1, 2

Fuchs, Daniel 1909-1993 **CLC 8, 22**
See also CA 81-84; 142; CAAS 5; CANR 40; DLB 9, 26, 28; DLBY 93

Fuchs, Daniel 1934- **CLC 34**
See also CA 37-40R; CANR 14, 48

Fuentes, Carlos 1928- **CLC 3, 8, 10, 13, 22, 41, 60, 113; DA; DAB; DAC; DAM MST, MULT, NOV; HLC 1; SSC 24; WLC**
See also AAYA 4; AITN 2; CA 69-72; CANR 10, 32, 68; DA3; DLB 113; HW 1, 2; MTCW 1, 2

Fuentes, Gregorio Lopez y
See Lopez y Fuentes, Gregorio

Fuertes, Gloria 1918- **PC 27**
See also CA 178; 180; DLB 108; HW 2; SATA 115

Fugard, (Harold) Athol 1932- **CLC 5, 9, 14, 25, 40, 80; DAM DRAM; DC 3**
See also AAYA 17; CA 85-88; CANR 32, 54; MTCW 1

Fugard, Sheila 1932- **CLC 48**
See also CA 125

Fukuyama, Francis 1952- **CLC 131**
See also CA 140; CANR 72

Fuller, Charles (H., Jr.) 1939- **CLC 25; BLC 2; DAM DRAM, MULT; DC 1**
See also BW 2; CA 108; 112; CANR 87; DLB 38; INT 112; MTCW 1

Fuller, John (Leopold) 1937- **CLC 62**
See also CA 21-24R; CANR 9, 44; DLB 40

Fuller, Margaret NCLC 5, 50
See also Fuller, Sarah Margaret

Fuller, Roy (Broadbent) 1912-1991 **CLC 4, 28**
See also CA 5-8R; 135; CAAS 10; CANR 53, 83; DLB 15, 20; SATA 87

Fuller, Sarah Margaret 1810-1850
See Fuller, Margaret
See also CDALB 1640-1865; DLB 1, 59, 73, 83, 223

Fulton, Alice 1952- **CLC 52**
See also CA 116; CANR 57, 88; DLB 193

Furphy, Joseph 1843-1912 **TCLC 25**
See also CA 163

Fussell, Paul 1924- **CLC 74**
See also BEST 90:1; CA 17-20R; CANR 8, 21, 35, 69; INT CANR-21; MTCW 1, 2

Futabatei, Shimei 1864-1909 **TCLC 44**
See also CA 162; DLB 180

Futrelle, Jacques 1875-1912 **TCLC 19**
See also CA 113; 155

Gaboriau, Emile 1835-1873 **NCLC 14**

Gadda, Carlo Emilio 1893-1973 **CLC 11**
See also CA 89-92; DLB 177

Gaddis, William 1922-1998 **CLC 1, 3, 6, 8, 10, 19, 43, 86**
See also CA 17-20R; 172; CANR 21, 48; DLB 2; MTCW 1, 2

Gage, Walter
See Inge, William (Motter)

Gaines, Ernest J(ames) 1933- **CLC 3, 11, 18, 86; BLC 2; DAM MULT**
See also AAYA 18; AITN 1; BW 2, 3; CA 9-12R; CANR 6, 24, 42, 75; CDALB 1968-1988; CLR 62; DA3; DLB 2, 33, 152; DLBY 80; MTCW 1, 2; SATA 86

Gaitskill, Mary 1954- **CLC 69**
See also CA 128; CANR 61

Galdos, Benito Perez
See Perez Galdos, Benito

Gale, Zona 1874-1938 **TCLC 7; DAM DRAM**
See also CA 105; 153; CANR 84; DLB 9, 78

Galeano, Eduardo (Hughes) 1940- **CLC 72; HLCS 1**
See also CA 29-32R; CANR 13, 32; HW 1

Galiano, Juan Valera y Alcala
See Valera y Alcala-Galiano, Juan

Galilei, Galileo 1546-1642 **LC 45**

Gallagher, Tess 1943- **CLC 18, 63; DAM POET; PC 9**
See also CA 106; DLB 212

Gallant, Mavis 1922- **CLC 7, 18, 38; DAC;
DAM MST; SSC 5**
See also CA 69-72; CANR 29, 69; DLB 53;
MTCW 1, 2

Gallant, Roy A(rthur) 1924- **CLC 17**
See also CA 5-8R; CANR 4, 29, 54; CLR
30; MAICYA; SATA 4, 68, 110

Gallico, Paul (William) 1897-1976 **CLC 2**
See also AITN 1; CA 5-8R; 69-72; CANR
23; DLB 9, 171; MAICYA; SATA 13

Gallo, Max Louis 1932- **CLC 95**
See also CA 85-88

Gallois, Lucien
See Desnos, Robert

Gallup, Ralph
See Whitemore, Hugh (John)

Galsworthy, John 1867-1933 **TCLC 1, 45;
DA; DAB; DAC; DAM DRAM, MST,
NOV; SSC 22; WLC**
See also CA 104; 141; CANR 75; CDBLB
1890-1914; DA3; DLB 10, 34, 98, 162;
DLBD 16; MTCW 1

Galt, John 1779-1839 **NCLC 1**
See also DLB 99, 116, 159

Galvin, James 1951- **CLC 38**
See also CA 108; CANR 26

Gamboa, Federico 1864-1939 **TCLC 36**
See also CA 167; HW 2

Gandhi, M. K.
See Gandhi, Mohandas Karamchand

Gandhi, Mahatma
See Gandhi, Mohandas Karamchand

Gandhi, Mohandas Karamchand 1869-1948
TCLC 59; DAM MULT
See also CA 121; 132; DA3; MTCW 1, 2

Gann, Ernest Kellogg 1910-1991 **CLC 23**
See also AITN 1; CA 1-4R; 136; CANR 1,
83

Garber, Eric 1943(?)-
See Holleran, Andrew
See also CANR 89

Garcia, Cristina 1958- **CLC 76**
See also CA 141; CANR 73; HW 2

Garcia Lorca, Federico 1898-1936 **TCLC 1,
7, 49; DA; DAB; DAC; DAM DRAM,
MST, MULT, POET; DC 2; HLC 2; PC
3; WLC**
See also Lorca, Federico Garcia
See also CA 104; 131; CANR 81; DA3;
DLB 108; HW 1, 2; MTCW 1, 2

Garcia Marquez, Gabriel (Jose) 1928- **CLC
2, 3, 8, 10, 15, 27, 47, 55, 68; DA; DAB;
DAC; DAM MST, MULT, NOV, POP;
HLC 1; SSC 8; WLC**
See also Marquez, Gabriel (Jose) Garcia
See also AAYA 3, 33; BEST 89:1, 90:4; CA
33-36R; CANR 10, 28, 50, 75, 82; DA3;
DLB 113; HW 1, 2; MTCW 1, 2

Garcilaso de la Vega, El Inca 1503-1536
See also HLCS 1

Gard, Janice
See Latham, Jean Lee

Gard, Roger Martin du
See Martin du Gard, Roger

Gardam, Jane 1928- **CLC 43**
See also CA 49-52; CANR 2, 18, 33, 54;
CLR 12; DLB 14, 161; MAICYA; MTCW
1; SAAS 9; SATA 39, 76; SATA-Brief 28

Gardner, Herb(ert) 1934- **CLC 44**
See also CA 149

Gardner, John (Champlin), Jr. 1933-1982
**CLC 2, 3, 5, 7, 8, 10, 18, 28, 34; DAM
NOV, POP; SSC 7**
See also AITN 1; CA 65-68; 107; CANR
33, 73; CDALBS; DA3; DLB 2; DLBY
82; MTCW 1; SATA 40; SATA-Obit 31

Gardner, John (Edmund) 1926- **CLC 30;
DAM POP**
See also CA 103; CANR 15, 69; MTCW 1

Gardner, Miriam
See Bradley, Marion Zimmer

Gardner, Noel
See Kuttner, Henry

Gardons, S. S.
See Snodgrass, W(illiam) D(e Witt)

Garfield, Leon 1921-1996 **CLC 12**
See also AAYA 8; CA 17-20R; 152; CANR
38, 41, 78; CLR 21; DLB 161; JRDA;
MAICYA; SATA 1, 32, 76; SATA-Obit 90

Garland, (Hannibal) Hamlin 1860-1940
TCLC 3; SSC 18
See also CA 104; DLB 12, 71, 78, 186

Garneau, (Hector de) Saint-Denys 1912-1943
TCLC 13
See also CA 111; DLB 88

Garner, Alan 1934- **CLC 17; DAB; DAM
POP**
See also AAYA 18; CA 73-76, 178; CAAE
178; CANR 15, 64; CLR 20; DLB 161;
MAICYA; MTCW 1, 2; SATA 18, 69;
SATA-Essay 108

Garner, Hugh 1913-1979 **CLC 13**
See also CA 69-72; CANR 31; DLB 68

Garnett, David 1892-1981 **CLC 3**
See also CA 5-8R; 103; CANR 17, 79; DLB
34; MTCW 2

Garos, Stephanie
See Katz, Steve

Garrett, George (Palmer) 1929- **CLC 3, 11,
51; SSC 30**
See also CA 1-4R; CAAS 5; CANR 1, 42,
67; DLB 2, 5, 130, 152; DLBY 83

Garrick, David 1717-1779 **LC 15; DAM
DRAM**
See also DLB 84

Garrigue, Jean 1914-1972 **CLC 2, 8**
See also CA 5-8R; 37-40R; CANR 20

Garrison, Frederick
See Sinclair, Upton (Beall)

Garro, Elena 1920(?)-1998
See also CA 131; 169; DLB 145; HLCS 1;
HW 1

Garth, Will
See Hamilton, Edmond; Kuttner, Henry

Garvey, Marcus (Moziah, Jr.) 1887-1940
TCLC 41; BLC 2; DAM MULT
See also BW 1; CA 120; 124; CANR 79

Gary, Romain CLC 25
See also Kacew, Romain
See also DLB 83

Gascar, Pierre CLC 11
See also Fournier, Pierre

Gascoyne, David (Emery) 1916- **CLC 45**
See also CA 65-68; CANR 10, 28, 54; DLB
20; MTCW 1

Gaskell, Elizabeth Cleghorn 1810-1865
NCLC 70; DAB; DAM MST; SSC 25
See also CDBLB 1832-1890; DLB 21, 144,
159

Gass, William H(oward) 1924- **CLC 1, 2, 8,
11, 15, 39, 132; SSC 12**
See also CA 17-20R; CANR 30, 71; DLB
2; MTCW 1, 2

Gassendi, Pierre 1592-1655 **LC 54**

Gasset, Jose Ortega y
See Ortega y Gasset, Jose

Gates, Henry Louis, Jr. 1950- **CLC 65;
BLCS; DAM MULT**
See also BW 2, 3; CA 109; CANR 25, 53,
75; DA3; DLB 67; MTCW 1

Gautier, Theophile 1811-1872 **NCLC 1, 59;
DAM POET; PC 18; SSC 20**
See also DLB 119

Gawsworth, John
See Bates, H(erbert) E(rnest)

Gay, John 1685-1732 **LC 49; DAM DRAM**
See also DLB 84, 95

Gay, Oliver
See Gogarty, Oliver St. John

Gaye, Marvin (Penze) 1939-1984 **CLC 26**
See also CA 112

Gebler, Carlo (Ernest) 1954- **CLC 39**
See also CA 119; 133

Gee, Maggie (Mary) 1948- **CLC 57**
See also CA 130; DLB 207

Gee, Maurice (Gough) 1931- **CLC 29**
See also CA 97-100; CANR 67; CLR 56;
SATA 46, 101

Gelbart, Larry (Simon) 1923- **CLC 21, 61**
See also CA 73-76; CANR 45

Gelber, Jack 1932- **CLC 1, 6, 14, 79**
See also CA 1-4R; CANR 2; DLB 7

Gellhorn, Martha (Ellis) 1908-1998 **CLC 14,
60**
See also CA 77-80; 164; CANR 44; DLBY
82, 98

Genet, Jean 1910-1986 **CLC 1, 2, 5, 10, 14,
44, 46; DAM DRAM**
See also CA 13-16R; CANR 18; DA3; DLB
72; DLBY 86; MTCW 1, 2

Gent, Peter 1942- **CLC 29**
See also AITN 1; CA 89-92; DLBY 82

Gentile, Giovanni 1875-1944 **TCLC 96**
See also CA 119

Gentlewoman in New England, A
See Bradstreet, Anne

Gentlewoman in Those Parts, A
See Bradstreet, Anne

George, Jean Craighead 1919- **CLC 35**
See also AAYA 8; CA 5-8R; CANR 25;
CLR 1; DLB 52; JRDA; MAICYA; SATA
2, 68

George, Stefan (Anton) 1868-1933 **TCLC 2,
14**
See also CA 104

Georges, Georges Martin
See Simenon, Georges (Jacques Christian)

Gerhardi, William Alexander
See Gerhardie, William Alexander

Gerhardie, William Alexander 1895-1977
CLC 5
See also CA 25-28R; 73-76; CANR 18;
DLB 36

Gerstler, Amy 1956- **CLC 70**
See also CA 146

Gertler, T. CLC 34
See also CA 116; 121; INT 121

Ghalib NCLC 39, 78
See also Ghalib, Hsadullah Khan

Ghalib, Hsadullah Khan 1797-1869
See Ghalib
See also DAM POET

Ghelderode, Michel de 1898-1962 **CLC 6, 11;
DAM DRAM**
See also CA 85-88; CANR 40, 77

Ghiselin, Brewster 1903- **CLC 23**
See also CA 13-16R; CAAS 10; CANR 13

Ghose, Aurabinda 1872-1950 **TCLC 63**
See also CA 163

Ghose, Zulfikar 1935- **CLC 42**
See also CA 65-68; CANR 67

Ghosh, Amitav 1956- **CLC 44**
See also CA 147; CANR 80

Giacosa, Giuseppe 1847-1906 **TCLC 7**
See also CA 104

Gibb, Lee
See Waterhouse, Keith (Spencer)

Gibbon, Lewis Grassic TCLC 4
See also Mitchell, James Leslie

Gibbons, Kaye 1960- **CLC 50, 88; DAM POP**
See also AAYA 34; CA 151; CANR 75;
DA3; MTCW 1; SATA 117

Gibran, Kahlil 1883-1931 **TCLC 1, 9; DAM
POET, POP; PC 9**
See also CA 104; 150; DA3; MTCW 2

Gibran, Khalil
See Gibran, Kahlil

Gibson, William 1914- **CLC 23; DA; DAB; DAC; DAM DRAM, MST**
See also CA 9-12R; CANR 9, 42, 75; DLB 7; MTCW 1; SATA 66

Gibson, William (Ford) 1948- **CLC 39, 63; DAM POP**
See also AAYA 12; CA 126; 133; CANR 52, 90; DA3; MTCW 1

Gide, Andre (Paul Guillaume) 1869-1951 **TCLC 5, 12, 36; DA; DAB; DAC; DAM MST, NOV; SSC 13; WLC**
See also CA 104; 124; DA3; DLB 65; MTCW 1, 2

Gifford, Barry (Colby) 1946- **CLC 34**
See also CA 65-68; CANR 9, 30, 40, 90

Gilbert, Frank
See De Voto, Bernard (Augustine)

Gilbert, W(illiam) S(chwenck) 1836-1911 **TCLC 3; DAM DRAM, POET**
See also CA 104; 173; SATA 36

Gilbreth, Frank B., Jr. 1911- **CLC 17**
See also CA 9-12R; SATA 2

Gilchrist, Ellen 1935- **CLC 34, 48; DAM POP; SSC 14**
See also CA 113; 116; CANR 41, 61; DLB 130; MTCW 1, 2

Giles, Molly 1942- **CLC 39**
See also CA 126

Gill, Eric 1882-1940 **TCLC 85**

Gill, Patrick
See Creasey, John

Gilliam, Terry (Vance) 1940- **CLC 21**
See also Monty Python
See also AAYA 19; CA 108; 113; CANR 35; INT 113

Gillian, Jerry
See Gilliam, Terry (Vance)

Gilliatt, Penelope (Ann Douglass) 1932-1993 **CLC 2, 10, 13, 53**
See also AITN 2; CA 13-16R; 141; CANR 49; DLB 14

Gilman, Charlotte (Anna) Perkins (Stetson) 1860-1935 **TCLC 9, 37; SSC 13**
See also CA 106; 150; DLB 221; MTCW 1

Gilmour, David 1949- **CLC 35**
See also CA 138; 147

Gilpin, William 1724-1804 **NCLC 30**

Gilray, J. D.
See Mencken, H(enry) L(ouis)

Gilroy, Frank D(aniel) 1925- **CLC 2**
See also CA 81-84; CANR 32, 64, 86; DLB 7

Gilstrap, John 1957(?)- **CLC 99**
See also CA 160

Ginsberg, Allen 1926-1997 **CLC 1, 2, 3, 4, 6, 13, 36, 69, 109; DA; DAB; DAC; DAM MST, POET; PC 4; WLC**
See also AAYA 33; AITN 1; CA 1-4R; 157; CANR 2, 41, 63; CDALB 1941-1968; DA3; DLB 5, 16, 169; MTCW 1, 2

Ginzburg, Natalia 1916-1991 **CLC 5, 11, 54, 70**
See also CA 85-88; 135; CANR 33; DLB 177; MTCW 1, 2

Giono, Jean 1895-1970 **CLC 4, 11**
See also CA 45-48; 29-32R; CANR 2, 35; DLB 72; MTCW 1

Giovanni, Nikki 1943- **CLC 2, 4, 19, 64, 117; BLC 2; DA; DAB; DAC; DAM MST, MULT, POET; PC 19; WLCS**
See also AAYA 22; AITN 1; BW 2, 3; CA 29-32R; CAAS 6; CANR 18, 41, 60, 91; CDALBS; CLR 6; DA3; DLB 5, 41; INT CANR-18; MAICYA; MTCW 1, 2; SATA 24, 107

Giovene, Andrea 1904- **CLC 7**
See also CA 85-88

Gippius, Zinaida (Nikolayevna) 1869-1945
See Hippius, Zinaida
See also CA 106

Giraudoux, (Hippolyte) Jean 1882-1944 **TCLC 2, 7; DAM DRAM**
See also CA 104; DLB 65

Gironella, Jose Maria 1917- **CLC 11**
See also CA 101

Gissing, George (Robert) 1857-1903 **TCLC 3, 24, 47; SSC 37**
See also CA 105; 167; DLB 18, 135, 184

Giurlani, Aldo
See Palazzeschi, Aldo

Gladkov, Fyodor (Vasilyevich) 1883-1958 **TCLC 27**
See also CA 170

Glanville, Brian (Lester) 1931- **CLC 6**
See also CA 5-8R; CAAS 9; CANR 3, 70; DLB 15, 139; SATA 42

Glasgow, Ellen (Anderson Gholson) 1873-1945 **TCLC 2, 7; SSC 34**
See also CA 104; 164; DLB 9, 12; MTCW 2

Glaspell, Susan 1882(?)-1948 **TCLC 55; DC 10**
See also CA 110; 154; DLB 7, 9, 78; YABC 2

Glassco, John 1909-1981 **CLC 9**
See also CA 13-16R; 102; CANR 15; DLB 68

Glasscock, Amnesia
See Steinbeck, John (Ernst)

Glasser, Ronald J. 1940(?)- **CLC 37**

Glassman, Joyce
See Johnson, Joyce

Glendinning, Victoria 1937- **CLC 50**
See also CA 120; 127; CANR 59, 89; DLB 155

Glissant, Edouard 1928- **CLC 10, 68; DAM MULT**
See also CA 153

Gloag, Julian 1930- **CLC 40**
See also AITN 1; CA 65-68; CANR 10, 70

Glowacki, Aleksander
See Prus, Boleslaw

Gluck, Louise (Elisabeth) 1943- **CLC 7, 22, 44, 81; DAM POET; PC 16**
See also CA 33-36R; CANR 40, 69; DA3; DLB 5; MTCW 2

Glyn, Elinor 1864-1943 **TCLC 72**
See also DLB 153

Gobineau, Joseph Arthur (Comte) de 1816-1882 **NCLC 17**
See also DLB 123

Godard, Jean-Luc 1930- **CLC 20**
See also CA 93-96

Godden, (Margaret) Rumer 1907-1998 **CLC 53**
See also AAYA 6; CA 5-8R; 172; CANR 4, 27, 36, 55, 80; CLR 20; DLB 161; MAICYA; SAAS 12; SATA 3, 36; SATA-Obit 109

Godoy Alcayaga, Lucila 1889-1957
See Mistral, Gabriela
See also BW 2; CA 104; 131; CANR 81; DAM MULT; HW 1, 2; MTCW 1, 2

Godwin, Gail (Kathleen) 1937- **CLC 5, 8, 22, 31, 69, 125; DAM POP**
See also CA 29-32R; CANR 15, 43, 69; DA3; DLB 6; INT CANR-15; MTCW 1, 2

Godwin, William 1756-1836 **NCLC 14**
See also CDBLB 1789-1832; DLB 39, 104, 142, 158, 163

Goebbels, Josef
See Goebbels, (Paul) Joseph

Goebbels, (Paul) Joseph 1897-1945 **TCLC 68**
See also CA 115; 148

Goebbels, Joseph Paul
See Goebbels, (Paul) Joseph

Goethe, Johann Wolfgang von 1749-1832 **NCLC 4, 22, 34; DA; DAB; DAC; DAM DRAM, MST, POET; PC 5; SSC 38; WLC**
See also DA3; DLB 94

Gogarty, Oliver St. John 1878-1957 **TCLC 15**
See also CA 109; 150; DLB 15, 19

Gogol, Nikolai (Vasilyevich) 1809-1852 **NCLC 5, 15, 31; DA; DAB; DAC; DAM DRAM, MST; DC 1; SSC 4, 29; WLC**
See also DLB 198

Goines, Donald 1937(?)-1974 **CLC 80; BLC 2; DAM MULT, POP**
See also AITN 1; BW 1, 3; CA 124; 114; CANR 82; DA3; DLB 33

Gold, Herbert 1924- **CLC 4, 7, 14, 42**
See also CA 9-12R; CANR 17, 45; DLB 2; DLBY 81

Goldbarth, Albert 1948- **CLC 5, 38**
See also CA 53-56; CANR 6, 40; DLB 120

Goldberg, Anatol 1910-1982 **CLC 34**
See also CA 131; 117

Goldemberg, Isaac 1945- **CLC 52**
See also CA 69-72; CAAS 12; CANR 11, 32; HW 1

Golding, William (Gerald) 1911-1993 **CLC 1, 2, 3, 8, 10, 17, 27, 58, 81; DA; DAB; DAC; DAM MST, NOV; WLC**
See also AAYA 5; CA 5-8R; 141; CANR 13, 33, 54; CDBLB 1945-1960; DA3; DLB 15, 100; MTCW 1, 2

Goldman, Emma 1869-1940 **TCLC 13**
See also CA 110; 150; DLB 221

Goldman, Francisco 1954- **CLC 76**
See also CA 162

Goldman, William (W.) 1931- **CLC 1, 48**
See also CA 9-12R; CANR 29, 69; DLB 44

Goldmann, Lucien 1913-1970 **CLC 24**
See also CA 25-28; CAP 2

Goldoni, Carlo 1707-1793 **LC 4; DAM DRAM**

Goldsberry, Steven 1949- **CLC 34**
See also CA 131

Goldsmith, Oliver 1728-1774 **LC 2, 48; DA; DAB; DAC; DAM DRAM, MST, NOV, POET; DC 8; WLC**
See also CDBLB 1660-1789; DLB 39, 89, 104, 109, 142; SATA 26

Goldsmith, Peter
See Priestley, J(ohn) B(oynton)

Gombrowicz, Witold 1904-1969 **CLC 4, 7, 11, 49; DAM DRAM**
See also CA 19-20; 25-28R; CAP 2

Gomez de la Serna, Ramon 1888-1963 **CLC 9**
See also CA 153; 116; CANR 79; HW 1, 2

Goncharov, Ivan Alexandrovich 1812-1891 **NCLC 1, 63**

Goncourt, Edmond (Louis Antoine Huot) de 1822-1896 **NCLC 7**
See also DLB 123

Goncourt, Jules (Alfred Huot) de 1830-1870 **NCLC 7**
See also DLB 123

Gontier, Fernande 19(?)- **CLC 50**

Gonzalez Martinez, Enrique 1871-1952 **TCLC 72**
See also CA 166; CANR 81; HW 1, 2

Goodman, Paul 1911-1972 **CLC 1, 2, 4, 7**
See also CA 19-20; 37-40R; CANR 34; CAP 2; DLB 130; MTCW 1

Gordimer, Nadine 1923- **CLC 3, 5, 7, 10, 18, 33, 51, 70; DA; DAB; DAC; DAM MST, NOV; SSC 17; WLCS**
See also CA 5-8R; CANR 3, 28, 56, 88; DA3; INT CANR-28; MTCW 1, 2

Gordon, Adam Lindsay 1833-1870 **NCLC 21**
Gordon, Caroline 1895-1981 **CLC 6, 13, 29, 83; SSC 15**
　　See also CA 11-12; 103; CANR 36; CAP 1; DLB 4, 9, 102; DLBD 17; DLBY 81; MTCW 1, 2
Gordon, Charles William 1860-1937
　　See Connor, Ralph
　　See also CA 109
Gordon, Mary (Catherine) 1949- **CLC 13, 22, 128**
　　See also CA 102; CANR 44; DLB 6; DLBY 81; INT 102; MTCW 1
Gordon, N. J.
　　See Bosman, Herman Charles
Gordon, Sol 1923- **CLC 26**
　　See also CA 53-56; CANR 4; SATA 11
Gordone, Charles 1925-1995 **CLC 1, 4; DAM DRAM; DC 8**
　　See also BW 1, 3; CA 93-96; 180; 150; CAAE 180; CANR 55; DLB 7; INT 93-96; MTCW 1
Gore, Catherine 1800-1861 **NCLC 65**
　　See also DLB 116
Gorenko, Anna Andreevna
　　See Akhmatova, Anna
Gorky, Maxim 1868-1936 **TCLC 8; DAB; SSC 28; WLC**
　　See also Peshkov, Alexei Maximovich
　　See also MTCW 2
Goryan, Sirak
　　See Saroyan, William
Gosse, Edmund (William) 1849-1928 **TCLC 28**
　　See also CA 117; DLB 57, 144, 184
Gotlieb, Phyllis Fay (Bloom) 1926- **CLC 18**
　　See also CA 13-16R; CANR 7; DLB 88
Gottesman, S. D.
　　See Kornbluth, C(yril) M.; Pohl, Frederik
Gottfried von Strassburg fl. c. 1210- **CMLC 10**
　　See also DLB 138
Gould, Lois CLC 4, 10
　　See also CA 77-80; CANR 29; MTCW 1
Gourmont, Remy (-Marie-Charles) de 1858-1915 **TCLC 17**
　　See also CA 109; 150; MTCW 2
Govier, Katherine 1948- **CLC 51**
　　See also CA 101; CANR 18, 40
Goyen, (Charles) William 1915-1983 **CLC 5, 8, 14, 40**
　　See also AITN 2; CA 5-8R; 110; CANR 6, 71; DLB 2; DLBY 83; INT CANR-6
Goytisolo, Juan 1931- **CLC 5, 10, 23; DAM MULT; HLC 1**
　　See also CA 85-88; CANR 32, 61; HW 1, 2; MTCW 1, 2
Gozzano, Guido 1883-1916 **PC 10**
　　See also CA 154; DLB 114
Gozzi, (Conte) Carlo 1720-1806 **NCLC 23**
Grabbe, Christian Dietrich 1801-1836 **NCLC 2**
　　See also DLB 133
Grace, Patricia Frances 1937- **CLC 56**
　　See also CA 176
Gracian y Morales, Baltasar 1601-1658 **LC 15**
Gracq, Julien CLC 11, 48
　　See also Poirier, Louis
　　See also DLB 83
Grade, Chaim 1910-1982 **CLC 10**
　　See also CA 93-96; 107
Graduate of Oxford, A
　　See Ruskin, John
Grafton, Garth
　　See Duncan, Sara Jeannette

Graham, John
　　See Phillips, David Graham
Graham, Jorie 1951- **CLC 48, 118**
　　See also CA 111; CANR 63; DLB 120
Graham, R(obert) B(ontine) Cunninghame
　　See Cunninghame Graham, Robert (Gallnigad) Bontine
　　See also DLB 98, 135, 174
Graham, Robert
　　See Haldeman, Joe (William)
Graham, Tom
　　See Lewis, (Harry) Sinclair
Graham, W(illiam) S(ydney) 1918-1986 **CLC 29**
　　See also CA 73-76; 118; DLB 20
Graham, Winston (Mawdsley) 1910- **CLC 23**
　　See also CA 49-52; CANR 2, 22, 45, 66; DLB 77
Grahame, Kenneth 1859-1932 **TCLC 64; DAB**
　　See also CA 108; 136; CANR 80; CLR 5; DA3; DLB 34, 141, 178; MAICYA; MTCW 2; SATA 100; YABC 1
Granovsky, Timofei Nikolaevich 1813-1855 **NCLC 75**
　　See also DLB 198
Grant, Skeeter
　　See Spiegelman, Art
Granville-Barker, Harley 1877-1946 **TCLC 2; DAM DRAM**
　　See also Barker, Harley Granville
　　See also CA 104
Grass, Guenter (Wilhelm) 1927- **CLC 1, 2, 4, 6, 11, 15, 22, 32, 49, 88; DA; DAB; DAC; DAM MST, NOV; WLC**
　　See also CA 13-16R; CANR 20, 75; DA3; DLB 75, 124; MTCW 1, 2
Gratton, Thomas
　　See Hulme, T(homas) E(rnest)
Grau, Shirley Ann 1929- **CLC 4, 9; SSC 15**
　　See also CA 89-92; CANR 22, 69; DLB 2; INT CANR-22; MTCW 1
Gravel, Fern
　　See Hall, James Norman
Graver, Elizabeth 1964- **CLC 70**
　　See also CA 135; CANR 71
Graves, Richard Perceval 1945- **CLC 44**
　　See also CA 65-68; CANR 9, 26, 51
Graves, Robert (von Ranke) 1895-1985 **CLC 1, 2, 6, 11, 39, 44, 45; DAB; DAC; DAM MST, POET; PC 6**
　　See also CA 5-8R; 117; CANR 5, 36; CD-BLB 1914-1945; DA3; DLB 20, 100, 191; DLBD 18; DLBY 85; MTCW 1, 2; SATA 45
Graves, Valerie
　　See Bradley, Marion Zimmer
Gray, Alasdair (James) 1934- **CLC 41**
　　See also CA 126; CANR 47, 69; DLB 194; INT 126; MTCW 1
Gray, Amlin 1946- **CLC 29**
　　See also CA 138
Gray, Francine du Plessix 1930- **CLC 22; DAM NOV**
　　See also BEST 90:3; CA 61-64; CAAS 2; CANR 11, 33, 75, 81; INT CANR-11; MTCW 1, 2
Gray, John (Henry) 1866-1934 **TCLC 19**
　　See also CA 119; 162
Gray, Simon (James Holliday) 1936- **CLC 9, 14, 36**
　　See also AITN 1; CA 21-24R; CAAS 3; CANR 32, 69; DLB 13; MTCW 1
Gray, Spalding 1941- **CLC 49, 112; DAM POP; DC 7**
　　See also CA 128; CANR 74; MTCW 2
Gray, Thomas 1716-1771 **LC 4, 40; DA; DAB; DAC; DAM MST; PC 2; WLC**

　　See also CDBLB 1660-1789; DA3; DLB 109
Grayson, David
　　See Baker, Ray Stannard
Grayson, Richard (A.) 1951- **CLC 38**
　　See also CA 85-88; CANR 14, 31, 57
Greeley, Andrew M(oran) 1928- **CLC 28; DAM POP**
　　See also CA 5-8R; CAAS 7; CANR 7, 43, 69; DA3; MTCW 1, 2
Green, Anna Katharine 1846-1935 **TCLC 63**
　　See also CA 112; 159; DLB 202, 221
Green, Brian
　　See Card, Orson Scott
Green, Hannah
　　See Greenberg, Joanne (Goldenberg)
Green, Hannah 1927(?)-1996 **CLC 3**
　　See also CA 73-76; CANR 59
Green, Henry 1905-1973 **CLC 2, 13, 97**
　　See also Yorke, Henry Vincent
　　See also CA 175; DLB 15
Green, Julian (Hartridge) 1900-1998
　　See Green, Julien
　　See also CA 21-24R; 169; CANR 33, 87; DLB 4, 72; MTCW 1
Green, Julien CLC 3, 11, 77
　　See also Green, Julian (Hartridge)
　　See also MTCW 2
Green, Paul (Eliot) 1894-1981 **CLC 25; DAM DRAM**
　　See also AITN 1; CA 5-8R; 103; CANR 3; DLB 7, 9; DLBY 81
Greenberg, Ivan 1908-1973
　　See Rahv, Philip
　　See also CA 85-88
Greenberg, Joanne (Goldenberg) 1932- **CLC 7, 30**
　　See also AAYA 12; CA 5-8R; CANR 14, 32, 69; SATA 25
Greenberg, Richard 1959(?)- **CLC 57**
　　See also CA 138
Greene, Bette 1934- **CLC 30**
　　See also AAYA 7; CA 53-56; CANR 4; CLR 2; JRDA; MAICYA; SAAS 16; SATA 8, 102
Greene, Gael CLC 8
　　See also CA 13-16R; CANR 10
Greene, Graham (Henry) 1904-1991 **CLC 1, 3, 6, 9, 14, 18, 27, 37, 70, 72, 125; DA; DAB; DAC; DAM MST, NOV; SSC 29; WLC**
　　See also AITN 2; CA 13-16R; 133; CANR 35, 61; CDBLB 1945-1960; DA3; DLB 13, 15, 77, 100, 162, 201, 204; DLBY 91; MTCW 1, 2; SATA 20
Greene, Robert 1558-1592 **LC 41**
　　See also DLB 62, 167
Greer, Germaine 1939- **CLC 131**
　　See also AITN 1; CA 81-84; CANR 33, 70; MTCW 1, 2
Greer, Richard
　　See Silverberg, Robert
Gregor, Arthur 1923- **CLC 9**
　　See also CA 25-28R; CAAS 10; CANR 11; SATA 36
Gregor, Lee
　　See Pohl, Frederik
Gregory, Isabella Augusta (Persse) 1852-1932 **TCLC 1**
　　See also CA 104; 184; DLB 10
Gregory, J. Dennis
　　See Williams, John A(lfred)
Grendon, Stephen
　　See Derleth, August (William)
Grenville, Kate 1950- **CLC 61**
　　See also CA 118; CANR 53
Grenville, Pelham
　　See Wodehouse, P(elham) G(renville)

Greve, Felix Paul (Berthold Friedrich)
1879-1948
See Grove, Frederick Philip
See also CA 104; 141, 175; CANR 79;
DAC; DAM MST

Grey, Zane 1872-1939 **TCLC 6; DAM POP**
See also CA 104; 132; DA3; DLB 212;
MTCW 1, 2

Grieg, (Johan) Nordahl (Brun) 1902-1943
TCLC 10
See also CA 107

Grieve, C(hristopher) M(urray) 1892-1978
CLC 11, 19; DAM POET
See also MacDiarmid, Hugh; Pteleon
See also CA 5-8R; 85-88; CANR 33;
MTCW 1

Griffin, Gerald 1803-1840 **NCLC 7**
See also DLB 159

Griffin, John Howard 1920-1980 **CLC 68**
See also AITN 1; CA 1-4R; 101; CANR 2

Griffin, Peter 1942- **CLC 39**
See also CA 136

Griffith, D(avid Lewelyn) W(ark)
1875(?)-1948 **TCLC 68**
See also CA 119; 150; CANR 80

Griffith, Lawrence
See Griffith, D(avid Lewelyn) W(ark)

Griffiths, Trevor 1935- **CLC 13, 52**
See also CA 97-100; CANR 45; DLB 13

Griggs, Sutton (Elbert) 1872-1930 **TCLC 77**
See also CA 123; 186; DLB 50

Grigson, Geoffrey (Edward Harvey)
1905-1985 **CLC 7, 39**
See also CA 25-28R; 118; CANR 20, 33;
DLB 27; MTCW 1, 2

Grillparzer, Franz 1791-1872 **NCLC 1; SSC
37**
See also DLB 133

Grimble, Reverend Charles James
See Eliot, T(homas) S(tearns)

Grimke, Charlotte L(ottie) Forten
1837(?)-1914
See Forten, Charlotte L.
See also BW 1; CA 117; 124; DAM MULT,
POET

Grimm, Jacob Ludwig Karl 1785-1863
NCLC 3, 77; SSC 36
See also DLB 90; MAICYA; SATA 22

Grimm, Wilhelm Karl 1786-1859 **NCLC 3,
77; SSC 36**
See also DLB 90; MAICYA; SATA 22

**Grimmelshausen, Johann Jakob Christoffel
von** 1621-1676 **LC 6**
See also DLB 168

Grindel, Eugene 1895-1952
See Eluard, Paul
See also CA 104

Grisham, John 1955- **CLC 84; DAM POP**
See also AAYA 14; CA 138; CANR 47, 69;
DA3; MTCW 2

Grossman, David 1954- **CLC 67**
See also CA 138

Grossman, Vasily (Semenovich) 1905-1964
CLC 41
See also CA 124; 130; MTCW 1

Grove, Frederick Philip TCLC 4
See also Greve, Felix Paul (Berthold
Friedrich)
See also DLB 92

Grubb
See Crumb, R(obert)

Grumbach, Doris (Isaac) 1918- **CLC 13, 22,
64**
See also CA 5-8R; CAAS 2; CANR 9, 42,
70; INT CANR-9; MTCW 2

Grundtvig, Nicolai Frederik Severin
1783-1872 **NCLC 1**

Grunge
See Crumb, R(obert)

Grunwald, Lisa 1959- **CLC 44**
See also CA 120

Guare, John 1938- **CLC 8, 14, 29, 67; DAM
DRAM**
See also CA 73-76; CANR 21, 69; DLB 7;
MTCW 1, 2

Gudjonsson, Halldor Kiljan 1902-1998
See Laxness, Halldor
See also CA 103; 164

Guenter, Erich
See Eich, Guenter

Guest, Barbara 1920- **CLC 34**
See also CA 25-28R; CANR 11, 44, 84;
DLB 5, 193

Guest, Edgar A(lbert) 1881-1959 **TCLC 95**
See also CA 112; 168

Guest, Judith (Ann) 1936- **CLC 8, 30; DAM
NOV, POP**
See also AAYA 7; CA 77-80; CANR 15,
75; DA3; INT CANR-15; MTCW 1, 2

Guevara, Che CLC 87; HLC 1
See also Guevara (Serna), Ernesto

Guevara (Serna), Ernesto 1928-1967 **CLC
87; DAM MULT; HLC 1**
See also Guevara, Che
See also CA 127; 111; CANR 56; HW 1

Guicciardini, Francesco 1483-1540 **LC 49**

Guild, Nicholas M. 1944- **CLC 33**
See also CA 93-96

Guillemin, Jacques
See Sartre, Jean-Paul

Guillen, Jorge 1893-1984 **CLC 11; DAM
MULT, POET; HLCS 1**
See also CA 89-92; 112; DLB 108; HW 1

Guillen, Nicolas (Cristobal) 1902-1989 **CLC
48, 79; BLC 2; DAM MST, MULT,
POET; HLC 1; PC 23**
See also BW 2; CA 116; 125; 129; CANR
84; HW 1

Guillevic, (Eugene) 1907- **CLC 33**
See also CA 93-96

Guillois
See Desnos, Robert

Guillois, Valentin
See Desnos, Robert

Guimaraes Rosa, Joao 1908-1967
See also CA 175; HLCS 2

Guiney, Louise Imogen 1861-1920 **TCLC 41**
See also CA 160; DLB 54

Guiraldes, Ricardo (Guillermo) 1886-1927
TCLC 39
See also CA 131; HW 1; MTCW 1

Gumilev, Nikolai (Stepanovich) 1886-1921
TCLC 60
See also CA 165

Gunesekera, Romesh 1954- **CLC 91**
See also CA 159

Gunn, Bill CLC 5
See also Gunn, William Harrison
See also DLB 38

Gunn, Thom(son William) 1929- **CLC 3, 6,
18, 32, 81; DAM POET; PC 26**
See also CA 17-20R; CANR 9, 33; CDBLB
1960 to Present; DLB 27; INT CANR-33;
MTCW 1

Gunn, William Harrison 1934(?)-1989
See Gunn, Bill
See also AITN 1; BW 1, 3; CA 13-16R;
128; CANR 12, 25, 76

Gunnars, Kristjana 1948- **CLC 69**
See also CA 113; DLB 60

Gurdjieff, G(eorgei) I(vanovich)
1877(?)-1949 **TCLC 71**
See also CA 157

Gurganus, Allan 1947- **CLC 70; DAM POP**
See also BEST 90:1; CA 135

Gurney, A(lbert) R(amsdell), Jr. 1930- **CLC
32, 50, 54; DAM DRAM**
See also CA 77-80; CANR 32, 64

Gurney, Ivor (Bertie) 1890-1937 **TCLC 33**
See also CA 167

Gurney, Peter
See Gurney, A(lbert) R(amsdell), Jr.

Guro, Elena 1877-1913 **TCLC 56**

Gustafson, James M(oody) 1925- **CLC 100**
See also CA 25-28R; CANR 37

Gustafson, Ralph (Barker) 1909- **CLC 36**
See also CA 21-24R; CANR 8, 45, 84; DLB
88

Gut, Gom
See Simenon, Georges (Jacques Christian)

Guterson, David 1956- **CLC 91**
See also CA 132; CANR 73; MTCW 2

Guthrie, A(lfred) B(ertram), Jr. 1901-1991
CLC 23
See also CA 57-60; 134; CANR 24; DLB
212; SATA 62; SATA-Obit 67

Guthrie, Isobel
See Grieve, C(hristopher) M(urray)

Guthrie, Woodrow Wilson 1912-1967
See Guthrie, Woody
See also CA 113; 93-96

Guthrie, Woody CLC 35
See also Guthrie, Woodrow Wilson

Gutierrez Najera, Manuel 1859-1895
See also HLCS 2

Guy, Rosa (Cuthbert) 1928- **CLC 26**
See also AAYA 4; BW 2; CA 17-20R;
CANR 14, 34, 83; CLR 13; DLB 33;
JRDA; MAICYA; SATA 14, 62

Gwendolyn
See Bennett, (Enoch) Arnold

H. D. CLC 3, 8, 14, 31, 34, 73; PC 5
See also Doolittle, Hilda

H. de V.
See Buchan, John

Haavikko, Paavo Juhani 1931- **CLC 18, 34**
See also CA 106

Habbema, Koos
See Heijermans, Herman

Habermas, Juergen 1929- **CLC 104**
See also CA 109; CANR 85

Habermas, Jurgen
See Habermas, Juergen

Hacker, Marilyn 1942- **CLC 5, 9, 23, 72, 91;
DAM POET**
See also CA 77-80; CANR 68; DLB 120

Haeckel, Ernst Heinrich (Philipp August)
1834-1919 **TCLC 83**
See also CA 157

Hafiz c. 1326-1389(?) **CMLC 34**

Hafiz c. 1326-1389 **CMLC 34**

Haggard, H(enry) Rider 1856-1925 **TCLC 11**
See also CA 108; 148; DLB 70, 156, 174,
178; MTCW 2; SATA 16

Hagiosy, L.
See Larbaud, Valery (Nicolas)

Hagiwara Sakutaro 1886-1942 **TCLC 60; PC
18**

Haig, Fenil
See Ford, Ford Madox

Haig-Brown, Roderick (Langmere)
1908-1976 **CLC 21**
See also CA 5-8R; 69-72; CANR 4, 38, 83;
CLR 31; DLB 88; MAICYA; SATA 12

Hailey, Arthur 1920- **CLC 5; DAM NOV,
POP**
See also AITN 2; BEST 90:3; CA 1-4R;
CANR 2, 36, 75; DLB 88; DLBY 82;
MTCW 1, 2

Hailey, Elizabeth Forsythe 1938- **CLC 40**
See also CA 93-96; CAAS 1; CANR 15,
48; INT CANR-15

Haines, John (Meade) 1924- **CLC 58**

See also CA 17-20R; CANR 13, 34; DLB 212

Hakluyt, Richard 1552-1616 **LC 31**

Haldeman, Joe (William) 1943- **CLC 61**
See also Graham, Robert
See also CA 53-56, 179; CAAE 179; CAAS 25; CANR 6, 70, 72; DLB 8; INT CANR-6

Hale, Sarah Josepha (Buell) 1788-1879 **NCLC 75**
See also DLB 1, 42, 73

Haley, Alex(ander Murray Palmer) 1921-1992 **CLC 8, 12, 76; BLC 2; DA; DAB; DAC; DAM MST, MULT, POP**
See also AAYA 26; BW 2, 3; CA 77-80; 136; CANR 61; CDALBS; DA3; DLB 38; MTCW 1, 2

Haliburton, Thomas Chandler 1796-1865 **NCLC 15**
See also DLB 11, 99

Hall, Donald (Andrew, Jr.) 1928- **CLC 1, 13, 37, 59; DAM POET**
See also CA 5-8R; CAAS 7; CANR 2, 44, 64; DLB 5; MTCW 1; SATA 23, 97

Hall, Frederic Sauser
See Sauser-Hall, Frederic

Hall, James
See Kuttner, Henry

Hall, James Norman 1887-1951 **TCLC 23**
See also CA 123; 173; SATA 21

Hall, Radclyffe
See Hall, (Marguerite) Radclyffe
See also MTCW 2

Hall, (Marguerite) Radclyffe 1886-1943 **TCLC 12**
See also CA 110; 150; CANR 83; DLB 191

Hall, Rodney 1935- **CLC 51**
See also CA 109; CANR 69

Halleck, Fitz-Greene 1790-1867 **NCLC 47**
See also DLB 3

Halliday, Michael
See Creasey, John

Halpern, Daniel 1945- **CLC 14**
See also CA 33-36R

Hamburger, Michael (Peter Leopold) 1924- **CLC 5, 14**
See also CA 5-8R; CAAS 4; CANR 2, 47; DLB 27

Hamill, Pete 1935- **CLC 10**
See also CA 25-28R; CANR 18, 71

Hamilton, Alexander 1755(?)-1804 **NCLC 49**
See also DLB 37

Hamilton, Clive
See Lewis, C(live) S(taples)

Hamilton, Edmond 1904-1977 **CLC 1**
See also CA 1-4R; CANR 3, 84; DLB 8

Hamilton, Eugene (Jacob) Lee
See Lee-Hamilton, Eugene (Jacob)

Hamilton, Franklin
See Silverberg, Robert

Hamilton, Gail
See Corcoran, Barbara

Hamilton, Mollie
See Kaye, M(ary) M(argaret)

Hamilton, (Anthony Walter) Patrick 1904-1962 **CLC 51**
See also CA 176; 113; DLB 191

Hamilton, Virginia 1936- **CLC 26; DAM MULT**
See also AAYA 2, 21; BW 2, 3; CA 25-28R; CANR 20, 37, 73; CLR 1, 11, 40; DLB 33, 52; INT CANR-20; JRDA; MAICYA; MTCW 1, 2; SATA 4, 56, 79

Hammett, (Samuel) Dashiell 1894-1961 **CLC 3, 5, 10, 19, 47; SSC 17**
See also AITN 1; CA 81-84; CANR 42; CDALB 1929-1941; DA3; DLBD 6; DLBY 96; MTCW 1, 2

Hammon, Jupiter 1711(?)-1800(?) **NCLC 5;**

BLC 2; DAM MULT, POET; PC 16
See also DLB 31, 50

Hammond, Keith
See Kuttner, Henry

Hamner, Earl (Henry), Jr. 1923- **CLC 12**
See also AITN 2; CA 73-76; DLB 6

Hampton, Christopher (James) 1946- **CLC 4**
See also CA 25-28R; DLB 13; MTCW 1

Hamsun, Knut TCLC 2, 14, 49
See also Pedersen, Knut

Handke, Peter 1942- **CLC 5, 8, 10, 15, 38; DAM DRAM, NOV**
See also CA 77-80; CANR 33, 75; DLB 85, 124; MTCW 1, 2

Handy, W(illiam) C(hristopher) 1873-1958 **TCLC 97**
See also BW 3; CA 121; 167

Hanley, James 1901-1985 **CLC 3, 5, 8, 13**
See also CA 73-76; 117; CANR 36; DLB 191; MTCW 1

Hannah, Barry 1942- **CLC 23, 38, 90**
See also CA 108; 110; CANR 43, 68; DLB 6; INT 110; MTCW 1

Hannon, Ezra
See Hunter, Evan

Hansberry, Lorraine (Vivian) 1930-1965 **CLC 17, 62; BLC 2; DA; DAB; DAC; DAM DRAM, MST, MULT; DC 2**
See also AAYA 25; BW 1, 3; CA 109; 25-28R; CABS 3; CANR 58; CDALB 1941-1968; DA3; DLB 7, 38; MTCW 1, 2

Hansen, Joseph 1923- **CLC 38**
See also CA 29-32R; CAAS 17; CANR 16, 44, 66; INT CANR-16

Hansen, Martin A(lfred) 1909-1955 **TCLC 32**
See also CA 167

Hanson, Kenneth O(stlin) 1922- **CLC 13**
See also CA 53-56; CANR 7

Hardwick, Elizabeth (Bruce) 1916- **CLC 13; DAM NOV**
See also CA 5-8R; CANR 3, 32, 70; DA3; DLB 6; MTCW 1, 2

Hardy, Thomas 1840-1928 **TCLC 4, 10, 18, 32, 48, 53, 72; DA; DAB; DAC; DAM MST, NOV, POET; PC 8; SSC 2; WLC**
See also CA 104; 123; CDBLB 1890-1914; DA3; DLB 18, 19, 135; MTCW 1, 2

Hare, David 1947- **CLC 29, 58**
See also CA 97-100; CANR 39, 91; DLB 13; MTCW 1

Harewood, John
See Van Druten, John (William)

Harford, Henry
See Hudson, W(illiam) H(enry)

Hargrave, Leonie
See Disch, Thomas M(ichael)

Harjo, Joy 1951- **CLC 83; DAM MULT; PC 27**
See also CA 114; CANR 35, 67, 91; DLB 120, 175; MTCW 2; NNAL

Harlan, Louis R(udolph) 1922- **CLC 34**
See also CA 21-24R; CANR 25, 55, 80

Harling, Robert 1951(?)- **CLC 53**
See also CA 147

Harmon, William (Ruth) 1938- **CLC 38**
See also CA 33-36R; CANR 14, 32, 35; SATA 65

Harper, F. E. W.
See Harper, Frances Ellen Watkins

Harper, Frances E. W.
See Harper, Frances Ellen Watkins

Harper, Frances E. Watkins
See Harper, Frances Ellen Watkins

Harper, Frances Ellen
See Harper, Frances Ellen Watkins

Harper, Frances Ellen Watkins 1825-1911 **TCLC 14; BLC 2; DAM MULT, POET; PC 21**

See also BW 1, 3; CA 111; 125; CANR 79; DLB 50, 221

Harper, Michael S(teven) 1938- **CLC 7, 22**
See also BW 1; CA 33-36R; CANR 24; DLB 41

Harper, Mrs. F. E. W.
See Harper, Frances Ellen Watkins

Harris, Christie (Lucy) Irwin 1907- **CLC 12**
See also CA 5-8R; CANR 6, 83; CLR 47; DLB 88; JRDA; MAICYA; SAAS 10; SATA 6, 74; SATA-Essay 116

Harris, Frank 1856-1931 **TCLC 24**
See also CA 109; 150; CANR 80; DLB 156, 197

Harris, George Washington 1814-1869 **NCLC 23**
See also DLB 3, 11

Harris, Joel Chandler 1848-1908 **TCLC 2; SSC 19**
See also CA 104; 137; CANR 80; CLR 49; DLB 11, 23, 42, 78, 91; MAICYA; SATA 100; YABC 1

Harris, John (Wyndham Parkes Lucas) Beynon 1903-1969
See Wyndham, John
See also CA 102; 89-92; CANR 84

Harris, MacDonald CLC 9
See also Heiney, Donald (William)

Harris, Mark 1922- **CLC 19**
See also CA 5-8R; CAAS 3; CANR 2, 55, 83; DLB 2; DLBY 80

Harris, (Theodore) Wilson 1921- **CLC 25**
See also BW 2, 3; CA 65-68; CAAS 16; CANR 11, 27, 69; DLB 117; MTCW 1

Harrison, Elizabeth Cavanna 1909-
See Cavanna, Betty
See also CA 9-12R; CANR 6, 27, 85

Harrison, Harry (Max) 1925- **CLC 42**
See also CA 1-4R; CANR 5, 21, 84; DLB 8; SATA 4

Harrison, James (Thomas) 1937- **CLC 6, 14, 33, 66; SSC 19**
See also CA 13-16R; CANR 8, 51, 79; DLBY 82; INT CANR-8

Harrison, Jim
See Harrison, James (Thomas)

Harrison, Kathryn 1961- **CLC 70**
See also CA 144; CANR 68

Harrison, Tony 1937- **CLC 43, 129**
See also CA 65-68; CANR 44; DLB 40; MTCW 1

Harriss, Will(ard Irvin) 1922- **CLC 34**
See also CA 111

Harson, Sley
See Ellison, Harlan (Jay)

Hart, Ellis
See Ellison, Harlan (Jay)

Hart, Josephine 1942(?)- **CLC 70; DAM POP**
See also CA 138; CANR 70

Hart, Moss 1904-1961 **CLC 66; DAM DRAM**
See also CA 109; 89-92; CANR 84; DLB 7

Harte, (Francis) Bret(t) 1836(?)-1902 **TCLC 1, 25; DA; DAC; DAM MST; SSC 8; WLC**
See also CA 104; 140; CANR 80; CDALB 1865-1917; DA3; DLB 12, 64, 74, 79, 186; SATA 26

Hartley, L(eslie) P(oles) 1895-1972 **CLC 2, 22**
See also CA 45-48; 37-40R; CANR 33; DLB 15, 139; MTCW 1, 2

Hartman, Geoffrey H. 1929- **CLC 27**
See also CA 117; 125; CANR 79; DLB 67

Hartmann, Sadakichi 1867-1944 **TCLC 73**
See also CA 157; DLB 54

Hartmann von Aue c. 1160-c. 1205 **CMLC 15**
See also DLB 138

Hartmann von Aue 1170-1210 **CMLC 15**

Haruf, Kent 1943- **CLC 34**
See also CA 149; CANR 91

Harwood, Ronald 1934- **CLC 32; DAM DRAM, MST**
See also CA 1-4R; CANR 4, 55; DLB 13

Hasegawa Tatsunosuke
See Futabatei, Shimei

Hasek, Jaroslav (Matej Frantisek) 1883-1923 **TCLC 4**
See also CA 104; 129; MTCW 1, 2

Hass, Robert 1941- **CLC 18, 39, 99; PC 16**
See also CA 111; CANR 30, 50, 71; DLB 105, 206; SATA 94

Hastings, Hudson
See Kuttner, Henry

Hastings, Selina CLC 44

Hathorne, John 1641-1717 **LC 38**

Hatteras, Amelia
See Mencken, H(enry) L(ouis)

Hatteras, Owen TCLC 18
See also Mencken, H(enry) L(ouis); Nathan, George Jean

Hauptmann, Gerhart (Johann Robert) 1862-1946 **TCLC 4; DAM DRAM; SSC 37**
See also CA 104; 153; DLB 66, 118

Havel, Vaclav 1936- **CLC 25, 58, 65; DAM DRAM; DC 6**
See also CA 104; CANR 36, 63; DA3; MTCW 1, 2

Haviaras, Stratis CLC 33
See also Chaviaras, Strates

Hawes, Stephen 1475(?)-1523(?) **LC 17**
See also DLB 132

Hawkes, John (Clendennin Burne, Jr.) 1925-1998 **CLC 1, 2, 3, 4, 7, 9, 14, 15, 27, 49**
See also CA 1-4R; 167; CANR 2, 47, 64; DLB 2, 7; DLBY 80, 98; MTCW 1, 2

Hawking, S. W.
See Hawking, Stephen W(illiam)

Hawking, Stephen W(illiam) 1942- **CLC 63, 105**
See also AAYA 13; BEST 89:1; CA 126; 129; CANR 48; DA3; MTCW 2

Hawkins, Anthony Hope
See Hope, Anthony

Hawthorne, Julian 1846-1934 **TCLC 25**
See also CA 165

Hawthorne, Nathaniel 1804-1864 **NCLC 39; DA; DAB; DAC; DAM MST, NOV; SSC 3, 29, 39; WLC**
See also AAYA 18; CDALB 1640-1865; DA3; DLB 1, 74, 223; YABC 2

Haxton, Josephine Ayres 1921-
See Douglas, Ellen
See also CA 115; CANR 41, 83

Hayaseca y Eizaguirre, Jorge
See Echegaray (y Eizaguirre), Jose (Maria Waldo)

Hayashi, Fumiko 1904-1951 **TCLC 27**
See also CA 161; DLB 180

Haycraft, Anna (Margaret) 1932-
See Ellis, Alice Thomas
See also CA 122; CANR 85, 90; MTCW 2

Hayden, Robert E(arl) 1913-1980 **CLC 5, 9, 14, 37; BLC 2; DA; DAC; DAM MST, MULT, POET; PC 6**
See also BW 1, 3; CA 69-72; 97-100; CABS 2; CANR 24, 75, 82; CDALB 1941-1968; DLB 5, 76; MTCW 1, 2; SATA 19; SATA-Obit 26

Hayford, J(oseph) E(phraim) Casely
See Casely-Hayford, J(oseph) E(phraim)

Hayman, Ronald 1932- **CLC 44**
See also CA 25-28R; CANR 18, 50, 88; DLB 155

Haywood, Eliza (Fowler) 1693(?)-1756 **LC 1, 44**

See also DLB 39

Hazlitt, William 1778-1830 **NCLC 29, 82**
See also DLB 110, 158

Hazzard, Shirley 1931- **CLC 18**
See also CA 9-12R; CANR 4, 70; DLBY 82; MTCW 1

Head, Bessie 1937-1986 **CLC 25, 67; BLC 2; DAM MULT**
See also BW 2, 3; CA 29-32R; 119; CANR 25, 82; DA3; DLB 117; MTCW 1, 2

Headon, (Nicky) Topper 1956(?)- **CLC 30**

Heaney, Seamus (Justin) 1939- **CLC 5, 7, 14, 25, 37, 74, 91; DAB; DAM POET; PC 18; WLCS**
See also CA 85-88; CANR 25, 48, 75, 91; CDBLB 1960 to Present; DA3; DLB 40; DLBY 95; MTCW 1, 2

Hearn, (Patricio) Lafcadio (Tessima Carlos) 1850-1904 **TCLC 9**
See also CA 105; 166; DLB 12, 78, 189

Hearne, Vicki 1946- **CLC 56**
See also CA 139

Hearon, Shelby 1931- **CLC 63**
See also AITN 2; CA 25-28R; CANR 18, 48

Heat-Moon, William Least CLC 29
See also Trogdon, William (Lewis)
See also AAYA 9

Hebbel, Friedrich 1813-1863 **NCLC 43; DAM DRAM**
See also DLB 129

Hebert, Anne 1916- **CLC 4, 13, 29; DAC; DAM MST, POET**
See also CA 85-88; CANR 69; DA3; DLB 68; MTCW 1, 2

Hecht, Anthony (Evan) 1923- **CLC 8, 13, 19; DAM POET**
See also CA 9-12R; CANR 6; DLB 5, 169

Hecht, Ben 1894-1964 **CLC 8**
See also CA 85-88; DLB 7, 9, 25, 26, 28, 86

Hedayat, Sadeq 1903-1951 **TCLC 21**
See also CA 120

Hegel, Georg Wilhelm Friedrich 1770-1831 **NCLC 46**
See also DLB 90

Heidegger, Martin 1889-1976 **CLC 24**
See also CA 81-84; 65-68; CANR 34; MTCW 1, 2

Heidenstam, (Carl Gustaf) Verner von 1859-1940 **TCLC 5**
See also CA 104

Heifner, Jack 1946- **CLC 11**
See also CA 105; CANR 47

Heijermans, Herman 1864-1924 **TCLC 24**
See also CA 123

Heilbrun, Carolyn G(old) 1926- **CLC 25**
See also CA 45-48; CANR 1, 28, 58

Heine, Heinrich 1797-1856 **NCLC 4, 54; PC 25**
See also DLB 90

Heinemann, Larry (Curtiss) 1944- **CLC 50**
See also CA 110; CAAS 21; CANR 31, 81; DLBD 9; INT CANR-31

Heiney, Donald (William) 1921-1993
See Harris, MacDonald
See also CA 1-4R; 142; CANR 3, 58

Heinlein, Robert A(nson) 1907-1988 **CLC 1, 3, 8, 14, 26, 55; DAM POP**
See also AAYA 17; CA 1-4R; 125; CANR 1, 20, 53; DA3; DLB 8; JRDA; MAICYA; MTCW 1, 2; SATA 9, 69; SATA-Obit 56

Helforth, John
See Doolittle, Hilda

Hellenhofferu, Vojtech Kapristian z
See Hasek, Jaroslav (Matej Frantisek)

Heller, Joseph 1923- **CLC 1, 3, 5, 8, 11, 36, 63; DA; DAB; DAC; DAM MST, NOV, POP; WLC**

See also AAYA 24; AITN 1; CA 5-8R; CABS 1; CANR 8, 42, 66; DA3; DLB 2, 28; DLBY 80; INT CANR-8; MTCW 1, 2

Hellman, Lillian (Florence) 1906-1984 **CLC 2, 4, 8, 14, 18, 34, 44, 52; DAM DRAM; DC 1**
See also AITN 1, 2; CA 13-16R; 112; CANR 33; DA3; DLB 7; DLBY 84; MTCW 1, 2

Helprin, Mark 1947- **CLC 7, 10, 22, 32; DAM NOV, POP**
See also CA 81-84; CANR 47, 64; CDALBS; DA3; DLBY 85; MTCW 1, 2

Helvetius, Claude-Adrien 1715-1771 **LC 26**

Helyar, Jane Penelope Josephine 1933-
See Poole, Josephine
See also CA 21-24R; CANR 10, 26; SATA 82

Hemans, Felicia 1793-1835 **NCLC 71**
See also DLB 96

Hemingway, Ernest (Miller) 1899-1961 **CLC 1, 3, 6, 8, 10, 13, 19, 30, 34, 39, 41, 44, 50, 61, 80; DA; DAB; DAC; DAM MST, NOV; SSC 1, 25, 36, 40; WLC**
See also AAYA 19; CA 77-80; CANR 34; CDALB 1917-1929; DA3; DLB 4, 9, 102, 210; DLBD 1, 15, 16; DLBY 81, 87, 96, 98; MTCW 1, 2

Hempel, Amy 1951- **CLC 39**
See also CA 118; 137; CANR 70; DA3; MTCW 2

Henderson, F. C.
See Mencken, H(enry) L(ouis)

Henderson, Sylvia
See Ashton-Warner, Sylvia (Constance)

Henderson, Zenna (Chlarson) 1917-1983 **SSC 29**
See also CA 1-4R; 133; CANR 1, 84; DLB 8; SATA 5

Henkin, Joshua CLC 119
See also CA 161

Henley, Beth CLC 23; DC 6
See also Henley, Elizabeth Becker
See also CABS 3; DLBY 86

Henley, Elizabeth Becker 1952-
See Henley, Beth
See also CA 107; CANR 32, 73; DAM DRAM, MST; DA3; MTCW 1, 2

Henley, William Ernest 1849-1903 **TCLC 8**
See also CA 105; DLB 19

Hennissart, Martha
See Lathen, Emma
See also CA 85-88; CANR 64

Henry, O. TCLC 1, 19; SSC 5; WLC
See also Porter, William Sydney

Henry, Patrick 1736-1799 **LC 25**

Henryson, Robert 1430(?)-1506(?) **LC 20**
See also DLB 146

Henry VIII 1491-1547 **LC 10**
See also DLB 132

Henschke, Alfred
See Klabund

Hentoff, Nat(han Irving) 1925- **CLC 26**
See also AAYA 4; CA 1-4R; CAAS 6; CANR 5, 25, 77; CLR 1, 52; INT CANR-25; JRDA; MAICYA; SATA 42, 69; SATA-Brief 27

Heppenstall, (John) Rayner 1911-1981 **CLC 10**
See also CA 1-4R; 103; CANR 29

Heraclitus c. 540B.C.-c. 450B.C. **CMLC 22**
See also DLB 176

Herbert, Frank (Patrick) 1920-1986 **CLC 12, 23, 35, 44, 85; DAM POP**
See also AAYA 21; CA 53-56; 118; CANR 5, 43; CDALBS; DLB 8; INT CANR-5; MTCW 1, 2; SATA 9, 37; SATA-Obit 47

Herbert, George 1593-1633 **LC 24; DAB; DAM POET; PC 4**

See also CDBLB Before 1660; DLB 126

Herbert, Zbigniew 1924-1998 **CLC 9, 43;
    DAM POET**
    See also CA 89-92; 169; CANR 36, 74;
    MTCW 1

Herbst, Josephine (Frey) 1897-1969 **CLC 34**
    See also CA 5-8R; 25-28R; DLB 9

Heredia, Jose Maria 1803-1839
    See also HLCS 2

Hergesheimer, Joseph 1880-1954 **TCLC 11**
    See also CA 109; DLB 102, 9

Herlihy, James Leo 1927-1993 **CLC 6**
    See also CA 1-4R; 143; CANR 2

Hermogenes fl. c. 175- **CMLC 6**

Hernandez, Jose 1834-1886 **NCLC 17**

Herodotus c. 484B.C.-429B.C. **CMLC 17**
    See also DLB 176

Herrick, Robert 1591-1674 **LC 13; DA;
    DAB; DAC; DAM MST, POP; PC 9**
    See also DLB 126

Herring, Guilles
    See Somerville, Edith

Herriot, James 1916-1995 **CLC 12; DAM
    POP**
    See also Wight, James Alfred
    See also AAYA 1; CA 148; CANR 40;
    MTCW 2; SATA 86

Herris, Violet
    See Hunt, Violet

Herrmann, Dorothy 1941- **CLC 44**
    See also CA 107

Herrmann, Taffy
    See Herrmann, Dorothy

Hersey, John (Richard) 1914-1993 **CLC 1, 2,
    7, 9, 40, 81, 97; DAM POP**
    See also AAYA 29; CA 17-20R; 140; CANR
    33; CDALBS; DLB 6, 185; MTCW 1, 2;
    SATA 25; SATA-Obit 76

Herzen, Aleksandr Ivanovich 1812-1870
    NCLC 10, 61

Herzl, Theodor 1860-1904 **TCLC 36**
    See also CA 168

Herzog, Werner 1942- **CLC 16**
    See also CA 89-92

Hesiod c. 8th cent. B.C.- **CMLC 5**
    See also DLB 176

Hesse, Hermann 1877-1962 **CLC 1, 2, 3, 6,
    11, 17, 25, 69; DA; DAB; DAC; DAM
    MST, NOV; SSC 9; WLC**
    See also CA 17-18; CAP 2; DA3; DLB 66;
    MTCW 1, 2; SATA 50

Hewes, Cady
    See De Voto, Bernard (Augustine)

Heyen, William 1940- **CLC 13, 18**
    See also CA 33-36R; CAAS 9; DLB 5

Heyerdahl, Thor 1914- **CLC 26**
    See also CA 5-8R; CANR 5, 22, 66, 73;
    MTCW 1, 2; SATA 2, 52

Heym, Georg (Theodor Franz Arthur)
    1887-1912 **TCLC 9**
    See also CA 106; 181

Heym, Stefan 1913- **CLC 41**
    See also CA 9-12R; CANR 4; DLB 69

Heyse, Paul (Johann Ludwig von) 1830-1914
    TCLC 8
    See also CA 104; DLB 129

Heyward, (Edwin) DuBose 1885-1940 **TCLC
    59**
    See also CA 108; 157; DLB 7, 9, 45; SATA
    21

Hibbert, Eleanor Alice Burford 1906-1993
    CLC 7; DAM POP
    See also BEST 90:4; CA 17-20R; 140;
    CANR 9, 28, 59; MTCW 2; SATA 2;
    SATA-Obit 74

Hichens, Robert (Smythe) 1864-1950 **TCLC
    64**
    See also CA 162; DLB 153

Higgins, George V(incent) 1939-1999 **CLC 4,
    7, 10, 18**
    See also CA 77-80; 186; CAAS 5; CANR
    17, 51, 89; DLB 2; DLBY 81, 98; INT
    CANR-17; MTCW 1

Higginson, Thomas Wentworth 1823-1911
    TCLC 36
    See also CA 162; DLB 1, 64

Highet, Helen
    See MacInnes, Helen (Clark)

Highsmith, (Mary) Patricia 1921-1995 **CLC
    2, 4, 14, 42, 102; DAM NOV, POP**
    See also CA 1-4R; 147; CANR 1, 20, 48,
    62; DA3; MTCW 1, 2

Highwater, Jamake (Mamake) 1942(?)- **CLC
    12**
    See also AAYA 7; CA 65-68; CAAS 7;
    CANR 10, 34, 84; CLR 17; DLB 52;
    DLBY 85; JRDA; MAICYA; SATA 32,
    69; SATA-Brief 30

Highway, Tomson 1951- **CLC 92; DAC;
    DAM MULT**
    See also CA 151; CANR 75; MTCW 2;
    NNAL

Higuchi, Ichiyo 1872-1896 **NCLC 49**

Hijuelos, Oscar 1951- **CLC 65; DAM MULT,
    POP; HLC 1**
    See also AAYA 25; BEST 90:1; CA 123;
    CANR 50, 75; DA3; DLB 145; HW 1, 2;
    MTCW 2

Hikmet, Nazim 1902(?)-1963 **CLC 40**
    See also CA 141; 93-96

Hildegard von Bingen 1098-1179 **CMLC 20**
    See also DLB 148

Hildesheimer, Wolfgang 1916-1991 **CLC 49**
    See also CA 101; 135; DLB 69, 124

Hill, Geoffrey (William) 1932- **CLC 5, 8, 18,
    45; DAM POET**
    See also CA 81-84; CANR 21, 89; CDBLB
    1960 to Present; DLB 40; MTCW 1

Hill, George Roy 1921- **CLC 26**
    See also CA 110; 122

Hill, John
    See Koontz, Dean R(ay)

Hill, Susan (Elizabeth) 1942- **CLC 4, 113;
    DAB; DAM MST, NOV**
    See also CA 33-36R; CANR 29, 69; DLB
    14, 139; MTCW 1

Hillerman, Tony 1925- **CLC 62; DAM POP**
    See also AAYA 6; BEST 89:1; CA 29-32R;
    CANR 21, 42, 65; DA3; DLB 206; SATA
    6

Hillesum, Etty 1914-1943 **TCLC 49**
    See also CA 137

Hilliard, Noel (Harvey) 1929- **CLC 15**
    See also CA 9-12R; CANR 7, 69

Hillis, Rick 1956- **CLC 66**
    See also CA 134

Hilton, James 1900-1954 **TCLC 21**
    See also CA 108; 169; DLB 34, 77; SATA
    34

Himes, Chester (Bomar) 1909-1984 **CLC 2,
    4, 7, 18, 58, 108; BLC 2; DAM MULT**
    See also BW 2; CA 25-28R; 114; CANR
    22, 89; DLB 2, 76, 143; MTCW 1, 2

Hinde, Thomas CLC 6, 11
    See also Chitty, Thomas Willes

Hine, (William) Daryl 1936- **CLC 15**
    See also CA 1-4R; CAAS 15; CANR 1, 20;
    DLB 60

Hinkson, Katharine Tynan
    See Tynan, Katharine

Hinojosa(-Smith), Rolando (R.) 1929-
    See Hinojosa-Smith, Rolando
    See also CA 131; CAAS 16; CANR 62;
    DAM MULT; DLB 82; HLC 1; HW 1, 2;
    MTCW 2

Hinojosa-Smith, Rolando 1929-
    See Hinojosa(-Smith), Rolando (R.)
    See also CAAS 16; HLC 1; MTCW 2

Hinton, S(usan) E(loise) 1950- **CLC 30, 111;
    DA; DAB; DAC; DAM MST, NOV**
    See also AAYA 2, 33; CA 81-84; CANR
    32, 62; CDALBS; CLR 3, 23; DA3;
    JRDA; MAICYA; MTCW 1, 2; SATA 19,
    58, 115

Hippius, Zinaida TCLC 9
    See also Gippius, Zinaida (Nikolayevna)

Hiraoka, Kimitake 1925-1970
    See Mishima, Yukio
    See also CA 97-100; 29-32R; DAM DRAM;
    DA3; MTCW 1, 2

Hirsch, E(ric) D(onald), Jr. 1928- **CLC 79**
    See also CA 25-28R; CANR 27, 51; DLB
    67; INT CANR-27; MTCW 1

Hirsch, Edward 1950- **CLC 31, 50**
    See also CA 104; CANR 20, 42; DLB 120

Hitchcock, Alfred (Joseph) 1899-1980 **CLC
    16**
    See also AAYA 22; CA 159; 97-100; SATA
    27; SATA-Obit 24

Hitler, Adolf 1889-1945 **TCLC 53**
    See also CA 117; 147

Hoagland, Edward 1932- **CLC 28**
    See also CA 1-4R; CANR 2, 31, 57; DLB
    6; SATA 51

Hoban, Russell (Conwell) 1925- **CLC 7, 25;
    DAM NOV**
    See also CA 5-8R; CANR 23, 37, 66; CLR
    3; DLB 52; MAICYA; MTCW 1, 2; SATA
    1, 40, 78

Hobbes, Thomas 1588-1679 **LC 36**
    See also DLB 151

Hobbs, Perry
    See Blackmur, R(ichard) P(almer)

Hobson, Laura Z(ametkin) 1900-1986 **CLC
    7, 25**
    See also CA 17-20R; 118; CANR 55; DLB
    28; SATA 52

Hochhuth, Rolf 1931- **CLC 4, 11, 18; DAM
    DRAM**
    See also CA 5-8R; CANR 33, 75; DLB 124;
    MTCW 1, 2

Hochman, Sandra 1936- **CLC 3, 8**
    See also CA 5-8R; DLB 5

Hochwaelder, Fritz 1911-1986 **CLC 36; DAM
    DRAM**
    See also CA 29-32R; 120; CANR 42;
    MTCW 1

Hochwalder, Fritz
    See Hochwaelder, Fritz

Hocking, Mary (Eunice) 1921- **CLC 13**
    See also CA 101; CANR 18, 40

Hodgins, Jack 1938- **CLC 23**
    See also CA 93-96; DLB 60

Hodgson, William Hope 1877(?)-1918 **TCLC
    13**
    See also CA 111; 164; DLB 70, 153, 156,
    178; MTCW 2

Hoeg, Peter 1957- **CLC 95**
    See also CA 151; CANR 75; DA3; MTCW
    2

Hoffman, Alice 1952- **CLC 51; DAM NOV**
    See also CA 77-80; CANR 34, 66; MTCW
    1, 2

Hoffman, Daniel (Gerard) 1923- **CLC 6, 13,
    23**
    See also CA 1-4R; CANR 4; DLB 5

Hoffman, Stanley 1944- **CLC 5**
    See also CA 77-80

Hoffman, William M(oses) 1939- **CLC 40**
    See also CA 57-60; CANR 11, 71

Hoffmann, E(rnst) T(heodor) A(madeus)
    1776-1822 **NCLC 2; SSC 13**
    See also DLB 90; SATA 27

Hofmann, Gert 1931- **CLC 54**

See also CA 128
Hofmannsthal, Hugo von 1874-1929 **TCLC 11; DAM DRAM; DC 4**
    See also CA 106; 153; DLB 81, 118
Hogan, Linda 1947- **CLC 73; DAM MULT**
    See also CA 120; CANR 45, 73; DLB 175; NNAL
Hogarth, Charles
    See Creasey, John
Hogarth, Emmett
    See Polonsky, Abraham (Lincoln)
Hogg, James 1770-1835 **NCLC 4**
    See also DLB 93, 116, 159
Holbach, Paul Henri Thiry Baron 1723-1789 **LC 14**
Holberg, Ludvig 1684-1754 **LC 6**
Holcroft, Thomas 1745-1809 **NCLC 85**
    See also DLB 39, 89, 158
Holden, Ursula 1921- **CLC 18**
    See also CA 101; CAAS 8; CANR 22
Holderlin, (Johann Christian) Friedrich 1770-1843 **NCLC 16; PC 4**
Holdstock, Robert
    See Holdstock, Robert P.
Holdstock, Robert P. 1948- **CLC 39**
    See also CA 131; CANR 81
Holland, Isabelle 1920- **CLC 21**
    See also AAYA 11; CA 21-24R, 181; CAAE 181; CANR 10, 25, 47; CLR 57; JRDA; MAICYA; SATA 8, 70; SATA-Essay 103
Holland, Marcus
    See Caldwell, (Janet Miriam) Taylor (Holland)
Hollander, John 1929- **CLC 2, 5, 8, 14**
    See also CA 1-4R; CANR 1, 52; DLB 5; SATA 13
Hollander, Paul
    See Silverberg, Robert
Holleran, Andrew 1943(?)- **CLC 38**
    See also Garber, Eric
    See also CA 144
Hollinghurst, Alan 1954- **CLC 55, 91**
    See also CA 114; DLB 207
Hollis, Jim
    See Summers, Hollis (Spurgeon, Jr.)
Holly, Buddy 1936-1959 **TCLC 65**
Holmes, Gordon
    See Shiel, M(atthew) P(hipps)
Holmes, John
    See Souster, (Holmes) Raymond
Holmes, John Clellon 1926-1988 **CLC 56**
    See also CA 9-12R; 125; CANR 4; DLB 16
Holmes, Oliver Wendell, Jr. 1841-1935 **TCLC 77**
    See also CA 114; 186
Holmes, Oliver Wendell 1809-1894 **NCLC 14, 81**
    See also CDALB 1640-1865; DLB 1, 189; SATA 34
Holmes, Raymond
    See Souster, (Holmes) Raymond
Holt, Victoria
    See Hibbert, Eleanor Alice Burford
Holub, Miroslav 1923-1998 **CLC 4**
    See also CA 21-24R; 169; CANR 10
Homer c. 8th cent. B.C.- **CMLC 1, 16; DA; DAB; DAC; DAM MST, POET; PC 23; WLCS**
    See also DA3; DLB 176
Hongo, Garrett Kaoru 1951- **PC 23**
    See also CA 133; CAAS 22; DLB 120
Honig, Edwin 1919- **CLC 33**
    See also CA 5-8R; CAAS 8; CANR 4, 45; DLB 5
Hood, Hugh (John Blagdon) 1928- **CLC 15, 28**
    See also CA 49-52; CAAS 17; CANR 1, 33, 87; DLB 53

Hood, Thomas 1799-1845 **NCLC 16**
    See also DLB 96
Hooker, (Peter) Jeremy 1941- **CLC 43**
    See also CA 77-80; CANR 22; DLB 40
hooks, bell CLC 94; BLCS
    See also Watkins, Gloria Jean
    See also MTCW 2
Hope, A(lec) D(erwent) 1907- **CLC 3, 51**
    See also CA 21-24R; CANR 33, 74; MTCW 1, 2
Hope, Anthony 1863-1933 **TCLC 83**
    See also CA 157; DLB 153, 156
Hope, Brian
    See Creasey, John
Hope, Christopher (David Tully) 1944- **CLC 52**
    See also CA 106; CANR 47; SATA 62
Hopkins, Gerard Manley 1844-1889 **NCLC 17; DA; DAB; DAC; DAM MST, POET; PC 15; WLC**
    See also CDBLB 1890-1914; DA3; DLB 35, 57
Hopkins, John (Richard) 1931-1998 **CLC 4**
    See also CA 85-88; 169
Hopkins, Pauline Elizabeth 1859-1930 **TCLC 28; BLC 2; DAM MULT**
    See also BW 2, 3; CA 141; CANR 82; DLB 50
Hopkinson, Francis 1737-1791 **LC 25**
    See also DLB 31
Hopley-Woolrich, Cornell George 1903-1968
    See Woolrich, Cornell
    See also CA 13-14; CANR 58; CAP 1; MTCW 2
Horace 65B.C.-8B.C. **CMLC 39**
    See also DLB 211
Horatio
    See Proust, (Valentin-Louis-George-Eugene-) Marcel
Horgan, Paul (George Vincent O'Shaughnessy) 1903-1995 **CLC 9, 53; DAM NOV**
    See also CA 13-16R; 147; CANR 9, 35; DLB 212; DLBY 85; INT CANR-9; MTCW 1, 2; SATA 13; SATA-Obit 84
Horn, Peter
    See Kuttner, Henry
Hornem, Horace Esq.
    See Byron, George Gordon (Noel)
Horney, Karen (Clementine Theodore Danielsen) 1885-1952 **TCLC 71**
    See also CA 114; 165
Hornung, E(rnest) W(illiam) 1866-1921 **TCLC 59**
    See also CA 108; 160; DLB 70
Horovitz, Israel (Arthur) 1939- **CLC 56; DAM DRAM**
    See also CA 33-36R; CANR 46, 59; DLB 7
Horton, George Moses 1797(?)-1883(?) **NCLC 87**
    See also DLB 50
Horvath, Odon von
    See Horvath, Oedoen von
    See also DLB 85, 124
Horvath, Oedoen von 1901-1938 **TCLC 45**
    See also Horvath, Odon von; von Horvath, Oedoen
    See also CA 118
Horwitz, Julius 1920-1986 **CLC 14**
    See also CA 9-12R; 119; CANR 12
Hospital, Janette Turner 1942- **CLC 42**
    See also CA 108; CANR 48
Hostos, E. M. de
    See Hostos (y Bonilla), Eugenio Maria de
Hostos, Eugenio M. de
    See Hostos (y Bonilla), Eugenio Maria de
Hostos, Eugenio Maria
    See Hostos (y Bonilla), Eugenio Maria de

Hostos (y Bonilla), Eugenio Maria de 1839-1903 **TCLC 24**
    See also CA 123; 131; HW 1
Houdini
    See Lovecraft, H(oward) P(hillips)
Hougan, Carolyn 1943- **CLC 34**
    See also CA 139
Household, Geoffrey (Edward West) 1900-1988 **CLC 11**
    See also CA 77-80; 126; CANR 58; DLB 87; SATA 14; SATA-Obit 59
Housman, A(lfred) E(dward) 1859-1936 **TCLC 1, 10; DA; DAB; DAC; DAM MST, POET; PC 2; WLCS**
    See also CA 104; 125; DA3; DLB 19; MTCW 1, 2
Housman, Laurence 1865-1959 **TCLC 7**
    See also CA 106; 155; DLB 10; SATA 25
Howard, Elizabeth Jane 1923- **CLC 7, 29**
    See also CA 5-8R; CANR 8, 62
Howard, Maureen 1930- **CLC 5, 14, 46**
    See also CA 53-56; CANR 31, 75; DLBY 83; INT CANR-31; MTCW 1, 2
Howard, Richard 1929- **CLC 7, 10, 47**
    See also AITN 1; CA 85-88; CANR 25, 80; DLB 5; INT CANR-25
Howard, Robert E(rvin) 1906-1936 **TCLC 8**
    See also CA 105; 157
Howard, Warren F.
    See Pohl, Frederik
Howe, Fanny (Quincy) 1940- **CLC 47**
    See also CA 117; CAAS 27; CANR 70; SATA-Brief 52
Howe, Irving 1920-1993 **CLC 85**
    See also CA 9-12R; 141; CANR 21, 50; DLB 67; MTCW 1, 2
Howe, Julia Ward 1819-1910 **TCLC 21**
    See also CA 117; DLB 1, 189
Howe, Susan 1937- **CLC 72**
    See also CA 160; DLB 120
Howe, Tina 1937- **CLC 48**
    See also CA 109
Howell, James 1594(?)-1666 **LC 13**
    See also DLB 151
Howells, W. D.
    See Howells, William Dean
Howells, William D.
    See Howells, William Dean
Howells, William Dean 1837-1920 **TCLC 7, 17, 41; SSC 36**
    See also CA 104; 134; CDALB 1865-1917; DLB 12, 64, 74, 79, 189; MTCW 2
Howes, Barbara 1914-1996 **CLC 15**
    See also CA 9-12R; 151; CAAS 3; CANR 53; SATA 5
Hrabal, Bohumil 1914-1997 **CLC 13, 67**
    See also CA 106; 156; CAAS 12; CANR 57
Hroswitha of Gandersheim c. 935-c. 1002 **CMLC 29**
    See also DLB 148
Hsun, Lu
    See Lu Hsun
Hubbard, L(afayette) Ron(ald) 1911-1986 **CLC 43; DAM POP**
    See also CA 77-80; 118; CANR 52; DA3; MTCW 2
Huch, Ricarda (Octavia) 1864-1947 **TCLC 13**
    See also CA 111; DLB 66
Huddle, David 1942- **CLC 49**
    See also CA 57-60; CAAS 20; CANR 89; DLB 130
Hudson, Jeffrey
    See Crichton, (John) Michael
Hudson, W(illiam) H(enry) 1841-1922 **TCLC 29**
    See also CA 115; DLB 98, 153, 174; SATA 35

Johnson, Lionel (Pigot) 1867-1902 **TCLC 19**
See also CA 117; DLB 19
Johnson, Marguerite (Annie)
See Angelou, Maya
Johnson, Mel
See Malzberg, Barry N(athaniel)
Johnson, Pamela Hansford 1912-1981 **CLC 1, 7, 27**
See also CA 1-4R; 104; CANR 2, 28; DLB 15; MTCW 1, 2
Johnson, Robert 1911(?)-1938 **TCLC 69**
See also BW 3; CA 174
Johnson, Samuel 1709-1784 **LC 15, 52; DA; DAB; DAC; DAM MST; WLC**
See also CDBLB 1660-1789; DLB 39, 95, 104, 142
Johnson, Uwe 1934-1984 **CLC 5, 10, 15, 40**
See also CA 1-4R; 112; CANR 1, 39; DLB 75; MTCW 1
Johnston, George (Benson) 1913- **CLC 51**
See also CA 1-4R; CANR 5, 20; DLB 88
Johnston, Jennifer 1930- **CLC 7**
See also CA 85-88; DLB 14
Joinville, Jean de 1224(?)-1317 **CMLC 38**
Jolley, (Monica) Elizabeth 1923- **CLC 46; SSC 19**
See also CA 127; CAAS 13; CANR 59
Jones, Arthur Llewellyn 1863-1947
See Machen, Arthur
See also CA 104; 179
Jones, D(ouglas) G(ordon) 1929- **CLC 10**
See also CA 29-32R; CANR 13, 90; DLB 53
Jones, David (Michael) 1895-1974 **CLC 2, 4, 7, 13, 42**
See also CA 9-12R; 53-56; CANR 28; CD-BLB 1945-1960; DLB 20, 100; MTCW 1
Jones, David Robert 1947-
See Bowie, David
See also CA 103
Jones, Diana Wynne 1934- **CLC 26**
See also AAYA 12; CA 49-52; CANR 4, 26, 56; CLR 23; DLB 161; JRDA; MAI-CYA; SAAS 7; SATA 9, 70, 108
Jones, Edward P. 1950- **CLC 76**
See also BW 2, 3; CA 142; CANR 79
Jones, Gayl 1949- **CLC 6, 9, 131; BLC 2; DAM MULT**
See also BW 2, 3; CA 77-80; CANR 27, 66; DA3; DLB 33; MTCW 1, 2
Jones, James 1921-1977 **CLC 1, 3, 10, 39**
See also AITN 1, 2; CA 1-4R; 69-72; CANR 6; DLB 2, 143; DLBD 17; DLBY 98; MTCW 1
Jones, John J.
See Lovecraft, H(oward) P(hillips)
Jones, LeRoi CLC 1, 2, 3, 5, 10, 14
See also Baraka, Amiri
See also MTCW 2
Jones, Louis B. 1953- **CLC 65**
See also CA 141; CANR 73
Jones, Madison (Percy, Jr.) 1925- **CLC 4**
See also CA 13-16R; CAAS 11; CANR 7, 54, 83; DLB 152
Jones, Mervyn 1922- **CLC 10, 52**
See also CA 45-48; CAAS 5; CANR 1, 91; MTCW 1
Jones, Mick 1956(?)- **CLC 30**
Jones, Nettie (Pearl) 1941- **CLC 34**
See also BW 2; CA 137; CAAS 20; CANR 88
Jones, Preston 1936-1979 **CLC 10**
See also CA 73-76; 89-92; DLB 7
Jones, Robert F(rancis) 1934- **CLC 7**
See also CA 49-52; CANR 2, 61
Jones, Rod 1953- **CLC 50**
See also CA 128
Jones, Terence Graham Parry 1942- **CLC 21**

See also Jones, Terry; Monty Python
See also CA 112; 116; CANR 35; INT 116
Jones, Terry
See Jones, Terence Graham Parry
See also SATA 67; SATA-Brief 51
Jones, Thom (Douglas) 1945(?)- **CLC 81**
See also CA 157; CANR 88
Jong, Erica 1942- **CLC 4, 6, 8, 18, 83; DAM NOV, POP**
See also AITN 1; BEST 90:2; CA 73-76; CANR 26, 52, 75; DA3; DLB 2, 5, 28, 152; INT CANR-26; MTCW 1, 2
Jonson, Ben(jamin) 1572(?)-1637 **LC 6, 33; DA; DAB; DAC; DAM DRAM, MST, POET; DC 4; PC 17; WLC**
See also CDBLB Before 1660; DLB 62, 121
Jordan, June 1936- **CLC 5, 11, 23, 114; BLCS; DAM MULT, POET**
See also AAYA 2; BW 2, 3; CA 33-36R; CANR 25, 70; CLR 10; DLB 38; MAI-CYA; MTCW 1; SATA 4
Jordan, Neil (Patrick) 1950- **CLC 110**
See also CA 124; 130; CANR 54; INT 130
Jordan, Pat(rick M.) 1941- **CLC 37**
See also CA 33-36R
Jorgensen, Ivar
See Ellison, Harlan (Jay)
Jorgenson, Ivar
See Silverberg, Robert
Josephus, Flavius c. 37-100 **CMLC 13**
Josiah Allen's Wife
See Holley, Marietta
Josipovici, Gabriel (David) 1940- **CLC 6, 43**
See also CA 37-40R; CAAS 8; CANR 47, 84; DLB 14
Joubert, Joseph 1754-1824 **NCLC 9**
Jouve, Pierre Jean 1887-1976 **CLC 47**
See also CA 65-68
Jovine, Francesco 1902-1950 **TCLC 79**
Joyce, James (Augustine Aloysius) 1882-1941 **TCLC 3, 8, 16, 35, 52; DA; DAB; DAC; DAM MST, NOV, POET; PC 22; SSC 3, 26; WLC**
See also CA 104; 126; CDBLB 1914-1945; DA3; DLB 10, 19, 36, 162; MTCW 1, 2
Jozsef, Attila 1905-1937 **TCLC 22**
See also CA 116
Juana Ines de la Cruz 1651(?)-1695 **LC 5; HLCS 1; PC 24**
Judd, Cyril
See Kornbluth, C(yril) M.; Pohl, Frederik
Juenger, Ernst 1895-1998 **CLC 125**
See also CA 101; 167; CANR 21, 47; DLB 56
Julian of Norwich 1342(?)-1416(?) **LC 6, 52**
See also DLB 146
Junger, Ernst
See Juenger, Ernst
Junger, Sebastian 1962- **CLC 109**
See also AAYA 28; CA 165
Juniper, Alex
See Hospital, Janette Turner
Junius
See Luxemburg, Rosa
Just, Ward (Swift) 1935- **CLC 4, 27**
See also CA 25-28R; CANR 32, 87; INT CANR-32
Justice, Donald (Rodney) 1925- **CLC 6, 19, 102; DAM POET**
See also CA 5-8R; CANR 26, 54, 74; DLBY 83; INT CANR-26; MTCW 2
Juvenal c. 60-c. 13 **CMLC 8**
See also Juvenalis, Decimus Junius
See also DLB 211
Juvenalis, Decimus Junius 55(?)-c. 127(?)
See Juvenal
Juvenis
See Bourne, Randolph S(illiman)

Kacew, Romain 1914-1980
See Gary, Romain
See also CA 108; 102
Kadare, Ismail 1936- **CLC 52**
See also CA 161
Kadohata, Cynthia CLC 59, 122
See also CA 140
Kafka, Franz 1883-1924 **TCLC 2, 6, 13, 29, 47, 53; DA; DAB; DAC; DAM MST, NOV; SSC 5, 29, 35; WLC**
See also AAYA 31; CA 105; 126; DA3; DLB 81; MTCW 1, 2
Kahanovitsch, Pinkhes
See Der Nister
Kahn, Roger 1927- **CLC 30**
See also CA 25-28R; CANR 44, 69; DLB 171; SATA 37
Kain, Saul
See Sassoon, Siegfried (Lorraine)
Kaiser, Georg 1878-1945 **TCLC 9**
See also CA 106; DLB 124
Kaletski, Alexander 1946- **CLC 39**
See also CA 118; 143
Kalidasa fl. c. 400- **CMLC 9; PC 22**
Kallman, Chester (Simon) 1921-1975 **CLC 2**
See also CA 45-48; 53-56; CANR 3
Kaminsky, Melvin 1926-
See Brooks, Mel
See also CA 65-68; CANR 16
Kaminsky, Stuart M(elvin) 1934- **CLC 59**
See also CA 73-76; CANR 29, 53, 89
Kandinsky, Wassily 1866-1944 **TCLC 92**
See also CA 118; 155
Kane, Francis
See Robbins, Harold
Kane, Paul
See Simon, Paul (Frederick)
Kanin, Garson 1912-1999 **CLC 22**
See also AITN 1; CA 5-8R; 177; CANR 7, 78; DLB 7
Kaniuk, Yoram 1930- **CLC 19**
See also CA 134
Kant, Immanuel 1724-1804 **NCLC 27, 67**
See also DLB 94
Kantor, MacKinlay 1904-1977 **CLC 7**
See also CA 61-64; 73-76; CANR 60, 63; DLB 9, 102; MTCW 2
Kaplan, David Michael 1946- **CLC 50**
Kaplan, James 1951- **CLC 59**
See also CA 135
Karageorge, Michael
See Anderson, Poul (William)
Karamzin, Nikolai Mikhailovich 1766-1826 **NCLC 3**
See also DLB 150
Karapanou, Margarita 1946- **CLC 13**
See also CA 101
Karinthy, Frigyes 1887-1938 **TCLC 47**
See also CA 170
Karl, Frederick R(obert) 1927- **CLC 34**
See also CA 5-8R; CANR 3, 44
Kastel, Warren
See Silverberg, Robert
Kataev, Evgeny Petrovich 1903-1942
See Petrov, Evgeny
See also CA 120
Kataphusin
See Ruskin, John
Katz, Steve 1935- **CLC 47**
See also CA 25-28R; CAAS 14, 64; CANR 12; DLBY 83
Kauffman, Janet 1945- **CLC 42**
See also CA 117; CANR 43, 84; DLBY 86
Kaufman, Bob (Garnell) 1925-1986 **CLC 49**
See also BW 1; CA 41-44R; 118; CANR 22; DLB 16, 41
Kaufman, George S. 1889-1961 **CLC 38; DAM DRAM**

See also CA 108; 93-96; DLB 7; INT 108; MTCW 2

Kaufman, Sue CLC 3, 8
See also Baroness, Sue K(aufman)

Kavafis, Konstantinos Petrou 1863-1933
See Cavafy, C(onstantine) P(eter)
See also CA 104

Kavan, Anna 1901-1968 CLC 5, 13, 82
See also CA 5-8R; CANR 6, 57; MTCW 1

Kavanagh, Dan
See Barnes, Julian (Patrick)

Kavanagh, Julie 1952- CLC 119
See also CA 163

Kavanagh, Patrick (Joseph) 1904-1967 CLC 22
See also CA 123; 25-28R; DLB 15, 20; MTCW 1

Kawabata, Yasunari 1899-1972 CLC 2, 5, 9, 18, 107; DAM MULT; SSC 17
See also CA 93-96; 33-36R; CANR 88; DLB 180; MTCW 2

Kaye, M(ary) M(argaret) 1909- CLC 28
See also CA 89-92; CANR 24, 60; MTCW 1, 2; SATA 62

Kaye, Mollie
See Kaye, M(ary) M(argaret)

Kaye-Smith, Sheila 1887-1956 TCLC 20
See also CA 118; DLB 36

Kaymor, Patrice Maguilene
See Senghor, Leopold Sedar

Kazan, Elia 1909- CLC 6, 16, 63
See also CA 21-24R; CANR 32, 78

Kazantzakis, Nikos 1883(?)-1957 TCLC 2, 5, 33
See also CA 105; 132; DA3; MTCW 1, 2

Kazin, Alfred 1915-1998 CLC 34, 38, 119
See also CA 1-4R; CAAS 7; CANR 1, 45, 79; DLB 67

Keane, Mary Nesta (Skrine) 1904-1996
See Keane, Molly
See also CA 108; 114; 151

Keane, Molly CLC 31
See also Keane, Mary Nesta (Skrine)
See also INT 114

Keates, Jonathan 1946(?)- CLC 34
See also CA 163

Keaton, Buster 1895-1966 CLC 20

Keats, John 1795-1821 NCLC 8, 73; DA; DAB; DAC; DAM MST, POET; PC 1; WLC
See also CDBLB 1789-1832; DA3; DLB 96, 110

Keble, John 1792-1866 NCLC 87
See also DLB 32, 55

Keene, Donald 1922- CLC 34
See also CA 1-4R; CANR 5

Keillor, Garrison CLC 40, 115
See also Keillor, Gary (Edward)
See also AAYA 2; BEST 89:3; DLBY 87; SATA 58

Keillor, Gary (Edward) 1942-
See Keillor, Garrison
See also CA 111; 117; CANR 36, 59; DAM POP; DA3; MTCW 1, 2

Keith, Michael
See Hubbard, L(afayette) Ron(ald)

Keller, Gottfried 1819-1890 NCLC 2; SSC 26
See also DLB 129

Keller, Nora Okja CLC 109

Kellerman, Jonathan 1949- CLC 44; DAM POP
See also BEST 90:1; CA 106; CANR 29, 51; DA3; INT CANR-29

Kelley, William Melvin 1937- CLC 22
See also BW 1; CA 77-80; CANR 27, 83; DLB 33

Kellogg, Marjorie 1922- CLC 2
See also CA 81-84

Kellow, Kathleen
See Hibbert, Eleanor Alice Burford

Kelly, M(ilton) T(errence) 1947- CLC 55
See also CA 97-100; CAAS 22; CANR 19, 43, 84

Kelman, James 1946- CLC 58, 86
See also CA 148; CANR 85; DLB 194

Kemal, Yashar 1923- CLC 14, 29
See also CA 89-92; CANR 44

Kemble, Fanny 1809-1893 NCLC 18
See also DLB 32

Kemelman, Harry 1908-1996 CLC 2
See also AITN 1; CA 9-12R; 155; CANR 6, 71; DLB 28

Kempe, Margery 1373(?)-1440(?) LC 6, 56
See also DLB 146

Kempis, Thomas a 1380-1471 LC 11

Kendall, Henry 1839-1882 NCLC 12

Keneally, Thomas (Michael) 1935- CLC 5, 8, 10, 14, 19, 27, 43, 117; DAM NOV
See also CA 85-88; CANR 10, 50, 74; DA3; MTCW 1, 2

Kennedy, Adrienne (Lita) 1931- CLC 66; BLC 2; DAM MULT; DC 5
See also BW 2, 3; CA 103; CAAS 20; CABS 3; CANR 26, 53, 82; DLB 38

Kennedy, John Pendleton 1795-1870 NCLC 2
See also DLB 3

Kennedy, Joseph Charles 1929-
See Kennedy, X. J.
See also CA 1-4R; CANR 4, 30, 40; SATA 14, 86

Kennedy, William 1928- CLC 6, 28, 34, 53; DAM NOV
See also AAYA 1; CA 85-88; CANR 14, 31, 76; DA3; DLB 143; DLBY 85; INT CANR-31; MTCW 1, 2; SATA 57

Kennedy, X. J. CLC 8, 42
See also Kennedy, Joseph Charles
See also CAAS 9; CLR 27; DLB 5; SAAS 22

Kenny, Maurice (Francis) 1929- CLC 87; DAM MULT
See also CA 144; CAAS 22; DLB 175; NNAL

Kent, Kelvin
See Kuttner, Henry

Kenton, Maxwell
See Southern, Terry

Kenyon, Robert O.
See Kuttner, Henry

Kepler, Johannes 1571-1630 LC 45

Kerouac, Jack CLC 1, 2, 3, 5, 14, 29, 61
See also Kerouac, Jean-Louis Lebris de
See also AAYA 25; CDALB 1941-1968; DLB 2, 16; DLBD 3; DLBY 95; MTCW 2

Kerouac, Jean-Louis Lebris de 1922-1969
See Kerouac, Jack
See also AITN 1; CA 5-8R; 25-28R; CANR 26, 54; DA; DAB; DAC; DAM MST, NOV, POET, POP; DA3; MTCW 1, 2; WLC

Kerr, Jean 1923- CLC 22
See also CA 5-8R; CANR 7; INT CANR-7

Kerr, M. E. CLC 12, 35
See also Meaker, Marijane (Agnes)
See also AAYA 2, 23; CLR 29; SAAS 1

Kerr, Robert CLC 55

Kerrigan, (Thomas) Anthony 1918- CLC 4, 6
See also CA 49-52; CAAS 11; CANR 4

Kerry, Lois
See Duncan, Lois

Kesey, Ken (Elton) 1935- CLC 1, 3, 6, 11, 46, 64; DA; DAB; DAC; DAM MST, NOV, POP; WLC

See also AAYA 25; CA 1-4R; CANR 22, 38, 66; CDALB 1968-1988; DA3; DLB 2, 16, 206; MTCW 1, 2; SATA 66

Kesselring, Joseph (Otto) 1902-1967 CLC 45; DAM DRAM, MST
See also CA 150

Kessler, Jascha (Frederick) 1929- CLC 4
See also CA 17-20R; CANR 8, 48

Kettelkamp, Larry (Dale) 1933- CLC 12
See also CA 29-32R; CANR 16; SAAS 3; SATA 2

Key, Ellen 1849-1926 TCLC 65

Keyber, Conny
See Fielding, Henry

Keyes, Daniel 1927- CLC 80; DA; DAC; DAM MST, NOV
See also AAYA 23; CA 17-20R, 181; CAAE 181; CANR 10, 26, 54, 74; DA3; MTCW 2; SATA 37

Keynes, John Maynard 1883-1946 TCLC 64
See also CA 114; 162, 163; DLBD 10; MTCW 2

Khanshendel, Chiron
See Rose, Wendy

Khayyam, Omar 1048-1131 CMLC 11; DAM POET; PC 8
See also DA3

Kherdian, David 1931- CLC 6, 9
See also CA 21-24R; CAAS 2; CANR 39, 78; CLR 24; JRDA; MAICYA; SATA 16, 74

Khlebnikov, Velimir TCLC 20
See also Khlebnikov, Viktor Vladimirovich

Khlebnikov, Viktor Vladimirovich 1885-1922
See Khlebnikov, Velimir
See also CA 117

Khodasevich, Vladislav (Felitsianovich) 1886-1939 TCLC 15
See also CA 115

Kielland, Alexander Lange 1849-1906 TCLC 5
See also CA 104

Kiely, Benedict 1919- CLC 23, 43
See also CA 1-4R; CANR 2, 84; DLB 15

Kienzle, William X(avier) 1928- CLC 25; DAM POP
See also CA 93-96; CAAS 1; CANR 9, 31, 59; DA3; INT CANR-31; MTCW 1, 2

Kierkegaard, Soren 1813-1855 NCLC 34, 78

Kieslowski, Krzysztof 1941-1996 CLC 120
See also CA 147; 151

Killens, John Oliver 1916-1987 CLC 10
See also BW 2; CA 77-80; 123; CAAS 2; CANR 26; DLB 33

Killigrew, Anne 1660-1685 LC 4
See also DLB 131

Killigrew, Thomas 1612-1683 LC 57
See also DLB 58

Kim
See Simenon, Georges (Jacques Christian)

Kincaid, Jamaica 1949- CLC 43, 68; BLC 2; DAM MULT, NOV
See also AAYA 13; BW 2, 3; CA 125; CANR 47, 59; CDALBS; CLR 63; DA3; DLB 157; MTCW 2

King, Francis (Henry) 1923- CLC 8, 53; DAM NOV
See also CA 1-4R; CANR 1, 33, 86; DLB 15, 139; MTCW 1

King, Kennedy
See Brown, George Douglas

King, Martin Luther, Jr. 1929-1968 CLC 83; BLC 2; DA; DAB; DAC; DAM MST, MULT; WLCS
See also BW 2, 3; CA 25-28; CANR 27, 44; CAP 2; DA3; MTCW 1, 2; SATA 14

King, Stephen (Edwin) 1947- CLC 12, 26, 37, 61, 113; DAM NOV, POP; SSC 17

See also AAYA 1, 17; BEST 90:1; CA 61-64; CANR 1, 30, 52, 76; DA3; DLB 143; DLBY 80; JRDA; MTCW 1, 2; SATA 9, 55

King, Steve
See King, Stephen (Edwin)

King, Thomas 1943- **CLC 89; DAC; DAM MULT**
See also CA 144; DLB 175; NNAL; SATA 96

Kingman, Lee CLC 17
See also Natti, (Mary) Lee
See also SAAS 3; SATA 1, 67

Kingsley, Charles 1819-1875 **NCLC 35**
See also DLB 21, 32, 163, 190; YABC 2

Kingsley, Sidney 1906-1995 **CLC 44**
See also CA 85-88; 147; DLB 7

Kingsolver, Barbara 1955- **CLC 55, 81, 130; DAM POP**
See also AAYA 15; CA 129; 134; CANR 60; CDALBS; DA3; DLB 206; INT 134; MTCW 2

Kingston, Maxine (Ting Ting) Hong 1940- **CLC 12, 19, 58, 121; DAM MULT, NOV; WLCS**
See also AAYA 8; CA 69-72; CANR 13, 38, 74, 87; CDALBS; DA3; DLB 173, 212; DLBY 80; INT CANR-13; MTCW 1, 2; SATA 53

Kinnell, Galway 1927- **CLC 1, 2, 3, 5, 13, 29, 129; PC 26**
See also CA 9-12R; CANR 10, 34, 66; DLB 5; DLBY 87; INT CANR-34; MTCW 1, 2

Kinsella, Thomas 1928- **CLC 4, 19**
See also CA 17-20R; CANR 15; DLB 27; MTCW 1, 2

Kinsella, W(illiam) P(atrick) 1935- **CLC 27, 43; DAC; DAM NOV, POP**
See also AAYA 7; CA 97-100; CAAS 7; CANR 21, 35, 66, 75; INT CANR-21; MTCW 1, 2

Kinsey, Alfred C(harles) 1894-1956 **TCLC 91**
See also CA 115; 170; MTCW 2

Kipling, (Joseph) Rudyard 1865-1936 **TCLC 8, 17; DA; DAB; DAC; DAM MST, POET; PC 3; SSC 5; WLC**
See also AAYA 32; CA 105; 120; CANR 33; CDBLB 1890-1914; CLR 39, 65; DA3; DLB 19, 34, 141, 156; MAICYA; MTCW 1, 2; SATA 100; YABC 2

Kirkland, Caroline M. 1801-1864 **NCLC 85**
See also DLB 3, 73, 74; DLBD 13

Kirkup, James 1918- **CLC 1**
See also CA 1-4R; CAAS 4; CANR 2; DLB 27; SATA 12

Kirkwood, James 1930(?)-1989 **CLC 9**
See also AITN 2; CA 1-4R; 128; CANR 6, 40

Kirshner, Sidney
See Kingsley, Sidney

Kis, Danilo 1935-1989 **CLC 57**
See also CA 109; 118; 129; CANR 61; DLB 181; MTCW 1

Kivi, Aleksis 1834-1872 **NCLC 30**

Kizer, Carolyn (Ashley) 1925- **CLC 15, 39, 80; DAM POET**
See also CA 65-68; CAAS 5; CANR 24, 70; DLB 5, 169; MTCW 2

Klabund 1890-1928 **TCLC 44**
See also CA 162; DLB 66

Klappert, Peter 1942- **CLC 57**
See also CA 33-36R; DLB 5

Klein, A(braham) M(oses) 1909-1972 **CLC 19; DAB; DAC; DAM MST**
See also CA 101; 37-40R; DLB 68

Klein, Norma 1938-1989 **CLC 30**
See also AAYA 2; CA 41-44R; 128; CANR 15, 37; CLR 2, 19; INT CANR-15; JRDA; MAICYA; SAAS 1; SATA 7, 57

Klein, T(heodore) E(ibon) D(onald) 1947- **CLC 34**
See also CA 119; CANR 44, 75

Kleist, Heinrich von 1777-1811 **NCLC 2, 37; DAM DRAM; SSC 22**
See also DLB 90

Klima, Ivan 1931- **CLC 56; DAM NOV**
See also CA 25-28R; CANR 17, 50, 91

Klimentov, Andrei Platonovich 1899-1951
See Platonov, Andrei
See also CA 108

Klinger, Friedrich Maximilian von 1752-1831 **NCLC 1**
See also DLB 94

Klingsor the Magician
See Hartmann, Sadakichi

Klopstock, Friedrich Gottlieb 1724-1803 **NCLC 11**
See also DLB 97

Knapp, Caroline 1959- **CLC 99**
See also CA 154

Knebel, Fletcher 1911-1993 **CLC 14**
See also AITN 1; CA 1-4R; 140; CAAS 3; CANR 1, 36; SATA 36; SATA-Obit 75

Knickerbocker, Diedrich
See Irving, Washington

Knight, Etheridge 1931-1991 **CLC 40; BLC 2; DAM POET; PC 14**
See also BW 1, 3; CA 21-24R; 133; CANR 23, 82; DLB 41; MTCW 2

Knight, Sarah Kemble 1666-1727 **LC 7**
See also DLB 24, 200

Knister, Raymond 1899-1932 **TCLC 56**
See also CA 186; DLB 68

Knowles, John 1926- **CLC 1, 4, 10, 26; DA; DAC; DAM MST, NOV**
See also AAYA 10; CA 17-20R; CANR 40, 74, 76; CDALB 1968-1988; DLB 6; MTCW 1, 2; SATA 8, 89

Knox, Calvin M.
See Silverberg, Robert

Knox, John c. 1505-1572 **LC 37**
See also DLB 132

Knye, Cassandra
See Disch, Thomas M(ichael)

Koch, C(hristopher) J(ohn) 1932- **CLC 42**
See also CA 127; CANR 84

Koch, Christopher
See Koch, C(hristopher) J(ohn)

Koch, Kenneth 1925- **CLC 5, 8, 44; DAM POET**
See also CA 1-4R; CANR 6, 36, 57; DLB 5; INT CANR-36; MTCW 2; SATA 65

Kochanowski, Jan 1530-1584 **LC 10**

Kock, Charles Paul de 1794-1871 **NCLC 16**

Koda Rohan 1867-
See Koda Shigeyuki

Koda Shigeyuki 1867-1947 **TCLC 22**
See also CA 121; 183; DLB 180

Koestler, Arthur 1905-1983 **CLC 1, 3, 6, 8, 15, 33**
See also CA 1-4R; 109; CANR 1, 33; CDBLB 1945-1960; DLBY 83; MTCW 1, 2

Kogawa, Joy Nozomi 1935- **CLC 78, 129; DAC; DAM MST, MULT**
See also CA 101; CANR 19, 62; MTCW 2; SATA 99

Kohout, Pavel 1928- **CLC 13**
See also CA 45-48; CANR 3

Koizumi, Yakumo
See Hearn, (Patricio) Lafcadio (Tessima Carlos)

Kolmar, Gertrud 1894-1943 **TCLC 40**
See also CA 167

Komunyakaa, Yusef 1947- **CLC 86, 94; BLCS**
See also CA 147; CANR 83; DLB 120

Konrad, George
See Konrad, Gyoergy

Konrad, Gyoergy 1933- **CLC 4, 10, 73**
See also CA 85-88

Konwicki, Tadeusz 1926- **CLC 8, 28, 54, 117**
See also CA 101; CAAS 9; CANR 39, 59; MTCW 1

Koontz, Dean R(ay) 1945- **CLC 78; DAM NOV, POP**
See also AAYA 9, 31; BEST 89:3, 90:2; CA 108; CANR 19, 36, 52; DA3; MTCW 1; SATA 92

Kopernik, Mikolaj
See Copernicus, Nicolaus

Kopit, Arthur (Lee) 1937- **CLC 1, 18, 33; DAM DRAM**
See also AITN 1; CA 81-84; CABS 3; DLB 7; MTCW 1

Kops, Bernard 1926- **CLC 4**
See also CA 5-8R; CANR 84; DLB 13

Kornbluth, C(yril) M. 1923-1958 **TCLC 8**
See also CA 105; 160; DLB 8

Korolenko, V. G.
See Korolenko, Vladimir Galaktionovich

Korolenko, Vladimir
See Korolenko, Vladimir Galaktionovich

Korolenko, Vladimir G.
See Korolenko, Vladimir Galaktionovich

Korolenko, Vladimir Galaktionovich 1853-1921 **TCLC 22**
See also CA 121

Korzybski, Alfred (Habdank Skarbek) 1879-1950 **TCLC 61**
See also CA 123; 160

Kosinski, Jerzy (Nikodem) 1933-1991 **CLC 1, 2, 3, 6, 10, 15, 53, 70; DAM NOV**
See also CA 17-20R; 134; CANR 9, 46; DA3; DLB 2; DLBY 82; MTCW 1, 2

Kostelanetz, Richard (Cory) 1940- **CLC 28**
See also CA 13-16R; CAAS 8; CANR 38, 77

Kostrowitzki, Wilhelm Apollinaris de 1880-1918
See Apollinaire, Guillaume
See also CA 104

Kotlowitz, Robert 1924- **CLC 4**
See also CA 33-36R; CANR 36

Kotzebue, August (Friedrich Ferdinand) von 1761-1819 **NCLC 25**
See also DLB 94

Kotzwinkle, William 1938- **CLC 5, 14, 35**
See also CA 45-48; CANR 3, 44, 84; CLR 6; DLB 173; MAICYA; SATA 24, 70

Kowna, Stancy
See Szymborska, Wislawa

Kozol, Jonathan 1936- **CLC 17**
See also CA 61-64; CANR 16, 45

Kozoll, Michael 1940(?)- **CLC 35**

Kramer, Kathryn 19(?)- **CLC 34**

Kramer, Larry 1935- **CLC 42; DAM POP; DC 8**
See also CA 124; 126; CANR 60

Krasicki, Ignacy 1735-1801 **NCLC 8**

Krasinski, Zygmunt 1812-1859 **NCLC 4**

Kraus, Karl 1874-1936 **TCLC 5**
See also CA 104; DLB 118

Kreve (Mickevicius), Vincas 1882-1954 **TCLC 27**
See also CA 170; DLB 220

Kristeva, Julia 1941- **CLC 77**
See also CA 154

Kristofferson, Kris 1936- **CLC 26**
See also CA 104

Krizanc, John 1956- **CLC 57**

Krleza, Miroslav 1893-1981 **CLC 8, 114**
See also CA 97-100; 105; CANR 50; DLB 147

Kroetsch, Robert 1927- **CLC 5, 23, 57, 132; DAC; DAM POET**
See also CA 17-20R; CANR 8, 38; DLB 53; MTCW 1

Kroetz, Franz
See Kroetz, Franz Xaver

Kroetz, Franz Xaver 1946- **CLC 41**
See also CA 130

Kroker, Arthur (W.) 1945- **CLC 77**
See also CA 161

Kropotkin, Peter (Aleksieevich) 1842-1921 **TCLC 36**
See also CA 119

Krotkov, Yuri 1917- **CLC 19**
See also CA 102

Krumb
See Crumb, R(obert)

Krumgold, Joseph (Quincy) 1908-1980 **CLC 12**
See also CA 9-12R; 101; CANR 7; MAICYA; SATA 1, 48; SATA-Obit 23

Krumwitz
See Crumb, R(obert)

Krutch, Joseph Wood 1893-1970 **CLC 24**
See also CA 1-4R; 25-28R; CANR 4; DLB 63, 206

Krutzch, Gus
See Eliot, T(homas) S(tearns)

Krylov, Ivan Andreevich 1768(?)-1844 **NCLC 1**
See also DLB 150

Kubin, Alfred (Leopold Isidor) 1877-1959 **TCLC 23**
See also CA 112; 149; DLB 81

Kubrick, Stanley 1928-1999 **CLC 16**
See also AAYA 30; CA 81-84; 177; CANR 33; DLB 26

Kueng, Hans 1928-
See Kung, Hans
See also CA 53-56; CANR 66; MTCW 1, 2

Kumin, Maxine (Winokur) 1925- **CLC 5, 13, 28; DAM POET; PC 15**
See also AITN 2; CA 1-4R; CAAS 8; CANR 1, 21, 69; DA3; DLB 5; MTCW 1, 2; SATA 12

Kundera, Milan 1929- **CLC 4, 9, 19, 32, 68, 115; DAM NOV; SSC 24**
See also AAYA 2; CA 85-88; CANR 19, 52, 74; DA3; MTCW 1, 2

Kunene, Mazisi (Raymond) 1930- **CLC 85**
See also BW 1, 3; CA 125; CANR 81; DLB 117

Kung, Hans 1928- **CLC 130**
See also Kueng, Hans

Kunitz, Stanley (Jasspon) 1905- **CLC 6, 11, 14; PC 19**
See also CA 41-44R; CANR 26, 57; DA3; DLB 48; INT CANR-26; MTCW 1, 2

Kunze, Reiner 1933- **CLC 10**
See also CA 93-96; DLB 75

Kuprin, Aleksander Ivanovich 1870-1938 **TCLC 5**
See also CA 104; 182

Kureishi, Hanif 1954(?)- **CLC 64**
See also CA 139; DLB 194

Kurosawa, Akira 1910-1998 **CLC 16, 119; DAM MULT**
See also AAYA 11; CA 101; 170; CANR 46

Kushner, Tony 1957(?)- **CLC 81; DAM DRAM; DC 10**
See also CA 144; CANR 74; DA3; MTCW 2

Kuttner, Henry 1915-1958 **TCLC 10**
See also CA 107; 157; DLB 8

Kuzma, Greg 1944- **CLC 7**
See also CA 33-36R; CANR 70

Kuzmin, Mikhail 1872(?)-1936 **TCLC 40**
See also CA 170

Kyd, Thomas 1558-1594 **LC 22; DAM DRAM; DC 3**
See also DLB 62

Kyprianos, Iossif
See Samarakis, Antonis

La Bruyere, Jean de 1645-1696 **LC 17**

Lacan, Jacques (Marie Emile) 1901-1981 **CLC 75**
See also CA 121; 104

Laclos, Pierre Ambroise Francois Choderlos de 1741-1803 **NCLC 4, 87**

Lacolere, Francois
See Aragon, Louis

La Colere, Francois
See Aragon, Louis

La Deshabilleuse
See Simenon, Georges (Jacques Christian)

Lady Gregory
See Gregory, Isabella Augusta (Persse)

Lady of Quality, A
See Bagnold, Enid

La Fayette, Marie (Madelaine Pioche de la Vergne Comtes 1634-1693 **LC 2**

Lafayette, Rene
See Hubbard, L(afayette) Ron(ald)

La Fontaine, Jean de 1621-1695 **LC 50**
See also MAICYA; SATA 18

Laforgue, Jules 1860-1887 **NCLC 5, 53; PC 14; SSC 20**

Lagerkvist, Paer (Fabian) 1891-1974 **CLC 7, 10, 13, 54; DAM DRAM, NOV**
See also Lagerkvist, Par
See also CA 85-88; 49-52; DA3; MTCW 1, 2

Lagerkvist, Par SSC 12
See also Lagerkvist, Paer (Fabian)
See also MTCW 2

Lagerloef, Selma (Ottiliana Lovisa) 1858-1940 **TCLC 4, 36**
See also Lagerlof, Selma (Ottiliana Lovisa)
See also CA 108; MTCW 2; SATA 15

Lagerlof, Selma (Ottiliana Lovisa)
See Lagerloef, Selma (Ottiliana Lovisa)
See also CLR 7; SATA 15

La Guma, (Justin) Alex(ander) 1925-1985 **CLC 19; BLCS; DAM NOV**
See also BW 1, 3; CA 49-52; 118; CANR 25, 81; DLB 117; MTCW 1, 2

Laidlaw, A. K.
See Grieve, C(hristopher) M(urray)

Lainez, Manuel Mujica
See Mujica Lainez, Manuel
See also HW 1

Laing, R(onald) D(avid) 1927-1989 **CLC 95**
See also CA 107; 129; CANR 34; MTCW 1

Lamartine, Alphonse (Marie Louis Prat) de 1790-1869 **NCLC 11; DAM POET; PC 16**

Lamb, Charles 1775-1834 **NCLC 10; DA; DAB; DAC; DAM MST; WLC**
See also CDBLB 1789-1832; DLB 93, 107, 163; SATA 17

Lamb, Lady Caroline 1785-1828 **NCLC 38**
See also DLB 116

Lamming, George (William) 1927- **CLC 2, 4, 66; BLC 2; DAM MULT**
See also BW 2, 3; CA 85-88; CANR 26, 76; DLB 125; MTCW 1, 2

L'Amour, Louis (Dearborn) 1908-1988 **CLC 25, 55; DAM NOV, POP**
See also AAYA 16; AITN 2; BEST 89:2; CA 1-4R; 125; CANR 3, 25, 40; DA3; DLB 206; DLBY 80; MTCW 1, 2

Lampedusa, Giuseppe (Tomasi) di 1896-1957 **TCLC 13**
See also Tomasi di Lampedusa, Giuseppe
See also CA 164; DLB 177; MTCW 2

Lampman, Archibald 1861-1899 **NCLC 25**
See also DLB 92

Lancaster, Bruce 1896-1963 **CLC 36**
See also CA 9-10; CANR 70; CAP 1; SATA 9

Lanchester, John CLC 99

Landau, Mark Alexandrovich
See Aldanov, Mark (Alexandrovich)

Landau-Aldanov, Mark Alexandrovich
See Aldanov, Mark (Alexandrovich)

Landis, Jerry
See Simon, Paul (Frederick)

Landis, John 1950- **CLC 26**
See also CA 112; 122

Landolfi, Tommaso 1908-1979 **CLC 11, 49**
See also CA 127; 117; DLB 177

Landon, Letitia Elizabeth 1802-1838 **NCLC 15**
See also DLB 96

Landor, Walter Savage 1775-1864 **NCLC 14**
See also DLB 93, 107

Landwirth, Heinz 1927-
See Lind, Jakov
See also CA 9-12R; CANR 7

Lane, Patrick 1939- **CLC 25; DAM POET**
See also CA 97-100; CANR 54; DLB 53; INT 97-100

Lang, Andrew 1844-1912 **TCLC 16**
See also CA 114; 137; CANR 85; DLB 98, 141, 184; MAICYA; SATA 16

Lang, Fritz 1890-1976 **CLC 20, 103**
See also CA 77-80; 69-72; CANR 30

Lange, John
See Crichton, (John) Michael

Langer, Elinor 1939- **CLC 34**
See also CA 121

Langland, William 1330(?)-1400(?) **LC 19; DA; DAB; DAC; DAM MST, POET**
See also DLB 146

Langstaff, Launcelot
See Irving, Washington

Lanier, Sidney 1842-1881 **NCLC 6; DAM POET**
See also DLB 64; DLBD 13; MAICYA; SATA 18

Lanyer, Aemilia 1569-1645 **LC 10, 30**
See also DLB 121

Lao-Tzu
See Lao Tzu

Lao Tzu fl. 6th cent. B.C.- **CMLC 7**

Lapine, James (Elliot) 1949- **CLC 39**
See also CA 123; 130; CANR 54; INT 130

Larbaud, Valery (Nicolas) 1881-1957 **TCLC 9**
See also CA 106; 152

Lardner, Ring
See Lardner, Ring(gold) W(ilmer)

Lardner, Ring W., Jr.
See Lardner, Ring(gold) W(ilmer)

Lardner, Ring(gold) W(ilmer) 1885-1933 **TCLC 2, 14; SSC 32**
See also CA 104; 131; CDALB 1917-1929; DLB 11, 25, 86; DLBD 16; MTCW 1, 2

Laredo, Betty
See Codrescu, Andrei

Larkin, Maia
See Wojciechowska, Maia (Teresa)

Larkin, Philip (Arthur) 1922-1985 **CLC 3, 5, 8, 9, 13, 18, 33, 39, 64; DAB; DAM MST, POET; PC 21**
See also CA 5-8R; 117; CANR 24, 62; CD-BLB 1960 to Present; DA3; DLB 27; MTCW 1, 2

Larra (y Sanchez de Castro), Mariano Jose de 1809-1837 **NCLC 17**

Larsen, Eric 1941- **CLC 55**
See also CA 132

Larsen, Nella 1891-1964 **CLC 37; BLC 2; DAM MULT**

See also BW 1; CA 125; CANR 83; DLB 51

Larson, Charles R(aymond) 1938- **CLC 31**
See also CA 53-56; CANR 4

Larson, Jonathan 1961-1996 **CLC 99**
See also AAYA 28; CA 156

Las Casas, Bartolome de 1474-1566 **LC 31**

Lasch, Christopher 1932-1994 **CLC 102**
See also CA 73-76; 144; CANR 25; MTCW 1, 2

Lasker-Schueler, Else 1869-1945 **TCLC 57**
See also CA 183; DLB 66, 124

Laski, Harold 1893-1950 **TCLC 79**

Latham, Jean Lee 1902-1995 **CLC 12**
See also AITN 1; CA 5-8R; CANR 7, 84; CLR 50; MAICYA; SATA 2, 68

Latham, Mavis
See Clark, Mavis Thorpe

Lathen, Emma CLC 2
See also Hennissart, Martha; Latsis, Mary J(ane)

Lathrop, Francis
See Leiber, Fritz (Reuter, Jr.)

Latsis, Mary J(ane) 1927(?)-1997
See Lathen, Emma
See also CA 85-88; 162

Lattimore, Richmond (Alexander) 1906-1984 **CLC 3**
See also CA 1-4R; 112; CANR 1

Laughlin, James 1914-1997 **CLC 49**
See also CA 21-24R; 162; CAAS 22; CANR 9, 47; DLB 48; DLBY 96, 97

Laurence, (Jean) Margaret (Wemyss) 1926-1987 **CLC 3, 6, 13, 50, 62; DAC; DAM MST; SSC 7**
See also CA 5-8R; 121; CANR 33; DLB 53; MTCW 1, 2; SATA-Obit 50

Laurent, Antoine 1952- **CLC 50**

Lauscher, Hermann
See Hesse, Hermann

Lautreamont, Comte de 1846-1870 **NCLC 12; SSC 14**

Laverty, Donald
See Blish, James (Benjamin)

Lavin, Mary 1912-1996 **CLC 4, 18, 99; SSC 4**
See also CA 9-12R; 151; CANR 33; DLB 15; MTCW 1

Lavond, Paul Dennis
See Kornbluth, C(yril) M.; Pohl, Frederik

Lawler, Raymond Evenor 1922- **CLC 58**
See also CA 103

Lawrence, D(avid) H(erbert Richards) 1885-1930 **TCLC 2, 9, 16, 33, 48, 61, 93; DA; DAB; DAC; DAM MST, NOV, POET; SSC 4, 19; WLC**
See also CA 104; 121; CDBLB 1914-1945; DA3; DLB 10, 19, 36, 98, 162, 195; MTCW 1, 2

Lawrence, T(homas) E(dward) 1888-1935 **TCLC 18**
See also Dale, Colin
See also CA 115; 167; DLB 195

Lawrence of Arabia
See Lawrence, T(homas) E(dward)

Lawson, Henry (Archibald Hertzberg) 1867-1922 **TCLC 27; SSC 18**
See also CA 120; 181

Lawton, Dennis
See Faust, Frederick (Schiller)

Laxness, Halldor CLC 25
See also Gudjonsson, Halldor Kiljan

Layamon fl. c. 1200- **CMLC 10**
See also DLB 146

Laye, Camara 1928-1980 **CLC 4, 38; BLC 2; DAM MULT**
See also BW 1; CA 85-88; 97-100; CANR 25; MTCW 1, 2

Layton, Irving (Peter) 1912- **CLC 2, 15; DAC; DAM MST, POET**
See also CA 1-4R; CANR 2, 33, 43, 66; DLB 88; MTCW 1, 2

Lazarus, Emma 1849-1887 **NCLC 8**

Lazarus, Felix
See Cable, George Washington

Lazarus, Henry
See Slavitt, David R(ytman)

Lea, Joan
See Neufeld, John (Arthur)

Leacock, Stephen (Butler) 1869-1944 **TCLC 2; DAC; DAM MST; SSC 39**
See also CA 104; 141; CANR 80; DLB 92; MTCW 2

Lear, Edward 1812-1888 **NCLC 3**
See also CLR 1; DLB 32, 163, 166; MAICYA; SATA 18, 100

Lear, Norman (Milton) 1922- **CLC 12**
See also CA 73-76

Leautaud, Paul 1872-1956 **TCLC 83**
See also DLB 65

Leavis, F(rank) R(aymond) 1895-1978 **CLC 24**
See also CA 21-24R; 77-80; CANR 44; MTCW 1, 2

Leavitt, David 1961- **CLC 34; DAM POP**
See also CA 116; 122; CANR 50, 62; DA3; DLB 130; INT 122; MTCW 2

Leblanc, Maurice (Marie Emile) 1864-1941 **TCLC 49**
See also CA 110

Lebowitz, Fran(ces Ann) 1951(?)- **CLC 11, 36**
See also CA 81-84; CANR 14, 60, 70; INT CANR-14; MTCW 1

Lebrecht, Peter
See Tieck, (Johann) Ludwig

le Carre, John CLC 3, 5, 9, 15, 28
See also Cornwell, David (John Moore)
See also BEST 89:4; CDBLB 1960 to Present; DLB 87; MTCW 2

Le Clezio, J(ean) M(arie) G(ustave) 1940- **CLC 31**
See also CA 116; 128; DLB 83

Leconte de Lisle, Charles-Marie-Rene 1818-1894 **NCLC 29**

Le Coq, Monsieur
See Simenon, Georges (Jacques Christian)

Leduc, Violette 1907-1972 **CLC 22**
See also CA 13-14; 33-36R; CANR 69; CAP 1

Ledwidge, Francis 1887(?)-1917 **TCLC 23**
See also CA 123; DLB 20

Lee, Andrea 1953- **CLC 36; BLC 2; DAM MULT**
See also BW 1, 3; CA 125; CANR 82

Lee, Andrew
See Auchincloss, Louis (Stanton)

Lee, Chang-rae 1965- **CLC 91**
See also CA 148; CANR 89

Lee, Don L. CLC 2
See also Madhubuti, Haki R.

Lee, George W(ashington) 1894-1976 **CLC 52; BLC 2; DAM MULT**
See also BW 1; CA 125; CANR 83; DLB 51

Lee, (Nelle) Harper 1926- **CLC 12, 60; DA; DAB; DAC; DAM MST, NOV; WLC**
See also AAYA 13; CA 13-16R; CANR 51; CDALB 1941-1968; DA3; DLB 6; MTCW 1, 2; SATA 11

Lee, Helen Elaine 1959(?)- **CLC 86**
See also CA 148

Lee, Julian
See Latham, Jean Lee

Lee, Larry
See Lee, Lawrence

Lee, Laurie 1914-1997 **CLC 90; DAB; DAM POP**
See also CA 77-80; 158; CANR 33, 73; DLB 27; MTCW 1

Lee, Lawrence 1941-1990 **CLC 34**
See also CA 131; CANR 43

Lee, Li-Young 1957- **PC 24**
See also CA 153; DLB 165

Lee, Manfred B(ennington) 1905-1971 **CLC 11**
See also Queen, Ellery
See also CA 1-4R; 29-32R; CANR 2; DLB 137

Lee, Shelton Jackson 1957(?)- **CLC 105; BLCS; DAM MULT**
See also Lee, Spike
See also BW 2, 3; CA 125; CANR 42

Lee, Spike
See Lee, Shelton Jackson
See also AAYA 4, 29

Lee, Stan 1922- **CLC 17**
See also AAYA 5; CA 108; 111; INT 111

Lee, Tanith 1947- **CLC 46**
See also AAYA 15; CA 37-40R; CANR 53; SATA 8, 88

Lee, Vernon TCLC 5; SSC 33
See also Paget, Violet
See also DLB 57, 153, 156, 174, 178

Lee, William
See Burroughs, William S(eward)

Lee, Willy
See Burroughs, William S(eward)

Lee-Hamilton, Eugene (Jacob) 1845-1907 **TCLC 22**
See also CA 117

Leet, Judith 1935- **CLC 11**

Le Fanu, Joseph Sheridan 1814-1873 **NCLC 9, 58; DAM POP; SSC 14**
See also DA3; DLB 21, 70, 159, 178

Leffland, Ella 1931- **CLC 19**
See also CA 29-32R; CANR 35, 78, 82; DLBY 84; INT CANR-35; SATA 65

Leger, Alexis
See Leger, (Marie-Rene Auguste) Alexis Saint-Leger

Leger, (Marie-Rene Auguste) Alexis Saint-Leger 1887-1975 **CLC 4, 11, 46; DAM POET; PC 23**
See also CA 13-16R; 61-64; CANR 43; MTCW 1

Leger, Saintleger
See Leger, (Marie-Rene Auguste) Alexis Saint-Leger

Le Guin, Ursula K(roeber) 1929- **CLC 8, 13, 22, 45, 71; DAB; DAC; DAM MST, POP; SSC 12**
See also AAYA 9, 27; AITN 1; CA 21-24R; CANR 9, 32, 52, 74; CDALB 1968-1988; CLR 3, 28; DA3; DLB 8, 52; INT CANR-32; JRDA; MAICYA; MTCW 1, 2; SATA 4, 52, 99

Lehmann, Rosamond (Nina) 1901-1990 **CLC 5**
See also CA 77-80; 131; CANR 8, 73; DLB 15; MTCW 2

Leiber, Fritz (Reuter, Jr.) 1910-1992 **CLC 25**
See also CA 45-48; 139; CANR 2, 40, 86; DLB 8; MTCW 1, 2; SATA 45; SATA-Obit 73

Leibniz, Gottfried Wilhelm von 1646-1716 **LC 35**
See also DLB 168

Leimbach, Martha 1963-
See Leimbach, Marti
See also CA 130

Leimbach, Marti CLC 65
See also Leimbach, Martha

Leino, Eino TCLC **24**
See also Loennbohm, Armas Eino Leopold
Leiris, Michel (Julien) 1901-1990 CLC **61**
See also CA 119; 128; 132
Leithauser, Brad 1953- CLC **27**
See also CA 107; CANR 27, 81; DLB 120
Lelchuk, Alan 1938- CLC **5**
See also CA 45-48; CAAS 20; CANR 1, 70
Lem, Stanislaw 1921- CLC **8, 15, 40**
See also CA 105; CAAS 1; CANR 32; MTCW 1
Lemann, Nancy 1956- CLC **39**
See also CA 118; 136
Lemonnier, (Antoine Louis) Camille 1844-1913 TCLC **22**
See also CA 121
Lenau, Nikolaus 1802-1850 NCLC **16**
L'Engle, Madeleine (Camp Franklin) 1918- CLC **12; DAM POP**
See also AAYA 28; AITN 2; CA 1-4R; CANR 3, 21, 39, 66; CLR 1, 14, 57; DA3; DLB 52; JRDA; MAICYA; MTCW 1, 2; SAAS 15; SATA 1, 27, 75
Lengyel, Jozsef 1896-1975 CLC **7**
See also CA 85-88; 57-60; CANR 71
Lenin 1870-1924
See Lenin, V. I.
See also CA 121; 168
Lenin, V. I. TCLC **67**
See also Lenin
Lennon, John (Ono) 1940-1980 CLC **12, 35**
See also CA 102; SATA 114
Lennox, Charlotte Ramsay 1729(?)-1804 NCLC **23**
See also DLB 39
Lentricchia, Frank (Jr.) 1940- CLC **34**
See also CA 25-28R; CANR 19
Lenz, Siegfried 1926- CLC **27; SSC 33**
See also CA 89-92; CANR 80; DLB 75
Leonard, Elmore (John, Jr.) 1925- CLC **28, 34, 71, 120; DAM POP**
See also AAYA 22; AITN 1; BEST 89:1, 90:4; CA 81-84; CANR 12, 28, 53, 76; DA3; DLB 173; INT CANR-28; MTCW 1, 2
Leonard, Hugh CLC **19**
See also Byrne, John Keyes
See also DLB 13
Leonov, Leonid (Maximovich) 1899-1994 CLC **92; DAM NOV**
See also CA 129; CANR 74, 76; MTCW 1, 2
Leopardi, (Conte) Giacomo 1798-1837 NCLC **22**
Le Reveler
See Artaud, Antonin (Marie Joseph)
Lerman, Eleanor 1952- CLC **9**
See also CA 85-88; CANR 69
Lerman, Rhoda 1936- CLC **56**
See also CA 49-52; CANR 70
Lermontov, Mikhail Yuryevich 1814-1841 NCLC **47; PC 18**
See also DLB 205
Leroux, Gaston 1868-1927 TCLC **25**
See also CA 108; 136; CANR 69; SATA 65
Lesage, Alain-Rene 1668-1747 LC **2, 28**
Leskov, Nikolai (Semyonovich) 1831-1895 NCLC **25; SSC 34**
Lessing, Doris (May) 1919- CLC **1, 2, 3, 6, 10, 15, 22, 40, 94; DA; DAB; DAC; DAM MST, NOV; SSC 6; WLCS**
See also CA 9-12R; CAAS 14; CANR 33, 54, 76; CDBLB 1960 to Present; DA3; DLB 15, 139; DLBY 85; MTCW 1, 2
Lessing, Gotthold Ephraim 1729-1781 LC **8**
See also DLB 97
Lester, Richard 1932- CLC **20**
Lever, Charles (James) 1806-1872 NCLC **23**

See also DLB 21
Leverson, Ada 1865(?)-1936(?) TCLC **18**
See also Elaine
See also CA 117; DLB 153
Levertov, Denise 1923-1997 CLC **1, 2, 3, 5, 8, 15, 28, 66; DAM POET; PC 11**
See also CA 1-4R, 178; 163; CAAE 178; CAAS 19; CANR 3, 29, 50; CDALBS; DLB 5, 165; INT CANR-29; MTCW 1, 2
Levi, Jonathan CLC **76**
Levi, Peter (Chad Tigar) 1931- CLC **41**
See also CA 5-8R; CANR 34, 80; DLB 40
Levi, Primo 1919-1987 CLC **37, 50; SSC 12**
See also CA 13-16R; 122; CANR 12, 33, 61, 70; DLB 177; MTCW 1, 2
Levin, Ira 1929- CLC **3, 6; DAM POP**
See also CA 21-24R; CANR 17, 44, 74; DA3; MTCW 1, 2; SATA 66
Levin, Meyer 1905-1981 CLC **7; DAM POP**
See also AITN 1; CA 9-12R; 104; CANR 15; DLB 9, 28; DLBY 81; SATA 21; SATA-Obit 27
Levine, Norman 1924- CLC **54**
See also CA 73-76; CAAS 23; CANR 14, 70; DLB 88
Levine, Philip 1928- CLC **2, 4, 5, 9, 14, 33, 118; DAM POET; PC 22**
See also CA 9-12R; CANR 9, 37, 52; DLB 5
Levinson, Deirdre 1931- CLC **49**
See also CA 73-76; CANR 70
Levi-Strauss, Claude 1908- CLC **38**
See also CA 1-4R; CANR 6, 32, 57; MTCW 1, 2
Levitin, Sonia (Wolff) 1934- CLC **17**
See also AAYA 13; CA 29-32R; CANR 14, 32, 79; CLR 53; JRDA; MAICYA; SAAS 2; SATA 4, 68
Levon, O. U.
See Kesey, Ken (Elton)
Levy, Amy 1861-1889 NCLC **59**
See also DLB 156
Lewes, George Henry 1817-1878 NCLC **25**
See also DLB 55, 144
Lewis, Alun 1915-1944 TCLC **3; SSC 40**
See also CA 104; DLB 20, 162
Lewis, C. Day
See Day Lewis, C(ecil)
Lewis, C(live) S(taples) 1898-1963 CLC **1, 3, 6, 14, 27, 124; DA; DAB; DAC; DAM MST, NOV, POP; WLC**
See also AAYA 3; CA 81-84; CANR 33, 71; CDBLB 1945-1960; CLR 3, 27; DA3; DLB 15, 100, 160; JRDA; MAICYA; MTCW 1, 2; SATA 13, 100
Lewis, Janet 1899-1998 CLC **41**
See also Winters, Janet Lewis
See also CA 9-12R; 172; CANR 29, 63; CAP 1; DLBY 87
Lewis, Matthew Gregory 1775-1818 NCLC **11, 62**
See also DLB 39, 158, 178
Lewis, (Harry) Sinclair 1885-1951 TCLC **4, 13, 23, 39; DA; DAB; DAC; DAM MST, NOV; WLC**
See also CA 104; 133; CDALB 1917-1929; DA3; DLB 9, 102; DLBD 1; MTCW 1, 2
Lewis, (Percy) Wyndham 1882(?)-1957 TCLC **2, 9; SSC 34**
See also CA 104; 157; DLB 15; MTCW 2
Lewisohn, Ludwig 1883-1955 TCLC **19**
See also CA 107; DLB 4, 9, 28, 102
Lewton, Val 1904-1951 TCLC **76**
Leyner, Mark 1956- CLC **92**
See also CA 110; CANR 28, 53; DA3; MTCW 2
Lezama Lima, Jose 1910-1976 CLC **4, 10, 101; DAM MULT; HLCS 2**

See also CA 77-80; CANR 71; DLB 113; HW 1, 2
L'Heureux, John (Clarke) 1934- CLC **52**
See also CA 13-16R; CANR 23, 45, 88
Liddell, C. H.
See Kuttner, Henry
Lie, Jonas (Lauritz Idemil) 1833-1908(?) TCLC **5**
See also CA 115
Lieber, Joel 1937-1971 CLC **6**
See also CA 73-76; 29-32R
Lieber, Stanley Martin
See Lee, Stan
Lieberman, Laurence (James) 1935- CLC **4, 36**
See also CA 17-20R; CANR 8, 36, 89
Lieh Tzu fl. 7th cent. B.C.-5th cent. B.C. CMLC **27**
Lieksman, Anders
See Haavikko, Paavo Juhani
Li Fei-kan 1904-
See Pa Chin
See also CA 105
Lifton, Robert Jay 1926- CLC **67**
See also CA 17-20R; CANR 27, 78; INT CANR-27; SATA 66
Lightfoot, Gordon 1938- CLC **26**
See also CA 109
Lightman, Alan P(aige) 1948- CLC **81**
See also CA 141; CANR 63
Ligotti, Thomas (Robert) 1953- CLC **44; SSC 16**
See also CA 123; CANR 49
Li Ho 791-817 PC **13**
Liliencron, (Friedrich Adolf Axel) Detlev von 1844-1909 TCLC **18**
See also CA 117
Lilly, William 1602-1681 LC **27**
Lima, Jose Lezama
See Lezama Lima, Jose
Lima Barreto, Afonso Henrique de 1881-1922 TCLC **23**
See also CA 117; 181
Limonov, Edward 1944- CLC **67**
See also CA 137
Lin, Frank
See Atherton, Gertrude (Franklin Horn)
Lincoln, Abraham 1809-1865 NCLC **18**
Lind, Jakov CLC **1, 2, 4, 27, 82**
See also Landwirth, Heinz
See also CAAS 4
Lindbergh, Anne (Spencer) Morrow 1906- CLC **82; DAM NOV**
See also CA 17-20R; CANR 16, 73; MTCW 1, 2; SATA 33
Lindsay, David 1878-1945 TCLC **15**
See also CA 113
Lindsay, (Nicholas) Vachel 1879-1931 TCLC **17; DA; DAC; DAM MST, POET; PC 23; WLC**
See also CA 114; 135; CANR 79; CDALB 1865-1917; DA3; DLB 54; SATA 40
Linke-Poot
See Doeblin, Alfred
Linney, Romulus 1930- CLC **51**
See also CA 1-4R; CANR 40, 44, 79
Linton, Eliza Lynn 1822-1898 NCLC **41**
See also DLB 18
Li Po 701-763 CMLC **2; PC 29**
Lipsius, Justus 1547-1606 LC **16**
Lipsyte, Robert (Michael) 1938- CLC **21; DA; DAC; DAM MST, NOV**
See also AAYA 7; CA 17-20R; CANR 8, 57; CLR 23; JRDA; MAICYA; SATA 5, 68, 113
Lish, Gordon (Jay) 1934- CLC **45; SSC 18**
See also CA 113; 117; CANR 79; DLB 130; INT 117

Lispector, Clarice 1925(?)-1977 **CLC 43;
HLCS 2; SSC 34**
See also CA 139; 116; CANR 71; DLB 113;
HW 2
Littell, Robert 1935(?)- **CLC 42**
See also CA 109; 112; CANR 64
Little, Malcolm 1925-1965
See Malcolm X
See also BW 1, 3; CA 125; 111; CANR 82;
DA; DAB; DAC; DAM MST, MULT;
DA3; MTCW 1, 2
Littlewit, Humphrey Gent.
See Lovecraft, H(oward) P(hillips)
Litwos
See Sienkiewicz, Henryk (Adam Alexander
Pius)
Liu, E 1857-1909 **TCLC 15**
See also CA 115
Lively, Penelope (Margaret) 1933- **CLC 32,
50; DAM NOV**
See also CA 41-44R; CANR 29, 67, 79;
CLR 7; DLB 14, 161, 207; JRDA; MAI-
CYA; MTCW 1, 2; SATA 7, 60, 101
Livesay, Dorothy (Kathleen) 1909- **CLC 4,
15, 79; DAC; DAM MST, POET**
See also AITN 2; CA 25-28R; CAAS 8;
CANR 36, 67; DLB 68; MTCW 1
Livy c. 59B.C.-c. 17 **CMLC 11**
See also DLB 211
Lizardi, Jose Joaquin Fernandez de
1776-1827 **NCLC 30**
Llewellyn, Richard
See Llewellyn Lloyd, Richard Dafydd Viv-
ian
See also DLB 15
Llewellyn Lloyd, Richard Dafydd Vivian
1906-1983 **CLC 7, 80**
See also Llewellyn, Richard
See also CA 53-56; 111; CANR 7, 71;
SATA 11; SATA-Obit 37
Llosa, (Jorge) Mario (Pedro) Vargas
See Vargas Llosa, (Jorge) Mario (Pedro)
Lloyd, Manda
See Mander, (Mary) Jane
Lloyd Webber, Andrew 1948-
See Webber, Andrew Lloyd
See also AAYA 1; CA 116; 149; DAM
DRAM; SATA 56
Llull, Ramon c. 1235-c. 1316 **CMLC 12**
Lobb, Ebenezer
See Upward, Allen
Locke, Alain (Le Roy) 1886-1954 **TCLC 43;
BLCS**
See also BW 1, 3; CA 106; 124; CANR 79;
DLB 51
Locke, John 1632-1704 **LC 7, 35**
See also DLB 101
Locke-Elliott, Sumner
See Elliott, Sumner Locke
Lockhart, John Gibson 1794-1854 **NCLC 6**
See also DLB 110, 116, 144
Lodge, David (John) 1935- **CLC 36; DAM
POP**
See also BEST 90:1; CA 17-20R; CANR
19, 53; DLB 14, 194; INT CANR-19;
MTCW 1, 2
Lodge, Thomas 1558-1625 **LC 41**
Lodge, Thomas 1558-1625 **LC 41**
See also DLB 172
Loennbohm, Armas Eino Leopold 1878-1926
See Leino, Eino
See also CA 123
Loewinsohn, Ron(ald William) 1937- **CLC
52**
See also CA 25-28R; CANR 71
Logan, Jake
See Smith, Martin Cruz
Logan, John (Burton) 1923-1987 **CLC 5**
See also CA 77-80; 124; CANR 45; DLB 5

Lo Kuan-chung 1330(?)-1400(?) **LC 12**
Lombard, Nap
See Johnson, Pamela Hansford
London, Jack TCLC 9, 15, 39; SSC 4; WLC
See also London, John Griffith
See also AAYA 13; AITN 2; CDALB 1865-
1917; DLB 8, 12, 78, 212; SATA 18
London, John Griffith 1876-1916
See London, Jack
See also CA 110; 119; CANR 73; DA;
DAB; DAC; DAM MST, NOV; DA3;
JRDA; MAICYA; MTCW 1, 2
Long, Emmett
See Leonard, Elmore (John, Jr.)
Longbaugh, Harry
See Goldman, William (W.)
Longfellow, Henry Wadsworth 1807-1882
**NCLC 2, 45; DA; DAB; DAC; DAM
MST, POET; PC 30; WLCS**
See also CDALB 1640-1865; DA3; DLB 1,
59; SATA 19
Longinus c. 1st cent. - **CMLC 27**
See also DLB 176
Longley, Michael 1939- **CLC 29**
See also CA 102; DLB 40
Longus fl. c. 2nd cent. - **CMLC 7**
Longway, A. Hugh
See Lang, Andrew
Lonnrot, Elias 1802-1884 **NCLC 53**
Lopate, Phillip 1943- **CLC 29**
See also CA 97-100; CANR 88; DLBY 80;
INT 97-100
Lopez Portillo (y Pacheco), Jose 1920- **CLC
46**
See also CA 129; HW 1
Lopez y Fuentes, Gregorio 1897(?)-1966 **CLC
32**
See also CA 131; HW 1
Lorca, Federico Garcia
See Garcia Lorca, Federico
Lord, Bette Bao 1938- **CLC 23**
See also BEST 90:3; CA 107; CANR 41,
79; INT 107; SATA 58
Lord Auch
See Bataille, Georges
Lord Byron
See Byron, George Gordon (Noel)
Lorde, Audre (Geraldine) 1934-1992 **CLC
18, 71; BLC 2; DAM MULT, POET; PC
12**
See also BW 1, 3; CA 25-28R; 142; CANR
16, 26, 46, 82; DA3; DLB 41; MTCW 1,
2
Lord Houghton
See Milnes, Richard Monckton
Lord Jeffrey
See Jeffrey, Francis
Lorenzini, Carlo 1826-1890
See Collodi, Carlo
See also MAICYA; SATA 29, 100
Lorenzo, Heberto Padilla
See Padilla (Lorenzo), Heberto
Loris
See Hofmannsthal, Hugo von
Loti, Pierre TCLC 11
See also Viaud, (Louis Marie) Julien
See also DLB 123
Lou, Henri
See Andreas-Salome, Lou
Louie, David Wong 1954- **CLC 70**
See also CA 139
Louis, Father M.
See Merton, Thomas
Lovecraft, H(oward) P(hillips) 1890-1937
TCLC 4, 22; DAM POP; SSC 3
See also AAYA 14; CA 104; 133; DA3;
MTCW 1, 2
Lovelace, Earl 1935- **CLC 51**

See also BW 2; CA 77-80; CANR 41, 72;
DLB 125; MTCW 1
Lovelace, Richard 1618-1657 **LC 24**
See also DLB 131
Lowell, Amy 1874-1925 **TCLC 1, 8; DAM
POET; PC 13**
See also CA 104; 151; DLB 54, 140;
MTCW 2
Lowell, James Russell 1819-1891 **NCLC 2**
See also CDALB 1640-1865; DLB 1, 11,
64, 79, 189
Lowell, Robert (Traill Spence, Jr.)
1917-1977 **CLC 1, 2, 3, 4, 5, 8, 9, 11, 15,
37, 124; DA; DAB; DAC; DAM MST,
NOV; PC 3; WLC**
See also CA 9-12R; 73-76; CABS 2; CANR
26, 60; CDALBS; DA3; DLB 5, 169;
MTCW 1, 2
Lowenthal, Michael (Francis) 1969- **CLC 119**
See also CA 150
Lowndes, Marie Adelaide (Belloc) 1868-1947
TCLC 12
See also CA 107; DLB 70
Lowry, (Clarence) Malcolm 1909-1957 **TCLC
6, 40; SSC 31**
See also CA 105; 131; CANR 62; CDBLB
1945-1960; DLB 15; MTCW 1, 2
Lowry, Mina Gertrude 1882-1966
See Loy, Mina
See also CA 113
Loxsmith, John
See Brunner, John (Kilian Houston)
Loy, Mina CLC 28; DAM POET; PC 16
See also Lowry, Mina Gertrude
See also DLB 4, 54
Loyson-Bridet
See Schwob, Marcel (Mayer Andre)
Lucan 39-65 **CMLC 33**
See also DLB 211
Lucas, Craig 1951- **CLC 64**
See also CA 137; CANR 71
Lucas, E(dward) V(errall) 1868-1938 **TCLC
73**
See also CA 176; DLB 98, 149, 153; SATA
20
Lucas, George 1944- **CLC 16**
See also AAYA 1, 23; CA 77-80; CANR
30; SATA 56
Lucas, Hans
See Godard, Jean-Luc
Lucas, Victoria
See Plath, Sylvia
Lucian c. 120-c. 180 **CMLC 32**
See also DLB 176
Ludlam, Charles 1943-1987 **CLC 46, 50**
See also CA 85-88; 122; CANR 72, 86
Ludlum, Robert 1927- **CLC 22, 43; DAM
NOV, POP**
See also AAYA 10; BEST 89:1, 90:3; CA
33-36R; CANR 25, 41, 68; DA3; DLBY
82; MTCW 1, 2
Ludwig, Ken CLC 60
Ludwig, Otto 1813-1865 **NCLC 4**
See also DLB 129
Lugones, Leopoldo 1874-1938 **TCLC 15;
HLCS 2**
See also CA 116; 131; HW 1
Lu Hsun 1881-1936 **TCLC 3; SSC 20**
See also Shu-Jen, Chou
Lukacs, George CLC 24
See also Lukacs, Gyorgy (Szegeny von)
Lukacs, Gyorgy (Szegeny von) 1885-1971
See Lukacs, George
See also CA 101; 29-32R; CANR 62;
MTCW 2
Luke, Peter (Ambrose Cyprian) 1919-1995
CLC 38
See also CA 81-84; 147; CANR 72; DLB
13

Lunar, Dennis
See Mungo, Raymond

Lurie, Alison 1926- **CLC 4, 5, 18, 39**
See also CA 1-4R; CANR 2, 17, 50, 88;
DLB 2; MTCW 1; SATA 46, 112

Lustig, Arnost 1926- **CLC 56**
See also AAYA 3; CA 69-72; CANR 47;
SATA 56

Luther, Martin 1483-1546 **LC 9, 37**
See also DLB 179

Luxemburg, Rosa 1870(?)-1919 **TCLC 63**
See also CA 118

Luzi, Mario 1914- **CLC 13**
See also CA 61-64; CANR 9, 70; DLB 128

Lyly, John 1554(?)-1606 **LC 41; DAM
DRAM; DC 7**
See also DLB 62, 167

L'Ymagier
See Gourmont, Remy (-Marie-Charles) de

Lynch, B. Suarez
See Bioy Casares, Adolfo; Borges, Jorge
Luis

Lynch, B. Suarez
See Bioy Casares, Adolfo

Lynch, David (K.) 1946- **CLC 66**
See also CA 124; 129

Lynch, James
See Andreyev, Leonid (Nikolaevich)

Lynch Davis, B.
See Bioy Casares, Adolfo; Borges, Jorge
Luis

Lyndsay, Sir David 1490-1555 **LC 20**

Lynn, Kenneth S(chuyler) 1923- **CLC 50**
See also CA 1-4R; CANR 3, 27, 65

Lynx
See West, Rebecca

Lyons, Marcus
See Blish, James (Benjamin)

Lyre, Pinchbeck
See Sassoon, Siegfried (Lorraine)

Lytle, Andrew (Nelson) 1902-1995 **CLC 22**
See also CA 9-12R; 150; CANR 70; DLB
6; DLBY 95

Lyttelton, George 1709-1773 **LC 10**

Maas, Peter 1929- **CLC 29**
See also CA 93-96; INT 93-96; MTCW 2

Macaulay, Rose 1881-1958 **TCLC 7, 44**
See also CA 104; DLB 36

Macaulay, Thomas Babington 1800-1859
NCLC 42
See also CDBLB 1832-1890; DLB 32, 55

MacBeth, George (Mann) 1932-1992 **CLC 2,
5, 9**
See also CA 25-28R; 136; CANR 61, 66;
DLB 40; MTCW 1; SATA 4; SATA-Obit
70

MacCaig, Norman (Alexander) 1910- **CLC
36; DAB; DAM POET**
See also CA 9-12R; CANR 3, 34; DLB 27

MacCarthy, Sir(Charles Otto) Desmond
1877-1952 **TCLC 36**
See also CA 167

**MacDiarmid, Hugh CLC 2, 4, 11, 19, 63; PC
9**
See also Grieve, C(hristopher) M(urray)
See also CDBLB 1945-1960; DLB 20

MacDonald, Anson
See Heinlein, Robert A(nson)

Macdonald, Cynthia 1928- **CLC 13, 19**
See also CA 49-52; CANR 4, 44; DLB 105

MacDonald, George 1824-1905 **TCLC 9**
See also CA 106; 137; CANR 80; DLB 18,
163, 178; MAICYA; SATA 33, 100

Macdonald, John
See Millar, Kenneth

MacDonald, John D(ann) 1916-1986 **CLC 3,
27, 44; DAM NOV, POP**

See also CA 1-4R; 121; CANR 1, 19, 60;
DLB 8; DLBY 86; MTCW 1, 2

Macdonald, John Ross
See Millar, Kenneth

Macdonald, Ross CLC 1, 2, 3, 14, 34, 41
See also Millar, Kenneth
See also DLBD 6

MacDougal, John
See Blish, James (Benjamin)

MacDougal, John
See Blish, James (Benjamin)

MacEwen, Gwendolyn (Margaret)
1941-1987 **CLC 13, 55**
See also CA 9-12R; 124; CANR 7, 22; DLB
53; SATA 50; SATA-Obit 55

Macha, Karel Hynek 1810-1846 **NCLC 46**

Machado (y Ruiz), Antonio 1875-1939 **TCLC
3**
See also CA 104; 174; DLB 108; HW 2

Machado de Assis, Joaquim Maria
1839-1908 **TCLC 10; BLC 2; HLCS 2;
SSC 24**
See also CA 107; 153; CANR 91

Machen, Arthur TCLC 4; SSC 20
See also Jones, Arthur Llewellyn
See also CA 179; DLB 36, 156, 178

Machiavelli, Niccolo 1469-1527 **LC 8, 36;
DA; DAB; DAC; DAM MST; WLCS**

MacInnes, Colin 1914-1976 **CLC 4, 23**
See also CA 69-72; 65-68; CANR 21; DLB
14; MTCW 1, 2

MacInnes, Helen (Clark) 1907-1985 **CLC 27,
39; DAM POP**
See also CA 1-4R; 117; CANR 1, 28, 58;
DLB 87; MTCW 1, 2; SATA 22; SATA-
Obit 44

Mackenzie, Compton (Edward Montague)
1883-1972 **CLC 18**
See also CA 21-22; 37-40R; CAP 2; DLB
34, 100

Mackenzie, Henry 1745-1831 **NCLC 41**
See also DLB 39

Mackintosh, Elizabeth 1896(?)-1952
See Tey, Josephine
See also CA 110

MacLaren, James
See Grieve, C(hristopher) M(urray)

Mac Laverty, Bernard 1942- **CLC 31**
See also CA 116; 118; CANR 43, 88; INT
118

MacLean, Alistair (Stuart) 1922(?)-1987 **CLC
3, 13, 50, 63; DAM POP**
See also CA 57-60; 121; CANR 28, 61;
MTCW 1; SATA 23; SATA-Obit 50

Maclean, Norman (Fitzroy) 1902-1990 **CLC
78; DAM POP; SSC 13**
See also CA 102; 132; CANR 49; DLB 206

MacLeish, Archibald 1892-1982 **CLC 3, 8,
14, 68; DAM POET**
See also CA 9-12R; 106; CANR 33, 63;
CDALBS; DLB 4, 7, 45; DLBY 82;
MTCW 1, 2

MacLennan, (John) Hugh 1907-1990 **CLC 2,
14, 92; DAC; DAM MST**
See also CA 5-8R; 142; CANR 33; DLB
68; MTCW 1, 2

MacLeod, Alistair 1936- **CLC 56; DAC;
DAM MST**
See also CA 123; DLB 60; MTCW 2

Macleod, Fiona
See Sharp, William

MacNeice, (Frederick) Louis 1907-1963 **CLC
1, 4, 10, 53; DAB; DAM POET**
See also CA 85-88; CANR 61; DLB 10, 20;
MTCW 1, 2

MacNeill, Dand
See Fraser, George MacDonald

Macpherson, James 1736-1796 **LC 29**
See also Ossian

See also DLB 109

Macpherson, (Jean) Jay 1931- **CLC 14**
See also CA 5-8R; CANR 90; DLB 53

MacShane, Frank 1927-1999 **CLC 39**
See also CA 9-12R; 186; CANR 3, 33; DLB
111

Macumber, Mari
See Sandoz, Mari(e Susette)

Madach, Imre 1823-1864 **NCLC 19**

Madden, (Jerry) David 1933- **CLC 5, 15**
See also CA 1-4R; CAAS 3; CANR 4, 45;
DLB 6; MTCW 1

Maddern, Al(an)
See Ellison, Harlan (Jay)

Madhubuti, Haki R. 1942- **CLC 6, 73; BLC
2; DAM MULT, POET; PC 5**
See also Lee, Don L.
See also BW 2, 3; CA 73-76; CANR 24,
51, 73; DLB 5, 41; DLBD 8; MTCW 2

Maepenn, Hugh
See Kuttner, Henry

Maepenn, K. H.
See Kuttner, Henry

Maeterlinck, Maurice 1862-1949 **TCLC 3;
DAM DRAM**
See also CA 104; 136; CANR 80; DLB 192;
SATA 66

Maginn, William 1794-1842 **NCLC 8**
See also DLB 110, 159

Mahapatra, Jayanta 1928- **CLC 33; DAM
MULT**
See also CA 73-76; CAAS 9; CANR 15,
33, 66, 87

Mahfouz, Naguib (Abdel Aziz Al-Sabilgi)
1911(?)-
See Mahfuz, Najib
See also BEST 89:2; CA 128; CANR 55;
DAM NOV; DA3; MTCW 1, 2

Mahfuz, Najib CLC 52, 55
See also Mahfouz, Naguib (Abdel Aziz Al-
Sabilgi)
See also DLBY 88

Mahon, Derek 1941- **CLC 27**
See also CA 113; 128; CANR 88; DLB 40

Mailer, Norman 1923- **CLC 1, 2, 3, 4, 5, 8,
11, 14, 28, 39, 74, 111; DA; DAB; DAC;
DAM MST, NOV, POP**
See also AAYA 31; AITN 2; CA 9-12R;
CABS 1; CANR 28, 74, 77; CDALB
1968-1988; DA3; DLB 2, 16, 28, 185;
DLBD 3; DLBY 80, 83; MTCW 1, 2

Maillet, Antonine 1929- **CLC 54, 118; DAC**
See also CA 115; 120; CANR 46, 74, 77;
DLB 60; INT 120; MTCW 2

Mais, Roger 1905-1955 **TCLC 8**
See also BW 1, 3; CA 105; 124; CANR 82;
DLB 125; MTCW 1

Maistre, Joseph de 1753-1821 **NCLC 37**

Maitland, Frederic 1850-1906 **TCLC 65**

Maitland, Sara (Louise) 1950- **CLC 49**
See also CA 69-72; CANR 13, 59

Major, Clarence 1936- **CLC 3, 19, 48; BLC
2; DAM MULT**
See also BW 2, 3; CA 21-24R; CAAS 6;
CANR 13, 25, 53, 82; DLB 33

Major, Kevin (Gerald) 1949- **CLC 26; DAC**
See also AAYA 16; CA 97-100; CANR 21,
38; CLR 11; DLB 60; INT CANR-21;
JRDA; MAICYA; SATA 32, 82

Maki, James
See Ozu, Yasujiro

Malabaila, Damiano
See Levi, Primo

Malamud, Bernard 1914-1986 **CLC 1, 2, 3,
5, 8, 9, 11, 18, 27, 44, 78, 85; DA; DAB;
DAC; DAM MST, NOV, POP; SSC 15;
WLC**

See also AAYA 16; CA 5-8R; 118; CABS 1; CANR 28, 62; CDALB 1941-1968; DA3; DLB 2, 28, 152; DLBY 80, 86; MTCW 1, 2

Malan, Herman
See Bosman, Herman Charles; Bosman, Herman Charles

Malaparte, Curzio 1898-1957 **TCLC 52**

Malcolm, Dan
See Silverberg, Robert

Malcolm X CLC 82, 117; BLC 2; WLCS
See also Little, Malcolm

Malherbe, Francois de 1555-1628 **LC 5**

Mallarme, Stephane 1842-1898 **NCLC 4, 41; DAM POET; PC 4**

Mallet-Joris, Francoise 1930- **CLC 11**
See also CA 65-68; CANR 17; DLB 83

Malley, Ern
See McAuley, James Phillip

Mallowan, Agatha Christie
See Christie, Agatha (Mary Clarissa)

Maloff, Saul 1922- **CLC 5**
See also CA 33-36R

Malone, Louis
See MacNeice, (Frederick) Louis

Malone, Michael (Christopher) 1942- **CLC 43**
See also CA 77-80; CANR 14, 32, 57

Malory, (Sir) Thomas 1410(?)-1471(?) **LC 11; DA; DAB; DAC; DAM MST; WLCS**
See also CDBLB Before 1660; DLB 146; SATA 59; SATA-Brief 33

Malouf, (George Joseph) David 1934- **CLC 28, 86**
See also CA 124; CANR 50, 76; MTCW 2

Malraux, (Georges-)Andre 1901-1976 **CLC 1, 4, 9, 13, 15, 57; DAM NOV**
See also CA 21-22; 69-72; CANR 34, 58; CAP 2; DA3; DLB 72; MTCW 1, 2

Malzberg, Barry N(athaniel) 1939- **CLC 7**
See also CA 61-64; CAAS 4; CANR 16; DLB 8

Mamet, David (Alan) 1947- **CLC 9, 15, 34, 46, 91; DAM DRAM; DC 4**
See also AAYA 3; CA 81-84; CABS 3; CANR 15, 41, 67, 72; DA3; DLB 7; MTCW 1, 2

Mamoulian, Rouben (Zachary) 1897-1987 **CLC 16**
See also CA 25-28R; 124; CANR 85

Mandelstam, Osip (Emilievich) 1891(?)-1938(?) **TCLC 2, 6; PC 14**
See also CA 104; 150; MTCW 2

Mander, (Mary) Jane 1877-1949 **TCLC 31**
See also CA 162

Mandeville, John fl. 1350- **CMLC 19**
See also DLB 146

Mandiargues, Andre Pieyre de CLC 41
See also Pieyre de Mandiargues, Andre
See also DLB 83

Mandrake, Ethel Belle
See Thurman, Wallace (Henry)

Mangan, James Clarence 1803-1849 **NCLC 27**

Maniere, J.-E.
See Giraudoux, (Hippolyte) Jean

Mankiewicz, Herman (Jacob) 1897-1953 **TCLC 85**
See also CA 120; 169; DLB 26

Manley, (Mary) Delariviere 1672(?)-1724 **LC 1, 42**
See also DLB 39, 80

Mann, Abel
See Creasey, John

Mann, Emily 1952- **DC 7**
See also CA 130; CANR 55

Mann, (Luiz) Heinrich 1871-1950 **TCLC 9**
See also CA 106; 164, 181; DLB 66, 118

Mann, (Paul) Thomas 1875-1955 **TCLC 2, 8, 14, 21, 35, 44, 60; DA; DAB; DAC; DAM MST, NOV; SSC 5; WLC**
See also CA 104; 128; DA3; DLB 66; MTCW 1, 2

Mannheim, Karl 1893-1947 **TCLC 65**

Manning, David
See Faust, Frederick (Schiller)

Manning, Frederic 1887(?)-1935 **TCLC 25**
See also CA 124

Manning, Olivia 1915-1980 **CLC 5, 19**
See also CA 5-8R; 101; CANR 29; MTCW 1

Mano, D. Keith 1942- **CLC 2, 10**
See also CA 25-28R; CAAS 6; CANR 26, 57; DLB 6

Mansfield, Katherine TCLC 2, 8, 39; DAB; SSC 9, 23, 38; WLC
See also Beauchamp, Kathleen Mansfield
See also DLB 162

Manso, Peter 1940- **CLC 39**
See also CA 29-32R; CANR 44

Mantecon, Juan Jimenez
See Jimenez (Mantecon), Juan Ramon

Manton, Peter
See Creasey, John

Man Without a Spleen, A
See Chekhov, Anton (Pavlovich)

Manzoni, Alessandro 1785-1873 **NCLC 29**

Map, Walter 1140-1209 **CMLC 32**

Mapu, Abraham (ben Jekutiel) 1808-1867 **NCLC 18**

Mara, Sally
See Queneau, Raymond

Marat, Jean Paul 1743-1793 **LC 10**

Marcel, Gabriel Honore 1889-1973 **CLC 15**
See also CA 102; 45-48; MTCW 1, 2

March, William 1893-1954 **TCLC 96**

Marchbanks, Samuel
See Davies, (William) Robertson

Marchi, Giacomo
See Bassani, Giorgio

Margulies, Donald CLC 76

Marie de France c. 12th cent. - **CMLC 8; PC 22**
See also DLB 208

Marie de l'Incarnation 1599-1672 **LC 10**

Marier, Captain Victor
See Griffith, D(avid Lewelyn) W(ark)

Mariner, Scott
See Pohl, Frederik

Marinetti, Filippo Tommaso 1876-1944 **TCLC 10**
See also CA 107; DLB 114

Marivaux, Pierre Carlet de Chamblain de 1688-1763 **LC 4; DC 7**

Markandaya, Kamala CLC 8, 38
See also Taylor, Kamala (Purnaiya)

Markfield, Wallace 1926- **CLC 8**
See also CA 69-72; CAAS 3; DLB 2, 28

Markham, Edwin 1852-1940 **TCLC 47**
See also CA 160; DLB 54, 186

Markham, Robert
See Amis, Kingsley (William)

Marks, J
See Highwater, Jamake (Mamake)

Marks-Highwater, J
See Highwater, Jamake (Mamake)

Markson, David M(errill) 1927- **CLC 67**
See also CA 49-52; CANR 1, 91

Marley, Bob CLC 17
See also Marley, Robert Nesta

Marley, Robert Nesta 1945-1981
See Marley, Bob
See also CA 107; 103

Marlowe, Christopher 1564-1593 **LC 22, 47; DA; DAB; DAC; DAM DRAM, MST; DC 1; WLC**

See also CDBLB Before 1660; DA3; DLB 62

Marlowe, Stephen 1928-
See Queen, Ellery
See also CA 13-16R; CANR 6, 55

Marmontel, Jean-Francois 1723-1799 **LC 2**

Marquand, John P(hillips) 1893-1960 **CLC 2, 10**
See also CA 85-88; CANR 73; DLB 9, 102; MTCW 2

Marques, Rene 1919-1979 **CLC 96; DAM MULT; HLC 2**
See also CA 97-100; 85-88; CANR 78; DLB 113; HW 1, 2

Marquez, Gabriel (Jose) Garcia
See Garcia Marquez, Gabriel (Jose)

Marquis, Don(ald Robert Perry) 1878-1937 **TCLC 7**
See also CA 104; 166; DLB 11, 25

Marric, J. J.
See Creasey, John

Marryat, Frederick 1792-1848 **NCLC 3**
See also DLB 21, 163

Marsden, James
See Creasey, John

Marsh, (Edith) Ngaio 1899-1982 **CLC 7, 53; DAM POP**
See also CA 9-12R; CANR 6, 58; DLB 77; MTCW 1, 2

Marshall, Garry 1934- **CLC 17**
See also AAYA 3; CA 111; SATA 60

Marshall, Paule 1929- **CLC 27, 72; BLC 3; DAM MULT; SSC 3**
See also BW 2, 3; CA 77-80; CANR 25, 73; DA3; DLB 157; MTCW 1, 2

Marshallik
See Zangwill, Israel

Marsten, Richard
See Hunter, Evan

Marston, John 1576-1634 **LC 33; DAM DRAM**
See also DLB 58, 172

Martha, Henry
See Harris, Mark

Marti (y Perez), Jose (Julian) 1853-1895 **NCLC 63; DAM MULT; HLC 2**
See also HW 2

Martial c. 40-c. 104 **CMLC 35; PC 10**
See also DLB 211

Martin, Ken
See Hubbard, L(afayette) Ron(ald)

Martin, Richard
See Creasey, John

Martin, Steve 1945- **CLC 30**
See also CA 97-100; CANR 30; MTCW 1

Martin, Valerie 1948- **CLC 89**
See also BEST 90:2; CA 85-88; CANR 49, 89

Martin, Violet Florence 1862-1915 **TCLC 51**

Martin, Webber
See Silverberg, Robert

Martindale, Patrick Victor
See White, Patrick (Victor Martindale)

Martin du Gard, Roger 1881-1958 **TCLC 24**
See also CA 118; DLB 65

Martineau, Harriet 1802-1876 **NCLC 26**
See also DLB 21, 55, 159, 163, 166, 190; YABC 2

Martines, Julia
See O'Faolain, Julia

Martinez, Enrique Gonzalez
See Gonzalez Martinez, Enrique

Martinez, Jacinto Benavente y
See Benavente (y Martinez), Jacinto

Martinez Ruiz, Jose 1873-1967
See Azorin; Ruiz, Jose Martinez
See also CA 93-96; HW 1

Nik. T. O.
See Annensky, Innokenty (Fyodorovich)
Nin, Anais 1903-1977 **CLC 1, 4, 8, 11, 14, 60, 127; DAM NOV, POP; SSC 10**
See also AITN 2; CA 13-16R; 69-72; CANR 22, 53; DLB 2, 4, 152; MTCW 1, 2
Nishida, Kitaro 1870-1945 **TCLC 83**
Nishiwaki, Junzaburo 1894-1982 **PC 15**
See also CA 107
Nissenson, Hugh 1933- **CLC 4, 9**
See also CA 17-20R; CANR 27; DLB 28
Niven, Larry CLC 8
See also Niven, Laurence Van Cott
See also AAYA 27; DLB 8
Niven, Laurence Van Cott 1938-
See Niven, Larry
See also CA 21-24R; CAAS 12; CANR 14, 44, 66; DAM POP; MTCW 1, 2; SATA 95
Nixon, Agnes Eckhardt 1927- **CLC 21**
See also CA 110
Nizan, Paul 1905-1940 **TCLC 40**
See also CA 161; DLB 72
Nkosi, Lewis 1936- **CLC 45; BLC 3; DAM MULT**
See also BW 1, 3; CA 65-68; CANR 27, 81; DLB 157
Nodier, (Jean) Charles (Emmanuel) 1780-1844 **NCLC 19**
See also DLB 119
Noguchi, Yone 1875-1947 **TCLC 80**
Nolan, Christopher 1965- **CLC 58**
See also CA 111; CANR 88
Noon, Jeff 1957- **CLC 91**
See also CA 148; CANR 83
Norden, Charles
See Durrell, Lawrence (George)
Nordhoff, Charles (Bernard) 1887-1947 **TCLC 23**
See also CA 108; DLB 9; SATA 23
Norfolk, Lawrence 1963- **CLC 76**
See also CA 144; CANR 85
Norman, Marsha 1947- **CLC 28; DAM DRAM; DC 8**
See also CA 105; CABS 3; CANR 41; DLBY 84
Normyx
See Douglas, (George) Norman
Norris, Frank 1870-1902 **SSC 28**
See also Norris, (Benjamin) Frank(lin, Jr.)
See also CDALB 1865-1917; DLB 12, 71, 186
Norris, (Benjamin) Frank(lin, Jr.) 1870-1902 **TCLC 24**
See also Norris, Frank
See also CA 110; 160
Norris, Leslie 1921- **CLC 14**
See also CA 11-12; CANR 14; CAP 1; DLB 27
North, Andrew
See Norton, Andre
North, Anthony
See Koontz, Dean R(ay)
North, Captain George
See Stevenson, Robert Louis (Balfour)
North, Milou
See Erdrich, Louise
Northrup, B. A.
See Hubbard, L(afayette) Ron(ald)
North Staffs
See Hulme, T(homas) E(rnest)
Norton, Alice Mary
See Norton, Andre
See also MAICYA; SATA 1, 43
Norton, Andre 1912- **CLC 12**
See also Norton, Alice Mary

See also AAYA 14; CA 1-4R; CANR 68; CLR 50; DLB 8, 52; JRDA; MTCW 1; SATA 91
Norton, Caroline 1808-1877 **NCLC 47**
See also DLB 21, 159, 199
Norway, Nevil Shute 1899-1960
See Shute, Nevil
See also CA 102; 93-96; CANR 85; MTCW 2
Norwid, Cyprian Kamil 1821-1883 **NCLC 17**
Nosille, Nabrah
See Ellison, Harlan (Jay)
Nossack, Hans Erich 1901-1978 **CLC 6**
See also CA 93-96; 85-88; DLB 69
Nostradamus 1503-1566 **LC 27**
Nosu, Chuji
See Ozu, Yasujiro
Notenburg, Eleanora (Genrikhovna) von
See Guro, Elena
Nova, Craig 1945- **CLC 7, 31**
See also CA 45-48; CANR 2, 53
Novak, Joseph
See Kosinski, Jerzy (Nikodem)
Novalis 1772-1801 **NCLC 13**
See also DLB 90
Novis, Emile
See Weil, Simone (Adolphine)
Nowlan, Alden (Albert) 1933-1983 **CLC 15; DAC; DAM MST**
See also CA 9-12R; CANR 5; DLB 53
Noyes, Alfred 1880-1958 **TCLC 7; PC 27**
See also CA 104; DLB 20
Nunn, Kem CLC 34
See also CA 159
Nye, Robert 1939- **CLC 13, 42; DAM NOV**
See also CA 33-36R; CANR 29, 67; DLB 14; MTCW 1; SATA 6
Nyro, Laura 1947- **CLC 17**
Oates, Joyce Carol 1938- **CLC 1, 2, 3, 6, 9, 11, 15, 19, 33, 52, 108; DA; DAB; DAC; DAM MST, NOV, POP; SSC 6; WLC**
See also AAYA 15; AITN 1; BEST 89:2; CA 5-8R; CANR 25, 45, 74; CDALB 1968-1988; DA3; DLB 2, 5, 130; DLBY 81; INT CANR-25; MTCW 1, 2
O'Brien, Darcy 1939-1998 **CLC 11**
See also CA 21-24R; 167; CANR 8, 59
O'Brien, E. G.
See Clarke, Arthur C(harles)
O'Brien, Edna 1936- **CLC 3, 5, 8, 13, 36, 65, 116; DAM NOV; SSC 10**
See also CA 1-4R; CANR 6, 41, 65; CD-BLB 1960 to Present; DA3; DLB 14; MTCW 1, 2
O'Brien, Fitz-James 1828-1862 **NCLC 21**
See also DLB 74
O'Brien, Flann CLC 1, 4, 5, 7, 10, 47
See also O Nuallain, Brian
O'Brien, Richard 1942- **CLC 17**
See also CA 124
O'Brien, (William) Tim(othy) 1946- **CLC 7, 19, 40, 103; DAM POP**
See also AAYA 16; CA 85-88; CANR 40, 58; CDALBS; DA3; DLB 152; DLBD 9; DLBY 80; MTCW 2
Obstfelder, Sigbjoern 1866-1900 **TCLC 23**
See also CA 123
O'Casey, Sean 1880-1964 **CLC 1, 5, 9, 11, 15, 88; DAB; DAC; DAM DRAM, MST; DC 12; WLCS**
See also CA 89-92; CANR 62; CDBLB 1914-1945; DA3; DLB 10; MTCW 1, 2
O'Cathasaigh, Sean
See O'Casey, Sean
Ochs, Phil(ip David) 1940-1976 **CLC 17**
See also CA 185; 65-68
O'Connor, Edwin (Greene) 1918-1968 **CLC 14**

See also CA 93-96; 25-28R
O'Connor, (Mary) Flannery 1925-1964 **CLC 1, 2, 3, 6, 10, 13, 15, 21, 66, 104; DA; DAB; DAC; DAM MST, NOV; SSC 1, 23; WLC**
See also AAYA 7; CA 1-4R; CANR 3, 41; CDALB 1941-1968; DA3; DLB 2, 152; DLBD 12; DLBY 80; MTCW 1, 2
O'Connor, Frank CLC 23; SSC 5
See also O'Donovan, Michael John
See also DLB 162
O'Dell, Scott 1898-1989 **CLC 30**
See also AAYA 3; CA 61-64; 129; CANR 12, 30; CLR 1, 16; DLB 52; JRDA; MAICYA; SATA 12, 60
Odets, Clifford 1906-1963 **CLC 2, 28, 98; DAM DRAM; DC 6**
See also CA 85-88; CANR 62; DLB 7, 26; MTCW 1, 2
O'Doherty, Brian 1934- **CLC 76**
See also CA 105
O'Donnell, K. M.
See Malzberg, Barry N(athaniel)
O'Donnell, Lawrence
See Kuttner, Henry
O'Donovan, Michael John 1903-1966 **CLC 14**
See also O'Connor, Frank
See also CA 93-96; CANR 84
Oe, Kenzaburo 1935- **CLC 10, 36, 86; DAM NOV; SSC 20**
See also CA 97-100; CANR 36, 50, 74; DA3; DLB 182; DLBY 94; MTCW 1, 2
O'Faolain, Julia 1932- **CLC 6, 19, 47, 108**
See also CA 81-84; CAAS 2; CANR 12, 61; DLB 14; MTCW 1
O'Faolain, Sean 1900-1991 **CLC 1, 7, 14, 32, 70; SSC 13**
See also CA 61-64; 134; CANR 12, 66; DLB 15, 162; MTCW 1, 2
O'Flaherty, Liam 1896-1984 **CLC 5, 34; SSC 6**
See also CA 101; 113; CANR 35; DLB 36, 162; DLBY 84; MTCW 1, 2
Ogilvy, Gavin
See Barrie, J(ames) M(atthew)
O'Grady, Standish (James) 1846-1928 **TCLC 5**
See also CA 104; 157
O'Grady, Timothy 1951- **CLC 59**
See also CA 138
O'Hara, Frank 1926-1966 **CLC 2, 5, 13, 78; DAM POET**
See also CA 9-12R; 25-28R; CANR 33; DA3; DLB 5, 16, 193; MTCW 1, 2
O'Hara, John (Henry) 1905-1970 **CLC 1, 2, 3, 6, 11, 42; DAM NOV; SSC 15**
See also CA 5-8R; 25-28R; CANR 31, 60; CDALB 1929-1941; DLB 9, 86; DLBD 2; MTCW 1, 2
O Hehir, Diana 1922- **CLC 41**
See also CA 93-96
Ohiyesa
See Eastman, Charles A(lexander)
Okigbo, Christopher (Ifenayichukwu) 1932-1967 **CLC 25, 84; BLC 3; DAM MULT, POET; PC 7**
See also BW 1, 3; CA 77-80; CANR 74; DLB 125; MTCW 1, 2
Okri, Ben 1959- **CLC 87**
See also BW 2, 3; CA 130; 138; CANR 65; DLB 157; INT 138; MTCW 2
Olds, Sharon 1942- **CLC 32, 39, 85; DAM POET; PC 22**
See also CA 101; CANR 18, 41, 66; DLB 120; MTCW 2
Oldstyle, Jonathan
See Irving, Washington
Olesha, Yuri (Karlovich) 1899-1960 **CLC 8**

Park, Jordan
  See Kornbluth, C(yril) M.; Pohl, Frederik
Park, Robert E(zra) 1864-1944 **TCLC 73**
  See also CA 122; 165
Parker, Bert
  See Ellison, Harlan (Jay)
Parker, Dorothy (Rothschild) 1893-1967 **CLC 15, 68; DAM POET; PC 28; SSC 2**
  See also CA 19-20; 25-28R; CAP 2; DA3; DLB 11, 45, 86; MTCW 1, 2
Parker, Robert B(rown) 1932- **CLC 27; DAM NOV, POP**
  See also AAYA 28; BEST 89:4; CA 49-52; CANR 1, 26, 52, 89; INT CANR-26; MTCW 1
Parkin, Frank 1940- **CLC 43**
  See also CA 147
Parkman, Francis Jr., Jr. 1823-1893 **NCLC 12**
  See also DLB 1, 30, 186
Parks, Gordon (Alexander Buchanan) 1912- **CLC 1, 16; BLC 3; DAM MULT**
  See also AITN 2; BW 2, 3; CA 41-44R; CANR 26, 66; DA3; DLB 33; MTCW 2; SATA 8, 108
Parmenides c. 515B.C.-c. 450B.C. **CMLC 22**
  See also DLB 176
Parnell, Thomas 1679-1718 **LC 3**
  See also DLB 94
Parra, Nicanor 1914- **CLC 2, 102; DAM MULT; HLC 2**
  See also CA 85-88; CANR 32; HW 1; MTCW 1
Parra Sanojo, Ana Teresa de la 1890-1936
  See also HLCS 2
Parrish, Mary Frances
  See Fisher, M(ary) F(rances) K(ennedy)
Parson
  See Coleridge, Samuel Taylor
Parson Lot
  See Kingsley, Charles
Parton, Sara Payson Willis 1811-1872 **NCLC 86**
  See also DLB 43, 74
Partridge, Anthony
  See Oppenheim, E(dward) Phillips
Pascal, Blaise 1623-1662 **LC 35**
Pascoli, Giovanni 1855-1912 **TCLC 45**
  See also CA 170
Pasolini, Pier Paolo 1922-1975 **CLC 20, 37, 106; PC 17**
  See also CA 93-96; 61-64; CANR 63; DLB 128, 177; MTCW 1
Pasquini
  See Silone, Ignazio
Pastan, Linda (Olenik) 1932- **CLC 27; DAM POET**
  See also CA 61-64; CANR 18, 40, 61; DLB 5
Pasternak, Boris (Leonidovich) 1890-1960 **CLC 7, 10, 18, 63; DA; DAB; DAC; DAM MST, NOV, POET; PC 6; SSC 31; WLC**
  See also CA 127; 116; DA3; MTCW 1, 2
Patchen, Kenneth 1911-1972 **CLC 1, 2, 18; DAM POET**
  See also CA 1-4R; 33-36R; CANR 3, 35; DLB 16, 48; MTCW 1
Pater, Walter (Horatio) 1839-1894 **NCLC 7**
  See also CDBLB 1832-1890; DLB 57, 156
Paterson, A(ndrew) B(arton) 1864-1941 **TCLC 32**
  See also CA 155; SATA 97
Paterson, Katherine (Womeldorf) 1932- **CLC 12, 30**
  See also AAYA 1, 31; CA 21-24R; CANR 28, 59; CLR 7, 50; DLB 52; JRDA; MAI-CYA; MTCW 1; SATA 13, 53, 92

Patmore, Coventry Kersey Dighton 1823-1896 **NCLC 9**
  See also DLB 35, 98
Paton, Alan (Stewart) 1903-1988 **CLC 4, 10, 25, 55, 106; DA; DAB; DAC; DAM MST, NOV; WLC**
  See also AAYA 26; CA 13-16; 125; CANR 22; CAP 1; DA3; DLBD 17; MTCW 1, 2; SATA 11; SATA-Obit 56
Paton Walsh, Gillian 1937-
  See Walsh, Jill Paton
  See also AAYA 11; CANR 38, 83; DLB 161; JRDA; MAICYA; SAAS 3; SATA 4, 72, 109
Patton, George S. 1885-1945 **TCLC 79**
Paulding, James Kirke 1778-1860 **NCLC 2**
  See also DLB 3, 59, 74
Paulin, Thomas Neilson 1949-
  See Paulin, Tom
  See also CA 123; 128
Paulin, Tom CLC 37
  See also Paulin, Thomas Neilson
  See also DLB 40
Pausanias c. 1st cent. - **CMLC 36**
Paustovsky, Konstantin (Georgievich) 1892-1968 **CLC 40**
  See also CA 93-96; 25-28R
Pavese, Cesare 1908-1950 **TCLC 3; PC 13; SSC 19**
  See also CA 104; 169; DLB 128, 177
Pavic, Milorad 1929- **CLC 60**
  See also CA 136; DLB 181
Pavlov, Ivan Petrovich 1849-1936 **TCLC 91**
  See also CA 118; 180
Payne, Alan
  See Jakes, John (William)
Paz, Gil
  See Lugones, Leopoldo
Paz, Octavio 1914-1998 **CLC 3, 4, 6, 10, 19, 51, 65, 119; DA; DAB; DAC; DAM MST, MULT, POET; HLC 2; PC 1; WLC**
  See also CA 73-76; 165; CANR 32, 65; DA3; DLBY 90, 98; HW 1, 2; MTCW 1, 2
p'Bitek, Okot 1931-1982 **CLC 96; BLC 3; DAM MULT**
  See also BW 2, 3; CA 124; 107; CANR 82; DLB 125; MTCW 1, 2
Peacock, Molly 1947- **CLC 60**
  See also CA 103; CAAS 21; CANR 52, 84; DLB 120
Peacock, Thomas Love 1785-1866 **NCLC 22**
  See also DLB 96, 116
Peake, Mervyn 1911-1968 **CLC 7, 54**
  See also CA 5-8R; 25-28R; CANR 3; DLB 15, 160; MTCW 1; SATA 23
Pearce, Philippa CLC 21
  See also Christie, (Ann) Philippa
  See also CLR 9; DLB 161; MAICYA; SATA 1, 67
Pearl, Eric
  See Elman, Richard (Martin)
Pearson, T(homas) R(eid) 1956- **CLC 39**
  See also CA 120; 130; INT 130
Peck, Dale 1967- **CLC 81**
  See also CA 146; CANR 72
Peck, John 1941- **CLC 3**
  See also CA 49-52; CANR 3
Peck, Richard (Wayne) 1934- **CLC 21**
  See also AAYA 1, 24; CA 85-88; CANR 19, 38; CLR 15; INT CANR-19; JRDA; MAICYA; SAAS 2; SATA 18, 55, 97; SATA-Essay 110
Peck, Robert Newton 1928- **CLC 17; DA; DAC; DAM MST**

  See also AAYA 3; CA 81-84, 182; CAAE 182; CANR 31, 63; CLR 45; JRDA; MAI-CYA; SAAS 1; SATA 21, 62, 111; SATA-Essay 108
Peckinpah, (David) Sam(uel) 1925-1984 **CLC 20**
  See also CA 109; 114; CANR 82
Pedersen, Knut 1859-1952
  See Hamsun, Knut
  See also CA 104; 119; CANR 63; MTCW 1, 2
Peeslake, Gaffer
  See Durrell, Lawrence (George)
Peguy, Charles Pierre 1873-1914 **TCLC 10**
  See also CA 107
Peirce, Charles Sanders 1839-1914 **TCLC 81**
Pellicer, Carlos 1900(?)-1977
  See also CA 153; 69-72; HLCS 2; HW 1
Pena, Ramon del Valle y
  See Valle-Inclan, Ramon (Maria) del
Pendennis, Arthur Esquir
  See Thackeray, William Makepeace
Penn, William 1644-1718 **LC 25**
  See also DLB 24
PEPECE
  See Prado (Calvo), Pedro
Pepys, Samuel 1633-1703 **LC 11, 58; DA; DAB; DAC; DAM MST; WLC**
  See also CDBLB 1660-1789; DA3; DLB 101
Percy, Walker 1916-1990 **CLC 2, 3, 6, 8, 14, 18, 47, 65; DAM NOV, POP**
  See also CA 1-4R; 131; CANR 1, 23, 64; DA3; DLB 2; DLBY 80, 90; MTCW 1, 2
Percy, William Alexander 1885-1942 **TCLC 84**
  See also CA 163; MTCW 2
Perec, Georges 1936-1982 **CLC 56, 116**
  See also CA 141; DLB 83
Pereda (y Sanchez de Porrua), Jose Maria de 1833-1906 **TCLC 16**
  See also CA 117
Pereda y Porrua, Jose Maria de
  See Pereda (y Sanchez de Porrua), Jose Maria de
Peregoy, George Weems
  See Mencken, H(enry) L(ouis)
Perelman, S(idney) J(oseph) 1904-1979 **CLC 3, 5, 9, 15, 23, 44, 49; DAM DRAM; SSC 32**
  See also AITN 1, 2; CA 73-76; 89-92; CANR 18; DLB 11, 44; MTCW 1, 2
Peret, Benjamin 1899-1959 **TCLC 20**
  See also CA 117; 186
Peretz, Isaac Loeb 1851(?)-1915 **TCLC 16; SSC 26**
  See also CA 109
Peretz, Yitzhok Leibush
  See Peretz, Isaac Loeb
Perez Galdos, Benito 1843-1920 **TCLC 27; HLCS 2**
  See also CA 125; 153; HW 1
Peri Rossi, Cristina 1941-
  See also CA 131; CANR 59, 81; DLB 145; HLCS 2; HW 1, 2
Perlata
  See Peret, Benjamin
Perrault, Charles 1628-1703 **LC 3, 52; DC 12**
  See also MAICYA; SATA 25
Perry, Anne 1938- **CLC 126**
  See also CA 101; CANR 22, 50, 84
Perry, Brighton
  See Sherwood, Robert E(mmet)
Perse, St.-John
  See Leger, (Marie-Rene Auguste) Alexis Saint-Leger
Perutz, Leo(pold) 1882-1957 **TCLC 60**

See also CA 147; DLB 81

Peseenz, Tulio F.
See Lopez y Fuentes, Gregorio

Pesetsky, Bette 1932- **CLC 28**
See also CA 133; DLB 130

Peshkov, Alexei Maximovich 1868-1936
See Gorky, Maxim
See also CA 105; 141; CANR 83; DA;
DAC; DAM DRAM, MST, NOV; MTCW
2

Pessoa, Fernando (Antonio Nogueira)
1888-1935 **TCLC 27; DAM MULT;**
HLC 2; PC 20
See also CA 125; 183

Peterkin, Julia Mood 1880-1961 **CLC 31**
See also CA 102; DLB 9

Peters, Joan K(aren) 1945- **CLC 39**
See also CA 158

Peters, Robert L(ouis) 1924- **CLC 7**
See also CA 13-16R; CAAS 8; DLB 105

Petofi, Sandor 1823-1849 **NCLC 21**

Petrakis, Harry Mark 1923- **CLC 3**
See also CA 9-12R; CANR 4, 30, 85

Petrarch 1304-1374 **CMLC 20; DAM POET;**
PC 8
See also DA3

Petronius c. 20-66 **CMLC 34**
See also DLB 211

Petrov, Evgeny TCLC 21
See also Kataev, Evgeny Petrovich

Petry, Ann (Lane) 1908-1997 **CLC 1, 7, 18**
See also BW 1, 3; CA 5-8R; 157; CAAS 6;
CANR 4, 46; CLR 12; DLB 76; JRDA;
MAICYA; MTCW 1; SATA 5; SATA-Obit
94

Petursson, Halligrimur 1614-1674 **LC 8**

Peychinovich
See Vazov, Ivan (Minchov)

Phaedrus c. 18B.C.-c. 50 **CMLC 25**
See also DLB 211

Philips, Katherine 1632-1664 **LC 30**
See also DLB 131

Philipson, Morris H. 1926- **CLC 53**
See also CA 1-4R; CANR 4

Phillips, Caryl 1958- **CLC 96; BLCS; DAM**
MULT
See also BW 2; CA 141; CANR 63; DA3;
DLB 157; MTCW 2

Phillips, David Graham 1867-1911 **TCLC 44**
See also CA 108; 176; DLB 9, 12

Phillips, Jack
See Sandburg, Carl (August)

Phillips, Jayne Anne 1952- **CLC 15, 33; SSC**
16
See also CA 101; CANR 24, 50; DLBY 80;
INT CANR-24; MTCW 1, 2

Phillips, Richard
See Dick, Philip K(indred)

Phillips, Robert (Schaeffer) 1938- **CLC 28**
See also CA 17-20R; CAAS 13; CANR 8;
DLB 105

Phillips, Ward
See Lovecraft, H(oward) P(hillips)

Piccolo, Lucio 1901-1969 **CLC 13**
See also CA 97-100; DLB 114

Pickthall, Marjorie L(owry) C(hristie)
1883-1922 **TCLC 21**
See also CA 107; DLB 92

Pico della Mirandola, Giovanni 1463-1494
LC 15

Piercy, Marge 1936- **CLC 3, 6, 14, 18, 27, 62,**
128; PC 29
See also CA 21-24R; CAAS 1; CANR 13,
43, 66; DLB 120; MTCW 1, 2

Piers, Robert
See Anthony, Piers

Pieyre de Mandiargues, Andre 1909-1991
See Mandiargues, Andre Pieyre de
See also CA 103; 136; CANR 22, 82

Pilnyak, Boris TCLC 23
See also Vogau, Boris Andreyevich

Pincherle, Alberto 1907-1990 **CLC 11, 18;**
DAM NOV
See also Moravia, Alberto
See also CA 25-28R; 132; CANR 33, 63;
MTCW 1

Pinckney, Darryl 1953- **CLC 76**
See also BW 2, 3; CA 143; CANR 79

Pindar 518B.C.-446B.C. **CMLC 12; PC 19**
See also DLB 176

Pineda, Cecile 1942- **CLC 39**
See also CA 118

Pinero, Arthur Wing 1855-1934 **TCLC 32;**
DAM DRAM
See also CA 110; 153; DLB 10

Pinero, Miguel (Antonio Gomez) 1946-1988
CLC 4, 55
See also CA 61-64; 125; CANR 29, 90; HW
1

Pinget, Robert 1919-1997 **CLC 7, 13, 37**
See also CA 85-88; 160; DLB 83

Pink Floyd
See Barrett, (Roger) Syd; Gilmour, David;
Mason, Nick; Waters, Roger; Wright, Rick

Pinkney, Edward 1802-1828 **NCLC 31**

Pinkwater, Daniel Manus 1941- **CLC 35**
See also Pinkwater, Manus
See also AAYA 1; CA 29-32R; CANR 12,
38, 89; CLR 4; JRDA; MAICYA; SAAS
3; SATA 46, 76, 114

Pinkwater, Manus
See Pinkwater, Daniel Manus
See also SATA 8

Pinsky, Robert 1940- **CLC 9, 19, 38, 94, 121;**
DAM POET; PC 27
See also CA 29-32R; CAAS 4; CANR 58;
DA3; DLBY 82, 98; MTCW 2

Pinta, Harold
See Pinter, Harold

Pinter, Harold 1930- **CLC 1, 3, 6, 9, 11, 15,**
27, 58, 73; DA; DAB; DAC; DAM
DRAM, MST; WLC
See also CA 5-8R; CANR 33, 65; CDBLB
1960 to Present; DA3; DLB 13; MTCW
1, 2

Piozzi, Hester Lynch (Thrale) 1741-1821
NCLC 57
See also DLB 104, 142

Pirandello, Luigi 1867-1936 **TCLC 4, 29;**
DA; DAB; DAC; DAM DRAM, MST;
DC 5; SSC 22; WLC
See also CA 104; 153; DA3; MTCW 2

Pirsig, Robert M(aynard) 1928- **CLC 4, 6,**
73; DAM POP
See also CA 53-56; CANR 42, 74; DA3;
MTCW 1, 2; SATA 39

Pisarev, Dmitry Ivanovich 1840-1868 **NCLC**
25

Pix, Mary (Griffith) 1666-1709 **LC 8**
See also DLB 80

Pixerecourt, (Rene Charles) Guilbert de
1773-1844 **NCLC 39**
See also DLB 192

Plaatje, Sol(omon) T(shekisho) 1876-1932
TCLC 73; BLCS
See also BW 2, 3; CA 141; CANR 79

Plaidy, Jean
See Hibbert, Eleanor Alice Burford

Planche, James Robinson 1796-1880 **NCLC**
42

Plant, Robert 1948- **CLC 12**

Plante, David (Robert) 1940- **CLC 7, 23, 38;**
DAM NOV
See also CA 37-40R; CANR 12, 36, 58, 82;
DLBY 83; INT CANR-12; MTCW 1

Plath, Sylvia 1932-1963 **CLC 1, 2, 3, 5, 9, 11,**
14, 17, 50, 51, 62, 111; DA; DAB; DAC;
DAM MST, POET; PC 1; WLC
See also AAYA 13; CA 19-20; CANR 34;
CAP 2; CDALB 1941-1968; DA3; DLB
5, 6, 152; MTCW 1, 2; SATA 96

Plato 428(?)B.C.-348(?)B.C. **CMLC 8; DA;**
DAB; DAC; DAM MST; WLCS
See also DA3; DLB 176

Platonov, Andrei TCLC 14; SSC 38
See also Klimentov, Andrei Platonovich

Platt, Kin 1911- **CLC 26**
See also AAYA 11; CA 17-20R; CANR 11;
JRDA; SAAS 17; SATA 21, 86

Plautus c. 251B.C.-184B.C. **CMLC 24; DC 6**
See also DLB 211

Plick et Plock
See Simenon, Georges (Jacques Christian)

Plimpton, George (Ames) 1927- **CLC 36**
See also AITN 1; CA 21-24R; CANR 32,
70; DLB 185; MTCW 1, 2; SATA 10

Pliny the Elder c. 23-79 **CMLC 23**
See also DLB 211

Plomer, William Charles Franklin 1903-1973
CLC 4, 8
See also CA 21-22; CANR 34; CAP 2; DLB
20, 162, 191; MTCW 1; SATA 24

Plowman, Piers
See Kavanagh, Patrick (Joseph)

Plum, J.
See Wodehouse, P(elham) G(renville)

Plumly, Stanley (Ross) 1939- **CLC 33**
See also CA 108; 110; DLB 5, 193; INT
110

Plumpe, Friedrich Wilhelm 1888-1931 **TCLC**
53
See also CA 112

Po Chu-i 772-846 **CMLC 24**

Poe, Edgar Allan 1809-1849 **NCLC 1, 16, 55,**
78; DA; DAB; DAC; DAM MST,
POET; PC 1; SSC 34; WLC
See also AAYA 14; CDALB 1640-1865;
DA3; DLB 3, 59, 73, 74; SATA 23

Poet of Titchfield Street, The
See Pound, Ezra (Weston Loomis)

Pohl, Frederik 1919- **CLC 18; SSC 25**
See also AAYA 24; CA 61-64; CAAS 1;
CANR 11, 37, 81; DLB 8; INT CANR-
11; MTCW 1, 2; SATA 24

Poirier, Louis 1910-
See Gracq, Julien
See also CA 122; 126

Poitier, Sidney 1927- **CLC 26**
See also BW 1; CA 117

Polanski, Roman 1933- **CLC 16**
See also CA 77-80

Poliakoff, Stephen 1952- **CLC 38**
See also CA 106; DLB 13

Police, The
See Copeland, Stewart (Armstrong); Sum-
mers, Andrew James; Sumner, Gordon
Matthew

Polidori, John William 1795-1821 **NCLC 51**
See also DLB 116

Pollitt, Katha 1949- **CLC 28, 122**
See also CA 120; 122; CANR 66; MTCW
1, 2

Pollock, (Mary) Sharon 1936- **CLC 50; DAC;**
DAM DRAM, MST
See also CA 141; DLB 60

Polo, Marco 1254-1324 **CMLC 15**

Polonsky, Abraham (Lincoln) 1910- **CLC 92**
See also CA 104; DLB 26; INT 104

Polybius c. 200B.C.-c. 118B.C. **CMLC 17**
See also DLB 176

Pomerance, Bernard 1940- **CLC 13; DAM**
DRAM
See also CA 101; CANR 49

Ponge, Francis 1899-1988 **CLC 6, 18; DAM POET**
See also CA 85-88; 126; CANR 40, 86

Poniatowska, Elena 1933-
See also CA 101; CANR 32, 66; **DAM MULT; DLB 113; HLC 2; HW 1, 2**

Pontoppidan, Henrik 1857-1943 **TCLC 29**
See also CA 170

Poole, Josephine **CLC 17**
See Helyar, Jane Penelope Josephine
See also SAAS 2; SATA 5

Popa, Vasko 1922-1991 **CLC 19**
See also CA 112; 148; DLB 181

Pope, Alexander 1688-1744 **LC 3, 58; DA; DAB; DAC; DAM MST, POET; PC 26; WLC**
See also CDBLB 1660-1789; DA3; DLB 95, 101

Porter, Connie (Rose) 1959(?)- **CLC 70**
See also BW 2, 3; CA 142; CANR 90; SATA 81

Porter, Gene(va Grace) Stratton 1863(?)-1924 **TCLC 21**
See also CA 112

Porter, Katherine Anne 1890-1980 **CLC 1, 3, 7, 10, 13, 15, 27, 101; DA; DAB; DAC; DAM MST, NOV; SSC 4, 31**
See also AITN 2; CA 1-4R; CANR 1, 65; CDALBS; DA3; DLB 4, 9, 102; DLBD 12; DLBY 80; MTCW 1, 2; SATA 39; SATA-Obit 23

Porter, Peter (Neville Frederick) 1929- **CLC 5, 13, 33**
See also CA 85-88; DLB 40

Porter, William Sydney 1862-1910
See Henry, O.
See also CA 104; 131; CDALB 1865-1917; DA; DAB; DAC; DAM MST; DA3; DLB 12, 78, 79; MTCW 1, 2; YABC 2

Portillo (y Pacheco), Jose Lopez
See Lopez Portillo (y Pacheco), Jose

Portillo Trambley, Estela 1927-1998
See also CANR 32; **DAM MULT; DLB 209; HLC 2; HW 1**

Post, Melville Davisson 1869-1930 **TCLC 39**
See also CA 110

Potok, Chaim 1929- **CLC 2, 7, 14, 26, 112; DAM NOV**
See also AAYA 15; AITN 1, 2; CA 17-20R; CANR 19, 35, 64; DA3; DLB 28, 152; INT CANR-19; MTCW 1, 2; SATA 33, 106

Potter, Dennis (Christopher George) 1935-1994 **CLC 58, 86**
See also CA 107; 145; CANR 33, 61; MTCW 1

Pound, Ezra (Weston Loomis) 1885-1972 **CLC 1, 2, 3, 4, 5, 7, 10, 13, 18, 34, 48, 50, 112; DA; DAB; DAC; DAM MST, POET; PC 4; WLC**
See also CA 5-8R; 37-40R; CANR 40; CDALB 1917-1929; DA3; DLB 4, 45, 63; DLBD 15; MTCW 1, 2

Povod, Reinaldo 1959-1994 **CLC 44**
See also CA 136; 146; CANR 83

Powell, Adam Clayton, Jr. 1908-1972 **CLC 89; BLC 3; DAM MULT**
See also BW 1, 3; CA 102; 33-36R; CANR 86

Powell, Anthony (Dymoke) 1905- **CLC 1, 3, 7, 9, 10, 31**
See also CA 1-4R; CANR 1, 32, 62; CDBLB 1945-1960; DLB 15; MTCW 1, 2

Powell, Dawn 1897-1965 **CLC 66**
See also CA 5-8R; DLBY 97

Powell, Padgett 1952- **CLC 34**
See also CA 126; CANR 63

Power, Susan 1961- **CLC 91**
See also CA 145

Powers, J(ames) F(arl) 1917-1999 **CLC 1, 4, 8, 57; SSC 4**
See also CA 1-4R; 181; CANR 2, 61; DLB 130; MTCW 1

Powers, John J(ames) 1945-
See Powers, John R.
See also CA 69-72

Powers, John R. **CLC 66**
See also Powers, John J(ames)

Powers, Richard (S.) 1957- **CLC 93**
See also CA 148; CANR 80

Pownall, David 1938- **CLC 10**
See also CA 89-92; 180; CAAS 18; CANR 49; DLB 14

Powys, John Cowper 1872-1963 **CLC 7, 9, 15, 46, 125**
See also CA 85-88; DLB 15; MTCW 1, 2

Powys, T(heodore) F(rancis) 1875-1953 **TCLC 9**
See also CA 106; DLB 36, 162

Prado (Calvo), Pedro 1886-1952 **TCLC 75**
See also CA 131; HW 1

Prager, Emily 1952- **CLC 56**

Pratt, E(dwin) J(ohn) 1883(?)-1964 **CLC 19; DAC; DAM POET**
See also CA 141; 93-96; CANR 77; DLB 92

Premchand **TCLC 21**
See also Srivastava, Dhanpat Rai

Preussler, Otfried 1923- **CLC 17**
See also CA 77-80; SATA 24

Prevert, Jacques (Henri Marie) 1900-1977 **CLC 15**
See also CA 77-80; 69-72; CANR 29, 61; MTCW 1; SATA-Obit 30

Prevost, Abbe (Antoine Francois) 1697-1763 **LC 1**

Price, (Edward) Reynolds 1933- **CLC 3, 6, 13, 43, 50, 63; DAM NOV; SSC 22**
See also CA 1-4R; CANR 1, 37, 57, 87; DLB 2; INT CANR-37

Price, Richard 1949- **CLC 6, 12**
See also CA 49-52; CANR 3; DLBY 81

Prichard, Katharine Susannah 1883-1969 **CLC 46**
See also CA 11-12; CANR 33; CAP 1; MTCW 1; SATA 66

Priestley, J(ohn) B(oynton) 1894-1984 **CLC 2, 5, 9, 34; DAM DRAM, NOV**
See also CA 9-12R; 113; CANR 33; CDBLB 1914-1945; DA3; DLB 10, 34, 77, 100, 139; DLBY 84; MTCW 1, 2

Prince 1958(?)- **CLC 35**

Prince, F(rank) T(empleton) 1912- **CLC 22**
See also CA 101; CANR 43, 79; DLB 20

Prince Kropotkin
See Kropotkin, Peter (Aleksieevich)

Prior, Matthew 1664-1721 **LC 4**
See also DLB 95

Prishvin, Mikhail 1873-1954 **TCLC 75**

Pritchard, William H(arrison) 1932- **CLC 34**
See also CA 65-68; CANR 23; DLB 111

Pritchett, V(ictor) S(awdon) 1900-1997 **CLC 5, 13, 15, 41; DAM NOV; SSC 14**
See also CA 61-64; 157; CANR 31, 63; DA3; DLB 15, 139; MTCW 1, 2

Private 19022
See Manning, Frederic

Probst, Mark 1925- **CLC 59**
See also CA 130

Prokosch, Frederic 1908-1989 **CLC 4, 48**
See also CA 73-76; 128; CANR 82; DLB 48; MTCW 2

Propertius, Sextus c. 50B.C.-c. 16B.C. **CMLC 32**
See also DLB 211

Prophet, The
See Dreiser, Theodore (Herman Albert)

Prose, Francine 1947- **CLC 45**
See also CA 109; 112; CANR 46; SATA 101

Proudhon
See Cunha, Euclides (Rodrigues Pimenta) da

Proulx, Annie
See Proulx, E(dna) Annie

Proulx, E(dna) Annie 1935- **CLC 81; DAM POP**
See also CA 145; CANR 65; DA3; MTCW 2

Proust, (Valentin-Louis-George-Eugene-) Marcel 1871-1922 **TCLC 7, 13, 33; DA; DAB; DAC; DAM MST, NOV; WLC**
See also CA 104; 120; DA3; DLB 65; MTCW 1, 2

Prowler, Harley
See Masters, Edgar Lee

Prus, Boleslaw 1845-1912 **TCLC 48**

Pryor, Richard (Franklin Lenox Thomas) 1940- **CLC 26**
See also CA 122; 152

Przybyszewski, Stanislaw 1868-1927 **TCLC 36**
See also CA 160; DLB 66

Pteleon
See Grieve, C(hristopher) M(urray)
See also DAM POET

Puckett, Lute
See Masters, Edgar Lee

Puig, Manuel 1932-1990 **CLC 3, 5, 10, 28, 65; DAM MULT; HLC 2**
See also CA 45-48; CANR 2, 32, 63; DA3; DLB 113; HW 1, 2; MTCW 1, 2

Pulitzer, Joseph 1847-1911 **TCLC 76**
See also CA 114; DLB 23

Purdy, A(lfred) W(ellington) 1918- **CLC 3, 6, 14, 50; DAC; DAM MST, POET**
See also CA 81-84; CAAS 17; CANR 42, 66; DLB 88

Purdy, James (Amos) 1923- **CLC 2, 4, 10, 28, 52**
See also CA 33-36R; CAAS 1; CANR 19, 51; DLB 2; INT CANR-19; MTCW 1

Pure, Simon
See Swinnerton, Frank Arthur

Pushkin, Alexander (Sergeyevich) 1799-1837 **NCLC 3, 27, 83; DA; DAB; DAC; DAM DRAM, MST, POET; PC 10; SSC 27; WLC**
See also DA3; DLB 205; SATA 61

P'u Sung-ling 1640-1715 **LC 49; SSC 31**

Putnam, Arthur Lee
See Alger, Horatio Jr., Jr.

Puzo, Mario 1920-1999 **CLC 1, 2, 6, 36, 107; DAM NOV, POP**
See also CA 65-68; 185; CANR 4, 42, 65; DA3; DLB 6; MTCW 1, 2

Pygge, Edward
See Barnes, Julian (Patrick)

Pyle, Ernest Taylor 1900-1945
See Pyle, Ernie
See also CA 115; 160

Pyle, Ernie 1900-1945 **TCLC 75**
See also Pyle, Ernest Taylor
See also DLB 29; MTCW 2

Pyle, Howard 1853-1911 **TCLC 81**
See also CA 109; 137; CLR 22; DLB 42, 188; DLBD 13; MAICYA; SATA 16, 100

Pym, Barbara (Mary Crampton) 1913-1980 **CLC 13, 19, 37, 111**
See also CA 13-14; 97-100; CANR 13, 34; CAP 1; DLB 14, 207; DLBY 87; MTCW 1, 2

Pynchon, Thomas (Ruggles, Jr.) 1937- **CLC 2, 3, 6, 9, 11, 18, 33, 62, 72; DA; DAB;**

See also CA 1-4R; CANR 6, 22, 38, 87;
CLR 24; JRDA; MAICYA; SATA 22, 75,
111

Reilly, William K.
See Creasey, John

Reiner, Max
See Caldwell, (Janet Miriam) Taylor
(Holland)

Reis, Ricardo
See Pessoa, Fernando (Antonio Nogueira)

Remarque, Erich Maria 1898-1970 **CLC 21;
DA; DAB; DAC; DAM MST, NOV**
See also AAYA 27; CA 77-80; 29-32R;
DA3; DLB 56; MTCW 1, 2

Remington, Frederic 1861-1909 **TCLC 89**
See also CA 108; 169; DLB 12, 186, 188;
SATA 41

Remizov, A.
See Remizov, Aleksei (Mikhailovich)

Remizov, A. M.
See Remizov, Aleksei (Mikhailovich)

Remizov, Aleksei (Mikhailovich) 1877-1957
TCLC 27
See also CA 125; 133

Renan, Joseph Ernest 1823-1892 **NCLC 26**

Renard, Jules 1864-1910 **TCLC 17**
See also CA 117

Renault, Mary CLC 3, 11, 17
See also Challans, Mary
See also DLBY 83; MTCW 2

Rendell, Ruth (Barbara) 1930- **CLC 28, 48;
DAM POP**
See also Vine, Barbara
See also CA 109; CANR 32, 52, 74; DLB
87; INT CANR-32; MTCW 1, 2

Renoir, Jean 1894-1979 **CLC 20**
See also CA 129; 85-88

Resnais, Alain 1922- **CLC 16**

Reverdy, Pierre 1889-1960 **CLC 53**
See also CA 97-100; 89-92

Rexroth, Kenneth 1905-1982 **CLC 1, 2, 6, 11,
22, 49, 112; DAM POET; PC 20**
See also CA 5-8R; 107; CANR 14, 34, 63;
CDALB 1941-1968; DLB 16, 48, 165,
212; DLBY 82; INT CANR-14; MTCW
1, 2

Reyes, Alfonso 1889-1959 **TCLC 33; HLCS 2**
See also CA 131; HW 1

Reyes y Basoalto, Ricardo Eliecer Neftali
See Neruda, Pablo

Reymont, Wladyslaw (Stanislaw)
1868(?)-1925 **TCLC 5**
See also CA 104

Reynolds, Jonathan 1942- **CLC 6, 38**
See also CA 65-68; CANR 28

Reynolds, Joshua 1723-1792 **LC 15**
See also DLB 104

Reynolds, Michael S(hane) 1937- **CLC 44**
See also CA 65-68; CANR 9, 89

Reznikoff, Charles 1894-1976 **CLC 9**
See also CA 33-36; 61-64; CAP 2; DLB 28,
45

Rezzori (d'Arezzo), Gregor von 1914-1998
CLC 25
See also CA 122; 136; 167

Rhine, Richard
See Silverstein, Alvin

Rhodes, Eugene Manlove 1869-1934 **TCLC
53**

Rhodius, Apollonius c. 3rd cent. B.C.- **CMLC
28**
See also DLB 176

R'hoone
See Balzac, Honore de

Rhys, Jean 1890(?)-1979 **CLC 2, 4, 6, 14, 19,
51, 124; DAM NOV; SSC 21**

See also CA 25-28R; 85-88; CANR 35, 62;
CDBLB 1945-1960; DA3; DLB 36, 117,
162; MTCW 1, 2

Ribeiro, Darcy 1922-1997 **CLC 34**
See also CA 33-36R; 156

Ribeiro, Joao Ubaldo (Osorio Pimentel)
1941- **CLC 10, 67**
See also CA 81-84

Ribman, Ronald (Burt) 1932- **CLC 7**
See also CA 21-24R; CANR 46, 80

Ricci, Nino 1959- **CLC 70**
See also CA 137

Rice, Anne 1941- **CLC 41, 128; DAM POP**
See also AAYA 9; BEST 89:2; CA 65-68;
CANR 12, 36, 53, 74; DA3; MTCW 2

Rice, Elmer (Leopold) 1892-1967 **CLC 7, 49;
DAM DRAM**
See also CA 21-22; 25-28R; CAP 2; DLB
4, 7; MTCW 1, 2

Rice, Tim(othy Miles Bindon) 1944- **CLC 21**
See also CA 103; CANR 46

Rich, Adrienne (Cecile) 1929- **CLC 3, 6, 7,
11, 18, 36, 73, 76, 125; DAM POET; PC
5**
See also CA 9-12R; CANR 20, 53, 74;
CDALBS; DA3; DLB 5, 67; MTCW 1, 2

Rich, Barbara
See Graves, Robert (von Ranke)

Rich, Robert
See Trumbo, Dalton

Richard, Keith CLC 17
See also Richards, Keith

Richards, David Adams 1950- **CLC 59; DAC**
See also CA 93-96; CANR 60; DLB 53

Richards, I(vor) A(rmstrong) 1893-1979 **CLC
14, 24**
See also CA 41-44R; 89-92; CANR 34, 74;
DLB 27; MTCW 2

Richards, Keith 1943-
See Richard, Keith
See also CA 107; CANR 77

Richardson, Anne
See Roiphe, Anne (Richardson)

Richardson, Dorothy Miller 1873-1957 **TCLC
3**
See also CA 104; DLB 36

Richardson, Ethel Florence (Lindesay)
1870-1946
See Richardson, Henry Handel
See also CA 105

Richardson, Henry Handel TCLC 4
See also Richardson, Ethel Florence
(Lindesay)
See also DLB 197

Richardson, John 1796-1852 **NCLC 55; DAC**
See also DLB 99

Richardson, Samuel 1689-1761 **LC 1, 44;
DA; DAB; DAC; DAM MST, NOV;
WLC**
See also CDBLB 1660-1789; DLB 39

Richler, Mordecai 1931- **CLC 3, 5, 9, 13, 18,
46, 70; DAC; DAM MST, NOV**
See also AITN 1; CA 65-68; CANR 31, 62;
CLR 17; DLB 53; MAICYA; MTCW 1,
2; SATA 44, 98; SATA-Brief 27

Richter, Conrad (Michael) 1890-1968 **CLC
30**
See also AAYA 21; CA 5-8R; 25-28R;
CANR 23; DLB 9, 212; MTCW 1, 2;
SATA 3

Ricostranza, Tom
See Ellis, Trey

Riddell, Charlotte 1832-1906 **TCLC 40**
See also CA 165; DLB 156

Ridge, John Rollin 1827-1867 **NCLC 82;
DAM MULT**
See also CA 144; DLB 175; NNAL

Ridgway, Keith 1965- **CLC 119**
See also CA 172

Riding, Laura CLC 3, 7
See also Jackson, Laura (Riding)

Riefenstahl, Berta Helene Amalia 1902-
See Riefenstahl, Leni
See also CA 108

Riefenstahl, Leni CLC 16
See also Riefenstahl, Berta Helene Amalia

Riffe, Ernest
See Bergman, (Ernst) Ingmar

Riggs, (Rolla) Lynn 1899-1954 **TCLC 56;
DAM MULT**
See also CA 144; DLB 175; NNAL

Riis, Jacob A(ugust) 1849-1914 **TCLC 80**
See also CA 113; 168; DLB 23

Riley, James Whitcomb 1849-1916 **TCLC 51;
DAM POET**
See also CA 118; 137; MAICYA; SATA 17

Riley, Tex
See Creasey, John

Rilke, Rainer Maria 1875-1926 **TCLC 1, 6,
19; DAM POET; PC 2**
See also CA 104; 132; CANR 62; DA3;
DLB 81; MTCW 1, 2

Rimbaud, (Jean Nicolas) Arthur 1854-1891
**NCLC 4, 35, 82; DA; DAB; DAC; DAM
MST, POET; PC 3; WLC**
See also DA3

Rinehart, Mary Roberts 1876-1958 **TCLC 52**
See also CA 108; 166

Ringmaster, The
See Mencken, H(enry) L(ouis)

Ringwood, Gwen(dolyn Margaret) Pharis
1910-1984 **CLC 48**
See also CA 148; 112; DLB 88

Rio, Michel 19(?)- **CLC 43**

Ritsos, Giannes
See Ritsos, Yannis

Ritsos, Yannis 1909-1990 **CLC 6, 13, 31**
See also CA 77-80; 133; CANR 39, 61;
MTCW 1

Ritter, Erika 1948(?)- **CLC 52**

Rivera, Jose Eustasio 1889-1928 **TCLC 35**
See also CA 162; HW 1, 2

Rivera, Tomas 1935-1984
See also CA 49-52; CANR 32; DLB 82;
HLCS 2; HW 1

Rivers, Conrad Kent 1933-1968 **CLC 1**
See also BW 1; CA 85-88; DLB 41

Rivers, Elfrida
See Bradley, Marion Zimmer

Riverside, John
See Heinlein, Robert A(nson)

Rizal, Jose 1861-1896 **NCLC 27**

Roa Bastos, Augusto (Antonio) 1917- **CLC
45; DAM MULT; HLC 2**
See also CA 131; DLB 113; HW 1

Robbe-Grillet, Alain 1922- **CLC 1, 2, 4, 6, 8,
10, 14, 43, 128**
See also CA 9-12R; CANR 33, 65; DLB
83; MTCW 1, 2

Robbins, Harold 1916-1997 **CLC 5; DAM
NOV**
See also CA 73-76; 162; CANR 26, 54;
DA3; MTCW 1, 2

Robbins, Thomas Eugene 1936-
See Robbins, Tom
See also CA 81-84; CANR 29, 59; DAM
NOV, POP; DA3; MTCW 1, 2

Robbins, Tom CLC 9, 32, 64
See also Robbins, Thomas Eugene
See also AAYA 32; BEST 90:3; DLBY 80;
MTCW 2

Robbins, Trina 1938- **CLC 21**
See also CA 128

Roberts, Charles G(eorge) D(ouglas)
1860-1943 **TCLC 8**
See also CA 105; CLR 33; DLB 92; SATA
88; SATA-Brief 29

Roberts, Elizabeth Madox 1886-1941 **TCLC 68**
See also CA 111; 166; DLB 9, 54, 102; SATA 33; SATA-Brief 27

Roberts, Kate 1891-1985 **CLC 15**
See also CA 107; 116

Roberts, Keith (John Kingston) 1935- **CLC 14**
See also CA 25-28R; CANR 46

Roberts, Kenneth (Lewis) 1885-1957 **TCLC 23**
See also CA 109; DLB 9

Roberts, Michele (B.) 1949- **CLC 48**
See also CA 115; CANR 58

Robertson, Ellis
See Ellison, Harlan (Jay); Silverberg, Robert

Robertson, Thomas William 1829-1871 **NCLC 35; DAM DRAM**

Robeson, Kenneth
See Dent, Lester

Robinson, Edwin Arlington 1869-1935 **TCLC 5; DA; DAC; DAM MST, POET; PC 1**
See also CA 104; 133; CDALB 1865-1917; DLB 54; MTCW 1, 2

Robinson, Henry Crabb 1775-1867 **NCLC 15**
See also DLB 107

Robinson, Jill 1936- **CLC 10**
See also CA 102; INT 102

Robinson, Kim Stanley 1952- **CLC 34**
See also AAYA 26; CA 126; SATA 109

Robinson, Lloyd
See Silverberg, Robert

Robinson, Marilynne 1944- **CLC 25**
See also CA 116; CANR 80; DLB 206

Robinson, Smokey CLC 21
See also Robinson, William, Jr.

Robinson, William, Jr. 1940-
See Robinson, Smokey
See also CA 116

Robison, Mary 1949- **CLC 42, 98**
See also CA 113; 116; CANR 87; DLB 130; INT 116

Rod, Edouard 1857-1910 **TCLC 52**

Roddenberry, Eugene Wesley 1921-1991
See Roddenberry, Gene
See also CA 110; 135; CANR 37; SATA 45; SATA-Obit 69

Roddenberry, Gene CLC 17
See also Roddenberry, Eugene Wesley
See also AAYA 5; SATA-Obit 69

Rodgers, Mary 1931- **CLC 12**
See also CA 49-52; CANR 8, 55, 90; CLR 20; INT CANR-8; JRDA; MAICYA; SATA 8

Rodgers, W(illiam) R(obert) 1909-1969 **CLC 7**
See also CA 85-88; DLB 20

Rodman, Eric
See Silverberg, Robert

Rodman, Howard 1920(?)-1985 **CLC 65**
See also CA 118

Rodman, Maia
See Wojciechowska, Maia (Teresa)

Rodo, Jose Enrique 1872(?)-1917
See also CA 178; HLCS 2; HW 2

Rodriguez, Claudio 1934- **CLC 10**
See also DLB 134

Rodriguez, Richard 1944-
See also CA 110; CANR 66; DAM MULT; DLB 82; HLC 2; HW 1, 2

Roelvaag, O(le) E(dvart) 1876-1931 **TCLC 17**
See also Rolvaag, O(le) E(dvart)
See also CA 117; 171; DLB 9

Roethke, Theodore (Huebner) 1908-1963 **CLC 1, 3, 8, 11, 19, 46, 101; DAM POET; PC 15**

See also CA 81-84; CABS 2; CDALB 1941-1968; DA3; DLB 5, 206; MTCW 1, 2

Rogers, Samuel 1763-1855 **NCLC 69**
See also DLB 93

Rogers, Thomas Hunton 1927- **CLC 57**
See also CA 89-92; INT 89-92

Rogers, Will(iam Penn Adair) 1879-1935 **TCLC 8, 71; DAM MULT**
See also CA 105; 144; DA3; DLB 11; MTCW 2; NNAL

Rogin, Gilbert 1929- **CLC 18**
See also CA 65-68; CANR 15

Rohan, Koda
See Koda Shigeyuki

Rohlfs, Anna Katharine Green
See Green, Anna Katharine

Rohmer, Eric CLC 16
See also Scherer, Jean-Marie Maurice

Rohmer, Sax TCLC 28
See also Ward, Arthur Henry Sarsfield
See also DLB 70

Roiphe, Anne (Richardson) 1935- **CLC 3, 9**
See also CA 89-92; CANR 45, 73; DLBY 80; INT 89-92

Rojas, Fernando de 1465-1541 **LC 23; HLCS 1**

Rojas, Gonzalo 1917-
See also HLCS 2; HW 2

Rojas, Gonzalo 1917-
See also CA 178; HLCS 2

Rolfe, Frederick (William Serafino Austin Lewis Mary) 1860-1913 **TCLC 12**
See also CA 107; DLB 34, 156

Rolland, Romain 1866-1944 **TCLC 23**
See also CA 118; DLB 65

Rolle, Richard c. 1300-c. 1349 **CMLC 21**
See also DLB 146

Rolvaag, O(le) E(dvart)
See Roelvaag, O(le) E(dvart)

Romain Arnaud, Saint
See Aragon, Louis

Romains, Jules 1885-1972 **CLC 7**
See also CA 85-88; CANR 34; DLB 65; MTCW 1

Romero, Jose Ruben 1890-1952 **TCLC 14**
See also CA 114; 131; HW 1

Ronsard, Pierre de 1524-1585 **LC 6, 54; PC 11**

Rooke, Leon 1934- **CLC 25, 34; DAM POP**
See also CA 25-28R; CANR 23, 53

Roosevelt, Franklin Delano 1882-1945 **TCLC 93**
See also CA 116; 173

Roosevelt, Theodore 1858-1919 **TCLC 69**
See also CA 115; 170; DLB 47, 186

Roper, William 1498-1578 **LC 10**

Roquelaure, A. N.
See Rice, Anne

Rosa, Joao Guimaraes 1908-1967 **CLC 23; HLCS 1**
See also CA 89-92; DLB 113

Rose, Wendy 1948- **CLC 85; DAM MULT; PC 13**
See also CA 53-56; CANR 5, 51; DLB 175; NNAL; SATA 12

Rosen, R. D.
See Rosen, Richard (Dean)

Rosen, Richard (Dean) 1949- **CLC 39**
See also CA 77-80; CANR 62; INT CANR-30

Rosenberg, Isaac 1890-1918 **TCLC 12**
See also CA 107; DLB 20

Rosenblatt, Joe CLC 15
See also Rosenblatt, Joseph

Rosenblatt, Joseph 1933-
See Rosenblatt, Joe
See also CA 89-92; INT 89-92

Rosenfeld, Samuel
See Tzara, Tristan

Rosenstock, Sami
See Tzara, Tristan

Rosenstock, Samuel
See Tzara, Tristan

Rosenthal, M(acha) L(ouis) 1917-1996 **CLC 28**
See also CA 1-4R; 152; CAAS 6; CANR 4, 51; DLB 5; SATA 59

Ross, Barnaby
See Dannay, Frederic

Ross, Bernard L.
See Follett, Ken(neth Martin)

Ross, J. H.
See Lawrence, T(homas) E(dward)

Ross, John Hume
See Lawrence, T(homas) E(dward)

Ross, Martin
See Martin, Violet Florence
See also DLB 135

Ross, (James) Sinclair 1908-1996 **CLC 13; DAC; DAM MST; SSC 24**
See also CA 73-76; CANR 81; DLB 88

Rossetti, Christina (Georgina) 1830-1894 **NCLC 2, 50, 66; DA; DAB; DAC; DAM MST, POET; PC 7; WLC**
See also DA3; DLB 35, 163; MAICYA; SATA 20

Rossetti, Dante Gabriel 1828-1882 **NCLC 4, 77; DA; DAB; DAC; DAM MST, POET; WLC**
See also CDBLB 1832-1890; DLB 35

Rossner, Judith (Perelman) 1935- **CLC 6, 9, 29**
See also AITN 2; BEST 90:3; CA 17-20R; CANR 18, 51, 73; DLB 6; INT CANR-18; MTCW 1, 2

Rostand, Edmond (Eugene Alexis) 1868-1918 **TCLC 6, 37; DA; DAB; DAC; DAM DRAM, MST; DC 10**
See also CA 104; 126; DA3; DLB 192; MTCW 1

Roth, Henry 1906-1995 **CLC 2, 6, 11, 104**
See also CA 11-12; 149; CANR 38, 63; CAP 1; DA3; DLB 28; MTCW 1, 2

Roth, Philip (Milton) 1933- **CLC 1, 2, 3, 4, 6, 9, 15, 22, 31, 47, 66, 86, 119; DA; DAB; DAC; DAM MST, NOV, POP; SSC 26; WLC**
See also BEST 90:3; CA 1-4R; CANR 1, 22, 36, 55, 89; CDALB 1968-1988; DA3; DLB 2, 28, 173; DLBY 82; MTCW 1, 2

Rothenberg, Jerome 1931- **CLC 6, 57**
See also CA 45-48; CANR 1; DLB 5, 193

Roumain, Jacques (Jean Baptiste) 1907-1944 **TCLC 19; BLC 3; DAM MULT**
See also BW 1; CA 117; 125

Rourke, Constance (Mayfield) 1885-1941 **TCLC 12**
See also CA 107; YABC 1

Rousseau, Jean-Baptiste 1671-1741 **LC 9**

Rousseau, Jean-Jacques 1712-1778 **LC 14, 36; DA; DAB; DAC; DAM MST; WLC**
See also DA3

Roussel, Raymond 1877-1933 **TCLC 20**
See also CA 117

Rovit, Earl (Herbert) 1927- **CLC 7**
See also CA 5-8R; CANR 12

Rowe, Elizabeth Singer 1674-1737 **LC 44**
See also DLB 39, 95

Rowe, Nicholas 1674-1718 **LC 8**
See also DLB 84

Rowley, Ames Dorrance
See Lovecraft, H(oward) P(hillips)

Rowson, Susanna Haswell 1762(?)-1824 **NCLC 5, 69**
See also DLB 37, 200

Roy, Arundhati 1960(?)- **CLC 109**

See also CA 163; CANR 90; DLBY 97

Roy, Gabrielle 1909-1983 **CLC 10, 14; DAB; DAC; DAM MST**
See also CA 53-56; 110; CANR 5, 61; DLB 68; MTCW 1; SATA 104

Royko, Mike 1932-1997 **CLC 109**
See also CA 89-92; 157; CANR 26

Rozewicz, Tadeusz 1921- **CLC 9, 23; DAM POET**
See also CA 108; CANR 36, 66; DA3; MTCW 1, 2

Ruark, Gibbons 1941- **CLC 3**
See also CA 33-36R; CAAS 23; CANR 14, 31, 57; DLB 120

Rubens, Bernice (Ruth) 1923- **CLC 19, 31**
See also CA 25-28R; CANR 33, 65; DLB 14, 207; MTCW 1

Rubin, Harold
See Robbins, Harold

Rudkin, (James) David 1936- **CLC 14**
See also CA 89-92; DLB 13

Rudnik, Raphael 1933- **CLC 7**
See also CA 29-32R

Ruffian, M.
See Hasek, Jaroslav (Matej Frantisek)

Ruiz, Jose Martinez CLC 11
See also Martinez Ruiz, Jose

Rukeyser, Muriel 1913-1980 **CLC 6, 10, 15, 27; DAM POET; PC 12**
See also CA 5-8R; 93-96; CANR 26, 60; DA3; DLB 48; MTCW 1, 2; SATA-Obit 22

Rule, Jane (Vance) 1931- **CLC 27**
See also CA 25-28R; CAAS 18; CANR 12, 87; DLB 60

Rulfo, Juan 1918-1986 **CLC 8, 80; DAM MULT; HLC 2; SSC 25**
See also CA 85-88; 118; CANR 26; DLB 113; HW 1, 2; MTCW 1, 2

Rumi, Jalal al-Din 1297-1373 **CMLC 20**

Runeberg, Johan 1804-1877 **NCLC 41**

Runyon, (Alfred) Damon 1884(?)-1946 **TCLC 10**
See also CA 107; 165; DLB 11, 86, 171; MTCW 2

Rush, Norman 1933- **CLC 44**
See also CA 121; 126; INT 126

Rushdie, (Ahmed) Salman 1947- **CLC 23, 31, 55, 100; DAB; DAC; DAM MST, NOV, POP; WLCS**
See also BEST 89:3; CA 108; 111; CANR 33, 56; DA3; DLB 194; INT 111; MTCW 1, 2

Rushforth, Peter (Scott) 1945- **CLC 19**
See also CA 101

Ruskin, John 1819-1900 **TCLC 63**
See also CA 114; 129; CDBLB 1832-1890; DLB 55, 163, 190; SATA 24

Russ, Joanna 1937- **CLC 15**
See also CA 5-28R; CANR 11, 31, 65; DLB 8; MTCW 1

Russell, George William 1867-1935
See Baker, Jean H.
See also CA 104; 153; CDBLB 1890-1914; DAM POET

Russell, (Henry) Ken(neth Alfred) 1927- **CLC 16**
See also CA 105

Russell, William Martin 1947- **CLC 60**
See also CA 164

Rutherford, Mark TCLC 25
See also White, William Hale
See also DLB 18

Ruyslinck, Ward 1929- **CLC 14**
See also Belser, Reimond Karel Maria de

Ryan, Cornelius (John) 1920-1974 **CLC 7**
See also CA 69-72; 53-56; CANR 38

Ryan, Michael 1946- **CLC 65**
See also CA 49-52; DLBY 82

Ryan, Tim
See Dent, Lester

Rybakov, Anatoli (Naumovich) 1911-1998 **CLC 23, 53**
See also CA 126; 135; 172; SATA 79; SATA-Obit 108

Ryder, Jonathan
See Ludlum, Robert

Ryga, George 1932-1987 **CLC 14; DAC; DAM MST**
See also CA 101; 124; CANR 43, 90; DLB 60

S. H.
See Hartmann, Sadakichi

S. S.
See Sassoon, Siegfried (Lorraine)

Saba, Umberto 1883-1957 **TCLC 33**
See also CA 144; CANR 79; DLB 114

Sabatini, Rafael 1875-1950 **TCLC 47**
See also CA 162

Sabato, Ernesto (R.) 1911- **CLC 10, 23; DAM MULT; HLC 2**
See also CA 97-100; CANR 32, 65; DLB 145; HW 1, 2; MTCW 1, 2

Sa-Carniero, Mario de 1890-1916 **TCLC 83**

Sacastru, Martin
See Bioy Casares, Adolfo

Sacastru, Martin
See Bioy Casares, Adolfo

Sacher-Masoch, Leopold von 1836(?)-1895 **NCLC 31**

Sachs, Marilyn (Stickle) 1927- **CLC 35**
See also AAYA 2; CA 17-20R; CANR 13, 47; CLR 2; JRDA; MAICYA; SAAS 2; SATA 3, 68; SATA-Essay 110

Sachs, Nelly 1891-1970 **CLC 14, 98**
See also CA 17-18; 25-28R; CANR 87; CAP 2; MTCW 2

Sackler, Howard (Oliver) 1929-1982 **CLC 14**
See also CA 61-64; 108; CANR 30; DLB 7

Sacks, Oliver (Wolf) 1933- **CLC 67**
See also CA 53-56; CANR 28, 50, 76; DA3; INT CANR-28; MTCW 1, 2

Sadakichi
See Hartmann, Sadakichi

Sade, Donatien Alphonse Francois, Comte de 1740-1814 **NCLC 47**

Sadoff, Ira 1945- **CLC 9**
See also CA 53-56; CANR 5, 21; DLB 120

Saetone
See Camus, Albert

Safire, William 1929- **CLC 10**
See also CA 17-20R; CANR 31, 54, 91

Sagan, Carl (Edward) 1934-1996 **CLC 30, 112**
See also AAYA 2; CA 25-28R; 155; CANR 11, 36, 74; DA3; MTCW 1, 2; SATA 58; SATA-Obit 94

Sagan, Francoise CLC 3, 6, 9, 17, 36
See also Quoirez, Francoise
See also DLB 83; MTCW 2

Sahgal, Nayantara (Pandit) 1927- **CLC 41**
See also CA 9-12R; CANR 11, 88

Saint, H(arry) F. 1941- **CLC 50**
See also CA 127

St. Aubin de Teran, Lisa 1953-
See Teran, Lisa St. Aubin de
See also CA 118; 126; INT 126

Saint Birgitta of Sweden c. 1303-1373 **CMLC 24**

Sainte-Beuve, Charles Augustin 1804-1869 **NCLC 5**

Saint-Exupery, Antoine (Jean Baptiste Marie Roger) de 1900-1944 **TCLC 2, 56; DAM NOV; WLC**
See also CA 108; 132; CLR 10; DA3; DLB 72; MAICYA; MTCW 1, 2; SATA 20

St. John, David
See Hunt, E(verette) Howard, (Jr.)

Saint-John Perse
See Leger, (Marie-Rene Auguste) Alexis Saint-Leger

Saintsbury, George (Edward Bateman) 1845-1933 **TCLC 31**
See also CA 160; DLB 57, 149

Sait Faik TCLC 23
See also Abasiyanik, Sait Faik

Saki TCLC 3; SSC 12
See also Munro, H(ector) H(ugh)
See also MTCW 2

Sala, George Augustus NCLC 46

Saladin 1138-1193 **CMLC 38**

Salama, Hannu 1936- **CLC 18**

Salamanca, J(ack) R(ichard) 1922- **CLC 4, 15**
See also CA 25-28R

Salas, Floyd Francis 1931-
See also CA 119; CAAS 27; CANR 44, 75; DAM MULT; DLB 82; HLC 2; HW 1, 2; MTCW 2

Sale, J. Kirkpatrick
See Sale, Kirkpatrick

Sale, Kirkpatrick 1937- **CLC 68**
See also CA 13-16R; CANR 10

Salinas, Luis Omar 1937- **CLC 90; DAM MULT; HLC 2**
See also CA 131; CANR 81; DLB 82; HW 1, 2

Salinas (y Serrano), Pedro 1891(?)-1951 **TCLC 17**
See also CA 117; DLB 134

Salinger, J(erome) D(avid) 1919- **CLC 1, 3, 8, 12, 55, 56; DA; DAB; DAC; DAM MST, NOV, POP; SSC 2, 28; WLC**
See also AAYA 2; CA 5-8R; CANR 39; CDALB 1941-1968; CLR 18; DA3; DLB 2, 102, 173; MAICYA; MTCW 1, 2; SATA 67

Salisbury, John
See Caute, (John) David

Salter, James 1925- **CLC 7, 52, 59**
See also CA 73-76; DLB 130

Saltus, Edgar (Everton) 1855-1921 **TCLC 8**
See also CA 105; DLB 202

Saltykov, Mikhail Evgrafovich 1826-1889 **NCLC 16**

Samarakis, Antonis 1919- **CLC 5**
See also CA 25-28R; CAAS 16; CANR 36

Sanchez, Florencio 1875-1910 **TCLC 37**
See also CA 153; HW 1

Sanchez, Luis Rafael 1936- **CLC 23**
See also CA 128; DLB 145; HW 1

Sanchez, Sonia 1934- **CLC 5, 116; BLC 3; DAM MULT; PC 9**
See also BW 2; CA 33-36R; CANR 24, 49, 74; CLR 18; DA3; DLB 41; DLBD 8; MAICYA; MTCW 1, 2; SATA 22

Sand, George 1804-1876 **NCLC 2, 42, 57; DA; DAB; DAC; DAM MST, NOV; WLC**
See also DA3; DLB 119, 192

Sandburg, Carl (August) 1878-1967 **CLC 1, 4, 10, 15, 35; DA; DAB; DAC; DAM MST, POET; PC 2; WLC**
See also AAYA 24; CA 5-8R; 25-28R; CANR 35; CDALB 1865-1917; DA3; DLB 17, 54; MAICYA; MTCW 1, 2; SATA 8

Sandburg, Charles
See Sandburg, Carl (August)

Sandburg, Charles A.
See Sandburg, Carl (August)

Sanders, (James) Ed(ward) 1939- **CLC 53; DAM POET**
See also CA 13-16R; CAAS 21; CANR 13, 44, 78; DLB 16

Scotland, Jay
See Jakes, John (William)
Scott, Duncan Campbell 1862-1947 **TCLC 6; DAC**
See also CA 104; 153; DLB 92
Scott, Evelyn 1893-1963 **CLC 43**
See also CA 104; 112; CANR 64; DLB 9, 48
Scott, F(rancis) R(eginald) 1899-1935 **CLC 22**
See also CA 101; 114; CANR 87; DLB 88; INT 101
Scott, Frank
See Scott, F(rancis) R(eginald)
Scott, Joanna 1960- **CLC 50**
See also CA 126; CANR 53
Scott, Paul (Mark) 1920-1978 **CLC 9, 60**
See also CA 81-84; 77-80; CANR 33; DLB 14, 207; MTCW 1
Scott, Sarah 1723-1795 **LC 44**
See also DLB 39
Scott, Walter 1771-1832 **NCLC 15, 69; DA; DAB; DAC; DAM MST, NOV, POET; PC 13; SSC 32; WLC**
See also AAYA 22; CDBLB 1789-1832; DLB 93, 107, 116, 144, 159; YABC 2
Scribe, (Augustin) Eugene 1791-1861 **NCLC 16; DAM DRAM; DC 5**
See also DLB 192
Scrum, R.
See Crumb, R(obert)
Scudery, Madeleine de 1607-1701 **LC 2, 58**
Scum
See Crumb, R(obert)
Scumbag, Little Bobby
See Crumb, R(obert)
Seabrook, John
See Hubbard, L(afayette) Ron(ald)
Sealy, I(rwin) Allan 1951- **CLC 55**
See also CA 136
Search, Alexander
See Pessoa, Fernando (Antonio Nogueira)
Sebastian, Lee
See Silverberg, Robert
Sebastian Owl
See Thompson, Hunter S(tockton)
Sebestyen, Ouida 1924- **CLC 30**
See also AAYA 8; CA 107; CANR 40; CLR 17; JRDA; MAICYA; SAAS 10; SATA 39
Secundus, H. Scriblerus
See Fielding, Henry
Sedges, John
See Buck, Pearl S(ydenstricker)
Sedgwick, Catharine Maria 1789-1867 **NCLC 19**
See also DLB 1, 74
Seelye, John (Douglas) 1931- **CLC 7**
See also CA 97-100; CANR 70; INT 97-100
Seferiades, Giorgos Stylianou 1900-1971
See Seferis, George
See also CA 5-8R; 33-36R; CANR 5, 36; MTCW 1
Seferis, George CLC 5, 11
See also Seferiades, Giorgos Stylianou
Segal, Erich (Wolf) 1937- **CLC 3, 10; DAM POP**
See also BEST 89:1; CA 25-28R; CANR 20, 36, 65; DLBY 86; INT CANR-20; MTCW 1
Seger, Bob 1945- **CLC 35**
Seghers, Anna CLC 7
See also Radvanyi, Netty
See also DLB 69
Seidel, Frederick (Lewis) 1936- **CLC 18**
See also CA 13-16R; CANR 8; DLBY 84
Seifert, Jaroslav 1901-1986 **CLC 34, 44, 93**

See also CA 127; MTCW 1, 2
Sei Shonagon c. 966-1017(?) **CMLC 6**
Séjour, Victor 1817-1874 **DC 10**
See also DLB 50
Sejour Marcou et Ferrand, Juan Victor
See S
Selby, Hubert, Jr. 1928- **CLC 1, 2, 4, 8; SSC 20**
See also CA 13-16R; CANR 33, 85; DLB 2
Selzer, Richard 1928- **CLC 74**
See also CA 65-68; CANR 14
Sembene, Ousmane
See Ousmane, Sembene
Senancour, Etienne Pivert de 1770-1846 **NCLC 16**
See also DLB 119
Sender, Ramon (Jose) 1902-1982 **CLC 8; DAM MULT; HLC 2**
See also CA 5-8R; 105; CANR 8; HW 1; MTCW 1
Seneca, Lucius Annaeus c. 1-c. 65 **CMLC 6; DAM DRAM; DC 5**
See also DLB 211
Senghor, Leopold Sedar 1906- **CLC 54, 130; BLC 3; DAM MULT, POET; PC 25**
See also BW 2; CA 116; 125; CANR 47, 74; MTCW 1, 2
Senna, Danzy 1970- **CLC 119**
See also CA 169
Serling, (Edward) Rod(man) 1924-1975 **CLC 30**
See also AAYA 14; AITN 1; CA 162; 57-60; DLB 26
Serna, Ramon Gomez de la
See Gomez de la Serna, Ramon
Serpieres
See Guillevic, (Eugene)
Service, Robert
See Service, Robert W(illiam)
See also DAB; DLB 92
Service, Robert W(illiam) 1874(?)-1958 **TCLC 15; DA; DAC; DAM MST, POET; WLC**
See also Service, Robert
See also CA 115; 140; CANR 84; SATA 20
Seth, Vikram 1952- **CLC 43, 90; DAM MULT**
See also CA 121; 127; CANR 50, 74; DA3; DLB 120; INT 127; MTCW 2
Seton, Cynthia Propper 1926-1982 **CLC 27**
See also CA 5-8R; 108; CANR 7
Seton, Ernest (Evan) Thompson 1860-1946 **TCLC 31**
See also CA 109; CLR 59; DLB 92; DLBD 13; JRDA; SATA 18
Seton-Thompson, Ernest
See Seton, Ernest (Evan) Thompson
Settle, Mary Lee 1918- **CLC 19, 61**
See also CA 89-92; CAAS 1; CANR 44, 87; DLB 6; INT 89-92
Seuphor, Michel
See Arp, Jean
Sevigne, Marie (de Rabutin-Chantal) Marquise de 1626-1696 **LC 11**
Sewall, Samuel 1652-1730 **LC 38**
See also DLB 24
Sexton, Anne (Harvey) 1928-1974 **CLC 2, 4, 6, 8, 10, 15, 53; DA; DAB; DAC; DAM MST, POET; PC 2; WLC**
See also CA 1-4R; 53-56; CABS 2; CANR 3, 36; CDALB 1941-1968; DA3; DLB 5, 169; MTCW 1, 2; SATA 10
Shaara, Jeff 1952- **CLC 119**
See also CA 163
Shaara, Michael (Joseph, Jr.) 1929-1988 **CLC 15; DAM POP**
See also AITN 1; CA 102; 125; CANR 52, 85; DLBY 83

Shackleton, C. C.
See Aldiss, Brian W(ilson)
Shacochis, Bob CLC 39
See also Shacochis, Robert G.
Shacochis, Robert G. 1951-
See Shacochis, Bob
See also CA 119; 124; INT 124
Shaffer, Anthony (Joshua) 1926- **CLC 19; DAM DRAM**
See also CA 110; 116; DLB 13
Shaffer, Peter (Levin) 1926- **CLC 5, 14, 18, 37, 60; DAB; DAM DRAM, MST; DC 7**
See also CA 25-28R; CANR 25, 47, 74; CDBLB 1960 to Present; DA3; DLB 13; MTCW 1, 2
Shakey, Bernard
See Young, Neil
Shalamov, Varlam (Tikhonovich) 1907(?)-1982 **CLC 18**
See also CA 129; 105
Shamlu, Ahmad 1925- **CLC 10**
Shammas, Anton 1951- **CLC 55**
Shandling, Arline
See Berriault, Gina
Shange, Ntozake 1948- **CLC 8, 25, 38, 74, 126; BLC 3; DAM DRAM, MULT; DC 3**
See also AAYA 9; BW 2; CA 85-88; CABS 3; CANR 27, 48, 74; DA3; DLB 38; MTCW 1, 2
Shanley, John Patrick 1950- **CLC 75**
See also CA 128; 133; CANR 83
Shapcott, Thomas W(illiam) 1935- **CLC 38**
See also CA 69-72; CANR 49, 83
Shapiro, Jane CLC 76
Shapiro, Karl (Jay) 1913- **CLC 4, 8, 15, 53; PC 25**
See also CA 1-4R; CAAS 6; CANR 1, 36, 66; DLB 48; MTCW 1, 2
Sharp, William 1855-1905 **TCLC 39**
See also CA 160; DLB 156
Sharpe, Thomas Ridley 1928-
See Sharpe, Tom
See also CA 114; 122; CANR 85; INT 122
Sharpe, Tom CLC 36
See also Sharpe, Thomas Ridley
See also DLB 14
Shaw, Bernard TCLC 45
See also Shaw, George Bernard
See also BW 1; MTCW 2
Shaw, G. Bernard
See Shaw, George Bernard
Shaw, George Bernard 1856-1950 **TCLC 3, 9, 21; DA; DAB; DAC; DAM DRAM, MST; WLC**
See also Shaw, Bernard
See also CA 104; 128; CDBLB 1914-1945; DA3; DLB 10, 57, 190; MTCW 1, 2
Shaw, Henry Wheeler 1818-1885 **NCLC 15**
See also DLB 11
Shaw, Irwin 1913-1984 **CLC 7, 23, 34; DAM DRAM, POP**
See also AITN 1; CA 13-16R; 112; CANR 21; CDALB 1941-1968; DLB 6, 102; DLBY 84; MTCW 1, 2
Shaw, Robert 1927-1978 **CLC 5**
See also AITN 1; CA 1-4R; 81-84; CANR 4; DLB 13, 14
Shaw, T. E.
See Lawrence, T(homas) E(dward)
Shawn, Wallace 1943- **CLC 41**
See also CA 112
Shea, Lisa 1953- **CLC 86**
See also CA 147
Sheed, Wilfrid (John Joseph) 1930- **CLC 2, 4, 10, 53**
See also CA 65-68; CANR 30, 66; DLB 6; MTCW 1, 2

15, 63; DA; DAB; DAC; DAM MST,
NOV; WLC
See also CA 5-8R; 25-28R; CANR 7;
CDALB 1929-1941; DA3; DLB 9; INT
CANR-7; MTCW 1, 2; SATA 9

Singer, Isaac
See Singer, Isaac Bashevis

Singer, Isaac Bashevis 1904-1991 **CLC 1, 3,
6, 9, 11, 15, 23, 38, 69, 111; DA; DAB;
DAC; DAM MST, NOV; SSC 3; WLC**
See also AAYA 32; AITN 1, 2; CA 1-4R;
134; CANR 1, 39; CDALB 1941-1968;
CLR 1; DA3; DLB 6, 28, 52; DLBY 91;
JRDA; MAICYA; MTCW 1, 2; SATA 3,
27; SATA-Obit 68

Singer, Israel Joshua 1893-1944 **TCLC 33**
See also CA 169

Singh, Khushwant 1915- **CLC 11**
See also CA 9-12R; CAAS 9; CANR 6, 84

Singleton, Ann
See Benedict, Ruth (Fulton)

Sinjohn, John
See Galsworthy, John

Sinyavsky, Andrei (Donatevich) 1925-1997
CLC 8
See also CA 85-88; 159

Sirin, V.
See Nabokov, Vladimir (Vladimirovich)

Sissman, L(ouis) E(dward) 1928-1976 **CLC
9, 18**
See also CA 21-24R; 65-68; CANR 13;
DLB 5

Sisson, C(harles) H(ubert) 1914- **CLC 8**
See also CA 1-4R; CAAS 3; CANR 3, 48,
84; DLB 27

Sitwell, Dame Edith 1887-1964 **CLC 2, 9, 67;
DAM POET; PC 3**
See also CA 9-12R; CANR 35; CDBLB
1945-1960; DLB 20; MTCW 1, 2

Siwaarmill, H. P.
See Sharp, William

Sjoewall, Maj 1935- **CLC 7**
See also CA 65-68; CANR 73

Sjowall, Maj
See Sjoewall, Maj

Skelton, John 1463-1529 **PC 25**

Skelton, Robin 1925-1997 **CLC 13**
See also AITN 2; CA 5-8R; 160; CAAS 5;
CANR 28, 89; DLB 27, 53

Skolimowski, Jerzy 1938- **CLC 20**
See also CA 128

Skram, Amalie (Bertha) 1847-1905 **TCLC 25**
See also CA 165

Skvorecky, Josef (Vaclav) 1924- **CLC 15, 39,
69; DAC; DAM NOV**
See also CA 61-64; CAAS 1; CANR 10,
34, 63; DA3; MTCW 1, 2

Slade, Bernard CLC 11, 46
See also Newbound, Bernard Slade
See also CAAS 9; DLB 53

Slaughter, Carolyn 1946- **CLC 56**
See also CA 85-88; CANR 85

Slaughter, Frank G(ill) 1908- **CLC 29**
See also AITN 2; CA 5-8R; CANR 5, 85;
INT CANR-5

Slavitt, David R(ytman) 1935- **CLC 5, 14**
See also CA 21-24R; CAAS 3; CANR 41,
83; DLB 5, 6

Slesinger, Tess 1905-1945 **TCLC 10**
See also CA 107; DLB 102

Slessor, Kenneth 1901-1971 **CLC 14**
See also CA 102; 89-92

Slowacki, Juliusz 1809-1849 **NCLC 15**

Smart, Christopher 1722-1771 **LC 3; DAM
POET; PC 13**
See also DLB 109

Smart, Elizabeth 1913-1986 **CLC 54**
See also CA 81-84; 118; DLB 88

Smiley, Jane (Graves) 1949- **CLC 53, 76;
DAM POP**
See also CA 104; CANR 30, 50, 74; DA3;
INT CANR-30

Smith, A(rthur) J(ames) M(arshall)
1902-1980 **CLC 15; DAC**
See also CA 1-4R; 102; CANR 4; DLB 88

Smith, Adam 1723-1790 **LC 36**
See also DLB 104

Smith, Alexander 1829-1867 **NCLC 59**
See also DLB 32, 55

Smith, Anna Deavere 1950- **CLC 86**
See also CA 133

Smith, Betty (Wehner) 1896-1972 **CLC 19**
See also CA 5-8R; 33-36R; DLBY 82;
SATA 6

Smith, Charlotte (Turner) 1749-1806 **NCLC
23**
See also DLB 39, 109

Smith, Clark Ashton 1893-1961 **CLC 43**
See also CA 143; CANR 81; MTCW 2

Smith, Dave CLC 22, 42
See also Smith, David (Jeddie)
See also CAAS 7; DLB 5

Smith, David (Jeddie) 1942-
See Smith, Dave
See also CA 49-52; CANR 1, 59; DAM
POET

Smith, Florence Margaret 1902-1971
See Smith, Stevie
See also CA 17-18; 29-32R; CANR 35;
CAP 2; DAM POET; MTCW 1, 2

Smith, Iain Crichton 1928-1998 **CLC 64**
See also CA 21-24R; 171; DLB 40, 139

Smith, John 1580(?)-1631 **LC 9**
See also DLB 24, 30

Smith, Johnston
See Crane, Stephen (Townley)

Smith, Joseph, Jr. 1805-1844 **NCLC 53**

Smith, Lee 1944- **CLC 25, 73**
See also CA 114; 119; CANR 46; DLB 143;
DLBY 83; INT 119

Smith, Martin
See Smith, Martin Cruz

Smith, Martin Cruz 1942- **CLC 25; DAM
MULT, POP**
See also BEST 89:4; CA 85-88; CANR 6,
23, 43, 65; INT CANR-23; MTCW 2;
NNAL

Smith, Mary-Ann Tirone 1944- **CLC 39**
See also CA 118; 136

Smith, Patti 1946- **CLC 12**
See also CA 93-96; CANR 63

Smith, Pauline (Urmson) 1882-1959 **TCLC
25**

Smith, Rosamond
See Oates, Joyce Carol

Smith, Sheila Kaye
See Kaye-Smith, Sheila

Smith, Stevie CLC 3, 8, 25, 44; PC 12
See also Smith, Florence Margaret
See also DLB 20; MTCW 2

Smith, Wilbur (Addison) 1933- **CLC 33**
See also CA 13-16R; CANR 7, 46, 66;
MTCW 1, 2

Smith, William Jay 1918- **CLC 6**
See also CA 5-8R; CANR 44; DLB 5; MAI-
CYA; SAAS 22; SATA 2, 68

Smith, Woodrow Wilson
See Kuttner, Henry

Smolenskin, Peretz 1842-1885 **NCLC 30**

Smollett, Tobias (George) 1721-1771 **LC 2,
46**
See also CDBLB 1660-1789; DLB 39, 104

Snodgrass, W(illiam) D(e Witt) 1926- **CLC 2,
6, 10, 18, 68; DAM POET**
See also CA 1-4R; CANR 6, 36, 65, 85;
DLB 5; MTCW 1, 2

Snow, C(harles) P(ercy) 1905-1980 **CLC 1, 4,
6, 9, 13, 19; DAM NOV**
See also CA 5-8R; 101; CANR 28; CDBLB
1945-1960; DLB 15, 77; DLBD 17;
MTCW 1, 2

Snow, Frances Compton
See Adams, Henry (Brooks)

Snyder, Gary (Sherman) 1930- **CLC 1, 2, 5,
9, 32, 120; DAM POET; PC 21**
See also CA 17-20R; CANR 30, 60; DA3;
DLB 5, 16, 165, 212; MTCW 2

Snyder, Zilpha Keatley 1927- **CLC 17**
See also AAYA 15; CA 9-12R; CANR 38;
CLR 31; JRDA; MAICYA; SAAS 2;
SATA 1, 28, 75, 110; SATA-Essay 112

Soares, Bernardo
See Pessoa, Fernando (Antonio Nogueira)

Sobh, A.
See Shamlu, Ahmad

Sobol, Joshua CLC 60

Socrates 469B.C.-399B.C. **CMLC 27**

Soderberg, Hjalmar 1869-1941 **TCLC 39**

Sodergran, Edith (Irene)
See Soedergran, Edith (Irene)

Soedergran, Edith (Irene) 1892-1923 **TCLC
31**

Softly, Edgar
See Lovecraft, H(oward) P(hillips)

Softly, Edward
See Lovecraft, H(oward) P(hillips)

Sokolov, Raymond 1941- **CLC 7**
See also CA 85-88

Solo, Jay
See Ellison, Harlan (Jay)

Sologub, Fyodor TCLC 9
See also Teternikov, Fyodor Kuzmich

Solomons, Ikey Esquir
See Thackeray, William Makepeace

Solomos, Dionysios 1798-1857 **NCLC 15**

Solwoska, Mara
See French, Marilyn

Solzhenitsyn, Aleksandr I(sayevich) 1918-
**CLC 1, 2, 4, 7, 9, 10, 18, 26, 34, 78; DA;
DAB; DAC; DAM MST, NOV; SSC 32;
WLC**
See also AITN 1; CA 69-72; CANR 40, 65;
DA3; MTCW 1, 2

Somers, Jane
See Lessing, Doris (May)

Somerville, Edith 1858-1949 **TCLC 51**
See also DLB 135

Somerville & Ross
See Martin, Violet Florence; Somerville,
Edith

Sommer, Scott 1951- **CLC 25**
See also CA 106

Sondheim, Stephen (Joshua) 1930- **CLC 30,
39; DAM DRAM**
See also AAYA 11; CA 103; CANR 47, 68

Song, Cathy 1955- **PC 21**
See also CA 154; DLB 169

Sontag, Susan 1933- **CLC 1, 2, 10, 13, 31,
105; DAM POP**
See also CA 17-20R; CANR 25, 51, 74;
DA3; DLB 2, 67; MTCW 1, 2

Sophocles 496(?)B.C.-406(?)B.C. **CMLC 2;
DA; DAB; DAC; DAM DRAM, MST;
DC 1; WLCS**
See also DA3; DLB 176

Sordello 1189-1269 **CMLC 15**

Sorel, Georges 1847-1922 **TCLC 91**
See also CA 118

Sorel, Julia
See Drexler, Rosalyn

Sorrentino, Gilbert 1929- **CLC 3, 7, 14, 22,
40**
See also CA 77-80; CANR 14, 33; DLB 5,
173; DLBY 80; INT CANR-14

Soto, Gary 1952- **CLC 32, 80; DAM MULT; HLC 2; PC 28**
See also AAYA 10; CA 119; 125; CANR 50, 74; CLR 38; DLB 82; HW 1, 2; INT 125; JRDA; MTCW 2; SATA 80

Soupault, Philippe 1897-1990 **CLC 68**
See also CA 116; 147; 131

Souster, (Holmes) Raymond 1921- **CLC 5, 14; DAC; DAM POET**
See also CA 13-16R; CAAS 14; CANR 13, 29, 53; DA3; DLB 88; SATA 63

Southern, Terry 1924(?)-1995 **CLC 7**
See also CA 1-4R; 150; CANR 1, 55; DLB 2

Southey, Robert 1774-1843 **NCLC 8**
See also DLB 93, 107, 142; SATA 54

Southworth, Emma Dorothy Eliza Nevitte 1819-1899 **NCLC 26**

Souza, Ernest
See Scott, Evelyn

Soyinka, Wole 1934- **CLC 3, 5, 14, 36, 44; BLC 3; DA; DAB; DAC; DAM DRAM, MST, MULT; DC 2; WLC**
See also BW 2, 3; CA 13-16R; CANR 27, 39, 82; DA3; DLB 125; MTCW 1, 2

Spackman, W(illiam) M(ode) 1905-1990 **CLC 46**
See also CA 81-84; 132

Spacks, Barry (Bernard) 1931- **CLC 14**
See also CA 154; CANR 33; DLB 105

Spanidou, Irini 1946- **CLC 44**
See also CA 185

Spark, Muriel (Sarah) 1918- **CLC 2, 3, 5, 8, 13, 18, 40, 94; DAB; DAC; DAM MST, NOV; SSC 10**
See also CA 5-8R; CANR 12, 36, 76, 89; CDBLB 1945-1960; DA3; DLB 15, 139; INT CANR-12; MTCW 1, 2

Spaulding, Douglas
See Bradbury, Ray (Douglas)

Spaulding, Leonard
See Bradbury, Ray (Douglas)

Spence, J. A. D.
See Eliot, T(homas) S(tearns)

Spencer, Elizabeth 1921- **CLC 22**
See also CA 13-16R; CANR 32, 65, 87; DLB 6; MTCW 1; SATA 14

Spencer, Leonard G.
See Silverberg, Robert

Spencer, Scott 1945- **CLC 30**
See also CA 113; CANR 51; DLBY 86

Spender, Stephen (Harold) 1909-1995 **CLC 1, 2, 5, 10, 41, 91; DAM POET**
See also CA 9-12R; 149; CANR 31, 54; CDBLB 1945-1960; DA3; DLB 20; MTCW 1, 2

Spengler, Oswald (Arnold Gottfried) 1880-1936 **TCLC 25**
See also CA 118

Spenser, Edmund 1552(?)-1599 **LC 5, 39; DA; DAB; DAC; DAM MST, POET; PC 8; WLC**
See also CDBLB Before 1660; DA3; DLB 167

Spicer, Jack 1925-1965 **CLC 8, 18, 72; DAM POET**
See also CA 85-88; DLB 5, 16, 193

Spiegelman, Art 1948- **CLC 76**
See also AAYA 10; CA 125; CANR 41, 55, 74; MTCW 2; SATA 109

Spielberg, Peter 1929- **CLC 6**
See also CA 5-8R; CANR 4, 48; DLBY 81

Spielberg, Steven 1947- **CLC 20**
See also AAYA 8, 24; CA 77-80; CANR 32; SATA 32

Spillane, Frank Morrison 1918-
See Spillane, Mickey
See also CA 25-28R; CANR 28, 63; DA3; MTCW 1, 2; SATA 66

Spillane, Mickey **CLC 3, 13**
See also Spillane, Frank Morrison
See also MTCW 2

Spinoza, Benedictus de 1632-1677 **LC 9, 58**

Spinrad, Norman (Richard) 1940- **CLC 46**
See also CA 37-40R; CAAS 19; CANR 20, 91; DLB 8; INT CANR-20

Spitteler, Carl (Friedrich Georg) 1845-1924 **TCLC 12**
See also CA 109; DLB 129

Spivack, Kathleen (Romola Drucker) 1938- **CLC 6**
See also CA 49-52

Spoto, Donald 1941- **CLC 39**
See also CA 65-68; CANR 11, 57

Springsteen, Bruce (F.) 1949- **CLC 17**
See also CA 111

Spurling, Hilary 1940- **CLC 34**
See also CA 104; CANR 25, 52

Spyker, John Howland
See Elman, Richard (Martin)

Squires, (James) Radcliffe 1917-1993 **CLC 51**
See also CA 1-4R; 140; CANR 6, 21

Srivastava, Dhanpat Rai 1880(?)-1936
See Premchand
See also CA 118

Stacy, Donald
See Pohl, Frederik

Stael, Germaine de 1766-1817
See Stael-Holstein, Anne Louise Germaine Necker Baronn
See also DLB 119

Stael-Holstein, Anne Louise Germaine Necker Baronn 1766-1817 **NCLC 3**
See also Stael, Germaine de
See also DLB 192

Stafford, Jean 1915-1979 **CLC 4, 7, 19, 68; SSC 26**
See also CA 1-4R; 85-88; CANR 3, 65; DLB 2, 173; MTCW 1, 2; SATA-Obit 22

Stafford, William (Edgar) 1914-1993 **CLC 4, 7, 29; DAM POET**
See also CA 5-8R; 142; CAAS 3; CANR 5, 22; DLB 5, 206; INT CANR-22

Stagnelius, Eric Johan 1793-1823 **NCLC 61**

Staines, Trevor
See Brunner, John (Kilian Houston)

Stairs, Gordon
See Austin, Mary (Hunter)

Stairs, Gordon
See Austin, Mary (Hunter)

Stalin, Joseph 1879-1953 **TCLC 92**

Stannard, Martin 1947- **CLC 44**
See also CA 142; DLB 155

Stanton, Elizabeth Cady 1815-1902 **TCLC 73**
See also CA 171; DLB 79

Stanton, Maura 1946- **CLC 9**
See also CA 89-92; CANR 15; DLB 120

Stanton, Schuyler
See Baum, L(yman) Frank

Stapledon, (William) Olaf 1886-1950 **TCLC 22**
See also CA 111; 162; DLB 15

Starbuck, George (Edwin) 1931-1996 **CLC 53; DAM POET**
See also CA 21-24R; 153; CANR 23

Stark, Richard
See Westlake, Donald E(dwin)

Staunton, Schuyler
See Baum, L(yman) Frank

Stead, Christina (Ellen) 1902-1983 **CLC 2, 5, 8, 32, 80**
See also CA 13-16R; 109; CANR 33, 40; MTCW 1, 2

Stead, William Thomas 1849-1912 **TCLC 48**
See also CA 167

Steele, Richard 1672-1729 **LC 18**
See also CDBLB 1660-1789; DLB 84, 101

Steele, Timothy (Reid) 1948- **CLC 45**
See also CA 93-96; CANR 16, 50; DLB 120

Steffens, (Joseph) Lincoln 1866-1936 **TCLC 20**
See also CA 117

Stegner, Wallace (Earle) 1909-1993 **CLC 9, 49, 81; DAM NOV; SSC 27**
See also AITN 1; BEST 90:3; CA 1-4R; 141; CAAS 9; CANR 1, 21, 46; DLB 9, 206; DLBY 93; MTCW 1, 2

Stein, Gertrude 1874-1946 **TCLC 1, 6, 28, 48; DA; DAB; DAC; DAM MST, NOV, POET; PC 18; WLC**
See also CA 104; 132; CDALB 1917-1929; DA3; DLB 4, 54, 86; DLBD 15; MTCW 1, 2

Steinbeck, John (Ernst) 1902-1968 **CLC 1, 5, 9, 13, 21, 34, 45, 75, 124; DA; DAB; DAC; DAM DRAM, MST, NOV; SSC 11, 37; WLC**
See also AAYA 12; CA 1-4R; 25-28R; CANR 1, 35; CDALB 1929-1941; DA3; DLB 7, 9, 212; DLBD 2; MTCW 1, 2; SATA 9

Steinem, Gloria 1934- **CLC 63**
See also CA 53-56; CANR 28, 51; MTCW 1, 2

Steiner, George 1929- **CLC 24; DAM NOV**
See also CA 73-76; CANR 31, 67; DLB 67; MTCW 1, 2; SATA 62

Steiner, K. Leslie
See Delany, Samuel R(ay, Jr.)

Steiner, Rudolf 1861-1925 **TCLC 13**
See also CA 107

Stendhal 1783-1842 **NCLC 23, 46; DA; DAB; DAC; DAM MST, NOV; SSC 27; WLC**
See also DA3; DLB 119

Stephen, Adeline Virginia
See Woolf, (Adeline) Virginia

Stephen, SirLeslie 1832-1904 **TCLC 23**
See also CA 123; DLB 57, 144, 190

Stephen, Sir Leslie
See Stephen, SirLeslie

Stephen, Virginia
See Woolf, (Adeline) Virginia

Stephens, James 1882(?)-1950 **TCLC 4**
See also CA 104; DLB 19, 153, 162

Stephens, Reed
See Donaldson, Stephen R.

Steptoe, Lydia
See Barnes, Djuna

Sterchi, Beat 1949- **CLC 65**

Sterling, Brett
See Bradbury, Ray (Douglas); Hamilton, Edmond

Sterling, Bruce 1954- **CLC 72**
See also CA 119; CANR 44

Sterling, George 1869-1926 **TCLC 20**
See also CA 117; 165; DLB 54

Stern, Gerald 1925- **CLC 40, 100**
See also CA 81-84; CANR 28; DLB 105

Stern, Richard (Gustave) 1928- **CLC 4, 39**
See also CA 1-4R; CANR 1, 25, 52; DLBY 87; INT CANR-25

Sternberg, Josef von 1894-1969 **CLC 20**
See also CA 81-84

Sterne, Laurence 1713-1768 **LC 2, 48; DA; DAB; DAC; DAM MST, NOV; WLC**
See also CDBLB 1660-1789; DLB 39

Sternheim, (William Adolf) Carl 1878-1942 **TCLC 8**
See also CA 105; DLB 56, 118

Stevens, Mark 1951- **CLC 34**
See also CA 122

Stevens, Wallace 1879-1955 **TCLC 3, 12, 45;**

Swados, Elizabeth (A.) 1951- **CLC 12**
See also CA 97-100; CANR 49; INT 97-100

Swados, Harvey 1920-1972 **CLC 5**
See also CA 5-8R; 37-40R; CANR 6; DLB 2

Swan, Gladys 1934- **CLC 69**
See also CA 101; CANR 17, 39

Swanson, Logan
See Matheson, Richard Burton

Swarthout, Glendon (Fred) 1918-1992 **CLC 35**
See also CA 1-4R; 139; CANR 1, 47; SATA 26

Sweet, Sarah C.
See Jewett, (Theodora) Sarah Orne

Swenson, May 1919-1989 **CLC 4, 14, 61, 106; DA; DAB; DAC; DAM MST, POET; PC 14**
See also CA 5-8R; 130; CANR 36, 61; DLB 5; MTCW 1, 2; SATA 15

Swift, Augustus
See Lovecraft, H(oward) P(hillips)

Swift, Graham (Colin) 1949- **CLC 41, 88**
See also CA 117; 122; CANR 46, 71; DLB 194; MTCW 2

Swift, Jonathan 1667-1745 **LC 1, 42; DA; DAB; DAC; DAM MST, NOV, POET; PC 9; WLC**
See also CDBLB 1660-1789; CLR 53; DA3; DLB 39, 95, 101; SATA 19

Swinburne, Algernon Charles 1837-1909 **TCLC 8, 36; DA; DAB; DAC; DAM MST, POET; PC 24; WLC**
See also CA 105; 140; CDBLB 1832-1890; DA3; DLB 35, 57

Swinfen, Ann CLC 34

Swinnerton, Frank Arthur 1884-1982 **CLC 31**
See also CA 108; DLB 34

Swithen, John
See King, Stephen (Edwin)

Sylvia
See Ashton-Warner, Sylvia (Constance)

Symmes, Robert Edward
See Duncan, Robert (Edward)

Symonds, John Addington 1840-1893 **NCLC 34**
See also DLB 57, 144

Symons, Arthur 1865-1945 **TCLC 11**
See also CA 107; DLB 19, 57, 149

Symons, Julian (Gustave) 1912-1994 **CLC 2, 14, 32**
See also CA 49-52; 147; CAAS 3; CANR 3, 33, 59; DLB 87, 155; DLBY 92; MTCW 1

Synge, (Edmund) J(ohn) M(illington) 1871-1909 **TCLC 6, 37; DAM DRAM; DC 2**
See also CA 104; 141; CDBLB 1890-1914; DLB 10, 19

Syruc, J.
See Milosz, Czeslaw

Szirtes, George 1948- **CLC 46**
See also CA 109; CANR 27, 61

Szymborska, Wislawa 1923- **CLC 99**
See also CA 154; CANR 91; DA3; DLBY 96; MTCW 2

T. O., Nik
See Annensky, Innokenty (Fyodorovich)

Tabori, George 1914- **CLC 19**
See also CA 49-52; CANR 4, 69

Tagore, Rabindranath 1861-1941 **TCLC 3, 53; DAM DRAM, POET; PC 8**
See also CA 104; 120; DA3; MTCW 1, 2

Taine, Hippolyte Adolphe 1828-1893 **NCLC 15**

Talese, Gay 1932- **CLC 37**
See also AITN 1; CA 1-4R; CANR 9, 58; DLB 185; INT CANR-9; MTCW 1, 2

Tallent, Elizabeth (Ann) 1954- **CLC 45**
See also CA 117; CANR 72; DLB 130

Tally, Ted 1952- **CLC 42**
See also CA 120; 124; INT 124

Talvik, Heiti 1904-1947 **TCLC 87**

Tamayo y Baus, Manuel 1829-1898 **NCLC 1**

Tammsaare, A(nton) H(ansen) 1878-1940 **TCLC 27**
See also CA 164; DLB 220

Tam'si, Tchicaya U
See Tchicaya, Gerald Felix

Tan, Amy (Ruth) 1952- **CLC 59, 120; DAM MULT, NOV, POP**
See also AAYA 9; BEST 89:3; CA 136; CANR 54; CDALBS; DA3; DLB 173; MTCW 2; SATA 75

Tandem, Felix
See Spitteler, Carl (Friedrich Georg)

Tanizaki, Jun'ichiro 1886-1965 **CLC 8, 14, 28; SSC 21**
See also CA 93-96; 25-28R; DLB 180; MTCW 2

Tanner, William
See Amis, Kingsley (William)

Tao Lao
See Storni, Alfonsina

Tarantino, Quentin (Jerome) 1963- **CLC 125**
See also CA 171

Tarassoff, Lev
See Troyat, Henri

Tarbell, Ida M(inerva) 1857-1944 **TCLC 40**
See also CA 122; 181; DLB 47

Tarkington, (Newton) Booth 1869-1946 **TCLC 9**
See also CA 110; 143; DLB 9, 102; MTCW 2; SATA 17

Tarkovsky, Andrei (Arsenyevich) 1932-1986 **CLC 75**
See also CA 127

Tartt, Donna 1964(?)- **CLC 76**
See also CA 142

Tasso, Torquato 1544-1595 **LC 5**

Tate, (John Orley) Allen 1899-1979 **CLC 2, 4, 6, 9, 11, 14, 24**
See also CA 5-8R; 85-88; CANR 32; DLB 4, 45, 63; DLBD 17; MTCW 1, 2

Tate, Ellalice
See Hibbert, Eleanor Alice Burford

Tate, James (Vincent) 1943- **CLC 2, 6, 25**
See also CA 21-24R; CANR 29, 57; DLB 5, 169

Tauler, Johannes c. 1300-1361 **CMLC 37**
See also DLB 179

Tavel, Ronald 1940- **CLC 6**
See also CA 21-24R; CANR 33

Taylor, C(ecil) P(hilip) 1929-1981 **CLC 27**
See also CA 25-28R; 105; CANR 47

Taylor, Edward 1642(?)-1729 **LC 11; DA; DAB; DAC; DAM MST, POET**
See also DLB 24

Taylor, Eleanor Ross 1920- **CLC 5**
See also CA 81-84; CANR 70

Taylor, Elizabeth 1912-1975 **CLC 2, 4, 29**
See also CA 13-16R; CANR 9, 70; DLB 139; MTCW 1; SATA 13

Taylor, Frederick Winslow 1856-1915 **TCLC 76**

Taylor, Henry (Splawn) 1942- **CLC 44**
See also CA 33-36R; CAAS 7; CANR 31; DLB 5

Taylor, Kamala (Purnaiya) 1924-
See Markandaya, Kamala
See also CA 77-80

Taylor, Mildred D. CLC 21

See also AAYA 10; BW 1; CA 85-88; CANR 25; CLR 9, 59; DLB 52; JRDA; MAICYA; SAAS 5; SATA 15, 70

Taylor, Peter (Hillsman) 1917-1994 **CLC 1, 4, 18, 37, 44, 50, 71; SSC 10**
See also CA 13-16R; 147; CANR 9, 50; DLBY 81, 94; INT CANR-9; MTCW 1, 2

Taylor, Robert Lewis 1912-1998 **CLC 14**
See also CA 1-4R; 170; CANR 3, 64; SATA 10

Tchekhov, Anton
See Chekhov, Anton (Pavlovich)

Tchicaya, Gerald Felix 1931-1988 **CLC 101**
See also CA 129; 125; CANR 81

Tchicaya U Tam'si
See Tchicaya, Gerald Felix

Teasdale, Sara 1884-1933 **TCLC 4**
See also CA 104; 163; DLB 45; SATA 32

Tegner, Esaias 1782-1846 **NCLC 2**

Teilhard de Chardin, (Marie Joseph) Pierre 1881-1955 **TCLC 9**
See also CA 105

Temple, Ann
See Mortimer, Penelope (Ruth)

Tennant, Emma (Christina) 1937- **CLC 13, 52**
See also CA 65-68; CAAS 9; CANR 10, 38, 59, 88; DLB 14

Tenneshaw, S. M.
See Silverberg, Robert

Tennyson, Alfred 1809-1892 **NCLC 30, 65; DA; DAB; DAC; DAM MST, POET; PC 6; WLC**
See also CDBLB 1832-1890; DA3; DLB 32

Teran, Lisa St. Aubin de CLC 36
See also St. Aubin de Teran, Lisa

Terence c. 184B.C.-c. 159B.C. **CMLC 14; DC 7**
See also DLB 211

Teresa de Jesus, St. 1515-1582 **LC 18**

Terkel, Louis 1912-
See Terkel, Studs
See also CA 57-60; CANR 18, 45, 67; DA3; MTCW 1, 2

Terkel, Studs CLC 38
See also Terkel, Louis
See also AAYA 32; AITN 1; MTCW 2

Terry, C. V.
See Slaughter, Frank G(ill)

Terry, Megan 1932- **CLC 19**
See also CA 77-80; CABS 3; CANR 43; DLB 7

Tertullian c. 155-c. 245 **CMLC 29**

Tertz, Abram
See Sinyavsky, Andrei (Donatevich)

Tesich, Steve 1943(?)-1996 **CLC 40, 69**
See also CA 105; 152; DLBY 83

Tesla, Nikola 1856-1943 **TCLC 88**

Teternikov, Fyodor Kuzmich 1863-1927
See Sologub, Fyodor
See also CA 104

Tevis, Walter 1928-1984 **CLC 42**
See also CA 113

Tey, Josephine TCLC 14
See also Mackintosh, Elizabeth
See also DLB 77

Thackeray, William Makepeace 1811-1863 **NCLC 5, 14, 22, 43; DA; DAB; DAC; DAM MST, NOV; WLC**
See also CDBLB 1832-1890; DA3; DLB 21, 55, 159, 163; SATA 23

Thakura, Ravindranatha
See Tagore, Rabindranath

Tharoor, Shashi 1956- **CLC 70**
See also CA 141; CANR 91

Thelwell, Michael Miles 1939- **CLC 22**
See also BW 2; CA 101

Theobald, Lewis, Jr.
See Lovecraft, H(oward) P(hillips)
Theodorescu, Ion N. 1880-1967
See Arghezi, Tudor
See also CA 116; DLB 220
Theriault, Yves 1915-1983 **CLC 79; DAC; DAM MST**
See also CA 102; DLB 88
Theroux, Alexander (Louis) 1939- **CLC 2, 25**
See also CA 85-88; CANR 20, 63
Theroux, Paul (Edward) 1941- **CLC 5, 8, 11, 15, 28, 46; DAM POP**
See also AAYA 28; BEST 89:4; CA 33-36R; CANR 20, 45, 74; CDALBS; DA3; DLB 2; MTCW 1, 2; SATA 44, 109
Thesen, Sharon 1946- **CLC 56**
See also CA 163
Thevenin, Denis
See Duhamel, Georges
Thibault, Jacques Anatole Francois 1844-1924
See France, Anatole
See also CA 106; 127; DAM NOV; DA3; MTCW 1, 2
Thiele, Colin (Milton) 1920- **CLC 17**
See also CA 29-32R; CANR 12, 28, 53; CLR 27; MAICYA; SAAS 2; SATA 14, 72
Thomas, Audrey (Callahan) 1935- **CLC 7, 13, 37, 107; SSC 20**
See also AITN 2; CA 21-24R; CAAS 19; CANR 36, 58; DLB 60; MTCW 1
Thomas, Augustus 1857-1934 **TCLC 97**
Thomas, D(onald) M(ichael) 1935- **CLC 13, 22, 31, 132**
See also CA 61-64; CAAS 11; CANR 17, 45, 75; CDBLB 1960 to Present; DA3; DLB 40, 207; INT CANR-17; MTCW 1, 2
Thomas, Dylan (Marlais) 1914-1953 **TCLC 1, 8, 45; DA; DAB; DAC; DAM DRAM, MST, POET; PC 2; SSC 3; WLC**
See also CA 104; 120; CANR 65; CDBLB 1945-1960; DA3; DLB 13, 20, 139; MTCW 1, 2; SATA 60
Thomas, (Philip) Edward 1878-1917 **TCLC 10; DAM POET**
See also CA 106; 153; DLB 98
Thomas, Joyce Carol 1938- **CLC 35**
See also AAYA 12; BW 2, 3; CA 113; 116; CANR 48; CLR 19; DLB 33; INT 116; JRDA; MAICYA; MTCW 1, 2; SAAS 7; SATA 40, 78
Thomas, Lewis 1913-1993 **CLC 35**
See also CA 85-88; 143; CANR 38, 60; MTCW 1, 2
Thomas, M. Carey 1857-1935 **TCLC 89**
Thomas, Paul
See Mann, (Paul) Thomas
Thomas, Piri 1928- **CLC 17; HLCS 2**
See also CA 73-76; HW 1
Thomas, R(onald) S(tuart) 1913- **CLC 6, 13, 48; DAB; DAM POET**
See also CA 89-92; CAAS 4; CANR 30; CDBLB 1960 to Present; DLB 27; MTCW 1
Thomas, Ross (Elmore) 1926-1995 **CLC 39**
See also CA 33-36R; 150; CANR 22, 63
Thompson, Francis Clegg
See Mencken, H(enry) L(ouis)
Thompson, Francis Joseph 1859-1907 **TCLC 4**
See also CA 104; CDBLB 1890-1914; DLB 19
Thompson, Hunter S(tockton) 1939- **CLC 9, 17, 40, 104; DAM POP**
See also BEST 89:1; CA 17-20R; CANR 23, 46, 74, 77; DA3; DLB 185; MTCW 1, 2

Thompson, James Myers
See Thompson, Jim (Myers)
Thompson, Jim (Myers) 1906-1977(?) **CLC 69**
See also CA 140
Thompson, Judith CLC 39
Thomson, James 1700-1748 **LC 16, 29, 40; DAM POET**
See also DLB 95
Thomson, James 1834-1882 **NCLC 18; DAM POET**
See also DLB 35
Thoreau, Henry David 1817-1862 **NCLC 7, 21, 61; DA; DAB; DAC; DAM MST; PC 30; WLC**
See also CDALB 1640-1865; DA3; DLB 1, 223
Thornton, Hall
See Silverberg, Robert
Thucydides c. 455B.C.-399B.C. **CMLC 17**
See also DLB 176
Thumboo, Edwin 1933- **PC 30**
Thurber, James (Grover) 1894-1961 **CLC 5, 11, 25, 125; DA; DAB; DAC; DAM DRAM, MST, NOV; SSC 1**
See also CA 73-76; CANR 17, 39; CDALB 1929-1941; DA3; DLB 4, 11, 22, 102; MAICYA; MTCW 1, 2; SATA 13
Thurman, Wallace (Henry) 1902-1934 **TCLC 6; BLC 3; DAM MULT**
See also BW 1, 3; CA 104; 124; CANR 81; DLB 51
Tibullus, Albius c. 54B.C.-c. 19B.C. **CMLC 36**
See also DLB 211
Ticheburn, Cheviot
See Ainsworth, William Harrison
Tieck, (Johann) Ludwig 1773-1853 **NCLC 5, 46; SSC 31**
See also DLB 90
Tiger, Derry
See Ellison, Harlan (Jay)
Tilghman, Christopher 1948(?)- **CLC 65**
See also CA 159
Tillich, Paul (Johannes) 1886-1965 **CLC 131**
See also CA 5-8R; 25-28R; CANR 33; MTCW 1, 2
Tillinghast, Richard (Williford) 1940- **CLC 29**
See also CA 29-32R; CAAS 23; CANR 26, 51
Timrod, Henry 1828-1867 **NCLC 25**
See also DLB 3
Tindall, Gillian (Elizabeth) 1938- **CLC 7**
See also CA 21-24R; CANR 11, 65
Tiptree, James, Jr. CLC 48, 50
See also Sheldon, Alice Hastings Bradley
See also DLB 8
Titmarsh, Michael Angelo
See Thackeray, William Makepeace
Tocqueville, Alexis (Charles Henri Maurice Clerel, Comte) de 1805-1859 **NCLC 7, 63**
Tolkien, J(ohn) R(onald) R(euel) 1892-1973 **CLC 1, 2, 3, 8, 12, 38; DA; DAB; DAC; DAM MST, NOV, POP; WLC**
See also AAYA 10; AITN 1; CA 17-18; 45-48; CANR 36; CAP 2; CDBLB 1914-1945; CLR 56; DA3; DLB 15, 160; JRDA; MAICYA; MTCW 1, 2; SATA 2, 32, 100; SATA-Obit 24
Toller, Ernst 1893-1939 **TCLC 10**
See also CA 107; 186; DLB 124
Tolson, M. B.
See Tolson, Melvin B(eaunorus)
Tolson, Melvin B(eaunorus) 1898(?)-1966 **CLC 36, 105; BLC 3; DAM MULT, POET**

See also BW 1, 3; CA 124; 89-92; CANR 80; DLB 48, 76
Tolstoi, Aleksei Nikolaevich
See Tolstoy, Alexey Nikolaevich
Tolstoy, Alexey Nikolaevich 1882-1945 **TCLC 18**
See also CA 107; 158
Tolstoy, Count Leo
See Tolstoy, Leo (Nikolaevich)
Tolstoy, Leo (Nikolaevich) 1828-1910 **TCLC 4, 11, 17, 28, 44, 79; DA; DAB; DAC; DAM MST, NOV; SSC 9, 30; WLC**
See also CA 104; 123; DA3; SATA 26
Tomasi di Lampedusa, Giuseppe 1896-1957
See Lampedusa, Giuseppe (Tomasi) di
See also CA 111
Tomlin, Lily CLC 17
See also Tomlin, Mary Jean
Tomlin, Mary Jean 1939(?)-
See Tomlin, Lily
See also CA 117
Tomlinson, (Alfred) Charles 1927- **CLC 2, 4, 6, 13, 45; DAM POET; PC 17**
See also CA 5-8R; CANR 33; DLB 40
Tomlinson, H(enry) M(ajor) 1873-1958 **TCLC 71**
See also CA 118; 161; DLB 36, 100, 195
Tonson, Jacob
See Bennett, (Enoch) Arnold
Toole, John Kennedy 1937-1969 **CLC 19, 64**
See also CA 104; DLBY 81; MTCW 2
Toomer, Jean 1894-1967 **CLC 1, 4, 13, 22; BLC 3; DAM MULT; PC 7; SSC 1; WLCS**
See also BW 1; CA 85-88; CDALB 1917-1929; DA3; DLB 45, 51; MTCW 1, 2
Torley, Luke
See Blish, James (Benjamin)
Tornimparte, Alessandra
See Ginzburg, Natalia
Torre, Raoul della
See Mencken, H(enry) L(ouis)
Torrence, Ridgely 1874-1950 **TCLC 97**
See also DLB 54
Torrey, E(dwin) Fuller 1937- **CLC 34**
See also CA 119; CANR 71
Torsvan, Ben Traven
See Traven, B.
Torsvan, Benno Traven
See Traven, B.
Torsvan, Berick Traven
See Traven, B.
Torsvan, Berwick Traven
See Traven, B.
Torsvan, Bruno Traven
See Traven, B.
Torsvan, Traven
See Traven, B.
Tournier, Michel (Edouard) 1924- **CLC 6, 23, 36, 95**
See also CA 49-52; CANR 3, 36, 74; DLB 83; MTCW 1, 2; SATA 23
Tournimparte, Alessandra
See Ginzburg, Natalia
Towers, Ivar
See Kornbluth, C(yril) M.
Towne, Robert (Burton) 1936(?)- **CLC 87**
See also CA 108; DLB 44
Townsend, Sue CLC 61
See also Townsend, Susan Elaine
See also AAYA 28; SATA 55, 93; SATA-Brief 48
Townsend, Susan Elaine 1946-
See Townsend, Sue
See also CA 119; 127; CANR 65; DAB; DAC; DAM MST
Townshend, Peter (Dennis Blandford) 1945- **CLC 17, 42**

See also CA 107

Tozzi, Federigo 1883-1920 **TCLC 31**
See also CA 160

Traill, Catharine Parr 1802-1899 **NCLC 31**
See also DLB 99

Trakl, Georg 1887-1914 **TCLC 5; PC 20**
See also CA 104; 165; MTCW 2

Transtroemer, Tomas (Goesta) 1931- **CLC 52, 65; DAM POET**
See also CA 117; 129; CAAS 17

Transtromer, Tomas Gosta
See Transtroemer, Tomas (Goesta)

Traven, B. (?)-1969 **CLC 8, 11**
See also CA 19-20; 25-28R; CAP 2; DLB 9, 56; MTCW 1

Treitel, Jonathan 1959- **CLC 70**

Trelawny, Edward John 1792-1881 **NCLC 85**
See also DLB 110, 116, 144

Tremain, Rose 1943- **CLC 42**
See also CA 97-100; CANR 44; DLB 14

Tremblay, Michel 1942- **CLC 29, 102; DAC; DAM MST**
See also CA 116; 128; DLB 60; MTCW 1, 2

Trevanian CLC 29
See also Whitaker, Rod(ney)

Trevor, Glen
See Hilton, James

Trevor, William 1928- **CLC 7, 9, 14, 25, 71, 116; SSC 21**
See also Cox, William Trevor
See also DLB 14, 139; MTCW 2

Trifonov, Yuri (Valentinovich) 1925-1981 **CLC 45**
See also CA 126; 103; MTCW 1

Trilling, Diana (Rubin) 1905-1996 **CLC 129**
See also CA 5-8R; 154; CANR 10, 46; INT CANR-10; MTCW 1, 2

Trilling, Lionel 1905-1975 **CLC 9, 11, 24**
See also CA 9-12R; 61-64; CANR 10; DLB 28, 63; INT CANR-10; MTCW 1, 2

Trimball, W. H.
See Mencken, H(enry) L(ouis)

Tristan
See Gomez de la Serna, Ramon

Tristram
See Housman, A(lfred) E(dward)

Trogdon, William (Lewis) 1939-
See Heat-Moon, William Least
See also CA 115; 119; CANR 47, 89; INT 119

Trollope, Anthony 1815-1882 **NCLC 6, 33; DA; DAB; DAC; DAM MST, NOV; SSC 28; WLC**
See also CDBLB 1832-1890; DA3; DLB 21, 57, 159; SATA 22

Trollope, Frances 1779-1863 **NCLC 30**
See also DLB 21, 166

Trotsky, Leon 1879-1940 **TCLC 22**
See also CA 118; 167

Trotter (Cockburn), Catharine 1679-1749 **LC 8**
See also DLB 84

Trotter, Wilfred 1872-1939 **TCLC 97**

Trout, Kilgore
See Farmer, Philip Jose

Trow, George W. S. 1943- **CLC 52**
See also CA 126; CANR 91

Troyat, Henri 1911- **CLC 23**
See also CA 45-48; CANR 2, 33, 67; MTCW 1

Trudeau, G(arretson) B(eekman) 1948-
See Trudeau, Garry B.
See also CA 81-84; CANR 31; SATA 35

Trudeau, Garry B. CLC 12
See also Trudeau, G(arretson) B(eekman)
See also AAYA 10; AITN 2

Truffaut, Francois 1932-1984 **CLC 20, 101**

See also CA 81-84; 113; CANR 34

Trumbo, Dalton 1905-1976 **CLC 19**
See also CA 21-24R; 69-72; CANR 10; DLB 26

Trumbull, John 1750-1831 **NCLC 30**
See also DLB 31

Trundlett, Helen B.
See Eliot, T(homas) S(tearns)

Tryon, Thomas 1926-1991 **CLC 3, 11; DAM POP**
See also AITN 1; CA 29-32R; 135; CANR 32, 77; DA3; MTCW 1

Tryon, Tom
See Tryon, Thomas

Ts'ao Hsueh-ch'in 1715(?)-1763 **LC 1**

Tsushima, Shuji 1909-1948
See Dazai Osamu
See also CA 107

Tsvetaeva (Efron), Marina (Ivanovna) 1892-1941 **TCLC 7, 35; PC 14**
See also CA 104; 128; CANR 73; MTCW 1, 2

Tuck, Lily 1938- **CLC 70**
See also CA 139; CANR 90

Tu Fu 712-770 **PC 9**
See also DAM MULT

Tunis, John R(oberts) 1889-1975 **CLC 12**
See also CA 61-64; CANR 62; DLB 22, 171; JRDA; MAICYA; SATA 37; SATA-Brief 30

Tuohy, Frank CLC 37
See also Tuohy, John Francis
See also DLB 14, 139

Tuohy, John Francis 1925-1999
See Tuohy, Frank
See also CA 5-8R; 178; CANR 3, 47

Turco, Lewis (Putnam) 1934- **CLC 11, 63**
See also CA 13-16R; CAAS 22; CANR 24, 51; DLBY 84

Turgenev, Ivan 1818-1883 **NCLC 21; DA; DAB; DAC; DAM MST, NOV; DC 7; SSC 7; WLC**

Turgot, Anne-Robert-Jacques 1727-1781 **LC 26**

Turner, Frederick 1943- **CLC 48**
See also CA 73-76; CAAS 10; CANR 12, 30, 56; DLB 40

Tutu, Desmond M(pilo) 1931- **CLC 80; BLC 3; DAM MULT**
See also BW 1, 3; CA 125; CANR 67, 81

Tutuola, Amos 1920-1997 **CLC 5, 14, 29; BLC 3; DAM MULT**
See also BW 2, 3; CA 9-12R; 159; CANR 27, 66; DA3; DLB 125; MTCW 1, 2

Twain, Mark TCLC 6, 12, 19, 36, 48, 59; SSC 34; WLC
See also Clemens, Samuel Langhorne
See also AAYA 20; CLR 58, 60; DLB 11, 12, 23, 64, 74

Tyler, Anne 1941- **CLC 7, 11, 18, 28, 44, 59, 103; DAM NOV, POP**
See also AAYA 18; BEST 89:1; CA 9-12R; CANR 11, 33, 53; CDALBS; DLB 6, 143; DLBY 82; MTCW 1, 2; SATA 7, 90

Tyler, Royall 1757-1826 **NCLC 3**
See also DLB 37

Tynan, Katharine 1861-1931 **TCLC 3**
See also CA 104; 167; DLB 153

Tyutchev, Fyodor 1803-1873 **NCLC 34**

Tzara, Tristan 1896-1963 **CLC 47; DAM POET; PC 27**
See also CA 153; 89-92; MTCW 2

Uhry, Alfred 1936- **CLC 55; DAM DRAM, POP**
See also CA 127; 133; DA3; INT 133

Ulf, Haerved
See Strindberg, (Johan) August

Ulf, Harved
See Strindberg, (Johan) August

Ulibarri, Sabine R(eyes) 1919- **CLC 83; DAM MULT; HLCS 2**
See also CA 131; CANR 81; DLB 82; HW 1, 2

Unamuno (y Jugo), Miguel de 1864-1936 **TCLC 2, 9; DAM MULT, NOV; HLC 2; SSC 11**
See also CA 104; 131; CANR 81; DLB 108; HW 1, 2; MTCW 1, 2

Undercliffe, Errol
See Campbell, (John) Ramsey

Underwood, Miles
See Glassco, John

Undset, Sigrid 1882-1949 **TCLC 3; DA; DAB; DAC; DAM MST, NOV; WLC**
See also CA 104; 129; DA3; MTCW 1, 2

Ungaretti, Giuseppe 1888-1970 **CLC 7, 11, 15**
See also CA 19-20; 25-28R; CAP 2; DLB 114

Unger, Douglas 1952- **CLC 34**
See also CA 130

Unsworth, Barry (Forster) 1930- **CLC 76, 127**
See also CA 25-28R; CANR 30, 54; DLB 194

Updike, John (Hoyer) 1932- **CLC 1, 2, 3, 5, 7, 9, 13, 15, 23, 34, 43, 70; DA; DAB; DAC; DAM MST, NOV, POET, POP; SSC 13, 27; WLC**
See also CA 1-4R; CABS 1; CANR 4, 33, 51; CDALB 1968-1988; DA3; DLB 2, 5, 143; DLBD 3; DLBY 80, 82, 97; MTCW 1, 2

Upshaw, Margaret Mitchell
See Mitchell, Margaret (Munnerlyn)

Upton, Mark
See Sanders, Lawrence

Upward, Allen 1863-1926 **TCLC 85**
See also CA 117; DLB 36

Urdang, Constance (Henriette) 1922- **CLC 47**
See also CA 21-24R; CANR 9, 24

Uriel, Henry
See Faust, Frederick (Schiller)

Uris, Leon (Marcus) 1924- **CLC 7, 32; DAM NOV, POP**
See also AITN 1, 2; BEST 89:2; CA 1-4R; CANR 1, 40, 65; DA3; MTCW 1, 2; SATA 49

Urista, Alberto H. 1947-
See Alurista
See also CA 45-48, 182; CANR 2, 32; HLCS 1; HW 1

Urmuz
See Codrescu, Andrei

Urquhart, Guy
See McAlmon, Robert (Menzies)

Urquhart, Jane 1949- **CLC 90; DAC**
See also CA 113; CANR 32, 68

Usigli, Rodolfo 1905-1979
See also CA 131; HLCS 1; HW 1

Ustinov, Peter (Alexander) 1921- **CLC 1**
See also AITN 1; CA 13-16R; CANR 25, 51; DLB 13; MTCW 2

U Tam'si, Gerald Felix Tchicaya
See Tchicaya, Gerald Felix

U Tam'si, Tchicaya
See Tchicaya, Gerald Felix

Vachss, Andrew (Henry) 1942- **CLC 106**
See also CA 118; CANR 44

Vachss, Andrew H.
See Vachss, Andrew (Henry)

Vaculik, Ludvik 1926- **CLC 7**
See also CA 53-56; CANR 72

Vaihinger, Hans 1852-1933 **TCLC 71**
See also CA 116; 166

Valdez, Luis (Miguel) 1940- **CLC 84; DAM MULT; DC 10; HLC 2**
See also CA 101; CANR 32, 81; DLB 122; HW 1

Valenzuela, Luisa 1938- **CLC 31, 104; DAM MULT; HLCS 2; SSC 14**
See also CA 101; CANR 32, 65; DLB 113; HW 1, 2

Valera y Alcala-Galiano, Juan 1824-1905 **TCLC 10**
See also CA 106

Valery, (Ambroise) Paul (Toussaint Jules) 1871-1945 **TCLC 4, 15; DAM POET; PC 9**
See also CA 104; 122; DA3; MTCW 1, 2

Valle-Inclan, Ramon (Maria) del 1866-1936 **TCLC 5; DAM MULT; HLC 2**
See also CA 106; 153; CANR 80; DLB 134; HW 2

Vallejo, Antonio Buero
See Buero Vallejo, Antonio

Vallejo, Cesar (Abraham) 1892-1938 **TCLC 3, 56; DAM MULT; HLC 2**
See also CA 105; 153; HW 1

Valles, Jules 1832-1885 **NCLC 71**
See also DLB 123

Vallette, Marguerite Eymery 1860-1953 **TCLC 67**
See also CA 182; DLB 123, 192

Valle Y Pena, Ramon del
See Valle-Inclan, Ramon (Maria) del

Van Ash, Cay 1918- **CLC 34**

Vanbrugh, Sir John 1664-1726 **LC 21; DAM DRAM**
See also DLB 80

Van Campen, Karl
See Campbell, John W(ood, Jr.)

Vance, Gerald
See Silverberg, Robert

Vance, Jack CLC 35
See also Vance, John Holbrook
See also DLB 8

Vance, John Holbrook 1916-
See Queen, Ellery; Vance, Jack
See also CA 29-32R; CANR 17, 65; MTCW 1

Van Den Bogarde, Derek Jules Gaspard Ulric Niven 1921-1999 **CLC 14**
See also CA 77-80; 179; DLB 19

Vandenburgh, Jane CLC 59
See also CA 168

Vanderhaeghe, Guy 1951- **CLC 41**
See also CA 113; CANR 72

van der Post, Laurens (Jan) 1906-1996 **CLC 5**
See also CA 5-8R; 155; CANR 35; DLB 204

van de Wetering, Janwillem 1931- **CLC 47**
See also CA 49-52; CANR 4, 62, 90

Van Dine, S. S. TCLC 23
See also Wright, Willard Huntington

Van Doren, Carl (Clinton) 1885-1950 **TCLC 18**
See also CA 111; 168

Van Doren, Mark 1894-1972 **CLC 6, 10**
See also CA 1-4R; 37-40R; CANR 3; DLB 45; MTCW 1, 2

Van Druten, John (William) 1901-1957 **TCLC 2**
See also CA 104; 161; DLB 10

Van Duyn, Mona (Jane) 1921- **CLC 3, 7, 63, 116; DAM POET**
See also CA 9-12R; CANR 7, 38, 60; DLB 5

Van Dyne, Edith
See Baum, L(yman) Frank

van Itallie, Jean-Claude 1936- **CLC 3**
See also CA 45-48; CAAS 2; CANR 1, 48; DLB 7

van Ostaijen, Paul 1896-1928 **TCLC 33**
See also CA 163

Van Peebles, Melvin 1932- **CLC 2, 20; DAM MULT**
See also BW 2, 3; CA 85-88; CANR 27, 67, 82

Vansittart, Peter 1920- **CLC 42**
See also CA 1-4R; CANR 3, 49, 90

Van Vechten, Carl 1880-1964 **CLC 33**
See also CA 183; 89-92; DLB 4, 9, 51

Van Vogt, A(lfred) E(lton) 1912- **CLC 1**
See also CA 21-24R; CANR 28; DLB 8; SATA 14

Varda, Agnes 1928- **CLC 16**
See also CA 116; 122

Vargas Llosa, (Jorge) Mario (Pedro) 1936- **CLC 3, 6, 9, 10, 15, 31, 42, 85; DA; DAB; DAC; DAM MST, MULT, NOV; HLC 2**
See also CA 73-76; CANR 18, 32, 42, 67; DA3; DLB 145; HW 1, 2; MTCW 1, 2

Vasiliu, Gheorghe 1881-1957
See Bacovia, George
See also CA 123; DLB 220

Vassa, Gustavus
See Equiano, Olaudah

Vassilikos, Vassilis 1933- **CLC 4, 8**
See also CA 81-84; CANR 75

Vaughan, Henry 1621-1695 **LC 27**
See also DLB 131

Vaughn, Stephanie CLC 62

Vazov, Ivan (Minchov) 1850-1921 **TCLC 25**
See also CA 121; 167; DLB 147

Veblen, Thorstein B(unde) 1857-1929 **TCLC 31**
See also CA 115; 165

Vega, Lope de 1562-1635 **LC 23; HLCS 2**

Venison, Alfred
See Pound, Ezra (Weston Loomis)

Verdi, Marie de
See Mencken, H(enry) L(ouis)

Verdu, Matilde
See Cela, Camilo Jose

Verga, Giovanni (Carmelo) 1840-1922 **TCLC 3; SSC 21**
See also CA 104; 123

Vergil 70B.C.-19B.C. **CMLC 9, 40; DA; DAB; DAC; DAM MST, POET; PC 12; WLCS**
See also Virgil
See also DA3; DLB 211

Verhaeren, Emile (Adolphe Gustave) 1855-1916 **TCLC 12**
See also CA 109

Verlaine, Paul (Marie) 1844-1896 **NCLC 2, 51; DAM POET; PC 2**

Verne, Jules (Gabriel) 1828-1905 **TCLC 6, 52**
See also AAYA 16; CA 110; 131; DA3; DLB 123; JRDA; MAICYA; SATA 21

Very, Jones 1813-1880 **NCLC 9**
See also DLB 1

Vesaas, Tarjei 1897-1970 **CLC 48**
See also CA 29-32R

Vialis, Gaston
See Simenon, Georges (Jacques Christian)

Vian, Boris 1920-1959 **TCLC 9**
See also CA 106; 164; DLB 72; MTCW 2

Viaud, (Louis Marie) Julien 1850-1923
See Loti, Pierre
See also CA 107

Vicar, Henry
See Felsen, Henry Gregor

Vicker, Angus
See Felsen, Henry Gregor

Vidal, Gore 1925- **CLC 2, 4, 6, 8, 10, 22, 33, 72; DAM NOV, POP**

See also AITN 1; BEST 90:2; CA 5-8R; CANR 13, 45, 65; CDALBS; DA3; DLB 6, 152; INT CANR-13; MTCW 1, 2

Viereck, Peter (Robert Edwin) 1916- **CLC 4; PC 27**
See also CA 1-4R; CANR 1, 47; DLB 5

Vigny, Alfred (Victor) de 1797-1863 **NCLC 7; DAM POET; PC 26**
See also DLB 119, 192

Vilakazi, Benedict Wallet 1906-1947 **TCLC 37**
See also CA 168

Villa, Jose Garcia 1904-1997 **PC 22**
See also CA 25-28R; CANR 12

Villarreal, Jose Antonio 1924-
See also CA 133; DAM MULT; DLB 82; HLC 2; HW 1

Villaurrutia, Xavier 1903-1950 **TCLC 80**
See also HW 1

Villehardouin 1150(?)-1218(?) **CMLC 38**

Villiers de l'Isle Adam, Jean Marie Mathias Philippe Auguste, Comte de 1838-1889 **NCLC 3; SSC 14**
See also DLB 123

Villon, Francois 1431-1463(?) **PC 13**
See also DLB 208

Vine, Barbara CLC 50
See Rendell, Ruth (Barbara)
See also BEST 90:4

Vinge, Joan (Carol) D(ennison) 1948- **CLC 30; SSC 24**
See also AAYA 32; CA 93-96; CANR 72; SATA 36, 113

Violis, G.
See Simenon, Georges (Jacques Christian)

Viramontes, Helena Maria 1954-
See also CA 159; DLB 122; HLCS 2; HW 2

Virgil 70B.C.-19B.C.
See Vergil

Visconti, Luchino 1906-1976 **CLC 16**
See also CA 81-84; 65-68; CANR 39

Vittorini, Elio 1908-1966 **CLC 6, 9, 14**
See also CA 133; 25-28R

Vivekananda, Swami 1863-1902 **TCLC 88**

Vizenor, Gerald Robert 1934- **CLC 103; DAM MULT**
See also CA 13-16R; CAAS 22; CANR 5, 21, 44, 67; DLB 175; MTCW 2; NNAL

Vizinczey, Stephen 1933- **CLC 40**
See also CA 128; INT 128

Vliet, R(ussell) G(ordon) 1929-1984 **CLC 22**
See also CA 37-40R; 112; CANR 18

Vogau, Boris Andreyevich 1894-1937(?)
See Pilnyak, Boris
See also CA 123

Vogel, Paula A(nne) 1951- **CLC 76**
See also CA 108

Voigt, Cynthia 1942- **CLC 30**
See also AAYA 3, 30; CA 106; CANR 18, 37, 40; CLR 13, 48; INT CANR-18; JRDA; MAICYA; SATA 48, 79, 116; SATA-Brief 33

Voigt, Ellen Bryant 1943- **CLC 54**
See also CA 69-72; CANR 11, 29, 55; DLB 120

Voinovich, Vladimir (Nikolaevich) 1932- **CLC 10, 49**
See also CA 81-84; CAAS 12; CANR 33, 67; MTCW 1

Vollmann, William T. 1959- **CLC 89; DAM NOV, POP**
See also CA 134; CANR 67; DA3; MTCW 2

Voloshinov, V. N.
See Bakhtin, Mikhail Mikhailovich

Voltaire 1694-1778 **LC 14; DA; DAB; DAC; DAM DRAM, MST; SSC 12; WLC**
See also DA3

von Aschendrof, BaronIgnatz
See Ford, Ford Madox
von Daeniken, Erich 1935- CLC 30
See also AITN 1; CA 37-40R; CANR 17, 44
von Daniken, Erich
See von Daeniken, Erich
von Hartmann, Eduard 1842-1906 TCLC 96
von Heidenstam, (Carl Gustaf) Verner
See Heidenstam, (Carl Gustaf) Verner von
von Heyse, Paul (Johann Ludwig)
See Heyse, Paul (Johann Ludwig von)
von Hofmannsthal, Hugo
See Hofmannsthal, Hugo von
von Horvath, Odon
See Horvath, Oedoen von
von Horvath, Oedoen -1938
See Horvath, Oedoen von
See also CA 184
von Liliencron, (Friedrich Adolf Axel) Detlev
See Liliencron, (Friedrich Adolf Axel) Detlev von
Vonnegut, Kurt, Jr. 1922- CLC 1, 2, 3, 4, 5, 8, 12, 22, 40, 60, 111; DA; DAB; DAC; DAM MST, NOV, POP; SSC 8; WLC
See also AAYA 6; AITN 1; BEST 90:4; CA 1-4R; CANR 1, 25, 49, 75; CDALB 1968-1988; DA3; DLB 2, 8, 152; DLBD 3; DLBY 80; MTCW 1, 2
Von Rachen, Kurt
See Hubbard, L(afayette) Ron(ald)
von Rezzori (d'Arezzo), Gregor
See Rezzori (d'Arezzo), Gregor von
von Sternberg, Josef
See Sternberg, Josef von
Vorster, Gordon 1924- CLC 34
See also CA 133
Vosce, Trudie
See Ozick, Cynthia
Voznesensky, Andrei (Andreievich) 1933- CLC 1, 15, 57; DAM POET
See also CA 89-92; CANR 37; MTCW 1
Waddington, Miriam 1917- CLC 28
See also CA 21-24R; CANR 12, 30; DLB 68
Wagman, Fredrica 1937- CLC 7
See also CA 97-100; INT 97-100
Wagner, Linda W.
See Wagner-Martin, Linda (C.)
Wagner, Linda Welshimer
See Wagner-Martin, Linda (C.)
Wagner, Richard 1813-1883 NCLC 9
See also DLB 129
Wagner-Martin, Linda (C.) 1936- CLC 50
See also CA 159
Wagoner, David (Russell) 1926- CLC 3, 5, 15
See also CA 1-4R; CAAS 3; CANR 2, 71; DLB 5; SATA 14
Wah, Fred(erick James) 1939- CLC 44
See also CA 107; 141; DLB 60
Wahloo, Per 1926-1975 CLC 7
See also CA 61-64; CANR 73
Wahloo, Peter
See Wahloo, Per
Wain, John (Barrington) 1925-1994 CLC 2, 11, 15, 46
See also CA 5-8R; 145; CAAS 4; CANR 23, 54; CDBLB 1960 to Present; DLB 15, 27, 139, 155; MTCW 1, 2
Wajda, Andrzej 1926- CLC 16
See also CA 102
Wakefield, Dan 1932- CLC 7
See also CA 21-24R; CAAS 7
Wakoski, Diane 1937- CLC 2, 4, 7, 9, 11, 40; DAM POET; PC 15
See also CA 13-16R; CAAS 1; CANR 9, 60; DLB 5; INT CANR-9; MTCW 2

Wakoski-Sherbell, Diane
See Wakoski, Diane
Walcott, Derek (Alton) 1930- CLC 2, 4, 9, 14, 25, 42, 67, 76; BLC 3; DAB; DAC; DAM MST, MULT, POET; DC 7
See also BW 2; CA 89-92; CANR 26, 47, 75, 80; DA3; DLB 117; DLBY 81; MTCW 1, 2
Waldman, Anne (Lesley) 1945- CLC 7
See also CA 37-40R; CAAS 17; CANR 34, 69; DLB 16
Waldo, E. Hunter
See Sturgeon, Theodore (Hamilton)
Waldo, Edward Hamilton
See Sturgeon, Theodore (Hamilton)
Walker, Alice (Malsenior) 1944- CLC 5, 6, 9, 19, 27, 46, 58, 103; BLC 3; DA; DAB; DAC; DAM MST, MULT, NOV, POET, POP; PC 30; SSC 5; WLCS
See also AAYA 3, 33; BEST 89:4; BW 2, 3; CA 37-40R; CANR 9, 27, 49, 66, 82; CDALB 1968-1988; DA3; DLB 6, 33, 143; INT CANR-27; MTCW 1, 2; SATA 31
Walker, David Harry 1911-1992 CLC 14
See also CA 1-4R; 137; CANR 1; SATA 8; SATA-Obit 71
Walker, Edward Joseph 1934-
See Walker, Ted
See also CA 21-24R; CANR 12, 28, 53
Walker, George F. 1947- CLC 44, 61; DAB; DAC; DAM MST
See also CA 103; CANR 21, 43, 59; DLB 60
Walker, Joseph A. 1935- CLC 19; DAM DRAM, MST
See also BW 1, 3; CA 89-92; CANR 26; DLB 38
Walker, Margaret (Abigail) 1915-1998 CLC 1, 6; BLC; DAM MULT; PC 20
See also BW 2, 3; CA 73-76; 172; CANR 26, 54, 76; DLB 76, 152; MTCW 1, 2
Walker, Ted CLC 13
See also Walker, Edward Joseph
See also DLB 40
Wallace, David Foster 1962- CLC 50, 114
See also CA 132; CANR 59; DA3; MTCW 2
Wallace, Dexter
See Masters, Edgar Lee
Wallace, (Richard Horatio) Edgar 1875-1932 TCLC 57
See also CA 115; DLB 70
Wallace, Irving 1916-1990 CLC 7, 13; DAM NOV, POP
See also AITN 1; CA 1-4R; 132; CAAS 1; CANR 1, 27; INT CANR-27; MTCW 1, 2
Wallant, Edward Lewis 1926-1962 CLC 5, 10
See also CA 1-4R; CANR 22; DLB 2, 28, 143; MTCW 1, 2
Wallas, Graham 1858-1932 TCLC 91
Walley, Byron
See Card, Orson Scott
Walpole, Horace 1717-1797 LC 49
See also DLB 39, 104
Walpole, Hugh (Seymour) 1884-1941 TCLC 5
See also CA 104; 165; DLB 34; MTCW 2
Walser, Martin 1927- CLC 27
See also CA 57-60; CANR 8, 46; DLB 75, 124
Walser, Robert 1878-1956 TCLC 18; SSC 20
See also CA 118; 165; DLB 66
Walsh, Jill Paton CLC 35
See also Paton Walsh, Gillian
See also CLR 2, 65

Walter, Villiam Christian
See Andersen, Hans Christian
Wambaugh, Joseph (Aloysius, Jr.) 1937- CLC 3, 18; DAM NOV, POP
See also AITN 1; BEST 89:3; CA 33-36R; CANR 42, 65; DA3; DLB 6; DLBY 83; MTCW 1, 2
Wang Wei 699(?)-761(?) PC 18
Ward, Arthur Henry Sarsfield 1883-1959
See Rohmer, Sax
See also CA 108; 173
Ward, Douglas Turner 1930- CLC 19
See also BW 1; CA 81-84; CANR 27; DLB 7, 38
Ward, E. D.
See Lucas, E(dward) V(errall)
Ward, Mary Augusta
See Ward, Mrs. Humphry
Ward, Mrs. Humphry 1851-1920 TCLC 55
See also DLB 18
Ward, Peter
See Faust, Frederick (Schiller)
Warhol, Andy 1928(?)-1987 CLC 20
See also AAYA 12; BEST 89:4; CA 89-92; 121; CANR 34
Warner, Francis (Robert le Plastrier) 1937- CLC 14
See also CA 53-56; CANR 11
Warner, Marina 1946- CLC 59
See also CA 65-68; CANR 21, 55; DLB 194
Warner, Rex (Ernest) 1905-1986 CLC 45
See also CA 89-92; 119; DLB 15
Warner, Susan (Bogert) 1819-1885 NCLC 31
See also DLB 3, 42
Warner, Sylvia (Constance) Ashton
See Ashton-Warner, Sylvia (Constance)
Warner, Sylvia Townsend 1893-1978 CLC 7, 19; SSC 23
See also CA 61-64; 77-80; CANR 16, 60; DLB 34, 139; MTCW 1, 2
Warren, Mercy Otis 1728-1814 NCLC 13
See also DLB 31, 200
Warren, Robert Penn 1905-1989 CLC 1, 4, 6, 8, 10, 13, 18, 39, 53, 59; DA; DAB; DAC; DAM MST, NOV, POET; SSC 4; WLC
See also AITN 1; CA 13-16R; 129; CANR 10, 47; CDALB 1968-1988; DA3; DLB 2, 48, 152; DLBY 80, 89; INT CANR-10; MTCW 1, 2; SATA 46; SATA-Obit 63
Warshofsky, Isaac
See Singer, Isaac Bashevis
Warton, Thomas 1728-1790 LC 15; DAM POET
See also DLB 104, 109
Waruk, Kona
See Harris, (Theodore) Wilson
Warung, Price 1855-1911 TCLC 45
Warwick, Jarvis
See Garner, Hugh
Washington, Alex
See Harris, Mark
Washington, Booker T(aliaferro) 1856-1915 TCLC 10; BLC 3; DAM MULT
See also BW 1; CA 114; 125; DA3; SATA 28
Washington, George 1732-1799 LC 25
See also DLB 31
Wassermann, (Karl) Jakob 1873-1934 TCLC 6
See also CA 104; 163; DLB 66
Wasserstein, Wendy 1950- CLC 32, 59, 90; DAM DRAM; DC 4
See also CA 121; 129; CABS 3; CANR 53, 75; DA3; INT 129; MTCW 2; SATA 94
Waterhouse, Keith (Spencer) 1929- CLC 47
See also CA 5-8R; CANR 38, 67; DLB 13, 15; MTCW 1, 2

Waters, Frank (Joseph) 1902-1995 **CLC 88**
See also CA 5-8R; 149; CAAS 13; CANR 3, 18, 63; DLB 212; DLBY 86
Waters, Roger 1944- **CLC 35**
Watkins, Frances Ellen
See Harper, Frances Ellen Watkins
Watkins, Gerrold
See Malzberg, Barry N(athaniel)
Watkins, Gloria Jean 1952(?)-
See hooks, bell
See also BW 2; CA 143; CANR 87; MTCW 2; SATA 115
Watkins, Paul 1964- **CLC 55**
See also CA 132; CANR 62
Watkins, Vernon Phillips 1906-1967 **CLC 43**
See also CA 9-10; 25-28R; CAP 1; DLB 20
Watson, Irving S.
See Mencken, H(enry) L(ouis)
Watson, John H.
See Farmer, Philip Jose
Watson, Richard F.
See Silverberg, Robert
Waugh, Auberon (Alexander) 1939- **CLC 7**
See also CA 45-48; CANR 6, 22; DLB 14, 194
Waugh, Evelyn (Arthur St. John) 1903-1966 **CLC 1, 3, 8, 13, 19, 27, 44, 107; DA; DAB; DAC; DAM MST, NOV, POP; WLC**
See also CA 85-88; 25-28R; CANR 22; CD-BLB 1914-1945; DA3; DLB 15, 162, 195; MTCW 1, 2
Waugh, Harriet 1944- **CLC 6**
See also CA 85-88; CANR 22
Ways, C. R.
See Blount, Roy (Alton), Jr.
Waystaff, Simon
See Swift, Jonathan
Webb, Beatrice (Martha Potter) 1858-1943 **TCLC 22**
See also CA 117; 162; DLB 190
Webb, Charles (Richard) 1939- **CLC 7**
See also CA 25-28R
Webb, James H(enry), Jr. 1946- **CLC 22**
See also CA 81-84
Webb, Mary Gladys (Meredith) 1881-1927 **TCLC 24**
See also CA 182; 123; DLB 34
Webb, Mrs. Sidney
See Webb, Beatrice (Martha Potter)
Webb, Phyllis 1927- **CLC 18**
See also CA 104; CANR 23; DLB 53
Webb, Sidney (James) 1859-1947 **TCLC 22**
See also CA 117; 163; DLB 190
Webber, Andrew Lloyd CLC 21
See also Lloyd Webber, Andrew
Weber, Lenora Mattingly 1895-1971 **CLC 12**
See also CA 19-20; 29-32R; CAP 1; SATA 2; SATA-Obit 26
Weber, Max 1864-1920 **TCLC 69**
See also CA 109
Webster, John 1579(?)-1634(?) **LC 33; DA; DAB; DAC; DAM DRAM, MST; DC 2; WLC**
See also CDBLB Before 1660; DLB 58
Webster, Noah 1758-1843 **NCLC 30**
See also DLB 1, 37, 42, 43, 73
Wedekind, (Benjamin) Frank(lin) 1864-1918 **TCLC 7; DAM DRAM**
See also CA 104; 153; DLB 118
Weidman, Jerome 1913-1998 **CLC 7**
See also AITN 2; CA 1-4R; 171; CANR 1; DLB 28
Weil, Simone (Adolphine) 1909-1943 **TCLC 23**
See also CA 117; 159; MTCW 2
Weininger, Otto 1880-1903 **TCLC 84**

Weinstein, Nathan
See West, Nathanael
Weinstein, Nathan von Wallenstein
See West, Nathanael
Weir, Peter (Lindsay) 1944- **CLC 20**
See also CA 113; 123
Weiss, Peter (Ulrich) 1916-1982 **CLC 3, 15, 51; DAM DRAM**
See also CA 45-48; 106; CANR 3; DLB 69, 124
Weiss, Theodore (Russell) 1916- **CLC 3, 8, 14**
See also CA 9-12R; CAAS 2; CANR 46; DLB 5
Welch, (Maurice) Denton 1915-1948 **TCLC 22**
See also CA 121; 148
Welch, James 1940- **CLC 6, 14, 52; DAM MULT, POP**
See also CA 85-88; CANR 42, 66; DLB 175; NNAL
Weldon, Fay 1931- **CLC 6, 9, 11, 19, 36, 59, 122; DAM POP**
See also CA 21-24R; CANR 16, 46, 63; CDBLB 1960 to Present; DLB 14, 194; INT CANR-16; MTCW 1, 2
Wellek, Rene 1903-1995 **CLC 28**
See also CA 5-8R; 150; CAAS 7; CANR 8; DLB 63; INT CANR-8
Weller, Michael 1942- **CLC 10, 53**
See also CA 85-88
Weller, Paul 1958- **CLC 26**
Wellershoff, Dieter 1925- **CLC 46**
See also CA 89-92; CANR 16, 37
Welles, (George) Orson 1915-1985 **CLC 20, 80**
See also CA 93-96; 117
Wellman, John McDowell 1945-
See Wellman, Mac
See also CA 166
Wellman, Mac 1945- **CLC 65**
See also Wellman, John McDowell; Wellman, John McDowell
Wellman, Manly Wade 1903-1986 **CLC 49**
See also CA 1-4R; 118; CANR 6, 16, 44; SATA 6; SATA-Obit 47
Wells, Carolyn 1869(?)-1942 **TCLC 35**
See also CA 113; 185; DLB 11
Wells, H(erbert) G(eorge) 1866-1946 **TCLC 6, 12, 19; DA; DAB; DAC; DAM MST, NOV; SSC 6; WLC**
See also AAYA 18; CA 110; 121; CDBLB 1914-1945; CLR 64; DA3; DLB 34, 70, 156, 178; MTCW 1, 2; SATA 20
Wells, Rosemary 1943- **CLC 12**
See also AAYA 13; CA 85-88; CANR 48; CLR 16; MAICYA; SAAS 1; SATA 18, 69, 114
Welty, Eudora 1909- **CLC 1, 2, 5, 14, 22, 33, 105; DA; DAB; DAC; DAM MST, NOV; SSC 1, 27; WLC**
See also CA 9-12R; CABS 1; CANR 32, 65; CDALB 1941-1968; DA3; DLB 2, 102, 143; DLBD 12; DLBY 87; MTCW 1, 2
Wen I-to 1899-1946 **TCLC 28**
Wentworth, Robert
See Hamilton, Edmond
Werfel, Franz (Viktor) 1890-1945 **TCLC 8**
See also CA 104; 161; DLB 81, 124
Wergeland, Henrik Arnold 1808-1845 **NCLC 5**
Wersba, Barbara 1932- **CLC 30**
See also AAYA 2, 30; CA 29-32R; 182; CAAE 182; CANR 16, 38; CLR 3; DLB 52; JRDA; MAICYA; SAAS 2; SATA 1, 58; SATA-Essay 103
Wertmueller, Lina 1928- **CLC 16**
See also CA 97-100; CANR 39, 78

Wescott, Glenway 1901-1987 **CLC 13; SSC 35**
See also CA 13-16R; 121; CANR 23, 70; DLB 4, 9, 102
Wesker, Arnold 1932- **CLC 3, 5, 42; DAB; DAM DRAM**
See also CA 1-4R; CAAS 7; CANR 1, 33; CDBLB 1960 to Present; DLB 13; MTCW 1
Wesley, Richard (Errol) 1945- **CLC 7**
See also BW 1; CA 57-60; CANR 27; DLB 38
Wessel, Johan Herman 1742-1785 **LC 7**
West, Anthony (Panther) 1914-1987 **CLC 50**
See also CA 45-48; 124; CANR 3, 19; DLB 15
West, C. P.
See Wodehouse, P(elham) G(renville)
West, (Mary) Jessamyn 1902-1984 **CLC 7, 17**
See also CA 9-12R; 112; CANR 27; DLB 6; DLBY 84; MTCW 1, 2; SATA-Obit 37
West, Morris L(anglo) 1916- **CLC 6, 33**
See also CA 5-8R; CANR 24, 49, 64; MTCW 1, 2
West, Nathanael 1903-1940 **TCLC 1, 14, 44; SSC 16**
See also CA 104; 125; CDALB 1929-1941; DA3; DLB 4, 9, 28; MTCW 1, 2
West, Owen
See Koontz, Dean R(ay)
West, Paul 1930- **CLC 7, 14, 96**
See also CA 13-16R; CAAS 7; CANR 22, 53, 76, 89; DLB 14; INT CANR-22; MTCW 2
West, Rebecca 1892-1983 **CLC 7, 9, 31, 50**
See also CA 5-8R; 109; CANR 19; DLB 36; DLBY 83; MTCW 1, 2
Westall, Robert (Atkinson) 1929-1993 **CLC 17**
See also AAYA 12; CA 69-72; 141; CANR 18, 68; CLR 13; JRDA; MAICYA; SAAS 2; SATA 23, 69; SATA-Obit 75
Westermarck, Edward 1862-1939 **TCLC 87**
Westlake, Donald E(dwin) 1933- **CLC 7, 33; DAM POP**
See also CA 17-20R; CAAS 13; CANR 16, 44, 65; INT CANR-16; MTCW 2
Westmacott, Mary
See Christie, Agatha (Mary Clarissa)
Weston, Allen
See Norton, Andre
Wetcheek, J. L.
See Feuchtwanger, Lion
Wetering, Janwillem van de
See van de Wetering, Janwillem
Wetherald, Agnes Ethelwyn 1857-1940 **TCLC 81**
See also DLB 99
Wetherell, Elizabeth
See Warner, Susan (Bogert)
Whale, James 1889-1957 **TCLC 63**
Whalen, Philip 1923- **CLC 6, 29**
See also CA 9-12R; CANR 5, 39; DLB 16
Wharton, Edith (Newbold Jones) 1862-1937 **TCLC 3, 9, 27, 53; DA; DAB; DAC; DAM MST, NOV; SSC 6; WLC**
See also AAYA 25; CA 104; 132; CDALB 1865-1917; DA3; DLB 4, 9, 12, 78, 189; DLBD 13; MTCW 1, 2
Wharton, James
See Mencken, H(enry) L(ouis)
Wharton, William (a pseudonym) CLC 18, 37
See also CA 93-96; DLBY 80; INT 93-96
Wheatley (Peters), Phillis 1754(?)-1784 **LC 3, 50; BLC 3; DA; DAC; DAM MST, MULT, POET; PC 3; WLC**

Wycherley, William 1641-1715 **LC 8, 21; DAM DRAM**
See also CDBLB 1660-1789; DLB 80

Wylie, Elinor (Morton Hoyt) 1885-1928 **TCLC 8; PC 23**
See also CA 105; 162; DLB 9, 45

Wylie, Philip (Gordon) 1902-1971 **CLC 43**
See also CA 21-22; 33-36R; CAP 2; DLB 9

Wyndham, John CLC 19
See also Harris, John (Wyndham Parkes Lucas) Beynon

Wyss, Johann David Von 1743-1818 **NCLC 10**
See also JRDA; MAICYA; SATA 29; SATA-Brief 27

Xenophon c. 430B.C.-c. 354B.C. **CMLC 17**
See also DLB 176

Yakumo Koizumi
See Hearn, (Patricio) Lafcadio (Tessima Carlos)

Yamamoto, Hisaye 1921- **SSC 34; DAM MULT**

Yanez, Jose Donoso
See Donoso (Yanez), Jose

Yanovsky, Basile S.
See Yanovsky, V(assily) S(emenovich)

Yanovsky, V(assily) S(emenovich) 1906-1989 **CLC 2, 18**
See also CA 97-100; 129

Yates, Richard 1926-1992 **CLC 7, 8, 23**
See also CA 5-8R; 139; CANR 10, 43; DLB 2; DLBY 81, 92; INT CANR-10

Yeats, W. B.
See Yeats, William Butler

Yeats, William Butler 1865-1939 **TCLC 1, 11, 18, 31, 93; DA; DAB; DAC; DAM DRAM, MST, POET; PC 20; WLC**
See also CA 104; 127; CANR 45; CDBLB 1890-1914; DA3; DLB 10, 19, 98, 156; MTCW 1, 2

Yehoshua, A(braham) B. 1936- **CLC 13, 31**
See also CA 33-36R; CANR 43, 90

Yellow Bird
See Ridge, John Rollin

Yep, Laurence Michael 1948- **CLC 35**
See also AAYA 5, 31; CA 49-52; CANR 1, 46; CLR 3, 17, 54; DLB 52; JRDA; MAI-CYA; SATA 7, 69

Yerby, Frank G(arvin) 1916-1991 **CLC 1, 7, 22; BLC 3; DAM MULT**
See also BW 1, 3; CA 9-12R; 136; CANR 16, 52; DLB 76; INT CANR-16; MTCW 1

Yesenin, Sergei Alexandrovich
See Esenin, Sergei (Alexandrovich)

Yevtushenko, Yevgeny (Alexandrovich) 1933- **CLC 1, 3, 13, 26, 51, 126; DAM POET**
See also CA 81-84; CANR 33, 54; MTCW 1

Yezierska, Anzia 1885(?)-1970 **CLC 46**
See also CA 126; 89-92; DLB 28, 221; MTCW 1

Yglesias, Helen 1915- **CLC 7, 22**

See also CA 37-40R; CAAS 20; CANR 15, 65; INT CANR-15; MTCW 1

Yokomitsu, Riichi 1898-1947 **TCLC 47**
See also CA 170

Yonge, Charlotte (Mary) 1823-1901 **TCLC 48**
See also CA 109; 163; DLB 18, 163; SATA 17

York, Jeremy
See Creasey, John

York, Simon
See Heinlein, Robert A(nson)

Yorke, Henry Vincent 1905-1974 **CLC 13**
See also Green, Henry
See also CA 85-88; 49-52

Yosano Akiko 1878-1942 **TCLC 59; PC 11**
See also CA 161

Yoshimoto, Banana CLC 84
See also Yoshimoto, Mahoko

Yoshimoto, Mahoko 1964-
See Yoshimoto, Banana
See also CA 144

Young, Al(bert James) 1939- **CLC 19; BLC 3; DAM MULT**
See also BW 2, 3; CA 29-32R; CANR 26, 65; DLB 33

Young, Andrew (John) 1885-1971 **CLC 5**
See also CA 5-8R; CANR 7, 29

Young, Collier
See Bloch, Robert (Albert)

Young, Edward 1683-1765 **LC 3, 40**
See also DLB 95

Young, Marguerite (Vivian) 1909-1995 **CLC 82**
See also CA 13-16; 150; CAP 1

Young, Neil 1945- **CLC 17**
See also CA 110

Young Bear, Ray A. 1950- **CLC 94; DAM MULT**
See also CA 146; DLB 175; NNAL

Yourcenar, Marguerite 1903-1987 **CLC 19, 38, 50, 87; DAM NOV**
See also CA 69-72; CANR 23, 60; DLB 72; DLBY 88; MTCW 1, 2

Yuan, Chu 340(?)B.C.-278(?)B.C. **CMLC 36**

Yurick, Sol 1925- **CLC 6**
See also CA 13-16R; CANR 25

Zabolotsky, Nikolai Alekseevich 1903-1958 **TCLC 52**
See also CA 116; 164

Zagajewski, Adam 1945- **PC 27**
See also CA 186

Zamiatin, Yevgenii
See Zamyatin, Evgeny Ivanovich

Zamora, Bernice (B. Ortiz) 1938- **CLC 89; DAM MULT; HLC 2**
See also CA 151; CANR 80; DLB 82; HW 1, 2

Zamyatin, Evgeny Ivanovich 1884-1937 **TCLC 8, 37**
See also CA 105; 166

Zangwill, Israel 1864-1926 **TCLC 16**

See also CA 109; 167; DLB 10, 135, 197

Zappa, Francis Vincent, Jr. 1940-1993
See Zappa, Frank
See also CA 108; 143; CANR 57

Zappa, Frank CLC 17
See also Zappa, Francis Vincent, Jr.

Zaturenska, Marya 1902-1982 **CLC 6, 11**
See also CA 13-16R; 105; CANR 22

Zeami 1363-1443 **DC 7**

Zelazny, Roger (Joseph) 1937-1995 **CLC 21**
See also AAYA 7; CA 21-24R; 148; CANR 26, 60; DLB 8; MTCW 1, 2; SATA 57; SATA-Brief 39

Zhdanov, Andrei Alexandrovich 1896-1948 **TCLC 18**
See also CA 117; 167

Zhukovsky, Vasily (Andreevich) 1783-1852 **NCLC 35**
See also DLB 205

Ziegenhagen, Eric CLC 55

Zimmer, Jill Schary
See Robinson, Jill

Zimmerman, Robert
See Dylan, Bob

Zindel, Paul 1936- **CLC 6, 26; DA; DAB; DAC; DAM DRAM, MST, NOV; DC 5**
See also AAYA 2; CA 73-76; CANR 31, 65; CDALBS; CLR 3, 45; DA3; DLB 7, 52; JRDA; MAICYA; MTCW 1, 2; SATA 16, 58, 102

Zinov'Ev, A. A.
See Zinoviev, Alexander (Aleksandrovich)

Zinoviev, Alexander (Aleksandrovich) 1922- **CLC 19**
See also CA 116; 133; CAAS 10

Zoilus
See Lovecraft, H(oward) P(hillips)

Zola, Emile (Edouard Charles Antoine) 1840-1902 **TCLC 1, 6, 21, 41; DA; DAB; DAC; DAM MST, NOV; WLC**
See also CA 104; 138; DA3; DLB 123

Zoline, Pamela 1941- **CLC 62**
See also CA 161

Zoroaster 628(?)B.C.-551(?)B.C. **CMLC 40**

Zorrilla y Moral, Jose 1817-1893 **NCLC 6**

Zoshchenko, Mikhail (Mikhailovich) 1895-1958 **TCLC 15; SSC 15**
See also CA 115; 160

Zuckmayer, Carl 1896-1977 **CLC 18**
See also CA 69-72; DLB 56, 124

Zuk, Georges
See Skelton, Robin

Zukofsky, Louis 1904-1978 **CLC 1, 2, 4, 7, 11, 18; DAM POET; PC 11**
See also CA 9-12R; 77-80; CANR 39; DLB 5, 165; MTCW 1

Zweig, Paul 1935-1984 **CLC 34, 42**
See also CA 85-88; 113

Zweig, Stefan 1881-1942 **TCLC 17**
See also CA 112; 170; DLB 81, 118

Zwingli, Huldreich 1484-1531 **LC 37**
See also DLB 179

Literary Criticism Series
Cumulative Topic Index

This index lists all topic entries in Gale's *Classical and Medieval Literature Criticism, Contemporary Literary Criticism, Literature Criticism from 1400 to 1800, Nineteenth-Century Literature Criticism,* and *Twentieth-Century Literary Criticism.*

Topic Index

NCLC Cumulative Nationality Index

NCLC–87 Title Index

ISBN 078764542-7

90000